Caffeine-Related Disorders

Cannabis-Related Disorders

Cocaine-Related Disorders

Hallucinogen-Related Disorders

Inhalant-Related Disorders

Nicotine-Related Disorders

Opioid-Related Disorders

Phencyclidine-Related Disorders

Sedative-, Hypnotic-, or Anxiolytic-
Related Disorders

Polysubstance-Related Disorder

Schizophrenia and Other Psychotic Disorders

Schizophrenia
Paranoid Type
Disorganized Type
Catatonic Type
Undifferentiated Type
Residual Type

Schizophreniform Disorder

Schizoaffective Disorder

Delusional Disorder

Brief Psychotic Disorder

Shared Psychotic Disorder

Psychotic Disorder Due to a General
Medical
With Delusions
With Hallucinations

Substance-Induced Psychotic Disorder

Mood Disorders

Depressive Disorders
Major Depressive Disorder
Dysthymic Disorder

Bipolar Disorders
Bipolar I Disorder

*Bipolar II Disorder (Recurrent
Major Depressive Episodes With
Hypomania)*
Cyclothymic Disorder

Mood Disorder Due to a General Medical
Condition

Substance-Induced Mood Disorder

Anxiety Disorders

Panic Disorder
Without Agoraphobia
With Agoraphobia

Agoraphobia Without History of Panic Disorder

Specific Phobia

Social Phobia (Social Anxiety Disorder)

Obsessive-Compulsive Disorder

Posttraumatic Stress Disorder

Acute Stress Disorder

Generalized Anxiety Disorder

Anxiety Disorder Due to a General
Medical Condition

Substance-Induced Anxiety Disorder

Somatoform Disorders

Somatization Disorder

Conversion Disorder

Pain Disorder

Hypochondriasis

Body Dysmorphic Disorder

Factitious Disorders

With Predominantly Psychological Signs
and Symptoms

With Predominantly Physical Signs
and Symptoms

With Combined Psychological and
Physical Signs and Symptoms

(continued on inside back cover)

Abnormal Psychology

Michael T. Nietzel
University of Kentucky

Matthew L. Speltz
University of Washington

Elizabeth A. McCauley
University of Washington

Douglas A. Bernstein
University of Illinois,
Urbana-Champaign

Allyn and Bacon
Boston • London • Toronto
Sydney • Tokyo • Singapore

Vice President, Social Sciences: *Sean W. Wakely*
Senior Development Editor: *Sue Gleason*
Development Editor: *Kathy Field*
Editorial Assistant: *Jessica Barnard*
Director of Field Marketing: *Joyce Nilsen*
Senior Editorial Production Administrator: *Susan McIntyre*
Editorial Production Service: *Marjorie Payne, Marbern House*

Composition and Prepress Buyer: *Linda Cox*
Manufacturing Buyer: *Megan Cochran*
Cover Administrator: *Linda Knowles*
Text Design: *Carol Somberg*
Electronic Composition: *Omegatype East*
Photo Research: *Laurie Frankenthaler*
Artist: *Jay Alexander, I-hua Graphics*

Library of Congress Cataloging-in-Publication Data

Nietzel, Michael T.
    Abnormal psychology / Michael T. Nietzel and Douglas Bernstein.
      p.   cm.
    Includes bibliographical references and index.
    ISBN 0-205-14721-6
    1. Psychology, Pathological. 2. Psychiatry. I. Bernstein.
  Douglas A. II. Title.
  RC454.N54   1997
616.89—dc21   96-52617

Credits appear on pp. 762–764, which constitute a continuation of the copyright page.

Printed in the United States of America
10 9 8 7 6 5 4 3 2 1   VHP   03 02 01 00 99 98 97

About the Chapter Opening Artists

We are pleased and privileged to offer as chapter opening illustrations creative works from Sistare, a nonprofit education institute, and from Creative Growth Art Center.

Sistare's first project was "Truth from Darkness," an exhibit of sculpture, prints, and paintings by artists with such mental disorders as schizophrenia, bipolar disorder, and obsessive-compulsive disorder. The exhibit opened in the Russell Senate Building Rotunda in Washington, D.C., in fall 1996 and traveled nationwide throughout the following year. The project was inspired by Susan Sistare Thorne, an artist who lost her battle with schizophrenia when she committed suicide in 1993. "The exhibit is committed to shedding light on the talents and intelligence of individuals who suffer from mental illnesses using fine art," says Sarah Thorne Mentock, president and founder of the namesake nonprofit organization. "It is simply one more avenue to bring the crisis of mental illness to the public, in hopes that awareness is raised and interest is heightened."

Creative Growth Art Center, a studio/gallery in the San Francisco Bay Area, provides creative art programs, educational and independent living training, counseling, and vocational opportunities for adults who are physically, mentally, and emotionally disabled. Yearly, over 4,000 people visit the Creative Growth Gallery, which was started with a National Endowment for the Arts grant as the first gallery of its kind in the country whose primary mission is to exhibit the art of people with disabilities. Creative Growth Art Center demonstrates that labels such as disability need not be barriers to high achievement and success in the arts.

Brief Contents

Contents

CHAPTER 4

Developmental Disorders
and Learning Disabilities   116

CHAPTER 5

Stress, Sleep, and
Adjustment Disorders   152

To the Student

A Guided Tour of *Abnormal Psychology*

Welcome to one of the most fascinating courses you'll ever take! Fascinating as it may be, however, this is no tabloid treatment of the subject matter. The text you have opened is grounded in research and steeped in clinical experience. You can trust what you're about to read!

We know from experience with our own students that you'll be especially interested in coverage of clinical disorders—depression, schizophrenia, obsessive-compulsive disorder, and so on. So, after a basic introduction to the nature and diagnosis of abnormal behavior, we begin our coverage of disorders in Chapter 3—much earlier than most other texts do.

Because there is evidence that many disorders have their roots in childhood, so the first disorders chapters deal with disorders of infancy, childhood, and adolescence. These chapters will give you important developmental background material for understanding the later disorders chapters in the text.

Our coverage of all disorders is organized in relation to the *Diagnostic and Statistical Manual of Mental Disorders,* Fourth Edition *(DSM-IV)*, published by the American Psychiatric Association. And, because prevention is quickly becoming as important in today's world as diagnosis and treatment, every disorders chapter includes a focus on how disorders might be prevented as well as treated.

Perhaps most important of all, you'll find the text peppered with real-life clinical stories of patients whom we and our colleagues have encountered.

So that you'll make the most of all the material in the following pages and chapters, we've incorporated a number of helpful features and ancillary items in this textbook package.

An Integrated View of the Field

Roots of Disorders

Underscoring the developmental theme that appears early in the text and recurs throughout:

Connections tabs appear in every chapter, giving you cross-references to other interesting coverage elsewhere in the text. Rather than presenting abnormal psychology's varied topics as isolated bits of information, we will help you tie them together meaningfully at every opportunity.

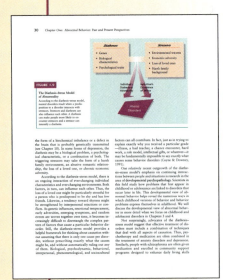

Diathesis–stress models are presented in carefully and consistently color-coded diagrams to show how the interaction of biological, psychological, and environmental factors can bring about disorders.

The Clinical and Research Base

Each chapter opens with **From the Case of . . .** , a dramatic case history to which the chapter text refers and to which we return at the end of the chapter in **Revisiting the Case of . . .** . Among other cases, you'll be especially interested in the stories of

- Nelson McGrath, whose diary provides a haunting introduction to abnormality;
- former Green Bay Packers defensive end Lionel Aldridge, diagnosed with schizophrenia; and
- serial killer Ted Bundy's antisocial personality disorder.

Specially highlighted **brief case histories** appear throughout each chapter, further bringing the clinical world of abnormal psychology to life.

How should mental disorders be diagnosed? Find at-a-glance summaries of the official terminology, criteria, and categories in special **DSM tables.**

The research base truly comes to life, as today's leading authorities in the specialty areas of abnormal psychology speak with us in **A Talk with . . .** features within each chapter. Among others, hear the words of

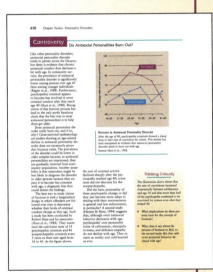

- Lee Sechrest, on the science of abnormal psychology;
- Elizabeth Loftus, on repressed memory and dissociative disorders;
- Irving Gottesman, on schizophrenia; and
- David Orlinsky, on psychotherapy.

Prevention

How can mental disorders be prevented? Check out each disorders chapter's **Prevention** feature on such topics as

- adolescent suicide;
- the FAST track approach to derailing childhood conduct disorder;
- promoting community health; and
- adolescent drinking.

Holding Your Interest and Stretching Your Thinking

There is a special section in each chapter on a **Controversy** that is capturing current scholarly, popular, or clinical attention. A set of **Thinking Critically** questions at the end of each Controversy will deepen your understanding of the material. Among the Controversies are:

- What are the implications of genetic causes of abnormality?
- Are diagnoses gender biased?
- Is Ritalin a safe treatment for hyperactivity?
- Can violence be socially inherited?

Masterful Teaching and Effective Learning

In the Textbook . . .

Chapter Outlines   help you preview and organize the material.

In Review   at the end of most major sections, brief reviews provide you with summaries that help you along the way.

Chapter Summaries   provide a paragraph of review for each of the chapter's main sections. You'll see the main headings from the chapter outline repeated here, for effective review and "chunking" of the material.

Key Terms   All of the chapter's boldfaced glossary terms are gathered at the end of the chapter for you to test your recall of the chapter's terminology. If you're having trouble with a term, check the page reference provided.

And beyond . . .

A variety of student ancillary items are also available from your bookstore. Check with your instructor.

Practice Tests   Multiple-choice tests, with answers, for all chapters, composed of real test items from the text's Test Bank, by Susan K. Fuhr of Weber State University, prepare you to take the real thing.

Study Guide   By John Foust of Parkland College, applies the tried-and-tested learning technique—SQ3R—to a variety of exercises for each chapter.

Website   Visit the Allyn & Bacon America Online home page (keyword: College Online) and this textbook's website (http://www.abacon.com/nietzel) for a wealth of information and assistance related to abnormal psychology. Interact with an online study guide, follow links to other useful sites, or just browse.

Casebook   *Case Studies in Abnormal Behavior,* Third Edition by Robert G. Meyer and Yvonne Hardaway Osborne, provides a wealth of actual, recent cases, accompanied by introductions and discussions.

To the Instructor

This book arose from a vision that we shared about a more exciting organization for an abnormal psychology textbook, as well as a new set of emphases on how disorders develop and can be prevented. This vision was focused by our experiences teaching abnormal psychology courses, by talking with other instructors about their classes, and, most important, by talking with students about what they wanted in an abnormal psychology textbook. We believe we have translated this vision into a book that students will enjoy reading and that instructors will appreciate assigning in their classes.

An Innovative Organization

The traditional abnormal psychology textbook begins with four to six chapters on the history of psychology and abnormality, an overview of theoretical approaches to abnormal behavior, a survey of classification and assessment techniques, and often a primer on research methods. In many cases, one quarter to one third of the book is devoted to these topics. In our experience, such an organization creates several problems that we have tried to eliminate in this text. First, students routinely become bored with so much background material and grow impatient, as they often put it, "to get to the interesting stuff"— the disorders themselves. Instructors frequently respond by not assigning all of the opening chapters, but this can result in an incomplete introduction to the course, inadequately explained content later, or both.

In this text, we compress what we believe to be the necessary preparatory content into the first two chapters. In those chapters, we survey major historical periods and their associated worldviews, summarize various theoretical perspectives on abnormality, describe the basics of assessment and classification, and introduce the logic of the scientific method. We confine ourselves to the fundamentals of this material, but we return to all of these issues later in the text, by discussing them in the context of specific disorders. By the end of the book, students will have been exposed to all the basic historical, psychological, and scientific concepts in a way that we believe is more interesting and less artificial than the typical abnormal text's format.

A second major innovation in this text lies in its placement of chapters on infancy, childhood, and ad-olescence. In the typical text, these problems are discussed in the last third of the text, usually after all the major adult disorders have been described. This standard organization does nothing to help students understand the many important links between childhood experiences and adult problems. In this text, disorders of infancy, childhood, and adolescence, and developmental disorders, are covered before all others. This arrangement helps students learn how, in many individuals, childhood experiences are linked to adult disorders.

The unique organization of this text makes possible some special features and themes. One repeated theme is **developmental psychopathology,** a perspective on mental disorders that is gaining ever-greater prominence. The origins and signs of many adult disorders emerge in childhood and adolescence. Understanding how early developmental factors increase the risk of mental disorders is crucial, and the organization of this text provides a framework for achieving this understanding.

Special attention to developmental contributions to mental disorder is enhanced by an emphasis on **prevention.** Each disorders chapter contains a highlighted section devoted to a specific prevention topic. Does family violence produce aggressive children who then become antisocial adults? What role do early thinking patterns play in creating anxiety and mood disorders, and can these patterns be altered? Do we know enough about the genetics of mental disorders to offer genetic counseling to prospective parents? Although our current knowledge of psychopathology does not yet permit the design of effective prevention programs for all disorders, considerable progress has been made in several areas. Our book is intended to portray what is currently known about prevention and to help students understand the importance of research in this vital area.

Various theoretical models have attempted to explain mental disorders by invoking a large number of biological, psychological, and social factors. Our text surveys these models, but, for each disorder, we emphasize the causal model that we believe is best supported by existing data. For many disorders, this turns out to be a **diathesis–stress model,** which emphasizes an interaction between a vulnerability or predisposition to disorder (diathesis) and the stressors and other triggering events that translate diathesis into disorder. In order to highlight the importance of the diathesis–stress model, we use carefully and consistently color-coded diagrams to depict the diatheses and stressors involved in specific disorders.

Why do men and women differ in the frequency with which they are diagnosed with certain disorders? What is the most effective form of treatment for a given disorder? Should we devote increased resources to preventing mental disorders or to treating them once they appear? For many of these questions, the answer remains unclear. Scholars often disagree about how to interpret empirical data about such questions or even about whether empirical data can resolve their disagreement. In order to acquaint students with these inevitable, and desirable, disputes, we have included a **Controversy** in each chapter that focuses on an unresolved diagnostic, causal, or treatment issue. The purpose of these Controversy sections is to point students toward some of the "big questions" that remain unanswered in the field of abnormal psychology while encouraging them to deepen their understanding of the issue by thinking critically about it. To this end, each Controversy concludes with **Thinking Critically** questions.

Just as childhood experiences are often linked to later problems, the symptoms, causes, and treatments of one type of disorder are often relevant to other conditions as well. Given the degree to which biological, psychological, and social factors interact with each other, this overlap should not be surprising. However, it is often overlooked. One key skill in learning about abnormal behavior is being able to see linkages between different disorders, causal factors, treatment methods, and outcomes. We attempt to promote this kind of insight in our readers by noting some of the connections between chapters. These **Connections** appear in the margins of the text and direct the reader to content on specific pages in other parts of the text that is related to the current topic under discussion.

Discoveries in abnormal psychology are unfolding at an astounding rate. New knowledge in the areas of diagnosis, causation, and treatment appears literally almost every day. To ensure that students are exposed to the most current and sophisticated thinking available, each chapter includes **A Talk with . . . ,** an interview with a world-renowned expert on a topic covered in that chapter. These experts also suggest some of the most crucial questions in need of future study.

Promoting Interest and Learning

To promote students' interest in the material and aid their understanding, we have employed a number of other pedagogical devices in all chapters. In addition to brief case histories liberally distributed throughout the text, we begin each chapter with a lengthy case history entitled **From the Case of . . . ,** which illustrates the clinical reality of a disorder discussed in that chapter. We return to these cases at the end of the chapter in **Revisiting the Case of . . . ,** which summarizes the course and outcome of the individual's problem. These introductory and revisited cases were selected to show how general concepts of cause and treatment operate in individuals most of whom are known personally by the authors.

Students' studying of the text should be facilitated by our use of several other learning tools, including:

- **In Review** summaries that highlight the key points of major sections in each chapter.

- **Chapter Summaries,** which identify and integrate the most important subject matter for chapters.

- **Key Terms,** which are boldfaced in the chapter, listed at the end of each chapter with page references, and defined in the book's Glossary.

Ancillaries for Instructors

No major college textbook today would be complete without a full complement of teaching materials to help make the instructor's job easier. Ours is no exception. We are pleased to offer:

- An **Instructor's Manual,** by Peggy Nash of Broward Community College, featuring chapter overviews, outlines, lecture makers, transparency lists, and various other helpful resources.

- A **Test Bank** of over 2,500 items, by Susan K. Fuhr of Weber State University, available in both hard copy and computerized form for DOS, Windows, and Macintosh computers.

- A **website** specifically for this textbook, which offers both students and instructors the opportunity to browse to other sites relevant to specific topics in this textbook, to chat with one another on our message boards, and to participate in an on-line study guide.

- **Transparencies,** in full color, of key figures from the textbook and other sources.

- A variety of video resources for you to choose from, including:
  —A 90-minute **case video,** featuring (1) Devon, an autistic boy, whose mother is interviewed by pediatric psychologist Sandra

D'Angelo; and (2) Lionel Aldridge, former Green Bay Packers defensive end, diagnosed with paranoid schizophrenia, interviewed by Mike Nietzel. Each case also provides a description of the disorder, as well as treatments each individual received.

—A series of videos from **American Psychiatric Press, Inc.**, on diagnostic issues and treatments for a variety of disorders.

Acknowledgments

We gratefully acknowledge the contributions of two colleagues who provided valuable assistance in the creation of this book:

Dr. *Ronald Kleinknecht,* of Western Washington University, wrote the initial drafts of Chapters 7 (Anxiety Disorders), 10 (Schizophrenia), and 15 (Biological Treatment of Mental Disorders);

Dr. *Arthur Nonneman,* of Asbury College, wrote the initial draft of Chapter 11 (Cognitive Disorders) and assisted with other sections of the text concerned with neuroanatomy and brain functioning.

In addition, we were fortunate to be able to interview and share the wisdom of the following leaders in the field of abnormal psychology. We thank them deeply.

Judith Becker, University of Arizona
Susan Campbell, University of Pittsburgh
Paul T. Costa, Gerontology Research Center, National Institute on Aging
Geraldine Dawson, University of Washington
David L. Dunner, University of Washington Medical School
Irving Gottesman, University of Virginia
Constance Hammen, University of California, Los Angeles
Robert Hodapp, University of California, Los Angeles
Danny Kaloupek, Boston Veterans' Administration Medical Center
Terrence Keane, Boston Veterans' Administration Medical Center
Elizabeth Loftus, University of Washington
William R. Markesbery, University of Kentucky
Alan Marlatt, University of Washington
Karen Matthews, University of Pittsburgh
David Orlinsky, University of Chicago

James Pennebaker, Southern Methodist University
Ron Roesch, Simon Fraser University, Vancouver, British Columbia
Lee Sechrest, University of Arizona
Tom Widiger, University of Kentucky
Melvin Wilson, University of Virginia

We also want to thank several other colleagues who provided extremely valuable advice and assistance at several points throughout this project. Whether we asked for a review of an initial draft, help with references, clarification of controversies in the field, opinions about treatments, or information that would fill gaps in our own knowledge, the following people were always generous with their time and their expertise. We owe them a lot.

Michael Bardo   Richard Milich
Susan Barron   Norm Pedigo
David Berry   Greg Smith
Charley Carlson   Martha Wetter
Daniel Kivlahan   Tom Widiger
Don Lynam

The following individuals provided detailed manuscript reviews at all stages of this book's development. Their advice and constructive criticism were of great value to us.

Carol Baldwin, University of Arizona
James F. Calhoun, University of Georgia
Scott J. Dickman, University of Massachusetts, Dartmouth
Anthony F. Fazio, University of Wisconsin—Milwaukee
John Foust, Parkland College
Robert E. Francis, North Shore Community College
Steven C. Funk, Northern Arizona University
Bernard S. Gorman, Nassau Community College
William G. Iacono, University of Minnesota
Richard L. Leavy, Ohio Wesleyan University
Alan J. Lipman, Temple University
Joseph Lowman, University of North Carolina at Chapel Hill
Richard D. McAnulty, University of North Carolina at Charlotte
Michael Rodman, Middlesex Community College
Linda J. Skinner, University of Arkansas
David A. Smith, Ohio State University
Michael D. Spiegler, Providence College
Norris E. Vestre, Arizona State University
John Vitkus, Barnard College

Fred W. Whitford, Montana State
  University
Logan Wright, University of Oklahoma
Eric A. Zillmer, Drexel University

The completion and coordination of this manuscript would have been impossible without the heroic efforts of Mike Nietzel's assistant, Shirley Jacobs, who, in this project as in many previous ones, proved to be efficient, tireless, tactful, patient, and dedicated. In short, Shirley was her usual indispensable self, the miracle worker of Kastle Hall.

We also want to thank the many individuals at Allyn and Bacon, who teamed up to help us write this book. Special praise must go to our developmental editor, Kathy Field, who was a wonderful source of advice, examples, teaching, and wisdom, and to Sue Gleason, senior developmental editor, who provided an abundance of suggestions, encouragement, and organizational skill to keep us on track. They both listened to our gripes, helped us out of tight spots, pushed us when they had to, and bolstered our confidence. To the extent that this text is successful, Kathy and Sue deserve much of the credit.

Our deep thanks also go to several others at Allyn and Bacon, including Sean Wakely, vice president and editor in chief, for his leadership and belief in our project; Sandi Kirshner, editorial director, and Bill Barke, president, for their support and confidence; Joyce Nilsen, director of field marketing, for her marketing insights and instincts; Susan McIntyre, senior production administrator, for her attention to all the details in bringing the manuscript together; Marjorie Payne, freelance production editor, for her meticulous reading of and corrections to the manuscript; Jay Alexander, graphic artist, for his knowledgeable preparation of the figures; and Laurie Frankenthaler, photo researcher, for her inspired eye in finding just the right photographs.

Finally, a word about some of the people who are closest to us. Writing this book meant there were many nights when we neglected our families, numerous weekends when we isolated ourselves from them, and countless times when we were distracted, curt, or downright boring. Writing a book is tough on families and loved ones. We want to thank ours for making it go more easily than we had any right to expect. So, to Sandy, Aaron, Katy, Matt, and Emory, our apologies for the inconveniences and absences, and our thanks for your tolerance and understanding.

About the Authors

MICHAEL T. NIETZEL earned his Ph.D. in clinical psychology at the University of Illinois at Urbana-Champaign in 1973. He joined the faculty at the University of Kentucky that same year. He is currently professor of psychology and chair of the department of psychology at the University of Kentucky. Throughout most of the 1980s, he served as the director of the clinical psychology program at the University of Kentucky. Mike's research and teaching interests are focused on abnormal psychology, psychotherapy, forensic psychology, origins of criminal behavior, the assessment of therapeutic outcomes, and the relationship of personality to mental disorders. He is a frequent consultant to law enforcement agencies and correctional facilities. Mike is the coauthor of leading textbooks on clinical psychology and psychology and the law.

Among Mike's favorite pastimes are playing golf, listening to jazz, following the Chicago Cubs, watching his son Aaron play hockey, and observing his wife Sandy unsuccessfully attempt to train their two Labrador retrievers, Axel and Bella.

MATTHEW SPELTZ received a B.S. in psychology from the University of Illinois and an M.S. in psychology from Western Washington University. He earned his Ph.D. in clinical psychology at the University of Missouri-Columbia in 1980. Matt then completed a postdoctoral fellowship in child clinical psychology at the University of Washington. He is currently the chief of child psychiatry outpatient services at Seattle's Children's Hospital and Medical Center, and associate professor of psychiatry and behavioral sciences at the University of Washington School of Medicine. Matt has taught introductory psychology to undergraduates and developmental psychopathology to graduate students in child clinical psychology. He also teaches clinical psychology interns and psychiatry residents about clinical work with children and families. Matt has published research on the early development of children with conduct problems, the assessment of children's risk for injury, and the psychosocial development of infants with craniofacial birth defects.

In his spare time, Matt enjoys skiing and hiking in the Cascade Mountains in Washington state, playing basketball with friends, and watching Puget Sound sunsets with wife, Katy, and cat, George.

ELIZABETH A. MCCAULEY completed her undergraduate studies at the University of Wisconsin at Madison and her Ph.D. at the State University of New York at Buffalo. She is currently an associate professor in the department of psychiatry and behavioral sciences, with an adjunct appointment in the department of psychology, at the University of Washington in Seattle. Elizabeth is the clinical director of the Inpatient and Partial Psychiatry Hospitalization Programs at the Children's Hospital and Medical Center and the psychology head for the University of Washington's Adolescent Health Training Program. She teaches and provides clinical supervision in the department of psychiatry and behavioral sciences. Elizabeth also lectures on adolescent development and psychopathology to pediatric residents and psychology students. Her research has focused on mood disorders in children and adolescents, and on the behavioral aspects of endocrine and sex chromosome anomalies. She is currently working on a federally funded study of a preventive intervention for at-risk high school students.

In her spare time, Elizabeth enjoys reading, gardening, and hiking. She and her husband are landscaping their back yard—bit by bit. She goes on a yearly backpacking trip into the wilds of the Pacific Northwest with a group of women and is planning a trip to Tanzania with Habitat for Humanity. She has enjoyed raising and coparenting three children—two stepdaughters, and a son—all of whom have now left home to explore the world of college and work.

DOUGLAS A. BERNSTEIN received his Ph.D. in clinical psychology frm Northwestern University in 1968. In that same year, he joined the faculty at the University of Illinois at Urbana-Champaign, where he is currently professor of psychology. His teaching responsibilities have included undergraduate courses in introductory psychology, abnormal psychology, clinical psychology, and behavior modification, as well as graduate courses in research methods and psychotherapy. He has won the University of Illinois Psychology Graduate Student Organization's teaching award, as well as the department's Mabel Kirkpatrick Hohenboken Memorial Teaching Award. Doug's research interests have centered on anxiety assessment and treatment (including programs to alleviate fear of dentistry), and the modification of smoking behavior. In recent years, he has focused most of his energies on directing the introductory psychology program at Illinois, on coauthoring textbooks in introductory and clinical psychology, and on promoting excellence in the teaching of psychology through his leadership of the National Institute on the Teaching of Psychology (now in its 20th year) and his founding, in 1994, of the APS Preconvention Institute on the Teaching of Psychology.

Doug enjoys travel, dancing, listening to classical and country music, and keeping a blinding shine on his car. He also loves to teach and has made a minor hobby out of collecting odd excuses from students. His only regret in life is his inability to teach Mike Nietzel how to train his dogs.

Abnormal Psychology

1

Abnormal Behavior: Past and Present Perspectives

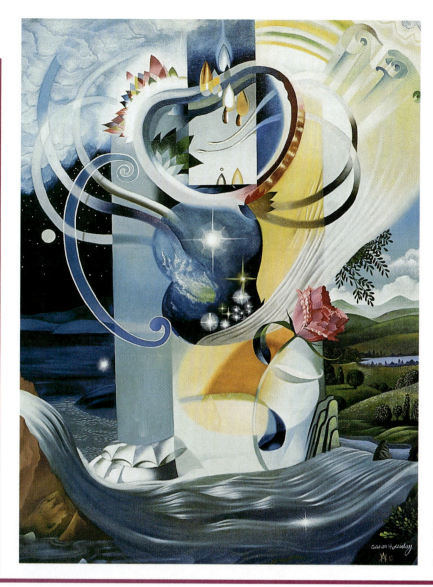

Stream of Time by Aaron Holiday. Oil on canvas, 30" x 40". Courtesy of Sistare and NARSAD Artworks.

From the Case of Nelson McGrath

Soon others will notice their discoloration. It's been going on for years but so slowly that only a few people are aware of it. Everyone gets a few more tiny spots every day—on their skin, their fingernails, everywhere—but they still don't see them. Lack of insight or hindsight. They are too far gone to save. Soon they will all be out of sight and out of mind.

I first noticed my own spots about five years ago, when I was 17. Little dots in the folds of my skin. I needed a magnifying glass to see them then and to study how the ink was filling up my pores. I burned my skin, salted it, rubbed myself with sand. But I couldn't stop the ink. Now I know I was looking in the wrong places. Spots come from the inside. All religions teach this lesson: evil is our tar. Eat pure and think sure; they were the cure. My contamination was carried by the poison of cooked animals and the unclean thoughts of the young girls always around me. No one else seemed to understand. Hospitals are the worst places you can be for these contagious contaminations.

They had to be stopped despite what my parents and the doctors thought. I had undergone their sterobic procedures for years, and they did no good. I didn't get any better, only more full of light rays and sophistry.

How could I be a sophist and a prophet? I knew the answer: stay away from the young girls and the cooked animals. I knew the answer. My brother and John the Baptist told me just as they had told others. But I listened when others didn't. I scared the girls away—even those who didn't scare easy—but they wouldn't be missed. And I eat the right stuff. White flour and cauliflower; they're the best. They keep you bright and clean. And I stay home, away from everyone who doesn't understand. Away from everybody. I lock myself in at night, and I put chairs against the door because you never can be sure when they might try to break through on you. Try to come in and wreck you. No wonder I can't sleep. I shouldn't sleep too deep. The girls are out there, and they're nothing but a dirty bunch of grotesqueries.

I could never have faced the terrors alone. I have guides who have gone before me. They talk to me. My older brother (who isn't dead like others say) warned me of my enemies. John the Baptist does too; being next to Christ on the cross made him sadder but wiser, and a good thing, too, for me. The rest of them can go to Hell. My mother, a whore if there ever was one. And all my fathers, always nagging me that I should work and wear cotton clothes. They don't know that I do work. I'm rich. I work on my inside. And that is a lot better than those s _ _ _ drugs they try to give me. Poking me with needles; left arm, then right. I put a stop to that. I told them I'd take the pills if they stopped the shots. Idiots. Hadn't they noticed how "well behaved and intact" the trash cans had been the last few months? Stop the spots. Stop the spots. I will stop the spots.

From the diary of Nelson McGrath ■

*Y*ou probably agree that Nelson McGrath's behavior is bizarre and that his thinking is disturbed. But what else do you think about Nelson? Would you fear him? Condemn him? Pity him? Envy his fantasy life? And how would you explain Nelson's thoughts and actions? Is he evil? Sick? Inspired? Mentally disordered?

These are just a few of the attitudes and ideas about abnormality that people have adopted in various parts of the world at various times in history. Prevailing attitudes tend to reflect a society's broader values, beliefs, and standards regarding issues such as the importance of science or religion and the degree to which people are responsible for their own problems. Which attitudes prevail at a given time and place strongly influence what happens to those who are labeled *abnormal*. As a result, people such as Nelson have been callously ignored, given cleansing baths, offered "talking therapy," confined in dismal cells, granted special privileges, drugged, operated on, or burned at the stake. In fact, your own background has shaped your reaction to people such

as Nelson, just as it shapes your interactions with the rest of the world.

Throughout time, every culture has struggled to define the forms of conduct that constitute abnormal behavior, also known as madness, mental illness, or mental disorders (the term used by most clinicians today). Like attitudes toward troubled people, these definitions grow out of historical and cultural contexts. In some settings, the most important criterion for defining abnormality has been whether behavior violates social expectations. In other settings, personal distress and suffering have been emphasized. Meanwhile, some people believe that the terms *crazy, mad,* or *ill* have always been no more than labels for behaviors that certain people dislike.

In Chapter 2, we will evaluate various definitions of abnormality that have been prominent throughout the ages. Although none of these definitions is completely objective or universally accepted, we believe that **abnormal behavior** is best defined as a disturbance of an individual's behavioral, psychological, or physical functioning that is not culturally

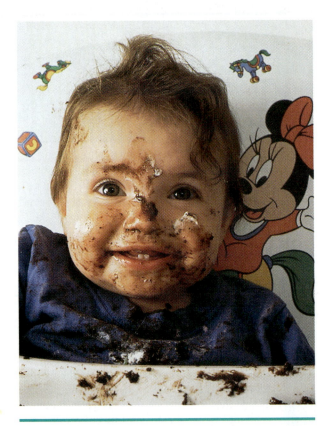

Definitions of abnormal behavior depend on certain characteristics of people such as their developmental stage and maturity. An adult who behaved in the same way as this baby might be considered abnormal because such behavior would violate social expectations about how "normal" adults behave.

expected and that leads to psychological distress, behavioral disability, or impaired overall functioning. In the sections that follow we will describe how societies throughout history have attempted to understand and treat abnormal behavior.

Making Sense of Abnormality: A Brief History

Several distinct themes appear in the way people in various cultures and historical eras have viewed and treated abnormality. To review these themes, this chapter will take a whirlwind tour through time to give you an idea of how a person such as Nelson McGrath might be received in different cultures and at different times in history.

Faraway Places, Ancient Times, and Supernatural Forces

There are no systematic, written records prior to the Egyptian and Mesopotamian cultures of around 3500–3000 B.C.E., so scholars depend on archeological discoveries and interpretations of oral myths to speculate about what our ancient ancestors would have made of someone such as Nelson McGrath. Some evidence suggests that they would have considered his behavior, and any other abnormality, as a reflection of the presence of evil spirits or other overpowering supernatural forces. Seen as an innocent victim of his affliction, Nelson might have been helped to expel his invader. Helping might have included *trephining,* a crude form of surgery practiced during the Stone Age in which a hole was bored through a person's skull, probably in order to give evil spirits a means of escape.

As ancient Chinese, Egyptian, and Hebrew civilizations developed, abnormal behavior was often blamed on evil spirits and demons, as were bad weather, earthquakes, physical illness, and other unexplainable events. For example, according to the Biblical account, Israel's first king, Saul, was said to be troubled by evil spirits and was treated with calming music. Indeed, when "David took the harp and played it . . . Saul was refreshed and was well, and the evil spirit departed from him" (I Samuel 16:14–23). However, abnormality was sometimes interpreted as divine punishment for disobedience or other misbehavior. For example, Nebuchadnezzar, King of Babylon, was said to be stricken with *lycanthropy* (the belief that one is a wolf) as divine retribution for his boastfulness (Daniel 4: 28–33). The king had to live in the wild until, after acknowledg-

ing God's power, his reason was restored, and he was reinstated.

Thus ancient civilizations might have dealt with Nelson in many ways. Prayer and faith healing were used to treat abnormal behaviors and may have been timed to coincide with the movement of planets or stars in hopes of enhancing the treatment. Some practitioners favored exorcism rituals designed to scare, drown, pummel, or whip evil spirits out of the host body; mixtures of animal excrement and blood also were concocted in order to poison evil spirits. But priests and religious healers supplemented incantations with treatments designed to correct problems in biological processes that were also seen as related to abnormality. If they had treated Nelson McGrath, they might have urged him to get more rest and prescribed exercise, peaceful activities, and an improved diet.

The Birth of the Medical Tradition: The Classical Period

The development of formal philosophy by the Greeks around 600–500 B.C.E. introduced the belief that humans were capable of understanding and taking control of themselves and their world. The Greek philosophic traditions of critical analysis and careful observation were refined during the third, fourth, and fifth centuries B.C.E. by the two greatest philosophers of the Classical Period: Plato and Aristotle. Plato believed that humans gained knowledge of the world rationally, through reasoning and recollection, and that people could discover universal concepts and truths that lay behind misleading appearances. Aristotle, on the other hand, claimed that people acquired knowledge through analyzing perceived events, thus laying the groundwork for the empirical method on which psychology and other sciences are based today.

These attempts to understand and to explain events in natural terms were compatible with the Greeks' increasing knowledge of the human body. Hippocrates (460?–377? B.C.E.), the early physician known as the "father of medicine," argued that all illnesses have natural, physical causes. Hippocrates concluded that mental disorders are also biological in nature and can be traced to imbalances among the four major fluids, or *humors,* of the body: yellow bile, black bile, blood, and phlegm. For example, excessive yellow bile was thought to cause the overexcitement of mania; too much black bile was related to melancholia, or depression. Treatment consisted of efforts to restore balance among the humors, usually through special diets, laxatives, and purgatives.

Hippocrates' views guided Greek and Roman physicians for several centuries. Galen, a famous Roman doctor who lived about A.D. 130–201, refined humoral theory and used it to describe human temperaments and "diseases of the soul." Galen also emphasized the role of the brain in controlling mental processes. To rebalance humors, Galen, like Hippocrates, prescribed medicine as well as special diets and physical therapy such as showers, sunbathing, and even sneezing bouts.

Similar ideas about the desirability of physical balance can be found in the Chinese culture of this era and the philosophy of Taoism. Normal behavior was thought to depend on the proper balance between *yin* and *yang,* the two major opposing forces in the universe. Yin is usually associated with nurturance, darkness, and femininity; yang, with power, light, and masculinity. Unifying these opposites is seen as the major task of life, requiring moderation in behavior and openness to nature's healing forces.

The Nelson McGraths of ancient times might also have received some sort of "talking cure." From antiquity, physicians, philosophers, and clerics have believed that the skillful use of words can soothe troubled minds and alter disordered behavior. In the fourth century B.C.E., for example, Stoic philosopher Epictetus argued that "Men are disturbed not by things, but by the view which they take of them." The Roman Emperor Marcus Aurelius noted in his *Meditations* that opinions are what lead to unhappiness: "Let opinion be taken away, and no man will think himself wronged. . . . It is in thy power absolutely to exclude all manner of conceit and opinion . . . and by the same means to exclude all grief and sorrow from thy soul." Galen himself subscribed to Plato's belief that the power of reason could control emotions and argued that a physician could, through persuasion and advice, help patients overcome anger, anxiety, and other emotional problems.

To summarize, thinkers in the Classical Period began to emphasize natural over supernatural causes of mental disorders, paving the way for later biological and psychological theories of abnormality. The Classical Period also established in Western minds the idea that medical doctors are the experts responsible for understanding and treating mental disorders. This idea ultimately led to the rise of psychiatry as the specialty that most people in modern Western cultures recognize as an important mental health profession.

From Demons to Instincts: The European Tradition

The Greek and Roman civilizations began to decline around A.D. 200 and continued to deteriorate until the fall of the Roman Empire in A.D. 476. During the next 500 years, a period known as the *early Middle Ages,* Europe experienced great political and economic upheaval. The feudal system replaced nation states, and wars were common. Reliance on rationalism and empiricism as sources of knowledge was replaced by the belief that, through faith and meditation, God would reveal divine truths.

We will concentrate on developments in Europe throughout this period because contemporary mental health fields grew largely from Western European origins. However, non-European cultures influenced the understanding and treatment of abnormal behavior as well. For example, in both the Middle East and Africa, beliefs about the causes of abnormal behavior vacillated between the supernatural and the physical. In both cultures, folk healers combined magic, herbal medicines, and common sense to treat the disturbed. Both also stressed the value of the local community in caring for people with mental disorders.

The Middle Ages and the Return of Demons. As the influence of Christian theology grew in Western Europe, science became less important. Once again, people began to believe that supernatural forces, especially the Devil and his demons and witches, were responsible for disordered behavior and that it should be treated with exorcisms or other religious rituals. Magical potions were concocted to purge evil forces. Nelson McGrath might have been given this one:

> Take a testicle of a goat that has been killed on a Tuesday midnight, during the first quarter of the moon, and the heart of a dog, mix with the excrement of a newborn babe, and after pulverizing, take an amount equivalent to half an olive twice a day. (Roback, 1961, p. 215)

Greek and Roman traditions did not disappear completely. For example, in his book, *The Canon of Medicine,* the Islamic physician Avicenna described humane procedures that preserved the philosophical traditions of Aristotle and the medical practices of Galen. Beginning in the eighth century, Islamic physicians pioneered the use of hospitals in which mentally disordered people received special treatment. In Europe, numerous monasteries served as sanctuaries for the mentally disordered. By providing a place where disturbed persons could be isolated from stress and treated kindly, these facilities represented a continuation of the Greek medical tradition.

There was certainly plenty of disturbance to deal with, including a phenomenon in which entire groups of people behaved in an extremely agitated fashion. In one form of this mass madness known as

In the Middle Ages, supernatural forms of intervention such as exorcism once again became a standard treatment for the mentally ill.

St. Vitus' Dance or *tarantism,* groups of men and women would suddenly begin frenzied jumping and dancing, tearing off their clothes as they frolicked in the streets. This bizarre behavior was widely blamed on demonic possession, but others attributed it to a naturalistic cause, the bite of the tarantula. Modern scholars still cannot agree on an explanation.

The late Middle Ages (from A.D. 1000 to the fourteenth century) saw harbingers of a new era. For one thing, the influence of the Christian Church on politics and philosophy began to weaken. However, the Church did not relinquish its dominant role in human affairs easily. As more secular world views gained influence, the Church intensified its use of power in a search for suspected heretics and witches. Thousands of suspects were tortured, and many were burned at the stake in the name of religious orthodoxy. Physician-priests "diagnosed" the "possessed" by looking for signs of the devil (*stigmata diaboli*) on their skin (Spanos, 1978). The search for the demon-possessed was guided by the publication of *Malleus Maleficarum,* or *Witches' Hammer,* about 1486, by the Dominican monks Heinrich Kraemer and Johan Sprenger. This book was regarded as the definitive treatise on the links between sin, demonic possession, witchcraft, and disordered behavior. It described magical methods for detecting demonic possession as well as many gruesome methods for extracting confessions from witches.

The Renaissance and the Rise of Humanism. The spirit of the European Renaissance appeared as early as the thirteenth and fourteenth centuries as intellec-

tual, cultural, and political life became more and more secular. The dawn of the Renaissance itself is generally marked as 1453, when the fall of Constantinople to the Turks ended the Byzantine Empire. The Renaissance saw a secularization of life and values known as *humanism* (Leahey, 1992). It was greatly facilitated by the advent of the printing press in 1440. As books became more accessible, people came in contact with ideas other than those authorized by the Church. For example, Copernicus's (1473–1543) theory that the sun, not the earth, was the center of the universe paved the way for later scientific discoveries that demystified all aspects of nature, from the heavens to the inner workings of human beings. People began to see the study of individuals and human nature—including behavior and social relations—not as a way to discover or honor God, but as a worthy topic in its own right. The Renaissance may have been the first era in which *psychological* concerns equalled or surpassed theological issues as the dominant questions of the day.

At the same time, physicians again came to view the human body as a biological machine to be studied empirically, not as an inviolate creation of God. The philosopher René Descartes (1596–1650) sought to explain a great deal of human mental activity in physical, mechanical terms. In fact, he suggested that we could learn about human minds by studying animal behavior, a view shared by many modern psychologists. The physicians Paracelsus (1493–1541) and Johann Weyer (1515–1588) championed naturalistic explanations of mental disorders that included both biological and psychological factors. Paracelsus never abandoned all supernatural preoccupations, however. He was convinced, for example, that the brain was influenced by the moon. Weyer is often considered the first **psychiatrist** (a medical doctor who specializes in the study and treatment of mental disorders) because of his careful descriptions of various mental disorders and his belief that treatment of these disorders required a "therapeutic relationship marked by understanding and kindness" (Brems, Thevenin, & Routh, 1991, p. 9). Weyer ridiculed beliefs in witches and condemned the brutal treatments supported by many theologians.

On the assumption that quarantine provided the best protection for both the public and the mentally disturbed, treatment of mental disorders during the Renaissance gradually took the form of confinement in hospitals and asylums, many of which had once been monasteries. If Nelson McGrath had lived in London, for example, he might have been admitted to the St. Mary of Bethlehem monastery, which had become a hospital in 1547. Local citizens referred to this "madhouse" as "Bedlam," a contraction of the word *Bethlehem.*

Unfortunately, Renaissance treatments for mental disorders were not much better than were those of the Middle Ages. Indeed, the "insane" in the hospitals of the Renaissance were usually treated as prisoners and had to endure abominable conditions. Jonathan Swift, a great novelist of the period, described the condition of a Bedlam inmate this way:

> Accost the hole of another Kennel, first stopping your Nose, you will behold a surley, gloomy, nasty slovenly Mortal, raking in his own Dung and dabling in his Urine. The best part of his Diet, is the reversion of his own Ordure, which expiring into Steams, whirls perpetually about, and at last reinfunds. His Complexion is of a dirty Yellow, with a thin scattered Beard, exactly agreeable to that of his Dyet upon its first Declination; like other Insects, who having their Birth and Education in an Excrement, from thense borrow their Colour and their Smell. (From Swift, J. (1704). *A Tale of a Tub.* London: J. Nutt.)

The Enlightenment and the Rise of Science. In the seventeenth and eighteenth centuries, the trend toward naturalistic world views blossomed. This era, known as the *Enlightenment,* was characterized by an unshakable confidence in human reason and in science, especially. During this era, Kepler (1571–1630) proposed the basic laws of planetary motion, and Newton (1642–1727) described the principle of gravity and developed calculus. It was assumed that empirical research would reveal mathematical or mechanical principles that governed all phenomena, including human behavior. This assumption made it possible, late in the 1800s, for psychology to become a scientific discipline.

Although modern science had begun, the deplorable conditions in European and North American asylums for the insane had not changed much. A group of reformers tried, in the last half of the 1700s, to improve the living conditions and treatment in asylums. Among these mental health "muckrakers" were Vincenzo Chiarugi (1759–1820) in Italy, William Tuke (1732-1822) in England, and Benjamin Rush (1745–1813) in the United States. Their work ushered in what became known as the *moral treatment era.*

The inspirational leader of the moral treatment movement was Phillipe Pinel (1745–1826), a French physician. When placed in charge of the Bicêtre asylum in Paris in 1793, Pinel unchained its inmates and insisted that they be treated with kindness and consideration. Pinel justified this risky, but courageous, experiment as follows: "It is my conviction that these mentally ill are intractable only because they are deprived of fresh air and liberty" (Ullmann & Krasner, 1975, p. 135). Moral treatment also tried to instill in patients the expectation that they could alter their disordered behavior, learn to manage daily stress, find useful employment, and get along better with others. After years of being treated as wild beasts and acting accordingly, many of the inmates at Bicêtre and other moral treatment centers seemed transformed almost overnight into well-behaved human beings.

Tony Robert-Fleury's 1876 painting of Philippe Pinel freeing the insane from shackles in the Bicêtre is one of the most famous artistic interpretations of the Moral Era's reformist spirit. Pinel pioneered other important methods such as taking notes to document his observations of patients.

However, moral treatment all but disappeared by the late 1800s, especially in the United States. Why? Ironically, its own success was partially responsible. Many assumed that hospital care could help more patients if hospitals were larger than traditional moral treatment centers. In mid-nineteenth century America, this assumption fueled the *mental hygiene movement,* led by crusaders such as Dorothea Dix (1802–1887), a Boston schoolteacher, and Clifford W. Beers (1876–1943), a former mental patient who helped to form the National Committee for Mental Hygiene. Dix became a tireless agitator for the construction of large, public mental hospitals. Unfortunately, these new state hospitals were so understaffed that they could offer little more than custodial care to the large number of patients they housed.

Moral treatment approaches were also overshadowed in the late 1800s because psychiatrists and other physicians working in mental health came to believe that disordered behaviors were caused by biological rather than social factors and thus required treatment based on biology and medicine. As one physician put it, there can be "no twisted thought without a twisted molecule" (Abood, 1960).

Indeed, even under the best circumstances, moral treatment approaches had only limited effects on severely disturbed patients—they often halted further deterioration but did not cure mental disorders. Some of these patients suffered a particularly severe disorder that involved ever-worsening delusions, muscle paralysis, and, ultimately, death. In 1825 this deteriorative brain syndrome was termed *general paresis,* and throughout the remainder of the nineteenth century, physicians searched for its cause. By the turn of the twentieth century, following basic discoveries of how bodily infections were caused, the puzzle was finally solved. The cause of general paresis turned out to be syphilitic infection of the brain. With this mental disorder traced to a biological cause, the search was on to find other links between mental disorders and physical causes. That search continues to this day, and we describe its findings throughout this book.

The presence of thousands of mental patients in public hospitals in the United States, Canada, and Europe allowed psychiatrists to compare individual patterns of disordered behavior. By the end of the nineteenth century, these comparisons had led to systems for classifying mental disorders. The most prominent of these systems was developed by Emil Kraepelin (1856–1926) in Germany and Eugen Bleuler (1857–1939) in Switzerland.

Better classification of disorders often helped practitioners apply treatments that were most effective for specific problems, but effective treatments for *any* problems were still scarce. Physicians simply did not know enough about organic causes to develop treatments that were much different from those of their predecessors. For example, American psychiatrist Benjamin Rush treated mental patients with bleedings and purges, and physicians often sought to tranquilize agitated patients by binding them in chairs, confining them in narrow cribs, dunking them in water, or wrapping them tightly in wet sheets. Believing that mental health depended on proper digestion, Horace Fletcher advocated chewing each mouthful of food hundreds of times before swallowing.

The Psychoanalytic Revolution. Of all the treatments for mental disorders used during the Enlightenment, *hypnotism* is best remembered, and it is still used today. First known as *mesmerism,* hypnotism was popularized as a quasi-magical cure by a French physician, Franz Anton Mesmer (1734–1815), who believed it could realign magnetic forces in the body.

Soon a number of reputable physicians were experimenting with hypnosis. For example, in India, James Esdaile pioneered hypnotic anesthesia during surgery. French psychiatrists such as Jean Charcot, Pierre Janet, and Hippolyte Bernheim discovered that hypnosis could be helpful in the treatment of **hysteria,** a disorder in which patients with normal physical abilities appear unable to see or hear or walk. This success helped to reawaken the idea that at least some mental disorders might be caused by psychological factors as well as, or even instead of, biological dysfunctions.

Enter Sigmund Freud, a Viennese neurologist who, with his colleague Joseph Breuer, successfully used hypnosis—and other "talking cures"—to treat cases of hysteria. Late in the 1800s Freud's clinical experience led him to conclude that many forms of abnormal behavior were caused by intense, prolonged, and largely unconscious mental struggles between instinctual desires and concern over social prohibitions against fulfilling those desires.

Freud was certainly not the first to focus on unconscious processes as the basis for abnormal behavior. Philosophers such as Johann Herbart (1776–1841) and Gottfried Wilhelm Leibniz (1646–1716) had discussed the importance of the unconscious, and writers and artists of the early nineteenth century had suggested that our most base passions are rooted in the unconscious and revealed in our dreams. It was

Connections

How do these early classification systems compare with those in use today? For a history of various systems used to classify mental disorders, see Chapter 2, pp. 60–61.

TABLE 1.1	The Mental Health Professions
Profession	Description
Psychiatrists	Psychiatrists are physicians who have completed additional years of training (called a *residency*) in the specialty of psychiatry. Psychiatrists are M.D.s.
Clinical psychologists	Psychologists have earned a doctoral degree (Ph.D. or Psy.D.) in psychology and specialize in applying scientific methods and psychological knowledge to the study, assessment, and treatment of mental disorders.
Psychiatric (clinical) social workers	Psychiatric social workers usually have completed a master's degree in social work and concentrate on treating mental disorders and family problems.
Psychiatric nurses, occupational therapists, and recreational therapists	These professionals have completed advanced training in their specialty areas and offer treatment services, usually as members of a mental health team.
Marriage and family counselors	These professionals have usually completed some post-graduate study in their specialties. They offer treatment for marital and family problems, which sometimes also involve mental disorders.

Freud, however, who synthesized these ideas into a coherent theory of personality and abnormal behavior that suggested *how* and *why* unconscious conflicts and other psychological processes create disordered behavior. Freud also applied his theory of abnormality in psychoanalysis, the first modern psychological treatment of mentally disturbed people.

Psychological explanations of abnormal behavior gained influence with the help of a new mental health profession known as **clinical psychology,** the branch of psychology devoted to scientifically studying mental disorders as well as assessing, diagnosing, and treating them. In the United States, the first psychological clinic was founded in 1896 (Nietzel, Bernstein, & Milich, 1998). When Freud came to the United States to deliver lectures at Clark University in 1909, he received a warm reception from American psychologists interested in mental disorders. Their response came partly because Freud's ideas suggested an important role for psychologists, not just psychiatrists, in assessing and treating psychological disorders (see Table 1.1). Many clinical psychologists began to apply their training in motivation, emotion, learning, social influences, and other areas to develop psychological theories about abnormal behavior that went beyond, and often conflicted with, Freud's.

Contemporary Approaches to Abnormality

Our historical review shows that there has always been competition among approaches or conceptual models to explain the abnormal behavior of people such as Nelson McGrath. **Models of abnormality** are comprehensive accounts of how and why abnormal behaviors develop and how best to treat them. They provide a conceptual map to help researchers and practitioners decide which aspects of abnormal behavior are most important to study—overt behavior or accompanying thoughts, for example—and which treatment methods—exorcism, drugs, talking—are most likely to succeed. The popularity of different models has waxed and waned from time to time and place to place throughout history. For example, in Western cultures today, the supernatural model of abnormality is largely overshadowed by the biological, physiological, sociocultural, and diathesis–stress models. In the following sections, we consider each of these models and how they seek to account for abnormal behavior.

In Review

Views of abnormal behavior are influenced by historical context, social attitudes, and cultural standards. Key figures in the history of the development of scientific approaches to abnormal behavior include:

- Hippocrates and Galen, physicians of ancient Greece and Rome who developed treatments of abnormal behavior derived from medical knowledge;

- Avicenna, an Islamic physician whose writings helped preserve Greek and Roman learning during the early Middle Ages;
- Pinel, a French physician and inspirational leader of the moral treatment movement who unchained the inmates of the *Bicêtre* asylum in Paris in 1793; and
- Sigmund Freud, who developed the first purely psychological model of abnormal behavior.

The Biological Model

The basic assumption of the **biological model** of abnormality is that the nervous system controls all thought and behavior, both normal and abnormal. From this perspective, any event or substance that affects the functioning of the nervous system also affects thinking and behavior. The abnormal behaviors and thought patterns displayed by Nelson Mc-Grath—and others who are diagnosed with mental disorders—are assumed to arise from changes in neural functioning triggered by traumatic life events, drugs, hormone imbalances, environmental toxins, head trauma, major infections, genetic defects, or other biological factors. Biological treatments attempt to change the patient's physical condition, usually through the use of therapeutic drugs (see Chapter 15).

The concept of a medical model is related to, but not always identical to, the biological model. A **med-** ical model of abnormal behavior considers that disturbed behavior involves *symptoms* of some underlying illness that is the result of specific causal or **etiological factors**. The person with the symptoms is considered a patient. The symptoms tend to go together in a pattern known as a *syndrome* that follows a well-recognized course, allowing professionals to diagnose a specific illness and to offer a prognosis of how the illness will unfold. The medical model often looks for biochemical or other physical causes of a syndrome. But in some theories, psychological factors are seen as analogous to biological processes. The basic assumptions and terminology of these theories are so similar to biological accounts that they are considered to be following a medical model. For example, Freud's system has sometimes been termed a medical model because of the parallels between his psychological explanations of abnormality and the strictly biological accounts of disturbed behavior.

Insights into the biological factors involved in abnormal behavior have expanded greatly in recent decades, thanks in large part to research in **neuroscience**, a set of disciplines that study the structure, organization, functions, and chemistry of the nervous system, especially the brain.

The Nervous System and Abnormality

As illustrated in Figure 1.1, the human nervous system consists of the *central nervous system (CNS)*—the brain and spinal cord—and the *peripheral nervous system*, which includes the somatic nervous system and the autonomic nervous system. The *so-*

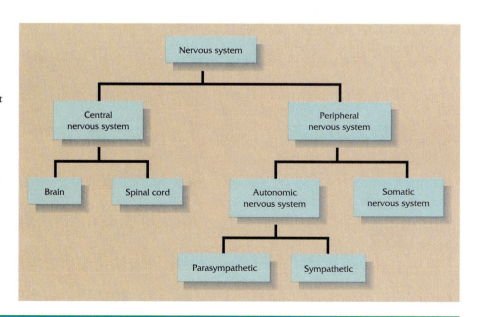

FIGURE 1.1

Organization of the Nervous System

The brain and spinal cord act as the body's organizer and central information processor. The peripheral nervous system's main role is to carry messages throughout the body. The somatic subsystem transmits sensory information from the outside world to the brain and carries messages from the brain to the muscles. The autonomic subsystem shuttles messages back and forth between the brain and organs and glands throughout the body.

matic nervous system (SNS) is largely concerned with voluntary control of the muscles. The *autonomic nervous system (ANS)* regulates motivational, emotional, and other physical reactions. The ANS controls the cardiovascular system, raises and lowers body temperature, and sends signals to other organs in the body. In this way, the brain receives information about what is happening in the outside world and within the body, and the muscles and organs receive instructions about how to respond.

The ANS contains sympathetic and parasympathetic divisions. Generally, the **sympathetic nervous system** prepares the body for action. It increases physiological arousal, usually by stimulating heart rate and increasing blood pressure as preparation for fighting or fleeing a threat (known as the fight-or-flight response). The **parasympathetic nervous system,** on the other hand, decreases arousal, conserving the body's energy and resources. It balances the sympathetic system by slowing heart rate and decreasing blood pressure, for example.

The spinal cord contains neural pathways that link the peripheral nervous system to the brain. The brain consists of three main parts: the hindbrain, the midbrain, and the forebrain (see Figure 1.2).

The Hindbrain. The **hindbrain** includes structures that maintain activities essential to life. For example, it includes the *medulla,* which maintains and regulates basic functions such as breathing, swallowing, heart rate, and blood pressure; the *reticular formation,* which controls arousal, attention, and sleep–wakefulness cycles; and the *cerebellum,* which maintains balance and posture and controls locomotion and finely coordinated movements such as threading a needle. Damage to parts of the hindbrain can leave a person comatose.

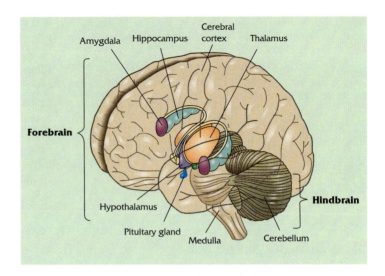

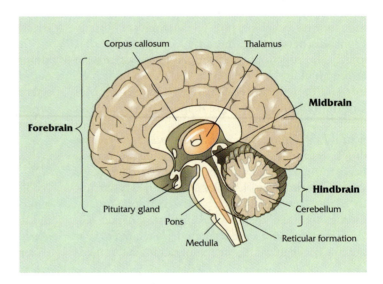

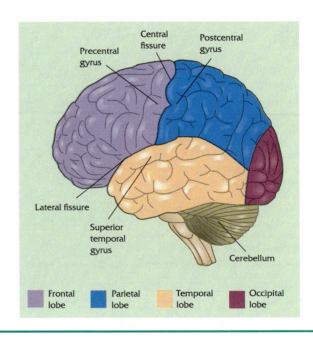

FIGURE 1.2

The Human Brain
These three figures show major regions of the brain, with a focus on the left cerebral hemisphere and the structures of the forebrain.

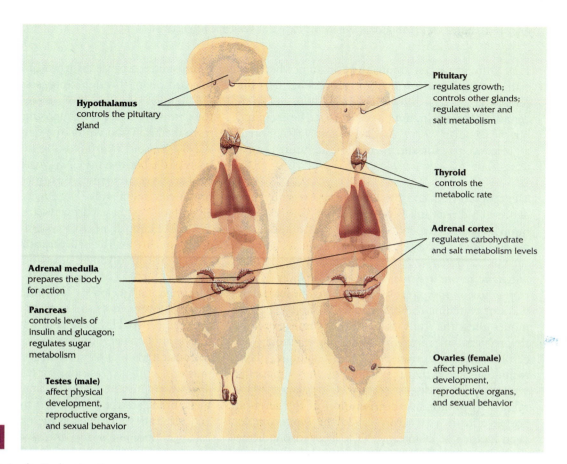

Major Glands in the Endocrine System

The glands of the endocrine system release their hormones directly into the bloodstream. The hypothalamus, exerts control over the pituitary, the master gland of the endocrine system.

The Midbrain. The **midbrain** helps coordinate head and eye movements and controls gross movements of the body and limbs. The midbrain is also involved in basic responses to visual, auditory, and tactile stimuli and regulates responsiveness to rewarding stimuli.

The Forebrain. The largest part of the brain, the **forebrain,** includes structures that are responsible for a wide variety of functions, from processing sensory information and guiding the body's movements, to accomplishing the most complex aspects of thought and imagination.

The thalamus, hypothalamus, and cerebrum are key structures in the forebrain. Figure 1.2 shows their location. The **thalamus** is a kind of relay station that receives, analyzes, and sends on information from all the senses (except the sense of smell). Located just below the thalamus is a small but vital structure called the **hypothalamus,** which regulates hunger, thirst, the sex drive, and other motivated behavior.

The hypothalamus receives information from the autonomic nervous system about the functioning of internal organs, and helps regulate the activity of those organs. It responds to chemical messengers called **hormones** that are secreted by the cortical (outer) portion of the adrenal glands and other parts of the **endocrine system,** a network of glands that affect organs throughout the body by releasing hormones into the bloodstream (see Figure 1.3). The hypothalamus connects to the **pituitary gland,** which in turn serves as the director of the endocrine system. As we will discuss in later chapters, activity in the hypothalamus and pituitary are key elements of our physiological responses to stressful events. The hypothalamus is also part of the *limbic system,* a group of interconnected forebrain structures that play important roles in regulating emotion and memory.

The Cerebrum and Cerebral Cortex. The **cerebrum,** and especially its outer covering, the **cerebral cortex,** is the part of the human brain that is the most distinct from the brains of other mammals and the most active in such distinctively human capabilities as abstract thought and complex language. The cortex is divided into two hemispheres, each of which is itself divided into regions, called *lobes* (see Figure

1.2). Different lobes are involved in somewhat specialized aspects of information processing. It is the cerebral cortex that allows humans to think and wonder about the world, not just react to it. We can plan, but we can also worry. As Carl Sagan (1977) noted, a "price we pay for anticipation of the future is anxiety about it."

Mental Disorders and the Brain. Until recently, evidence of a direct link between mental disorders and brain structures depended on autopsies or, perhaps, neurosurgery. Today, however, imaging techniques such as *computerized axial tomography (CT scans), magnetic resonance imaging (MRI scans),* and *positron emission tomography (PET scans)* provide new ways of watching the brain at work. Imaging techniques allow the study of how brain damage or subtle problems in brain functioning might account for certain mental dysfunctions. For example, these techniques show that the mental decline in patients with Alzheimer's disease (described in Chapter 11) is related to progressive degeneration in the cerebral cortex and in a structure called the *hippocampus* (Van Hoesen & Damasio, 1987). They also indicate that some cases of schizophrenia (discussed in Chapter 10) are related to atrophy of brain tissue and to irregularities in the flow of blood to the brain (Gur & Pearlson, 1993).

The Role of Neurotransmitters. Researchers have also investigated the possibility that disorders such as schizophrenia might be linked not only to problems in particular brain structures but also to breakdowns in communication among the brain's millions of nerve cells or **neurons.** All normal activity, from moving an arm to thinking rationally, depends on smooth and organized communication among neurons in the brain. This communication occurs when electrochemical activity in one neuron causes it to *fire,* thus releasing chemicals called **neurotransmitters** that carry messages between neurons.

As Figure 1.4 shows, neurotransmitters are released from the end of an **axon,** a long fiber on the neuron; they flow across the **synapse,** a tiny gap between neurons, and come in contact with branchlike structures called **dendrites** on the next neuron. If the neurotransmitter binds with *receptor sites* on the dendrite, a signal is sent up the dendrite; the signal makes this neuron either more or less ready to fire. After affecting other neurons, neu-

rotransmitters are reabsorbed into the neurons that released them, through a process called **reuptake.**

Bundles of axons from many neurons make up the pathways along which information travels to and from the brain and within the central nervous system (CNS). Sensory neurons bring information from all parts of the body to the CNS where it is processed and then sent via motor neurons to control the response of muscles and glands. The effects of communication along many of these pathways are well-known.

For example, neuron systems in the brain that communicate via the neurotransmitter acetylcholine (ACH) are involved in learning (Deutsch, 1983), memory (Buzsaki & Gage, 1988), and sleep (Sitaram, Moore, & Gillin, 1978). The muscles involved in voluntary movement of the arms or legs contract when they receive ACH. In the parasympathetic branch of the autonomic nervous system (ANS), this same neurotransmitter acts to slow heart rate, lower blood pressure, and increase digestion. **Norepinephrine** is another important neurotransmitter. In the sympathetic branch of the ANS, it acts to increase heart rate and respiration. Systems in the brain that communicate via norepinephrine are involved in sleep and arousal (Aston-Jones & Bloom, 1981), attention (Waterhouse et al., 1988), mood (Sulser & Sanders-Bush, 1989), and eating behavior (Leibowitz, et al., 1985).

It is no wonder that drugs that alter neurotransmitters can produce complex psychological and behavioral effects. As you will see in Chapters 3–15, most of the drugs used to treat mental disorders have a strong effect on the level or activity of some neurotransmitter.

Genetic Influences on Abnormality

Why would neurotransmitters operate abnormally? Why do brain structures deteriorate? In some cases, genes may hold the answer. **Genes,** the basic units of heredity, determine many aspects of who and what we are, from eye color and skin tone to body type and vulnerability to disease. At conception, the new cell formed by the fertilization of an egg by sperm contains 23 pairs of chromosomes—half from the father and half from the mother. As the new cell divides and redivides into millions of cells, a human being is formed out of a unique combination of genes from both parents.

What Are Genes and What Do They Do? Human heredity is determined by an estimated 100,000 genes, each of which rests at a specific location, or *locus,* along a chromosome. Chemically, genes are

Connections

What do neurotransmitters have to do with mental disorders? *GABA* affects anxiety disorders, (see Chapter 7, p. 222), and *dopamine* is involved in schizophrenia (see Chapter 10, p. 358).

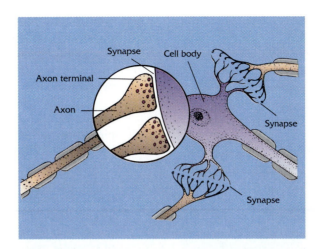

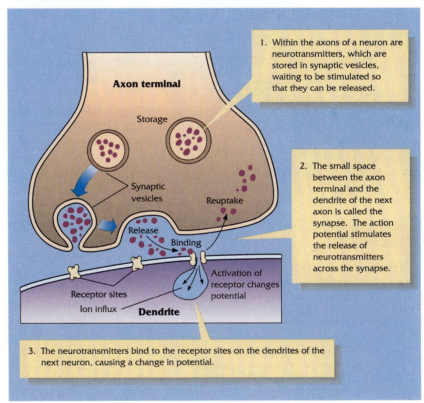

1. Within the axons of a neuron are neurotransmitters, which are stored in synaptic vesicles, waiting to be stimulated so that they can be released.

2. The small space between the axon terminal and the dendrite of the next axon is called the synapse. The action potential stimulates the release of neurotransmitters across the synapse.

3. The neurotransmitters bind to the receptor sites on the dendrites of the next neuron, causing a change in potential.

FIGURE 1.4

The Synapse and Communication Between Neurons

When a neuron fires, the nervous impulse is carried along the axon, which triggers release of a neurotransmitter across the synapse, where it may bind to a receptor on the dendrite of another neuron. The result is the spread of an electrical impulse on the dendrite of the second neuron. This impulse may stimulate or inhibit this neuron from firing and releasing its own neurotransmitters.

strands of **deoxyribonucleic acid,** or **DNA** (see Figure 1.5 on page 16), which is made up of nucleotides. Each **nucleotide** consists of sugar, phosphate, and bases containing nitrogen. Through a complex series of steps, DNA directs chemical reactions that assemble amino acids into proteins. Which proteins are produced depends on the particular order in which the nitrogen-containing bases occur in the nucleotides. Proteins, in turn, form and direct the structure of human cells. In short, DNA provides the genetic code that, during prenatal de-

velopment, determines how proteins are used to build each cell in the body, including the brain.

Note that genes affect physical features and behavior indirectly, by determining the production of proteins. Figure 1.6 on page 17 summarizes the process. However, not every gene is expressed in a person's physical characteristics or behavior. Whether a gene is expressed depends on which other genes are present. At a particular locus, alternative forms, or **alleles,** of the gene are inherited—one from the mother and one from the father. If the alleles are

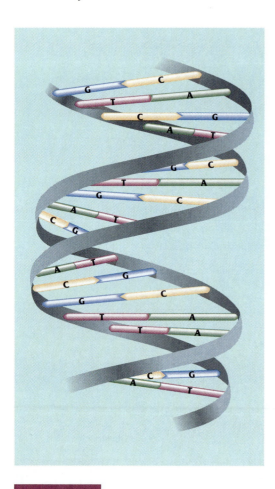

The Structure of DNA

A segment of DNA consists of two strands twisted in a double spiral. The sides of the spiral are composed of sugar and phosphate. The connecting "rungs" that keep the spiral together are four nitrogen-containing bases: adenine (A), thymine (T), cytosine (C), and guanine (G). Adenine always binds with thymine and cytosine with guanine. These four bases form the genetic alphabet that translates into proteins.

governed by *polygenic inheritance,* involving multiple, interacting genes. The degree to which a genetically determined predisposition is actually expressed in behavior or physical features is called **penetrance.**

A faulty gene or a problem with genetic expression can cause serious dysfunctions. For example, *phenylketonuria (PKU)* is a rare disorder that has been traced to the malfunction of a single gene (see Chapter 4). This malfunction creates a deficiency in the enzyme that metabolizes phenylalanine, an amino acid found in many foods. Unless given a special diet that excludes foods containing phenylalanine, individuals with PKU suffer a variety of physical problems and progressive mental deterioration. PKU illustrates the fact that a person's genetic makeup, or **genotype,** interacts with the environment, in this case a nutritional environment, to determine one's **phenotype,** the characteristics and traits actually displayed.

The expression of genetic predispositions is also influenced by such prenatal factors as hormones, drugs, maternal nutrition, and health; by childhood illnesses; by the home and school environment; and by a variety of other social experiences and relationships. In short, genetic endowment (often referred to as *nature*) is always interacting with past and present environmental factors (often called *nurture*) to shape physical and behavioral characteristics.

Behavioral Genetics.   Scientists in the field of **behavioral genetics** use specialized research methods to study genetic influences on behavior and to understand the combined influences of nature and nurture on normal and abnormal behavior (Plomin, 1989). For example, to explore a possible genetic predisposition to a particular form of abnormal behavior, behavioral geneticists often conduct **family studies** that examine the pattern of disorder in members of the same family. These studies capitalize on the fact that the closer the relationship between people the more genes they share. Identical, or *monozygotic,* twins share 100 percent of their genes; parents and their children as well as fraternal—or *dizygotic* twins —and other siblings share about 50 percent of their genes. Nieces, nephews, aunts, and uncles who are genetically related share about 25 percent, first cousins about 12.5 percent. Thus, if a trait is based entirely on genetic heritage, we should be able to predict the likelihood that two individuals will share that trait from a knowledge of their genetic similarity. For example, *Huntington's disease,* a genetically determined disorder that causes severe behavioral and mental problems (Emerich, Cahill, & Sanberg, 1994), is caused by a single dominant gene. Thus,

alike, the person is said to be **homozygous** for that gene; if the alleles are different, the person is said to be **heterozygous.** Some alleles are **recessive,** which means that they can be expressed only when they are paired with a similar allele from the other parent. Other alleles are **dominant** and can be expressed whenever they are present.

The path from genes to physical characteristics or behavior is further complicated by the fact that many genes at different locations influence most characteristics. No single gene controls height or skin color, for example; these characteristics are

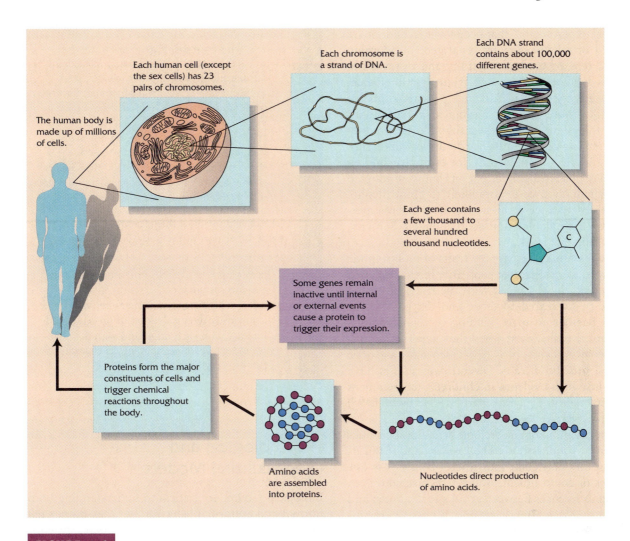

FIGURE 1.6

Genes and Their Function

Segments of a DNA molecule such as that shown in Figure 1.5 make up the thousands of genes that transfer hereditary messages. As the bottom portion of this figure shows, the genes exert their influence by directing the synthesis of proteins. Proteins, in turn, direct the creation of new cells and regulate their functioning.

the child of a parent with the Huntington's gene has a 50 percent likelihood of having this gene, too.

However, genetic influences are seldom as clear as in Huntington's disease. For one thing, closer kin tend to share more similar environments as well as more similar genes. Finding high **concordance**—or sharing—of a trait or disorder in close relatives cannot by itself prove that the trait or disorder is inherited. Siblings might display the same disorder because they are eating the same food or living near the same toxic waste dump, not because they share genes. This possibility is gruesomely illustrated by *kuru,* a fatal disease of the central nervous system found only in cannibalistic tribes in the highlands of New Guinea.

Some of the symptoms of kuru are similar to those of Huntington's disease, and because those most closely related to kuru victims are most likely to develop the disease themselves, it was long considered a genetic disorder. Recent research suggests, however, that the cause may be a virus that is transmitted when individuals eat the brains of recently deceased relatives in a respectful attempt to acquire the relative's traits. Closer family members were allowed to consume the part of the brain most likely to contain the virus. With the decline of cannibalism among these tribes, kuru has almost disappeared.

The interaction of nature and nurture can be explored more powerfully by observing results of the "natural experiments" that occur when children are adopted or when twins are separated. In **adoption studies,** researchers look at traits and disorders in persons who were separated from their biological parents at very early ages. If such persons' traits are more like those of their biological parents (with whom they share many genes) than like their adoptive parents, a genetic influence on those traits is supported. In one adoption study, for example, children who were born to alcoholic parents but were adopted by nonalcoholics were more likely to abuse alcohol themselves than were children of nonalcoholic parents reared by alcohol abusers (Cloninger, Bohman, & Sigvardsson, 1981).

Twin studies compare the traits of monozygotic twins who were separated soon after birth and raised in different environments with the traits of monozygotic twins reared together and dizygotic twins reared together or apart. Finding very similar traits in identical twins, even when they experienced different environments, provides evidence for a genetic influence on those traits. Several twin studies have found just such evidence in children's temperament and personality (e.g., Bouchard, 1984; Buss, 1995; Loehlin, 1989; Tellegen et al., 1988).

The meaning of research on behavioral genetics is often misunderstood. The results cannot tell us whether any particular individual's behavior is due to genes or environment. And the research does not explain differences between groups such as men and women or Black Americans and White Americans. What behavioral genetics research can do is *estimate the average influence* that genes and environment exert on *individual differences within a group of people.*

We will describe evidence from numerous studies of behavioral genetics in later chapters as we discuss genetic and environmental influences on a variety of abnormal behavior patterns. As this chapter's Controversy section on pages 34 and 35 suggests, claims about genetic influences on abnormal behavior often lead to passionate debates about the relative importance of nature and nurture.

In Review

The biological model explains abnormal behavior in terms of physical malfunctions of the nervous system. Of particular interest are:

- the cerebral cortex, the part of the brain that is involved in abstract thought and language;

- the hypothalamus, a structure of the forebrain that receives information from the autonomic nervous system, which determines physiological arousal; connects to the pituitary gland, which directs the endocrine system; is part of the system that responds to stress; and is part of the system that regulates emotion and memory; and

- the neurotransmitters, chemical messengers that, when released by neurons, stimulate or inhibit the firing of other neurons.

The development of the nervous system, and every other part of the body, is controlled by the genes, which:

- are composed of DNA and are located on the chromosomes;

- influence an organism's characteristics by orchestrating the production of proteins; and

- interact with each other and with the environment to produce the unique characteristics of every human being.

Psychological and Sociocultural Models

Biological factors are critical to understanding both normal and abnormal behavior, but they do not tell the whole story. Many mental disorders occur without any apparent biological reason. To understand abnormality fully, clinicians recognize that they must also consider the influence of psychological and sociocultural variables. These variables play a prominent role in psychodynamic, behavioral, cognitive, phenomenological, interpersonal, and sociocultural theories of abnormality.

Psychodynamic Theories

Formal psychological models of abnormal behavior began with the work of Sigmund Freud. Freud's **psychoanalysis** is defined by the idea that both normal and abnormal behaviors are influenced by *unconscious forces*—especially sexual and aggressive instincts. From this perspective, even apparently such innocent events as forgetting a friend's name or writing the word *date* instead of *data* can be interpreted as expressing feelings of anger or lust of which the person is unaware. Freud believed that, because sexual or aggressive instincts often conflict with the moral demands and the realistic constraints of society, each individual faces a lifelong struggle to find ways of expressing these instincts without suffering punishment, anxiety, or guilt. As a result, said Freud, a hidden war among aspects of personality that represent instinct, reason, and morality rages within us. From the Freudian perspective, Nelson McGrath's behavior problems, like all other psychological disorders, result from this war, and they are best treated by psychoanalysis, a "talking cure" that is designed to help people become aware of, understand, and resolve unconscious conflicts.

Freudian Personality Structures. As shown in Figure 1.7, Freud identified three personality structures: id, ego, and superego. The **id** is the location of the most basic, unconscious instincts. Present at birth, the id provides the energy (which Freud called **libido**) that motivates us to satisfy our need for food, water, and other basic requirements of life. Id operates on the **pleasure principle** ("if it feels good, do it"), seeking immediate gratification of its desires and impulses. Around the age of 2, however, infants begin to learn that cultural rules place limits on their behavior, and they require "appropriate" patterns of eating, speaking, toileting, and the like. The child's **ego**, or "self," said Freud, begins to develop in response to these limits. The ego operates on the **reality principle**. It constrains the id by seeking rational compromises between the blind demands of the id and the limits im-

posed by other people. We can see the workings of the ego when, instead of simply grabbing a cookie, a child asks permission to have one. Eventually, often by the age of 5 or so, the child begins to adopt, or *introject,* the rules taught by the culture, and young children can often be heard scolding themselves for wrongdoing. **Superego** is the name Freud gave to the part of the personality that becomes the repository of cultural rules, models of ideal behavior, and moral values. The superego is a stern taskmaster; it insists on socially acceptable, even perfect behavior.

Freud believed that the constant conflicts among the id, ego, and superego can cause anxiety, guilt, and many other unpleasant emotional problems, especially if unconscious desires reach consciousness. He said that the ego employs a variety of **defense mechanisms** that operate mostly outside our awareness to minimize these conflicts and keep them from reaching consciousness. One of the most important defense mechanisms is **repression,** a form of motivated forgetting by which the ego keeps us unaware of threatening impulses from the id.

Like trying to hold an inflated beach ball underwater, defense mechanisms take a lot of energy and can ultimately fail. If they do, said Freud, the person retreats (or *regresses*) to even more primitive, immature behaviors reminiscent of early childhood. In extreme cases, the regression may result in incon-

FIGURE 1.7

The Psychoanalytic Personality Structure

Sigmund Freud (1856–1939), shown here with his daughter Anna, was the founder of psychoanalysis, the first comprehensive psychological theory of abnormal behavior. At right is Freud's own drawing of his three-part conception of personality, showing id, ego, and superego and the influence of repression on the unconscious.

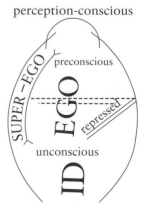

tinence, mutism, and other infantile behaviors associated with severe mental disorders.

Stages of Psychosexual Development. Because his clients reported many sexual events from their childhoods, Freud initially believed that their problems stemmed from sexual molestation by parents or other relatives. Various forms of this idea enjoy contemporary empirical support (Trickett & Putnam, 1993), but within a few years of proposing this theory, Freud abandoned it (Masson, 1983). Instead, he claimed that these sexual recollections were not memories of real events, but of taboo sexual wishes and fantasies from childhood. Freud further believed that the symptoms of mental disorders are lingering surrogates of long-repressed sexual fantasies that the id, ego, and superego still battle over. The specific nature of the symptoms, said Freud, are determined largely by the psychosexual stage during which the original conflicts are experienced.

According to Freud, all children pass through **psychosexual stages of development.** He named each stage for the part of the body most involved with pleasurable experiences at the time. The first year or so is called the **oral stage** because eating, sucking, and biting are the main sources of pleasure. If oral needs are neglected or overindulged, the child may fail to pass through this stage without clinging to, or becoming *fixated* on, oral behavior patterns. Freud believed that the stronger the fixation at a given stage, the more behaviors typical of that stage would be evident later in life, and the more likely it would be that the person would regress to that level when under stress or in a crisis. Oral fixation is reflected, according to Freud, in habitual smoking, overeating, intemperate drinking, and excessive talking.

The **anal stage** begins in the second year, when the anus and stimuli associated with elimination and retention of feces become the focus of pleasure. Toilet training is the critical feature of this stage. When parents and their child clash over the time and place of elimination, the relative passivity of the oral stage is replaced by defiance, as the term "terrible twos" suggests. Toilet training that is too strict or too lax can result, said Freud, in adults who are "tight" and overly controlled or "loose" and disorderly. Thus, Freudians view excessive cleanliness, orderliness, and organization, as well as carelessness and disorganization, as anal characteristics.

Connections

Does the sexual abuse of children have links to later abnormal behavior? For contemporary answers to this question, see Chapter 8, pp. 264–266 and Chapter 12, p. 429.

Freud said that the genitals become the focus of a child's pleasure in the third or fourth year, so he marked this as the onset of the **phallic stage.** Freud argued that at this time young boys begin to feel sexual desire for their mothers and wish to eliminate their fathers as sexual competitors. He called this situation the **Oedipus complex** because it recapitulates the plot of the Greek tragedy, *Oedipus Rex.* The boy fears that his desires will be discovered and that his father will punish him with castration. Normally, the boy resolves the conflict and reduces his anxiety by repressing his sexual urges and forming an identification with his father. **Identification** involves the boy's imitating the father's behavior, emulating obvious aspects of his gender role, and, as an adult, finding an appropriate female sex partner.

Little girls resolve the Oedipus complex differently. Freud claimed that female children feel inferior because they feel they have already been castrated and therefore, experience *penis envy.* To overcome these feelings, girls develop a desire to have a baby as a kind of "substitute penis" and, as a result, identify with their mother's gender role.

Freudians see fixation at the phallic stage as responsible for many adult problems, especially those involving anxiety in dealing with parents and other authority figures, confusion about sex roles, and sexual dysfunctions. Indeed, Freud believed that Oedipal problems were the core of all neuroses and many personality disorders.

A **latency stage** ensues around the age of five or six as the turmoil of resolving the Oedipus complex subsides. Children spend the next several years focusing on academic skills and same-sex friendships. The **genital stage** begins in adolescence when physical maturity is nearly complete, and it continues through adulthood. Pleasure is once again focused on the genital area, but, if earlier development has gone well, the pursuit of pleasure is not characterized by the selfishness of the phallic stage. Instead, sexuality is fused with love for another and finds expression within a long-term relationship.

Contemporary Psychodynamic Theories. Many of Freud's colleagues and students—not to mention the general public—have been dissatisfied with his emphasis on the unconscious, his belief in childhood sexuality, his emphasis on male rather than female sexuality, his focus on instincts as the major motivation behind human behavior, and other aspects of his work. Consequently, several theorists suggested revisions to Freud's theory of personality development and mental disorders. Some of these revisions involved a change in emphasis; others, such as Carl Jung's (1875–1961), altered or even rejected many of

Freud's main principles. We will mention only a few modified psychoanalytic theories here (more comprehensive coverage can be found in Eagle, 1984; Munroe, 1955; Slipp, 1981).

One of Freud's earliest followers, Alfred Adler (1870–1937), argued that the most important psychological motivator of human behavior was not instinct, but a "striving for superiority" aimed at compensating for the sense of inferiority everyone feels as a helpless child. The particular way a child pursues superiority, first in the family, then in the wider social world, constitutes what Adler called a *style of life.*

Adaptive lifestyles, said Adler, are characterized by *social interest,* a blend of cooperation, common sense, and an interest in promoting the welfare of others. Maladaptive lifestyles involve extreme competitiveness, excessive dependency or withdrawal, preoccupation with selfish worries, and other problems. Thus, if a little girl discovers that she can control others by pleading for assistance in everything from eating to dressing, she might develop the misconceptions that she is entitled to special consideration and that she cannot solve her own problems. As an adult, her dependent lifestyle might be reflected in symptoms of depression or anxiety as she seeks new ways of getting others to attend to and assist her.

Ego analysts assign a larger role than Freud did to conscious personality factors and see the ego as an autonomous force, not just a mediator of unconscious conflicts. Erik Erikson (1946), for example, proposed eight stages of *psychosocial* (not psychosexual) development that stress an individual's interactions with others rather than conflict over instincts. At each stage, the person faces a social crisis that is either resolved or left partly unfinished. Positive outcomes at each stage help the person deal with the crisis of the next stage; unsettled problems interfere with continued development. For example, if infants do not develop the feeling that parents can be trusted to take care of their needs, they will be unlikely to feel secure enough to try new behaviors on their own as is expected around the age of 2.

One of the more important modern variants on psychoanalysis is object relations theory, associated with analysts such as Ronald Fairbairn (1952), Donald Winnicott (1965), Margaret Mahler (Mahler, Pine, & Bergman, 1975), and Melanie Klein (1975). Closely related to object relations views are the theories of Otto Kernberg (1976) and Heinz Kohut (1977). The fundamental assumption of **object relations theory** is that the adult personality is based on the nature and quality of interpersonal relationships, especially in the early interactions between infant and caregiver. If these interactions do not allow infants to feel pride in themselves or to develop a secure sense of self-esteem, for example, they cannot achieve a stable sense of self; the result will be disturbed behavior in childhood and adulthood. Another theme of many object relations theorists is that parents must allow or encourage infants to move from a state of complete dependency to one in which the child feels secure as a separate and independent adult. Failure to achieve adequate separation and individuation can lead to serious personality problems in adulthood.

Psychodynamic Treatment.   The primary goal of Freudian psychoanalysis is to help clients gain insight into the unconscious origins of their behavior so that they can eventually gain control over their impulses through a strengthened ego. Freud believed that clients gain this insight through an analyst's skillful use of techniques such as *free association* ("say whatever comes into your mind without trying to control it") and the *interpretation* of dreams, slips of the tongue, and everyday mistakes that might reveal a hidden motive. The most important technique is *transference,* in which clients, responding to the analyst, relive emotional reactions that are actually reenactments of early emotional conflicts with their parents. Because the transference reveals how past conflicts are still influencing their lives, clients can clearly recognize the importance of these conflicts and then gradually begin to resolve them. Therefore, the psychoanalyst first allows the transference to emerge and then helps clients understand what it means for their current lives.

Variations on Freud's psychoanalytic theories have led to variations of his treatment techniques. Because ego analysts assume that people are more capable of actively controlling their behavior than Freud believed them to be, their treatments concentrate more on exploring clients' egos and helping clients understand how they rely too heavily on defense mechanisms to cope with personal conflicts and environmental demands. Object relations therapists, on the other hand, use the therapeutic relationship to repair the psychological defects and insults that clients suffered as very young children. The goal is not so much to understand the real or imagined traumas of childhood as it is to give clients a second chance at forming the secure and healthy relationships that they missed in childhood.

Behavioral Theories

Psychoanalytic theories of disorder grew out of nineteenth-century therapists' efforts to treat disturbed individuals. During the first half of the twentieth century, several alternative psychological theories emerged that sought to explain abnormal behavior in terms of the laws of learning being mapped out by academic psychologists' laboratory research on human and animal behavior. These **behavioral theories** (also called **learning theories**) are based on the assumption that genetic and biological factors provide an individual's basic physical structures and general tendencies but that specific behaviors, normal and abnormal, are shaped by people's experiences with the world. Behaviorists place special emphasis on how people *learn* to behave as a result of these experiences.

Behavioral theorists differ among themselves primarily in terms of the learning processes they emphasize. *Operant* theorists stress the functional relationships between behavior and its environmental consequences, especially rewards and punishments. Others concentrate on *respondent,* or classical, conditioning and the associations that develop between stimuli and responses (such as between being bitten by a dog and later developing a fear of dogs). *Cognitive–behavioral* theorists see behavior as guided not only by consequences and associations, but also by the thoughts and expectations people acquire as they grow. They emphasize differences in the way people process and understand information about their lives.

Operant Conditioning.

Operant conditioning is rooted in the work of Edward L. Thorndike (1874–1949), an American psychologist who proposed that learning follows the *law of effect:* behaviors followed by pleasurable outcomes are more likely to be repeated, while behaviors that lead to unpleasant effects are less likely to be repeated. Expanding on this basic idea, psychologist B. F. Skinner (1904–1990) argued that it is not necessary to focus on conscious or unconscious mental activity in order to understand human behavior, because all behavior is learned as a function of the *antecedent conditions* in which it is displayed and the *consequences* that follow it. Thus, said Skinner, behavior can be explained by looking at the functional relationships between *operant behavior*—acts, such as crying, that "operate" on the environment—and its observable antecedents and consequences. According to Skinner, the act of ordering a pizza can be explained by noting the number of hours since the person last ate and whether pizza-ordering behavior has been rewarded in the past. There is no need to invoke the mentalistic concept of "hunger."

Behavior is strengthened through **reinforcement,** that is, when positive consequences follow the behavior. Positive consequences can take two forms: the appearance of something pleasant, such as food or praise, or the disappearance of something unpleasant, such as an annoying sound. Being paid for shoveling a snowy sidewalk is an example of the first form of reinforcement, called *positive reinforcement;* getting rid of a headache after taking a pain reliever illustrates the second kind of reinforcement, called *negative reinforcement.* Any type of reinforcement makes behavior such as shoveling snow or taking aspirin *more* likely to occur on appropriate occasions in the future. Thus, some behaviorists might suggest that Nelson McGrath's aversion to young women was based on negative reinforcement because the act of avoiding them reduced his anxiety.

Behavior is *less* likely to occur when it is followed by negative consequences; this process is called **punishment.** Negative consequences can take two forms: the appearance of something unpleasant, such as pain, or the loss of something valued, such as privileges. Behavior can also be made less likely to occur through **extinction,** or the absence of *any* notable consequences. Extinction is at work when we give up calling someone on the telephone after repeatedly getting no answer.

Often, behavior is not reinforced or punished every time it occurs. Employees, for example, may be paid once a month, not after each task they do. Skinner noted that such *schedules of reinforcement* often hold the key to understanding certain aspects of behavior. Intermittent reinforcement results in remarkably persistent behavior; note how long some people will gamble or play golf even though the rewards may be infrequent.

Classical Conditioning.

Another behavioral theory of abnormality has its roots in the work of Ivan Pavlov (1849–1936). Pavlov and other Russian scientists in the early twentieth century believed that behavior was based on reflexes that were automatically elicited by the environment. In his famous experiments with dogs, Pavlov repeatedly paired an *unconditioned stimulus* such as food, which elicits a reflexive (or *unconditioned response*) such as salivation, with a neutral stimulus such as a tone. Eventually, the neutral stimulus became a *conditioned stimulus* that elicits salivation as a *conditioned response;* the dogs learned to salivate in response to the tone. This process of **classical conditioning** is depicted in Figure 1.8 on page 23.

Behavioral psychologists soon began to apply the laws of classical conditioning to the study and treatment of abnormal behavior. The most famous early example of this work was the case of "Little Albert," reported by John Watson and Rosalie Rayner (Watson & Rayner, 1920).

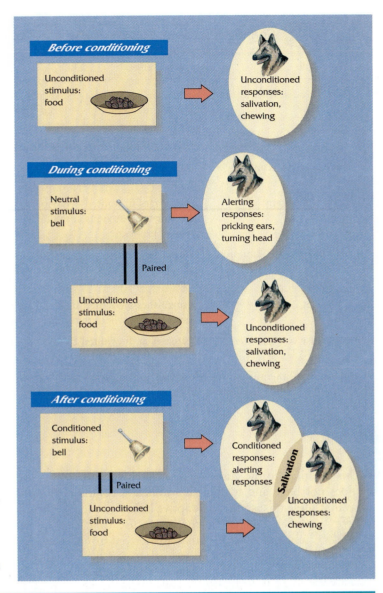

FIGURE 1.8

Pavlovian Conditioning

In classical conditioning, the bell (the neutral stimulus) is sounded just before food (the unconditioned stimulus) is presented to the animal. After several pairings, the bell becomes a conditioned stimulus and elicits a set of responses that resemble the unconditioned responses that the food alone elicited. Behavioral psychologists believe that certain phobias can develop through classical conditioning.

*W*atson and Rayner first showed a 9-month-old infant, Albert B., several stimuli, including a white rat, a dog, a rabbit, a monkey, masks, and a burning newspaper. He showed no fear of these objects, but he did display a reflexive fear response to a sudden loud noise. To determine whether fear, like salivation, could become a conditioned response to a conditioned stimulus, Watson and Rayner repeatedly paired the loud noise with the sight of the white rat. After about a week, Albert did indeed show fear when he saw the rat.

Behavioral Treatment. A few years after the case of "Little Albert" was reported, Mary Cover Jones used classical conditioning to *reduce* children's learned fears by pairing the feared stimulus (such as a rabbit) with a pleasant activity such as eating (Jones, 1924). Researchers have applied both classical and operant conditioning methods to a wide range of problems, including fears, sexual disorders, and substance abuse disorders. By the 1960s, an arsenal of new behavioral techniques had been developed and tested (Eysenck & Rachman, 1965; Wolpe, 1958). Table 1.2 on page 24 describes some of these.

As discussed in Chapter 16, behavioral treatments, also known as **behavior therapy** or **behavior modification**, are aimed at helping clients decrease specific maladaptive behaviors and increase adaptive ones. The focus of behavior therapy is on the here and now. Less attention is paid to early psychologi-

TABLE 1.2 Common Behavior Therapy Treatment Techniques

Technique	How it is used
Systematic desensitization	Reduces anxiety by having clients visualize a graded series of anxiety-provoking stimuli while maintaining a relaxed state.
Exposure	Reduces anxiety by having clients maintain real or imagined contact with anxiety-provoking stimuli until the fear dissipates.
Social skills training	Teaches anxious or socially ineffective clients how to interact more confidently and competently with others.
Aversive therapy	Discourages unwanted behavior by pairing the behavior or cues that lead to the behavior with noxious stimuli such as electric shock, nausea, or imaginary aversive events.
Successive approximation	Teaches new behavior by initially reinforcing any act that resembles the desired behavior and then increasing the standards for reinforcement until the behavior meets a final criterion.
Time out	Extinguishes unwanted behavior by temporarily removing the person, usually a child, from a setting where reinforcers exist.
Response cost	Decreases an unwanted behavior by removing a reward or privilege following the behavior; fines are an example.
Self-control therapy	Teaches people how to modify their own behaviors by first observing the conditions under which behaviors occur and then manipulating the contingencies that apply to the behaviors.

cal history than to the current skills the client does or does not have and to the environmental conditions that serve to sustain maladaptive behaviors. In brief, behavior therapists use treatment techniques that are derived from the same basic laws of learning that led to problem behaviors in the first place. These interventions are aimed at specific changes that can be quantitatively measured.

Cognitive Theories

To many observers, operant or classical conditioning explanations of human behavior and behavior disorders seem incomplete because they pay too little attention to what people *think* about the world and themselves. By the 1970s, psychologists who agreed with this critique had developed cognitive, or social learning, theories of development and behavior modification. These theories are actually part of a larger movement known as the cognitive revolution that began to sweep through all of psychology in the late 1960s.

Connections

For what mental disorders are behavioral treatments particularly useful? For a discussion of their effectiveness in treating childhood disorders, see Chapter 3, pp. 96–97.

According to **cognitive** and **social learning theories,** learning occurs not only as a result of operant and classical conditioning, but also through the way people process information about the world—what they attend to, perceive, think about, and remember.

Important Cognitive Processes. One prominent social learning theorist, Albert Bandura, emphasizes **observational learning** (Bandura, 1969, 1986). In his view, behavior develops not only through first-hand conditioning, but also as a result of observing other people—known as *models*—and the consequences of their behavior. For example, if a preschooler observed a parent repeatedly showing a fear of snakes, avoiding outdoor activities whenever there might be a chance of encountering snakes, and refusing to read about or view scenes containing snakes, the child might develop a phobia of snakes. According to Bandura, observational learning can stimulate new responses, inhibit or disinhibit already learned responses (as when a person violates a "Don't Walk" sign after watching someone else do so), and prompt behavior (as when people in an airport line up at an unattended check-in counter after a single prankster stands in front of it).

Expectancies also play a major role in social learning theories. For example, Julian Rotter (1954) has argued that the probability that a given behavior will occur depends on (1) what the person has learned to expect will happen after the response, and (2) the value the person places on that outcome. One type of expectancy is **self-efficacy,** the belief that one can successfully perform a given behavior, such as meeting new people at a party. Bandura (1977, 1982, 1986) believes that overt behavior is controlled by an individual's perceived self-efficacy: the higher the level of self-efficacy, the greater a person's aspirations and accomplishments will be. Other important cognitive processes include appraisals, attributions, and long-standing beliefs or assumptions.

Appraisals are individuals' evaluations of their own behavior and the behavior of others. They often precede and influence emotional reactions automatically and outside of a person's awareness. According to psychiatrist Aaron Beck (1976), individuals who always evaluate their performance as inadequate will interpret compliments as a sign that others are merely being polite. People who see the world in such a negative light see themselves as worthless and inadequate and are predisposed to depression.

Attributions are explanations for behavior and other events. They have three key characteristics: internality—whether we see the cause of an event as due to something about ourselves or something about the environment; stability—whether we see the cause as enduring or temporary; and globalness—whether we see the cause as specific to a given situation or affecting all situations. Thus, a student who explains having failed a test by saying "it was too hard" is employing an external, temporary, and specific attribution, whereas the statement "I am stupid" reflects an internal, stable, and global attribution (Abramson, Seligman, & Teasdale, 1978).

Albert Ellis has emphasized the role of enduring negative expectancies and especially what he calls *irrational beliefs* in the development of behavior disorders (Ellis, 1962). These irrational beliefs, said Ellis, are often associated with "should" statements (e.g., "Everyone should like me") and unrealistically high standards that leave a person doomed to failure or disappointment.

Connections

How do cognitive therapists target the distortions underlying anxiety disorders and depression? For answers, see Chapter 7, pp. 230–231, and Chapter 9, pp. 316–317.

Cognitive and Social-Learning Therapies. As described in Chapter 16, cognitive therapists attempt to modify maladaptive behavior by encouraging clients to consider new information and change the way they think about themselves, other people, and the world in general. They assume that psychological problems are largely caused by irrational or distorted thinking; correcting these misconceptions should therefore be therapeutic. Cognitions about the self—about a person's abilities or the degree to which a person is liked by others—are particularly important therapy targets because such cognitions affect how people react to success and failure, not only in love but also in work.

Across different cultures, children pay close attention to and model the behavior of their parents. They are able to imitate a wide range of behavior precisely.

For example, Beck's original version of cognitive therapy was developed to help depressed clients correct cognitive distortions to which they are prone—pessimistic, self-deprecating, catastrophizing beliefs about themselves and their future. Ellis, on the other hand, developed *rational-emotive therapy* as a way to attack, and help clients alter, chronic irrational beliefs such as "I must be perfect in everything I do" or "It is horrible when things do not work out as I planned."

Phenomenological Theories

A third psychological approach to abnormality, known as the **phenomenological,** or **humanistic, model,** asserts that human behavior is determined not by instincts, conflicts, or environmental consequences, but by each person's unique perception of the world at any given moment. Either these perceptions allow the person to live an emotionally authentic and behaviorally effective life or they constrain the person to a life that is based on false assumptions and excessive desires to meet others' expectations.

Carl Rogers's Self Theory. Carl Rogers (1902–1987) believed that people have an innate drive toward personal growth that he called *self-actualization.* And he saw all human behavior, normal and abnormal, as a reflection of the individual's efforts at self-actualization in the world the person perceives. Thus, aggression might be seen as seeking personal goals in a world that must be conquered, while speech anxiety might reflect personal growth stunted by the perceived threat of negative evaluations from others. Even Nelson McGrath's bizarre ideas would be viewed not as illness but as his attempt to cope with a world that he perceives as horribly dangerous.

According to Rogers, all experiences are evaluated as positive or negative, depending on whether they are consistent or inconsistent with the self-actualizing tendency. These evaluations are made partly on the basis of direct feelings and partly on the basis of other people's judgments. People value the positive regard of others so highly that they will seek it even if it means thinking and acting in ways that are *incongruent* with their own experience and even if it thwarts self-actualization. This tendency is encouraged, beginning in childhood, by *conditions of worth,* circumstances in which children get positive regard from others *only if* they display certain behaviors and attitudes. These conditions, first set up by parents, family, and others, eventually become part of the person's belief system in a manner similar to Freud's concept of superego.

Rogers said that when people try to please others at the expense of personal growth, they become uncomfortable with the incongruity, and they try to reduce their discomfort by distorting reality. For example, men whose early conditions of worth made crying or fearfulness unacceptable may distort their emotional experience by denying genuine feelings of sadness or fear (and perhaps ridiculing these feelings in others). According to Rogers, the greater the discrepancy between real feelings and self-concept, the more severe the resulting problems.

Maslow and Humanistic Psychology. Like Rogers, Abraham Maslow, one of the founders of humanistic psychology, saw people as capable of self-actualization, but he suggested that people's failure to realize their full potential is caused by unmet needs. Maslow (1954, 1962) believed that human needs form a hierarchy. At the base of the hierarchy are basic physiological requirements (such as food and water); needs for safety, security, love, belongingness, self-esteem, and self-actualization appear at successively higher levels. According to Maslow, lower-level needs must be at least partially satisfied before people can focus on higher-level needs. Thus, a starving person is unlikely to be concerned with fulfilling the need for love or belongingness.

Phenomenological Therapies. Phenomenologically oriented therapists view therapy as an opportunity for clients to discover how they have allowed themselves to become restricted or hemmed in by the expectations of others. As a result, they have stopped growing and do not take full responsibility for their lives. The therapist's main task, therfore, is to create a context in which clients feel free to explore their potential and to express a full range of emotions. In Chapter 16, we discuss how this is done in Rogers's client-centered therapy and in Fritz Perls's (1893–1970) Gestalt therapy.

Interpersonal Theories

Associated primarily with the American psychiatrist Harry Stack Sullivan, **interpersonal theory** explains abnormal behavior as the result of interaction styles that become so rigid and extreme that they are maladaptive. These fossilized interpersonal styles develop in people who are too anxious to behave flexibly and thus insist on interacting in one fixed way with everyone. Sullivan (1953) believed that psychological disorders result from interpersonal relationships that have become so disturbed that constructive interactions with others become impossible. Like Freud, Sullivan saw personality developing in a series of stages in which important skills and tasks appeared. But unlike Freud, Sullivan concentrated on major *interpersonal*, rather than psychosexual, issues typical of each stage.

Sullivan (1953) believed that adult relationships are governed by a rule of reciprocity. In relationships that work well, people negotiate their complementary needs so smoothly that they remain largely unaware of why they interact easily. Smooth transactions occur, for example, when both parties share a friendly attitude toward each other or when a dominant person interacts with someone who is submissive. However, if one person approaches others with anxiety and inordinately strong needs for security, for example, that person will inevitably frustrate relationships until they are either terminated or filled with desperation and unhappiness.

According to Sullivan, people try to feel secure and prevent anxiety through repeated interpersonal ploys (Carson, 1969). They elicit, or "pull" certain behaviors from others by using a typical interpersonal style (Leary, 1957). Interpersonal theory appears to account especially well for *personality disorders*, which are extreme and inflexible behaviors that cause substantial difficulties in a person's social life (see Chapter 12).

From the interpersonal perspective, treatment of disordered behavior involves helping people to develop more flexible, less extreme ways of relating to others. Take, as an example, the antisocial client whose style of interaction is to be hostile and dominant toward everyone. This style "invites" others, including therapists, to be hostile and submissive in return. The interpersonal therapist would try to act in a consistently friendly and dominant manner, thus counteracting, foiling, and forcing the antisocial client to give up this coercive interpersonal strategy. Interpersonal therapists also help clients try out new behaviors in the safety of therapy sessions and then encourage them to use these new behaviors with other people.

The Sociocultural Model

All the models we have discussed so far focus on internal dysfunctions, conflicts, or deficits that ultimately result in abnormal behavior. They share an assumption that something *inside* a person is disturbed and needs to be repaired. Without necessarily denying the role of such factors, the **sociocultural model** of abnormality emphasizes *external* factors, such as harmful environments, adverse social policies, powerlessness, and cultural traditions as causes of behavior disorders. Because it highlights the need to view people's behavior in relation to the socio-cultural environment in which it occurs, this approach is sometimes referred to as the **ecological model** (Rappaport, 1977). Some proponents of this model see social and cultural forces as being so dominant that they question whether mental illnesses really exist or whether they are merely a set of labels that a particular culture attaches to certain persons or behaviors.

Traces of the sociocultural model can be found throughout history, especially during the Moral Era in the 1800s, when evidence about the potentially harmful effects of living in an industrializing society began to be considered. The sociocultural model would suggest, for example, that a person such as Nelson McGrath may have developed his bizarre and dysfunctional behaviors largely as a result of living in a complex, stressful culture.

Epidemiological studies, which look at the patterns and frequency of disorders in certain populations, do suggest that the nature and frequency of abnormal behavior are related to environmental, socioeconomic, ethnic, and cultural variables. For example, in the United States, where aggressive behavior is accepted and often encouraged, particularly among boys, problems involving poor control of behavior such as disobedience and excessive attention-seeking are more frequent than in societies such as Thailand or Jamaica, where respect for parental authority and submissiveness are promoted. In Thailand and Jamaica, however, there are higher rates of "overcontrol" problems such as withdrawal and physical complaints (Lambert, Weisz, & Knight, 1989; Weisz, Suwanlert, Chaiyasit, & Walter, 1987). Sociocultural explanations for such differences in disorder patterns include social causation, social drift, and cultural relativism.

Social Causation or Social Drift.

It could be that social, environmental, or cultural hardships put people at greater risk for a disorder, thereby increasing the rates of disorder in certain populations. This **social causation theory** suggests that stress, poverty, racism, inferior education, unemployment, and social changes are sociocultural risk factors for abnormal behavior.

A number of studies suggest, for example, that children who are chronically exposed to high levels of violence suffer higher rates of disordered behavior (Osofsky, 1995). As another example, Helzer et al. (1990) assessed rates of alcohol addiction among adults in St. Louis, Missouri, Edmonton, Alberta (Canada), Puerto Rico, Taiwan, and Korea. Alcohol consumption tends to be more discouraged by cultural values in most Asian countries than in most Western communities. However, in contrast to Taiwan,

TABLE 1.3	Lifetime Percentage Rates of Alcohol Abuse by Sex in Five Countries		
	Alcohol Abuse		
	Men	*Women*	*Total*
St. Louis, Missouri	16.1	3.0	9.2
Edmonton, Alberta, Canada	18.5	3.9	11.3
Puerto Rico	15.7	1.6	8.2
Taiwan			
Metropolis	2.9	0.1	1.5
Townships	3.2	0.2	1.8
Korea	20.4	1.0	10.4

Source: Based on Helzer et al., 1990.

heavy consumption is encouraged in Korea, especially among men, who often compete with one another to see who can drink the most. In Edmonton, at the time of the research, stress arising from unemployment and an unpredictable economy was especially high. As shown in Table 1.3, the results are consistent with predictions derived from social causation theory. The highest overall rate of problem drinking was in Edmonton where economic adversity was greatest, and the lowest rate was in Taiwan where excessive drinking is culturally discouraged.

An alternative explanation of social and cultural differences in psychological disorders is that people with certain mental disorders gravitate to certain locations or status levels within a culture. This **social drift,** or **social selection, hypothesis** explains higher rates of some disorders among lower socioeconomic groups as the inevitable consequence of disordered people falling to lower socioeconomic levels *because* of their disorders. The fact that mental disorders are associated with different demographic and social factors is consistent with social causation, social drift, or both. Scholars continue to debate the issue of which explanation is better. (e.g., Faris & Dunham, 1939; Jarvis, 1844; Robins & Regier, 1991; Srole et al., 1962).

Social Relativism. A third explanation of social and cultural differences in abnormality holds that disorders are defined or diagnosed in different ways in different places by different groups. This **social rela-** tivism viewpoint involves the idea that the same standards and definitions of abnormal behavior do not apply in all cultures. For example, a clinician who is not sensitive to a client's cultural values and traditions can easily mistake that person's devoutly held religious beliefs or averting of the eyes for delusions, inordinate shyness, or depression.

Some forms of abnormality are found only in certain cultures. For example, in *koro,* a condition seen only in Southeast Asia, a man believes his penis is about to retract into his stomach and kill him. *Windigo* is an anxiety disorder among North American Indians in which victims believe that monsters will possess them and turn them into homicidal cannibals. Anorexia nervosa, an eating disorder that will be discussed in Chapter 3, is most common in Western societies that place a premium on thinness as a criterion for physical beauty. Immigrants to these societies appear to be at increased risk for the disorder as they adopt the Western aversion to fatness (Ritenbaugh et al., 1996).

Even when the basic nature of a disorder is similar across cultures, its predominant symptoms may vary a great deal from one culture to another. For example, the content of hallucinations and delusions tends to vary among schizophrenics depending on the society in which they live (Al-Issa, 1977).

Social Labeling. The most extreme version of cultural relativism suggests that mental disorders are merely labels applied to behavior that is unpopular or troubling at a given time or place. A prominent contemporary advocate of this position is Thomas Szasz (1961; 1986), an American psychiatrist who maintains that mental illness is a myth created by medical professionals to legitimize their coercive treatment of people who simply have "problems in living." According to Szasz, these problems in living are usually due to economic hardships, political oppression, or a crisis in personal values. Calling these problems "illness" or "disorder," says Szasz, makes them more burdensome by subjecting their victims to the stigma of being perceived as "mentally ill" and therefore not fully responsible members of society (see also Sarbin, 1969; Scheff, 1966).

Social labeling theory forces us to think seriously about the possible dangers of labeling problematic behavior as a disorder or illness. Labels can be demeaning, often producing prejudice and discrimination, and even making it more likely that people will behave in accordance with a label. However, most mental health professionals see social labeling theory as incomplete, first because it fails to explain how problematic behaviors begin. Second, it

The symptoms of some mental disorders depend, in part, on sociocultural influences. This drawing depicts symbols that are unique to the artist's background just as a drawing by someone from another culture might focus on different images.

ignores the fact that people's problems tend to persist and worsen even if they are not officially labeled, and that these problems are often relieved following diagnosis and treatment.

The various versions of the sociocultural model reflect the idea that maladaptive behavior develops when people's needs and abilities are not well suited to their environment. By implication, people can be helped either by improving their living skills or by making their environments more supportive. Developing and studying interventions that modify environments or build individual competencies defines the field of *community psychology,* (discussed in Chapter 17). Many community psychologists argue that *preventing* abnormal behavior is preferable to *treating* it. We believe that the goal of preventing mental disorders is so important that we will return to it throughout this book in a special section of each chapter called Prevention.

In Review

Psychological and sociocultural variables play an important role in several theories of abnormality, including:

- psychodynamic theories;
- behavioral theories;
- cognitive theories;
- phenomenological theories;
- interpersonal theories; and
- the sociocultural model.

Each of these theories:

- emphasizes a different set of psychological or sociocultural factors that contribute to abnormal behavior; and
- is associated with interventions designed to change those factors the theory specifies as leading to abnormal behavior.

The Diathesis–Stress Model

The idea that abnormal behavior results from the interaction of particular people with specific environments is given the fullest expression in the **diathesis–stress model** of abnormality. The basic assumption of the diathesis–stress model, illustrated in Figure 1.9 on page 30, is that a behavior disorder results from the combined effects of two influences: (1) a *predisposition* for that disorder—called a **diathesis,** and (2) a **stressor,** which is any event that causes a person to adjust to it. According to this model, stressors are the triggers that convert a predisposition for a disorder into the actual appearance of that disorder.

The specific nature of the diathesis and the particular triggering events vary according to the disorder in question. Research suggests that in schizophrenia, for example, the predisposition may take

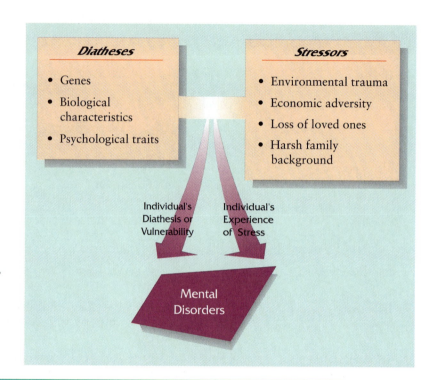

FIGURE 1.9

The Diathesis–Stress Model of Abnormality

According to the diathesis–stress model, mental disorders result when a predisposition to a disorder interacts with stressors. Stressors and diatheses can also influence each other. A diathesis can make people more likely to encounter stressors and a stressor can intensify a diathesis.

the form of a biochemical imbalance or a defect in the brain that is probably genetically transmitted (see Chapter 10). In some forms of depression, the diathesis may be a biological problem, a psychological characteristic, or a combination of both. The triggering stressors may take the form of a harsh family environment, an abusive romantic relationship, the loss of a loved one, or chronic economic adversity.

According to the diathesis–stress model, there is an ongoing interaction of ever-changing individual characteristics and ever-changing environments. Both factors, in turn, can influence each other. Thus, the loss of a loved one might be particularly stressful for a person who is predisposed to be shy and has few friends. Likewise, a tendency toward shyness might be strengthened by interpersonal rejections or conflicts. As genetic influences, emotional temperament, early adversities, emerging symptoms, and random events are woven together over time, it becomes increasingly difficult to disentangle the complex pattern of factors that cause a particular behavior disorder. Still, the diathesis–stress model provides a helpful framework for thinking about causation without assuming that there is only one cause per disorder, without prescribing exactly what the causes might be, and without automatically ruling out any of them. Biological, psychodynamic, behavioral, interpersonal, phenomenological, and sociocultural

factors can all contribute. In fact, just as in trying to explain exactly why you received a particular grade —illness, a bad teacher, a chance encounter, hard work, a role model, intellectual gifts, or whatever—it may be fundamentally impossible to say *exactly* what causes some behavior disorders (Coyne & Downey, 1991).

One relatively recent outgrowth of the diathesis–stress model's emphasis on continuing interactions between people and situations is research in the area of **developmental psychopathology**. Scientists in this field study how problems that first appear in childhood or adolescence are linked to disorders that occur later in life. This developmental view of abnormal behavior helps reveal the numerous ways in which childhood versions of behavior and behavior problems express themselves in adulthood. We will discuss the developmental view of abnormal behavior in more detail when we focus on childhood and adolescent disorders in Chapters 3 and 4.

Not surprisingly, advocates of the diathesis–stress model suggest that effective treatment of disorders must include a combination of techniques that deal with all aspects of causation. Thus, psychotherapy and medication are often combined in the treatment of anxiety disorders and depression. Similarly, people with schizophrenia are often given medication and enrolled in community support programs designed to enhance daily living skills

TABLE 1.4	Major Psychological and Sociocultural Theories of Abnormal Behavior
Theory	**Basic assumption about abnormality**
Psychoanalysis	Abnormality is determined by unconscious conflicts between social rules and personal impulses. Other versions of this theory stress unconscious disturbances in early relationships between infants and caregivers that later affect adult development.
Behavioral	Abnormality is caused by learning experiences involving operant contingencies and classical conditioning. These same forms of learning are responsible for normal behavior and provide the basis for treatment.
Cognitive	Abnormality results from biased or irrational thinking by which people distort their perceptions or understanding of themselves and events around them, leading to emotional disturbances.
Phenomenological	Abnormality develops from subjective perceptions that lead people to feel constrained in their ability to live authentic, autonomously directed lives.
Interpersonal	Abnormality involves extreme and rigid styles of interpersonal behavior in which a person tries to induce others to behave in ways that protect the person from anxiety.
Sociocultural	Abnormality is the result of external forces such as poverty, environmental stress, harsh family background, and cultural traditions that influence the frequency and form of disorders.
Diathesis–stress	Abnormality is the product of two interacting factors: a biological or psychological predisposition to disorder and stressors arising from the family, environment, or the person's own behavior that translates the diathesis into an actual disorder.

and reduce the effects of stressful experiences. The diathesis–stress model also has implications for how best to prevent disorders, as the Prevention section on page 32 illustrates.

The major principles of the diathesis–stress model and the other models of abnormality we have discussed are summarized in Table 1.4.

Scientific Methods and Models of Abnormality

Which model of abnormality provides the "correct" explanation for mental disorders? There is no easy answer to this question. In their search for the causes of mental disorders and for optimal treatments, psychologists—like other scientists—are guided by the **scientific method,** a set of research principles and methods that help them to draw valid conclusions.

Psychologists test their ideas about the origins and treatment of abnormal behavior by collecting empirical data designed to show whether those ideas are true or false. The process usually starts when the researcher states a **hypothesis,** a proposition de-

scribing how two or more variables are related (e.g., "depression is caused by lack of pleasant social interaction"). Usually, hypotheses are based on whatever model of disorder the researcher finds most convincing–in this case, the psychological model. In any case, as evidence accumulates in support of a hypothesis, the researcher may organize his or her explanations into a **theory,** a set of propositions used to predict and explain certain phenomena. Psychodynamic, behavioral, and phenomenological accounts of mental disorders are examples of such theories. But even theories are only tentative explanations, or sets of hypotheses that must be subjected to further scientific evaluation before they can be accepted as valid explanations and guides to future research (see Figure 1.10 on page 33).

To test a hypothesis empirically, researchers must use methods that allow the hypothesis to be confirmed *or* disconfirmed. Accordingly, the hypothesis must be specific, clear, and stated in terms that have been operationally defined. An **operational definition** is a statement that equates a concept with the exact methods used to represent or measure it. An operational definition of depression, for example, might be a high score on a test that is

Prevention   Improving Environments, Strengthening People

What happens to people who live in harmful environments that are known to increase the risk of abnormal behavior? Do children who show early psychological difficulties develop more severe problems later in life? These questions are at the root of attempts to prevent abnormal behavior. We can never know for certain which person will fall victim to a pernicious environment and develop a mental disorder. Neither can we predict which child will outgrow an early behavior problem and which will go on to suffer a more lasting disorder. However, we do know that small problems in the early years have a tendency to grow into larger difficulties unless something is done to alter their course. This knowledge, gained by the careful scientific study of how various disorders develop, is the foundation for the science of prevention and its attempts to reduce the onset or severity of disorders.

Prevention of abnormal behavior can occur at three levels (Caplan, 1964). **Primary prevention** attempts to reduce the onset of disorders or eliminate them entirely by bringing about a *universal* change that affects everyone in a specific population. **Secondary prevention** seeks a *selective* impact by focusing on persons who are judged to be "at risk" based on an assessment that they possess or are exposed to factors known to increase the occurence of a disorder. **Tertiary prevention** aims to reduce the severity or consequences of a disorder. It is restricted to people who have already been found to have a disorder; consequently, it is really a form of treatment rather than prevention. In a term paper, a student once gave the following analogy to explain the levels of prevention:

If a lot of people drowned along a particular stretch of an ocean beach, the lifeguards could try three strategies to cut down on the deaths. They could swim out and try to rescue every person as they began to sink; that would be tertiary prevention. They could give a swimming test to everyone who came to the beach and then make sure that only the strongest swimmers were allowed in the ocean; that would be secondary prevention. Or they could close the beach to all swimmers during strong tides, bad weather, and at other risky times; that would be primary prevention.

Many mental health professionals believe that we should pay increased attention to preventing rather than treating abnormal behavior. Effective prevention can improve the lives of large numbers of people, reduce the overall frequency of disorders, and may, in the long run, be less costly to society than attempting to treat every new case of disorder. Researchers are gaining a greater understanding of how early factors are related to later disorders, and mental health professionals are becoming more interested in developing prevention programs for mental disorders. These programs are often centered in schools, families, and neighborhoods; in some cases, they involve major changes in national health or education policies.

Regardless of the disorder in question, effective prevention targets one of two major goals. First, prevention programs can work to change environments so that they are less harmful, stressful, and disruptive. Making schools and neighborhoods safer and ensuring adequate health care for all children are illustrations of this approach. Second, prevention

programs can try to strengthen individuals' **resilience**—the ability to solve problems, cope with stressors, and overcome adversity. To accomplish this goal, psychologists might want to train the general population in skills known to build resilience, such as good parenting, or to try to improve the problem-solving skills of all youngsters. In other cases, it may be necessary to use an early assessment to identify the warning signs of a problem so that those people who would benefit from a strengthening program can be reached. As Prevention sections in the remaining chapters indicate, all effective prevention programs accomplish one—sometimes both—of these objectives.

Poor social skills, shyness, and uncertainty about how to solve problems are often the focus of person-centered prevention. Poverty, chronic exposure to violence, and urban decay are targets of environmentally oriented prevention programs.

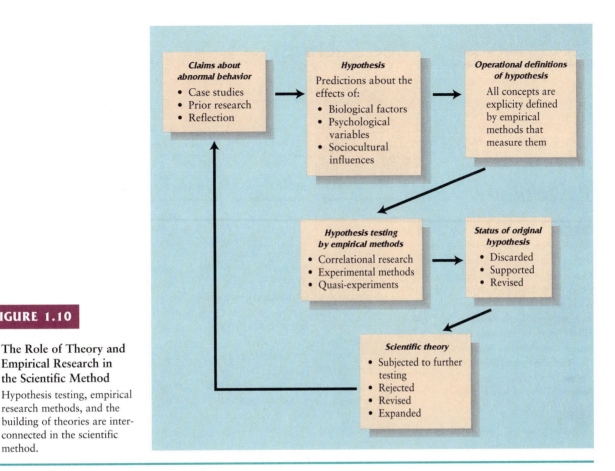

The Role of Theory and Empirical Research in the Scientific Method

Hypothesis testing, empirical research methods, and the building of theories are interconnected in the scientific method.

known to measure depression. Two of the most important methods for testing hypotheses are correlational research and experiments.

Correlational Research

Correlation is a measure of the degree to which one variable is related to another. When two variables change together in the same direction, they are *positively correlated*. For example, height and weight tend to be positively correlated; taller people usually weigh more than shorter people. When two variables move in opposite directions, they are *negatively correlated*. For example, as more snow falls on a highway, motorists tend to drive slower. If the correlation between two variables is large, knowing about one variable allows for accurate predictions about the second variable.

To test the hypothesis that people feel depressed as a result of having too few pleasant social interactions, a researcher might operationally define "depression" as a score of, say, greater than 50 on a depression test, and "pleasant social interactions" as the number of conversations during which a person is observed smiling at another person. If these two variables are negatively correlated (the higher the de-

pression score, the fewer smiling conversations), the hypothesis has been supported.

Correlational studies help researchers describe and predict abnormal behavior and evaluate hypotheses about its causes. However, these correlations cannot inform us about *why* two variables are related; they cannot establish that one variable *caused* a change in another. Thus, we do not know whether (a) lack of pleasant social interaction caused depression; (b) depression made people less likely to have pleasant social interactions; or (c) some third factor caused both depression and social withdrawal.

Experiments

To help them draw cause–effect conclusions about relationships between variables—and thus to choose the most likely explanation for these relationships—researchers conduct experiments. In an **experiment**, the researcher manipulates one variable and measures the effect of this manipulation on a second variable, while holding all other influences constant. The variable that is manipulated by the experimenter is called the **independent variable (IDV)**; the variable that is observed for the effect of the manipulation is called the **dependent variable (DV)**.

A Talk with Lee Sechrest

Dr. Lee Sechrest is Professor of Psychology at the University of Arizona. He is known widely for his many contributions to research methodology and is regarded as a leading spokesperson for ensuring that clinical psychology is based on scientific principles and findings.

Abnormal Psychology

Q *Abnormal psychology texts typically cover psychodynamic, biological, behavioral, cognitive, phenomenological, interpersonal, sociocultural, and diathesis–stress explanations of abnormal behavior. Which of these explanations of abnormality do you see as most influential today and why? Which approaches do you see as being most influential in the next century?*

A "Most influential" could mean the ideas that are most widely prevalent and that affect the most people; on the other hand it could mean the ideas that are scientifically most important. In my view the ideas that have been most influential in determining our views of abnormal behavior are the psychodynamic, biological, and diathesis–stress explanations. That is because the psychodynamic explanation was so widely adopted, but also because it had such substantial correspondence with people's own experiences. Consequently, it became widely influential both among professionals and in the public mind—an influence that was unmerited on the basis of evidence. The biological views of abnormal behavior have existed for centuries, so they have always been influential in determining the views of professionals and the lay public. Finally, diathesis–stress explanations are influential because

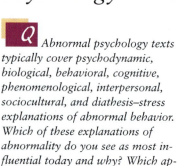

The idea of labeling every human frailty . . . as psychopathology . . . is simply wrong.

they square with our everyday experience. It is easy to believe that stress has an important impact on abnormal behavior. In the future I think a combination of a biological and a sociocultural view of abnormal behavior will be most influential. The biological influence on abnormal behavior can't be avoided and I suspect that we will continue to be influenced by the notion that abnormal behaviors are conditioned by social expectations and that a variety of social conditions and pressures come together in some instances to produce phenomena we think of as abnormal behavior.

Q *What do you see as the value and the limitations of scientific methods in making professional decisions about abnormal behavior?*

A The value of scientific methods in making professional decisions about abnormal behavior is that they provide clinicians with relative certainty that their decisions are the best available under the circumstances. Scientific methods also provide uniformity with respect to the treatment of patients or clients. It may be true that some individual clinicians are astonishingly good at what they do, but a great many are not, or would not be if they did not have guidance from the scientific literature. It is still possible for the best clinicians to go beyond what the written prescriptions might be from the literature and to elaborate on them in useful ways and to try new things.

The two greatest limitations of reliance on scientific methods are, first

of all, that clinical acts and clinical decisions are made in real time and science can be slow and plodding; therefore, it takes a long time for science to produce information that is useful. Second, there is often a considerable difference between the nature of scientific studies and the work that clinicians actually have to do. Science cannot guarantee that it will produce findings that are immediately relevant and that will answer questions that clinicians have, such as, "Well, what exactly should I do now?"

Q *Should clinicians be allowed to use only therapy techniques that are empirically validated in controlled experimental research?*

A We have to have better theory so that, if clinicians are using interventions or following plans that are not substantiated by research, they should at least be closely guided by the theory toward which the research is contributing. Whether they should stick to empirically validated methods depends, in my view, on two things: (1) who is paying for their work, and (2) how their work is presented to their clients and the public. If clinicians do not ask the public—either through public legislation or through insurance—to pay for what they do, then I have no objection to anything they do, whether it is empirically validated or not, as long as it isn't harmful. I have sometimes referred to this in relation to the FTC regulations regarding toys. Toys must be safe; they need not necessarily be any fun. But clinicians should not be allowed to pretend that what they are doing has been scientifically validated when there is no basis for their clinical work. When clinicians engage in experimental treatments, even within the context of a generally scientific approach, patients or clients should know that the interventions they are receiving are experimental in nature, that they are not validated. Furthermore, if clinicians want to be paid by public funds or through insurance companies, I think that their work should be based directly on what has been evaluated and what has been shown to be effective. They should not simply follow their own theoretical bent or other predilections without regard for whether they have been validated.

Q *Where do you stand on the question of what is abnormal behavior?*

A I have a fairly restricted view of abnormal behavior. I don't believe that all behavior that we call abnormal because it is statistically infrequent or because it bothers us should be regarded as psychopathology. Much of what we see as abnormal behavior and even psychopathology is really a manifestation of the range of human behaviors; that is, that people differ–some people are more intact, some people are more effective, some people are easier to deal with than others. The idea of labeling every human frailty and every human foible and every difficulty that people have as psychopathology and suppose that it could be cured or even

substantially altered by psychologically oriented clinicians I think is simply wrong. We may be able to effect changes in people's behavior over brief periods of time and under special conditions, but we're not changing the people, themselves, fundamentally. We are not capable of taking, let's say, an introverted person who is shy and unresponsive to people and change that person into a party animal, someone who is outgoing and expansive. People are just different in this way so I want to confine clinical efforts to what I see as the major forms of psychopathology that most closely resemble what we would think of as diseases.

Q *In historical perspective, from Hippocrates to today, what do you see as the three most important developments in efforts to explain psychopathology?*

A The three most important developments in understanding psychopathology are the discovery of the mind, the discovery of the brain, and the discovery of religion. The discovery of the mind and the idea that behavior is related to people's views of the world and to their perceptions must have been a slow process, but once that process led to the discovery that people had minds, their abnormal behaviors came to be seen in a different kind of way. The discovery of the brain—by that I mean the discovery that what goes on in the brain has implications for behavior—is also a fairly profound discovery because it led to the connection of behavior to what's going on in the

body and the notion that we might intervene at the somatic level in order to produce changes at the behavioral level and maybe vice versa. Finally, one of the critical things that is related to religion is the recognition and the generation of guilt, and I think that was an important element in our views of psychopathology, the notion that people's behavior could be influenced by their morale, and that internal states such as guilt resulting from misbehavior and so on could result in psychopathology.

In another way, the three most important developments could be seen as Freud, the DSM (the official classification system of mental disorders in North America), and the explosion of knowledge about the brain. Freud was important because he conditioned the views of psychopathology for nearly a century. His influence was enormous, although I think wrong. The DSM was an important development in framing our approach to psychopathology because it provided a set of diagnostic categories suggesting that disordered behaviors could be classified as diseases are classified. This had great influence on our approaches to explaining and treating psychopathology, and it threatens to continue to distort our views. Finally, brain science has been important because it is increasing our understanding of the workings of the brain and of the relationships between events in the brain and events in the rest of the body and in behavior. I think that it is tremendously important to know that behavior stems from biological sources.

In the simplest experiment, the researcher manipulates the independent variable by randomly assigning people to an **experimental group** (which, say, receives treatment for a phobia) or to a **control group** (which receives no treatment). The independent variable in this experiment is whether or not the subjects receive treatment. The dependent variable here is the degree to which the subjects' phobias improved following treatment or the mere passage of time. **Random assignment** of subjects to each condition is vital because it makes it likely that factors such as age, personality characteristics, severity of phobia, and other variables that might affect the dependent variable will be distributed randomly, and therefore about equally, between the experimental and control groups. Random assignment, in other words, decreases the chance that variables other than the independent variable will influence the experimenter's results.

Variables that *do* act to confuse or distort results are called **confounding variables.** Their presence makes it harder for researchers to be sure whether the independent variable, the confounding variable, or some combination of the two, was responsible for the observed effects on the dependent variable. For example, suppose depressed subjects who were randomly assigned to receive a drug treatment improved more than equally depressed subjects in a no-treatment control group. Was the difference due to the drug itself or to the fact that the treated subjects had stronger *expectations* for improvement? Perhaps *any* treatment, from drugs to back rubs, that raised their expectations would have the same effect. Even the *experimenter's* expectations about the drug's benefit might have caused them to act in a way that gave the treated group greater motivation to improve. Improvement stemming solely from expectations or other factors beyond a treatment's active ingredient is known as a **placebo effect.**

In order to assess the role of placebo effects on the dependent variable, researchers often randomly assign some subjects to a **placebo control group** that receives an impressive, but inert or phony treatment; the progress of the placebo subjects is then compared to that of subjects in treatment and no-treatment control groups. Of course, if the subjects or the therapists know who is receiving real treatment and who is getting placebos, differing expectations for improvement could still bias the results. To minimize such bias, a **double-blind study** is often used: only the director of the experiment knows who is in which group. Everyone else is kept "blind" to the subjects' group assignment.

Quasi-Experiments

Researchers testing the hypothesis that a lack of pleasant social interactions leads to depression might conduct a true experiment by randomly assigning some subjects to an experimental group whose lives are manipulated to ensure that they experienced few pleasant interactions; subjects assigned to a control group would be allowed to have normal interactions. The subjects' level of depression (the dependent variable) would then be measured to determine whether reduced social enjoyment had the hypothesized effect.

This experiment could indeed help evaluate the researchers' hypothesis, but it could not be conducted because it violates basic ethical standards for psychological research. Among other things, researchers are obliged to protect subjects from physical or psychological harm, including that which might come from manipulating the quality of social interactions. (Other requirements of ethical research are discussed in relation to other studies throughout this book.)

A far more ethical alternative in this case would be to conduct a **quasi-experiment,** a study that resembles or "comes close" to being a true experiment. Generally, quasi-experiments lack one or more of the elements of a true experiment: subjects are not randomly assigned to groups, the independent variable is not manipulated, or a control group is not included (Campbell & Stanley, 1966). For example, a quasi-experimental test of our depression–interaction hypothesis might be to measure (not manipulate) the social interactions experienced by a large group of people and identify a group of individuals who tend to enjoy many pleasant interactions and a group who tend to have few such interactions. The researcher could then compare the two groups on their levels of depression. If the low-pleasant group is more depressed than the high-pleasant group, the researcher's hypothesis will have been supported.

The conclusions that can be drawn from such quasi-experiments are usually not as strong as those from true experiments because quasi-experiments permit less control over extraneous variables; without random assignment to groups or careful manipulation of independent variables, quasi-experiments are far less able to rule out or measure the effect of confounding variables. Still if the results of a quasi-experiment are subject to **replication**—that is, if the results are duplicated many times with new groups of subjects, the researcher can have greater confidence that the observed relationship between the independent and dependent variables may be a cause–effect relationship.

Human Diversity and Research Methods

Replication of research results is important for another reason, as well. Researchers need to know how well their results represent or generalize to people in general, not just their research sample. Do conclusions about social interaction and depression apply to men as well as women? Does the relationship hold among Black Americans as well as Asian Americans and White Americans?

To study the effects of human diversity on abnormal behavior, researchers must pay special attention to *sampling*, the methods used for selecting research participants. Ideally there would be utterly random sampling in which all people on Earth have an equal chance of being included in a study. In reality, it is impossible to draw a truly random sample from the world population, so researchers usually aim for **representative samples** in which participants are selected so as to represent all levels of important subject variables such as age, gender, and ethnicity. Another option is to focus on a specific subject characteristic and select people as randomly as possible from that group alone. Thus, if researchers are studying whether a treatment that works with adults will also benefit children, they would select their next sample from a diverse population of children.

Researchers can also study the impact of human diversity by sampling in such a way that its effects can be analyzed. For example, suppose we are interested in the impact of age or ethnicity on the relationship between social interaction and depression. We can explore these questions by selecting subjects in a way that ensures that there are equal numbers of people from each of several age groups and each of several ethnic backgrounds. We can then determine whether the correlation between pleasant social interactions and depression is stronger for people of a particular age or for those in a particular ethnic group.

Resolving Controversy Through Scientific Methods

Not surprisingly, the field of abnormal psychology is filled with controversies. Researchers disagree about how best to diagnose mental disorders, what their major causes and consequences are, and how they should be treated. Is schizophrenia inherited? Why are women diagnosed with depression more often than men? Should hyperactive children be given drugs? Do mental disorders cause people to be dangerous? Can clinicians predict who will be dangerous?

Final answers to questions such as these are difficult to come by because even though each study provides part of an answer, it also raises new questions and controversies that spur researchers to do more research and make new discoveries. Even basic theories about abnormal behavior are constantly being tested, revised, abandoned, and refined. Yet a field without uncertainty and controversy would be a field without progress. Accordingly, each chapter of this book includes a special Controversy section such as the one beginning below and continuing on page 38 that deals with a major dispute about some aspect of abnormal behavior, discusses existing research, and points to gaps in current knowledge. Each Controversy section also invites you to think critically about the dispute.

Controversy

Should We Study Genetic Causes of Abnormality?

Genes influence many prominent physical features—weight, eye color, and whether we ultimately grow bald. Genes also help account for diseases such as high blood pressure or diabetes. Although the mechanics of how genes control physical features and processes are still not completely understood, little controversy exists about whether genes are necessary for understanding the biological qualities of people.

More controversial is the role that genetic factors play in shaping mental abilities, behavior, personality traits, and mental disorders. Although few mental disorders appear to be caused solely by genetic inheritance, and certainly not by the inheritance of a single gene, research consistently suggests that some combination of genes may increase people's vulnerability to such disorders as schizophrenia, depression, and alcoholism.

When genetic factors are considered as contributors to a disorder, controversy often follows (Alper & Natowicz, 1993; Lewontin, Rose, & Kamin, 1984). In some cases, attempts to study the genetics of behavior problems have been condemned or blocked because of concerns that even asking questions about genes and abnormality is risky or improper. One example of

(continued)

Controversy *(continued)*

what many scientists regard as a kind of academic censorship was the fate of a national conference on the relationship between crime and genes. Originally scheduled for 1992 by the University of Maryland with funding from the National Institutes of Health, the conference was postponed after critics charged that it might encourage a racist view of crime. The conference was ultimately held in 1995, despite protests.

What accounts for such controversy? Why are genetic theories of abnormality so unpopular? What makes it so difficult for some people to look objectively at the tangled issues involving the possible genetic roots of abnormal behavior? Does the problem reflect honest scientific disagreements or the pursuit of political agendas?

One concern appears to be that if scientists find that genetics play a causal role in mental disorders, they will neglect social and environmental factors, along with social programs designed to correct them. This concern reflects the misconception that either nature *or* nurture is responsible for disorders; in fact, they always interact. Consistent with the diathesis–stress model, inheriting a vulnerability to a disorder should *increase* attention to the importance of the environment. Just as the person who is genetically predisposed to high blood pressure might need to be especially cautious about diet, the person who is genetically vulnerable to schizophrenia might need extra social support and guidance to cope with environmental threats.

A second concern about studying the genetics of abnormality is that it will lead to certain people being designated as genetically "inferior." As horribly exemplified by the Nazi era in Europe, genetic research has led to awful abuses, including forced sterilization, genocide, coerced abortions, and discriminatory immigration poli-

cies—all conducted to get rid of supposedly inferior people. Although critics of contemporary genetic research often associate it with past sins, most genetic researchers are cautious not to overstate the role of genetic contributions to mental disorders and not to argue that purely biological treatments are sufficient.

A third reason for negative reactions to genetic theories is that they can imply racist or discriminatory practices. For example, Richard Herrnstein and Charles Murray's book *The Bell Curve* (1994) sparked a firestorm of criticism, not so much because of its claim that intellectual abilities were genetically influenced (a contention with which many psychologists agree) but because of its argument that genetic factors account for most of the measured IQ differences among different ethnic groups (a contention *not* endorsed by most psychologists).

Scientists must always be concerned that a person's genotype not be used as a basis for deciding whether that person is hired for a job, given a promotion, accepted to a school, or stigmatized in any way. Behavioral genetics cannot explain whether any given individual's behavior is due to genes or environment; it can only estimate the average influence that both genes and environment exert on individual differences within a group of people. Furthermore, the average degree to which a behavior is inheritable *within one group* of people cannot explain behavioral differences *between groups*.

A simple example will illustrate this important principle. Height is clearly inheritable. Assume that a large group of people are raised in a culture in which they are chronically underfed; on average, the taller parents in this culture will still have taller children. However, the children in

this culture might be a few inches shorter on average than children raised in another culture where food is plentiful and diet is adequate. Height is genetically determined in both cultures, but the difference between children from the two cultures is not due to genetic differences. Likewise, even though height is linked to genes, a purely environmental intervention—better diet for the first culture—would be an effective treatment. Throughout this book, we often note the role of genetic influences on mental disorders, but this does not mean that environmental factors or interventions are unimportant.

Thinking Critically

As noted earlier, scientific methods have an important role to play in resolving controversies about abnormal behavior, including those about the role of genetics. The scientific method provides public, agreed-upon procedures for engaging in *critical thinking* about a dispute. The steps in this critical thinking process are based on the following questions:

1. What assertion or phenomenon is to be evaluated or explained?

2. What is the evidence for the explanation or assertion?

3. Can a study be designed that will support one explanation over others?

4. What other hypotheses are not ruled out as alternative explanations for the results? What additional research could clarify the initial results?

5. Based on existing evidence, what is the most reasonable conclusion to be drawn about the assertion or phenomenon?

In each of the Controversy sections in the chapters to come, we invite you to ask questions such as these in order to think critically about the controversy discussed.

Revisiting the Case of Nelson McGrath

Nelson McGrath's fate would have been different in other times and societies. Had Nelson lived in ancient Egypt or Asia, his disorder would probably have been viewed as a sign of demonic possession and he would have been treated with exorcism or some other religious ritual. In Classical Greece or in the early Roman Empire, he might have received a prescription for moderation in behavior, along with special diets, calming words, and physical therapy. In medieval Europe, Nelson might have been treated as a religious heretic. In the fifteenth century Renaissance, Nelson might have been isolated from society in a large asylum where he would have received little in the way of treatment.

By the eighteenth century, Nelson might have benefitted from the humanitarian treatments introduced by such reformers as Pinel. But as more and larger hospitals were built, Nelson would more than likely have been confined in an institution for an indefinite period. By the late 1800s, as the specialties of psychiatry and clinical psychology developed, medical or psychological treatments might have been used with Nelson. In the absence of a scientific understanding of the biology or psychology of most disorders, however, these treatments would probably not have been effective.

Today, Nelson's problems would be explained as due to a combination of biological, psychological, and sociocultural factors. In fact, his disorder was diagnosed as a form of schizophrenia, and he was treated with medication and behaviorally oriented techniques aimed at helping him live effectively in society rather than in a hospital. For most of the past 5 years, Nelson has been able to remain out of the hospital. His disorder, while not fully understood, is now the subject of research studies around the world. These studies continue to yield important information about the causes and treatment of schizophrenia.

Why was Nelson diagnosed with schizophrenia? In the next chapter we will review the processes and criteria by which abnormal behavior is diagnosed and classified by mental health professionals. In Chapters 3–14 we will discuss the various categories of disorder in more detail. We will describe the major characteristics of each disorder, along with some case examples, and a summary of research on causal factors and the most effective methods of treatment. To give added perspective to this material, each of these chapters will also include a brief interview with a leading expert on the disorder under discussion.

Chapters 15–17 offer a general overview of the major approaches to treatment used by mental health professionals today. Then, in Chapter 18, we will explore the larger social context in which abnormal behavior is displayed, and we consider some of the legal, ethical, and social policy issues that clinicians must deal with as they study and treat abnormal behavior.

SUMMARY

Making Sense of Abnormality: A Brief History

We have reviewed the major explanations for abnormal behavior that have prevailed across much of recorded history. From the most ancient civilizations, through the early Greek and Roman periods, and throughout the Middle Ages, supernatural and natural explanations vied for dominance. Depending on which view was most popular, religious rituals or naturalistic therapies were the treatments of choice. Neither proved to be effective. Beginning in the Renaissance and extending through the Enlightenment to the beginning of the twentieth century, views of abnormality became more and more naturalistic in orientation, mainly because of the influence of the scientific method. Current models of abnormality combine biological, psychological, and sociocultural explanations, each of which has been supported by results of scientific research.

The Biological Model

Abnormal behavior can be explained in terms of disturbances in the nervous system caused by illness, trauma, or genetic factors. The nervous system has two main parts: the central nervous system (spinal cord and brain) and the peripheral nervous system (composed of the somatic nervous system and the autonomic nervous system). In the autonomic nervous system, the sympathetic division generally increases physiological arousal, preparing the body for action, and the parasympathetic division usually decreases arousal. Malfunctions can occur in any of the main structures of the nervous system, but the forebrain is particularly important because it helps regulate emotion, planning, and thinking and because it is linked to other regulators of the body's functions, such as the glands that make up the endocrine system. Much research has also focused on the role of disturbances in chemical messengers known as neurotransmitters and on the influence of genes. Although genes control the development of every cell and organ of the body, the unique physical and psychological characteristics of each person reflect the interaction between genetic predispositions and the environment. To understand this interaction, behavioral geneticists conduct family, twin, and adoption studies.

Psychological and Sociocultural Models

The first formal psychological theory of abnormal behavior was Sigmund Freud's psychoanalysis. By the middle of the twentieth century, several alternative psychological theories had been proposed, including variations on psychoanalysis, as well as behavioral, cognitive, interpersonal, and phenomenological theories. Although biological and psychological models of abnormality emphasize internal causes of disor- der, sociocultural models point to external factors such as poverty, stress, and family hardships as the major causes.

The Diathesis–Stress Model

The diathesis–stress model combines internal factors (the diathesis) with external factors (stressors) to explain abnormal behavior. When a predisposing diathesis is aggravated by a stressor, the risk of a disorder increases.

Scientific Methods and Models of Abnormality

Scientists collect empirical data to test hypotheses about various models and theories of abnormal behavior. To verify hypotheses, scientists use operational definitions, describing concepts in terms of the operations used to measure them. They then employ correlational and experimental research methods to test their hypotheses. Correlational studies help describe and predict abnormal behavior, but cannot explain why two variables are related or confirm that a change in one variable actually caused a change in another. To draw causal conclusions, scientists conduct experiments, studies in which one variable—the independent variable—is manipulated and its effect on a second variable—the dependent variable—is observed. To guard against the distortion of placebo effects and other confounding variables, true experiments include random assignment of subjects to experimental and various control groups. Especially in treatment studies, double-blind designs are vital to protect against experimenter bias. When it would be impossible or unethical to conduct true experiments, quasi-experimental designs approximating experimental controls are employed. Regardless of the designs used, researchers try to study samples of people who represent the full range of human diversity. This effort makes it more likely that research results will be widely applicable.

KEY TERMS

abnormal behavior, p. 4	axon, p. 14	cerebral cortex, p. 13
adoption study, p. 18	behavioral genetics, p. 16	cerebrum, p. 13
allele, p. 15	behavior modification, p. 23	classical conditioning, p. 22
anal stage, p. 20	behavioral theory, p. 22	clinical psychology, p. 10
appraisal, p. 25	behavior therapy, p. 23	cognitive theory, p. 24
attribution, p. 25	biological model, p. 11	concordance, p. 17

2

Assessment and Diagnosis

From the Case of Bill

When Bill contacted the clinician, he told her that he had been constantly nervous for the past year or so. She learned that he was a 58-year-old business executive at a national computer company. Bill grew up in a working-class family, the oldest of three brothers. He was an average student through school and never gave his parents any trouble, but he also remembered never "having much fun." He was slightly overweight as a teenager and always felt slighted by other boys who were more interested in and successful at sports.

Bill married his high-school girlfriend while both were attending the same college. They had been married for 35 years and had two grown children. In addition to his salary of about $150,000 per year, Bill had reaped excellent profits from rental properties and business ventures. Despite his material success, Bill has felt restless and unhappy for the past 2 years.

Now, Bill says, his stomach is "always upset," and often he feels he can't "get his breath." According to his physician, Bill has Crohn's disease, a potentially dangerous intestinal disorder. Bill also says that he feels so agitated he can't sit still, can't concentrate at work, and has trouble remembering things. One night he drove out of the parking lot at work and left his briefcase on the pavement where he had parked his car. His success at work has begun to decline. He can't fall asleep until 3 A.M. most nights because his mind is "spinning" with constant worry about work and marital problems. He reports being sexually "impotent," a problem that has caused so much conflict with his wife that, 2 months ago, they "just gave up" trying to have sex. He describes their marriage as "extremely tense and uncomfortable"; he and his wife avoid each other as much as possible. He has been carrying on an affair with a co-worker for over a year and has kept this relationship a secret from everyone, a deception that he recognizes is beginning to take a toll on him.

Bill is also worried because his company is downsizing its work force. Other mid-level executives have recently been fired, and Bill is sure it is just a matter of time before he gets his pink slip. At his age, he is convinced that no one else will hire him. Increasingly, when he thinks about the future, Bill feels depressed and desperate. In fact, he becomes so obsessed with the fear that he will die an early death that he sometimes wonders whether he just shouldn't kill himself and put an end to his insecurity and fear. ■

*B*ill's complaints are familiar to most clinicians. Like many clients, he complains of a mixture of anxiety, depression, physical symptoms, and marital discord. What has caused Bill's problems? Is he suffering from a mental disorder, or is he just going through a rough time in his life? Are Bill's problems the cause or the result of his marital difficulties? How could a clinician decide? If Bill does have a mental disorder, which diagnosis would be most accurate? What methods should a clinician use to diagnose Bill? Will his treatment differ depending on his diagnosis? These are some of the questions that mental health professionals try to answer through clinical assessment and diagnostic classification.

In this chapter, we will review several definitions of mental disorders, discuss their advantages and disadvantages, and then offer a working definition to be used throughout the book. We will then describe how mental health professionals assess and classify mental disorders in North America, how they distinguish disorders from nondisorders, and how they differentiate one disorder from another. We will also discuss the frequency with which different mental disorders are diagnosed and how diagnoses are affected by various real-world considerations, including financial concerns and cultural differences. Finally, we will return to the case of Bill and see how his clinician assessed and diagnosed his problem.

Identifying Mental Disorders: Some Basic Issues

Think back to the diary of Nelson McGrath, which opened Chapter 1. What was it about Nelson that made you believe he was abnormal and that he suffered from a mental disorder? Was it his strange behavior alone, or was it because others were surprised by and disapproved of it? Was it because Nelson was so anguished? Perhaps it was because Nelson had

previously been treated for his bizarre behavior. Maybe you concluded that Nelson's disturbed behavior was harmful to himself and others. Or did you question whether Nelson actually had a mental disorder? Each of these views reflects a different perspective on what constitutes a mental disorder.

Before we review these perspectives, we need to comment briefly on terminology. In Chapter 1, we used the term *abnormal behavior* to refer to the subject matter of this book. We used this term because it is general enough to fit the different theoretical perspectives—religious, biological, psychological, and sociocultural—that we surveyed. Several other synonyms have been used for abnormal behavior— mental illness, deviant behavior, psychological abnormality, psychopathology, and psychiatric illness are the most common. Beginning in this chapter and for the rest of the book, we will use the term that mental health professionals today employ most often: *mental disorder*.

What Is a Mental Disorder?

Mental disorder has been defined in five general ways throughout history:

1. as a deviation from social expectations;
2. as what mental health professionals treat;
3. as subjective distress;
4. as a label for disliked actions; and
5. as a dysfunction that causes harm.

An alternative to defining mental disorder is defining what is normal. Unfortunately, defining normality is as complicated as defining abnormality, so it is not really a practical solution (Offer & Sabshin, 1991).

Disorder as a Deviation from Social Expectations. *Mental disorder* can be defined as a deviation from social expectations. Typically, the deviation is in the negative direction from expectations; otherwise, all unusual qualities, including high intelligence or outstanding memory abilities, for example, would be classified as disorders. Usually, a behavior that deviates from social expectations is also statistically rare. In fact, when a formerly unusual behavior becomes too frequent, it stops being a sign of nonconformity or a violation of expectations and starts becoming an expected behavior or norm.

Several serious problems make this social-deviation definition incomplete. First, it ignores characteristics that are not rare but that are still problematic and require treatment. For example, if many people in a community suffer severe anxiety following a devastating hurricane, should the high fre-

Michael Kearney has an IQ that reportedly exceeds 200; he graduated from the University of South Alabama with honors when he was only 10 years old, the age at which most children are finishing fifth grade. These characteristics are extremely rare, but because they are valued achievements in our culture, they are not viewed as signs of mental disorder.

quency of the symptoms rule out a diagnosis of disorder? Second, how rare must a condition be before qualifying as a disorder? For schizophrenia, which affects about 1 percent of adults in North America, a statistical approach works fairly well because 1 percent is a reasonable definition of "rare." However, a deviation-based definition is less adequate for alcohol abuse or alcoholism, which may affect 10 percent of American adults. Third, deviation-based definitions imply that conformity to social expectations is synonymous with mental health, but this is not necessarily the case. Not everyone who meets a society's expectations is mentally healthy, nor are those—such as creative artists—who challenge those expectations necessarily mentally disordered.

Disorder as What Clinicians Treat. A second, pragmatic definition is that mental disorders are whatever problems or symptoms clinicians treat. This definition is occasionally used in **epidemiology,** the scientific study of the onset and frequency of disorders in certain populations. Its greatest strength is its simplicity, but it has several disadvantages. First, not everyone who consults a clinician is suffering symptoms. Many people consult mental health professionals because they want to learn how to communicate better with their spouses, be more effective parents, or to be happier in their jobs. Obviously, people can pursue such goals without having a mental disorder. Second, this definition assumes that everyone—regardless of the disorder they suffer, the availability of treatment, or their ability to pay for it—is equally likely to seek professional treatment. However, this assumption is incorrect, so the definition of disorder on which it is based would be misleading. It would underestimate, for example, the frequency of disorder among the poor, who are least likely to receive treatment.

Connections

Is schizophrenia rare in all cultures? To learn about the frequency of this disorder in different countries, see Chapter 10, pp. 344–346.

Disorder as Subjective Distress or Unhappiness. Personal distress and unhappiness often accompany mental disorders; indeed, these feelings frequently lead people to seek treatment. Although subjective distress is a symptom of some mental disorders, distress alone cannot define disorder. People feel unhappy over many events in their lives. They worry over finances, become jealous of lovers, and get angry at bosses. In fact, *not* feeling emotionally upset in the face of a devastating loss or a callous insult might be interpreted as a sign of disorder. In addition, this definition does not distinguish between the temporary upset that accompanies stressful events and distress that is chronic, intense, and seemingly unrelated to external stressors. Finally, certain patterns of behavior, such as some of the personality disorders that will be described in Chapter 12, cause little or no distress for individuals displaying them, but they create problems for the people around them. Few would argue that such behavior patterns should be disqualified as mental disorders.

Disorder as a Label. There are those who argue that most mental disorders represent nothing more than labels bestowed by mental health professionals on people whose behavior is disturbing to others. As noted in Chapter 1, Thomas Szasz argued that mental illness should refer only to those relatively few behavioral problems that are clearly traceable to organic causes. Skeptics such as Szasz believe that labeling people who fall outside this category as mentally ill harms them by stigmatizing them. In addition, the labels often lead to the imposition of treatment, which invades people's privacy and limits their freedom.

As noted in Chapter 1, this skeptical view has a declining influence today, mainly because it appears to trivialize the problems of people in whom no specific biological malfunction has been found but whose troubles are very real to them. It also fails to account for the fact that behavior problems often do not go away and sometimes worsen if unlabeled, and they often improve when treated.

Disorder as Dysfunction That Causes Harm. A useful definition is provided by Jerome Wakefield (1992) who said that **mental disorders** are dysfunctions that cause harm. Defining mental disorders as harmful dysfunctions is similar to the definition employed in the fourth edition of the *Diagnostic and Statistical Manual of Mental Disorders (DSM-IV)*, which is published by the American Psychiatric Association (1994) and serves as the official diagnostic system used in North America.

Dysfunction refers to the failure of a biological or psychological mechanism to operate as it should; there is a breakdown in the way a person thinks, feels, or perceives the world. When Nelson McGrath perceived that the world was growing spots, he was experiencing a perceptual dysfunction. Likewise, when Bill experienced problems in concentration and memory, he was experiencing cognitive dysfunctions.

The concept of *harm* in this definition refers to the consequences of dysfunction that a society or an individual considers to be negative. Because not every dysfunction produces harm, not every dysfunction would be considered a disorder by this definition. Nelson's hallucinated spots reflected a disorder because they led him to burn his skin and to lock himself in his room each night. Bill's cognitive lapses also produced harm because they led to growing problems at work.

Defining mental disorders as harmful dysfunctions is not ideal for all circumstances and purposes, and it is not always entirely clear (Lilienfeld & Marino, 1995). For example, how much impairment must appear before it becomes "dysfunction"? Are some psychological conditions dysfunctional in one culture, but functional in others? And when do the consequences of dysfunction cease to be merely annoying and become harmful? One parent, for example, might tolerate a child's misbehavior as "just a phase" of rambunctiousness while another might see the same behavior as a symptom of a disorder requiring medication. Clearly, there is room for bias to creep into the definition. And, like all other definitions, this one can be misused and misapplied. Still, defining mental disorder as harmful dysfunction appears to be the most workable, least arbitrary definition, and the one that best captures both the objective impairment and the subjective harm that is usually associated with the concept of mental disorders.

Assessment and Classification

Imagine that nothing happens when you turn on your television set. You check to see whether it has been unplugged; if not, has an electric switch in the room been flipped off? If not, is a circuit breaker tripped? If the answer to all these questions is no, you check whether other electrical devices in the house are working, whether your neighbors have power, and so on. These steps are all part of **assessment,** the collection of information for the purpose of making an informed decision. In the case of the malfunctioning TV, you are assessing the situation in order to classify or to make a **diagnosis** of the problem. Unless you can classify the problem with your TV, it will be hard to understand or fix it. The relationship between assessment and diagnosis is the same when trying to understand mental disorders. Clinical assessment is the foundation on which accurate diagnosis of mental disorders rests.

Assessment proceeds in three steps. Clinicians first gather assessment information. Next, they organize and process this information into a description or understanding of the person they are assessing. Finally, they compare this description with what is known about various disorders in order to arrive at a diagnosis of the problem. This last step in diagnosis is guided by a **nosology,** a classification system containing a set of categories of disorder and rules for categorizing disorders based on the signs and symptoms that appear (Millon, 1991). As noted earlier, the *Diagnostic and Statistical Manual of Mental Disorders (DSM-IV)* is the main diagnostic nosology in North America; clinicians in other parts of the world use the World Health Organization's *International Classification of Diseases (ICD-10)*.

Clinicians use a variety of sources to gather assessment information, from interviews and observations to psychological tests and personal diaries. The quality of assessment sources and the information they provide is evaluated on two dimensions: reliability and validity.

Reliability and Validity. Reliability, which refers to consistency or agreement among assessment data, can be measured in several ways. If an assessment is repeated at different times with essentially the same results, the assessment instrument is said to have high *test-retest reliability*. Another form of reliability that is especially important for psychological tests is *internal consistency,* which is judged to be high if one portion of a test provides information that is similar to that coming from other parts of the test. A third type of reliability that is especially important for diagnosis is interrater reliability. High *interrater reliability* means that different clinicians reach the same diagnosis, description, or conclusion about a person after using the same assessment tools.

The **validity** of an assessment instrument reflects the degree to which the instrument measures what it is supposed to measure. It provides an estimate of an instrument's accuracy or meaning. There are several types of validity. *Content validity* refers to the extent to which a tool measures all aspects of the domain it is supposed to measure. For example, an intelligence test that measures only math skills would be low in content validity because intelligence involves more than mathematical ability. If an assessment procedure accurately forecasts a person's behavior (e.g., grade point average, suicide attempts), it is said to have high *predictive validity.* When the results of one procedure agree closely with the results of another assessment method that was given at about the same time, the two methods are said to have high *concurrent validity.*

A final form of validity is construct validity (Cronbach & Meehl, 1955). An assessment method has high *construct validity* when its results coincide with what a theory about some construct would predict. For example, theories of anxiety predict that people's anxiety levels will increase under stressful circumstances. Thus, an anxiety assessment tool would have construct validity if it yields higher scores when people are in situations they fear, such as speaking in public. If not, the tool may not be measuring anxiety. Its construct validity is suspect. Construct validity cannot usually be established with a single experiment or demonstration; it requires a series of studies. The availability of assessment devices with good construct validity is important for identifying factors that place a person at risk for certain disorders and, in turn, for guiding the development of prevention programs, as discussed in the Prevention section on page 48.

The reliability and validity of assessments are typically expressed as **correlation coefficients,** which summarize the relationship between two variables. The size of a correlation, noted by the symbol r, ranges from 0.00 to +1.00 or −1.00. As Figure 2.1 illustrates, an r of 0.00 means that there is no relationship between two variables. A correlation of +1.00 or −1.00 is a perfect correlation, which means that if you know the value of one variable, you can predict the value of the second one with certainty. The larger the correlation (whether positive or negative), the stronger the relationship between the variables. In psychological assessment, adequate reliability is usually indicated by correlation coefficients in the .70 to .90 range. In most psychological research, validity correlations are in the .20 to .60 range, indicating that two variables are related to some less-than-perfect degree.

The validity of an assessment device can be no higher than its reliability, but it can be lower, some-

---

FIGURE 2.1

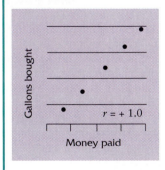 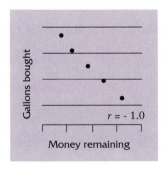 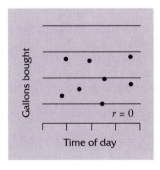

Correlations Showing Different Relationships Between Two Variables

In the first panel, the cost of a gasoline purchase shows a *perfect positive correlation* (+1.00) with the number of gallons purchased; the more you buy, the more you pay. In the second panel, the amount of money remaining in your wallet shows a *perfect negative correlation* (−1.00) with your purchase; the more you buy, the less cash you have left. The third panel illustrates a *zero correlation* in which the number of gallons purchased is unrelated to the time of day the purchase is made.

Prevention   The Role of Early Detection

One key to many forms of prevention is early detection of risks or behavior problems before they appear or worsen. Assessment instruments that yield reliable and valid information about the risk factors preceding a disorder are essential for aiming prevention programs at people who will most benefit from them. Reliability and validity of these assessments are also crucial in order to avoid subjecting people to interventions they do not actually need.

Juvenile delinquency and crime is one of society's most pressing problems. During the 1980s, arrests for persons younger than 18 increased 60 percent compared with a 5 percent increase for persons over 18 (Yoshikawa, 1994). The costs of these crimes is enormous, as is the fear they cause. Can juvenile delinquency be prevented? An answer to this question depends, first, on whether we can

- pinpoint early risk factors that lead to delinquency;
- assess which children actually possess or have been exposed to these risk factors; and
- design preventive interventions to reduce these risks.

Recent research by behavioral scientists has uncovered a valid set of early childhood risk factors for later aggression and chronic delinquency (Tolan, Guerra, & Kendall, 1995). Children at greatest risk are those who (1) have a difficult temperament, (2) are subject to abusive, hostile, or inconsistent parental discipline, (3) experience family adversity, (4) do poorly at school, and (5) come from a low socioeconomic background (Yoshikawa, 1994). Several of these risk factors can be detected during the preschool or elementary school years with special assessment techniques.

If you want to know about children, children are sometimes the best source of information. Asking children about their peers is one method for identifying highly skilled children as well as children who might need professional intervention.

The most common screening techniques involve asking parents, teachers, and other children to rate the aggressiveness of elementary school children. Aggressive behavior is a strong predictor of later problems, in part because aggressiveness turns out to be remarkably stable through the elementary, middle-school, and adolescent years. For example, one review found that between one third and one half of the boys who were excessively aggressive at ages 4 to 11 continued or intensified the same behavior over the next 4 to 9 years (Loeber & Dishion, 1983). Aggressive children can be readily identified by peers; children as young as 10 have been shown to reliably answer questions such as "Who never gets in trouble at school?" or "Who lies, cheats, or steals things in your class?" (Cole & White, 1993), and third-grade peer nominations of aggressive children have been found to predict problem behavior during high school (Coie et al., 1992).

Early detection, in turn, allows interventions to be put in place before problems become entrenched. Peer or teacher nomination techniques have been used to select children who would benefit most from early preventive interventions. The prevention programs that have proved most successful with early-aggression children combine extra educational assistance (such as Head Start) to improve commitment to school with training of parents to use more consistent and nurturing child-rearing methods (Yoshikawa, 1994; Zigler, Taussig, & Black, 1992). The newest delinquency prevention programs recognize that early aggression and later delinquency are caused by multiple factors arising in homes, schools, and peer systems and that changes must be achieved in each of these settings for prevention to be successful (Borduin et al., 1995; Tremblay et al., 1995).

times much lower. In other words, high reliability does not guarantee validity. Consider the example provided by the movie *The Crying Game*. The leading male character, Fergus, becomes obsessed with a beautiful nightclub singer named Dil. In one of the most surprising scenes in movie history, Fergus (and the audience) discovers that Dil is not a woman, but a male cross-dresser. Up to that point, the audience members' judgment about Dil's gender would have produced high interrater reliability; they would have agreed that Dil was an attractive woman. This high reliability did not make their assessment correct or valid, however.

Diagnostic Errors. It is fun to be fooled in the context of entertainment, but there is nothing funny about diagnostic errors in real life. Because people's lives can be drastically affected by clinicians' diagnostic judgments, the validity of those judgments is crucial. A clinician can reach two kinds of correct diagnostic conclusions: true positives and true negatives. In the case of a *true positive*, the clinician correctly concludes that a disorder is present; a *true negative* conclusion occurs when the clinician correctly states that the person does not have a disorder. The **sensitivity** of diagnosis is the probability that a person with a mental disorder will be diagnosed as having a disorder. Diagnostic **specificity** is the probability that a person without any mental disorder will indeed be seen to have no disorder.

Unfortunately, clinicians can also make two kinds of diagnostic errors: false positives and false negatives. A *false positive* occurs when the clinician concludes that the person suffers a disorder when no disorder is present; a *false negative* occurs when the clinician diagnoses no mental disorder when the person is actually suffering a disorder. Both kinds of errors can have severe consequences. False positives can lead to unnecessarily labeling, and possibly stigmatizing persons with no disorders. False negatives can keep troubled people from receiving the professional help they need.

In Review

Mental disorders have been defined as:

- deviations from social expectations;
- conditions that clinicians treat;
- conditions causing subjective distress and unhappiness;
- labels applied to unpopular behavior; and
- dysfunctions or breakdowns in a biological or psychological process that lead to harm.

The three major steps in assessment and diagnosis are:

- to gather information;
- to organize the information into a clinical description of the person; and
- to use this description and a nosology to reach a diagnosis.

The quality and utility of diagnoses depend on:

- the reliability and validity of the assessment tools used; and
- the sensitivity and specificity of the diagnoses.

Assessment Tools

To avoid false positives and false negatives, clinicians need reliable sources of information. They gather assessment information from five sources: life records, interviews, tests, observations, and biological measures.

Life records are documents associated with important events and milestones in a person's life, such as school grades, court records, police reports, and medical records. This information can be helpful in determining whether, when, and how often a certain problem has occurred. Because life records are usually made for reasons other than a formal assessment, they are unlikely to be distorted by a person's attempt to create a certain impression.

In practice, clinicians usually combine information from one or more assessment tools. When they use multiple channels of information, clinicians can compare the results from all sources, thus strengthening their confidence in their findings. Next, we consider the reliability and validity of the most commonly used assessment tools—interviews, tests, observations, and biological measures—and how each is used by clinicians in reaching diagnoses.

Interviews

Interviews are the most widely used assessment tool for classifying mental disorders. Because they resemble other forms of conversation, interviews are a natural way of gaining personal information. In addition, they are relatively inexpensive and flexible with respect to their content.

Modern diagnostic interviewing usually follows a structured format. In a **structured interview,** the interviewer asks questions in a predetermined sequence so the procedure is essentially the same from one respondent to another. Consistent rules are provided for scoring respondents' answers or for using additional probes designed to obtain scorable

TABLE 2.1	Structured Interviews Frequently Used to Assess Clinical Conditions

Interview	Purpose
The Schedule of Affective Disorders & Schizophrenia (SADS)	Differential diagnosis of more than 20 categories of mental disorder.
The Diagnostic Interview Schedule (DIS)	Used by nonprofessionals in large-scale epidemiological studies of mental disorder.
Structured Clinical Interview for DSM (SCID)	Broad-scale differential diagnoses tied to DSM criteria.
Diagnostic Interview Schedule for Children-Revised (DISC-R)	Parallel formats for children and parents for making differential diagnoses of childhood disorders.
Anxiety Disorders Interview Schedule-Revised (ADIS-R)	Differential diagnoses among anxiety disorders.
Personality Disorders Interview-IV	Differential diagnoses among DSM-IV Personality Disorders.
The Referral Decision Scale (RDS)	Preliminary screening of mental illness in jails.
Interdisciplinary Fitness Interview (IFI)	Evaluation of competence to stand trial.
Rogers Criminal Responsibility Assessment Scale (RCRAS)	Assess criminal responsibility against specific legal criteria.
Psychopathy Checklist Revised (PCL-R)	Evaluation of major dimensions of psychopathic (antisocial) behavior.

responses. Usually the interviewer is also given detailed guidelines for what to ask when the respondent answers questions in a given manner (for example, "If the respondent answers 'no,' skip to question 32 and continue with the interview."). Of course, interviewers are permitted some flexibility in how they word questions and in the number of questions they ask, but they are expected to indicate such changes whenever they deviate from the standard format so that the effects of any changes can be studied.

Table 2.1 describes a few of the many structured interviews in use today (see also Rogers, 1995). Several of these interviews are coordinated with DSM criteria in order to help the interviewer arrive at a diagnosis. The Personality Disorders Interview-IV (Widiger et al., 1995) is one example. Clinicians use it to determine whether a given client meets criteria for any of the personality disorders in DSM-IV. For example, one criterion for diagnosing someone with *borderline personality disorder* is whether the person has acted impulsively in at least two areas that could be personally damaging. An interviewer assesses this criterion with the following questions:

1. Did you ever spend so much money that you had trouble paying it off?
2. Have you ever gone on a drinking or eating binge?
3. Have you ever taken any major chances or risks with drugs?
4. Have you ever done anything impulsive that was risky or dangerous?
5. Have you ever become sexually involved with someone in a risky or dangerous way?

Another type of structured interview is the **mental status examination (MSE)**, a brief, specialized, and very focused interview designed to assess a person's memory, mood, orientation, thinking, and ability to concentrate. The MSE is analogous to the brief physical exam that physicians employ at the beginning of patient assessments. The questioning is direct, as suggested by the following excerpt:

Clinician: Good morning. I would like to ask you some questions. Is that all right?

Client: Fine.

Clinician: How long have you been here?

Client: Since yesterday morning.

Clinician: What are you here for?

Client: I don't know. I think my wife called the police and here I am.

Clinician: Well, what did you do to make her call the police?

Client: I don't know.

Clinician: What day is today?

Client: Tuesday, the twelfth.

Clinician: What year is it?

Client: 1997.

Clinical interviews also assess a person's **social history,** including educational achievements, occupational positions, family history, marital status, physical health, and prior contacts with mental health professionals. An accurate social history is crucial to the correct diagnosis of mental disorders because it helps establish whether the person has experienced symptoms of mental disorders in the past and, if so, which of the symptoms have been most prominent.

Interrater and test–retest reliability generally exceed +.70 for structured diagnostic interviews and mental status examinations, although, as the interval between interviews becomes longer, test–retest reliability sometimes decreases (Olin & Zelinski, 1991). The validity of structured interviews has been studied less often than their reliability has, but they are believed to be superior to any other diagnostic assessment tool. Occasionally, they serve as the standard against which to judge the diagnostic validity of other assessment methods such as tests or observations.

Unfortunately, many clinicians do not routinely use structured diagnostic interviews, preferring instead to "play their interviews by ear." Often they say that structured interviews are too bothersome to learn or that less structured interviews increase flexibility and save time. However, unstructured interviews are almost always less reliable than structured ones. Thus, what clinicians gain in flexibility and efficiency tends to be offset by what they lose in reliable and comprehensive information (Rogers, 1995).

Psychological Tests

A **psychological test** is a systematic procedure for observing and describing a person's behavior in a standardized situation. **Standardization** means that the test is administered and scored using uniform procedures for all respondents. Tests require a person to respond to a set of stimuli such as inkblots, true/false statements, or multiple-choice questions. These responses are then scored and compared with **norms,** scores obtained from large numbers of people who have taken the test previously under the same conditions.

Almost all of the thousands of psychological tests now in use can be grouped into one of five categories: achievement and aptitude tests, attitude and interest tests, intelligence tests, neuropsychological tests, and personality tests. **Aptitude tests** measure the accumulated effects of educational or training experiences and attempt to forecast future performance; the Scholastic Aptitude Test (SAT) is a familiar example. **Achievement tests** measure how much a person knows or can do in a specific area; the Wide Range Achievement Test-Revised (WRAT-3) is the

best-known example. Although achievement and aptitude tests are often used in diagnosing learning disorders and occasionally disorders that have an organic cause, they do not play a major role in diagnosing most mental disorders. Similarly, **attitude and interest tests**—which measure the range and strength of a person's interests, attitudes, preferences, and values—are seldom used in diagnostic classification, although they can add important information to a general psychological assessment.

Intelligence Tests. **Intelligence tests** measure general mental ability and various specific intellectual abilities such as verbal reasoning, quantitative skills, abstract thinking, visual recognition, and memory. The Stanford Binet Intelligence Scale (Thorndike, Hagen, & Sattler, 1986), the Wechsler Intelligence Scale for Children (WISC-III) (Wechsler, 1991), and the Wechsler Adult Intelligence Scale (WAIS-R) (Wechsler, 1981) are the best-known intelligence tests in the world today. Although originally written in English, these tests have all been translated into several languages, and norms are available for many different countries. Intelligence tests are used in the assessment and clas-

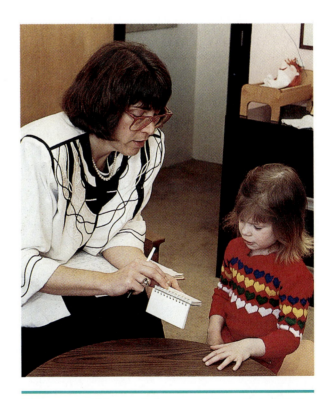

This young girl is completing one of the tasks included in the Stanford Binet Intelligence Scale. Individualized tests give psychologists an opportunity to observe clients' behavior, allowing them to compare and integrate information from two different, but simultaneous, assessment sources.

sification of brain damage, mental retardation, and other developmental disorders (see Chapter 4 for more on their use and limitations).

Neuropsychological Tests.

Neuropsychological tests measure deficits in behavior, cognition, or emotion that are known to correlate with brain dysfunction and damage. They are valuable tools for determining whether a person is suffering brain damage or deterioration, or for assessing how well a person has recovered following neurosurgery (Prigatano, Parsons, & Bortz, 1995). Neuropsychological testing often consists of a standardized set, or *battery,* of tests, but, as the following case illustrates, it may also be individualized, beginning with a few standard tests followed by tests selected with questions specific to the patient in mind (Lezak, 1995.)

*J*oyce, a 25-year-old woman, was knocked unconscious by an outdoor gas grill explosion that threw her 50 feet across the backyard into the wall of her house. She also sustained third-degree burns to her legs and arms when the propane gas ignited and engulfed her in flames. She reports almost no memory of the explosion.

Joyce spent two weeks in the hospital, receiving skin grafts and whirlpool therapy for her burns. About a year later, Joyce's physician referred her to a psychologist for diagnostic testing because of a variety of lingering symptoms including sleeplessness, loss of memory and concentration, and unusual outbursts of impulsivity and anger.

After taking a social history and learning about Joyce's accident, the psychologist was especially interested in determining whether Joyce might be suffering from some sort of head injury or from an anxiety disorder due to the stress of the accident. A host of neuropsychological tests were selected to measure Joyce's attention, memory, perceptual accuracy, and language skills. When they all yielded normal results, the psychologist concluded that Joyce's symptoms were the result of posttraumatic stress and recommended brief psychotherapy.

The most widely used neuropsychological test battery in North America is one developed by Ward Halstead and later modified by his student, Ralph Reitan. Table 2.2 summarizes some of the tests included in the Halstead-Reitan Battery. The results of one client's aphasia screening test are shown in Figure 2.2. Another popular battery is the Luria-Nebraska Neuropsychological Battery (Golden, Purisch, & Hammeke, 1985). Many neuropsychologists question the validity of the Luria-Nebraska, but its major advantage is that it can be administered in 3 to 4 hours, about half the time required for the Halstead-Reitan battery.

Personality Tests.

Personality tests measure an individual's predominant personality traits and charac-

TABLE 2.2   Some Tests Used in the Halstead-Reitan Battery

Test	Description
Categories test	Consists of 208 slides that require a subject to form correct categorizations of the visual stimuli in the slides. The test measures mental efficiency and the ability to form abstract concepts.
Tactual performance test	Consists of a board with spaces into which ten blocks of various shapes can be fitted, somewhat like a large jigsaw puzzle. The subject is blindfolded and then asked to fit the blocks into the spaces as quickly as possible. This test measures abilities such as motor speed, tactile and kinesthetic perception, and incidental memory.
Rhythm test	Presents thirty pairs of rhythmic beats. The subject says whether the rhythms are the same or different. It is a measure of nonverbal auditory perception, attention, and concentration.
Speech-sounds perception test	Requires that the subject match spoken nonsense words to words on written lists. Language processing, verbal auditory perception, attention, and concentration are measured by this task.
Finger tapping test	A simple test of motor speed in which the subject depresses a small lever with the index finger as fast as possible for 10 seconds. Several trials with each hand are used, allowing comparison of lateralized motor speed.

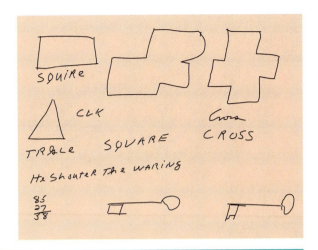

FIGURE 2.2

Results of an Aphasia Screening Test

These results are from a test given to a 60-year-old, college-educated, right-handed, independent businessman with suspected diffuse brain damage due to a metabolic disorder. His drawings of a square and two attempts at drawing a cross and key are much more primitive than expected for someone of his education. He could perform a basic subtraction problem but could not spell simple words such as *square, clock, triangle,* or *warning.* He could accurately copy the words *square* and *cross* when they were placed in front of him.

teristics. There are objective and projective personality tests. **Objective tests** require answers or ratings to specific questions or statements (for example, "Have you ever felt depressed?"); the responses can be scored quantitatively. **Projective tests** present ambiguous stimuli such as inkblots, incomplete sentences, or vague drawings to which people are asked to respond in any way they choose, often by telling a story or filling in a blank (see Figure 2.3 on page 54). Users of projective tests assume that these responses will reflect the meaning people "project" onto the ambiguous stimuli—that is, the way they perceive and interpret them—and thus reveal important characteristics about their personalities. Recently developed

scoring systems designed to provide quantitative summaries of projective tests have increased the tests' reliability (e.g., Exner, 1993), but they are still not as reliable as the best objective personality tests (Rogers, 1995; Wood, Nezworski, & Stejskal, 1996). Accordingly, projective tests tend to be less useful (and less often used) for diagnostic classification.

The most widely used objective test of personality is the Minnesota Multiphasic Personality Inventory (MMPI). Originally developed in the 1930s, it was revised in the 1980s and is now known as the MMPI-2 (Butcher et al., 1989). A separate form of the MMPI has been developed for adolescents (the MMPI-A) (Butcher et al., 1992).

Test	Description
Trail making test	A kind of "connect-the-dots" task involving a set of circles that are numbered or lettered. The circles must be connected in a consecutive sequence requiring speed, visual scanning, and the ability to use and integrate different sets.
Strength of grip test	A right-side versus left-side comparison of strength. The subject simply squeezes a dynamometer twice with each hand.
Sensory–perceptual exam	Assesses whether the subject can perceive tactile, auditory, and visual stimulation when presented on each side of the body.
Tactile perception tests	Various methods to assess the subject's ability to identify objects when they are placed in the right and left hand, to perceive touch in different fingers of both hands, and to decipher numbers when they are traced on the fingertips.
Aphasia screening test	A short test that measures several aspects of language usage and recognition, as well as abilities to reproduce geometric forms and pantomime simple actions.

FIGURE 2.3

Inkblot Such as Those Used in the Rorschach
What does this inkblot look like to you? Your response to this question might be determined by the shape of the blot ("It looks like a pelvis."), the whole blot ("It's a crab."), just some part of it ("Two smiling bears, on the sides"), or even the white spaces in the middle ("Cat's eyes, looking out at me"). Some people might even perceive movement taking place ("Those two bears are leaving their cave to get something to eat.").

The MMPI-2 consists of 567 true/false statements that were included in the test because they (1) distinguished between people who do and do not display mental disorders, and (2) differentiated people with different mental disorders. For example, one group of items tends to be answered in the same way by persons with schizophrenia; a different set of items tends to be answered similarly by depressed persons; a third set is answered in a typical way by people who are socially introverted. Based on these empirical differences, ten groups of differentiating items, called *clinical scales,* were named for the groups of people with which they were originally associated.

Table 2.3 summarizes the MMPI-2 clinical scales, along with four *validity scales,* groups of items on the MMPI-2 that help detect test-taking attitudes and distortions that may influence clinical scale scores. For example, the *F* (or infrequency) scale contains items that are rarely endorsed by members of any diagnostic group. High *F* scores suggest that a respondent was careless, attempted to exaggerate symptoms, or displayed a severe disorder.

To interpret an MMPI-2, clinicians create a *scale profile* showing a client's scores, such as the one shown in Figure 2.4 on page 56. They then conduct a *profile analysis* by comparing the client's scale profile with the profiles of other clients. Based on

that comparison, they form hypotheses about the person's psychological condition. The comparison can be based on the clinician's own experience with the MMPI-2 or on published norms showing the profiles of patients with various kinds of disorders. Increasingly, clinicians rely on computerized scoring and interpretation of the MMPI-2, in which a given client's profile is compared with thousands of other clients using actuarial formulas applied by a computer.

Despite widespread use, the MMPI-2 has been criticized for having been developed without reference to any underlying psychological theory about mental disorders (Helmes & Reddon, 1993). Items were included on the test as long as they differentiated people with different disorders, but the items themselves may not possess much construct validity or explain much about the nature of the disorders with which they correlate. Several other objective personality tests have attempted to overcome the perceived weaknesses of the MMPI-2 and to conform more closely to the DSM. Among the more influential of these newer tests are the Millon Clinical Multiaxial Inventory-II (Millon, 1987), the Basic Personality Inventory (Jackson, 1989), and the Personality Assessment Inventory (Morey, 1991). In addition, tests of normal personality such as the California Personality Inventory (Gough, 1987) and the NEO Personality Inventory-R (Costa & McCrae, 1992a) are also used to assess characteristics associated with mental disorders (Costa & McCrae, 1992b), usually as supplements to other objective measures of psychopathology (Ben-Porath & Waller, 1992).

Objective personality tests tend to have good reliability and adequate validity. For example, test–retest reliabilities for MMPI and MMPI-2 scales range from .60 to .90, even when retesting intervals span several years (Matz, Altepeter, & Perlman, 1992). Several studies have also demonstrated that the clinical scales of the MMPI and MMPI-2 possess good validity for the assessment of different mental disorders and clinical conditions (Ben-Porath, Butcher, & Graham, 1991; Keller & Butcher, 1991).

Nonetheless, objective test results are not foolproof indicators of mental disorders. They can be distorted by clients who are motivated to appear either overly healthy or extremely disturbed. Furthermore, test publishers sometimes assert claims for the test's predictive powers that go beyond the findings of empirical research. Accordingly, most clinicians are careful not to use psychological tests in isolation. Such tests should be just one element in a comprehensive evaluation that includes several assessment methods as cross-checks.

TABLE 2.3   MMPI-2 Scales and Simulated Items

Validity (or test-taking attitude) scales

Scale	Description
? (Cannot Say)	Number of items left unanswered.
L (Lie)	Fifteen items of overly good self-reports, such as "I smile at everyone I meet." (Keyed True)
F (Infrequency)	Sixty items answered in the scored direction by 10 percent or less of normals, such as "There is an international plot against me." (True)
K (Correction)	Thirty items reflecting defensiveness in admitting to problems, such as "I feel bad when others criticize me." (False)

Clinical Scales	Description
1 or Hs (Hypochondriasis)	Thirty-two items derived from patients showing abnormal concern with bodily functions, such as "I have chest pains several times a week." (True)
2 or D (Depression)	Fifty-seven items derived from patients showing extreme pessimism, feelings of hopelessness, and slowing of thought and action, such as "I usually feel that life is interesting and worthwhile." (False)
3 or Hy (Conversion Hysteria)	Sixty items from patients using physical or mental symptoms as a way of unconsciously avoiding difficult conflicts and responsibilities, such as "My heart frequently pounds so hard I can feel it." (True)
4 or Pd (Psychopathic Deviate)	Fifty items from patients who show a repeated and flagrant disregard for social customs, an emotional shallowness, and an inability to learn from punishing experiences, such as "My activities and interests are often criticized by others." (True)
5 or Mf (Masculinity-Femininity)	Fifty-six items from patients showing homoeroticism and items differentiating between men and women, such as "I like to arrange flowers." (True, scored for femininity.)
6 or Pa (Paranoia)	Forty items from patients showing abnormal suspiciousness and delusions of grandeur or persecution, such as "There are evil people trying to influence my mind." (True)
7 or Pt (Psychasthenia)	Forty-eight items from patients showing obsessions, compulsions, abnormal fears, and guilt and indecisiveness, such as "I save nearly everything I buy, even after I have no use for it." (True)
8 or Sc (Schizophrenia)	Seventy-eight items from patients showing bizarre or unusual thoughts or behavior, who are often withdrawn and experiencing delusions and hallucinations, such as "Things around me do not seem real" (True) and "It makes me uncomfortable to have people close to me." (True)
9 or Ma (Hypomania)	Forty-six items from patients characterized by emotional excitement, overactivity, and flight of ideas, such as "At times I feel very 'high' or very 'low' for no apparent reason." (True)
0 or Si (Social Introversion)	Sixty-nine items from persons showing shyness, little interest in people, and insecurity, such as "I have the time of my life at parties." (False)

Source: Adapted from Sundberg, 1977; p. 183.

Observations

Observational data often contribute to clinical assessment and diagnosis. Observational assessments are especially popular with clinicians who follow a behavioral model of mental disorders. In combination with other methods, observations can lead to a more comprehensive view of mental disorders, particularly when other instruments produce conflicting results. Observation is also useful when it helps clin-

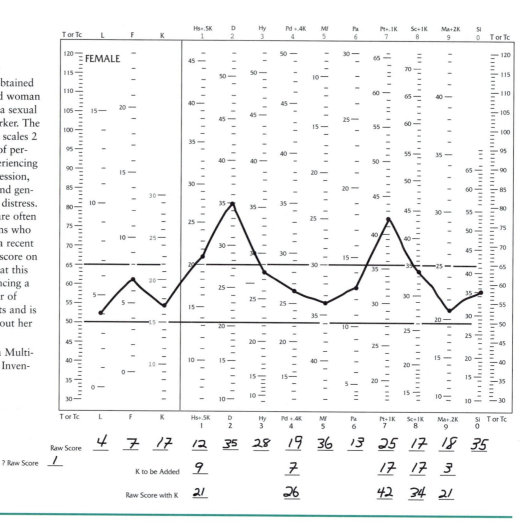

FIGURE 2.4

MMPI-2 Profile

This profile was obtained from a 38-year-old woman who had suffered a sexual assault by a coworker. The elevated scores on scales 2 and 7 are typical of persons who are experiencing symptoms of depression, tension, anxiety, and general psychological distress. These two scales are often elevated for persons who have experienced a recent trauma. The high score on scale 1 suggests that this woman is experiencing a fairly large number of physical complaints and is very concerned about her health.

Source: Minnesota Multiphasic Personality Inventory-2.

icians learn how changes in the environment might affect a problem behavior. These advantages are illustrated by the following case:

*J*enny was 10 when she was referred by her fifth-grade teacher to a psychologist because of behavior problems at school. According to the teacher, every time she asked Jenny a question or gave her a direction, Jenny talked back to her, saying things such as "I hate school, and you can't make me like it" or "You're picking on me. The other kids don't have to work so hard." Jenny's mother disputed the teacher's account. She said that Jenny never misbehaved at home and that the teacher did not know how to manage Jenny, who was bored with school because she was "too smart" for the fifth grade. The psychologist gave Jenny an intelligence test and found her IQ to be in the normal range. She then obtained permission to observe Jenny at school and also arranged for Jenny and her mother to come to the clinic where she could watch them through a one-way mirror.

The classroom observation revealed that, compared with her classmates, Jenny spent more time talking to other children, completed fewer tasks, and was often inattentive. During the play assessment, Jenny frequently contradicted her mother or ignored her suggestions. Jenny's mother tried to persuade her to cooperate by reasoning with her or threatening to cancel their planned trip to the mall. Based on these observations, which are summarized on the form shown in Figure 2.5, the psychologist concluded that Jenny was noncompliant in both settings, but in different ways.

Observations can be conducted in many different settings. Clinicians use *naturalistic* observation to look at people's behavior as it occurs spontaneously in a school, home, hospital, or office. In *controlled observation,* a clinician arranges for people to be observed reacting to controlled and standardized events such as a video about a feared stimulus. In *participant observation,* the observer is not only visible to those being watched, but may also interact

Name *Jenny*   Date_____   Rater _____

Math Class — 30-second intervals

Behavior						
Talking with children	✔	✔		✔		✔
Working on problem			✔		✔	
Paying attention					✔	
Walking around room			✔	✔	✔	
Looking out window	✔	✔		✔		

Play Period with Mother — 30-second intervals

Jenny

Behavior							
Follows mother's advice	✔				✔		
Contradicts mother		✔	✔		✔		
Plays with mother	✔			✔			
Ignores mother						✔	✔

Mother

Behavior							
Gives advice	✔	✔	✔		✔	✔	✔
Threatens		✔	✔		✔		
Ignores							
Rewards					✔		

FIGURE 2.5

Behavior Observation Form

The psychologist who observed Jenny used this form to record how often Jenny engaged in several behaviors during 30-second intervals in math class: paying attention to the teacher, talking with other children, working on problems, walking around room. The lower half of the chart was used to record interactions between Jenny and her mother during their play period.

with them. Usually, *nonparticipant* observers are not even in the same room with clients.

Self-monitoring is a special form of observation in which clients record the frequency, duration, intensity, or quality of their own behaviors, such as their smoking, eating, mood, or thoughts (Nietzel, Bernstein, & Milich, 1998).

Naturalistic observations are often impractical because of the obvious difficulty of following people around in their everyday environments. In addition, most people would not give clinicians permission to watch them in this fashion, creating an ethical barrier to many observations. As a result, direct observation for the purpose of assessing or diagnosing mental disorders is used mainly with children in school, daycare, or at play, and with severely disturbed patients in mental hospitals (Paul & Lentz, 1977).

Most modern observational approaches using well-trained observers achieve excellent interrater reliabilities. Self-monitoring clients often attain correlations in the .90s between their observations and those of external observers. Observations can also be highly valid if they meet three important criteria (Nietzel, Bernstein, & Milich, 1998). First, the observed behavior (e.g., a parent speaking in a raised voice to a child) must provide a satisfactory example of the construct being assessed (e.g., aggression). Second, the format for summarizing the observations (e.g., counting the number of voice raisings) must fairly represent the behaviors observed. Finally, the summary must provide a fair representation of the client's behavior when it is not being observed (the presence of an observer might cause a parent to be more controlled than usual).

Biological Measures

Biological methods allow a special kind of observation of changes in a client's body chemistry or other internal functioning that are almost never available to the naked eye (Tomarken, 1995). Also, these changes are seldom revealed through self-reports. Biological assessment is especially important because genetic and biological factors are becoming more prominent in explaining mental disorders.

Several mental disorders can now be assessed through the measurement of the biological changes that are uniquely associated with those disorders. These *biological markers*

Connections

Are measures of sexual arousal reliable enough to use in diagnosing specific sexual disorders? For the pros and cons, see Chapter 14, p. 518.

include counting fat cells that are associated with obesity (Brownell & Wadden, 1992); monitoring elevations in liver enzymes or blood cell size to detect alcoholism (Allen & Litten, 1993); measuring changes in the immune system following exposure to stressors (Kielcolt-Glaser & Glaser, 1992); or monitoring neurochemical and endocrinological changes in depression (Depue & Iacono, 1989) and schizophrenia (Hazlett et al., 1993).

Biological measurements are also useful for assessing anxiety, mood, sexual, and other disorders that have clear physiological components. For example, in patients with anxiety disorders, heart rate, respiration, blood pressure, muscle tension, and skin conductance are often measured as a way of studying the relationships between physiological arousal,

subjective distress, and behavioral dysfunction (McNeil et al., 1993). Physiological measures are also important in assessing sexual arousal, especially for clients who are attracted to socially deviant stimuli. Several studies, for example, have found that rapists show more arousal to rape stimuli than to scenes of consensual sex, while nonrapists show the opposite pattern (Hall, 1990).

The most widely used biological measures of mental disorders are techniques for studying the brain and its functions. Some direct neurodiagnostic procedures are summarized in Table 2.4; others involve brain imaging procedures. These latter procedures, most of which have been introduced during the past 20 years, identify abnormalities in the structure or functioning of certain areas of the brain. For

TABLE 2.4   Some Neurodiagnostic Procedures

Procedure	Description
Neurological clinical exam	The physician screens the patient's sensory abilities, eye movements, cognitive and perceptual abilities, language, motor and postural irregularities, and symptom history as a preliminary investigation of brain disturbance.
Lumbar puncture	Spinal fluid is extracted from the spinal cord through a needle. Examination of the fluid can help diagnose brain infections, hemorrhages, and some tumors. It has some complications, the most common of which is headaches.
Electroencephalogram (EEG)	The EEG monitors the electrical activity of the cerebral cortex. EEGs are useful in diagnosing seizure disorders and vascular diseases affecting large blood vessels in the brain, but they yield a relatively high rate of false positives. EEG recordings as a person sleeps—*polysomnographic measures*—are used to assess sleep disorders and can be collected in a person's home (Lacks & Morin, 1992).
Other electrical tests— electromyogram (EMG), evoked potentials, and nerve conduction velocities	All three tests measure electrical activity of some sort: in muscles (EMG), in the brain when elicited by an external stimulus (evoked potentials), or in peripheral nerves (nerve conduction velocities). They are useful in the diagnosis of muscle disease, nerve disease caused by conditions such as diabetes, sensory deficits, and serious headaches (Blanchard, 1992). Evoked potentials also have shown recent promise as a substitute for the polygraph in lie detection (Bashore & Rapp, 1993).
Arteriography	Dye is injected into arteries, and a series of X-rays are taken of the arteries as the dye passes through them. It is used to diagnose cerebrovascular disease, especially strokes and hemorrhages. Arteriograms can be uncomfortable and sometimes dangerous.
Biopsies and exploratory surgery	Both of these procedures involve direct examination of suspect tissue. Although they are risky, they can give definite diagnoses of some neurological conditions.
Computerized topographic mapping of EEGs	Uses computers to synthesize EEG more efficiently. This technique relies on a computer to analyze EEG signals, code their different frequencies with different colors, and then print a multicolored map of the brain showing differences in EEG activity.

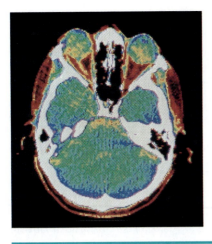 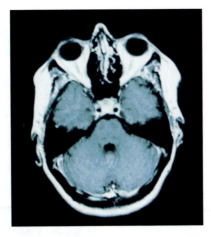 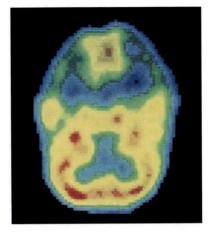

Mapping the geography of the brain: CT, MRI, or PET? Each type of brain scan has advantages and disadvantages. CT (left) scans show detailed pictures of the brain, but they cannot distinguish a live brain from a dead one. MRIs (middle) can resolve structures that are only a fraction of an inch apart, but they cannot picture the activity of these structures. PET (right) scans allow neuroscientists to watch different areas of the brain "light up" as they go about their work, but they cannot picture structure.

example, **computerized tomography** (**CT** scan) provides computer-enhanced, three-dimensional images of successive slices of the brain. CT scans are valuable in diagnosing tumors, traumatic damage, and degenerative diseases such as Alzheimer's and cerebrovascular disease.

Positron emission tomography (**PET** scan) shows changes not just in the structure of the brain, but also in its metabolic functioning. PET scans do this by tracking the rate at which radioactive glucose injected into the brain is consumed by brain cells. Since diseased tissue uses glucose at a different rate than normal tissue, the PET scan can reveal specific areas of abnormal brain physiology, as shown in the photograph. **Single photon emission computed tomography** (**SPECT**) is a similar procedure using a radioactive chemical that lasts longer than those used in PET scans. Therefore, SPECT can take pictures of the brain from several angles.

Another technique, called **magnetic resonance imaging** (**MRI**), works by tracking the activity of atoms in the body as they are "excited" by magnets in a chamber or coil placed around the patient (see the photograph). MRI involves no X-ray exposure. A newer version of magnetic resonance imaging called **magnetic resonance spectroscopy** (**MRS**) allows the simultaneous imaging of the brain's structure and function.

The reliability of biological measures is generally good, although each is sensitive to the effects of such factors as medication, circadian cycles, smoking, and overall fitness (Tomarken, 1995). These factors can also lower the validity of biological measures by misleading the diagnostician or researcher about a client's biological functioning. For example, most patients with severe mental disorders receive medication, often for months or years. The effects of such medication may make it impossible to obtain a valid assessment of the original biological factors that might have contributed to the patient's disorder. Further, the validity of biological assessments can vary from one disorder to the next, or one population to the next. Children, for example, often display abnormal EEGs despite the absence of any brain damage. Like other assessments, biological methods are fallible, and their relationship to psychological variables is often ambiguous.

In Review

Clinicians collect assessment data from five sources, which are then usually combined to help them diagnose mental disorders. Each of these assessment sources have unique strengths:

- life records are relatively immune to deliberate attempts by individuals to create particular impressions;
- interviews are flexible sources of information that, when sufficiently structured, yield highly reliable diagnoses;
- psychological tests are standardized instruments that allow accurate comparisons of a person's scores to those of others;

(continued)

- observations permit clinicians to assess the effects of situations on a person's behavior and to resolve discrepancies among other assessment sources; and
- biological measures permit assessment of internal changes that are neither observable nor reportable by clients themselves.

Diagnostic Classification

Accurate diagnosis is a necessary first step for the treatment and scientific study of mental disorders. Diagnosing disorders helps bring order to what would otherwise be a confusing welter of individual symptoms. Classifying mental disorders makes it possible to study them, to better understand their likely course, and to look for common causal factors in the backgrounds, experiences, and other characteristics of people with similar disorders. Diagnosis also allows clinicians to describe mental disorders with a common language that is efficient and easy to understand.

A Brief History

Although efforts to classify mental disorders began as early as Hippocrates' humoral system, scientifically based classification schemes did not appear until the nineteenth century. Several European physicians in that era proposed classification systems, beginning with Wilhelm Griesinger (1817–1868) who argued that mental disorders should be understood as biological diseases of the brain. The most influential classification scheme of this era was developed by Emil Kraepelin, a German psychiatrist. Kraepelin believed that the thousands of mental patients he observed throughout the world could be placed in three categories: *dementia praecox* (now called schizophrenia), *manic-depressive psychosis* (now called bipolar disorder), and *organic brain disorders* (now called dementia, delirium, amnestic and other cognitive disorders).

By 1917, a simple classification system for mental disorders was being used to gather hospital statistics in the United States. It did not prove clinically useful, however, so other classification schemes were developed in the 1930s and 1940s, including systems by the military to classify the many veterans who suffered mental disorders as a result of combat in World War II (see Widiger et al., 1991 for an historical review of this period). In 1948, the World Health Organization (WHO) published the sixth edition of the *Manual of the International Statistical Classification of Diseases, Injuries, and Causes of Death (ICD-6).*

The four temperaments, described by Hippocrates, formed an early classification system. Hippocrates believed that all disorders were biologically caused, and he linked different mental disorders to body fluids, or humors. Mania or irritability was the result of an excess of yellow bile (lower left); melancholy or depression was caused by too much black bile (lower right); sluggishness or lethargy was caused by too much phlegm (upper left); and an optimistic or a changeable temperament resulted from too much blood (upper right).

The ICD-6 included some mental disorders—classified essentially in the same way as in the U.S. military's system—but, because the expanding number of classification schemes were often in substantial disagreement with one another, the American Psychiatric Association decided to create its own system. In 1952, it published the first edition of the *Diagnostic and Statistical Manual of Mental Disorders (DSM-I)* (APA, 1952). To make the DSM conform more closely with the eighth edition of the ICD (World Health Organization, 1968), a second version of the DSM (DSM-II) was published in 1968 (APA, 1968).

The DSM-I and DSM-II had several major weaknesses. They lacked a uniform principle for assigning diagnoses. Some diagnoses were based on theories of causation (often psychoanalytic), others concentrated on symptoms that tended to cluster, and some reflected an assortment of criteria. Many disorders were defined so vaguely that it was difficult to obtain adequate reliability for them. Low reliability, in turn, insured low validity for many diagnoses. Furthermore, early DSM systems focused almost exclusively on a single label. They failed to consider background factors that influence the severity and prognosis of disorders, such as a client's medical problems, psychosocial stress, and cultural influences. Ultimately, and ironically, these systems had little effect on how different clients were treated, and they did not predict the course of disorders the way that a valid classification system should.

To correct these and other problems, in 1980 the APA published the DSM-III, a radically revised edition of the DSM (APA, 1980). Seven years later, it published another slightly revised edition, known as the DSM-III-R (APA, 1987). The advent of the DSM-III and DSM-III-R signalled a major change in how the North American classification system was constructed. The DSM-III was the first edition of DSM to provide specific, clearly defined criteria, some combination of which had to be present for a disorder to be diagnosed. These operational definitions uncoupled DSM diagnoses from theoretical assumptions about the cause and nature of disorders. By focusing instead on the observable signs and symptoms of various disorders, the DSM-III and DSM-III-R greatly improved the reliability of diagnoses by clinicians regardless of their theoretical model of psychopathology (APA, 1980, 1987).

The DSM-III also introduced **multiaxial classification,** which means that a person is described along several dimensions or *axes* (the plural of axis), such as physical health and social and occupational functioning, as well as the presence of mental disorders. Multiaxial classification provides a more complete picture of a client than any single label can.

Despite their many improvements, the DSM-III and DSM-III-R continued to have serious weaknesses. Several diagnostic criteria were still too vague and sometimes inconsistent, and interrater reliabilities were low for some of the axes. Furthermore, the influence of patients' gender, age, and cultural factors on diagnosis was not emphasized. Finally, many clinicians believed that too little attention was paid to the construct validity of many diagnoses (see Bellack & Hersen, 1988; Kaplan, 1983; McReynolds, 1989; Millon & Klerman, 1986; Nathan, 1987a; and Vaillant, 1984 for these and other critiques of the DSM-III and DSM-III-R).

One year after the publication of the DSM-III-R, the American Psychiatric Association formed a task force to develop the DSM-IV. The task force was charged with correcting many of the weaknesses in the DSM-III-R, but there were other reasons for the revision as well. For one thing, the WHO was ready to publish the latest edition of its ICD (ICD-10) in 1993, and the United States is under a treaty obligation to maintain classification systems that are consistent with those of the WHO. Also, there was a desire to build a better empirical foundation for DSM criteria. In the DSM-III and DSM-III-R, many

diagnostic criteria were based on the opinions of experts, not on empirical findings, because an insufficient number of diagnostic research studies were available. Finally, the DSM-III and DSM-III-R did not clearly document the rational or empirical support for their diagnostic criteria.

In preparing the DSM-IV, 13 groups of researchers and clinicians studied specific disorders and recommended the best way to diagnose them (Widiger et al., 1991). To resolve specific diagnostic controversies, the groups also conducted a series of field trials. A **field trial** is a research study conducted in the natural environment. The DSM-IV field trials were conducted with more than 6,000 subjects at more than 70 locations throughout the United States (APA, 1994). The final decisions of each group were reviewed by as many as 100 advisors who were not formally involved in developing the DSM-IV. Documentation of all this activity is contained in a five-volume *DSM-IV Sourcebook* (Widiger et al., 1994).

Diagnoses with the DSM-IV

Diagnosis of mental disorders in the United States and Canada is guided by the DSM-IV, while ICD-10 is officially used in the rest of the world. However, as a result of WHO's decision to also use specific operational definitions of mental disorders, the two systems have moved closer together in their approaches to diagnosis, making greater international cooperation possible and reducing cross-cultural variations in diagnostic practices (Sartorius et al., 1995). International contributions to classification is important, given that about 75 percent of psychiatric populations live in developing countries, primarily in Asia, Africa, and South America (Mezzich & von Cranach, 1988).

In truth, the DSM-IV is used unofficially by clinicians around the world, many of whom believe its diagnostic criteria are better validated than those of the ICD-10. One barrier to even wider international use of the DSM-IV is that, in the majority of developing countries, nonprofessional mental health workers render most of the care. They need a classification system that is simple to use, and the DSM-IV's relatively long lists of criteria for different disorders makes it less "user friendly" than would be ideal for these settings.

The DSM-IV retained a multiaxial approach to classification, but it modified the format of some of the axes.

- **Axis I** contains 16 general groupings of major mental disorders. Included on this axis are most of the disorders described in this book.
- **Axis II** contains mental retardation as well as 10 *personality disorders,* extreme styles of behavior that appear early in life and tend to

continue relatively unchanged through adulthood. The personality disorders were originally placed on a separate axis to ensure that they are not overlooked when a more obvious Axis I disorder is also present. However, this rationale is not very convincing because some personality disorders can be as obvious as most Axis I disorders. Axis II diagnoses continue mostly because of custom.

- **Axis III** lists general medical conditions that could be relevant to the understanding or treatment of mental disorders (see the DSM table below).
- **Axis IV** is a checklist for recording psychosocial and environmental stressors that could affect

the diagnosis, treatment, and course of a mental disorder. These stressors may be an acute problem, a chronic strain, a lack of social support, or any combination of these adversities. Generally, the clinician will focus on those stressors that have been present during the prior year unless there is some long-term stressor of obvious relevance (see the DSM table below).

- **Axis V** provides a scale on which clinicians rate the person's overall level of functioning at the time of the evaluation. This rating gives a summary assessment of the person's general clinical status and provides a gauge for how well the person has responded to treatment (see Figure 2.6).

DSM-IV

Axes III and IV

Axis III: General Medical Conditions

Infectious and Parasitic Diseases

Neoplasms

Endocrine, Nutritional, and Metabolic Diseases and Immunity Disorders

Diseases of the Blood and Blood-Forming Organs

Diseases of the Nervous System and Sense Organs

Diseases of the Circulatory System

Diseases of the Respiratory System

Diseases of the Digestive System

Diseases of the Genitourinary System

Complications of Pregnancy, Childbirth, and the Puerperium

Diseases of the Skin and Subcutaneous Tissue

Diseases of the Musculoskeletal System and Connective Tissue

Congenital Anomalies

Certain Conditions Originating in the Perinatal Period

Symptoms, Signs, and Ill-Defined Conditions

Injury and Poisoning

Axis IV: Psychosocial and Environmental Problems

Problems with primary support group

Problems related to the social environment

Educational problems

Occupational problems

Housing problems

Economic problems

Problems with access to health care services

Problems related to interaction with the legal system/crime

Other psychosocial and environmental problems

Source: American Psychiatric Association; *Diagnostic and Statistical Manual of Mental Disorders,* Fourth Edition. Washington, DC, American Psychiatric Association, 1994.

Global Assessment of Functioning (GAF) Scale

Consider psychological, social, and occupational functioning on a hypothetical continuum of mental health-illness. Do not include impairment in functioning due to physical (or environmental) limitations.

Code   (**Note:** Use intermediate codes when appropriate, e.g., 45, 68, 72.)

100 | Superior functioning in a wide range of activities, life's problems never seem to get out of hand, is sought out by others because of his or her many positive qualities.
91 | No symptoms.

90 | Absent or minimal symptoms (e.g., mild anxiety before an exam), good functioning in all areas, interested and involved in a wide range of activities, socially effective, generally satisfied with life, no more than everyday problems or concerns (e.g., an
81 | occasional argument with family members).

80 | If symptoms are present, they are transient and expectable reactions to psychosocial stressors (e.g., difficulty concentrating after family argument); no more than slight impairment in social, occupational, or school functioning (e.g.,
71 | temporarily falling behind in schoolwork).

70 | Some mild symptoms (e.g., depressed mood and mild insomnia) OR some difficulty in social, occupational, or school functioning (e.g., occasional truancy, or theft within the household), but generally functioning pretty well, has some meaningful
61 | interpersonal relationships.

60 | Moderate symptoms (e.g., flat affect and circumstantial speech, occasional panic attacks) OR moderate difficulty in social, occupational, or school functioning (e.g.,
51 | few friends, conflicting with peers or co-workers).

50 | Serious symptoms (e.g., suicidal ideation, severe obsessional rituals, frequent shoplifting) OR any serious impairment in social, occupational, or school
41 | functioning (e.g., no friends, unable to keep a job).

40 | Some impairment in reality testing or communication (e.g., speech is at times illogical, obscure, or irrelevant) OR major impairment in several areas, such as work or school, family relations, judgment, thinking, or mood (e.g., depressed man avoids friends, neglects family, and is unable to work; child frequently beats up
31 | younger children, is defiant at home, and is failing at school).

30 | Behavior is considerably influenced by delusions or hallucinations OR serious impairment in communication or judgment (e.g., sometimes incoherent, acts grossly inappropriately, suicidal preoccupation) OR inability to function in almost
21 | all areas (e.g., stays in bed all day, no job, home, or friends).

20 | Some danger of hurting self or others (e.g., suicide attempts without clear expectation of death, frequently violent, manic excitement) OR occasionally fails to maintain minimal personal hygiene (e.g., smears feces) OR gross impairment in
11 | communication (e.g., largely incoherent or mute).

10 | Persistent danger of severely hurting self or others (e.g., recurrent violence) OR persistent inability to maintain minimal personal hygiene OR serious suicidal act
1 | with clear expectation of death.

0 | Inadequate information.

FIGURE 2.6

Axis V of the DSM-IV

Clinicians rate an individual's overall level of functioning on Axis V. Axis V can be useful in tracking how much impairment a disorder may be causing at different times or how much clinical progress an individual has made in treatment.

Source: American Psychiatric Association; *Diagnostic and Statistical Manual of Mental Disorders,* Fourth Edition. Washington, DC, American Psychiatric Association, 1994.

Axis I: The Mental Disorders. The DSM-IV defines a mental disorder as a

> clinically significant behavioral or psychological syndrome or pattern that occurs in an individual and that is associated with present distress or disability or with a significantly increased risk of suffering death, pain, disability, or an important loss of freedom. In addition, this syndrome or pattern must not be merely an expectable and culturally sanctioned response to a particular event. . . . Whatever its original cause, it must be currently considered a manifestation of a behavioral, psychological, or biological dysfunction in the individual. Neither deviant behavior . . . nor conflicts that are primarily between the individual and society are mental disorders unless the deviance or conflict is a symptom of a dysfunction in the individual, as described above. (APA, 1994)

This definition of disorder is similar to Wakefield's "harmful dysfunction" definition described earlier. It emphasizes dysfunction that is internal to the individual, and it gives an operational definition to the idea of harm by referring to examples such as distress, disability, and other negative outcomes. It does not specify, however, what is meant by "mental." The term *mental disorder* suggests something other than a physical problem, but this distinction is arbitrary. In many cases that we will discuss, physical and mental causes and manifestations of disorders are so entwined as to be inseparable.

The DSM-IV diagnoses of mental disorders are arranged on Axis I in the following 16 major categories.

1. Disorders Usually First Diagnosed in Infancy, Childhood, or Adolescence. Although there is no set age limit for these disorders, they usually appear at least by adolescence. Included here are mental retardation (which is coded on Axis II), learning disorders, disruptive behaviors, attentional problems, tics, communication disorders, and several other problem behaviors associated with childhood.

2. Delirium, Dementia, Amnestic and Other Cognitive Disorders. These disorders all involve impairment in a person's cognitive functioning. They can be the result of substance abuse, disease, trauma, or age-related deterioration.

3. Mental Disorders Due to a General Medical Condition. This category includes certain mental disorders for which historical, physical, or laboratory findings point to a medical condition as the

cause. In DSM-IV, many such disorders are placed in categories whose symptom picture they share. For example, the criteria for a Mood Disorder Due to a General Medical Condition are listed and described in the Mood Disorder category.

4. Substance-Related Disorders. Included in this category are mental disorders arising from dependence on or abuse of alcohol, amphetamines, caffeine, cannabis, cocaine, hallucinogens, inhalants, nicotine, opioids, phencyclidine, and other drugs.

5. Schizophrenia and Other Psychotic Disorders. Schizophrenia and other psychoses typically involve serious disturbances in a person's perception and thinking, emotional responsiveness, and behavioral appropriateness. Several bizarre symptoms can be present in a psychosis: the most prominent usually involve distorted perceptions and thinking.

6. Mood Disorders. Mood disorders involve disturbances in emotion and usually fall into one of two patterns: (1) prolonged periods of depression and (2) shifts between periods of depression and periods of highly elevated mood and energy known as *manic episodes.*

7. Anxiety Disorders. Strong "irrational" feelings of fear, anxiety, and panic along with avoidance of feared situations typify the anxiety disorders. Various anxiety disorders are defined by the nature of the feared stimulus and the primary way the anxiety is expressed, such as through panic attacks, chronic worry, or avoidance of specific stimuli.

8. Somatoform Disorders. The central feature of these disorders is the existence of physical complaints or symptoms that suggest a physical disorder but that are, in fact, caused by psychological factors. The temporary loss of a sensory ability such as vision is a common example.

9. Factitious Disorders. This category refers to the intentional creation or feigning of physical or psychological symptoms in the absence of an obvious external incentive for doing so.

10. Dissociative Disorders. These disorders involve a disturbance or alteration in the normally integrated functions of identity, consciousness, or memory. Examples include multiple personality disorder (now called dissociative identity disorder) and psychologically caused memory disruptions.

11. Sexual and Gender Identity Disorders. Included in this category are *paraphilias* (experiencing sexual arousal in response to nonhuman objects or nonconsenting partners), dysfunction in sexual desire or sexual responses, and strong, persistent discomfort with one's gender and a preference to be the other sex.

Connections

How do personality disorders differ from Axis I disorders? Are they simply less severe? Are they the causes or the results of some mental disorders? See Chapter 12, pp. 412–413.

12. Eating Disorders. *Anorexia nervosa* (self-starvation) and *bulimia nervosa* (binging and purging) are the main disorders in this category.

13. Sleep Disorders. Insomnia, excessive sleepiness, recurrent nightmares and sleep terrors, and other sleep-related difficulties are included here. These problems are not considered disorders when they occur only occasionally.

14. Impulse-Control Disorders Not Elsewhere Classified. This category includes disorders involving repeated failure to resist impulses to steal, set fires, or gamble. Episodes of extreme aggressiveness are also classified under this heading.

15. Adjustment Disorders. Adjustment disorders appear as brief periods (not longer than 6 months) of poor adaptation and psychological symptoms in response to one or more psychological stressors that have occurred within the previous 3 months.

16. Other Conditions That May Be a Focus of Clinical Attention. This category includes a variety of clinical conditions that do not meet the criteria for being a mental disorder but are problematic conditions nonetheless and may be the focus of professional treatment; therefore, they are coded on Axis I. Examples include psychological symptoms that lead to a medical problem, that make a medical condition worse, or that delay a person's recovery from the condition; interpersonal conflicts involving romantic partners or family members; academic and occupational problems; bereavement; and other life crises.

Criteria for Diagnosis. Like the DSM-III and DSM-III-R, the DSM-IV lists specific operational criteria that must be met before a given disorder can be diagnosed. And like the DSM-III and DSM-III-R, the DSM-IV retains a **polythetic approach** to classification, meaning that, to be diagnosed with a mental disorder, a person must meet a particular number of criteria out of a larger set of possible criterion symptoms. For example, Table 2.5 shows that even though Nelson McGrath (whose case was discussed in Chapter 1) does not display all possible symptoms of schizophrenia, he meets enough DSM-IV diagnostic criteria for schizophrenia to be diagnosed. The polythetic approach contrasts with the **classical method** of classification in which every disorder is assumed to be a distinct, unique condition for which each and every attribute must be present for a diagnosis to be made.

Classical models are commonly used to diagnose physical illnesses, and they usually yield *homogeneous* categories. In other words, all individuals given the same diagnosis appear very similar to one another. Polythetic systems, on the other hand, produce greater variability among people receiving the same diagnosis. They generate *heterogeneous* categories; the same diagnosis can be given to patients who have a similar, *but not identical,* set of symptoms.

In addition, a person may be diagnosed with more than one DSM-IV disorder at the same time if he or she meets the criteria for each disorder. In fact, there are several reasons why mental disorders are likely to coexist, a condition known as **comorbidity** (Kendall & Clarkin, 1992). First, different disorders can result from the same cause or from different, but simultaneous, causes. For example, exposure to a violent stressor, such as the 1994 bombing of the World Trade Center in New York City, could lead to both an anxiety disorder and to depression. Second, the appearance of one disorder can lead to the development of another disorder. Third, comorbidity may merely reflect the fact that different disorders

TABLE 2.5   A DSM-IV Diagnosis of Nelson McGrath

DSM-IV criteria for schizophrenia	Nelson McGrath's behavior
At least two of the following symptoms during a one-month period: delusions, hallucinations, disorganized speech, disorganized or catatonic behavior, "flat" moods or lack of motivation.	Saw spots on himself and everyone else; numerous false beliefs involving contamination, threats from young girls; disorganized "speech" in diary; would not work.
Associated with symptoms is markedly poor performance in work, interpersonal relations, and self-care.	Mutilated his own skin; locked himself in room at night; health-impairing eating habits.
Disturbance has lasted at least six months.	Hallucinations present for at least five years.
Other mental disorders have been ruled out as explanation.	No symptoms indicated of exclusionary disorder.
Disturbance is not due to substance abuse or a medical condition.	No evidence of either.

often share similar criteria, resulting in an increased probability that diagnosis of one disorder will be accompanied by diagnosis of another disorder with overlapping criteria.

The comorbidity of mental disorders, which is discussed again later in this chapter and in several other chapters, has numerous implications for how clinicians diagnose and treat mental disorders (Clarkin & Kendall, 1992). Does each disorder require different, but simultaneous, treatment, or should the more serious disorder be treated first? Does the presence of a comorbid disorder make the targeted disorder more difficult to treat? These are some of the questions that researchers will study as comorbid mental disorders are fully investigated in the future.

The DSM-IV also contains new supplementary material that accompanies the criteria for many disorders. For example, one special section provides descriptions on specific cultural, age, and gender features that might accompany a particular diagnosis. Another section lists physical examination or general medical findings that might be associated with a disorder. These portions of the DSM-IV reflect two modern directions in the study of abnormal behavior—an increasing interest in discovering the biological foundations of disorders and a recognition that mental disorders need to be understood in their larger cultural and social context.

Criticisms of DSM Diagnoses

Despite continued improvement in the empirical foundations for diagnoses and greater sophistication in the way the diagnostic system is organized, the DSM-IV is still a target of several criticisms (Clark, Watson, & Reynolds, 1995). We discuss some of the most important of these next and in the Controversy section.

Labeling Produces Stereotypes, Prejudice, and Harm. It is easy to forget that diagnoses apply to disorders, not individuals. When people overlook this fact, diagnoses can have many adverse effects, including rejection and discrimination.

The potential dangers of labeling were suggested more than 20 years ago by a famous study conducted by David Rosenhan (1973). Rosenhan and seven other people, *none of whom suffered from a mental disorder,* presented themselves to psychiatric hospitals in five states and asked to be admitted as patients. Each person complained of the same, single symptom: hearing voices saying the words "thud," "empty,"

and "hollow." In almost every instance, the hospital's staff admitted these people and diagnosed them as schizophrenic, a serious disorder. Following their admissions to the hospitals, these pseudopatients behaved as normally as possible. Nonetheless, their actions were often interpreted as signs of disorder. For example, behaviors intended to relieve their boredom, such as keeping a personal journal, were interpreted by the hospital staff as symptoms of mental illness. Despite their normal behavior, the researchers were kept in the hospitals anywhere from 7 to 52 days. After being discharged, they were usually given the diagnosis "schizophrenia, in remission," suggesting that the disorder (which they never had!) might return someday.

One should be careful not to make too much of this study. As many critics pointed out (e.g., Spitzer, 1975), hospital staff are rarely confronted by normal people who report hearing nonexistent voices and ask to be admitted. Usually, something is wrong, and the clinician's wisest and safest course is to take the complaint seriously and admit the patient to the hospital. In fact, failing to do so might well be negligent, so legal considerations make the staff's reactions appear more reasonable. Still, the Rosenhan study did dramatically demonstrate how labels can exert too much influence, distorting the interpretation of a labeled person's behavior.

Labels can also lead to detrimental changes in the labeled person's behavior, especially when the label involves mental disorders. If a person were to be incorrectly diagnosed as having diabetes, this false-positive diagnosis may be frightening and could lead to additional, costly medical procedures. But the label itself will not cause diabetes. With mental disorders, false labels can sometimes make the conditions they describe more likely, an outcome known as a *self-fulfilling prophecy*. This concern is particularly strong with some childhood disorders. For example, children incorrectly diagnosed as having learning disabilities may decrease their academic effort because they believe that no amount of effort can ever overcome their "disabilities." Tragically, decreased motivation might increase the risk of academic difficulties, until the diagnosis finally appears accurate.

Do such dilemmas mean that diagnoses should not be made? No. Consider cases of Acquired Immunodeficiency Syndrome (AIDS). There is no doubt that patients diagnosed with AIDS often face prejudice and discrimination, a problem compounded by the fact that the prevalence of AIDS is disproportionately high among minority groups. Still, few would suggest that AIDS should not be diagnosed.

Controversy

Are DSM Diagnoses Biased by Gender?

One of the most heated controversies regarding the diagnosis of mental disorders is the criticism that the DSM is gender biased. For example, some charge that its diagnostic criteria codify "masculine-based assumptions about what behaviors are healthy and what behaviors are crazy" (Kaplan, 1983). Others object that society encourages women to be submissive and dependent, but then labels them as mentally disordered if they show too much of these qualities. In the DSM-IV, for example, one criterion for Histrionic Personality Disorder (which is much more commonly diagnosed in women than men) is "consistently uses physical appearance to draw attention to self." Our male-dominated society appears to want women to be physically beautiful so they are more sexually desirable, but it then condemns them with a diagnostic label if they show what men think to be too much of this quality.

The existence of gender bias in DSM diagnoses would be a major scientific, social, and clinical problem. However, the mere fact that one gender is diagnosed with certain disorders more often than the other does not necessarily mean the diagnosis is biased. Consider the obvious case of breast cancer, a disease diagnosed almost exclusively in women. This difference does not reveal a bias, however; it simply reflects a biological consequence associated with gender. Similarly, the fact that antisocial personality disorder is more frequently diagnosed in males than in females might reflect real sex-linked differences rather than a socially constructed bias.

Gender bias can be defined in several ways (Widiger & Spitzer, 1991). One type occurs when a disorder is misdiagnosed for one sex more often than for the other. For example, if females are more often diagnosed with a disorder they do not in fact have (a false-positive diagnosis), gender bias is present. Likewise, if men are more often not diagnosed with a disorder they really do have (a false-negative diagnosis), bias is again present.

Such errors might stem from two sources. First, clinicians could be using different standards in applying diagnostic criteria to males and females. If a clinician required that male clients show more sadness, dejection, and suicidal concern to be diagnosed as depressed than they required of female clients, the clinician's diagnoses are gender biased. Second, the diagnostic criteria themselves could be biased. If a criterion resulted in one sex's being diagnosed with a disorder more often than the other *and* this criterion had not been proved to be related to what is known about the cause or course of the disorder, the criterion itself is gender biased.

At present, evidence that clinicians make gender-biased diagnoses is stronger than the evidence that the criteria themselves are biased (Widiger & Spitzer, 1991). In one study (Ford & Widiger, 1989), psychologists read one of three case histories that illustrated antisocial personality disorder (APD; diagnosed more often in males), histrionic personality disorder (HPD; diagnosed more often in females), or an ambiguous mixture of the two. One third of the psychologists were told that their case involved a female client, one third were told it was a male, and one third were not informed of the client's gender. A second group of psychologists rated the extent to which each symptom presented in the cases represented a criterion for antiso-

cial or histrionic diagnosis. For the antisocial case, the psychologists failed significantly more often to diagnose APD for the female (15 percent) than for the male (42 percent). The reverse was true for the HPD case; the psychologists significantly underdiagnosed this disorder in males (44 percent) compared with females (76 percent). The ambiguous case was not affected by the gender of the client, and the gender of the psychologists themselves made little difference to their diagnoses. Little, if any, bias was shown in the ratings of individual criterion symptoms. Regardless of the gender of the client, psychologists rated individual criteria as representative of the correct diagnosis.

Either type of bias, whether in criteria or in diagnostic practices, is important, however, and clinicians have much more to learn about the validity of disorders that are diagnosed at different rates for males and females.

Thinking Critically

On the basis of this study, it appears that clinicians are more likely to be biased than diagnostic criteria are. But take a closer look at this conclusion and the study we described.

- How else could a researcher distinguish biased diagnosis from biased criteria?

- What other sources of gender bias might exist besides clinicians' decisions and the diagnostic criteria themselves?

- Should identical criteria be applied to diagnosing men and women, regardless of the results of research studies?

Whatever the problem—AIDS or a mental disorder—learning more about it and caring adequately for those who suffer from it require its accurate detection.

Mental Disorders Occur on a Continuum, Not in Discrete Categories. DSM-based diagnoses imply that a person either does, or does not, have a disorder. This categorical, all-or-none approach to classification has been challenged by mental health professionals who argue that mental disorders are not arranged so neatly in real life (Carson, 1991). Many argue as well that the line separating disorder from nondisorder in the DSM—in terms of the particular number of symptoms needed to define a disorder—is usually rather arbitrary.

One alternative is for clinicians to think of disorders occurring along different dimensions (Widiger et al., 1987). In a **dimensional approach,** a person would receive scores on several dimensions of personality such as extraversion, openness to different kinds of experience, conscientiousness, and emotional stability. When taken together, these scores produce a profile that summarizes the person's standing on those dimensions.

How would Nelson McGrath have been described by a dimensional system? Using the most common personality dimensions—sometimes called "The Big Five"—a clinician might describe Nelson as highly introverted, extremely emotionally unstable, and very prone to odd, eccentric experiences. He also would probably be rated as interpersonally disagreeable and very low on conscientiousness and achievement.

Although the multiaxial organization of the DSM-IV reflects an appreciation of dimensional approaches, the overall logic of DSM-IV diagnoses is still categorical. The categorical approach has remained dominant for several reasons: (1) the medical tradition of diagnosis emphasizes discrete illnesses; (2) clinicians find it easier to use categorical systems; and (3) theorists have not been able to agree on the nature or number of personality dimensions necessary to describe psychopathology adequately (Millon, 1991).

The DSM-IV Pays Too Much Attention to Reliability, Not Enough to Validity. In order to ensure high interrater reliability, the diagnostic criteria for DSM-IV disorders were simplified and made specific enough that clinicians could agree on them. However, this simplification may have distorted the true nature of some disorders (Carson, 1991; Widiger & Trull, 1991). Imagine that you used the same approach in setting up a movie review system to help different movie critics agree on whether a particular film is good enough to earn four stars. You might re-

quire that only movies with French subtitles be rated four stars. This four-star criterion would produce excellent agreement among movie critics but would not be valid because it excludes many potentially excellent movies from consideration. Likewise, too much simplification in diagnostic criteria may enable clinicians to agree, but their diagnoses may not adequately reflect the core features or implications of many mental disorders.

DSM Diagnoses Imply That Disorder Is the Result of Causal Factors Internal to the Person Rather Than of External, Environmental Problems. Despite the presence of Axis IV (psychosocial stressors), the DSM-IV emphasizes individual dysfunction far more than the effects of harmful environments and social policies that impair people's psychological adjustment. Some critics believe this emphasis on internal factors is one of the most harmful effects of the medical model of mental disorders. By focusing diagnoses exclusively on individual problems, mental health professionals run the risk of blaming the victims of poverty, discrimination, undereducation, unemployment, and abuse. In a country such as the United States, where one in every five children lives in poverty, the potential significance of considering the external factors contributing to psychopathology is obvious. If destructive environments and social policies are the true culprits behind some mental disorders, diagnostic practices that distract mental health professionals from working on these external problems do a disservice to persons with mental disorders and to society at large.

Diagnosis in the Real World

When clinicians conduct assessments and assign specific diagnoses, their decisions are affected by many factors other than a person's social history, test responses, or clinical interview. Consider again the case of Bill that opened this chapter. Based on Bill's history and current symptoms, what diagnosis do you think a clinician would give him?

Money, Privacy, and Diagnoses. Bill's symptoms satisfy the criteria for an anxiety disorder; the amount of conflict in his marriage points to a marital problem; and the psychological stress of an impending job loss indicates the likelihood of an adjustment disorder. (Assume that the results of psychological testing are consistent with any of these diagnoses.) The clinician may assign any or all of these diagnoses, but the final decision will be influenced by additional factors that are distinct from, and go beyond, Bill's clinical complaints.

First, like the majority of Americans, Bill has health insurance, paid for in part by his employer. The policy will pay 50 percent of the cost of up to 20 sessions of psychotherapy for most Axis I disorders, including anxiety disorders, but does not cover treatment of marital problems or adjustment disorders. There is an obvious *financial* incentive for the clinician (and Bill) to diagnose an anxiety disorder.

In order to make Bill's treatment financially feasible, the clinician could decide to diagnose anxiety disorder, but Bill is concerned that his insurance company will review the diagnosis and treatment before reimbursement is made. He wants assurance from the clinician that the diagnosis will be kept confidential; otherwise, he is convinced that his employer will use the anxiety disorder diagnosis to hasten his dismissal. The clinician cannot, in good conscience, provide this assurance because this insurance carrier has not previously protected clients' privacy.

In addition to Bill's financial and social considerations, the clinician's professional interests may influence the diagnosis. Clinicians who have expertise in treating one disorder may construe ambiguous cases in a way that results in the favored diagnosis. Some clinicians try to build a reputation for specializing in specific disorders, so marketing considerations might also influence diagnoses.

Another factor that influences diagnosis is that many people with mental disorders do not go first to mental health professionals, but to a hospital emergency room, their family physician, or a health maintenance organization (HMO). Compared with mental health specialists, primary care physicians tend to underdiagnose mental disorders (Muñoz et al., 1994). If Bill had first consulted his primary physician, he might well have been diagnosed with, and treated for, a physical rather than a mental disorder.

Diversity and Assessment Measures. When you first read about Bill, how did you visualize him? If you are like most of the people who have read this case, you probably assumed that Bill is White. But in fact, Bill is Black. Your assumptions about Bill's ethnicity illustrate another major influence on the way clinical diagnosis is conducted in the real world. Human diversity affects the manifestation and diagnosis of mental disorders in several ways. For example, most psychological tests, structured interviews, and observational systems were developed and normed on European American samples. Are these measures biased against ethnic minorities as a result?

A test can be biased in at least two ways. First, people from a certain ethnic group may do poorly on a test relative to other groups *for reasons that have nothing to do with what the test is measuring.* For example, a person whose first language is not English will probably not perform as well on an IQ test administered in English as a person who has always spoken English. Many popular IQ and personality tests have been translated into different languages to overcome this bias, but we still must be cautious that the translation does not introduce subtle differences in meaning that distort the interpretation of test scores.

A second type of bias occurs when scores on a test lead to valid predictions for one ethnic group but invalid predictions for another group. For example, if subjects from different ethnic groups take a personality test, do their scores lead to equally accurate predictions? If not, the test is biased. In one study (Timbrook & Graham, 1994), Blacks and Whites completed the MMPI-2, and their spouses or partners rated them on a variety of traits and behaviors that should correlate with the test scores. No ethnic differences were found for the accuracy of MMPI-2 scores in predicting the partners' ratings. At least on the basis of this preliminary study, the MMPI-2 was not biased in its ability to predict outcomes for White and Black subjects.

Another possible problem is that members of various ethnic groups may respond differently to interviews. To take just one example, being surveyed about symptoms of mental disorder over the telephone by a stranger probably has a unique meaning for an older Chinese woman whose traditions suggest that personal problems are matters to be kept within the family (Ying, 1989). At the same time, she might see refusing to cooperate with an interviewer as unacceptably rude. Many traditional Chinese women appear to resolve this dilemma by not acknowledging to interviewers that they have experienced certain symptoms.

Diversity and Definitions of Mental Disorders. Ethnic or cultural factors are most likely to distort diagnoses when clinicians do not understand a person's cultural or ethnic background. For example, Asian Americans may express psychological problems through physical complaints, a tendency known as **somaticizing.** This form of complaint may be less embarrassing to people from an Asian background than admitting to emotional problems. Therefore, clinicians need to consider how cultural tolerance for different kinds of problems may affect the way clients experience distress.

Connections

How could social adversity and poverty contribute to the incidence of mental disorders? See Chapter 1, pp. 27–28, or how socioeconomic stressors affect health behaviors in Chapter 6.

The dress of teenagers is often consistent with the values that prevail in their culture. Japanese youth often dress in a way that reflects traditional Asian values of group conformity and collectivism. These values affect the form of some mental disorders in Eastern cultures.

To foster an appreciation of how diversity affects the expression of mental disorders, the DSM-IV includes a glossary of **culture-bound syndromes,** patterns of abnormal behavior that appear only in certain localities or cultures. In some cases, these syndromes closely resemble DSM-IV disorders. In other cases, the syndrome is limited almost exclusively to one cultural setting; koro and Windigo, described in Chapter 1, are examples.

Diversity and Interactions Between Clients and Clinicians. The effect of ethnic or cultural factors on diagnosis stems in part from their impact on how clinicians and clients interact. At the most obvious level, if they have difficulty understanding each other's spoken language, the clinician will have difficulty understanding the client's psychological functioning. In particular, clinicians must be cautious about how they interpret idioms such as "My nerves are shot" or "I'm having my spells again."

Cultural values can also affect a person's willingness to disclose personal problems to a professional. The cultural background of many Hispanic Americans, for example, tends to discourage seeking help from outside professionals, so it is not surprising that Hispanic Americans use formal mental health services less than other ethnic groups (Sue, Zane, & Young, 1994).

Failure to understand the influences of clients' cultural background and experience can lead clinicians to make two fundamental mistakes (Lopez, 1989). First, clinicians can misconstrue a certain behavior as a symptom of a mental disorder when in fact the behavior is considered desirable in the client's culture. An example of this **overpathologiz-**ing error is seen when some Hispanic American's deference to family authority figures is interpreted as a sign of anxiety or immaturity. The opposite of this tendency is the **underpathologizing** error in which clinicians dismiss some bizarre behavior as merely the reflection of a cultural difference when in fact it is the symptom of a mental disorder. This mistake sometimes occurs when clinicians try too hard to prove their cultural sensitivity and can result in people being denied the treatment they clearly need.

In Review

Scientific classification of mental disorders was first widely established in the United States with the introduction of the DSM in 1952. In DSM-IV diagnoses:

- a person's behavior is compared with a set of clearly specified criteria for each disorder;
- the person's behavior must satisfy a predetermined number of these criteria for a disorder to be diagnosed; and
- a person is assessed on several axes including medical conditions, exposure to stressors, and overall functioning, as well as the presence of mental disorders.

Major criticisms of the DSM-IV are:

- that psychiatric labels can be biased and harmful;
- that mental disorders are not "either/or" categories as much as they are extremes along continuous dimensions;

- that too much attention to the reliability of diagnoses has detracted from their validity; and
- that DSM diagnoses imply that mental disorders are caused by internal factors alone, thus ignoring important social causes.

Diagnoses of mental disorders in the real world are influenced by:

- financial considerations;
- concerns over privacy; and
- ethnic and cultural factors that shape the way clinicians and clients understand and interact with each other.

The Frequency of Mental Disorders

How many people currently suffer from a mental disorder or have suffered from one at some point in their lives? These are among the questions addressed by the field of epidemiology. The total number of people who suffer from a disorder in a specific population is called the **prevalence** of a disorder; lifetime prevalence is the percentage of people in a population who have had a disorder at any time in their lives. The number of people who develop a disorder in a specific time period (usually the previous 6 or 12 months) is known as the **incidence** of a disorder.

Epidemiologists have studied the prevalence and incidence of mental disorders in the United States and other parts of the world throughout the latter half of the twentieth century. Their studies are usually based on interviews with large numbers of people who have been selected to represent a larger population. For example, researchers conducting the Midtown Manhattan Study (Srole et al., 1962) interviewed more than 1,600 people in New York City. Based on these interviews, the authors estimated that about 26 percent of the population had a mental disorder.

The most comprehensive study of mental disorders in the United States was the Epidemiologic Catchment Area (ECA) Project sponsored by the National Institute of Mental Health (Robins & Regier, 1991). In this study, trained interviewers used a structured interview (the Diagnostic Interview Schedule or DIS) to collect information about 30 major mental disorders in five large "catchment" areas: Los Angeles, California; St. Louis, Missouri; New Haven, Connecticut; Baltimore, Maryland; and Durham, North Carolina. More than 20,000 subjects were selected so that their age, gender, economic status, education, and place of residence made them as representative as possible of the United States population in general. Interviews were conducted not only with community residents, but with people living in prisons, nursing homes, hospitals, and other institutions.

What can the ECA Project tell us about mental health in the United States? Some of the most important of the study's many findings were these:

1. The lifetime prevalence of any of 30 major mental disorders was 32 percent. About one in four people had suffered an active mental disorder in the prior year. Results from the National Comorbidity Survey (NCS), another recent large-scale epidemiological study, suggest that even these figures may underestimate the extent of mental disorders in our society (Kessler et al., 1994). Based on structured interviews with a national sample of more than 8,000 adults, ages 15–54, this survey found that 48 percent of this sample reported at least one lifetime mental disorder, and 29 percent indicated that they had experienced a disorder in the prior year.

2. The lifetime prevalence of mental disorders was frequently related to demographic or social variables, as Figure 2.7 on page 72 shows. Higher rates of disorder were associated with being poor and not completing high school. Black Americans showed higher rates of mental disorder than European Americans or Hispanic Americans did. However, according to more detailed ECA and NCS results, if cognitive symptoms that are strongly correlated with social class are excluded, Black Americans actually show a lower prevalence of several disorders, including mood disturbances and substance abuse, than did European Americans (Kessler et al., 1994). Rates of disorder also varied considerably among different ECA sites, from a high of 41 percent of the sample suffering a disorder in Baltimore to a low of 28 percent in New Haven.

3. The most common disorders are phobias and alcohol abuse, followed by generalized anxiety disorder, major depression, and drug abuse or dependence (see Table 2.6 on page 72).

4. About 38 percent of people with a history of disorder were in **remission** (defined as being free of symptoms during the year prior to the interview). Over half of the persons who had suffered drug abuse/dependence, generalized anxiety disorder, alcohol abuse, or antisocial personality disorder had been without symptoms of these disorders during the prior year.

5. Remission rates far exceeded the percentage of people seeking treatment for a disorder. Indeed,

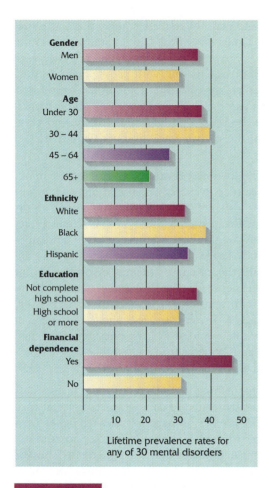

Lifetime prevalence rates for any of 30 mental disorders

FIGURE 2.7

Demographic Characteristics and the Prevalence of Mental Disorders in the ECA Study

Overall prevalence was greater among men, and large sex differences were also found for rates of specific disorders. Anxiety and mood disorders were more frequent in women; antisocial personality disorder and substance abuse problems were more common in men. Surprisingly, older people did not show higher prevalence rates although they have had more years to develop a disorder. Poverty and lower levels of education were associated with higher prevalence rates.

Source: Robins & Regier, 1991.

| TABLE 2.6 | Prevalence of Specific Disorders (Percent of Sample with Disorders) |

Disorder	Lifetime	Active (one-year)
Phobia	14.3	8.8
Alcohol abuse/dependency	13.8	6.3
Generalized anxiety	8.5	3.8
Major depressive episode	6.4	3.7
Drug abuse/dependence	6.2	2.5
Antisocial personality	2.6	1.2
Obsessive compulsive disorder	2.6	1.7
Panic	1.6	0.9
Schizophrenia or schizophreniform disorder	1.5	1.0

Source: Adapted from Robins and Regier, 1991.

served, meaning that they do not receive interventions that are needed.

6. Comorbidity of mental disorders was common. If we define comorbidity simply as having at least two different diagnoses, 18 percent of the ECA sample would be classified as comorbid, and 60 percent of people with one disorder in their lifetime had at least one additional diagnosed mental disorder. The comorbidity results from the NCS are even more striking. Among respondents with a history of at least one disorder, 56 percent had suffered one or more other disorders in their lifetime, and over half of all lifetime disorders occurred in the 14 percent of the sample having a history of three or more comorbid disorders. In other words, the major burden of mental disorders is concentrated in a group of comorbid people who constitute less than one sixth of the population.

7. In the ECA study, the first symptoms of most mental disorders occur at a surprisingly early age. Considering all disorders, the average age for noticing the first symptoms of a disorder was 16. This finding helps explain the dual emphases throughout this book on understanding the developmental origins of mental disorders and on the need for preventive programs that focus on children and adolescents.

only 19 percent of community residents with a current disorder reported receiving recent treatment for it, usually from general physicians rather than mental health professionals. Children, the elderly, ethnic minorities, the poor and homeless, and people with physical disabilities are especially likely to be *under-*

A Talk with Thomas Widiger

Dr. Thomas Widiger, Professor of Psychology at the University of Kentucky, is a leading expert on the diagnosis of mental disorders. Dr. Widiger has written extensively about classification issues, and he served as the Research Coordinator for the DSM-IV.

Diagnosis

Q *Why do we need a classification system such as the DSM-IV?*

A The main reason is the one you discuss in this chapter. We have to have a common language so we can discuss what we are studying. Classification allows us to communicate about mental disorders. Without it, meaningful communication would be impossible. Even though diagnosis carries risks of bias and stigmatization, these risks are outweighed by the communication advantage that formal classification provides. On the other hand, careful construction of a system such as the DSM is crucial because, like any language, it governs how clinicians think about their clients.

> . . . all people suffer a mental disorder at some point in their lives.

Q *What is the role of psychological assessment in diagnosis?*

A Beginning with the DSM-III, the use of well-defined classification criteria has resulted in an increased emphasis on structured and semistructured diagnostic interviews. Although psychological testing remains an important element in assessment, its role in diagnosis is diminishing. Obviously, this trend means that students need much better training in interviewing techniques than they have typically received so that they are competent in using the new structured interviews.

Q *How prevalent are mental disorders?*

A I actually think they are much more prevalent than studies such as the NIMH ECA suggest. I am convinced that all people suffer a mental disorder at some point in their lives. We recognize this to be true for our neighbors or roommates or friends, but we find it difficult to admit ourselves. If we acknowledged that mental disorders are more common in ourselves, it would have the added advantage of decreasing their stigma. People are less stigmatized by physical illnesses, in part, because we recognize they are just a part of life. Mental disorders are really no different. Nobody is entirely physically healthy, and nobody is entirely psychologically healthy.

Q *How will diagnosis change in the future?*

A The biggest change in the future will be an increasing reliance on neurochemical models of disorder. You can already see this trend in the progress and emphasis on medication treatments and in the DSM-IV itself, which includes a special section for listing any lab and physical exam findings that are associated with the disorder. This emphasis is, of course, part of larger trend within psychiatry, which is betting more and more of its money on biological horses. However, I believe the pendulum is swinging too far in the biological direction. We are psychosocial beings as well as biochemical animals, and our understanding of mental disorders needs to reflect this fact.

I also think we will see dimensional approaches to mental disturbance becoming more accepted. This trend is revealed by the number of newly suggested disorders, many of which are intended to fill in the gaps between existing disorders. So we now have new disorders being discussed such as mixed anxiety-depressive disorder and bipolar 2 disorder (filling the gap between bipolar disorder and cyclothymia). In my opinion, it would be much better to recognize that many of these categories do not refer to distinct conditions but rather to different slices or forms of underlying dimensions that usually shade into normality.

The case of Bill, which began this chapter, is typical of what clinicians encounter in their everyday practice. Bill's symptoms are common, and his concerns about being diagnosed are also familiar to most clinicians. His case illustrates how clinicians must constantly balance knowledge about disorders and official classifications with the many practical consequences of a diagnosis.

The clinical psychologist who assessed Bill conducted a comprehensive psychological assessment that included a social history and review of Bill's medical and work records, an extensive structured interview geared to measure DSM-IV diagnostic criteria, and psychological testing with the MMPI-2 and the Wechsler Adult Intelligence Scale. The clinician also conducted one session in which, after obtaining Bill's permission, she interviewed Bill's wife to gain additional information about the couple's marital problems.

Based on these assessment data, the clinician concluded that Bill was experiencing a generalized anxiety disorder, which, as we will discuss in Chapter 7, is a common type of disorder found a bit more often among non-White than among White populations. Bill's nervous stomach and shortness of breath are examples of the physical symptoms that are often associated with generalized anxiety disorder, as is the marital dissatisfaction that Bill reported.

In order to provide a thorough diagnostic evaluation, Bill's psychologist completed a DSM-IV multiaxial classification as follows:

Axis I	300.02	Generalized Anxiety Disorder
Axis II	V71.09	No diagnosis
Axis III	555.9	Crohn's disease
Axis IV		Threat of job loss, marital difficulties
Axis V	GAF = 53	(current functioning)

Before reporting the diagnosis to Bill's health insurance company, the psychologist discussed with Bill the implications of the diagnosis. She explained that she would do all that she could to protect against unnecessary disclosures of information about his condition but that she was almost certain that his diagnosis would be known to the claims manager of the insurance company. She also explained that generalized anxiety disorder can be effectively treated with cognitive-behavioral techniques, which we will discuss in Chapter 7.

Because he concluded that the risks of breaches of confidentiality were outweighed by the reimbursement offered by his insurance, Bill decided to continue in psychotherapy. Like most good clinicians, Bill's therapist took the time to explain what is known about the cause of his disorder. His treatment lasted 14 sessions, after which he reported that most of his symptoms had declined considerably, that he no longer felt suicidal, and that he was doing better at work. He said that his marital problems had not changed much, but that neither he nor his wife were ready to work on them.

As Bill's case illustrates, diagnoses seldom help clients understand how or why they developed a disorder. This is both a strength and weakness of systems such as the DSM. Because it bases diagnoses on specific symptoms rather than on presumed causes, the DSM allows clinicians of different theoretical persuasions to agree on most diagnoses. However, this agreement sometimes comes at the price of not indicating enough about the origins or implications of a disorder. In the remaining chapters, we will describe what clinicians know about the causes and treatment of mental disorders.

SUMMARY

Identifying Mental Disorders: Some Basic Issues

Mental disorders have been defined in various ways, but the definition that we prefer is that mental disorders involve a dysfunction or failure of biological or psychological processes to operate as they should, resulting in some harm to the individual. Clinical assessment is the process that clinicians follow to gather the information necessary for diagnosing mental disorders. The quality of clinical assessment is judged along two dimensions: reliability and validity.

Assessment Tools

Clinicians use life records, interviews, psychological tests, behavioral observations, and biological measures as their primary sources of information. Data from these sources are usually then combined to help clinicians diagnose mental disorders.

Diagnostic Classification

Although attempts to classify mental disorders have been made from antiquity, formal nosological systems are a product of the twentieth century. The two systems in widest use—the DSM in North America and the ICD in the rest of the world—have been revised many times. In their most recent versions, these two nosologies base diagnoses on specific, operational criteria. The DSM-IV also allows for multiaxial evaluations of other dimensions that contribute to mental disorders.

Criticisms of the DSM include concerns that official labels can have harmful effects; that disorders do not constitute clear categories that are distinct from other variations in behavior; that too much attention has been paid to the reliability of diagnoses at the expense of their validity; and that most diagnostic labels imply that mental disorders are caused by individual, internal factors, thus minimizing the role of possible social causes. Diagnoses may also be affected by such real-world factors as the reimbursement requirements of health insurance companies, clients' concerns about the confidentiality of their diagnoses, clinicians' personal preferences and interests, and the ethnic and cultural backgrounds of both clinicians and clients.

The Frequency of Mental Disorders

According to major epidemiological surveys, about one third to almost one half of adults have experienced a mental disorder at some point in their lives, and about one quarter have suffered a disorder in the prior year. Mental disorders often coexist or are comorbid; in fact, most people with one disorder in their lifetimes have had at least one other diagnosed mental disorder. The prevalence of mental disorders is associated with various demographic factors, including age, gender, educational level, and ethnicity.

KEY TERMS

achievement test, p. 51

aptitude test, p. 51

assessment, p. 46

attitude and interest test, p. 51

Axis I, II, III, IV, V, p. 61–62

classical method, p. 65

comorbidity, p. 65

computerized tomography (CT), p. 59

correlation coefficient, p. 47

culture-bound syndrome, p. 70

diagnosis, p. 46

dimensional approach, p. 68

epidemiology, p. 45

field trial, p. 61

incidence, p. 71

intelligence test, p. 51

life record, p. 49

magnetic resonance imaging (MRI), p. 59

magnetic resonance spectroscopy (MRS), p. 59

mental disorder, p. 46

mental status examination (MSE), p. 50

multiaxial classification, p. 61

neuropsychological test, p. 52

norm, p. 51

nosology, p. 46

objective test, p. 53

overpathologizing, p. 70

personality test, p. 52

polythetic approach, p. 65

positron emission tomography (PET), p. 59

prevalence, p. 71

projective test, p. 53

psychological test, p. 51

reliability, p. 46

remission, p. 71

self-monitoring, p. 57

sensitivity, p. 49

single photon emission computed tomography (SPECT), p. 59

social history, p. 51

somaticizing, p. 69

specificity, p. 49

standardization, p. 51

structured interview, p. 49

underpathologizing, p. 70

validity, p. 47

3

Disorders of Infancy, Childhood, and Adolescence

Outside by Camille Holvoet, 1988. Oil pastel on paper, 18" x 24". Courtesy of Creative Growth Art Center.

From the Case of Tom

Tom was 8 when his mother called a child psychiatry clinic asking for an evaluation of what she referred to as an "attentional disorder." She told the intake worker that Tom's teacher had complained all year about his "tuning out" in the classroom and not finishing assignments.

As Tom seemed to have at least average intelligence, his teacher believed that an attention deficit was causing his failing academic work. At home, he never listened to his parents. Tom's mother had read a magazine article about children with attentional problems, and, according to her, Tom had every single one of the 10 warning signs. She had heard that medication could eliminate these problems. She didn't like the idea of her son's needing medication to behave like other kids, but what else could she do? She was desperate.

During their first visit to the clinic, Tom and his parents were interviewed by a clinical child psychologist, and many of the mother's concerns were verified. Tom *did* have significant problems getting things done. He was forgetful, and he was always losing his lunch and homework. But this wasn't the whole story. The psychologist discovered that Tom also worried excessively about many things, especially about his parents' getting hurt or dying, something that

made him reluctant to be away from home. Often he would protest strongly about being left with a baby-sitter, complaining that his parents shouldn't leave because he had stomach pains or a headache.

It wasn't just Tom's inattention that was a problem, it was also what he did and thought about when he wasn't paying attention. Usually he was thinking about his favorite activity—fishing! When Tom wasn't doing his work at school, he was drawing pictures of fish or daydreaming about fishing, or pretending that his pencils were fishing poles and his paper clips were fish. At home, Tom would spend hours playing with his dad's fishing gear, casting his line into an imaginary stream in the backyard. Sometimes he would refuse to go to school, wanting to stay home and "fish." When he played with other children—which wasn't often—he always wanted to talk about fishing, a topic that quickly grew boring to others.

Tom's problems, the psychologist learned, had begun years before. As a baby, he had been difficult, often fussy, and unusually fearful of new situations. As a preschooler, he was reluctant to join the other kids in play. His family life had not been easy either. When Tom was 10 months old, his mother returned to full-time work, and he was placed in day care about 40 hours a week. He cried and screamed when his mother left him in the morning, and he was angry and resistant when she came to get him at the end of the day. His parents had experienced considerable marital friction during Tom's early years, including a couple of arguments that got out of hand in front of him. Shortly after the birth of Tom's younger brother, when Tom was 3, his parents separated. Tom's mother was subsequently treated for depression.

As the initial clinic visit drew to a close, Tom's parents bombarded the psychologist with questions: Was the teacher right about an attention-deficit disorder? Was it normal for Tom to worry so much about their safety? Could their marital conflicts have had anything to do with this? Were Tom's problems the early signs of something really serious, or simply a difficult phase that he would grow out of? Was medication the answer? ■

*I*f Tom's clinic visit had taken place in 1970 instead of in the 1990s, his parents' questions would have been very difficult for the psychologist to answer. Only within the past quarter century has research been conducted that is capable of answering these questions. In previous years, clinical research focused far more on *adult* psychopathology than on children's problems. Children were regarded simply as miniature adults, and their problems were viewed as less intense versions of adult disorders.

A dramatic change in this situation has occurred in the last two decades, as psychologists and other mental health specialists began to conduct *prospective, longitudinal studies.* In a **longitudinal study,** investigators repeatedly assess the same people at different ages; they may follow the same children for several months or even into adulthood. These studies can be distinguished from the once more common method—**retrospective,** or follow-back, **research**—in which adults with a given disorder were asked to recall information about their childhoods. Thus, knowledge about children's disorders was based largely on inferences from adults' often-biased accounts of childhood experiences (Achenbach, 1974). The prospective, longitudinal method is superior because it allows researchers to examine the many outcomes that are associated with childhood problems and to analyze the conditions that make positive and negative outcomes likely. Mental health professionals have also made advances in the classification and measurement of children's behaviors using better-defined diagnostic categories and improved methods of collecting information. Thanks in part to these advances, and to increased attention to various theories

of child development, a new discipline called *developmental psychopathology* has emerged (Sroufe & Rutter, 1984).

To emphasize the importance of factors underlying the *development* of psychopathology and the role these factors play in adult disorders, our coverage of mental disorders begins with this chapter on disorders seen early in life. In it, we will show how psychologists involved in the discipline of developmental psychopathology seek the origins and early signs of many adult mental disorders in childhood and adolescence. For example, in one investigation, nearly 90 percent of adult mental disorders were found to have started in childhood or adolescence (Newman et al., 1996).

We will first provide a developmental perspective on children's disorders, followed by a description of how psychopathology in children has been classified and measured. Then we will discuss specific disorders of childhood and adolescence typically assessed and treated in mental health settings; these include disruptive behavior and attention disorders, mood and anxiety disorders, and elimination and eating disorders. (Chapter 4 is devoted to disorders usually treated in specialized educational settings: mental retardation, learning disorders, autism, and other pervasive developmental disorders.) Finally, we will review what has been learned about the questions Tom's parents asked, discuss how we might explain Tom's problems, and describe the treatments he received and how well they worked.

A Developmental Perspective

Concepts about child development provide a framework for understanding how experiences in infancy and early childhood are linked to disorders appearing during middle childhood, adolescence, and even adulthood. It is unlikely, for example, that Tom's school problems at age 8 emerged spontaneously without connection to previous events. His temperament as an infant, his distress and resistant reunions with his mother at daycare, and difficulties with his peers in preschool all seem to foretell later problems. But exactly *how* might they be related to these problems? By what pathways might these earlier events influence later behavior?

Some possibilities are suggested by Alan Sroufe and Michael Rutter (1984) in a now-classic essay on the basic propositions of developmental psychopathology. In it, they listed important **developmental tasks** that children must accomplish as they grow

TABLE 3.1	Developmental Tasks Crucial to Later Competence

Age (years)	Tasks
0–1	Regulating biological needs such as hunger and thirst; forming effective attachment to parents
1–3	Exploring the environment; experimenting and manipulating objects; using parents as a "secure base" while developing autonomy; responding to external (parental) control of impulses; using language
3–5	Developing self-reliance and flexible self-control of impulses; learning to take initiatives; identifying with same-sex parent to form sense of gender; establishing effective peer contacts; learning to empathize
6–12	Acquiring an understanding of fairness and equity; developing gender constancy; forming same-sex friendships; gaining a sense of "industry" or competence; adjusting to demands of school
13+	Learning to take different perspectives and engage in "as if" thinking; forming loyal friendships; separating from family and developing a unique identity.

Source: Adapted from Sroufe & Rutter, 1984.

from infancy to adolescence. These tasks, originally described by such well-known developmental theorists as Erik Erickson, Jean Piaget, John Bowlby, and Lawrence Kohlberg, are the foundation on which a child's later adjustment depends. Examples of these tasks include forming an effective *attachment relationship* with the parent during infancy, attaining *empathy* and *self-reliance* during the preschool years, developing *academic competence* during the middle-school years, and *emancipating* (or separating) from the family during later adolescence. All are critical in setting the stage for normal social and emotional development (see Table 3.1).

Many of the most frequently studied developmental tasks were defined by researchers in Europe and the United States. Are these same tasks important in other cultures? There are certainly some variations in developmental tasks from one culture to another. For example, does cognitive development proceed on the same timetable in countries that do not have compulsory schooling as in countries that do? In general, research indicates that the amount of required, formal schooling affects children's success on perceptual tasks and memory problems (Rogoff & Chavajay, 1995). Also, children do better on problem-solving tasks when they use materials that they find in their everyday worlds. Children from Zambia build better patterns with wire, but children from England excel when they make patterns with paper and pencils (Serpell, 1979). In short, developmental tasks do not occur in a vacuum; they are embedded in everyday cultural practices that help define how children

respond to the expectations of parents, teachers, and peers.

Developmental Tasks and Psychopathology

A child's quality of adaptation or "fit" with the environment can be expressed in terms of how well and in what manner developmental tasks have been mastered. The major link between developmental tasks and psychopathology is that a *child's failure to effectively handle an early developmental task will impair the capacity to handle later tasks successfully.* For example, an infant who is unable to attract care from a parent and cannot use the parent as a source of comfort during stressful situations is less likely to become self-reliant as a preschooler. In turn, the preschooler who has trouble attaining self-reliance is likely to struggle with academic work during middle school.

However, an early failure to adapt does not necessarily lead to failures at later ages. Early problems in completing a developmental task simply increase the likelihood of later maladaptation and the child's need for support from the environment in order to succeed with later tasks. Think again about Tom: His developmental trajectory through age 8 suggests an increased risk for adolescent difficulties, perhaps in the area of family emancipation. This is a critical transition in which adolescents begin the process of leaving the family, sometimes by wearing outrageous clothes, fashioning an unusual hair style, or listening to music that their parents hate. Given Tom's pattern of poor adaptation in early life, he—more than teenagers with less troubled histories—might require a parent who can understand and tolerate adolescent rebellion.

Viewing child psychopathology in relation to developmental tasks allows us to see more clearly how a child's efforts to adapt to an unfavorable or threatening care-giving environment might lead to problems later on (Cicchetti & Toth, 1991). For example, some infants learn that it is best to avoid or minimize contact with an abusive parent. Although this might be an adaptive short-term response, in the long term the lost opportunity to use an adult care giver as a secure base from which to gather emotional support may cripple that child's ability to become close to others (Sroufe & Fleeson, 1986).

Developmental psychopathologists believe that a child's progress with important developmental tasks should be a powerful predictor of later functioning, perhaps even more predictive than surface behaviors or specific emotional symptoms. For example, the probability that a preschooler will develop conduct problems in later life may be better predicted by the quality of attachment to a parent or the degree of self-reliance than by the child's compliance with parental directions. For this reason, it is important to consider not only the symptoms listed in the DSM-IV but also a child's patterns of adaptation to specific developmental tasks (Sroufe & Rutter, 1984).

Analyzing Development: The Example of Attachment

To study the consequences of problems in accomplishing developmental tasks, researchers must first have reliable methods for studying performance on these tasks. One such method is the **Strange Situation,** a 20-minute laboratory assessment of infant–parent attachment developed by psychologist Mary Ainsworth in the mid-1970s (Ainsworth, Blehar, Waters, & Wall, 1978).

The Strange Situation allows an experimenter to observe how an infant responds to separations from a parent, usually the mother. It begins when the parent and infant are brought into a room containing toys. A stranger then enters the room, and after a couple of minutes, the parent is cued to depart, leaving the infant with the stranger. The parent then returns for a reunion with the child. Later, the parent leaves the infant alone in the room again and then returns once more for a final reunion.

Infants respond to this series of separations and reunions in a variety of ways. Most explore the room and the toys at first, but their interest in exploration wanes when the stranger enters. Most infants also protest strongly when the parent first leaves, and they make strong efforts to regain physical contact when the parent returns. Some infants, though, become upset when the parent leaves and cannot be comforted when the parent returns. Others show little emotional distress when the parent

This child is showing the emotional upset typical of being left alone with a stranger during the Strange Situation. If this girl has formed a secure attachment with the parent, she will be soothed by the parent's return. If the attachment is insecure (a risk factor for later developmental problems), the child's distress will not be easily calmed by a reunion with the parent.

leaves and actually *avoid* the parent when she returns to the room.

Ainsworth and later researchers used these variations in how infants respond to the Strange Situation to describe several attachment patterns. The most common pattern—in which infants show moderate separation distress, coupled with a strong approach to the parent during reunions—is called **secure attachment**. Researchers have also identified three patterns of **insecure attachment:** (1) minimal separation distress and avoidance of the parent during reunion; (2) excessive and unrelenting separation distress manifested by resistance and anger that is not relieved when the parent returns to the room; and (3) contradictory, undirected, or confused behaviors during reunion (Main & Hesse, 1990). Secure attachment is the most frequent response to the Strange Situation in all cultures (van Ijzendoorn & Kroonenberg, 1988), but children from various countries differ in the types of insecure attachments they show. For example, Japanese babies display unusually frequent resistant responses, perhaps because Japanese infants are not accustomed to their mothers' leaving them in the care of strangers (Berk, 1991).

What do infants' responses to the Strange Situation mean? In longitudinal studies, children who as infants showed secure behavior during the Strange Situation function better later in life than children who showed any of the three insecure attachment patterns (Urban, et al., 1991). Because insecure infants are at greater risk for behavior problems in childhood (Greenberg, Speltz, & DeKlyen, 1993), many clinicians are convinced that early attachment difficulties play a major role in the development of child psychopathology.

Additional clues about the consequences of troubled attachments come from animal research. Stephen Suomi and his colleagues conducted a series of studies on how baby rhesus monkeys respond to various caregiver conditions (Suomi, 1991). Because rhesus monkeys develop strong attachments to one another, they provide an opportunity for controlled studies of how separating a baby from its mother might affect later behavior.

In general, separating a baby monkey from its mother for a few days elicits immediate emotional and behavioral distress in the baby, much as human infants initially respond to separations in the Strange Situation. Most monkeys do not remain distressed very long, but about 20 percent show longer-term negative behaviors and emotions. Additional research by Suomi and his colleagues has suggested that the baby monkeys who show the greatest disruption and distress have levels of stress-related chemicals in their bodies that may leave them biologically predisposed

to overreact to separations and many other kinds of stressors.

Suomi's research thus illustrates a diathesis–stress model for how human emotional problems might develop. Perhaps disturbed attachments are most likely to cause psychological problems for infants who are biologically hyperreactive to stressors.

Children's problems with early developmental tasks such as attachment can be related to later mental disorders in several ways. For example, a developmental problem may stem from having a difficult temperament, which itself can be the foundation for a later disorder. Or the problem with the developmental task may indicate that the child will have difficulty coping with later stressors, thereby leaving the child especially vulnerable to developing a disorder. More research is necessary for isolating exactly how early development predicts later disorders.

Classification and Diagnosis of Children's Disorders

Efforts to classify children's disorders follow one of two strategies: the first reflects a categorical approach, the second, a dimensional approach. As noted in Chapter 2, the *categorical approach* assumes that mental disorders, like physical disorders, have relatively clear boundaries that distinguish normal behavior from abnormal behavior and one disorder from another. Disorders are like "boxes" into which an individual can be placed, depending on the particular behaviors (or symptoms) shown. In contrast, the *dimensional approach* assumes that most forms of psychopathology are *not* categorically different from normal behavior, so psychopathology is described along one or more continuous dimensions that reflect the degree to which the child shows a maladaptive behavior or emotion.

As discussed in Chapter 2, the DSM-IV is the most widely used categorical approach to mental disorders in North America. The DSM table on page 82 lists the disorders that the DSM-IV categorizes as "disorders usually first diagnosed in infancy, childhood, or adolescence." Clinicians using the DSM-IV begin the diagnostic process with hypotheses about which disorders (or disorder categories) are most relevant to the child's main problems. Then the clinician interviews the child, the parents, and, sometimes, teachers or daycare workers to confirm or rule out the presence of various symptoms. One strategy for improving the reliability of children's diagnostic categories is to use *structured interviews* in which the order and wording of diagnostic questions are standardized. The clinician might also administer formal psychological tests to the child.

DSM-IV

Overview of Disorders Usually First Diagnosed in Infancy, Childhood, or Adolescence

Mental retardation (Chapter 4)

Learning disorders (Chapter 4)

Motor skills disorder

Pervasive developmental disorders (Chapter 4)
  Autistic disorder
  Rett's disorder
  Childhood disintegrative disorder
  Asperger's disorder

Attention-deficit and disruptive behavior disorders (Chapter 3)
  Attention-deficit/hyperactivity disorder
  Conduct disorder
  Oppositional defiant disorder

Feeding and eating disorders of infancy or early childhood (Chapter 3)
  Pica
  Rumination disorder

Feeding disorder of infancy or early childhood

Tic disorders (Chapter 7)
  Tourette's disorder
  Chronic motor or vocal tic disorder
  Transient tic disorder

Communication disorders

Elimination disorders (Chapter 3)
  Encopresis
  Enuresis

Other disorders of infancy, childhood, or adolescence (Chapter 3)
  Separation anxiety disorder
  Selective mutism
  Reactive attachment disorder of infancy or early childhood
  Stereotypic movement disorder

Source: American Psychiatric Association; *Diagnostic and Statistical Manual of Mental Disorders,* Fourth Edition. Washington, DC, American Psychiatric Association, 1994.

Clinicians or researchers who employ a dimensional approach favor different methods. They usually assess the child's psychopathology by asking parents or teachers to complete behavior checklists that rate the extent to which the child shows specified problem behaviors or social competencies in the home or in the classroom. The resulting data are subjected to a statistical procedure called *factor analysis* in which coherent subgroups of behaviors are identified that are relatively independent of one another. For example, the behaviors "fidgets" and "runs about" might co-occur in parental reports and end up in the same subgroup; behaviors such as "cries a lot" or "keeps to self" are likely to end up in another subgroup. Unlike the categorical approach, this method uses *statistical criteria,* rather than clinical experience or theory, to determine which maladaptive behaviors should be grouped together.

One widely used and well-researched dimensional method is the Child Behavior Checklist, or CBCL (Achenbach, 1997). Factor analyses of the CBCL have uncovered two broad dimensions and several more specific scales. The two broad dimensions are called *externalizing* and *internalizing.*

■ **Externalizing problems** (or *undercontrolled* behaviors) represent an excess of undesirable behavior.

They are primarily disruptive behaviors that are a nuisance to others, such as aggression, hyperactivity, impulsivity, and inattention. The externalizing dimension can be divided into two scales: aggressive and delinquent.

■ **Internalizing problems** (or *overcontrolled* behaviors) refer to maladaptive problems in which there are deficits in desired behaviors, usually accompanied by subjective distress in the child; for example, failing to interact with peers or avoiding school because of anxiety or a depressed mood. The internalizing dimension can be broken down into three scales: withdrawn, somatic complaints, and anxious/depressed (Achenbach et al., 1991).

In addition, there are three scales that do not correlate highly enough to be included with either the internalizing or externalizing dimensions:

■ attention problems, such as daydreams and inability to concentrate;

■ thought problems, such as hearing or seeing nonexistent things and harboring strange ideas; and

■ social problems, such as being teased often and not being liked by peers.

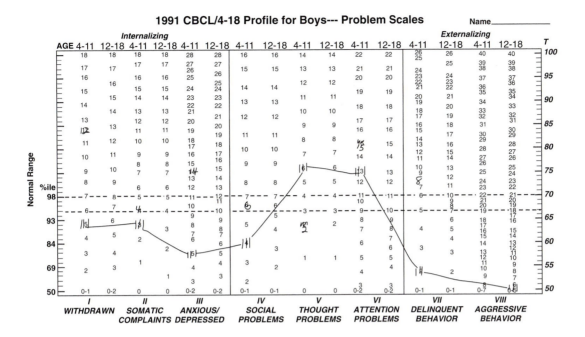

1991 CBCL/4-18 Profile for Boys--- Problem Scales   Name_____

FIGURE 3.1

CBCL Profile for Tom

The scores on the right side of the graph are T scores that are standardized so that the mean score for all scales is 50 and the standard deviation is 10. Scores greater than 70 are considered to be clinically significant; those between 68 and 70 are in the borderline range; scores below 68 are considered in the normal range. Note that Tom has elevated scores on two scales: Attention Problems and Thought Problems. These two scales capture Tom's difficulty in concentrating on and completing school work and his preoccupation with the solitary activity of fishing.

A CBCL profile representing Tom's mother's reports is shown in Figure 3.1. Notice the elevation on the Thought Problems and Attention Problems scales. High scores on these two scales are often found for children diagnosed with attention-deficit disorders. These scores also suggest that a child would be having significant academic difficulties, as was the case with Tom.

Clinicians can classify children's disorders using:

■ a categorical approach such as the DSM-IV; or
■ a dimensional approach.

The primary dimensions of childhood psychopathology are:

■ the externalizing dimension, involving excesses or undercontrol of unwanted or disruptive behaviors; and
■ the internalizing dimension, involving deficits or overcontrol of desirable behaviors.

In Review

A developmental perspective on psychopathology requires:

■ prospective longitudinal studies of the effects of childhood experiences;
■ understanding of how mastery of major developmental tasks provides the building blocks for adolescent and adult competence; and
■ tracing the long-term consequences of problems in developmental tasks such as infant attachment through research methods such as the Strange Situation.

Disruptive Behavior and Attention-Deficit Disorders

The most common reasons for a child's referral to a mental health service are disruptive behaviors and attention deficits. In many mental health facilities, 60 to 70 percent of child and adolescent cases involve these problems (Beitchman, Inglis, & Schachter, 1992).

In the general American population, the prevalence of officially diagnosed disruptive behavior may exceed 10 percent; the overall rate for attentional problems is about 5 percent (see Figure 3.2). Boys are at least 2 to 3 times more likely than girls to exhibit and be diagnosed with these problems (Szatmari, Offord, & Boyle, 1989).

In the DSM-IV, the term *disruptive* applies to two disorders involving antisocial behavior: (1) **oppositional defiant disorder (ODD)**, a pattern of negativistic, disobedient, and defiant behavior usually shown at home and sometimes at school, and (2) **conduct disorder (CD)**, characterized by more serious antisocial behavior at home or in the community, including significant physical aggression, property damage, deceitfulness, or rule violations. Children with **attention-deficit/hyperactivity disorder (ADHD)** may be disruptive, but their behavior is not necessarily antisocial; rather it is marked by inattention, impulsivity, or high motor activity.

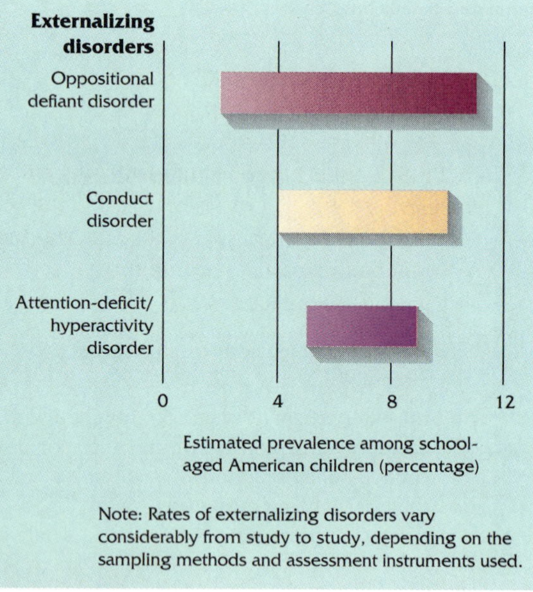

Connections

Does comorbidity indicate a flaw in the DSM system, or does it describe the way disorders occur? For possible explanations of comorbidity, see Chapter 2, pp. 65–66, 72.

ODD, CD, and some aspects of ADHD are all examples of behaviors described by the externalizing dimension of the Child Behavior Checklist. These disorders show high levels of co-occurrence, or *comorbidity;* in one study, for example, as many as 90 percent of children with CD were also diagnosed as having ADHD (Hinshaw, 1987). The symptoms of ODD usually precede those of CD; in fact, many clinicians view ODD as a less mature form of conduct disorder (Rey et al., 1988). Despite frequent overlap among ODD, CD, and ADHD, all these disorders, but especially ADHD, can occur independently.

Oppositional Defiant Disorder

ODD can be diagnosed in a person of any age, but the diagnosis is usually given to children aged 3 to 7. Typically, these children have poor control of their emotions, are extremely noncompliant and argumentative with parents and teachers, and have repeated conflicts with peers as a result of provocative and hostile interactions (Campbell, 1990). They blame other people for their mistakes and always seem to have a chip on their shoulders. These behaviors seem to reflect a high need for control of social interaction, as if the oppositional child is forever thinking "Everything must go MY WAY, all the time." Many parents of ODD children report that being around them requires "walking on eggs": any little conflict can escalate into a full-blown tantrum, as was the case with Nick.

*N*ick is a 9-year-old boy brought to a mental health center by his mother because of his increasing disobedience at home and school. Within the last month, Nick has been sent to the principal's office three times for swearing at his teacher in front of other children. At home, Nick can be an affectionate child, but, more often, he is argumentative and spiteful. He has to be told again and again to do the smallest of household chores, and even then he bickers and complains about all the work that is expected of him. Nick has received fairly good grades in school, but his parents report that they have to argue with him about finishing his homework almost every night. His mother says she is fed up with Nick, claiming that "it's just one battle after the next with him; I've had it up to here. It's time for him to grow up."

FIGURE 3.2

Externalizing Disorders and Their Prevalence
The externalizing disorders are among the most prevalent of childhood mental disorders. Estimates of the frequency of these disorders vary considerably, depending on the methodology of the research. However, all the externalizing disorders are diagnosed much more often in boys than in girls.

A major problem in diagnosing ODD is that some of its symptoms occur at a very high base rate in the general population, particularly during the preschool and adolescent years when concerns over self-assertion come to the fore. Many, if not most, youngsters in the United States argue with their parents, do not follow rules, try to avoid their household chores, act angry and spiteful, and could thus be potentially diagnosed with a mental disorder.

The DSM-IV attempts to solve the problem of overdiagnosing ODD by stipulating that, before a youngster can be diagnosed with ODD, the clinician must find evidence that the individual's oppositional behavior—not some other disorder or condition—is producing impairment in social relations, school performance, or other aspects of adaptive functioning expected of someone of the child's age.

Most of us have encountered an oppositional toddler or preschooler (most likely a boy) and wondered whether he'll ever grow out of it. Longitudinal research suggests that a significant minority of preschoolers continue to engage in troublesome disobedience. Susan Campbell (1990) found that about 50 percent of the preschool children referred to her mental health clinic for externalizing behavior problems continued to have significant difficulties through their early grade school years. About one third of these children still had significant problems at age 9. Other studies suggest that the majority of grade schoolers (particularly boys) referred for ODD will show later conduct problems, usually aggression and other antisocial behaviors during adolescence (Verhulst et al., 1993). We now know that, for a significant subgroup of very young children referred to clinics with ODD, this early pattern will persist and increase over time (Robins, 1991).

How do we distinguish between young children who are likely to have continuing problems and those with temporary problems? Continuing problems are more likely when

- they are observed in more than one setting (i.e., home and school);
- aggression and hyperactivity co-occur with core ODD features;
- the child engages in covert behaviors such as lying and stealing in addition to overt behaviors such as excessive arguing and aggression; and
- there is a high level of stress in the family.

Conduct Disorder

Compared with ODD, a diagnosis of conduct disorder (CD) requires the presence of more serious antisocial behaviors that substantially infringe on the basic rights of others and that violate community rules. It is not enough to throw tantrums and disobey rules. In order to be diagnosed with conduct

Conduct disorder can take many forms, depending on social and cultural factors. These boys are engaging in the kind of vandalism that is typical of conduct disorder.

disorder, a child must exhibit behaviors that are potentially harmful to the child, to others, or to property. The DSM-IV symptoms of CD are shown in the DSM table on page 86. The majority of symptoms pertain to physically aggressive action; other items describe vandalism, truancy, or taking advantage of others for personal gain. The diagnosis of CD requires a repetitive and persistent pattern consisting of at least three of these symptoms during the previous 12 months and at least one symptom in the previous 6 months.

Conduct disorder is exemplified by a 14-year-old boy ("Eric") recently seen in one of the authors' clinic.

*E*ric had a history of unusually violent temper tantrums at age 4, followed by a series of shoplifting incidents at age 8. In the eighth grade he began to miss school regularly as a result of truancy or being suspended for fights that he usually started. Eric was known as a mean fighter who went out of his way to hurt his adversaries. His parents tried desperately to change his behavior. They paid him to attend classes; took him to a counselor; and hired a tutor to help him with his reading, which had

DSM-IV

Symptoms of Conduct Disorder

The DSM-IV criteria for conduct disorder require that three or more of the following symptoms be present in the previous 12 months, with at least one of the symptoms present in the previous 6 months; and that the disturbance in behavior causes clinically significant impairment in social, academic, or occupational functioning. (If the person is older than 18, criteria for Antisocial Personality Disorder must not be met.)

Aggression to people and animals

(1) often bullies, threatens, or intimidates others
(2) often initiates physical fights
(3) has used a weapon that can cause serious physical harm to others (e.g., a bat, brick, broken bottle, knife, gun)
(4) has been physically cruel to people
(5) has been physically cruel to animals
(6) has stolen while confronting a victim (e.g., mugging, purse snatching, armed robbery)
(7) has forced someone into sexual activity

Destruction of property

(8) has deliberately engaged in fire setting with the intention of causing serious damage
(9) has deliberately destroyed others' property (other than by fire setting)

Deceitfulness or theft

(10) has broken into someone else's house, building, or car
(11) often lies to obtain goods or favors or to avoid obligations (i.e., "cons" others)
(12) has stolen items of nontrivial value *without* confronting a victim (e.g., shoplifting, but without breaking and entering; forgery)

Serious violations of rules

(13) often stays out at night despite parental prohibitions, beginning before age 13
(14) has run away from home overnight at least twice while living in parental or parental surrogate home (or once without returning for a lengthy period)
(15) is often truant from school, beginning before age 13

Source: American Psychiatric Association; *Diagnostic and Statistical Manual of Mental Disorders,* Fourth Edition. Washington, DC, American Psychiatric Association, 1994.

---

always been poor. None of these strategies worked. Just prior to being brought to the clinic, Eric was discovered in a school bathroom where he had cut another student's arm with a knife. When questioned about this incident, Eric first blamed the other student, but later admitted to instigating the fight. When asked why he did it, Eric said the victim—a boy in his shop class—had looked at him "the wrong way." Although the two had never spoken, Eric was convinced that this boy planned to harm him. The only regret Eric expressed about this incident was that he didn't get the chance "to do some real damage."

Children and adolescents with CD vary greatly in social class, age, and characteristic types of antisocial behavior. For example, an adolescent member of an inner-city gang who has stolen, used weapons, and broken into cars with his buddies is very different from the socially isolated, suburban 9-year-old who has set fires, skipped school, and tortured the family cat. But both individuals might be diagnosed with CD. To get around this problem, some clinicians identify subtypes of CD. For example, they might distinguish between aggressive and non-aggressive children with CD or between children who engage in antisocial behavior by themselves and those who do this only in a peer group.

Longitudinal Course. Several longitudinal studies suggest that youngsters who show *childhood onset* of conduct disorder (before age 10) are more likely to experience academic failure and to develop adult antisocial problems than those with *adolescent onset* (after age 10) do. Adolescent-onset CD is more likely to dissipate by the end of the teenage years (White et al., 1990). Children with childhood onset, such as Eric, are often called "early starters" (Patterson, DeBaryshe & Ramsey, 1989).

What happens to teenagers such as Eric? About one quarter of the children who meet the DSM-IV criteria for CD before age 15 go on to be diagnosed with antisocial personality disorder as adults (Robins, Tipp, & Przybeck, 1991). Antisocial personality disorder shares so many characteristics of conduct disorder (e.g., aggressiveness, irresponsibility, deceitfulness) that the two conditions are essentially the same; the antisocial label is simply applied to people older than 18. Adolescents with CD are also at higher risk than normal peers for substance abuse and emotional disorders such as depression and anxiety in adulthood (Robins, 1991). Even when CD does not lead to later psychiatric dysfunction, it is associated with major life problems such as divorce, joblessness, abusive parenting, and higher death rates due to risky or self-destructive behaviors (Rydelius, 1988). Clearly, CD has negative adult consequences that are pervasive and long-standing. It is one of the most valid early warning signs of serious problems of aggression in adulthood.

Causes of Conduct Disorder: Biological Factors. What causes some children to engage in long-term antisocial or aggressive behavior? Studies have shown that the offspring of criminal or alcoholic parents—even when raised by adoptive parents without these problems—have higher-than-expected rates of criminality themselves, pointing to a possible genetic basis for some forms of criminal behavior (e.g., Cloninger & Gottesman, 1987).

A biological influence is also suggested by the fact that boys show a much higher prevalence of conduct problems than girls do. Some theorists attribute this pattern to the correlation between aggression and the male hormone *testosterone*. Animal studies suggest that higher levels of testosterone are linked to greater aggressiveness, but human studies have produced inconsistent results. In any event, it is still unclear whether elevated testosterone levels precede and cause later aggressiveness or whether they merely result from an aggressive lifestyle (Robbins, 1991).

Aggression may also be related to certain *neurotransmitters*, the chemicals mentioned in Chapter 1 that facilitate communication between cells in the brain. One such neurotransmitter is *serotonin*, which is implicated in the brain's control over emotions and behavior. Low levels of serotonin are associated with high levels of aggression—particularly impulsive aggression—in adults (Linnoila et al., 1983) and children (Kruesi et al., 1992). However, the direction of causality is as yet unknown; like testosterone, abnormal levels of serotonin could either precede or follow aggressive patterns of behavior.

Physiological arousal may also play a causal role in CD. Perhaps individuals with low general levels of arousal—a low heart rate and reduced respiration rate, for example—have less capacity to experience the fear responses that discourage most people from engaging in risky behaviors such as criminal acts (Eysenck, 1964; Mednick, Gabrielli, & Hutchings, 1984). In support of this idea, one study found that children with conduct disorder had lower resting heart rates than did children with ADHD or internalizing behavior problems such as anxiety or shyness (Raine & Jones, 1987). Another prospective study measured physiological arousal in 101 15-year-old boys in England. About 10 years later, these researchers checked court records to determine which boys had been arrested in the interim; 17 of the subjects had a criminal record. As shown in Figure 3.3, the criminals had also had significantly lower heart rates and skin conductance levels than the nonoffenders when they were measured at age 15 (Raine, Venebles, & Williams, 1990).

Connections

Is there a genetic basis for criminal behavior? Is just one gene involved? See the discussion of behavioral genetics in Chapter 1, pp. 16–18.

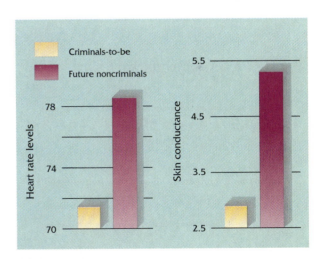

FIGURE 3.3

Adolescent Underarousal and Adult Criminality

A study in England used court records to determine which of the teenagers examined had criminal records 10 years later. Both heart rate and skin conductance (a perspiration index of arousal) were significantly lower for criminals-to-be than for noncriminals when measured at age 15. These results provide evidence that physiological underarousal during childhood is one risk factor for externalizing disorders.

Source: Raine et al., 1990.

Causes of Conduct Disorder: Cognitive and Psychosocial Factors. Deficits in neuropsychological abilities (such as memory, problem solving, language facility) may also contribute to disruptive behavior. Tests of these abilities in children with disruptive behavior have revealed deficiencies in the ability to comprehend, retain, and utilize language and in **executive functioning,** the ability to attend to relevant information in the environment and to make thoughtful decisions based on that information. Neuropsychologist Terrie Moffit and her colleagues have shown that deficits in these areas are correlated with children's antisocial behaviors, even after controlling for the influence of low socioeconomic status, poor test motivation, or school failure (Lynam, Moffitt, & Stouthamer-Loeber, 1993). She believes that problems in language processing and executive functioning are the primary causal factors in cases where there is early onset of disruptive behavior. However, these factors may be less important in children who first show disruptive behavior in early adolescence (an age when peer group influences are more likely to be the determining factor).

Parenting skills may also play a causal role in CD. According to Gerald Patterson and his colleagues, parent–child interactions in families of aggressive boys are characterized by *coercive cycles,* in which one person's aversive behavior is reinforced by *termination* of the other's aversive behavior (Patterson, 1982, 1986). Here is an example of a coercive cycle from the opening case of Tom:

---

*T*om whines and becomes verbally abusive when his parents won't turn on the TV. His father yells at him to stop whining and talking back, but Tom continues more intensely. Eventually the father gets tired of this interchange and allows Tom to turn on the TV. Tom abruptly stops his negative behavior.

In this example, Tom's aversive behavior is reinforced when his father stops yelling and gives in to Tom's request. The father's giving in is, in turn, reinforced when Tom stops whining. Because both parties are reinforced for their behavior, it is likely to become well entrenched in the family's interactions during conflicts, leading to parent–child relationships that emphasize the exchange of negative behavior.

Parents of disruptive children are more likely than the parents of nonproblem children to behave in ways that encourage the development of coercive cycles. For example, they criticize more often, react more strongly to negative child behavior, and issue more frequent commands (Campbell et al., 1986). It is tempting to conclude that such parental behaviors cause child conduct problems, but this might not be the case. In one study, interactions between problem mothers and their disruptive boys were compared with interactions between nonproblem mothers and their nondisruptive boys (Anderson, Lytton, & Romney, 1986). As expected, the problem mothers were more bossy and critical. However, in a second phase of the study, problem mothers interacted with a *nonproblem* boy, and nonproblem mothers interacted with a disruptive boy. In this phase, the problem mothers were *less* critical and directive than the nonproblem mothers, suggesting that parental interaction styles may be, at least in part, the *result* of having a difficult-to-manage child.

In addition to skills in conflict management, parents' abilities to anticipate and respond promptly to their child's needs and their warmth and closeness to the child may reduce the likelihood of conduct problems (Greenberg, Speltz, & DeKlyen, 1993). A positive, warm bond between parent and child tends to be associated with greater child compliance to the parent (Baumrind, 1971; Crockenberg & Littman, 1990). Observations of families in their homes have shown that parents who initiate more positive conversations with their child, stay physically closer to their child, and spend more time in interactive play are less likely to have children with significant behavior problems (Pettit & Bates, 1989).

Research using the Strange Situation tells a similar story. Infants and toddlers in high-risk environments who show signs of an insecure attachment to their parents are more likely to have behavior problems in their preschool and elementary school years than infants with secure attachment (e.g., Urban et al., 1991). According to other studies, about 80 percent of preschool boys referred to a mental health clinic for ODD show insecure attachment, as opposed to only 25 percent of nonproblem boys with equivalent family backgrounds and learning abilities (Greenberg et al., 1991).

Adverse environmental factors can make it difficult for parents to use effective child-rearing skills or to foster secure attachment in their child. These factors include negative parental characteristics (such as low education or substance abuse), poor family functioning (marital distress, family violence), limited resources (poverty, social isolation), and stressful events (death of a family member, divorce, job loss). Some researchers use a **family adversity index** to represent the total number of negative factors that a family has experienced (e.g., Sameroff et al., 1987; Rutter, Tizard, & Whitmore, 1970). This index consists of six risk factors: (1) severe marital discord, (2) low socioeconomic class, (3) large family size, (4) criminality by the father, (5) mental disorder in the mother, and (6) placement of the child in foster care. Generally, the higher the index, the more likely it is that the child will engage in antisocial behavior, which is consistent with the idea that these factors have a causal effect on conduct problems (Biederman et al., 1990).

One final causal factor in the development of conduct disorder is the child's *social-cognitive skills*. Aggressive children tend to have trouble thinking of nonaggressive ways of solving the problems they encounter (Spivack & Shure, 1974). They tend to jump to the conclusion that if something negative happens it is because someone else did it to them on purpose. Ken Dodge and his colleagues have shown that aggressive elementary school children can be distinguished from nonaggressive peers by the way they handle social information during conflicts (Dodge & Coie, 1987; Lochman & Lenhart, 1993). Aggressive children are less able to remember relevant social cues in many interactions and more likely to perceive hostile intentions in the everyday behaviors of peers. Thus, they may interpret any accidental phys-

ical contact by a peer as a deliberate act of aggression. They are also more inclined to believe that aggression on their part will result in positive outcomes (Dodge, Pettit, McClaskey, & Brown, 1986). Some disruptive children are very poor at communicating their sides of an issue in conflict situations. In short, disruptive children may be ill-equipped to handle the *cognitive demands* of interpersonal conflict, making physical aggression the most accessible strategy for them.

Figure 3.4 summarizes the factors that are the most likely contributors to the development of conduct disorder. In most cases, the presence of just one causal factor is probably not sufficient to result in a disruptive behavior disorder. For most children who develop severe disruptive behavior problems—especially early starters who persist in their antisocial behavior—two or more factors are usually at work. Therefore, disruptive behavior disorders are best understood as arising from a combination of biological, psychological, and social factors. Consistent with this theory, Moffitt (1990) found that boys who had both low neuropsychological test scores and high family adversity were 4 times more aggressive than were boys with either risk condition alone.

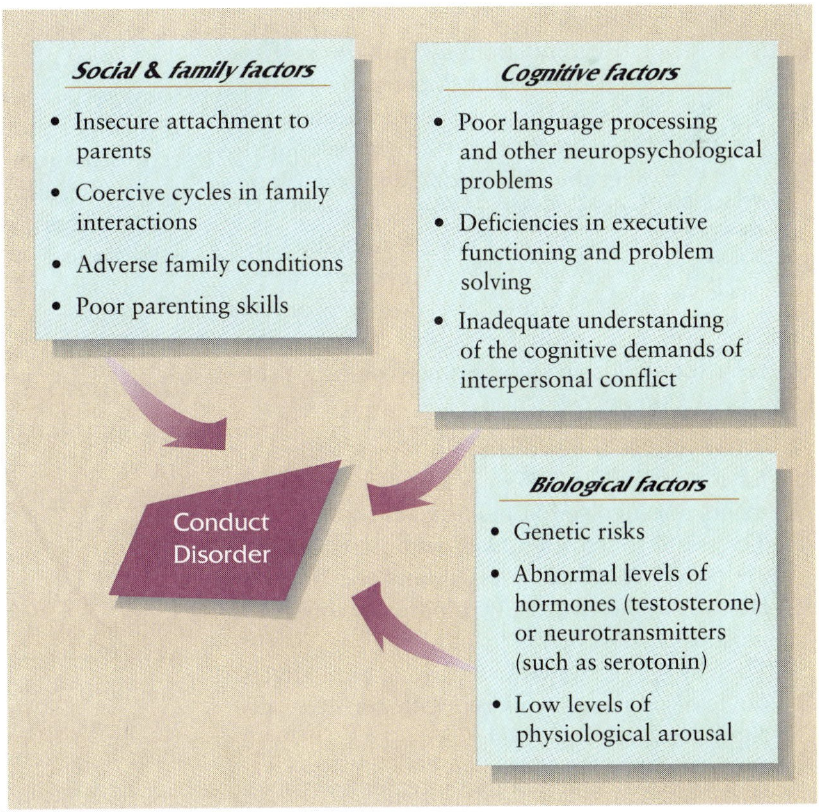

FIGURE 3.4

Multiple Factors in the Causes of Conduct Disorder

These biological, cognitive, and social factors are all associated with aggressiveness, disruptive behavior, and other aspects of conduct disorder. To date, however, research has not determined exactly how these factors combine to cause the disorder.

Social & family factors
- Insecure attachment to parents
- Coercive cycles in family interactions
- Adverse family conditions
- Poor parenting skills

Cognitive factors
- Poor language processing and other neuropsychological problems
- Deficiencies in executive functioning and problem solving
- Inadequate understanding of the cognitive demands of interpersonal conflict

Biological factors
- Genetic risks
- Abnormal levels of hormones (testosterone) or neurotransmitters (such as serotonin)
- Low levels of physiological arousal

Conduct Disorder

Treatment of Disruptive Behavior Disorders

The most widely used and best researched treatment for childhood disruptive behavior aims to improve specific parenting skills. For example, clinicians may teach parents to use praise to reinforce the child's prosocial behavior and encourage parents to reserve the use of negative consequences only for serious problem behaviors (Forehand & McMahon, 1981).

In Sheila Eyberg's (1988) Parent–Child Interaction Therapy, a therapist coaches parents on how to play and talk effectively with their children. In a typical session, the family plays together in a room while the therapist observes them through a one-way mirror. The therapist gives immediate instructions and feedback to parents through tiny electronic listening devices in the parents' ears. For example, if a young child is banging a toy on the table, the therapist, using the "bug in the ear," will tell the parent to ignore this attention-getting ploy but to enthusiastically praise and play with the child as soon as more appropriate play begins. Parents are also taught how to give clear, simple instructions to their children, how to talk to their children without nagging them, and how to discipline them without losing their tempers.

Parent training programs have led to significant changes in parenting skills and, to some degree, in children's behavior, at least as observed immediately after treatment (Patterson, Chamberlain, & Reid, 1982). In some programs, changes have been maintained for up to a year (Webster-Stratton, 1984). However, several problems limit the long-term utility of parent training interventions for children with serious conduct problems. For example,

1. These interventions often fail to produce behavior changes at school or in other environments not involved in the original training.
2. They tend to work less well with parents who are poorly educated, stressed, and socially isolated—in other words, with parents who are most in need of help.
3. They have not shown strong, long-term effects on "early starting" children with persistent disruptive behavior problems.

In an effort to make these interventions more effective, especially for children from lower socio-economic backgrounds, clinicians have introduced several innovations. In some cases, therapists conduct much of the treatment in the family's home in order to bring about better transfer of skills. They may help poor families arrange transportation, purchase a telephone, or acquire baby-sitting services so that they can participate more regularly in treatment. Special training in how to play pleasantly and noncritically with children has also been introduced to increase parent sensitivity, warmth, and positive attachment patterns (Speltz, 1990).

Other treatments for disruptive behavior focus more on the individual child than on family interactions. Cognitive-behavioral programs, for example, attempt to change the child's perceptual inaccuracies, biased expectations of hostile intent, limited awareness of nonaggressive solutions to problems, and language deficits during conflict situations. Children are taught to monitor their emotions, double-check their assumptions about others' behavior, and use specific problem-solving steps to avoid physical confrontations (e.g., Lochman & Lenhart, 1993).

Research on the use of such programs with disruptive children has shown encouraging evidence of increased social skills and reduced disruptive behavior across different settings (Kolko, Loar, & Sturnick, 1990) and over at least a 1-year period (Kazdin et al., 1987). However, the skill levels of treated children often still lag behind those of normal peers (Kazdin et al., 1989). Thus, cognitive-behavioral training may have only limited effects on the long-term trajectory of severe conduct disorder. Because of the difficulty of treating conduct disorder and the long-term risks associated with it, many clinicians believe that more effort must be devoted to programs that try to prevent this disorder, as we discuss in the Prevention section.

Attention-Deficit/Hyperactivity Disorder (ADHD)

No other childhood disorder has generated as much interest and controversy as ADHD. Popular magazines and talk shows periodically list the symptoms of ADHD, and it is not uncommon for a parent coming to a children's mental health clinic to remark that a friend, relative, or teacher "thinks my child has ADHD." Critics worry that a diagnosis of ADHD may medicalize problems unnecessarily and that both the label and medication-based treatments are oversimplified, short-term solutions to a complex, long-term problem.

Exactly what is ADHD? The core symptoms are inattention, hyperactivity, and impulsivity. The symp-

Connections

How do psychologists know whether any therapy is effective? For a discussion of methods for evaluating treatments, see Chapter 16, pp. 575–577.

Prevention   Derailing Conduct Disorder—The FAST Track Approach

As noted earlier, children at greatest risk for conduct disorder in adolescence can be identified early in life, usually by the time they enter grade school. Are such children destined to become troublemakers for the rest of their lives, or can something be done to prevent a problematic future?

A number of investigators have developed school-based prevention programs for children believed to be at risk for behavioral and educational problems. An early example of this approach was the Primary Mental Health Project (PMHP) (Cowen, Gesten, & Wilson, 1979). The PMHP first identified primary schoolers with potential conduct problems. These at-risk children were then seen in schools by trained, nonprofessional child aides, who taught the children new skills for coping with stressors and controlling impulsive behavior.

Children participating in the PMHP and similar projects experience behavioral and educational gains, but these improvements tend to be modest and often do not generalize well to settings outside of school. Numerous attempts to prevent conduct disorder suggest an important lesson: preventing or changing major aspects of serious childhood disorders requires lengthy interventions that simultaneously target social, familial, economic, and psychological difficulties.

Some of these requirements are met by a nationwide prevention project called FAST Track. Developed by a group of scholars called the Conduct Problems Prevention Research Group (1994), and funded by the National Institute of Mental Health, FAST Track is offering a variety of psychological and social services to over 400 families of high-risk chil-

dren. The program begins in the first grade and is scheduled to continue for 6 years. It is based on a developmental model that claims that the probability of conduct disorder in a high-risk child can be lowered if

1. the child's parents are actively involved in the child's school program and develop trust in the school system;
2. the child experiences some measure of academic success, particularly in reading;
3. the child acquires social-cognitive skills that promote the development of friendships and cooperative relationships;
4. the child learns to regulate emotions effectively; and
5. the child develops a mentoring relationship with a same-sex adult.

To accomplish these goals, FAST Track provides services to parents, teachers, and children, and it focuses on two critical time periods: school entry and transition to middle school. FAST Track staff members go to the child's school to teach social-cognitive skills such as anger management, to run "friendship groups," and to work with teachers. They also make regular visits to the family's home to help parents acquire child-rearing skills and to become more skilled at managing daily hassles and major stressors ranging from overdue rent to joblessness. FAST Track is attempting to measure how much prevention can be achieved when families are given a broad range of intensive treatments in multiple settings and are supported for remaining in the program.

Is FAST Track working? A definitive answer won't be available until these children reach their mid-teenage years. Early results are encouraging, however. After 1 year,

Prevention programs are most effective when interventions such as conflict resolution are staged in schools or other settings where problem behaviors are most likely to develop.

almost all of the children and parents were participating regularly. In addition, parents expressed a great deal of satisfaction with many aspects of the program, and they reported improvements in their children's school work, social skills, and problem behavior at school and home (Conduct Problems Prevention Research Group, 1994). The investigators hope that similar effects will be sustained during the entire project and will produce a large, cost-effective difference in these children's futures.

Results of the FAST Track program will be followed closely by clinicians and public policy makers alike. Many believe that programs such as FAST Track may offer the best chance of stemming the tide of crime and serious antisocial behaviors in adolescents and young adults. Even the most expensive prevention programs may be a bargain when weighed against the enormous social costs of increasing rates of crime, imprisonment, and wasted lives.

toms are most readily observed when the child is required to perform structured activities such as academic tasks. Like Tom, children with ADHD usually fail to finish school assignments or do them carelessly. They appear not to listen, and they are easily distracted and seem disorganized. Children with ADHD are fidgety and restless. They squirm in their seats, fiddle with objects, misplace toys and clothes, climb over furniture, and run through the house. These children have trouble waiting their turn, often blurt out comments, may grab at other people, or interrupt others' activities. ADHD children always seem to have their "engines revved up, ready to go" to the point that they wear their parents and teachers to a frazzle.

When so many symptoms are associated with a single disorder, there is always the danger of over-diagnosing it. One review found little agreement by practicing clinicians on the defining features of this disorder (Goodman & Poillion, 1992), suggesting that the term *ADHD* is so broad that it could be applied to just about any child with academic and behavior problems.

Partly in response to criticisms such as this, the developers of the DSM-IV made significant improvements in the definition of this disorder. For example, symptoms must now produce problems in at least two settings in which the child functions (e.g., at school and at home), and these problems must result in "clinically significant impairment" in the child's day-to-day functioning. It is not enough for the child to show levels of inattention, activity, or impulsiveness that are excessive when compared to those of age-mates; such behavior must also be a primary cause of functional problems. Thus, a child who is highly active and often impulsive, but who does school work consistent with his or her ability and has reasonably good peer relations, would not meet ADHD diagnostic criteria, no matter how much the child annoys adults. The DSM table opposite summarizes the DSM-IV criteria for a diagnosis of ADHD.

The prevalence of ADHD is affected by demographic and cultural factors. Between 3 and 9 percent of school-aged children in the United States meet formal DSM-IV criteria for ADHD (Richters et al., 1995). Boys are 4 to 9 times more likely to be diagnosed than girls. Although ADHD is diagnosed in children from all socioeconomic backgrounds, it is slightly more common among children in lower socioeconomic groups. This relationship may reflect differences in the way children's activity is tolerated or controlled by adults, or it may be due to the fact that lower social class families have higher rates of pregnancy complications, inadequate health care, and

instability in general (Barkley, 1990). ADHD is seen worldwide, and, although cross-national differences in rates have been found, they are not consistent enough to suggest what factors might be responsible for them.

Three subtypes of ADHD have been distinguished: ADHD primarily marked by *inattention,* ADHD primarily characterized by *hyperactivity or impulsivity,* and *combined ADHD* in which both inattention and hyperactivity-impulsivity are present. Both ADHD/inattentive and ADHD/hyperactive-impulsive children display academic underachievement (Barkley, DuPaul, & McMurray, 1990), but the underlying reasons for these problems may differ. Research has documented several consistent differences between ADHD/inattentive and ADHD/hyperactive children (Goodyear & Hynd, 1992). In particular, ADHD children with hyperactivity are more likely to have

- other externalizing behavior problems (non-compliance, aggression);
- low popularity among peers; and
- comorbid conduct disorder.

ADHD children without hyperactivity are more likely to have

- internalizing behavior problems (anxiety, depression);
- a slow pace of solving problems; and
- comorbid sensory–motor problems and learning disorders.

ADHD/hyperactivity is 4 to 5 times more common than the ADHD/inattention subtype. It is suspected that girls are more likely to show the inattentive type than the hyperactive type.

Which subtype does Tom represent? His inattention and off-task behavior at school suggest a diagnosis of ADHD, inattentive type. Learning disabilities are frequently associated with this subtype, and they may contribute to some of Tom's off-task behavior in school. If additional testing confirmed that Tom had a learning disability, the therapist could recommend that Tom's teachers see whether he would comply better when given instructions in both written and oral form.

Longitudinal Course. The primary symptoms of ADHD are highly persistent over time (Klein & Mannuzza, 1991). About 70 percent of children who are diagnosed with ADHD in elementary school still meet criteria for this disorder in mid-adolescence (Barkley et al., 1990). By adolescence, about half meet criteria for a conduct disorder as well; but this may be a consequence of the high level of comorbid-

Symptoms of Attention-Deficit/Hyperactivity Disorder

The DSM-IV criteria for a diagnosis of ADHD include the symptoms described in either of the two categories below. Clear evidence of clinically significant social, academic, or occupational impairment from these symptoms must be present in two or more settings.

Inattention: Six (or more) of the following symptoms of inattention have persisted for at least 6 months to a degree that is maladaptive and inconsistent with developmental level:

(a) often fails to give close attention to details or makes careless mistakes in schoolwork, work, or other activities
(b) often has difficulty sustaining attention in tasks or play activities
(c) often does not seem to listen when spoken to directly
(d) often does not follow through on instructions and fails to finish schoolwork, chores, or duties in the workplace (not due to oppositional behavior or failure to understand instructions)
(e) often has difficulty organizing tasks and activities
(f) often avoids, dislikes, or is reluctant to engage in tasks that require sustained mental effort (such as schoolwork or homework)
(g) often loses things necessary for tasks or activities (e.g., toys, school assignments, pencils, books, or tools)

(h) is often easily distracted by extraneous stimuli
(i) is often forgetful in daily activities

Hyperactivity/Impulsivity: Six (or more) of the following symptoms of hyperactivity/impulsivity have persisted for at least 6 months to a degree that is maladaptive and inconsistent with developmental level:

(a) often fidgets with hands or feet or squirms in seat
(b) often leaves seat in classroom or in other situations in which remaining seated is expected
(c) often runs about or climbs excessively in situations in which it is inappropriate (in adolescents or adults, may be limited to subjective feelings of restlessness)
(d) often has difficulty playing or engaging in leisure activities quietly
(e) is often "on the go" or often acts as if "driven by a motor"
(f) often talks excessively
(g) often blurts out answers before questions have been completed
(h) often has difficulty awaiting turn
(i) often interrupts or intrudes on others (e.g., butts into conversations or games)

Source: American Psychiatric Association; *Diagnostic and Statistical Manual of Mental Disorders,* Fourth Edition. Washington, DC, American Psychiatric Association, 1994.

ity between ADHD and conduct and oppositional defiant disorders (Lilienfeld & Waldman 1990). When ADHD is comorbid with a disruptive behavior disorder, the child's prognosis is poorer.

In many cases of ADHD, the severity of symptoms does not diminish until the mid-20s to early 30s. In fact, an increasing number of people are suspected of having an adult form of ADHD, although insufficient research has been conducted to establish the validity of this diagnosis in adults. People who displayed ADHD as children have a higher-than-average risk for adult substance abuse and antisocial personality disorder (Mannuzza et al., 1991). For most, however, these disorders do not appear and the core symptoms of ADHD eventually dissipate. Still, many of these people experience residual negative effects of poor school performance and previous parent–child conflicts.

Causes of ADHD: Biological Factors One review of the ADHD literature (Goodman & Poillion, 1992) uncovered 38 suggested causal factors, ranging from the plausible (such as low birth weight) to the debatable (including excess sugar, lead poisoning, food additives, poor self-esteem) to the highly improbable (TV radiation leaks, ill-fitting underwear). Research has shown that most of the debatable and improbable factors found to be *correlated* with ADHD actually have little or no *causal* effect on the disorder (e.g., Kaplan, Wamboldt, & Barnhardt, 1986; Wolraich et al., 1994).

Scientists were once so convinced that some form of brain damage was the culprit behind ADHD that they called the condition *minimal brain dysfunction.* However, evidence for this view is also mainly correlational. ADHD has been associated with three problems in early life that could affect brain growth:

■ Infants with low birth weight (associated primarily with premature birth) are at elevated risk for attentional problems in early childhood, presumably due to central nervous system damage (Klein, 1988).

■ Prolonged oxygen deprivation at birth is commonly thought to increase the risk of attentional problems, but evidence for its doing so in children who do not have a major developmental disability is lacking.

■ There is considerable evidence that maternal alcohol consumption during pregnancy has detrimental effects on a child's attention and activity (Streissguth, 1994). However, when a child's problems are tied to the mother's use of alcohol during pregnancy, it is more likely that the child shows a combination

of problems known as *fetal alcohol syndrome (FAS)* rather than ADHD. (We will discuss FAS in Chapter 4.)

Numerous other possible biological causes of ADHD have been examined. For example, because stimulant medications that reduce ADHD symptoms increase the availability of *catecholamines* such as *dopamine* and *norepinephrine* in the brain, it was thought that ADHD might result from a deficit of these neurotransmitters. However, research has not consistently supported this idea. Because the rate of ADHD among biological relatives of children with ADHD is higher than among the general population, some children may be genetically predisposed to develop ADHD. Some cases of ADHD may arise from a mutation of a gene that is known to lead to a form of thyroid disease in which the thyroid hormone is generally ineffective (Weiss et al., 1993). As a result, the body may compensate by producing more thyroid hormone, which accelerates the body's metabolism rate and therefore may stimulate higher levels of activity (Elia et al., 1994).

Yet another possible biological source of ADHD involves a brain structure called the **reticular activating system (RAS),** pictured in Figure 3.5. Some theorists have speculated that abnormally low RAS activity in children with ADHD leaves them underaroused (Satterfield & Dawson, 1971) and therefore in need of extra stimulation from the environment, which they obtain through hyperactive, rapidly shifting, im-

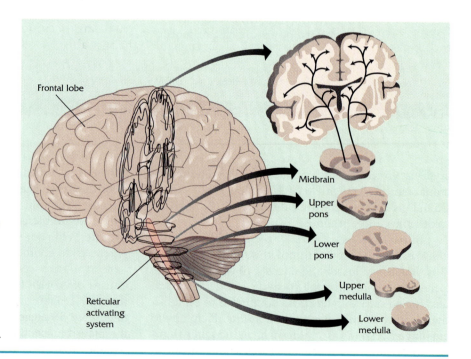

FIGURE 3.5

Brain Structures and ADHD
Both deficits of the frontal lobe of the cerebral cortex and underarousal of the reticular activating system (RAS) have been implicated in ADHD. The RAS is a complex network of neurons in the core of the brain stem that regulates arousal level.

pulsive behaviors. Evidence in support of this idea is inconclusive, due in part to problems associated with the measurement of RAS activity (Hynd et al., 1991).

ADHD has also been related to deficits in the **frontal lobe** of the cerebral cortex (Figure 3.5). This area of the brain controls executive functions such as planning and carrying out goal-directed activities. Two sources of data suggest that problems in this part of the brain might have a causal effect on ADHD (Hynd et al., 1991). First, ADHD children do not perform as well as non-ADHD children on neuropsychological tests commonly used to evaluate frontal lobe functioning. Second, magnetic resonance imaging (MRI) studies of the brain have shown that the frontal lobes of children with ADHD differ in size from those of normal children (Hynd, Semrud-Clikeman, & Lyytinen, 1991) and that other regions of the brain that connect to the frontal lobes and control motor activity are less active in ADHD children (Lou, Henrikson, & Bruhn, 1984).

These intriguing findings are subject to several limitations and cautions, however. For example, some neuropsychological tests used in this research may not be appropriate for children. Moreover, brain imaging has so far been performed on very few children. In other studies involving disorders that overlap with ADHD (e.g., learning disabilities), initially promising brain imaging findings have been difficult to replicate (Coles, 1987). Nevertheless, as methods for the measurement of brain activity become more sophisticated, evidence continues to mount that neurobiological processes play a role in the etiology of ADHD.

Causes of ADHD: Psychological Factors. Evidence for a biological cause of a disorder does not rule out a causal role for psychological factors as well. There are probably many children with atypically sized frontal lobes who are not inattentive or hyperactive, and a significant subgroup of children with ADHD have normal brain anatomy. A diathesis–stress model may be useful in explaining ADHD. Perhaps the presence of neurobiological vulnerability aggravated by psychosocial risk factors leads to a significantly increased likelihood of ADHD. Unfortunately, the tendency to emphasize biological factors in ADHD has resulted in relatively few research studies on possible psychological causes.

One exception is a fascinating longitudinal investigation by Deborah Jacobvitz and Alan Sroufe (1987). Starting with the hypothesis that RAS underarousal might provide a diathesis for ADHD, they considered the different ways in which a parent might respond to an infant or toddler whose RAS problems lead to irregular arousal. An optimal

Babies may need an optimal level of stimulation in order to learn how to control their arousal. Too much stimulation can lead to overexcitement; too little can cause underarousal. Most parents learn to be sensitive to the level of stimulation their infants need.

response might be to provide stimulation when the baby is underaroused and to reduce stimulation when the baby becomes overexcited. On the other hand, an interaction pattern characterized by parental *intrusiveness* and *overstimulation* when the baby is already aroused might overwhelm the child and make it less likely that he or she will learn to exert *self*-control over arousal.

Jacobvitz and Sroufe (1987) tested this idea by first measuring mothers' intrusive and stimulating behaviors during interactions with their children at ages 6 months, 24 months, and 42 months. They then examined the extent to which these interactions were related to hyperactivity when the child entered kindergarten. Results showed that the mothers of hyperactive children were more intrusive when the child was 6 months of age and more stimulating at 42 months of age than were the mothers of non-hyperactive children. These interactional measures were stronger predictors of later hyperactivity than were assessments of the child's activity level and difficulty of care at birth. These results suggest that hyperactivity may arise when an infant's hyperarousal (a diathesis) is combined with parental overstimulation (an environmental stressor).

Treatment of ADHD

The most common treatment for ADHD is to use one of three types of stimulant medications. These include *methyphenidate (MPH)* sold as *Ritalin; dextroamphetamine,* sold as *Dexedrine;* and *pemoline,* sold as *Cylert.* Although all are equally effective, Ritalin has been by far the most frequently used and studied. **Ritalin** facilitates the release, and blocks the reuptake, of norepinephrine and dopamine, amplifying the impact of these neurotransmitters in the brain. The result is that children taking Ritalin are better able to focus on relevant stimuli. This change also reduces the core symptoms of ADHD (inattention, hyperactivity, impulsivity) and leads to improved classroom work and social relationships (e.g., Buhrmester et al., 1992). About 70 percent of elementary school children with ADHD who take medication show a positive response; younger children and adolescents respond less consistently to medication (Spencer, 1996). Preliminary research also suggests that the results are less positive for ADHD children who display symptoms of anxiety or depression (Richters et al., 1995).

As treated children become more attentive, they appear calmer, less demanding, and more in control of their behavior, thus allowing teachers and parents to interact more pleasantly with them. Children receiving Ritalin tend to demonstrate improvement not only compared with their premedicated condition, but also compared with normal peers. Medication is thus said to normalize a child's attention and academic efficiency (DuPaul & Rapport, 1993).

Giving stimulants to children as young as 3 raises special caution flags, however. The side effects of these stimulants can include decreased appetite, insomnia, abdominal pains, headaches, crying spells, nervous habits and tics, and increased heart rate and blood pressure (Julien, 1992). A tendency to eat less can also result in a child's rate of weight and height gain lagging behind age-mates. However, concerns that stimulants cause permanent growth retardation or long-term emotional problems have proved to be unfounded when stimulant medications are monitored carefully. Use of periodic *drug holidays* (suspending medication on weekends or during school vacations) helps prevent substantial growth stunting, and reductions in dosage levels can counter such common side effects as sleep disturbance and emotional irritability.

The major problem with stimulant medications is that their effects last only about 4 to 5 hours. If the drug is discontinued, ADHD children often experience a *rebound effect* in which inattention, hyperactivity, and impulsivity come back stronger than ever (Evans & Pelham, 1991). Thus, it is common for ADHD children to continue taking stimulant medication into adolescence or adulthood. Furthermore, while this medication has beneficial effects on classroom work in the short-run, it does not appear to produce long-term academic gains (Klein & Mannuzza, 1991). Finally, follow-up samples of grown children with ADHD show that duration of drug therapy is unrelated to the quality of psychological and social adjustment later in life (Fischer et al., 1993). Ritalin can increase attention, but it cannot teach children the academic or social skills they will children need to succeed. Additional questions regarding the proper use of stimulant medications are addressed in the Controversy section.

Psychological treatments for ADHD are similar to those described earlier for disruptive behaviors. In behavior management programs, children are rewarded by parents or teachers for listening to directions carefully, remaining on task, staying in their seats during classroom projects, or performing other behaviors that are incompatible with primary ADHD symptoms. For example, a child might earn extra free time for remaining seated, or peers might be included in *group contingencies,* in which the ADHD child *and* classmates earn bonus free time when the ADHD child remains seated (Speltz, Shimimura, & McReynolds, 1982). Coordinated home–school procedures, where parent and teacher use the same behavior program to increase compliance and attentiveness, have also been used. In cognitive-behavioral interventions, children with ADHD are taught to ask and then answer a series of questions that direct their behavior toward completion of a specific task (e.g., How do I begin? How am I doing? Who can I ask to check my work?). Unfortunately, reviews of both behavior management procedures (e.g., Pelham & Murphy, 1986) and cognitive-behavioral training (Whalen, Henker, & Hinshaw, 1985; Baer & Nietzel, 1991) suggest they have weak or only temporary effects on core ADHD symptoms.

Some evidence suggests that a combination of behavior management and medication is superior to medication alone in reducing core symptoms (Pelham & Murphy, 1986) and that the dosage of medication needed in combined treatments is lower than when medication is used alone (Carlson, Pelham, Milich, & Dixon, 1992). According to other studies, however, combined programs are not more effective in reducing core symptoms than either medication alone (Horn et al., 1991) or cognitive therapy alone (Abikoff et al., 1987). Furthermore, the cost-effectiveness of combined programs has been questioned (Abikoff & Klein, 1992). However, ADHD is a mul-

Weighing the Risks of Ritalin

Prescribing Ritalin for children with ADHD has long been controversial, in large part because of the steady increase in its use during the 1970s and 1980s (Safer & Krager, 1988). In the late 1980s representatives of the Church of Scientology claimed that Ritalin was a dangerous drug that was being used as a "chemical straitjacket" by unskilled or intolerant adults to control normal, "feisty" children (Barkley, 1990). These accusations led to extreme polarization of the issues; parents were told that Ritalin was either a miracle drug or a virtual poison for their children.

Today, research has permitted a more clear-headed examination of the issues. There is no longer any doubt that stimulants reduce the core symptoms of ADHD in the majority of children who receive them, at least in the short term. Current concerns focus on the drug's physical and psychological costs to children and on the broader social implications of using medications that can so effectively control children's behavior.

First, there is concern that medicated children will come to believe that medication, not personal effort, controls their behavior. Critics worry that this attribution could erode a child's self-confidence and motivation to persist at challenging tasks. In fact, evidence from special ADHD summer camp programs suggests that medicated children experience *enhanced* self-confidence and attribute post-medication improvements to their own efforts (Pelham et al., 1992). It is unclear, however, whether these results hold up for the majority of children with ADHD who do not participate in intensive educational programs.

A second concern focuses on the sheer number of children receiving medication for ADHD. One study in Baltimore, Maryland, found that the rate of stimulant prescriptions doubled every 5 to 7 years. By 1988, more than 7 percent of third graders and 6 percent of all the county's elementary school children were taking stimulants (Safer & Krager, 1988). Has this trend continued? We do not know for sure, because there is no national database on stimulant drug use among children (Gadow, 1993). If, as suspected, stimulant medication prescriptions are still increasing, it would be important to know why. Does increasing use reflect increased prevalence of ADHD, improved detection of the disorder, or merely a diminishing capacity for parents and teachers to manage children's behavior, due perhaps to overcrowded classrooms, family disintegration, or parenting stress?

A third concern pertains to the possibility that children who take medication for ADHD might be at increased risk for drug abuse later in life. Follow-up studies of children with ADHD do reveal high rates of adult substance abuse. However, substance abuse in grown ADHD children could well be the result of other factors such as school failure or comorbidity with conduct disorder.

Finally, there is concern about how careful doctors are (1) in determining that a child needs stimulant medication and (2) in monitoring the effects of that medication. Treatment decisions are sometimes based on parents' reports rather than on standardized behavior checklists, parents often make haphazard dosage adjustments, and there is frequently a lack of communication between physicians and teachers about proper medication use. The prevalence of such problems today is unknown.

The controversy over drug therapy for ADHD continues. Although some suspected problems have proved to be of little concern, others linger and require more information to resolve. Questioning the psychological cost and social implications of a drug so widely used with children seems a healthy response. Still, this examination should not obscure the fact that stimulants are the only available treatment with the demonstrated capacity to normalize the primary symptoms of ADHD (Barkley, DuPaul, & Costello, 1993).

Thinking Critically

We noted that one study found that medicated children attending an ADHD summer camp experienced enhanced self-confidence and attributed their improved behavior to their own efforts. Why can't we say for sure that this result would generalize to all children who receive stimulant medication for ADHD? Consider the following questions:

- Might children attending a special camp program for ADHD react differently to medication than other ADHD children? Why?

- What other kinds of research studies could shed light on how children interpret changes in their behavior following drug therapy?

- Is it desirable that children attribute their improvements to their own efforts rather than a medication? Why or why not?

tifaceted disorder with several complications, such as poor communication skills, peer relationship problems, and anger management difficulties. These associated problems must be treated in addition to the core symptoms, and ADHD youngsters have responded well to behavioral interventions for them (Barkley et al., 1992). For this reason, most clinicians regard programs that combine medication and nonmedication treatments as essential to long-term improvement (Whalen & Henker, 1991).

In Review

ODD, CD, and ADHD are externalizing disorders that:

- are diagnosed much more often in boys than girls;
- show high levels of comorbidity, although they can occur independently, especially ADHD; and
- indicate a risk for continuing antisocial problems into adulthood, especially if the child shows signs of these disorders at an early age.

Disruptive behavior disorders and attention deficits are caused by a combination of etiological factors, which may include:

- biological or neuropsychological deficits;
- family stress and adversity;
- limited cognitive and social skills;
- insecure attachment to parents; and
- poor parenting skills.

Effective treatments include:

- programs that teach parenting skills for dealing with disruptive behavior disorders, although the long-term effects of these treatments have not been established;
- stimulant medications for the core symptoms of ADHD; and
- behavior modification programs for problems associated with ADHD (such as poor social skills).

Anxiety and Mood Disorders of Childhood and Adolescence

Children suffer anxiety and mood disorders that are very similar to those diagnosed in adults although, especially in younger children, the symptoms of these internalizing disorders more often include somatic symptoms such as stomachaches, headaches, and breathing problems. Although childhood mood and anxiety disorders may not be as socially disruptive or upsetting to adults as children's externalizing problems, they can leave children feeling profoundly unhappy and isolated.

The impact of anxiety and mood disorders is compounded by their frequent comorbidity with other problems. Up to 60 percent of anxious young-

sters also meet the criteria for depression (Brady & Kendall, 1992), and nearly 25 percent display ADHD and/or oppositional disorder (Strauss, 1990). When depression and anxiety overlap, the occurrence of anxiety usually precedes the onset of depression (Kovacs et al., 1989). The co-occurrence of depression and anxiety is so frequent that some researchers have suggested that both represent a single underlying disturbance of negative reactivity (Kendall & Watson, 1989).

Anxiety Disorders

Most adults can recall periods of intense anxiety in childhood that lasted for more than a day or two, stemming from conflict between parents, a dreaded confrontation with a neighborhood bully, a scary new class, or anticipation of a piano recital or classroom speech. These are normal experiences. For anxiety to reach the severity required for diagnosing a mental disorder, it must be persistent (lasting weeks or months) and it must interfere significantly with age-expected activities, responsibilities, or developmental tasks. For example, a child's anxiety about parental marital conflict is normal, but when this anxiety prevents the child from going to school or making friends, an anxiety disorder may be diagnosed. Anxiety of this magnitude is not uncommon. Anxiety disorders, including specific fears (called *phobias*), represent one of the most common forms of childhood psychopathology, with an estimated prevalence rate of 9 percent (Bernstein & Borchardt, 1991).

Until recently children's anxieties received less attention from clinicians and researchers than disruptive disorders and attention deficit disorders did. The reasons for this situation illustrate some basic differences between externalizing and internalizing problems. First, children's anxieties tend to have less impact on adults than disruptive or hyperactive behaviors do. Second, children's anxiety states are more difficult than disruptive behaviors to assess and diagnose; internal experiences, such as thoughts and feelings, are often difficult for children to put into words. Third, anxiety is a more normal part of everyday experience than are serious disruptive behaviors (Last & Strauss, 1990). The boundaries between normal and abnormal anxiety are therefore not as distinct. Moreover, unlike most disruptive behaviors, fear can be important to survival. For example, fear of strangers is a clearly adaptive response for young children because it minimizes the likelihood of victimization by dangerous adults (Hodiamont, 1991).

Although externalizing problems are almost impossible for most parents to ignore, equally serious internalizing problems often escape the notice of the adult world because they are seen as signs of a "nice" or "compliant" child.

Types of Anxiety Disorders. Anxiety is a multifaceted phenomenon, consisting of (1) observable behaviors such as trembling and avoidance, (2) physiological arousal such as upset stomach or sweating, and (3) cognitions such as persistent thinking or worrying about a dreaded event. One kind of anxiety symptom may be more prominent than others, depending on the specific type of anxiety disorder.

Older children, especially preadolescents, may develop *generalized anxiety disorder;* their anxiety is not associated with a specific stimulus but is experienced as diffuse apprehension about numerous, everyday occurrences such as a new bus driver, a guest at home, or any future event. Adolescents and, sometimes, younger children may also show some aspects of the anxiety disorders more commonly diagnosed in adulthood, including *panic attacks* and a pattern of intrusive thoughts and ritualistic behaviors called *obsessive-compulsive disorder.* These disorders are described in detail in Chapter 7. Here we look at a type of anxiety disorder that is specific to children.

Separation Anxiety Disorder. From about age 6 months to age 3 or 4 years, most infants and children show some anxiety when separated briefly from their parents or other attachment figures. In fact, some separation anxiety is a sign of good early adjustment. For this reason, the diagnosis of a separation anxiety disorder is not usually made until children reach 8 or 9 years. **Separation anxiety disorder** refers to developmentally inappropriate fear of separation from home or from those to whom the child is most closely attached, usually parents.

Children who suffer separation anxiety are often clingy and dependent on adults. They appear to need their parents' help to complete even the simplest tasks, including getting dressed, brushing their teeth, or going to bed. They worry about their parents' getting sick or injured, believing, for example, that the parent is certain to have an auto accident if the child is not along for the ride. Such children also show excessive fear of being left alone and often have nightmares that reflect their most prominent worries. Some insist on sleeping with their parents. Separation anxiety is often associated with frequent headaches, stomachaches, and other physical complaints.

According to the DSM-IV, a child must show three or more of these behaviors for at least 4 weeks in order to be diagnosed with a separation anxiety disorder. The disorder may be present in as many as 4 percent of children and young adolescents. It is prevalent throughout the world and is believed to be somewhat more common among girls than boys (Last et al., 1987). However, clinicians may tend to underdiagnose separation anxiety disorder in boys because anxious boys are more likely to also show disruptive behavior that directs attention away from their anxiety symptoms.

One of the most serious consequences of separation anxiety is the child's refusal to attend school, which occurs in about 75 percent of these cases (Last et al., 1987). School refusal leads to such secondary problems as academic failure and isolation from peers, problems that further increase the child's dependence on adults and maintain the child's motivation to stay home.

School refusal by children with separation anxiety can be distinguished from the school refusal commonly associated with two other disorders: social phobia and specific phobias. The child with **social phobia** is afraid of situations that involve close social contact and scrutiny by others. These children usually feel embarrassed or humiliated in groups. Since school is a place where close social contact naturally occurs, the socially phobic child will resist going to school. In cases of **specific phobia,** children resist school because they fear and want to avoid a *specific object or circumstance* associated with the school, such as dogs encountered on the way to school or a specific school activity. Neither social nor specific phobia is driven by the child's fear of being away from the parent, a distinction that is difficult to make and often leads to incorrect diagnoses (Phelps, Cox, & Bajorek, 1992).

Longitudinal Course of Childhood Anxiety Disorders.

A predisposition for fearfulness can be observed early in life. In toddlers, this is evidenced by unusually shy, quiet, and withdrawn behavior, a pattern referred to as *behavioral inhibition* (Kagan, 1989). This pattern is usually regarded as a temperamental characteristic of the child. In other words, **inhibition** is considered an inborn, biologically determined tendency to experience higher-than-average levels of fearfulness in unfamiliar situations.

Longitudinal studies have found that inhibited toddlers are more likely than their uninhibited peers to develop phobias and other anxiety disorders by school age (Biederman et al., 1990), especially if their parents have also had anxiety problems (Hirshfeld et al., 1992). During the preschool and kindergarten years, inhibited children are usually compliant and agreeable but withdrawn from peers (Rubin et al., 1991). By the late grade school years, such children tend to be rejected by their peers and report feeling lonely and sad. It is at this age that the severity of their inhibition is usually noticed by adults, and an anxiety disorder, most often separation anxiety disorder, is diagnosed. About 50 percent of these children are expected to have continuing anxiety problems through adolescence (Cantwell & Baker, 1989; Rosenbaum, et al., 1991; Strauss, 1990). In

Parents can inadvertently strengthen a child's anxiety about separation or school attendance by reinforcing the child's avoidance of peers and encouraging the child to stay at home.

adults, high levels of inhibition are associated with social introversion, timidity, and a tendency toward social anxiety.

Causes of Childhood Anxiety Disorders.

One view of the cause of childhood anxiety disorders focuses on the relationship between these disorders and inhibition. Compared with other children, inhibited children have heightened signs of physiological arousal such as accelerated heart rate and higher levels of norepinephrine. These characteristics suggest that anxious children are predisposed to react to many different stressors with greater physiological arousal (Kagan, 1989). These differences in arousal may reflect differences in the anatomy and functioning of the brain (Davidson, 1991).

Whether a biological diathesis actually leads to an anxiety disorder depends on a host of environmental and family factors including (1) the frequency and type of stressors that the child encounters; (2) the degree of match (or "goodness of fit") between the child's inhibited temperament and the parents' style of parenting; and (3) social relationships that reinforce or discourage fearful behavior. The interplay of biological and psychosocial factors (diathesis and stress) in the development of an anxiety disorder is clear in the case of Mike.

> *M*ike, a 9-year-old boy with severe separation anxiety and school refusal, was described as shy and withdrawn since toddlerhood. Separation anxiety developed 2 years before he came to the clinic, soon after the youngster witnessed his mother having a heart attack and being removed from his home by emergency medical staff. Mike's mother never fully regained her health, and she inadvertently reinforced the child's desire to remain at home with her.

Cognitive factors may also contribute to the development of children's anxiety disorders (see Figure 3.6). Anxious children are prone to several cognitive distortions that heighten their fears unnecessarily. For example, they expect that bad things will happen, blame themselves for all sorts of misfortunes, lack self-confidence, criticize their past performances excessively, and express pessimism about the future. Their attention to the environment is often biased, so they exaggerate the threatening aspects of unfamiliar situations (Grossman & Hughes 1992). As a result of these cognitive biases, anxious children can talk themselves into becoming and staying unduly frightened about many aspects of their world.

Treatment of Children's Anxiety Disorders. When children's (or adults') anxiety disorders are focused on a relatively specific object or situation, a treatment called *systematic desensitization* is often used. In **systematic desensitization** the client learns to use an anxiety-inhibiting technique such as muscle relaxation or deep breathing in the presence of the feared object or situation. Exposure to the feared situation is gradual and occurs either *in vivo* (i.e., through a live presentation of the feared stimulus) or through mental imagery, in which the client imagines increasingly intense versions of a feared stimulus.

For example, *in vivo* desensitization for school refusal in a child with separation anxiety might begin by first taking the child to the front door of the school and having the child practice relaxed breathing exercises until all signs of anxiety dissipate. Next, the child would walk to an interior hallway, then to an

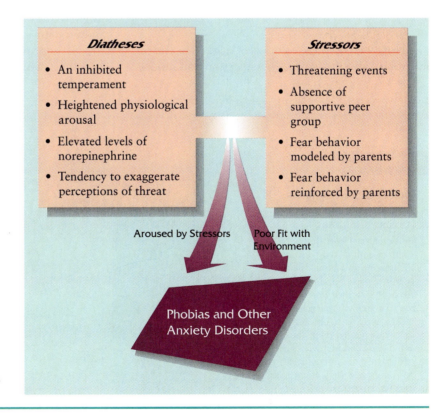

FIGURE 3.6

Diathesis–Stress Model of Childhood Anxiety Disorders

Diatheses can be triggered into anxiety disorders by several kinds of stressors. The diatheses can make certain stressors more likely, and stressors can exacerbate the strength of some diatheses.

empty classroom, and finally to a classroom containing a few other students. Relaxation breathing techniques would reduce or prevent anxiety at each of these steps.

Desensitization is often used in conjunction with other learning-based methods. For example, a child with separation anxiety might be rewarded with special privileges for attending school. In some cases, therapists might use a modeling approach, in which the anxious child observes a peer interacting with a feared stimulus before the child tries to do so.

Desensitization can also be combined with cognitive-behavioral treatments in which the child is taught to alter the biased thinking that precipitates or maintains anxiety (Grossman & Hughes, 1992). These treatments use several techniques including:

1. **Cognitive restructuring.** Distorted and biased thoughts (e.g., "If I don't get every question right on this test, I'm stupid.") are identified and replaced with more adaptive self-statements ("It's okay to make mistakes as long as I try my best.").

2. **Coping skills training.** The child is taught to use a cognitive plan and a behavioral strategy to control a negative emotion (e.g., "Count to 10, relax, and read the first test question slowly.").

3. **Self-reinforcement.** The child is taught to create and use positive self-evaluative statements (e.g., "I did a good job on that question, now on to the next one.").

How well do these techniques work? For the reduction of specific fears, desensitization and modeling are very effective, at least in terms of immediate posttreatment gains (Thyer, 1991; Grossman & Hughes, 1992). However, their long-term effects and their efficacy with more severe and diffuse forms of anxiety are less certain (King & Ollendick, 1989).

Philip Kendall (1994) reported the first controlled study of cognitive-behavioral treatments for children with debilitating forms of anxiety (including separation anxiety disorders and generalized anxiety disorders). His subjects were males and females from various ethnic groups, and he used a combination of desensitization, cognitive restructuring, coping skills training, and self-reinforcement. According to Child Behavior Checklists completed by parents, 60 percent of the treated children improved enough to be indistinguishable from normal peers (see Figure 3.7). These results suggest both optimism and caution. Although slightly more than half of the treated children improved dramatically, the rest did not—a result attesting to the persistence of childhood anxiety disorders.

Medications have also been used to treat anxiety disorders in children and adolescents. Antidepressants, antianxiety drugs, neuroleptics (drugs that reduce some symptoms of psychosis), and even antihistamines and stimulants have been prescribed. The effects of these medications have not been established in controlled research, even though antidepressant treatment has been examined in three well-designed studies. One of these, a study of young children with separation anxiety, found clear indications of improvement (Gittelman & Klein, 1980). The other two, which studied older children with

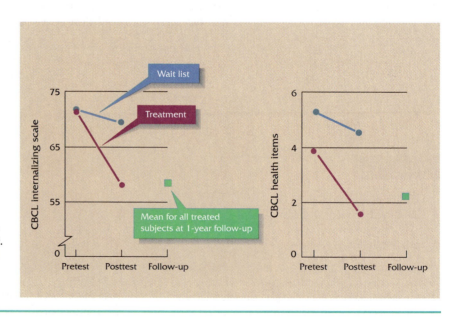

FIGURE 3.7

Outcomes for Cognitive-Behavioral Treatment of Anxious Children

In Kendall's (1994) study of children with anxiety disorders, the treatment combined several cognitive–behavioral techniques. According to their parents, anxious children who received treatment improved significantly more than did children on a waiting list. Among the children who received treatment, both internalizing scores on the CBCL and physical complaints decreased.

mixed generalized anxiety and depressive symptoms, did not (Berney et al., 1981; Bernstein, Garfinkel, & Borchardt, 1990). Overall, medication currently has a limited role in the treatment of children's anxiety.

Depression in Childhood and Adolescence

A person of any age—from early childhood to late adulthood—can experience a depressed mood that is severe enough to justify a diagnosis of depression. Unfortunately, depression is quite persistent across the life span: there is a fourfold increase in the risk of adult depression for those who have experienced persistent depressed mood as children or adolescents (Harrington, 1992). However, the specific ways in which depression is manifested change with age. Here, we describe the nature of depressed mood as it typically occurs in children and adolescents. Chapter 9 focuses on the depressive patterns seen in adults.

Symptoms of Depression. The DSM-IV does not list childhood depression separately from adult mood disorders. Instead, it describes children's mood disorders using adult criteria, then specifies some symptoms that are particularly common in depressed children. For example, in children and adolescents, depressed mood is usually experienced as a mixture of strong negative feelings including irritability, sadness, hopelessness (e.g., "What's the use of going to school today?"), and guilt (e.g., "My parents fight because of me."). This *negative affect* can last several weeks or months. In adolescents, an episode of serious depression typically lasts for 6 or 7 months (Strober et al., 1993). The outward expression of these emotions often takes on an irritable, angry tone. Sudden demonstrations of anger can be triggered by the smallest stressor.

Complaints of physical ailments such as stomach pains and headaches are also common in children with depressed mood (Mitchell et al., 1988). In younger children, such as 8-year-old Michelle, reports of physical symptoms without a clear organic basis often lead the clinician to suspect depression.

*M*ichelle was brought to the clinic on the recommendation of her pediatrician, who had found no medical reason for the girl's complaints of head and stomach pain. Although this youngster talked a lot about "worries" and had other signs of anxiety, she also displayed a pronounced sadness, "flat" emotions, and obvious lack of energy. Her parents noted that she often woke up during the night and could not get back to sleep. Michelle had shown this pattern of emotions for the last 4 or 5 months at home and in school, and both her parents and teachers saw it as a clear departure from her "usual self." Michelle's mother stated that she knew something was wrong when Michelle lost interest in gymnastics and no longer wanted to play with her friends, presumably because of her headaches and stomach pain.

Another feature of depressed mood in children is low self-esteem (Renouf & Harter, 1990). Their thinking is often dominated by exaggerated self-deprecation ("I'm the dumbest kid in my class; I'll never amount to anything."). Depressed children seem especially sensitive to normal, day-to-day variations in the quality of interactions with others; minor incidents such as a classmate's critical remark can become the basis for deciding that "nobody likes me" (Hammen & Goodman-Brown, 1990). Children experiencing depression often engage in cognitive distortions in which they set unrealistically high standards for themselves and then evaluate their behavior negatively, no matter how well they actually do (Grossman & Hughes, 1992).

Childhood depression is also associated with problems making and maintaining friendships and with academic difficulties. Impairments such as these typically occur only while the child or adolescent is experiencing depressed mood (McCauley & Myers, 1992). Michelle, for example, resumed playing with her friends and performed well during the following school year when her mood returned to normal.

A particularly serious consequence of childhood and adolescent depression is suicidal thoughts and suicide attempts. One longitudinal study of 8- to 13-year-old children with depressive disorders found that 1 out of 3 made at least one suicide attempt in the 7 years following their initial diagnosis (Kovacs, Goldston, & Gatsonis, 1993). Self-destructive tendencies in depressed children and adolescents can also take the form of substance abuse, reckless play, reckless driving, or other high-risk behaviors.

Case studies suggest that children and adolescents are capable of showing any of the mood disorders found in the DSM-IV, but most are still relatively rare in children. (We will discuss these specific disorders and their diagnoses for children in Chapter 9.)

Connections

What are the major antidepressant and antianxiety drugs, and how do they affect the brain? See Chapter 15 for explanations.

Susan Campbell

Dr. Susan Campbell is Professor of Psychology and Director of the Clinical Psychology Training Program at the University of Pittsburgh. She is a leading expert in the area of assessing and treating children's mental disorders.

Childhood Disorders

Q *Treatments for some childhood disorders have shown good short-term effects, but long-term efficacy is generally poor or not established. Will this change? How?*

A So many treatments target symptoms rather than the underlying causes of a disorder, probably because currently we know so little about what the causes are. As a result, we treat different disorders in much the same way. There is not good specificity between a diagnosis and its corresponding treatment.

We are often dealing with children who have *chronic* behavioral and emotional problems, yet we expect to see positive effects in a short period of time. Treatments such as medication or structured behavior programs in the classroom may need to be used continuously for many children.

> *. . . providers do not usually see children . . . until the problem is well out of hand.*

Another factor that complicates treatment is that mental health providers do not usually see children and their families until the problem is well out of hand. Often the child is brought to treatment only after there has been a serious antisocial incident at home or school. When problems have become that full-blown, the mental health practitioner is simply propping up the child and family. By then, it is often too late for treatment to bring about dramatic change.

Q *Which treatments do you think are most effective?*

A The most effective are multimodal—treatments containing multiple components that address different aspects of the problem and involve several individuals in the child's environment, such as peers, teachers, and parents. For example, some treatment programs include a parent training component, social skills training for the child, and a behavior management program in the classroom. But of course this gets us into political issues regarding the cost. Many people question the worth of this investment.

Q *Do high rates of comorbidity for most children's disorders threaten the validity of the DSM-IV?*

A It seems that everything is comorbid with everything. As noted in this chapter, 70 percent or more of children with ODD and CD also have ADHD. It leads me to wonder whether the main issue is really the *number* of problems that a child has, rather than the type of problem. That is, if you have many problems, you have a much worse prognosis.

Q *What's the solution?*

A I'm very sympathetic to the dimensional approach to diagnosis. I'm really troubled by a categorical approach that tries to force children into diagnostic boxes. For example, many studies compare children with only ADHD to children having ADHD and ODD or CD. But often the pure ADHD groups contain oppositional children who didn't quite meet criteria for ODD because they were one or two symptoms short of the diagnosis. A dimensional approach would be a more powerful way of understanding the relationship between a child's behavior problems and other characteristics.

Q *Do you think there is any reason for concern over the use of medication for children with ADHD?*

A There is a tendency to prescribe stimulant medication too freely. In my experience, many children are getting Ritalin who do not have ADHD. Even for children with ADHD, medication is all too often the only treatment used, and no effort is made to teach the child new skills.

Q *Do you think other treatments really help?*

A At the very least, use of other therapies sometimes permits a lower dosage or a shorter duration of medication treatment. This is important because we know very little about the long-term use of Ritalin and other stimulant medications. It also doesn't feel right to work with the family of an ADHD child and give only medication to the child. Unfortunately though, as I look into the future, I believe that medications will be used with greater and greater frequency.

Among younger children, boys are somewhat more likely than girls to show significant depression, but by mid-adolescence girls show higher rates than boys. Childhood mood disorders are marked by a high degree of comorbidity. Separation anxiety disorder is a coexisting disorder in nearly half of depressed children and adolescents, and conduct disorder has been found in nearly a quarter of them (McCauley & Myers, 1992). Such comorbidity generally has the effect of making the symptoms of childhood depression worse, and it tends to make recovery from the disorder more difficult.

Causes of Children's Depression. Episodes of serious depression in adults are often marked by biological abnormalities (described in Chapter 9). So far, however, studies of depressed children and adolescents have not revealed similar abnormalities (e.g., Kutcher et al., 1991), perhaps because the systems that regulate emotional expression are not yet fully developed (Ryan, 1992).

One promising direction for future research is on the role of brain activity during different emotional states. Richard Davidson (1991) and his colleagues found that when adults are experiencing depressive symptoms, there is decreased activity in the left frontal region of the brain relative to that in the right frontal region. Furthermore, 10-month-old infants who show this same kind of **cerebral asymmetry** are more likely to display negative emotions during separation from their mothers than infants with normal patterns of brain activity (Davidson & Fox, 1989). These findings suggest that cerebral asymmetry might be a useful marker of an early predisposition for depressed mood.

Children of depressed parents have a significantly higher risk for depression (Downey & Coyne, 1990). Genetic transmission probably accounts for part of this risk, but the family environment is also an important contributor. Depressed mothers display less positive affect than nondepressed mothers; they are more critical, rejecting, and overcontrolling toward their children, and are generally less attuned to their children's emotional needs (e.g., Cohn et al., 1990). Families with depressed parents also tend to be less cohesive and supportive and more stress-filled than other families (Billings & Moos, 1985), and they are more often marked by parental discord and hostility toward the children (Rutter & Quinton, 1984). Families with depressed youngsters are less supportive than are families with either well-functioning children (Garber, Braafladt, & Zeman, 1991) or nondepressed but psychiatrically impaired children (McCauley et al., 1991). Thus, research evidence consistently points to both heredity and family experiences as substantial contributors to the development of childhood depression.

Another factor that may make a child more susceptible to depression is poor **affect regulation,** the process by which individuals use thought and action to prevent or reduce strong negative emotions. Depressed children and adolescents are more likely than their nondepressed peers to use avoidant, aggressive, or passive strategies when experiencing sadness, anger, or fear (Garber et al., 1991). They also tend to devalue active problem-solving methods when experiencing these emotions. Perhaps their repeated interactions with a depressed and unresponsive parent have convinced them that they do not have the power to bring about positive changes. The few studies in this area indicate that maladaptive affect regulation is more evident in depressed girls than in depressed boys (McCauley, Kendall, & Pavlidis, 1995).

Treatment of Childhood Depression. Drugs known as *tricyclic antidepressants* (e.g., imipramine or Tofranil) have been the medications most commonly prescribed for childhood depression. Early studies of the effectiveness of these medications with children generated quite a bit of optimism, but they lacked adequate methodology. When better-designed studies compared the tricyclics with a placebo (pills containing no active ingredient) in double-blind trials (in which neither the patient nor the doctor knows which pill is being taken), the results were far less encouraging (Strober, Freeman, & Rigali, 1990). These findings, combined with the fact that tricyclics can cause negative side effects, have led to the recommendation that these medications should be given only to children with severe depression who fail to respond to other treatments (Harrington, 1992).

Some of the cognitive-behavioral treatments discussed earlier (cognitive restructuring, coping skills training, and self-reinforcement) are also commonly used to treat childhood depression. These procedures have produced significant improvement in children with mild depression (e.g., Kahn et al., 1990). In one study of children with more severe depression, group therapy using cognitive-behavioral interventions also produced positive results (Lewinsohn et al., 1990). Obviously, more research is still needed on the effects of cognitive-behavioral treatments with severely depressed children and adolescents.

Connections

If children cannot enlist the help of a depressed parent, might they develop a sense of helplessness? For the learned helplessness model of depression, see Chapter 9, pp. 304–305.

Family environments play a role in childhood depression. Parents who do not respond to a youngster's emotional needs with empathy and understanding may increase their feelings that they are worthless, that no one cares about them, and that they are powerless.

In Review

Anxiety and mood disorders during childhood and adolescence share several characteristics:

■ overcontrolled or internalized problems;
■ frequent comorbidity;
■ a limited role for medication in their treatment;
■ responsiveness to cognitive-behavioral techniques; and
■ similarity to DSM categories that also indicate mood and anxiety disorders in adults.

Anxiety disorders and depression during childhood and adolescence differ from adult forms of these disorders in several ways:

■ childhood anxiety often takes the form of separation anxiety disorder;
■ sad or depressed mood often takes the form of pronounced irritability in children and adolescents; and
■ more frequent complaints of physical symptoms, such as stomachaches, headaches, and breathing problems.

Other Disorders of Childhood and Adolescence

Feeding and Eating Disorders

Most feeding and eating disorders are first noticed in childhood and adolescence, which is why we are discussing these problems in this chapter, even though the DSM-IV lists the major eating disorders such as anorexia nervosa and bulimia nervosa in a separate "Eating Disorders" section. Eating disorders and accompanying problems of excessive weight loss or gain often continue into the adult years when they may be accompanied by other mental disorders that complicate our understanding and treatment of these conditions.

Anorexia Nervosa. Unreasonable fear of gaining weight, disturbances in the perception of one's body shape or size, and the relentless pursuit of thinness, no matter what the consequences, are the main characteristics of **anorexia nervosa.** Affected individuals insist on keeping their weight below a normal level. Some remain obsessed with food, despite their reluctance to eat it, devoting enormous amounts of time to reading about food or cooking large amounts of it for others. Anorexia is a serious disorder that sometimes requires hospitalization. Severe malnutrition, skin disease, and even death are some of its possible consequences.

Some individuals with anorexia try to reduce their weight by extreme dieting, fasting, excessive exercise, or some combination of all three strategies. This subtype of anorexia nervosa is called the *restricting type*. In the *binge-eating/purging type,* binge eating may be followed by purging, which involves self-induced vomiting or misuse of laxatives or diuretics to prevent ingested food from adding to body weight. In adolescence, outright refusals to eat, or eating only a few preferred items, are the most prevalent thinness strategies.

Anorexic adolescents often have extremely distorted images of their bodies. Carol is a case in point.

*C*arol, a 17-year-old who was recently treated in one of the authors' clinic, frequently complained of "looking dumpy" and "feeling fat" despite being well below the average weight for her age and height. Before developing an anorexic pattern, Carol recalled that normal satiety cues (feeling full just after eating) would lead to extremely self-deprecating thoughts such as "I'm fat and ugly," along with guilt. "Eating made me feel like a bad person, as if I had done something wrong," she said. Consequently, Carol began to refuse all foods except rice cakes and pickles. Shortly before her parents brought her to the clinic, this 5'3"

young woman weighed only about 80 pounds. Although Carol said she felt healthy at this weight, she still believed that her legs and ankles were "too thick."

Like Carol, anorexic persons typically believe they can never be quite thin enough. Even though other people might perceive them as looking emaciated and unhealthy, anorexic persons are preoccupied with any sign of fat, no matter how small, on any part of their bodies.

Anorexia should not be confused with the tendency to be extremely weight conscious or overly concerned about caloric intake and exercise. Thinness alone, or wanting to be thin, is insufficient to diagnose anorexia. All the symptoms in the DSM table below must be observed in post-menarcheal females,

DSM-IV

Diagnostic Criteria for Eating Disorders

Anorexia Nervosa

A. Refusal to maintain body weight at or above a minimally normal weight for age and height (e.g., weight less than 85 percent of that expected)

B. Intense fear of gaining weight or becoming fat, even though underweight

C. Disturbance in the way in which one's body weight or shape is experienced, undue influence of body weight or shape on self-evaluation, or denial of the seriousness of the current low body weight

D. In postmenarcheal females, amenorrhea, i.e., the absence of at least three consecutive menstrual cycles

Bulimia Nervosa

A. Recurrent episodes of binge eating. An episode of binge eating is characterized by both of the following:

(1) eating (within about a 2-hour period) an amount of food that is definitely larger than most people would eat during a similar period of time and under similar circumstances, and

(2) a sense of lack of control over eating during the episode (e.g., a feeling that one cannot stop eating or control what or how much one is eating)

B. Recurrent inappropriate compensatory behavior in order to prevent weight gain, such as self-induced vomiting; misuse of laxatives, diuretics, enemas, or other medications; fasting; or excessive exercise

C. The binge eating and inappropriate compensatory behaviors both occur, on average, at least twice a week for 3 months

D. Self-evaluation is unduly influenced by body shape and weight

E. The disturbance does not occur exclusively during episodes of Anorexia Nervosa

Note: The DSM-IV also lists, in an appendix, Binge-Eating Disorder as a proposed new category for future study. In contrast to Bulimia, the person with Binge-Eating Disorder uses no inappropriate strategies such as purging to compensate for binge eating.

Source: American Psychiatric Association; *Diagnostic and Statistical Manual of Mental Disorders,* Fourth Edition. Washington, DC, American Psychiatric Association, 1994.

including weight that is 85 percent or less of ideal, and *amenorrhea,* the suppression of the menstrual cycle due to weight loss. In males, or in females prior to menses, only the first three symptoms are necessary. Depression commonly accompanies anorexia, but it is not known whether depression is a cause of anorexia or a result of the physical effects of malnourishment.

The prevalence of anorexia among late adolescent or adult females is estimated to be about 0.5 percent to 1.0 percent, but the rate has increased substantially in North America over the last half of the twentieth century. It is estimated that anorexic females outnumber males at least 10 to 1 (Leichner & Gertler, 1988).

A variety of causal factors for anorexia have been proposed (Hsu, 1988). Sociocultural interpretations have focused on societal factors in North America and Europe that influence perceptions of ideal appearance and body weight. Television commercials, magazines, and beauty pageants encourage an almost obsessive pursuit of slimness by women, a trend that has become prominent since the middle part of the twentieth century. For example, *Playboy* centerfolds and Miss America Pageant contestants showed decreasing average body weight from 1959 to 1978,

while the number of diet articles in women's magazines increased substantially (Garner et al., 1980). During this same period, Miss America Contest winners had body weights that were about 82 percent of average, lower than the DSM-IV criterion for anorexia.

This constant publicity about thinness as a standard of beauty may lead many women to hold unreasonable expectations about how thin they should be in order to be attractive. In a classic study (Fallon & Rozin, 1985), undergraduates rated their current and ideal body sizes compared with the size they thought people of the opposite sex would find attractive. As shown in Figure 3.8, men's ratings of these two sizes were very close to one another, and all were *heavier* than the figure that women actually found most attractive for men. The results were dramatically different for the female students. As Figure 3.8 shows, females' ideal figure and the figure they assumed men would find most attractive were both substantially *thinner* than their current weight, and their current weight was greater than the figure men rated as most attractive.

Psychoanalysts have interpreted anorexia as a "flight from adult sexuality" in which the individual equates food and eating with "forbidden sexual ob-

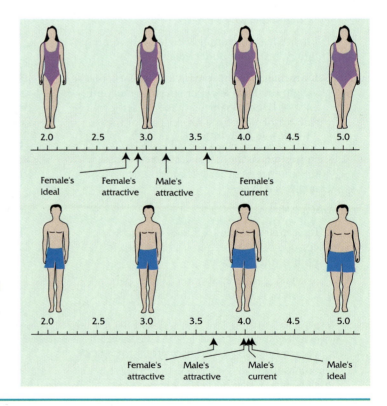

FIGURE 3.8

Perceptions of Body Shapes

When male and female undergraduates rated various body shapes, their responses were strikingly different (Fallon & Rozin, 1985). The students indicated the figure that represented their ideal body shape, the figure they thought would be attractive to the opposite sex, and their own current figure. The ratings show how males and females differ in their satisfaction about their weight.

Source: The scale is adapted from Stunkard, Sorensen, & Shulsinger, 1980.

jects and activities" (Wilson, 1988). Other theorists have looked to the family for causes. Families having an adolescent with anorexia have been found to be less skilled at conflict resolution and communication, more traditional, rigid, and likely to shift blame from one family member to another and to establish covert alliances (Palazzoli, 1985). In Carol's family, for example, a strong but unacknowledged alliance existed between her mother and her younger sister. This alliance excluded Carol as well as her father, who had recently become increasingly removed from the family. Her father even had an extramarital affair that, although supposedly a secret, was known to the whole family. Many clinicians believe that this type of family situation provides fertile ground for the development of eating disorders in already vulnerable and unstable adolescents (Minuchin, Rosman, & Baker, 1978). In these cases, anorexia may divert attention from trouble spots, such as an unhappy marriage, thereby maintaining the family's equilibrium. It is not yet clear, however, to what extent these family patterns are causes of anorexia or part of the family's reaction to a child's eating disorder. Thus, it is important to emphasize that, although family factors may have contributed to Carol's eating disorder, they almost certainly were not its original cause.

Biological explanations for anorexia have centered on the role of the *hypothalamus,* which controls feeding, drinking, and sexual drive and plays a role in regulating the menstrual cycle. Hypothalamic dysfunction is suspected because some anorexic women evidence amenorrhea *prior* to weight loss, suggesting that menstrual cycle suppression may result from something other than weight loss (Katz et al., 1978). However, emotional distress can also cause amenorrhea, and hypothalamic dysfunction alone would not explain the increased prevalence of anorexia seen in the last few decades (Hsu, 1988). Thus, although support for a hypothalamic cause of anorexia, as well as for other biological causes, is not compelling, research in this area continues.

Bulimia Nervosa. The eating disorder known as **bulimia nervosa** is characterized by recurrent binge eating, in which large quantities of food are consumed in one sitting, followed by efforts to prevent weight gain. A *purging subtype* of bulimia refers to people who regularly induce vomiting or use laxatives, diuretics, or enemas after binge eating. *Nonpurging subtypes* primarily use fasts or stringent exercise (even if it causes them injury or medical problems) to compensate for binges.

Persons with bulimia nervosa, primarily young women, believe that they cannot control their eat-

ing. Their anxiety and remorse after binge eating are relieved somewhat by purging. Unfortunately, purging usually brings about even stronger feelings of shame and disgust, and the bulimic person is caught in a downward spiral of emotional distress. Often, binge eating occurs in an attempt to cope with the emotional aftermath of purging, but it leads only to more purging. This pattern can accelerate to the point that bulimic individuals spend the majority of their days locked in binge–purge cycles.

DSM-IV criteria for the diagnosis of bulimia are listed in the DSM table on page 107. As in anorexia nervosa, depression is an associated feature of bulimia nervosa. Unlike anorexics, individuals with bulimia tend to be of normal weight or even somewhat overweight. They are not usually trying to achieve low weight; rather, the motivating force behind bulimia seems to be the avoidance of fatness rather than the desire to be extremely thin. Adolescents referred for treatment of bulimia sometimes state that they only want to lose weight.

Many of the same causal factors suspected in anorexia have been implicated in bulimia, including pathogenic family interactions and dysfunction of the hypothalamus (Kaye & Weltzin, 1991). However, learning processes also appear to play an explicit role in bulimia. For example, the reduction of anxiety brought about by purging may help maintain the act of purging through negative reinforcement.

Longitudinal Course of Eating Disorders. Although anorexia nervosa and bulimia nervosa are usually diagnosed in adolescence, they have been found in children as young as age 8. Among preadolescent anorexic children, females outnumber males, but not to the extent observed in adolescence (about 3 out of 10 grade school cases are males; Gislason, 1988). In a few cases, anorexia and bulimia plague individuals throughout most of their adult lives.

Like other disorders discussed in this chapter, eating disorders are often preceded by other problems. Most preadolescent anorexics had one or more *internalizing* problem behaviors (shyness, low mood, anxiety) prior to their eating disturbance. In many cases the onset of eating problems was preceded by a stressful event such as the birth of a sibling, peer teasing about body weight, or separation from or loss of a parent. Similarly, both anorexia and bulimia during adolescence have been associated with eating problems in earlier childhood, although each is predicted by different problems (Marchi & Cohen, 1990). Bulimia is related to childhood *pica* (eating nonfood substances such as dirt, paint chips, etc.) and to "problem meals" in which mealtimes are

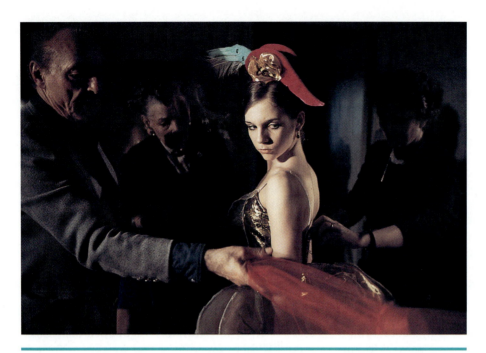

Anorexia nervosa was first described by the physician Sir William Gull in 1868. But only recently has public awareness of eating disorders soared as many celebrities have described their travails with these problems. The pop singer Karen Carpenter died as a result of anorexia; Olympic gymnast Cathy Rigby suffered from bulimia. In her 1986 autobiography Dancing on My Grave, *the ballerina Gelsy Kirkland (shown above) described how she became anorexic in order to achieve what she perceived as the ideal proportions for a classic dancer: "an almost skeletal frame, accentuating the collarbone and length of the neck." Unlike most people with eating disorders, Kirkland faced explicit pressure to lose weight:*

> *I had an encounter with Mr. B [George Balanchine] in class which underscored his demand for starvation, a memory that is etched in my mind with all the pain of a fingernail being scraped across a blackboard. He halted class and approached me for a kind of physical inspection. With his knuckles, he thumped on my sternum and down my ribcage, remarking, "Must see the bones." I was less than a hundred pounds even then. . . . He did not merely say "Eat less." He said repeatedly, "Eat nothing."*

a battle between parents and their children over eating. Anorexia is related to earlier picky eating and digestive problems, including frequent vomiting, diarrhea, and stomachaches.

Treatment of Eating Disorders. The treatment objective in cases of anorexia nervosa is to increase body weight; for bulimia nervosa, it is to decrease binge-eating episodes. Both disorders can have serious, life-threatening consequences, and both are difficult to change. Most treatment research has been conducted with young adults rather than with children.

For anorexia, a variety of drugs with *appetite-enhancing* characteristics—including *cyproheptadine* and *THC*, the active ingredient in marijuana—have been tried, but with little success. Patients with bu-

limia were once given anticonvulsant medications, but this treatment was also ineffective (Kaplan et al., 1983). Because of the link between low mood and eating disorders, antidepressant medications have been tried, with mixed success for bulimic patients and with little success for anorexia (Walsh, 1988). In one study, group psychotherapy was superior to the antidepressant *imipramine* in reducing bulimic eating patterns, but medication led to more improvement in associated depressive and anxiety symptoms (Mitchell et al., 1990). Another drug, *fluoxetine* (Prozac) has shown promise in the treatment of bulimia (Goldbloom & Olmstead, 1993; Fichter et al., 1991). (We will discuss these drugs and their effects further in Chapters 9 and 15.) New research is focusing on various brain chemicals such as *cerocortin* that appear to suppress appetite; scientists are now trying to develop drugs that either induce production of cerocortin in overeaters or block its production in people with anorexia.

Behavior therapy procedures for eating disorders include desensitization (i.e., to the fear of gaining weight), as well as self-administered rewards and punishments. Cognitive-behavioral approaches teach clients to eat small amounts of food at regularly scheduled times, to quantify and record their eating to gain a sense of control over it, and to use specific statements to themselves or other strategies to counter the irrational thinking that precedes abnormal eating.

The results of behavior therapy for eating disorders have been mixed. Self-reward programs have led to success in some studies, but self-administered punishment has not been effective (Kuechler & Hampton, 1988). In the treatment of bulimia, cognitive-behavioral therapy has had considerable success, producing better overall results than rewards and punishers (Fairburn et al., 1993), and leading to significant improvements when used in groups (Kettlewell, Mizes, & Wasylyshyn, 1992; Wolf & Crowther, 1992). Interpersonal therapy has produced improvements equal to those of cognitive-behavioral therapy (Fairburn et al. 1993).

Family therapy is sometimes used in conjunction with the reinforcement of weight change (Crisp et al., 1992). In therapy based on the work of Salvador Minuchin (Minuchin et al., 1978) anorexic adolescents and their families attend sessions (sometimes while eating lunch) at which discussion and role-playing are aimed at (1) clarifying relationships, (2) developing distinct boundaries between and among relationships in order to give the adolescent breathing room from an overprotective parent, and (3) improving communication among family members. Improved communication is thought to make disordered eating behaviors unnecessary. For example, adolescents might express anger directly to a rejecting or overprotective parent, rather than doing so by refusing food.

Using these methods, Minuchin and his colleagues reported improvement in 83 percent of 53 patients whose progress had been followed for up to 5 years after family therapy. Unfortunately, there was no comparison group of untreated clients, so the validity of these findings is unclear. In a better-designed study (Crisp et al., 1991), 90 patients with severe anorexia were randomly assigned to one of four conditions—behavioral, individual, or family therapy, or a no-treatment control group. A year after therapy, the three treated groups were equally successful in terms of weight gain and the return of menstruation; all did better than the control group.

Elimination Disorders

When children show a marked departure from socially defined and developmentally appropriate toileting practices, elimination disorders are diagnosed. Repeated release of urine into bedding or clothes is called **enuresis,** and the repeated passage of feces in inappropriate places is called **encopresis.** Both may be involuntary or intentional. In either case, they generate a great deal of misery for the family and the child and make the treatment of co-occurring problems such as anxiety or oppositional behaviors much more difficult. Often the elimination incident is embedded in elaborate clean-up and punishment rituals that can escalate into severe conflict. If the problem occurs at school as well as at home, the child is often scorned and ridiculed by peers.

Elimination problems are considered abnormal only in children older than 4 years (for encopresis) or 5 years (for enuresis). Difficulties prior to these ages probably reflect normal variations in the acquisition of toileting skills.

Enuresis. In order to meet the DSM-IV criteria for enuresis, a child's problem with control of urination must occur at least twice a week for at least 3 months or have clear negative effects on social development. These problems are not uncommon in young children (about 10 percent of the general population has them at age 5) but become increasingly rare with age, showing about 1 percent prevalence by age 18. Boys are more likely than girls to be diagnosed with this disorder. Children do not easily outgrow an enuretic disorder; only about 1 out of 8 enuretic children between ages 5 and 19 will show spontaneous remission within a year. On average it takes about 3 years for enuresis to subside (Houts, 1991).

The causes of enuresis are not clearly understood. Various theories have focused on biological factors (sleep pattern difficulties, small bladder size), learning processes, and emotional problems as possible explanations, but research has not consistently supported any of them. Contemporary research has revealed two promising factors, however (Houts, 1991): (1) lack of normal coordination of bladder muscles during urination, resulting in residual urine in the bladder that then leaks out, and (2) a deficiency in the daily rhythm at which *arginine vasopressin,* an **antidiuretic hormone,** is released. This hormone controls the kidney's regulation of urine production in relation to bladder capacity.

Even though clinicians do not fully understand its cause, enuresis can be effectively treated. A behavior therapy technique for nocturnal enuresis uses an alarm that is set off by initial drops of urine on a special mattress pad. The alarm awakens the sleeping child, who can be taken to the bathroom to complete urination. This device is effective in stopping nocturnal enuresis in about 75 percent of treated children. Although relapse occurs frequently, it can be avoided with the use of additional behavior therapy procedures such as parental reinforcement of appropriate toileting or giving the child responsibility for self-monitoring of toileting successes and failures (Houts, Peterson, & Whelan, 1986). Nathan Azrin and his colleagues (e.g., Azrin, Hontos, & Besalel-Azrin, 1979) have also had success with a procedure called *dry-bed training* in which the child (1) practices getting up from the bed and using the toilet, (2) receives reinforcement from parents for avoiding accidents, and (3) must remake the bed and change clothing following an accident.

Medications, including imipramine, have also been used to treat enuresis, but they have not proved to be as generally effective as urine alarms in the long term. Some evidence indicates that the combination of medication and an alarm leads to more rapid reduction of bed-wetting than the alarm alone (Sukhai, Mol, & Harris, 1989).

Encopresis. Less common than enuresis, encopresis affects about 1 to 2 percent of children in the grade school years; 3 to 4 times as many boys as girls are diagnosed with the disorder (Thapar et al., 1992). In most cases, encopresis disappears by adolescence without any formal intervention.

Theories emphasizing the psychological origins of encopresis have implicated dysfunctional family relationships, excessive parental control, and children's anger or stress. Physiological explanations have centered on the contribution of muscle tension and relaxation in the rectum and the anal sphincters. For example, about 35 to 45 percent of encopretic children demonstrate a paradoxical tightening of the external anal sphincter when trying to defecate (Loening-Baucke & Cruikshank, 1986).

One approach to treating encopresis applies *biofeedback training,* a technique that uses technology to allow people to monitor physiological processes such as blood pressure and muscle tension. Encopresis has responded well to a biofeedback procedure in which the child learns to control the sphincter through reinforcement (Loening-Baucke, 1990). The most common and successful treatments for encopresis include parental reinforcement of appropriate toileting or loss of privileges for accidents as well as multicomponent programs that offer some combination of behavior management, education, dietary modifications, and treatment for the constipation that is a common complicating factor (Thapar et al., 1992).

Revisiting the Case of Tom

What do the theories and research discussed in this chapter tell a psychologist about how to help Tom, the boy described at the beginning of this chapter? His inattention and off-task behaviors at school suggest a diagnosis of ADHD, probably the inattentive subtype. His worries about the safety of his parents and frequent stomachaches suggest a concurrent anxiety disorder, probably separation anxiety disorder, although further questioning would be required to confirm the presence of other symptoms of this disorder. Thus, the combination of ADHD/inattentive type and separation anxiety disorder is a likely tentative diagnosis of Tom's problems. This particular combined diagnosis suggests that stimulant medication is less likely to be effective than if Tom had the more typical hyperactive type of ADHD without a comorbid disorder.

What treatment is indicated? To the psychologist at the clinic, Tom's case history suggested some possible goals for treatment, as well as some probable explanations for his difficulties. Tom's fearful behavior during infancy and the preschool years are reminiscent of behavioral inhibition (Kagan, 1989) and suggest a biological diathesis for his anxiety. This vulnerability may have been made worse by Tom's rocky family life, which featured unresponsive parenting, his mother's depression, and his parents' severe marital conflict. These early problems probably led to and were exacerbated by Tom's troubled relationships with his peers. Although none of these factors alone is likely to have caused problems, their cumulative effects are the probable causes of Tom's abnormal behavior.

For 8 months, Tom and his family participated in a multicomponent treatment that involved family therapy and parent training. For example, his parents were taught how to organize their time so they could regularly engage in child-directed play with Tom and his younger brother (see Eyberg, 1988). When it became evident that Tom's parents did not have an effective system for sharing child-care responsibilities, some sessions were devoted to marital communication skills.

In addition, a behavior management program was instituted in which Tom earned points for productive 30-minute work intervals; the points could be exchanged for special privileges such as going to the movies. This program worked well enough that medication was unnecessary. Because Tom experienced severe social anxiety and had few effective coping strategies, a cognitive-behavioral intervention was undertaken in which the therapist taught Tom how to join a group of children who were playing and to remain calm while doing so.

At the end of about 6 months, Tom showed improvements in some areas but not in others. His off-task behavior at school decreased substantially, and conflict with his mother diminished. However, his peer interactions did not improve, and problems remained in communication between his parents. Nevertheless, the psychologist and the family decided to stop treatment temporarily, mainly because the family had exhausted its insurance benefits for mental health services. At last report, Tom was getting better grades at school, but he was still socially awkward and had no close friends.

Tom is typical of cases seen in child mental health clinics today. He is a boy, he was referred for an externalizing behavior problem and academic failure, and his parents and teacher believed that ADHD was responsible for his difficulties. Tom's problems were complex and reflected a suspected biological predisposition for inhibition coupled with adverse family conditions and an unstable caregiving environment during critical periods. Unfortunately, Tom is typical of most children referred to clinics in yet another way: treatment alleviated some difficulties but by no means effected a cure. Only time will tell how well Tom will be able to master the increasingly challenging developmental tasks that lie ahead.

SUMMARY

A Developmental Perspective

The quality of a child's adaptation to the social environment is determined by the manner in which the child approaches and masters certain developmental tasks, such as the formation of secure attachments during infancy and the development of effective peer relationships during the early school years. Difficulties in resolving early tasks will adversely affect the child's accomplishment of later tasks, elevating the probability of psychopathology. Children's disorders rarely emerge in fully developed form but are preceded by earlier patterns of poor adaptation: oppositional behavior often precedes conduct disorder; social inhibition and fearfulness often lead to anxiety and depression; and childhood eating problems often predate the onset of adolescent eating disorders. Among children with disorders, a significant minority will have continuing difficulties in social adjustment well into their adult years.

Classification and Diagnosis of Children's Disorders

A categorical approach to classifying childhood mental disorders such as the DSM-IV assumes that mental disorders are discrete entities that can clearly be distinguished from normal behavior and other disorders. By contrast, a dimensional approach to classification organizes children's various problems along a few continuous dimensions that are identified by the statistical procedure of factor analysis. The Child Behavior Checklist, a leading example of this approach, identifies two major dimensions of childhood psychopathology—externalizing problems involving disruptive, undercontrolled behaviors and internalizing problems involving subjective distress and overcontrolled behaviors.

Disruptive Behavior and Attention-Deficit Disorders

Oppositional defiant disorder (ODD), conduct disorder (CD), and attention-deficit/hyperactivity disorder (ADHD) are examples of the externalizing dimension of the Child Behavior Checklist. Comorbidity is common among these disorders, although each can occur independently. There are multiple causes of ODD and CD including biological or neuropsychological deficits, cognitive limitations, adverse conditions in the family, the child's insecure attachment to the parent, and poor parenting skills. Usually a combination of two or more of these factors is necessary to produce a full-blown disorder. ADHD has been attributed to a similar range of causal factors, although neurobiological factors have received the most attention thus far. ODD and CD are treated most effectively with interventions that focus on the family interactions that reinforce and maintain the child's disruptive behavior. These interventions usually produce changes in parenting skills shortly after treatment, but their long-term effects on the child have not been established. ADHD is best treated with stimulant medications. These produce good, immediate results but have questionable effects on the child's long-term functioning. Stimulants are often combined with behavior modification techniques that teach the child new social and academic skills.

Anxiety and Mood Disorders of Childhood and Adolescence

Symptoms related to children's anxieties and depression are best captured by the internalizing dimension of the Child Behavior Checklist. Separation anxiety is a common form of anxiety in the early school years, leading to school refusal in most cases. Although children's specific fears respond well to behavioral treatments, more diffuse and severe anxieties (such as separation anxiety) are more difficult to treat. The most effective treatments combine systematic desensitization with modeling or cognitive-behavioral therapies in which self-talk and self-reinforcement are emphasized.

Persistent low mood is the hallmark of depression. It includes sadness, hopelessness, or guilt. In young children, such feelings often take the form of pronounced irritability. Antidepressant medications have not proved to be effective with most depressed children, but there is preliminary support for the use of cognitive-behavioral therapy.

Other Disorders of Childhood and Adolescence

Anorexia nervosa is characterized by an unreasonable fear of gaining weight and the relentless pursuit of thinness, even at the cost of serious malnutrition. Individuals with anorexia will try to reduce their weight by engaging in extreme diet restrictions and/or excessive exercise. Bulimia nervosa is a pattern of excessive binge eating followed by purging (e.g., self-induced vomiting) or other inappropriate strategies intended to prevent weight gain. Both anorexia and bulimia are more frequent among girls than among boys. A variety of medications and psychological treatments for eating disorders have been studied and several have shown promise (e.g., cognitive-behavioral interventions for bulimia), although none has yet emerged as clearly superior.

Elimination disorders are developmentally inappropriate toilet habits involving lack of control over urination (enuresis) or defecation (encopresis). Although their causes are not completely understood, elimination disorders have often been successfully treated with learning-based therapy.

KEY TERMS

affect regulation, p. 105

anorexia nervosa, p. 106

antidiuretic hormone, p. 111

attention-deficit/hyperactivity
    disorder (ADHD), p. 84

bulimia nervosa, p. 109

cerebral asymmetry, p. 105

cognitive restructuring, p. 102

conduct disorder (CD), p. 84

coping skills training, p. 102

developmental task, p. 78

encopresis, p. 111

enuresis, p. 111

executive functioning, p. 88

externalizing problem, p. 82

4

Developmental Disorders and Learning Disabilities

Contemplating Artist by Genevieve Burnett, 1970. Oil on canvas, 30" x 22". Courtesy of Sistare.

From the Case of Jordan

ordan crawled slowly across the living room floor, hesitating as he neared the couch. His heart was pounding; his eyes were wide and unfocused. He could barely see where he was going, guided only by the light coming from under the closed kitchen door. He heard his mother yelling in the kitchen, "Why couldn't you have *called* if you were going to be this late! I was scared half to death!"

"I'm tired of being treated like a kid," Jordan's father shouted back, "always needing to check in, getting *your* permission to see a ball game with my friends. Maybe if you had a little more to *do* around here, you'd have less time to check up on *me!*"

Jordan heard something fly across the kitchen counter and explode against the door, followed by the sounds of shattering glass. He was terrified. He began to groan, making the low "eh-eh" noises he made whenever something really bad was happening. But his parents continued to shout at each other.

"And what exactly do *you* do around here?" Jordan's mother demanded. "You're never around, always out with your friends, supposedly *working late* . . . but I know better. I know you don't want to be at home!"

Back in the living room, Jordan clumsily reached for the lamp cord, pulling the lamp over the back of the couch. It hit the floor

117

with a crash. The yelling in the kitchen stopped abruptly. Jordan's mother threw open the kitchen door, casting a wide beam of light across the living room floor, the broken lamp, and Jordan.

"Jordan! What are you doing? How did you get out of bed!"

Jordan began to bite the back of his hand furiously, making a high-pitched screeching sound at the same time.

"Jordan, stop that. No!" his mother said firmly. "No biting!"

She sat down on the floor, grabbing Jordan's hand while pulling him up into her lap.

"Are you okay? What happened in here?" she asked. Her voice softened. Jordan stopped biting himself and looked up at his mother unsteadily, giving her a big, lopsided grin.

Jordan's father stood over the two of them, looking down. His anger quickly dissipated, replaced by feelings of guilt. Jordan's mother stared vacantly into the dark corners of the living room, her anger gone, absently running her hand through Jordan's hair as she rocked him back and forth. "What are we going to do about Jordan?" she asked. "He seems to be getting worse all the time." Jordan's father didn't know what to say. He just sighed and turned around, heading for the bedroom down the hallway. ■

*J*ordan's parents described this incident to a psychologist during a family therapy session. Jordan is an 11-year-old child with profound mental retardation and cerebral palsy. He is unable to talk or use sign language. He is unable to walk, feed or dress himself, or use the toilet. He is confined to a wheelchair for all but 1 hour a day, when he is allowed to crawl freely around the house.

Jordan also has behavior problems that have become almost as debilitating as his physical and mental disabilities. At home and school, he can be very destructive, often throwing or breaking things when angry. Of greatest concern is his tendency to engage in *self-injurious behavior,* such as hand biting and head banging, when he is under stress or does not get what he wants.

Jordan's case illustrates several important aspects of developmental disabilities. Like many people with such disabilities, Jordan has multiple areas of dysfunction, including deficits in cognitive skills, communication, and motor abilities. Also common —at least among individuals with severe disabilities—is the co-occurrence of significant behavioral and emotional problems that often pose a greater threat to long-term adaptation than the primary areas of disability do. Finally, as is true in most if not all cases of developmental disabilities, Jordan's family interactions influence his behavior, and his disability shapes his family life.

If you know any children like Jordan, you know some of the difficulties they and their families face. The disorders described in this chapter—mental retardation, autistic disorders, and learning disabilities (called *learning disorders* in the DSM-IV)—are almost always diagnosed early in childhood, but their effects usually persist through the rest of an individual's life and can have profound effects on a person's overall development.

The term *developmental disability* was first used in Public Law 95-602 (1978), which specified the services to which persons with disabilities would be legally entitled. This law defined a **developmental disability** in terms of three criteria: (1) *lifelong* impairment in mental or physical functioning that is first evident *prior to* adulthood; (2) substantial limitations in daily living skills such as communication and self-care; and (3) the necessity for extended specialized care, usually well beyond the normal age of schooling. Nearly all the disabilities described in this chapter meet these criteria. The one exception is *learning disabilities,* which originate in childhood but have less impact on daily living skills than developmental disabilities and require interventions that are usually limited to the school years.

Most developmental disabilities are diagnosed in infancy and early childhood. Although some disabilities become apparent at birth or shortly thereafter, most are more subtle and become evident only after the infant or young child shows consistently poor progress or growth.

As discussed in Chapter 3, a child's psychological development usually follows a sequence in which simple cognitive or social skills are the building blocks for more sophisticated skills later in life. Interruptions or delays in the development of these early skills can prevent a child's being able to acquire necessary language or socialization abilities. Language and socialization difficulties, in turn, can increase the risk for later mental disorders. It is important for clinicians to understand both the normal course of human development and how disruptions in that course might lead to the disorders discussed in this chapter. Appreciating the potential impact of developmental disorders is also essential because it promotes early treatment of these problems, thereby reducing their impact on later development.

To set the stage for our discussion of developmental and learning disabilities, we will begin by providing a brief overview of the different areas or *domains* of growth in a child's developmental progress and the ages at which normal infants and young children are expected to master certain skills. These expectations illustrate the usual sequence of progressively developing more advanced skills that build on each other, and they define approximate standards for diagnosing a developmental or learning disability. We will discuss mental retardation next, focusing first on matters of classification, followed by a review of causal factors. We will then review some promising treatments and prevention programs for retardation. Next, we will describe autism as well as disorders characterized by partial manifestations of autism, and we will review suspected causal factors and possible treatments for these disorders. Finally, we will turn to learning disabilities and discuss their causes and treatment. The chapter will conclude with a return to the case of Jordan.

Domains of Development

Research by developmental psychologists has helped establish the ages at which normal infants and children typically reach important developmental milestones such as smiling, talking, and walking. For example, studies have shown that infants typically begin to talk at about 11 months. However, there is considerable variation in the rate of development, both among children and for the same child across different developmental domains. Consequently, a sizeable minority of normal children will not achieve a particular milestone at the same age that the "average" child does. Nevertheless, age norms provide a rough gauge of whether a given child is significantly behind or ahead of schedule.

Table 4.1 outlines the typical course of a child's development in two domains: motor skills and language. Motor skills include **gross motor skills,** which refer to success in controlling large movements involving body posture and moving from one place to another, and **fine motor** and **visual–motor skills,** which include upper extremity and hand and finger movements as well as eye–hand coordination. Early language development involves progress in both **expressive language,** the use of language to communicate one's thoughts or needs, and **receptive language,** the understanding of language. In most infants, receptive abilities precede expressive skills. The babbling and other vocalizations heard during an infant's first year are forerunners of expressive language. By age 2, the typical infant knows at least 50 words.

Skills in another key domain, cognition, are more difficult to assess in infancy and early childhood. **Cognition** refers to a variety of mental processes that determine the individual's capacity to

---

TABLE 4.1   Developmental Milestones: Motor and Language Skills

Average age	Language milestones	Motor milestones
6 months	Cooing, changes to distinct babbling by introduction of consonants	Sits using hands for support; unilateral reaching
1 year	Beginning of language understanding; one-word utterances	Stands; walks when held by one hand
12–18 months	Words used singly; repertoire of 30–50 words that cannot as yet be joined in phrases but are used one at a time; does not use words such as "the," "and," "can," "be."	Grasping and release fully developed; walking; creeps downstairs backward
18–24 months	Two-word (telegraphic) phrases are ordered according to syntactic rules; vocabulary of 50 to several hundred words.	Runs (and falls); walks stairs with one foot forward
2–5 years	New words nearly every day; three or more words in many combinations; functors begin to appear; many grammatical errors and idiosyncratic expressions; good understanding of language	Jumps with both feet; builds tower of six cubes
3 years	Full sentences; few errors; vocabulary of around 1,000 words	Tiptoes; walks stairs with alternating feet
4 years	Close to adult speech competence	Jumps over rope; hops on one foot; walks on a line

Source: Adapted from Kandel et al., 1995; p. 638.

learn, to retain acquired information, and to use such information to solve problems in a flexible and creative way. This is essentially what we mean by *intelligence,* although psychologists have struggled for decades to define the exact meaning of this term.

Before children can speak, assessment of cognitive skills depends on the child's progress in other related areas. For example, a preverbal toddler's ability to solve problems is inferred from the child's performance on tasks that require motor or visual–motor ability, such as completing a 2- or 3-piece puzzle. If infants have significant motor limitations, their performance on such tasks may lead to an underestimation of their cognitive ability.

Generally, in the first 3 years, information about the family is a better predictor of a child's later cognitive abilities than is information about the infant or child (Kochanek, Kabacoff, & Lipsitt, 1990). However, during the first year, an unusually good predictor of later cognitive performance is **habituation speed,** the amount of time it takes an infant to habituate, or lose interest in, a repetitively presented stimulus. Six-month-old infants with relatively long habituation times are more likely to have low IQs in later childhood than are infants with shorter habituation times (Bornstein & Sigman, 1986).

After age 3, measurements of a child's skill are probably superior to information about the family as a predictor of later cognitive performance (Kochanek et al., 1990). Psychologists typically assess cognitive ability in post-infancy children, adolescents, and adults with standardized intelligence tests such as the Stanford-Binet Intelligence Scale (Thorndike, Hagen, & Sattler, 1986) and the Weschler Intelligence Scale for Children (WISC-III) (Wechsler, 1991). Such tests are essentially a series of problem-solving tasks ordered by difficulty. Some of the tasks require verbal abilities such as identifying the way in which two words are conceptually similar; other tasks emphasize visual–motor or spatial skills (e.g., putting together a puzzle).

Research with large samples of individuals has established the average number of items passed by persons at different ages. These norms allow for the computation of an individual's **mental age.** For example, if 50 were the average number of items passed by 10-year-olds on a particular test, then a score of 50 would represent a mental age of 10 for that test. If both an 8-year-old and a 12-year-old passed 50 items on such a test, they would each have a mental age of 10.

Performance on intelligence tests is usually described by so-called IQ scores. Today, intelligence tests use *deviation IQ scores;* that is, they indicate the child's relative standing in a group of same-aged children. The score distribution has a mean of 100 and a standard deviation of 15. Thus, if a 5-year-old child obtained a *raw score* (the number of correctly answered test items) 1 standard deviation below the *average* raw score for 5-year-olds, that child would receive an IQ score of 85 (100 − 15 = 85).

Intelligence tests are widely used to assess children, and IQ scores figure prominently in definitions of mental retardation and learning disabilities. However, these tests have been criticized for measuring a narrow range of skills. Critics argue that IQ tests fail to capture both what is important for everyday survival and what is truly exceptional achievement (Gardner, 1993). They may also underestimate the cognitive abilities of individuals from cultures that differ substantially from that of the test developers (MacMillian, Gresham, & Siperstein, 1993). For example, a picture-recognition test that assesses a child's ability to name various farm animals would probably be biased against children from an urban background; conversely, a child who grew up in a country without mandatory schooling would do poorly on tests designed to measure factual knowledge taught in school.

Children's understanding of concepts depends to some extent on their familiarity with certain tools and experiences. For example, one consequence of frequently using an abacus is a superior ability to remember a series of 15 digits, either forward or backward. This skill apparently transfers from having to imagine several digits while calculating with an abacus. Memory for words or letters is not facilitated, however, only numbers, the specific activity that was practiced.

Adaptive behaviors represent yet another developmental domain; they enable an individual to meet the cultural expectations for independent functioning associated with a particular age. At the age of 5, children in the United States, for example, are expected to be toilet trained, to use utensils to feed themselves, and to be emotionally capable of being away from their parents for several hours a day at school. Although adaptive behavior is clearly influenced by other skills (e.g., using money correctly requires the ability to count), it cannot be fully explained by intelligence or other types of skills. For example, most of us know someone who is intellectually skilled but lacks common sense in handling the challenges of everyday life.

Measurement of adaptive behavior usually involves observations by parents or teachers. Tests of adaptive behavior include the Vineland Adaptive Behavior Scales (Sparrow, Balla, & Cicchetti, 1984) and the American Association on Mental Retardation Adaptive Behavior Scale (Nihira, Leland, & Lambert, 1993). Both tests use a structured interview in which detailed questions about an individual's behavior are used to establish the level of adaptive skill. Research with large samples of children, adolescents, and adults has established the ages at which most individuals display specific adaptive skills. The number of items successfully passed on these tests can be converted to a score distribution that, like IQ tests, has a mean of 100 and a standard deviation of 15. Table 4.2 gives a few examples of adaptive behaviors and the ages at which they usually first appear.

Standardized tests such as the Vineland that quantify the level of adaptive skill help establish realistic expectations about development, but even these tests have problems in reliability, and they tend to overclassify children as impaired (MacMillian et al., 1993). It is essential to remember that different children develop adaptive skills at different rates; just because a child is slow to acquire a certain skill does not mean that the child will inevitably remain delayed or show deficits in that skill in adulthood. Not every developmental delay is a symptom of a disorder. Many children go through periods when their speech is a bit hard to understand or they reverse letters when spelling certain words. These behaviors are usually a normal part of development, not a sign of disorder. As long as clinicians and parents keep these caveats in mind, the concept of adaptive behavior is a useful supplement to IQ in the definition of mental retardation.

Mental Retardation

The term **mental retardation** refers to significantly subaverage intellectual functioning occurring before the age of 18. There is a long history of debate about how to best distinguish "average" and "subaverage" intelligence and whether mental retardation is better defined by cognitive deficits or problems in adaptive behavior. Even small changes in the definition can alter the services provided to thousands of children and adults with below- but near-average intelligence.

Most definitions of mental retardation use IQ scores, but during the past 40 years, the score used to distinguish retarded from normal functioning has fluctuated. Mental retardation was once defined as an IQ score below 85 (Heber, 1961) and then as an IQ score below 70 (Grossman, 1973). More recently, the American Association on Mental Retardation (AAMR) defined the cutoff for mental retardation as a score between 70 and 75 (Luckasson et al., 1992), resulting in a near doubling of the number of potentially diagnosable individuals (e.g., MacMillian et al., 1993). However, both the DSM-IV and ICD-10 have retained an IQ cutoff score of 70 for the definition of mental retardation. Thus, the determination of mental retardation in borderline cases may depend, in part, on which diagnostic system is used.

Fortunately, IQ is not the sole criterion for defining mental retardation. AAMR, DSM-IV, and ICD-10 definitions list specific areas of adaptive functioning such as skills in communication, self-care,

TABLE 4.2	Sample Behaviors from the Vineland Adaptive Behavior Scales
Approximate age	**Adaptive behavior**
By 1 year	Smiles in response to caregiver
	Eats solid food
	Picks up small object with hands
Over 1 year	Names at least 20 familiar objects
	Feeds self with fork or spoon
	Calls at least 2 familiar people by name
Over 2 years	Uses at least 100 recognizable words
	Asks to use toilet
	Engages in elaborate make-believe activities

home living, health, and safety that need to be considered as well. Impairment in at least two of these areas is necessary for mental retardation to be diagnosed using the DSM-IV, although the DSM does not clearly define what is meant by *impaired*.

A Classification

How many people are mentally retarded? The answer, of course, depends on the criteria used to reach a diagnosis, but the worldwide prevalence is probably between 1 and 3 percent. People with mental retardation differ considerably in intellectual impairment and personality characteristics. Researchers have organized this diversity by developing subgroups of mental retardation. Some classifications identify subgroups by their presumed potential to benefit from educational programs (e.g., "educable" versus "trainable"); others by the presumed cause of the retardation. The most prominent approach to classification is based on *level of retardation* as measured by IQ score. Typically, four categories are specified throughout the world: mild, moderate, severe, and profound.

Mild Mental Retardation. Subtle deficits in adaptive behavior and an IQ of 50 to approximately 70 to 75 (depending on which classification criteria are used) characterize mild mental retardation. About 85 percent of all persons with mental retardation fall into this category.

Children with mild mental retardation are delayed in their acquisition of basic language and cognitive abilities. However, their slower-than-average rate of development may not become obvious until middle childhood or adolescence. Before middle childhood, their near-normal social and communication skills allow children with mild mental retardation to get by and acquire basic academic skills, albeit with intense effort. These children can usually acquire what Americans consider fifth- or sixth-grade skills. However, in middle childhood (10 to 12 years) when typical children show more complex cognitive and communication skills (such as advanced problem solving), the limitations of children with mild mental retardation become more obvious. It is at this point that many show problems in their thinking skills, awkwardness in social relationships, and poor emotional control.

As adults, most persons with mild mental retardation hold semiskilled jobs and get married, al-

though during stressful periods their parenting skills and ability to take care of themselves may suffer. In one longitudinal study of persons with mild retardation, 64 percent were found to be capable of independent adult functioning, but 24 percent were partially dependent on others, and 12 percent were totally dependent, a distinction that had less to do with IQ than with levels of adaptive behavior (Ross et al., 1985). Persons with mild retardation are also at increased risk of psychopathology, especially attention-deficit disorders, disruptive behavior disorders, and substance abuse. The term **dual diagnosis** is used to describe individuals who meet criteria for mental retardation and some other psychiatric disorder.

Moderate Mental Retardation. Moderate retardation is associated with IQs from 35 to 40 through 50 to 55 and significantly limited adaptive behavior. About 10 percent of mentally retarded people function in this range of impairment. In early childhood they often show significant delays in language and cognitive skills and sometimes in motor abilities. Most eventually develop expressive language, although speech dysfluencies and articulation errors remain common. Most persons with moderate mental retardation can learn to read and do simple addition and subtraction problems. In adult life, the majority can perform unskilled jobs in a closely supervised setting; a few are able to work under less-supervised conditions when job tasks are routine and the goal is well specified (e.g., lawn mowing, laundry, assembly-line work). Most adults with moderate mental retardation live in supervised group homes where assistance with personal finances and health care is provided. Very few persons with moderate mental retardation marry and even fewer bear children.

Severe Mental Retardation. Severe impairment is indicated by IQs of 20 to 25 through 35 to 40. About 3 to 4 percent of persons with mental retardation are in this category. In early childhood, their verbal communication is limited. By late middle childhood, the majority can talk, although articulation may be compromised, and the content of speech is simple. Although some severely retarded people can be taught to recognize survival words on road signs, store signs, and product labels, most do not learn to read. Motor and visual–motor deficits are common and may limit capabilities for self-care and vocational training. Even in the absence of motor problems, however, cognitive limitations usually lead to poor adaptive behaviors, and help with self-care is often required. Vocational opportunities are usually

Connections

What disorders might cause a person to show impaired cognition and adaptation for the first time after the age of 18? See Chapter 11.

limited to simple assembly work in so-called sheltered workshops.

Profound Mental Retardation. About 1 to 2 percent of persons with mental retardation are profoundly retarded, displaying IQs below 20 or 25. Pervasive neurological damage is almost always present, and it has significant adverse effects on all developmental domains. Gross motor deficits usually limit locomotion; many are wheelchair bound. Constant supervision is required, and self-care is nearly impossible without assistance.

Profoundly retarded people do not usually acquire speech, but many develop a repertoire of vocalizations for use in greeting others and signaling basic needs. Sometimes, disruptive behaviors seem to serve as a last resort in the attempt to communicate. Did Jordan, for example, *deliberately* pull down the lamp to interrupt his parents' fighting? It seems unlikely, but during counseling sessions Jordan almost always began some form of disruptive behavior whenever his parents began to argue—for example, by knocking a cup over, hitting the back of his head against his wheelchair, or biting his hand. Jordan's mother would immediately stop arguing, attend to Jordan, and then change the topic of conversation, often talking about Jordan rather than the issue that started the argument. We can never know for certain whether Jordan's disruptive behaviors were influenced by their effect on his parents' fighting. Whatever the cause, his behavior served to terminate his parents' arguments.

Variation in Motor Development. Motor development varies across and within the four levels of mental retardation and greatly affects adaptive functioning and quality of life. Generally, the lower the IQ, the more likely it is that a significant motor dysfunction will be present.

Many persons with mental retardation have **cerebral palsy,** a group of motor disorders that result from cerebral insult or injury, usually during the perinatal or postnatal period of early childhood when brain development is most active. Cerebral palsy can severely impair muscle activity and muscle tone in one, two, or all four extremities, sometimes producing a complete loss of function. The most common form of cerebral palsy is *hemiplegic spasticity,* which involves the arm and leg on one side of the body (Capute & Accardo, 1996). In our case example, Jordan has the more severe *quadriplegia* that affects all four extremities,

Mental retardation occurs in about 60 percent of cases of cerebral palsy (Capute & Accardo, 1996). Perhaps the most important aspect of this statistic is that 40 percent of individuals with cerebral palsy do *not* have retardation and are capable of totally normal intellectual achievement. All too often, however, people assume that persons with cerebral palsy are intellectually compromised and ignore them or treat them with disrespect.

Causes of Mental Retardation

The causes of mental retardation can be grouped into two broad categories, *organic* and *nonorganic.* The organic category includes any of the approximately 300 known biological causes of mental retardation, including genetic disorders, prenatal problems, and a vast array of perinatal and postnatal diseases and injuries. Such factors account for 25 to 50 percent of all cases of mental retardation, especially those with IQs below 50 (Zigler & Hodapp, 1986). The remaining 50 to 75 percent of cases without a clear biological cause are said to have *cultural–familial* causes. These cases are much more likely to have IQs in the mild range of retardation than are those with organic origins.

We will look first at organic factors. The prevalence of organically caused mental retardation is not appreciably affected by demographic or cultural differences. Among the known organic causes are genetic errors (including abnormalities in how chromosomes are paired), deletions or additions of genes to chromosomes, and mutations in genes.

Chromosomal Abnormalities: Down Syndrome. The nuclei of human cells normally contain 46 chromosomes, arranged in 23 pairs (see Figure 4.1 on page 124). One member of each chromosome pair comes from the reproductive cells of the mother, the other from the father. The most common genetic malfunction leading to mental retardation occurs when the splitting of reproductive cells in one or both parents goes awry, and the developing fetus receives too few or too many chromosomes.

For example, most cases of **Down syndrome** result when the 21st pair of chromosomes fails to separate during maturation of the egg. If this egg is fertilized by sperm, the resulting fetus will have cells with three instead of the usual two 21st chromosomes. For this reason, Down syndrome is also known as **trisomy 21.** The extra chromosome disrupts cell metabolism, producing a variety of anomalies in physical growth and damage to the central nervous system. The incidence of trisomies increases dramatically with the age of the mother, suggesting that aging makes eggs increasingly vulnerable to chromosomal damage. For example, mothers giving birth before the age of 30 have only about 1 chance

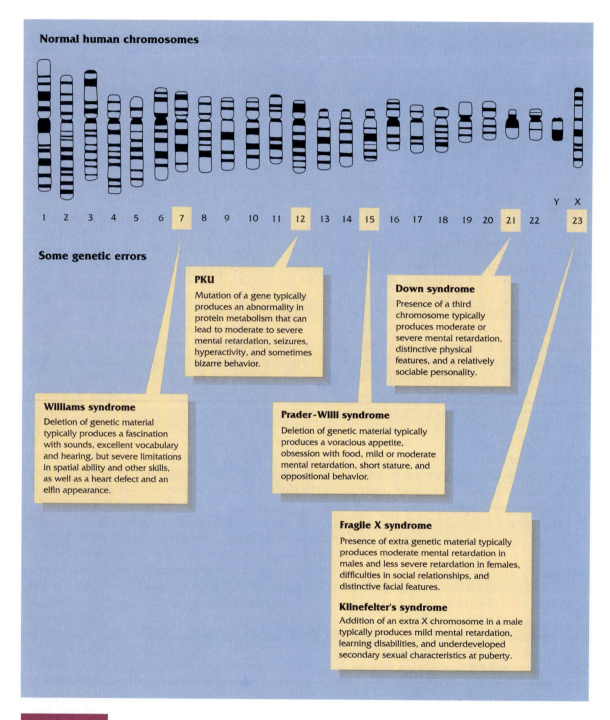

Normal human chromosomes

1 2 3 4 5 6 7 8 9 10 11 12 13 14 15 16 17 18 19 20 21 22   Y X   23

Some genetic errors

PKU

Mutation of a gene typically produces an abnormality in protein metabolism that can lead to moderate to severe mental retardation, seizures, hyperactivity, and sometimes bizarre behavior.

Down syndrome

Presence of a third chromosome typically produces moderate or severe mental retardation, distinctive physical features, and a relatively sociable personality.

Williams syndrome

Deletion of genetic material typically produces a fascination with sounds, excellent vocabulary and hearing, but severe limitations in spatial ability and other skills, as well as a heart defect and an elfin appearance.

Prader-Willi syndrome

Deletion of genetic material typically produces a voracious appetite, obsession with food, mild or moderate mental retardation, short stature, and oppositional behavior.

Fragile X syndrome

Presence of extra genetic material typically produces moderate mental retardation in males and less severe retardation in females, difficulties in social relationships, and distinctive facial features.

Klinefelter's syndrome

Addition of an extra X chromosome in a male typically produces mild mental retardation, learning disabilities, and underdeveloped secondary sexual characteristics at puberty.

FIGURE 4.1

Chromosomal Abnormalities and Mental Retardation

This map shows one member of each pair of the normal human chromosomes as they appear when they are collected midway through cell division and react with a biological stain. Marked on the map are some of the genetic aberrations that cause mental retardation.

in 1500 of having a child with Down syndrome. If the mother is between 40 and 44 years old, however, the chances increase to 1 in 130 (Smith & Wilson, 1973).

Trisomy 21 accounts for about 10 percent of all cases of moderate and severe mental retardation and occurs once in approximately 700 to 800 births. The syndrome is named after the British physician

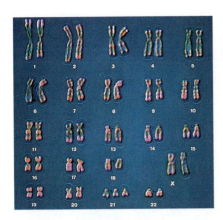 

The first photograph shows the trisomy 21 associated with most cases of Down syndrome. Infants with Down syndrome usually show normal sociability early in life. In fact, Cichetti and Beeghly (1990) found that 12-month-old infants with Down syndrome are as likely as normal babies to be securely attached to their mothers in the Strange Situation, described in Chapter 3. Children with Down syndrome have special trouble comprehending and remembering auditory information. They are able to overcome some of these limitations by being trained to use computers to write out their thoughts. Children with Down syndrome, like the boy in the right-hand photo, can be successfully trained in many skills. However, the brains of people with Down syndrome seem to deteriorate early, particularly the hippocampus, which is heavily involved in memory. Many adults with Down syndrome lose the ability to care for themselves at relatively young ages.

Langdon Down, who first identified this cluster of symptoms in the late nineteenth century. Down syndrome is the result of an error during the reproductive process, but it is *not* inherited from one generation to another.

The diagnosis of Down syndrome is almost always made shortly after birth on the basis of the newborn's physical features, particularly the eyes, which tend to slant upward with small folds of skin in the inside corners. Individuals with Down syndrome are also likely to be shorter than average and stocky, with small hands and short fingers. Another characteristic of Down syndrome is premature aging, including the development of wrinkled skin and, in many cases, *dementia* (poor memory and confusion) by middle age. Postmortem examinations have found that, by age 40, many adults with Down syndrome show a pattern of brain cell deterioration similar to that found in nonretarded adults with Alzheimer's disease (Brugge et al., 1994).

Most children with Down syndrome have IQs of approximately 50. Their intellectual deficits are particularly evident in higher-level cognitive skills such as concept formation and flexible problem solving. Children with Down syndrome usually show expressive language deficits that are disproportionally more severe than their mental age would suggest and more severe than their receptive language problems. They have relatively well-developed rote learning and visual–motor abilities (Pueschel et al., 1987) that enable them to acquire many daily living skills with relative ease. Persons with Down syndrome are known for their sociability, relatively stable emotions, and good mental health, at least in comparison with other individuals with mental retardation.

Over time, children with Down syndrome show an interesting pattern of alternating periods of relatively fast and slow progress. During preschool and early grade school, their increases in grammatical skill approximate the growth rate for nonretarded peers (Fowler, 1988). During the middle-school years their rate of progress in these skills slows down but returns to a faster rate during adolescence (Hodapp & Dykens, 1994). A similar pattern has been observed in their acquisition of adaptive behaviors (Dykens, Hodapp, & Evans, 1994).

Genetic Additions or Deletions: Fragile X and Williams Syndromes. Mental retardation can also result from the addition or deletion of genes. In fragile X syndrome, the aberration involves chromosome 23. This is known as the **sex-linked chromosome** because it consists of duplicate chromosomes in the female (designated XX) but not the male, who normally has an X and a Y chromosome. In **fragile X syndrome,** an excess of genetic material on one tip of the X chromosome makes it appear thin and threadlike—or "fragile."

First identified in the 1970s by Robert Lehrke, a doctoral student at the University of Wisconsin, fragile X is second only to Down syndrome as the most common biological cause of retardation. All six children in this family have fragile X syndrome. No treatment is currently available.

Fragile X syndrome is the result of a genetic error that—unlike Down syndrome—*is* heritable. In fact, it is the most commonly inherited cause of mental retardation. The problem begins in an unaffected individual as a genetic premutation on the X chromosome (Dykens, Hodapp, & Leckman, 1994). This vulnerability worsens as it is passed from one generation to another, eventually leading to offspring affected with fragile X syndrome.

Fragile X occurs in about 1 in 750 to 1,000 males, and 1 in 500 to 750 females (Dykens, Hodapp, & Leckman, 1994). Most males and about one third of females with fragile X experience moderate mental retardation. Females, because they have two X chromosomes, still have an undamaged X when the other is defective, so their retardation tends to be less severe. Males, on the other hand, tend to experience more severe effects when their single X chromosome is damaged. Certain physical features are associated with the disorder—more commonly in affected males than females—including a long, thin face with a broad, flat nose, and large ears. Affected males also tend to have enlarged testicles.

Although children with fragile X and Down syndrome suffer the same average level of retardation, the two syndromes lead to different learning abilities and social behaviors (Hodapp et al., 1992). For example, children with fragile X cannot perform tasks that require them to learn information presented in a sequential order, such as imitating a series of hand movements. Children with Down syndrome can perform this task quite well (Hodapp et al., 1992). Whereas children with Down syndrome are often quite sociable, children with fragile X have difficulties in social relationships. In fact, so many children with fragile X avoid or show disinterest in social relationships that fragile X is considered to be a genetic cause of a small proportion of the autistic disorders described later in this chapter. And unlike the typical case of Down syndrome, children with fragile X often develop oppositional and disruptive behavior, sometimes in combination with attention deficits and hyperactivity.

The deletion of a gene is the cause of a puzzling combination of strengths and weaknesses known as **Williams syndrome,** a rare disorder found in only one of every 20,000 births. This syndrome results from a deleted gene on chromosome 7. The case of Ann, an 8-year-old girl referred to a psychologist for an intellectual assessment, illustrates some typical symptoms of Williams syndrome.

According to her parents, Ann could "talk your ear off," telling imaginative and entertaining stories with good grammar and vocabulary. But she was unable to tie her shoes, dress herself, or draw even the simplest pictures. She was almost obsessed with certain sounds, especially the sound of wind chimes, which she could detect from remarkable distances. Test results and assessment of adaptive behaviors indicated that Ann was functioning in the moderate range of mental retardation, but her verbal communication was in the normal range. Even though she did extremely well on some tests of verbal abilities—such as vocabulary—Ann's verbal skills more closely matched her IQ on tasks that required more complex language such as using words to solve a novel problem.

Typically individuals with Williams syndrome demonstrate vocabulary and grammar skills, but not other aspects of language, that exceed their IQ. Their hearing is extremely good. They are fascinated with sounds and have a flair for dramatic storytelling (Reilly, Klima, & Bellugi, 1990), but their spatial ability, including drawing, is severely limited. Because of the wide gap between vocabulary and other intellectual skills, children with Williams syndrome have been described as having "language in the relative absence of thought" (Hodapp & Dykens, 1994). Physical anomalies are also common. Children with Williams syndrome have an elfin appearance marked by a small, upturned nose, full lips, and a small chin. All have a heart defect. Brain-imaging studies have found that these children have a smaller-than-normal cerebral cortex but a normal-sized *neocerebellum* (a part of the brain that controls some language functions) and a normal-sized *auditory cortex* (which might explain their hearing acuity and fascination with sounds) (Galaburda et al., 1994).

Genetic Mutations: PKU. Mutations in a single gene can also cause mental retardation. Such errors can be passed on to future generations. Usually, the mutations that lead to mental retardation involve recessive genes.

An example is a rare condition called **phenylketonuria,** or **PKU,** in which an abnormality in protein metabolism is carried by a recessive gene. If the infant inherits this gene from both parents, the newborn infant will be literally poisoned by the intake of an amino acid called *phenylalanine*—common in foods such as meat and cow's milk. Normally, phenylalanine is converted to another harmless amino acid, *tyrosine,* but in infants with PKU, the enzyme required for this conversion is missing and phenylalanine is instead converted to *phenylpyruvic acid*—a substance that is toxic to the central nervous system and that produces moderate-to-severe mental retardation, marked hyperactivity, and, sometimes, extremely fearful or bizarre behavior.

Today, newborns are routinely screened for this condition. Identified cases are immediately placed on a diet low in phenylalanine, preventing toxicity and permitting normal development. Untreated children with PKU have average IQs of about 25, whereas children who follow a low-phenylalanine diet from early infancy are likely to have IQs in the 90s (Zigler & Hodapp, 1986).

Environmental Damage to the Central Nervous System. Genetic problems represent only one of the organic sources of mental retardation. Many cases can be traced to insults to the central nervous system that occur before, during, or after birth.

Prenatal hazards include viral and bacterial infections in the mother that cross the placental barrier and harm the fetus, sometimes permanently. One example is German measles—also known as *rubella.* When occurring during the first trimester, rubella can cause mental retardation, deafness, retarded physical development, microcephaly, cardiac disease, cataracts, and glaucoma. Herpes virus is another example. Herpes is relatively benign for adults and older children, but a mothers' herpes can have devastating effects on the fetus, including mental retardation.

Another potential prenatal hazard comes from chemical substances, such as alcohol and other drugs, that are ingested by the mother during pregnancy. Substances that cross the placenta and damage the fetus are known as **teratogens.** For example, cocaine, tobacco, and marijuana are suspected teratogens. Negative effects of maternal cocaine use on infants' physical health have been demonstrated (e.g., Frassica et al., 1994), but it is less clear whether prenatal cocaine exposure has long-term effects on cognitive and social development (Hurt et al., 1995). Maternal tobacco use has been associated with increased likelihood of lung problems in infants and children (Cunningham, Dockery, & Speizer, 1994), but neither tobacco nor marijuana has been consistently shown to harm other aspects of development (e.g., Day et al., 1994).

Alcohol is the most thoroughly studied teratogen. As few as two drinks per day in the midcourse of pregnancy can produce an average drop of 7 IQ points in children (Streissguth et al., 1990). Maternal alcohol binges (usually defined as five or more drinks per day) during and just before pregnancy have been associated with mild to severe mental retardation and a distinctive pattern of abnormal features. This pattern includes small head circumference, shortened eyelids, a flattened jaw line, and a poorly developed philtrum and thin upper lip. The term **fetal alcohol syndrome (FAS)** is used to describe these facial abnormalities when they occur in conjunction with retarded physical growth and any of several signs of neurological deficit including mental retardation, attentional problems, or learning disabilities. Most FAS children are mentally retarded. Some infants do not show all the effects of the full FAS syndrome, often because their mothers drank less heavily during pregnancy than mothers of FAS infants did; when

Connections

In cases of severe maternal alcoholism, newborns may actually be addicted to alcohol. How widespread is such alcoholism? Can it be prevented? See Chapter 13, pp. 450 and 464–465.

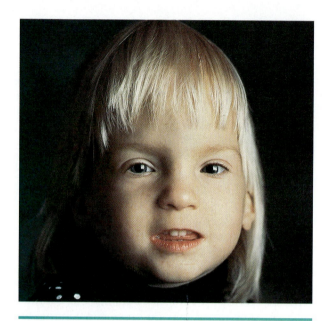

This child's mother drank heavily during her pregnancy. The child's face shows the widely spaced eyes, small upturned nose, and thin upper lip that are characteristic of FAS. Because alcohol moves swiftly through the placenta, it can cause extensive damage to fetal tissue.

they have abnormalities in any *two* of these areas (facial deformity, growth retardation, or neurological dysfunction), children are said to have *fetal alcohol effect (FAE).* Older children with FAS/FAE can have a variety of social and emotional problems in addition to cognitive impairment.

Several factors associated with labor and delivery can result in mental retardation for infants, although the damage to their central nervous system is usually less extreme than that associated with maternal substance abuse. Premature birth and low birth weight can cause slower-than-normal development of many skills, but these are usually temporary delays rather than permanent deficits (Crnic et al., 1983). Oxygen deprivation, or **hypoxia,** at birth was once thought to be a common cause of cerebral palsy and associated mental retardation, but most studies have not supported this belief (Shonkoff & Marshall, 1990).

Head injuries, brain tumors, and infectious diseases such as encephalitis are the leading causes of mental retardation after birth. Each year nearly 30,000 children in the United States suffer permanent disability from an accidental injury (Rodriguez, 1990); many of these are head injuries that result in mental retardation. The most hazardous circumstances for children include automobile travel, bicycle riding, and pedestrian travel near busy streets. Consequently, school-based programs have been developed to encourage the use of seat belts and bicy-

cle helmets and to teach pedestrian safety (Peterson & Brown, 1994; Rivara et al., 1991).

Psychosocial Adversity. Adversity in a child's psychosocial environment can also limit intellectual development, although such effects are usually confined to the mild range of retardation. As we noted earlier, the term *cultural–familial* is used to describe mild mental retardation with no known organic cause. The term suggests that the retardation is due to psychosocial disadvantage, and, not surprisingly, the prevalence of mild retardation is affected by social and demographic characteristics. Boys are more often diagnosed than girls, for example, and Black children receive the diagnosis more often than Whites, a difference that probably reflects the influence of socioeconomic class on cognitive attainments.

The specific mechanisms that are responsible for cultural–familial retardation are still debated. It is possible that some cases are related to yet-undiscovered genetic syndromes or prenatal accidents or conditions that affect fetal or infant growth (Hodapp, 1994). But most cases are almost certainly linked to the greater number of adversities faced by individuals from lower socioeconomic classes, where moderate retardation is much more prevalent than in other segments of society.

One view of how adverse psychosocial conditions might lead to retardation focuses on parents with limited intellectual skills or little education. These parents may interact with their children in ways that slow down cognitive and social development (Keltner, 1994). Parents with limited skills are more likely to be critical of the child's efforts and to be less attentive and responsive to the child during interactions (Barnard & Kelly, 1990). Less-educated parents talk less frequently and elaborately to their children, thus limiting the child's development of verbal abilities (Chaney, 1994; Walker et al., 1994). Such parents are also less able to provide homes containing stimulating items such as educational toys, games, music, or books.

These limitations in parent–child interaction and in the quality of the home environment may be regarded as a form of *environmental deprivation.* Experiments with animals have clearly demonstrated that environmental deprivation early in life can harm CNS development. Experimentally induced environmental deprivation limits the number and length of neurons in the developing brains of rats (e.g., Pascual et al., 1993). Conversely, extra environmental stimulation can produce measurable increases in the growth of neurons and synapses (Anastasiow, 1990).

Ethical factors obviously preclude such experimentation with humans, but several studies provide indirect support for similar effects in human infants.

Premature infants raised in attentive and responsive home environments have significantly higher IQs than similar infants raised in less-responsive homes (Beckwith & Parmelee, 1986). In addition, premature newborns given daily, 45-minute massages in the nursery had higher survival rates, greater weight gain, and higher scores on a test of early developmental skills than did nonstimulated premature newborns (Field et al., 1986). Studies of extreme parental neglect or poor institutional care have also shown that environmental deprivation adversely affects the physical and psychological development of young children (Kaler & Freeman, 1994).

In many cases, both organic and psychosocial factors contribute to mild mental retardation (Baumeister, Kupstas, & Klindworth, 1991). For example, young, poorly educated mothers living in poverty are more vulnerable to illness and disease and are less likely to receive adequate prenatal health care. They are also more likely to use or abuse alcohol or other drugs during their pregnancies. Whatever damage to the infant's CNS might result from these organic factors is likely exacerbated by additional limitations in the postnatal care-giving environment. Thus, as Figure 4.2 illustrates, mild mental retardation can probably best be viewed as having multifaceted origins, similar to other disorders that we can explain from a diathesis–stress perspective.

Detecting and Preventing Mental Retardation

Efforts at detecting and preventing mental retardation can take place at each stage in the process of raising a child, beginning with planning for conception and arranging for prenatal health care.

Prenatal Detection and Prevention. Prospective parents who want to know their chances of having a child with a genetic disorder can seek this information through genetic counseling. They can complete a detailed interview to give the family's history and submit a blood sample for analysis of their chromosomes. A relatively good estimate of the probability of having a child with a known genetic syndrome can be obtained in this way. Under some circumstances, parents may decide that an abortion is their wisest course of action at this point. Similar screening information can be collected early in a pregnancy by obtaining samples of blood or **amniotic fluid** (the fluid surrounding the fetus). The procedure for extracting amniotic fluid, known as **amniocentesis**, does pose a

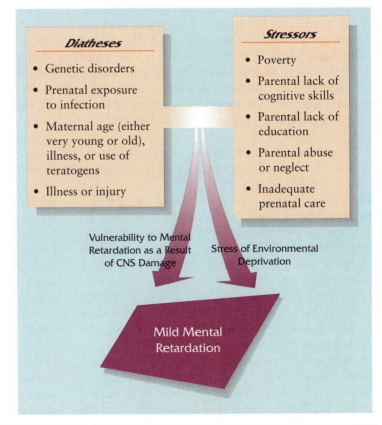

FIGURE 4.2

Diathesis–Stress Model of Mild Mental Retardation

Many cases of mild mental retardation may be best explained by a diathesis–stress model. Genetic and other biological factors may create vulnerabilities to subaverage intellectual development, but a child's actual development is also strongly influenced by psychosocial factors such as parental skills, socioeconomic resources, and overall adequacy of child care.

risk to the fetus, however, and it cannot be performed until about the fourth month of pregnancy.

Some prevention strategies during the prenatal period aim at fostering good physical and psychological health in young mothers. These efforts try to prevent the maternal illness, malnutrition, and prolonged emotional distress that can increase the chances of fetal complications or premature birth, which in turn increase the likelihood of mental retardation. Another approach attempts to modify the behavior of prospective parents in order to reduce teratogenic effects. For example, television ads and warnings on bottles and posters have been used to increase awareness of the dangers of maternal alcohol consumption (Baumeister et al., 1991).

Postnatal Detection and Early Childhood Education. After a child is born, mental retardation associated with a genetically determined metabolic deficiency can sometimes be prevented by early detection. In one example described earlier—PKU—mental retardation can be prevented or lessened if dietary modifications are made early in life (Zigler & Hodapp, 1986). Similarly, controlling the diets of infants who show a genetic intolerance of lactose (found in milk products) or fructose (found in fruits, vegetables, and sugar) can also prevent mental retardation.

The infants and young children who are most likely to show mild mental retardation can be identified on the basis of both familial high-risk characteristics and cognitive tests that were described earlier (see pages 120–121). Once identified, children at risk for poor intellectual development can be helped through nursery or preschool programs that provide an intellectually enriched environment. The best-known example of this approach in the United States is Project Head Start, a federally funded program begun in the 1960s.

Head Start exemplifies a two-generational intervention that provides services to both children and their parents (Zigler & Styfco, 1993). For example, while the child is trained in early reading skills, the parent is taught how to read effectively to the child, to stimulate the child's interest, and to teach important letter–sound associations. Parent groups that focus on topics ranging from nutrition to behavior management are included in many Head Start programs, both to educate parents and to provide them with much-needed social support. Many Head Start programs also provide medical checkups and dental exams as routine parts of the program.

The effectiveness of Project Head Start has been evaluated in several longitudinal programs (e.g., McKey et al., 1985; Schweinhart, Weikart, & Larner, 1986). The findings have varied, in part because the quality of Head Start programs across the country is uneven (Zigler & Styfco, 1993), but also because different studies have used different measures to determine outcome. Most studies have found that Head Start children *initially* do better than comparison children on developmental tests, but that these effects tend to diminish during the first couple of years after the child leaves the program (McKey et al., 1985). However, studies using long-term measures of school progress have reported that Head Start children are more likely than those in comparison groups to complete high school and are less likely to require special education (McKey et al., 1985). Studies of other approaches to prevention have yielded even more optimistic results, as discussed in the Prevention section.

Treatment of Mental Retardation

Treatment of mental retardation is not usually aimed at cures. Instead, the goals of most interventions are to maximize children's developmental progress and adaptive behavior skills, eliminate or reduce disruptive or self-injurious behavior, and help families adjust to their children's disabilities. These various interventions can be distinguished by their specific techniques and the settings in which they are used.

Treatment Techniques. Procedures based on operant learning principles are the most widely used techniques for individuals with mental retardation, especially those with moderate, severe, or profound retardation. The term **applied behavior analysis** describes an operant teaching process in which complex skills are broken down into a series of smaller units. For example, the process of eating with utensils might be divided into four or five specific steps or *target behaviors,* beginning with picking up a spoon, centering the spoon over a bowl, and so on. Positive consequences are then used as part of a process called **shaping,** that is, rough approximations of the target behavior are first reinforced, and, as performance improves, better approximations are required for reinforcement. Reinforcement is eventually given less often or in smaller amounts, and, when possible, finally removed altogether, with the expectation that the target behavior will persist (called **maintenance**) and will occur in new situations (called **generalization**).

Formal applications of these procedures are called behavior modification programs. For example, such a program was needed for a profoundly retarded, blind, 6-year-old girl. She was incontinent, lacked speech, and could not walk or feed herself. In addition, the child often stuck her fingers into her eye sockets with such force that she bruised the skin

The Head Start program targets children whose risk for retardation is primarily associated with poverty, not with the intellectual skills of the parent. However, parental IQ is a better predictor of the developmental quality of the home environment than family income (Keltner, 1994). For this reason, several programs have targeted infants whose parents have limited intellectual skills. These programs provide a more direct test than Head Start of whether the intergenerational transmission of cultural–familial retardation can be interrupted by early intervention.

One such program is the Abecedarian Project, established in 1972 at the Frank Porter Graham Child Development Center in North Carolina (Ramey & Smith, 1977). The word *abecedarian* refers to one who learns the fundamentals of some area of skill, such as the alphabet. The Abecedarian intervention begins in the first 3 months of life and lasts at least until the child's entry into kindergarten. Toddlers participate 6 to 8 hours a day in a nursery school setting, 50 weeks per year. For children 3 and under, the curriculum focuses on motor, social, and cognitive skills, often provided in one-to-one instruction. Between ages 3 and 5, small group instruction is devoted to science, arithmetic, music, prereading, and reading. In order to test the hypothesis that children in this curriculum would show improved development, selected families were randomly assigned to an intervention or control group. Both groups received free nutritional supplements and health care, but only the intervention group was given the school-based curriculum just described.

Numerous studies have traced the progress of these two groups of children, the oldest of whom are now adolescents (Ramey & Ramey, 1992). By age 3, the intervention group had IQs that were, on average, 20 points higher than those of children in the control condition. Among control-group mothers with IQs below 70, all but one of their children had IQs in the mentally retarded or borderline range of intelligence. In contrast, *all* children in the intervention group tested in the normal range of IQ at age 3. The effect of intervention at this age suggested that even children whose intelligence may be influenced partially by heredity are able to benefit from early intervention.

Assessments of the Abecedarian children at age 12 have shown continuing superiority for the intervention group, although the magnitude of the difference is smaller than it was during the preschool years. The intervention group had IQs that averaged about 5 points higher than the control group. Nearly half of the children in the control group had IQs less than 85, compared with only 13 percent of the intervention group. And, as shown in the accompanying figure, the intervention led to a 50 percent reduction in the rate of grade failure and to significantly higher reading and mathematical skills.

The success of the Abecedarian project and others like it cast doubt on the idea proposed by some theorists that ethnic and class differences in intelligence and achievement are immutable facts of life (e.g., Herrnstein & Murray, 1994). We can now be more hopeful that early interventions can prevent intergenerational patterns of cognitive disability (Ramey, 1993). Un-

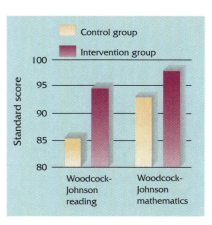

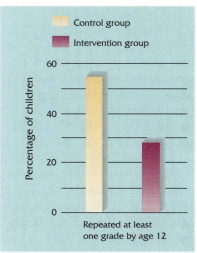

Outcomes of Abecedarian Interventions

By age 12, children who had participated in the preschool Abecedarian Project had higher reading and math achievement scores than the control children. Over half of the control children had repeated at least one grade. By contrast, only about one in four intervention children had done so.

fortunately, the positive results of early intervention programs are not matched by the public's will to pay for these interventions.

around her eyes. How could she be stopped from harming herself? After observing the child for 5 days, therapists noted that she engaged in eye-gouging behavior approximately 75 percent of the time. They then devised a two-part treatment program: overcor-

rection and direct reinforcement of other behavior (DRO). Overcorrection consisted of the therapist's guiding and extending the girl's arms over her head in an exercise that resembled jumping jacks for 15 minutes every time she attempted to put her hands to her

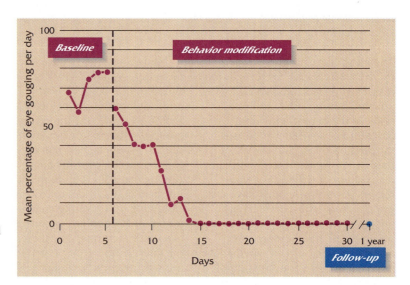

FIGURE 4.3

An Operant Treatment Program for a Mentally Retarded Child

After 10 days of the behavior modification treatment, eye gouging behavior had stopped completely. At a 1-year follow-up, this self-injurious behavior had not resumed.

Source: Wesolowsi & Zawlocki, 1982.

eyes. DRO consisted of rewarding her with food every time she performed any behavior other than eye gouging within certain intervals of time based on the initial 5-day observation. Figure 4.3 shows the results.

Behavior modification programs are used to teach self-care (e.g., toileting, washing, dressing, eating), communication, social, and vocational skills. For example, through such programs, adolescents with mild and moderate retardation have been taught to fill a soda machine and use a duplicating machine or a photocopier (Chandler, Schuster, & Stevens, 1993); younger children with mild or moderate retardation have been taught to give a toy to a peer or make a specific request to play (Odom et al., 1982).

These programs have consistently succeeded in teaching individuals with severe and profound retardation to acquire the basic, life-enhancing skills. These interventions have been most successful in their initial stages, when reinforcers are presented frequently. Less success has been achieved in maintaining initial gains when reinforcers are removed or in obtaining generalization of the behaviors beyond the training or teaching environment. To improve generalization and maintenance, the school environments of children with mental retardation must often be reengineered to provide ongoing reinforcement of the child's adaptive skills. Parents have also been trained to implement behavioral programs at home that replicate the teachers' efforts at school (Egel & Powers, 1989).

Another strategy called *self-instruction* trains children with retardation to monitor their performance on a task and to follow a set of rules that help them complete the task in the absence of an instructor. For example, the person might be taught to repeat simple instructions out loud as he or she follows a sequence of pictures that describes the task.

Of course, the effectiveness of these procedures depends on the cognitive abilities of the person being treated (Ferretti et al., 1993).

Behavior modification programs are also used to eliminate self-injurious and disruptive behaviors. These applications may use punishment to discourage undesirable behavior along with positive reinforcers to support alternative behaviors. Recall that, in our opening case, Jordan would frequently bite his hand or bang his head. Because Jordan's teacher noticed that he was most likely to bang his head in the first 2 or 3 minutes after he sat in his wheelchair, Jordan was given a special music box on his wheelchair tray when he first sat in the chair. He was allowed to keep the box as long as he did not bang his head; but at the first instance of head banging, the box was immediately removed. This program worked for a while, but it eventually lost its effectiveness. The teachers then added a new, aversive consequence for head banging: when head banging occurred, they removed the box and sprayed a fine mist of water in Jordan's face, something he disliked. This also worked for a while, but it, too, lost its power, and Jordan's teachers once again had to redesign his behavior modification program.

Special Problems in the Treatment of Self-Injurious Behavior. Why is self-injurious behavior so difficult to eliminate in persons with mental retardation? First, researchers suspect that some children with mental retardation suffer abnormal regulation of *endogenous opiates,* the brain's pain-relieving chemicals. Children with mental retardation may have an excess of endogenous opiates in their brains, or these opiates may be released after self-injurious behavior, thus functioning as biochemical reinforcers for self-injury (Osman & Loschen, 1992). This hypothesis is supported by the fact that *naltrexone,* a drug that keeps endogenous opiates from reaching the receptor sites where they have their pain-killing effects has shown promise in controlling self-injurious behavior (Thompson, Weiner, & Myers, 1994).

Second, self-injurious and other disruptive behaviors influence the *social* environment. Nonverbal persons with mental retardation have limited opportunities for communication, and self-injurious behaviors command a lot of attention and action. For example, for Jordan, being placed in the wheelchair was probably unpleasant, but he could not express his displeasure, negotiate an alternative, or resist his teacher's wishes. By banging his head, Jordan communicated distress and modified the behavior of his teachers—they were forced to do something to prevent his hurting himself, sometimes by removing him from his wheelchair. "Escape from task demands" is a powerful reinforcer of self-injurious behavior, and teaching alternative methods for gaining attention often reduces this behavior (Durand & Carr, 1987). In Jordan's case, better results were obtained when his teachers eliminated all verbal and nonverbal communication with Jordan while they punished him and never removed him from his chair after he banged his head.

Use of aversive consequences for self-injurious behavior has ignited vigorous debate (Bailey, 1992; McGee, 1992). Some experts argue that, in cases in which severe, self-inflicted mutilation would result, the end justifies the means even when electric shock or similar stimuli are necessary to stop the behavior. Others claim that such procedures are both degrading and abusive and cannot be morally justified, no matter what behavior occurs (Hobbs & Goswick, 1977). Fortunately, nonaversive alternatives, such as positive reinforcement for behaviors that are incompatible with self-injury, can often be used to reduce self-injurious behavior (Koegel & Koegel, 1989).

Institutionalization and Normalization.

In the United States prior to the 1970s, children such as Jordan were usually placed in an institution for long-term care. Even many children with moderate retardation were institutionalized from their early years. This practice was supported by the belief that a residential program staffed with professionals could provide better care and education than untrained parents could and that out-of-home placement would protect the family from psychological distress.

In the 1970s, these beliefs were supplanted by the idea that service delivery should be "normalized" as much as possible. The **normalization** movement was based on the idea that persons with mental retardation should experience the "norms and patterns of the mainstream society" in their everyday lives

(Wolfensberger, 1972). Normalization thus involved a retreat from large, centralized institutions and a new emphasis on family care for persons with mental retardation, on the education of children with disabilities in public school settings, and on providing community-based facilities for residential care.

For persons with severe and profound retardation who require nearly continual supervision, the normalization movement led to creative alternatives to institutional living. For example, programs that provide supervised apartment dwelling allow persons with mental retardation to live in their own units (Burchard et al., 1991), and frequent monitoring by trained staff enables them to receive immediate assistance when needed. Other alternatives include family-like group homes in residential neighborhoods and specialized foster homes in which a family is trained to care for one or two individuals with severe mental disabilities.

Living in normalized community settings offers many persons with mental retardation a chance to enjoy increased variety in their daily activities, greater community interaction, and a more normal lifestyle (Cumins et al., 1990; Lord & Pedlar, 1991). However, institutional living offers some advantages over other arrangements. For example, interviews with young adults with mental retardation indicated that those living in the community were more satisfied with their ability to make personal choices, but those in an institution were more satisfied with their social lives (Barlow & Kirby, 1991). Both groups were generally positive about their current living arrangement

Special Education and Mainstreaming.

Normalization and deinstitutionalization put increased responsibility on neighborhood schools to educate all children with disabilities, including those with severe and profound mental retardation. In the United States, the 1975 Individuals with Disabilities Education Act (IDEA) made special educational services for children with disabilities mandatory. These services were to be available in the least-restrictive environment possible.

In the early years of special education, most children with mental retardation were placed in self-contained classrooms in regular public schools. IQ testing was emphasized as a means of determining which of these classrooms was most appropriate for a given child (Ysseldyke, Algozzine, & Epps, 1983). More specific assessment data—for example, scores

Connections

Does the deinstitutionalization of mentally retarded children share similarities with other changes in the treatment of mentally disordered persons? See Chapters 17, pp. 602–604, and 18, pp. 620–623.

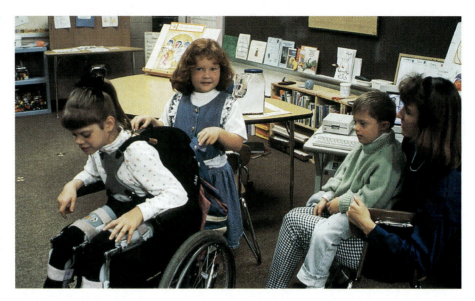

Children with disabilities were once segregated from much of society, including its schools. In many schools today, mainstreaming means that the child with mental retardation can spend part or most of the day in a regular classroom—usually with assistance from a special education teacher or teacher's assistant. Some educators advocate for the full inclusion of students with disabilities in regular education, and call for the complete abolishment of special education (Stainback & Stainback, 1992).

on tests of motor ability, language, social skills, and so on—were also used to determine a child's *individualized education program,* or *IEP,* a formal record of the goals for a child and teaching strategies for reaching those goals.

Opposition to self-contained special education has steadily increased during the past two decades. Many self-contained programs take place in buildings that are removed from regular classrooms, and critics warn that such segregation works against normalization and promotes antidisability biases in nondisabled students (e.g., Heller, Holtzman, & Messick, 1982). The testing process—especially when it involves the measurement of IQ—is also seen as creating labels that "pigeonhole children into educationally questionable classifications" (Fuchs & Fuchs, 1994). A related problem is that reliance on IQ tests has led to a disproportionate number of Black American children being assigned to special education classrooms in many schools. Several reasons might explain this overrepresentation, including the effects of discrimination, higher levels of poverty and family disturbance among ethnic minorities, and educational practices or biases that disadvantage certain children. Finally, many educators are concerned about the costs of ever-expanding special education departments for students with disabilities.

Most school districts have developed alternatives to self-contained programs in which children with disabilities—primarily those with mild or moderate mental retardation—are partially served in regular classrooms for nondisabled students, a process known as **mainstreaming** (Dunn, 1968). Some schools have eliminated their special education programs altogether, instead, serving students of all ability levels in the same general program (Stainback & Stainback, 1992). In this more extreme version of mainstreaming, called **inclusion,** teachers, rather than children, move from one classroom to another, providing extra help to needy students or consulting with regular teachers.

It is unclear to what extent mainstreaming has actually occurred in American education and whether all of its effects are desirable. Segregated programs are still widely used, even for students with mild disabilities who would seem to be the most easily mainstreamed (McLeskey & Pacchiano, 1994). Critics worry that many students with disabilities will receive inadequate instruction in full inclusion programs and that such programs sacrifice students' academic progress for the social–political goals of normalization (Fuchs & Fuchs, 1994). Although educators continue to debate the relative merits of mainstreaming and inclusion, most agree that self-contained classrooms should be used on a limited basis for students with severe disruptive behavior.

In Review

Mental retardation refers to:

- significantly subaverage intelligence occurring during childhood, as defined by an IQ score of approximately 70 or below; and
- deficits in adaptive behaviors such as feeding, dressing, and basic social skills.

Organic causes of mental retardation:

- account for 25 to 50 percent of all retardation cases, most with IQs below 50; and
- include genetic disorders, prenatal problems, perinatal and postnatal diseases, and childhood head injuries.

Cultural–familial causes of retardation:

■ account for the majority of cases of mild retardation; and

■ involve parental limitations, family hardships, and other kinds of psychosocial disadvantage, although the specific causal mechanisms are still unclear.

Services for persons with mental retardation:

■ include attempts at both prevention and treatment; and

■ have often been guided by the principles of normalization and mainstreaming.

Autistic Disorders

Kathy Mills sits at her kitchen table, watching her 3-year-old son, Devon, play in the den. For the last hour, Devon has been sitting on the floor peering intently at his right hand, which he holds over his head as he slowly opens and closes his fingers. Devon is looking at changes in the lighting that he makes by waving his fingers in front of the ceiling light. He has been going through this exercise every day for months, creating his own private kaleidoscope, so fascinated with it that he pays attention to nothing else.

Kathy dreads what she knows is coming next. Devon will stay so absorbed in his finger-and-light ritual that soon he will defecate in his pants. As soon as Kathy tries to pick him up to change his clothes, he will fly into a tantrum, and Kathy might get kicked before she can get Devon changed.

Sometimes Kathy feels as if she won't be able to cope with Devon's strange behavior another day. Even before Devon was a year old, Kathy had begun to notice all sorts of problems. Devon would never reach out for toys or babble like other babies. He wouldn't even splash around in the water when she gave him a bath. He refused to eat solid food until Kathy devised maneuvers to trick him into eating. By the time he was 18 months old, Devon no longer slept through the night. After a hurricane destroyed the family's house in Florida, they lived in a hotel room for almost 2 months. Then, when Devon was about 2 years old, his parents separated; 6 months later they got a divorce.

Perhaps most upsetting of all, Devon didn't use language and didn't seem to notice other people. If another child walked over to him, Devon would shrink back and begin to cry. If his mother called his name, he usually ignored

her. The only words he ever uttered were "hi," "off," and "bye-bye." Sometimes he used these words correctly, but more often he merely seemed to be chanting them to himself.

Most of the time, Devon would just sit by himself and stare off into space. He'd gaze at the lights or shadows on the wall, or he'd spin objects around and around on the floor, completely absorbed by their movement. The only time Devon seemed to notice other people was when he got upset. Then he would cry and cling to his mother, who could usually comfort him by holding him on her lap and singing to him.

Devon was diagnosed with autistic disorder before he was 3. The term *autism* is derived from the Greek word *autos* (self) and literally means a preoccupation with the self. Psychiatrist Leo Kanner first used this term in 1943 to describe a group of 11 infants that he followed in his clinical practice at Harvard. These infants seemed incapable of relating to their parents or to other people; they often engaged in repetitive, purposeless activities called *stereotyped behavior* or *stereotypies;* they seemed more interested in objects than in their parents. At ages 2 and 3, these infants either failed to develop language or made only bizarre speech sounds.

Contemporary guidelines for the diagnosis of autism are remarkably consistent with the characteristics identified by Kanner over 50 years ago. These characteristics fall into three categories (Rutter & Schopler, 1992):

1. severe deficits in establishing *reciprocal* social relationships;
2. nonexistent or poor language skills; and
3. stereotyped patterns of behavior, activities, or interests.

Although some children show autistic symptoms in all three of these areas, others show only partial manifestations. A child with stereotyped behaviors (e.g., rocking or unusual hand movements) who does not develop social relationships might have normal language skills. Another child with undeveloped language and socialization deficits might not show stereotyped behavior. Because of these variations, autism is sometimes described as a **spectrum disorder:** at one end of the spectrum is **typical autism** that is marked by disturbances in social relationships, language, *and* stereotypies; at the other end of the spectrum are incomplete or atypical versions of the full syndrome (Rutter & Schopler, 1992).

Other disorders with autistic features include *Rett's disorder, child disintegrative disorder, Asperger's disorder,* and *pervasive developmental disorder not otherwise specified (PDD-NOS).* The DSM-IV uses the term **pervasive developmental disorder (PPD)** to describe disorders with autistic features, along with typical autism, but the term has not been widely accepted. Experts such as Michael Rutter and Eric Schopler (1992) suggest *autistic spectrum disorders* as a more understandable label.

Typical Autism

Depending on the diagnostic criteria used, autistic disorder is found in only 2 to 5 children per 10,000 (APA, 1994). In about 75 percent of cases, the autistic child has significant mental retardation as well, most often in the moderate range. Autistic disorder tends to be a lifelong condition with unremitting effects on social adjustment.

The rate of autism is 4 to 5 times higher in males than in females. When present in females, it is more likely to co-occur with mental retardation. Autism has been diagnosed throughout the world, but its prevalence appears to vary in different countries. China reports an extremely low rate; Japan has a rate that is 3 to 5 times greater than most other countries. Whether these rates reflect varying diagnostic practices or different exposure to causal factors is not yet known.

The DSM-IV criteria for autistic disorder are shown in the DSM table below. Problems in at least

---

DSM-IV

Diagnostic Criteria for Autistic Disorder

A. A total of six (or more) items from (1), (2), and (3), with at least two from (1), and one each from (2) and (3):

(1) qualitative impairment in social interaction, as manifested by at least two of the following:

(a) marked impairment in the use of multiple nonverbal behaviors such as eye-to-eye gaze, facial expression, body postures, and gestures to regulate social interaction

(b) failure to develop peer relationships appropriate to developmental level

(c) a lack of spontaneous seeking to share enjoyment, interests, or achievements with other people (e.g., by a lack of showing, bringing, or pointing out objects of interest)

(d) lack of social or emotional reciprocity

(2) qualitative impairments in communications as manifested by at least one of the following:

(a) delay in, or total lack of, the development of spoken language (not accompanied by an attempt to compensate through alternative modes of communication such as gesture or mime)

(b) in individuals with adequate speech, marked impairment in the ability to initiate or sustain a conversation with others

(c) stereotyped and repetitive use of language or idiosyncratic language

(d) lack of varied, spontaneous make-believe play or social imitative play appropriate to developmental level

(3) restricted repetitive and stereotyped patterns of behavior, interests, and activities, as manifested by at least one of the following:

(a) encompassing preoccupations with one or more stereotyped and restricted patterns of interest that is abnormal either in intensity or focus

(b) apparently inflexible adherence to specific, nonfunctional routines or rituals

(c) stereotyped and repetitive motor mannerisms (e.g., hand or finger flapping or twisting, or complex whole-body movements)

(d) persistent preoccupation with parts of objects

B. Delays or abnormal functioning in at least one of the following areas, with onset prior to age 3 years: (1) social interaction, (2) language as used in social communication, or (3) symbolic or imaginative play.

C. The disturbance is not better accounted for by Rett's Disorder or Childhood Disintegrative Disorder.

Source: American Psychiatric Association; *Diagnostic and Statistical Manual of Mental Disorders,* Fourth Edition. Washington, DC, American Psychiatric Association.

one of these areas *must be present prior to the age of 3.* Autism is ordinarily recognized in the first year of life, and the majority of cases are detected by age 2; however, some cases of autism may not be recognized until the child enters school.

Social Relationship Problems. "Gross and sustained" impairment in reciprocal social interaction is the defining feature of autism. Autistic children lack many of the *nonverbal* behaviors that regulate social discourse, such as eye contact, "open" facial expression, and the body postures and hand gestures that facilitate interaction. These children have trouble using gestures and eye contact to coordinate attention with another person, a process called **joint attention** (Mundy, Sigman, & Kasari, 1994). Many nonverbal cues ordinarily used to share the experience of an interesting object or event with another person—showing, pointing, head nodding, eyebrow raising—are absent or poorly developed in persons with autism. Autistic children often seem unaware of others or view them as objects rather than people. One 13-year-old boy with autism, while playing with the fingers of the examining psychologist, began to bend one of them back at an impossible angle—not maliciously, but seemingly unaware that the finger was part of a person, or that such an action would hurt the person. Children with autism are often said to "look through" rather than "look at" other people. Similarly, the DSM-IV notes that some children with autism might involve peers in games, but merely as "tools or mechanical aids."

The nature of these social problems changes as the child grows older. Infants with autism are disinclined to cuddle or smile directly at their parents (Kanner, 1943). Autistic preschoolers seldom show any observable interest in peers, although they may be quite dependent on close contact with their parents. Older children with autism will begin to show discernible interest in peers, but only in a mechanical, detached style.

Expressive Language Deficits. Spoken language is absent or minimal in about half of the individuals with autism (Volkmar, 1992). In the other half, vocabulary size is close to mental age expectations, but the pragmatic use of language—for communication or self-expression—is extremely limited. Speech may have an unusual tone, rate, or rhythm. Certain words or phrases may be stated repeatedly, sometimes borrowed from television commercials or songs, or formed from idiosyncratic associations that make sense only to those who know the autistic person well. For example, an autistic teenager constantly repeated the phrase "antenna head goes down" whenever he saw his father drive up to the family's home.

It took his parents several weeks to discover that this phrase stemmed from a song their son heard on the radio ("Antenna Head" by ZZ Top) and his fascination with the retractable radio antenna on his father's car!

Stereotypic Behavior. Autistic stereotypies often take the form of inflexible adherence to a specific routine, such as dressing in a particular order that never changes, or lining up toys in an exact way at the end of every play period. These routines reflect a pervasive *insistence on sameness* in the physical and psychological environment. Many autistic children seem to rely on unspoken rules that they regard as unbreakable. For example, the parents of an autistic 4-year-old boy complained about his insistence that every light in a room be turned off before anyone could leave the room. These parents had long ago learned that confronting his inflexibility was futile; any deviation from the "lights off" rule sent him into extreme tantrums.

Repetitive or stereotyped behavior may also be manifested as an all-encompassing preoccupation with a particular activity, object, or special interest. Some autistic children maintain an abnormal fascination with mechanical devices or other objects (clocks, vacuum cleaners, stereo equipment). Others are preoccupied with a special topic (e.g., trains, animals, a particular sport) about which they know a surprising number of specific facts, although the expression of knowledge is usually repetitive and uninformative.

The body movements of children with autism may also be stereotyped. Odd hand movements (clapping, flapping, finger flicking), whole body activity (rocking or swaying), and abnormal body posture or limb positioning (moving the hands and arms in an unusual way) are common. Stereotyped body movements can also take the form of self-injurious head banging, biting, scratching, and hitting, sometimes leaving permanent scars and injuries.

Distinguishing Autism from Mental Retardation. Most autistic persons have some degree of mental retardation, and many persons with mental retardation show limited language development and stereotyped behaviors such as rocking and self-injurious behavior. Still, clear differences between these two developmental disabilities are evident when autistic and mentally retarded persons of the same mental age are compared. Children with mental retardation usually engage others socially and show reciprocal interaction skills that are commensurate with their mental age. They also use whatever language they possess to communicate with others. Finally, whereas most children with mental retardation have uniformly low scores on subtests that tap various abilities measured by an IQ test, autistic children are likely to show extreme variability in their scores. In particular, children with autism generally have notable weaknesses in language and abstract reasoning, but some are near average in nonverbal intellectual skills.

Causes of Autistic Disorder

Experts once believed that autism was due to inadequate parenting. This view was based on theories that parents of autistic children were often overly formal in their social interactions (Kanner & Lesser, 1958). It was thought that cold parenting produced the social and emotional deficits seen in autism. However, subsequent studies showed few differences between the personalities of parents of autistic and those of normal children (Cantwell, Baker, & Rutter, 1978; McAdoo & DeMeyer, 1978), and theories that focus on parenting are no longer in favor. In the last decade research has suggested that autism may be related to both biological and psychological factors.

Biological Factors. Could autistic disorder be genetically transmitted? A definitive answer is not yet known, but it appears that at least some cases may be inherited. Genetic syndromes such as fragile X produce autistic characteristics, although the proportion of autistic individuals with fragile X is too small for this particular genetic abnormality to be a major causal factor. More generally, a genetic basis for autism is suggested by twin studies showing that the concordance rate for autism (i.e., the rate at which both twins have autism) is higher among identical (monozygotic) than fraternal (dizygotic) twins (e.g., Rutter et al., 1990). However, many of these studies are conducted with very small samples, primarily because autistic disorder is so rare. For example, in one well-known study 11 autistic people with a monozygotic twin were compared with 10 autistic people with a dizygotic twin. The concordance rate for the identical twins was 36 percent compared with a 0 concordance rate for the fraternal twins (Folstein & Rutter, 1977). The rate of autism among siblings of autistic children also appears to be higher than in the general population (Smalley, Asarnow, & Spence, 1988; Szatmari et al., 1993). Although we do not yet know the specific genetic mechanisms that lead to autism, some kind of genetic predisposition seems to be involved.

Autism may result from several different biological factors that produce brain damage. Individuals with autism have higher rates of physical anomalies, EEG abnormalities, and seizures (Golden, 1987). Autism has also been associated with various complications of pregnancy and birth (Tsai, 1987). However, recent work suggests that when maternal parity (the number of children previously born) is taken into account, the association between birth complications and autism is not significant (Piven et al., 1993).

Other studies indicate that the brains of some people with autism have structural or functional abnormalities. Some researchers using brain imaging techniques have found that the cerebellum and the frontal lobes are less well developed in some autistic persons than in normal controls (Courchesne et al., 1988; Gaffney et al., 1989). Other studies have found that levels of the neurotransmitter serotonin are significantly higher in about one third of autistic persons than in control subjects (Anderson & Hosino, 1987). However, elevated serotonin has been found in several other disorders (including mental retardation without autism), so it is still unclear whether this neurotransmitter is uniquely related to autism (Volkmar, 1992).

In short, research on specific neurobiological causes of autistic disorder is still in its infancy. We know that different kinds of brain damage are involved in different cases, but we still do not understand the biology of autism well enough to explain just how biological factors might cause this disorder.

Psychological Factors. Research on potential psychological causes of autism has focused on the cognitive and social disabilities shown by most autistic children. These deficits suggest that psychological differences interact with biological differences to produce the disorder.

One view, with roots in Kanner's (1943) original work, proposes that the primary deficit in autism is the inability to form attachments. However, observations of autistic children in the Strange Situation (described in Chapter 3) have indicated that, although they may take longer to develop attachments, their attachments eventually resemble those of other children with disabilities (e.g., Rogers, Ozonoff, & Maslin-Cole, 1991).

Research results regarding other causal hypotheses are mixed. For example, some scientists have suggested that an inability to imitate is the primary deficit in autism (e.g., Meltzoff & Gopnik, 1993). However, the research has been equivocal about differences in this area, partly because of the difficulty of measuring imitation in experimental settings. Another proposal suggests that autistic children suffer a deficit in their understanding or expression of emotional states (Hobson, 1989). However, it may be linguistic impairment, rather than emotional unexpressiveness, that distinguishes autistic children from others of similar mental age (Loveland et al., 1994).

 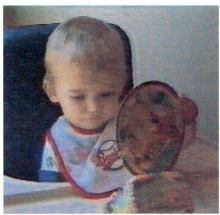

Many parents of children with autistic disorder notice that something is different about their children even before they are a year old. What clue do these parents detect? As these photos indicate, children with autism tend not to look at faces or share emotional expressions with others. In fact, in Osterling and Dawson's (1994) study, the researchers correctly guessed the diagnosis of children with or without autism in 77 percent of the cases just by rating whether the child looked at another person's face. In these photos, the child on the left is not autistic; the child on the right was diagnosed with the disorder.

Geraldine Dawson and her colleagues (1989) have proposed that the fundamental deficit in autism is the infant's failure to attend to social stimuli such as the mother's face and voice. As a result, the infant cannot assign emotional meaning to social stimuli. Rather, the autistic infant seems to prefer and attach importance to nonsocial stimulation such as the sounds of a rattle or bell. To examine this hypothesis, Julie Osterling and Geraldine Dawson (1994) compared videotapes of autistic children at their first birthday parties with those of matched normal children. There were clear differences between the two groups. For example, the autistic infants were far less likely to orient to someone calling their names and to engage in joint attention (pointing and showing). Dawson believes that attentional deficits of this nature operate from the earliest days of life and prevent the infant from developing normal social behavior.

Another group of researchers suggests that autistic children have a deficit in their **theory of mind**, a cognitive process that allows an individual to infer the mental states of others. They are unable to anticipate what other people are thinking and to understand that others may have intentions, beliefs, and desires that are different from their own.

This ability can be tested by asking children to predict what another person will think. For example, children with a mental age of about 3 or 4 years are given a task in which the child discovers that an M&M box actually contains a pencil (Perner et al., 1989). The child is then asked to predict what another child, who has never seen the box, will think it contains. The correct response is "M&Ms," indicating that the child has understood that another child would likely interpret the cover of the box in the same way as he or she did. More difficult versions of this task require subjects to make more complex inferences about the beliefs of characters in stories. In several studies, autistic children have been unable to predict the beliefs of others on these tasks, while persons of comparable mental age can (e.g., Baron-Cohen, 1989; Leekam & Perner, 1991). Other studies of theory of mind have found that autistic children cannot tell lies (Russell et al., 1991; Sodian & Frith, 1992), have difficulty solving mental problems (Shulman et al., 1995), and find it hard to understand that different people can have access to different sources of information (Perner et al., 1989).

Another line of research indicates that autistic persons do very poorly on neuropsychological tests of *executive functioning*, such as planning, flexible problem solving, and inhibition of off-task behavior in a goal-directed situation (Ozonoff et al., 1994). These operations are primarily controlled by the frontal cortex. As noted previously, the frontal lobes of some autistic persons are undersized. In a longitudinal study comparing the performance of autistic adolescents on measures of executive function and theory of mind (Ozonoff & McEvoy, 1994), researchers found that deficits in these two areas were strongly related, suggesting that they are interdependent, rather than separate, cognitive functions. This research suggests a potential link between psychological and biological factors: underdeveloped brain

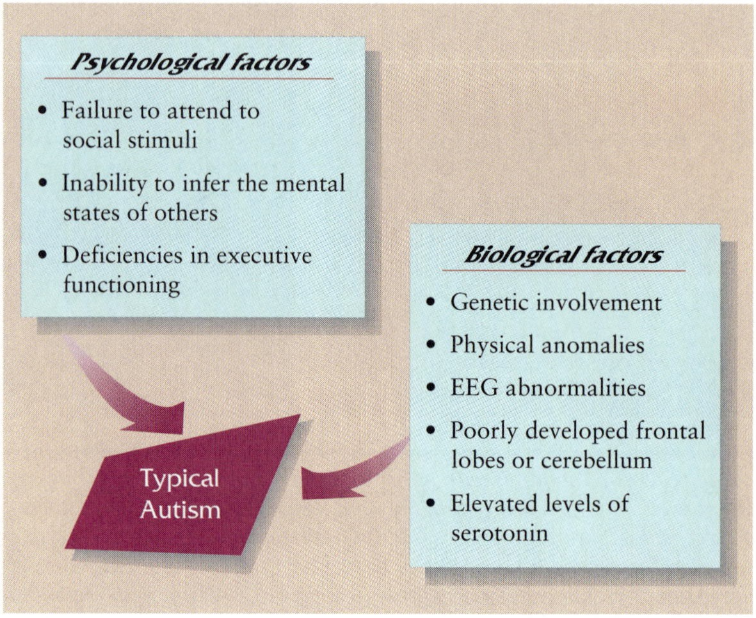

FIGURE 4.4

Multiple Factors in the Etiology of Autistic Disorder

Over the years, researchers have explored numerous hypotheses about the causes of autism. To date, empirical studies show that the factors listed here are all associated with autism. Whether these factors actually cause or help cause the disorder and the mechanisms by which they act are still unknown.

structures may produce executive function deficits and may preclude a theory of mind, thereby accounting for the social interaction problems of autistic individuals (Baron-Cohen et al., 1994).

Taken together, studies of the psychological factors in autism suggest that autistic persons operate in the dark during social interactions, unable to decipher the social codes that enable most people to understand what others are thinking and feeling. These deficits may result from disturbed biological, cognitive, emotional, or attentional processes. Although it is still unclear how autistic disorder is caused by these processes, it does seem likely that, as Figure 4.4 suggests, the social, behavioral, and cognitive deficits of autism result from an interaction of multiple factors.

Other Pervasive Developmental Disorders (Atypical Autistic Disorders)

Relatively little is known about the incidence and course of other pervasive developmental disorders—Asperger's disorder, Rett's disorder, and childhood disintegrative disorder. Even their defining features are still unclear (Klin et al., 1993). Whether they remain in the next version of the DSM as they are now defined will depend on the results of further study.

Asperger's disorder was first described by Hans Asperger (1944) as *autistic psychopathy*. Initial investigations of the syndrome were published primarily in European medical journals, but the disorder became widely known in the United States only during the past decade. Occurring in only about 1 in 10,000 individuals, **Asperger's disorder** is similar to autism except that Asperger's cases show higher intellectual skills and normal or near-normal expressive language. Compared with autistic persons of the same mental age, individuals with Asperger's disorder show much greater interest in others and are much more knowledgeable about social conventions, although they still seem unable to use these assets on an everyday basis (Klin, 1993). Asperger's disorder differs from autism in other ways, including a later age of onset and initial diagnosis (usually after age 2) and the presence of mild motor deficits that give the impression of general clumsiness.

Children with Asperger's disorder often chatter on and on about their special interests (e.g., trains, TV programs, Greek mythology, dinosaurs), initially impressing adults with their excellent memory and knowledge. However, they usually offer this information in an intrusive and egocentric way that has been described as an "unrelenting monologue" (Klin et al., 1993). Their *nonverbal* communication skills are often poor; they do not maintain good eye contact, and their facial expressions are not very communicative.

Like typical autism, Asperger's disorder persists throughout life. Adults with this disorder can live independently and hold jobs, although vocational failure is common (Klin, 1993). The same causal factors suspected for typical autism are relevant to Asperger's disorder.

Rett's disorder, first described by Andreas Rett in the 1960s, is much less common than autism, occurring in about 1 in 15,000 individuals. Thus far, it has been found almost exclusively in females, suggesting an influence from an X-linked dominant gene. Children with **Rett's disorder** develop normally at least midway through the first year of life; then, rather suddenly, between 6 and 18 months, there is a deceleration in head growth and a loss of previously acquired motor skills, primarily involving the hands. These changes are followed by severely impaired language development, loss of interest in others, and stereotypical hand-wringing or hand-washing movements. These autistic behaviors diminish over time, but other aspects of development continue to deteriorate, including severe mental retardation, weight loss, and loss of the ability to walk. There is not yet a treatment for Rett's disorder.

Like Rett's disorder, **childhood disintegrative disorder** appears after a period of normal development. The child develops normally for at least the first 2 years, but by age 10 autistic symptoms appear that are identical to those of typical autism. And like autism, childhood disintegrative disorder is more common among males, but it is much less common than autism. No biological or psychological cause for the relatively late onset of this disorder has yet been determined.

Another category in the DSM-IV, *pervasive developmental disorder, not otherwise specified (PDD-NOS),* covers patterns of autistic behavior that are not described by the other pervasive developmental disorders or that are better classified as other psychiatric disorders (such as schizophrenia or a personality disorder). Although PDD-NOS is more common than typical autism (Volkmar, 1992), its exact prevalence is uncertain. A typical case is one in which the child shows various behavioral stereotypies and expressive language problems but exhibits normal interest in social interaction. The causes and outcomes of PDD-NOS are not well understood.

Treatment of Pervasive Developmental Disorders

Autistic disorder and other pervasive developmental disorders are difficult to treat. In one longitudinal study, only 1 of 64 autistic adults was able to hold a job, live independently, and maintain normal social relationships (Rutter, 1970). Still, a great deal of energy has been devoted to creating treatment methods, primarily involving medication, behavior modification, and special educational programs. None of these treatments is a cure-all, but some—primarily behavior modification programs and educational programs for pre-school-aged children—can improve certain aspects of the disorder (Dawson & Osterling, 1996).

The most extensive and thoroughly researched behavior modification program for autistic individuals is described by Ivar Lovaas and his colleagues (Lovaas & Smith, 1989). This training program requires intensive training sessions that occur every day for 2 years, in the child's home and other environments, and includes the child's parents and peers. The treatment focuses on language development and cooperative play with peers. Efforts are also made to curtail stereotyped behaviors, tantrums, and aggressive behavior. In one study of this intervention for children who began treatment prior to age 4, Lovaas (1987) found that treated children gained an average of 20 IQ points by age 7 and about 50 percent were able to attend a regular (non–special education) first-grade class. Children in an untreated control group did significantly worse; less than 5 percent were able to attend regular education. A 5-year follow-up of these children indicated that the impressive, early gains seen in the treated children were maintained (McEachin, Smith, & Lovaas, 1993).

Devon, described on page 135, took part in a Lovaas-type behavior modification program.

Connections

The pervasive developmental disorders have sometimes been described as psychoses but they are not. For the differences, see Chapter 10, p. 332.

*W*hen Devon was about 4, Kathy and Devon moved, and she found a home-care setting for Devon that he was able to accept. She also enrolled him in an intensive behavior modification program developed by Dr. Lovaas. A team of psychology graduate-student therapists worked with Devon about 30 hours a week. They used reinforcement techniques to help Devon increase his attention, play, and social skills. Devon also began to learn how to use language to communicate. After 3 months of this program, in conjunction with private speech therapy, Devon learned how to imitate the behavior of an adult, and his ability to understand and use language increased considerably. His mother also reported that Devon began to show a better attention span, to control his bowels, and to comply with instructions more easily.

Medications have been used along with behavior modification and educational programs, usually when there are severe problems of hyperactivity, aggressiveness, and self-injurious behavior. Unfortunately, the stimulants that so often improve the behavior of hyperactive, nonautistic children often worsen the functioning of autistic children. Other medications such as the antipsychotic *haloperidol*

Robert Hodapp
and *Geri* Dawson

Dr. Robert Hodapp is Associate Professor in the School of Education at UCLA. He is nationally recognized for his research on children with different genetic forms of mental retardation and for studies of families of children with mental retardation. Dr. Geraldine Dawson is professor of Psychology at the University of Washington, Seattle. She is well known for her research on how psychological factors contribute to autistic disorders.

Developmental Disorders and Mental Retardation

Q *You have been cautious about the effects of early intervention programs for mental retardation, especially the Abecedarian Project. Now that we have longer follow-up data, what do you think?*

A **Dr. Hodapp:** I have always been cautious about the effects of early intervention programs, particularly the Abecedarian Project. The problem is not so much with IQ gains, but with what IQ gains alone mean. The Abecedarian Project shows that, given an incredibly long-lasting, intensive, school-based intervention program, one can increase the IQ of low-income, at-risk children 10 or 15 points. My concern is to what extent these children do well in school and in after-school life. The evidence from other projects is that helping mothers to parent their children may be more effective than getting children to have higher IQs. By giving services to mothers, they learn how to help themselves and their children. The children's lives improve immensely.

...helping mothers to parent their children may be more effective...

Q *What's your opinion about the use of aversive consequences for self-injurious behavior?*

A **Dr. Hodapp:** Some courts have ordered programs to stop using aversive procedures such as ammonia nasal sprays for children with severe, self-injurious behaviors. Incredible care needs to be taken that aversive methods are not overused, are well monitored, and are the treatment of last resort. But, given those conditions—and if they really do work as effectively as some claim—I would reluctantly favor their use.

Q *We reviewed several psychological theories about the social interaction deficits of autistic children. What's the latest on this issue?*

A **Dr. Dawson:** Since autism was first defined by Leo Kanner, people have been speculating about what deficit accounts for the syndrome. As you discuss in the chapter, some have suggested that autism involves an impairment in the way the child responds emotionally to people; others have suggested that autism is a cognitive impairment that interferes with the processing of social information. We are beginning to recognize that it is impossible to separate these aspects of psychological cognition and affect, especially early in life.

Also, it is extremely unlikely that a complex disorder such as autism is the result of only one problem. Rather, autism probably involves a cluster of problems that affect many domains.

Q *What advances in neurobiology and genetics do you expect in the field of autism over the next decade?*

A **Dr. Dawson:** New technologies, such as functional brain imaging and genetic linkage analysis, will lead to important discoveries about the biological and genetic bases of autism. In addition, the establishment of a brain bank used to collect brains for autopsy studies is an important step toward understanding the disorder. We hope that the different methods will lead to converging evidence—that the results of the autopsy studies will be consistent with those of imaging studies. For example, of the 10 autopsy cases Margaret Bauman has examined, all have shown neuronal abnormalities in the limbic regions of the brain, especially the amygdala. If we also find that this region is not functioning properly in imaging studies, we will start to have confidence that we are beginning to isolate one brain region responsible for autism.

Q *What progress are we making in the treatment of autism?*

A **Dr. Dawson:** The optimistic news in the area of intervention is that early intervention appears to be quite effective for many children with autism. One of my former graduate students, Julie Osterling, and I recently reviewed the outcome data from eight model early-intervention programs for children with autism. Regardless of the particular philosophy of the program, across the board early intervention resulted in a large percentage of children being mainstreamed by the time they were 5 years of age. Substantial IQ gains were also made.

have been used with some success in reducing hyperactivity and disruptive behavior in autistic persons (Anderson et al., 1989). However, when used for long periods these medications can induce serious side effects, including *tardive dyskinesia* in which there are irreversible neurological problems such as muscle tremors and impaired gait. Researchers have evaluated several medication alternatives to antipsychotic drugs (including fenfluramine and naltrexone), but further research is needed before their widespread use can be warranted (Campbell et al., 1993; Volkmar, 1992).

In short, the long-term prognosis for autistic disorder and other pervasive developmental disorders remains poor. Behavior modification programs can lead to substantial gains in language and self-maintenance skills, but, in adulthood, most persons with autistic disorder remain seriously handicapped in their abilities to interact with others and to live independently. People who develop language skills and have higher overall intellectual levels show the best improvements.

As is often the case with severe conditions that do not respond to conventional treatments, the field of autism is ripe for techniques that promise quick and dramatic results. People who care for those with severe disabilities can reach a point of despair and hopelessness that makes them especially vulnerable to claims that some new treatment will produce unexpected, even miraculous, results. As this chapter's Controversy section on pages 144 and 145 demonstrates, innovative treatments should be judged on the basis of scientific research, not testimonials or promotional statements.

In Review

Autism is characterized by:

- severe deficits in reciprocal social relationships;
- nonexistent or poor language skills;
- stereotyped patterns of behavior, activities, or interests; and
- multiple causal factors including genetic transmission, neurobiological deficits, and social and cognitive disturbances.

One view of how these factors might work to produce autism suggests that:

- underdevelopment of the frontal cortex produces deficits in executive functioning and prevents development of a theory of mind;
- because of these cognitive deficits, the child cannot decipher the social stimuli that guide interactions; and

- these problems in turn produce the deficits in attention, emotional understanding, and social behavior that characterize autistic children.

Treatment of pervasive developmental disorders:

- often relies on behavior modification procedures to teach communication and socialization skills; and
- seldom overcomes the severe impairments in social interaction and independent living skills associated with these disorders.

Learning Disabilities

It was oral reading time in Carl's fourth-grade classroom. He grew increasingly uncomfortable as the teacher made her way around the room, calling on students to take a turn. It wasn't Carl's lucky day. His name was called.

Carl slowly rose to his feet, vaguely aware of laughter coming from the back of the classroom. He began to read, John . . . cam . . . him from the . . . stair?" The laughter grew a little louder.

"No, Carl, that's 'John came home from the store.' Can you say that?" asked Carl's teacher, glaring in the direction of the laughter.

Carl tried, but he could not improve on his first attempt. The teacher corrected him again and he tried once more but finally gave up, too frustrated and angry to continue. His teacher was sympathetic. "That's okay Carl, we'll try again tomorrow," she said, before calling on another student.

Carl's reading difficulties were puzzling. He seemed at least average in intelligence, and he came from an educated and apparently well-functioning family. What could account for his inability to read?

To answer this question, Carl was sent to the school psychologist for IQ and achievement testing. The results indicated that Carl had an average overall IQ, but he was reading at only a beginning second-grade level. He was also behind his grade level in spelling but was close to average for his age and grade in math. A multidisciplinary assessment team concluded that Carl had a learning disability. Consequently, he was placed, for part of each school day, in a special education class for individualized reading and spelling instruction.

The term *learning disabilities* originated in the early 1960s to describe underachieving children who did *not* have mental retardation, psychopathology, or impoverished or abusive care-giving environ-

The histories of many chronic illnesses and disabilities are marked by "miracle cures" that initially generate enormous enthusiasm but eventually prove to be ineffective (Jacobson, Mulick, & Schwartz, 1995). Treatments for mental retardation and autism provide some particularly fascinating examples (Zigler & Hodapp, 1986). For example, in the 1960s, Glenn Doman and Carl Delacato introduced a motor "patterning" technique to help children with mental retardation (Doman et al., 1960). It was based on the theory that having children engage intensively in early motor patterns and exposing them to strong sensory stimulation would strengthen the brain cells associated with sensory–motor functions and reverse the effects of retardation. The technique required as many as four or five trainers to move the child's limbs and head in a rhythmic fashion, encourage the child to crawl about, or expose the child to flashing lights, varied textures, and unusual sounds.

Case studies reported "miraculous recoveries" following motor patterning treatment. An article by Doman and colleagues even appeared in a respected medical journal in 1960. But as the method became known to more and more scientists, major problems with the research came to light. These included the absence of appropriate control groups, the use of nonstandardized measures of progress, and questionable statistical methods (Zigler & Hodapp, 1986). A well-designed study failed to find any evidence that the Doman-Delacato method worked (Sparrow & Zigler, 1978). Today, the Doman-Delacato method is regarded as worthless by most professional organizations (Zigler & Hodapp, 1986).

Despite widespread claims of producing miraculous improvements in autistic children's literacy, facilitated communication training has been found in controlled research studies to be neither a reliable nor valid technique. These studies indicate that the content of communications is determined by the facilitator, not the child.

The present decade has witnessed the emergence of an equally controversial treatment, called *facilitated communication*. Proponents of this procedure claim that it unlocks the communicative abilities of children with autism or mental retardation (Biklen & Schubert, 1991). The term **facilitated communication** is derived from the use of an adult "facilitator," who sits next to the child and physically assists the child to type or point to letters on a keyboard or letterboard.

The history of facilitated communication begins with Rosemary Crossley, who began using the technique with handicapped children in Australia in the early 1970s. In 1989 Douglas Biklen introduced the technique to speech pathologists and teachers in the United States. Proponents of the method quickly claimed that children, who were once unable to communicate at all, could suddenly express themselves, often in very sophisticated ways. According to one author, "Many [children] who previously showed no indication of communication skills now need only light arm support to type on a keyboard" (Spake, 1992).

Early case studies of facilitated communication reported impressive improvements in communication and other skills by children with severe disabilities (Bilken & Schubert, 1991; Bilken et al., 1992)—but did not include control groups or other experimental precautions that would allow for the testing of alternative hypotheses. Nevertheless, the popularity of facilitated communication has grown. In many cases, facilitated communication has replaced proven methods of communication such as sign lan-

ments. For the first time in the twentieth century in the United States, relatively large numbers of White, middle-class children—with apparently average intelligence—were doing poorly in school. All the diagnostic labels that had been previously used to describe the school problems of *non*retarded children (e.g., "emotionally disturbed," "culturally deprived") did not really capture the nature of these problems,

guage and communication boards that use pictorial messages. One mother is reported to have removed her daughter's hearing aids because she believed they were not needed for facilitated communication (Levine, Shane, & Wharton, 1994).

The major problem with facilitated communication is that research consistently has shown that the messages originate with the facilitator rather than with the child. Apparently, facilitators consciously or unconsciously guide the child's hand to create a coherent message. For example, in one study, four students with autism and mental retardation were shown cards with fill-in or short-answer questions and were asked to respond with the assistance of a trained facilitator (Cabay, 1994). The facilitator was allowed to see some of the questions but not others. Nearly all of the students' responses were correct when the facilitator knew what the questions were, but only 19 percent were correct when the facilitator was unaware of the questions. Other studies have reported similar findings, or found no effect whatsoever of facilitated communication (Hudson et al., 1993; Starr, 1994; Regal et al., 1994; Eberlin et al., 1993; Smith & Belcher, 1993). But facilitated communication continues to have its supporters, who dismiss experimental research as an unnatural test of the method or argue that, when researchers are too confrontational about facilitated communication, it undermines children's confidence and ability to perform well.

Facilitated communication might be dismissed merely as an ineffective way to interact with a disabled child were it not for several harmful effects (Levine et al., 1994). For one thing, the time spent on this activity reduces the opportunity for appropriate instruction; in many instances the child's academic goals are abandoned because the facilitated messages are assumed to indicate that the child now has exceptional skills and knowledge. Although advocates defend facilitated communication as a means by which the true wishes and intentions of the disabled person can be made known and acted on, the reverse may actually be the case. Consider, for example, this interaction between an autistic boy and his facilitator, Claudia:

> As Ian's requests for honey [via facilitated communication] had continued, Claudia decided to experiment and offer him a teaspoonful one afternoon. He had assured her by typing that she should put it in his mouth even if he fought her, and fight he did—shrieking, kicking, biting her hand hard enough to draw blood before a bit of honey finally made its way into his mouth. "We shouldn't try that anymore," she said to him, crying. Ian was still distraught also, but his response suggested otherwise: YES YES RREALLY [sic] REALLY GPOOD [sic], he typed. (Martin, 1994; cited in Levine et al., 1994)

Without facilitated communication, Ian's care givers would have interpreted his resistance as an indication that he did not want honey, and they would not have forced him to eat any. But because the typed message—probably emanating from the facilitator—was regarded as a valid communication of Ian's wishes, his obvious cues of distress and fear were overlooked.

Another harmful consequence of facilitated communication is the false hope raised in parents who are desperate for any means of helping their child. When a child fails to respond to the "miracle cure," parents often suffer extreme guilt or depression (Levine et al., 1994; Zigler & Hodapp, 1986). Perhaps the greatest risk is revealed by the case of a 7-year-old autistic child who allegedly communicated to his facilitator that he had been sexually abused by another adult (Heckler, 1994). Allegations of child abuse have surfaced during other facilitated communication sessions at a startling rate; 13 percent of the children in Biklen's (1990) sample "communicated" such allegations. Should such reports be taken seriously?

Other "miracle cures" have plagued the field of mental retardation and autism, including vitamin therapies, special diets, and sensory stimulation devices. As long as there are clinicians untrained in the scientific method and parents desperate for a cure, such "miracles" will emerge regularly. The only defenses are well-trained practitioners who know how to evaluate the scientific merits of treatment techniques and well-informed "consumers" who demand information about the methods by which innovative treatments have been validated.

Thinking Critically

We noted that supporters of facilitated communication believe that empirical research is an unnatural and unfair test of the treatment. How do you evaluate such criticisms?

- What is there about Cabay's (1994) study that is "unnatural"?
- How much confidence should we have in treatments that cannot be supported by empirical research?

and they tended to imply causes that many people found unacceptable, if not inaccurate. According to Gerald Coles (1987), the concept of a learning *disability* became the perfect solution because it implied that something *within* the child was responsible for academic failure, thereby sparing families or schools from admitting their possible contributions to these problems.

Defining and Identifying Learning Disabilities

Many organizations use their own definitions of *learning disability.* Some definitions emphasize a particular presumed cause, even though no specific cause of learning disabilities has received convincing empirical support. For example, the definition of learning disability proposed by the National Joint Committee for Learning Disabilities (Hammill et al., 1981) states that these disorders are intrinsic to the individual and are presumed to be due to central nervous system dysfunction. However, there is no reliable way to assess the presumed CNS deficit in individual cases (Berninger, 1994).

Many other definitions of learning disability revolve around indicating what the term does *not* mean. For example, Public Law 94-142 states that the term *learning disability* does not include children whose learning problems are primarily the result of mental retardation, physical handicaps, emotional disturbances, or disadvantaged environments. Of course, most underachieving children do have emotional, social, and family problems (Silver, 1992), making it impossible in most cases to determine whether emotional and social problems are the result or the cause of the child's learning difficulties.

More recent definitions of learning disabilities focus on the severity of academic deficiencies. Many school districts define learning disabilities by comparing a child's scores on an achievement test with his or her score on an IQ test. If the achievement test score is more than 1 or 2 standard deviations below the IQ score, a learning disability is said to exist. Other school districts define learning disabilities as a deviation from grade level, without regard to IQ.

The DSM-IV states that a **learning disorder** is diagnosed when "achievement in reading, writing or mathematics is substantially below that expected for age, schooling, *and* level of intelligence." *Substantially below* is defined as a discrepancy of 2 or more standard deviations between achievement and IQ.

The case of Carl illustrates the IQ discrepancy method. All the tests given to Carl were based on an average population score of 100 with a standard deviation of 15. He received an IQ score of 100, and scores of 65 and 89 on tests of reading and mathematics, respectively. Because the reading score was more than 2 standard deviations below the mean (i.e., 2 × 15, or 30 points below average), Carl was diagnosed as having a learning disability.

Variability in definitions and diagnostic criteria make a precise determination of the overall prevalence of learning disabilities impossible. However, estimates of the prevalence of learning disabilities range from 2 to 10 percent of the general population, with approximately 5 percent of public school students receiving educational services under this diagnosis (APA, 1994). Regardless of how learning disability is defined, diagnosed males outnumber females by a 3:1 to 5:1 ratio (McGuinness, 1985). However, this gender difference may reflect a certain amount of bias in referrals. Because they are less apt than boys to show inattentive, hyperactive, or disruptive behaviors, girls with learning problems may receive less help and attention than their male peers do (Berry, Shaywitz, & Shaywitz, 1985).

The DSM-IV differentiates learning disabilities by area of academic deficit, specifying disorders of reading, mathematics, and written expression. There is considerable overlap among these areas of poor achievement, especially in reading and writing deficits. Another, *nonverbal* type of learning disability is characterized by relatively normal reading and spelling, but difficulties in visual–motor skills, mathematics, and social skills (Semrud-Clikeman & Hynd, 1991).

Reading Disabilities

Reading disabilities, often called *dyslexia,* are the most frequent learning problem, accounting for about 80 percent of learning disabilities in U.S. schools (APA, 1994). Contrary to popular belief, poor readers do not perceive letters and words as reversed (e.g., mistaking *was* for *saw*) any more often than good readers do (Black, 1973; Kaufman & Biren, 1977). And poor readers do not make abnormal eye movements, nor do they benefit from special glasses (Coles, 1987).

The most consistent differences between good and poor readers are *linguistic.* Poor readers tend to use shorter and less complex sentences and make more grammatical errors when speaking. These differences do not necessarily indicate that language deficits lead to reading problems. Poor expressive language may simply be one negative consequence of limited exposure to reading material.

Other linguistic differences, more closely related to the reading process, may have causal significance. Poor readers have more difficulty remembering verbal information than good readers do (Vellutino & Scalon, 1985). They also have problems in *phonetic decoding,* the ability to decipher and use the smallest sound units of language, called *phonemes* (e.g., the *sh* sound in *show*). Good readers probably learn to read by first sounding out words, holding those sounds in memory, and then blending the sounds to form words (e.g., *sh* + *o* = *show*). Poor readers, like Carl, seem less able than good readers to use phonemes to help them read (Waterman & Lewandowski, 1993). Limited phonological awareness in preschoolers predicts subsequent poor reading and spelling in elementary school (Stuart & Masterson, 1992).

Causes of Reading Disabilities

Problems in phonetic decoding are regarded by many reading specialists as the primary deficit in most cases of reading disability. But it is unclear whether such problems stem from genetic factors, neurological dysfunction, the nature or quality of teaching strategies, or parent–child interactions that influence the child's motivation to learn.

Genetic and Neurological Factors. Reading problems tend to run in families. The probability of a reading disability is higher than average in the offspring and other first-degree relatives of poor readers (Berninger, 1994). Fathers and sons in poor-reading families show similar patterns of specific deficits (Hoien et al., 1989). Consistently, research has shown a higher concordance of reading disability in monozygotic twins than in dizygotic twins (DeFries, Fulker, & Labuda, 1987; Olson et al., 1989). Finally, about 30 to 40 percent of the difference in reading achievement throughout the population appears to be due to genetic factors, with the remaining 60 to 70 percent due to environmental influences (Berninger, 1994).

Investigators have tried to find the specific locations of genes that might influence reading ability by using a statistical procedure called **linkage analysis.** This procedure is based on the fact that, when two genes are located near each other, they are likely to be inherited together. Researchers study the behavior of multiple generations to see whether the presence of learning disability is associated with any traits

with known genetic locations, such as eye color or blood type. If the association between reading disability and another trait exceeds chance levels, it is likely that the gene influencing reading disability is on the same chromosome as the gene controlling the other trait. The few linkage analysis studies conducted so far suggest that genes on chromosomes 1, 6, and 15 may be involved in reading ability (Cardon et al., 1994), so it is likely that multiple genes influence reading problems (Berninger, 1994).

How might genes affect reading? As indicated earlier, genes influence behavior by producing enzymes that ultimately determine the structure and functioning of the central nervous system, including the brain. Do the brains of good and poor readers differ? Several brain-imaging studies suggest that the brains of poor readers show unusual patterns of hemispheric asymmetries. In about 70 percent of normal adults, the *planum temporale* (the back and upper region of the temporal lobe) is larger and longer on the left side of the brain than on the right (Geschwind & Levitsky, 1968), as Figure 4.5 shows. (Note that the left temporal lobe is specialized to handle language.) In contrast, the brains of poor readers occasionally either show planum *symmetry* (both sides are approximately the same size and shape) or reversed asymmetry in which the left planum is smaller than the right (e.g., Hynd et al., 1990). A third pattern in which there are atypical planum characteristics on only the right hemisphere has recently been discovered (Leonard et al., 1993). The symmetry of neurons in the *medial geniculate nuclei,* a part of the thalamus that relays auditory information to the temporal lobe, has also been investigated. Poor readers have been found to have smaller

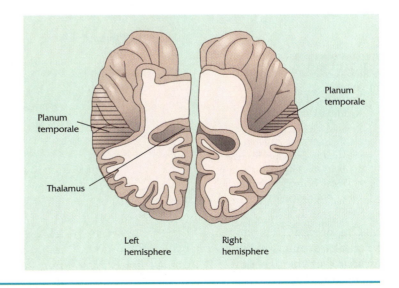

FIGURE 4.5

Brain Asymmetries and Reading Disabilities

For most adults, the planum temporale is larger in the left hemisphere than in the right. However, this pattern is sometimes not seen in adults who are poor readers. In some of these cases, the planum temporale on both sides of the brain are of equal size, and in other cases, the planum temporale is larger in the right hemisphere than in the left.

neurons on the left side than on the right; normal readers show no such difference (Galaburda, Menard, & Rosen, 1994).

These findings should be interpreted cautiously. Many neuroimaging studies are marred by major problems—chiefly, the absence of control groups, small numbers of subjects, and inadequate measures of reading ability (Hynd et al., 1991). Moreover, only about 7 percent of the brains of poor readers examined before 1990 were considered abnormal by pathologists (Filipek & Kennedy, 1991). Indeed, the differences between the brains of good and poor readers are usually subtle and rarely indicate abnormal brain development. Finally, a significant number of relatives of poor readers who have brain asymmetries or other subtle neurological anomalies read normally (Leonard et al., 1993), suggesting that environmental factors play a large role in determining reading skill.

The Role of Schooling and Parenting. Reading problems may reflect failures in how reading is taught. Most students receive group instruction in reading, which is notoriously ineffective for pinpointing reading problems, giving corrective feedback, or providing opportunities for rehearsal. The average learner spends less than 1 minute each day reading aloud (Graden, Thurlow, & Ysseldyke, 1983). As the school year progresses in most classrooms, poor readers are given fewer and fewer opportunities to read orally (Berninger, 1994). Furthermore, reading curricula tend not to be matched to individual needs and learning styles.

Parents, too, may influence reading problems by affecting children's readiness to learn and by reinforcing progress and effort. **Learning readiness** refers to cognitive and emotional factors that aid or deter the learning process. These factors include the child's expectations of success or failure (self-efficacy), motivation to persist in the face of obstacles, and emotional responses to corrective feedback. One child may approach the learning task with confidence, undaunted by initial failure and correction; another may become emotionally fragile and resistant after making the first mistake. These characteristics of the child have been related to the quality and quantity of parent–child interaction. Parents who foster secure attachment, play in a child-directed manner, buffer family stress, and frequently reinforce academic gains are more likely to have children who succeed in school (Hess & McDevitt, 1984).

Based on the limited evidence now available, reading disability appears to develop from a combination of biological and environmental factors, none of which is the single cause of reading problems. Suppose a child inherits a predisposition for phonological dysfunction because of left temporal lobe anomalies. If the child then experiences poor parenting or teaching that ignores phonological awareness, reading disability becomes highly probable. As Figure 4.6 suggests, however, this outcome is not inevitable. If this child were instead to receive optimal parenting and reading instruction in phonological strategies

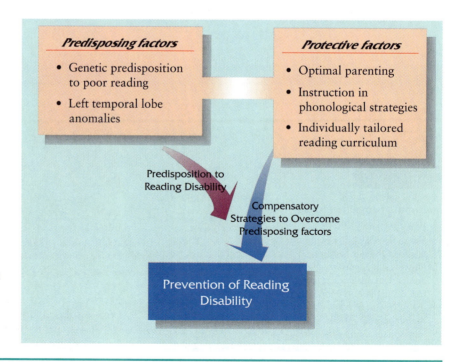

FIGURE 4.6

Protective Factors Against Reading Disabilities

Even if a child is genetically predisposed or neurobiologically prepared to develop a reading disability, the chances of a disorder can be reduced by parents who work closely with the child to promote good reading through careful phonological reading instruction and by a reading curriculum in school that is tailored to the needs of the individual student.

(e.g., how to divide a word into its phonetic parts), he or she could develop *compensatory strategies* that would lessen the impact of biological vulnerabilities. Young children can be taught to overcome phonological weaknesses (Alexander et al., 1991; Ball & Blackman, 1991). Thus, learning disabilities are not explained by neurology alone; they result from the interplay of biological features and teaching and parenting variables.

Prevention and Treatment of Learning Disabilities

Reading specialists have hypothesized that there is a critical period of development between ages 5 and 7 in which reading and writing skills are most easily learned; thereafter, these skills are acquired with increasing difficulty (Berninger, 1994). Receptiveness to instruction during this period is associated with phonological awareness; therefore, an ideal program for preventing reading disabilities would first screen children for deficits in phonetic decoding. Once they are identified, these children could then be given individual, intensive training in how to divide words into their phonetic parts.

The only treatment for academic deficiencies with clear positive effects is educational intervention. Various noneducational treatments have been explored over the years—medication, dietary modifications, special glasses, visual exercises—all of which have been found to lack scientific credibility.

Educational interventions for learning disabilities have usually focused on reading problems, although recent programs are beginning to stress the teaching of writing skills and mathematics (e.g., Parmar, Cawley, & Miller, 1994). Two methods of reading instruction have been emphasized: one is a *whole language* approach that teaches the child to recognize whole words based on the meaning of the material being read, and the other is a *sound-based* approach that teaches word recognition in terms of phonetic decoding. Many children learn to read regardless of the teaching method used, and the minority that require special help benefit from an individualized approach that combines phonetic and meaning-based procedures (Lyon, 1985). Many problem readers also benefit from direct instruction in the comprehension of reading passages (Berninger, 1994).

In Review

Current definitions of learning disabilities:
- avoid assumptions about the causes of the disability; and
- focus on the discrepancy between the child's academic achievement and IQ or grade level.

Reading disabilities:
- are the most frequent learning problem;
- may be due to an impaired ability to decipher and effectively use the smallest sound units of language, called *phonemes;* and
- might best be understood as arising from a combination of a genetic predisposition for phonological dysfunction exacerbated by parenting and teaching practices that ignore the child's phonological problems.

Revisiting the Case of Jordan

Throughout this chapter, we have focused on children with developmental disabilities, saying little about their families. The families of these children have higher rates of divorce and single parenthood than families of nondisabled children (Gath, 1977; Hodapp & Krasner, 1995), and the normal siblings of children with disabilities experience higher-than-average levels of psychosocial problems (e.g., Gold, 1993). These complications have led to the realization that treatment must address the family as well as the individual with the disability (Egel & Powers, 1989). Furthermore, clinical experience suggests that family relationships shape the way these children respond to stressful situations and to treatment.

Jordan's case demonstrates the importance of the family in the treatment of children with disabilities. Despite the development of a successful school program for self-injurious behavior, Jordan's behaviors continued to worsen at home. He often threw or broke things when he was angry or began to bite his hands or bang his head when he was under stress or was unable to get his way. Meanwhile, his parents' conflicts escalated, and Jordan's adolescent sister was resentful of the time her mother devoted to Jordan. Jordan's parents wanted the psychologist to devise a home-based behavior modification program similar to the one at school, but the family environment was not conducive to such a program, which required consistency and emotional stability from the participants.

In Jordan's case, the family participated in a short series of sessions focusing on marital communication and problem solving, some family sessions aimed at improving communication between the daughter and her parents, and in-home parent training in applied behavior analysis. Because this family had close attachments and loving relationships, major improvements occurred. Eventually, a behavioral program for self-injurious and destructive behavior was successfully implemented at home.

The outcome for Jordan has been mixed. The initial interventions (with periodic updating) kept Jordan's behavior under reasonable control at home and at school through his early and middle-adolescent years. He made few gains, however, in cognition, language, or adaptive behaviors, which were severely limited by his cerebral palsy. Jordan developed a severe seizure disorder in late adolescence that did not respond to antiseizure medications. At the same time, his destructive and self-injurious behavior returned, a possible effect of the seizures or a side effect of the medications used to treat the seizures. Caring for Jordan at home became increasingly difficult, and at age 17 he was moved to a group home in the community. At age 21, Jordan was relatively free of seizures and was responding well to a behavior modification program.

What does the future hold for children who, like Jordan, have severe multiple disabilities? Behavioral programs for reducing self-injurious behavior will likely become more sophisticated, with a continuing trend toward less frequent use of aversive consequences. Studies are needed to better understand the developmental course of self-injurious behaviors, how they are related to various environmental conditions, and how nonverbal persons use them to communicate (Koegel & Koegel, 1989). There are also large gaps in our understanding of how the family system affects the social and emotional development of children with retardation and how such children affect the family environment (Hodapp, Burack, & Zigler, 1990).

The current state of research in mental retardation, pervasive developmental disorders, and learning disabilities offers hope for progress on several fronts. Future studies of autism will likely clarify the relationship between specific brain structures and psychological processes. New interventions may be developed that teach autistic children to engage in joint attention or to guess about what another person is thinking during social interchanges. Meanwhile, preschool children may soon be routinely screened for phonetic decoding skills and provided with early phonological instruction as a strategy for preventing reading disabilities. Research may lead to the identification of new genetic causes of reading disabilities or mental retardation.

Advances in the diagnosis of genetic syndromes are likely to present new dilemmas for parents and professionals (Dykens, Hodapp, & Leckman, 1994; Sherman, 1992). For example, we can now screen for premutations of fragile X—essentially identifying a genetic vulnerability one or two generations in advance of the full expression of the syndrome. This raises several practical and ethical questions: What risk factors should be emphasized when scientists select families to screen: the presence of mild mental retardation, an autistic spectrum disorder, or something as common as a learning disability? Who should have access to such information, with its possibly stigmatizing effects? These questions will occupy researchers and policymakers in the years ahead.

SUMMARY

Domains of Development

A developmental disability is a lifelong impairment in mental or physical functioning originating in childhood. Substantial limitations in adaptive behaviors are also required to diagnose a developmental disability. Cases of mental retardation and autism meet these criteria. Learning disabilities also originate in childhood and can have lifelong effects; however, they have less impact on adaptive behaviors than mental retardation and autism do. A developmental disability is often identified with the help of standardized tests of a child's progress in key domains of development, which include motor skills, language, cognition, and adaptive behavior.

Mental Retardation

Mental retardation is a developmental disability characterized by subaverage intellectual functioning and impairments in adaptive behavior. The vast majority of persons with mental retardation are in the mild range of retardation, about 10 percent are in the moderate category, and the remainder are in the severe or profound categories. Organic causes—such as genetic disorders, prenatal problems, perinatal and postnatal diseases, and childhood head injuries—account for 25 to 50 percent of all cases of mental retardation, with most children having IQs below 50. The most common genetic disorder involving mental retardation is Down syndrome; it results from an error during reproduction that is not passed on to future generations. Fragile X is the most common heritable form of mental retardation.

About 50 to 75 percent of cases of mental retardation are without clear biologic cause and are typically in the mild range; they are said to have cultural–familial causes, presumably related to multiple psychosocial disadvantages. Behavior modification programs can be effective in teaching people with retardation a wide range of basic skills. In the United States, normalization and mainstreaming have been promoted recently as principles for the education of people with mental retardation.

Autistic Disorders

Autism, in its typical form, is characterized by (1) severe deficits in reciprocal social relationships, (2) poor language skills, and (3) stereotyped patterns of behavior, activities, or interests. Some individuals show deficits in all of these areas, but others show partial or atypical versions of the full syndrome. A genetic basis for autism is suggested both by twin studies and an elevated rate of autism among siblings of autistic children. Several psychological deficits are associated with autism, including selective inattention to faces and other social stimuli, theory of mind deficits, and problems in executive functions. Behavior modification programs and educational interventions can enhance the academic and social functioning of autistic children, and medications have had some success in reducing disruptive or self-injurious behavior. However, the overall prognosis for people with pervasive developmental disorders is usually guarded at best.

Learning Disabilities

Definitions of learning disabilities have focused on the discrepancy between a child's academic achievement and IQ or grade level, usually requiring a discrepancy of 2 standard deviation units. Reading deficits are the most common learning disability. Poor readers have problems in phonetic decoding, that is, the use of phonemes to help them read. The causal basis for reading disability involves a combination of factors. There may be a genetic vulnerability for phonological dysfunction that leads to significant reading problems if environmental risk factors are present as well.

KEY TERMS

adaptive behavior, p. 121

amniocentesis, p. 129

amniotic fluid, p. 129

applied behavior analysis, p. 130

Asperger's disorder, p. 140

childhood disintegrative disorder, p. 141

cerebral palsy, p. 123

cognition, p. 119

developmental disability, p. 118

Down syndrome, p. 123

dual diagnosis, p. 122

expressive language, p. 119

facilitated communication, p. 144

fetal alcohol syndrome (FAS), p. 127

fine motor skill, p. 119

fragile X syndrome, p. 125

generalization, p.130

gross motor skill, p. 119

habituation speed, p. 120

hypoxia, p. 128

inclusion, p. 134

joint attention, p. 137

learning disorder, p. 146

learning readiness, p. 148

linkage analysis, p. 147

mainstreaming, p. 134

maintenance, p. 130

mental age, p. 120

mental retardation, p. 121

normalization, p. 133

pervasive developmental disorder (PDD), p. 136

phenylketonuria (PKU), p. 127

receptive language, p. 119

Rett's disorder, p. 141

sex-linked chromosome, p. 125

shaping, p. 130

spectrum disorder, p. 135

teratogens, p. 127

theory of mind, p. 139

trisomy 21, p. 123

typical autism, p. 135

visual–motor skill, p. 119

Williams syndrome, p. 126

5

Stress, Sleep, and Adjustment Disorders

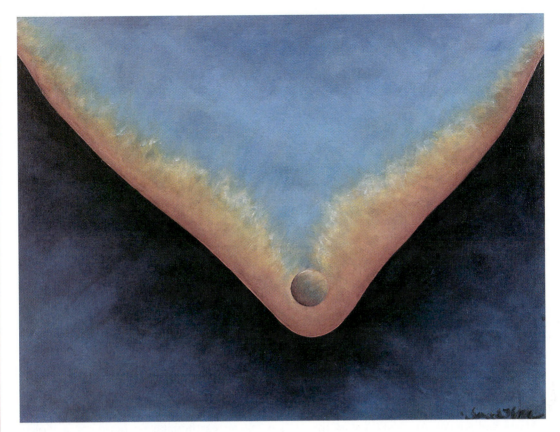

Canyon Planet by Susan Sistare Thorne, 1981. Oil on canvas, 23" x 30". Private Collection. Courtesy of Sistare.

From the Case of Officer Schuler

Within 30 minutes on the afternoon of October 17, 1993, four citizens of Louisville, Kentucky, called the police. They all complained about a man walking up and down their street with a bandana covering his face, shouting "The war's over, come out of your homes, the war's over." The callers noted that the man was well known in the area as an oddball who frequently acted "crazy." One caller added, "People are getting pretty afraid of him; he's real bad this time."

After the second call, two Louisville police officers were dispatched to check on the man. Officers Marty Harris and Sandy Schuler arrived at the scene within seconds of each other. They parked their cruisers and approached the subject, who jogged away from them. Officer Schuler shouted at the man to stop, but he continued to trot toward a house at the end of the street. He reached the house and jumped to the porch; both officers slowly walked up the steps to the porch and asked the man to stop and talk with them.

As the man opened the door of the house, Officer Schuler stepped to the porch, and the man suddenly turned and flailed his arms, hitting her in the face. Officer Harris leapt to the porch to assist Schuler, and they wrestled with the subject. He was uncontrollably strong, and both officers absorbed several hard blows. Suddenly, the man pulled a knife from his waistband and slashed Officer Harris. Schuler backed off the porch and drew her revolver, shouting at Harris to get away from the suspect.

Officer Harris lost control of the subject's arm and tried to roll away as the man again swung at him with the knife. The knife cut Harris's left ear; another blow broke his nose. With Officer Harris still within arms' reach of the subject, Officer Schuler fired four times at the subject, who crumpled at Harris's feet, dropping the knife as he fell. Officer Harris ran to his cruiser and radioed for an emergency care unit. The subject, pronounced dead at the University Medical Center, was identified as Drexel Root, 35, who had been hospitalized several times for treatment of schizophrenia.

Immediately after the incident, Officers Harris and Schuler were temporarily relieved of their patrol duties, as required by departmental policy. They received brief (but mandatory) psychological counseling authorized by the department for officers involved in "critical incidents" because, often, psychological problems arise from them. In this case, the local media were soon swarming over the houses of Officers Harris and Schuler. TV reporters kept a vigil outside Officer Schuler's duplex for 3 days, hoping to interview her. One enterprising newspaper reporter asked several of Officer Harris's neighbors whether he had a hot temper or stirred up trouble in the neighborhood. The barrage of media attention to the police officer's shooting of Drexel Root went on for more than 3 months, finally dying down after a coroner's jury ruled the shooting justifiable.

Officers Harris and Schuler remained off work for almost 1 month. Marty Harris attended his three mandated counseling sessions but denied to his counselor that he was suffering any psychological difficulties. Privately, however, he admitted to other officers that he was having a lot of trouble sleeping, that he and his wife were arguing more often, and that he dreaded coming to work because of the chance that someone would "bring up that damned Root thing again." But after a while, Marty seemed to forget about the shooting. His life returned to its normal routine.

Sandy Schuler was a willing participant in her counseling. She admitted having two or three nightmares a week about the shooting. Even more upsetting to her was the fact that her stomach was "knotted up" all the time; she couldn't remember the last time she had really felt hungry. At her last counseling session, Sandy broached a subject she thought she would never consider—maybe police work just wasn't worth it. She was going to give some thought to quitting the force. ■

*S*evere trauma such as this incident usually leaves psychological marks on its victims, and Officers Schuler and Harris were no exceptions. Their sleep problems, physical complaints, and personal insecurities were all signs of stress. What is stress, and how does it affect people? Are some stressors more disruptive than others? What are the best ways to cope with stress? What emotions do people feel when experiencing stress? Can stress cause mental disorders? We

will consider these questions in this chapter. In Chapter 6 we will focus on the relationship between stress, psychological factors, and physical illnesses and health.

What Is Stress?

Stress is a process that occurs when environmental or social threats (called *stressors*) place demands on individuals. Stress is an ongoing process that involves interactions between environments and people. The way in which an individual experiences stress depends on (1) the nature and timing of the stressors, (2) the person's psychological characteristics and social situation, and (3) biochemical variables that influence stress responses. Figure 5.1 presents a summary of this process.

Types of Stressors

Stressors can include unpredictable traumas—experiencing an earthquake or flood, or a violent encounter such as the one involving Officers Harris and Schuler. Even if such events happen only once in a person's lifetime, they are often so powerful that they can leave lasting psychological scars. Attempts to prevent such traumas from happening in the first place are, as the Prevention section on page 156 indicates, the best intervention strategy.

Traumatic events are surprisingly frequent. In one nationwide telephone survey of 4,008 adult women (Resnick et al., 1993), over 35 percent had been victimized by one of four major crimes (rape, other sexual assault, physical assault with a weapon, or the killing of a family member). An additional one third of the women had suffered a noncrime trauma such as a serious accident, a natural disaster, encounters in which the woman was seriously injured, and situations in which the woman feared being injured or killed or saw someone else seriously injured or killed.

Children are also frequently exposed to violent trauma. When a national sample of adolescents were asked about their experiences with serious trauma (Boney-McCoy & Finkelhor, 1995),

- 18 percent of boys between the ages of 10 and 16 reported being victimized by an assault that involved a weapon or resulted in physical injury;
- 15 percent of girls reported victimization in the form of sexual assault; and
- 6 percent of children reported being the victims of attempted kidnappings.

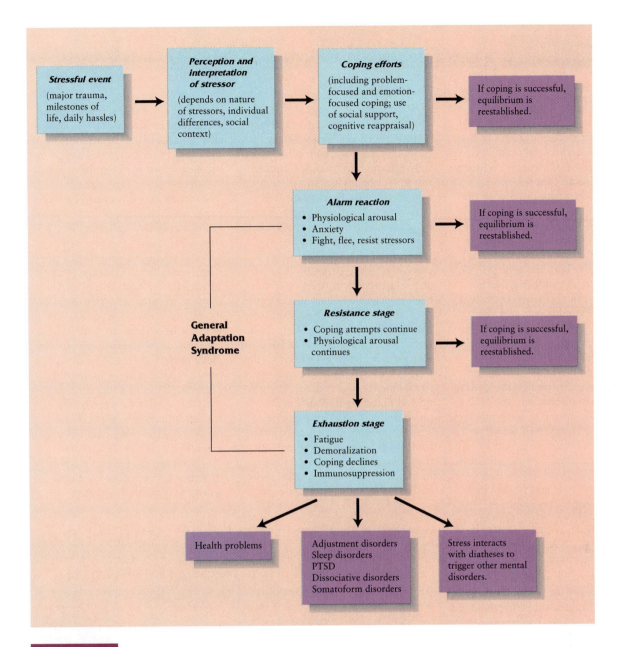

FIGURE 5.1

The Process of Stress

More predictable stressors arise from life's milestones such as getting married, having children, starting college, or beginning a new job. Other common stressful events include academic setbacks, financial losses, occupational failures, marital difficulties, unemployment, and the illness or death of loved ones. These events happen regularly as people live their lives.

Many stressors are linked to occupational demands. For example, air-traffic controllers are under constant pressure to make quick, life-and-death decisions; waitresses are urged by customers to hurry; and underground miners live with the constant danger of cave-ins. In general, jobs that make many demands but allow little control over how and when to meet these demands generate the greatest stress (Karasek, 1979).

Finally, even relatively minor events such as car trouble, getting stuck in a traffic jam, or losing your lecture notes the night before an exam can be

Prevention   Stopping Stressors Before They Start: The Case of Sexual Assault

National surveys suggest that over half of all college women have suffered a sexual assault involving forced sexual contact or activity (Koss, Gidycz, & Wisniewski, 1987) and that the majority of victims were acquainted with their assailants before the assault. Research has uncovered several risk factors associated with sexual assault. For example, rape victims tend to have suffered a disproportionately high number of sexual assaults prior to their most recent assault. Acquaintance rapes are more frequent (1) when both the victim and the assailant have been drinking or using drugs, (2) on dates when the man pays all the expenses, and (3) when the date is at an isolated location. Several colleges and universities have incorporated this information into rape prevention programs aimed at changing attitudes about sexuality, challenging rape myths and sex-role stereotypes, and improving women's coping responses in potentially dangerous situations.

In the typical rape prevention program, participants discuss several facts and myths about rape, learn how to avoid situations involving heavy use of alcohol, practice resisting pressure for unwanted sexual activity, and role-play other strategies for protecting themselves. The programs try to help women change behaviors and to dispel the notion that victims cause sexual assault. They also strive to minimize the blaming of women as the cause of sexual trauma. Evaluation of the success of these programs in preventing assaults is just beginning.

In one large experimental study (Hanson & Gidycz, 1993), 181 college women participated in a 9-week acquaintance rape prevention program while 165 others were assigned to a no-program control group. The prevention program was designed to debunk common

myths about rape, educate women about how to protect themselves against rape, alter risky dating practices, improve communication between men and women concerning sexual behavior, and prevent sexual assaults. Participants discussed rape myths and protective behaviors, watched videotapes that depicted risky situations and the protective behaviors that women can use in these situations, and shared general information about how to prevent acquaintance rape.

The effects of the program were assessed 9 weeks later. The prevention program appeared effective for women who had never been victimized before the study; 14 percent of the women in the control group reported that they had suffered a sexual victimization during the period studied compared with only 6 percent of the women in the prevention program. However, as the figure shows, among women who had histories of various types of

sexual victimization, there was no difference in the victimization rates of the program and control groups.

These results suggest that previous sexual assaults can be a potent risk factor for future assaults. What they do not explain is why prior sexual assault is such a strong risk for repeated victimization. Perhaps victimization lowers self-esteem so that a woman thinks she has already been so damaged that subsequent victimizations don't matter. Alternatively, victimization may convince a woman that she will not be wanted for any reason other than sex so she continues to place herself in sexually risky situations. Whatever the explanation, these results send a clear message for other prevention programs: the earlier the attempt at prevention, the better. If women participate in assault prevention services before they are ever victimized, it appears that the success of such services will be substantially greater.

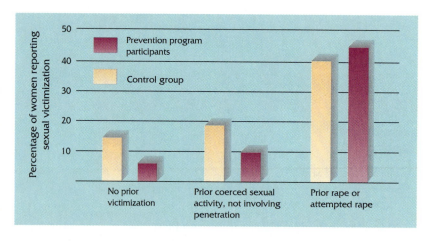

Prior Victimization and the Effects of a Sexual Assault Prevention Program

Nine weeks after participating in a rape prevention program, women were asked whether they had been sexually victimized (Hanson & Gidycz, 1993). Women in the prevention program who had not been previously victimized were half as likely to have been sexually victimized during this period as women who did not take part in the program. However, the program was not effective in reducing sexual revictimization for women with a history of victimization.

significant stressors. The effect is worse when several of these daily hassles pile up in a short period of time.

Individual Differences and Potential Stressors

Stress is the result of interacting biological, psychological, and sociocultural forces. It is not possible to understand stressful events and the effects they have on people unless the social and cultural environments in which stressors occur are also understood. People differ in the ways they respond to a stressful event, depending, in part, on the meaning they give to the event. These meanings are shaped by their personal histories as well as by numerous social and cultural forces.

Exposure to Stressors: Individual and Cultural Differences. Certain people seem more likely than others to repeatedly experience stressful events. What accounts for their greater risk of adversity? Perhaps some people just have more bad luck than others. However, other explanations are more probable. First, it is possible that certain people, as a result of poor social skills or long-term psychological handicaps, unintentionally bring about stressful events in their lives. Another possibility is that repeated financial or interpersonal setbacks have a cumulative effect so that one bad event (e.g., getting fired) leads to more problems (e.g., divorce) later on. Finally,

severe stressors such as violence might even cause changes in brain chemistry that could contribute to future problems. Experiments in which young hamsters were repeatedly attacked by older animals have shown that the brains of the youngsters became less sensitive to serotonin, a neurotransmitter involved in the restraint of aggression (Melloni, Delville, & Ferris, 1995). Depending on the environments they encountered as adults, these traumatized hamsters tended to be either overly aggressive or timid, bringing more stress into their lives in either case. Obviously all these factors might also interact, resulting in a series of life problems that are the result of biological processes, personal limitations, and previous adversities.

Ethnic differences, gender, and age can affect the frequency and types of stressors people encounter. Black Americans, for example, must confront a host of cultural and social stressors more frequently than White Americans (Anderson, 1989). Members of minority groups are more likely than White Americans to face poverty, discrimination in housing and jobs, difficulties in single parenting, and pressure to conform to the norms of the majority culture. Similarly, women are much more likely than men to suffer sexual assaults, a major source of trauma related to psychological problems in the United States. Women are also more likely to be single, custodial parents, a sta-

Connections

What role do stressors play in depression and suicide? See Chapter 9, pp. 308–309, 323.

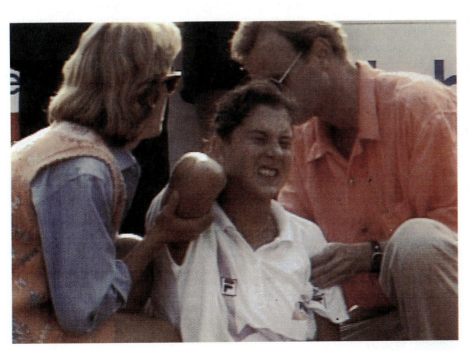

Because violent trauma destroys assumptions of security that most people enjoy, emotional scars often are slower to heal than physical wounds. Monica Seles had to take an indefinite leave from competitive tennis because of the emotional effects associated with being stabbed by a fan of her rival Steffi Graf.

tus accompanied by numerous major stressors. Older persons may be particularly likely to face the stressors of economic setbacks, deaths of loved ones, chronic illnesses, and gradual loss of physical abilities. Given the premium that American society places on physical beauty and a youthful countenance, older people often face the stress of discrimination against their changing appearance. Aging women are especially apt to encounter this stressor.

Reactions to Stressors: Individual and Cultural Differences. Individual and cultural differences also influence the impact that stressors have on people's lives. The harmful impact (and even the definition) of stressors seem to exist largely in the minds of those who experience them. The amount of *subjectively perceived* stress is more strongly correlated with later adjustment problems than is the sheer frequency of negative life events (Coyne & Downey, 1991). Not getting an A in a course may be demoralizing to one student; being turned down for a date may be much more upsetting to another. Unexpected stressors take more of a toll on a person than stressors that are expected and prepared for. Accordingly, many researchers who study stress ask individuals to describe their subjective feelings in order to learn as much as possible about how each person perceives upsetting life experiences. For example, Officer Schuler was interviewed at length about how she perceived the shooting incident, how she tried to cope with it, and how others responded to her afterward.

A host of factors determine how a person reacts to and copes with potential stressors. In addition to the stronger impact of unexpected events, several other characteristics tend to amplify the impact of stressors. For example, people usually feel more harmed by stressors

- when they have to cope alone rather than with the aid of social support;
- when they feel helpless or unable to control what is happening to them; and,
- when they believe that their stress was caused by the intentional or careless behavior of another.

In addition, people who are generally more optimistic and have greater self-esteem tend to be less threatened by stressors. A confident person may view many stressors as challenges or opportunities for growth. By contrast, an introverted or shy person, or one who lacks self-assurance may be traumatized by the same stressors. The point is that identical events affect individuals in different ways. Not all stressors are created equal, and neither are people's capacities for coping with them.

Measuring Stress

Psychologists have developed several scales to measure how much stress a person has suffered (Zimmerman, 1983). For example, the Schedule of Recent Experience (SRE) (Amundson, Hart, & Holmes, 1986) lists 42 events involving health, work, family, and social and financial difficulties. Examples include

- major changes in eating or sleeping habits;
- being fired from work;
- death of a relative or close friend;
- a violation of the law; and
- a major business readjustment.

Respondents check the events they have experienced during the previous 6, 12, 24, and 36 months. Each event is then given a predetermined weight based on prior research in which subjects rated the amount of adjustment that was needed to cope with it (1 = very little adjustment; 100 = maximal adjustment). These weights are added to give a total *Life Change Units* score, which provides an overall index of how much stress the person experienced in a given time period. In the 57-item Life Experiences Survey (LES) (Sarason, Johnson, & Siegel, 1978), the respondents themselves rate the positive or negative impact of an event. Allowing individualized ratings of events should make instruments such as the LES more sensitive to some of the individual and cultural influences described previously.

With the Hassles Scale (Kanner et al., 1981), subjects rate how much they have been hassled in the prior month by minor problems such as "misplacing or losing things," "unexpected company," "too many meetings," and "filling out forms." Small stressors such as these can have significant cumulative effects, especially when they happen to someone who is primed to react strongly. A woman who is paid an hourly wage might be much more upset by waiting in traffic jams on her way to work than is a woman who is paid a fixed salary. Other hassles may be especially upsetting to a person who has tried and failed to eliminate them, because each new occurrence serves as a reminder of another failure. For example, intrusions that make it hard to meet a deadline may be particularly upsetting to a chronic procrastinator who is trying to break this habit.

Effects of Stressors

Although stressors differ in many ways, they produce an amazingly similar pattern of closely entwined physiological and psychological reactions. Some of these reactions occur so quickly and automatically that we are unaware of them. Others extend over longer periods of time.

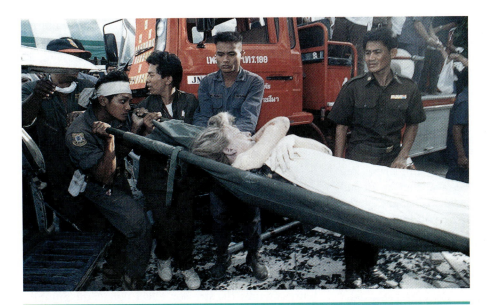

In stressful situations, time distortion is a common reaction. A faster-than-normal rate of psychological processing following a rapid stressor conveys an impression that more time has elapsed; a decreased rate of psychological activity during an extended stressor suggests that less time has passed. Both kinds of distortions may facilitate coping. With quick stressors, a sense of slowed time may suggest that evasive action is possible, despite the speed of the threat. With prolonged stressors, a feeling of shortened time may suggest to victims that they can "hold out" a little longer.

The physiological reactions to stress include hundreds of biochemical changes, but a clear pattern underlies them all. This pattern is *adaptive*; it helps people adjust to stressors. Hans Selye (1936) described this system of reactions as the **general adaptation syndrome** or **GAS.** He identified three stages of response to stressors:

1. The first stage is the *alarm reaction,* which Selye (1982) said is a "general call to arms of the body's defensive forces." This stage is sometimes called the **fight-or-flight response** because the autonomic nervous system is jolted into activity either to fight or to escape the stressor.

2. If a stressor lasts only a short time, the alarm reaction and its aftereffects are little more than an unpleasant reminder of how close disaster came. But if the stressor persists, or if new stressors are piled on top of old ones, alarm is followed by a **stage of resistance,** in which coping mechanisms are used to defend against the continuing effects of stress.

3. Eventually, if stressors continue long enough, the **stage of exhaustion** begins as a result of the long-term effects of resistance. Physical signs of exhaustion include indigestion, loss of weight, insomnia, and fatigue. When a person's energy is finally depleted, the ability to cope with stressors is lost, and the person suffers a "breakdown." In extreme situations, the stage of exhaustion can end in death.

In Review

Individuals undergo stress when they are exposed to environmental or social threats called *stressors*. Stressors can involve:

- severe traumatic events;
- milestones of development;
- occupational demands; and
- daily hassles.

Individuals' exposure and reactions to stressors can vary greatly depending on:

- ethnic differences, gender, and age;
- subjective differences in how people perceive and define a stressor; and
- differences in the timing, severity, or social context of a stressor.

Selye's General Adaptation Syndrome:

- is a description of the sequence of physiological changes occurring in response to a stressor; and
- consists of alarm, resistance, and exhaustion stages.

Reactions to Stress

Selye's description of the GAS was an attempt to organize the physiological changes underlying stressful experiences. It is a rough approximation of these changes, not a precise schedule. Selye did not focus on the psychological or behavioral changes that take place during stress, but, since the GAS was first described, other research has shed more light on these aspects of stress reactions. Table 5.1 summarizes key physical, emotional, behavioral, and cognitive reactions that typically occur during the stages of the GAS sequence. In this section, we will look at these reactions in more detail.

Physiological Reactions

Recall from Chapter 1 that the autonomic nervous system (ANS) regulates both the emotions and the body's responses to stressors. The ANS is divided into two branches—the sympathetic and parasympathetic nervous systems—that stimulate the endocrine glands, the heart, and many other organs. The two branches of the ANS usually work to balance each other; what one system speeds up, the other slows down. As Figure 5.2 shows, the sympathetic nervous system helps mobilize the body for fighting or fleeing stressors by releasing *epinephrine*, quickening the heartbeat, dilating the pupils of the eyes, sending more blood to the muscles, and inhibiting digestion. The parasympathetic branch conserves the body's supplies by constricting the pupils, slowing the heart, and stimulating digestion. It may also be activated during stress, but it generally does not help in coping with immediate stressors.

The Alarm Reaction. The alarm stage of the GAS is really a two-alarm alert, involving separate but integrated systems (Chrousos & Gold, 1992), as Figure 5.3 on page 162 illustrates. In response to a sudden stressor, a chemical relay system, known as the **hypothalamic-pituitary-adrenocortical (HPAC) axis,** swings into action. The hypothalamus first secretes a substance known as **corticotropin-releasing hormone (CRH).** CRH, in turn, jump starts a chain of coordinated physiological and biochemical defenses against the stressor. CRH signals the pituitary to secrete **adrenocorticotrophic hormone (ACTH),** which in turn directs the cortical (outer) portion of the adrenal glands to release **adrenal corticosteroids.** These chemical messengers, sometimes referred to as **stress hormones,** intensify the alarm and prepare the body to cope with the stressor. Activity in the parasympathetic division of the autonomic nervous system temporarily shuts down, directing energy away from the digestive and reproductive systems in favor of more immediately vital functions. Heart rate increases, as does blood pressure, respiration,

TABLE 5.1	Typical Reactions to Stress		
Stage	**Physiological reactions**	**Emotional reactions**	**Cognitive and behavioral reactions**
Alarm	• HPAC axis is activated; hypothalamus releases CRH • Sympathetic nervous system aroused • Epinephrine and norepinephrine activate organs throughout the body	• Fear • Excitement • Panic • Anger	• Mental activity increases, particularly attention and concentration • Fight or flee stressors
Resistance	• Body expends its energy supplies, but more slowly to resist stressors • Immune system weakens	• Tension • Anxiety • Defense mechanisms • Insomnia	• Cognitive appraisal of stressor • Organize efforts at coping • Emotion-focused coping • Problem-focused coping • Elicit social support
Exhaustion	• Immunosuppression • Physical energies depleted • Weight loss • Organ damage • Death	• Hopelessness • Desperation • Insomnia • Helplessness	• Disorganized thinking • Impaired attention and concentration • Weakened coping efforts

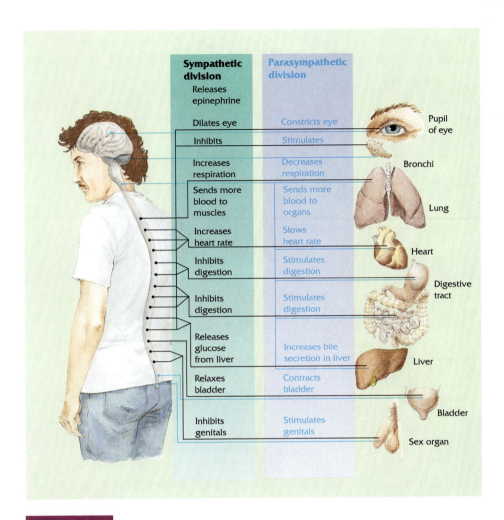

Sympathetic division

- Releases epinephrine
- Dilates eye
- Inhibits
- Increases respiration
- Sends more blood to muscles
- Increases heart rate
- Inhibits digestion
- Inhibits digestion
- Releases glucose from liver
- Relaxes bladder
- Inhibits genitals

Parasympathetic division

- Constricts eye
- Stimulates
- Decreases respiration
- Sends more blood to organs
- Slows heart rate
- Stimulates digestion
- Stimulates digestion
- Increases bile secretion in liver
- Contracts bladder
- Stimulates genitals

Pupil of eye
Bronchi
Lung
Heart
Digestive tract
Liver
Bladder
Sex organ

FIGURE 5.2

Activation of the Autonomic Nervous System
These are some of the changes involved when the sympathetic and parasympathetic divisions of the autonomic nervous system are activated.

and production of glucose. Pupils dilate, and muscles tense. At the same time, immune responses are slowed down in order to conserve energy for answering the immediate threat. The corticosteroids also direct the hypothalamus to inhibit further production of CRH, thereby completing a *negative feedback loop* in the HPAC axis.

The second initial alarm originates in the hypothalamus, which influences the brain stem and spinal cord to stimulate the adrenal medulla (inner part of the adrenal glands) to release the *catecholamines*, epinephrine and norepinephrine. The catecholamines stimulate heart rate and raise blood pressure; at the same time, they stimulate the central nervous system, increasing attention and concentration. These

changes make the alarmed person more vigilant to danger, but feelings of heightened anxiety, or even panic, may accompany these changes.

The two stress alarms interact to produce other biological changes. For example, they activate the production and release of *endogenous opioids*, opiates that exist naturally in the body. **Endorphins** are a special type of endogenous opioid that help regulate cardiovascular activity, relieve pain, and facilitate psychological coping with stress (McCubbin, 1993). The body "prescribes" endogenous opioids following a stressor to help people cope with intense threat. The stress-coping benefits of physical exercise may be linked to the fact that exercise helps release extra endorphins.

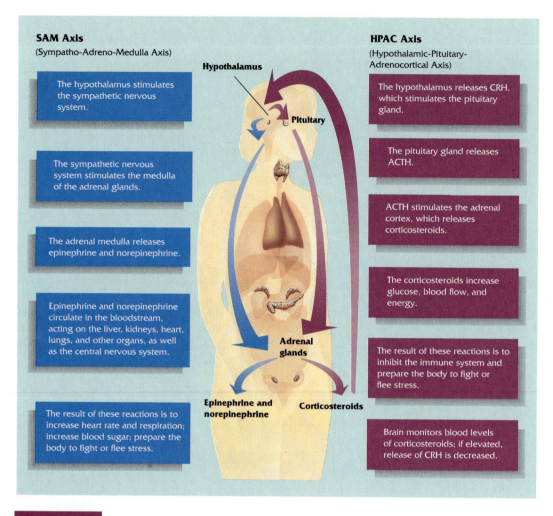

SAM Axis
(Sympatho-Adreno-Medulla Axis)

Hypothalamus

The hypothalamus stimulates the sympathetic nervous system.

Pituitary

The sympathetic nervous system stimulates the medulla of the adrenal glands.

The adrenal medulla releases epinephrine and norepinephrine.

Epinephrine and norepinephrine circulate in the bloodstream, acting on the liver, kidneys, heart, lungs, and other organs, as well as the central nervous system.

Adrenal glands

The result of these reactions is to increase heart rate and respiration; increase blood sugar; prepare the body to fight or flee stress.

Epinephrine and norepinephrine

HPAC Axis
(Hypothalamic-Pituitary-Adrenocortical Axis)

The hypothalamus releases CRH, which stimulates the pituitary gland.

The pituitary gland releases ACTH.

ACTH stimulates the adrenal cortex, which releases corticosteroids.

The corticosteroids increase glucose, blood flow, and energy.

The result of these reactions is to inhibit the immune system and prepare the body to fight or flee stress.

Corticosteroids

Brain monitors blood levels of corticosteroids; if elevated, release of CRH is decreased.

FIGURE 5.3

Physiological Stress Responses
The physiological reactions to stress involve a coordinated activation of the body via the brain, the sympathetic nervous system, and the endocrine glands.

Experiencing the Alarm Reaction. It is not uncommon to feel these short-term adjustments to a stressor after a near-accident in an automobile. Arms and legs shake; the heart thumps against the chest; and breaths come in gasps. Dizziness or lightheadedness is common. All these sensations are by-products of the sympathetic nervous system's rush to protect against threat. Likewise, if sickness and a knotted up stomach follow, it is partly because of rapid changes in the digestive system, which has become less relevant during the emergency.

During the alarm reaction, several perceptual, cognitive, and behavioral adjustments—all intended to increase the immediate ability to cope with a stressor—are quickly made. First, as noted earlier, attention is riveted on the stressor so it can be perceived more clearly. This heightened vigilance and concentration can take extreme forms. Survivors of automobile accidents commonly recall the experience as unfolding in slow motion; police officers who have been shot may remember seeing the bullet coming toward them. At the same time, focused attention is a distraction from many other stimuli. Shooting victims often report that they did not hear the blast of the gun, and assault victims may not recall suffering some of their injuries.

Reactions to Prolonged Stress. If a stressor persists long enough for a person to enter the resistance phase, the biological reactions can become harmful. Prolonged release of stress hormones can cause chronically high blood pressure, damage muscle tissue, and inhibit the body's ability to heal after injury. Sustained secretion of corticosteroids also produces wear and tear on various parts of the nervous system such as the hippocampus, and, because it suppresses the body's immune system, prolonged stress reduces the immune system's strength (Herbert & Cohen, 1993a). If the immune system remains suppressed for too long, the body becomes more vulnerable to various diseases (see Chapter 6). Many experts believe this **immunosuppression** is the basis for the association between stress and increased risks of physical illness such as cancer and certain autoimmune diseases (O'Leary, 1990).

Stress and the Immune System

Over 30 years of research have demonstrated that exposure to stressors can interfere with certain aspects of the immune response (Maier, Watkins, & Fleshner, 1994). This research initially relied on demonstrations with animals in which loud noises, electric shocks, cold temperatures, separation of newborns from mothers, and crowding suppressed aspects of the animals' immune systems. More recent research with human beings has found compromised immunity resulting from sleep deprivation, final examinations, divorce, loss of a loved one, and caring for chronically ill relatives (Herbert & Cohen, 1993a; Kiecolt-Glaser & Glaser, 1992). In addition, depressed or angry mood, negative thinking, and conditioned stimuli have been linked to altered immunity (Herbert & Cohen, 1993b).

Components of the Immune System. The immune system is the body's defense network against invading viruses and bacteria, known as **pathogens,** and against enemies originating in the body such as renegade cells that turn into tumors.

The immune defenses are divided into two main branches: innate immunity and specific immunity (Maier et al., 1994). *Innate immunity* is present from birth and is a first line of defense against pathogens in general. For example, the skin wards off all sorts of invader germs, and, internally, mucus contains chemicals that wipe out many viruses. If a pathogen should slip by the innate immunity trip line, *specific immunity* is called to arms. Specific immunity is acquired rather than innate, and it involves two defensive processes: (1) detection of the invading pathogen, and (2) destruction of these pathogens, mainly by T and B lymphocytes or **T cells** and **B cells,** as they are more commonly known.

Detection is accomplished mostly by special white blood cells called **macrophages.** Macrophages seek out pathogens by looking for specific proteins, called **antigens,** on their surfaces. When these antigens are found, macrophages devour them and spit out a digested form of the invader that can be killed off by T cells that are uniquely receptive to that invader. The macrophages use a chemical messenger called **interleukin-1** that summons various kinds of T cells and activates them for battle. Some of the T cells, called *T helpers,* secrete *interleukin-2,* which in turn calls more T cells and B cells to the battleground. Just the right killer T cell must be called in to destroy the pathogen, which is why it may take the body several days to gain sufficient specific-immunity troops to wage a successful fight.

T cells are produced in the thymus and B cells in the bone marrow. Their battle against pathogens is coordinated by the interleukins, and they play different roles in the battle. For example, B cells divide into plasma cells that release **antibodies** into the blood for widespread deployment throughout the body. Killer T cells use chemical warfare to destroy pathogens. Also, special **memory T cells** and B cells are brought into the fray. If any pathogens try to sneak back into the body days after their initial foray, these memory cells are ready to destroy them quickly. The success of inoculations in preventing various infections depends on their ability to introduce just enough of the enemy pathogen to trigger the activity of memory cells.

Suppressor T cells call off the troops once the battle against a pathogen has been won. Suppressor cells stop killer cells from going too far and turning against the body itself, a condition described as **autoimmune disease.** However, if suppressor cells come to outnumber helper and killer cells, they will ultimately weaken the immune system to the point that its defenses are essentially useless. Table 5.2 on page 164 summarizes some of the main components of the immune system.

The Relationship Between Stress Responses and Immune Functioning. How does the immune system respond to stressors? The nervous system and the immune system have two lines of connection. First, the autonomic nervous system innervates major immune system organs such as the spleen, bone marrow, and lymph nodes. Sympathetic nervous system neurons release the catecholamines, which are then received by receptors on immune cells. The second line involves the hypothalamic-pituitary-adrenocortical axis (HPAC). The HPAC axis is activated by stressors in a chemical chain reaction that results in the

| TABLE 5.2 | Some Key Elements of the Immune System |

Component	Function
Macrophage	Seek out, devour, and spit out digested pathogens
Interleukins	Used by macrophages to summon other immune system defenders such as T cells
B cells	Release antibodies into the blood to kill pathogens
T cells	
Killer T cells	Destroy pathogens by deploying chemicals in cells themselves
Helper T cells	Use interleukin-2 to recruit other B cells and T cells.
Memory T cells	Allow immune system to activate more quickly when it recognizes familiar antigens
Suppressor T cells	Stop killer cell activity

cortical part of the adrenal glands secreting **gluco-corticoids,** the steroid hormone that the body uses to fight stress. T cells and B cells have receptors for the glucocorticoids, thereby creating a specific mechanism by which stress can exert an influence on immune functioning.

The relationship between a stressor and changes in the immune system is delicate and selective. Identical stressors affect people in different ways (Krantz & Manuck, 1984). For example, a socially isolated person often suffers a substantially greater amount of immunosuppression than does someone who can turn to close friends for aid (Andersen, Kiecolt-Glaser, & Glaser, 1994). The nature of the stressor can also make a difference. Brief stressors, such as the kind studied in most research laboratories, often increase killer cells, but exposure to long-term naturalistic stressors usually results in a decline in immunological strength (Andersen et al., 1994). Finally, the same stressor may affect only selected aspects of immunity (e.g., the number of T cells), leaving other aspects (the amount of antibody released) untouched.

Some defenses of the immune system are redundant. If a stressor disrupts one aspect of immunity, some other part of the system may be able to compensate for the suppressed function so that the endpoint level of immunity is maintained.

The biochemical foundations of stress responses and immune defenses help explain how stressors suppress immune functioning, in turn increasing the risk for illness. Both stress responses and immune system defenses require large amounts of energy. The fight-or-flight nature of the alarm reaction calls for energy to be transferred to the muscles and brain immediately. The immune defenses, on the other hand, require that energy be directed almost entirely to other systems, such as white blood cell production and temperature increases, involved in inflammation at

the site of an injury or infection. Faced with both the immediate threat of a stressor and the more leisurely progress of a pathogen, the body responds to the imminent danger first, thus depriving the immune system. Stress-induced immunosuppression is usually adaptive in the short run, but, when stress responses are maintained for too long, the costs of continued immunosuppression appear in the form of greater susceptibility to disease and slowed recovery from illness.

Coping with Stressors

Individuals cope with stress in many ways (Lazarus, 1993). **Coping** refers to people's efforts at modifying or tolerating stressors (Folkman & Lazarus, 1980). How successfully a person copes with a stressor depends on the individual, the stressor itself, and the context in which the stressor is experienced. People often change their coping strategies from one situation to another. They may even select different coping strategies as a single, stressful event unfolds.

Types of Coping. People who try to reduce stress by directly solving a problem are using **problem-focused coping.** Problem-focused coping is aimed at changing the stressor itself. For example, if daily arguments between roommates are a major source of stress, one roommate might try to change the stressor by moving out, by asking the other roommate to move out, by trying to resolve the disagreements, or by trying new activities that would help them become better friends.

People also attempt to change the way they think about a stressor so that, even if they cannot eliminate it, they can at least make it less upsetting. This strategy is known as **cognitive reappraisal,** and it is often a powerful tool for reducing stress responses.

The person on the left has just learned that she has not been offered the job she was seeking. Depending on how the woman views this event, she may or may not feel stressed. Cognitive reappraisals are a major way some people deal with potentially stressful experiences.

Freud describes another type of cognitive coping, called defense mechanisms, which are psychological maneuvers that help protect a person from anxiety. If *denial* is used to cope with a roommate, a person might claim that, for roommates, they actually get along pretty well compared with other people. Another defensive strategy would be to *project* the blame for the conflict onto the other roommate, concluding that no one could get along with someone *this* obnoxious. A more mature form of psychological defense involves *humor* (Vaillant, 1994a), in which one roommate might make jokes about the other, or even about him- or herself, as a way of lessening the conflict while subtly expressing his or her feelings about it.

People who try to reduce stress by managing the emotional effects of the stressor are using **emotion-focused coping.** Their efforts are not aimed at eliminating the stressor itself but at changing their emotional responses to it. If one roommate responded to the other roommate's conflicts by talking to a friend about how angry he or she is, or by trying to cheer him- or herself up by concentrating on the other roommate's good qualities, or by practicing meditation to reduce feelings of tension, he or she would be using an emotion-focused strategy.

Another way of coping with stressors is to seek or use **social support.** Social support requires more than just the presence of other people; it involves feeling that every individual belongs to a valued per-

son or group (Baumeister & Leary, 1995). Even more important than the sheer number of social contacts is the belief that one is cared for and valued.

Social support can take the form of advice, guidance, feedback, and direct help. A friend can provide social support by offering advice, by listening to vented feelings, or by taking the person under stress out for the evening to get a break from the stressor. In a sense, social support often provides a combination of problem-focused and emotion-focused coping resources, which is why social support is so important in helping people cope with stressors. The *perception* of social support enhances self-esteem and increases feelings of optimism about handling stressful events (Heller, Swindle, & Dusenbury, 1986). Experiencing social support helps people feel esteemed, loved, and part of a community of people who care for one another (Schradle & Dougher, 1985).

Effects of Coping Strategies. Are certain stressors managed better with one type of coping than another? In general, most people are flexible in how they cope, therefore it is difficult to identify the "best" coping style (Stone & Neale, 1984). Men tend to use direct problem solving a little more often than women do. Women tend to rely a little more on distraction, venting emotions, and social support than men do (Stone & Neale, 1984).

Coping via defense mechanisms such as denial is a reasonably effective response to short-term, isolated stressors, but it is an ineffective strategy with longer-term stressors, such as that of the troublesome roommate (Mullen & Suls, 1982). In fact, for years, many psychologists believed that defense mechanisms would ultimately harm a person's adjustment because they might lead to misperceptions of reality and to an inability to behave adaptively. In some cases, however, distraction from trauma might be the most effective form of coping. For example, throughout the Persian Gulf war, thousands of Israeli school children were forced to take shelter in sealed rooms during a series of missile attacks. Children who used avoidance and distraction during the attacks (e.g., by making fun of the missiles or reading a book in the shelter) experienced less serious stress reactions than children who tried to cope actively with the attacks (e.g., by constantly checking to see whether their masks or the seals on the room were secure) (Weisenberg et al., 1993).

People tend to cope best with the adversities of a protracted stressor (e.g., a painful, chronic illness such as arthritis) by seeking information about the stressor so they can anticipate and control it better (Revenson

& Felton, 1989) or at least convince themselves that they can control it. On the other hand, when faced with a truly uncontrollable condition, emotion-focused coping might be the most effective strategy (Meyerowitz, Heinrich, & Schag, 1983).

Several studies suggest that stressors are less likely to have harmful effects on people who enjoy high levels of social support (Mitchell, Billings, & Moos, 1982). Why is this so?

One possibility is that social support acts as a *buffer* against the harmful effects of stressors. By serving as an additional resource in a person's attempts to manage stressors, social support bolsters coping efforts (Thoits, 1986). Support may also deter a person from responding to stressors with harmful behaviors, such as excessive drinking. Several studies have shown that married men suffer fewer psychological difficulties after a traumatic event than do their widowed counterparts (e.g., Siegel & Kuykendall, 1990), and a few investigations suggest that married women live somewhat longer than unmarried women do (Hibbard & Pope, 1993).

A second explanation for the beneficial effects of social support is that it exerts *direct effects*. In this view, social support is seen as helpful regardless of the stressors a person experiences because there are general benefits to being embedded, and feeling that one belongs, in supportive relationships (Baumeister & Leary, 1995).

A third possible answer is that higher levels of social support and lower levels of stress reflect the influence of a common underlying characteristic such as social competence. Socially competent persons are more likely to have friends, to manage their lives effectively, and to encounter fewer major adversities (Adler & Matthews, 1994). Social competence may be a general characteristic of some individuals that accounts for both supportive relationships and good adjustment.

Of course, a combination of all three models may be at work. In reality it is difficult to separate the effects of personal competence, social support, and exposure to fewer stressors. Each of these qualities makes the others more likely. What does seem clear is that a lack of social support generally puts people at higher risk for both physical and psychological disorders (Cohen & Wills, 1985) and even mortality (House, Robbins, & Metzner, 1982).

Social support does not always produce positive results, however. It can create guilt and discomfort if recipients feel overly indebted or dependent because the support is one-sided. In other instances, well-intentioned helpers may give too much help or behave in other ways that lead recipients to see themselves as weak or incompetent (Wortman & Lehman, 1985). When assistance starts to feel like supervision, it may no longer be helpful.

Connections

Can social support help protect people against illness when they are under stress? For a discussion of this possibility, see Chapter 6, pp. 203–204.

One of the most serious stressors a person can face is the death of a loved one. Funerals facilitate the coping process by serving as a ritual that mobilizes both social support and emotion-focused coping.

Stress and Psychological Disorders

Just as physical reactions to stressors are adaptive in the short run but harmful if they become chronic, some psychological reactions can become maladaptive if they continue too long. Heightened attentiveness and concentration can become obsessiveness and restlessness. Concern about a stressor may intensify into constant anxiety, depression, or feelings of helplessness. Preparation and planning can become so preoccupying that a person is unable to sleep. Memories of the details of a stressful incident may turn into terrifying flashbacks or nightmares. Indeed, anxiety, helplessness, frustration, hostility, sleeplessness, and demoralization are the most common psychological effects of stress. Severe stress also contributes to several specific mental disorders, including:

   1. *sleep disorders,* which involve disturbances in latency, amount, or quality of sleep that are serious enough to cause social or occupational impairments;

   2. *adjustment disorders,* which are maladaptive behavioral and psychological reactions to a stressor occurring within 3 months of a stressor;

   3. *posttraumatic stress disorder (PTSD),* which is an anxiety disorder triggered by an unusually severe stressor. PTSD involves several distinct symptoms of disturbance that last for at least 1 month. Posttraumatic stress disorder, as well as a related condition, *acute stress disorder,* will be described in Chapter 7.

   4. *dissociative and somatoform disorders* (discussed in Chapter 8), which are often preceded by intense stressors or emotional conflict but involve symptoms that mask or substitute for feelings of anxiety;

   5. physical illnesses triggered or worsened by stress. Prior to the DSM-III, physical illnesses that appeared to be influenced by stress and associated psychological factors were termed *psychophysiological* or *psychosomatic disorders.* Hypertension, heart disease, chronic headaches, ulcers, and asthma are prime examples of illnesses influenced by both physical and psychological factors. Psychophysiological disorders are now called **psychological factors affecting medical condition.** This change reflects the belief that singling out certain illnesses as psychosomatic would be misleading because almost all physical disorders have a psychological component.

   6. the onset or recurrence of other psychological disorders. The role of stress in depression, bipolar disorder, as well as schizophrenia has received special research attention. Stressful events have been implicated as triggers for the onset of these disorders and for repeated episodes of them.

   The significance of stress in mental disorders is also reflected in Axis IV of the DSM-IV, which allows clinicians to describe the stressors that may be contributing to a diagnosed mental disorder. These problems may contribute to the development or worsening of a mental disorder, or they may develop as a consequence of mental disorders. In either case, a comprehensive intervention should help a person cope with these stressors.

In Review

The initial physiological responses to a stressor consist of two chemical alarms:

- the HPAC axis and the corticosteroids; and
- the sympathetic nervous system and the catecholamines.

When continued over long periods of time, stress can lead to:

- immunosuppression, a weakening of the immune system;
- extreme emotional and behavioral changes; and
- certain mental disorders.

People undergoing stress can cope with it through various strategies, including:

- cognitive reappraisal and defense mechanisms;
- problem-focused and emotion-focused coping; and
- eliciting social support.

Sleep Disorders

One of the most frequent complaints reported to physicians and mental health professionals is disturbed sleep. This is not surprising given that people spend about one third of their lives asleep. Infants sleep about 16 hours a day; by the time people reach their 70s, they sleep only 6 hours a day. Any activity that commands that much time is certain to be subject to problems, and almost everyone knows how a sleepless night feels. Over 90 percent of adults report having trouble sleeping on occasion. Lying in bed and not being able to sleep can be extremely

A Talk with James Pennebaker

Dr. James Pennebaker is Professor of Psychology at Southern Methodist University and a leading researcher in the area of stress and coping. His work has focused on how people can most effectively cope with the emotional consequences of trauma and on the benefits of writing about trauma, or as he calls it, "putting our feelings into words."

Stress and Adjustment Disorders

Q *Is Selye's General Adaptation Syndrome an accurate description of stress reactions?*

A Selye's GAS is still a very useful description of the stress process. However, I think Selye, and many stress researchers since, neglected one important aspect of stress and that is what happens when a stressor stops. Too little attention has been paid to "stressor offset." I have noticed in my research that very often people do not break down or become sick until after the stressor ends. For example, remember the American hostages who had been held in Iran for over a year? When they were released, most of them were in reasonably good physical health, but when they returned home, a lot of them got sick. The same pattern holds for college students. They make it through final exam week without becoming ill, but as soon as vacation starts, they come down with something. Is there a physical and psychological letdown after the stressor is over that leaves people more susceptible to sickness? Or do people become so used to the stressor that when it is finally over, the change feels like a new stressor?

> *. . . very often people do not break down . . . until after the stressor ends.*

Q *What is the key to effectively coping with a stressor?*

A I think the key is for persons to put their emotional life into words somehow so that they both acknowledge the emotions they are feeling and begin to coherently understand these emotions. You are correct in the text when you say that denial works sometimes, especially in the short run, as a coping strategy, but, with major stressors, the person who focuses on his or her deepest thoughts and feelings and consequently understands them better will cope more effectively.

Q *Is writing about feelings more effective than talking to someone about them?*

A Either method can be effective as long as the person actually does it. One advantage that writing has over talking is that writing does not require an audience. When we talk to someone about our troubles, we usually notice that person's reactions, and, if we are socially sensitive at all, we may begin to alter what we say so as not to upset or bore the listener. As a result, talking may not allow as deep a processing of our feelings as writing unless we are lucky enough to have someone to talk to who is a very good listener.

Q *Do certain kinds of people benefit more than others from writing about their traumas?*

A My research suggests that about 60 percent of all people who write about a personally meaningful trauma derive physical and psychological benefits from it. People who are highly repressed and therefore think it is silly to write about personal feelings do not usually benefit. Those who tend to be helped the most by writing about their feelings are those for whom the trauma is still psychologically active, i.e., they are still living with the emotions about the stressor.

Q *What are the most important questions that stress researchers should address in the future?*

A I can think of at least four areas that will be exciting to study. First, we need to study the nature of language itself so that we can learn what it is about writing or speaking that can be therapeutic for people. Second, we are witnessing an explosion in biotechnology. We need to harness this technology to learn how the different systems in the body change in real-life situations. Third, most major stressors are interpersonal in nature; they involve arguments between friends, breakups in relationships, deaths of loved ones. As a result, we need to understand the social dynamics of stressors much better than we currently do. Finally, we need to broaden our research perspectives by focusing on cultural shifts and differences as influences on stress. Early childhood experiences clearly influence people's needs, emotions, and thoughts. I suspect that the cultures in which these experiences are embedded are far more important than we currently give them credit for being.

frustrating, and usually the harder a person tries to fall asleep, the less likely sleep becomes. The day after a sleepless night can be miserable, and, after a sleepless night, most people go to bed earlier than usual the next night to catch up on the missed sleep. For millions of people, however, it's not that easy. They may struggle with disturbed or inadequate sleep night after night, for years on end, becoming desperately preoccupied with the one thing they can't achieve—a good night's sleep. The chronic misery of the poor sleeper was described by the English novelist Iris Murdoch who said, "There is a gulf fixed between those who sleep and those who cannot. It is one of the greatest divisions of the human race."

Troubled sleep may stem from several causes. When the disturbance lasts for a few nights or as long as a couple of weeks, the most likely explanation is that an individual is going through a stressful period. About 75 percent of people with insomnia report that their first attack occurred when facing major stressors (Dunkell, 1994). The connection between stress and sleep problems is one that most people experience at some time in their lives. People have trouble falling or staying asleep the night before a big trip, an important test, a major speech, or an important game. Worry about finances, children, or relationships often leads to disrupted and restless sleep.

Sleep disturbance is often tied to other mental disorders. **Insomnia** (in which a person complains of difficulty falling asleep or staying asleep) is common among those diagnosed with schizophrenia, anxiety disorders, and mood disorders. In one study, insomniacs were three times more likely to have a mental disorder than were those without sleep complaints (Ford & Kamerow, 1989). Although sleep disturbances can be produced by mental disorders, it is also possible that sleep problems sometimes cause mental disorders. Another possibility is that sleep problems and mental disorders are connected because they share a common biological cause. The evidence for this possibility has grown as more is discovered about the biological underpinnings of mental disorders and the process of sleep.

The Process of Sleep

The poet Percy Shelley referred to sleep as the "brother of death" (Shelley, 1813), but sleep, unlike death, is not a passive state; it is a dynamic process made up of physical and behavioral changes. Much of our understanding of these changes comes from research using the **electroencephalogram (EEG),** which measures changes in the electrical activity of the brain. The EEG is one measure used in a **polysomnographic (PSG) assessment,** in which a person sleeps for a night or two in a sleep laboratory while being observed. During sleep, several biological measures (EEG, muscle movements, heart activity, and eye movements) are monitored. Based on these measures, researchers have identified 5 distinctive stages of sleep, each with different behavioral and biological qualities.

Stages of Sleep. When a person falls asleep, muscles relax, body temperature begins to drop, and the person drifts into a light sleep from which he or she can be easily awakened. This *stage 1* sleep lasts from 30 seconds to 10 minutes. In *stage 2* sleep, the EEG shows some distinctive changes in brain activity as sleep deepens. A single phase of stage 2 sleep lasts, on average, 30 to 45 minutes; on most nights, half of the sleep time is spent in stage 2. *Stage 3* and *Stage 4* sleep are sometimes called **deep** or **delta sleep** because of a predominance of delta brain waves, a slower wave pattern recorded during these stages. These two stages account for about 10 to 20 percent of total sleep time, and they are the most restorative and revitalizing periods of our sleep. The immune system is thought to replenish itself during deep sleep. It is relatively difficult to wake someone in stage 4 sleep. One complete cycle through these first 4 stages takes about 90 minutes.

After 30 to 40 minutes in stage 4, the sleeper ascends into a special phase of lighter sleep in which the eyes dart back and forth quickly under closed lids. This stage, called **rapid eye movement (REM) sleep,** is differentiated from stages 1 to 4, which are called **non-REM (NREM) sleep.** Physiologically, REM sleep looks similar to stage 1 sleep; heart rate, breathing, and brain waves all increase. Paradoxically, however, the muscles become so relaxed during REM sleep that a person is essentially paralyzed, with the exception that penile erections are most likely to occur during REM sleep. On about 80 percent of awakenings during REM sleep, people report that they had been dreaming. Almost all dreams appear to take place during REM sleep. In fact, the eye movements of this stage may be coordinated with the actions taking place in dreams.

When people are deprived of REM sleep for a few nights, they will compensate by entering REM more quickly and remaining in it about twice as long on subsequent nights. This rebound suggests that REM sleep has some important functions. First, the *locus coeruleus,* which releases norepinephrine during the waking state, is almost totally inactive during REM sleep. The nervous system becomes less sensitive to norepinephrine if it is released steadily for too long; therefore, one function of REM sleep may be to shut down production of norepinephrine long enough to allow the brain to reset its receptive-

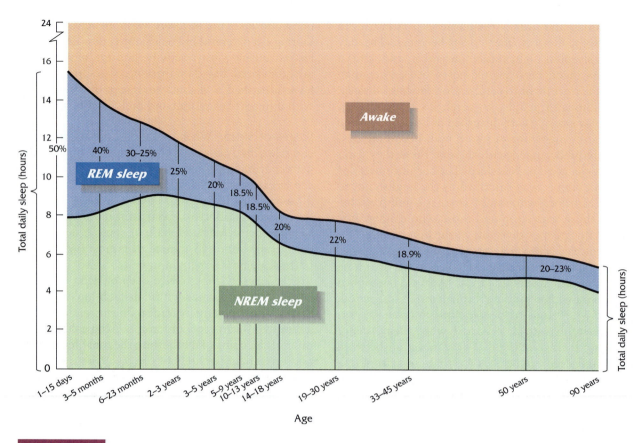

FIGURE 5.4

Sleep Changes with Age

As people age, the amount of REM and NREM sleep change. The percentages in the figure indicate the percentage of total sleep that is spent in REM sleep. REM sleep declines sharply in the first 10 years of life and continues to drop off more slowly after that. The amount of NREM sleep changes less dramatically, falling from about 8 hours during infancy to 5 hours in old age.

Source: Based on Roffwarg, Muzio, & Dement, 1966.

ness to this neurotransmitter. Several studies have shown that people who are deprived of REM sleep have poorer retention of material learned the day before than do people who are allowed to sleep normally or who are deprived of NREM sleep (Mc-Grath & Cohen, 1978). Therefore, REM sleep may also help individuals consolidate and fortify important learning experiences.

During a night's sleep, most people pass through the full sleep cycle 4 to 6 times. Most deep sleep (stages 3 and 4) occurs in the first 3 to 5 hours of sleep. As a night's sleep continues, more and more time is spent in the shallower stage 2 and REM sleep. Total sleep declines with age, particularly REM sleep, which, as Figure 5.4 shows, declines by about 50 percent between infancy and old age.

Biological Regulation of Sleep. Sleep, like many other biological functions, takes place on a rhythmic schedule that repeats roughly every 24 hours. These **circadian rhythms** (from the Latin *circa dies,* meaning "about a day") are partially linked to external cues such as light, but they are maintained even when people are isolated from external cues. Apparently, the body is equipped with a biological clock that maintains circadian rhythms even when external cues are missing. This clock appears to be in the **suprachiasmatic nucleus (SCN)** of the hypothalamus. The eyes send signals to the SCN to link it to external cues of the light/dark cycle. In addition, when the eyes sense darkness, the pineal gland soon begins to produce **melatonin,** a hormone that also informs the hypothalamus of darkness. The SCN then sends signals to areas of the hindbrain such as the locus coeruleus that activate either wakefulness or sleep.

Types of Sleep Disorders

The DSM-IV classifies sleep disorders in four major categories that are organized according to the presumed cause of the problem. **Sleep disorders related to another mental disorder** refers to sleep disturbances that are symptoms of some other diagnosed mental problem, most often a mood disorder or anxiety disorder. Disturbed sleep is the single most common physical symptom of people with depression, so common, in fact, that researchers often study depressed people in sleep laboratories to learn more about normal and abnormal sleep patterns.

Sleep disorders due to a general medical condition and **substance-induced sleep disorders** refer to problems of sleep that are either the direct physiological result of a medical problem or of ingestion of medication or a drug of abuse. For example, sleep problems often develop from endocrine disorders (e.g., hyperthyroidism), chronic pain (e.g., rheumatoid arthritis), or neurological disease (e.g., Parkinson's disease). The substance most often associated with sleep disorders is alcohol, but amphetamines, caffeine, cocaine, and opioids are other frequent culprits. Sleep disorders can occur either during the intoxication phase or the withdrawal phase of drug use. The use of several medications prescribed for anxiety and sleep problems can ultimately contribute to sleep disorders. For example, although sedatives and tranquilizers produce the desired increase in sleepiness when they are first taken, when used repeatedly, they lead to **tolerance,** meaning that more and more of the drug must be taken to achieve the desired result. If a person discontinues the drug, a sleep disorder may appear rapidly.

According to the DSM-IV, **primary sleep disorders** arise from the interaction of biological, psychological, behavioral, and cultural factors. The primary sleep disorders are subdivided into two categories: **dyssomnias,** which are disturbances in the amount, quality, or timing of a person's sleep, and **parasomnias,** which involve unusual behaviors or abnormal physiological events during sleep.

Dyssomnias. The most common dyssomnia is **primary insomnia,** in which individuals have such trouble falling asleep or staying asleep that they suffer significant distress or impairment. Insomnia affects about one third of the population annually, with women affected twice as often as men. Many insomniacs complain of sleep disturbance without showing all the expected indicators or impairments such as frequent sleep interruptions or daytime sleepiness. In fact, self-identified insomniacs may not get much less sleep than the 7 hours reported by most adults (see Figure 5.5). As reported in a large number of studies, on average, insomniacs take only about 35 minutes longer to fall asleep than good sleepers do, and 70 percent of insomniacs appeared to have no appreciable delay in onset of sleep (Chambers & Keller, 1992). Many insomniacs do engage in more active thinking at night; in particular they report more negative thoughts, perhaps in anticipation of another night of troubled sleep.

Primary insomnia can be caused by several factors, including irregularities in the timing of the internal biological clock. It can also be caused by such bad sleep habits as consuming alcohol or caffeine before bedtime, going to bed or getting up at irregular times, trying to go to sleep without first winding down or relaxing, and using the bedroom for studying, problem solving, watching TV, or other nonsleep-related activities.

Connections

Why is insomnia such a common symptom of depression? For some possible answers, see Chapter 9, pp. 290–291.

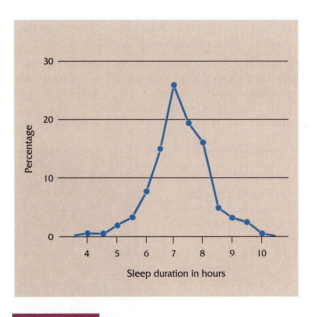

FIGURE 5.5

How Much Do People Sleep?

Individuals vary greatly in the amount of sleep they need. Most people sleep between 5 and 9 hours a night, with 7 hours being the most common amount.

Source: Browerman et al., 1977.

When these activities begin to affect sleep, a person starts to worry that it will be hard to fall asleep. Once this pattern of worry sets in, the person approaches going to bed with apprehension, thereby making sleep more difficult.

For some people, poor sleeping begins in infancy. **Infant sleep disturbance (ISD)** affects 15 to 25 percent of infants and usually includes having trouble falling asleep, nighttime waking and distress, and secondary problems such as parental discord and even child abuse (France & Hudson, 1992). One risk factor for ISD is a fussy or overactive temperament, which in turn causes parents to be too responsive or stimulating, making it harder for the child to fall asleep. In the United States, children's sleep problems might be more likely because of demands that they go to bed earlier than in other cultures where children go to sleep with their parents for the first several years.

Other prominent dyssomnias include

1. **primary hypersomnia,** in which the person complains of excessive sleepiness and engages in prolonged episodes of sleep on an almost daily basis;

2. **narcolepsy,** in which a person suffers sudden attacks of REM sleep, usually accompanied by **cataplexy,** a period of muscle paralysis that causes the person to collapse and be immobile for several seconds to a few minutes. (Narcolepsy affects less than 1 percent of the population.); and

3. **circadian rhythm sleep disorder,** involving a pattern of sleep disturbance caused by a mismatch between a person's natural circadian sleep/wake cycle and the demands of the environment. The most common causes of this disorder are changing shifts at work and air travel across time zones. In such cases, a person feels ready for sleep at the wrong time or tries to sleep when the body is not ready.

Parasomnias. The most common parasomnias are nightmare disorder, sleep terror disorder, and sleepwalking disorder. **Nightmare disorder** involves repeated frightening dreams that interrupt sleep, usually during REM stages. In occasional cases, multiple nightmares occur in the same night, sometimes revolving around a common theme. Disturbing nightmares occur in about 50 percent of children younger than 5, but the overall prevalence of nightmare disorder is not known. In **sleep terror disorder,** the person awakes during the first third of a sleep cycle, in NREM sleep, with a terrified scream or panicky cry. It may be difficult to comfort or reassure the person, who often remains upset for several minutes. The next morning, the person may have no memory of the terror. Sleep terrors do not involve story-length nightmares, but they may include frightening images or dreamlike segments. About 5 percent of children and 1 percent of adults suffer sleep terror disorder; most childhood cases spontaneously disappear in adolescence. **Sleepwalking disorder** occurs during NREM sleep and involves the person's leaving the bed and moving about; simply sitting up in bed, talking, or gesturing may also occur. During the episode, the person is unresponsive and can be awakened only with great difficulty. After the episode, the person usually has no memory of what transpired.

The well-known phenomenon of "jet lag" is particularly difficult following travel eastward, when time "is lost." For example, the records of professional sports teams are worse for games played immediately after eastward travel than for games played the day after traveling westward.

Treatment of Sleep Disorders

The most common treatment for insomnia is medication, particularly prescription drugs such as Halcion, Dalmane, and Valium. These drugs have several disadvantages, however. They produce unwanted side effects such as sleepiness during the daytime; they often induce dependence; and when they are discontinued, insomnia often becomes worse than before medication was begun. Other dyssomnias such as hypersomnia, tend to be treated with stimulants such as Ritalin, while narcolepsy is often treated with antidepressants.

Several psychological treatments have been used for insomnia. The specific method depends on the nature of an individual's problem. Relaxation techniques can be used to counter physical tension; cognitive therapies can help people reduce tendencies to ruminate and worry, especially about being able to fall asleep. Sleep hygiene counseling is among the most effective psychological approaches. The person is taught to develop good sleep habits, such as not using caffeine or alcohol before bedtime, going to bed at the same time every night, rising at the same hour in the morning, and restricting activities in the bedroom to sleep and sex rather than work and TV viewing.

In Review

The normal process of sleep involves:

- repeating stages of progressively deeper NREM sleep and one stage of rapid eye movement sleep (REM) during which dreams occur;
- a circadian rhythm that is regulated by an internal clock in the brain; and
- major decreases in the amount of REM sleep as people age.

The DSM-IV classifies several categories of sleep disorders, including:

- disturbances in the duration, timing, or quality of sleep known as *dyssomnias;* and
- abnormal behavioral or physiological events taking place during sleep known as *parasomnias.*

Adjustment Disorders

A person with an **adjustment disorder** suffers significant behavioral or psychological symptoms in response to a stressor. To be classified as an adjustment disorder according to the DSM-IV, these symptoms must occur within 3 months after the stressor's appearance and last no longer than 6 months after the stressor or its consequences have ended. With chronic stressors or those that have enduring consequences (e.g., the financial setbacks associated with divorce), the symptoms may last longer than 6 months. The symptoms must also exceed what would normally be expected from exposure to the stressor or be serious enough to impair the person's occupational, social, or academic functioning. On the other hand, the symptoms should not be so severe as to constitute one of the other Axis I disorders. If, as is sometimes the case, the symptoms last more than 6 months after the stressor or its consequences end, the diagnosis is changed, usually to a mood disorder or anxiety disorder.

All stressors cause some disruption, so it is often difficult to distinguish between reactions that are normal consequences of a stressor (such as grief over the death of a loved one) and those causing enough impairment to constitute an adjustment disorder. Generally, if a person believes that he or she is handling the stressor adequately, no diagnosis is made. If, however, the person cannot maintain normal functioning or experiences enough distress to seek professional help, an adjustment disorder will probably be diagnosed.

Usually, an adjustment disorder appears as a milder version of some other mental disorder. Depending on the nature of the symptoms, five subtypes of adjustment disorders can be specified: adjustment disorder with anxiety, with depressed mood, with disturbance of conduct, with mixed disturbance of emotions and conduct, and with mixed anxiety and depressed mood. (A sixth, unspecified, subtype is used for cases that do not fit any of the five main subtypes.) For example, if the primary symptoms are nervousness and tension, adjustment disorder with anxiety would be diagnosed. If symptoms involve both emotional upset and behavioral difficulties (such as not meeting financial responsibilities, missing work frequently, or illegal activities), adjustment disorder with mixed disturbance of emotions and conduct would be the diagnosis. The mixed subtype is common among adolescents; among adults the depressed subtype is most common.

Adjustment disorders, posttraumatic stress disorder, and acute stress disorder (Chapter 7) are all linked to a precipitating stressful event, but adjustment disorders differ from the others in two important respects. First, adjustment disorders can arise in response to stressors of any magnitude, while PTSD and acute stress disorder are diagnosed only in response to unusually severe stressors. Second, PTSD and acute stress disorder involve a specific set of symptoms including heightened anxiety and disruptions in behavior as well as disruptions in the autonomic nervous system. The symptoms of adjustment disorders range widely in form, but are typically mild and of limited duration.

Adjustment disorders are diagnosed frequently (Mezzich et al., 1989); as many as 20 percent of clients in outpatient mental health clinics receive this diagnosis (APA, 1994). Clinicians often use this diagnosis to indicate that a person's symptoms are mild, are unlikely to last a long time, and are not the result of a more serious condition. Therefore, the adjustment disorder label carries few of the negative stereotypes often associated with other mental disorders. It appears to be diagnosed about equally in males and females.

Unfortunately, adjustment disorder diagnoses tend to be unreliable, probably because the diagnosis is often made to avoid using a more serious diagnosis. Adjustment disorder is also something of a "wastebasket" category, which is used when symptoms do not fit well elsewhere in the DSM-IV. Thus, clinicians may not be as rigorous in assessing individual criteria for adjustment disorder as they should be.

Triggers for Adjustment Disorders

The stressors that give rise to adjustment disorders may be one-time events such as divorce or multiple setbacks such as repeated occupational failures. They may last a short time (e.g., an earthquake) or stretch on for what seems like forever (e.g., the chronic illness of a loved one). Most adjustment disorders develop following marital, academic, or occupational problems, but people differ so much in their responses to stressors that it is impossible to predict how a particular individual will react to a given stressor. Likewise, even though the DSM-IV indicates that adjustment disorders occur within 3 months of a triggering stressor and improve within 6 months after the stressor is over, clinicians treat many cases that do not follow this temporal pattern.

Adjustment Disorders and Natural Disasters.

*M*anuel Díaz was driving to his home in Oakland, California, around 5 P.M. on October 17, 1989, when his car was suddenly swept off the road and thrown into a road sign. Dazed, but not seriously injured, Manuel sat, gripping the steering wheel in terror, while his car

bounced wildly from side to side for what seemed like 2 endless minutes. Manuel had just lived through the worst earthquake to strike the United States in decades, resulting in 60 deaths and property damage exceeding $5 billion. Manuel's home was spared any structural damage, and his family escaped serious injury. But over the next several weeks, he just did not feel like himself. He was reluctant to leave home for fear that something would happen while he was gone. At work, he was seized by the idea that something horrible had happened to one of his children. He was forgetful about little tasks, and he often found himself bickering with coworkers with whom he had never before had problems. Manuel began waking up at 3 A.M. and could not get back to sleep; often, it seemed as if he had been awakened by a nightmare. He began to make plans to move someplace where he would feel safer.

Manuel's distress was shared by thousands of victims of the 1989 earthquake. His reactions are an example of an adjustment disorder with mixed anxiety and depressed mood, and they illustrate a common type of adjustment disorder following a natural disaster.

The question of how common one of Manuel's symptoms—nightmares—might be was investigated in a study in which undergraduate students from the San Francisco Bay area (San Jose State and Stanford Universities) were asked to write a description of their nightmares every morning for 3 weeks after the earthquake. Undergraduates from another area not affected by the earthquake (University of Arizona) served as a control group.

Students from the three universities did not differ in the frequency of nightmares they experienced during the year before the earthquake. However, after the earthquake, the San Jose State students experienced about twice as many nightmares, and the Stanford students about 1.5 times as many nightmares as the Arizona students (Wood et al., 1992). The content of the students' nightmares was also affected. More than 25 percent of the nightmares reported by students from the Bay area were about earthquakes compared with only 3 percent of the nightmares for the Arizona students. These nightmares did not differ, however, in their overall intensity.

Adjustment Disorders and Technological Disasters.

*N*olan Berry had lived on the Cumberland River in southeast Kentucky for more than 20 years. His home was located on 3 acres of bottomland that backed up to the river. His five children had bathed, swum, and fished in the river all their lives. He and his wife cooked with water from the river, raised a garden on the bottomland, and rebuilt their home twice after the floods of 1978 and 1984. One day toward the end of 1991, an official from the Environmental Protection Agency knocked on Nolan's front door to tell him that the river water he and his family had been using for two decades contained excessive levels of several toxic chemicals (some of which were known carcinogens) dumped by an electric plant 1 mile upstream. Nolan was told to stop using the water immediately, and the next day, the state of Kentucky brought a truckload of safe water to his home. Within 2 months, Nolan's land and that of several of his neighbors was declared a Superfund site by the EPA, meaning that its cleanup was one of the highest priorities among environmental hazards in the United States.

Nolan was unable to sell his home, nor could he use it as collateral for a loan to buy new property. He and his wife began to worry about every ache and pain. They talked constantly about their health and were terrified that sooner or later they would be stricken with cancer. The family members argued more and more among themselves; they became suspi-

cious of outsiders and remained increasingly isolated at home despite the fact that they grew to hate being there. Nolan and his wife were enraged at the electric plant for secretly dumping its chemicals in their water for 20 years. Along with their neighbors, they filed a lawsuit against the corporation that owned the plant. However, as litigation dragged on for more than 2 years without any resolution, they became almost as frustrated with the justice system as with the corporation's negligence. Nolan began to drink more heavily, he and his wife stopped sleeping together, and they stopped going to church.

Nolan's case illustrates how an adjustment disorder can last a long time in response to a persistent stressor or one with long-term consequences. Substantial psychological and physiological stress has been linked to other, even more notorious accidents and environmental disasters in the United States (Baum & Fleming, 1993). The nuclear accident at Three Mile Island, Pennsylvania (Baum, Gatchel, & Schaeffer, 1983), the chemical exposure at Love Canal, Niagara Falls, New York (Levine & Stone, 1986), the fire at the Beverly Hills Supper Club near Cincinnati, Ohio (Green, Grace, Titchener, & Lindy, 1983), and the exposure of California farm workers

Victims of major disasters may suffer a host of psychological reactions. Stressful reactions are an occupational hazard of emergency rescue workers who are often vicariously traumatized by their contact with victims' suffering.

Controversy

Which Is Worse—Natural or Technological Disasters?

Within the past decade, the United States has seen a rash of disasters that have caused widespread loss of life and property. The July, 1989, crash of a DC-10 at Sioux City, Iowa, killed 112 people. Two months later, Hurricane Hugo struck the Caribbean and the southeastern United States. These disasters were followed in rapid succession by the Loma Prieta earthquake in northern California, the bombing of the World Trade Center in New York City, the Midwest floods of 1993, the bombing of the Murrah Federal Building in Oklahoma City in 1995, and the explosion of TWA flight 800 in 1996. These emergencies led to the development of a Disaster Response Network coordinated by the American Red Cross and the American Psychological Association that can mobilize a team of psychologists to answer the imme-

diate mental health needs of communities affected by disasters (Jacobs, 1995). The field of disaster mental health has also stimulated research that examines different disaster and survivor characteristics and evaluates emergency mental health interventions.

One of the major questions being addressed by this research is whether the characteristics of a disaster influence how people react to it. Do some disasters cause greater psychological damage than others? Trauma researchers have been particularly interested in whether natural catastrophes such as floods and earthquakes are more traumatic than disasters such as airplane crashes, bombings of buildings, or urban riots. The question is complicated because the psychological effects of a disaster depend on several factors, such as how much warning was provided, how long

the emergency lasted, how many people were affected, and how visible and extreme the physical injuries were. The impact of a disaster is often also affected by the perceptions of individual victims. If a person does not feel victimized by an event, its psychological effects may be minimal even though the disaster inflicted great damage on a community or group. Likewise, psychological damage from a disaster can be measured in several ways—frequency of mental disorders, subjective unhappiness, missed work days—resulting in varying estimates of the psychological toll that a disaster has taken.

This controversy has not yet been resolved, but several researchers have come to believe that accidents or disasters of human origin are more distressing than natural disasters (Baum & Fleming, 1993; Smith, North, & Price,

to harmful pesticides (Vaughan, 1993) are primary examples.

In both natural and technological disasters, the severity of psychological problems is related to the extent or length of direct exposure to the danger (Vernberg et al., 1996). In floods, for example, the higher the waters submerge a person's body or the longer a person stays in them, the more serious the psychological aftermath tends to be. Israeli school children subjected to missile attacks during the Persian Gulf war experienced greater stress reactions if the missiles landed near their homes or neighborhoods or if they felt personally close to someone who was actually injured in an attack (Schwarzwald et al., 1993). As this chapter's Controversy section discusses, some researchers believe that, among all types of trauma, technological disasters cause the most serious stressful reactions.

Adjustment Disorders and Interpersonal Stressors.

Margerie Still has just discovered that Bob, her husband of more than 10 years, has been

having an affair with a female coworker. Bob confessed that this relationship had been going on for 4 months, and that, although he still cared for Margerie and their two daughters, he "needs more space" and would like to move out and live on his own. Although Bob promised that he would end his affair, Margerie discovered that he is still living with his new lover.

Margerie felt that her world has been shattered. She had trusted her husband completely. She had never been romantically involved with anyone except Bob from the time they had begun dating in high school; now she felt alone. She was too embarrassed to tell her friends or parents about Bob's affair so she stayed at home as much as possible. Margerie found her girls were getting on her nerves constantly, acting as if it were her fault that their father had left the family. Margerie lost 15 pounds in 5 weeks, feeling sick to her stomach all the time. Her future seemed totally empty. She could not concentrate at work. Two weeks after Bob left, Margerie was driving too fast, lost control of her car, and smashed into a parked pickup truck. She

1988). One reason may be that humans expect to be able to control their own inventions and products, but not weather or earthquakes. Because we think human technology *should* be controlled, we are particularly prone to feel a *loss of control* during technological disasters. Loss of perceived control is a common contributor to psychological distress, just as the perception of being in control helps promote a sense of psychological well-being (Taylor & Brown, 1988).

A second explanation for the greater effects of technological disasters is that, unlike floods or hurricanes, they often occur with little or no warning, giving victims less time to prepare. A considerable amount of research has demonstrated that people usually cope better with stressors that they can anticipate as opposed to those that appear without advance notice (Averill, 1973). Natural disasters usually also have a "low point,"

after which victims feel that the worst is over. Technological disasters may not have such clearly discernible stages, leading to more prolonged feelings of dread and uncertainty.

A final reason why victims of technological disasters may feel especially distressed is that they tend to blame someone for their plight. Blaming, in turn, may increase hostility, suspiciousness, and aggressiveness toward others, making social support less available to victims at the very time it could be most beneficial. Loss of control and blaming may also lead victims to give up trying to cope with a disaster. Whatever the trauma, when people blame others for their misfortune, they tend to adjust poorly (Tennen & Affleck, 1990).

None of these hypotheses has been clearly confirmed, and research on this controversy is difficult to conduct. Obviously, people cannot be randomly assigned to

suffer a technological versus a natural disaster so that scientists can measure how traumatized they feel after either kind. Also, it is not possible, or ethical, to simulate in laboratory settings the level of trauma that disasters usually create. At this point, then, the suspicion that technological disasters are more psychologically harmful than natural disasters is a reasonable, but as yet unconfirmed, hypothesis.

Thinking Critically

We suggested several complications in studying the effects of technological versus natural disasters. Can you think of any others?

- Is it always clear whether a disaster is natural or technological in nature?
- If a person's home is built on a floodplain or barrier beach and is destroyed by a flood is the loss technological or natural?

told herself that the wreck was "just an accident," but she realized that she was endangering herself and, shortly afterward, she called a psychologist for help.

Margerie's adjustment disorder is typical of people experiencing severe marital problems. In the development of the Social Readjustment Rating Scale subjects rated divorce and marital separation as the second and third most upsetting life events possible, exceeded only by the death of a spouse (Holmes & Rahe, 1967).

Why do interpersonal stressors, such as Margerie's marital difficulties, so often lead to psychological and physical problems? One reason is that interpersonal problems are often chronic, and they can have a substantial impact on all family members (Coyne & Downey, 1991); children raised in adverse family environments run higher than normal risks of suffering even more stressors in the future. Indeed, the correlation between marital stressors and subsequent maladjustment may actually reflect a long series of interpersonal stressors. Furthermore, people

who experience a series of stressors often become more difficult to get along with, thus actually creating additional stressors. Finally, interpersonal stressors, such as a troubled marriage, usually have a double impact. They are stressors, and they involve a loss of the partner's social support. In addition, in Margerie's case, shame over her problems also prevented her using her social support network.

Treatment of Adjustment Disorders

Although we lack definitive data on the course of adjustment problems, most mild adjustment disorders probably resolve themselves in a few months without formal treatment. Many persons with adjustment disorders turn to friends or family for support, or they just "wait it out," assuming that once the stressor is over they will feel better and function normally again. In many cases, this assumption proves correct and the person regains a satisfactory level of adjustment. Although some sadness or uneasiness may linger long after the stressor is gone, it usually does not significantly impair the person's functioning.

More serious adjustment disorders may progress into another mental disorder, usually an anxiety disorder or mood disorder. Still, even serious adjustment disorders have a generally favorable prognosis.

Adjustment disorders can be eased by any intervention that enhances environmental or psychological stress mediators (Dohrenwend, 1978). Whether the intervention is delivered by a mental health professional or nonprofessional is less important than the fact that it enhances a person's coping resources. Increasing a person's resistance to specific stressors can help ward off the stressors themselves or at least their most harmful effects.

Enhancing Problem-Focused Coping. Strengthening a person's ability to solve problems is an effective strategy for preventing or lessening adjustment disorders. This goal can be attained through family or friends, or through formal counseling in which a client learns effective problem solving (D'Zurilla & Goldfried, 1971).

Problem-solving therapy has been used with many types of clients and has generally proved successful in helping people cope with a wide range of life difficulties, including divorce, occupational stressors, interpersonal problems, and financial setbacks (Spiegler & Guevremont, 1993). It has had particular success in boosting the coping skills of children and adolescents who face many serious challenges (Kazdin, 1994a; Spivack & Shure, 1974).

Effective problem-solving therapy programs follow seven steps:

1. Define the problem clearly. This step usually requires the person to identify the major goals that need to be achieved and the obstacles or conflicts blocking the path to these goals.

2. Identify alternative strategies for solving the problem. The goal of this brainstorming is to discover as many general solutions as possible.

3. Evaluate the short-term and long-term consequences of the alternative strategies and select a general strategy for attempting to solve the problem.

4. List several specific alternative tactics for implementing the general strategy that has been chosen.

5. Choose a tactic that appears to have the best chance of resolving the problem.

6. Act on the decisions reached in the previous steps.

7. Assess the effectiveness of these actions. If the problem is resolved, the problem-solving sequence has been successful. If the problem remains, the person must return to one of the earlier stages and go through the sequence again, selecting different strategies or tactics to solve the problem.

Enhancing Emotion-Focused Coping. People often cope more effectively with a stressful event if they have the opportunity to express their feelings about the event and gain a better understanding of it (Greenberg, Elliott, & Lietaer, 1994). Expressing feelings about a stressor is helpful, first, because it unburdens people of the negative thoughts and emotions they have kept bottled up, and, second, because it allows them to think about the stressor in new and more effective ways.

Research by James Pennebaker and his associates (Pennebaker & Beall, 1986; Pennebaker, Kiecolt-Glaser, & Glaser, 1988; Petrie et al., 1995) has examined the effects of writing about one's thoughts and feelings after a stressful experience. Writing provides the opportunity to vent negative feelings, clarify and explore them more fully, and consider various methods for coping with them.

In one study (Pennebaker et al., 1988), 25 undergraduate students wrote for 20 minutes on 4 consecutive days about traumatic events in their lives. Another 25 students wrote for the same amount of time about more trivial events such as a recent social activity. Before and after completing their daily writing assignments, the students rated their moods and reported any symptoms of physical illness. The researchers also measured the students' immune system functioning and the number of visits they made to the student health center during the study. Students who wrote about personal traumas showed better immune system functioning, made fewer visits to health centers, and reported less emotional distress than did students who wrote about trivial matters. In another study, college students who either wrote about traumatic events or spoke into a tape recorder about them for 20 minutes a week showed better immune system control over latent Epstein-Barr antibodies than did students who wrote about trivial topics (Esterling et al., 1994).

Writing or talking about a stressful event can improve a person's psychological and physical functioning even years after the event (Pennebaker, Barger, & Tiebout, 1989). For example, survivors of the Nazi Holocaust during World War II who disclosed strong negative feelings in an interview 40 years after their trauma demonstrated greater improvements in health than those who expressed milder feelings.

Even though writing or talking about a negative event may cause a short-term surge in negative emotions (Donnelly & Murray, 1991), the long-term effects of emotion-focused coping appear to be largely positive. Emotional disclosures seem to give people an opportunity to rid themselves of negative feelings while simultaneously increasing confidence that they can cope with future stressors. As this confidence grows, individuals may gradually replace a general pessimism about themselves and the future with a more optimistic, upbeat style of thinking. A tendency to take an optimistic perspective on most events has been linked to better physical health and improved psychological adjustment during stress (e.g., Peterson, Seligman, & Vaillant, 1988; Scheier & Carver, 1985). A stable optimistic outlook in which a person believes that good things will generally or eventually happen in the future has been termed **dispositional optimism** (Scheier & Carver, 1985). This trait may be genetically influenced to some extent, but it is also likely that a person's unique interpersonal experiences and real-life accomplishments can increase its strength.

Enhancing Social Support.   Therapists often try to help their clients become more receptive to social support opportunities. Some clients place a premium on keeping up an image of sturdy independence and regard turning to others as a sign of weakness that will cause others to lose respect for them. Therapists may challenge this attitude by asking clients how they feel when others solicit help from them. Generally, clients will admit they feel closer to people who occasionally look to them for assistance. Therapists then ask clients to consider whether the same positive feelings might not come to those whose support they accept (Nietzel, Guthrie, & Susman, 1991). As we will discuss further in Chapter 16, helping clients increase the social support in their lives may be one of the common beneficial effects of most forms of therapy (Cross, Sheehan, & Kahn, 1980).

Connections

Is writing about personal problems anything like the expression of feelings in psychotherapy? Do certain therapies emphasize such expression? See Chapter 16, pp. 565–566.

Revisiting the Case of Officer Schuler

Officers Schuler and Harris were lucky in the sense that they did not develop an adjustment disorder or posttraumatic stress disorder, which is described in Chapter 7. They did not escape unscathed, however. Schuler continued in counseling for about 2 months, far longer than required by the police division's formal policy. The counseling focused on helping her understand that the immediate reactions she felt were normal and predictable consequences of being under stress. But her counseling also helped her examine more carefully the way she typically coped with stress. Sandy discovered that she relied almost exclusively on problem-focused coping; she wanted to fix problems that came her way as soon as possible. When she was unable to do so, as in the aftermath of the Drexel Root shooting, she became frustrated and despondent. Schuler gradually began to learn that she needed to accept help from others as she attempted to cope with stressors. She discovered that if she disclosed her fears and disappointments to friends and didn't always try to act like a hero, she felt more relaxed and in charge of her life. Ultimately, she decided to stay on the force, and, 2 years later, she was promoted to Sergeant.

SUMMARY

What Is Stress?

Stress is a process that results when environmental or social threats place demands on a person. Stressors come in many forms, including predictable challenges and sudden, unpredictable crises. Stress reactions occur in a three-stage pattern of physiological, behavioral, and psychological changes that Selye termed the *general adaptation syndrome (GAS)*.

Reactions to Stress

In the alarm stage of the GAS, the person is jolted into action, and the body prepares to fight or flee the stressor. In the resistance stage, the person attempts to cope with the stressor. In the final exhaustion stage, the person's capacity to resist breaks down and the ability to cope with stressors is ultimately lost.

Physical and psychological reactions to stressors are usually adaptive in the short run because they are aimed at coping with stressors in some way. However, if these defenses must be employed for too long, people begin to experience harmful physical and psychological effects. Prolonged stressors lead to suppression of the immune system, which in turn results in greater susceptibility to illness.

People use a variety of strategies to cope with stressful events in their lives. Cognitive reappraisals involve thinking about stressors in less upsetting ways. Problem-focused coping is aimed at modifying stressors themselves. Emotion-focused coping consists of attempts to manage the feelings one has about a stressful event. Enlisting social support is a fourth general strategy that people use to cope with stress. Depending on the nature and context of a stressful event, any or all coping strategies can be successful. In general, people who are flexible in the strategies they use are most effective at coping with stress.

If coping efforts fail and stressors continue, the possible consequences include sleep disorders, adjustment disorders, dissociative and somatoform disorders, posttraumatic stress disorder, acute stress disorder, other psychological disorders, certain physical illnesses, and the recurrence of prior disorders.

Sleep Disorders

A common consequence of stress is sleep disorders. Stress can disrupt the biological regulators of sleep, resulting in disturbances in the amount, timing, or quality of sleep (dyssomnias) or in abnormal behavioral and physiological events that take place during sleep (parasomnias). Medications are often used to treat insomnia and other dyssomnias, despite several disadvantages and side effects. Counseling people about proper sleep habits is often an effective psychological intervention.

Adjustment Disorders

Adjustment disorders are common diagnoses for the temporary problems that people suffer following a stressor. Often the symptoms of an adjustment disorder resemble a mild version of other mental disorders, particularly mood disorders and anxiety disorders. Adjustment disorders are commonly diagnosed following natural disasters, technological catastrophes, and chronic problems in relationships or work. Interventions that bolster a person's perceived social support or strengthen problem-focused and/or emotion-focused coping strategies will usually help resolve an adjustment disorder.

KEY TERMS

adjustment disorder, p. 173
adrenal corticosteroid, p. 160
adrenocorticotrophic hormone (ACTH), p. 160
antibody, p. 163
antigens, p. 163
autoimmune disease, p. 163
B cell, p. 163
cataplexy, p. 172
circadian rhythm, p. 170
circadian rhythm sleep disorder, p. 172
cognitive reappraisal, p. 164
coping, p. 164
corticotropin-releasing hormone (CRH), p. 160

deep sleep, p. 169
delta sleep, p. 169
dispositional optimism, p. 179
dyssomnia, p. 171
electroencephalogram (EEG), p. 169
emotion-focused coping, p. 165
endorphin, p. 161
fight or flight response, p. 159
general adaptation syndrome (GAS), p. 159
glucocorticoid, p. 164
hypothalamic-pituitary-adrenocortical (HPAC) axis, p. 160
immunosuppression, p. 163

infant sleep disturbance (ISD), p. 172
insomnia, p. 169
interleukin-1, p. 163
macrophage, p. 163
melatonin, p. 170
memory T cell, p. 163
narcolepsy, p. 172
nightmare disorder, p. 172
non-REM (NREM) sleep, p. 169
parasomnia, p. 171
pathogen, p. 163
polysomnographic (PSG) assessment, p. 169
primary hypersomnia, p. 172

primary insomnia, p. 171

primary sleep disorder, p. 171

problem-focused coping, p. 164

psychological factors affecting
   medical condition, p. 167

rapid eye movement (REM) sleep,
   p. 169

sleep disorder due to a general
   medical condition, p. 171

sleep disorder related to another
   mental disorder, p. 171

sleep terror disorder, p. 172

sleepwalking disorder, p. 172

social support, p. 165

stage of exhaustion, p. 159

stage of resistance, p. 159

stress, p. 154

stress hormone, p. 160

substance-induced sleep disorder,
   p. 171

suppressor T cell, p. 163

suprachiasmatic nucleus (SCN),
   p. 170

T cell, p. 163

tolerance, p. 171

6

Psychological Factors and Health

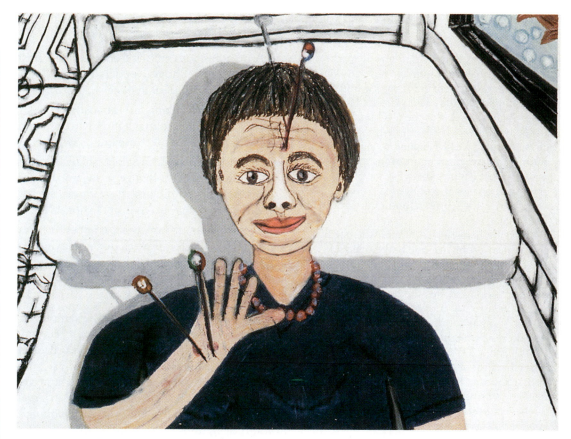

Untitled by Camille Holvoet, 1993. Oil pastel on paper, 22" x 30". Courtesy of Creative Growth Art Center.

From the Case of Beth

Beth, a 34-year-old businesswoman, is a married mother of two small children. Her first job after college was as an account agent in a large travel agency. Beth was an energetic, "all business" executive who enjoyed official recognition of her many achievements.

Beth always drove herself to reach high goals, and within 3 years she was promoted to assistant manager of the agency. Beth couldn't remember failing at anything. Most of her colleagues seemed to crumble under pressure, but Beth relished the challenges that came with increasing responsibilities. She knew that some of her coworkers resented her, but as Beth liked to say, "They have the rest of their lives to get over it."

At 32, with both of her children in elementary school, Beth borrowed the money to buy a 50 percent share in a small travel agency. Her goal was to double the agency's business in 2 years. Within a year of buying the business, Beth found she was on the run constantly. She got up at 5:30 every morning, fixed breakfast for the kids, packed them off to the school bus, and headed for work. She installed a phone in her car so she could get work done on the way to the office and save a few minutes of down time during the traffic jams she found so intolerable.

Beth hired several new employees and devoted her full attention to supervising them. She demanded that her staff work as hard as she did. She was particularly impatient with anyone who missed a deadline or made excuses about being too busy, often belittling them in public for being "lazy." Within the first 6 months, Beth fired three of the nine people she had hired because they "just couldn't cut it." Two others quit, and most of the remaining employees disliked or feared her.

183

As her business grew, Beth found herself working almost every night. She gave up her regular exercise class, and she and her husband dropped out of the gourmet cooking circle they had started. The kids were no problem; she'd rent them a bunch of movies and they would watch TV till bedtime. But after a while Beth found herself having to stay up until 2 or 3 almost every morning in order to get all her paperwork done. When she wasn't working, she was worrying about what still needed to be done. More and more she felt tense and guilty about her work.

Beth kept driving herself even though she began experiencing physical problems. She had gained 15 pounds in the past few months and was now 30 pounds overweight. She rationalized that this was because of all the fast-food lunches she ate at her desk and told herself she'd return to a better diet and start exercising just as soon as she straightened things out at work. She said the same thing about her smoking; she was up to a pack a day now, but she was sure she could quit whenever she really needed to. Beth also noticed that she was having a lot more headaches, which she controlled by taking three or four strong pain relievers every day. She vowed to go to her HMO and get a checkup just as soon as things settled down.

Beth could minimize her physical problems, but she had more trouble with the fact that she simply felt alone much of the time. Beth didn't have a best friend anymore, someone she could talk to or just have fun with. She knew her employees couldn't be too friendly with her because it would look as if they were currying favor with the boss, but where was everyone else? She thought that if she worked a little harder, she wouldn't feel quite as lonely.

Beth's symptoms took an alarming turn when one day she fainted in the shower and cut her head. She told her husband she had merely slipped, but secretly Beth worried that something was seriously wrong. It was the fourth time in the past month that she had passed out. If one of these spells happened while she was driving, she might kill herself or the kids.

Beth knew she needed to see a physician, but she was afraid. Her father had died from heart disease, and her mother was diabetic. She made and cancelled several appointments, claiming that she was too busy. When she had finally had a thorough physical examination, her physician diagnosed Beth's problem as high blood pressure. She prescribed some medication and advised Beth to make several changes in her lifestyle. Unless she made these changes, the doctor warned, her hypertension would probably worsen. ■

*B*eth's case illustrates a basic fact about illness: *being sick* involves more than physical disease, and good health requires more than the absence of physical sickness. Consider these examples:

■ A man has a greater risk of suffering a heart attack as a result of intense anxiety than as a result of smoking cigarettes (Kawachi et al., 1993).

■ Heart attack victims are almost twice as likely to have a second heart attack if they live alone rather than with a companion (Case et al., 1992).

■ Cancer patients who are able to blame their disease on something they can change show a better prognosis than patients who blame it on causes over which they believe they have no control (Taylor, 1983, 1989).

■ Persons who are impatient, competitive, and feel pressured to get a lot of work done quickly are more likely to experience elevated blood pressure in frustrating situations than are persons with a more relaxed style of life (Lyness, 1993).

These findings represent a few examples of how psychological and physical factors are entwined in many medical disorders. About one third of all patients visit a physician because of physical symptoms caused by psychological distress, and another third go for physical problems that develop largely because of unhealthy behaviors such as smoking, alcohol and drug abuse, or an unhealthy diet. The remaining third have conditions such as heart trouble or arthritis that are strongly affected by psychological factors. How can we explain these relationships? Can psychological differences help explain differences in health and susceptibility to disease? Do social factors play a role in sickness?

Mind, Body, and Health Psychology

Questions of the interaction of mind, body, and health are the concern of **health psychology,** a specialty that emerged in the 1970s and is devoted to studying "psychological influences on how people stay healthy, why they become ill, and how they respond when they do get ill" (Taylor, 1995, p. 3). Health psychologists concentrate on four activities:

1. understanding how psychological and physiological factors interact to influence illness and health;
2. identifying *risk factors* for sickness (influences that lead to or exacerbate illness) as well as *protective factors* for health;
3. developing and evaluating techniques for promoting healthy behaviors and preventing unhealthy ones; and
4. developing and evaluating psychological interventions that contribute to the effective treatment of illness (Blumenthal, Matthews, & Weiss, 1994).

Closely related to health psychology is a broader discipline called **behavioral medicine,** which integrates behavioral science and biomedical knowledge into an interdisciplinary effort to understand, treat, and prevent illness. Health psychology and behavioral medicine both follow a **biopsychosocial model,** which holds that physical illnesses are the outgrowth of biological vulnerability, psychological processes, and social conditions. In this chapter, we take a closer look at how psychological and social factors contribute to illness and health.

Health psychology is founded on the idea that mind and body are so intricately merged that, as Aristotle said of body and soul, "We can wholly dismiss as unnecessary the question of whether [they] are one: it is as meaningless to ask whether the wax and the shape given to it by the stamp are one" (see McKeon, 1941). In the same vein, Socrates noted that "Just as you ought not to attempt to cure eyes without head, or head without body, so you should not treat body without soul" (quoted in Blumenthal, 1994). During the Renaissance, this view gave way to dualistic thinking, in which the body and mind were considered to be separate domains. But the dualistic position was, itself, challenged in the late 1800s by the rise of psychiatry, and especially by the influence of Sigmund Freud. Because Freud's psychoanalytic theory suggested a strong tie between unconscious psychological conflicts and physical changes, it offered a bold alternative to dualistic thinking.

Sir William Osler (1849–1919) is generally considered the father of modern behavioral medicine. He insisted that psychological and emotional factors must be considered in order to understand and treat various diseases. For example, in a lecture delivered in 1910 Osler suggested that many symptoms of heart disease "are brought on by anger, worry, or sudden shock." These ideas are remarkably similar to contemporary proposals about how key psychological factors may be linked to heart disease.

Meanwhile, the nature of illness itself was changing in Western cultures. As recently as 100 years ago, most Americans, for example, died of acute infectious diseases such as pneumonia, typhoid fever, and tuberculosis. Advances in education, sanitary conditions, and vaccinations have reduced these diseases dramatically. Today, as Table 6.1 on page 186 shows, chronic illnesses such as heart disease, cancer, and various forms of violence pose the greatest threats to life (Blumenthal, 1994). Furthermore, the major risk factors for developing chronic illnesses are behaviors such as smoking, unhealthy eating habits, and alcohol abuse.

These shifts in the source of major threats to health, along with changes in ideas about illness,

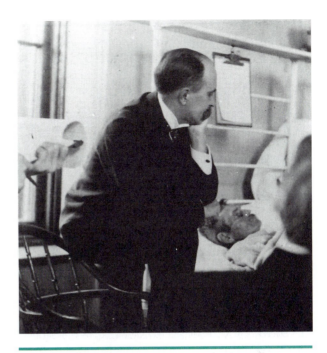

William Osler, the father of behavioral medicine, claimed that the prognosis for heart disease depended on the lifestyle of the patient. "The ordinary high-pressure business or professional man may find relief, or even cure, in the simple process of slowing the engines, reducing the speed from the 25 knots an hour of a Lusitania to the 10 knots of a [tramp steamer]."

spurred the growth of knowledge about the meshing of psychological and medical conditions. We have known for some time that psychological factors contribute to the onset or severity of heart disease, ulcers, asthma, stomach disorders, cancer, arthritis, headaches, and hypertension. Indeed, until recently, these illness were called *psychophysiological* or *psychosomatic disorders*, in recognition of the mixture of psychological and biological determinants that operate in them. But categorizing a few select illnesses as psychosomatic implies that psychological factors contribute only to these conditions. Modern behavioral medicine considers psychological factors as potential influences on almost all diseases.

Connections

Does Freud's theory that unconscious emotional problems are responsible for physical symptoms have relevance to mental disorders? See Chapter 8, pp. 252–253.

Classifying Psychological Factors Affecting Health

The more we learn about any human disorder, the more difficult it becomes to sharply divide those that are "physical" from those that are "mental." For ex-

TABLE 6.1	Leading Causes of Death in the United States, 1900 and 1990

1900		1990	
Cause	Death rate per 100,000	*Cause*	Death rate per 100,000
Influenza and pneumonia	202.2	Diseases of the heart	152.2
Tuberculosis, all forms	194.4	Cancers	135.0
Gastroenteritis	142.7	Unintentional injuries	32.5
Diseases of the heart	137.4	Cerebrovascular diseases (stroke)	27.7
Vascular lesions of the central nervous system	106.9	Chronic obstructive pulmonary disease	19.7
All accidents	72.3	Pneumonia and influenza	14.0
Cancers	64.0	Suicide	11.5
Certain diseases of early infancy	62.6	Homicide	10.2

Source: Sexton, 1979, and the National Center for Health Statistics, 1992; cited by Taylor, 1995.

ample, schizophrenia and major depression, two of our most serious mental disorders, almost always entail a mixture of physical and psychological causes and symptoms. Furthermore, depression often adversely affects the course of diseases such as diabetes; and many cases of diabetes ultimately lead to clinical depression.

The DSM-IV deals with this dilemma in at least three ways. First, Axis III concentrates on general medical conditions that are related to a mental disor-der. Second, the DSM-IV provides special rules for classifying mental disorders caused by drugs and medical conditions. Third, it directs clinicians to use multiple diagnoses to classify *all* the conditions that might apply to a given patient. Psychological contributions to physical illnesses are coded under the special category, *Psychological Factors Affecting Medical Condition*, which appears under the broader designation *Other Conditions That May Be a Focus of Clinical Attention*. These psychological factors are coded on

At various times in history, large numbers of people have appeared to suffer a disorder in which they are always tired, feel run down and drained of energy, experience low-grade fevers, and complain of many aches, pains, and flu-like symptoms. The diagnosis and explanation for this condition has varied according to historical and cultural factors. In the nineteenth century it was termed neurasthenia, *while in the twentieth century it has been called* chronic fatigue syndrome. *In both cases, high levels of stress and evolving social roles for women (who are more likely to be diagnosed with these conditions) appear to be contributing factors. Cher has battled chronic fatigue syndrome for several years. At one point, she reported, she was so tired that she had to sit down in the shower to wash her hair.*

TABLE 6.2	DSM-IV Classification of Conditions Involving an Interaction of Physical and Psychological Features

Disorder	Major characteristics/symptoms
Psychological factors affecting medical condition	1. Presence of a medical condition or illness. 2. Psychological factor worsens prognosis, poses additional health risk, or interferes with treatment of illness.
Somatoform disorders	1. Presence of physical symptoms that suggest an illness but are not fully explained by any medical problem or physical cause. 2. Psychological factors play a substantial role in explaining the development/course of the symptoms.
Mental disorders due to a general medical condition	1. A mental disorder is the direct physical result of a general medical condition. 2. These conditions were formerly called "organic" mental disorders.
Factitious disorders	1. Physical or psychological symptoms are intentionally produced; they are not due to a true illness or medical condition. 2. The motivation for producing symptoms is a psychological need to assume the role of sick person.
Malingering	1. Physical or psychological symptoms are intentionally produced or exaggerated; they are not due to a true illness or medical condition. 2. The motivation for intentionally producing or faking symptoms is to gain an external incentive such as financial compensation or to avoid a punishment or obligation such as work or military service.

Source: APA, 1994.

Axis I because Axis I (and Axis II) is used to describe conditions that are the focus of clinicians' attention.

Note that this category is used for cases in which there are genuine physical symptoms and real damage to the body due to a medical condition. These cases are sometimes confused with somatoform and factitious disorders (see Table 6.2). *Somatoform disorders* involve physical symptoms that appear to be caused by a physical disease but in fact are largely due to psychological determinants. As will be described in Chapter 8, no diagnosable medical condition can explain the physical symptoms seen in somatoform disorders. *Factitious disorders* are diagnosed when a person intentionally fakes or exaggerates physical or psychological symptoms in order to play the role of someone who is sick. Factitious disorders are classified as mental disorders because the pretense is assumed to be motivated by psychological needs. In contrast, *malingering*, which is not a mental disorder, involves deliberately faking symptoms in order to obtain some tangible gain such as financial compensation or the avoidance of unwanted obligations.

Still, the DSM-IV is sometimes inconsistent in how it deals with conditions that involve both phys-

ical and psychological causes and symptoms. For example, male erectile disorder, a condition in which a man is chronically unable to attain or maintain an adequate erection during sexual activity, is classified as a mental disorder; so, too, are sleep disorders. Both involve obvious physical dysfunction, often caused exclusively by psychological factors. So why are they classified as mental disorders instead of as psychological conditions affecting medical condition?

When a condition straddles the fuzzy boundary between medical (physical) and mental (psychological) disorders, tradition usually determines how that disorder is classified. If a problem has traditionally been understood as a psychological condition treated primarily by mental health professionals, formal diagnostic systems are likely to define it as a mental disorder.

Linking Psychosocial Factors and Illness

Are some people psychologically disposed to physical sickness? Can psychological factors influence whether a person becomes sick? If the answer is yes, what mechanisms account for the relationship?

In his 1950 book, *Psychosomatic Medicine,* the psychoanalyst Franz Alexander extended Freud's thinking by proposing that various illnesses result from specific unconscious emotional problems. He believed, for example, that ulcers were linked to oral conflicts; hence the expression "I'm fed up with you." He attributed the cause of migraine headaches to repressed hostility, an idea captured by the phrase "He's a pain in the neck." Alexander was a key figure in advancing the field of behavioral medicine, but empirical support for most of his ideas has been weak (Friedman & Booth-Kewley, 1987). It does appear, however, that certain emotional states—particularly depression, hostility, and anxiety—are related to illness in general.

In fact, hundreds of studies have found a correlation between some measure of personality or emotion and a measure of health (Adler & Matthews, 1994; Taylor, 1995). The important question is not *whether* psychological factors are linked to illness, but *how* are they linked. Several types of connection are possible (Rodin & Salovey, 1989).

1. Disease can cause psychological changes. Even a simple case of the flu can be emotionally upsetting, and being diagnosed with a serious disease such as cancer or AIDS can lead to profound feelings of depression, demoralization, and social isolation that can, in turn, aggravate the disease. Furthermore, activity in the immune system can cause temporary behavioral and psychological changes that closely resemble the stress responses described in Chapter 5. For example, the immune system's responses to an invading pathogen may be responsible for frequent mood swings that appear unrelated to anything going on in the environment (Maier et al., 1994).

2. Disease and psychological conditions may both be influenced by a common, underlying biological process. For example, an overly reactive nervous system might increase feelings of anxiety *and* lead to a heightened risk for heart disease. In such cases, anxiety would be associated with heart disease, even though it did not cause the disease.

3. Psychological and social influences may exert a direct influence on biological processes that, in turn, are implicated in the cause of disease.

4. Psychological and social influences may indirectly lead to diseases because they encourage unhealthy behaviors.

In this chapter we will focus on the last two of these mechanisms because extensive research has established their importance (Taylor, 1995). In addi-

tion, they point to many ideas for prevention and treatment. We will concentrate on two basic questions. First, how do psychological and environmental variables cause illness in some people but not in others? Second, can changes in psychological and environmental variables prevent illness and promote recovery and better health?

In Review

Psychological Factors Affecting Medical Condition is a category in the DSM-IV that includes conditions that:

- are characterized by genuine physical symptoms and real damage to the body due to a medical condition;
- were once called *psychosomatic* or *psychophysiological disorders;* and
- are distinct from somatoform and factitious disorders.

A disease and a psychological condition may be linked because the disease:

- causes the psychological condition;
- is influenced by a process that also shapes the psychological condition;
- reflects the effect of the psychological condition on a biological process; and
- results from unhealthy behaviors.

The Psychology of Getting Sick

Personality and social factors almost certainly influence health through overlapping and interacting pathways. Figure 6.1 illustrates a model of these pathways (Adler & Matthews, 1994). The double-headed arrow between the social environment and individual dispositions suggests the numerous interactions between personality and social factors that can affect health. For example, a health-related behavior such as aggression is likely to lead to competitive situations producing physiological arousal. This arousal may ultimately increase the risk of illness. At the same time, aggressiveness may make it less likely that a person will receive social support from the environment. Because such a person is often competitive and in a hurry, he or she is also less likely to keep appointments with a physician. In summary, a personality trait such as aggressiveness can make three contributions to an illness: by increasing physiological arousal, by suppressing social support, and by interfering with healthy behavior.

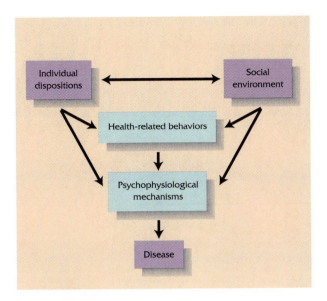

FIGURE 6.1

Personality and Environmental Influences on Disease

The social environment and individual psychological dispositions can interact to affect health behaviors and change psychophysiological processes. The result is often physical disease.

This same multifaceted influence is seen in several other illnesses. A psychological trait leads certain individuals into specific types of social environments, which in turn have stronger effects on particular types of people. In many cases these person–situation interactions culminate in unhealthy behaviors (people smoke more often when feeling nervous), physiological hyperactivation (the threat of a social evaluation increases shy people's blood pressure), or both. When these interactions occur, particularly in individuals who are genetically predisposed to any of several illnesses, the risk of sickness is heightened. In the following sections, we will examine how psychologists have applied this model of sickness to cardiovascular diseases, AIDS, and cancer.

Psychological Factors in Cardiovascular Diseases

Evidence for the adverse effects of psychological variables on physical health is particularly strong for cardiovascular diseases, which include diseases of the heart and the circulatory system. About half the deaths each year in the United States are the result of cardiovascular diseases, and their financial costs may exceed $100 billion annually.

Coronary Heart Disease. Over half a million Americans die from **coronary heart disease (CHD)**—diseases of the heart—every year. The main cause of coronary heart disease is **atherosclerosis,** in which the flow of blood to the heart is reduced due to cholesterol and other fatty substances forming **plaque** inside the walls of blood vessels. As people age, plaque builds up and clogs the flow of blood-carried supplies, primarily oxygen, to organs and muscles until serious, sometimes fatal, tissue damage results. These deposits gradually damage the arterial walls themselves, leading to clots and **aneurysms,** which are bulges in the artery walls that may rupture.

The two most serious clinical consequences of CHD are angina pectoris and myocardial infarctions. **Angina pectoris** involves periodic serious chest pains that sometimes radiate down the left arm or up the neck. In other cases, the patient experiences a squeezing, pressing sensation in the chest. Angina results from an insufficient supply of oxygen to the heart or inadequate removal of carbon dioxide from the heart. It is often made worse by emotional upset or too much physical exertion. More serious are **myocardial infarctions,** commonly known as *heart attacks*. People experiencing heart attacks often feel as if their chests are being squeezed in a vice so that they must gasp for every breath. In a heart attack the supply of blood to the heart muscle is cut off completely or nearly completely. As a result, the heart muscle can be seriously and permanently damaged, or even destroyed.

Scientists and physicians have discovered several risk factors for CHD. It is more common among men, in older people, and in people whose parents have had the disease. Cigarette smoking, high blood pressure, and high levels of low-density lipoprotein cholesterol (the so-called "bad" cholesterol) also contribute to the disease. Ethnic differences in CHD are also fairly well established; for example, it is about half as common among Chinese or Japanese Americans as among White or Black Americans.

Hypertension. High blood pressure, or **hypertension,** is another correlate of atherosclerosis. Blood pressure is measured by comparing the force of blood against the blood vessels at its highest pressure (*systole*) to its force at the lowest pressure (*diastole*). Normal blood pressure level is approximately 120/80. High blood pressure (140/90 or higher) develops either when the output of the heart is too high or when the resistance to blood flow in the vessels is too great because of atherosclerotic changes. High blood pressure puts a strain on the heart and, if left untreated, can lead to kidney problems, heart failure, and **strokes,** in which brain tissue and functioning

Lack of exercise, poor diet, and smoking are all well-known risk factors for cardiovascular diseases, but they still do not explain most instances of these diseases. Personality factors and levels of psychological stress also play important roles.

are damaged by a loss of blood (and therefore oxygen) to the brain.

As many as one-third of adult Americans may suffer high blood pressure. Over 85 percent of cases of high blood pressure are not caused by any obvious organic factor, as in the case of Beth; these cases are termed **essential hypertension.** The disorder is about twice as common among Black Americans as White Americans. Black women are at particular risk for high blood pressure; over 80 percent of those over age 60 have it. What might explain these patterns? Some biological differences have been discovered. For example, Blacks excrete less sodium than Whites do (Anderson, 1989), and retention of higher levels of sodium in the body increases the risk of hypertension.

Stress and Cardiovascular Diseases. Important as they are, risk factors such as genetics and sociocultural variables cannot explain the majority of cases of CHD or hypertension. Accordingly, scientists have studied the role of stress and personality characteristics in these disorders.

Some of the first strong evidence about the role of stress in cardiovascular activity came from a team of scientists working collaboratively at the University of Pittsburgh and Wake Forest University's Bowman Gray School of Medicine on a study of monkeys' responses to different types of stress. Stephen Manuck and his colleagues were interested in testing the idea that environmental stressors can cause increases in cardiovascular and endocrine reactivity. This heightened, stressor-induced reactivity, if repeated many times over several years, might ultimately produce

the kinds of damage in the heart or peripheral arteries seen in various cardiovascular diseases.

In one of the first of these studies (Manuck, Kaplan, & Clarkson, 1983), monkeys were exposed to a threatening stimulus (a glove that had been used in the capture of the animal), and changes in their heart rates were measured. Over time, the monkeys showing the greatest increase in heart rate in response to the glove had significantly more atherosclerosis than animals whose reactivity was less extreme.

In another study, the researchers examined the effects of social stressors on monkeys (Manuck et al., 1988). This study relied on the fact that monkeys develop social hierarchies in which dominant animals dictate the terms of existence to more submissive animals. In general, "life at the top" is thought to be preferable because the dominant animals enjoy more control over their lives and greater access to resources. Introducing new animals into the group disrupts the existing hierarchy and creates stress. The animals fight more often until a new hierarchy of dominance is established.

Does this social stress affect the monkeys' hearts? Does it affect dominant and subordinate animals differently? In this experiment, cynomolgus monkeys were assigned to one of two living conditions over a 22-month period. In the "unstable" condition, the monkeys lived in groups whose composition was changed every few months, forcing them to deal with continual disruptions of their social hierarchies. Monkeys in the "stable" condition lived with the same group of animals throughout the experiment. The monkeys were fed a diet moderately rich in choles-

Norman Anderson, director of the Office of Behavioral and Social Sciences Research at the National Institutes of Health, has called hypertension "perhaps the number-one health problem of Black Americans." Anderson has studied how stress affects the nervous systems of Blacks and Whites differently. He has discovered that Blacks are more likely to experience lower heart rate reactivity to stressors and to show a tendency toward greater constriction of peripheral arteries compared with Whites.

terol to simulate the diet of humans at higher risk for heart disease. Each monkey was also classified as dominant or subordinate based on its aggressiveness toward other monkeys.

Examination of the monkeys' coronary arteries revealed that dominant monkeys living in the unstable groups developed significantly more arterial plaque than any other monkeys. It appears as if repeated social disruptions exerted the most harm on animals who had the greatest stake in maintaining competitive advantages over their peers. In the stable group, however, it was the dominant monkeys—the ones consistently in control—who had the least arterial plaque.

As discussed in Chapter 5, people, like the monkeys in Manuck's first experiment, react to threatening stimuli and other stressors with increases in heart rate—as well as pronounced changes in blood pressure, blood levels of epinephrine and norepinephrine, and sodium secretion (Anderson, 1989; Krantz & Manuck, 1984). In the short run, these changes usually have little significance for cardiovascular functioning, which returns to normal soon after a stressor ends. Over time, however, if stressors con-

tinually stimulate cardiac activity, the small arteries at the body's periphery may undergo permanent constrictions that result in increased blood pressure (Obrist, 1981).

Psychological factors can also affect the meaning—and therefore the impact—of various stressors. At some time, all people have felt a surge in heart rate or "butterflies in the stomach" in the face of a sudden stressor, such as a near car crash or a pop quiz. When people think that they have little control over a stressful event, they are likely to experience these physiological changes as anxiety or fear, leading to more physiological reactivity and emotional upset. On the other hand, if they believe that they can cope adequately with the stressor and therefore view it as a challenge, they are more likely to interpret physiological changes as excitement or readiness, which helps reduce subsequent reactivity (Lazarus & Folkman, 1984). And, like the monkeys in the second experiment described above, many people show the greatest reactivity to interpersonal stressors that provoke hostility or competitiveness. In short, stressors are more harmful to health when they are chronic and when they exceed a person's perceived ability to cope.

Several demographic variables—ethnicity, gender, and age—are related to a tendency to overreact physiologically to stressors (Adler & Matthews, 1994), explaining why certain people are at greater risk for heart disease than others. Black Americans, men, and older people all suffer higher-than-average rates of heart disease—*and* have greater-than-average blood pressure responses to certain stressors.

Why these responses occur is not yet clear, although physical factors (such as diet) and cultural factors (such as living in stressful environments) are certainly important contributors. In one study, persons who lived in crowded, urban environments (defined by the presence of a high number of both commercial and residential properties) showed more cardiovascular reactivity to laboratory stressors than did residents of lower stress areas (Fleming et al., 1987). Because Black Americans are more likely to be exposed to this kind of living arrangement, their heightened risk of cardiovascular disease may be due in part to higher levels of chronic stress.

Various psychological characteristics may be linked to demographics as well as to greater health risks. Men may be more likely to behave aggressively or competitively in social situations. Older people may suffer a gradual erosion in social sup-

Connections

How are people's health, stressful experiences, and perceptions of coping abilities related to dispositional optimism? See Chapter 5, pp. 178–179.

Type As dislike tasks that require a slow, patient approach such as driving in heavy traffic. They become frustrated and angry with such a pace, thereby linking their hurried tempo to frequent hostility.

port, thereby decreasing the extent to which others can help them cope. As a result of facing more social adversity and obstacles, Black Americans may feel or express more anger, which may be an especially important psychological risk factor.

Identifying the Type A Behavior Pattern. The most intensively studied psychological risk factor for cardiovascular diseases is the Type A Behavior Pattern (Friedman & Rosenman, 1974). This pattern was named by Meyer Friedman and Ray Rosenman, two California cardiologists whose office receptionist made an offhand comment that the upholstery on the front edges of their waiting room chairs were worn off and needed to be replaced. The significance of this observation about patients squirming, literally on the edge of their seats, was later confirmed by a woman who told the physicians:

> If you really want to know what is going to give our husbands heart disease, I'll tell you. . . . It's stress, the stress they have to face in their business, day in, day out. Why, when my husband comes home at night, it takes at least one martini just to unclench his jaws. (Friedman & Ulmer, 1984, p. 4)

When Friedman and Rosenman studied the lives of their patients more carefully, they discovered a specific emotional and behavioral pattern that seemed to

heighten the risk of CHD. In 1958, for the first time, they termed this the **Type A behavior pattern,** or the "hurry sickness."

What are the psychological characteristics of the Type A behavior pattern? Type A persons tend to be highly competitive, driving hard to achieve maximum outcomes in minimum time, and defining success in terms of the quantity of work they finish or the amount of recognition they receive. Their pursuit of visible success is relentless, leading others to see them as rude, hostile, and aggressive. Type A persons also show a heightened sense of *time urgency,* a feeling that time is passing too quickly and that they must always hurry to get things done. They seem restless, edgy, and nervous, and consequently do poorly on tasks that require sustained attention. They become enraged at drivers in front of them who go too slowly. They cannot stand to wait in line and become impatient with obstacles to their progress. Type A speech is often loud, fast, and pressured. Their overall tempo of life is sometimes just short of frantic, yet they are always dissatisfied with what they have accomplished.

Type A individuals strive to maintain control over as much of their environment as possible. They do not like to feel unprepared, and they dislike ambiguity or uncertainty. In general, they seem preoccupied with maintaining a high sense of self-esteem by always striving to do better than others (Matthews, 1982). They are usually willing to put achievement goals ahead of social interactions. Although most initial research on Type A behavior was conducted with men, the Type A behavior pattern appears to be similar in women.

In contrast to Type A behavior, persons with **Type B behavior patterns** are more relaxed and feel less time pressure in their lives. They also appear less controlling, hostile, and competitive. They thrive on tasks that require careful analysis and sustained concentration.

Researchers have used several assessment devices to identify Type A individuals, but different measures of Type A behavior do not agree well in their classifications (Matthews & Haynes, 1986), a fact that complicates research on the pattern. For convenience, many studies have relied on a 50-item questionnaire called the *Jenkins Activity Schedule* (Jenkins, Zyzanski, & Rosenman, 1979) that contains questions such as "Do you ever have trouble finding time to get your hair cut or styled?" However, this questionnaire has not proved to be a sensitive measure of Type A behavior.

A more valid measure of Type A behavior is a special structured interview (Rosenman, 1978) that consists of questions that measure not only the content of what people say but also how they respond to frustrating incidents in the interview itself. For example, the interviewer might ask whether the person always shows up on time for appointments and how he or she feels if the appointment is delayed. During the person's answer, the interviewer might interrupt or challenge the candor of the answer. The interviewer may deliberately try to provoke hostility and impatience by asking questions in a slow, distracted manner—a behavior designed to annoy the average Type A person. Tapes of these interviews are scored for both verbal and nonverbal signs of Type A behavior.

Does Type A Behavior Cause CHD? The first large-scale study of Type A behavior as a risk factor for CHD was the Western Collaborative Group Study (WCGS), an 8½ year study of 3,500 men between the ages of 39 and 59 (Rosenman, et al., 1975). At the beginning of the study, the men were assessed for three risk factors: a test of blood clotting, a measure of different kinds of cholesterol, and a measure of Type A or Type B behavior (about half the men were one or the other).

Within 1 year, 113 men had been diagnosed with CHD, and 80 of them were Type A individuals. By the end of the study, 257 men had suffered heart attacks, and 178 (69 percent) were Type As. In other words, over these 8½ years, Type A men were more than twice as likely to have heart attacks as Type B men were. Even after controlling for several other risk factors, including family history of heart disease, high cholesterol, high blood pressure, and cigarette smoking, Type A behavior substantially increased the risk of CHD.

A second major epidemiological study involved about 1,600 healthy men and women who participated in the Framingham (Massachusetts) Heart Study, begun over 40 years ago to evaluate a wide array of CHD risk factors. The investigators (Haynes, Feinleib, & Kannel, 1980) classified subjects as Type A or Type B; they then followed their health status for the next 8 years. More than twice as many Type A participants developed CHD as Type B persons did.

Enough evidence about Type A behavior had accumulated by 1981 that a special review panel from the National Heart, Lung, and Blood Institute concluded that the Type A behavior pattern was a risk factor equal in magnitude to smoking and high levels of LDL cholesterol. However, we now know that the links that tie Type A behavior to CHD are much more complicated than was originally believed.

First, being a Type A person does not mean that you are highly likely to suffer a heart attack or other form of CHD. The vast majority of people catego-

rized as Type A in either the WCGS or Framingham study never developed CHD. Instead, they were simply about twice as likely as Type B persons to develop CHD.

Second, more recent prospective studies, which involved additional follow-up of the WCGS (Ragland & Brand, 1988), or were conducted with Asian men rather than Europeans (Cohen & Reed, 1985), or that carefully reanalyzed the Framingham study (Eaker et al., 1989, 1992) suggest that Type A behavior is not necessarily a significant risk factor for heart trouble (see Matthews, 1988; Miller et al., 1991 for reviews). A few studies, have even found the reverse relationship: Type B persons were at higher risk than Type As (Ragland & Brand, 1988).

How can we explain these contradictory findings? One possibility is that different research methodologies produce different outcomes. For example, studies that use the structured interview report stronger relationships between Type A and CHD than studies using questionnaire measures. Another possible explanation of the conflicting findings may lie in the fact that not all of the various components of the Type A behavior pattern are equally damaging to health.

Negative Affect and CHD. Recent research suggests that the most health-risky component of the Type A pattern are negative emotions such as hostility, anger, and cynicism (Williams & Barefoot, 1988). Although Type A behavior might be related to poor health in general (Adler & Matthews, 1994), hostility, especially when it involves cynicism and a chronic suspiciousness or distrust of others, seems to pose the greatest risk for CHD (Dembroski et al., 1985). Other investigators believe that the research is not yet clear enough to single out hostility as the major CHD risk factor (Thoresen & Powell, 1992).

It may be that chronic negative emotions, whether part of Type A behavior or not, carry the greatest risks for CHD, and for physical illness in general. For example, after controlling for age, obesity, smoking, and alcohol use, one team of researchers found that anxiety significantly predicted the 20-year incidence of hypertension in middle-aged men in the Framingham Heart Study (Markowitz et al., 1991). Separate large-scale studies (Appels & Otten, 1992; Appels & Schouten, 1991) have found that men who reported fatigue, dejection, defeat, and increased irritability—a condition termed **vital exhaustion,** or what is commonly called *burnout*—were at higher risk for later angina and heart attacks. A comprehensive review of the literature on psychological predictors of CHD found that persons with one or more negative emotions such as depression, aggressive competitiveness, and anger were more likely to develop CHD than were hurried, impatient work-aholics, the traditional Type A people (Booth-Kewley & Friedman, 1987).

Some Tentative Conclusions About Type A and CHD.
If we combine the findings about negative emotions with studies of the physiology of Type As, an interesting picture begins to take shape (see Figure 6.2). When encountering a stressor, Type As experience faster heart rate, higher diastolic blood pressure, and higher systolic blood pressure than Type Bs do (Harbin, 1989; Lyness, 1993). These differences in physiological reactivity are strongest in response to stressors that generate interpersonal conflict, mobilize competitiveness, or involve criticism. Of course, these are the types of situations most likely to lead to anger and hostility. Likewise, chronically hostile people experience high levels of cardiovascular reactivity, most notably in response to interpersonal stressors (Suls & Wang, 1993).

Perhaps Type A behavior or chronic negative emotions are linked to CHD because people with these characteristics consistently overreact physiologically to situations that threaten them or make them angry. In addition, their competitiveness and hostility create more and more opportunities for conflict, to which they then overreact. In the long run, the physiological overarousal could put a strain on arteries and increase the chances of other cardiovascular defects. The link between these characteristics and CHD might also be forged in another way. Frequent angry outbursts or other negative emotions may be accompanied by rapid swings in the levels of stress hormones such as the corticosteroids and catecholamines. A constant barrage of hormonal changes could, in turn, bring about various chemical changes that weaken arteries.

Hypotheses about these psychological–biological mechanisms still need much more evaluation. They may contribute to the link between psychological

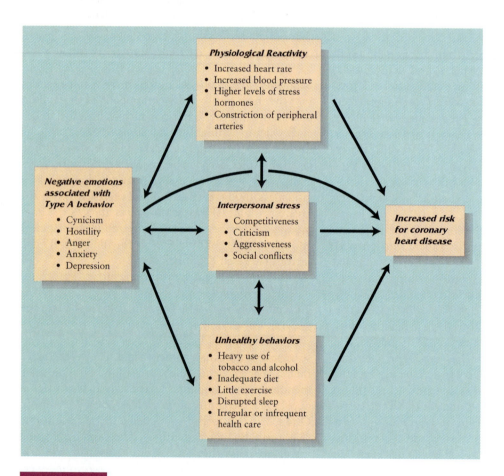

FIGURE 6.2

Type A Risks for Coronary Heart Disease
The negative emotions associated with Type A behavior interact with physiological reactivity, interpersonal stress, and harmful behaviors to increase a person's risks for CHD.

Karen Matthews

Dr. Karen Matthews is Professor of Psychiatry, Epidemiology, and Psychology at the University of Pittsburgh. Her research focuses on the study of behavioral risk factors for cardiovascular disease. Dr. Matthews is a past editor of Health Psychology. *In 1992, she received the Distinguished Contributions to Health Psychology Award from the Health Psychology Division of the American Psychological Association.*

Health Psychology

Q *You have been studying Type A behavior for years. Why do you think Type A behavior is a risk factor for heart disease?*

A Our knowledge about Type A behavior and heart disease has changed a lot over the 30 years we have studied it. The original idea that hard-driving competitiveness and a fast pace of life were the main culprits might have been true for the men who were first studied back in the 1960s and 1970s. They were a different population from the people we study today. Society and families certainly have also changed since then. The men in the original studies were largely sole breadwinners, trying to accomplish a lot professionally because they had returned from fighting in World War II and were catching up on life's activities. It is easy to see how they could have become frustrated and annoyed by obstacles. Today, those professional priorities may be less closely related to feelings of annoyance and distrust. Nonetheless, negative emotions, in and of themselves, still appear to be quite important.

> *. . . socioeconomic class (SES) "acts as a proxy" for psychological and social health risks.*

Q *We discuss socioeconomic factors in this chapter [page 199] and how they are often associated with greater risk for illness. How important are socioeconomic factors to a health psychologist?*

A They are absolutely critical because they usually signal the influence of several other processes that compromise health. That is what we mean when we say that socioeconomic class (SES) "acts as a proxy" for psychological and social health risks. For example, consider gender and educational attainment and imagine an adolescent female who quits school in the 10th grade because of an unexpected pregnancy. Early childbirth will limit her opportunity to return to school at the same time that it reduces her occupational alternatives. These limits impose serious financial restraints on a woman, who, in turn, now has few resources for coping with difficult circumstances and for leisure time activities.

Q *Let's talk about intervention and prevention. What makes for a successful health psychology intervention?*

A Interventions, whether they involve treatment or prevention, have the greatest potential when done early. When I say "early," I mean in the childhood years. Most health habits are established by middle school so, if you want to instill health-protective behaviors with lasting impact, you have to start at this age, and your programs must involve both the school curriculum and families. If families are not trained to support the behaviors their children learn in school, these changes will not be maintained.

The same thing is true for psychological variables. Negative emotions begin to stabilize in middle childhood so if we strive to increase feelings of trust or conscientiousness—both of which are associated with better health—we must encourage these traits in families when their children are young.

Q *Why do you think conscientiousness has an important influence on health?*

A Actually, evidence about its potential importance can be gleaned from several sources. One is your "Termites" study discussed in the Controversy section [202–203]. A recent analysis by Ralph Horowitz examined the effects of people regularly taking the medication they were prescribed in clinical research trials. This involves the issue of adherence or compliance that you also describe in the chapter. Horowitz found that not only was adhering to the active medication schedule important for improvement, but also that those people who adhered better *even when taking a placebo* improved more than those who did not. There must be something healthful about the act of adherence itself, which brings us back to the matter of conscientiousness. Conscientious people may be more willing to commit themselves to taking medication and maintaining schedules. Ultimately, they may develop more effective living skills in general.

variables and CHD, but they may not be the only, or even the most important, link. Type A people tend to experience more negative emotions, but they also are often too busy to go to a doctor, to eat a balanced diet, to get enough sleep, or to engage in regular exercise. They may eat on the run, consume excessive caffeine, and smoke tobacco. These unhealthy behaviors may turn out to be even more critical to the development of CHD than any of the biological effects we have discussed. In all likelihood, the interaction of unhealthy behaviors with emotionally driven wear and tear on the cardiovascular system will prove to be the most complete explanation of the risks for CHD.

Psychological Factors and the Immune System

*K*eri is a college senior with a double major in biology and computer science. She has her heart set on attending medical school and consequently takes her academic work very seriously. Keri normally maintains an active social life and enjoys good physical health, except during final exams, when she pulls out all the stops to ensure that she does well. At those times, Keri devotes all her time to studying, even renting a motel room during finals week so she will have a quiet place to study for as long and as late as she wants every night. This strategy has worked well when it comes to her grades, but for the last four semesters, Keri has gone home for semester break and has immediately come down with a cold. Her "vacation sickness" is something of a family joke, but Keri can't understand why she always gets sick after her exams are over.

Keri's case is another example of how psychological characteristics can increase disease risks via a biological mechanism—this time through their influence on the *immune system,* the body's defense network. A description of how the *macrophages* of the immune system detect invading bacteria and viruses and how *T cells* and *B cells* then attack the invaders was presented in Chapter 5.

Although immunologists once thought that the brain and the immune system operated independently, we now know that they are connected in important ways. In fact, a new field of study, called **psychoneuroimmunology,** has come into being to study how the brain, the immune system, and psychological processes affect each other (Ader & Cohen, 1993).

One of the most convincing demonstrations of these interconnections is a study in which rats learned to inhibit immune responses through Pavlovian con-

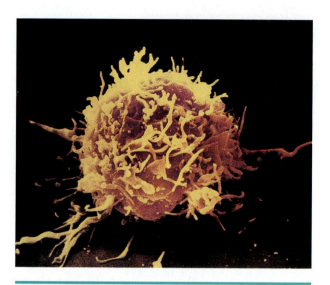

Killer T-cells such as the ones shown here fight illness by encircling a diseased cell, bacterium, or virus and destroying it.

ditioning (Ader & Cohen, 1982). The rats drank saccharine-flavored water and were then immediately injected with *cyclophosphamide,* a drug that is used to treat cancer or lupus but that also suppresses the immune system. After experiencing several such pairings, the rats were given the flavored water without the drugs being injected. Much as Pavlov's dogs showed conditioned salivation to the sound of a bell, these rats showed decreased immune functioning when they tasted the flavored water. Immunosuppression had become a conditioned response to a taste.

Not only did this experiment show that psychological processes—in this case, learning—could influence immunity, it also suggested an explanation for an important problem in treating cancer patients. Chemotherapy is the treatment of first choice for the majority of cancer patients, but, unfortunately, drugs such as cyclophosphamide are toxic and produce many side effects such as severe nausea and vomiting, jaundice, and hair loss in addition to immunosuppression. In fact, it is common to discover that cancer patients undergoing chemotherapy develop these symptoms (including immunosuppression) merely upon traveling to the clinic or hospital where they receive their treatments.

Almost half of adult cancer patients treated with chemotherapy vomit or become nauseated in the 24 hours *preceding* drug administrations (Burish & Carey, 1986), a condition called **anticipatory nausea.** These side effects are extremely stressful and embarrassing for many patients, and they start to dread anything associated with their treatment. Ultimately, many patients stop chemotherapy because they are overwhelmed by its aversive side effects.

The most likely explanation for anticipatory nausea is that patients learn to associate the chemotherapy drug's physical side effects (unconditioned responses) with the sights, sounds, and smells of the hospital (conditioned stimuli). Just as rats can learn to associate flavored water with immunosuppression, a few pairings of hospital stimuli with chemotherapy-induced nausea may be enough to create conditioned nausea (Andrykowski & Redd, 1987; Carey & Burish, 1988).

Stress, the Immune System, and Illness. Disruptions in the immune system can lead to illnesses in two ways. First, a hyperreactive immune system can damage healthy tissue, leading to autoimmune diseases such as rheumatoid arthritis, which affects millions of older people. Second, as described in Chapter 5, stress can suppress the functioning of the immune system, and, when the stress response is maintained for too long, continued immunosuppression leads to greater susceptibility to disease and slower recovery from illness. Researchers have repeatedly documented links between stress and compromised immunity. In one study, researchers injected volunteers with cold viruses or with a placebo pathogen and then measured the amount of stress the volunteers experienced over a set time (Cohen, Tyrell, & Smith, 1991). The results showed that the number of colds and infections was correlated with the amount of stress the subjects encountered. Rates of children's infections increase when their families are under stress (Boyce et al., 1977), and the risk of diseases associated with herpes virus infections is increased for people experiencing more stress (Kiecolt-Glaser & Glaser, 1987). Residents living near the Three Mile Island nuclear reactor experienced significantly lower B cell and T cell activity following exposure to the nuclear accident that occurred there compared with a similar group of people who did not live near the disaster site (McKinnon et al., 1989). Similar results have been predicted for technological disasters such as the 1986 nuclear accident at Chernobyl in the Soviet Union or the 1984 gas leak in Bhopal, India. Interpersonal stressors such as marital conflict and hostility can also impair immunological functioning (Kiecolt-Glaser et al., 1993).

One of the stressors most often linked to lowered immunity (and perhaps more illness) is an event with which all students are familiar—examinations. Some empirical studies (Workman & LaVia, 1987) have shown that, as with the case of Keri, healthy students suffer a decline in the effectiveness of their immune systems while taking finals.

If stress and psychological factors adversely affect immune system functioning, it is possible that they might also worsen or complicate such diseases

Half of all Americans over 65 suffer from arthritis or other painful bone or joint conditions. One of the most severe of these is rheumatoid arthritis (RA), an autoimmune disease involving pain and swelling in the joints and progressive deformity and disability. The main medical treatments of RA are antiinflammatory drugs (which often have severe side effects) or surgical replacement of deteriorated joints (which is very expensive). Several well-controlled studies have shown that a combination of cognitive behavioral techniques and biofeedback training can decrease RA patients' pain, psychological distress, and overall impairment (Young, 1992).

as acquired immune deficiency syndrome (AIDS) and cancer, two lethal conditions that involve impaired immunity.

AIDS. The first case of AIDS in the United States was diagnosed in 1981, although the disease originated in the rain forests of central Africa a few years earlier (Preston, 1994). **AIDS** is caused by the **human immunodeficiency virus type 1 (HIV-1)**, which destroys the immune system's T cells, leaving an infected person susceptible to all sorts of secondary, opportunistic infections, central nervous system damage, and malignancies that ultimately may result in death. HIV is a particularly formidable enemy to the immune system because it can convert itself so adroitly into mutant strains that are highly resistant to drug treatments. The course of AIDS is variable; many people die within the first year of developing the disease, others may survive for 5 years or more; some individuals test positive for HIV and go as long as a decade with almost no symptoms.

It is estimated that 650,000 to 1 million Americans are HIV positive, and over 20 million people worldwide are infected with HIV. By the year 2000, 30 million people (including 10 million children) around the world could be infected with AIDS (Shariff, 1995). In African and Asian countries, HIV infections are transmitted primarily through heterosexual contact and via mother–child transmission; HIV seroprevalence is now approaching 25 percent in some of these areas (Kelly & Murphy, 1992). During the 1980s, the two highest-risk groups in the United States were homosexual males and intravenous drug users. These two groups still account for the largest number of AIDS cases in the United States, but the incidence of HIV infections is growing especially fast among low-income Black Americans and Hispanic American adolescents. AIDS is also spreading among young women at a particularly alarming rate. HIV/AIDS is now the fourth leading killer of American women between 18 and 44, ranking behind only cancer, accidents, and heart disease. According to World Health Organization estimates, by the year 2000, HIV/AIDS is expected to become the world's second-leading cause of death for women. The HIV epidemic among women in the United States appears to be linked to increases in women's poverty, use of intravenous drugs, and sexual abuse victimization.

Psychological factors are implicated in AIDS in two major ways. First, most cases of AIDS can be prevented by avoiding three high-risk sexual behaviors: (1) heavy use of alcohol or drugs before sexual activity; (2) sexual activity with multiple partners and/or partners with an unknown sexual history; and (3) sexual activity without condoms. A fourth risk behavior for many HIV infections is the sharing of needles used to inject drugs.

The second way in which psychological factors are implicated in AIDS is that they can influence the overall course of the disease, particularly if those factors bring about changes in immunity. For example, if people can learn to cope with stress more effectively, it may be that improvements in their overall psychological functioning will be accompanied by a fortification of the immune system. Later in this chapter we will discuss psychological interventions aimed at changing high-risk behaviors as well as a program to protect immune functions.

Cancer. Normally, the cells in our body divide in an orderly fashion, directed by the right match of pro-

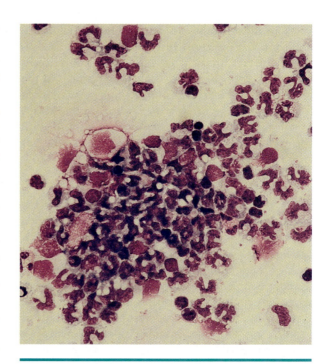

Healthy and cancerous cells in the human body. The healthy cells are small and dark; the cancerous cells are lighter.

teins and protein receptors. This match is a little like a key fitting just the right lock; if the fit is right, the key clicks in and the lock turns. But if certain mutations occur in a cell, the cell can begin to reproduce itself without any direction, spreading wildly throughout the body like a skeleton key that turns almost any lock (Bodmer & McKie, 1994). This out-of-control reproduction leads to tumors or *metastasized* growth throughout the body. The initial causes of cell mutations are not yet fully understood, but we do know that age, radiation, chemicals, and other environmental hazards are some of the triggers that can fire a cell into the chaotic and deadly division that becomes a cancer.

Cancer is actually a collection of diseases that begin with a malfunction in the way DNA controls cell growth. It is the second leading cause of death in the United States. About 1 million Americans are diagnosed with cancer each year, and one of every three Americans will be diagnosed with some form of cancer in his or her lifetime. Psychosocial factors are related to the risk of cancer in several ways. First, the incidence of cancer in the United States is mildly related to ethnicity and gender, as shown in Figure 6.3. Second, and perhaps most obvious, cancers are linked to environmental events; unhealthy habits such as smoking tobacco or eating a high-fat diet increase the risk of several types of cancer by increas-

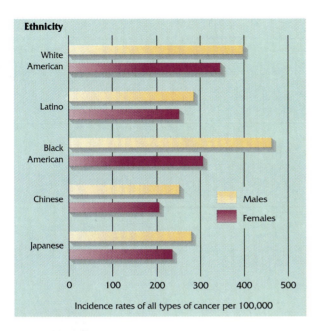

Ethnicity

Incidence rates of all types of cancer per 100,000

Males
Females

FIGURE 6.3

Cancer Rates According to Gender and Ethnicity
Across most ethnic groups in the United States, men are at slightly greater risk for contracting cancer than women are. These rates have been adjusted slightly to rule out the effects of age.

ing a person's exposure to potential hazards (Bodmer & McKie, 1994).

Another question about psychology and cancer is whether certain personality types are more susceptible to cancer or more likely to suffer a worse prognosis once cancer is diagnosed. The so-called **Type C personality,** or cancer-prone personality, has often been described as an overly conforming, emotionally blunted person who appears calm and collected on the outside but is trying to deny and repress emotional turmoil. Type C persons are also thought to feel hopeless and relatively powerless in controlling their lives. Although this theory has been in circulation for many years (Kissen & Eysenck, 1962), the empirical evidence supporting it is quite weak. Longitudinal studies that have attempted to predict cancer onset from personality variables measured earlier in a person's life have produced conflicting findings. At this point, the relationship between personality traits and cancer risk is best regarded as unproved.

Social Factors and Illness

As noted in Chapter 5, stressors are less likely to adversely affect the physical health of people who enjoy high levels of social support. Several explanations for the beneficial effects of social support were discussed: it may buffer the negative effects of stressors; it may increase individuals' sense of well-being and overall physical health regardless of its effects on stressors; or it may reflect the fact that socially competent persons are more likely to have many friends and maintain better health. Whatever the explanation, the lack of social support increases the risk for physical illnesses (Cohen & Wills, 1985) and even death (House et al., 1982).

The impact of social factors on health is also seen in the consistently strong relationship between socioeconomic status and health. **Socioeconomic status (SES)** reflects a person's standing relative to others in a society. It is measured by the combination of a person's income, education, and occupation.

Figure 6.4 on page 200 summarizes the findings of two studies that measured **standardized mortality ratios**—the ratio of deaths that actually occur to deaths that are naturally expected—at different SES levels. SES classes were defined slightly differently in these studies so the comparisons are not exact, but the relationship is clear. Whether a study considered males or females, whether SES was measured by education in the United States (Kitagawa & Hauser, 1973) or by occupation in the United Kingdom (Adelstein, 1980), the lower people's socioeconomic standing, the greater their chances of unexpected death. This relationship is not limited to comparisons between people at the bottom of the SES ladder with those at the top; it holds up between every pair of levels of the hierarchy (Adler et al., 1994). Looking at the frequency of chronic illnesses, rather than death rates, at different SES levels tells the same story: the lower the SES, the higher the rates of sickness.

How can we explain this SES–health gradient? One possibility is the social drift hypothesis described in Chapter 1. According to this theory, the multiple impairments resulting from a mental disorder may cause people to gradually slide down the SES ladder. However, this explanation does not work when we consider physical health. For example, if illness leads to lower SES, we should find no SES–illness association for older people in studies that computed SES on the basis of education. People's health in their 70s obviously cannot have affected their education when they were teenagers. However, research shows a reliable link between the current health of elderly people and their SES measured by prior attainments (see Adler et al., 1994).

Connections

What other adverse consequences might a lower SES have on adjustment or psychological functioning? For a discussion of the effects of *social causation,* see Chapter 1, pp. 27–28.

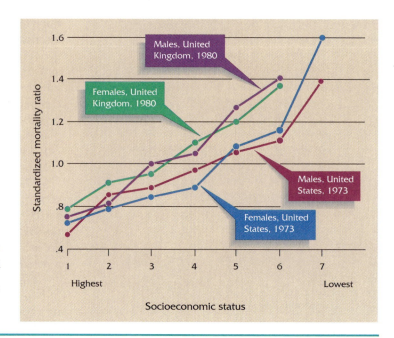

FIGURE 6.4

Effects of SES on Unexpected Death Rates
The rate of unexpected deaths (the standardized mortality ratio) increases as the SES level decreases. This relationship is true regardless of gender or country, and it is consistent at each step down the SES ladder.

Another possibility is that SES affects biochemical processes—such as physiological reactivity and immune system impairments—that, in turn, lead to poor health. Low SES is linked to poorer basic nutrition, more exposure to environmental hazards, and less adequate medical care. If these problems are severe and continue for long periods, they can contribute to a greater number of biologically based problems. However, these factors are more likely to explain the health disadvantages suffered by poor people compared with rich, rather than the differences between middle and upper SES levels, where nutritional, environmental, and health care differences are not as great.

The most likely explanation of the health–SES link is that there are SES differences in psychological functioning, environmental stressors, and everyday behavior that can affect people's vulnerability to illness.

1. *Psychological functioning.* As already noted, negative emotions are significantly linked to greater risks for serious illnesses. Social class is inversely related to certain strong negative emotions. For example, depressive symptoms and the formal diagnosis of depression are more likely to occur among lower-SES populations. Likewise, hostility and chronic antagonism tend to be higher among the less educated (Scherwitz et al., 1992). Therefore, an association between SES and poorer health may be mediated through their common relationship to increased levels of chronic negative emotion.

If negative emotions are linked to the risk of illness, might certain positive traits or emotions be linked to good health? The Controversy section on pages 202–203 explores this possibility.

2. *Stressors.* People of lower SES face more negative life events than do higher-SES individuals (McLeod & Kessler, 1990), thereby increasing the adversities with which they must cope. Of course, lower income and educational status make it likely that people will also have fewer resources at hand to cope with these stressors, thereby further increasing their impact.

3. *Unhealthy behaviors.* The practice of many unhealthy behaviors tends to be inversely related to socioeconomic status. Smoking is consistently more common among less-educated people, and people who work in lower-status occupations are less likely to engage in physical exercise. These habits have direct effects on health, but they also often act in concert with each other, and with other variables, to magnify health problems. For example, lack of physical exercise is associated with obesity, which itself is more common among low-SES groups (Ernst & Harlan, 1991). Obesity significantly increases risks for such serious illnesses as hypertension, diabetes, and CHD (Brownell & Wadden, 1992; Foster & Kendall, 1994). Similarly, people who drink alcohol excessively or abuse illegal drugs are also much more likely to smoke (Sobell, Toneatto, & Sobell, 1994), thereby constituting a double behavioral risk.

Worse yet, smoking prevention or cessation programs are less likely to be effective with impoverished or poorly educated people. Poor people may have less time available to attend such programs, and less-educated people may not be fully aware of the health implications of smoking or other behaviors. Social pressures for practicing certain health habits may be fewer among lower-SES groups, thus contributing to a lack of motivation to stop smoking or to lose weight.

The relationship between SES and risky health habits may help explain how SES builds psychological and stressful links to poor health. Beyond their obvious harmful physiological effects, a combination of unhealthy behaviors involving substance abuse and poor nutrition is also likely to lead to greater depression, increased levels of stress, and less adequate coping skills (Valliant, 1994b). For people in lower socioeconomic classes, years of engaging in harmful behaviors may slowly but surely lead to a cluster of bad outcomes that include greater levels of stress, poorer mental health, and more frequent physical diseases.

In Review

Personality and social factors can increase the risks of physical illness by:

- causing changes in physiological reactivity, immune system functioning, or other biological processes; and
- leading to changes in health-related behaviors such as smoking, diet, physical exercise, and following medical advice.

Research on psychosocial risk factors in cardiovascular diseases has focused on:

- the role of stress in generating chronically exaggerated physiological reactivity that can ultimately damage the cardiovascular system; and
- Type A behavior, particularly those components that involve negative emotions such as anger, anxiety, and cynicism.

When an organism must cope with stressful conditions for long periods:

- the functioning of the immune system may be suppressed; and
- the risk of diseases that involve impairments in immunity such as cancer may become more likely.

Lower socioeconomic status is related to a greater risk of illness and premature death; this relationship appears to be due to a combination of:

- biological factors associated with poverty;
- greater exposure to stressors;
- higher levels of negative emotions; and
- more unhealthy behaviors such as smoking.

The Psychology of Getting Well and Staying Well

If psychosocial factors are implicated in the onset or course of chronic illnesses, perhaps these factors could also be manipulated as part of the prevention or treatment of disease. For example, improved mood, increased social support, or better coping skills might enhance the immune system and therefore help prevent or fight diseases that involve serious immunological deficiencies. Some diseases or injuries might also be prevented if people could learn to give up unhealthy behaviors or practice healthy behaviors more regularly. Finally, the pain or severity of certain medical conditions might be reduced if people could use psychological techniques to gain better control over disabling symptoms.

We will evaluate these possibilities by again considering coronary heart disease, AIDS, and cancer. However, treatments arising from behavioral medicine and health psychology have been directed at many other targets as well, including gastrointestinal problems, respiratory illnesses, pediatric conditions, recovery from surgery, prevention of accidents and violence, and pain disorders (Blan-

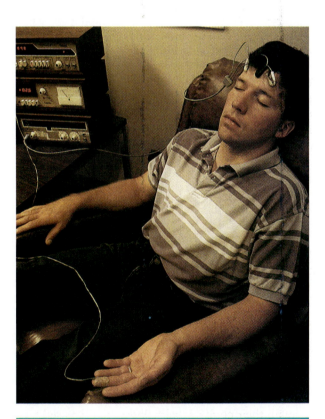

If given feedback about a physiological activity such as heart rate or blood pressure, individuals can learn to reduce their arousal in order to reduce stress.

Controversy   Is Virtue Good for You?

Social and psychological stressors have surprisingly strong effects on physical health, even among people who are not socially or economically disadvantaged. One of the more remarkable demonstrations of these effects is a long-term follow-up of participants in L. M. Terman's famous study of young, intellectually gifted students. Beginning in 1921, as part of his examination of the genetics of intelligence, Terman recruited 1,528 primary-school boys and girls in California who had measured IQs of at least 135. He then followed these children, nicknamed the "Termites," into adulthood, measuring their emotional and intellectual development at 5- to 10-year intervals (Terman & Oden, 1947).

In the early 1990s, when about half the Termites had died, Howard Friedman and his associates (Friedman et al., 1995) used Terman's data as part of an ingenious study of the effects of stress and personality on physical health and longevity. Friedman and his coinvestigators tracked down the death certificates of the deceased members of the sample and coded when and how each Termite had

died. They then examined Terman's original archives to find measures of early social stress, childhood and adolescent patterns of personality, and various health behaviors that might predict longevity and various illnesses.

They first discovered results for this sample that were consistent with the well-known fact that women tend to outlive men; female Termites lived, on average, about 6 years longer than males. More relevant to our interests, however, is that, when the researchers divided the Termites into two groups—those whose parents either had or had not divorced before their children reached 21—they discovered that the children of divorced parents had a one-third greater mortality risk than those whose parents remained married. Instability in the Termites' own marriages was also related to mortality. Those who had been married more than once and those who had been separated, widowed, or divorced were all at higher risk for an earlier death than Termites who remained married.

Finally, the researchers found that measures of personality col-

lected when these people were as young as 11 years old were also related to mortality. Children who were rated by parents and teachers as conscientious, truthful, and dependable were about 30 percent less likely to die in any given year than children who had been described as impulsive and immature. As might be expected, conscientious children grew up to smoke and drink less; was this lower rate of unhealthy behaviors the real reason for their longevity? Apparently not. Even after controlling for drinking and smoking, conscientiousness remained a strong predictor of longevity.

In summary, for this sample, the experience of parental or personal divorce predicted premature death. As the accompanying figure shows, personality did so as well; adults who were impulsive and troublesome as children tended to die earlier than those who had been more conscientious as children. Family stability and personal dependability appear to be good for your health, or in the words of Friedman et al. (1995), "In terms of the rush toward death, the en-

chard, 1994; Taylor, Ironson, & Burnett, 1990; Taylor, 1995).

Regardless of the illness under study, the most effective interventions usually involve a combination of treatment techniques. One particular trio of techniques has repeatedly demonstrated superior effects. The first component is training in a stress-reduction technique such as relaxation training, biofeedback, hypnosis, or meditation. These techniques are often effective in reducing the physiological arousal and anxiety that can complicate a serious illness.

The second technique is cognitive restructuring, which is frequently effective in combating feelings of depression and hopelessness in the face of a serious illness. Patients are taught more adaptive ways to think about problem solving in general, their specific

illnesses, and their ability to exert control over their lives. An increased sense of control is particularly important in helping patients recover promptly from surgery, which about 25 million Americans undergo annually. Because the length of a hospital stay after an operation is a main determinant of the cost of surgical care, considerable savings in health care costs would be realized if the length of hospitalization could be safely reduced. This application of health psychology began many years ago when psychologist Irving Janis (1958) discovered that surgery patients who held realistic expectations about what their surgery would be like showed the best postoperative recovery. These "realistic" patients appeared to engage in just the right amount of worry to prepare themselves for their surgeries.

couraging news may be that good guys finish last" (p. 76).

Of course Terman's sample is not representative of the American population as a whole. The Termites were a bright and well-educated group of people who probably enjoyed at least adequate medical care throughout their lives and lived comfortably above poverty levels. On the one hand, these characteristics make it un-likely that social adversity would contribute to poor health, thereby maximizing the chance that personal and family characteristics could play a larger role. On the other hand, the fact that Terman's subjects were relatively successful suggests that they might have possessed several kinds of resources to buffer the negative effects of personal or family difficulties on their health. Individuals with fewer resources might have been more strongly affected by life's stressors and trauma. It will take additional research to help resolve these differing interpretations and to learn how well this study's conclusions apply to other groups.

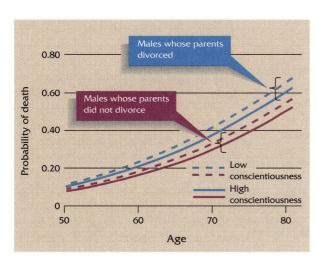

Childhood Conscientiousness, Parental Divorce, and Longevity

Children of divorced parents faced a greater risk of early death than did children whose parents had remained married. Children who were rated as conscientious—high in dependability and trustworthiness—survived longer than children who were rated low in conscientiousness. (The data depicted are for males; females had significantly different survival rates, but showed the same effect.)

Thinking Critically

The beneficial effects of conscientiousness were due not only to the fact that conscientious people smoked and drank less.

- What other health-related behaviors might be involved?
- Do the measures of conscientiousness that were collected in childhood guarantee that personality differences caused the health differences?

Since Janis's discovery, several researchers have found that informing surgical patients about the course of an operation and its usual aftereffects improves their postsurgery adjustment. For example, if patients are told how much pain to expect and are instructed in how to reduce this pain, they tend to need less pain medication and leave the hospital sooner than patients who receive no instructions (e.g., Egbert et al., 1964). Even placing a patient who is about to undergo surgery in a room with a patient who has already had a successful operation leads to shorter hospital stays (Kulik & Mahler, 1989). Presumably, the chance to observe the roommate gives the patient valuable information about what to expect regarding his or her own surgery, thereby increasing an overall sense of control.

The third technique is to offer behavioral medicine interventions in a group context, which provides ongoing social support for members as they share their strategies for coping with an illness. As discussed in Chapter 5, various types of stressors are less harmful to people who have high levels of social support (Kulik & Mahler, 1989; House, Umberson, & Landis, 1988; Shumaker & Czajkowski, 1994). Social support may also provide the modeling and social reinforcement people need to maintain healthy behaviors in a crisis (Adler & Matthews, 1994). Finally, social support sometimes takes the form of tangible aid—providing food, transportation, child care, financial assistance—in which the literal "helping hand" can make the difference to a person's survival. Whatever the mechanisms (and they are not yet fully understood), feelings of being socially connected appear to be a crucial element to many successful psychological interventions.

Interventions for Cardiovascular Diseases

Because obesity, smoking, high sodium levels, high LDL cholesterol levels, lack of aerobic fitness, and major stressors are risk factors for hypertension and CHD, behaviors related to them have been targeted for psychological intervention. Evaluative studies often report that these interventions have short-term benefits, but may not lead to clinically significant effects in the long run (Blanchard, 1994). For example, most psychologically oriented weight-reduction interventions can achieve reductions of about 1 pound per week, but it is much more difficult to maintain these reductions beyond 1 or 2 years (Brownell & Wadden, 1992). Similarly, smoking cessation can often be achieved for a time, but relapse rates remain discouragingly high.

Many studies have evaluated whether Type A behavior can be altered, and whether the changes will lead to improved health (Nunes, Frank, & Kornfeld, 1987; Thoresen & Powell, 1992). In general, despite the many questions about Type A behavior as a risk factor for CHD, Type A behavior can be changed, and doing so can yield health benefits. For example, in the Recurrent Coronary Prevention Project (Friedman et al., 1986), over 800 patients who had already suffered heart attacks received counseling about the importance of diet, exercise, smoking, and adherence to prescribed medications. Some patients received this counseling along with advice on how to reduce Type A behavior. The counseling groups met periodically over 3 years. By the end of the 3 years, patients who regularly attended the Type A counseling sessions were 3 times more likely to achieve substantial Type A reductions than were those who received only cardiological counseling. The most dramatic finding, however, was that at the end of the program, only 7.2 percent of the patients who regularly attended the counseling-plus-Type A modification sessions had another heart attack. The rate of heart attacks was 13.2 percent for those who had received counseling alone.

Preventing and Coping with AIDS

Cognitive-behavioral techniques have helped people at risk for HIV/AIDS modify high-risk behaviors that often lead to infections. In one program gay men participated in 12 group sessions of role-playing, behavioral rehearsal, and problem-solving techniques (Kelly et al., 1989). In these sessions the men were taught how to lower their AIDS risks by practicing safe sex or following safe needle injection practices, resisting coercive efforts by partners to get them to engage in high-risk behaviors, and using self-control techniques to cope with situations that triggered risky behaviors. Compared with a control group of gay men who did not receive training, the participants significantly increased their use of condoms, their resistance to sexual coercion, and their knowledge of AIDS risks.

Another successful program developed by Janet St. Lawrence and her colleagues (St. Lawrence et al., 1995) was aimed at Black American teenagers at risk for HIV infection. The teenagers were randomly assigned to one of two risk-reduction programs. One group attended a single class that provided basic facts about HIV transmission and prevention. The other attended eight sessions that combined HIV information with behavioral skill training, role playing, and group support. The goal of this intervention was to train participants to resist pressure to engage in unsafe sexual practices and to encourage them to practice either sexual abstinence or safer forms of sexual activity. Teenagers in the behavioral skills group decreased their rate of unprotected intercourse significantly more than did the youngsters in the educational class, a difference that was maintained at a 1-year follow-up. In addition, among those youths who had been sexually abstinent when the study began, 88.5 percent of those in the behavioral training program remained so during the follow-up, while only 69 percent of the one-session information group were still abstinent.

Many large American cities have established educational programs about AIDS, clean needle exchanges, condom distribution, and publicity campaigns encouraging safe sex (Kelly & Murphy, 1992). The overall success of these efforts is difficult to gauge. Among gay men, particularly those who live in large American cities, marked reductions in unsafe sexual practices such as anal intercourse have been reported over recent years following special campaigns (Ekstrand & Coates, 1990). However, among inner-city men and women, gay men in smaller communities, and lower-SES and minority adolescents, HIV prevention efforts have not been nearly as successful (Kelly & Murphy, 1992).

AIDS prevention programs have been set up in many countries around the world, including those of sub-Saharan Africa, Asia, and parts of the Caribbean, where women's AIDS risks are skyrocketing. Women

Economic and social empowerment of women in conjunction with the creation of social support networks are critical to effective health programs in developing countries.

in these cultures face numerous obstacles to lowering their AIDS risks. They lack economic or social power, so they are unable to exert control over their sexual lives. In many cultures, women find it difficult to convince partners to use condoms because they are afraid their sexual fidelity will be questioned. In other situations, women lack basic knowledge about how AIDS is transmitted and about how they can lower their risks of infection. Therefore, a basic goal of many of these programs is to empower women

- to learn more about HIV transmission;
- to take more control of their sexual lives;
- to obtain forms of protection such as female condoms or vaginal microbicides; and
- to become less economically dependent on men and therefore less subject to coerced or commercialized sex.

These gender-sensitive policies are all aimed at helping women develop HIV prevention methods that they understand, control, and can support one another for using. They are based on an apparently universal psychological principle, namely that people cope better when they believe that they can exert control over stressors.

Other psychological interventions attempt to help patients cope with HIV/AIDS itself. For example, in a study conducted at the University of Miami 47 gay men who were not aware of their HIV status when they began the study agreed to be tested for HIV and informed of their HIV antibody status (Antoni et al., 1991; LaPerriere et al., 1990). Five weeks before being notified of whether they were infected with HIV, the men were randomly assigned to one of three conditions: (1) a cognitive-behavioral stress management (CBSM) program; (2) a group aerobic exercise program; or (3) a no-treatment control group. Measures of psychological distress and immune system functioning were collected for all the men, both before and after they were notified of their HIV test results.

The exercise and CBSM programs met for 10 weeks. Their main goals were to buffer the anxiety and depression associated with being notified of HIV infection and to lessen the immunological impairments that often occur with the

Connections

What other kinds of prevention programs emphasize empowerment, and why is empowerment important? For some answers, see Chapter 17, pp. 602–604.

stress of being notified that one has HIV. Men in the CBSM training group participated in assertiveness role playing and received training in muscle relaxation, cognitive restructuring to help reduce feelings of stress and helplessness, and information about HIV risks and transmission.

Preliminary results for the men in the aerobic exercise program showed that aerobic exercise lessened the emotional distress and protected against a decline in natural killer cells for men who were informed that they had tested positive for HIV (LaPerriere et al., 1990). CBSM men who were notified that they were HIV positive also showed less postnotification depression and fewer adverse effects on immune system functioning than did no-treatment controls who learned that they had tested positive for HIV. Two kinds of cells that are attacked specifically by HIV and a general measure of immunity showed increases for CBSM participants; these measures either decreased or showed no change in the controls. (Two other measures of immune system functioning revealed no significant effects.) The more often the CBSM men practiced relaxation training at home, the lower their postnotification depression scores and the higher their HIV-specific measures of immune competence. Relaxation training appears to be an especially important part of this treatment package, but the reasons for its specific effectiveness need further study. The long-term implications of this intervention are still unknown. In particular, we still need to learn how permanent and how large a change such treatments can bring about in immune functioning and whether such a change can alter the course of AIDS.

Psychological Interventions and Cancer

A number of psychological interventions, including educational programs, group therapy, individual psychotherapy, and behavioral therapy, can improve the psychological and physical well-being of cancer patients (Fawzy et al., 1995). Behavioral techniques such as relaxation training, hypnosis, stress management, and cognitive restructuring have proved especially useful.

One of the most influential studies of behavioral interventions for cancer patients found that a year of weekly group meetings supplemented by training in self-hypnosis improved the survival of women with metastatic breast cancer (Spiegel et al., 1981; Spiegel & Bloom, 1983). A total of 86 women were randomly assigned either to no psychological treatment or to group therapy that emphasized group support,

self-disclosure, and discussions of death and dying; half of the treatment group members were randomly assigned to receive additional training in self-hypnosis for pain reduction. Because many of these women were in the advanced stages of cancer, not all of them completed the 12-month treatment. However, among those who did, patients receiving group therapy reported significantly less emotional distress and fatigue, a higher energy level, and fewer maladaptive efforts at coping with cancer than did the no-treatment controls. These differences actually increased through the year as the intervention continued. The hypnosis component also appeared to have its own analgesic benefit. Women who received group therapy without hypnosis reported increased pain during the year, while those who received hypnosis with the group therapy reported no change in pain. Ten years later, the only three patients from the original sample who were still alive had all been in the group therapy condition. Measured from the time the study began until time of death, group therapy patients lived about twice as long (36.6 months of survival) as control subjects (18.9 months of survival).

In another major study (Fawzy et al., 1990), 80 patients who had recently undergone surgical treatment for malignant melanoma (a serious form of skin cancer) were randomly assigned either to a no-treatment control group or to a six-week group program that consisted of education about skin cancer, stress management including relaxation training, enhancement of personal coping strategies, and social support from the group. Six months later, patients who had received the psychosocial treatments showed significantly more effective coping skills, less emotional distress, and greater antipathogen activity in the immune system than control patients did. Even more impressive, 5 or 6 years after surgery, the death rate among the 34 control patients was 29.4 percent (3 others had suffered recurrences of their cancer). Significantly fewer, 8.8 percent, of the 34 group treatment subjects had died, though 4 had recurrences of cancer. What could account for these effects? Generally, treatments that help patients reduce feelings of anxiety and inadequacy, that increase their sense of personal control over the illness, and that improve active participation in their overall treatment plan produce the most benefits.

Claims that behaviorally oriented psychotherapy can help prevent cancer or prolong the lives of people suffering from cancer have also been made (Grossarth-Maticek & Eysenck, 1991; Eysenck & Grossarth-Maticek, 1991), but the data in support of such claims are scanty. Using a form of behavior therapy that they call *creative novation therapy* or *autonomy training*, Hans Eysenck and his colleagues attempted to help cancer-prone people become more autonomous and assertive, to increase their skills in reducing feelings of stress, and to express emotions more freely. Many of these components are aimed at changing the psychological characteristics of the so-called Type C personality.

In one study, 100 adults, all of whom had been classified as having a Type C personality but no active cancer, were randomly assigned to a no-therapy group or were offered individual autonomy training. About 13 years after the experiment began, 32 percent of control subjects were reported to have died from cancer (there were no cancer deaths among the psychotherapy group); another 30 percent of the controls were listed as having died from causes other than cancer compared with 10 percent of the therapy subjects (Eysenck & Grossarth-Maticek, 1991).

The published descriptions of these studies are too sketchy to allow a confident judgment about the validity of the reported results. We are also not aware of other investigators' being able to replicate these outcomes. Before concluding that any form of psychotherapy can reduce or even delay the incidence of cancer, much more well-controlled research will be necessary.

Increasing Compliance with Treatment Regimens

Whether a prescribed treatment for a medical illness is effective depends on two factors. First, the treatment needs to be correct. Second, the patient needs to follow through with the treatment. The extent to which patients follow medical advice is called **adherence** or **compliance** (Rodin & Salovey, 1989).

Up to 50 percent of patients who are prescribed medications are thought to be noncompliant, at times, with instructions for taking their medicine. They may not take the medicine at all, they may take it less frequently or more frequently than recommended, or they may ignore rules about not mixing the medication with alcohol or taking it on an empty stomach. As Figure 6.5 shows, noncompliance tends to increase in relation to treatments that are more complicated or that involve substantial changes in lifestyle.

Table 6.3 on page 208 summarizes key reasons for noncompliance as well as conditions that make compliance more probable. Systematic attempts to increase patients' medical compliance fall into one of three categories: (1) educating patients about the importance of compliance so that they will take a more active role in maintaining their own health; (2) modifying treatment plans to make compliance easier; and (3) using behavioral and cognitive-behavioral techniques to increase patients' ability to maintain compliance (Masur, 1981).

Health psychologists have studied the value of behavioral compliance techniques extensively. Compliance can be prompted by *environmental cues* such as postcard reminders, telephone calls, or wristwatches set to emit a tone when a pill should be taken. Written *contingency contracts* between patient and physician can specify what compliance behaviors the patient must perform to earn rewards (e.g., future appointments scheduled at more convenient times). Such contracts have demonstrated success in improving compliance (Swain & Steckel, 1981), al-

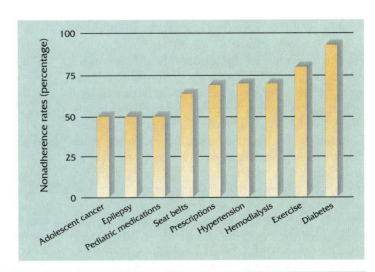

FIGURE 6.5

Saying No to What the Doctor Ordered

People often resist complying with various health-related behaviors and medical treatments. The more cumbersome or inconvenient the treatment, the higher the rate of nonadherence tends to be.

Source: Kirschenbaum & Fitzgibbon, 1995.

TABLE 6.3	Medical Noncompliance: Causes and Cures

Causes of noncompliance

Communication problems between physicians and patients

Frustration and emotional conflicts between patients and physicians

Treatments that are complex, that demand great changes in lifestyle, that are longlasting, that are painful or produce adverse side effects

Behavioral and environmental influences that make it difficult for patients to develop the habits needed for compliance. Examples include overinvolvement in occupational activities or cultural norms that discourage certain behaviors (e.g., taking medication is "just a crutch")

Aids to compliance

Clear cues and rewards for desirable behaviors, such as precise written instructions

Prompts for compliance that fit in with a patient's daily routines, such as medication schedules that coincide with a daily ritual such as tooth brushing

Cues, desired behaviors, and rewards that all occur within a short time of one another, with minimal delay

Cues and rewards for compliance that are meaningful to the patient

though at least one study of hypertensives (Hoelscher, Lichstein, & Rosenthal, 1986) found that a written contract produced less compliance in practicing relaxation at home than a noncontract condition did. *Token economies* have also been employed to encourage compliance. In a study by Magrab and Papadopoulou (1977), three children with renal failure were given points for maintaining recommended weight, potassium, and nitrogen levels. These points could then be exchanged for rewards in the hospital. Compared with baseline levels, these children were able to make substantial weight gains, and two of them showed improvements in the other indices.

Many patients avoid essential medical procedures because they are painful or they produce aversive side effects. Behavioral therapies have often been used to reduce these side effects, thereby increasing compliance with necessary interventions. The best-known examples of these methods are those used to

counter the anticipatory nausea experienced by cancer chemotherapy patients.

Standard antiemetic drugs have not proved successful for treating learned side effects, so attention has turned to psychological treatments such as hypnosis, relaxation training with guided imagery, and biofeedback as alternatives. In one well-controlled study at Vanderbilt University, patients receiving chemotherapy were randomly assigned either to a psychological treatment group or a no-treatment control (Burish et al., 1987). Before their first session of chemotherapy, patients in the treatment group were trained to use muscle relaxation and calming imagery to cope with the stress of their upcoming chemotherapy. No-treatment patients were told about the advantages of staying relaxed during chemotherapy and were urged to do so, but they were given no training in relaxation or coping skills. Patients receiving the training reported significantly less nausea, vomiting, and anxiety than did control subjects. These improvements were still apparent as long as 3 days after chemotherapy sessions. The benefit of relaxation probably stems from the fact that it helps distract patients from focusing on aversive stimuli and promotes patients' confidence that they can control their reactions to these stimuli.

Interventions for Promoting Health

Psychological approaches to promoting health and preventing illness are two sides of the same coin. On one side are efforts to prevent illness by helping people break unhealthy habits or avoid developing them in the first place. In fact, experts estimate that about half of the 2 million deaths that occur every year in the United States could be prevented by changes in six behavioral risk factors: (1) use of tobacco, (2) abuse of alcohol and illegal drugs, (3) unhealthy eating habits, (4) infrequent use of seat belts, (5) failure to obtain and comply with necessary medical treatment such as immunizations, and (6) risky sexual practices.

On the other side of the coin is health promotion, which can be accomplished by helping people develop and maintain good health habits to achieve a state of wellness. Eating a balanced diet, getting adequate sleep, engaging in physical exercise, and using seatbelts are examples of healthy behaviors that promote wellness. Ideally, these habits would be instilled during childhood so that they give a person the benefit of a lifelong pattern of healthy behavior.

Serious questions remain about how successful we can realistically expect health-promotion efforts to be, about who should be the target audiences for wellness and prevention programs, and what methods are best for promoting good health (Winett, 1995). Long-term adherence to a schedule of health-enhancing behavior is difficult to maintain, partly because many changes in lifestyle are downright inconvenient. For example, engaging in regular physical exercise is time-consuming; if it isn't a daily priority, other demands will take over and dampen people's commitment to an exercise program. See the Prevention box on this and the following page.

Furthermore, the consequences of most changes in health behaviors are usually so remote that people have no sense that the changes produced any real benefits. Research on the effects of reinforcement consistently show that, the more delayed the consequences of an act, the less impact they will have. Compared with the strong, immediate reinforcement that smoking a cigarette brings a smoker, the long-term negative consequences of an increased risk of cancer simply don't have much chance of influencing behavior.

Finally, it must be remembered that engaging in unhealthy behavior does not guarantee that a disease will develop, any more than avoiding that behavior guarantees good health. Most behavioral risks change the odds of illness a little, but it is still the case that most smokers do not get lung cancer and that more than 90 percent of people classified as exhibiting Type A behavior do not develop a heart condition.

Whether a person wants to make the effort to change the odds and practice healthy behaviors depends on how vulnerable he or she feels to a certain illness and how confident he or she is that any changes in lifestyle would reduce risks in the long run. These are key factors in the **health belief model (HBM),** the most influential theory about why people do or do not engage in healthy behaviors (Rosenstock, 1966). According to the HMB, the probability that individuals will change a risky behavior depends on

1. how susceptible to a given illness they believe themselves to be and how severe they think the illness would be;

2. how effective and feasible versus how costly and difficult they perceive a prescribed treatment to be; and

3. how much they are bothered by internal cues (physical symptoms or distress from the illness) and motivated by external cues (pressure from friends or advertisements in the media) that promote lifestyle changes.

Prevention   Promoting Community Fitness

Because illnesses such as heart disease are so widespread and dangerous and because population-wide prevention may be more cost effective than targeting only those people at high risk, health psychologists have developed community-wide programs aimed at decreasing harmful habits and promoting healthy habits such as regular exercise and good diet (Jeffery, 1988; Perry, Klepp, & Schultz, 1988). Although such programs can be expensive, they can be worth the cost in the long run because of the lives that are saved and the improvements in overall health that are realized. Increasingly, therefore, health officials are looking to large-scale programs to change lifestyle

attitudes and habits. Some large-scale prevention programs target a specific risk factor such as obesity; others address several risk factors at the same time.

A leading example of a community-based project aimed at preventing multiple risk factors for cardiovascular disease is the Stanford Heart Disease Prevention Program (SHDPP) (Meyer et al., 1980). Approximately 500 persons at high risk for heart disease were identified in three Northern California towns of similar size. In Community #1 (Watsonville), 56 subjects were simply exposed to a mass media campaign (TV and radio spots) designed to acquaint listeners with probable causes of

heart disease and specific behaviors that could reduce risk factors (smoking cessation, healthy diet, and exercise). More than 100 other Watsonville subjects received the same media campaign supplemented with intensive face-to-face counseling about how to change diet, smoking, and exercise habits. In Community #2 (Gilroy), 139 subjects received a media campaign like the one in Watsonville. In Community #3 (Tracy) 136 citizens served as the control group who received neither the media campaign nor the instructional counseling.

All groups of treated subjects reduced their risk factors for cardiovascular disease and increased their

(continued)

Prevention (continued)

knowledge of behavioral factors that contribute to heart disease. But as the figure shows, larger and longer-lasting reductions in overall risk scores occurred in the Watsonville group that received the mass media campaign combined with intensive instruction. For example, half of them quit smoking and those who did not quit were smoking 51 percent fewer cigarettes per day—significantly greater reductions than in any other group. On other measures (e.g., physical exercise), no significant intervention effects were found.

The Stanford investigators concluded that "intensive media plus face-to-face instruction had greater impact on cardiovascular disease risk and related knowledge and behavior than did the media-only treatment or control." In addition, the intensive instruction resulted in more durable changes in these factors over the 3-year follow-up.

Other community-based prevention programs have also shown that they can lower health risks using mass media (MRFIT, 1982). These programs have been successful with children (Blackburn et al., 1984) and in other countries such as Fin-

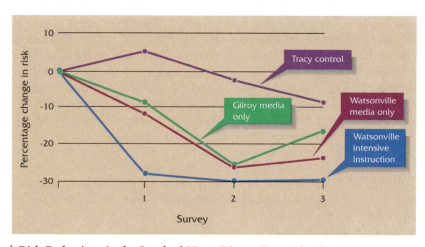

Risk Reductions in the Stanford Heart Disease Prevention Program
The citizens in Watsonville who received both media campaigns and individual counseling showed the largest reductions in health risks and steadily maintained these reductions over a 3-year period.

land (Williams, Arnold, & Wynder, 1977). However, community-based programs must still overcome some serious limitations if they are to achieve their maximum impact. For example, a major difficulty in the SHDPP was the dropout rate of about 25 percent. When dropouts were taken into account in the Watsonville intensive instruction group, its smoking cessation rate dropped

from 50 to 32 percent. In addition, the media campaign and behavioral counseling had significant effects only on smoking; the other risk factors were barely affected. Finally, it is still unclear whether community programs mostly affect people who are already motivated to change their behavior or whether they persuade some hard-to-reach people to lower their risks.

Several studies have shown that the health belief model predicts people's willingness to engage in health-promoting behavior such as periodic breast self-examinations (Champion, 1990). However, demographic and societal variables appear to limit the generalizability of the model (Taylor, 1995; Winett, 1995). The HBM tends to apply to the health-related behaviors of upper socioeconomic people who are already fairly well informed about illness and health issues; it does less well at predicting the behavior of poor people who lack basic knowledge about the causes and treatment of many diseases and who therefore may also lack confidence that they can perform necessary health-promoting behaviors.

Who is the most appropriate target audience for interventions aimed at health promotion and disease prevention? Should we encourage physicians to

try to convince each of their patients that there are benefits to a healthy lifestyle? Should we aim our efforts at groups who appear most vulnerable to a given disease? Should we try to influence attitudes and knowledge about health in elementary schools, when children are just beginning to form their health habits? Should we create worksite interventions that transmit health messages to adults who spend a lot of time together and might be able to reinforce one another for making healthy changes? Or should we create community-based programs that rely, in part, on the mass media to influence the health habits of entire populations?

Each of these interventions has been attempted, with mixed success (Taylor, 1995). Individual physicians can persuade their patients to adopt positive health habits *if* the physicians themselves are genuinely convinced of the importance of such changes. Interventions aimed at high-risk groups tend to focus limited resources on the people who may need them the most, but confronting individuals about their high-risk status might unnecessarily alarm them or give them a false sense of security if they were to adopt improved health habits. School-based programs have the advantage of reaching children before unhealthy behaviors have become habitual, but these programs must be designed so that children are able to understand them. Also, for effects to be maintained for any length of time, parents need to be convinced of the importance of the changes their children may be motivated to make. As the Prevention section suggested, community-based prevention programs can be successful, particularly when they combine a mass media campaign with individual counseling on how to change health habits.

Revisiting the Case of Beth

After prescribing some hypertension medication for Beth, her physician recommended that she join an HMO-sponsored counseling group to help her develop a more healthy lifestyle and cope with stress better. The HMO started this group after discovering that other health care organizations had been able to save money by offering such services to their patients. These savings are known as *medical offsets,* because patients who attend behavioral counseling sessions for conditions in which psychological factors play a causal role often reduce their use of more expensive medical procedures.

Beth attended these sessions once a week for 2 months. She learned how to use relaxation skills to cope with tension and to reduce her headaches; she committed herself to a new diet; she started a smoking cessation program; and she made a contract with the other group members to attend an aerobic exercise class three nights a week. Beth also received feedback from the other members of her group about how she pushed people away from her and always appeared a bit hostile or "on edge." They encouraged her to try to relax a little more often and to take some extra time to cultivate friendships.

After eight sessions, Beth had lost 7 pounds, she was using her relaxation skills on a fairly regular basis, she was smoking less, and she noticed that her headaches had decreased somewhat. She felt in better shape than she had in years. But Beth was discouraged that her blood pressure was still high; in fact, it hadn't decreased a bit. Frustrated with her slow progress, Beth began to miss group sessions now and then. Within a couple of months she stopped going completely. Soon she had gained back almost all of the weight she had lost, and she was smoking just as much as before.

Beth told her physician she quit the counseling group because the lifestyle changes were too hard for her. At one point she admitted, "I know this group is exactly what I need, but I just don't have time for it. I'd rather take the pills." Several times Beth tried to make the recommended behavior changes on her own, but she could never stick with the program for more than a couple of weeks. Three years later, she is taking a higher dose of medication to keep her blood pressure under control.

SUMMARY

Mind, Body, and Health Psychology

Health psychologists study how psychological factors influence the maintenance of health as well as the onset, course, and treatment of physical illnesses.

Health psychology and its closely related discipline, behavioral medicine, are both based on a biopsychosocial model that suggests that illnesses result from interactions between biological vulnerability, psychological factors, and social conditions. Psychological, physical, and social factors are implicated in both sickness and health.

As acute illnesses came under better control in the twentieth century, more attention was paid to chronic illnesses, such as heart disease, high blood pressure, and cancer, and the roles that behavioral factors play in these conditions. Among the factors most often linked to physical illnesses and premature death are the use of tobacco, abuse of alcohol and illegal drugs, unhealthy diet, risky sexual behavior, and failure to obtain and comply with medical treatments. Many of the conditions discussed in this chapter were historically described as psychosomatic illnesses, but the DSM-IV classifies most of them under a category called psychological factors affecting medical condition.

The Psychology of Getting Sick

Personality and social factors can be related to illnesses in several ways, but health psychologists are primarily interested in two possible connections: (1) direct effects on the biological processes that underlie disease, and (2) indirect links with poor health through their association with unhealthy behaviors. These two influences may interact with each other to increase the risk of disease.

High levels of stress may be linked to physiological hyperreactivity, which in turn may increase the chances of hypertension and coronary heart disease (CHD). The most direct evidence for this link comes from animal studies showing that increases in arterial plaque correlate with exposure to stressful environments. In humans, the most-studied psychological risk factor for CHD is Type A behavior, a pattern that involves a sense of impatience and time urgency, chronic hostility, competitiveness, and a strong desire for achievement. Recent research suggests that only certain components of Type A behavior, namely negative emotions, are the major culprits leading to CHD risks.

Psychological factors might also increase disease risk by suppressing the immune system. Research in the field of psychoneuroimmunology is leading to new discoveries about how psychological processes, the brain, and the immune system affect each other. Several lines of research have shown that psychosocial factors can adversely affect the immune system, at least temporarily. Two diseases for which many of these discoveries have obvious relevance are AIDS and cancer.

A large amount of empirical research indicates that socioeconomic status (SES) is consistently related to physical illness and death; the lower a person's SES, the greater his or her chance of serious illness and premature death. It is likely that this relationship stems from a combination of negative emotions, stress, and unhealthy habits, all of which are more frequent in lower-SES samples.

The Psychology of Getting Well and Staying Well

Because psychological factors are implicated in the cause and course of several chronic illnesses, these factors might also be manipulated as part of the prevention or treatment of these diseases. Effective health psychology interventions usually involve several integrated treatment components. The typical intervention package involves three elements: (1) training in a stress-reduction technique; (2) cognitive restructuring to increase coping capacity and to correct mistaken health beliefs; and (3) increasing a sense of social support by delivering interventions in a group context. Interventions involving these elements have produced improvements for patients with coronary heart disease, cancer, and AIDS. Other interventions address noncompliance with prescribed treatments, a major medical problem. Efforts to increase compliance take the form of educating patients about the importance of compliance, making treatments easier to follow, and applying behavioral techniques such as contingency contracts and token economies to change behaviors.

Finally, health psychologists have designed programs aimed at promoting health and preventing illness. These programs aim to help people develop healthy habits and to break or avoid unhealthy ones, but such goals have proved difficult to achieve for a number of reasons. The Health Belief Model explains that the probability of people changing risky behaviors depends on how susceptible to an illness they perceive themselves to be, how effective they perceive a treatment to be, and how motivated they are by internal distress and external pressures to change.

Health promotion/illness prevention programs have been delivered through the mass media to entire communities, offered to groups of adults at worksites, or introduced in school curricula. How cost-effective or durable the changes produced by these prevention programs are is still open to question.

KEY TERMS

adherence (compliance), p. 207

AIDS, p. 197

angina pectoris, p. 189

aneurysm, p. 189

anticipatory nausea, p. 196

atherosclerosis, p. 189

behavioral medicine, p. 185

biopsychosocial model, p. 185

coronary heart disease (CHD),
    p. 189

essential hypertension, p. 190

health belief model (HBM),
    p. 209

health psychology, p. 184

human immunodeficiency virus
    type 1 (HIV-1), p. 197

hypertension, p. 189

myocardial infarction, p. 189

plaque, p. 189

psychoneuroimmunology, p. 196

socioeconomic status (SES),
    p. 199

standardized mortality ratio,
    p. 199

stroke, p. 189

Type A behavior pattern, p. 192

Type B behavior pattern, p. 192

Type C personality, p. 199

vital exhaustion, p. 193

7

Anxiety Disorders

Nancy's Love by Michael Kort, 1991. Oil on canvas, 12" x 9". Private Collection. Courtesy of Sistare and NARSAD Artworks.

From the Case of Jim

When Jim appeared for treatment at age 40, he had been suffering from anxiety and depressive symptoms for 8 years. He dated his problems to one fall day when he foiled a burglary attempt across the street from where he was working. A distance runner, Jim decided to follow the fleeing burglar and to attempt to attract help along the way. After a chase, Jim slowed and looked around for help. Turning again to the burglar, he found himself staring down the barrel of a handgun. The burglar shot him. Jim was hit in the legs with three bullets and immobilized. He begged the young man to spare his life and stop shooting. Instead, the assailant continued firing until the gun was empty. He then fled, leaving Jim to die.

Fortunately, Jim was found and rushed to the hospital and to surgery. After 8 days in the hospital, he knew he would recover. He felt elated just to be alive.

Soon, the elation wore off, and Jim began thinking of what might have occurred had he not been found in time. More and more frequently, sights and sounds began to evoke the memory of the shooting and the panic he had experienced. The sight of guns or depictions of violence on TV or in the movies triggered waves of strong emotion. Sirens and the sight of ambulances would startle him, then panic and despair would set in. By the following year, even the cool dampness of autumn could reactivate the event in his mind. He had frequent nightmares of looking into a gun barrel.

As time went on, Jim felt more on edge. He became wary of people, and he kept to himself. He no longer experienced life's joy and excitement. Due to injury-related leg pain, he was forced to stop running, giving up one of his major pleasures and outlets for stress. Leg pain brought up images of the shooting that, in turn, brought fear, hyperventilation, and a wildly racing heart. Episodes in which Jim felt deeply depressed and suicidal would sometimes follow exposure to various triggering stimuli. After 8 years of nightmares and daily reminders of the trauma, Jim sought treatment. ■

*F*ear of dying, which Jim experienced after being shot, is probably the most primitive emotion experienced by humans beings. This fear is a normal, inborn response to the perception of threat. As discussed in Chapter 5, people who suddenly perceive threats are energized by rushes of chemicals that increase their energy, endurance, and strength, and help them escape or fight off attackers. This alarm system, so crucial in saving people from danger, can also be triggered as a false alarm; sometimes, as in Jim's case, the responses can persist long after the danger has passed. When anxiety or fear is experienced so pervasively, intensely, and uncontrollably that it interferes with a person's ability to perform normal daily tasks, to maintain important role functions, and to enjoy the pleasures of life, the conditions are called **anxiety disorders.**

Jim was diagnosed as suffering from *posttraumatic stress disorder,* which falls in the category of anxiety disorders. Anxiety disorders are the most prevalent of all mental disorders in the United States (Kessler et al., 1994; Myers et al., 1984; Robins &

Regier, 1991) and perhaps throughout the world (Chen et al., 1993; Amering & Katschnig, 1990). Current epidemiological research shows that one fourth of American adolescents and adults have experienced one or more of these disorders during their lifetime, and 17 percent, roughly 28 million people, either have had an anxiety disorder within the past year or are currently experiencing one (Kessler et al., 1994). In this chapter we will describe the main anxiety disorders as they are classified in the DSM-IV: specific and social phobias, agoraphobia, panic disorder (with or without agoraphobia), obsessive-compulsive disorder, generalized anxiety disorder, posttraumatic stress disorder, and acute stress disorder (see Figure 7.1). Although the rate of comorbidity among anxiety disorders is quite high (Brown & Barlow, 1992), each disorder has distinct clinical features. Following the clinical description of each disorder, we will discuss theories that explain it and the most effective treatments for alleviating it.

Fear and Anxiety Gone Awry

Fear and anxiety lie at the core of anxiety disorders. Both emotions are expressed through three channels:

1. cognitive distress, distortions, and ruminations;
2. physiological arousal; and
3. behavioral disruptions and avoidance.

Although people often talk about fear and anxiety as if they were identical, researchers have found it useful to distinguish between the two emotions. **Fear** refers to a set of responses to a specific perceived danger. It is thought to be a biologically primitive alarm

These facial expressions show fear in a human being and a monkey. Of the 44 muscles in the human face, 40 are devoted to facial expression. Some facial muscles are activated by positive thoughts, others by negative thoughts such as those involving fear. The brains of primates are also highly sensitive to faces and their messages. Scientists can now read our emotional feelings by measuring changes in facial expression.

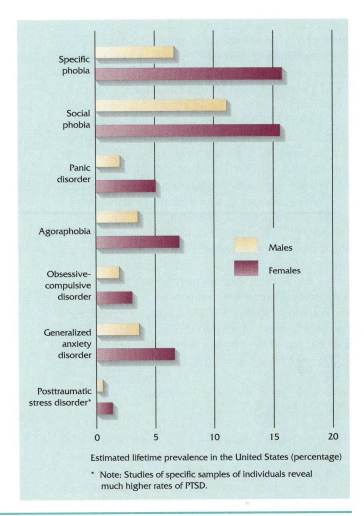

FIGURE 7.1

Prevalence of Anxiety Disorders

Based on the results of one large-scale survey, prevalence rates of all anxiety disorders are higher for women than for men (Kessler et al., 1994). The estimated prevalence for posttraumatic stress disorder is based on figures from the Epidemiological Catchment Area studies (Helzer et al., 1987); other studies tend to find much higher rates of this anxiety disorder among groups who have suffered a trauma.

system that sets off a series of cognitive, physiological, and behavioral responses designed to deliver a person from impending harm. A person would likely feel "fear" in a car that is stalled on a railroad track as a train approaches.

Anxiety is a more diffuse or vague sense of apprehension that some aversive event will occur. David Barlow (1988) uses the term *anxious apprehension* to convey the idea that anxiety is a future-oriented concern about events that might happen and over which a person appears to have little or no control. The result is a gnawing sense of foreboding. A person would probably feel anxiety after completing an interview for a job that he or she wanted very badly, recalling several answers that, in hindsight, seemed incomplete or inaccurate, and then having to wait 2 weeks to find out whether he or she got the job.

In Sigmund Freud's psychoanalytic theory, anxiety played a central role in causing several mental disorders. Freud concentrated on conditions that he and others called the *neuroses*. In general, **neurosis** refers to chronic anxiety, unhappiness, and guilt that

reduces a person's overall effectiveness. According to Freud, anxiety resulted from conflicts among the id, ego, and superego, and served as a warning that repressed traumatic or instinctual content was about to become conscious. Different expressions of anxiety defined different types of neurosis. In some cases, said Freud, persons do not consciously experience anxiety because they repress it. He contended, however, that it still caused problems. Freud believed, for example, that physical problems that we now call *somatoform disorders* (see Chapter 8) are caused by excessive repressed anxiety.

In recent years, clinicians have used the term *neurosis* less frequently, perhaps because the DSM no longer includes it as an official diagnosis; the DSM-IV lists as anxiety disorders only specific conditions in which fear or anxiety and their associated avoidance behaviors are clearly experienced as the core of the disturbance.

How do we view these disorders today? The core emotions, anxiety and fear, can be adaptive when they serve as alarms that enable people to avoid danger or escape harm. In fact, evolutionary theory suggests that natural selection made it advantageous for individuals to be highly fearful of predators and other potentially lethal stimuli because those animals whose fears led to successful escape or avoidance would be the most likely to survive (Kendler et al., 1992a). Few scientists today, however, believe that all human fears of specific objects or situations are acquired solely by inheritance. Nonetheless, certain stimuli—such as sudden, loud noises and loss of physical support—are innately fearful to infants.

When historically useful alarm systems are triggered by stimuli that are not dangerous, they become false alarms that may lead to anxiety disorders. In this chapter we will describe anxiety disorders as disturbances in biologically based danger response systems that were of evolutionary importance in helping our ancestors survive the threat of predators. As the coming sections show, these anxiety response systems are further shaped into specific patterns by learning and conditioning experiences, by cognitive processes, and by cultural norms and expectations.

The Phobias

The term *phobia* comes from the name of the Greek deity, Phobos, a fearsome creature who was a son of Ares, the god of war. A **phobia** is an irrational, excessive fear that causes intense emotional distress and interferes significantly with everyday life. In the midst of a phobic reaction, a person feels engulfed by a terror that blots out almost all other experience. The fear usually grips an individual with a rush of physiological symptoms including trembling, a racing heart, sweating, choking, and dizziness or lightheadedness. The phobic person may "freeze" or may run from the frightening situation. Phobias are among the most commonly diagnosed mental disorders in the United States (Kessler et al., 1994; Robins & Regier, 1991). They are diagnosed twice as often in women as in men, and Black Americans and Hispanics are diagnosed more frequently than White Americans. In the DSM-IV, phobias are classified as specific phobias, social phobias, and agoraphobia without history of panic disorder. We discuss agoraphobia—the fear of public places, crowds, or forms of transportation from which escape is difficult—in the section on panic disorder because the two so often occur together (APA, 1994; Horwath, Johnson, & Hornig, 1993).

Specific Phobias

Intense, persistent fear of specific objects or situations that objectively pose little or no actual threat charac-

terize **specific phobias.** Of course, most people fear and prefer to avoid some stimulus or situation. It is not unusual for a person to fear swimming in the ocean or flying, for example. For a fear to meet the DSM-IV diagnostic criteria for a specific phobia, however, it must cause intense distress each time the person is, or anticipates being, exposed to the feared situation. Furthermore, the fear must be intense enough that the resulting cognitive and physiological distress and behavioral avoidance interfere significantly with the person's educational, occupational, or social life. As many as 11 percent of adults and children have true specific phobias (Agras et al., 1969; Costello et al., 1988; Kessler et al., 1994; Myers et al., 1984), but perhaps twice as many people report specific fears that fall short of being diagnosed as phobias.

Specific phobias are named by placing the Greek word for the feared object or situation before the word *phobia*. Table 7.1 lists some common phobias.

TABLE 7.1   Specific Phobias

Type	Phobia
Animals	
Bees	Apiphobia
Spiders	Arachnophobia
Snakes	Ephidiophobia
Mice	Musophobia
Animals	Zoophobia
Natural environment	
Stars	Siderophobia
Wind	Anemophobia
Rain	Ombrophobia
Thunder	Brontophobia
Darkness	Nyctophobia
Blood, illness, and injection	
Blood	Hematophobia
Needles	Belonephobia
Injury	Traumatophobia
Pain	Algophobia
Contamination	Mysophobia
Situations	
Enclosed places	Claustrophobia
Travel	Hodophobia
Bridges	Gephyrophobia
Empty rooms	Kenophobia

Animal phobias are the most common of the specific phobias and include (among others) snakes, mice, spiders, cats, and dogs. Animal phobias usually develop in early childhood, with the majority first appearing between the ages of 4 and 10 and only rarely occurring after the early teens (Öst, 1987). Even if they are not treated, most animal phobias tend to diminish over the years so that by the time a person reaches the age of 60 or 70, relatively few remain (Agras, Oliveau, & Chapin, 1972).

*B*ecause of her snake phobia, Martha had nearly become a prisoner in her own house. She, her husband, and small child had moved to a new home in the country during the winter. By late spring she discovered snakes in her yard. She would not allow her child out alone nor would she venture into the yard herself. When she had to leave the house, she would run to the car carrying her child, lock the doors, and speed away before she could see a snake. While in the house, she was constantly vigilant for snakes, and she would not eat vegetables from the garden for fear that snakes might have touched them. (After Kleinknecht, 1991)

Another common cluster of phobias involves fears of *blood, injections,* and *injury.* The majority of these phobias develop by the early teens and are seen in females more often than in males (Kleinknecht & Lenz, 1989; Öst, 1987). Specific fears within this group include receiving injections, seeing blood or having it drawn, and having stitches to close a wound. This cluster has at least two distinctive features. First, these fears may lead people to delay seeking needed medical attention and thus impair their health (Kleinknecht & Lenz, 1989). Second, approximately 80 percent of blood and injury phobics faint when they are exposed to the critical stimuli. This anxiety disorder is the only one in which fainting occurs readily (Öst, 1992; Öst & Hugdahl, 1984). Although as many as 15 percent of adults have experienced a blood- or injury-related fainting spell, (Kleinknecht & Lenz, 1989), they are considered phobic only if their reaction is severe enough to cause significant avoidance, disrupt their daily lives, or impair their health.

Situational phobias are also relatively common and include fear of closed places such as elevators, tunnels, airplanes, and small rooms. *Natural environment* phobias involve exaggerated fears of storms, deep water, heights, or other aspects of the physical world. All infants and many animals, such as dogs, pigs, and cats, have an intense fear of heights. In most cases, this phobia probably involves the fear of falling rather than of height itself. Fortunately, with maturation and experience, this seemingly innate fear eventually abates. When it does not or if it is reactivated, victims may be unable to walk down flights of stairs, look through high windows, or walk across bridges.

*A*t 9 years old, Jessica's fear of heights was so strong she was unable to attend schools with more than one story. She was panic stricken when her class went on field trips where there were steps. She was both frightened and embarrassed in front of her classmates on their trip to a museum. Jessica was able to climb the stairs to the second floor with only a little assistance. However, she had to lie face down and slide on her stomach to get back down.

Social Phobia

Excessive fear of situations in which a person might be evaluated and possibly embarrassed marks **social phobia.** Social phobics, such as Maria, fear situations in which they believe that they will be exposed to scrutiny by others and that they might humiliate or embarrass themselves.

*M*aria was a substitute school teacher who blushed easily when embarrassed. When students or others whom she did not know well asked her a question that she was unable to answer immediately, her face turned bright red, and she felt hot all over. She feared that others would conclude that she was embarrassed because she did not know what she was doing and would evaluate her negatively. As her anxiety grew and she became less able to think and to speak, her fear became a self-fulfilling prophesy. The fear of negative evaluation kept her from accepting jobs that she knew she was competent to perform.

The most common situations that evoke social phobias involve speaking or performing in public, meeting strangers (particularly authorities and members of the opposite sex), using public rest rooms or dressing rooms, and eating or writing in public. In each case, people with social phobia fear that others will find them lacking in some way, that they will be ridiculed, or that they will become the target of public scrutiny. This fear either keeps them from situations that include possible public scrutiny, or causes them to live in fear of self-humiliation.

Often, only a single situation, such as public speaking, is the focus of concern. Many people with such specific social phobias function adequately by avoiding their phobic situations. For some, however, virtually all public or social situations elicit intense anxiety. These *generalized* social phobias affect most aspects of the person's life and are extremely distressing and disruptive. Individuals with generalized social phobia often underachieve at school or at work and are less likely to marry than nonphobics.

Social phobias are about as prevalent as specific phobias. As many as 13 percent of the population in the United States have had a social phobia at some period in their lives, and 7.9 percent have suffered social phobia in the past year (Kessler et al., 1994).

Social phobias differ from specific phobias in that they develop later in life, typically during mid-teenage years. There also appear to be smaller gender differences for social phobias compared with specific phobias. Some studies find a slightly increased prevalence of social phobia among females (Kessler et al., 1994; Myers et al., 1984; Öst, 1987), but others suggest that this difference is insignificant (American Psychiatric Association, 1987).

Social phobias appear in all cultures and are thus referred to as *culture-general.* However, because cultural norms and standards shape the expression of fear, the disorder may look different from one culture to another. For example, the culture of Japan as well many other Asian countries tend to emphasize an *interdependent* or *collective* social orientation in which individuals' identities are intimately tied to their families or close friends; in other words, personal identity is defined largely by others. Many Westerners, on the other hand, have more *independent* identities and are concerned with how others think of them as individuals. A *culture-specific* form of social phobia commonly seen in Japan is *Tia-jin kyofusho* or *TKS* (Takahashi, 1989). Japanese people with TKS fear that they will do something to offend another person from their social group, that they will emit offensive odors, have a displeasing blemish, or speak in an offensive fashion. Thus, Japanese social phobics fear that they will offend others, whereas those from an independent cultural orientation fear that they themselves will be embarrassed by others' scrutiny. Like social phobias in Western cultures, TKS typically begins during the teenage years, but it is predominantly a male phenomenon (Takahashi, 1989).

Causes of Phobias

Behavioral, cognitive, and biological theories currently provide the most influential accounts of how

phobias develop. However, psychoanalysis has an historically important perspective on phobias so we will begin our discussion of how phobias develop with a review of Freud's ideas on this topic.

Psychoanalytic Formulations. Sigmund Freud proposed that phobias, especially animal phobias in young males, were due to an unconscious fear of castration (Freud, 1936/1963). (According to Freud, a snake can be a symbolic reminder to a male that he might lose his penis, or, to a female, that she already has.) Freud believed that, when unconscious sexual impulses threaten to emerge in consciousness, the ego transfers the anxiety to another object, such as a snake, that can be rationalized as truly dangerous.

Freud's most famous phobia case was Little Hans, the son of one of Freud's medical colleagues (Freud, 1936/1963). Little Hans developed a fear of horses and would not go into the street for fear of being bitten by one. Freud conjectured that, during the Oedipal period, Little Hans had incestuous desires for his mother and wished to destroy his father, whom he feared would castrate him if he discovered Hans's desire for his mother. Hans unconsciously transferred his castration anxiety into a fear of horses, which symbolically represented his father.

According to Freud, social phobias also resulted from unconscious impulses stemming from sexual urges. For example, he believed that fear of crowds stemmed from an unconscious fear that one might expose oneself in public (Freud, 1933/1965). Freud's analysis of phobias has not been well supported by empirical research, and psychoanalytic treatment is no longer a preferred intervention for phobias.

Behavioral and Cognitive Factors. An alternative to the Freudian conception of phobias was proposed early in this century by John B. Watson, an American behaviorist. Watson believed that all emotional learning developed from conditioning processes. In his view, a phobia develops because of a direct traumatic experience with a formerly neutral object. For example, suppose a youngster locks a younger sibling in a dark closet and terrifies the trapped child with menacing noises or threats. This experience sets the stage for the traumatized child to avoid closets or other confining places at all costs, thereby reducing feelings of anxiety but also leaving the child convinced that all such situations are dangerous. As a result of this avoidance, the child remains afraid of enclosed spaces and develops into an adult who suffers claustrophobia.

It is now clear, however, that direct conditioning is an incomplete explanation of phobias (Menzies & Clarke, 1995). For one thing, many phobic persons

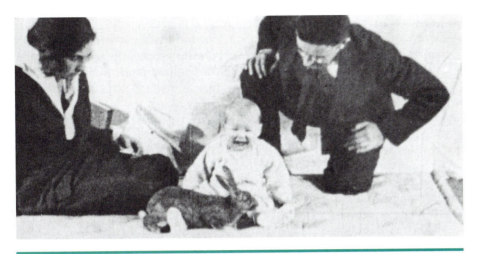

Watson set out to prove his behavioral theory of fear by conditioning an 11-month-old child, Albert B., affectionately called "little Albert," to fear a white rat (Watson & Rayner, 1920). Watson and his assistant, Rosalie Rayner, first tested Albert to be sure that he had no fear of white rats or other furry objects. Then, as Albert reached for the rat to play with it, Watson struck a steel bar with a hammer that frightened Albert. After six pairings of the frightening sound with Albert's close proximity to the rat, the rat and any other white or furry objects caused Albert to recoil in fear. From this demonstration, Watson concluded that fears and phobias were conditioned responses.

appear not to have suffered a traumatic conditioning experience that could account for their fears. Second, Watson believed that phobias could be relatively easily extinguished by deconditioning; if the person were reexposed to the frightening stimulus under conditions in which nothing traumatic happened, he or she would realize that the stimulus was not dangerous and no longer needed to be feared. However, once acquired, phobias are not extinguished as easily as Watson suggested they ought to be; in fact, they are often highly resistant to deconditioning. Finally, there are dramatic differences in the ease with which people can be conditioned to fear various stimuli. People develop fears of the dark or of small enclosed spaces far more easily than they do of electric outlets or automobiles, even though they experience many more traumatic events with the latter stimuli.

In light of these problems with the direct conditioning explanation for phobias, what other mechanisms might account for them? We now know that cognitive processes play an important role in causing some phobias. As described in Chapter 1, learning occurs not only through direct conditioning but also through observation—that is, through modeling and vicarious conditioning. Some people report that their phobias developed after observing others undergo a trauma (Mineka et al., 1984). In fact, Bandura (1986) argued that modeling processes could explain Little Hans's fear of horses better than Freud's

original psychoanalytic account could: Hans had witnessed a number of incidents that sensitized him to horses, and he had been repeatedly warned that horses were dangerous and could hurt him. Here is another case of how modeling can lead to a phobia.

Johnny was 10 years old when he and his classmates lined up in the school gym for vaccinations. The boy in front of Johnny screamed and jumped when he got his shot and pulled the syringe off the needle, which remained lodged in his arm. Having observed this traumatic incident, Johnny ran screaming from the gym and avoided needles for 12 years. He missed dental appointments on several occasions. When he finally had to go to the dentist for severe tooth pain, he was clearly phobic and would not allow the dentist to give him an anesthetic injection. (after Kleinknecht, 1991)

People can also develop phobias by hearing or reading vivid accounts of the dangers associated with certain stimuli. Phobias of air travel are typically acquired in this way; few people who fear flying have actually experienced a plane crash. They have often, however, seen pictures or heard stories of horrible air disasters. And yet, despite the fact that almost everyone has read or seen the gruesome details of plane crashes, relatively few people become phobic as a result. Other factors—probably involving an inherited biological sensitivity to anxiety—must be involved as well.

Biological Theories. If there is a genetic component to phobias, then they should appear more often in both members of monozygotic twin pairs than in members of dizygotic twin pairs; in other words, the **concordance rate** should be higher among monozygotic pairs. Indeed, when Kenneth Kendler and his colleagues interviewed 2,163 female twin pairs about their histories of phobias and other anxiety disorders, the concordance rate was higher in monozygotic than in dizygotic pairs for animal phobias, social phobias, and agoraphobia (Kendler et al., 1992a).

What neurobiological factors might be associated with a genetic vulnerability to phobias? Several possibilities have been proposed, but they all emphasize the idea that the phobic person is particularly prone to excessive physiological activity in certain situations. This overreactivity, which is probably first manifested in the temperamentally inhibited children described in Chapter 3, might arise from several sources. One possibility is that levels of one or more of the brain's neurotransmitters are disturbed. For example, **gamma aminobutyric acid (GABA)** is a neurotransmitter that inhibits postsynaptic activity. When the level of GABA is low, neurons tend to fire more rapidly, thereby increasing physiological arousal and anxiety. The hypothesis that low levels of GABA might be associated with anxiety is bolstered by the fact that the **benzodiazepines,** a class of drugs that reduces anxiety, increases the activity of GABA. Animal studies (Davis, 1994) indicate that intense fear appears to originate with signals from the **amygdala,** a mass of gray matter in the **limbic system,** a complex circuit of brain structures (including the thalamus, hippocampus, cingulate gyrus, hypothalamus, amygdala, septum, and parts of the cortex) that regulates emotions. When activated in mammals, the amygdala can trigger the adrenal gland to produce epinephrine, thereby increasing the physiological arousal related to fear. A tendency for this system to be overactivated may also be due to deficiencies in those neurotransmitters whose primary function is to inhibit neuron activity (Merckelbach et al., 1996).

Although there is evidence that phobias have a genetic component, the genetic contribution does not automatically determine the presence of a phobia. In Kendler's study (Kendler et al., 1992a), genetic make-up was estimated to account for only 30 to 40 percent of the variation in who ultimately became phobic;

thus, environmental experiences such as individual traumas, vicarious influences, informational processes, and family history were primarily responsible for triggering most phobias. This combination of genetic predisposition (a diathesis) and environmental experiences (stressors) illustrates how the diathesis–stress model (described in Chapter 1) applies to many phobias.

Preparedness theory proposes that people are *biologically prepared* to develop fears of certain classes of stimuli, such as snakes and spiders, that were potentially dangerous to our ancestors (Seligman, 1971; Cook & Mineka, 1987). In other words, some stimuli are more easily associated with fears than are others because, in past eras, these stimuli could threaten a person's survival. According to Martin Seligman, who originated this theory, these fears are not inherited directly; rather, it is the capacity to acquire certain fears through traumatic or vicarious conditioning that is inherited. The theory proposes that a single traumatic exposure to a "prepared stimulus" such as snakes or high places is sufficient for a phobia to develop. It is much more difficult to develop fears of "unprepared stimuli" such as electrical outlets or microwave ovens that have no history of evolutionary threat.

Preparedness theory has focused primarily on phobias of snakes and spiders (Seligman, 1971; Cook & Mineka, 1987) and on social phobias involving fear of stares or potentially threatening facial expressions (Öhman, 1985). Experimental research with humans has provided only partial support for preparedness theory (McNally, 1987), but Susan Mineka and Michael Cook have reported some remarkable supportive evidence from studies of vicarious conditioning of fear in young rhesus monkeys (Cook & Mineka, 1987; Mineka & Cook, 1986; Zinbarg & Mineka, 1991). For example, when a monkey, referred to as the "demonstrator," displayed a fear reaction to a snake, a previously fearless "observer" monkey became strongly and persistently fearful of snakes on the basis of seeing this single fear reaction (Mineka et al., 1984). However, when a fearless monkey observed a demonstrator monkey displaying fear in the face of a "nonprepared stimulus" such as flowers, no fear reaction developed (Cook & Mineka, 1987). These results have been replicated in numerous experiments, supporting the claim that monkeys can readily learn fears to prepared, but not to unprepared, stimuli.

To summarize, a person is mostly likely to develop a phobia when the conditions illustrated in Figure 7.2 are in place. First, certain people have an inborn neurological capacity to physiologically over-

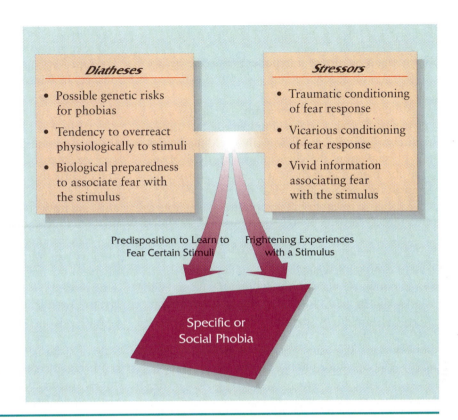

FIGURE 7.2

A Diathesis–Stress Model of Phobias

Phobias are most likely to occur when a person who is genetically prone to overreact physiologically to prepared stimuli has some form of frightening experience with one of these stimuli.

react to specific stimuli and therefore feel anxious. If such people directly undergo or vicariously learn about a traumatizing experience with an object or situation, they are at increased risk to become phobic of that stimulus. Their chances of becoming phobic are heightened even further if the stimulus has a history of evolutionary importance that "prepares" them for the development of a fear.

Treatment of Phobias

Phobias are the most treatable of the anxiety disorders and perhaps of all mental disorders; over 90 percent of specific phobias (particularly animal phobias) respond well to treatment (Bandura, Blanchard, & Ritter, 1969). Among the many approaches to treating phobias, those using learning-based procedures have proved most consistently successful (Rachman, 1990). These procedures include systematic desensitization, exposure techniques, and modeling.

Systematic Desensitization. The first treatment that was found to be effective for specific phobias was systematic desensitization, developed by Joseph Wolpe (Wolpe, 1958). The procedure begins by teaching the phobic client to become proficient at muscle relax-

ation, which in turn, leads to calmness and reduced physiological arousal. The client and therapist then construct an **anxiety hierarchy,** a graded list of fear-provoking stimuli or situations ranging from the least to the most threatening. For example, the following is an anxiety hierarchy for a person with an injection and blood phobia (Kleinknecht, 1993):

1. feeling the hypodermic needle in my arm and watching blood pump out when having blood drawn;
2. feeling the needle in my arm for injection;
3. waiting for injection during "countdown";
4. seeing the nurse come toward me with the hypodermic needle;
5. feeling the rubber tourniquet on my arm;
6. getting my arm swabbed with alcohol;
7. waiting in a room to get an injection or to have blood drawn;
8. watching someone else get blood drawn;
9. watching someone else get an injection;
10. being told I'll need blood drawn now;
11. being told I'll need an injection now;
12. being told I'll need blood drawn in the future;
13. being told I'll need an injection in the future;
14. holding a hypodermic needle;

15. seeing a picture of someone holding a hypodermic needle;
16. seeing a picture of a hypodermic needle by itself in a magazine.

While in a deeply relaxed state, the client is asked to imagine the least frightening item on the anxiety hierarchy. Once able to do so without losing the feelings of relaxation, the client moves up the list, successively imagining each item until able to imagine the most threatening item while remaining relaxed.

Extensive research has shown that being able to remain relaxed while imagining items in a hierarchy generalizes to live, or *in vivo*, situations (Rachman & Wilson, 1980). If a person with acrophobia can remain calm while visualizing standing at the top of a tall building, chances are good that the person will also be able to climb to the top floor of the building without becoming terrified. Although it is highly effective, systematic desensitization is time consuming and laborious. Exposure procedures provide more efficient treatments for phobic clients.

Exposure Procedures. The principle of extinction is the basis for exposure procedures. Once a conditioned fear response has been acquired by directly pairing or vicariously associating a fear-provoking, unconditioned stimulus (US) with a previously neutral stimulus (CS, or conditioned stimulus), the fear response can be extinguished by arranging for multiple exposures to the CS in the absence of the US.

One version of this procedure is **graduated exposure,** in which clients are given live, rather than imagined, exposure to items from an anxiety hierarchy similar to those used in systematic desensitization. Using the needle phobia hierarchy, for example, the client would first view a picture of a hypodermic syringe, then observe another person holding one, and eventually actually receive an injection and have blood drawn. New technologies, such as virtual reality, are now being used to create vivid, but safe, exposures to feared stimuli.

A more intense exposure procedure called **flooding** involves immediate and prolonged presentation of the most intense version of the feared stimulus. This procedure results in an initial increase in anxiety, followed by relatively rapid fear reduction. Lars-Goran Öst (1992) has shown significant fear reduction in needle phobics using this procedure in a single 3-hour session. A 20-session flooding program has also been found to be superior to anti-anxiety medication in the treatment of social phobias (Turner, Beidel, & Jacob, 1994).

Modeling Procedures. Just as phobias can be acquired by observing another person undergo a traumatic experience, vicarious learning can be used to reduce fears. Albert Bandura has extensively studied

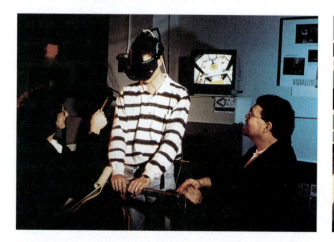 

The phobic client (left) *wears a virtual reality (VR) headset that presents a simulated, controlled exposure to feared stimuli. The client sees in the headset the scene shown at the right and can vary the exposure by moving back from or closer to the edge of the balcony. Acrophobic clients exposed to such scenes with VR experience the same fear sensations as they would in real-life situations including racing heart, nausea, and weak knees. One participant even vomited from motion sickness during the simulated elevator ride.*

the effectiveness of modeling treatments in which fearful clients observe a model interacting with the feared stimuli. Someone fearful of heights, for example, would observe another person (perhaps the therapist) gradually ascend a flight of stairs, climb a ladder, or peer out a high window. A dog phobic would observe another person happily playing with dogs. The repeated observation of others displaying fearlessness communicates to phobic persons that the situation is safe for them.

Participant modeling, a combination of *in vivo* exposure and modeling, is one of the most effective of all treatments for specific phobias. This procedure begins with the therapist's demonstrating the feared behavior until the client's fear has diminished somewhat. Next, the therapist helps the client approach the feared situation step by step, each time arranging the circumstances to maximize the client's success and confidence about further progress. In treating a child for dog phobia, for example, the therapist might hold the child while, together, they pet a friendly, calm dog. The child would gradually be encouraged to pet the dog independently, and the therapist would eventually move away as the child's fear diminishes.

The fact that all these behavioral treatments work well, even though their rationales and details differ considerably, has lead to speculation that a common underlying mechanism is responsible for fear reduction in all of them. Albert Bandura, who developed the modeling and participant modeling procedures, believes that the common mechanism is the enhancement of clients' sense of **self-efficacy,** their confidence that they can approach and tolerate their feared objects or situations. Behavioral progress, whether gradual or concentrated (as in flooding), engenders this confidence (Bandura, 1986). Each accomplishment builds clients' self-efficacy so that they can take the next step. Thus, any procedure that enhances self-efficacy should reduce fear behavior.

In Review

Phobias, the most common form of anxiety disorder, are:

- irrational, excessive fears of specific objects or situations that cause intense distress and interfere with everyday life;
- usually focused on animals, blood or injections, events in the natural environment, specific situations, or social encounters involving potential evaluations;

- most likely in persons who are predisposed to overreact physiologically to stimuli and who have had or have heard of some frightening experiences with a stimulus; and
- effectively treated by procedures that expose the person to the feared stimulus so that he or she gains confidence about being able to control or tolerate it.

Panic Disorder and Agoraphobia

Earlier diagnostic systems such as the DSM-II included a condition called *anxiety neurosis* as a prominent anxiety disorder. Anxiety neurosis was described as a chronic state of *free-floating* anxiety, that is, anxiety not clearly tied to specific stimuli (Beck, 1976; Freud, 1933/1965). This ongoing anxiety was periodically punctuated by intense attacks of panic. Beginning with the DSM-III (APA, 1980), anxiety neurosis was divided into separate disorders, such as generalized anxiety disorder, panic disorder, and agoraphobia. Because panic disorder and agoraphobia are usually considered to be connected (Goisman et al., 1995; Horwath et al., 1993), we will describe them together.

Characteristics and Prevalence

The hallmark of **panic disorder** is periodic and unexpected attacks of intense, terrifying anxiety, called **panic attacks,** that leave victims feeling as if they are going crazy or are about to die. The attacks come on suddenly, reach peak intensity within a few minutes, and may last for minutes or hours (APA, 1994; Barlow, 1988). The person then develops persistent anxiety that another attack will occur or that such attacks will be uncontrollable should they recur. Most cases have their onset between adolescence and the mid-30s. The course of untreated panic disorder is variable. An individual may go months or even years without an attack and then suddenly experience an episode.

The DSM table on page 226 lists the symptoms of a panic attack, which resemble the fear experienced in phobias, including physical symptoms such as a racing heart (tachycardia), sweating, trembling, choking or smothering sensations, chills, dizziness, nausea, and shortness of breath (Craske et al., 1993). In panic disorder, however, at least some of the attacks appear to come on suddenly for no apparent

---

DSM-IV

Criteria for Panic Attack

A discrete period of intense fear or discomfort, in which four (or more) of the following symptoms developed abruptly and reached a peak within 10 minutes:

1. Palpitations, pounding heart, or accelerated heart rate;

2. Sweating;

3. Trembling or shaking;

4. Sensations of shortness of breath or smothering;

5. Feeling of choking;

6. Chest pain or discomfort;

7. Nausea or abdominal distress;

8. Feeling dizzy, unsteady, lightheaded, or faint;

9. Derealization (feelings of unreality) or depersonalization (being detached from oneself);

10. Fear of losing control or going crazy;

11. Fear of dying;

12. Paresthesias (numbness or tingling sensations); and

13. Chills or hot flashes

Source: American Psychiatric Association; *Diagnostic and Statistical Manual of Mental Disorders,* Fourth Edition. Washington, DC, American Psychiatric Association, 1994.

---

reason and with little warning. Other panic attacks seem to be elicited by specific aspects of a situation, but, unlike the fear associated with phobias, they occur only intermittently. For example, being in a crowded shopping mall may often, but not always, precipitate a panic attack. Panic attacks are sometimes so strong that they leave a person feeling as if the surrounding objects or events are not real (derealization) or as if they have become detached from themselves (depersonalization).

Connections

In what other disorders do people experience symptoms of derealization and depersonalization? For the answer, see Chapter 8, pp. 253–254.

Agoraphobia. Panic disorder can occur on its own, but the majority of serious panic disorder cases include agoraphobia. Indeed, the DSM-IV contains a special category, *panic disorder without agoraphobia.* **Agoraphobia** means fear of open spaces (*agora* is Greek for *marketplace.*) Persons with agoraphobia, which is the single most common phobia treated by clinicians, typically fear leaving home alone, being in public, and traveling. Their most basic fear, however, is having a panic attack while being away from a place they consider safe. They fear having an attack in a situation in which they will be embarrassed and from which they cannot readily escape (Barlow, 1988; Faravelli et al., 1992). The following case illustrates panic disorder with agoraphobia.

Joseph had triple bypass surgery and was recuperating at home. When he felt well enough, he went outside to walk, but after a few minutes, his heart began to flutter and race. He felt a wave of terror sweep over him, and he thought he was dying. He had an overwhelming urge to run but did not know why or from what, and, besides, he was too weak. He could only sit down and shake in terror. After what seemed like hours (actually only minutes), the panic passed. He staggered home, shaken by the experience. His cardiologist suspected panic disorder since his patient's newly repaired heart was working fine. Within a week, a second panic attack occurred while Joseph was driving his car, and a third occurred while he was waiting in line at a store. Eventually, Joseph was reluctant to go out of the house, and, when he did, he would no longer drive for fear of having another attack. Despite his wife's urging, he would venture only a couple of blocks from home to ensure that he could return quickly in case of another attack.

As in Joseph's case, most clients' agoraphobia develops following a series of unpredictable and uncontrollable panic attacks (Barlow, 1988; Faravelli et al., 1992). They begin to avoid places where the attacks occurred, or places like them, until they come to suffer what has been called a "fear of fear" (Arrindell, 1993; Goldstein & Chambless, 1978). Panic attacks can occur in so many places or with such severity in a few places that agoraphobics often become totally housebound.

Although clinicians usually assume that most cases of agoraphobia are accompanied by a history of panic attacks (Goisman et al., 1995; Horwath et al., 1993), some researchers (Eaton & Keyl, 1990) report that cases of agoraphobia without a history of panic disorder are not uncommon. The confusion over the frequency of agoraphobia without panic disorder may be due to differences in the way clinicians and epidemiologists have assessed this condition. Obviously, the relationship between agoraphobia and panic disorder is controversial and requires much more research.

Persons displaying panic disorder with agoraphobia are vulnerable to problems that go beyond restricted activities and fear of panic attacks. Their frequent use of alcohol and other drugs as self-prescribed anxiety medications places them at risk for substance abuse (Kushner, Sher, & Beitman, 1990; Pollard et al., 1990). Self-medication and prescription medications for anxiety are potentially addictive and can add to the agoraphobic's misery (Rickels et al., 1993). People who suffer from panic disorder with agoraphobia also frequently suffer depression (Weissman et al., 1989) and have a significantly increased risk of premature death from various causes, including suicide (Markowitz et al., 1989; Weissman et al., 1989).

Prevalence. Recent estimates of the lifetime prevalence of panic disorder (with or without agoraphobia) is between 1.5 to 3.5 percent throughout the world (APA, 1994); in the general U.S. population, estimates run as high as 9 percent of adults (Burnam et al., 1987; Katerndahl & Realini, 1993; Kessler et al., 1994; Robins et al., 1984). In most epidemiological studies, females are found to suffer panic disorder more frequently than males (Burnam et al., 1987; Katerndahl & Realini, 1993; Robins et al., 1984; review Figure 7.1 on page 217). Estimates of panic disorder in other countries, such as Germany and Switzerland (Amering & Katschnig, 1990), yield similar figures. One exception to this pattern was found in Hong Kong. Using a methodology similar to that reported in American and European research, Char-Nie Chen and his colleagues found panic disorder occurring in only 0.26 percent of the Hong Kong population (Chen et al., 1993).

Rates of panic disorder have not been found to differ among ethnic groups in the United States (Burnam et al., 1987; Canino et al., 1987; Horwath, Johnson, & Hornig, 1993; Katerndahl & Realini, 1993); however, agoraphobia appears to occur at a higher rate among Black Americans than among White Americans (Neal & Turner, 1991). Black Americans may also experience different symptoms of panic than do White Americans. Specifically, Black Americans with panic disorder tend to show sleep paralysis, a symptom that is uncommon in other ethnic groups. **Sleep paralysis** occurs when a person is waking up or falling asleep, and it involves an inability to move; it is often accompanied by visual hallucinations, hyperventilation, and acute fear. Sleep

Earl Campbell, a Heisman Trophy winner in college and then a professional football running back, experienced his first panic attack about 5 years after retiring from football while taking a short trip in his car. The attacks continued, and Campbell went to eight different doctors trying to find out what was wrong. After each attack, Campbell grew more worried about what was happening to him. "I'd go to bed at night and just lie there because I knew that if I went to sleep, I'd have an attack. I used to cherish being by myself," he said. "I used to jog, hunt deer and work out, but I stopped. I'd enjoyed running my own company, but instead, I stayed home."

paralysis is also associated with hypertension in Black Americans, leading researchers to look for possible causal links between these conditions (Neal & Turner, 1991).

Prevalence of agoraphobia is similar to that for panic disorder, since the two are so closely related. Lifetime prevalence figures in the United States and Puerto Rico, for example, range from 5.3 to 6.8 percent. Again, females outnumber males about 2 to 1 (Canino et al., 1987; Robins et al., 1984). Agoraphobia is found in most parts of the world, but it accompanies panic disorder in the northern more often than in the southern latitudes (Amering & Katschnig, 1990).

Causes of Panic Disorder and Agoraphobia

Panic disorder and agoraphobia have been attributed to both psychological and biological factors.

Psychodynamic Formulations. Freud theorized that agoraphobia had its roots in fears tied to an unresolved Oedipal complex (Freud, 1936/1963). He believed that the anxiety generated by being alone and away from home derived from an unconscious temptation to act out sexual impulses in public. A companion serves to inhibit those urges (Free, Winget, & Whitman, 1993; Freud, 1933/1965).

A more recent psychodynamic theory explanation comes from object relations theory, which claims that agoraphobia has its origins in unresolved *separation anxiety* (Gittelman & Klein, 1985), the fear of losing or being separated from a protective or nurturant person, usually the mother. This fear is first seen around 4 months of age and is a perfectly normal sign that an infant is emotionally attached to a parent and feels distressed when separated from that parent.

In some cases, however, parents may not have adequately fulfilled an infant's needs for physical security and emotional closeness. This problem may arise from a physical loss of or separation from a parent, or it can develop when parents are emotionally distant and unresponsive to an infant. In such cases the child is thought to develop long-lasting fears of being abandoned or being away from home. These children may be diagnosed with a *separation anxiety disorder*. These fears can be reactivated later in life when a person is forced to move or loses a loved one or a close friend (Free et al., 1993). Some studies have

Connections

How are childhood fears and phobias related to anxiety disorders in adulthood? For a discussion of this issue, see Chapter 3, pp. 98–102.

reported that agoraphobics experience more loss-related events in the year preceding the onset of agoraphobia than do nonagoraphobics (Free et al., 1993). Other studies, however, have not found this difference (Thyer et al., 1986). At present, a more serious limitation of the object relations theory is that there is no convincing evidence that agoraphobics were more likely than nonagoraphobics to have been separated from their parents or to have experienced disturbed object relations in early childhood. However, there is evidence that a history of childhood sexual or physical abuse is more common in adults with anxiety disorder than in nondisordered adults; 45 percent of women with anxiety disorder were sexually abused before the age of 18, compared with 15.4 percent of women without a disorder (Stein et al., 1996).

Biological Factors. Panic disorder and agoraphobia tend to run in families. In one study, Raymond Crowe and his colleagues found that over 17 percent of the family members of panic-disordered patients also had panic disorder. The percentage was even greater for female relatives: 46 percent also had panic disorder, compared with less than 2 percent in the general population (Crowe et al., 1983). Similar findings have been reported for relatives of agoraphobics (Noyes et al., 1986). Twin studies of panic disorder typically find greater concordance between monozygotic than dizygotic twins (Torgersen, 1983). Most researchers today acknowledge a genetic contribution to panic disorder and agoraphobia, and they have proposed several inherited neurophysiological and biochemical mechanisms that could make a person vulnerable to panic attacks.

The intense terror of the panic experience must be a basic, primitive alarm mechanism (Barlow, 1988; Gorman et al., 1989). The neurological underpinnings of this alarm system center in a small area of the brainstem called the **locus coeruleus (LC)** (see Figure 7.3). Artificial stimulation of this area in animals results in panic-like behavior (Gorman et al., 1989). If the LC is removed, the animal does not show panic. Hypersensitivity of this alarm system could be the basis for panic disorder, and this hypersensitivity could have a genetic base. Other areas of the brain, especially the amygdala and the frontal and temporal lobes, are also involved in panic and anxiety experiences as a result of the limbic system's being part of a circuit with the locus coeruleus.

How might LC sensitivity lead to panic disorder? One possibility is that, in people with LC hypersensitivity, certain substances are more likely to trigger panic attacks. There is evidence that many panic disordered patients are particularly sensitive to such

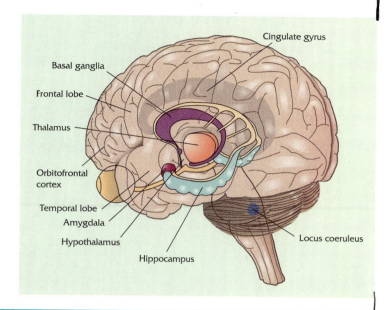

FIGURE 7.3

Brain Structures Involved in Anxiety and Panic

Emotions such as fear, anxiety, and panic are mediated by various brain circuits that involve the structures shown here.

substances. For example, *hyperventilation* (rapid breathing) or injection of lactic acid, a natural by-product of muscle activity during exercise, results in panic attacks in 54 to 90 percent of panic clients. Fewer than 25 percent of nonpsychiatric patients experience attacks under these conditions (Barlow, 1988). A similar hypersensitivity also occurs to substances such as caffeine, carbon dioxide, and noradrenalin (Papp et al., 1993).

Hypersensitivity to these substances cannot completely explain panic disorder, however. For one thing, lactate does not cross the blood–brain barrier in lower primates, and thus it might not directly affect the LC as some have theorized (Coplan et al., 1992). Furthermore, if panic-disordered clients are led to believe that they can control the amount of carbon dioxide they inhale, they are no more likely to have panic attacks than those not inhaling it (Carter et al., 1995; Rapee et al., 1992; Sanderson, Rapee, & Barlow, 1989). It has also been demonstrated that, when patients with panic disorder are given a placebo they think was sodium lactate, they respond with panic attacks that are virtually identical to those of patients who *are* given sodium lactate (Goetz et al., 1993).

Although neuroscientists are identifying brain areas that are implicated in panic attacks, just how the attacks are triggered in clients with panic disorder is not yet established (Goetz et al., 1993). Because a person's perception of control seems to affect responses to these biochemicals, the onset of panic attacks must involve psychological processes as well.

Diathesis–Stress Models. Cognitive theorists such as Aaron Beck (1976) and David Clark (1986) claim that panic attacks result from misperceptions that benign bodily sensations or harmless external stimuli are actually very dangerous. In some clients, these misperceptions can escalate into repetitive thoughts about potentially dangerous events. The more convinced they become that normal sensations are really dangerous, the more their anxiety grows. This anxiety then drives the activation of the sympathetic nervous system even higher. Therefore, according to Beck (1976), panic attacks really begin as *false alarms*.

A more comprehensive view of panic disorder comes from David Barlow (1988). Barlow incorporates aspects of biological theories with the cognitive theories of Beck and Clark (see Figure 7.4 on page 230). He begins with the assumption that people can have a hereditary predisposition to panic in the form of a highly reactive autonomic nervous system and/or a tendency to be highly sensitive to anxiety symptoms.

When biologically vulnerable individuals are exposed to major life stressors, they are prone to experience a panic attack because they interpret the stressor as a signal of mortal danger. The attack is a false alarm (there is no immediate danger from which to escape), but when cues and sensations associated with this attack occur again, they can trigger panic. The cues and sensations have become *learned alarms*. As the attacks continue, clients become highly vigilant for their early warning signs. Barlow calls this anticipatory "on guard" state *anxious apprehension*. Anxious apprehension leaves the person on edge all

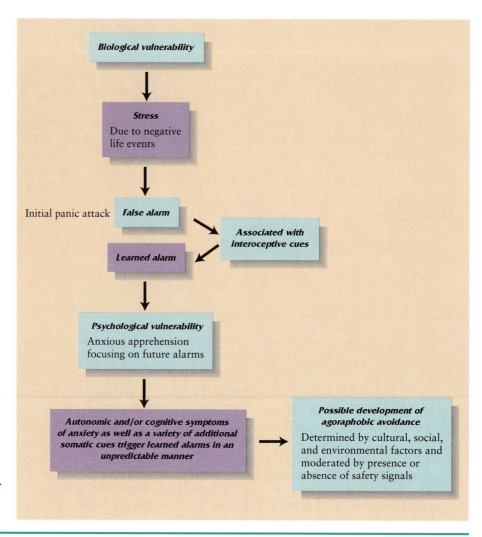

FIGURE 7.4

Barlow's Model of the
Causes of Panic Disorder
and Agoraphobia
Source: Barlow, 1988.

the time and ready to interpret many different bodily sensations as signs of an impending attack (Asmundson & Norton, 1993). Individuals who are easily upset by anxiety symptoms—shortness of breath, sweaty palms—tend to score high on a trait called *anxiety sensitivity* (McNally, 1994).

Barlow's theory suggests that the triggering role of substances such as lactic acid stems from the fact that these substances create physiological sensations that mimic the early internal cues associated with previous panic attacks. If a person mistakenly believes that these sensations are signs of an impending attack, worry, anxiety, and a real attack may ultimately follow. A similar process may occur when panic-disordered patients hyperventilate, misinterpret the resulting physiological sensations as the beginning of an attack, and thereby hasten its actual occurrence (Ley, 1985). One important implication of Barlow's model is that effective treatments for panic disorder and agoraphobia should address both

the physiological and psychological contributions to these disorders.

Treatment of Panic Disorder and Agoraphobia

Both cognitive-behavioral and drug treatments are effective therapies for panic disorder (Clum, Clum & Surls, 1993).

Cognitive Behavioral Treatments. Cognitive-behavioral treatments for panic disorder and agoraphobia stem directly from the view that these problems reflect a misinterpretation of physical sensations as signs of danger. These treatment packages typically contain three basic elements:

1. *breathing retraining* that teaches clients to reduce their breathing rate, thus promoting relaxation and combating hyperventilation;

2. *interoceptive exposure* to somatic cues (such as changes in heart rate or dizziness) that often trigger an attack. This graded exposure is intended to reduce clients' anxiety about physical sensations; and

3. *cognitive restructuring* geared to correct clients' chronic misinterpretations of benign bodily sensations (Gould & Clum, 1995; Margraf et al., 1993; Zinbarg et al., 1992).

Cognitive behavioral treatment packages have been reported to eliminate panic attacks in 80 to 90 percent of treated clients over follow-up periods as long as 4 years (Chambless & Gillis, 1993; Margraf et al., 1993). These procedures are equally effective whether used in group or individual therapy (Telch et al., 1993).

A specific cognitive-behavioral intervention known as *panic control treatment* (Craske & Barlow, 1993) has an especially good track record not only in relieving the symptoms of panic disorder, but also in reducing symptoms of other anxiety disorders that are often comorbid with panic disorder (Brown, Antony, & Barlow, 1995). This treatment usually entails a combination of the three components described above—breathing retraining, interoceptive exposure, and cognitive restructuring—plus educating clients about how panic arises from their tendency to overreact to and *catastrophize* physical sensations. In one study, clients who completed 12 sessions of panic control treatment experienced a significant decrease in panic-related symptoms, and a majority maintained their improvements over a 2-year follow-up. However, even among clients who improved, many still had setbacks; more than half of them occasionally suffered panic attacks during the 2-year period, and more than one quarter sought additional treatment (Brown & Barlow, 1995). One

lesson to learn from these results is that panic disorder can be difficult to treat; even the most powerful treatments do not guarantee lasting benefits to all clients.

Cognitive-behavioral treatment of agoraphobia is similar to that used for panic attacks, but additional techniques may be necessary to eliminate agoraphobic avoidance behavior, even after panic attacks have diminished. The most effective procedure for treating avoidance involves the kinds of exposure methods used for specific phobias. Agoraphobic clients are encouraged and assisted to confront such feared situations as leaving home, going to department stores or shopping malls, or using public transportation. Exposure can be carried out in graduated fashion or in more intense flooding procedures (Zinbarg et al., 1992).

Drug Treatments. Certain antidepressants and anxiolytics (antianxiety drugs) have been found useful for treating panic disorder. Antidepressants can be therapeutic for panic regardless of whether the person is depressed. Table 7.2 describes several of these drugs (their benefits and side effects are discussed in Chapter 15).

The main type of anxiolytic used to treat panic disorder is the class of drugs called benzodiazepines. As described earlier, these drugs facilitate the action of inhibitory neurotransmitters such as GABA. As a result, they reduce anxiety by slowing down the activity of neurons in the brain. Benzodiazepines work rapidly to relieve anxiety, but they also produce undesirable side effects such as drowsiness and reduced motor coordination. In addition, clients can quickly become dependent on, or even physically addicted to, these drugs. Antidepressants such as imipramine or phenelzine are effective in reducing panic symptoms,

---

TABLE 7.2   Drugs Used in Treating Panic Disorder

Type of drug	Biochemical action	Key benefit
Benzodiazepines Alprazolam (Xanax) Diazepam (Valium) Oxazepam (Serax)	Facilitates the binding of inhibitory neurotransmitters such as GABA, augmenting inhibitory effects of the neurotransmitter and thus decreasing the activity of certain neurons	Physical relaxation, calmer mental processes, less worry
Antidepressants: Monoamine oxidase inhibitors Phenelzine (Nardil)	Slows the decomposition of norepinephrine and serotonin, augmenting their action in the brain	Aborts panic attacks
Antidepressants: Tricyclics Imipramine (Tofranil)	Blocks the reuptake of norepinephrine and serotonin, increasing their availability to the brain	Aborts panic attacks

but they too have troubling side effects, such as dizziness, impotence, and extreme thirst, which often cause patients to stop taking them.

In one study, 44 percent of panic disordered patients receiving imipramine and 57 percent of those given the anxiolytic alprazolam (sold as Xanax) were panic free after 8 weeks of treatment (Schweizer et al., 1993). In a study comparing the effectiveness of alprazolam with cognitive-behavioral therapy in the treatment of panic disorder, Janet Klosko and her colleagues found that, after 12 weeks of treatment, 87 percent of those receiving CBT were panic free compared with 50 percent of drug-treated clients (Klosko et al., 1990).

Some clinicians believe that a combination of psychological and pharmacological treatments might be more effective than either one by itself (Marks et al., 1993; Mavissakalian & Michelson, 1986), but recent research has not found combined treatment to be superior to cognitive-behavioral treatment alone (Gould, Otto, & Pollack, 1995). Proponents of combined treatment suggest that drugs should be used to treat the panic attacks and that cognitive-behavioral approaches should be aimed at agoraphobic avoidance (e.g., Zitrin, Klein, & Woerner, 1980). More definitive studies of combined treatments are currently under way. (The effects of other drug treatments are described in greater detail in Chapter 15.)

In Review

Panic disorder:

- consists of intense, unexpected attacks of panic coupled with the dread of having more attacks;
- is often linked with agoraphobia because many panic disordered clients try to avoid situations in which they might have an attack and might not be able to escape to safety;
- appears in most parts of the world and is more prevalent in females than males;
- appears to be caused by a biological predisposition to overreact physically to stressors, followed by a tendency to misinterpret bodily sensations as signs of danger, leading to constant apprehension about further attacks; and
- can usually be treated with antidepressant and antianxiety drugs or cognitive-behavioral treatment packages.

Obsessive-Compulsive Disorder

Obsessive-compulsive disorder (OCD) involves recurrent obsessions or compulsions that are serious enough to adversely affect a person's life (see the DSM table opposite for the DSM-IV criteria for this diagnosis). **Obsessions** are unwanted, disturbing, often irrational thoughts, feelings, or images that people cannot get out of their minds. When clinicians use the term *obsession,* they are not referring to the preoccupation a person might feel about a romantic partner or the daydreams a person has about an upcoming weekend. Such repeated thoughts are usually experienced with some pleasure. Most people experience intrusive thoughts such as these once in a while, and such thoughts are perfectly normal. Clinical obsessions, however, seem to force their way into the mind, and usually involve frightening images or aggressive urges. Obsessions are often termed **ego-dystonic,** meaning that the person believes them to be entirely out of his or her control.

Most people have experienced a minor, temporary obsession in the form of a tune or advertising jingle that they cannot get out of their minds. Others may frequently worry when they are away from home that they have forgotten to lock a door or turn off an appliance. In OCD, however, the obsessions are much more distressing. Among the most common obsessions are

- fear of contacting dirt, germs, or of touching infected people or objects;
- disgust over body waste or secretions;
- undue concern that a job has not been done adequately, even when the person knows that it was done well;
- fear of committing a crime or hurting someone;
- fear of shouting obscenities or insults; and
- fear of thinking antireligious or sexual thoughts.

About 80 percent of clients with OCD find their obsessions so uncomfortable that they feel compelled to take some action to suppress them or to ease the anxiety and guilt caused by them (Rachman & Hodgson, 1980). **Compulsions** are repetitive, nearly irresistible acts that temporarily neutralize obsessions or relieve the anxiety they cause. Common compulsive rituals include

- repetitively washing the hands or other objects that may be a source of contamination;
- checking doors or windows, water or gas taps;

DSM-IV

Diagnostic Criteria for Obsessive-Compulsive Disorder

A. Either obsessions or compulsions:

Obsessions as defined by (1), (2), (3), and (4):

1. recurrent and persistent thoughts, impulses, or images that are experienced, at some time during the disturbance, as intrusive and inappropriate and that cause marked anxiety or distress
2. the thoughts, impulses, or images are not simply excessive worries about real-life problems
3. the person attempts to ignore or suppress such thoughts, impulses, or images, or to neutralize them with some other thought or action
4. the person recognizes that the obsessional thoughts, impulses, or images are a product of his or her own mind (not imposed from without as in thought insertion)

Compulsions as defined by (1) and (2):

1. repetitive behaviors (e.g., hand washing, ordering, checking) or mental acts (e.g., praying, counting, repeating words silently) that the person feels driven to perform in response to an obsession, or according to rules that must be applied rigidly
2. the behaviors or mental acts are aimed at preventing or reducing distress or preventing some dreaded event or situation; however, these behaviors or mental acts either are not connected in a realistic way with what they are designed to neutralize or prevent or are clearly excessive

B. At some point during the course of the disorder, the person has recognized that the obsessions or compulsions are excessive or unreasonable.
Note: This does not apply to children.

C. The obsessions or compulsions cause marked distress, are time consuming (take more than 1 hour each day), or significantly interfere with the person's normal routine, occupational (or academic) functioning, or usual social activities or relationships.

D. If another Axis I disorder is present, the content of the obsessions or compulsions is not restricted to it (e.g., preoccupation with food in the presence of an Eating Disorder; hair pulling in the presence of Trichotillomania; concern with appearance in the presence of Body Dysmorphic Disorder; preoccupation with drugs in the presence of a Substance Use Disorder; preoccupation with serious illness in the presence of Hypochondriasis; preoccupation with sexual urges or fantasies in the presence of Paraphilia; or guilty ruminations in the presence of Major Depressive Disorder).

E. The disturbance is not due to the direct physiological effects of a substance (e.g., a drug of abuse, a medication) or a general medical condition.

Source: American Psychiatric Association; *Diagnostic and Statistical Manual of Mental Disorders,* Fourth Edition. Washington, DC, American Psychiatric Association, 1994.

- counting objects a precise number of times or repeating certain actions (such as going through a doorway) a set number of times; and
- hoarding old newspapers, mail, and other used and useless objects (DeSilva & Rachman, 1992; Rachman & Hodgson, 1980).

Sometimes compulsions take the form of performing some small act in exactly the same manner, time after time, so that the individual labors through each day at an extremely slow pace. Putting dishes and silverware away in a precisely aligned pattern, hanging clothes in a closet so that exactly the same gap is maintained between hangers, sorting food on shelves according to their caloric content, or insisting that books be always maintained in alphabetical order on shelves are typical compulsive routines. Although clients try to resist performing these ritu-

Hoarding of objects—as shown in this photo of the home of the Collyer brothers, who lived in Harlem and packed their house full of newspapers, pianos, and even an old car—is one of the common compulsive rituals seen in obsessive-compulsive disorder.

als and understand them to be unreasonable and excessive, the impulse to use them to reduce mounting tension eventually wins out.

Characteristics and Prevalence

The lack of pleasure in compulsive behavior and the fact that it is performed in response to obsessional thoughts differentiate OCD from other conditions commonly thought to be compulsive in nature, such as overeating, gambling, and alcohol and drug abuse. People displaying these conditions seek the opportunity to engage in the behaviors and, at least in the short run, derive pleasure from doing so. OCD rituals, on the other hand, can be highly debilitating. For example, persons with contamination obsessions and its accompanying washing compulsions might wash their hands for several hours each day, leaving little time for other activities. Hand washers have been known to continue their compulsion even after they have rubbed skin off or seriously bruised themselves.

*H*oward Hughes, the famous industrialist, aviator, and movie producer suffered OCD related to his dread of contamination. His obsessive behavior led to virtual total isolation from the world. Anything that came into his penthouse apartment had to be wrapped in special paper. His attempts at cleanliness became so involved that he was unable to continue them, and, eventually, he abandoned all efforts to cleanse himself. (CIBA-GIEGY, 1991)

OCD can sometimes be merely annoying rather than debilitating. Dr. Samuel Johnson, the eighteenth-century English lexicographer, essayist, and biographer, apparently had a version of OCD. One of his contemporaries described his behavior as he approached a door: "Johnson would take a prescribed number of steps from a certain point in the room and just before crossing the threshold he would twist, turn, and make strange gesticulations. Finally, he would leap over the threshold . . . " (Rapoport, 1989).

OCD-Related Disorders. Clinical researchers have noted similarities between OCD and other conditions. For example, a condition known as **Tourette's disorder,** originally noted by Gilles de la Tourette in the nineteenth century, is characterized by both repetitive vocal tics or vocalizations (teeth clicking, coughing, grunting) *and* motor acts and tics such as rapid eye blinking, retracing footsteps or twirling around, and facial grimaces. Because Tourette's disorder usually begins in childhood or early adolescence, the DSM-IV classifies it as a Disorder Usually First Diagnosed in Infancy, Childhood, or Adolescence. In addition to motor tics, which many children have at some point in their development but then outgrow, about one third of children with Tourette's disorder also display **coprolalia,** the involuntary shouting or repeating of obscene words. They also tend to have problems involving impulsive behavior and socially annoying actions.

Gilles de la Tourette himself noted a possible association between Tourette's disorder and obsessive-compulsive behavior, and many contemporary clinicians have observed increased rates of OCD among patients with Tourette's disorder as well as among their relatives (George et al., 1993; Leckman & Cohen, 1994; Pauls, Raymond, & Robertson, 1991). Based on these findings and the fact that the motor rituals of Tourette's often appear similar to OCD, several researchers currently believe that people with Tourette's and OCD share a genetic vulnerability. Despite these similarities, there are important differences between OCD and Tourette's. For example, Tourette's patients who also have OCD symptoms report more violent and sexual images than OCD-only patients, and they display more counting and hoarding rituals (George et al., 1993).

Prevalence of Obsessive-Compulsive Disorder.

Between 2 and 3 percent of U.S. adults and 1 percent of children and adolescents suffer OCD at some time in their lives (Rapoport, 1989; Robins et al., 1984; Robins & Regier, 1991). Up to half of the cases begin in childhood or adolescence, with some compulsive behaviors starting as young as 3 years of age (Rapoport, 1989).

In her extensive studies of children with OCD, Judith Rapoport found that gender distribution varies by age (Rapoport 1989; Rapoport et al., 1981). In particular,

- those with onset in early childhood are predominantly male;
- the gender distribution is fairly even among patients who develop OCD during adolescence; and
- adult-onset cases are predominantly female (Rapoport, 1989).

Males and females are equally represented among those whose compulsions involve counting and checking, but the majority of "washers" are female (Minichiello et al., 1990; Rachman & Hodgson, 1980). Paul Emmelkamp, an anxiety disorders specialist from the Netherlands, has proposed that this phenomenon reflects an extension of traditional gender role differences in which women are typically cast as cleaners (Emmelkamp, 1982). Overall, among all adults with OCD, there is only a slight predominance of females (Minichiello et al., 1990; Robins & Regier, 1991; Robins et al., 1984).

Causes of Obsessive-Compulsive Disorder

Biological and cognitive-behavioral theories are the leading explanations of how OCD develops.

The Role of Genetics.

In addition to the genetic clues derived from OCD's association with Tourette's syndrome, genetic contributions to OCD have been examined in both family studies and twin studies. For example, Donald Black and his colleagues (1992) examined 120 relatives of 32 OCD patients for the presence of OCD and other anxiety disorders and compared them with 129 relatives of 33 normal control subjects. No difference was found in the rate of OCD among family members of OCD patients and those of the normal controls. However, significantly more OCD family members compared with controls (30 percent versus 17.1 percent) had one or more anxiety disorders. These data are consistent with findings from a twin study (Torgersen, 1983) in which concordance rates of OCD in monozygotic (MZ) and dizygotic (DZ) twins did not differ, but there was greater concordance between MZ twins compared with DZ twins, for "any anxiety disorder." This research suggests that anxiety disorders may have a genetic component, but it probably takes the form of an inherited general diathesis rather than genetic transmittal of specific symptoms (Black et al., 1992).

Neurobiological Factors.

Other research on OCD implicates **serotonin,** a neurotransmitter that is thought to influence emotions and regulate sleep. At this point, the evidence is circumstantial, resting largely on the fact that the drugs found most effective in treating OCD are antidepressants such as Prozac, which inhibit the reuptake of serotonin (e.g., Lickey & Gordon, 1991; Rapoport, 1989). The stronger the blockage, the more effective the drug is (Lickey & Gordon, 1991). The suggestion from this evidence is that OCD may be triggered by low levels of serotonin, but exactly how serotonin systems in the brain affect OCD symptoms is still unknown (Insel, 1992; Lickey & Gordon, 1991).

A separate line of research regarding serotonin involves OCD-type symptoms in dogs. Many of the compulsive behaviors observed in people with OCD involve excessive grooming, washing, and cleaning rituals. As veterinarians and many dog owners can testify, a common behavioral disorder seen in several larger breeds of dogs, especially Labrador retrievers, is incessant licking of the paws and sides, officially known as *canine acral lick dermatitis.*

Although we obviously cannot know for sure how biologically or psychologically similar canine acral lick is to OCD, its behavioral similarity to OCD makes it an excellent model for exploring the causes of OCD. In one study (Rapoport, Ryland, & Kriete, 1992), 42 dogs who had suffered canine acral lick dermatitis for at least 6 months were treated with one of several drugs. Three of these medications were serotonin reuptake inhibitors, the category of drugs that has proved particularly effective in treating OCD. A fourth drug was an antidepressant that did not affect serotonin; a fifth drug released serotonin rather than inhibiting its reuptake, and a sixth drug was a placebo. Based on owners' ratings, only the drugs that inhibited serotonin reuptake significantly decreased dogs' licking behaviors. Of the 37 dogs who completed treatment with one of the serotonin reuptake inhibitors, 13 showed a 50 percent or greater reduction in their licking symptoms. The fact that the serotonin reuptake inhibitors were effective while the serotonin releaser was not illustrates the complexity of the relationships between behavior and neurotransmitters. Both kinds of drugs increased the availability of serotonin, but inhibiting the reuptake of serotonin may cause neuronal receptors to change or adapt in a way that is therapeutic, while simply releasing more serotonin into the synapse may not.

Biological research also points to differences in brain activity in OCD patients compared with normals. Although the evidence is far from conclusive, researchers believe that several interconnected brain areas are implicated in OCD symptoms. These include the *orbitofrontal cortex* (a portion of the frontal lobes just above the eyes), *basal ganglia* (particularly the head of the *caudate nucleus* just under the cortex), and the *cingulate gyrus* (a region of the cortex just overlaying the caudate nucleus; review Figure 7.3 on page 229). These areas are thought to form a circuit that, when overactivated, results in the repetitious symptoms seen in OCD (Insel, 1992; Rapoport, 1989). Brain imaging studies have shown these areas to have higher-than-normal metabolism in OCD patients before treatment and more normal activity following successful behavior therapy or drug therapy (Baxter et al., 1992; Swedo et al., 1992). However, researchers do not yet agree on just which areas are involved in these overactive circuits and what the observed metabolic changes mean (Baxter et al., 1992; Insel, 1992). Additional support for neurological contributions to OCD comes from studies showing that a large proportion of patients with head injuries and neurological diseases such as Huntington's, Sydenham's chorea, and Tourette's disorder also have obsessive or compulsive symptoms (Insel, 1992; Rapoport, 1989).

Cognitive-Behavioral Factors. Cognitive behaviorists believe that OCD involves a vicious cycle in which (1) physiological reactivity and obsessive thinking increase during times of heightened stress; (2) the obsessive thoughts are experienced as anxiety provoking; (3) ritualistic behaviors or thoughts are used to neutralize the anxiety; and (4) these compulsive responses are then reinforced and become persistent because of their anxiety-reducing ability.

This model begins with a component that is implicated in the cause of other anxiety disorders—physiological overreactivity to events. However, unlike persons with panic disorder, for example, who become distressed over increased physical sensations, the person with OCD becomes particularly upset about intrusive thoughts. Why do certain people feel intense anxiety about their own thoughts? The answer might be found in early experiences that teach people that some thoughts are so dangerous that they must be avoided at all costs. It is almost as if the person with OCD believes that thinking aggressive or destructive thoughts is as bad as performing the acts themselves. Therefore, persons prone to OCD constantly strive to undo such thoughts as soon as they occur, typically through compulsive behavior.

There is evidence that the specific form of obsessions and compulsions is influenced by early family experiences that dictate which thoughts and behaviors are particularly unacceptable. For example, Gail Steketee and her colleagues found that parents of "checkers" are more meticulous and strict than parents of "washers," who tend to stress cleanliness (Steketee & White, 1990). In general, the parents of adults with OCD appear to have held rigid expectations for proper conduct and placed strict controls on their children's behavior.

When these cognitive factors are combined with what is known about the neurobiological underpinnings of anxiety, the following explanation for OCD emerges. Certain individuals are prone to overreact physiologically to many events and to experience anxiety as a result. Furthermore, although people are generally prone to think a bit more obsessively after stressful events, those who are more physiologically reactive to stress are more likely to experience obsessions than are less reactive people (Barlow, 1988; Rachman & Hodgson, 1980). Even though many people experience obsessions from time to time, OCD patients are predisposed to become extremely distressed by their obsessions. These predispositions, acquired through early learning experiences that established specific thoughts or ideas as taboo, convince the OCD person that certain thoughts are dangerous, immoral, or threatening (Rachman, 1993; Rachman & Hodgson, 1980). When these thoughts occur, they cause great anxiety, which the person feels must be nullified by compulsive rituals.

Treatment of Obsessive-Compulsive Disorder

Obsessive-compulsive disorder is one of the more difficult anxiety disorders to treat. In fact, some patients become so desperate to rid themselves of OCD symptoms that they undergo a special form of psychosurgery known as a *cingulotomy,* in which a small amount of tissue in the cingulum is destroyed. Unfortunately, this extreme form of treatment is successful in only a minority of patients (Cosgrove et al., 1995; Jenike et al., 1991; Sachdev, Hay, & Cumming, 1992). To date, only two approaches have shown consistent success as treatments of OCD: a form of cognitive-behavior therapy and a new class of drugs that affect the neurotransmitter serotonin.

Drug Therapy. Clomipramine (sold as Anafranil), another drug that inhibits the reuptake of serotonin, was the first effective pharmacological treatment for OCD (Lickey & Gordon, 1991). Indeed, only drugs that inhibit serotonin reuptake (such as Prozac, Zoloft, and Anafranil) seem to reduce OCD symptoms (Leonard et al., 1989; Lickey & Gordon, 1991). Enthusiasm for these drugs must be tempered, however, because they produce clear improvement in only 50 to 75 percent of OCD patients (Lickey & Gordon, 1991; Freund et al., 1991), symptoms return quickly after discontinuation of the drugs (Pigott et al., 1990), and the drugs produce notable side effects such as nausea, fatigue, and loss of sexual desire.

Cognitive-Behavioral Therapy. Behavioral treatments for OCD are the only psychological treatments consistently shown to reduce OCD symptoms. These procedures, sometimes combined with drug treatments, are based on the principle of extinction described for treating phobias. Two treatment components are usually combined: *exposure* to the stimulus that elicits obsessive rumination and anxiety, and *response prevention,* in which the person is kept from performing an anxiety-reducing ritual (Steketee & White, 1990).

Suppose a client compulsively washes as a way of allaying fear of contracting the AIDS virus. The therapist might arrange for the client to go to a local health department or hospital where HIV testing is done. The client would fear that the AIDS virus might be lurking on door knobs or table tops, so exposure would require having the client touch or even rub these surfaces. This exposure would generate anxiety and set up a strong urge to wash the contamination away. However, the therapist would help the client resist washing at this point. In some cases the therapist can prevent the compulsion by

simply being present and reminding the client not to give in to the urge to wash. In more severe cases, the client might need to be locked out of all areas where water is available. In either case, the client's anxiety will rise and might remain high for 30 to 60 minutes, after which it begins to decline, along with the urge to wash. Repeated exposure and response prevention trials at different locations and for different stimuli eventually help the client learn that the obsessions are exaggerated concerns and that the rituals related to them are not necessary.

Exposure and response prevention can be effective treatments whether administered to individuals or to a group (Fals-Stewart, Marks, & Schafer, 1993). When direct exposure is impossible, *imaginal exposure* can be substituted. For example, a client's fear of making an error at work can lead to anxiety-provoking obsessions about being fired and anxiety-reducing compulsions to check all work over and over. Here, the client would be asked to imagine making errors while resisting the urge to perform compulsive checking (Steketee & White, 1990). In some cases, clients can carry out effective exposure and response prevention programs on their own.

In Review

Individuals who suffer obsessive-compulsive disorder:

- experience recurring intrusive thoughts (obsessions) or repetitive behaviors (compulsions) that are time consuming and disruptive to normal life; usually, both symptoms are present;
- are thought to be predisposed to overreact physiologically and cognitively to stressors and then to become anxious about any unacceptable thoughts they experience; and
- are difficult to treat, although some success has been achieved with cognitive-behavioral therapy or drugs that inhibit the reuptake of serotonin.

Generalized Anxiety Disorder

In contrast to the disorders previously described, anxiety may not be focused on any particular object, situation, or person. Rather, people with **generalized anxiety disorder (GAD)**, as in the case of Bill in Chapter 2 (p. 43) and the case of Alica on page 238, are chronic worriers who experience "free-floating anxiety" that is sufficiently pervasive to dominate their lives and interfere with their daily functioning.

---

*A*lica was a 19-year-old Black American in her first semester of college. Ever since she arrived on campus, Alica noticed that she became more and more agitated about a seemingly endless list of things. She spent most of her day worrying about whether she would do well enough in her classes to maintain her scholarship, whether the other students in her dorm liked her, whether she said the right thing in various conversations throughout the day. Alica replayed these situations and conversations in her mind, fretting about how she should have behaved. She found it impossible to fall asleep most nights because her mind was racing with worries; she just couldn't turn them off. Alica also noticed that her neck and back always ached and that she felt tense almost constantly.

Like Alica, people with generalized anxiety disorder worry endlessly over numerous minor events and are generally overwhelmed by anxious expectations (Barlow, 1988). They are often keyed up, irritable, tense, and easily fatigued. They report a large number of physical complaints, have trouble concentrating, and often have difficulty getting to sleep.

Generalized anxiety disorder is predominantly a cognitive disorder in that its major symptoms involve worry and other negative thought processes. Although GAD clients worry about the same things as most other adults—family, money, work, and illness—their worry is constant and extreme. One sample of GAD patients reported that, on average, they spent over half their time worried and anxious (Barlow, 1988). Typically, this worrying is not productive because it interferes with their ability to concentrate and to arrive at good solutions for life's problems.

Figures on the prevalence of GAD are highly variable because the definition of this disorder has changed considerably in recent years. Although GAD can occur at any age, it is most prevalent in persons under 30. Like other anxiety disorders, GAD is more prevalent among females; the Controversy section on pages 240–241 discusses possible reasons for this gender difference. Current estimates suggest that about 6.6 percent of females and 3.6 percent of males in the adult population of the United States suffer from GAD at some time in their lives (Blazer et al., 1991; Kessler et al., 1994). The highest rate overall is among young Black Americans (Blazer et al., 1991).

Individuals of lower socioeconomic status seem to be particularly vulnerable to chronic anxiety.

Causes of Generalized Anxiety Disorder

Theories about the causes of GAD are less well developed than those for other anxiety disorders. Indeed, debate continues over whether it is a discrete disorder at all (Blazer et al., 1991; Brown, Moras, Zinbarg, & Barlow, 1993; Massion et al., 1993; Noyes et al., 1992). For example, Ann Massion and her colleagues (1993) found that, among a group of 123 clients with GAD, only two did not have either another anxiety disorder or major depression. Some clinicians suggest that GAD is not a separate disorder, but a basic anxiety state from which other disorders develop (Massion et al., 1993; Noyes et al., 1992). Others suggest that since GAD is so strongly associated with social and economic factors it should be considered more a response to chronic economic stressors than a true anxiety disorder (Blazer et al., 1991).

Genetic research also presents a confused picture. For example, one twin study found no evidence for genetic factors in GAD (Torgersen, 1983), but another found a moderate genetic effect among a large sample of female twins (Kendler et al., 1992b).

Most psychological theories of GAD have focused on the role of chronic and excessive worrying because it is this symptom that most clearly distinguishes GAD from other anxiety disorders. In most anxiety disorders, anxiety is focused on specific fear experiences, such as the panic attacks in panic disorder or the obsessive thoughts in obsessive-compulsive disorder. But in GAD, the anxiety is spread across many situations. Perhaps the tendency to worry over almost everything is an attempt to maintain tight control over all aspects of life. Chronic worriers believe that, if they stay alert enough to anything that could possibly go wrong, all mistakes or mishaps can be prevented. Of course, this constant "on alert" status carries a heavy price; people with GAD believe that they can never let down their guard or they will be victimized by a bad event. Consequently they stay on edge, tense, and nervous, always ready to confront the next threat. Worrying may also function as a way to avoid the emotional or physical feelings of anxiety. Consistent with this idea are studies showing that people who worry excessively experience *less* physiological arousal (e.g., increases in heart rate) to a feared stimulus than do nonworriers (Borkovec & Hu, 1990). A person who is always *thinking* about threats may have less opportunity to *feel* upset or to visualize vivid images that are physiologically arousing. Worrying may therefore be a means of avoiding strong feelings of fear by concentrating on more abstract concerns. However, because chronic worriers do not actively confront the situations they find distressing, their high levels of anxiety continue.

Although this model accounts for most of what is known about GAD, it requires further study before it is accepted as a valid explanation of how GAD develops. Whatever GAD's formal status, people who worry chronically and excessively suffer diminished quality of life and can benefit from treatment.

Treatment of Generalized Anxiety Disorder

Both cognitive-behavioral treatment and drug therapy have shown promise in reducing GAD.

Cognitive-Behavioral Treatment. Virtually all data on psychological treatment for GAD come from cognitive-behavioral methods. These methods include *cognitive restructuring*, in which clients are trained to identify and challenge irrational anxiety-generating thoughts and to replace them with more rational beliefs that are then applied in everyday life (Beck & Emery, 1985). Most treatment programs also include relaxation training designed to reduce excessive physiological arousal (Barlow et al, 1992; Chambless & Gillis, 1993).

In one of the most comprehensive studies of GAD treatment to date, Barlow and his associates (1992) compared cognitive restructuring, relaxation training, and a combination of the two treatments with a no-treatment control group. Clients in all three active treatment groups improved relative to the controls, and most of the differences had remained in place at a 2-year follow-up. The three treatment groups did not differ among themselves in terms of success, and the vast majority of treated clients who had been taking antianxiety medications before treatment had discontinued using them after treatment (Barlow et al., 1992). However, not all the results were so positive. Several clients dropped out of treatment, and among those who completed treatment, many were still suffering substantial anxiety.

In another large-scale study of treatment for GAD, Borkovec and Costello (1993) evaluated three different therapies: nondirective therapy (involving self-reflection on general life experiences in a calm, relaxed atmosphere), relaxation training, and a combined relaxation and cognitive-behavioral therapy that taught clients alternatives to worrying as a way of coping with stressors. The latter two treatments tended to be somewhat more effective than the nondirective therapy, and the combined treatment showed some advantages over relaxation therapy alone at a longer-term follow-up. Those clients who responded well to treatment also were more likely to experience improvement in the other anxiety disorders that accompanied their GAD (Borkovec, Abel, & Newman, 1995).

Although studies such as Barlow's and Borkovec's demonstrate that certain types of treatment can reduce some GAD symptoms (such as chronic worry), no psychological treatment has yet proved highly effective with GAD, and it is not clear how much better they are than nonspecific or "psychological placebo" treatments in which therapists simply provide understanding and reassurance (Borkovec & Mathews, 1988; Borkovec et al., 1991).

Drug Treatments. Drugs are the most widely used treatment for generalized anxiety disorder. Antidepressant medications have occasionally been used with some success (Kahn et al., 1986), but it is not clear whether they affect GAD specifically or simply relieve the depression that often accompanies it. The most commonly prescribed medications for GAD are the benzodiazepines, such as Valium, Xanax, and Serax (Julien, 1995; see also Chapter 15). In fact, prior to the advent of psychological treatments for GAD, benzodiazepines were the only treatment offered to individuals with GAD. Initially, these drugs were believed to provide significant relief for this disorder, but recent evidence has called this conclusion into question.

The benzodiazepines begin to relieve symptoms of anxiety in about 20 minutes. This rapid calming effect reduces worry and tension and facilitates sleep in the short run. However, the long-term effects of the benzodiazepines are problematic. First, as previously described, these drugs produce several adverse side effects such as drowsiness, reduced motor coordination, and physical dependence. Second, the benzodiazepines do not seem to produce lasting reductions in anxiety. In one large-scale study in Scotland, diazepam (Valium) taken alone or in combination with cognitive-behavior therapy (CBT) was compared with placebo medication alone, or placebo medication combined with cognitive-behavioral therapy (Power et al., 1990). During 10 weeks of treatment,

Connections

Are depression and anxiety disorders distinct conditions, or are they different labels for a negative emotion? See Chapter 9, p. 290.

Controversy

Explaining Gender Differences in Anxiety

Significantly more females than males are diagnosed with anxiety disorders. Figure 7.1 on page 217 shows that, for most disorders, females' anxiety-disorder prevalence exceeds that of males (Bourdon et al., 1988; Kessler et al., 1994). The female-to-male difference for some specific phobias (such as fear of storms) is nearly 4 to 1 (Bourdon et al., 1988). The female-to-male ratios for panic disorder, agoraphobia, generalized anxiety disorder, and obsessive-compulsive disorder are at least 2 to 1.

Are females more anxious, more fearful, and more vulnerable to anxiety disorders than males are? Or do clinicians diagnose anxiety disorders in females more often because of differences in the way males and females report their fears? The nature of gender differences in the prevalence of anxiety disorders is controversial. Three explanations for the observed differences have been offered: (1) biological differences between the genders; (2) differential socialization and gender role

expectations for males and females; and (3) response style differences in which males portray themselves in accordance with a typically masculine role, which includes fearlessness.

It has been suggested that hormonal differences between males and females are one source of differential fearfulness. Isaac Marks (1987) has suggested that males' greater exposure to the class of hormones known as *androgens* makes them more aggressive and less reticent in potentially fear-provoking situations, especially after puberty when much of the gender difference emerges. Another relevant finding is that the onset of several anxiety disorders in females is often associated with hormonal fluctuations. For example, the onset of panic disorder, agoraphobia, and obsessive-compulsive disorder has been observed to occur during or closely following pregnancy, miscarriage, or hysterectomy (Last et al., 1984; Neziroglu et al., 1992; Shulman et al., 1994). These correlational data are in-

triguing, but they offer little direct evidence that hormonal differences explain the gender differences in the prevalence of anxiety disorders.

Some researchers argue that gender differences in the prevalence of anxiety disorders are due to differences in the types of behaviors that are expected and encouraged in males and females. For example, boys are often expected to play rougher than girls, to experience more cuts and bruises, and to play with spiders, snakes, and insects. Repeated exposure to these stimuli might help extinguish fears that boys initially experience. Girls, who are often discouraged from many of these activities, may therefore have fewer opportunities to extinguish early fears. Indeed, some of the largest gender differences in phobia prevalence are related to fears of snakes, spiders, and the like (Bourdon et al., 1988; Marks, 1987).

Further evidence for sociocultural factors in gender differences among anxiety disorders comes from examining disorders in which

---

GAD patients receiving the CBT—whether alone, with Valium, or with a placebo—showed the greatest anxiety reduction. The effects of diazepam alone were no greater than the placebo alone.

The search for effective treatments for GAD continues. On the medication front, a nonbenzodiazepine anxiolytic known as **buspirone** (sold as BuSpar) has shown some success in bringing about slower, but more durable, reductions in anxiety and tension. However, the chronic worrying seen in GAD is resistant to change, particularly during stressful times. More powerful treatments are needed for improving the functioning of people with this anxiety disorder.

Posttraumatic Stress Disorder

Individuals who have experienced a severe trauma and, weeks later, continue to experience intense, fear-related reactions when reminded of the trauma, are

experiencing **posttraumatic stress disorder (PTSD)**. Usually, the trauma threatened the victim, or someone close to the victim, with mortal danger or serious bodily harm. In the case that opened this chapter, it was Jim's experience with the armed robber that precipitated his PTSD.

According to the DSM-IV, symptoms of PTSD fall into three broad classes:

1. frequent reexperiencing of the event through intrusive thoughts, flashbacks, and repeated nightmares and dreams;

2. persistent avoidance of stimuli associated with the trauma and a general numbing or deadening of emotions (feeling detached or estranged from others); and

3. increased physiological arousal resulting in exaggerated startle responses or difficulty sleeping. (Orr et al., 1995)

these differences are small or are reversed. For example, in the United States, gender differences in shyness and social phobias are typically insignificant (Bourdon et al., 1988; Kessler et al., 1994; Robins et al., 1984), possibly because gender role expectations in many social situations are often similar for American males and females. Social phobia in Japan, however, is reported to be more common in males than in females. Cross-cultural differences in gender ratios are, therefore, more likely a result of differences in social and cultural expectations rather than in biological makeup.

A social explanation of gender differences is also indicated by prevalence data on obsessive-compulsive disorder. As noted earlier, there are slightly more females than males with OCD (Robins et al., 1984), but females are clearly predominant among compulsive washers, a behavior associated with the traditional female role as housekeeper. There is no gender difference among people whose compulsion involves gender-neutral behaviors such as checking and counting (Rachman & Hodgson, 1980; Emmelkamp, 1982). Thus, at least some of the differences among certain anxiety disorders appear to be sociocultural in origin.

Some psychologists believe that observed gender differences in anxiety disorders do not reflect true differences in fear, but rather, a combination of male reluctance to admit to fear and female willingness to do so. Although there is little direct evidence for this theory, one ingenious study provided some support. Kent Pierce and Dwight Kirkpatrick (1992) administered a questionnaire in which university students rated how much they feared a variety of stimuli. As is typically found, females reported significantly more fear than males. Later, Kirkpatrick invited the students to retake the questionnaire, this time while attached to a polygraph that, they were told, would be able to tell whether their reports were true. Under the threat of "lie detection," males reported significantly more fear than they had the first time, whereas females' second fear reports were unchanged. Perhaps some of the differential in reported fears might be due to males' trying to live up to gender-role expectations of fearlessness. However, even in the lie-detection condition, males reported fewer fears than females.

Each of the preceding explanations probably contributes to gender differences in the prevalence of anxiety disorders. Further research is necessary to clarify the psychological and biological mechanisms through which they exert their effects.

Thinking Critically

- The onset of several anxiety disorders is often associated with pregnancy, miscarriage, and hysterectomy. How do you evaluate this finding?

- Does this relationship indicate that gender differences in anxiety disorders are created by hormonal differences between the sexes? What factors other than hormones might be involved?

Reviewing Jim's case description reveals that he experienced each of these diagnostic criteria: he was shot and left to die; guns and related stimuli would trigger a reexperiencing of the trauma; he avoided stimuli associated with the trauma; and he was hyperaroused and reactive. The DSM table on page 242 lists the full range of symptoms diagnostic of PTSD.

According to the DSM-IV, these symptoms must last longer than 1 month to qualify as PTSD. Trauma-related symptoms beginning within 1 month after the trauma and lasting more than 2 days but less than 1 month are diagnosed as acute stress disorder (ASD; APA, 1994), a new diagnostic category in the DSM-IV. However, there are some cases of PTSD in which trauma-related symptoms may not emerge for months or even years following the actual event.

Traumatic events known to precipitate PTSD include war, natural disasters (such as tornados, earthquakes, and floods), serious accidents, torture, and various forms of abuse, including physical and sexual assault. All of these situations directly threaten a person's bodily integrity or life. They would cause distress in almost anyone who experienced them.

The prevalence of PTSD is not entirely clear. The Epidemiological Catchment Area studies, consisting of randomized, door-to-door diagnostic surveys of thousands of residents of the United States, found PTSD in about 0.5 percent of males, most of whom were veterans of the Vietnam war. Approximately 1.3 percent of females were found to have this diagnosis, most of whom had suffered sexual or physical assault or had witnessed others being assaulted (Helzer et al., 1987). However, estimates of PTSD prevalence from other studies are much higher. For example, Heidi Resnick and her colleagues (1993) conducted a diagnostic survey of 4,008 females and found that 12 percent of the sample had had the symptoms of PTSD at some time in their lives and 4.6 percent were currently suffering PTSD symptoms. These percentages suggest that, in the United States alone,

DSM-IV

Diagnostic Criteria for Posttraumatic Stress Disorder

A. The person has been exposed to a traumatic event in which both of the following were present:

1. the person experienced, witnessed, or was confronted with an event or events that involved actual or threatened death or serious injury, or a threat to the physical integrity of self or others
2. the person's response involved intense fear, helplessness, or horror.
    Note: In children, this may be expressed instead by disorganized or agitated behavior.

B. The traumatic event is persistently reexperienced in one (or more) of the following ways:

1. recurrent and intrusive distressing recollections of the event, including images, thoughts, or perceptions.
    Note: In young children, repetitive play may occur in which themes or aspects of the trauma are expressed.
2. recurrent distressing dreams of the event.
    Note: In children, there may be frightening dreams without recognizable content.
3. acting or feeling as if the traumatic event were recurring (includes a sense of reliving the experience, illusions, hallucinations, and dissociative flashback episodes, including those that occur on awakening or when intoxicated).
    Note: In young children, trauma-specific reenactment may occur.
4. intense psychological distress at exposure to internal or external cues that symbolize or resemble an aspect of the traumatic event.
5. physiological reactivity on exposure to internal or external cues that symbolize or resemble an aspect of the traumatic event.

C. Persistent avoidance of stimuli associated with the trauma and numbing of general responsiveness (not present before the trauma), as indicated by three (or more) of the following:

1. efforts to avoid thoughts, feelings, or conversations associated with the trauma
2. efforts to avoid activities, places or people that arouse recollections of the trauma
3. inability to recall an important aspect of the trauma
4. markedly diminished interest or participation in significant activities
5. feeling of detachment or estrangement from others
6. restricted range of affect (e.g., unable to have loving feelings)
7. sense of a foreshortened future (e.g., does not expect to have a career, marriage, children, or a normal life span)

D. Persistent symptoms of increased arousal (not present before the trauma), as indicated by two (or more) of the following:

1. difficulty falling or staying asleep
2. irritability or outbursts of anger
3. difficulty concentrating
4. hypervigilance
5. exaggerated startle response

E. Duration of the disturbance (symptoms in Criteria B, C, and D) is more than 1 month

F. The disturbance causes clinically significant distress or impairment in social, occupational, or other important areas of functioning.

Specify if:

Acute: if duration of symptoms is less than 3 months

Chronic: if duration of symptoms is 3 months or more

Specify if:

With Delayed Onset: if onset of symptoms is at least 6 months after the stressor

Source: American Psychiatric Association; *Diagnostic and Statistical Manual of Mental Disorders,* Fourth Edition. Washington, DC, American Psychiatric Association, 1994.

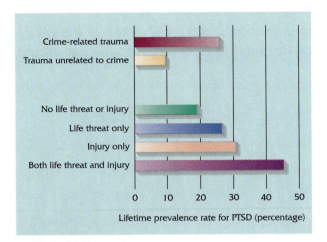

PTSD Following Crimes and Other Traumas

As the top part of this figure shows, women who experienced crime-related trauma are nearly 3 times more likely to suffer PTSD than are women who suffered non-crime trauma. In addition, among the women who were crime victims, those who believed that their lives were in danger were more likely to develop symptoms than those who did not. Furthermore, those who received an injury *and* perceived their lives to be threatened were significantly more likely to develop PTSD.

Source: From Resnick et al., 1993.

11,800,000 women have had PTSD at some time in their lives and that 4,400,000 currently suffer from it (Resnick et al., 1993). The survey also found, however, that only 18 percent of women who had suffered a trauma also experienced PTSD symptoms. Why might this be? Why do some people undergo horrible trauma and remain relatively free of symptoms, while others who are exposed to similar or less severe stressors develop severe PTSD? Research on the causes of PTSD provides some possible answers.

Causes of PTSD

PTSD is the only anxiety disorder in which a specific causal agent (trauma) serves as a diagnostic criterion. Although trauma is a necessary cause of PTSD, its occurrence does not tell the whole causal story. Among other factors that contribute to symptom development are characteristics of the trauma itself, what happens to the victim after the trauma, and the personality and stress-coping style of the trauma victim.

Traumatic Experiences. Resnick et al. (1993) found that 26 percent of women whose trauma was crime related developed PTSD, whereas only 9 percent of noncriminal trauma victims developed PTSD symptoms (see Figure 7.5). The extent of injury during trauma also predicts subsequent symptom development. Women who were injured by a trauma appear more likely to develop PTSD symptoms than those who were not (see Figure 7.5). Another study found war-related PTSD to be 7 times more likely for Vietnam veterans who spent more time in combat and who were wounded (CDC, 1988) than for other veterans. Victims' perceptions of trauma are also important in determining the likelihood of PTSD. The belief that the victim's life is in danger and that he or she has no control over the trauma appears to contribute to PTSD symptoms (Foa et al., 1989; Foa & Kozak, 1986; Green et al., 1990; Kilpatrick et al., 1989; Kushner et al., 1992).

Posttrauma Events. Several studies have shown that the risk of developing PTSD is inversely related to the amount of social support that trauma victims have. As discussed in Chapter 5, the more embedded in helpful relationships a person feels and the larger the network of friends or relatives the person can call on in time of need, the better the person's ability to cope with severe stressors (Cohen & Wills, 1985). One study found that the male Vietnam veterans most likely to suffer PTSD were those who, upon returning from the war, experienced significant reductions in the size of their social network and the quality of social support they received (Keane et al., 1985). Indeed, the social rejection that was experienced by many returning Vietnam veterans may be one reason why rates of PTSD following combat in Vietnam were so high compared to veterans of earlier wars.

PTSD symptoms are also more likely to occur if the victim comes to believe that the world is a dangerous place and then generalizes danger signs from one traumatic incident to all situations (Kushner et al., 1992). Such overgeneralization may be particularly problematic for persons who believe that there is no one to whom they can turn for help or no one with whom they can discuss their fears and coping strategies.

Individual Differences. With regard to coping strategies, Paula Schnurr and her colleagues (1993) looked for differences in the prewar personalities of 136

Connections

Why does social support help people cope with stress? For a discussion of the benefits of social support, see Chapter 5, pp. 165–167.

Vietnam veterans who did and did not develop combat-related PTSD. Those who developed PTSD symptoms were more likely than non-PTSD veterans to have:

1. been overly concerned with bodily functions such as stomach or head pains;

2. exhibited social maladjustments and irresponsibility, including legal difficulties;

3. been more passive, inner directed, and have had more aesthetic interests; and

4. been highly sensitive to criticism and suspicious of others.

Within the PTSD group, those who were more socially introverted had more severe symptoms.

Other studies, however, have not found differences among the prewar personalities of veterans who did or did not develop PTSD (e.g., Foy et al., 1984), so the role of personality predispositions to PTSD remains uncertain. Based on what we know about how people cope with common stressors, the risk of PTSD should be greater among people who have a prior history of (1) depression, (2) social withdrawal, and (3) a sense of being unable to control stressors (Joseph, Williams, & Yule, 1995).

Are some people biologically predisposed to develop PTSD? William True and his colleagues (1993) studied reports of 4,042 twin pairs, in which both members had seen military service during the Vietnam era. Concordance rates for PTSD symptoms between twins led to the conclusion that a genetic predisposition contributes substantially to nearly all symptoms of PTSD. Other research has pointed out that PTSD reactions appear to originate from excessive surges of neurotransmitters such as norepinephrine or from hypersensitivity in the same brain structures (e.g., the locus coeruleus) that are involved in panic attacks (Southwick, Yehuda, & Morgan, 1995).

Over the years PTSD has gone by many names, each one usually linked to the specific trauma giving rise to symptoms. In war it is called "shell shock" or "war neurosis." In sexual assault it is called "rape trauma syndrome." Indeed, two major phenomena brought PTSD to the attention of mental health professionals: frequent psychological complications for veterans of the Vietnam war and recognition of the deep trauma experienced by victims of sexual assault. Extreme and unexpected personal tragedies are also leading causes of PTSD.

Behavioral and Cognitive Factors in PTSD. So far we have looked at risk factors for developing PTSD symptoms. Behavioral and cognitive theorists have proposed a couple of mechanisms by which symptoms might develop. Behavioral theories focus on a **two-factor conditioning** model originated by Hobart Mowrer (1939) that involves both classical conditioning and operant conditioning. According to this explanation, during a trauma such as rape, previously neutral stimuli become conditioned emotional stimuli (CSs) through their association with fear and pain (unconditioned stimuli or USs). Later, the CSs (such as the sight of a hunting knife) can elicit terror as memories of being raped at knifepoint come flooding back. Through stimulus generalization, related stimuli, such as a table knife, may also elicit anxiety (Keane et al., 1985). Even the time of day or type of weather associated with the trauma may, through classical conditioning and stimulus generalization, come to elicit PTSD symptoms. Once these emotional responses become conditioned to an array of stimuli, the victim tries to avoid these stimuli. These avoidance behaviors are further strengthened by operant conditioning; they are reinforced by their ability to reduce anxiety.

This two-factor conditioning theory is similar to some behavioral explanations of phobias, and, in

A Talk with Danny Kaloupek and Terrence Keane

Dr. Danny Kaloupek is the Deputy Director and Dr. Terence M. Keane is the Director of the Behavioral Science Division of the National Center for Post-Traumatic Stress Disorder, Boston Veterans Administration Medical Center, Boston, Massachusetts.

PTSD

Q *What, if any, typical PTSD symptoms were missing from Jim's case?*

A *Dr. Keane:* Each individual with PTSD presents unique symptoms. Jim's waking thoughts about the event appear to be triggered by specific, albeit widely generalized, reminders such as sirens, TV shows, autumn weather. In contrast, some individuals experience repeated intrusive thoughts and memories about their traumatic events in the absence of reminders. Jim also seems to have vivid recall of the event, unlike many who suffer from PTSD who find themselves unable to recall important details. Jim reports few arousal symptoms, and doesn't identify sleep disturbance other than nightmares. Heightened vigilance for danger and problems concentrating are also largely absent.

> *. . . PTSD can last 20 years or longer.*

Q *Is the fear that one will die a typical experience in PTSD and, if so, is it a necessary condition for PTSD to develop?*

A *Dr. Kaloupek:* The belief that one will die or be seriously injured is a common basis for the development of PTSD. However, it is not the only mechanism that leads to PTSD; evidence that witnessing a death or serious injury to others can also lead to the disorder emphasizes that experiencing direct physical harm is not necessary.

Q *How typical is it for PTSD clients to have backgrounds involving multiple traumas?*

A *Dr. Keane:* Recent research evidence indicates that a significant portion of Americans experience potentially traumatizing events and that these individuals have an increased chance of experiencing more of them in the future. There is also emerging evidence that individuals who develop PTSD after a particular event have, on average, more prior experience with potentially traumatizing events than do unaffected individuals. These findings are consistent with the view that PTSD is a chronic condition that develops when individuals are unable to recover from acute effects of successive, highly stressful life experiences.

Q *What psychological and physiological processes maintain the symptoms of PTSD over years?*

A *Dr. Kaloupek:* The continuation of Jim's symptoms over 8 years is consistent with evidence that, in the absence of treatment, PTSD can last 20 years or longer. At least two factors are responsible for this chronicity, both of which are evident for Jim. First, he began to remove himself from contact with the world. This behavior had the immediate effect of preventing distress, but it probably had the long-term effect of preserving his sensitivity to reminders about the shooting. Persistent confronting of these reminders seems to be the best approach to reducing their impact in the long term. Second, Jim's depression and the loss of running as a stress-reducing activity probably made him more vulnerable to ongoing life stresses.

Q *Given a severe trauma, what factors determine who develops PTSD and who does not?*

A *Dr. Keane:* Prior exposure to potentially traumatizing events, especially if they result in PTSD, may create vulnerability for later development of the disorder if new stressors are encountered. Alternatively, there are suggestions that prior success in overcoming the effects of severe stressors can prevent such vulnerability and may even provide a measure of resiliency. With respect to Jim, vulnerability may have been created by his unresolved grief and the stress symptoms that were produced by the accidental deaths of his family members. Treatment of preexisting symptoms would be one means for reducing or preventing later PTSD. Furthermore, once a severe stressor has been encountered, efforts to confront reminders and to find some element of personal meaning in the experience are both means for lessening long-term distress. On the other hand, prolonged avoidance of reminders runs the risk of making the problem chronic.

some ways, PTSD is like an intense, pervasive phobia. However, several elements of PTSD differ from phobias and are not readily explained by conditioning theory. For example, Edna Foa (Foa et al., 1992) points out that, unlike other anxiety disorders, PTSD involves two paradoxical extremes of consciousness: (1) reliving the traumatic event in nightmares, flashbacks, and intrusive thoughts, and (2) experiencing a numbing of emotional response and denial of the trauma. According to Foa and others, these features of PTSD are better accounted for by cognitive-behavioral theory (Foa et al., 1992; Creamer, Burgess, & Pattison, 1992).

Foa and her colleagues have drawn on network theories of cognition and emotion to posit a theory of **fear networks** for PTSD (Foa & Kozak, 1986; Foa et al., 1989; Foa et al., 1992; Lang, 1985; Litz & Keane, 1989). They propose that, following a traumatic event, a memory network be set up that interconnects all the fear stimuli and response elements associated with the trauma. The network contains information about trauma-related *stimuli* and *responses* (including verbal, physiological, and behavioral activity), along with information about the *meaning* of the event to the person. These fear networks also include escape and avoidance programs designed to protect people from harm in situations similar to those in which they experienced life-threatening trauma. When any part of the fear network is accessed and activated, escape and avoidance programs are set in motion to remove the person from danger. Activation of these responses constitutes the PTSD symptoms. For example, flashbacks, in which the victim mentally reexperiences the trauma, can be explained as activation of the whole fear network including its stimulus and response elements. Experimental validation of these hypothetical networks has not yet been accomplished, but the network model has considerable appeal because of its implications for treatment and prevention as noted in the Prevention section.

Treatments for PTSD

Like OCD, PTSD is difficult to treat, and it is not unusual for its symptoms to persist for 20 years or more (Bremner et al., 1996). The best results so far have come from behavioral and cognitive approaches. *Direct exposure treatment,* similar to that used for phobias, follows from the idea that the PTSD symptoms are a series of conditioned responses that were acquired at the time of the trauma and have

generalized to related stimuli. And, as in phobia cases, exposure to feared stimuli can be either imaginal or in vivo. In one study, the effects of exposure treatment in reducing depression and reexperiencing of the trauma were greater than in a no-treatment control group (Keane et al., 1989). Exposure treatments often include other components such as relaxation training. These added elements help the client develop new coping skills while extinguishing emotional reactions to the fear-provoking stimuli.

Cognitive Therapy. Following from their cognitive view of PTSD, Foa and her colleagues suggest that treatment of PTSD should both (1) activate the fear memory network and (2) provide experiences that are incompatible with the information stored in it (Foa et al., 1989). Foa believes that repeatedly exposing PTSD victims to feared stimuli in the absence of negative consequences challenges the fear of danger and allows new, more rational information to become part of the network.

A variant of this treatment has been proposed and tested by Patricia Resick and Monica Schnicke (1992). They extended Foa's methods to include homework such as writing about the meaning of the event (see also Chapter 5) and identifying and challenging beliefs that might maintain the symptoms. One recent study found the effectiveness of this *cognitive processing therapy* (CPT) to be superior to a no-treatment control group (Resick & Schnicke, 1992). Additional clinical research to evaluate the components of cognitive processing therapy is clearly necessary.

Other PTSD treatment programs incorporate several procedures that target different aspects of the PTSD symptoms. These procedures include cognitive restructuring to improve the client's efforts to manage symptoms of cognitive intrusion, systematic desensitization to decrease physiological arousal, and training in specific coping strategies to deal with daily stressors (Fairbanks & Brown, 1987; Zinbarg et al., 1992). Such combined treatment programs have only recently been studied in outcome research, so final evaluation of their clinical effects requires further research.

Drug Treatments. At present, no single drug has been discovered that will reduce all the symptoms found in PTSD. However, different drugs may each be useful in alleviating specific PTSD symptoms. Reexperienc-

Prevention   Can PTSD Be Prevented?

Natural disasters and other traumas are unfortunate facts of life, but there is reason to believe that PTSD, in some trauma victims at least, can be prevented. For one thing, although many persons experiencing severe trauma may develop acute stress disorder, most do not go on to develop PTSD. One reason may be that those experiencing trauma, but not PTSD, tend to receive high levels of social support from family, friends, or counselors immediately following the event (e.g., Barlow, 1988; Madakasira & O'Brien, 1987; Perry et al., 1992; Sutker et al., 1995). Thus, providing immediate social support for trauma victims may prevent their experiences from triggering an acute stress disorder or progressing into a posttraumatic stress disorder.

Two other characteristics tend to distinguish people who develop PTSD from those who do not. Individuals who suffer chronic PTSD often perceive the world as a dangerous place from which they must retreat, and they usually come to view themselves as incompetent and helpless to deal with stressors. If these two misconceptions could be eliminated after a trauma, full-blown cases of PTSD might be prevented in many victims. Edna Foa has developed a 4-session prevention course designed to attack these two misconceptions in women who have been raped or assaulted.

Based on her fear network model of PTSD, Foa includes the following elements in her prevention course:

1. education about the common psychological reactions to assault in order to help victims realize that their responses are normal;
2. training in skills such as relaxation so that the women are better prepared to cope with stress;
3. emotionally reliving the trauma through imaginal exposure methods to allow victims to defuse their lingering fears of the trauma; and
4. cognitive restructuring to help the women replace negative beliefs about their competence and adequacy with more realistic appraisals.

Ten women who had recently been raped or assaulted completed the 4-week course. Their PTSD symptoms were then compared with 10 other women who had also been assaulted or raped but who did not take part in the course. As the figure below shows, at 2-month and 5.5-month postassault assessment, victims who completed the prevention course had fewer PTSD symptoms than did the no-treatment controls. Two months after their trauma, 70 percent of the untreated women, but only 10 percent of the treated women met the DSM-IV criteria for PTSD (Foa, Hearst-Ikeda, & Perry, 1995). These results suggest that a brief program that facilitates emotionally reexperiencing trauma *and* correcting beliefs about personal inadequacy can reduce the incidence of PTSD.

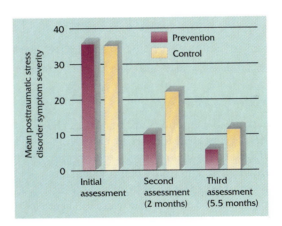

Prevention of PTSD in Rape and Assault Victims

Compared with controls, women participating in a PTSD prevention course experienced fewer symptoms of the disorder at assessments conducted at 2 and 5.5 months after their assaults.

ing symptoms seem to respond best to antidepressants; avoidant/numbing symptoms may respond to selective serotonin reuptake inhibitors; and arousal symptoms seem to improve most with antiadrenergics such as propranolol (Friedman & Southwick, 1995).

Revisiting the Case of Jim

im received cognitive-behavioral therapy for his PTSD. He attended 8 therapy sessions over 4 months before his intense anxiety attacks were reduced. Chronic cases of PTSD such as Jim's often require multicomponent interventions to address the broad range of symptoms involved. One key element in Jim's treatment was imaginal exposure in which he repeatedly visualized all aspects of his assault. This helped him relive the cognitive, emotional, and physiological reactions to the traumatic event in the safety of a supportive therapeutic relationship.

The therapist also provided Jim with relevant information about PTSD, including the common problems that people report after being traumatized so that Jim would understand that his reactions were not unusual. Jim was also trained in coping skills he could use to manage stress; for example, he was encouraged to resume an aerobic exercise regimen. The aim was to help Jim develop a noncatastrophic perspective on his disorder and to foster a sense of greater personal control over the stresses of his daily life.

Jim's treatment also examined some old wounds that may well have contributed to his symptoms. Four years prior to the shooting incident, Jim had been involved in an auto accident in which his wife and unborn child were killed. Over the intervening years, Jim had suffered other life-threatening and traumatic stresses that may have increased the crippling symptoms that he later experienced. Therapy also helped Jim resolve the grief that remained from these events (Kleinknecht & Morgan, 1992).

SUMMARY

Fear and Anxiety Gone Awry

Fear and anxiety are the emotions at the core of the anxiety disorders. Fear refers to a set of physiological, behavioral, and emotional responses to a specific danger. It is an adaptive emotion when it signals an organism to avoid or escape danger. Anxiety is a diffuse sense of apprehension about some aversive event in the future that people fear they cannot control.

The Phobias

Phobias of circumscribed objects or situations are classified as specific phobias. Social phobias are those in which people fear that they will embarrass themselves or attract negative attention from others. Phobias are the most common anxiety disorders. They can be acquired by direct or vicarious conditioning and through information about the alleged danger of an object or situation. Preparedness theory postulates that we are biologically predisposed to become afraid of objects or situations that were dangerous to our evolutionary ancestors and therefore had significance for survival.

Effective treatment of phobias usually involves systematic desensitization, extinction procedures such as exposure and flooding, and different types of modeling. The key to successful treatment of phobias appears to be increasing the client's sense of self-efficacy about coping with the feared stimulus.

Panic Disorder and Agoraphobia

Panic disorder consists of intense attacks of panic that are unexpected and not triggered by phobic stimuli. Repeated attacks, and the dread of having more attacks, leads many panic disordered victims to avoid situations in which they have previously had an attack or in which they believe they might have one. This avoidance constitutes agoraphobia. Panic and agoraphobia usually co-occur.

Panic disorder appears in some form in most parts of the world. It is more prevalent among females. Biologically based theories suggest a genetic contribution to panic disorder. It is becoming more clear that specific areas of the brain, such as the locus coeruleus, may be involved in panic attacks, but just how these attacks are triggered is still unclear. Cognitive behavioral theorists propose that misinterpretation of bodily sensations as signs of danger escalate into panic attacks. Antidepressant and antianxiety drugs decrease panic attacks, as do cognitive-behavioral treatment programs.

Obsessive-Compulsive Disorder

In obsessive-compulsive disorder, unwanted thoughts, images, or urges (obsessions) compel people to engage in repetitive behaviors (compulsions) to reduce anxiety. Similarity between OCD symptoms and those of disorders caused by brain dysfunction has led to a hypothesis that OCD is due to neurological malfunction. However, behavior therapy and drug therapy appear to be equally successful as treatments for OCD.

Generalized Anxiety Disorder

Chronic worriers whose anxiety is free floating and persistent are said to have generalized anxiety disorder. Since GAD overlaps with other conditions such as panic disorder and depression, some have questioned whether GAD is a separate disorder. However, other evidence indicates that people with GAD do not experience the same type of physiological arousal that is seen in other anxiety disorders. So far, the only effective treatments for GAD are antianxiety or antidepressant drugs and cognitive-behavioral therapy.

Posttraumatic Stress Disorder

Some people exposed to intense, life-threatening traumas develop posttraumatic stress disorder in which they periodically reexperience the trauma, suffer deadened emotions, and are easily startled and physiologically reactive. Natural disasters, war, and physical and sexual assault are the major traumas that precipitate PTSD. Although some people may be genetically vulnerable to PTSD, the disorder cannot be fully explained without considering the cognitive and learning processes that exacerbate and perpetuate PTSD symptoms. Although treatments for PTSD have not been as successful as with some other anxiety disorders, exposing clients to triggering stimuli and helping them change the way they think about those stimuli are the most promising.

KEY TERMS

acute stress disorder, p. 241
agoraphobia, p. 226
amygdala, p. 222
anxiety, p. 217
anxiety disorder, p. 216
anxiety hierarchy, p. 223
benzodiazepines, p. 222
buspirone, p. 240
clomipramine, p. 237
compulsion, p. 232
concordance rate, p. 222
coprolalia, p. 234
ego-dystonic, p. 232
fear, p. 216

fear networks, p. 246
flooding, p. 224
gamma aminobutyric acid (GABA), p. 222
generalized anxiety disorder (GAD), p. 237
graduated exposure, p. 224
limbic system, p. 222
locus coeruleus (LC), p. 228
neurosis, p. 217
obsession, p. 232
obsessive-compulsive disorder (OCD), p. 232
panic attacks, p. 225

panic disorder, p. 225
participant modeling, p. 225
phobia, p. 218
posttraumatic stress disorder, p. 240
preparedness theory, p. 222
self-efficacy, p. 225
serotonin, p. 235
sleep paralysis, p. 227
specific phobia, p. 218
social phobia, p. 219
Tourette's disorder, p. 234
two-factor conditioning, p. 244

Dissociative and Somatoform Disorders

My Special People in My Dreams by Camille Holvoet,
1991. Oil pastel on paper, 30" x 36". Courtesy of Creative
Growth Art Center.

From the Case of Louise

Louise is a 30-year-old account representative for an up-and-coming telecommunications company. Her job involves a fair amount of travel, and she works mostly on her own, checking into the office only once or twice a week. Although she is successful in her work, she has only a few close friends and has been estranged from her family since she left home after high school. As soon as a romantic relationship becomes at all serious she feels panicky and cuts it off. She has struggled with depression as well as terrible headaches for years and has consulted many doctors, with no real relief. She has finally decided to seek psychotherapy because her difficulties have begun to interfere with her work productivity.

In therapy Louise tried to provide a complete history of her past but could recall only a few memories from her childhood. She remembered having not gotten along with her stepfather, which led to friction with her mother. When she left home for college, everyone seemed relieved. Her memory problems extended into her adult life—she described having to post lists and written reminders to keep her on target at work. She admitted that she sometimes lost track of time and could not remember what she had done or where she had been. She complained of finding things in her apartment she could not remember buying.

The first 6 months of therapy focused on reducing Louise's somatic complaints and feelings of depression and anxiety. As Louise began to feel more relaxed and trusting in the therapeutic relationship, the therapist noticed some striking changes. Typically, Louise came to sessions in simple, casual dress, but now she began to appear in flamboyant outfits. Moreover, her behavior seemed to change with her dress. Within the same therapy session Louise would switch from talking and acting like a mature, outspoken adult, to behaving like a little girl with a child's voice and demeanor. These changes occurred as Louise started to talk about childhood memories that were coming back to her, first in dreams and then during the day. Many of these memories involved frightening interactions with her stepfather, such as when he punished her by locking her in a closet.

The therapist began to suspect that Louise might have been the victim of physical abuse during her childhood. As therapy continued, Louise began to talk about different personalities that sometimes took charge of her; at other times, she said she could hear all their voices in her head. The therapist finally diagnosed Louise's problems as a dissociative identity disorder. ■

*D*issociative disorders involve disruptions in a person's memory, consciousness, or identity. In this chapter we will explore dissociative disorders, along with **somatoform disorders,** in which people show symptoms of a *somatic,* or physical, disorder that has no physical cause. We will cover these two disorders in the same chapter because, historically, clinicians have thought of them as involving similar symptoms and processes. For example, in earlier classification systems such as the DSM-II, dissociative disorders and some types of somatoform disorders were classified under the heading *hysterical neuroses.* This practice reflected long-standing interest in individuals who complained of physical problems that seemed to have no physical cause. The ancient Egyptians blamed such symptoms (which they believed occurred only in women) on a "wandering" uterus. Later, the Greeks used the term *hysteria* (after the Greek word for *uterus*) to refer to a condition in which a person had multiple somatic complaints without any obvious medical explanation. In subsequent centuries, the term *hysteria* gradually took on additional connotations; it often suggested behavior that was exaggerated or overly dramatic.

In the nineteenth century, Freud used the term *conversion hysteria* to describe conditions in which he believed overwhelming anxiety had been converted into physical symptoms. Freud presumed that many people dealt with emotional conflicts regarding sexual and aggressive impulses through *repression* (an unconsciously motivated form of forgetting personally threatening material). In some cases, repressed conflicts ultimately were expressed through physical problems rather than through direct displays

of anxiety. These views were strengthened by Freud's knowledge of how Joseph Breuer had treated one of his most famous patients, Anna O., who suffered from a variety of symptoms including headaches, neck and arm paralysis, a severe cough, and difficulty swallowing and speaking. A physical cause of these symptoms could not be identified so Breuer and Freud concluded that Anna's problems had to be disguised expressions of emotional conflicts surrounding her ailing father. Their logic was that Anna had repressed these conflicts, but that they still continued to wreak havoc through physical symptoms. Adding support to these ideas were the benefits Anna seemed to experience when, after being hypnotized by Breuer, she would talk—often very emotionally—about past conflicts. Despite Breuer's and Freud's conclusions, the exact nature of Anna's disorder has been in dispute ever since they first reported it.

According to Breuer, hypnotizing Anna O. helped her bypass repression and relive important emotional conflicts. After undergoing these cathartic sessions, Anna usually experienced relief. Based on Breuer's and Freud's account, the unusual physical symptoms experienced by Anna O., whose real name was Bertha Pappenheim, have been interpreted as indicating either a dissociative or a somatoform disorder. However, scholars are still divided on Anna's diagnosis; some have insisted that her problems were due to meningitis rather than to a mental disorder.

Somatoform and dissociative disorders both appear to involve dramatic, unexpected, and involuntary reactions to trauma and other emotionally charged situations. As a result, these disorders were initially classified as neuroses in the DSM-II. Historically, a neurosis was defined as a psychological disorder brought about largely by unconscious emotional conflicts and expressed mainly through anxiety-related symptoms. However, in cases of somatoform and dissociative problems, various defense mechanisms were seen as converting anxiety into physical problems (somatoform disorders) or disturbances in memory or identity (dissociative disorders).

In the DSM-III, the somatoform and dissociative disorders were separated into distinct categories, where they remain in the DSM-IV. However, the disorders share several similarities—both with each other and with posttraumatic stress disorder (PTSD), which, as discussed in Chapter 7, is classified as an anxiety disorder. PTSD is also triggered by exposure to an unusually stressful experience, and it includes a mixture of physical complaints, disruptions in memory, and discontinuities in emotions and behavior. Different combinations of these symptoms (plus other problems) are present in the somatoform and dissociative disorders.

The dissociative and somatoform disorders are relatively rare conditions whose names are derived from the psychological processes presumed to underlie them. **Dissociation** is a process by which the normally integrated processes of consciousness, memory, and personal identity become splintered. In some cases, dissociation takes the form of not being able to remember important personal experiences. In other cases, individuals become confused about their identity or act as if they have a new identity. During some dissociated experiences, people describe feeling as if they, or objects around them, are not real. They feel emotionally detached from ongoing events, like an outsider watching a movie, rather than a person actively participating in real life.

Somatization is a process in which physical symptoms that suggest a medical disorder appear without an adequate medical explanation. In many cases, consistent with Freud's early ideas, clinicians assume that the symptoms are an expression of underlying emotional conflicts or are intensified by such conflicts. The symptoms may mimic actual medical disorders, and affected individuals are convinced that an illness is responsible. Some of these patients undergo expensive and invasive medical procedures or visit one physician after another in an attempt to relieve their symptoms.

We will examine the characteristics, causes, and treatment of these two disorders in this chapter, beginning with the dissociative disorders.

Dissociative Disorders

Dissociative experiences are not necessarily pathological. In fact, mild forms of dissociation are common and perfectly normal. For example, we dissociate when we focus our attention on one aspect of experience and ignore another. When students daydream during a boring class or fantasize about being a movie star or a Nobel laureate, they are engaging in mild dissociation. At times, people can become so absorbed in these fantasies that they lose track of events around them until something snaps them back to awareness, such as a professor repeating their name louder and louder in class. Similarly, while driving for several hours at a stretch, some people briefly lose awareness that they have been steering their vehicles.

Children often engage in dissociation. They invent imaginary playmates and temporarily assume new identities during play. When frightened by an event, some children report "pretending it was happening to someone else" as a way of coping when no other form of help is available.

Most examples of dissociation are passing experiences that offer brief, even pleasurable, respites in the day and do not interfere with work or relationships. But in other instances dissociation involves complex and disturbing processes in which people temporarily forget where or who they are or what they have been doing. In extreme cases, people behave as if they possess more than one identity, and these identities appear to have unique memories and personal histories.

Cultural Perspectives on Dissociation

There have been examples of dissociation described throughout history and across many cultures. Ancient Greek and Roman mythology is replete with stories of humans assuming different personalities to act out the will of the gods or to make up for past wrongs (Ross, 1989). Early Christianity emphasized the belief that a person's soul could be possessed by evil spirits. Beliefs in Satanic possession have been popular at other points in history; for example, the witch hunts conducted by sixteenth-century settlers in colonial America were driven by the conviction that some women's personalities had been taken over by demons.

In many religions, achieving a trancelike state is welcomed because it indicates that an important religious experience has been attained. It is only when these trances are involuntary and lead to emotional distress and impairment that they are considered mental disorders.

In many contemporary cultures, dissociative experiences such as trance states, "speaking in tongues," or spirit possession are accepted, even valued, ways of coping with stress or expressing strong emotions. For instance, in a common form of spirit possession in parts of India, another self temporarily "takes over" a person's body and leaves the person with no memory of what transpired (Spanos, 1994). *Ataque de Nervios,* another culturally defined form of dissociation, is commonly seen as a response to stress in Latin American cultures. It involves uncontrollable shouting or crying, displays of seizurelike behavior, and failure to recall the episode afterward. When such episodes are brief and leave no residual problems, they are considered a form of normal distress. More extreme attacks may be considered a symptom of a mental disorder.

Other forms of dissociation occur as part of religious ceremonies or medical rituals and are therefore viewed as desirable achievements. In many cultures native healers, or *shamans,* induce trance states to allow communication with spirits or to bring about a hypnotic anesthesia against the pain of branding the skin (Kirmayer, 1994; Ross, 1989).

In other words, culturally accepted dissociative experiences often occur, do not lead to impairment, and are perceived as beneficial within the culture and by the individual (Lewis-Fernandez, 1994). Some dissociative experiences are shared by significant portions of a population. For instance, more than half of the women between 35 and 55 years of age in a traditional community in northern Sudan reported experiencing spirit possession (Boddy, 1988). When

dissociation does not lead to impairments or produce personal distress, it is not considered a disorder.

Symptoms and Types of Dissociative Disorders

Fantasizing, daydreaming, and culturally bound rituals form the normal end of a continuum of dissociative experiences; dissociative disorders represent the dysfunctional end of the spectrum. Five key symptoms are found in most dissociative disorders (Steinberg, 1994):

Amnesia: the loss of a person's memory, including memory of identity or of periods of the person's past. Dissociative amnesia does not include simple forgetfulness of isolated facts (e.g., a car's license number or the capitol of North Dakota) or loss of memory caused by an organic injury or illness.

Depersonalization: persistent feelings of detachment as if a person were observing him- or herself from outside the body. During such experiences, a person loses a sense of being real and may feel as if someone else is in control of his or her body or voice.

Derealization: a sense that objects in the external world are strange or unreal or have suddenly changed shape, size, or location. A person may feel that his or her home is unfamiliar, or that the trees in the yard have become smaller or look farther away than usual.

Identity confusion: an uncertainty about the nature of a person's own identity, of who he or she is.

Identity alteration: behavior patterns suggesting that a person has assumed a new identity.

These symptoms may develop rapidly or gradually and may be present only during certain periods, or they may be chronic. Depending on the combination of symptoms, the DSM-IV classifies four main dissociative disorders: (1) dissociative amnesia, (2) dissociative fugue, (3) depersonalization disorder, and (4) dissociative identity disorder. A fifth category, "dissociative disorder not otherwise specified" is included for dissociative conditions in which there is significant psychopathology but the criteria for other disorders are not met. Examples include **dissociative trance disorder,** which refers to involuntary trance states that are not an accepted expression of cultural or religious beliefs; this disorder is typically associated with trauma or long confinement without adequate sensory stimulation (Kaplan, Saddock, & Grebb, 1994).

Most dissociative disorders are exceedingly rare; when they do occur, they often disappear in a matter of hours or days. As a result, clinicians do not have many opportunities to study these conditions. We know very little, for example, about ethnic variations in the prevalence of these disorders. The two most common dissociative disorders appear to be dissociative amnesia and depersonalization disorder, but the one that attracts the most attention is dissociative identity disorder.

Dissociative Identity Disorder

Dissociative identity disorder, known as **multiple personality disorder** prior to the DSM-IV, is one of the most perplexing of all mental disorders. In 1791, Gmelin, a German physician, reported the first detailed case history of a person experiencing multiple identities after being hypnotized (North et al., 1993). Sporadic reports of cases of what was called "dual personality" occurred throughout the 1800s, a period that also saw a marked increase in spiritualism in Europe and the United States. The spiritualism of that era included beliefs in communing with the dead, spirit possession, and the power of devices such as the Ouija board and divining rod (North et al., 1993). Reports of multiple personalities became less frequent in the early 1900s, as spiritualism declined among the general population and naturalistic explanations of unusual behavior gained popularity.

A resurgence of interest in multiple personalities occurred gradually over the middle of the twen-

tieth century, stimulated by the dramatic cases described in books and movies such as *Three Faces of Eve* (Thigpen & Cleckley, 1957), *Sybil* (Schreiber, 1973), and *The Minds of Billy Milligan* (Keyes, 1981). In each of these accounts, stories of childhood trauma—often in the form of child abuse—played a central role in the author's explanation of why multiple personalities subsequently emerged.

While some mental health experts strongly believe that dissociative identity disorder is a *bona fide* clinical condition, others either question its status as a real clinical phenomenon or doubt that it belongs in a unique diagnostic category. Is it actually possible for a person's sense of identity to disintegrate into several pieces? Could this transformation really take place without the person's being aware of it?

Connections

How does derealization differ from visual hallucinations? For examples of some differences, see Chapter 10, p. 337.

Symptoms and Prevalence of Dissociative Identity Disorder. In dissociative identity disorder an individual's personality appears as separate identities or parts rather than being integrated into a cohesive whole. All of us have multifaceted personalities and, as we go through life, we express these differing parts of ourselves in various situations. Sometimes we feel ambitious, other times lazy; sometimes outgoing, sometimes shy. We also struggle to balance the many roles we are asked to play—husband, mother, student, child, lover, employee. On occasion we may feel confused about who we really are, but we remain conscious of this confusion and retain a cohesive set of memories and behavior patterns. In short, our identity stays unified. Individuals with **dissociative identity disorder,** however, experience a shattering of a unified identity into at least two separate, but coexisting, personalities with different memories, behavior patterns, and emotions.

As the DSM table on page 256 indicates, the presence of different personalities is the core symptom of dissociative identity disorder. These different personalities, called **alters,** appear to assume control over the individual's functioning in different situations. Some alters seem not to know about the existence of other alters and do not usually remember what the others have done. As with Louise, whose case opened this chapter, people with dissociative identity disorder report finding objects in their homes that they don't remember buying. Sometimes, these people turn up in places with no memory of how they got there or why.

Alters often differ widely among themselves in how they dress, move, talk, and interact with the

DSM-IV

Diagnostic Criteria for Dissociative Identity Disorder

A. The presence of two or more distinct identities or personality states (each with its own relatively enduring pattern of perceiving, relating to, and thinking about the environment and self).

B. At least two of these identities or personality states recurrently take control of the person's behavior.

C. Inability to recall important personal information that is too extensive to be explained by ordinary forgetfulness.

D. The disturbance is not due to the direct physiological effects of a substance (e.g., blackouts or chaotic behavior during Alcohol Intoxication) or a general medical condition (e.g., complex partial seizures).

Note: In children, the symptoms are not attributable to imaginary playmates or other fantasy play.

Source: American Psychiatric Association; *Diagnostic and Statistical Manual of Mental Disorders,* Fourth Edition. Washington, DC, American Psychiatric Association, 1994.

world. One alter may be prim and proper; another flamboyant and promiscuous. Many times both male and female alters appear in the same individual. The person usually displays a **host personality,** who is the primary identity in charge most of the time. The host typically is the personality who seeks psychological treatment. The host personality usually does not represent the person's original personality and is frequently troubled by low self-esteem, depression, and recurrent nightmares. Suicidal or self-mutilative thoughts are also common, as are headaches and other physical concerns.

In some cases **personality fragments** also occur. Personality fragments are not as well-developed as alters. They do not have a sense of a full personal history; instead, fragments typically represent one emotion, such as rage, that the person displays only in certain situations.

Certain kinds of alters are found in almost all cases. As illustrated in the case of Louise, one alter is usually a child who may report a series of early traumas or upsetting memories not reported or recognized by other alters. Other typical alters include a personality that acts out impulses and forbidden behaviors, such as promiscuous sexual activity or substance abuse, and an alter who engages in suicidal or self-mutilative behavior. Often, one of the alters is a powerful, dominant figure who seems to serve as a protector for the host.

In the late 1800s, most cases of dissociative identity disorder described in France and the United

States involved only two personalities. However, since the early 1900s, the average number of reported alters has increased gradually, then leaped dramatically during the past decade. Currently, the typical case averages about 15 alters; reports of 100 or more alters have been described (North et al., 1993). This explosion in the number of alternate personalities adds to some clinicians' skepticism about the reality of dissociative identity disorder.

Switching, the process of changing from one personality to another, is thought to be stimulated by anxiety (Putnam, 1988). Some switches are triggered by flashback memories of prior trauma. Others are linked to stressful events, such as a reprimand by a boss or a request for increased sexual intimacy by a partner. Therapists sometimes witness switching when clients begin to gradually recall childhood traumas.

Persons with dissociative identity disorder generally do not exert voluntary control over the switching of alters. They may be aware of periods of lost time but not of the alter's appearance or actions. Observers may recognize a switch because of changes in the individual's facial expression, body language, or manner of speaking. At times, the changes can be dramatic. The person might suddenly switch from being quiet and depressed to aggressive and angry or might adopt markedly diverse ways of dressing and grooming to suit the alter in control.

Dissociative identity disorder was once thought to be extremely uncommon, but the number of re-

The most famous case of a dual personality is undoubtedly Robert Louis Stevenson's depiction of Dr. Jekyll and Mr. Hyde. Henry Jekyll described his dual nature this way:

(M)an is not truly one, but truly two. I say two, because the state of my own knowledge does not pass beyond that point. Others will follow, others will outstrip me on the same lines, and I hazard the guess that man will be ultimately known for a mere polity of multifarious, incongruous and independent denizens. . . . I learned to recognize the thorough and primitive duality of man; I saw that, of the two natures that contended in my field of consciousness, even if I could rightly be said to be either, it was only because I was radically both; and from an early date . . . I had learned to dwell with pleasure, as a beloved daydream, on the thought of the separation of these elements. If each, I told myself, could but be housed in separate identities, life would be relieved of all that was unbearable.

ported cases in North America has jumped dramatically in the past two decades. Similar increases have not occurred in other countries, raising many questions about the validity of this trend. Does the growing incidence in North America reflect a true increase in the disorder, a growing preference among clinicians to use the diagnosis, or the effects of greater publicity in the media? We do not know for sure.

The overall prevalence of dissociative identity disorder is difficult to ascertain; one small-scale study placed it at a little over 1 percent (Ross, 1991). It occurs up to 9 times more frequently in women than in men. Although the disorder is thought to develop in childhood, the typical age of first diagnosis is the late 20s to early 30s. Because of the problematic behaviors displayed by the alternate personalities, many dissociative identity disorder patients have al-

ready been treated for a wide variety of symptoms by the time the diagnosis is first made. A large proportion of persons with dissociative identity disorder have been previously diagnosed with mood disorders, somatization disorders, or personality disorders. At certain times the key features of schizophrenia—including delusions, hallucinations, disorganized speech, grossly disorganized behavior, and lack of affect—may also be present. In fact, some clinicians believe that, in the past, dissociative identity disorder was often misdiagnosed as schizophrenia (Putnam, 1989).

Is Dissociative Identity Disorder a Real Clinical Disorder? A major controversy among mental health professionals concerns the question of whether dissociative identity disorder is a true mental disorder or whether it is a condition that some clinicians inadvertently create in suggestible clients. Those mental health professionals who doubt the existence of dissociative identity disorder point to several kinds of evidence in support of their skepticism. First, dissociative identity disorder appears to be a culture-bound syndrome that does not meet the necessary criteria to be considered a distinct clinical condition. Even though sexual and physical abuse of children occurs in most cultures, dissociative identity disorder is usually diagnosed in North America and in Western Europe. A recent survey failed to discover a single case in Japan (Takahashi, 1990), but in Switzerland (Modestin, 1992) and the Netherlands (Boon & Draijer, 1993) a number of cases resembling the usual picture found in American clients have been reported. Furthermore, the symptoms of dissociative identity disorder include a vast array of somatic, psychological, and cognitive features that overlap with other disorders such as depression, borderline personality disorder, somatization disorders, and posttraumatic stress disorder. Because of this overlap, some clinicians have speculated that dissociative identity disorder symptoms represent a severe variant or complication of one of these disorders rather than a discrete diagnostic entity (Mersky, 1995). As previously noted, many symptoms of posttraumatic stress disorder are remarkably similar to those of dissociative identity disorder, consequently, some clinicians believe that dissociative identity disorder is actually a severe subtype of PTSD.

Critics also suggest that many features of the disorder can be created through suggestions from overzealous therapists or mass media coverage in a culture that has become fascinated with the disorder. They argue that increases in the appearance of dissociative identity disorder may be a result of extensive media coverage; high-profile cases may encourage both vulnerable and suggestible patients as well as some clinicians to explain certain psychiatric symptoms as manifestations of multiple identities. As discussed in the Controversy section, it is possible that clinicians can create certain features of dissociative disorder by inadvertently coaching clients to enact multiple roles. The widespread use of hypnosis to elicit recall by clients suspected of having dissociative identity disorder may be a source of therapist contamination in that memories recalled under hypnosis are particularly subject to distortions and inaccuracies, especially if the client is trying to please the therapist.

Connections

How do posttraumatic stress disorder (PTSD) and dissociative identity disorder differ? For a reminder of the clinical picture of PTSD, see Chapter 7, pp. 240–242.

Therapist influence may account for two well-established facts: (1) most clients who are diagnosed with dissociative identity disorder did not begin therapy complaining about multiple personalities, and (2) some therapists diagnose the condition frequently while others report never having seen a single case.

Even strong proponents of dissociative identity disorder acknowledge that therapists can exacerbate a client's symptoms by inappropriately using hypnosis or becoming naïvely fascinated with the client's presentation (Kluft, 1995). However, they also point to several physiological or behavioral differences that would be difficult (although not impossible) for clients to fake or simulate. For example, alter personalities within the same person have been shown to differ in

- handedness (some alters are left handed while others are right handed);
- visual acuity (some alters need glasses while others do not);
- allergic reactions (some alters are allergic to pollen while others are allergic to cat hair);
- brain wave activity (the EEGs of the alters are often different); and
- physical limitations (one alter may be color-blind while others can accurately perceive colors).

Many of these claims remain controversial, however. In some cases, the alleged differences between alters have not been confirmed by independent observers. In other instances, equally dramatic differences have been achieved by people who were simply asked to role-play the condition. For example, in one study (Coons, Milstein, & Marley, 1982), a person who role-played multiple personalities showed larger EEG differences between the simulated personalities than the EEG differences seen across alters in persons diagnosed with dissociative identity disorder. The Controversy section on pages 260–261 provides other evidence of the power of role-playing.

Like many questions in the field of abnormal psychology, the dispute about whether dissociative identity disorder is real cannot be answered with a simple "yes" or "no." The disruptive effects of severe trauma—a key causal factor cited by proponents of the diagnosis—should not be underestimated. Some traumas are probably severe enough to lead to dissociation. Neither should we doubt that psychologically important ideas and emotions can exist without a person's always being fully conscious of them. The splintering of consciousness and loss of autobiographical memories reported in dissociative identity disorder are clearly possible. By the same token, simply because some mental activity can take place outside of awareness does not mean that all—or even most—claims of dissociated identity are caused by severe trauma. Many cases might involve a small degree of genuine dissociation, which an individual then exaggerates either to confirm a therapist's expectations or to provide the person with an explanation for psychological problems.

Other Dissociative Disorders

Several of the symptoms that characterize dissociative disorders are observed in other clinical conditions or can be caused by *bona fide* medical problems. Therefore, clinicians must be careful to rule out alternative explanations before concluding that such symptoms indicate a dissociative condition. We will next discuss three dissociative disorders—dissociative amnesia, dissociative fugue, and depersonalization disorder—in which careful clinical assessment of possible medical causes is necessary before rendering a final diagnosis.

Dissociative Amnesia. The key symptom of **dissociative amnesia** is the sudden loss of memory for personally important information that is not caused by a medical condition or other mental disorder. This memory loss usually follows a stressful event such as a suicide attempt or violent assault, as in the case of John.

*J*ohn was a college-aged man who showed up in a New York City hospital emergency room at 11 P.M. on a Saturday night. His clothes were torn, and he had fresh cuts and bruises on his face and arms. He was able to tell the physician his name and that he came to New York City with a group of college friends for the weekend, but he could not recall anything about where he had been for the past several hours, what had happened to his friends, how he was injured, or how he got to the hospital. Medical tests ruled out most of the possible physical explanations for his condition. John was admitted for further observation and fell asleep for the rest of the night. The next morning John still felt "fuzzy" about many details. He remembered being separated from his friends somewhere outside a bar in Greenwich Village. He also recalled looking for them near a subway station at which point he vaguely remembered being accosted at gunpoint by a group of teenagers. He thinks he must have been robbed and beaten but he really doesn't know for sure. He knows he started the evening with $100 in his billfold, but he had no money when he entered the hospital. When John's friends were eventually contacted, they confirmed that they had been separated from John the night before. When John finally left the hospital, he still could not remember anything more about his assault.

The memory loss in dissociative amnesia can take several forms. **Localized amnesia** refers to loss of memory for a distinct period of time, usually the few hours immediately after a specific trauma. With **selective amnesia,** a person can remember only some of the events surrounding a trauma; the remainder are forgotten. Less common forms of dissociative memory loss include generalized, continuous, and systematized amnesia. **Generalized amnesia** involves total loss of memory for a person's entire life. **Continuous amnesia** refers to the loss of memory for events from a particular time or trauma up to the present, and **systematized amnesia** describes the loss of memory for certain classes of information, such as all memories of a person's father, or of life in the military. Most localized and selective amnesias lift rapidly and completely, but the other forms of amnesia are often accompanied by other dissociative symptoms and may signal a more complex dissociative disorder.

During World War II, dissociative amnesia or other dissociative episodes accounted for 5 to 14 percent of all psychiatric casualities (Ross, 1989), and 35 percent of soldiers exposed to heavy combat in World War II could not recall major aspects of these experiences (Davis, 1993). (Many veterans of the Vietnam war also reported amnesia for battleground experiences, but they were usually diagnosed with posttraumatic stress disorder.)

Dissociative amnesia is most common in young adults, especially men. The relatively high prevalence among young adult males may simply reflect the fact that they are most likely to have faced violent stressors such as combat. The United States is seeing an increasing incidence of reported dissociative amnesia, often in the form of lost and then recovered memories for childhood trauma. These claims remain highly controversial among clinicians. As suggested earlier, some therapists believe that greater awareness of child abuse has sensitized clinicians to identify more cases of trauma-related dissociation, and to develop special treatments for it. Others believe that dissociative problems are being overdiagnosed or even suggested by overzealous clinicians.

Evaluation of amnesic patients should include a careful assessment to rule out medical conditions that might explain the memory loss, such as neurological illnesses, brain trauma, and substance abuse (Brna & Wilson, 1990). The patient's history, a neurological examination, and neuropsychological test-

Controversy

The Hillside Strangler: Malingerer, Murderer, or Multiple?

Many people find dissociative disorders difficult to understand and wonder whether these clients might be faking their symptoms and merely pretending to be disturbed. This suspicion is particularly pronounced in the case of people charged with serious crimes who then plead not guilty by reason of insanity. The case of Kenneth Bianchi, the "Hillside Strangler," provides an example in which experts differed publicly in their opinions about dissociative identity disorder. Some were convinced that Bianchi acted while in a dissociative state; others concluded he was malingering as part of his antisocial personality disorder.

In 1979, Kenneth Bianchi was arrested for the murder of two female college students in Bellingham, Washington. The evidence supporting the arrest was conclusive, but Bianchi insisted he was innocent and had no memory for the nights the murders took place. Furthermore, he described frequent memory lapses but denied that he was mentally ill. Bianchi presented himself as a polite young man, and despite subsequently discovered evidence that he had a long record of antisocial conduct (including faking a college transcript and posing as a psychologist), he steadfastly denied previous criminal or violent behavior.

Nationally known experts representing the defense and the prosecution as well as evaluators appointed by the judge evaluated Bianchi's mental health. John G. Watkins (1984), a psychologist with expertise in hypnosis and

dissociative identity disorder, was called by the defense to evaluate Bianchi and help him recall the nights when the murders occurred. In a videotaped hypnotic session Dr. Watkins gave Bianchi the following instructions:

> I've talked quite a bit to Ken but I think that perhaps there might be another part of Ken that I haven't talked to. And I would like to communicate with that part. And I would like that other part to come and talk to me . . . And when you are here, lift the left hand off the chair to signal me that you are here . . . Would you please come, part, so that I can talk to you . . . Part, would you please come and lift Ken's hand to indicate to me that you are here? . . . " (Spanos, 1994, p.153)

In the course of being hypnotized by Watkins, Bianchi revealed a second identity named Steve whose demeanor was strikingly different from Ken's. He was strident and angry while Ken was quiet and cooperative. Steve described taking part in a number of killings in the Los Angeles area. The details corresponded with 10 then-unsolved murders of young women in the late 1970s in the hills surrounding Los Angeles. Steve implicated Kenneth Bianchi as well as his cousin, Angelo Buono, as being responsible for what had become known as the "Hillside Strangler Murders."

Is it possible that Dr. Watkins' use of hypnosis helped Bianchi create an excuse in the form of multiple personalities? Some mental

health and law enforcement experts believed that Dr. Watkins had created the other personality through hypnotic suggestion; others argued that Bianchi was simply a clever criminal who manipulated the system to avoid punishment. Bianchi pleaded not guilty to the crimes by reason of insanity, citing multiple personalities as the basis for his claim. Three of the seven mental health experts involved in the case argued vehemently that Bianchi had antisocial personality disorder; the other four concluded he was insane and suffering from some sort of dissociative disorder.

Could the appearance of alternate personalities result from a hypnotist's suggestions? Could Bianchi fool so many professionals? An ingenious experiment by Nicholas Spanos and colleagues (Spanos, Weekes, & Bertrand, 1985) investigated whether hypnotic techniques such as those used with Bianchi could provide enough information to enable a group of naïve college students to make up convincing multiple personalities. The students were asked to pretend that they were an accused murderer and to role-play how they thought such a defendant would respond in a hypnosis session. They were given no information regarding dissociative personality disorder. One group of students then participated in a hypnotic interview that mimicked the one used with Bianchi. A second group was also hypnotized but was given less explicit suggestions about different personality "parts." A third group was not hypnotized and was given

ing help clinicians determine the possible causes of a loss of memory.

In many cases people deliberately *malinger,* or fake, a loss of memory in order to avoid punishment. For example, 27 to 65 percent of murderers report no memory of their criminal actions (Parkin,

1987; Taylor & Kopelman, 1984), an extraordinary and unlikely rate of amnesia. How can amnesia be differentiated from malingering? Malingerers are typically less concerned about their memory loss and less cooperative with efforts to foster recall. Sometimes, interviewing patients while they are hypno-

only the information that personalities are "complex" and often contained thoughts that were "walled off" in different parts of the mind.

The vast majority of students in the Bianchi hypnosis condition responded by describing alternate personalities, including using a different name, referring to their primary identities in the third person, and claiming amnesia for their alter personalities after the hypnotic session ended. The students given the less-directive interviews provided little or no evidence of alter personalities in their role-plays. In a second session, the students who had previously introduced personality alters during hypnosis did so again and exhibited large differences between their various personalities on several psychological tests.

In other studies, Spanos asked subjects who were role-playing dissociative identity disorder to describe the kinds of childhoods they would have had. In these interviews the subjects described childhoods that closely resemble the backgrounds reported by dissociative patients—a negative and abusive childhood in which the alter personalities emerged early in life as a way of dealing with stressful situations and strong emotions (Spanos et al., 1986).

In Bianchi's case, clever investigative work revealed that his multiple personality defense was a fraud. The prosecution hired a noted expert on hypnotism, Martin Orne, to test Bianchi's claims. Orne proceeded to hypnotize Bianchi, but only after telling him that most people with true multiple personality disorder revealed three, rather than two, alters. As if on cue, after Orne hypnotized Bianchi, a third alter named Billy suddenly emerged. The ruse had fooled Bianchi into confirming Orne's incorrect statement. Furthermore, although Bianchi claimed to know nothing about multiple personality disorder, a search of his room uncovered numerous textbooks on hypnosis and abnormal psychology from which he presumably learned much about the disorder.

Ken Bianchi eventually withdrew his insanity defense and pleaded guilty to murder. The prosecutor dropped his request for the death penalty in exchange for Bianchi's agreeing to testify against his cousin Angelo. Bianchi and Buono are currently serving life sentences.

Ken Bianchi during a hypnotic session. Was Bianchi really in a hypnotized state, or was he merely play acting?

Thinking Critically

Research suggests that people can role-play dissociative identity disorder. But what these role-plays mean in terms of whether dissociative identity disorder is a genuine disorder is uncertain.

■ Some studies have shown greater physiological or psychological discrepancies between the alter personalities of people with dissociative identity disorder and the alters of people who are asked to role-play the disorder. What might explain these larger discrepancies?

tized or under the influence of **sodium amytal**, the so-called truth serum, helps determine the validity of the amnesia. Dissociating patients willingly accept these techniques to gain access to forgotten material, but malingering patients usually resist attempts to increase recall (Brna & Wilson, 1990).

Dissociative Fugue. In **dissociative fugue** a person suddenly leaves home or work and travels to a new location. While in a fugue, a person does not remember the pre-fugue life; after the fugue, the episode may or may not be remembered. Most fugue states last only a few days, but they can go on for several months. In some fugues, an individual may become confused about his or her identity and, in a few instances, as in the case of Burt (reported by Spitzer et al., 1994), he or she may assume a new identity.

A 42-year-old white male was brought to a hospital emergency room by the police after being in a fight at the diner where he worked. He told the police his name was Burt Tate and that he had drifted into town several weeks earlier and had begun working as a cook. He could not remember where he had worked or lived before arriving in town. The police persuaded him to stay in the emergency room for an evaluation. When questioned by a physician, Burt knew what town he was in and the current date. He admitted it was odd that he could not recall the details of his life, but he did not seem very upset about it. No evidence of substance abuse, head injury, or other physical illness was found.

When the police ran a missing-persons check, they found that "Burt" fit the description of a person named Gene Saunders, who had disappeared about a month earlier from a city 200 miles away. A visit by Mrs. Saunders confirmed his identity. She told the police that, for 18 months before his disappearance, her husband had gone through a lot of trouble at work. He had been passed over for a promotion, and several of his staff had left the company, leaving him far behind in his production goals. Previously an outgoing and friendly person, Mr. Saunders had become increasingly withdrawn and hostile toward his family. Right before his disappearance, he and his teenage son had had a violent argument. Two days later, he left home and had not been heard from since. When brought into the room to meet his wife, Mr. Saunders said he did not recognize her.

Although fugues most often occur after an individual has faced an overwhelming trauma such as combat, they can also be prompted by events that are interwoven into everyday life. Fugue states have been triggered by traumatic memories, financial crises, extramarital affairs, or overwhelming suicidal or homicidal urges (Kaplan, Sadock, & Grebb, 1994; Riether & Stoudemire, 1988). In a series of World War II cases, Stengel (1943) found that many fugues followed a period of depression or mania (excitement), suggesting that an underlying mood disorder might be a risk factor. As described in Chapter 9, excessive travel to pursue grandiose schemes is sometimes seen in manic episodes, but, unlike a fugue, a manic person does not assume a different identity. During most dissociative fugues, the person behaves normally and displays few symptoms suggestive of a mental disorder.

Although few data are available on its prevalence or characteristics, dissociative fugue is not common. The DSM-IV estimates the overall prevalence to be 0.2 percent. Clinical reports suggest that dissociative fugue occurs approximately twice as often in men as in women (Davis, 1993). It is rarely reported before adolescence.

As with dissociative amnesia, clinicians need to rule out neurological injuries, organic brain disease, or "blackouts" due to heavy alcohol or drug use before diagnosing a fugue disorder. The prognosis for complete recovery from a dissociative fugue is good. Recovery frequently happens spontaneously and quickly, and recurrence is rare (Kaplan, Sadock, & Grebb, 1994).

Depersonalization Disorder. Depersonalization and derealization are usually experienced together in **depersonalization disorder.** The person may feel like a robot or like an actor in a dream or movie; others report feeling as if they have left their bodies and are hovering above them. Sometimes the person feels so detached that movement or speech seem to be outside of personal control. Objects in the external world may seem unreal or bizarre. Both depersonalization and derealization often accompany a number of other physical and mental disorders, so depersonalization disorder is diagnosed only when there is no evidence of a medical illness, mood disorder, schizophrenia, anxiety disorder, substance abuse, or neurological disorder.

Depersonalization disorder usually first occurs in adolescence or young adulthood, and it affects women more often than men. Isolated depersonalization experiences are common in the general population, often in the form of fleeting reactions to a severe stressor. In such cases little, if any, psychiatric impairment is suffered. The presence of persistent depersonalization, particularly in the absence of other psychiatric symptoms, demands careful evaluation to rule out a neurological problem. Both brain tumors and some forms of epilepsy can produce depersonalization symptoms.

In Review

Dissociation is a process in which:

- periods of divided attention and concentration, amnesia, uncertain or confused identity, and feelings of unreality may occur; and
- cultural factors often play an important role.

The dissociative disorders include:

- periods in which two or more identities appear to take control of an individual's personality, accompanied by a loss of memory for or recognition of these alter personalities (dissociative identity disorder);
- episodes of amnesia that are not caused by medical conditions (dissociative amnesia);
- sudden, unexpected travel from a person's customary environment, sometimes accompanied by the assumption of a new identity (dissociative fugue); and
- recurring feelings of being unreal or being detached from the body and of feeling that the outside world is unreal (depersonalization disorder).

Clinicians are divided about whether dissociative identity disorder is:

- a real disorder with a distinct cause and set of symptoms; or
- a condition that might in some cases be unintentionally created in suggestible individuals.

Causes and Treatment of Dissociative Disorders

Although psychoanalytic theorists have long contended that unconscious anxiety is the root cause of dissociative disorders, this view lacks empirical support and is no longer considered an adequate explanation. What does cause these puzzling conditions? We do not yet know for sure, but most clinicians agree that unexpected trauma or severe emotional threats are the immediate triggers for some dissociative experiences. Rates of hospitalization for dissociative amnesia, for example, increase significantly in the aftermath of earthquakes, tornadoes, and floods (Davis, 1993). But the majority of people who have been traumatized do not suffer a dissociative disorder. Therefore, other factors must also be involved.

Vulnerability to Dissociative Disorders

Individuals differ in the ease with which they engage in dissociation and, thus, in their vulnerability to dissociative disorders. Among the many factors contributing to an individual's tendency to dissociate, three have received most of the attention so far: imaginative involvement or absorption, hypnotizability, and a history of abuse during childhood.

Imaginative Involvement. Does daydreaming come easily to everyone? Can we all become equally absorbed in a novel or movie? Apparently not. Some people find it easy to get completely caught up in what they are doing, and they lose track of time and of what is going on around them. They can become so immersed in fantasies that they occasionally have trouble distinguishing fantasized events from real ones. Others, even when trying hard to attend fully to a movie or book, remain fully aware of their surroundings and are easily distracted. In short, people differ along a dimension of personality known as **imaginative involvement, absorption,** or **fantasy proneness.** The ability to become absorbed in private reveries or imaginings may be one factor that contributes to dissociation (Spiegel & Vermutten, 1994).

Steven Lynn and his colleagues have investigated whether people who score high on measures of fantasy proneness are also more likely to experience dissociative symptoms. Table 8.1 on page 264 compares items that are drawn from two different questionnaires used in this research—one that measures fantasy proneness and one that measures dissociative events. In one study, college students who scored in the upper 4 percent on the measure of fantasy proneness were compared with students scoring in the average range on this measure (Rauschenberger & Lynn, 1995). Both groups responded to a structured diagnostic interview to determine whether they suffered any past or present mental disorders. They also completed interviews and questionnaires about dissociative symptoms and experiences. Two thirds of the high fantasy-prone students met the criteria for a past or present mental disorder compared with only 31 percent of the medium fantasy-prone students. Even more striking was the fact that 50 percent of the high fantasizers, but only 12 percent of the medium fantasizers, had experienced an episode of major depression. High fantasizers also reported 3 to 4 times as many dissociative symptoms as medium fantasizers, although no student in either group qualified for a diagnosis of a dissociative disorder.

Clearly, fantasy proneness is related to general psychopathology, but the exact nature of the relationship is not clear. Perhaps a tendency to fantasize increases recollection of past negative experiences or a tendency to exaggerate the potential negative aspects of future events. These characteristics could, in turn, lead to demoralization and greater vulnerability to stressors. Another possibility is that high fantasizers are more prone to report symptoms of mental disorders, whether they actually occurred or were merely fantasized.

Hypnotizability. Hypnosis is a procedure during which alterations in sensations, perception, behavior,

---

TABLE 8.1   Fantasy Absorption and Dissociative Experiences

Fantasy absorption items	Dissociative experience items
The sound of a voice can be so fascinating to me that I can just go on listening to it.	I sometimes have the experience of finding myself dressed in clothes that I don't remember putting on.
I can sometimes recollect certain past experiences in my life with such clarity and vividness that it is like living them again, or almost so.	I sometimes find that when I am alone, I talk out loud to myself.
If I wish, I can imagine (or daydream) some things so vividly that they hold my attention in the way a good movie or story does.	I sometimes remember a past event so vividly that I feel as if I were reliving the event.
I am sometimes able to forget about my present self and get absorbed in a fantasy that I am someone else.	I sometimes find myself in a familiar place but find it strange and unfamiliar.
	I sometimes look in a mirror and do not recognize myself.

---

and memory are suggested to a person who then often displays the suggested changes. The ease with which a person can be hypnotized is called **hypnotizability** (Lynn & Ruhe, 1986). People differ in how hypnotizable, or *suggestible,* they are (Spiegel & Vermutten, 1994). Some can be hypnotized easily and are responsive to suggestions made to them while hypnotized. Individuals with dissociative disorders score higher on measures of hypnotic responsivity than do people who display other psychological problems or no disorders (Frischholz et al., 1992). These data lead some investigators to argue that high hypnotizability increases the risk that a person will use hypnotic-like dissociation as a defense in anxiety-provoking situations.

Childhood Trauma. The third factor thought to increase the risk for dissociation is a history of trauma, specifically a history of trauma during early childhood. Because dissociative symptoms such as amnesia, fugue, and depersonalization typically occur following an acute trauma, it has been suggested that they reflect a pattern of coping through dissociation that was established during early childhood. Once a child learns that dissociation can provide an avenue of psychological escape from severe abuse, the child becomes more and more likely to dissociate in the face of stressors throughout his or her lifetime.

Conclusions. The three vulnerability factors we have described might contribute to a diathesis for dissociative disorders that may or may not appear, depending on how much stress an individual encounters. Appealing as it is, a diathesis–stress model of disso-

ciation (see Figure 8.1) has not yet been consistently supported by experimental research (Spanos, 1994). For example, certain dissociative disorders are diagnosed primarily in the United States and among women. However, hypnotizability, trauma, and child abuse rates do not differ enough between men and women or between people in the United States and other countries to explain the differing prevalence rates. Furthermore, in the early part of the twentieth century, dissociative disorders were much less likely than modern cases to be linked to reports of childhood trauma, casting doubt on whether prior trauma is a necessary predisposing factor.

Causes of Dissociative Identity Disorder

Just as clinicians are divided on whether dissociative identity disorder is a real condition, so too, are they divided on what causes the behavior that leads to the diagnosis. Two major theories have been proposed. According to one theory, which we call the **trauma-dissociation model,** dissociative identity disorder originates from severe trauma during childhood that produces a splitting of personalities as a defense against the trauma. The second theory, which we call the **sociocultural model,** suggests that patients diagnosed with dissociative identity disorder learn to present themselves as possessing multiple personalities, often in response to suggestions from therapists.

Trauma-Dissociation Model. Childhood trauma was considered a possible contributor to dissociative

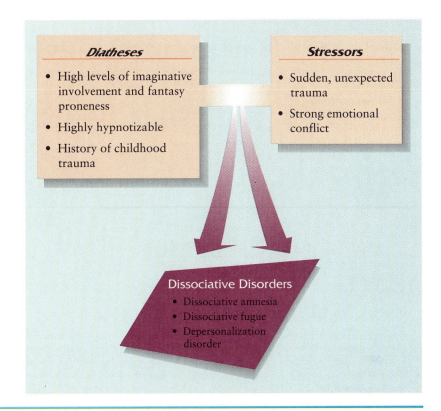

FIGURE 8.1

Diathesis–Stress Model of Dissociative Disorders

Dissociative amnesias and fugues and depersonalization disorder can be explained using a diathesis–stress model. According to this view, following a sudden trauma or a strong emotional conflict, dissociative disorders are most likely to occur in persons who are prone to becoming absorbed in fantasies, are easily hypnotized, or who experienced severe trauma in childhood.

states as early as the 1920s, but its role started to receive far more emphasis in the 1970s, when therapists began to link severe childhood abuse to dissociative identity disorder.

According to Frank Putnam (1988, 1989; Putnam et al., 1995), dissociative identity disorder almost always begins with severe childhood trauma (see Figure 8.2 on page 266). Putnam studied 100 cases and reported that 97 percent of the patients had suffered extreme trauma during childhood. Sexual abuse, particularly incest, was the most common type of abuse reported, followed by a combination of sexual and physical abuse. The participants frequently described ritualistic abuse that was repetitive, lurid, and sadistic. Examples included inserting objects into the child's vagina or anus, binding and torturing the child, and locking the child up in small spaces such as closets. In some cases, the patients had not endured direct abuse but had witnessed terrifying scenes such as the murder of a family member.

Putnam argues that exposure to such unrelenting and cruel trauma forced these children to rely on one of the few coping processes at their disposal: psychological escape, usually by imagining themselves to be someone else, often someone strong or smart enough to defeat the abuser or outsmart the assailant. Many children have an excellent ability to engage in spontaneous dissociation such as fantasy games played with imaginary friends. If repeatedly traumatized, these children become adroit at mental escape through dissociation. A related explanation suggests that children who are prone to being easily hypnotized enter hypnotized states during extreme trauma. The hypnotized state then facilitates the emergence of alter personalities whose existence is kept out of normal consciousness (Bliss, 1986).

Because children are still forming integrated identities, dissociation represents an effective way for them to cope with trauma. Dissociation allows children to escape the constraints of reality, to keep traumatic memories and emotions outside of conscious awareness, to feel detached from the traumas (i.e., "It happened to someone else."), and, by providing an analgesic effect, to avoid feeling the actual physical pain of the abuse. Every time children enter a dissociative state, they accrue memories, feelings, and behaviors that are unique to that state. These episodes form the beginnings of an alternate personality or personality fragment.

According to Putnam, early to middle childhood is the critical period during which trauma is most likely to lead to the formation of multiple personalities. After middle childhood, the ability to spontaneously dissociate begins to wane. Thus, a person

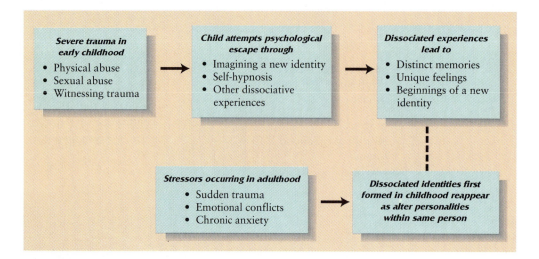

FIGURE 8.2

Dissociation-Trauma Model of Dissociative Identity Disorder

According to the dissociation-trauma model, a major risk for dissociative identity disorder is severe trauma in early childhood, which some children deal with through dissociative forms of coping. These dissociative experiences form the beginning of one or more new identities, which reappear as personality alters when the person is subjected to severe stressors in adulthood.

first exposed to severe trauma during middle to late adolescence or adult life would be less likely to use a dissociated identity as a coping mechanism. However, less complex forms of dissociation such as amnesia might still come into play.

In adulthood, following stressful situations, the separate personalities dissociated from childhood periodically reappear as alter identities who express strong emotions or engage in extreme behaviors that the person would normally disavow.

Evaluating the Trauma Dissociation Model. The value of the trauma-dissociation model is uncertain, mainly because the cause–effect relationship between child trauma and dissociative identity disorder has not been established. First of all, many individuals with well-documented histories of abuse do not develop dissociative identity disorders. In other cases, the occurrence of abuse is difficult to prove because it is documented only by adults' retrospective recall of childhood events. Such memories may or may not be accurate.

We are not, of course, suggesting that child abuse does not occur. Not only does it occur, it is much more common than was originally thought (Finkelhor, 1994), and it appears to be associated with men-

tal disorders in adulthood. The most important question, however, is whether memories of childhood abuse that surface only after intensively searching for them in therapy are a trustworthy foundation for explaining dissociative identity disorder (Lindsay & Read, 1995).

Can we really be sure that these alleged abuses took place? Is it possible that some memories, especially those that appear to have been repressed for years only to be recovered through aggressive "memory work" therapy, are imagined or made up to satisfy the expectations of therapists? Although it is always difficult to know the authenticity of any individual's memories, evidence is accumulating that false memories can be implanted, that people can be led through suggestion and misinformation to believe that the memories are real, and that third parties such as therapists find it difficult to distinguish authentic from unauthentic recollections (Loftus, 1993; Loftus & Ketcham, 1994; Piper, 1994). In addition, many individuals with well-documented histories of abuse do remember their abuse quite vividly, yet they experience no dissociative symptoms.

Trauma-dissociation theorists defend their emphasis on the role of early trauma by pointing to the fact that in some cases a history of abuse has been

A Talk with Elizabeth Loftus

Dr. Elizabeth Loftus is Professor of Psychology at the University of Washington. She is one of the world's leading experts on memory and has written and lectured widely on issues relating to sex abuse charges stemming from claims of repressed and recovered memories.

Repressed Memory and Dissociative Disorders

Q *There is considerable controversy in the United States about "repressed" memories of childhood sexual abuse. Do you think delayed recall of childhood trauma occurs?*

A It depends on what you mean by "delayed recall." Can people remember things that they haven't thought about for a long time? Can they be reminded of experiences that they once had, but haven't recalled in many years? Of course! Go to a high school reunion and you can experience that. But, do people take massive traumas and routinely banish them and recover them later? There is no good scientific proof for that.

> *. . . you can make people believe they had childhood experiences they never actually had.*

Q *From your perspective as a cognitive psychologist, how do you view dissociative identity disorder?*

A There is no question that something is going on with individuals diagnosed with dissociative iden-tity disorder. But it's simplistic to ask, is it real? The question is whether these symptoms are caused by a history of violent, prolonged, early childhood trauma, or by something else, such as suggestion from a thera-pist or the culture. While I have be-come convinced that in some of these cases the effects are caused by sug-gestion, I can't say whether there are other cases that are actually caused by a long history of violent abuse.

Q *Is there basic research that might be relevant to the hypothesis that traumatized children build sepa-rate banks of memories?*

A One line of research in cognitive psychology is work on implicit versus explicit memory. Explicit memory is involved when I ask you to remember a specific episode from your life. Implicit memory is a residual of a prior experience that occurs in the absence of conscious awareness that you even had the prior experience. There is proof that we show a residual from past experiences when we are not even aware we had those experi-ences. It's possible that a child could be exposed to something traumatic, store a residual of the experience, and express that without explicitly remembering the incident. It's a stretch to see how it would lead to alters and multiple personalities but it doesn't mean it couldn't happen.

There is a pretty large literature that demonstrates that you can create amnesias and then restore memories with hypnosis. It is possible that gen-uine trauma could operate this way and create some amnesias that could be restored. But you really have to stretch to make these things fit with existing theory.

Q *Does your work tell about how or whether a therapist or evalu-ator can determine whether a mem-ory is real?*

A Yes, the work tells us that, without independent corroboration, there is no way to know whether a memory is real or whether it's a product of imagination, suggestion, amnesia, or some other mental process.

Q *Do you think social or historical factors have contributed to increases in recalled memories of abuse?*

A In our culture we have a re-cent history in which reports of abuse coming primarily from women and children were ignored or not be-lieved. There has been a very useful social movement to bring recognition of and belief in these reports. But in the interest of advancing belief in and respect for victims, the pendulum has swung too far. Now, we tend to be-lieve every single story, no matter how dubious.

(continued)

Q *Where is research on "repressed memory" going?*

A My collaborators and I are trying to test the limits of memory creation and the power of suggestion to create false memories. We have recently shown that you can make people believe they had childhood experiences that they never actually had. For example, by suggesting events to them we can make them believe that they were lost in a shopping mall, that they were crying and frightened and ultimately rescued by an elderly person, even when that never happened. We are currently conducting a research project to see whether you can get people to think they can remember what their hospital room was like the day after they were born.

I have another series of studies in which we are looking at the effects of inducing people to imagine their past differently than it might have really been. If you get people to imagine something mildly traumatic—for example, that they broke a window with their hand—does it increase the chances that they believe that something like this really happened? We're finding that even a single act of this creative imagination exercise is enough to affect feelings about past experiences.

Q *How does this fit with characteristics, such as the ability*
to become absorbed in things or the ability to become hypnotized, that are thought to increase risk for dissociative identity disorder?

A Another investigator, Professor Ira Hyman, is working on similar experiments to those that I've been doing. He has shown that the people who are the most susceptible to having memory implantation are people who score high on the DES (Dissociative Experiences Scale), and the CIS (Creative Imagination Scale), which is a measure of hypnotizability. So there is preliminary evidence that these characteristics are associated with greater susceptibility to memory implantation.

confirmed by other family members or child protection records (Kluft, 1984; Williams, 1994). In addition, recent studies employing magnetic resonance imaging have found reductions in the size of the hippocampus in adults who had been severely abused during childhood and who show current evidence of PTSD and dissociative symptoms (Mukerjee, 1995). The hippocampus is the part of the brain responsible for transferring information between short- and long-term memory; therefore, hippocampal changes may constitute a biological consequence of physical abuse that also influences memory disturbance. Further research is necessary to explore this possibility, however, because it has not been established that abuse is the cause of the brain changes.

Sociocultural Model. Nicholas Spanos (1994) offers a sociocultural explanation of why and how people might learn to present multiple selves. He notes that the *enactment* of multiple identities usually serves specific personal goals. Spanos claims that, across history and different cultures, multiple identities have typically been enacted by individuals who are culturally or socially disadvantaged. In some cultures, acting as if one is possessed by spirits is one of the few acceptable ways of expressing distress or disagreement. In these cultures, brief epidemics of spirit possession occur in times of stress or upheaval. For instance, spirit "possessions" increased dramatically among female factory workers in Malaysia following a tightening of policies that made their tedious and low-paying jobs even more difficult (Spanos, 1994). Spanos argues that, in the last 20 years in the United States, dissociative identity disorder has become a socially acceptable way to "express failures and frustrations as well as a covert tactic by which to manipulate others and attain succor and other rewards" (Spanos, 1994, p. 143).

Second, if people have been abused as children, the chances that they will be given information about enacting multiple personalities increase (Bowers & Farvolden, 1996). Many patients with mental disorders have been physically or sexually abused as children. Because many therapists are convinced that a history of childhood abuse is a primary cause of dissociative disorders, they are likely to ask questions and convey ideas about dissociative identity disorder to clients who were abused, thus becoming a key source of information about enactment of multiple identities. Therapists who are committed to the diagnosis of dissociative identity disorder typically use highly leading interviewing techniques to encourage patients to report a disorder that might not otherwise appear. Finally, as we have seen, through the use of hypnotic procedures, therapists can encourage alter personalities to emerge in therapy. In response to these suggestive techniques, clients may enact alters and ultimately become convinced that they suffer dissociative identity disorder.

Evaluating the Sociocultural Model. Spanos (1994) has marshalled considerable evidence to support his claim that dissociative identity disorder is a role that is enacted by persons with psychological problems, often with the encouragement of naïve therapists who use leading techniques. However, finding evidence that some people enact dissociated identities and that some therapists suggest and reinforce these enactments does not confirm that *all* cases of dissociated identity disorder are fabrications (Gleaves, 1996). The jury is still out on questions of whether dissociative identity disorder is authentic and, if it is authentic, how best to explain it. At this point, it is probably best to remain open to all possibilities while being skeptical of simplistic answers.

Treatment of Dissociative Identity Disorder

The long-term prognosis for dissociative identity disorder is not favorable. Most patients experience chronic impairments from the condition, which, unlike other dissociative disorders, seldom improves spontaneously. Many therapists are convinced that the patient's "real" personality will emerge only after the alters have been *fused* or integrated in therapy. In the last two decades, specially tailored treatment approaches have been developed to reach this goal. These treatments focus on helping clients clarify the alter system, explore emotionally upsetting material, and work through the consequences of childhood trauma.

One highly structured approach requires 2 to 3 years of individual psychotherapy (Ross, 1995). Four stages of treatment are delineated. The initial phase, like most forms of psychotherapy, involves developing a trusting relationship and working alliance with the client. During this phase, clients are educated about dissociation and trauma and helped to map the system of alters. The therapist also helps the client strengthen support systems and addresses comorbid problems such as substance abuse or depression.

The second phase of treatment involves working to establish communication and cooperation among the alter personalities. This, in turn, allows the individual to begin to recognize and cope with past trauma. Hypnosis is used to facilitate access to allegedly unconscious memories, communicate with

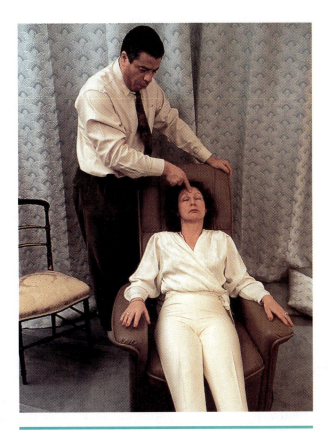

Hypnosis is often used to help people with dissociative identity disorder bring repressed memories of abuse to the surface and to facilitate awareness of the various alters that are competing for control of the person's identity.

alter personalities, and allow the client to confront and then release painful emotions related to early trauma. In addition to using hypnosis, the therapist uses cognitive-behavioral techniques to teach clients about the thinking errors often found in dissociative disorders and to develop non-dissociative ways of coping with stress. The client is asked to give up dissociative defenses and allow painful memories into conscious awareness so that he or she can gain a sense of control over them.

The third phase of therapy emphasizes incorporating gains made in the preceding phase. The client strengthens new coping mechanisms through practice, works through the grief that comes with acknowledging past trauma and relegating it to the distant past, and begins to build an integrated personality that subsumes the former alters.

Connections

Why is a trusting relationship so important to the success of most forms of psychotherapy? For a discussion of some reasons, see Chapter 16, p. 560.

Prevention   Childhood Abuse and Therapist Suggestions: Reducing the Risks for Dissociative Disorders

As the number of reported cases of dissociative identity disorder has increased, so too have concerns about how the disorder can be prevented. One of two approaches is called for, depending on one's theoretical perspective toward dissociative identity disorder. If we assume, along with the proponents of the trauma-dissociation hypothesis, that sexual and physical abuse of young children contributes to the disorder, prevention of child abuse and treatment of abusers are obvious prevention strategies. If, on the other hand, we agree with the skeptics who believe that some therapists encourage clients to enact multiple roles and diagnose these enactments as dissociated identities, then prevention requires educating therapists about the need to be cautious when using hypnosis and other suggestive techniques to explore memories of trauma or to "speak" with a client's different identities.

Both strategies have been attempted, but the priority has been to prevent abuse. This is understandable. Even if child abuse proves to be irrelevant to dissociative disorders, preventing such violence is a worthwhile goal.

Several risk factors have been isolated for child abuse (Bauer & Twentyman, 1985; Friedman et al., 1981). As examples, abusive parents tend to:

- possess little knowledge about normal child development;

- hold unrealistic expectations for their children, such as the age by which they should be toilet trained;

- become easily annoyed when under stress;

- choose aggressive means of resolving conflicts;

- have limited access to social support and help with child care; and

- disagree with each other about childrearing and discipline standards.

Parents who are poor, were abused themselves as children, give birth to children with congenital defects, have children while they are still teenagers, or are embroiled in their own marital conflicts are also at greater risk to be abusers (Nietzel & Himelein, 1986). Can these risks be reduced or overcome?

Several studies have shown that parents can learn more effective child management skills and that abusive interactions with children can also be reduced. For example, Joseph Denicola and Jack Sandler (1980) developed a 12-session program that (1) taught parents basic principles of child management such as using reinforcement rather than punishment to control their children's behavior, and (2) helped parents reduce their own feelings of stress, anger, and frustration through the use of relaxation training exercises and stress inoculation as new coping skills. Two families, which had been referred to the courts for legal action concerning abuse, were referred to the program. The figure shows the results for one family, indicating that the techniques were successful in decreasing the mother's aversive behavior and increasing her positive interactions.

Abusive parents can be taught to change their behavior, if they learn the necessary skills for managing their children. However, child abuse is not caused solely by the problems of individual parents. Social factors play a role as well. A comprehensive plan to reduce child abuse should combine parent training with several larger scale interventions aimed at helping families. Community daycare centers to occasionally relieve mothers of child care demands and crisis intervention to help parents cope with personal stress are two examples of needed social services.

Sociocognitive theorists do not deny the horrors of child abuse, and they do not oppose efforts to prevent it. However, because they argue that dissociative identity disorder is an *iatrogenic* condition (one that is inadvertently caused by treatment), they believe it is essential that therapists avoid implanting ideas of abuse and multiple identities in suggestible clients. Scientists such as psychologist Elizabeth Loftus (1993) at the University of Washington and sociologist Richard Ofshe (at the University of California, Berkeley) have studied claims of repressed memories and the techniques used to retrieve them. They have used laboratory research and real-life cases to document how memories—sometimes for incredibly brutal acts—can be built from the suggestions of others.

Ofshe's involvement in the case of Paul Ingram provides a chilling example. Ingram, a sheriff's deputy in Olympia, Washington, was arrested for child abuse in 1988. He steadfastly denied the allegations, but the police continued to question and pressure him over the next 5 months even though there was very little evidence to support the allegations of sexual abuse that Ingram's children had lodged against him. To help Ingram's memory, a psychologist or a detective would repeatedly describe an act of abuse, such as Ingram and a bunch of

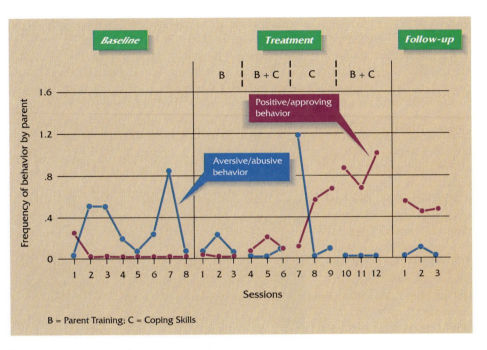

A Parent Retraining Program

After establishing a baseline for abusive and positive parental behavior, a therapy program that involved training parents to manage their children's behavior and to cope with stress better was introduced. The program resulted in decreased abuse and increased positive interactions, and these changes were maintained up to 3 months after the end of the program.

other men raping his daughter. Ingram would at first have no memory for such incidents, but after concerted effort, including praying and being hypnotized to help his memory, he started to "recall" some details. Ultimately, Paul Ingram confessed to not just the charges of incest but to rapes, assaults, sexual abuse, and participation in a Satanic cult that was believed to have killed 25 babies. To check the accuracy of Ingram's memory, Ofshe, who the prosecutor had hired as a consultant, asked him to recall an event that Ofshe had totally fabricated—that Ingram had forced his son and daughter to have sex in front of him. Just as with the police interrogation, Ingram could not remember anything at first but after thinking and praying about it, he gradually formed images of the event and, within a matter of hours, endorsed a three-page confession to the scene Ofshe had made up. Ofshe concluded that, rather than being a sex offender or a Satanic cult member, Paul Ingram was a vulnerable man with a strong need to please authorities, a highly suggestible nature, and the ability to fall easily into a trance. Ultimately, Paul Ingram decided to plead guilty to six counts of third-degree rape. He is currently in prison and now insists that he never abused his children. Was Paul Ingram duped into confessing on the basis of false memories, or was he a guilt-ridden abuser who finally admitted his crime? Questions such as these are at the heart of the controversy over whether therapists should aggressively try to help clients recover memories of abuse that they suspect have been repressed, and the outcome of trials such as this make it clear that therapists need to be more responsible and careful about their diagnoses.

In the final phase, the client learns a new way of living in which the menace of trauma no longer lurks in memory as a threat to the personality. The client continues to focus on facing problems without using dissociative strategies. Difficulties with depression, substance abuse, or anxiety may still require attention in this phase of treatment.

Not all clinicians endorse long-term psychotherapy that focuses on uncovering alternate personalities and uses hypnosis to promote recall of early trauma. In light of our earlier discussion of how hypnosis might implant memories of trauma, we tend to agree with this position.

Rather than directly addressing the issue of alter personalities, some clinicians use cognitive-behavioral therapy or interpersonal psychotherapy to treat the depression and anxiety that is usually present. Others employ a behavioral approach in which they respond to only one personality, refusing to reinforce behavior associated with supposed alters. Case reports of clients treated with a behavioral approach document a gradual decline in references to personality alters, coupled with increased willingness to focus on other problems (Fahey, Abas, & Brown, 1989; Kohlenberg, 1973). However, controlled research has not been conducted on any type of psychotherapy for dissociative identity disorder, so we don't really know whether any specific type of psychotherapy is effective. Whether and how the disorder can be prevented are also open questions, as the Prevention section on pages 270–271 makes clear.

Systematic research on drug treatments for dissociative identity disorder is as scarce as psychotherapy studies. So far, no medication has been found that addresses the core symptoms of the disorder. Medications are commonly used, however, to address related symptoms such as depression and anxiety, and the little evidence available suggests that antidepressant medications may be useful in some cases (Coons, 1986; Ross, 1995).

Treatment of Other Dissociative Disorders

Most individuals who suffer dissociative amnesia, fugues, or depersonalization disorder improve without any formal treatment once the triggering stressor is removed or resolved. In cases that require psychotherapy, the goal is to help the person cope better with the trauma that led to the amnesia or fugue. Attention is usually also devoted to helping clients deal with their loss of memory and sense of identity and to teaching them new skills for coping with stress. The patient is sometimes hypnotized to promote the retrieval of memory, but, as noted, this approach risks the implantation of false memories. Antianxiety medications are also sometimes useful because reduced anxiety may allow clients to think about the stressful situations they have encountered, and perhaps forgotten. In most cases, brief interventions are very effective. Clients usually regain their memories and return to their prior levels of functioning.

Specific treatments for depersonalization and derealization have received little attention because both problems most often accompany a more global problem, such as depression, which is treated with medication, psychotherapy, or both. These methods frequently result in a decline in the depersonalization or derealization symptoms as well.

In Review

Sudden trauma or strong emotional conflicts can trigger dissociative disorders in individuals who are vulnerable as a result of:

- a tendency to be highly absorbed in imaginative activity;
- a tendency to be suggestible and easily hypnotized; and
- a childhood history of trauma or physical abuse.

Two very different theories have been proposed to explain dissociative personality disorder, emphasizing either:

- a history of early childhood trauma that causes certain people to fall into a repetitive pattern of dissociated identities as a form of defensive coping; or
- a pattern of enacting multiple identities as a result of expectations and suggestions from clinicians and cultural support from modern Western society.

Most treatments for dissociative identity disorder:

- focus on helping the person come to terms with past traumas and to integrate the various alters into one personality; and
- have not been evaluated in controlled studies, so their overall effectiveness is not known.

Treatment for other dissociative disorders focuses on helping the person cope with the triggering trauma, if it has not been otherwise resolved.

Somatoform Disorders

Rebecca was referred to the pediatric neurologist by her family doctor after she experienced a brief period of unconsciousness followed by an inability to move her legs. She is a pleasant 10-year-old girl with no history of medical or behavioral problems or mental health concerns. Her family is closely knit and active in church. They live in a semirural setting where Rebecca is admired as a good student and a "model child." She and three younger siblings attend a small church school where she is making excellent academic progress. Rebecca was carefully evaluated, and no physical problems were identified. Her thinking and memory were clear, and she cooperated with the physician. She seemed a bit withdrawn, but she could not identify any psychological stressors in her life.

Rebecca's parents were adamant that Rebecca had to be suffering a physical, not a mental, problem. They believed that feelings were private and that emotional distress was best resolved through prayer and hard work. Nevertheless, they agreed to let Rebecca enter a child psychiatry unit.

During her time on the unit, Rebecca continued her schooling, received physical therapy to help her regain muscle strength and walk again, and participated in group therapy that focused on education about feelings, coping with stress, problem solving, and anger-management skills. At first, Rebecca was afraid to try walking, but she was soon doing better each day. She also began to talk more about her feelings. She admitted to being intensely afraid of leaving her small school to attend the regional middle school—a move she was scheduled to make at the end of her summer break. By the time she was discharged from the hospital, Rebecca was completely mobile and expressed a more positive outlook toward her new school.

Apparently, Rebecca's inability to move her legs was triggered by her unexpressed fears about changing schools and moving into a larger community. She was diagnosed with a conversion disorder, which is one of the *somatoform disorders.* These disorders involve physical complaints or disabilities that suggest a medical problem but have no known biological cause and are not voluntarily produced by patients. The disabilities associated with several of these disorders are assumed to arise from somatization—a process by which emotional distress is converted into physical symptoms. Not all somatoform disorders involve the expression of disguised emotions or conflicts, however. Some are grouped in this category simply because it provides a convenient label for several types of patients who consult physicians about physical complaints that are not due to a medical illness.

Somatization is a widespread and not necessarily pathological condition. Bodily symptoms often serve as a barometer of emotional well-being. Some people get stomach cramps or diarrhea when pressures increase at work; others complain of tension headaches or migraines when emotionally upset. Instances of somatization fall along a continuum from ordinary muscle tension after a difficult day to persistent physical symptoms that interfere with a happy and productive life.

Somatoform disorders include clinical conditions such as

- expression of psychological distress via physical symptoms;

- heightened sensitivity to or preoccupation with bodily cues; and

- misinterpretation of emotions and bodily sensations as signs of physical illness. (Barsky, Barnett, & Cleary, 1994)

In all these conditions, however, the physical symptoms feel real to the patient. A diagnosis of somatoform disorder does not apply to individuals who are deliberately faking (malingering) symptoms to achieve some sort of reward or avoid some problem or responsibility. Somatoform disorders also differ from *factitious disorder,* in which individuals exaggerate or pretend to have symptoms in order to be seen as sick by others. Factitious disorder is seen in people who appear to have a psychological need to assume the role of a patient and who go to extraordinary lengths to prove their claims.

Somatoform disorders can be difficult to diagnose because the symptoms tend to mimic medical disorders, and the patient experiences real pain or discomfort. Many somatizing persons have had a physical problem that leads to excessive worry about and elaboration of authentic symptoms. Because physicians do not want to miss a real organic problem, they often respond to the person's distress with extensive testing to rule out even the most esoteric disorders. Furthermore, to many people—including patients and physicians—medical illness is more acceptable than mental illness, so they are reluctant to consider psychological explanations for physical symptoms. This bias can lead to unnecessary testing, excessive use of medications, and invasive medical procedures that can produce serious side effects.

Currently, somatoform disorders are receiving more attention than ever because of growing concern about medical costs. Patients with somatoform disorders are expensive to treat, up to 9 times more expensive than the typical patient (Groth-Marnat & Edkins, 1996). They are frequently referred from doctor to doctor for extensive testing, so they use a disproportionate share of health care resources. In one study, 10 percent of the patients in a large health care cooperative used one third of all the services (Katon et al., 1990). These high utilizers are more likely than low utilizers to have undiagnosed emotional problems. In the Katon et al. (1990) study, half of the high-utilizing patients met the criteria for a psychiatric diagnosis, usually a mood, anxiety, or somatoform disorder. By one estimate, patients with somatization disorder use 10 percent of every health care dollar spent in the United States, amounting to about $30 billion dollars each year (Ford, 1995).

In the DSM-IV, there are six specific somatoform disorders: somatization disorder, undifferentiated somatoform disorder, hypochondriasis, conversion disorder, pain disorder, and body dysmorphic disorder. One additional diagnosis—somatoform disorder not otherwise specified—is included for conditions that do not meet the criteria for any of the specific disorders. In the following sections we will examine the characteristics, causes, and treatment of the somatoform disorders.

Somatization Disorder

In 1859, French physician Pierre Briquet provided the first formal description of patients who consulted him about a seemingly endless list of physical complaints that he could not explain medically. These patients kept coming back for one type of treatment after another, even though none were successful. The condition was known as **Briquet's syndrome** until 1980 when the DSM-III relabeled it *somatization disorder.*

Patients diagnosed with **somatization disorder** show a chronic pattern of physical complaints that begin before age 30 and are serious enough to warrant medical treatment or interfere with the ability to work and fulfill social or family responsibilities. As the DSM table below indicates, the core feature of somatization disorder is complaints of several difficulties affecting various systems of the body. The typical patient reports pain in different parts of the

---

DSM-IV

Diagnostic Criteria for Somatization Disorder

A. A history of many physical complaints beginning before age 30 years that occur over a period of several years and result in treatment being sought or significant impairment in social, occupational, or other important areas of functioning.

B. Each of the following criteria must have been met, with individual symptoms occurring at any time during the course of the disturbance:

 (1) a history of pain related to a least four different sites or functions
 (2) two gastrointestinal symptoms other than pain
 (3) one sexual or reproductive symptom other than pain
 (4) one symptom or deficit suggesting a neurological condition not limited to pain

C. Either (1) or (2):

 (1) after appropriate investigation, each of the symptoms in Criterion B cannot be fully explained by a known general medical condition or the direct effects of a substance
 (2) when there is a related general medical condition, the physical complaints or resulting social or occupational impairment are in excess of what would be expected from the history, physical examination, or laboratory findings

D. The symptoms are not intentionally produced or feigned

Source: American Psychiatric Association; *Diagnostic and Statistical Manual of Mental Disorders,* Fourth Edition. Washington, DC, American Psychiatric Association, 1994.

body, complains of gastrointestinal distress, experiences neurological symptoms, and claims to have problems in sexual or reproductive functioning.

Initial assessments to rule out true organic pathology are complicated by the countless examinations, hospitalizations, and medications that most of these patients have already received. Adding to this problem is the fact that people with somatization disorder often exaggerate their symptoms or fail to report past treatments because they fear being dismissed by their new physicians.

Earlier versions of the DSM required the clinician to diagnose somatization disorder if the patient displayed at least 13 of 35 possible symptoms. However, research has revealed few differences between patients who met these criteria and those whose symptoms were less numerous. The DSM-IV includes two disorders that differ in number of symptoms: somatization disorder, which requires the presence of at least 8 symptoms, and **undifferentiated somatoform disorder,** which is used for individuals who report fewer than 8 somatic complaints, not caused by a medical condition, lasting at least 6 months.

The prevalence of somatization disorder in the United States is less than 1 percent of the population (Samuels, 1995), but the rate may be as high as 4 percent when undifferentiated somatoform disorders are included (Bridges & Goldberg, 1985). Both prevalence rates and the kinds of symptoms reported are affected by cultural factors. Somatization disorder is seldom diagnosed in men in the United States, but in Greece and certain Latin American countries, males and females are about equally affected. In the United States, the most-reported symptoms mimic medical complaints that are common in our culture, such as fatigue, headache, stomach pain, erectile or ejaculatory dysfunction, and dizziness. However, in Africa a typical symptom is the "experience of worms in the head," and in India men are concerned about *dhat*, in which severe anxiety is accompanied by involuntary discharge of semen and discoloration of urine.

Most patients are first diagnosed in their 30s or 40s, but their somatizing complaints usually began in adolescence, frequently with the report of severe *dysmenorrhea* (painful menses) in the case of females. In the United States, unmarried, poorly educated women of color from rural areas are those most likely to be diagnosed with somatization disorder (Ford, 1995). Indeed, somatization may be the primary way some disenfranchised women express dissatisfaction or frustration with their social situation without having to face negative repercussions (Samuels, 1995). Others may simply lack the vocabulary to discuss feelings. Some patients who lack so-

cial support may be driven to seek medical attention and use medical care providers as a surrogate social network (Ford, 1995).

Although patients with somatization disorder focus on physical complaints, they also report many other symptoms of mental disorders (Wetzel et al., 1994). In fact, a past or present episode of major depression is found in up to 90 percent of somatization disorder patients (Katon, 1993). Comorbid phobias and panic disorder are often present, as is a history of suicide attempts and antisocial behavior.

Somatization disorder is generally a chronic problem. The typical patient's life always seems to be in upheaval, and it is rare for much time to go by without a medical consultation being sought. In fact, physical complaints seem to be the one constant that these people depend on, almost as if their complaints give meaning and organization to their otherwise chaotic lives.

Hypochondriasis

Whereas somatization disorder involves complaints about a wide variety of physical ailments, the person with **hypochondriasis** focuses on a few select symptoms and is preoccupied with the fear of having a serious medical illness. This belief usually originates from a misinterpretation of a bodily sensation or physical change, and it persists even after medical evaluations and reassurance by physicians confirm that nothing is wrong. The preoccupation that a headache is a sign of a brain tumor or that a fast heartbeat is a sign of an impending heart attack can become so consuming that the person cannot work or manage interpersonal relationships. In some cases these unwarranted fears are limited to a certain organ or disease; in others, several illnesses are feared.

Hypochondriacal fears, however, never reach delusional proportions, which would be the case if the person could never entertain the possibility that the feared illness was not present. Some hypochondriacs realize their fears are exaggerated, but they still cannot control them. Others become frustrated with doctors and family members who do not take their complaints seriously, as shown in the following case.

A 38-year-old radiologist was referred to a psychiatrist by a gastroenterologist who had "reached the end of the line" with him. The patient had undergone physical, laboratory, and X-ray examinations of the entire gastrointestinal tract, esophagoscopy, gastroscopy, and colonoscopy. Although he was told that the results were negative for physical disease, he was resentful and disappointed rather than relieved at the findings.

The patient described occasional mild abdominal pain, sensations of "fullness," "bowel rumblings," and a "firm abdominal mass" that he could sometimes feel. Over recent months, as he had become more aware of these sensations, he was convinced that they were due to a carcinoma of the colon. He tested his stool weekly for occult blood, and he palpated his abdomen every 2 to 3 days. He had secretly performed X-ray studies on himself.

Although he was successful in his work and active in the community, the patient spent much of his leisure time at home alone in bed. His wife was bitter about this behavior, which had strained their marriage.

When the patient was 13, a heart murmur had been detected during a school physical (he also had a younger brother who had died of congenital heart disease). His heart murmur had proved to be benign, but the patient continued to worry that the evaluation might have "missed something," particularly in light of occasional sensations of his heart's "skipping a beat." He had kept his fears to himself, and they subsided over the next 2 years.

The patient told his story with a sincere, discouraged tone, brightened only by a note of pleasure as he detailed the discovery of a genuine, but clinically insignificant, urethral anomaly as the result of one evaluation he had ordered himself. He explained that his coming in for psychiatric evaluation was precipitated by an encounter with his 9-year-old son. The boy had accidentally walked in while he was palpating his abdomen for "masses" and asked, "What do you think it is this time, Dad?" (Based on Spitzer et al., 1994)

Hypochondriacs seek health care consultations repeatedly, provide detailed descriptions of specific symptoms, and resist psychological explanations of their symptoms. Relationships with family, friends, and health care professionals are often strained because these patients routinely disagree with physicians' feedback and become easily angered when the feedback does not support their opinions. Many hypochondriacs read about medical disorders, self-diagnose their symptoms, and are prone to developing symptoms similar to those in media accounts of trendy new disorders.

The prevalence of hypochondriasis among patients in medical clinics varies between 4.2 and 6.3 percent (Barsky et al., 1990). The true rate of hypochondriasis in the general population is not known, but it is probably lower. Onset typically occurs between the ages of 20 and 30 (Katon, 1993), but hypochondriasis is diagnosed in children and adolescents as well as older adults. Men and women are at equal risk.

Many people temporarily experience hypochondriacal feelings after a major health scare such as a heart attack. In these cases, the preoccupation with symptoms gradually fades as the person returns to normal activities. In contrast, hypochondriasis is more chronic, as the diagnostic criteria in the DSM table opposite indicate. Symptoms may wax and wane, but the core excessive preoccupation with health persists (Noyes et al., 1994).

Hypochondriacal symptoms often appear during episodes of depression, and they usually abate as the depression lifts. Fear of illness and the misinterpretation of innocent bodily changes as life threatening are also associated with anxiety disorders, especially phobias and panic disorder. The overlap of these symptoms has led to debate about whether hypochondriasis should be considered a type of anxiety disorder. In both hypochondriasis and anxiety disorders, routine sensations, such as breathing irregularities or digestive upset, are misinterpreted, leading to excessive alarm or arousal (Barsky, Barnett, & Cleary, 1994).

Can hypochondriasis be distinguished from anxiety disorders? In one study that compared 100 panic disorder and 60 hypochondriasis patients, 25 percent of those with panic disorder also displayed hypochondriasis and 13.3 percent of those with hypochondriasis had a comorbid panic disorder (Barsky et al., 1994). However, several important differences between the two groups were discovered. Patients with hypochondriasis had a history of more frequent and severe somatic symptoms than the panic group and had less positive social and occupational functioning (Barsky et al., 1994). The two disorders also showed different patterns of psychiatric comorbidity. Depression, phobias, and obsessive-compulsive disorder were less common among patients with hypochondriasis than among those with panic disorder.

In addition to these differences, the specific complaints of hypochondriacal persons differ from those with illness phobias or panic disorders. Hypochondriacs are convinced they have a serious disease, and no amount of reassurance can dissuade them. They keep consulting physicians, convinced that sooner or later an expert will confirm that they were right all along. Phobics, on the other hand, are afraid that they might develop a disease and therefore try to avoid situations that would expose them to risks. In people with panic disorder, the fearful overreaction

DSM-IV

Diagnostic Criteria for Hypochondriasis

A. Preoccupation with fears of having, or the idea that one has, a serious disease based on the person's misinterpretation of bodily symptoms.

B. The preoccupation persists despite appropriate medical evaluation and reassurance.

C. The belief in Criterion A is not of delusional intensity and is not restricted to circumscribed concern about appearance.

D. The preoccupation causes clinically significant distress or impairment in social, occupational, or other important areas of functioning.

E. The duration of the disturbance is at least 6 months.

F. The preoccupation is not better accounted for by Generalized Anxiety Disorder, Obsessive-Compulsive Disorder, Panic Disorder, a Major Depressive Episode, Separation Anxiety, or another Somatoform Disorder.

Source: American Psychiatric Association; *Diagnostic and Statistical Manual of Mental Disorders,* Fourth Edition. Washington, DC, American Psychiatric Association, 1994.

to physical symptoms is mostly confined to the experience of panic attacks; they do not go "doctor shopping" to prove or disprove that they are in good health.

Conversion Disorder

In **conversion disorder,** the individual experiences problems with motor or sensory abilities that suggest a neurological impairment, but no such impairment exists. As illustrated by the case of Rebecca on page 273, these *pseudoneurological* symptoms usually develop suddenly after some stressful event or emotional conflict, although this connection is not apparent to the person in distress. Three types of symptoms are common:

- *motor* deficits such as difficulties swallowing, poor balance or coordination, paralysis or weakness of the arms or legs, loss of the voice, and urinary retention;
- *sensory* deficits such as the loss of sensation to touch or pain, double vision, blindness, and deafness; and
- *seizurelike* symptoms (Katon, 1993).

Although the symptoms of conversion disorder can be temporarily disabling, they differ from disabilities caused by actual neurological disorders. For example, in conversion disorder, the symptoms may come and go depending on the activity the person is performing. A person might inadvertently use a "paralyzed" arm to get dressed or scratch an itch. Furthermore, many conversion anesthesias make no anatomical sense because the complaint does not correspond to the body's sensory systems. A common example is **glove anesthesia,** depicted in Figure 8.3 on page 278, in which the person experiences a loss of sensation and sometimes paralysis only in a hand, despite the fact that the "wiring" of nerves in the area dictates that the paralysis should run the entire length of the arm and hand. Conversion disorder symptoms often reflect how much the patient knows about the body. For instance, it was Rebecca's sudden inability to walk in the absence of any evidence of spinal cord damage that suggested a conversion disorder. An older, more medically sophisticated person might experience just localized weakness, making it more difficult to rule out illnesses, such as multiple sclerosis.

About one third of persons displaying conversion disorders appear strangely indifferent to their symptoms, a nonchalant attitude known as *la belle indifférence.* The person may chat away about the problem without showing any serious concern over its potential adverse consequences. In contrast, most malingerers are apprehensive about discussing their "symptoms" and remain on guard against being tripped up by an interviewer and having their ruse discovered.

The prevalence of conversion disorder in the general population of the United States is about 0.5 percent, but conversion disorder may account for up

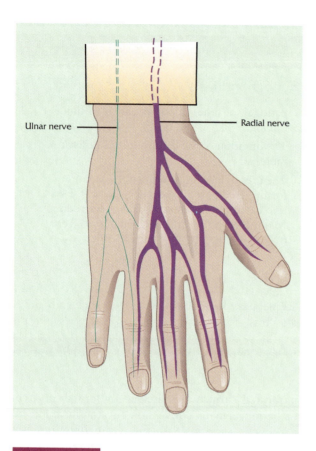

FIGURE 8.3

Glove Anesthesia

In glove anesthesia, an individual experiences a loss of sensation in the hand. However, the hand is enervated by nerves that run from the fingers along the length of the arm. Therefore, it does not make anatomical sense for the numbness to stop at the wrist.

terms of physical and mental health, and in carrying out their normal social roles (Kent, Tomasson, & Coryell, 1995).

Pain Disorder

Complaints about pain are the number one reason that motivates people to seek medical attention, but there are significant individual differences in the experience and expression of pain. Some people "grin and bear it" and go on with little change in their daily routines. Others focus on pain and sometimes become incapacitated and socially isolated.

In most cases, pain is adaptive because it signals that something is harming the body. However, pain signals are not always reliable indicators of physical condition. If distracted, as are athletes in competition or soldiers in combat, people can tolerate a lot of pain, or not feel pain at all. Likewise, people who feel that they can control a potentially painful stimulus or are optimistic about their ability to deal with pain report feeling less pain when exposed to a painful stimulus (Turk & Rudy, 1990). The experience of pain is intensified when people feel anxious or depressed or when they believe that they can exert no control over a painful stimulus.

to 5 percent of referrals to hospital mental health services. Still, the incidence of this disorder has been declining over the past 100 years, a trend thought to be due to increased education and medical sophistication in the population. Conversion disorder is observed more often among women, in rural populations, and in lower socioeconomic groups; it is the somatoform disorder most likely to affect children.

The course of conversion symptoms is typically short lived; most symptoms disappear, although, in up to a quarter of cases, they may recur. A recent longitudinal study documented better long-term adjustment among patients who initially displayed conversion symptoms compared with patients with somatization disorder. The patients with conversion disorder had a lower rate of divorce, fewer psychiatric symptoms, and reported better adjustment in

Physical, psychological, and social factors affect the experience of pain. Individuals can often withstand severe pain if they are willing to put up with it in the pursuit of other activities or goals.

A diagnosis of **pain disorder** is made when a person's predominant clinical complaint is pain and psychological factors are thought to play a significant role in causing or maintaining the pain. The pain is not intentionally produced, nor can it be accounted for by another mental disorder. If the duration of pain disorder is less than 6 months, it is called *acute pain disorder;* if the pain lasts 6 months or longer, it is termed *chronic pain disorder.* Pain disorder is also diagnosed when both psychological and medical factors have contributed to the disorder, as when an individual has a back injury but suffers unusually intense pain and seeks an excessive amount of medical treatment.

Pain disorder is a fairly common condition among adults. Based on the number of people who apply for worker's compensation on the basis of pain, the rate of pain disorder may be as high as 10 to 12 percent in the general population of the United States. It is estimated that the direct and indirect costs of pain total $90 billion a year in the United States alone; Americans consume as much as 20 million tons of aspirin annually for pain (Groth-Marnat & Edkins, 1996). Several psychosocial and economic variables influence pain. For example, pain tends to be more chronic when victims are receiving worker's compensation or are pursuing an injury-related lawsuit. The rate of pain disorder does not seem related to ethnicity. Individuals diagnosed with pain disorder often suffer a variety of related problems. Abuse of alcohol, narcotics, and over-the-counter pain killers is common, as are depression and anxiety disorders.

Body Dysmorphic Disorder

Most of us can point to features of our appearance that we would change if we could. A "too-big" nose, freckles, acne, feeling too short, too tall, too heavy, or too slight are a few typical complaints. Sensitivity about physical appearance and excess attention to minor physical imperfections are most intense in adolescence, but for most people these worries gradually decline as they come to accept their appearance. Others, however, harbor a focused, dysfunctional preoccupation about one particular physical aspect of themselves. In **body dysmorphic disorder** the preoccupation becomes so all-consuming that the person avoids social contact or even employment because of acute self-consciousness about a real or imagined physical imperfection.

Individuals suffering form body dysmorphic disorder repeatedly check their looks in the mirror or spend hours each day engaging in self-devised remedies, such as extensive hair removal, or excessive use of makeup. Their behavior exceeds mere vanity; indeed, the preoccupation can lead to paranoid ideas that others are scrutinizing or talking about their appearance. They may try to camouflage a defect or seek repeated surgical interventions to correct perceived faults, but they seldom feel satisfied with the results. Individuals with body dysmorphic disorder account for about 2 percent of those who seek cosmetic surgery (Barsky, 1992).

Concern over appearance and the focal defect often begins with normal, adolescent self-consciousness, but then it builds over a period of years until the concern is far out of proportion to reality. Many people are not diagnosed until they are in their 30s or early 40s, even when they have been plagued by their preoccupation for many years. Affected individuals suffer considerable anguish, which sometimes leads to suicide attempts. Western society's emphasis on physical attractiveness may contribute to this problem, which is diagnosed about equally in men and women.

Causes of Somatoform Disorders

Although different causal factors have been emphasized for specific somatoform disorders, we believe a diathesis–stress model provides the most useful framework for organizing these factors into a general explanation of somatoform disorders. This model, pictured in Figure 8.4 on page 280, contains the following three elements:

- A predisposition to somatoform disorders is conveyed by a combination of biological and psychological vulnerabilities, including higher levels of negative emotions, deficiencies in the ability to inhibit behavior, neurological abnormalities, hypersensitivity to physical sensations, traits such as private self-consciousness and neuroticism, a history of physical illnesses, and family members who display illness.

- One or more of these factors interacts with long-term stressors, intense emotional conflicts, or a severe trauma to increase the probability that a person will experience physical symptoms associated with emotional arousal.

- These symptoms are likely to be interpreted and experienced as signs of an illness rather than a mental disorder if sociocultural conditions support such interpretations, if the individual lacks sufficient medical knowledge, or if the environment provides reinforcement for this interpretation.

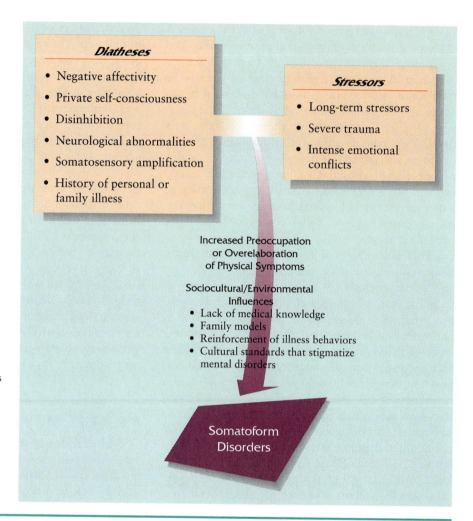

FIGURE 8.4

Diathesis–Stress Model of Somatoform Disorders

Somatoform disorders can be explained using a diathesis–stress model in which physical or psychological vulnerabilities interact with various kinds of stressors to produce an increase in and preoccupation with physical symptoms. Various kinds of reinforcement and social conditions can then transform this preoccupation into an actual somatoform disorder.

We will now consider the evidence pertaining to each element of this diathesis–stress model. In most cases the available research pertains to one specific somatoform disorder, but other factors have been associated with a general tendency to engage in somatization. Because different vulnerabilities might be at work for different disorders, we will indicate whether each factor is linked to a specific disorder or to somatoform patterns in general.

Biological and Psychological Vulnerabilities. There is conflicting evidence about the role of genetics in somatization disorder and hypochondriasis. Some twin and family studies suggest that both disorders run in families. For example, 10 to 20 percent of first-degree female relatives of individuals with somatization disorder also have the disorder (Guze, 1993). In contrast, another study that examined concordance for somatoform disorders among twins found no support for a genetic influence (Torgerson, 1986). Even if family aggregation is the rule, it is unclear whether genetic or environmental factors are more important. Just being raised by a parent (either bio-

logical or adoptive) with somatization disorder could increase the risk of developing the disorder.

Many studies have shown that the male relatives of people with somatization disorder have higher rates of antisocial personality disorder and substance abuse disorders than do males in control families. This relationship has led to the hypothesis that persons diagnosed with somatization disorder or antisocial personality disorder share an underlying physiological or psychological disturbance. For example, people with these disorders might suffer an impaired ability to inhibit impulsive behavior (Lilienfeld, 1992). Antisocial personalities manifest this problem through an aggressive and manipulative pursuit of immediate thrills and excitement at the expense of later punishment (see Chapter 12). People with somatization disorder, on the other hand, impulsively seek out attention through manipulative pleas for help and sympathy. They, too, appear to be relatively unaffected by long-term consequences.

The fact that conversion disorders cluster within families might be due to neurological abnormalities that constitute a vulnerability to these disorders. One intriguing finding is that conversion symptoms tend to be located on the left side of the body (Galin, Diamond, & Braff, 1977). Because the right hemisphere of the brain usually controls functions on the left side of the body, some abnormality in the right hemisphere, which is prominently involved in the experience of negative emotions, might play an important role in somatoform disorders. It also appears that the prevalence of conversion disorders may be higher than expected among persons who have some sort of organic brain disease or neuropsychological abnormality. Thus, organic factors may increase vulnerability to conversion disorder (Katon, 1993).

Biological factors might also contribute to the tendency of people with somatoform disorders to be **somatosensory amplifiers,** meaning that they perceive normal bodily sensations as more intense and disturbing than the general population does. Hypochondriacs, for instance, have a lower threshold for physical discomfort than other people do. Thus, "what the normal person perceives as abdominal pressure the hypochondriac experiences as pain" (Barsky, 1989). What accounts for the amplification is still unknown. One possibility is that some people have greater physiological sensitivity—they actually feel certain sensations more strongly than the average person.

An alternative explanation is that amplification occurs as a result of a tendency to selectively concentrate on or overinterpret bodily cues (Katon, 1993). Some individuals are prone to concentrate on internal sensations and private thoughts, a tendency called **private self-consciousness.** If this tendency were extreme and prolonged so that a person were chronically self-absorbed (Ingram, 1990), the person might be more likely to notice physical changes that would usually be missed by a less vigilant individual. Heightened physical sensitivity and self-absorption could act together to create a vicious cycle in which heightened sensations lead to an increased focus on and apprehension about the body, which in turn makes the original sensations seem all the more intense and worrisome.

A personality trait known as **negative affectivity** might also convey a vulnerability to somatoform disorders. People high in negative affectivity tend to worry, be pessimistic, fear uncertainty, feel guilt, tire easily, have poor self-esteem, and be shy and depressed (Gray, 1981). When combined with physiological sensitivity, negative affectivity may enhance the likelihood that people will make unduly negative attributions about benign bodily sensations on which they are constantly focused; in a sense, their worries are "specialized" to the area of health (Lecci et al., 1996). In a recent study (Russo et al., 1994), greater negative affectivity—particularly worry and pessimism—predicted increased severity of somatization. In addition, a separate trait—impulsivity or "novelty seeking"—was associated with a higher number of unexplained medical symptoms. Thus, when people who are high on negative affectivity become overly concerned about bodily sensations, they may find it difficult to restrain repeated urges to seek medical care if they are also relatively impulsive.

Family attitudes and behaviors concerning physical illness may also play a role in shaping somatoform disorders. Many people who display these disorders have experienced a serious illness during childhood or observed an illness or painful condition in a family member. Furthermore, many individuals who develop a somatoform disorder describe growing up in families where illness was a primary way to gain attention and affection. In a European study of 84 children with conversion symptoms, 62 percent had a history of prior illness as well as high rates of illness within their families (Spierings et al., 1990). More than a quarter of these children had a model within the family for the symptoms that they later displayed. Finally, children with a history of developmental or injury-related problems in a specific part of the body typically displayed conversion symptoms in the same area.

Other support for the influence of early family experiences comes from studies of children with *recurrent abdominal pain (RAP),* persistent stomachaches for which no organic cause can be identified. Children with RAP do not differ from other children on most psychological or behavioral variables, but they are more likely to grow up in families in which multiple illnesses are common, to have mothers who describe themselves as sickly, and to have been rewarded for illness-related behavior (Walker, Garber, & Green, 1994). Mothers of children with RAP also report more depression than do mothers of other children.

The Role of Stress and Trauma. Historically, psychoanalytic theorists have viewed somatization as a way of deflecting strong emotions. Because conversion disorder, in particular, has long been viewed as a way to express repressed conflicts, many clinicians have speculated that this condition and other somatoform disorders are often triggered by a personal conflict or stressor. In the late 1800s, when Freud used the term "conversion" to refer to the

Connections

Why might more males be diagnosed with antisocial personality disorder and more females with somatization disorder? For answers, read Chapter 12, pp. 430–433.

substitution of physical symptoms for repressed negative emotions, he became one of the first clinicians to link physical symptoms with a history of trauma or conflict (Tomasson, Kent, & Coryell, 1991).

Associated with this view is the hypothesis that adult somatizers are more likely to have been exposed to abuse as children. Because the average preschooler lacks the verbal and cognitive abilities necessary to understand and express emotions, physical symptoms might be one vehicle available to the child for conveying emotional distress, analogous to the make-believe processes that are hypothesized to precede dissociative identity disorder in traumatized children. Early instances of trauma-triggered somatization might make it more likely that a person will display emotional upsets via physical symptoms later in life.

Is there evidence to support an association between somatization and childhood abuse? In one study (Morrison, 1989), the early sexual experiences of 60 women diagnosed with somatization disorder were compared with 31 women diagnosed with a mood disorder. The two groups did not differ in terms of early voluntary sexual experiences, but the women with somatization disorder were more than 3 times as likely to report having been sexually molested; the average age at the time of this abuse was 10 years. However, this study was based on a small sample of women, and it lacked a normal control group, so it does not provide convincing evidence that childhood abuse is a risk factor for somatization disorder.

Theories about the origins of pain disorder also emphasize the potential role of childhood abuse. In one study, 45 patients who were receiving treatment for chronic oral-facial pain answered an anonymous survey about whether they had ever suffered sexual or physical abuse (Curran et al., 1995). Nearly 70 percent of the patients reported a history of abuse. These abused patients also suffered greater pain severity and higher levels of negative affectivity than nonabused patients did.

Of course, a link between stressors and somatization can be explained without reference to repression or conversion. As discussed in Chapters 5 and 6, exposure to stressors gives rise to increased physiological reactivity. This arousal is stronger in some individuals than in others, and it might be that these individuals are at greatest risk for becoming preoccupied with physical reactions and then gradually elaborating them into a somatoform disorder.

Reinforcement of Somatization. Once somatoform symptoms have been displayed, they are likely to be maintained or strengthened if they are reinforced by social or cultural factors in the environment. Somatizing patients often complain of symptoms that turn out to be similar to, and possibly modeled on, those of other family members. Somatizing individuals may learn from their families that illness is a legitimate way to garner attention, to avoid stressful responsibilities, or to express otherwise unacceptable negative feelings. These consequences are sometimes referred to as **secondary gain,** and they may play a major role in maintaining a somatizing style. (**Primary gain,** by contrast, refers to the reduction of anxiety that Freud believed was accomplished by the conversion of conflict into physical symptoms.) So, for example, pain behavior can be learned as a result of inadvertent reinforcement by health care providers who attempt repeated medical interventions and by family members and friends who offer sympathy and assistance (Fordyce, 1976).

The fact that the prevalence of somatoform patterns varies considerably among different cultures also points to the importance of social factors. In general, somatoform disorders are more prevalent in cultures that discourage open discussion of psychological problems and that stigmatize mental disorders. Not surprisingly, physical symptoms might take on special significance in these cultures because they provide an acceptable way for a person to communicate unhappiness or distress.

Treatment of Somatoform Disorders

Psychotherapy tends to be ineffective for some somatoform disorders—such as somatization disorder and hypochondriasis—because clients typically resist psychological interpretations of their problems. Many experts believe, therefore, that the best strategy is to prepare physicians to work with these patients within the general medical care system (Katon, 1993; Samuels, 1995). The general goals of treatment are to help patients cope better with the stressors that trigger somatization and to wean them from their chronic dependence on medical providers.

In order to reduce "doctor shopping" and constant help seeking, a single case manager may be designated to schedule all of the patient's medical appointments. In this way, the patient can receive support and attention without coming up with one complaint after another to justify medical visits. Each visit might include a brief physical exam, but tests and medications should be ordered only if necessary. Attempts might also be made to teach the patient alternative ways of communicating emotional needs, and gentle encouragement might be given for the patient to seek personal counseling.

For conversion disorder, hypnosis and behavioral interventions are often combined with supportive psychotherapy to help the patient overcome physical symptoms and cope with triggering stressors.

Body dysmorphic disorder has frequently been treated with medication. The antipsychotic drug Primozide (Orap) reduces some symptoms, but it has negative side effects that require careful monitoring (Barsky, 1989). In severe cases, antidepressants such as Prozac and Zoloft, which tend to have fewer side effects than Primozide, have proved effective (Phillips et al., 1993).

Based on the similarity of body dysmorphic disorder to obsessive-compulsive disorder (OCD), treatments that have proved successful with OCD have been adopted for body dysmorphic clients. A combination of cognitive therapy, which challenges clients' negative beliefs about their appearance, and exposure-response prevention techniques, which force clients to confront defects but prevent them from repeated mirror checking and camouflaging, has significantly reduced preoccupations with perceived physical defects (Neziroglu et al., 1996).

Contemporary treatment for pain disorder usually takes place in a medical setting and combines behavioral interventions, psychotherapy, and pharmacotherapy. The drugs that are used most often are nonsteroidal anti-inflammatory drugs and antidepressants (Dworkin & Wilson, 1993). Reinforcement of pain behavior is avoided, and more adaptive functioning is encouraged through techniques such as

- biofeedback and relaxation techniques to help patients learn how to reduce pain;
- rehabilitation programs to increase physical activity;
- cognitive behavioral therapy to help patients and family members better understand how cognitions and emotions affect physical health; and
- family or marital therapy to help patients and family members see how pain behaviors can serve as a dysfunctional form of communication.

Revisiting the Case of Louise

Louise continued weekly psychotherapy for 2 more years. Her therapist told her about the diagnosis of dissociative identity disorder and what clinicians believe can cause it. Thereafter, Louise began to talk more about her childhood and the abuse she suffered. Her dreams and memories of the past also became more intense. Two alters appeared in therapy, usually when Louise was hypnotized. One was a child who acted panicky and emerged only when Louise was involved in an angry conflict in which she felt she was "in trouble." The other was a teenage girl who dressed and acted provocatively and seemed to take pride in breaking as many rules or expectations as she could.

As Louise revealed more about her memories of childhood, she reported more about how her drunken stepfather often verbally abused her, sometimes beat her, and would lock her in a closet for several hours at a time. Since her mother was usually at work during these episodes, she never stood up for Louise and even blamed Louise for the arguments with her stepfather.

As a result of therapy, Louise attempted to talk with her mother about the past, but her mother refused to do so, saying, "You didn't have it any worse than most kids. We tried our best." However, Louise was able to talk to her younger brother about their childhood, and she felt some relief from these talks.

After over 2 years of therapy, Louise was transferred to a new job and discontinued therapy. At that point she was no longer plagued by separate alters. She was still hesitant about romantic relationships, but she was active in church and had begun making some female friends, although she had trouble trusting them. She maintained only a superficial relationship with her mother, mostly through phone calls or visits at holidays. Louise continued to struggle with bouts of depression, but she did not contact a therapist after she moved.

SUMMARY

Dissociative Disorders

Abrupt disruptions in the normally integrated processes of memory, consciousness, and awareness are typical of the dissociative disorders. Dissociative symptoms must be understood within a cultural context. In some cultures, amnesia and trance states are an accepted form of religious experience and, at other times, useful ways to express discontent. Contemporary North American culture has also played an important role in shaping our current understanding and acceptance of dissociative phenomena.

The most extreme and puzzling of the dissociative disorders is dissociative identity disorder, in which a person's identity appears to fragment into alternate personalities that exert control over the person's behavior at different times and without awareness of the others. Clinicians disagree on the extent to which dissociative identity disorder is a genuine, distinct disorder arising out of early trauma during childhood or a condition unintentionally created by therapists' suggestions.

Dissociative amnesia involves the sudden loss of memory without an organic cause. In dissociative fugue, a person suddenly and unexpectedly leaves home and travels to a new place where a new identity is often enacted. A person's recurrent feelings of being detached from him- or herself or feelings that the outside world is unreal are characteristic of depersonalization disorder.

Causes and Treatment of Dissociative Disorders

Dissociative amnesias and fugues and depersonalization disorder are thought to be triggered by sudden severe trauma or strong emotional conflicts occurring in a person who is prone to dissociation as a result of any of three vulnerabilities: a tendency to be easily absorbed in imagination, high levels of hypnotizability, and a history of childhood abuse.

One theory of dissociative identity disorder is that it originates from early severe childhood abuse experienced by individuals who are prone to dissociative-like experiences as a form of defense or psychological escape. Another theory is that the disorder is diagnosed in clients who learn to enact multiple identities from the leading and suggestive techniques used by psychotherapists and from modern cultural expectations.

Psychotherapy for dissociative identity disorder usually aims at helping clients come to terms with past trauma and integrate alters into a unified identity. However, the efficacy of these treatments has not been carefully evaluated. Many people with other dissociative disorders improve without formal treatment, once the triggering stressor has been resolved.

Somatoform Disorders

The somatoform disorders involve physical complaints or disabilities for which no organic cause can be found. In somatization disorder, patients chronically complain of a long list of physical symptoms. Hypochondriasis involves a preoccupying fear of having a serious medical illness. Individuals who are diagnosed with conversion disorder experience motor or sensory disabilities that have no organic cause; the symptoms usually appear after a stressful event. The main feature of pain disorder is preoccupation with pain in which psychological factors play a substantial role. Individuals who become obsessed with some imperfection in their physical appearance to the point of suffering serious distress or impairment are diagnosed with body dysmorphic disorder.

Historically, most somatoform disorders have been assumed to result from a tendency of individuals to express emotional distress through physical symptoms, a process known as somatization. A diathesis–stress model of somatoform disorders emphasizes the role of biological or psychological vulnerabilities to experience heightened arousal or to focus excessively on internal experiences. Coupled with trauma or long-term stressors, this vulnerability results in a tendency to experience emotional distress as physical illness, particularly in environments that reinforce such interpretations.

Because most people who have a somatoform disorder resist psychological explanations of their difficulties, standard psychotherapy is often not a successful form of intervention. Specialized treatments, along with drug therapies, may be more helpful.

KEY TERMS

absorption, p. 263

alter, p. 255

amnesia, p. 254

body dysmorphic disorder, p. 279

Briquet's syndrome, p. 274

continuous amnesia, p. 259

conversion disorder, p. 277

depersonalization disorder, p. 262

depersonalization, p. 254

derealization, p. 254

dissociation, p. 253

dissociative amnesia, p. 259

dissociative disorder, p. 252

dissociative fugue, p. 261

dissociative identity disorder, p. 255

dissociative trance disorder, p. 255

fantasy proneness, p. 263

generalized amnesia, p. 259

glove anesthesia, p. 277

host personality, p. 256

hypnotizability, p. 264

hypochondriasis, p. 275

identity alteration, p. 255

identity confusion, p. 255

imaginative involvement, p. 263

la belle indifference, p. 277

localized amnesia, p. 259

multiple personality disorder, p. 255

negative affectivity, p. 281

pain disorder, p. 279

personality fragment, p. 256

primary gain, p. 282

private self-consciousness, p. 281

secondary gain, p. 282

selective amnesia, p. 259

sociocultural model, p. 264

sodium amytal, p. 261

somatization, p. 253

somatization disorder, p. 274

somatoform disorder, p. 252

somatosensory amplifier, p. 281

switching, p. 256

systematized amnesia, p. 259

trauma-dissociation model, p. 264

undifferentiated somatoform disorder, p. 275

9

Mood Disorders and Suicide

View South of Dallas, Oregon by Ruth McDowell,
1987. Watercolor, 28" x 35". Courtesy of Sistare and
NARSAD Artworks.

From the Case of Margaret

Margaret had been a little scared about leaving home for college. She grew up in a small town where she had always excelled at everything she attempted. Success was important to Margaret. Her parents expected it, and she believed it was the key to her popularity.

At first, Margaret worried that college might not prove as easy for her as high school, but she made friends quickly and soon began enjoying campus life. She dated several men during her freshman year, then she met Jack early in her sophomore year. They spent more and more time together over the next several months and eventually became sexually involved. When summer came, they each went to their own home towns to work. When they returned to school in the fall, their relationship began to sour. They quarreled often and felt increasingly tense when they were together. Jack suggested that they start dating other people,

try to stay friends, and "see what happens." Margaret was upset but also relieved. She had thought about suggesting the same thing but had never had enough courage to do so.

Despite her relief, Margaret did not bounce back emotionally. Now a 21-year-old college junior, she has been plagued with frequent headaches and stomach pains for about three months. She has no energy, has periods of feeling "down in the dumps," and sometimes feels hopeless and overwhelmed. Typically a competent and motivated student, Margaret's grades during the previous term were lower than usual, and she has fallen further and further behind in her current work. She has started to skip classes, especially early in the morning, because she finds it difficult to get out of bed. Much of the time she feels too tired to study. When she tries, her mind wanders, and she wastes time reading the same pages over and over. Even though she feels exhausted, on

287

some nights she has difficulty falling asleep. Recently, she has begun to avoid her friends because she has to "fake it" in order to act like her former, happier self.

Most nights, Margaret stays in her room alone; she knows this is abnormal and has at several times resolved to "turn things around," but when the next day comes, Margaret feels even more demoralized and discouraged about her life. As she confided to her roommate, "it's as if I can't move; my body feels pulled down by some extra gravity in the room." She has also stopped calling her parents every week because she feels that they will just nag at her to "snap out of it." In fact, she is increasingly annoyed with her parents for pushing her so hard all her life. If they keep it up, she fears that she'll end up a moody, bitter woman just as her mother seems to be.

Margaret finally went to the Student Health Service for help because of her physical problems, but a physical examination and initial lab tests revealed nothing amiss. Are Margaret's symptoms a normal response to the end of a relationship, or do they reflect something more serious? After interviewing Margaret and having her complete an MMPI-2 personality test, a psychologist at the Health Center concluded that Margaret's feelings of depression were serious enough to qualify as a mood disorder. ■

*M*ood disorders refer to a group of emotional disturbances associated with serious and persistent difficulty maintaining an even, productive emotional state. (The term *affective disorders* is also used for these conditions.) However, mood disorders usually involve more than just emotional symptoms; they also interfere with individuals' ability to work, to stay involved in relationships, to enjoy family life, and even to maintain good physical health. A mood disorder can ruin almost all aspects of a person's functioning, and it can come and go many times in a person's life.

The most common mood disorder in Western cultures involves episodes of **depression**—a low, miserably unhappy mood—but mood disorders can also include extremely high or agitated moods—known as **mania**—in which the person feels excessively and unrealistically positive. In some cases, individuals experience both episodes of depression and periods of mania. This pattern is called *manic-depressive* or *bipolar disorder*. The term *unipolar depression* is sometimes used to refer to cases such as Margaret's in which only depressive symptoms are present.

Mood disorders affect people from all socioeconomic classes, ethnic groups, and occupations, but its victims seem to include an unusually large number of well-known creative people. Handel, Tchaikov-sky, Vincent van Gogh, Jack London, Ernest Hemingway, Sylvia Plath, Ingmar Bergman, and Virginia Woolf are prominent examples. The incidence of mood disorders among successful artists and writers appears to be higher than among the general population (Goodwin & Jamison, 1990; Jamison, 1989). Major political figures such as Napoleon, Abraham Lincoln, and Winston Churchill also have suffered mood disorders.

Are mood disorders and creativity somehow linked? Could creativity lead to an increased risk for mood disorders, or could mood disorders lead to increased creativity? Perhaps after prolonged creative concentration and introspection on emotional material or after a particularly productive burst of achievement, artists' moods intensify to the point that they are maladaptive. Or perhaps the intense emotions of the mood disorder, when they are at manageable levels, lead some artists to creative or dramatic insights or to prolonged periods of absorption in a creative task. We do not know, but the evidence does suggest that creative people are generally not able to work productively during periods of clinical depression or mania.

Another possibility is that creativity and mood disorders share common roots. One study of 30 creative writers who had attended the prestigious University of Iowa Writers' Workshop found that, not only was the rate of mood disorders significantly higher among the writers than among a control group of socioeconomically similar adults, but also that the prevalence of mood disorders among the writers' first-degree relatives was 9 times greater than among the relatives of the control group (Andreasen, 1987). This pattern fits with the well-established finding that mood disorders run in families and are probably genetically influenced to some extent.

Researchers have not solved the puzzle of the apparent relationship between creativity and mood disorders, but they have learned a great deal about mood disorders themselves.

In this chapter, we will consider the mood disorders in detail—their physical, emotional, and cognitive symptoms; the main theories about their causes; the research data available to support these theories; and efforts at prevention and treatment. We will also discuss suicidal behavior, because suicide is more common when a person is depressed or is undergoing a disabling cycle of intense mood swings. [More than half of all suicides are committed by depressed persons (Hirshfield & Goodwin, 1988)]. Finally, we will revisit the case of Margaret to see how she fared and what her experience can tell us about mood disorders.

William Styron is one of the many celebrated artists and leaders known to have suffered from a mood disorder. Mood disorders are no less painful for the famous. It would be a mistake to think that they are a pleasure or a unique advantage enjoyed by talented people. William Styron called his depression a "storm of murk." In Darkness Visible: A Memoir of Madness, *Styron (1990) described the depression that overtook him in 1985 and brought him to the brink of suicide:*

> [The] gray drizzle of horror induced by depression takes on the quality of physical pain. But it is not an immediately identifiable pain, like that of a broken limb. It may be more accurate to say that despair, owing to some evil trick played upon the sick brain by the inhabiting psyche, comes to resemble the diabolical discomfort of being imprisoned in a fiercely overheated room. And because no breeze stirs this cauldron, because there is no escape from this smothering confinement, it is entirely natural that the victim begins to think ceaselessly of oblivion. (p. 76)

Depressive Disorders

Most people have bad moods, days when, for no apparent reason, they feel especially sad or unusually irritable. And most people feel a bit dejected and demoralized when their grades are disappointing or their friends let them down. Usually, these moods don't last long, disappearing once individuals get past a difficult deadline, do something fun with a friend, or just catch up on their sleep. They bounce back and move on. What differentiates these common experiences from a depressive disorder?

1. The depressed mood seen in depressive disorders is, like Margaret's, not temporary or easily shaken off. It typically persists for weeks, months, or even years.
2. A depressive disorder is severe enough to impair an individual's ability to work or interact with friends or family.
3. People suffering from depressive disorders show a cluster of other physical and behavioral symptoms, such as reduced appetite, sleep disturbance, or loss of interest in, or pleasure from, their usual pursuits.

Depressive disorders are one of the most common mental health problems seen in Western cultures (Robins & Regier, 1991). It is estimated that one in five adults in the United States will experience at least one episode of significant depression at some time in life, and many of these individuals will have recurrent episodes (Hamilton, 1989). Females are twice as likely as males to experience a significant depression (a difference to which we will return when we consider the causes of depression). However, depressive disorders appear evenly across various ethnic or socioeconomic groups and in many cultures of the world (Weissman et al., 1991). Being rich or successful or beautiful does not protect a person from depressive disorders. Depressive disorders can occur across the entire life span (Hamilton, 1989). Usually first appearing when people are in their late twenties—and especially common between ages 20 and 45—depressive disorders have also been identified in children and adolescents (Klerman, 1988), and they are a significant problem among older people (Teri & Gallagher, 1991). In children and adolescents, the typical symptoms of depression differ somewhat from those seen in adults, but the overall clinical picture in both age groups is similar enough that clinicians believe they stem from the same basic disorder.

As in other mental disorders, depression is often exacerbated by comorbid problems (Tollefson, 1993). For example, many depressed individuals abuse alcohol or other drugs. Indeed, substance abuse may reflect depressed people's efforts to relieve their depressive symptoms. Such relief is only temporary, however, and the long-term complications

Connections

What are the major symptoms of mood disorders in children, and how do they differ from those seen in adults? See Chapter 3, pp. 103–105.

of substance abuse multiply the impairments that mood disorders cause and often lead to legal problems and financial ruin. In other cases, people develop mood disorders as a result of their chronic struggles with substance abuse. Depressive disorders are often accompanied by significant anxiety and panic attacks (Watson & Kendall, 1989). In such cases, individuals feel overwhelmed with negative emotions—despair and guilt over past problems, apprehension and fear about future threats—and they frequently have difficulty sleeping. In fact, the overlap between depression and anxiety is so extensive that some investigators believe they are both parts of a larger emotional state known as **negative affect,** made up of a mixture of anxious and depressive symptoms (Kendall & Watson, 1989). The most serious consequence of depression is suicide; about 15 percent of people suffering from severe depression take their own lives (Dowart & Chartock, 1989; Hamilton, 1989).

Individuals experience, express, and respond to depression in different ways, but depressive disorders tend to fall into two major categories: major depressive disorder and dysthymic disorder. The core symptoms associated with these two categories overlap considerably, but they differ in severity and course. Major depressive disorder is typically more severe

and episodic, whereas dysthymic disorder is milder but more chronic. The diagnosis of major depression is less common in children than it is in adolescents; depressed children are more likely to be diagnosed with dysthymic disorder. Some people experience both types of depression, with dysthymic disorder either preceding an episode of major depressive disorder or developing as a residual condition afterward (Winokur, 1986). These individuals are described as having **double depression** (Wells et al., 1992).

Major Depressive Disorder

Major depressive disorder is the term applied to the most severe forms of depression. At any one time, about 5 to 9 percent of women in the United States and about 2 to 3 percent of men have major depressive disorder. The key indicator of major depressive disorder is the presence of a major depressive episode, the criteria for which are described in the DSM-IV table below. Not everyone diagnosed with this disorder experiences all of the symptoms listed; however, it is common to see the first two, namely, depressed mood and **anhedonia,** the loss of the ability to enjoy activities central to the person's life. Thus, the avid basketball fan loses interest in the game; the involved and active parent finds it difficult to attend

DSM-IV

Symptoms of a Major Depressive Episode

A. Five (or more) of the following symptoms have been present during the same 2-week period and represent a change from previous functioning; at least one of the symptoms must be either depressed mood or loss of interest or pleasure.

(1) depressed mood most of the day, nearly every day. **Note:** In children and adolescents, can be irritable mood.
(2) markedly diminished interest or pleasure in all, or almost all, activities most of the day, nearly every day
(3) significant weight loss when not dieting or weight gain (e.g., a change of more than 5% of body weight in a month), or decrease or increase in appetite nearly every day

Note: In children, consider failure to make expected weight gains.
(4) insomnia or hypersomnia nearly every day
(5) psychomotor agitation or retardation nearly every day (observable by others)
(6) fatigue or loss of energy nearly every day
(7) feelings of worthlessness or excessive or inappropriate guilt nearly every day
(8) diminished ability to think or concentrate, or indecisiveness, nearly every day
(9) recurrent thoughts of death (not just fear of dying), recurrent suicidal ideation without a specific plan, or a suicide attempt or a specific plan for committing suicide

Source: American Psychiatric Association; *Diagnostic and Statistical Manual of Mental Disorders,* Fourth Edition. Washington, DC, American Psychiatric Association, 1994.

to child care; the once-productive employee becomes disengaged from work.

The predominant emotion in major depressive disorder is a dull despair, a constant sadness that leaves the person feeling as if nothing is worthwhile. These feelings may be accompanied by bitterness, a short temper, and guilt. A passage from Samuel Coleridge's "Dejection: An Ode" captures the oppressive sadness that engulfs the depressed person.

A grief without a pang, void, dark, and drear,
A stifled, drowsy, unimpassioned grief,
Which finds no natural outlet, no relief,
In word, sigh, or tear—

Physical symptoms often accompanying major depressive disorder include loss of appetite, persistent fatigue, and complaints about an upset stomach or a variety of aches and pains. Depression may cause the person to feel so drained of energy that body movements are slowed or reduced to the point of near immobility. Depressed people may have trouble falling asleep, but their most common sleep disturbances involve waking up during the night—or too early in the morning—and being unable to return to sleep. Although it is not an official criterion of major depressive disorder, depressed persons also tend to suffer impairment in immune system functioning, which increases their vulnerability to infections and other illnesses (Herbert & Cohen, 1993b; Weisse, 1992). Such impairment is particularly apparent among depressed older people and among people whose depression is severe.

Cognitive symptoms associated with depression include a sense of guilt and worthlessness and difficulty concentrating on such simple daily activities as reading the paper or watching TV. People who are depressed often postpone decisions for fear of making mistakes. They feel demoralized and hopeless. They are self-critical, blaming themselves for their problems and feeling pessimistic about their lives and futures. Their recollection of the past is also grim and unforgiving. This kind of thinking often leads to suicide or suicide attempts.

The most severely depressed individuals may experience psychotic symptoms, including delusions (false beliefs about being persecuted, for example) or hallucinations (e.g., seeing or hearing things that are not there). Usually, these symptoms are *mood congruent*, meaning that they are consistent with the person's depressed thinking. For example, depressed people preoccupied with death and dying might think that others are trying to kill them, or they might hear a voice telling them to kill themselves. *Mood incongruent* psychotic symptoms might involve the delusion that someone is trying to insert thoughts in their minds through electromagnetic airwaves.

Because of their somatic symptoms and preoccupation with physical well-being, many depressed individuals first seek relief from their physicians. In fact, major depressive disorder is one of the most common problems encountered in family practice and by primary care physicians (Katon & Russo, 1989). However, these practitioners must be careful in their diagnoses because the physical symptoms associated with major depressive disorder can also stem from other conditions including

- malignancies, such as lung cancer;
- impairments of the central nervous system, including tumors;
- infections such as viral pneumonia, hepatitis, and viral mononucleosis;
- endocrine disorders;
- deficiencies in nutrients such as niacin and folic acid; and
- numerous drugs, including steroids and narcotics (Tollefson, 1993).

Course and Recurrence. Most major depressive episodes clear up even without treatment in a matter of months. Some episodes last only a couple of weeks; others can last for years. The average duration of an untreated episode is between 8 to 10 months (Tollefson, 1993). Of greater clinical interest is whether the person will experience repeated episodes. Current research suggests that the chances of a recurrence are, unfortunately, rather high. Fewer than half of the adults who experience one episode of major depressive disorder recover fully and never have another. In many of these cases the person had no previous psychological problems but became severely depressed in the face of major life stressors, such as a divorce or the loss of a job.

More commonly, perhaps in as many as three quarters of the cases, episodes of major depressive disorder are recurrent, meaning that a depressed person recovers or improves for a period of time only to suffer another episode at a later time. In some cases the recurrences are separated by years during which there is no significant depression. In others, the episodes occur in clusters; and, in still others, the recurrences happen more and more frequently as the person grows older. Longitudinal research over periods as long 20 years find depressed patients suffering an average of five to six episodes in their lifetimes (Winokur, 1986). As might be expected, recurrent depressive episodes take an ever-growing toll on a person's relationships and productivity.

Major depressive disorder can begin at any age, but the most typical period of onset is the mid-twenties. A number of studies suggest that the average age of onset has decreased in recent years and that increasing numbers of young people are being diagnosed with depression. Both of these trends have been discovered in several countries throughout the world (e.g., Cross-National Collaborative Group, 1992).

Many people experience double depression, in which a major depressive disorder is preceded or followed by dysthymic disorder (Keller et al., 1992; Wells et al., 1992). As many as one quarter of all people with major depressive disorder have preexisting dysthymic disorder. Full recovery from double depression is much less likely than from major depression alone, and relapse is much more common. In one study of 431 people with depressive symptoms (Keller et al., 1992), it was found that those people with more severe initial symptoms and with double depression had more frequent and prolonged episodes of depression during a 5-year follow-up period.

Subgroups of Major Depressive Disorder.

Differences in the pattern of depressive episodes and in their predominant symptoms have led diagnosticians to propose subcategories of major depressive disorder. These subtypes may have different causes and prognoses and may respond best to different treatments.

DSM-IV diagnoses of major depression can include **specifiers,** which describe patterns of features that indicate the likely course of the disorder, its severity, and specific symptoms characteristic of a particular subtype of the disorder. These specifiers help clinicians tailor the treatment to the person and predict the course of the depression. Of the many specifiers available in the DSM-IV, clinicians often use one of the following six to describe the current or most recent episode of major depressive disorder:

1. *Chronic.* This specifier is used for cases of major depressive disorder that have lasted continuously for 2 years.

2. *With atypical features.* This specifier applies to about 15 percent of individuals diagnosed with major depressive disorder or dysthymic disorder. They show a pattern of symptoms that are slightly different from those outlined so far (Stewart et al., 1993). Rather than losing their appetite or having difficulty sleeping, these people sleep and eat more than usual, often gaining a lot of weight. They may even cheer up briefly following some positive event, such as a phone call from an old friend. Many of these individuals also show such intense sensitivity to rejection that it disrupts their social relationships. This variant on major depressive disorder is more likely to occur among younger patients, and it frequently has a more chronic, less episodic course than typical depression.

3. *With melancholic features.* This specifier is often used to differentiate severely depressed individuals. This type of depression was once termed *endogenous depression,* suggesting that it was caused by internal, biological causes. Patients with melancholic features tend to display severe anhedonia, a sleep disturbance that involves being unable to get back to sleep after awakening as early as 4 or 5 A.M., a change in bodily activity characterized either by extreme agitation or slowness, and significant weight loss. Melancholic symptoms are equally frequent in men and women, but they are more likely to be seen in older patients.

4. *With catatonic features.* This specifier is used for depression marked by extreme psychomotor disturbances; similar problems are also observed in some cases of schizophrenia. The person may stay immobile for long periods or stay fixed in bizarre postures, sometimes showing a *waxy flexibility* that allows them to be manipulated like a toy action figure. Others may engage in agitated, purposeless behavior; may resist any attempt to move them; or may mimic every movement someone else has made, a condition called *echopraxia.* Some become mute or engage in *echolalia,* a parrotlike repetition of other people's speech.

5. *With seasonal pattern.* This specifier refers to depressive episodes that have a clear seasonal pattern (Lewy, 1993). The term **seasonal affective disorder** is also used for mood disorders that are linked to a particular season of the year. For example, some individuals experience depressive episodes only during the winter months, then spontaneously recover in the spring. This type of depressive disorder is most commonly seen in locations where winter days are short and exposure to daylight is limited. Winter depression is associated with a unique set of symptoms including low energy, extreme fatigue, and greater than normal amounts of sleeping. People with a seasonal pattern to their disorder frequently experience increased appetite, often characterized by a craving for carbohydrates.

6. *With postpartum onset.* This specifier is used for cases of depressive disorder that begin within 4

Connections

What form does catatonic behavior take in schizophrenia? See, Chapter 10, pp. 339, 348.

Depression with melancholic features, a severe variety of major depressive disorder, occurs frequently in older people. The person suffering this disorder is unable to feel pleasure from almost any activity, and the feelings of depression are usually worse in the morning.

weeks after the birth of a child. The symptoms are similar to typical depressive disorder, but they tend to fluctuate more often and are frequently accompanied by attacks of severe anxiety and obsessive worries about harm befalling the baby. Women with postpartum episodes often feel guilty because their symptoms are at odds with the joy they were taught to expect following the birth of a baby. This shame often makes these women less willing to talk about their problems, thus making successful treatment less likely.

The existing empirical evidence casts doubt on whether postpartum onset depression actually constitutes a special category of disorder. Several studies have failed to find unique symptoms or characteristics that distinguish postpartum depressive disorder from other forms of major depressive disorder (Whiffen, 1992; Whiffen & Gotlib, 1993). Other researchers question whether the postpartum period is associated with any increased rate of depressive disorders (O'Hara et al., 1990). What does seem clear is that, if a mother suffers a mood disorder shortly after delivering one child, she is at greater

risk for mood disorders following future deliveries (Depression Guideline Panel, 1993).

Dysthymic Disorder and Other Types of Depression

In adults, the diagnosis of **dysthymic disorder** is reserved for individuals who have had difficulties with chronically depressed mood and related symptoms for at least 2 years, but dysthymic disorder can, and usually does, last substantially longer. The DSM table on page 294 lists the key criteria for this diagnosis. (In children, the prominent mood is often irritability rather than depression, and the minimum duration of symptoms is 1 year.) Dysthymic disorder tends to develop more gradually than major depression and typically does not involve an acute disruption of the person's life. It is analogous to a nagging cold that is never severe but, over time, can drag a person down. People with dysthymic disorder often feel inadequate and brood about the past. They appear almost accustomed to their demoralized feelings, and, in some cases, will say such things as "I've always felt like this." Dysthymic disorder is associated with increased risk for major depression (Keller, Baker, & Russell, 1993), which suggests that the two disorders may share a common causal pathway.

People may suffer symptoms of depression that do not last as long, are too few in number, or are not sufficiently severe to meet the criteria for either major depressive disorder or dysthymic disorder. The DSM-IV includes the diagnosis of *depressive disorder not otherwise specified* to cover these cases. In other cases, when a brief period of depressive symptoms develops after a stressor, clinicians might diagnose an *adjustment disorder*, as discussed in Chapter 5.

Many people develop symptoms of depression following the death of a loved one. In most of these cases, depressive symptoms are apparent for about 3 months—in some cases up to a year—but they then gradually diminish (Clayton et al., 1974). The DSM-IV refers to this process as **bereavement;** it is not considered a mental disorder, although people often do seek professional help while they cope with their grief. In approximately 2 to 5 percent of grieving individuals, however, this normal grief reaction evolves into a form of major depressive disorder characterized by persistent thoughts of suicide; a marked slowing of movement, speech, and reaction time; a desire to cling to the deceased person's belongings; and a strong reaction to the anniversary of the person's death (Winokur, 1986). Some clinicians call this condition a *pathological grief reaction.*

DSM-IV

Diagnostic Criteria for Dysthymic Disorder

A. Depressed mood for most of the day, for more days than not . . . for at least 2 years. **Note:** In children and adolescents, mood can be irritable and duration must be at least 1 year.

B. Presence, while depressed, of two (or more) of the following:

   (1) poor appetite or overeating
   (2) insomnia or hypersomnia
   (3) low energy or fatigue
   (4) low self-esteem
   (5) poor concentration or difficulty making decisions
   (6) feelings of hopelessness

C. During the 2-year period (1 year for children or adolescents) of the disturbance, the person has never been without the symptoms in Criteria A and B for more than 2 months at a time.

D. No major depressive disorder has been present during the first two years of the disturbance (1 year for children and adolescents).

E. There has never been a manic, mixed, or hypomanic episode, and criteria have never been met for cyclothymic disorder.

F. The disturbance does not occur exclusively during the course of a chronic psychotic disorder.

G. The symptoms are not due to the direct physiological effects of a substance or a general medical condition.

H. The symptoms cause clinically significant distress or impairment.

Source: American Psychiatric Association; *Diagnostic and Statistical Manual of Mental Disorders,* Fourth Edition. Washington, DC, American Psychiatric Association, 1994.

In Review

Depressive disorders, among the most common mental disorders in the world:

- affect women about twice as often as men;
- can occur at any age, but develop most frequently when people are in their twenties; and
- are so often accompanied by anxiety that some experts believe that depression and anxiety are both components of one emotional state called *negative affect.*

The two most common depressive disorders are:

- major depressive disorder, characterized by at least one, but usually several, major depressive episodes, and
- dysthymia, characterized by chronically depressed mood lasting for at least 2 years in adults, 1 year in children;
- often experienced together or in sequence, a condition known as *double depression.*

Bipolar Disorder

People suffering from **bipolar disorder** usually experience periods of depression as well as periods of either extremely elevated mood known as *mania,* or mixed episodes in which mania and depression alternate so rapidly that both are experienced within the same day.

*E*rnest is a 37-year-old married man who has been unemployed for several years. He was brought to the hospital by his wife following a week in which he had been partying every night and shopping every day. Ernest's troubles had begun 7 years earlier when, while working as an insurance adjuster, he suffered symptoms of depression and anxiety for a few months. He blamed these problems on stress, and, within a couple of months, they declined, and Ernest was back to his usual self. A few years later, following thyroid surgery, Ernest experienced some dramatic mood changes. He would go for 2 or 3 weeks feeling so full of energy that he was hyperactive and euphoric; these periods would then be followed by several days through which he slept almost constantly and felt deeply depressed. This pattern of alternating elation and depression repeated itself continuously over the next several years.

During his energetic periods, Ernest was full of self-confidence, but he became short-tempered easily. He often spent large sums of money on unnecessary purchases such as high-priced stereo systems and expensive pedigreed dogs. He has also had several impulsive sexual flings. During his depressed periods, he stayed in bed all day, feeling unmotivated and guilty about his irresponsibility and previous excesses. He frequently refused to eat, bathe, or shave during these period of withdrawal. (Based on Spitzer et al., 1994)

It is unclear whether bipolar disorder is independent of, or a variant of major depressive disorder (Clayton, 1986). The two disorders obviously overlap since the depression experienced in each looks the same, clinically. However, some features of the two are quite different. For example:

- Major depressive disorder is more common in women, while men and women are at about equal risk for bipolar disorder (Hamilton, 1989).
- Bipolar disorder usually starts in the late teens to early twenties, earlier than the age at which major depressive disorder usually first appears.
- Bipolar disorder seems to be more frequent among higher socioeconomic status groups (Weissman et al., 1991).
- Compared with unipolar depression, bipolar disorder is less often triggered or worsened by such psychosocial stressors as the breakup of a relationship.
- Bipolar disorder may have a greater genetic basis than major depressive disorder. Still, relatives of both unipolar and bipolar patients frequently display unipolar depression, suggesting an overlap in genetic risk factors (Goodwin & Jamison, 1990).

Characteristics of Bipolar Disorder

In most cases, women with bipolar disorder experience depression before the first manic phase. Men with bipolar disorder, however, are more likely to have manic episodes first. Approximately 10 to 20 percent of people who have more than one episode of major depressive disorder go on to display bipolar disorder (Post, 1993). Lifetime risk for bipolar disorder in the general population has been estimated at between 0.4 to 1.6 percent, with higher risk associated with a family history of bipolar disorder, early onset of major depression, and a history

of manic symptoms in response to antidepressant medication (Strober et al., 1988). Bipolar disorder is a recurring disorder. The vast majority of patients experience several episodes of depression or mania during their lives, interspersed with periods of relatively normal functioning.

Manic episodes can develop rapidly, in some cases in a matter of hours, but more typically over a few days. (The DSM table on page 296 lists the key criteria in defining a manic episode.) During these episodes, which must last at least 1 week to be officially defined as a manic episode, the person displays an abnormally elevated, expansive, or irritable mood, along with unlimited energy and enthusiasm for unrealistic goals. One woman's housecleaning became so extreme that she began cleaning the outside of her house with a toothbrush; one man shined his car headlights on his home so that he could begin painting it at 2 A.M. Manic persons may try to strike up intense conversations with strangers on the street only to become irritated if they are ignored or rebuffed. Sometimes, in mixed episodes of bipolar disorder, the person feels invincible and omnipotent one minute and in utter despair the next.

It is not unusual for people in a manic episode to go for days with only a few hours of sleep each night. Their speech becomes rapid and "pressured"; they talk on and on as if they cannot stop, seldom taking into account the remarks or needs of the listener. In addition, as in the case of Ernest, their judgment tends to be poor, leading in some cases to wild spending sprees, questionable business ventures, or sexual promiscuity. Many patients experience racing thoughts, and they are so easily distracted that their attention and conversational topics shift rapidly.

In bipolar disorder, as in major depressive disorder, mood disturbance is only part of the clinical picture. During manic episodes, there is an inflated sense of self-esteem known as *grandiosity*. Individuals may feel they possess special powers or are invulnerable to harm. For example, one man who had few technical or mechanical skills became convinced that he could invent a machine to eradicate the earth's trash disposal problems. Exhausted after working day and night, he became more and more agitated until, wildly out of control, he crashed through a plate glass window because he was sure that it could do him no harm.

Grandiosity can take on delusional proportions with religious, political, financial, or sexual themes predominating. The patient working on the trash disposal machine believed he was receiving instructions from God, and another man who talked incessantly about having special powers to solve all the world's problems became convinced that he had far-reaching political connections. Confusion, memory loss, and

---

DSM-IV

Criteria for a Manic Episode

A. A distinct period of abnormally and persistently elevated, expansive, or irritable mood, lasting at least 1 week (or any duration if hospitalization is necessary).

B. During the period of mood disturbance, three (or more) of the following symptoms have persisted (four if the mood is only irritable) and have been present to a significant degree:

  (1) inflated self-esteem or grandiosity
  (2) decreased need for sleep (e.g., feels rested after only 3 hours of sleep)
  (3) more talkative than usual or pressure to keep talking
  (4) flight of ideas or subjective experience that thoughts are racing
  (5) distractibility (i.e., attention too easily drawn to unimportant or irrelevant external stimuli)
  (6) increase in goal-directed activity (either socially, at work or school, or sexually) or psychomotor agitation

  (7) excessive involvement in pleasurable activities that have a high potential for painful consequences (e.g., engaging in unrestrained buying sprees, sexual indiscretions, or foolish business investments)

C. The symptoms do not meet the criteria for a mixed episode.

D. The mood disturbance is sufficiently severe to cause marked impairment in occupational functioning or in usual social activities or relationships with others, or to necessitate hospitalization to prevent harm to self or others, or there are psychotic features.

E. The symptoms are not due to the direct physiological effects of a substance or a general medical condition.

Source: American Psychiatric Association; *Diagnostic and Statistical Manual of Mental Disorders,* Fourth Edition. Washington, DC: American Psychiatric Association 1994.

---

fear of death are also frequently seen in a manic episode. The psychotic features typical of some manic episodes may interfere so seriously with an individual's functioning that psychiatric hospitalization is required. If left untreated, manic episodes typically last from a couple of days to about 3 months (Grof, Angst, & Haines, 1974) and, for any one patient, may occur from 2 to more than 30 times in a lifetime, with a median of 9 (Angst, Felder, & Frey, 1979).

It is important to distinguish mania from two other conditions with which it is sometimes confused: hyperactivity and psychosis. Although mania and hyperactivity share a tendency to excessive behavior, mania involves many additional disturbances in mood and thinking. Mania and psychosis also share some superficial similarities, but **psychosis** refers to a general level of mental disorder that produces severe disorganization in behavior and gross impairment in the ability to comprehend and accurately perceive events. Several disorders, including major depressive disorder, schizophrenia, and bipolar disorder, may reach psychotic proportions.

Classification of Bipolar Disorder

As with depressive disorders, there are variations in how bipolar disorders manifest themselves. Many bipolar patients experience separate episodes of both depression and mania, others have mixed episodes of depression and mania within the same day, and about 10 percent have only recurring episodes of mania (Clayton, 1986; Keller et al., 1993). Figure 9.1 summarizes how the DSM-IV classifies bipolar and other mood disorders.

Bipolar I and Bipolar II. For cases in which there are severe, full-blown manic symptoms, usually accompanied by one or more periods of major depression, the DSM-IV uses the label **bipolar I disorder.** About two thirds of bipolar patients are diagnosed as bipolar I. **Bipolar II** disorder refers to cases in which a major depressive episode has occurred in addition to a period in which the manic episodes are mild, or **hypomanic,** not serious enough to interfere with the person's social functioning, or to require hospitaliza-

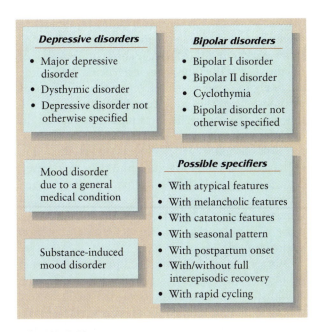

FIGURE 9.1

Overview of DSM-IV Major Mood Disorders
The specifiers do not apply to all of the disorders.

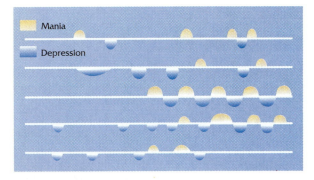

FIGURE 9.2

Typical Clinical Patterns in Mood Disorders
There is a vast amount of variability in the cycles of depression and mania in bipolar disorder. This figure shows cycles for five different patients.

tion, even though they are obvious and sometimes irritating to others.

To identify other key variations in these disorders, clinicians use two specifiers:

1. *with rapid cycling.* This specifier is used when four or more discrete, full-blown mood episodes are experienced within a 1-year period. It is applied to women much more frequently than to men.

2. *with/without full interepisode recovery.* Between depressive or manic phases, many bipolar patients experience periods of relatively normal mood—a full interepisode recovery—during which they function well (see Figure 9.2). However, about one third of these individuals have nearly constant social and emotional problems, including moodiness, impulsivity, and irritability associated with their mood cycles. These problems lead to difficulties in keeping a job and maintaining intimate relationships (Welner, Welner, & Leonard, 1977).

Cyclothymic Disorder. In another form of bipolar disorder, known as **cyclothymic disorder**, moods fluctuate over a long period—2 or more years in adults, 1 year or more in children and adolescents—but neither the depressive nor the manic phase is as severe as in bipolar I or II disorder. Cyclothymic disorder is a parallel term with dysthymic disorder; both suggest less severe but more chronic mood disturbances.

In cyclothymic disorder, periods of elevated mood never reach the state of elation commonly associated with mania, and low moods neither warrant a diagnosis of major depressive disorder nor interfere significantly with daily functioning. Cyclothymic disorder, which occurs in 3 to 4 percent of young adults (Akiskal, 1992) and about 1 percent of all adults (APA, 1994), is characterized by irritability and oscillations between behavioral extremes such as pessimism and optimism, low and high self-esteem, and sleeping much more, then much less, than usual (Akiskal, 1992; Depue et al., 1981). Individuals with cyclothymic disorder are at increased risk for eventually developing a bipolar disorder.

In Review

Bipolar disorder:
- is characterized by periods of depression and mania, often in a recurring, sometimes alternating period, over many years;
- occurs about equally in males and females; and
- appears to have a stronger genetic component than does major depressive disorder.

When bipolar disorder:
- includes periods of mania, it is diagnosed as bipolar I disorder;
- includes hypomanic episodes, it is diagnosed as bipolar II disorder; and when it
- involves swings between mild episodes of depression and mania over a 2-year period, it is diagnosed as cyclothymic disorder.

Biological Causes of Mood Disorders

Mood disorders can be caused by medical conditions such as strokes, vitamin deficiencies, or infections; they can also develop as a consequence of the abuse of drugs or alcohol. In such cases, the particular diagnosis of *mood disorder due to a general medical condition* or *substance-induced mood disorder* would be made, indicating the likely physical cause of the disorder. More often, the roots of mood disorder are less clear. Like most other mental disorders, mood disorders result from the complex interplay of biological (including genetic), psychological, environmental, and sociocultural factors. And, as in most other disorders, the relative contribution of each of these factors is probably slightly different in each case.

Most researchers view mood disorders as stemming at least partly from biological causes. This conclusion is suggested by data from studies of genetic influences on mood disorders, from research on biological processes and symptoms accompanying these disorders, and from the results of drug treatments. Biological findings regarding depression and bipolar disorders show some interesting differences as well as similarities.

Genetic Influences on Mood Disorders

In the 1980s, several scientific teams appeared to have found clear-cut evidence linking bipolar disorder to a specific genetic culprit. The evidence came from examining the unusually high rates of bipolar disorder in certain families. One team, for example, concentrated on a small set of families in a Pennsylvania Amish community of about 12,000 (Egeland et al., 1987; Kolata, 1987). Because the Amish are a close-knit group who tend to marry only within their group and whose religious values strongly discourage the use of alcohol or other addictive substances (the abuse of which often accompanies mood disorders), they provide an ideal population in which to study genetic transmission of a disorder. The researchers discovered that most of the active cases of bipolar disorder in this particular community involved descendants of just a few couples and that many of the ancestors of the bipolar patients had also suffered bipolar symptoms (Egeland et al., 1987). Hoping to pinpoint a specific gene that would account for this finding, these researchers conducted a **linkage analysis.** As described in Chapter 4, this type of study traces the occurrence of a disorder and some *genetic marker* across several generations. This genetic

marker is some characteristic (color blindness, for example) for which the genetics are well understood. If the marker and the disorder show similar patterns of inheritance, then the genes influencing the disorder are likely to occur at a similar location on the same chromosome as the genes controlling the marker. In this case, the researchers claimed that bipolar disorder was linked to two genetic markers on the tip of the 11th chromosome. However, several other studies have consistently failed to find the same pattern (Hodgkinson et al., 1987) or have reported different genetic linkages involving genes on the X chromosome (Baron et al., 1987). As yet, no specific genetic cause of bipolar disorder (or depression) has been demonstrated.

Other studies, however, do support the idea that, whatever their location, genes play a role in creating a predisposition to mood disorders. Recall that one way to explore the contribution of genetic factors to disorders is to contrast the appearance of a disorder in identical *(monozygotic)* twins who have exactly the same genes versus nonidentical *(dizygotic)* twins who share only about 50 percent of their genetic endowment. If a depressive or bipolar disorder appears in both members of monozygotic twin pairs more frequently than in dizygotic pairs, there is evidence of a genetic contribution to the disorder.

Indeed, major depressive disorder is about 4 times more likely to occur in both members of identical twins, compared with nonidentical twins (Bowman & Nurnberger, 1993); if one identical twin displays bipolar disorder, there is about a 79 percent chance that the other twin will also have some kind of mood disorder (not necessarily bipolar disorder, however). These findings have been interpreted to suggest that people can have a genetic predisposition to depression and that overlapping, rather than distinct, genetic factors underlie both unipolar and bipolar mood disorders.

Evidence for a genetic component in mood disorders has also been found in family studies comparing the risk of mood disorders for various relatives of people with such disorders (see Figure 9.3). These studies have consistently shown that close relatives of adults with major depressive disorder are at higher risk for such disorders than are more distant relatives.

Of course, greater environmental similarities in the lives of close relatives might help account for the results of family studies, so researchers have also used adoption studies to determine the relative contributions of genetic versus environmental factors. If mood disorders are determined to any significant degree by genetic factors, depression should be more frequent among the biological relatives of a de-

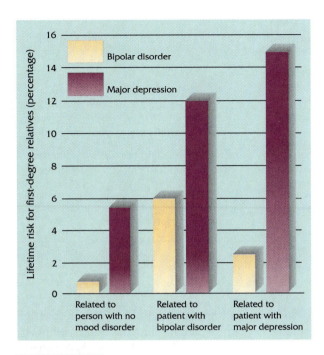

FIGURE 9.3

Mood Disorders Run in Families

First-degree relatives of patients with bipolar disorder have about eight times the normal risk of developing bipolar disorder compared with those related to persons with no mood disorders, and their risk of developing major depression is about twice the normal rate of those related to persons with no major depression. The risk of developing either bipolar disorder or depression among the relatives of patients with major depression is approximately three times the normal rate.

Source: Barondes, 1993.

pressed individual, even if that individual were raised in an adoptive family. Compared with twin and family studies, adoption studies provide less clear-cut evidence for a genetic contribution to mood disorders. One adoption study found that 31 percent of the biological parents of adoptees with bipolar disorder also had a mood disorder, compared with only 2 percent of the parents of adoptees with no psychiatric disturbance (Mendelwicz & Rainer, 1977). However, several other adoption studies have found little evidence for a genetic component in mood disorder (Von Knorring et al., 1983; Wender et al., 1986).

Taken together, twin, adoption, and family studies suggest that genetic factors play a role in mood disorders but that their influence is stronger in bipolar than in unipolar depression, and that there is a much more clearly defined genetic risk for unipolar

depression than for dysthymia. Clearly, however, genetics alone do not tell the whole causal story of mood disorders. For one thing, not everyone who is closely related to a depressed person becomes depressed, and some depressed people are the only people in their families to display the disorder. Furthermore, genetic models do not tell us *how* genetic endowment leads to depression. To understand that link, we must look at how alterations in biological functioning can affect mood.

Neurobiological Influences on Mood Disorders

Mood disorders are accompanied by a number of abnormalities in the central nervous system. These include abnormalities in the body's regulatory functions—especially in the production and utilization of the chemical messengers in the brain known as *neurotransmitters* and in the production and impact of stress hormones. Much research on the relationship between neurotransmitters and depression has focused on dopamine, serotonin, and the *catecholamines,* norepinephrine and epinephrine. These neurotransmitters are thought to regulate several important behavioral systems relevant to mood disorders, including motivation, concentration, and interest in others (Rogeness, Javors, & Pliszka, 1992). Table 9.1 on page 300 summarizes some of these key relationships.

Neurotransmitters and Depression. Theories about the biological processes underlying depression first appeared in the 1950s when physicians noted symptoms of depression in patients being treated for high blood pressure with reserpine—a drug that lowers catecholamine levels. Other research confirmed an association between depression and lowered catecholamines, specifically norepinephrine and its byproducts (Henn, 1986). Further evidence for this theory came from studies showing that medications that *increased* levels of norepinephrine in the brain diminished depressive symptoms. The links between high levels of norepinephrine and mania supported the catecholamine theory, as did research showing that antidepressant medications that increase catecholamine levels trigger mania in some individuals. In brief, according to the original **catecholamine theory,** low levels of norepinephrine lead to depression and high levels of norepinephrine lead to mania.

It turns out, however, that relationships between neurotransmission and depression are more complex than the original catecholamine theory envisioned (Rush, 1993). For example, later research

TABLE 9.1	Possible Characteristics Associated with Neurotransmitter System Activity	
	High	Low
Dopamine	Increased motor activity, aggressive, extroverted, reward driven	Decreased motor activity, nonaggressive, low interest in others, poor motivation
Norepinephrine	Good concentration and selective attention, conditions easily, internalizes values, easily becomes anxious, overly inhibited, introverted	Inattentive, conditions poorly, internalizes poorly, low anxiety, underinhibited
Serotonin	Good impulse control, low aggression	Poor impulse control, high aggression, increased motor activity

Source: From Rogeness et al., 1992; 765–781.

discovered that low levels of norepinephrine are not characteristic of all depressed patients. Furthermore, not all depressed patients improve after taking drugs that increase norepinephrine levels.

Since the catecholamine theory was first proposed, scientists have discovered that many other neurotransmitters and related chemicals may be involved in mood disorders. Furthermore, mood-related neural activity may be affected not only by the amount of a neurotransmitter at a synapse but also by a neurotransmitter's effects on other neurotransmitters and on the number and receptivity of receptor sites. Finally, long-term effects of a change in the amount of a neurotransmitter may differ from the short-term effects, and the amount of chemical available can be affected at several steps in the life cycle of the neurotransmitter. These discoveries help explain why there is no simple, direct correspondence between moods and the amount of any one neurotransmitter in the brain.

Current evidence suggests that dysregulation of serotonin, dopamine, and norepinephrine is also associated with depression. One theory holds that low serotonin levels may allow other neurotransmitters such as dopamine and norepinephrine to swing increasingly out of control, leading to extreme moods. Levels of serotonin are usually assessed by measuring how much of its main metabolite, 5-hydroxyindoleacetic acid (5-HIAA), is present in spinal fluid. Most studies reveal relatively low levels of 5-HIAA in depressed patients (McNeal & Cimbolic,

Connections

What other mental disorders are treated with medications that affect neurotransmitters? See Chapters 7, pp. 231–232, 237, and 10, pp. 366–367, and Chapter 15.

1986). Furthermore, medications such as fluoxetine (sold as Prozac), which inhibits the brain's reuptake of serotonin, and bupropion (sold as Wellbutrin), which selectively blocks reuptake of dopamine, have both proved to be effective antidepressants. These medications do not have the same effect on all patients, however. Some people gain relief only from medications that increase norepinephrine levels while others respond only to medications that influence serotonin.

Such findings have led some researchers to suggest that depressed patients may fall into subtypes according to whether their problems are related mainly to dysregulated norepinephrine, dopamine, or serotonin. Because it is unlikely that depression is related to only one neurotransmitter or another, even in a particular person, interactions among various biochemicals may ultimately prove to be the key causal factor in mood disorders.

Researchers are also using sophisticated technology—particularly magnetic resonance imaging (MRI) and positron emission tomography (PET)—to explore differences in the brain activity of depressed and nondepressed people. They have found, for example, that blood flow appears to be increased in the frontal cortex and decreased in the parietal and posterior temporal lobes of depressed people relative to nondepressed individuals. PET scans of depressed persons have also revealed increased blood flow in the amygdala and thalamus. These structures form brain circuits that are involved in attention, alertness, and emotion and are influenced by the neurotransmitters we have described.

Neurotransmitters and Bipolar Disorder. Imbalances in neurotransmitters have also been associated with

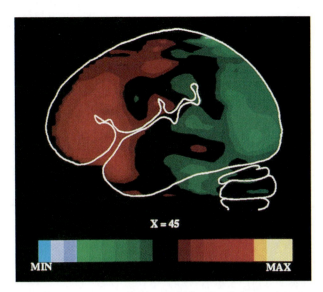

This PET scan is formed by subtracting the composite scans of a group of nondepressed subjects from the composite scans of depressed patients. It shows that depression is associated with substantial blood flow increases in the frontal lobes (red) along with blood flow decreases in the parietal and temporal lobes (green).

bipolar disorder. The catecholamine theory would lead us to expect that norepinephrine levels should be elevated during manic episodes. Consistent with this hypothesis is evidence that lithium, the most effective medication for bipolar disorder, lowers norepinephrine activity in the brain (Bunney & Garland, 1983).

We might expect a similar pattern for serotonin, which tends to be depleted in depression and therefore should be elevated during manic periods. However, as with unipolar depression, matters are not so simple. The principle metabolite of serotonin, 5-HIAA, is sometimes lower in the spinal fluids of bipolar patients than in control subjects, and lithium increases serotonin levels in many patients, leading to the puzzling conclusion that both depression and mania are accompanied by low levels of serotonin.

How can this seeming contradiction be resolved? One possibility is that low levels of serotonin introduce the risk of a mood disorder in general, but that the specific form of the disorder is shaped by either lowered (depression) or heightened (bipolar disorder) norepinephrine activity.

Another possibility is that mood disorders occur when the neurons themselves, rather than the chemicals they use to communicate, are not working properly. We know that lithium is chemically similar to sodium and that sodium ions are critical in controlling how neurons fire their messages back and forth across the nervous system. Some researchers suspect that disruptions in sodium ions may make neurons fire irregularly. If they fire too quickly or easily, manic symptoms would result; if they are too sluggish, depressive symptoms would occur. Some tentative findings support this hypothesis (Hirshfield & Goodwin, 1988), but, like other biological abnormalities, firm evidence that this factor specifically causes mood disorders is lacking.

Depression and the Endocrine System. Depression has also been related to the functioning of the endocrine system. This system includes the hypothalamus, which regulates functions such as sleep and appetite; the pituitary gland, which regulates growth; and the adrenal glands. As described in Chapter 5, a key part of the endocrine system is the hypothalamic-pituitary-adrenal (HPAC) axis, which plays a critical role in the body's response to stress (see Figure 5.3 on page 162). In times of stress, the adrenal glands respond to messages from the hypothalamic-pituitary system by increasing their output of cortisol and adrenaline, hormones that help the body cope with stressors.

Depressed patients often show elevated levels of cortisol, abnormal daily variations in cortisol secretion, and increased levels of cortisol metabolites (Sachar et al., 1973). These data have been used to support the theory that disruptions in the regulation of the hypothalamic-pituitary-adrenal axis contributes to depression. If, as some researchers believe, the dysregulation occurs in the hypothalamus, it would help explain the relationship between catecholamines and depression because the hypothalamus is strongly influenced by catecholamines.

The relationships between the endocrine system and depression have also been explored through *biological challenge tests*. These tests involve giving depressed patients **dexamethasone,** a substance that temporarily suppresses the production of cortisol in healthy adults. Initial dexamethasone challenges showed that, when given a nighttime dose of dexamethasone, depressed patients failed to show normal cortisol suppression the next day. This outcome was interpreted to mean that depressed patients must have an overactive HPAC system. However, further research revealed that similar "nonsuppression" effects occur in nondepressed psychiatric patients as well as in individuals who had suffered broken bones or other physical trauma (Carroll, 1986). Therefore, despite its early promise, the *dexamethasone suppression test* is no longer considered a specific or reliable tool for exploring the neuroendocrinological aspects of depression.

Psychological Causes of Mood Disorders

Psychological and biological theories do not necessarily compete with each other as explanations of mood disorders. In fact, most current psychological theories view biological factors as one of many risks that predispose some people to develop mood disorders. But beyond these risks, what factors influence the development of mood disorders?

Most psychological theories about mood disorders focus on unipolar depression, mainly because—unlike bipolar depression—it has proven treatable via psychological methods. In one way or another, psychological theories assert that depression results from a person's sense of lost control and diminished power (Gilbert, 1992). When people believe they have lost the ability to direct their own lives, they feel hopeless and become demoralized. Eventually, their actual power does diminish, and they give up many of their former productive or enjoyable activities.

Intimate Relationships and Depression

Some psychological theories suggest that problems with intimate relationships can create a predisposition or act as a trigger for depression.

Psychoanalytic Theories. Psychoanalytic theories of depression are based on a classic paper by Sigmund Freud called *Mourning and Melancholia* (1917/1957) and on the ideas of his student Karl Abraham (1911). In Freud's model, persons prone to depres-

sion harbor unresolved conflicts involving relationships with their caregivers in infancy and childhood. Freud said that, in childhood, these people were overindulged, suffered the loss of caregivers, or were disappointed by them in some way. As a result, they became abnormally dependent on others to make them feel adequate, and were prone to anger when their dependency needs were not met. They may also come to feel worthless and have fragile self-esteem.

People with this developmental background are hypersensitive to later losses or disappointments because these later events reactivate the feelings of anger and powerlessness experienced in childhood. After the death of a loved one, for example, depression-prone people will strongly identify with or *introject* the lost person, perhaps as a way of denying the loss. But people who mourn this way may also feel abandoned by and angry at the deceased. Freud said that depression results when this anger is turned inward against the introjected loved one and is coupled with a sense of inadequacy from unfulfilled early needs. Freud also suggested that depression stems in part from a tendency to maintain excessively high standards, or *ego-ideals*. Failure to live up to these standards adds to the person's sense of guilt, failure, and worthlessness (Becker & Schmaling, 1991).

Attachment Theories. Modern psychoanalytic theorists, including those favoring the object-relations models described in Chapter 1, have downplayed the importance of Freud's "anger turned inward" view of depression. Instead, they have emphasized the importance of social and cognitive factors, such as impaired self-esteem, needs for external gratification, and distorted cognitive processing, within a revised psychoanalytic model (Arieti & Bemporad, 1978).

For example, John Bowlby (1980, 1988a, b) proposed a model of psychopathology that draws on biological and social research on animals and humans. Like Freud, Bowlby stressed the importance of early mother–infant attachment. He noted that the nature of this attachment serves as the child's working model of the world and helps the child learn to regulate emotions. As discussed in Chapter 3, disturbance of this attachment can lead to impaired emotional adaptation (Cassidy, 1988; Kobak & Sceery, 1988). Children with secure attachments, said Bowlby, learn how to recognize their own distress and how to seek support from caregivers. Children with various kinds of insecure attachments may inhibit their support-seeking when distressed, either because they have learned that support will not be

Stack Sullivan, laid the groundwork for current interpersonal theories about the origins of depression. These theories emphasize social, cultural, and family causes of psychopathology (Karasu, 1990; Klerman, Weissman, & Rounsaville, 1984) and suggest that unsatisfactory relationships during childhood or adult life place people at increased risk for depression. Intimate interpersonal relationships can protect against depression; however, divorce, loss of friendships, and other deterioration in social support are seen as potential triggers for depression (Karasu, 1990; Monroe & Depue, 1991).

But does loss of social support precede or follow depression? James Coyne's (1976) interactional model of depression suggests that depressed persons may actually alienate those who could provide social support. Although submissiveness and help-seeking initially elicits attention and nurturing from others, the depressed individual's unceasing dependency, negative attitudes, and tendency to ignore or sabotage helpful advice eventually leads to criticism and rejection. In short, the depressed person may provoke exactly the interpersonal encounters that are most threatening and aversive, thus assuring that interpersonal relationships become increasingly unstable and contentious (Coyne & Downey, 1991).

Several experiments have shown that people who interact with a depressed person, either face to face or on the telephone, become more depressed, rejecting, and hostile themselves. Although some researchers have had trouble replicating these findings (King & Heller, 1984) or regard them as trivial because they usually involve interactions with strangers (Doerfler & Chaplin, 1985), some studies have found that the behavior of depressed people adversely affects the mood and behavior of their family members and friends, thereby decreasing the social support they might otherwise provide to the depressed person (e.g., Coyne et al., 1987).

In all likelihood, decreased social support is both a contributor to and a consequence of depression. The lack of a close confidant to whom one can turn in stressful times can cause a person to feel alone and hopeless, feelings that are common experiences in depression. At the same time, as a depressed person withdraws and shuts off contact with friends (as shown in the opening case of Margaret), fewer and fewer people are available to provide the support and understanding that could lessen depressed feelings.

Because baby rhesus monkeys form close attachments to their mothers, they provide an excellent opportunity for researchers to study the consequences of disrupted attachment. Steven Suomi has found, for example, that some baby monkeys suffer an emotional reaction similar to depression after being briefly separated from their mothers.

> **Connections**
>
> What kinds of family relationships might place children at risk for depression? See Chapter 3, pp. 81, 103 for some answers.

forthcoming or because they are fearful of what form the support might take (Kobak & Sceery, 1988; McCauley, Kendall, & Pavlidis, 1995).

Additional support for Bowlby's view comes from the results of animal research. In a series of studies, Stephen Suomi has demonstrated that separating baby rhesus monkeys from their mothers can produce symptoms of depression and anxiety in the infants that mimic the signs of insecure attachment in children (Suomi, 1991). Bowlby suggested that insecure attachments provide a basis for depression because the individual fails to develop successful methods for dealing with the stressors of life and negative emotions such as anxiety.

Interpersonal Theories. Bowlby's ideas, along with earlier contributions by Adolf Meyer and Harry

Learning, Cognition, and Depression

Behavioral and cognitive-behavioral theories seek to explain depression by focusing on current patterns of thinking and reinforcement rather than on early childhood events. Some of these theories begin with the idea that past learning experiences, including early experiences of loss, can sensitize a person to later losses, but they place greater emphasis on how such losses influence a person's current cognitive processes. These theories are most concerned with explaining how depression develops and is maintained by inadequate reinforcement or distorted thinking. Most prominent among these theories are Lewinsohn's (1974) reinforcement model, Rehm's (1977) self-control model, Beck's (1987) cognitive theory, and Pyszczynski and Greenberg's (1987) self-awareness theory.

The Role of Reinforcement. Peter Lewinsohn and his colleagues (1974, 1979, 1984) proposed that depression develops when people stop receiving adequate positive reinforcement from their environments, while also having many "punishing" experiences. Lewinsohn suggests three general reasons for the development of such reinforcement patterns.

1. An individual's environment may actually contain few positive elements and many negative ones; for example, living in an isolated area would be a deprivation for someone who craves many friendships.

2. Even more important, the individual may lack the skills necessary to obtain positive results or cope with negative consequences; a person who desires friendships may be too shy or fearful of criticism to talk to strangers.

3. The individual may interpret events in a way that minimizes the positive and accentuates the negative, as when a person who desires friendships avoids new acquaintances because they all seem to be "snobs."

If some combination of these environmental and personality characteristics triggers a decrease in people's efforts to obtain life's rewards, a downward spiral of depressed behavior and reduced reward may appear. As the depressed behavior interferes with reward-seeking efforts, the likelihood of finding positive reinforcement is further reduced, causing depression to deepen and eventually to eliminate efforts to find rewards (Lewinsohn, Youngren, & Grosscup, 1979).

The Importance of Self-Control. Perception and other cognitive factors play an even larger role in Lynn Rehm's (1977) *self-control* model of depression. According to Rehm, depressed people (1) establish ex-

cessively high standards for evaluating their own performance; (2) concentrate on negative events and on immediate as opposed to delayed consequences of their behavior; (3) provide too little self-reinforcement and too much self-punishment for their behavior; and (4) explain events in their lives in terms consistent with their negative self-images.

Because depressed persons can never live up to their own standards, they can never take pleasure in what they *do* accomplish. Caught in a cycle of constant self-criticism, their performance—and their self-evaluation—continues to decline until they give up on their long-term goals and feel worse and worse about themselves (Rehm, 1984).

Learned Helplessness and Depression. The **learned helplessness model** of depression suggests that if people feel they are unable to control life events—especially stressful events—they learn a sense of helplessness that will eventually lead to depressive symptoms. Learned helplessness theory grew out of research on the response of animals to uncontrollable stressors. In this research, dogs were exposed to episodes of electric shock from which they could not escape. When these animals later experienced shocks from which they *could* escape, many did not even try to do so; they just tolerated the shock, looking helpless and miserable (Seligman & Maier, 1967).

Similar results were observed in humans who had been exposed to sessions of inescapable aversive noise (Hiroto & Seligman, 1975). These and other results led Martin Seligman (1975) to hypothesize that learned helplessness in humans (1) interferes with the ability to learn responses that could solve or help them cope with life's problems; (2) causes them to give up even trying to solve such problems; and (3) eventually so impairs motivation, mood, and self-efficacy as to leave them in a state of depression.

More recent versions of the learned helplessness model of depression have stressed the importance of the individual's interpretation of aversive events in determining whether a sense of helplessness occurs (Abramson, Seligman, & Teasdale, 1978). People at risk for depression are thought to have a characteristic way of interpreting events, known as a **negative attributional style.** They consistently attribute their successes in life to luck or other external, temporary factors beyond their control but attribute their failures to lack of intelligence or to other stable, global, factors within them. When people with a negative attributional style fail to achieve a highly desired goal or to prevent some negative outcome, they may begin to think of themselves as unable to control anything in their lives, now or ever. This pattern of thinking can deflate their self-esteem, mood, and motivation, and lead to depression. When a couple breaks up, for example, a partner who thinks the breakup was simply the result of a bad match is far less likely to be seriously depressed than one who feels responsible for the failure of the relationship and who then wonders if anything in life—relationships, grades, career—will ever turn out right.

People who adopt a negative attributional style may display what Lynn Abramson and her colleagues (1989) have called *hopelessness*. **Hopelessness** occurs when an individual views negative events as inevitable, positive events as unlikely, and sees no prospect for changing this pattern. According to Abramson, three factors contribute to the development of hopelessness. First, there is a tendency to attribute negative outcomes to enduring and general causes ("I'm a *total* loser and always will be."). Second, there is a tendency to focus on the most negative possible consequences of events ("A low score on the GRE means I'll never get into any graduate school."). Third, there is a tendency to draw negative inferences about overall self-worth from negative events. Thus, some people who are laid off at work begin to think of themselves as worthless, even though an entire category of staff was similarly affected, regardless of performance. (Martin Seligman notes that people whose thinking is characterized by optimism tend to explain bad events in terms of external, unstable, and specific causes, thereby making hopelessness and depression less likely.) Abramson's version of helplessness theory provides yet another application of a *diathesis–stress model*. Here, a negative attributional style is the diathesis or predisposition, which leads to depression in the face of significant negative life events (Metalsky et al., 1993).

Beck's Cognitive Triad. One of the most influential theories of depression is Aaron Beck's (1987) *cognitive theory* (see Figure 9.4). According to this theory,

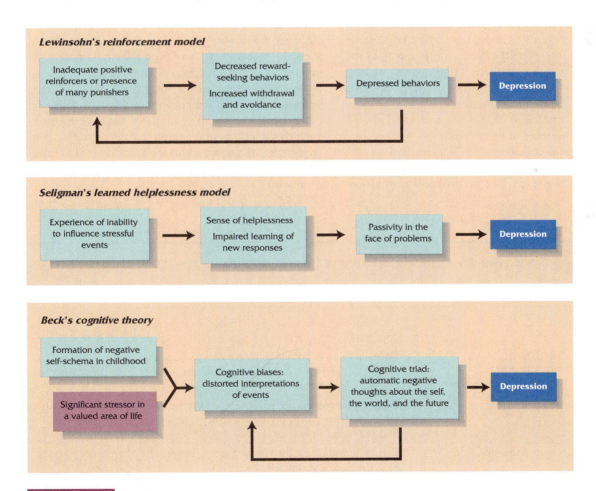

FIGURE 9.4

Psychological Mechanisms Involved in Depression
Peter Lewinsohn, Martin Seligman, and Aaron Beck developed three of the most important psychological theories describing the development of depression. Each theory has received considerable empirical support, and each has spurred important psychotherapeutic approaches to depression.

vulnerability to depression develops during childhood when basic beliefs about the self are formulated. Beck says that basic beliefs about the self—a person's **self-schemas**—such as "I'm likable" or "I'm unlikable" are determined by the quality of the developing child's interactions with the environment.

Negative self-schemas have little influence until they are activated by the threat that accompanies significant life stressors. The salience of a stressful life event depends, in part, on an individual's personality (Hammen et al., 1985). Beck (1983) and others (Blatt & Zuroff, 1992) have hypothesized that vulnerability to depression is greatest in individuals who place great importance on either interpersonal relationships or independence and achievement. When a person suffers a loss in the arena that he or she values most, negative self-schemas become activated. In line with the negative schemas, the person's thinking and interpretation of events becomes distorted, producing what Beck terms "automatic thoughts." Soon, the person begins to see neutral or even pleasant events in a negative light. For example, the clerk interprets the boss's compliments as insincere or a friend's cancellation of dinner plans as a sign of rejection. As a consequence of these cognitive processes, the person begins to experience sadness and other symptoms of depression, including loss of motivation and interest in activities.

Beck and his colleagues (1979) identified several cognitive distortions or "thinking errors" that characterize how depressed people process information

(see Table 9.2). These cognitive distortions make it difficult for depressed people to make realistic judgments about events, often causing them to ignore positive feedback, which in turn perpetuates their depression. This style leads to what Beck and his colleagues (1979) refer to as primitive modes of organizing reality. **Primitive thinking** is characterized by global judgments that are absolute, invariant, and irreversible. Examples of primitive versus more mature thinking are presented in Table 9.3. Ultimately, the thinking of depressed persons is characterized by a **cognitive triad** of automatic, repetitive, and negative thoughts about the self, the world, and the future. Depressed individuals see themselves as inadequate and, therefore, worthless; they perceive the world's demands as overwhelming; and they dread that the future will bring nothing but more of the same.

In general, research supports Beck's ideas that depressed people engage in an excess of negative thinking, are prone to the negative triad of beliefs, and tend to distort even positive feedback as negative. It is less clear, however, whether these dysfunctional cognitions precede or follow the onset of depression (Haaga, Dyck, & Ernst, 1991), so it is not appropriate to conclude that the cognitive dysfunctions Beck describes actually cause depression. Such dysfunctions may simply be the cognitive consequences of being depressed rather than long-term styles of thinking that predispose persons to depression.

TABLE 9.2	Systematic Errors in the Thinking of Depressed Persons
Type of Error	Description
Arbitrary inference	Drawing a specific conclusion in the absence of evidence to support the conclusion or when the evidence is contrary to the conclusion.
Selective abstraction	Focusing on a detail taken out of context, ignoring other, more salient features of the situation, and conceptualizing the whole experience on the basis of this fragment.
Overgeneralization	Drawing a general rule or conclusion on the basis of one or more isolated incidents and applying the concept across the board to related and unrelated situations.
Magnification and minimization	Errors in evaluating the significance or magnitude of an event that are so gross as to constitute a distortion.
Personalization	Relating external events to oneself when there is no basis for making such a connection.
Absolutistic, dichotomous thinking	Placing all experiences in one of two opposite categories, such as flawless or defective, saint or sinner.

Source: Adapted from Beck, Rush, Shaw, & Emery, 1979.

TABLE 9.3	Primitive and Mature Modes of Thought

Primitive Thinking	Mature Thinking
Nondimensional and global	*Multidimensional*
I am fearful.	I am moderately fearful, quite generous, and fairly intelligent.
Absolutistic and moralistic	*Relativistic and nonjudgmental*
I am a despicable coward.	I am more fearful than most people I know.
Invariant	*Variable*
I have been and always will be a coward.	My fears vary from time to time and from situation to situation.
Character diagnosis	*Behavioral diagnosis*
I have a defect in my character.	I avoid situations too much and I have many fears.
Irreversibility	*Reversibility*
Since I am basically weak, there's nothing that can be done about it.	I can learn ways of facing situations and fighting my fears.

Source: Reprinted from Beck et al., 1979.

Self-Awareness. **Self-awareness theory** represents an effort to integrate psychoanalytic, behavioral, and cognitive theories into a comprehensive explanation of unipolar depression (Pyszczynski & Greenberg, 1987). While acknowledging the role of genetic and biological factors in the cause and course of depression, self-awareness theory focuses on two psychological processes: self-focused attention and self-regulation.

Self-focused attention describes the process of private self-reflection and evaluation that people engage in as they work toward their goals. Self-focused persons concentrate most of their attention on internal feelings or sensations rather than on events taking place around them. **Self-regulation** refers to the actions that result from this reflection that are meant to bring people closer to their goals (Carver & Scheier, 1981). For example, a swimmer wants to improve her time in a particular event. Self-focused attention is the process of comparing her best previous times to some goal, perhaps as she thinks about possible reasons why she fell short of her objective. Self-regulation would involve the swimmer's increasing her workout time, getting more coaching, or the like.

When, as is often the case, there are discrepancies between personal goals and the limits imposed by reality, people engage in a period of self-reflection, during which they reassess the goal and either abandon it in favor of a more attainable one or devalue it. Either option allows the person to adapt to the situation. For instance, many students begin a

course with the goal of earning an A, only to realize that the course material and requirements are much more difficult than first anticipated. After a period of reflection, most students realign their goals—often accepting the possibility of a lower grade—or they drop the course and move on.

But what happens to students who perseverate, or remain focused, on their original goal or on their inability to meet it? Self-awareness theory suggests that, when people become trapped in an ongoing and unresolved self-reflective process, negative affect and self-criticism increase. Eventually, a negative cycle develops in which persistent self-focus coupled with negative affect leads to more and more self-criticism and eventually to a depressive self-focusing style.

People who have a depressive self-focusing style tend to display persistent self-focus about negative events—leading to self-blame—while avoiding self-focus after positive ones, thus preventing self-reinforcement. As a result, these people develop a negative self-image, which, in turn, provides a reason for feeling depressed. Although considerable research supports some elements of this intuitively appealing model (Pyszczynski & Greenberg, 1987), its validity as an explanation of depression has not yet been established.

Does Realism Produce Depression? The cognitive models reviewed so far suggest that depression is associated with problems in cognitive processing, particularly with distorted, negatively biased thinking. Other research suggests, however, that distortion or bias may be more characteristic of *non*depressed people.

Shelley Taylor (1994) and her colleagues (Taylor & Brown, 1988) have found that most nondepressed people have views of themselves, their accomplishments, and their futures that are slightly unrealistic. They also tend to selectively remember the positive aspects of their lives, a style similar to what Seligman called "optimism." This tendency to see themselves and the future in a positive, if slightly illusory, light appears to promote feelings of happiness (Gibbons, 1986; Taylor & Brown, 1988), adaptive social functioning (Diener, 1984), the capacity for productive work (Isen, Daubman, & Nowicki, 1987), and a measure of protection from the stress of life (Taylor & Brown, 1988). Those with depressive tendencies, however, appear to be more accurate—often relentlessly so—in appraising their abilities, accomplishments, and prospects.

Taylor believes that depression may result from perceiving life without the protective benefits of rose-colored glasses. Thus, depressed people's negative cognitive processes may simply reflect an unforgivingly accurate pattern of self-judgment. For this reason, some investigators refer to depressed people as "sadder but wiser" (Alloy & Abramson, 1979; 1988). This view is controversial, however, and others still question whether positive illusions really do foster better mental health (Colvin & Block, 1994).

Stressors as Triggers of Depression

As noted, many theorists view depression from a diathesis–stress perspective in which depressive symptoms do not emerge until a diathesis such as genetic risk or disturbances in early parent–child relationships combines with stressful events or harmful environments. Although most individuals exposed to severe stressors do not become depressed, the onset and, especially, the relapse of depression is often associated with a significant negative life event (Monroe & Depue, 1991).

Differences in the prevalence of depression across cultures and generations underscores the potentially important role of the environment. For example, the cohort of people born since 1940 have a higher lifetime prevalence of mood disorders and suicide than those born in earlier years. Furthermore, as Figure 9.5 reveals, the onset

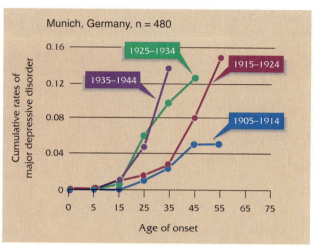

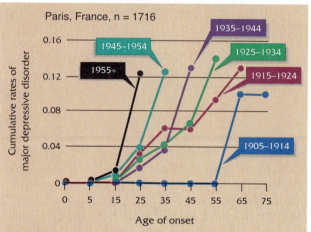

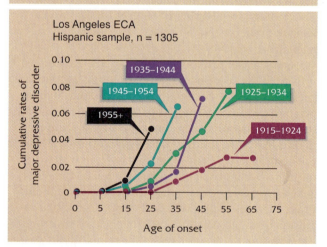

FIGURE 9.5

Age Changes in Depression

According to one large-scale, cross-cultural study, more people are becoming depressed and are experiencing their first major depressive episodes at increasingly earlier ages. This second trend holds true for all the countries shown.

of mood disorders is occurring at younger ages than previously documented. These changes have occurred over too brief a time span to be explained by genetic factors. Instead, they are thought to reflect the growing influence of social stressors such as disintegration of the family, unemployment, increased mobility, rising violence, and the resulting disillusionment found particularly in urban populations (Gershon et al., 1987).

But researchers are still not sure whether stressors cause depression or vice versa; being depressed is itself stressful and can have a negative impact on a person's interactions with other people. And, even when stressors do trigger depression, is it their type, timing, frequency, or severity that is most responsible? Investigators would also like to know whether stressful events increase the risk of mental or physical health problems in general or whether specific stressors are related to the development of particular disorders such as depression.

In a classic study of social environment and depression, George Brown and Tirril Harris (1978) compared English women being treated in a psychiatric clinic for depression with a control group of nondepressed women from similar backgrounds. They found that depression was more likely, given certain vulnerability factors and specific stressors or "provoking agents." These vulnerability factors included lack of a close confidant or friend, death of mother before one is age 11, having four or more children under the age of 14 living at home, and lack of employment outside of the home. Recent loss of a significant person or events that posed a serious threat of loss were the most common provoking factors, while chronic problems, such as longstanding poverty, were factors in some cases. The greater the number of stressors experienced by a woman in the previous several months, the greater her chances of being depressed. Subsequent research has consistently documented that onset or relapse of depression is more likely following a major loss, either of a significant relationship through death or divorce or loss of self-worth related to unemployment or the like (Brown, Adler, & Bifulco, 1988; Monroe & Depue, 1991).

Stressful environments also influence the course of a mood disorder (Davila et al., 1995). For example, depressed individuals who live with highly critical, nonsupportive families with poor problem-solving skills are more likely to suffer recurrent episodes of depression and be less able to get back to a productive life than those whose families have a more positive emotional climate (Hooley, 1987; Miller et al., 1992). The triggering function of significant stressful events is most obvious for initial episodes of depression; subsequent episodes may arise following less severe events (Ezquiaga, Gutierrez, & Lopez, 1987). Perhaps after repeated depressions, the individual becomes so vulnerable that even minor life events can lead to a relapse.

Major life stressors, especially in the form of loss, appear to be one factor that can trigger depressive reactions. They do not always do so, however. Why do some people become depressed after a trauma while others do not? In the previously mentioned study, Brown and Harris (1978) found that certain aspects of the women's current social situations—especially a lack of social support—increased the risk of depression following a loss. In addition to the social context, the individual's personality also makes a difference. For example, a divorce might be a devastating blow for one person but a welcomed end to a destructive relationship for another. Being fired from a job may seem like the end of the world to one individual but may be seen as a chance for a new start by a different person.

Coping Style, Personality, and Depression

The way people define and cope with stressors also appears to be important in determining the severity and length of a depressive episode (Nolen-Hoeksema, Morrow, & Fredrickson, 1993). For example, using *distraction* as a way of coping with stressful events appears to soften their impact and helps ameliorate depression. Distracting responses, such as doing something fun with a friend, may be beneficial because they allow people to temporarily get their minds off their depression while also providing an opportunity for positive feedback from others. However, *ruminative* responses tend to amplify and prolong periods of depression as the individual obsesses about the causes, symptoms, or consequences of depression (Nolen-Hoeksema, Morrow, & Fredrickson, 1993). These responses include endlessly thinking, writing, or talking about the depression in an effort to understand it. As suggested by Pyzsczynski and Greenberg's (1987) self-awareness model, excessive ruminative responses may keep the individual so obsessed with depression as to alienate those who

Connections

Does a negative emotional climate in families contribute to relapses of other types of mental disorders? For more on this subject, see Chapter 10, pp. 362–364.

might provide social support and, at the same time, may preclude more rewarding social interactions.

Susan Nolen-Hoeksema (1987) has proposed that men and women differ in their characteristic responses to stressors and that these differences may explain why women are more prone to depression. She notes also that, in many cultures, socialization throughout childhood teaches boys to emphasize action rather than feelings and teaches girls to be introspective and passive. Consequently, when faced with stressors, men are more likely than women to employ beneficial distracting strategies while women fall into ruminative patterns that accentuate personal responsibility for the problems at hand and therefore facilitate depression. Indeed, research indicates that, in both men and women, learning to decrease ruminative responses and increase distracting strategies leads to improvement in depressed mood (Morrow & Nolen-Hoeksema, 1990; Nolen-Hoeksema et al., 1993).

Does the relationship between coping styles and depression suggest that depression may be related to other, more general aspects of personality? Some researchers say yes and point to two clusters of personality characteristics that may serve as psychological predispositions for depression (Beck, 1983; Blatt, 1982, 1995), as Figure 9.6 shows. The first, known as the **sociotropic (dependent) personality,** includes heightened sensitivity to isolation, fear of abandonment, and a strong need for love from others. The second, called the **autonomy-oriented (achievement) personality** includes perfectionism, guilt over failure and shortcomings, frequent self-criticism, and a feeling of not living up to standards.

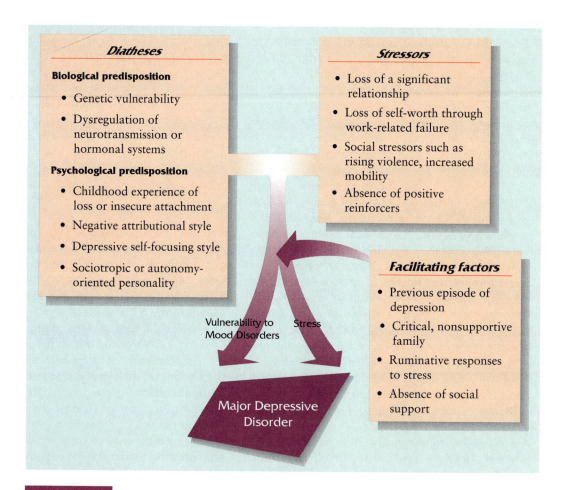

FIGURE 9.6

A Diathesis–Stress Perspective on Depression
There are a multitude of theories about major depressive disorder, and a multitude of factors that might be involved in its etiology. Perhaps there are also many ways in which the disorder develops. Shown here are the major factors we have discussed that seem to play a role.

Are these, then, depressive personalities? Perhaps, but it seems more likely that certain personality characteristics simply make people especially sensitive to certain types of stressors. If those particular stressors appear, the person with these characteristics is more likely to become depressed than someone with different characteristics (Hammen, 1992; Nietzel & Harris, 1990). Thus, dependent people may be more likely to be distressed over setbacks in their personal relationships, while achievement-oriented people might be more shaken and demoralized by work-related failures or a loss of status. Or, in Beck's terms, a loss in the most-valued domains triggers negative self-schemas. Thus, merely counting up the number of stressful events that a given person has experienced will not allow as accurate a prediction of subsequent mood disorders as understanding the unique meaning that a stressful event holds for that person. The role of personality as a causal factor in depression is still unclear, but the question of predisposing personality factors will surely be the focus of future research.

Psychological Theories of Bipolar Disorder

Because biological causes appear to play a larger role in bipolar disorder than in unipolar depression, psychological and environmental factors have not been emphasized as explanations of bipolar disorder. One early psychoanalytic theory suggested that bipolar disorder represented a flight from depressed feelings (Freeman, 1971). According to this view, manic behavior serves as a kind of defense mechanism that helps a person escape or avoid pain or loss. While this account fits with the commonsense notion that one way to cheer yourself up is to go on a spending spree or vigorously pursue a distracting activity, it has failed to win any scientific support. At this point, there is little empirical evidence that psychological factors play a major role in causing bipolar disorder.

Psychological or social factors have some effect on the *course* of bipolar disorder, although their roles appear less consistent and central than in unipolar depression (Monroe & Depue, 1991). Stressful events, especially those that disrupt social schedules or upset biological rhythms, exert some not yet fully understood influence on the course of bipolar disorders (Johnson & Roberts, 1995). For example, the birth of a child, frequent changes in work schedules, or hectic jet travel have all been suggested as particularly disruptive of the social and biological schedules that are usually affected in bipolar disorder. Stressful events seem to be more important in affecting initial rather than later episodes of bipolar disorder (Post, 1992), perhaps because, once the disorder has begun, each repeated episode itself weakens the person and makes later episodes more likely. Robert Post (1992) has argued that repeated or chronic stressors ultimately lead to biological changes that cause neurotransmitter systems to become increasingly sensitive to stressors. As a result of this process, the brain becomes more easily affected by stressors until eventually even minor events can trigger the mood swings seen in bipolar disorder.

In Review

Mood disorders are influenced by several psychological factors, including:

- early experiences with loss or disappointment that make a person unusually sensitive to later adversities;
- insecure attachments that leave a child less able to feel worthwhile, regulate emotions, and be satisfied in intimate relationships;
- a relative lack of positive reinforcement and an excess of punishment;
- a perceived lack of control over important events, leading to feelings of helplessness;
- distorted thinking in which a person exaggerates negative aspects about the self, the world, and the future and ignores or minimizes positive information; and
- a tendency to perseverate about the self, particularly about faults or failures.

Mood disorders also appear to occur more frequently following exposure to major stressful events, especially if these events:

- occur to someone lacking in social support;
- involve some kind of loss; and
- are matched to certain personality styles that make the person sensitive to a particular kind of stressor.

Treatment of Mood Disorders

During the last decade, clinicians have made significant progress in developing both biological and psychological treatments for mood disorders. Much of this progress has stemmed from research sponsored by the U.S. National Institute of Mental Health, which has compared the effectiveness of medication, psychotherapy, and combinations of the two for large numbers of depressed patients. Here, we consider

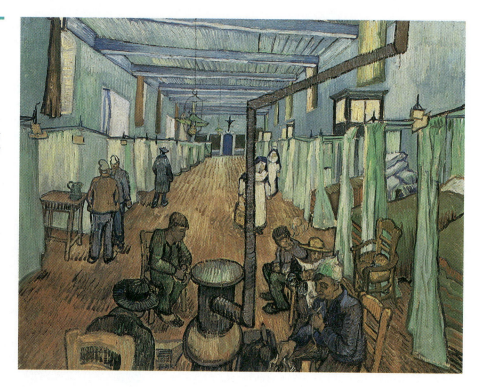

Vincent Van Gogh was hospitalized several times in his life for mental disorders, including depression. This famous painting by Van Gogh depicts a ward for the mentally ill in the late nineteenth century. Shortly before dying from a self-inflicted gunshot wound, Van Gogh told his brother why he no longer desired to live: "The sorrow will last for ever."

the results of some of this work, along with similar research on the treatment of bipolar disorder.

Drug Treatments for Depressive Disorders

Drugs have been used to treat depressive disorders for over three decades, with considerable effectiveness. Various studies suggest that 60 to 70 percent of depressed adults are helped by *antidepressant* medications (Andreasen & Black, 1991; Richelson, 1993). Typically, antidepressants bring about various therapeutic effects, including brightened mood, improved sleep, and increased energy. However, as indicated in Chapter 3, antidepressants tend not to be as effective for younger people as for adults. Studies of preadolescent children suggest that drug effects are not superior to those of placebo treatment, and little support exists for the efficacy of antidepressant medications for adolescents (Ambrosini et al., 1993).

The net effect of antidepressant drug action is to alter activity in the brain cells that use norepinephrine, serotonin, and other mood-related neurotransmitters. The best-known antidepressants fall into three categories.

- **Monoamine oxidase (MAO) inhibitors,** such as phenelzine, sold as Nardil; and tranylcypromine, sold as Parnate. MAO inhibitors block monoamine oxi-

dase, an enzyme that breaks down neurotransmitters such as serotonin and norepinephrine, resulting in greater availability of these neurotransmitters at neural synapses.

- **Tricyclics,** such as imipramine, sold as Tofranil; amitriptyline, sold as Elavil; or desipramine, sold as Norpramin also increase levels of neurotransmitters such as norepinephrine and serotonin, but they do so by blocking the reuptake of these neurotransmitters.

- **Selective serotonin reuptake inhibitors (SSRIs)** include fluoxetine, sold as Prozac; sertraline, sold as Zoloft, and paroxetine, sold as Paxil. These drugs slow the reabsorption of serotonin by the neurons that secrete it, thus keeping more of it in the synapse longer.

Another antidepressant, bupropion, sold as Wellbutrin, acts by blocking reuptake of dopamine.

Although the chemical action of many antidepressants is known, it is still unclear how they actually alter depressive symptoms. For example, antidepressants have an immediate impact on neurotransmitter levels, but alleviation of depressive symptoms usually does not appear until after at least 2 weeks of treatment, and, in some cases, it may take up to 8 weeks before improvements are noted. Scientists speculate that this delay may reflect the time it takes for neuronal receptors to adapt to changes in neurotransmitter levels. In other words, it may be a change in how neurotransmitters are used by brain cells, not simply the levels of available neurotransmitters, that is critical to symptom reduction.

The major types of antidepressants are all about equally effective so the choice of which one to prescribe depends on a variety of other considerations. As in all drug treatments, antidepressants have a variety of side effects, several of which are undesirable. For example, the tricyclics have cardiac side effects and therefore are not appropriate for patients with a history of cardiovascular disease. Tricyclics can also trigger manic episodes and therefore must be used cautiously in individuals with a family history of bipolar disorder or hypomanic episodes (Geller, Fox, & Fletcher, 1993; Prien & Potter, 1993). Some antidepressants, such as trazodone (sold as Desyrel) are sedating; trazodone might therefore be the medication of choice for agitated depression but inappropriate for a patient who already suffers from psychomotor retardation and sleepiness.

A major difficulty with some MAO inhibitors is that they create high blood pressure if combined with certain foods. Patients taking these drugs must follow a special diet and avoid many over-the-counter medications. Such precautions limit the usefulness of MAO inhibitors, especially with adolescents who are unlikely to adhere to dietary restrictions. Some of the newer antidepressants, such as Prozac, have been touted as creating fewer, less severe, side effects. However, as the Controversy section on page 314 discusses, the issue of side effects remains hotly debated. We will take a closer look at the side effects of these and other drugs in Chapter 15.

Ideally, drug treatment of depressive disorders begins with the gradual introduction of medication followed by a period of active treatment lasting for 4 to 6 months after depressive symptoms have been alleviated (Andreasen & Black, 1991). At that time the medication may be gradually reduced; sudden withdrawal can cause several unpleasant side effects (Prien & Potter, 1993). Increasingly, however, antidepressants are being used *prophylactically,* meaning that they are prescribed for periods as long as several years to prevent relapses of depression.

Drug Treatments for Bipolar Disorder

Because an acute manic episode can be so severe, hospitalization and drugs are often required to bring the symptoms under control. Since the 1970s, the primary drug treatment for acute manic episodes has been **lithium carbonate,** commonly known as lithium. Lithium's mechanism of action is not yet known, but the drug's effects usually begin 5 to 7 days after treatment commences. During this time, extremely agitated patients are sometimes also given antipsychotic or anticonvulsant drugs for sedation.

Patients receiving lithium must be monitored closely for two reasons. First, lithium can be toxic, particularly to the kidneys and thyroid. Therefore, lithium blood levels must be watched closely to guard against organ damage. Second, patients must be followed to determine whether, after a manic episode "breaks," a depressive episode is emerging. If so, antidepressant medication may also be started.

Lithium treatment often requires the patient to take maintenance dosages of the drug for years, sometimes for life. However, either as a result of side effects—such as tremors or weight gain—or feelings of invulnerability that occur during manic episodes, many bipolar patients do not comply with long-term lithium therapy regimens and thus experience a relapse of manic episodes (Clayton, 1986).

The overall effectiveness of lithium is a bit unclear. Initial studies suggested that two thirds to three quarters of patients receiving lithium improved and that patients who took maintenance doses of the drug were much less likely to relapse than patients not receiving lithium (Goodwin & Jamison, 1990; Suppes et al., 1991). More recent studies, however, have not been quite as encouraging, suggesting that as many as half of the patients taking lithium suffer relapses (Smith & Winokur, 1991). Alternative medications are therefore being used.

Recent years have seen increased use of the anticonvulsant *carbamazepine* to treat mania because it has fewer side effects and can be used for long periods with patients who respond poorly to lithium (Post, 1990, 1993). *Valproate,* another anticonvulsant, also acts rapidly to reduce manic symptoms and is effective for some patients—especially those with prominent depressive features—who have not been helped by lithium or carbamazepine (Pope et al., 1991).

Other Biological Treatments for Mood Disorders

More than 60 years ago, clinicians noted the remission of psychotic and depressive symptoms in some patients who experienced spontaneous seizures. On the assumption that the convulsions were responsible for the improvement, **electroconvulsive therapy (ECT)** was developed to purposely induce brief seizures in severely disturbed patients by passing an electric current through their brains.

The early ECT treatments were frightening procedures associated with many negative side effects

Ever since it was introduced in the late 1980s, Prozac has been at the center of a storm of controversy. Heralded by some as a wonder drug, condemned by others as a dangerous substance, Prozac had, by the mid-1990s, been prescribed to over 12 million people. Headlined in major news publications and the topic of countless TV talk shows, the debate over Prozac rages on.

Advocates for Prozac, including Peter Kramer, the psychiatrist whose book *Listening to Prozac* (1993) popularized the drug for millions of readers, claim that it relieves depression and is also safer than other antidepressants. More important, Prozac is credited with bringing about many other positive changes. According to a large number of case reports, Prozac can improve basic personality features. It helps shy introverts become assertive extroverts; it enables people with low self-esteem to become self-assured; it converts pessimists into optimists. All this, and it can often help people lose weight. No wonder Prozac is known in some circles as the drug that can help people become "better than well."

Critics of Prozac blame it for a number of problems, including what they claim is a heightened risk for suicide and violent behavior among people taking the drug. They point to incidents such as the one on the morning of September 14, 1989, when Joseph Wesbecker walked into the Standard Gravure printing plant in Louisville, Kentucky, and opened fire on his coworkers with an AK-47 assault rifle. By the end of his rampage,

Wesbecker had killed eight people and wounded twelve more before turning the gun on himself and taking his own life. When it was subsequently discovered that Wesbecker, who had a long history of depression, assaults, and emotional upheavals, had begun taking Prozac about 1 month before the shootings, families of the victims filed a lawsuit against Eli Lilly and Co., the manufacturer of Prozac. This lawsuit, the first of hundreds like it across the nation, claimed that Prozac causes previously nondangerous people to turn violent. The Westbecker case was resolved late in 1994 when a Kentucky jury decided that Prozac was not responsible for his killing spree. Still, the risk of possible dangerous side effects, plus the ethical concerns about a drug that offers the false promise of making over personalities, is the topic of *Talking Back to Prozac* (Breggin, 1994), a book intended to refute Kramer's book.

What evidence is there for the pro- and anti-Prozac positions? First, thoughts about suicide do sometimes increase in a small number of patients who are treated with antidepressant medication. After individuals take their medicine and begin to feel less depressed, their energy level rises, thereby increasing, at least temporarily, their risk for harming themselves. However, according to well-controlled studies (see Mann & Kapur, 1991), Prozac does not appear to be associated with any greater risk of suicide or suicidal thinking than other antidepressants. Second, in clinical trials, Prozac has consistently been shown

to be effective in reducing symptoms of depression, in some studies with fewer side effects than other antidepressants; the most commonly reported side effects of Prozac have been nervousness, insomnia, and nausea. Third, Prozac *increases* the availability of serotonin at the synapse, but aggressive behavior has reliably been linked to *reduced* levels of serotonin. Biochemically, Prozac should reduce aggression, not increase it, although the possibility that a few people might have a peculiar paradoxical reaction to Prozac cannot be ruled out.

In our view, both sides in this controversy have often relied on dramatic anecdotes and uncontrolled case histories rather than well-designed scientific studies to support their arguments. As a result, both proponents and opponents of Prozac have exaggerated the powers of the drug, and the public has been too influenced by the latest incident reported in the media.

Thinking Critically

- What other factors besides medication might account for suicides by depressed patients?

- How often does any adverse effect of a medication need to occur before it is considered a serious side effect? Is once enough, or should we require several examples before we decide that the risks of the drug outweigh its advantages?

(Winokur, 1986), including broken bones due to muscle stiffening during the ECT-induced seizures, marked memory loss, periods of disorientation, and even some deaths. Consequently, throughout the 1960s and 1970s, clinicians and hospitals began to limit or abandon the use of ECT.

To minimize problematic side effects, ECT is now administered only on one side of the head (a procedure known as *unilateral ECT*) and is accompanied by medication to control heart rate and relax muscles. Oxygen is also administered, because most patients stop breathing on their own during the seizure activity (Avery, 1993; Winokur, 1986). These precautions have eliminated ECT's most serious long-term side effects, although temporary memory loss and disorientation are still common. (See Chapter 15 for more on ECT.)

The use of ECT persists in spite of these difficulties because physicians know it is effective, especially for patients whose depression is severe or who do not respond to antidepressant medication. Improvement rates of 50 to 90 percent are reported for these patients when treated with ECT (Avery, 1993; Homan et al., 1982; Nobler et al., 1994). However, relapse remains a problem. Without continuing treatment of some sort, over half of the patients who initially respond well to ECT will suffer a recurrence of mood disorder (Depression Guidelines Panel, 1993). ECT is also an effective treatment for acute mania, but it is usually prescribed only for patients who should not take or do not respond to lithium or other antimanic drugs (Post, 1993).

It is still not clear just why ECT works, although it appears that the seizure, not the shock itself, is somehow responsible and that ECT affects the activity of neurotransmitters. The uncertainty surrounding its mechanism of action, its inherently frightening nature, and its negative side effects makes ECT one of the most controversial treatments currently in use for mood disorders.

Finally, light therapy is being used to treat depressive disorders that have a seasonal pattern. Individuals with these disorders appear to develop a phase delay in their circadian rhythms due to reductions in the amount of early morning light they experience (Avery et al., 1990; Lewy et al., 1987). **Light therapy,** which consists of exposing patients to a bright light source during the early morning hours, has been associated with remission of the symptoms of seasonal pattern depression; it also appears to correct phase delays in functions such as body temperature and hormone output (Lewy, 1993; Sack et al., 1990). Recent research suggests that use of a light source that provides gradually increasing light exposure or "dawn simulation" for the 2 hours before normal wakening is an especially effective treatment (Avery et al., 1994).

Psychotherapy for Mood Disorders

Although drugs are an important aspect of treatment for mood disorders, especially for severe depression and bipolar disorder, medication alone does not address the social, emotional, or personality factors that may also underlie patients' problems. Therefore, psychotherapy that emphasizes psychodynamic, behavioral, cognitive, or interpersonal approaches are also used to treat adults with mood disorders. Most psychotherapies focus on depressive disorders, but several have been applied to the depressive aspects of bipolar disorder as well. When used alone or in conjunction with drug treatments, these therapies have been found to be of significant benefit to adults (Antonuccio, Danton, & DeNelsky, 1995; Regier et al., 1988).

Psychotherapies for depressed children and adolescents are in a more formative stage; most of them focus on school-based, group interventions. As noted in Chapter 3, a variety of behavioral and cognitive-behavioral interventions including problem-solving, social-skills training, and cognitive restructuring (Butler et al., 1980); relaxation and cognitive-behavioral restructuring (Kahn et al., 1990; Reynolds & Coats, 1986); and self-monitoring skills (Stark, Reynolds, & Kaslow, 1987) have provided significant help to children with mild depression. However, more research is needed on the efficacy of these treatments in clinical settings with children who have more severe depression. One preliminary study of this kind (Fine et al., 1991) compared a social-skills training group intervention with a therapeutic support group. Results indicated greater initial improvement for the support-group youth but equal gains for both groups after 9 months. In another study using clinical patients, Peter Lewinsohn and colleagues (Lewinsohn et al., 1990) compared their Coping with Depression course, modified for adolescents (CDCA), to a no-treatment control group. The CDCA clients showed significant improvement compared with the controls, and these benefits were maintained up to 2 years after treatment.

Psychodynamic Approaches. Traditionally, psychodynamic therapies have attempted to alter the patient's personality structure—usually by exposing and working through various unconscious conflicts—rather than to treat a specific problem such as depression. Contemporary versions of psychodynamic treatment seek to address depression specifically and more directly. Examples of these therapies are *time-limited dynamic psychotherapy* (Strupp & Binder, 1984), *short-term dynamic psychotherapy* (Davanloo, 1994), and *supportive-expressive therapy* (Luborsky, 1984). Compared with traditional psychodynamic therapies, these methods take less time and require the therapist to play a more active role, focusing more on specific depression-related matters such as loss of self-esteem and current symptoms. Although widely used, there is still insufficient research on the efficacy of these newer, brief, psychodynamic therapies (Hollon, 1993). Accordingly, it is difficult at present to draw firm conclusions about their value in the treatment of mood disorders.

Depressed people tend to engage in negative, self-critical thinking. They are prone to blame themselves for every mistake, setback, or disappointment. Cognitive therapists try to help depressed clients evaluate their behavior more realistically.

Behavioral Approaches. As might be expected from the discussion of theories of depression, behavior therapists seek to reduce clients' depressive symptoms by helping them increase or gain access to positive events in their lives. Sometimes, this means teaching or enhancing the skills clients need to experience support and other rewards in social situations. Training in relaxation and assertiveness may be included as well. The most prominent behavioral therapies are Lewinsohn's *Coping with Depression* course (Lewinsohn & Clarke, 1984) and Lynn Rehm's (1977) *self-management* program. Although these approaches have been empirically evaluated more often than psychodynamic approaches have been, there is still not enough research on their value to draw final conclusions regarding their efficacy for either depressive or bipolar disorder (Hollon, 1993).

Cognitive-Behavioral Therapy. Cognitive-behavioral treatments for depression usually include educational, behavioral, and cognitive techniques. One of the most prominent of these therapies is a short-term intervention based on Beck's (1987) cognitive model of depression.

In this cognitive therapy, the client and therapist work together as collaborators to identify and change the client's maladaptive thinking patterns. The therapist first introduces the cognitive-behavioral model of depression, explaining that how people interpret events influences how they feel. Next the therapist helps the client keep track of, or monitor, daily activities and mood to clarify which thoughts and activities are associated with changes in mood. Clients learn, for example, that, even when they are depressed, their moods fluctuate during the course of the day. They may also begin to see links between brighter moods and certain activities, companions, or thoughts.

Finally, clients are helped to identify and test the validity of their "automatic thoughts" and underlying assumptions about the world. Since these thoughts and assumptions guide how clients interpret their experiences, this phase of treatment usually challenges clients' personal belief systems, as illustrated by the case of Ramon.

Ramon is a 30-year-old Cuban American who has suffered periods of depression over the last 5 years. The youngest of four children in his family, Ramon has always felt as if he has lived in the shadows of his older brothers, each of whom has his own family and has already been successful in the business world. Ramon believes he has been a disappointment to his parents, who had hoped he would attend medical school. Ramon himself wonders whether he settled for too little when he decided not to go to college and accepted a job as an insurance salesman in Miami. In cognitive therapy, Ramon has begun to learn that his depressive episodes often seem to follow events in which he feels like a failure. As an example, the therapist asked Ramon to concentrate on a recent incident in which a coworker wordlessly walked by Ramon in the hallway. Because of Ramon's underlying sense of inferiority, he automatically assumed that the coworker was ignoring him, thus adding to his feelings of inferiority and insecurity. However, the therapist asked Ramon to think of other explanations for his coworker's behavior, and she further asked him to test these explanations by talking to the coworker about the event and by watching the interactions of other coworkers. The goal was to help Ramon recognize that the coworker could have been preoccupied, might not have seen him, or was perhaps too ill to be sociable. The therapist also helped Ramon see that, had he automatically assumed one of these explanations, he would have experienced different, nondepressed feelings.

Most studies evaluating cognitive therapy have found it to be an effective treatment approach for depression, and some preliminary findings suggest that it may also reduce the risk of relapse (Hollon, 1993; Hollon, Shelton, & Loosen, 1991). In almost all reports, the effects of cognitive therapy have equalled or exceeded those of behavioral treatments (Hollon, Shelton, & Davis, 1993). In addition, several studies suggest that, although both medication and cognitive therapy are effective treatments for depression, cognitive therapy may have a slight advantage over medication in terms of long-term benefits (Antonuccio et al., 1995).

Interpersonal Therapy. The interpersonal approach to treating mood disorders focuses on the client's current social support system (Klerman et al., 1984). In the case of a depressive disorder, the therapist begins by asking the client to view depression as an illness so as to minimize any sense of guilt over being depressed. Then, attention is directed to one of four interpersonal problems presumed to be central to depression: (1) severe or prolonged grief reactions; (2) role conflicts in interpersonal relationships (as when a woman tries to excel in occupational, marital, and parental roles, all at the same time); (3) role transitions (such as becoming a widow or widower); and (4) deficits in interpersonal skills (such as extreme shyness).

The specific treatment strategies depend on which interpersonal problem is most important. For instance, if the core problem is a role transition, attention might center on exploring the losses associated with the change and on preparing for the new role. Overall, the goal is to reduce dependency and increase self-esteem by helping patients improve their relationships in family and work environments (Karasu, 1990).

The efficacy of interpersonal therapy has been tested in a number of studies that compared it with antidepressant medications, placebo medication, or cognitive therapy. Based on initial studies, interpersonal therapy appears to be as effective as cognitive therapy and antidepressant medications and may also have a longer-term, positive impact on patients' social adjustment (Hollon, 1993).

The largest and best-controlled comparison of alternative treatments for depression was the National Institute of Mental Health's Treatment of Depression Collaborative Research study, which compared the effects of the antidepressant imipramine, placebo medication, cognitive therapy, and interpersonal psychotherapy (Elkin, 1994; Elkin et al., 1989; see also Klein, 1990). In this study, conducted at three clinical sites in the United States, 250 adults who had been diagnosed with depression were randomly assigned to one of the four treatments. An enormous amount of data were collected on patients' progress, and it is therefore difficult to summarize the results in one or two statements. However, among the most important findings was that most patients tended to improve, regardless of whether they received the antidepressant drug, cognitive therapy, or interpersonal therapy. In addition, antidepressants were superior to cognitive therapy for severely depressed patients (Elkin et al., 1995). The long-term effectiveness of the treatments was less impressive, but there were tendencies for the psychotherapies to slightly outperform imipramine. At an 18-month follow-up, only 30 percent of the original cognitive therapy clients, 26 percent of the interpersonal therapy clients, 19 percent of the antidepressant drug clients, and 20 percent of the placebo clients had recovered and not suffered any relapses.

Combining Treatments

Some researchers suggest that the optimal treatment program for depression may be a combination of antidepressants and either cognitive or interpersonal psychotherapy (Hollon, 1993). The logic of this advice is that drugs can quickly relieve physical symptoms such as sleep disturbance, while psychotherapies address the cognitive and behavioral patterns that perpetuate depressive symptoms and increase the risk of recurrence. As appealing as this logic seems, several studies have found that combining drugs and psychotherapy does not give much of a boost to the effectiveness of what is achieved by either treatment alone (Wexler & Cicchetti, 1992).

Medication and psychotherapy are often combined in the treatment of bipolar disorder. After medication has controlled the symptoms of acute mania, psychotherapy is employed to help the patient cope with its aftermath and to prevent recurrences.

A Talk with Constance Hammen

Mood Disorders

Dr. Constance Hammen is Professor of Psychology at UCLA. She is a leading researcher in the area of mood disorders, particularly the development of depressive disorders.

Q *What do you think underlies the growing rates of depression in our population?*

A This phenomenon is not limited to just our population. It's a pattern, sometimes called the *birth cohort effect,* of increasing rates of depression worldwide, particularly in young people. And it's not just a phenomenon of people becoming more aware of depression and able to label it more accurately.

The increases are probably because young people have more to be depressed about, and fewer resources to buffer or combat the depression. Young people have more exposure to stress now. Their lives are full of family disruption and social mobility. I think they also have many more negative cognitions about themselves and their ability to control circumstances. Certainly families and social support are very important in helping people deal with stressful circumstances. Young people today have fewer of those ties, and many do not have resources such as a good education or a good job.

> *...women are lightning rods for stressors of other people...*

Q *Depression is still more common among women. Any thoughts about why?*

A In my view, three separate factors contribute to the gender differences. One factor has to do with the expression of the symptomatology itself. We know that women are more willing to admit to emotional difficulties, to express emotions, to play the role of the weak and needy. So in that sense, they are more likely to admit and feel the symptoms of depression than men are. But there is more to it than that.

A second factor has to do with causal factors that may be more prevalent with women. Women have greater exposure to stress because women experience not only their own stressors but also those of people they are close to. In a sense, women are lightning rods for stressors of other people as well as feeling their own greater exposure to stress. Women are raised to value close relationships, while men are raised to value achievement. Because women tend to value social relationships, they feel stressed when those relationships are threatened.

A third factor would be differences in how people cope with stress. Men and women cope somewhat differently with provoking situations. Men's coping methods may reduce the likelihood of depression. Men, generally speaking, are more active copers. They are more likely to go out and do things to solve the problem, avoid the problem, or distract themselves. Men also may turn to pathological forms of coping, such as drugs and alcohol; nonetheless, they try not to let themselves experience depressive symptoms.

Women on the other hand are somewhat less active copers, more likely to use what we call *emotion-focused coping;* that is, they'll think about their problems, they'll cry, they'll talk about their problems with other people, they'll focus on their feelings. Women tend to ruminate about their problems and feelings and may consequently exaggerate the symptoms of depression.

Q *What new directions should clinicians and researchers take to better understand and treat depression?*

A One fruitful approach might be to study how stressful experiences may alter the brain or neurochemistry to make people susceptible to depression. One strong finding in our field is that past depression predicts future depression. One explanation might be that past depression alters the organism in ways that make the person more susceptible to depression.

I think we are also going to see more research on the heterogeneity of depression. It really is a group of different disorders. The better we can describe the specific subtypes, the more we might be able to tailor treatment for those specific disorders.

Finally, we must conduct a lot more research on the problem of lower-grade chronic depression. It may be subclinical depression, but, if it is enduring, if it persists or recurs, it can still cause a lot of disruption in people's lives and in the lives of those around them.

Continued contact with the psychotherapist also allows for the monitoring of a bipolar patient's compliance with medication (Post, 1993). *Life charting,* a therapist-guided review of the history of patients' illness episodes and the impacts they have had on patients' lives, often helps them understand the importance of drug compliance. Psychotherapy is also aimed at helping bipolar disorder patients minimize and cope with stress and, ideally, prevent relapse. Bipolar disorder patients are sensitive to variations in their sleep–wake cycles, so another important goal of psychotherapy is to set up procedures for regulating daily schedules and to make plans for handling schedule disruptions caused by travel or seasonal changes in sleep–wake patterns (Post, 1993). Finally, family therapy may give close relatives of bipolar disorder patients important support and education about bipolar disorder (Clarkin et al., 1990).

Overall, the prognosis for people suffering from mood disorders is mixed. Most patients recover, even without any treatment, from an episode of depression or mania. Unfortunately, the risk of relapse is high. Therefore, if they remain untreated, many patients face a life of repeated episodes that result in heavy financial and personal burdens. Overall, treatment with psychotherapy or medication is effective for about 70 percent of adults. However, relapse is still a concern even among effectively treated patients. Whether psychotherapy or medication is the preferred treatment for adult depression remains a hotly debated topic among mental health professionals. The fact that psychotherapy carries fewer side effects and medical risks and achieves equal or even slightly superior long-term effects than medication suggests that it might be the treatment of first choice in mild or moderate cases. Medication has the advantages of being less expensive than psychotherapy and more effective with severe depression.

In Review

The three main categories of antidepressant medications are:

- MAO inhibitors, the tricyclics, and selective serotonin reuptake inhibitors; and are
- about equally effective, producing improvements in up to approximately 70 percent of adults.

Depression can also be treated effectively with psychotherapy (particularly cognitive therapy and interpersonal therapy) that:

- achieves improvement rates that do not usually differ from those of medication; and

- leads to relapse rates that may actually be a bit lower than with medication.

Some cases of depression that do not respond well to medication or psychotherapy may improve following electroconvulsive therapy or light therapy. Bipolar disorder is treated:

- primarily with lithium, often supplemented with psychotherapy; and
- with carbamazepine or valproate, in cases in which lithium has not been successful.

Suicide

Approximately 15 percent of depressed individuals eventually commit suicide, making it one of the most serious problems associated with mood disorders. However, suicide is not associated solely with depression. It is also linked to a host of other mental disorders, health difficulties, and social problems. In the remainder of this chapter, we will review the current knowledge about suicide, with special attention to warning signs, causes, and prevention.

Who Is Suicidal?

The traditional definition of suicide is the willful taking of one's own life. By this definition, approximately 40,000 suicides occur in the United States each year, making it one of the nation's "top ten" causes of death. However, any statistics on suicide may be underestimates for several reasons. First, many deaths that are thought to be accidental (one-car crashes, for example) might actually have been suicides. In addition, high-risk behavior, such as driving at excessive speed or using dangerous drugs, may be a form of suicide even though the person's intention to end his or her life is not obvious. Finally, social and religious prohibitions still make some relatives, police, and physicians reluctant to identify a death as a suicide.

A Profile of Suicide Attempts. Far more people make suicide attempts than actually kill themselves. There are approximately 300,000 suicide attempts every year in the United States. About one in eight of these attempts results in a completed suicide (Bongar, 1991; Goldsmith, Fyer, & Frances, 1990). Although a suicide attempt is the best predictor of a subsequent suicide, the profile of suicide attempters is different from that seen in people who actually kill themselves. Unlike completed suicides, attempted suicides are more frequent among females than males by a ratio of about 3 to 1. Attempted suicides are also more common in younger people. In older age groups, the frequency of attempted suicides actually declines, but the number of completed suicides increases. About 70 to 90 percent of attempted suicides involve drug overdoses or self-poisoning (Jacob, 1989, quoted in Bongar, 1991); wrist cutting is the next most common method of attempted suicide. In completed suicides, the act usually involves a gunshot, hanging, or carbon monoxide inhalation.

To assess the seriousness of a person's suicidal intent, suicide researchers have introduced the notion of a **risk/rescue ratio,** which compares the riskiness of the person's behavior to the availability of rescue or help in the situation. In the case of a man who goes to an isolated spot and shoots himself in the head, the risk/rescue ratio indicates a much higher suicide intent than does the case of a person who drinks too much at a party and takes a dare to swim out to some remote rocks. Both people have put themselves at grave risk for death but in very different ways.

The risk/rescue ratio in most attempted suicides suggests that the individual hoped to be saved; such attempts are often a call for help or attention from others. For example, suicide attempts frequently follow the breakup of romantic relationships, motivated apparently by the hope of regaining the affection of the estranged loved one. Suicide attempts are also associated with anxiety disorders, especially panic disorder, and with borderline or antisocial personality disorders (Goldsmith et al., 1990; Weissman et al., 1989).

Some people respond to an onslaught of stressors with thoughts of death and self-harming behaviors. Their reactions may include mild drug overdosing, mixing alcohol and other drugs, or minor cutting of the wrists. These actions, called **parasuicidal behaviors,** are especially common among those who have experienced early abuse or trauma or who display certain personality disorders (see Chapter 12). Although not as risky as more overt suicide attempts, parasuicidal behaviors may eventually lead to more lethal attempts.

Completed Suicide: Who Is at Risk? Completed suicide is strongly associated with mental disorder. Studies of the characteristics of individuals at the time of their suicides—known as *psychological autopsies*—indicate that the vast majority of people who kill themselves displayed either depression or alcoholism (Bongar, 1991). Suicide risk is also associated with the presence of schizophrenic symptoms, especially among young men (Black & Winokur, 1990).

There are substantial differences in completed suicide rates across cultural groups. In some northern European countries and Japan, for example, the suicide rate is estimated to be as high as 25 per 100,000 individuals. In countries with stronger religious prohibitions against suicide, such as Greece, Italy, and Ireland, the rate is more like 6 per 100,000. In the United States, the estimated suicide rate is 12 per 100,000.

Suicide rates among ethnic groups within the United States also vary considerably. Completed suicides are more common in Whites than in other ethnic groups. Suicide has been relatively uncommon among Blacks, but there has been a twofold increase in suicide rates in this group over the past 25 years, especially among young males who are 20 to 34 years old and living in urban settings (Bongar, 1991). The Alcohol, Drug Abuse, and Mental Health Administration (1989) reported 10.5 suicides per 100,000 people among African American males and 2.2 per 100,000 among African American females. Among American Hispanics, suicide is rare, but, when it does occur, the victims are likely to be young males. The overall rate of suicide among Native Americans is high—19.4 per 100,000 overall. For 10- to 24-year-old Native American males, the risk is as high as 24 per 100,000 (Bongar, 1991). Suicide among Native Americans is associated with significant alcohol use; cluster suicides are also common among Native American youth (Earls, Escobar, & Manson, 1990).

Completed suicide is more common for men than women. In most industrialized countries, including the United States, completed suicide is most common among White males over the age of 65, many of whom had developed significant problems relating to health, loss of family and friends, social isolation, and a sense of hopelessness (Osgood & Thielman, 1990).

In short, key risk factors for suicide include

- being a psychiatric patient, particularly with a diagnosis of depression, alcoholism, or schizophrenia;
- being male;
- being older;
- being of European American background;
- having a history of prior suicide attempts; and
- experiencing stressful life events, particularly events involving loss of loved ones and social support.

However, the demographics of suicide are changing. Over the past decade, rates of suicide among older adults, especially males, have increased, but the largest increase has been among adolescents and young adults, especially white males between the ages of 15 and 24 (Rosenberg, Smith, & Davidson, 1987). Since 1980, half of the suicides in the United States have occurred among individuals 40 years old or younger (Bongar, 1991).

Adolescent Suicide

There was a dramatic increase in suicide rates among adolescents in the United States between 1960 and 1990 (Garland & Zigler, 1993), as Figure 9.7 illustrates. Current estimates are that about 2,000 teenagers commit suicide in the United States every year; for boys, the rate is approximately 15 per 100,000 and for girls, about 3 per 100,000 (Robins & Rutter, 1990). The greatest increase has been among White males in their late teens and early twenties. This alarming change has come at a time when suicide rates among some segments of our population have actually declined.

The factors associated with adolescent suicide differ in many ways from those seen in adult suicides. Whereas social isolation and hopelessness characterize the older person at risk for suicide, young suicide victims often appear to have responded impulsively to an acute stressor (Shaffer et al., 1988). Thus, it is not surprising that adolescents who com-

mit suicide are less likely than adults to leave notes explaining their motives or to give away their belongings as signs of potential suicide risks.

The most common scenario involves a youngster who has gotten into trouble or was humiliated in public (Shaffer, 1990). Maybe a young boy was dropped by a girlfriend at a party or lost a fight in front of peers. The youngster who commits suicide typically does so impulsively, shortly after the stressful event, without seeking support or help from friends or family. Gunshot wounds have become the most frequent cause of death in youth suicide, but hanging, jumping from a window or bridge, and carbon monoxide poisoning are frequently used methods.

Suicide among young people has other unique characteristics, including the so-called contagion effect. A common precipitating factor in youth suicide attempts is hearing about another person's suicide. Even the death of another teen reported on the news or talked about at school has been associated with increased suicidal behavior among adolescents (Gould, 1990). Clusters of teen suicides have been described in which one adolescent's death seemed to set off the same behavior in others. Research on the impact of the media's portrayal of suicide also points to a possible contagion effect. Programs aired on TV depicting youth suicide have been associated with an increase in suicides within the viewing area (Gould, 1990).

Suicide pacts also distinguish suicide in the young. Historically, in times of war or in pursuit of shared religious or political beliefs, groups of people have accepted suicide as a necessary means to an end. However, this motive is different from what has been observed in contemporary United States where young people discuss suicide with friends, gather medications in their school lockers, and plan to die together for no clearly identified reason.

About 80 percent of adolescents who kill themselves had longstanding mental health problems (Shaffer, 1990). Although depression is associated with suicide in some young people, the majority of boys who kill themselves had externalizing behavior disorders often accompanied by substance abuse problems. Some studies suggest that as many as 50 percent of all youths who commit suicide had an immediate relative with a history of suicide or suicide attempts.

A small percentage of youth suicides are committed by high achievers who were in no apparent trouble emotionally, socially, legally, or academically. These young people appear to have set extremely high expectations for themselves and have rigid and perfectionistic tendencies (Blatt, 1995; Shaf-

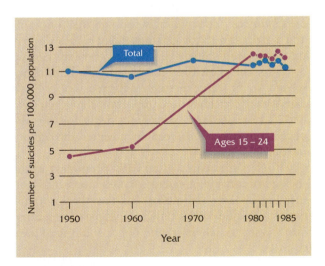

FIGURE 9.7

Increasing Rates of Suicide Among Young Americans

Although the overall rate of suicide among Americans has remained relatively stable since 1950, rates for Americans aged 15 to 24 have steadily increased.

Source: Adapted from *Report of the Secretary's Task Force on Suicide: Vol. 1;* cited in Bongar, 1991.

fer, 1990). Their suicides tend to be triggered by a poor grade, a sports injury, or some other setback that they saw as interfering with achieving important goals.

Like completed suicides, suicide attempts by adolescents are also on the rise. A recent study of high schoolers in a U.S. West coast community found that 21 percent reported suicidal thinking and 7.1 percent had made at least one suicide attempt (Lewinsohn, Rohde, & Seeley, 1993). As with adults, suicide is attempted about three times more often by young females than by young males. Adolescent attempts most frequently involve drug overdoses.

Causes of Suicide

As is true of the mood disorders associated with it, suicide can stem from multiple causes. Characteristics of people's social environments and their prevailing belief systems appear to play a more central role in suicide than in, say, depression, but genetic and biochemical factors cannot be ignored.

Biological Factors in Suicide. Although there are too few twin studies of suicide to provide conclusive findings, the data available indicate greater concordance for suicide among monozygotic than dyzgotic twin pairs (Kety, 1990). Adoption studies also suggest a higher incidence of suicide among biological relatives in contrast to adopted relatives (Kety, 1990; Wender et al., 1986). The results of twin and adoption studies are difficult to interpret, however, because of the overlap of suicide with mental disorders such as depression and schizophrenia. Thus, it is impossible to determine whether the genetic loading is related to suicidal behavior itself or to the mental disorder that often accompanies it. And because the risk of suicide is especially common in depressed people who are also impulsive and aggressive, any genetic component of suicide may not even be related to depression or schizophrenia per se but to the tendency to engage in violent or impulsive behavior (Kety, 1990).

Similar questions surround the interpretation of biochemical abnormalities found in individuals who attempted or completed suicide. Initial studies identified unusually low concentrations of 5-HIAA (the main metabolite of serotonin) in the cerebrospinal fluid (CSF) of suicidal, depressed patients (Bongar, 1991; Brown, Goodwin, & Bunney, 1982; Winchel, Stanley, & Stanley, 1990). Low CSF concentrations of *homovanillic acid (HVCA)*, a dopamine by-product, have also been documented in suicidal adults. These findings make it appear that suicide is associated with a slightly different pattern of neurotrans-

mitter abnormalities than that seen in nonsuicidal, depressed people. However, decreased 5-HIAA is also found in patients with schizophrenia and personality disorders (Brown et al., 1982) as well as in violent criminals (Virkkunen & Narvanen, 1987). Thus, these biochemical abnormalities may be more closely related to impulsive, aggressive behavior than to suicide itself.

Even if abnormalities in neurotransmitter systems are tied to suicide, we do not know how they operate to make suicide more likely. Nor do we know why artificially lowering serotonin levels in a healthy person does not give rise to suicidal impulses. Nevertheless, some researchers suggest that suicidal behavior may be a separate syndrome that frequently co-occurs with mental disorders such as depression (Winchel et al., 1990). If this is true, it would be important to develop diagnostic and treatment strategies specific to those persons with depression, schizophrenia, and other mental disorders who are also at risk for suicide. Unfortunately, no biological test capable of assessing suicide risk exists at this time.

Environmental Factors in Suicide. Social and cultural influences appear to be much more strongly related to the prevalence of suicide than biological factors are. In fact, over the years, many cultures have viewed suicide as a respectable response to social disgrace or public failure. In World War II, for example, Japanese *kamikaze* pilots willingly took on the honorable and patriotic duty of crashing their planes directly into American ships, even though it meant certain death for the pilot. Even today, individuals set themselves afire or starve themselves for social or political causes they consider more important than their own lives. The willingness to embrace death for the sake of religious beliefs has been documented throughout history.

Emile Durkheim was an early proponent of the sociocultural view of suicide. In late nineteenth-century France, Durkheim proposed that there are four types of suicide, each related to people's integration into the social, religious, and political fabric of their cultures.

- **Egoistic suicides** are committed by those who are poorly integrated into society. Suicides by lonely, isolated people, especially the elderly, may be the clearest example of egoistic suicides.

- **Altruistic suicides** occur when people choose suicide because they place a social goal or group ahead of personal survival. The *kamikaze* suicides are an example.

- **Anomic suicides** are committed by people who feel lost or abandoned by society, often because of social upheaval such as divorce or loss of a job.

- **Fatalistic suicides** are accomplished by those, such as prisoners or slaves, who experience severe social isolation or rejection and who hold little hope for social integration.

Studies conducted since Durkheim's time have consistently found that rates of attempted and completed suicide are indeed related to social changes and social mores. Among Native Americans, tribes that are loosely structured and stress greater individuality tend to see higher rates of youth suicide than do more traditional tribes that emphasize the importance of community over individuals (Earls et al., 1990). The rising tide of suicide among young, urban African Americans appears closely linked to the growing violence and poverty in many cities. Young African American men living in those cities may come to devalue life, to fear being killed before they reach adulthood, and to doubt that life has much to offer.

The relatively low rate of suicide among Hispanics appears to be due in part to strong family systems and the predominance of Catholicism, which strongly prohibits suicide. For Mexican Americans, specifically, individuals with strong cultural ties to Mexican culture rather than an orientation toward assimilation into American culture are at lower risk for suicide (Earls et al., 1990).

Stressors are also related to suicide. Suicidal behavior tends to be positively correlated with unemployment, marital instability, legal problems, and limited social support. The strength of these correlations has varied over time. High unemployment during the U.S. Depression in the 1930s was associated with an increased suicide rate, but, during more recent periods of increased unemployment, suicide rates have not risen markedly. It may be that only prolonged, widespread unemployment leads to the hopelessness and decreased self-esteem that are known to contribute to the risk of suicide.

Social support appears to reduce the risk of suicide, and social isolation appears to increase it. For example, suicide is more common among single, divorced, separated, or widowed people than among married people. (The one exception to this generalization appears to be among people who married very early, especially during their teenage years; their suicide rate is higher than for other married people.) Suicide is also less common among people who have children living in their homes.

Most suicides are committed by people who maintain little regular contact with their family or friends. Suicide is especially common in older men who have lost their spouses through divorce or death and have not developed alternative social support systems. Even a temporary loss of social support—through an argument with a family member or friend, or a breakup with a lover—is strongly associated with suicidal behavior in both adults and adolescents.

Developmental Factors in Suicide. Individuals vary greatly in their psychological vulnerability to stressors, leading some theorists to suggest that extreme vulnerability to stress could predispose a person to

Dr. Jack Kevorkian, a Michigan pathologist, developed a "suicide machine" that allows individuals to give themselves a fatal injection. Although use of this device was outlawed, Dr. Kevorkian continues to aid terminally ill adults in accomplishing their suicides.

When an individual faces a painful and terminal illness, does he or she have the right to choose suicide instead of continued suffering? Does a medical professional or relative have the right to assist in a suicide?

suicide. They trace these vulnerabilities to the quality of a child's early experiences with parents. Various models of abnormality offer different views of how suicide might be linked to these early experiences.

■ Traditional psychoanalysts view suicidal thoughts as reflecting intense, unresolved, internalized anger at the primary parent figure. Such thoughts are activated when a person feels unable to maintain a sense of self-worth and self-caring.

■ Object-relations and interpersonal theories stress the role of disturbed family relationships in suicide. Recall that these theories see family dysfunction early in life as hampering the child's ability to cope with negative affect, develop a positive sense of self, and master the skills necessary to develop and sustain relationships throughout life. These problems, in turn, may generate interpersonal conflicts, social isolation, and, eventually, too little of the support that makes it easier to deal with life's stressors.

■ From the cognitive perspective, early negative experiences can increase a person's tendency to feel hopelessness in the face of significant stress. Hopelessness, or a sense of overwhelming pessimism about the future, is one of the best predictors of suicide attempts.

Is there empirical support for these ideas? Although cause–effect links have not been established, numerous studies do indicate that early loss of a parent as well as chaotic, neglectful family life is associated with suicide in later life (Adam, 1990).

Suicide Prevention

Figure 9.8 presents a summary of how the factors we have discussed might lead to suicide. Can they explain the rise in adolescent suicides, and do they point to ways to reverse this trend? The Prevention section discusses these questions.

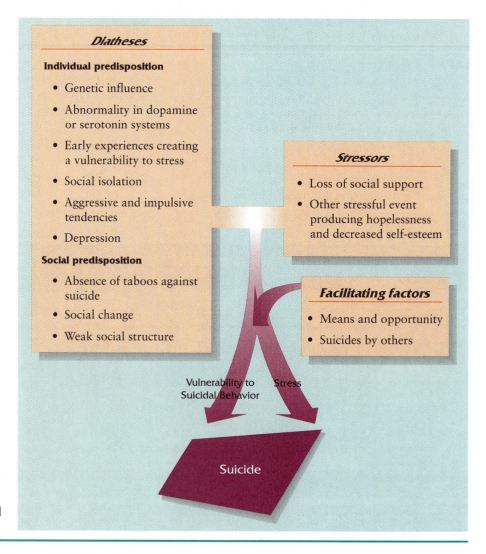

FIGURE 9.8

A Diathesis–Stress Model of Suicide

Prevention   Curbing Adolescent Suicide

Suicide is now the third leading cause of death of people between the ages of 15 and 19, accounting for 14 percent of all deaths among this age group. Rates of attempted suicides have also increased; somewhere between 6 percent and 13 percent of adolescents report they have attempted suicide at least once in their lives (Garland & Zigler, 1993).

What explains these troubling trends? Many clinicians point to increases in substance abuse and major stressors as possible factors. But experts in the area of adolescent suicide suggest that a more significant factor might be that society has inadvertently lowered its taboos about suicide (Shaffer et al., 1988). Ironically, some of this effect may stem from school-based curricula that attempt to prevent suicide by educating young people on how to detect risk factors for suicide and how to talk to others about problems such as suicide. Another goal of these educational programs is to reduce the stigma of suicide by depicting the problem as a normal response to stress rather than as a serious difficulty that is usually tied to mental disorders. These efforts may have backfired because troubled and vulnerable youth now seem more likely to see suicide as an acceptable solution to life's difficulties. In other words, some curriculum-based suicide-prevention programs may have unintentionally contributed to these harmful attitudes.

Another critical factor may be the growing availability of firearms. Most teen suicide is the result of an impulsive gesture. Access to a deadly weapon allows this impulsive behavior to have deadly consequences even if the youth may not have been totally resolved to die.

Because guns are used in the majority of teen suicides, many experts believe that stricter control over the availability of guns would reduce suicide rates.

These findings have clear implications for prevention programs. First, family and societal taboos against suicide must be reiterated. Suicide is not an acceptable alternative for a young person faced with stressors, even when they are of overwhelming proportions, and adolescents should not be given any message, even inadvertently, that suicide is acceptable.

Second, successful prevention programs should target those specific behaviors or psychological variables that research has shown to be the most significant risk factors for teen suicide. Included among these factors are adolescent depression and alcohol use, both of which have been found to predict adolescents' suicidal behavior (Reifman & Windle, 1995).

Finally, access to weapons should be restricted. At the social policy level, stricter gun-control laws may be an effective form of prevention. For example, one study found that the stricter the gun-control laws in a state, the lower the rate of suicides and the smaller the increase in suicides over a 10-year period (Lester & Murrell, 1980). In a second study, Lester (1988) correlated rates of suicide with the extent of gun ownership and the strictness of gun-control laws in nine major regions of the United States. Those regions with higher levels of gun ownership had higher rates of suicide, and the more lenient the region's gun-control legislation, the higher the suicide rate.

When mental health professionals determine that a young person is at risk of self-harm, they should work with parents to provide adequate supervision and to remove firearms or other dangerous items from the home.

Efforts to prevent suicide often seek to change social factors that increase suicide risks in the general population and to increase public awareness about suicide. As part of a suicide prevention program, the Netherlands, for example, used a mass media campaign to educate the public about the early signs of depression and what family and friends could do to obtain help for individuals displaying those signs. In the United States, school-based programs to increase self-esteem and academic success and to decrease substance abuse are thought to have preventive potential because they address the hopelessness and alienation that can lead young people to contemplate suicide. Other programs provide companions for elderly or recently widowed people in order to guarantee social support during a high-risk period. Finally, some mental health professionals are strong advocates of gun control legislation, in part because they believe that any policy that decreases the availability of guns—the most lethal means of self-inflicted death—will also ultimately lower the risks of suicide.

Most individually oriented efforts to prevent suicide have three basic components: (1) assessing the risk of suicide, (2) helping the person cope with the immediate crisis, and (3) treating any behavior disorders that increase a person's risk for later suicide attempts.

Crisis Interventions. Unfortunately, there is no foolproof way to predict whether an individual will or will not commit suicide. However, as we have seen, studies of the characteristics of suicidal people have identified the risk factors typically associated with suicide. This information helps police officers, 911 operators, and telephone hotline workers to respond to suicidal people more effectively. For example, when crisis workers for suicide hotlines take emergency calls, they try to provide support to callers while also determining the degree to which there is an imminent danger of suicide. They ask questions to determine the callers' demographic characteristics, whether they are alone, whether they have someone they can contact for support, whether they are being treated for their problems, whether they have a suicide plan or a weapon in hand, and whether they are intoxicated.

Data about the effectiveness of suicide hotline services are difficult to gather, but what information exists is mostly disappointing (Lester, 1993). Studies that have compared the rates of suicide in communities before and after the establishment of suicide hotlines have not found an overall reduction in suicides (e.g., Miller et al., 1984), but there is some evidence that certain groups of people who call hotlines most frequently (e.g., younger, white females) may benefit more from their availability.

If the individual's suicide risk is high, the crisis worker will often summon the police, who will then bring acutely distressed callers to a crisis intervention program or to a hospital emergency room. Here, the immediate goal is to assess the suicide risk, thwart suicidal impulses, and help restore the individual's hope for the future.

At this point, the person may or may not be hospitalized. This decision depends on factors such as the amount of support available in the environment, the person's overall mental status, whether there is a suicide plan and the means to execute it, the person's willingness to seek help if suicidal ideation again becomes overwhelming, and of course the person's history of prior suicide attempts. If hospitalization is not deemed necessary, arrangements will usually be made to give the patient access to a care provider on a 24-hour-call basis. A program of treatment may also be offered that includes helping family or friends appreciate the severity of the patient's situation and assuring that they will be ready to provide support and supervision.

Treating Suicidal Tendencies. Antianxiety and antipsychotic medications can reduce some symptoms that contribute to suicidal tendencies. It is ironic that antidepressants are not particularly helpful with acutely suicidal patients because their effects are too delayed. In fact, some antidepressants may actually increase risk for suicide during the initial treatment period. However, antidepressants can be valuable in the long-term management of suicidal patients.

The choice of medications is especially important with suicidal patients because of the obvious risk of overdose. For example, because some antidepressants can cause severe cardiac problems if taken in excess, physicians typically prescribe only small supplies—usually no more than 1 week's dosage at a time—so that the patient will never have a lethal dose on hand. It is sometimes necessary to place parents in charge of dispensing medication to their adolescent children.

Psychotherapy sessions with suicidal patients are designed to alleviate the problems that prompt suicidal urges. Because depressed, suicidal patients report greater feelings of hopelessness, more dysfunctional assumptions and cognitive distortions, and fewer reasons for living than do depressed, nonsuicidal patients, cognitive-behavioral therapies are often used to help patients feel more hopeful and more connected to others (Weishaar & Beck, 1990). Some therapists insist on a *suicide contract,* in which the client promises to seek immediate help if suicidal urges become overwhelming. Unfortunately, signing such a contract does not assure that the patient will comply with it.

As shown in Table 9.4, the cognitive-behavioral approach focuses on five key characteristics of the suicidal person: hopelessness, cognitive rigidity, dichotomous thinking, ineffective problem solving, and viewing suicide as a desirable solution. For example, the therapist helps the patient understand that hopelessness stems from negative expectations and interpretations of events rather than an inevitable reality and encourages efforts to identify alternative solutions to life's problems. The therapist also aims to re-duce patients' tendencies to think in rigid, either/or terms (e.g., "I will *never* succeed at anything.") by encouraging them to think more flexibly (e.g., "I am not as good at some things as I am at others."). As problem-solving skills are honed, the patient is less likely to view suicide as a desirable solution.

Are formerly suicidal patients out of danger once they start on the road to recovery? Often, but not always. Clinicians have contended for many years that depressed persons' risks of suicide actually increase as they first begin to improve. This may be especially true for people who have been severely depressed. As these individuals begin to feel a bit less depressed, they may regain enough energy to carry out a suicide plan. Thus therapists must continue to assess clients' suicide risks, even during periods of perceived improvement.

TABLE 9.4   Cognitive Techniques for the Treatment of Suicidal Behavior

Cognitive characteristic	Intervention
Dichotomous thinking	Build a continuum between extreme points of view.
	Specify criteria used to categorize things in all-or-nothing terms.
	Find "shades of gray" in judgments.
	Use conditional, or less absolute, language.
Problem-solving deficits	Apply problem-solving training, including accepting problems as a normal part of life, precisely defining the problem, generating alternatives, and implementing solutions.
	Minimize cognitive distortions that interfere with this process.
Cognitive rigidity	Employ collaborative empiricism: test the patient's assumptions logically and empirically.
	Role play with role reversal to generate alternatives.
	Look for evidence of alternative interpretations.
Hopelessness	View hopelessness as a symptom and not as an accurate reflection of the situation.
	List all the problems making the patient feel hopeless.
	Reduce cognitive distortions to define problems clearly.
	Share optimism with the patient about finding solutions.
	Use problem-solving training.
	Use skills training to aid implementation of solutions (e.g., assertiveness).
View of suicide as desirable	Elicit reasons for dying and reasons for living.
	Describe advantages and disadvantages of suicide relative to other solutions.
	Correct cognitive distortions about advantages of dying.

Source: Weishaar & Beck, 1990.

Revisiting the Case of Margaret

*T*he decades of research reflected in the findings we have discussed proved to be helpful in Margaret's treatment. Depression can take many forms, and Margaret had many of the common symptoms. She felt hopeless and overwhelmed; she could not sleep or eat well. She withdrew from her friends.

The psychologist who treated Margaret was aware of research suggesting that cognitive or interpersonal psychotherapy is at least as effective as medication in treating moderate depression such as Margaret's. Based on that knowledge, she recommended that Margaret receive eight to ten sessions of cognitively oriented therapy, to be focused on Margaret's excessively high standards and expectations for herself. Gradually, Margaret learned that she did not have to be perfect to be happy. After eight sessions of therapy, Margaret reported feeling much better. She began going out with her friends again and, by the end of the semester, she had caught up on her academic work. Although her grades were not as good as in the past, Margaret was satisfied with them. Her parents were disappointed, but for once in her life, Margaret decided that she would not apologize to her parents because of their disappointment. Two years after her treatment concluded, Margaret has not suffered a relapse of depression.

SUMMARY

Depressive Disorders

The two major categories of mood disorder are depressive disorders and bipolar disorders. The most serious depressive disorder, major depressive disorder, involves prolonged periods of sad moods and demoralized, hopeless feelings, a loss of interest in almost all activities, and disturbances in appetite, sleep, and energy levels. Dysthymic disorder is a depressive disorder in which depressed feelings and low self-esteem are present for at least 2 years but not as intensely as in major depressive disorder.

Bipolar Disorder

People diagnosed with bipolar disorder suffer periods of depression as well as episodes of highly elated mood and grandiosity, known as mania. Bipolar I disorder is typified by one or more manic episodes or mixed episodes (in which both depression and mania are experienced nearly every day), and usually accompanied by periods of major depression. Bipolar II disorder involves at least one major depressive episode along with at least one hypomanic period (a period of elevated or irritated mood that is not as pronounced as a full manic episode).

Biological Causes of Mood Disorders

Mood disorders are caused by an interplay of biological, psychological, and social factors. Genetic factors play an important role in both depressive and bipolar disorders, perhaps because they are linked to disturbances in chemical neurotransmitters such as norepinephrine, serotonin, and dopamine. Mood disorders have also been related to problems in the endocrine system.

Psychological Causes of Mood Disorders

Several psychological variables have been proposed as causes of depressive disorders, including heightened sensitivity to loss or failure, problems in early attachment relationships, interpersonal conflicts, learned helplessness, deficient reinforcement, cognitive distortions, excessive self-focused attention, and depression-prone personality traits. Environmental and sociocultural factors involving stressful events and the lack of adequate social support have also been implicated. Psychological and environmental factors have not yet been shown to be strongly related to bipolar disorders.

Treatment of Mood Disorders

Both medication and various kinds of psychotherapy are effective treatments for depressive disorders. Antidepressant medications such as MAO inhibitors, tricyclics, and selective serotonin reuptake inhibitors are effective for about 70 percent of adult patients, but they are less useful for children and adolescents. Some cases of severe depression, especially those that do not respond well to medication, are helped by electroconvulsive therapy (ECT). Lithium carbonate remains the treatment of choice for people with bipolar disorder.

In many instances, psychotherapy and medications are used in combination to treat mood disorders. Cognitive therapy and interpersonal therapy have been particularly successful in cases of depression, but well-controlled comparison studies have not clearly established any one therapy to be consistently superior.

Suicide

Several of the risk factors that predict attempted suicide differ from those predicting completed suicides. The most important risk factors for completed suicides are having attempted suicide previously, being male, older, and unmarried, and suffering from mental disorders such as depression, alcoholism, or schizophrenia. Like most mental disorders, suicide has been linked to multiple, interacting causes. Suicide is associated with a moderate genetic vulnerability, possible neurotransmitter abnormalities, social instability and isolation, and a chronic sense of hopelessness and pessimism. Prevention of suicide depends on the accurate assessment of a person's risk for suicidal behavior, helping resolve the immediate crisis that surrounds most suicide attempts, and providing additional treatment that addresses the social and psychological problems that often lead to repeated suicide attempts.

KEY TERMS

altruistic suicides, p. 322

anhedonia, p. 290

autonomy-oriented (achievement) personality, p. 310

anomic suicides, p. 323

bereavement, p. 293

bipolar disorder, p. 294

bipolar I disorder, p. 296

bipolar II disorder, p. 296

catecholamine theory, p. 299

cognitive triad, p. 306

cyclothymic disorder, p. 297

depression, p. 288

dexamethasone, p. 301

double depression, p. 290

dysthymic disorder, p. 293

egoistic suicides, p. 322

electroconvulsive therapy (ECT), p. 313

fatalistic suicide, p. 323

hopelessness, p. 305

hypomanic, p. 296

learned helplessness model, p. 304

light therapy, p. 315

linkage analysis, p. 298

lithium carbonate, p. 313

major depressive disorder, p. 290

mania, p. 288

monoamine oxidase inhibitors, p. 312

mood disorders, p. 288

negative affect, p. 290

negative attributional style, p. 304

parasuicidal behaviors, p. 320

primitive thinking, p. 306

psychosis, p. 296

risk/rescue ratio, p. 320

seasonal affective disorder, p. 292

selective serotonin reuptake inhibitors (SSRIs), p. 312

self-awareness theory, p. 307

self-focused attention, p. 307

self-regulation, p. 307

self-schemas, p. 306

sociotropic (dependent) personality, p. 310

specifiers, p. 292

tricyclics, p. 312

10

Schizophrenia

Flesh & Spirit #23 by Kate Monson, 1994. Acrylic on paper, 19" x 22". Courtesy of Sistare.

From the Case of Lionel Aldridge

During the 1960s, the Green Bay Packers were the dominant team in professional football. Under the leadership of their legendary coach, Vince Lombardi, they won three world championships and the first two Super Bowls. Key to the Packers' success was Lionel Aldridge, a defensive end who was a stalwart of the Packers' defense for almost a decade. Chosen as an All-Pro and elected to the Green Bay Packers' Hall of Fame, Lionel Aldridge was one of the best ever to play his position.

Born in the bayou country of Louisiana on St. Valentine's Day in 1941, Lionel was raised by his grandparents until he was a teenager. They were poor, but Lionel remembers his childhood as a normal and stable period of life. As a teenager, Lionel moved to California to live with other relatives. It was in California that Lionel was introduced to football. He became a star

player and ultimately won a football scholarship to Utah State University. While there, he majored in sociology. After college, Lionel joined the Packers and helped them dominate professional football throughout the 1960s.

After retiring from football in 1973, Lionel began to work in broadcasting. Eventually, he joined NBC as a national sports analyst, and in 1978 Lionel Aldridge helped announce Super Bowl XII.

But Lionel Aldridge's life was slowly falling apart. One year after retiring from football, he began to hear voices telling that he was a fraud and a con man and that his past would catch up with him. Lionel heard the voices even while announcing sports on TV. He tried to ignore them, but they did not stop. He grew increasingly paranoid that people were out to get him, a fear that was magnified by his nightly appearance on TV where all his "enemies" could see him.

The voices told Lionel that his boss was after him, that his wife was a witch, and that his dog was causing all his problems and had to be killed. Then Lionel began to see things that were not there—the wind chased him, the food on his dinnerplate transformed itself into a mass of worms, and his children's balloons became snakes trying to bite him.

At the age of 33, Lionel Aldridge had developed paranoid schizophrenia. There had been few, if any, warning signs of the disorder earlier in his life. In fact, he had enjoyed a life of remarkable success. However, over the next several years, delusions and hallucinations robbed Lionel of his grasp of reality. He lost his job, his family, his financial security, and his home. He began to live on the street, pawning his possessions, as he fought or ran from enemies he was sure were surrounding him.

Lionel Aldridge had become trapped in the grip of schizophrenia. He was hospitalized more than 20 times during the 1980s with a disorder that left him impoverished and alone. His condition would improve when he took his prescribed medications, but he so hated their side effects (they left him unable to speak for hours at a time) that he often refused to take them. ■

*W*hat could make Lionel Aldridge and millions of other people around the world hear voices, see visions, cower in terror, think that loved ones want to kill them, and retreat into desperate solitude? What causes this devastating and bewildering condition known as schizophrenia, and how can it be treated? This chapter examines the current knowledge about schizophrenia, a psychosis that can impair almost all aspects of psychological functioning.

Clinicians employ differing definitions of *psychosis,* but, in general, the term refers to a serious mental disorder in which individuals lack an accurate perception or understanding of reality and have little insight into how their behavior appears to others. Narrowly defined, a psychosis includes periods of **hallucinations,** sensory experiences that seem real to the person but are not based on any external stimulation of the relevant sensory organ, and **delusions,** false beliefs about reality that are so firmly held that no evidence or argument can convince the person to give them up. Often, psychoses also involve thinking and behavior that are so jumbled and disorganized that onlookers conclude that the person is crazy or insane. Several disorders are accompanied by one or more of these psychotic symptoms; schizophrenia is often marked by the presence of many such symptoms at once.

Lionel Aldridge developed schizophrenia in his 30s, after completing his career as an All-Pro football player.

In this chapter we will examine several disorders for which the presence of psychotic symptoms is a defining feature, but our main focus is on schizophrenia. First we will discuss the concept, describing how schizophrenia has been defined over the past 200 years, how the DSM-IV describes it today, and how it differs from other psychotic disorders. Then we will discuss the lives of people afflicted with schizophrenia—who they are, how they are similar, and how they differ. Next we will turn to an examination of the biological, psychological, and social factors that appear to contribute to the development of schizophrenia, followed by descriptions of the treatments that are most effective in controlling the disorder.

What Is Schizophrenia?

Schizophrenia is not, as popular culture sometimes suggests, a split or multiple personality, which, as was described in Chapter 8, is called *dissociative identity disorder.* Instead, **schizophrenia** is a psychosis that is marked by a fragmentation of basic psychological functions—attention, perception, thought, emotion, and behavior—that are normally integrated so that people can adjust to the demands of reality. People with schizophrenia misperceive what is happening around them, often hearing or seeing things that are not there. They have trouble maintaining attention to what is going on around them, and their thinking is often so confused and disorganized that they have difficulty communicating with others. Some people with this disorder display a blunting of emotional feelings and a lack of motivation that leaves them immobile and unresponsive. Or their emotions may be highly inappropriate, which may result in uproarious laughter at events that are not funny, or uncontrollable crying when nothing sad has taken place. Bizarre behavior is another common symptom, sometimes involving an outlandish or disheveled appearance and odd mannerisms. In other cases, the person avoids social contact as much as possible, withdrawing into private fantasy.

What holds this collection of symptoms together? Not all of them occur in all cases of schizophrenia, and many of them are displayed by people with other disorders. Does it make sense to talk about one disorder called *schizophrenia*? Or is schizophrenia a label that is applied to several different disorders? The concept of schizophrenia is anything but simple, as its history shows.

The Evolving Concept of Schizophrenia

The first formal description of mentally disordered patients that unequivocally matches the current conception of schizophrenia is less than 200 years old (Gottesman, 1991). It was not until 1809 that the classic symptoms of schizophrenia were first documented in descriptions of patients written by John Haslam at London's Bethlehem Hospital and by Philippe Pinel at Paris's Bicêtre (Gottesman, 1991). Another 50 years passed before Belgian psychiatrist Benedict Morel grouped a constellation of symptoms into a description of a specific syndrome (Kolb, 1968). Morel described the case of a previously bright 14-year-old boy whose intellectual and emotional abilities gradually deteriorated until he lost all of his prior knowledge and many mental functions. Morel called this condition *demence precoce* (or *dementia praecox*, in Latin) meaning premature loss of rational thought.

By the late 1800s, dementia praecox and several related psychoses had been documented by a number of German psychiatrists. The most influential of this group was Emil Kraepelin, a psychiatrist at Heidelberg Clinic who had examined thousands of mental patients by the 1890s. Through his systematic observations, Kraepelin concluded that three forms of psychosis were all variations or subtypes of a single syndrome he called dementia praecox. The subtypes were (1) *hebephrenia,* in which the person behaved in a silly, immature, and disorganized manner; (2) *catatonia,* in which the person held rigid, immobile postures and was mute for long periods; and (3) *paranoia,* in which the person had delusions of grandeur or persecution. Later, Kraepelin added the *simplex* or *simple* subtype, marked by gradual withdrawal and lack of responsiveness to the environment. Kraepelin differentiated these conditions from what he believed

Emil Kraepelin (1856–1926) was a student of Wilhelm Wundt, one of the first experimental psychologists. He was a leading psychiatrist in the 1800s, who pioneered an early classification scheme of psychoses based on careful observation of hundreds of patients.

was the other major mental disorder, manic depression (known today as bipolar disorder). He thought that dementia praecox was a progressive, deteriorating disease that terminated in "mental weakness" (Gottesman, 1991, p. 7).

Originally, Kraepelin based a diagnosis of dementia praecox on (1) the early onset of the disorder, typically during adolescence, and (2) the progressive, incurable deterioration of the patient's condition. By the beginning of the twentieth century, however, the Swiss psychiatrist Eugen Bleuler espoused different ideas. Bleuler recognized (as Kraepelin ultimately admitted) that dementia praecox did not always begin at an early age; therefore, the term *praecox* was not always appropriate. Furthermore, some patients got better; so *dementia* was not an appropriate description either. The central problem, said Bleuler, was a loosening or disharmony among various mental processes. There was a split ("schizen") in the mind's ("phren") normally integrated processes of affect and intellect, creating a condition he called *schizophrenia* (Bleuler, 1911/1950).

In his classic 1911 book, *Dementia Praecox: The Group of Schizophrenias,* Bleuler categorized schizophrenia's symptoms as either primary or secondary. According to Bleuler, four primary symptoms are responsible for the split of mental functions:

1. *loosening of associations,* such that thoughts and ideas are not coherently linked;
2. *ambivalence,* wanting two contradictory things at once and being unable to choose between them;
3. *autism,* or total self-centeredness in which reality is replaced by a fantasy life; and
4. *affective disturbance,* in which emotional responses are inconsistent with actions.

These symptoms—sometimes known as Bleuler's four As—force the patient to try to adapt to a chaotic mental life. The adaptations, said Bleuler, lead to other common symptoms of schizophrenia: delusions, hallucinations, mutism, and rigid postures.

Bleuler's conception of schizophrenia broadened Kraepelin's original criteria. By Bleuler's definition, a diagnosis of schizophrenia did not require early onset, continuous deterioration, or hallucinations or delusions. Thus, compared with Kraepelin's view of the disorder, many more cases met Bleuler's definition of schizophrenia. For example, Lionel Aldridge would not have satisfied Kraepelin's criteria for schizophrenia, but he did fit Bleuler's more flexible conception of the disorder.

During the first part of the twentieth century, Kraepelin's definition of schizophrenia remained dominant among diagnosticians in Europe while Bleuler's ideas found favor in North America. Over time, the two conceptualizations became increasingly divergent. A landmark study comparing the practices of psychiatrists in London and New York (Cooper et al., 1972) found that patients who were diagnosed as schizophrenic according to North American (Bleulerian) criteria were likely to be diagnosed with manic depression (bipolar disorder), major depression with delusions, or neurosis by British clinicians. Obviously, such differences in diagnosis hindered communication and reduced the comparability of research by North American and European scientists.

Partly in order to resolve this discrepancy, American mental health professionals began to search for an approach that would allow an operational definition of schizophrenia. The solution was derived from the work of the German psychiatrist Kurt Schneider (1959), who believed that particular kinds of delusions and hallucinations were the "first rank" or defining features of schizophrenia. Schneider's first-rank symptoms were relatively easy to observe and agree on; however, he ignored the quieter features of schizophrenia that we now know are also important

(Andreasen & Carpenter, 1993). A synthesis of the definitions of Kraepelin, Bleuler, and Schneider was eventually achieved in the DSM-III and remains the basis for the DSM-IV definition.

Schizophrenia According to the DSM-IV

According to the DSM-IV, there are no specific symptoms that must always be present for a diagnosis of schizophrenia to be made, nor is the presence of any one symptom enough to diagnose schizophrenia. Rather, as the DSM table shows, there are several characteristic psychotic symptoms, some combination of which must be present for a diagnosis. Furthermore, according to the DSM-IV's criteria (see the DSM table opposite), the symptoms must have been active for a minimum of 1 month along with other signs of disturbance that have lasted for at least 6 months. These symptoms must be accompanied by marked deterioration in the person's ability to function at work, engage in social relationships, and maintain self-care, and they must not be due to another mental disorder, substance abuse, or a medical condition.

The symptoms of schizophrenia are often classified as either positive or negative. **Positive symptoms** are distortions of normal psychological functions that produce excess behaviors, such as hallucinations, delusions, bizarre behavior, confused thinking, and disorganized speech. (Obviously, the term *positive* in this context does not mean that these behaviors are desirable.) **Negative symptoms** involve a diminution, absence, or loss of normal function; examples include apathy, flat emotions, lack of self-help skills, and social withdrawal. Positive symptoms tend to respond to antipsychotic medications better than negative symptoms. Negative symptoms are associated with higher levels of long-term impairment. As will be noted later in this chapter, there is some evidence that positive and negative symptoms might have different causes.

Positive Symptoms of Schizophrenia

Most schizophrenic patients exhibit both positive and negative symptoms at one time or another. Although a greater number of negative symptoms bodes ill for the patient's overall prognosis, positive symptoms are often more bizarre and therefore more immediately noticeable, even frightening, to observers. Positive symptoms can be further divided into two symptom clusters—psychoticism (primarily delusions and hallucinations) and disorganization (primarily formal thought disorder and bizarre behavior) (Andreasen et al., 1995).

DSM-IV

Diagnostic Criteria for Schizophrenia

A. *Characteristic symptoms:* Two (or more) of the following, each present for a significant portion of time during a 1-month period (or less if successfully treated):

  (1) delusions
  (2) hallucinations
  (3) disorganized speech (e.g., frequent derailment or incoherence)
  (4) grossly disorganized or catatonic behavior
  (5) negative symptoms, i.e., affective flattening, alogia, or avolition

  Note: Only one . . . symptom is required if delusions are bizarre or [if] hallucinations consist of a voice keeping up a running commentary . . . , or two or more voices conversing.

B. *Social/occupational dysfunction:* For a significant portion of the time since the onset of the disturbance, one or more major areas of functioning such as work, interpersonal relations, or self-care are markedly below the level achieved prior to the onset (or when the onset is in childhood or adolescence, failure to achieve expected level of interpersonal, academic, or occupational achievement).

C. *Duration:* Continuous signs of the disturbance persist for at least 6 months. This 6-month period must include at least 1 month of symptoms (or less if successfully treated) that meet Criterion A (i.e., active-phase symptoms) and may include periods of prodromal or residual symptoms.

D. *Exclusions:* Schizoaffective disorder and mood disorder with psychotic features have been ruled out . . . , [t]he disturbance is not due to the direct physiological effects of a substance . . . or a general medical condition.

Source: American Psychiatric Association; *Diagnostic and Statistical Manual of Mental Disorders,* Fourth Edition. Washington, DC, American Psychiatric Association, 1994.

Delusions. Usually, delusions involve misinterpretations of normal perceptual experiences. In other words, a person experiences the world as others do but forms obviously incorrect interpretations of those experiences. For example, if a police officer waves to pedestrians at a busy street corner, a delusional person might interpret this not as a sign to cross the intersection, but as a signal to a would-be assassin. Other delusions probably arise as attempted explanations for the peculiar sensory experiences that people with schizophrenia frequently suffer (Maher & Spitzer, 1993).

The range of beliefs that mental health professionals accept as normal is quite broad. Flagrant, bizarre delusions are fairly easy to identify, but, in other instances, distinguishing a delusion from a mistaken belief can be difficult. Generally, the clinician tries to determine whether a given belief is odd enough to qualify as a delusion. Truly implausible beliefs—such as that a person's heart has been removed by aliens or that Tom Brokaw is spying on a person's home every time he broadcasts the evening news—are easily recognized as delusions. On the other hand, a second-rate boxer's belief that he can still win a championship runs contrary to a lot of evidence, but it is not so extreme that it would be considered delusional.

Religious beliefs that are not endorsed by a clinician's culture or are not familiar to the clinician present particular diagnostic problems. Are such beliefs delusional or just rare conclusions accepted as the truth by some group? Most Westerners consider beliefs in the healing powers of witch doctors to be misguided, but many groups endorse such beliefs, and it would typically be improper to label them delusions. Usually, a delusion can be distinguished from a false belief on the basis that the delusion is recognized by almost everyone in a given society as obviously false.

Some delusions are classified by specific content. For example, in *somatic delusions* people believe that something is wrong with their bodies. They may be convinced that they are infested with parasites or that they are being bombarded with poisonous rays. In other cases, a man may believe he is losing his penis, or a woman may be convinced she is pregnant despite clear evidence to the contrary.

Delusions of persecution, the most common delusions in schizophrenia, are beliefs that a person is being tormented or harassed by an individual or group such as the FBI, a foreign government, or extraterrestrials. Lionel Aldridge's belief that enemies were tracking him while he was on TV was a persecutory delusion. Persecutory delusions lead the person to always be on guard lest an enemy sneak up undetected. Ambiguous events are usually interpreted in the most threatening terms, as in the case of a young man named Jimmy.

---

*J*immy lived with his parents and worked part-time as a high school janitor. He often overslept and reported late to work. He blamed his parents for this problem, accusing them of inserting "beaners" (his term for any substance that induced sleep) under his skin while he slept and of "wranging" his alarm clock so that it wouldn't work. When his parents pointed out that his alarm clock always showed the correct time, Jimmy insisted that this just showed that "you are all in cahoots with the government anyway so you have probably wranged all the clocks against me."

Delusions of reference are also relatively common and occur when people misinterpret sounds or other stimuli as having special reference only to them. For example, static from a radio may be interpreted as a sign that someone is trying to communicate with the listener. A newspaper article about a celebrity's troubles may be viewed as an exposé of a personal foible. Delusions of reference may also be triggered by highway billboards, song lyrics, and movies.

Delusions of control involve beliefs that an enemy or foreign entity is controlling a person's thoughts, feelings, or behavior. One patient was convinced that his mind was manipulated by deceased relatives who were living on Jupiter and "controlling earth's equipment as well as its people." Another believed that a dentist had implanted a microchip in his tooth, causing his bowels to lock up (Brown & Lambert, 1995). Related delusions include *thought withdrawal,* the belief that thoughts are being stolen out of a person's brain; *thought insertion,* the belief that bad thoughts are being forced into the delusional person's head; and *thought broadcasting,* the belief that a person's thoughts are being transmitted so that others can hear them.

Connections

Are delusions an excuse for criminal behavior? For a discussion of the relationship between legal concepts of responsibility and mental disorders, see Chapter 18, pp. 640–643.

People displaying *delusions of grandeur* believe that they are famous or important, often someone who can save the world from famine or war. Religious themes are prominent in many delusions of grandeur. Perhaps the most famous example occurred in the 1960s when three male patients at different mental hospitals in Michigan all claimed to be Jesus Christ. Ultimately, they were transferred to the same ward of a state hospital in Ypsilanti, Michigan, where they lived together for 2 years. Their encounters are described in Milton Rokeach's classic book, *The Three Christs of Ypsilanti* (1964). In the book, the three men are referred to by the fictitious names of Clyde, Joseph, and Leon. They met for the first time on July 1, 1959, in a small room at the Ypsilanti State Hospital. According to Rokeach, the first meeting began with a round of routine introductions.

---

*A*fter giving his real name, Joseph was asked if there was anything else he wanted to tell the group. "Yes, I'm God," he replied. Clyde introduced himself next, also giving his straight name first, and then proceeding, "I have six other names, but that's my vital side and I made God five and Jesus six . . . I made God, yes. I made it seventy years old a year ago. Hell! I passed seventy years old." Last came Leon.

"Sir," Leon began, "it so happens that my birth certificate says that I am Dr. Domino Dominorum et Rex Rexarum, Simplis Christianus Pueris Mentalis Doktor. [This is all the Latin Leon knows: Lord of Lords, and King of Kings, Simple Christian Boy Psychiatrist.] It also states on my birth certificate that I am the reincarnation of Jesus Christ of Nazareth, and I also salute, and I want to add this. I do salute the manliness in Jesus Christ also, because the vine is Jesus and the rock is Christ, pertaining to the penis and testicles; and it so happens that I was railroaded into this place because of prejudice and jealousy and duping that started before I was born, and that is the main issue why I am here. I want to be myself. I do not consent to their misuse of the frequency of my life."

When asked "Who are 'they' that you are talking about?" Leon said "Those unsound individuals who practice the electronic imposition and duping. I am working for my redemption. And I am waiting patiently and peacefully, sir, because what has been promised to me I know is going to come true. I want to be myself; I don't want this electronic imposition and duping to abuse me and misuse me, make a robot out of me. I don't care for it."

As this first session wound down, Clyde and Joseph became very annoyed, each believing the other was an imposter, each shouting divine warnings and orders to the other. Leon, who had sat quietly throughout much of the diatribe, announced he was not coming back to any more meetings, which he claimed were "mental torture." However, the very next day when Rokeach told the men it was time to get together again, they all assembled in the same room without the slightest protest. This went on for 2 years, and none of the men relinquished his delusional identity.

Hallucinations. Seventy percent of people diagnosed with schizophrenia experience hallucinations at some point in the course of their disorders (Bentall, 1990). Hallucinators have difficulty discriminating between real events and their own subvocalizations, thoughts, daydreams, or mental images. They often misattribute these sensations to external sources; therefore, hallucinations give people the "illusion of reality," that seems to exist outside of their control (Bentall, 1990).

It is important to distinguish hallucinations from illusions, which are more common. **Illusions** occur when an actual sensory experience is misperceived or misinterpreted; the "man in the moon," for example, is an illusion, not a hallucination; likewise, mistaking a cat's meow for a human voice is an illusion. Hallucinations should also be distinguished from a range of unusual experiences that occur among mentally healthy people (Holroyd et al., 1994). After driving for an extended time without sleep, for example, people might begin to see things swimming in front of their eyes; or if they are alone in a strange building, they might easily be convinced that they hear noises that are not there. Unusual sensory experiences such as these are not considered hallucinations unless the person acts as if they were real, is unable to stop them, and reports that they persist no matter what the person does (Bentall, 1990; Heilbrun, 1993).

About 60 percent of schizophrenics report *auditory hallucinations,* usually hearing hallucinated voices. In some cases, the voices sound as if they were coming from inside the person's head; in other instances, the voices seem to speak out of thin air. Typically, the voices accuse the person of wrongdoing, belittle the person, or command the person to perform some act (as they did with Lionel Aldridge). At times, two or more voices may seem to be conversing about the person, as was the case with Mark.

*M*ark reported hearing the voices of a man, a woman, and a child, all telling him that he was Harry Truman and that he was responsible for killing thousands of Japanese. They warned him that if he "was ever out of his house after 11 PM," he would be set on fire and burned to death. The voices usually taunted him, saying, "go out and burn," "come take your turn" over and over again.

About 40 percent of schizophrenics report *tactile hallucinations,* in which the person feels as if

This painting, by a patient with schizophrenia, capures the vividness, power, and, in some cases, the terror, of visual hallucinations.

something is touching the skin or moving underneath its surface. The most common forms of tactile hallucination involve the sensation of being electrically shocked and *formication,* in which the person feels as if bugs or other creatures are creeping under the skin.

Visual hallucinations are experienced in about one third of cases of schizophrenia. They usually involve visions of people or faces, although less distinct figures, objects, or flashes of light may be experienced as well. One schizophrenic reported seeing a computer screen behind her that displayed orders from her "higher in command" to audit the tax forms of her high-school classmates. One common visual hallucination involves the faces of devils and demons, who also serve as the sources of hallucinated voices (Brewerton, 1994).

Gustatory (taste) and *olfactory* (smell) *hallucinations* are less common schizophrenic experiences that almost always have an unpleasant character. One patient reported that he knew his food had been poisoned because he could taste arsenic in it. Others claim that their flesh smells as if it were rotting. *Somatic hallucinations* in which the person feels bizarre sensations within the body—such as electricity shooting through the limbs—are the least common schizophrenic hallucination.

Researchers are making progress in understanding the biological and psychological conditions that give rise to hallucinations. Brain-imaging studies are consistent with the hypothesis that hallucinators have trouble discriminating between real events and imaginary ones. These images show that several areas of the brain become unusually active during hallucinations. Other research shows that hallucinations are less likely to occur if a person is socially engaged or busy with some task, suggesting that schizophrenics' excessive focus on what is going on inside their heads may give rise to altered perceptions.

Disordered Thought Processes. Whereas delusions are disturbances in the *content* of thoughts, other positive symptoms of schizophrenia involve fundamental disturbances in the *form* of thought—in how thoughts are organized, controlled, and processed (Marengo, Harrow, & Edell, 1993). Almost all experts on schizophrenia agree that disordered thinking and faulty attention are key features of schizophrenia. Symptoms involving disturbances in the form of thought are therefore known as **formal thought disorder.** Because clinicians cannot directly observe how people think, they must infer thought processes from how people communicate through speech. Therefore

the DSM-IV focuses on the presence of disorganized speech as evidence of formal thought disorder.

In thought disorder, which is present in up to 85 percent of hospitalized schizophrenics, the speaker cannot maintain a specific train of thought. While conversing or answering a question, the patient "slips off track," leaving the listener trying to follow a wandering stream of talk. Such speech makes little or no sense and has consequently been called *derailment, cognitive slippage,* or *loosening of associations.* At extreme levels, speech becomes a *word salad,* in which words seem to be mixed, tossed, and flung out at random. The following excerpt from the comments of a patient with schizophrenia illustrates some of the common characteristics of schizophrenic speech:

> *I*f things turn by rotation of agriculture or levels in regards and "timed" to everything: I am referring to a previous document when I made some remarks that were also tested and there is another that concerns my daughter has a lobed bottomed right ear, her name being Mary Lou. . . . Much of abstraction has been left unsaid and undone in this product/milk syrup and others, due to economics, differentials, subsidies, bankruptcy, tools, buildings, bonds, national stocks, foundation crap, weather, trades, government in levels of breakages and fuse in electronics too all formerly "stated" not necessarily factuated. (Maher, 1968, p. 395)

Although most of the words in this passage are familiar, their arrangement does not make sense or communicate meaning. Patients often show little awareness that they cannot be understood when speaking this way.

Another sign of disordered thought processes is the creation of words, or *neologisms,* the meaning of which appears to be known only to the speaker. Two neologisms are italicized in the following example:

> *T*he players and boundaries have been of different colors in terms of black and white and I do not intend that the *futuramas* of supersonic fixtures will ever be in my life again because I believe that all known factors that would have its effect on me even the chemical reaction of ameno (sic) acids as they are in the process of *combustronability* are known to me. (Maher, 1968, p. 395)

Recall also the prior example of Jimmy who used the neologisms "beaners" and "wranged."

Disordered thought process may also be revealed through *perseveration*. The person seems to get stuck on a word or concept and repeats it over and over. Another sign of disordered thought is the presence of *clang associations*—words that are spoken apparently only because they sound alike. For example, a patient might repeatedly utter the sound of " . . . ation" or " . . . ating."

> Could we be afraid of not responding such as contracted hypothalami in women indicating by the ingestion of controlled substances and sovereign equality against administration not terminating contracted gestations and filing charges of treason and genocide against women using controlled substances prior to conceptions which gestating or while lactating?

Disorders of Behavior. Another class of symptoms associated with schizophrenia (as well as other mental and neurological disorders) is peculiar motor behavior. Patients may make odd movements, hold themselves in contorted postures, walk in a peculiar fashion, and make absurd or obscene gestures. The most dramatic behaviors range across a dimension of **catatonia,** or disordered behavior. At one end of this dimension, the person becomes virtually immobile, maintaining an awkward body position for hours at a time, often to the point of appearing stuporous. At the opposite extreme of catatonia, patients may display great excitement, extreme motor activity, repetitive gestures and mannerisms, and undirected violent behaviors (Manschreck, 1993).

Some schizophrenic patients also display *disorganized behavior* that makes it impossible for them to get dressed properly, prepare food, or take care of other daily needs. These patients may also giggle or sob inappropriately or uncontrollably. Inappropriate sexual behavior such as masturbating in public is not uncommon.

Some less dramatic behavioral anomalies associated with schizophrenia include facial grimaces, lip smacking, and other stereotyped behavior. One older male patient known to the authors would stuff all his pockets with magazine advertisements of attractive female models, while repeating again and again, "Oh, so that's what I'm doing." By the end of each day, so much ink from the magazines had rubbed off on him that his clothes were filthy.

Psychomotor disturbances such as poor eye–hand coordination or clumsiness in walking also occur on occasion (Manschreck, 1993). Some movement disorders represent the side effects of antipsychotic medications, but others are associated with

Disturbed movements and postures are observed in some individuals with schizophrenia. Some patients passively resist any attempt to move them, a condition known as extreme negativism; *some allow their arms and legs to be molded into contorted positions that they hold for hours (called* waxy flexibility).

schizophrenia itself. The presence of motor anomalies is correlated with greater overall severity of the disorder, but the origins of these anomalies and how they are related to other symptoms of schizophrenia remain unclear (Manschreck, 1993).

Negative Symptoms of Schizophrenia

Deficit schizophrenia is another name sometimes given to the negative symptoms of schizophrenia. Some negative symptoms such as social withdrawal and *anhedonia* (the inability to enjoy almost anything) are commonly associated with schizophrenia but are not considered diagnostic symptoms. Three negative symptoms—flat affect, alogia, and avolation—are among the criteria for diagnosing schizophrenia.

Flat Affect. Many patients with schizophrenia often stare straight ahead with an empty or glazed look. Even when spoken to, they make no eye contact with the speaker. Their faces are like emotionless masks. Their facial muscles appear slack, and they often speak in a voice so toneless it sounds robotic. Their entire demeanor is drab and listless. This **flat affect** or blunted affect is one of the more obvious negative symptoms of schizophrenia, and it is found in about two thirds of schizophrenic patients. Flat affect is an important symptom because it often suggests a poor prognosis.

Does flat affect indicate that the person is not experiencing emotions, or just not expressing them? Scientists are still not sure, but recent research suggests that flat affect reflects a problem mainly at the level of expression rather than experience. In one study (Berenbaum & Oltmanns, 1992), schizophrenic

The negative symptoms of schizophrenia—including social withdrawal, apathy, and dulled emotions—are among its most disabling features. Suicide attempts, although not officially listed as a negative symptom of schizophrenia, is a frequent complication of the disorder. Among people with schizophrenia, suicide is the leading cause of premature death, occurring in 10 to 15 percent of individuals with the disorder (Caldwell & Gottesman, 1990).

patients and normal subjects were videotaped as they watched clips from a variety of popular movies (e.g., *Marathon Man* and the cartoon *Ali Baba Bunny*) that usually create strong emotional reactions in viewers. The patients whose symptoms included flat affect showed few facial reactions to the movie scenes. However, when they were later asked to describe how they felt as they watched the films, they reported feeling emotions that were no different from those of the normal subjects.

Alogia. The failure to say much, if anything, in response to questions or comments is called **alogia.** Patients with alogia do not appear especially negativistic; they just seem to have little to say. Trying to talk with a patient who is alogic often leaves a person wondering, "Is that all there is?" In other patients, alogia takes the form of slow or delayed responses that become so frustrating that people finally give up trying to sustain the conversation.

Avolition. The behavioral counterpart to alogia is **avolition.** Avolitional patients may simply sit for hours on end making no attempt to do anything. If they do begin some activity, they wander off in the middle of it, seeming to lose interest or forget what they were doing.

Avolition may be accompanied by anhedonia. Anhedonic patients are chronically indifferent to events around them, as if all their energy has been sapped. They may stare blankly at a television or become agitated by a hallucination, but otherwise they seem to lack any capacity to be engaged by the environment. Sensitivity to painful stimulation is even reduced in some cases. Although some patients with schizophrenia feel the physical sensations of pain, their emotional component is diminished to the point where they do not find pain as aversive as other people do (Dworkin, 1994).

Distinguishing Schizophrenia from Other Psychotic Disorders

Before diagnosing schizophrenia, a clinician should consider other possible sources of the symptoms observed. As noted in Chapter 9, for example, severe mood disorders can produce some of the symptoms described here. Psychotic symptoms can also be produced by intoxication from alcohol or other drugs and by several medical conditions. For example, hallucinations and delusions can result from brain tumors, cerebral vascular disease, temporal lobe epilepsy, migraine headaches, central nervous system infections, endocrine disorders such as hypo- or hyperthyroidism, metabolic disorders such as hypoglycemia, and liver or kidney disease (APA, 1994). In these cases the disorder is classified as **psychotic disorder due to a general medical condition.**

Clinicians also need to distinguish schizophrenia from **schizophrenic spectrum disorders.** These are disorders that are schizophrenia-like but they do not meet all the diagnostic criteria for schizophrenia, and they tend to be less severe. Common spectrum disorders include the schizotypal, schizoid, and paranoid personality disorders discussed in Chapter 12. Spectrum disorders also include several disorders classified by the DSM-IV as **other psychotic disorders:** schizophreniform disorder, schizoaffective disorder, delusional disorder, brief psychotic disorder, and shared psychotic disorder (substance-induced psychotic disorder is also classified under "other psychotic disorders," but it is not part of the schizophrenia spectrum). Most of these disorders are relatively rare, and research on their characteristics and causes is scant. Their symptoms are usually more limited in duration and less intense than those of schizophrenia.

Brief Psychotic Disorder. "Nervous breakdown" and "falling to pieces" are familiar phrases used to describe people whose psychological functioning has rapidly deteriorated, usually after they have experienced a severe stressor. These cases are best described by what the DSM-IV classifies as brief psychotic disorder.

Unlike most cases of schizophrenia, **brief psychotic disorder** is characterized by the sudden onset of an episode marked by intense emotional turmoil and confusion and the appearance of positive psychotic symptoms such as hallucinations, delusions, incoherent speech, and catatonic or disorganized behavior. During this episode, the person is at high risk for attempting suicide. By definition, the episode must last at least 1 day but less than 1 month, after which the individual returns to a normal level of functioning. If the symptoms last longer than 1 month, the diagnosis should be changed to one of the other psychotic disorders.

Often, brief psychotic disorder is a reaction to a severe stressor such as the death of a loved one, but occasionally no precipitating stressor can be identified. When brief psychotic disorder follows childbirth, it is specified as having a **postpartum onset.**

Schizophreniform Disorder. People who experience the symptoms of schizophrenia for only a few months are given the diagnosis of **schizophreniform disorder.** There are two major differences between schizophrenia and schizophreniform disorder. First, impaired social or occupational functioning is not required for schizophreniform disorder. Second, in schizophreni-

form disorder, the symptoms are present for at least 1 but not more than 6 months. About one third of people with schizophreniform disorder recover and go on to live reasonably normal lives; the other two thirds eventually warrant a diagnosis of schizophrenia or schizoaffective disorder.

Schizoaffective Disorder. In **schizoaffective disorder,** people display either hallucinations or delusions that resemble those experienced in schizophrenia, but during the same psychotic episode, the symptoms of a mood disorder are also present. The prognosis for schizoaffective disorder is generally better than for schizophrenia but worse than for mood disorders. Schizoaffective disorder is less prevalent than schizophrenia and is more often diagnosed in females than males.

Should schizoaffective disorder be considered a separate category of psychosis, a subtype of schizophrenia, or a mood disorder? Exactly where this disorder, with its mixture of symptoms, belongs diagnostically remains a matter of debate (Coryell et al., 1984; Tsuang & Coryell, 1993).

Delusional Disorder. People who display a rare form of psychosis known as **delusional disorder** show no obvious impairment apart from the presence of at least one nonbizarre delusional belief (in the DSM-IV, *nonbizarre* means that the delusion involves a belief that would not be totally implausible within a person's culture). Usually the delusion is persistent and causes the person to organize much of his or her life around it. Other than the delusional belief and its consequences, the person may appear normal most of the time. Perhaps for this reason, and because these people usually avoid clinicians, this disorder tends to be diagnosed later in life than schizophrenia. Table 10.1 on page 342 describes some of the main types of delusional disorder.

Shared Psychotic Disorder. One of the most peculiar psychotic conditions is **shared psychotic disorder,** in which one person, termed the *inducer,* develops a psychotic disorder and then influences another person or persons (called *receivers*) to act on it as well. If the receiver is separated from the inducer, his or her delusions will usually fade away. The disorder is also known as *folie à deux* or "madness of two," but sometimes three (*folie à trois*) or more persons can become involved.

In some cases whole families have come to share a delusional system (Cryan & Ganter, 1992). In other cases shared delusional phenomena have occurred in groups, such as religious cults whose leader-inducer attracts members who all eventually embrace the

TABLE 10.1	Types of Delusional Disorder	
Type	**Description**	**Typical Behaviors**
Erotomanic	Believe that some other person, typically someone of notoriety or higher status, is secretly in love with them.	Stalk the love object, send annoying letters or gifts, make unwanted phone calls or take other steps to contact the loved object. (Such as the woman who insisted that she was the secret lover of David Letterman.)
Jealous	Believe that their romantic partners are being unfaithful, despite very skimpy evidence.	Follow the partner or constantly check on the partner's whereabouts through phone calls or repeated demands for partner's attention.
Grandiose	Believe that they have a special talent, have made an important discovery, know someone of great importance, or have a special relationship with God beyond that associated with established religion.	May try to convert others into followers or provoke confrontations with authorities. (Such as David Koresch, leader of the Branch Davidian sect.)
Persecutory	Believe that they are being spied on, cheated, followed, or otherwise taken advantage of.	May become increasingly isolated and bitter; often try to bring about opportunities to fight their alleged persecutors, often try to obtain legal remedies for problems.
Somatic	Hold beliefs about their bodies, such as the delusion that a rancid odor is seeping out, that their ears are grossly misshapen or that they have foreign organisms under the skin.	May become preoccupied with hiding the defect or hypersensitive to signs that someone else has noticed it.

inducer's delusional beliefs (Sirkin, 1992). When delusional systems take a paranoid turn, they can result in disasters. It is possible that shared delusional systems are involved in some cases of mass suicide or murder, as in the Branch Davidian slayings in Waco, Texas, in 1994 or the 1995 Tokyo nerve gas attack by members of the doomsday sect *Aum Shinri Kyo* ("Supreme Truth").

Substance-Induced Psychotic Disorder. Hallucinations and delusions can result from ingestion of various substances, including drugs of abuse (such as cocaine), medications (such as corticosteroids), or toxins (such as organophosphate insecticides). When people experience hallucinations or delusions beyond what is expected from intoxication with the substance or during withdrawal from it and they are not aware that the substances are producing the hallucinations or delusions, then they qualify for the diagnosis of **substance-induced psychotic disorder.**

In Review

The current definition of schizophrenia evolved from:

- Morel's original description, in the mid-1800s, of dementia praecox as a syndrome marked by the premature loss of the ability to reason;
- Kraepelin's identification, in the late 1800s, of dementia praecox as a major mental disorder with several subtypes;
- Bleuler's broader definition of the disorder, which he named *schizophrenia,* because he viewed the splitting of psychological functions as the core of the problem;
- Schneider's listing of certain delusions and hallucinations as the first-rank, or defining, criteria for the disorder; and
- the DSM-IV's compromise among the views of Kraepelin, Bleuler, and Schneider.

The symptoms of schizophrenia can be divided into two categories:

- positive symptoms, which include delusions, hallucinations, disturbances in the content and the form of thinking, and disorganized and grossly inappropriate behavior; and
- negative symptoms, which include flat affect, alogia, and avolition.

In addition to schizophrenia, psychotic symptoms can be associated with:

- severe mood disorders;
- intoxication from alcohol or other drugs;
- certain medical conditions and interventions;
- disorders along a dimension known as the *schizophrenia spectrum*; and
- disorders classified as other psychotic conditions, which usually involve symptoms that are less intense and less persistent than those of schizophrenia.

Life with Schizophrenia: Patterns and Variations

Schizophrenia comes in many shapes and forms. It can appear suddenly as it did with Lionel Aldridge, or it can develop slowly over several years. It can affect teenagers, or it can first occur in people who are over 50. In some cases the most prominent symptoms are hallucinations or delusions; other patients suffer primarily negative symptoms. Some patients make a complete recovery, others a partial recovery. About a quarter of patients continue to suffer symptoms of the disorder even when they take medications, and a few remain hospitalized for years, unimproved by any treatment. In truth, the term schizophrenia encompasses several disorders that vary dramatically in onset, symptoms, impairment, and prognosis. To highlight these differences, contrast the case of Lionel Aldridge with that of Louise.

Louise is a pale, stooped woman of 39 years, whose childlike face is surrounded by scraggly blond braids tied with pink ribbons. She was referred for a psychiatric evaluation by her family doctor, who was concerned about her low level of functioning. Her only complaint to him was, "I have a decline in self-care and a low life level." Her mother says that there has indeed been a decline that has occurred over many years. In the last few months Louise has remained in her room, mute and still.

Twelve years ago Louise was a supervisor in the occupational therapy department of a hospital, living in her own apartment, and engaged to a young man. After he broke off the engagement, she became increasingly disorganized, wandering aimlessly in the street wearing mismatched clothing. She was fired from her job, and eventually the police were called to hospitalize her. They broke into her apartment, which was a shambles, filled with papers, food, and broken objects. This hospitalization lasted 3 months, after which Louise was discharged to her mother's house.

After her discharge, her family hoped that Louise would pull herself together and get back on track, but, over the years, she became more withdrawn. She spent most of her time watching TV and cooking with bizarre combinations of ingredients, such as broccoli and cake mix, which she then ate by herself because no one else in the family would eat them. She hoarded stacks of cookbooks and recipes. Often when her mother entered her room, Louise would grab a magazine and pretend to be reading, when in fact she had just been sitting and staring into space. She stopped bathing and brushing her hair or her teeth. She ate less and less, although she denied losing her appetite, and, over a period of several years, she lost 20 pounds. She slept at odd hours. Eventually she became enuretic, wetting her bed frequently.

On admission to the psychiatric hospital, Louise sat with her hands clasped in her lap and avoided looking at the doctor who interviewed her. She answered questions and did not appear suspicious, but her mood was shallow. She denied having depressed mood, delusions, or hallucinations. However, her answers became more and more odd as the interview progressed. In response to a question about her cooking habits, she replied that she did not wish to discuss recent events in Russia. When discussing her decline in functioning, she said, "There's more of a take-off mechanism when you're younger." Asked about ideas of reference, she said, "I doubt it's true, but if one knows the writers involved, it could be an element that would be directed in a comical way." Between answers she repeated the mantra, "I'm safe. I'm safe." (Based on Spitzer et al., 1994)

The Course of Schizophrenia

Only about 4 percent of all diagnosed cases of schizophrenia develop before age 15. After that age, the rate of onset increases rapidly, reaching a peak in the early 20s. Males tend to be diagnosed with schizophrenia at earlier ages than females (Remschmidt et al., 1994), as Figure 10.1 shows. The average age of people first admitted to a hospital because of schizophrenia is about 30; by age 55, the majority of people who are going to develop schizophrenia have done so (Castle & Murray, 1993; Gottesman, 1991). Contrary to early views, schizophrenia (as defined by the DSM) can develop when people are as old as 50 to 60 years (Castle & Murray, 1993).

Schizophrenia can occur in young children, but it rarely does so. Childhood-onset schizophrenia bears similarities to pervasive developmental disorders such as autistic disorder. Both conditions involve disturbances in mood, language, and the ability to relate normally to other people. However, two important differences between childhood schizophrenia and autistic disorder are that (1) hallucinations and delusions are prominent in schizophrenia but not in autistic disorder and (2) speech is absent or limited in autistic disorder, whereas it tends to be present but disorganized or bizarre in schizophrenia. Children who have autistic disorder occasionally develop schizophrenia, in which case both disorders are diagnosed.

Although schizophrenia may begin abruptly, most cases start with a **prodromal phase**, in which affected persons show an insidious onset of problems that suggests that something is going wrong with them. They may start to avoid meals with their families or stop paying attention to their appearance and hygiene. Often, they start to talk in unusual ways, behave just a little strangely, and seem easily irritated and frustrated. As a general rule, the longer this prodromal phase lasts, the poorer the prognosis.

Eventually, but usually after some crisis, prodromal symptoms progress to an **active phase,** in which one or more psychotic symptoms such as delusions and hallucinations break into the open. The disorder appears most serious and obvious to other people during this phase.

Following the active phase is a **residual phase**, during which the psychotic symptoms subside in frequency and intensity. This stage of the disorder may resemble the prodromal phase; the patient is withdrawn, apathetic, behaves strangely at times, and continues to show social and occupational impairments.

Schizophrenia does not inevitably result in permanent disability, but most people who have schizophrenia continue to suffer recurring symptoms. In some cases, the symptoms improve so that patients can live almost completely on their own. In other

Connections

What are the symptoms of autistic disorder? How do its suspected causes differ from those of schizophrenia? See Chapter 4, pp. 135–140.

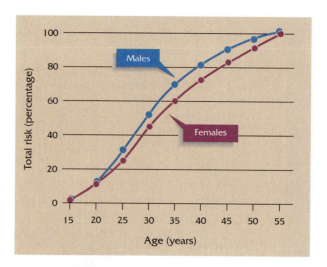

FIGURE 10.1

Hospitalization for Schizophrenia

Hospitalization for schizophrenia tends to occur at earlier ages for men than for women. Half of all males with schizophrenia are hospitalized for the disorder by age 28; females, by age 33. This difference in age at first hospitalization has been found worldwide.

Source: Based on Gottesman, 1991.

cases, the patient improves for a while and then suffers a relapse in which the symptoms can be serious enough to require rehospitalization. This pattern may be repeated several times, but, as patients age, they are hospitalized less often. The prognosis is not bleak for all schizophrenics, as Figure 10.2 shows. According to one review of six international studies (Watt & Saiz, 1991), about 25 percent of all patients hospitalized for schizophrenia recover enough so that they do not need rehospitalization. Another 25 percent enjoy an almost complete recovery, although they may still display some symptoms.

Who Is Affected by Schizophrenia?

Worldwide, about 20 million people suffer from schizophrenia, approximately 1.2 million of whom are in the United States. Obviously the prevalence of schizophrenia depends on how it is defined. A Kraepelinian or Schneiderian definition of schizophrenia yields a lower rate than does the broader, Bleulerian definition. Using criteria such as those in the DSM-IV, which is considered a middle-of-the-road compromise, clinicians diagnose schizophrenia in approximately 1 percent of the world's population

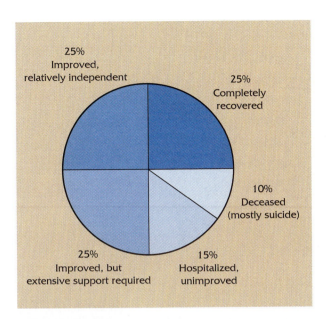

The Course of Schizophrenia

Outcomes for patients with schizophrenia 10 years after initial diagnosis.

Source: Based on Torrey, 1988.

(Gottesman, 1991). This figure is generally accepted as an average or standard; the range is about 0.2 to 2.0 percent.

Cultural Background. Does culture make a difference in the risk for schizophrenia? Interest in this question dates back to the late 1800s, when Kraepelin himself explored it by touring several countries to examine their mental patients. After traveling to Singapore, where he examined patients from Java, China, and Malaya, Kraepelin concluded that their symptoms were remarkably similar to those of his patients in Germany. Such experiences convinced Kraepelin that the disorder was transmitted genetically and was universal.

The strongest support for the universality of schizophrenia comes from a series of studies sponsored by the World Health Organization (WHO) called the "International Pilot Study on Schizophrenia" (IPSS) and the "Determinants of Outcome of Severe Mental Disorders" (DOSMD) (WHO, 1978). Begun in the 1960s, these studies were conducted in 12 research centers in 10 countries: Denmark, India, Nigeria, Columbia, Russia, China, Czechoslovakia, Japan, the United Kingdom, and the United States.

The WHO studies reached several conclusions. First, the descriptions of symptoms for schizophrenic patients in the various countries were similar; in fact, based on symptom patterns alone, it was not possible to identify the country from which patients were drawn (WHO, 1978)—a finding confirmed by other research (Murphy, 1976). Second, the **morbidity risk,** defined as the risk that a given person has of developing the disorder over his or her lifetime, averaged 1 percent. Third, at each site the prevalence of schizophrenia (whether defined by broad or narrow criteria) was significant, as Figure 10.3 on page 346 shows.

However, other studies spanning a greater number of cultures show larger variations in schizophrenia prevalence than those found by the WHO studies. For example, just 0.3 cases per 1,000 population were reported among the Amish in the United States (Torrey, 1987). Unusually low rates have also been found in Ghana and in New Guinea, but disproportionately high rates have been found among residents of rural Ireland and the former Yugoslavia (Torrey, 1987).

All researchers acknowledge geographic and cultural variations in rates of schizophrenia, but they differ in their opinions about the importance of this variation. Some argue that, overall, the differences amount to only a few cases per thousand people and are therefore of little significance (Gottesman, 1991), especially when compared with the large geographic variations observed for diseases such as diabetes and multiple sclerosis. For example, schizophrenia occurs at about equal rates among different ethnic groups in the United States; whatever variations are found are slight.

On the other hand, culture does seem to matter when it comes to the prognosis for schizophrenia, and it matters in a surprising way. Patients from so-called developing or Third World countries show *higher* rates of improvement than patients from developed countries. Why this should occur is not yet known, but the Controversy section on page 347 explores some possible explanations.

Even if cultural variation in the prevalence of schizophrenia is deemed insignificant, culture might make a difference in other ways. For one thing, it might affect the form of some hallucinations. For example, visual hallucinations have declined since the nineteenth century whereas auditory hallucinations have increased. The content of hallucinations also tends to reflect themes that are prominent in a person's culture (Al-Issa, 1977). Among younger patients in Western societies, hallucinations often include technological features—neon lights explode, loud noises

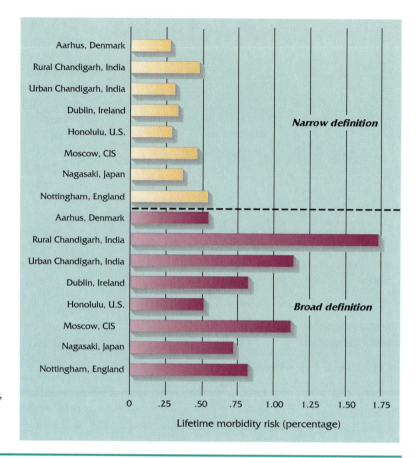

Worldwide Risks of Schizophrenia
The morbidity risk (i.e., the risk of a given person's developing a disorder in his or her lifetime) for schizophrenia varies depending on whether a broad or narrow definition of the disorder is used. However, schizophrenia is found in all countries that have been studied.
Source: Based on Gottesman, 1991.

buzz, and computer screens flash. In contrast, the voices of ghosts, dragons, or animals are likely to appear in the hallucinations of people in cultures with less modern technology.

Social Background. Schizophrenia occurs not only in all geographic areas but also among all social classes. However, in the United States at least, a disproportionate number of cases come from poorer classes living in inner cities. For example, the Epidemiologic Catchment Area (ECA) studies—a large-scale, interview-based investigation of the epidemiology of mental disorders in the United States—show that the relative risk of becoming schizophrenic for persons in the lowest quartile of socioeconomic status is nearly 8 times higher than for persons in the highest quartile and 2 times higher than for persons from the middle classes (Holzer et al., 1986). Similar findings were reported 60 years ago, when studies of admissions to Chicago mental hospitals found that 4 times as many admissions came from high-poverty urban areas as from more affluent areas (Faris & Dunham, 1939). This pattern is not restricted solely to the United

States. A relationship among urban living, lower social class, and higher rates of schizophrenia has been found in England, Sweden, and Germany (Freeman, 1994). Notable exceptions also occur, however; in India, Japan, and in certain areas of western Europe the expected correlation is not found (Freeman, 1994; Torrey, 1987).

Gender and Morbidity Risk. The morbidity risk for schizophrenia is essentially equal for males and females. However, the initial onset of symptoms averages at least 5 years earlier for males than females (Castle & Murray, 1993). As a result, males account for the majority of cases of schizophrenia with onset before age 30; females predominate among cases with later onset (Remschmidt et al., 1994). Men are also hospitalized for schizophrenia more often than women, and their prognosis is poorer (Goldstein, 1988). We do not know for certain why schizophrenia begins earlier for males than females, but this pattern is seen in virtually all countries where the disorder has been studied (Castle & Murray; 1993; Häfner et al., 1994; Harris & Jeste, 1988).

Controversy

Why Do Schizophrenics in Nonindustrialized Countries Have Better Prognoses Than Those in Industrialized Countries?

It is now well accepted that patients diagnosed with schizophrenia in developed countries, including the United States, have significantly poorer chances of recovery than those from "developing" countries (WHO, 1978; Lin & Kleinman, 1988; Torrey, 1987). For example, in the 2-year follow-up of patients from the IPSS, 57 percent of patients from Ibadan, Nigeria, and 48 percent from Agra, India, were fully recovered. In contrast, only 23 percent of patients from the industrialized countries had recovered in this time period. This difference was maintained up to 9 years later (Dube, Kumar, & Dube, 1984). Identical results have been found in other cross-cultural studies (Lin & Kleinman, 1988).

Two types of explanations have been offered to account for these differential recovery rates: one is biological; the other relies on sociocultural differences.

One biological hypothesis is that there are two strains of schizophrenia. The virulent strain is found more often in the industrial societies and results in poorer prognosis, while a more benign strain constituting many of the cases in nonindustrial societies has a better prognosis. For example, Leff (1994) notes that, when a narrow definition of schizophrenia is used to identify a hardcore group of patients, no substantial differences in prevalence of schizophrenia is found across cultures. However, using a broader definition consistently leads to more schizophrenia

being reported in the developing nations. Leff believes that this increased prevalence using the broader definition includes a mild form of schizophrenia that has a better prognosis.

An alternative biological explanation focuses on the hypothesis that some cases of schizophrenia develop from prenatal or perinatal injuries or illness (viral infections). These factors are more likely to lead to cases of schizophrenia involving damaged brain structures. Such cases should be more serious, chronic, and have poorer prognoses. In developing, as opposed to developed, societies, such individuals would also be more vulnerable to early death because of poorer medical care. Therefore, a larger proportion of brain-injured schizophrenics would survive in the industrial societies, but the poor prognoses of these patients would lower the average rate of recovery in these countries (Lin & Kleinman, 1988).

Several social or cultural factors might also account for the differences. For example, developing, nonindustrialized countries are more likely to be organized as *collectivist* societies in which a person's identity is bound up with others in collective groups, such as families or villages (Brislin, 1991). When a person in these societies becomes ill, the responsibility for the problem belongs to the group as a whole. Group members are available to support the person through the crisis, which is seen more as a community rather than

an individual problem. In contrast, most industrialized countries are organized as *individualistic* societies in which the person is seen as the center of the problem and is held responsible for the solution. Less community support may be provided for the individual's recovery in such societies. Posthospital employment is another element associated with recovery. After being released from a hospital, patients in a collectivist society might be more likely to have work opportunities available that accommodate their disabilities than are patients in individualistic societies (Lin & Kleinman, 1988).

Presently, the data necessary to choose among these various explanations are not available. The diathesis–stress model of schizophrenia would predict that cultural differences in recovery rates reflect some aspect of the ways in which different social practices or organizations can modify biological vulnerabilities to schizophrenia.

Thinking Critically

Recovery rates for schizophrenia appear to vary according to overall cultural setting, but the reasons for this difference remain unclear.

- What explanations, besides those we have discussed, might account for this difference?
- How would you design a study to investigate whether different mortality rates between countries explain the difference?

DSM-IV Subtypes and Other Classifications

The variations in the constellation of symptoms, personal histories, demographic characteristics, and impairments among people diagnosed with schizophre-

nia can be dizzying. In fact, many clinicians refer to *schizophrenias* rather than to *schizophrenia*. As we have seen, the effort to categorize subtypes of schizophrenia goes back to Kraepelin. The DSM-IV recognizes five types of schizophrenia. These types are based on clusters of observed symptoms that seem to go together. The diagnosis of a subtype is made on the basis of the symptoms that are most prominent when the patient is being evaluated, so the diagnosis can change over time. Indeed, it is not unusual for a patient to display symptoms that are indicative of more than one type of schizophrenia. When this occurs, the DSM-IV lists specific rules for which diagnoses take precedence.

Paranoid Type. The defining symptoms of the **paranoid type** are prominent, persistent, and elaborate delusions, usually involving themes of persecution. Auditory hallucinations are also common, and, as in the case of Lionel Aldridge, they are typically related to delusional beliefs. Compared with other types of schizophrenia, intellectual and cognitive functions are generally well preserved in the paranoid type. People with this type of schizophrenia are less likely than other types to exhibit disordered speech, disorganized behavior, or negative symptoms such as flat affect (Strauss, 1993).

Lionel Aldridge's case also illustrates that the onset of paranoid schizophrenia usually occurs later in life than for other types and is more likely to have been preceded by relatively normal adjustment. The symptoms usually appear relatively suddenly, and the prognosis is generally better than for the other types (Fenton & McGlashan, 1991a). Unfortunately, patients diagnosed as paranoid types are more likely to behave aggressively than people diagnosed with other types, and male paranoid schizophrenics have the highest suicide risk (13 percent) of all subtypes (APA, 1994; Fenton & McGlashan, 1991a).

Disorganized Type. Originally called *hebephrenia* by Kraepelin, the **disorganized type** of schizophrenia is defined by grossly inappropriate and disorganized speech, behavior, and affect. Speech may be incoherent at times. Emotional responses are usually either flat or flagrantly inappropriate. Persons with this type of schizophrenia often display a childlike silliness, and they may need help to perform the most basic of daily tasks. Even their delusions or hallucinations, if they have them, are poorly organized and fragmented.

In contrast to the paranoid type, disorganized schizophrenia usually involves serious intellectual incapacities. This subtype develops gradually, often beginning in the early teens, followed by a chronic, deteriorating course with a poor prognosis (Fenton & McGlashan, 1991a).

Catatonic Type. Less is known about the **catatonic type** than others because it is so rare, but it is distinctive. It is defined by extremely disordered, odd motor movements (Fenton & McGlashan, 1991a).

The person may show catatonic excitement, relentless activity, and wild flailing about, or catatonic stupor to the point that the person develops **catalepsy** (immobility) and maintains the same posture for extended periods of time. These postures may be rigid, or involve the molding and holding of limbs in bizarre positions, known as **waxy flexibility.** Other features of the catatonic type include *mutism,* (refusal or inability to speak), *echopraxia* (a semiautomatic, repetitive imitation of others' movements), and *echolalia* (a parrotlike repetition of words or phrases just spoken by others). Like the disorganized type, severe cases of the catatonic type can require almost constant supervision to protect the patient from self-harm or from endangering others during episodes of catatonic excitement.

Undifferentiated Type. The **undifferentiated type** includes persons who meet the diagnostic criteria for schizophrenia but who do not satisfy the specific criteria for any of the first three subtypes. This is probably the largest subtype of schizophrenia, and its members often present a mixture of positive and negative symptoms found in other subtypes. In fact, some patients, initially classified as one of the other subtypes, are eventually reclassified as undifferentiated when their symptoms become less distinct over time.

Residual Type. Patients are classified with the **residual type** if they have had at least one prior episode of schizophrenia, but do not currently display any major positive symptoms. These patients are still judged to be suffering from schizophrenia if they experience either negative symptoms or a minor form of at least two positive symptoms. Some residual cases represent a transition from an active episode of schizophrenia to a marked improvement or remission. In other cases, patients with schizophrenia who have been institutionalized for many years are diagnosed with the residual label. Such cases are known among clinicians as *burned out schizophrenia,* suggesting that, although most positive symptoms have died down, these patients have become extremely withdrawn and dependent on others for basic care.

A type of schizophrenia proposed for future study in the DSM-IV is *simple deteriorative disorder* (also known as *simple schizophrenia*). This subtype appears similar to the type of schizophrenia that Morel first described and that Kraepelin classified as "simplex." Symptoms of the simple subtype include a noticeable decline in occupational or academic functioning and the gradual appearance and worsening of negative symptoms. As this subtype develops, the person withdraws from others and becomes asocial. Some clinicians believe this subtype represents a form of "pure" negative-symptom schizophrenia.

Additional research will determine whether this disorder is listed as a formal type of schizophrenia in the future.

Other Classifications of Schizophrenia. In addition to the formal DSM-IV subtypes of schizophrenia that are based on different clusters of observed symptoms, researchers have proposed several other systems for classifying schizophrenia. The most prominent of these systems involves the distinction, described earlier, between positive and negative symptoms. Other systems are organized around hypothesized causes of schizophrenia or on the basis of onset or prognosis.

For example, the *process-reactive dimension* was proposed by Bleuler (1911). Patients with **process schizophrenia** tend to have onset at an early age and show a progressive deterioration in functioning. They are thought to have had *poor premorbid adjustment*, meaning that their social, educational, and occupational functioning was not well developed before the onset of full schizophrenia (Zigler, Levine, & Zigler, 1976). On the other end of this dimension is **reactive schizophrenia** whose symptoms come on suddenly, often in reaction to a traumatic situation. Typically, reactive types have *good premorbid adjustment*. Reactive types with good premorbid adjustment also have a better chance of recovery than process types do.

A related subtyping system combines distinctions between positive and negative symptoms with other criteria. According to British psychiatrist Timothy Crow (1985), people with *Type I schizophrenia* show mostly positive symptoms, have good premorbid functioning, including normal intelligence, experience an acute onset of symptoms, and respond to treatment with psychotropic drugs. *Type II schizophrenia* is characterized by predominantly negative symptoms, poor premorbid functioning, intellectual problems, and progressive and insidious onset and is less responsive to psychotropic drugs. Type I has a relatively good prognosis, while Type II has a poorer chance of recovery (Fenton & McGlashan, 1991b).

In Review

Schizophrenia occurs:

- worldwide at a prevalence rate of about 1 percent;
- equally in males and females;
- earlier for males than females;
- usually in the late teens or early 20s, but as late as the 50s.

Schizophrenia usually follows a course of three stages:

- the prodromal phase;
- the active phase; and
- the residual phase.

Five subtypes of schizophrenia are diagnosed, depending on the most prominent symptoms observed. The five subtypes are:

- paranoid;
- disorganized;
- catatonic;
- undifferentiated; and
- residual.

Other classification systems for schizophrenia include:

- the process-reactive dimension; and
- Type I and Type II schizophrenia.

Biological Causes of Schizophrenia

Schizophrenia has always been considered a complex disorder of many subtypes, and most modern researchers agree that it has no single cause. When it comes to causation, schizophrenia is like mental retardation (discussed in Chapter 4). Genetic forms of the disorder might exist, as might other forms arising from brain trauma, environmental handicap and stress, and chronic social adversity (Andreasen & Carpenter, 1993). Most cases probably reflect a combination of genetic, biochemical, structural, environmental, and social factors.

The explosion of knowledge in the biological sciences in recent decades has created particular interest in the biological factors in this mix. Our examination of these biological factors begins with those that might create a vulnerability to schizophrenia.

Genetic Factors and Schizophrenia

Kraepelin's examination of mental patients in various countries persuaded him that dementia praecox was not due to differences in childrearing, food, climate, or the environment. Because the disorder occurred in widely varying cultures, Kraepelin argued that it must be a biological disease transmitted genetically. Today, scientists have far better evidence that genetics play an important role in the development of schizophrenia.

The closer a person's biological relationship to someone diagnosed with schizophrenia, the greater that person's risk of developing schizophrenia or one of the schizophrenia spectrum disorders. This is the starting point for considering the role of genetics in this disorder. Overall, the evidence is clear on several other points as well:

- Schizophrenia "runs" or aggregates in families.
- This aggregation is found regardless of the type of research methodology (family, adoption, or twin studies) used or the country in which the study is performed.
- In many cases a vulnerability that predisposes a person to schizophrenia (scientists don't know exactly what) is genetically transmitted.
- Genes alone are not sufficient to account for the development of schizophrenia.

The evidence for these conclusions comes from three major lines of investigation.

Family Aggregation Studies. Family aggregations of schizophrenia have been examined since the early part of the twentieth century. These studies begin with identified schizophrenic patients, called *proband* or *index cases*. The percentage of their family members who are also diagnosed with schizophrenia is then compared with the percentage diagnosed among family members of control (nonschizophrenic) cases,

matched for age and other relevant variables. The results of family studies tell researchers the extent to which the disorder runs in families, but not why it does so. What else do these studies show?

Family studies agree on one fundamental point: the closer an individual's genetic relationship to a person with schizophrenia, the higher the risk of developing schizophrenia. This relationship is dramatically illustrated in Figure 10.4, which shows data compiled by Irving Gottesman, a psychologist at the University of Virginia, from 40 of the most reliable family studies conducted between 1920 and 1987 in Germany, Switzerland, Scandinavia, and the United Kingdom. The progression of increasing risk for schizophrenia with an increasing degree of family relationship is striking. Equally striking, however, is the fact that, even at the highest degree of genetic relationship, the majority of relatives to an index case are *not* diagnosed with schizophrenia. As noted below, for example, among identical, or monozygotic (MZ), twins, when one twin is diagnosed with schizophrenia, the cotwin, a virtual genetic clone, is similarly diagnosed in only about half the cases.

However, many older family aggregation studies, including some in Gottesman's compilation, suffered serious methodological flaws. For example, it cannot be assumed that researchers used the same criteria to

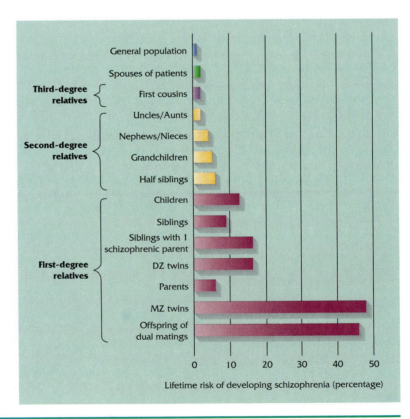

FIGURE 10.4

Family Risks for Developing Schizophrenia

The degree of risk for developing schizophrenia increases with the extent of shared genes.

Source: From Gottesman, 1991.

The Genain Quadruplets were born in the 1930s. Because their parents promoted them as a song and dance act while they were still young children, they received a great deal of public attention. Although genetically identical, the girls differed considerably in their behavior, but each began to experience several psychological problems. By their twenties, all four had developed schizophrenia—albeit at different times and with different symptoms. In the 1950s, the Genain quads were the subject of intensive study at the National Institute of Mental Health. Their backgrounds hinted at several possible causes for their schizophrenia: genetic (a number of family members on the father's side had psychological problems); birth-related complications (they were premature, low-birth weight babies); and environmental (their father was highly suspicious of outsiders and restricted the girls' activities; he was also reported to have sexually molested some of them). What caused the Genains' schizophrenias— genetics, neurological problems, a chaotic family life? Perhaps, as in many cases of schizophrenia, all these factors were involved.

diagnose schizophrenia from one study to the next, or that diagnosticians' knowledge of a person's family history did not bias the diagnoses. Finally, little is known about the procedures used to determine who was included in these studies. Without better methods, confidence that these results prove a genetic basis for schizophrenia is seriously compromised.

One recent study of residents of Roscommon County, Ireland, avoided many flaws of the older studies. Working with Kenneth Kendler, researchers in the *Roscommon Family Study* (Kendler et al., 1993a, b, c), conducted face-to-face structured interviews with relatives of schizophrenics diagnosed between 1980 and 1988, with relatives of a control group selected from registered voters, and with relatives of persons with severe affective disorders. The interviewers did not know the diagnoses, if any, of the probands of the relatives they were interviewing.

The results replicated findings from previous family studies (Kendler & Diehl, 1993). The risk for schizophrenia among members of families containing a schizophrenic proband was 13 times that of members of the control families. In 15.7 percent of families with a schizophrenic proband, one or more other family members were diagnosed with schizophrenia. Siblings of schizophrenic probands had a 9.2 percent risk of being diagnosed schizophrenic themselves, virtually identical to Gottesman's estimate shown in Figure 10.4 opposite. However, only 1.3 percent of the parents of probands were diagnosed as schizophrenic, considerably less than that shown in earlier studies.

Thus, family studies demonstrate that very few relatives of individuals with schizophrenia are themselves diagnosed with the disorder, but that coming from a family in which at least one first-degree relative has schizophrenia does increase a person's chances of being diagnosed schizophrenic as well. But family members share more than genes. They experience many environmental events in common as well, and there are a host of unique environmental factors that could affect some family members but not others. How can researchers evaluate these possible contributors to schizophrenia? As they have for other disorders, twin studies provide one way of exploring the roles of genetic and environmental factors.

Twin Studies. Because monozygotic twins are virtual genetic clones of one another, if one MZ twin becomes schizophrenic, then the other should also become schizophrenic *if* schizophrenia were due solely to genetic transmission. Similarly, because nonidentical or dizygotic (DZ) twins share only half of their genes, if schizophrenia were due only to genetic factors, and if a DZ twin develops schizophrenia, the cotwin should have a 50 percent chance of becoming schizophrenic. To the extent that observed rates of *concordance* (sharing the disorder) differ from these anticipated percentages, factors other than genes must contribute to the disorder.

There are some variations in the rates actually observed. For example, differences in how schizophrenia is defined affect concordance rates. Broad definitions of schizophrenia yield higher concordance rates than narrow definitions do (Gottesman, 1991). A second factor that affects concordance rates is the severity of the index twin's disorder. In one study of patients from London's Maudsley-Bethlehem hospital (Gottesman & Shields, 1972), for example, concordance rates for MZ twins were higher (75 percent) if the index twin had been hospitalized within the previous 6 months than if the index twin had been working during that time (17 percent).

Still, concordance rates for schizophrenia are consistent enough to justify some basic conclusions. As Figure 10.4 on page 350 indicates, averaged across several studies, the schizophrenia concordance rate is 48 percent for MZ twins and 17 percent for DZ twins (Gottesman, 1991). A study in Norway (Onstad et al., 1991) found the same 48 percent concordance rate for MZ twins, compared with 3.6 percent for DZ twins. Thus, the difference between MZ and DZ rates supports a role for genetic influence, but the fact that only about half of the identical twins of schizophrenic patients develop schizophrenia themselves means that genetics alone cannot account for schizophrenia.

Might the nonschizophrenic twins of patients with schizophrenia carry, but not express, a genetic predisposition for schizophrenia? Another form of twin study looks at this question by focusing on the children of these discordant twin pairs. One study found that the risk of developing schizophrenia among the children of discordant identical twins was virtually the same regardless of whether the parent was the twin who was diagnosed with schizophrenia: 16.8 percent of the children of schizophrenic MZ cotwins, and 17.4 percent of the children of nonschizophrenic cotwins eventually developed schizophrenia (Gottesman & Bertelsen, 1989). Apparently, even though the normal cotwins in MZ pairs do not exhibit schizophrenia themselves, they still carry and pass on some genetic vulnerability to their children at the same rate as their schizophrenic cotwins.

Adoption Studies. Another method for evaluating the genetic contribution to schizophrenia examines children born to schizophrenic parents who are then adopted and raised by families without schizophrenia in the home. Such adoption studies have usually been conducted in Europe because of the superior adoption records maintained there. Adoption studies can proceed in a couple of ways, but the most common method compares the rate of schizophrenia among adopted children who were born to schizophrenic parents with the rate of schizophrenia among adopted children whose biological parents were not diagnosed as schizophrenic. If children born to schizophrenic parents but then raised by normal adoptive families later develop schizophrenia at a higher rate than do adopted children born to nonschizophrenic parents, there is support for a genetic contribution to schizophrenia.

The first published adoption study of schizophrenia examined the adult offspring of 47 female patients at the Oregon State Mental Institution (Heston, 1966). These children had been placed in adoptive families within 3 days of birth. By age 36, 5 of them had been diagnosed with schizophrenia. In contrast, not one member of a comparison group of 50 adopted children born to nonschizophrenic mothers had developed schizophrenia by age 36.

The most comprehensive adoptive study of schizophrenia is currently under way in Finland and seems to be yielding similar results (Tiernari, 1991). Starting with a sample of over 20,000 women with schizophrenia, the authors located a group of mothers who had given up their children for adoption. A recent report from this study showed that:

■ Among 144 adoptees born to schizophrenic mothers, 9 percent had become psychotic; 7 of these 13 psychotic children met the DSM-III-R diagnostic criteria for schizophrenia, 2 for schizophreniform disorder, 2 for delusional disorder, and 2 for bipolar disorder.

■ Among adopted children who had been born to nonschizophrenic mothers, only about 1 percent were diagnosed with schizophrenia, a statistically significant difference. In short, even when children were not raised by a schizophrenic parent, having a schizophrenic parent increases the risk of developing the disorder.

A Model of Genetic Influence. For years scientists have been trying to pinpoint a gene or pattern of genes that might explain how genetic transmission of schizophrenia occurs. One method used is *linkage analysis*. As noted in previous chapters, researchers using linkage analysis study the behavior of multiple generations to see whether a disorder is associated with any traits with known genetic locations, such as eye color. If the association between the disorder and that other trait exceeds chance levels, it is likely that the gene influencing the disorder is on the same chromosome as the gene controlling the other trait. To date, linkage analyses of schizophrenia have not produced well-replicated findings (Gottesman, 1991; Kendler & Diehl, 1993).

The difficulty in finding the sites of genes influencing schizophrenia is probably due in part to the complexity of genetic influence. The genes that contribute to schizophrenia do not operate as simply as those determining hair color. For example, if you have brown hair, there is a very high probability that at least one of your parents has brown hair also. However, almost 90 percent of schizophrenics do *not* have a parent with schizophrenia, and most people who have a first-degree relative (parent or sibling) with schizophrenia never develop the disorder themselves.

What kind of genetic model can explain such patterns? Today, most investigators believe that the genetic contribution to the majority of cases of schizophrenia is *polygenic,* meaning that a mosaic of different genes act in concert to influence the development, probability, and severity of schizophrenia. No single dominant gene or no two recessive genes determine vulnerability in most cases of schizophrenia, although certain genes probably play a major role in the presence of several lesser genetic influences.

One of the great mysteries of schizophrenia is identifying the inherited liability that puts people at risk for the disorder. What is controlled by genetic factors? A schizophrenic-like personality? A general tendency to mental disorders? A deficit in language or information processing? Or a malfunction in brain chemistry? Whatever is inherited, it is not the diagnosis of schizophrenia per se, because concordance rates fall far short of what such transmission would require (Meehl, 1990).

Many authorities in the field believe that a diathesis–stress model probably best explains most cases of schizophrenia (Zubin & Spring, 1977) and that genes are at least one major source of the diatheses. In other words, schizophrenia may be a disorder that results from the interacting effects of a predisposition for the disorder (the diathesis) and stressors that trigger the diathesis into a full clinical disorder. The diathesis could be a characteristic of the central nervous system or a feature of a person's basic personality that makes up the core of schizophrenia, a kind of fuel that is inert until a match brings about combustion.

The first and best-known candidate for an inherited diathesis was described in Paul Meehl's (1962, 1990) diathesis–stress model of schizophrenia. According to Meehl, a single schizogene, operating against a backdrop of many other genetic influences, conveys the core schizophrenic vulnerability, known as **schizotaxia.** People who carry this predisposition are called *schizotypes,* and they display a variety of mild, psychotic-like qualities including cognitive slippage, poor emotional rapport, blunted affect, social withdrawal, passivity, and peculiar mannerisms and behaviors (Tyrka et al., 1995). Some schizotypes ultimately decompensate into schizophrenia when they are subjected to physical, social, or familial stressors. Other schizotypes can escape schizophrenia if their environments help them compensate for their inherited risk or protect them from extreme stressors. They may, however, still show signs of psychological impairment along the schizophrenia spectrum.

Schizotypy can be assessed through five self-report measures developed by Loren and Jean Chapman (1980) to tap suspected *psychosis proneness*. The five scales, along with a sample item from two of the most frequently used scales, are summarized below.

1. The Physical Anhedonia Scale consists of 61 items inquiring about the pleasure or lack of pleasure a person gains from eating, drinking, having sex, and so forth.

2. The Perceptual Aberration Scale contains 35 items tapping tendencies toward misperceptions of the body or external events ("Sometimes people whom I know well begin to look like strangers.").

3. The Magical Ideation Scale has 30 items that assess beliefs in causes that are generally believed to be impossible ("I sometimes have a feeling of fainting or losing energy when certain people look at me or touch me.").

4. The Impulsive Nonconformity Scale has 51 items that measure a lack of empathy toward others and a tendency to give in to impulses.

5. The Social Anhedonia Scale has 40 items that measure a pervasive indifference to other people.

These instruments were given to 7,800 undergraduates at the University of Wisconsin in the late 1970s and early 1980s. From this sample, a group of 375 students who scored very high on one or more of the five scales constituted the so-called psychosis-prone sample. A group of 159 students who scored below average on the scales served as a control group.

Ten to 15 years later, 508 of the original 534 subjects were located and completed diagnostic interviews (Chapman et al., 1994). The rate of psychosis (schizophrenia and mood disorders) during the 10-year follow-up was 3.4 percent for the "psychosis-prone" subjects compared with 0.8 percent for the controls. Those subjects who had scored high on measures of perceptual aberration and magical ideation were particularly likely to give more reports of psychotic-like experiences and to have relatives who had become psychotic. Notice, however that although the "psychosis-prone" students had a heightened risk for psychosis, very few actually became psychotic.

These results also suggest that the diathesis was not specific to schizophrenia, an outcome that goes against the trend of other studies that have found that whatever a person might inherit from schizophrenic relatives does not seem to increase the risk of mood disorders (Gottesman, 1991; Parnas et al., 1993; Kendler et al., 1993c), anxiety disorders (Kendler et al., 1993c), or alcoholism (Kendler et al., 1993c).

Several research teams have been searching for a behavior that could serve as a *genetic marker* for schizophrenia, thereby allowing identification of people who are at risk for the disorder. Ideally, such a marker would be easily detected and highly correlated with incidence of schizophrenia, but would not actually be a symptom of the disorder itself. One of the leading behavioral candidates involves the inability to follow or track a stimulus such as a spot of light as it moves across the visual field. The rate of dysfunctions in *smooth-pursuit eye tracking* has been found to be much higher among people with schizophrenia and their relatives than among normal persons (Clementz & Sweeney, 1990; Iacono, 1988). In addition, smooth-pursuit eye-tracking dysfunction is not common in other mental disorders (Iacono et al., 1992), but it is seen in patients whose schizophrenia is in remission.

Various genetic models have been proposed to account for the joint manifestation of dysfunctional smooth-pursuit eye tracking and schizophrenia (Holzman et al., 1988), but none of them has yet been clearly supported. However, scientists have also linked schizophrenia to several differences in the functioning and structures of various areas of the brain, which might be genetically transmitted or might be brought about by other functional and structural causes.

Early Physical Trauma

Genetic vulnerability is not the only biological factor that might produce a predisposition to schizophrenia. Evidence for another possible source comes from studies of structural differences in the brains of identical twins who are discordant for schizophrenia. The typical finding is that the twin diagnosed with schizophrenia has decreased brain volume, density, or function more often than the unaffected cotwin (Reveley et al., 1987; Suddath et al., 1990; Weinberger et al., 1992). These observed brain differences between identical twins are almost certainly the result of some nongenetic factor such as physical trauma to the brain that occurs prenatally, during the birth process, or shortly thereafter. Other evidence that early brain trauma sometimes contributes to schizophrenia comes from studies that show correlations between certain early traumas to the brain and an increased risk for schizophrenia.

Prenatal exposure to a viral infection such as influenza may be one specific risk factor for schizophrenia (Cannon, Mednick, & Parnas, 1989; Davis, Phelps, & Bracha, 1995; Mednick et al., 1988; Torrey et al., 1994; Torrey & Yolkin, 1995). Indirect support for this contention comes from findings that, compared with nonschizophrenics, a greater proportion of schizophrenics are born during the winter or early spring months (e.g., Bradbury & Miller, 1985; Paliast et al., 1994). Presumably, during these times of year, pregnant women and their fetuses are more likely to be exposed and succumb to viral infections. Especially if the fetus is exposed during the second trimester of pregnancy, viral infections might affect brain development in ways that ultimately result in schizophrenic behavior (Mednick et al., 1988). This **season-of-birth effect** is relatively small (less than a 10 percent differential [Kirch, 1993] is found), but there is evidence that children who were exposed to influenza epidemics have developed schizophrenia more frequently than expected (e.g., Mednick et al., 1990) or score higher on measures of proneness to schizophrenia (Venables, 1996). One other clue to the possible contribution of viral infections to schizophrenia is that the number of recorded stillbirths correlates with the number of people born who later become schizophrenic—and both are greater in winter months (Torrey et al., 1993). One explanation for this pattern is that a virus is responsible for both outcomes but that it affects different organs in the body. However, not all investigators find a relationship between the increased risk for schizophrenia and either season-of-birth effects or heightened exposure to infection (Kirch, 1993), so the seasonal hypothesis remains controversial.

Other sources of trauma that might affect development and ultimately increase the risk of schizophrenia are complications during pregnancy and birth. Such complications include prolonged delivery, hypoxia, breech delivery, forceps delivery, and excessive bleeding (Cannon et al., 1989; Cantor-Graae et al., 1994; Torrey et al., 1994). Several studies report an excess of birth complications in infants who eventually become schizophrenic relative to nonschizophrenic controls (Cannon et al., 1989), but, others have not (e.g., Buka, Tsuang, & Lipsitt, 1993).

How might these traumas—alone or in tandem with genetic predispositions—lead to schizophrenia? All of these traumas are capable of affecting the functioning of critical brain structures, and, in recent years, evidence linking schizophrenia with abnormalities in the structure and functioning of the brain has mounted.

Brain Structures and Functions

Recent research has begun to isolate structural deficits in the brains of schizophrenic patients, particularly those with pronounced negative symptoms (Andreasen et al., 1990; Andreasen et al., 1992). In the 1800s, Kraepelin speculated about structural abnormalities in the brains of people with schizophrenia (Bruton et al., 1990), and in the 1920s it was reported that some schizophrenics have enlarged **ventricles,** the cavities in the center of the brain that are filled with cerebrospinal fluid. But structural problems in the brain could not be documented clearly until recently. Today, methods for studying brain structures include not only postmortem examinations of the brains of deceased schizophrenics but also several *neuroimaging* techniques that provide "live," fine-grained pictures of the brain in action. As described in Chapter 2, these neuroimaging methods include CT scans, MRIs, PET scans, and the SPECT technique.

Initial neuroimaging studies of brain structure were able to document the claim that the brains of some schizophrenics have enlarged lateral ventricles.

This abnormality does not appear to be the result of a simple aging process, because it has been observed even in young patients. The ventricle enlargement suggests that the cortical tissue in surrounding areas has been diminished; in other words, ventricle enlargement points to the possibility of either abnormal neurological development or pathological brain deterioration. Ventricle enlargement is not observed in every patient with schizophrenia (Andreasen, 1988). It is usually encountered in a particular subset of schizophrenic patients, lending further support to the theory that different subtypes of schizophrenia stem from different causes.

Where do structural deficits occur, and what are their results? In recent years, researchers have focused on three areas of the brain that most consistently show structural problems: (1) the frontal lobe, (2) the temporal lobe and parts of the limbic system that lie beneath the temporal lobe, and (3) the thalamus (see Figure 10.5 on page 356).

Evidence of Hypofrontality. Recall that the frontal lobes play a critical role in executive functions such as planning, decision making, and abstract thinking. Using neuroimaging techniques, scientists have found both decreased frontal lobe volume (Andreasen et al., 1986) and diminished neuronal and blood flow activity (Buschbaum et al., 1992) in some schizophrenics. This diminished activity is called **hypofrontality,** and it appears to have important consequences. Hypofrontality has been associated with lowered performance on neuropsychological and problem-solving tests by people with schizophrenia and in children at risk for schizophrenia as a result of having a schizophrenic parent (Andreasen et al., 1992; Cohen & Servan-Schreiber, 1992.

In one study, Nancy Andreasen and her colleagues found that schizophrenic and normal control

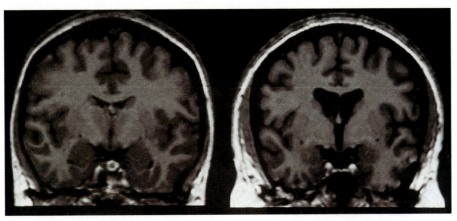

Normal   Schizophrenia

Brain structure of a normal control subject and a patient with schizophrenia. The ventricles are the black areas in the center of the brain. Note how they are enlarged in the case of schizophrenia, indicating that the cortex has been diminished.

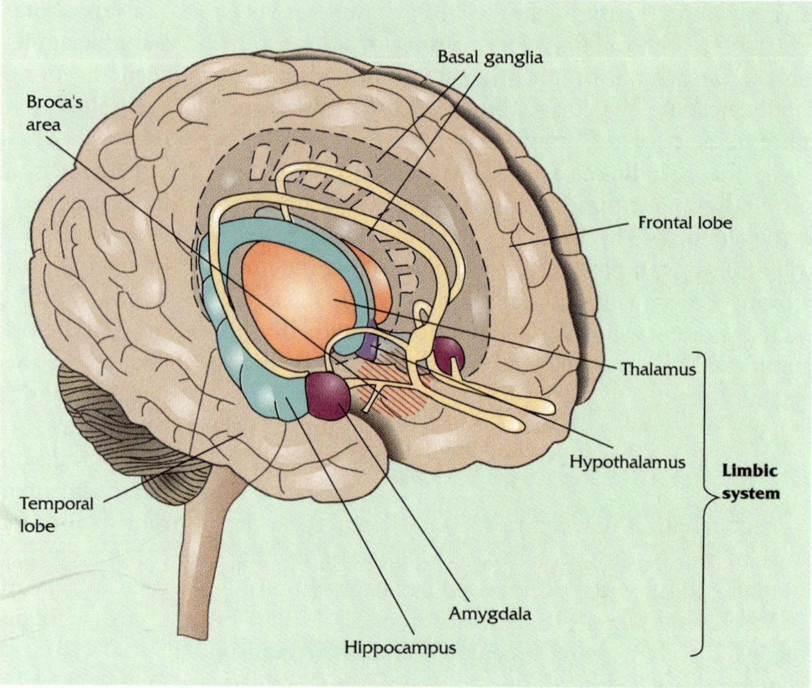

FIGURE 10.5

Brain Structures Involved in Schizophrenia

Areas of the brain that control cognitive, behavioral, and emotional functions are important in the development of some cases of schizophrenia. Abnormalities of the areas shown in this figure have been linked to schizophrenia.

participants did not differ in blood flow to various brain regions when simply watching undulating colored shapes. However, when the subjects were trying to solve a challenging task such as that shown in Figure 10.6, the blood flow to the frontal lobes increased in the normal control subjects, but not in the schizophrenic subjects. Furthermore, this underactivation was seen only in patients with negative symptoms such as apathy and withdrawal.

Other studies also indicate that hypofrontality does not occur in all cases of schizophrenia. It is more common in men, and it is associated with negative symptoms, poor premorbid adjustment, and poor prognosis (Andreasen et al., 1990; 1992; Wolkin et al., 1992).

These data suggest that the negative symptoms of schizophrenia may reflect diminished activity in the frontal lobe, which is normally heavily involved in problem solving, planning, and thinking. These findings are exciting because they begin to link particular brain regions to specific symptoms of schizophrenia. However, scientists must remain cautious about concluding that hypofrontality is a cause of schizophrenia. First, the extent of hypofrontality among those with schizophrenia tends to be small compared with normal subjects. Further-

Connections

Have abnormalities of the frontal lobes been linked to other disorders? For answers, see Chapter 4, p. 139 and Chapter 11, pp. 394–395.

more, not all studies have found schizophrenia associated with hypofrontality (Gur & Gur, 1995), perhaps because they have used different scanning techniques and different subject samples. At this point, it is best to consider the hypofrontality hypothesis as having only moderate support.

Temporal Lobe Abnormalities. The second brain area under intense investigation is the temporal lobe and certain structures of the limbic system underneath it. For example, MRI studies have found that the amount of abnormal activity in parts of the auditory association cortex is associated with the severity of schizophrenic patients' auditory hallucinations (Barta et al., 1990). In general, greater temporal abnormalities have been found in the left rather than in the right hemispheres of schizophrenic patients (Gur & Pearlson, 1993). Other studies have detected blood flow abnormalities in the basal ganglia and within the structures of the limbic system, a brain system that helps regulate emotions, aggression, and social behavior. Irregularities in these areas, particularly in the hippocampus and amygdala, are associated with auditory hallucinations and other positive symptoms such as formal thought disorder and delusions (Liddle et al., 1992).

Thalamic Irregularities. Linked to the limbic system is the thalamus, a kind of information relay station in the midline of the brain. An important function of

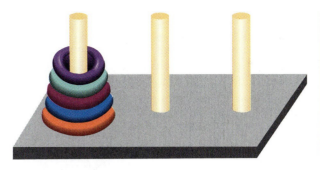

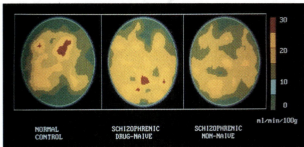

FIGURE 10.6

Hypofrontality in Schizophrenia

When patients with schizophrenia try to solve the tower task (*left*), they show less activation of the frontal region of their brains than do normal control subjects trying to solve the same puzzle (the puzzle requires the rings to be transferred from the first to the third peg so they end up in the same order (largest to smallest) as they were at the start). The summary PET scan images (*right*) show that the patients—both those who had received prior medications and those who had not—had less blood flow in the left frontal lobe than the controls.

Source: From Andreasen et al., 1992.

the thalamus is that it filters, sorts, and transmits sensory information to the entire cortex, including the frontal lobes. Irregularities in the thalamus have also been found in schizophrenic patients. Andreasen and her colleagues (1994) combined MRI scans of 47 normal subjects to form a composite "average brain." They then compared this normal composite with a composite of the scans of 39 schizophrenic patients. The schizophrenic brain composite was "subtracted" from the normal brain composite, and the differences replicated earlier studies that showed less overall brain volume and larger ventricles for the schizophrenic group. The specific brain structure that was the most diminished for the schizophrenic group was the thalamus.

If further research confirms these findings, defects in the thalamus and its function could help explain many of the symptoms of schizophrenia. For example, if the thalamus does not adequately filter out irrelevant information and sends a scrambled signal to the frontal or temporal lobes, the person could suffer attentional lapses, lose the ability to process information clearly, become overwhelmed by sensory input, and experience hallucinations or delusions (Andreasen et al., 1994).

Hallucinations and the Brain. Neuroimaging studies have also begun to reveal which areas of the brain are involved in hallucinations. The connections can be studied by having patients lie in a brain-scanning machine and then asking them to push a button when they experience auditory or visual hallucina-

tions. Pictures taken at the time the button is pushed reveal activation of the brain's surface and certain subcortical areas where thoughts, emotions, and perceptions are usually integrated. It seems as if activity in these areas—primarily the temporal cortex, the thalamus, and limbic structures such as the amygdala and hippocampus—simulates external sensory input so convincingly that the person believes it is coming from the outside world. When normal controls hear real noises, the same surface areas of the brain tend to become activated, but fewer subcortical areas are turned on. Other studies have shown that, when schizophrenic patients "hear" hallucinated voices, a substantial change in blood flow takes place in Broca's area (McGuire, Shah, & Murray, 1993), a part of the brain that helps control the production of speech.

Some Preliminary Conclusions. As exciting and promising as they are, the results of brain imaging research remain speculative and must be interpreted with great caution. First, even though differences in brain structures and functions are reliably found by various research teams, these differences do not appear in all schizophrenic patients; they are not even seen consistently within relatively homogeneous schizophrenic subgroups, such as those who display primarily positive or negative symptoms. Second, the bulk of earlier brain-scanning studies used older patients who had taken antipsychotic drugs for many years. These potent drugs may have been responsible for some of the observed brain abnormalities.

Recent studies have tried to correct this flaw by using only drug-naïve patients, studied early in their first schizophrenic episodes (e.g., Andreasen et al., 1992; Buschbaum et al., 1992; Wolkin et al., 1992). Third, many of the observed brain deficits are not specific to schizophrenia but occur also in mood disorders and in various medical diseases affecting the brain (Raz & Raz, 1990).

If the findings reported here continue to hold up after further research, then scientists will have made tremendous progress in understanding how the multiple disturbances observed in schizophrenia are related to activity in, and interactions among, various brain structures. At this point the available data suggest that the positive symptoms of schizophrenia are linked to abnormalities in the limbic system whereas disturbances in the frontal cortex are more strongly associated with the negative symptoms of the disorder.

The Role of Biochemical Processes

Another historically influential theory holds that positive symptoms of schizophrenia are associated with problems in a particular neurotransmitter system. The neurotransmitter receiving the most research support over the past 40 years is dopamine. It is now fairly clear that dopamine systems are implicated in at least some cases of schizophrenia. Several well-established lines of evidence support this conclusion.

1. Early studies found that the tissues and fluids of patients with schizophrenia had higher levels of certain dopamine by-products than did those of control subjects, suggesting that an excess of dopamine was a primary culprit in schizophrenia. This excess has been hypothesized to arise either from an over-abundance of dopamine receptors at the synapses or hypersensitivity of these receptors.

2. Drugs that increase dopamine activity in the brain (such as L-dopa and amphetamines) tend to intensify schizophrenic symptoms and may even induce paranoid, schizophrenic-like symptoms in nonschizophrenics (Lieberman & Koreen, 1993; Syvalahti, 1994).

3. Drugs that block the action of dopamine in the brain are effective in relieving many symptoms of schizophrenia, particularly its positive symptoms (Syvalathi, 1994).

4. The degree to which these drugs, called *neuroleptics,* block dopamine is correlated with their clinical ability to reduce symptoms of schizophrenia (Seeman, 1987).

Although these findings suggest a role for dopamine in schizophrenia, scientists now know that the situation is much more complicated than the initial dopamine-excess hypothesis suggested. First, although neuroleptic drugs block dopamine receptors shortly after being consumed, the full clinical effects of these drugs do not occur for days or even weeks in some cases (Syvalahti, 1994). Furthermore, only 70 percent of schizophrenics improve after taking these dopamine-blocking neuroleptics, and their negative symptoms are minimally affected (Davis et al., 1991).

Of greater interest is that studies designed to measure the concentration of dopamine in the brains of schizophrenic patients produce conflicting results (Davis et al., 1991). Some brain areas such as the limbic system show excess dopamine activity, but other areas, notably the frontal lobes, show *deficiencies.* Excessive activity may occur largely in Type I schizophrenia with its predominantly positive symptoms, while deficits in dopamine activity in the frontal lobes may be more typical in Type II schizophrenia with its predominantly negative symptoms.

The neurotransmitter serotonin has also been implicated in schizophrenia, either on its own or in interaction with dopamine (Laruelle et al., 1993; Lieberman & Koreen, 1993; Syvalahti, 1994). Alterations in the levels or functioning of norepinephrine and glutamate, two other neurotransmitters, have also been documented in schizophrenia, leading to speculation that they, too, might play a role in the disorder.

Obviously, until scientists learn much more about the complexities of the brain's neurotransmitter systems, a final conclusion about the significance of dopamine is not possible. Still, it is likely that different types or symptoms of schizophrenia are related in some way to neurotransmitter malfunctions. For example, the common finding that schizophrenia tends to begin earlier in males than in females might be because sex hormones act on the neurotransmitters that are thought to underlie schizophrenia. Perhaps androgens, such as testosterone (which men have at about 10 times the concentration that women have) stimulate psychosis through interaction with neurotransmitters, while estrogens (which women have more of relative to men) provide some protection for females (Hafner et al., 1994). Another possibility, of course, is that males who shows signs of schizophrenia are referred for treatment more quickly than females with similar symptoms.

Evidence from High-Risk Studies

Additional evidence for the role of biological factors in schizophrenia comes from a fascinating series of prospective, high-risk studies. Recall that *prospective designs* identify research participants at an early age and then follow them to track the factors that differentiate people who eventually become schizophrenic from those who do not. Prospective designs are usually more difficult to conduct than retrospective designs, but they provide more information on possible causal factors. *High-risk (HR) studies* employ a prospective design that focuses on children who are thought to be predisposed to schizophrenia by virtue of having been born to a parent with schizophrenia.

One such study, begun in Denmark in 1962 by Sarnoff Mednick from the United States and Fini Schulsinger from Denmark, selected a high-risk (HR) sample of 207 children of schizophrenic mothers. At the time, the children were between 10 and 18 years of age. None were schizophrenic. A low-risk (LR) comparison sample composed of 104 children of nonschizophrenic mothers was matched to the high-risk group on sex, age, rural versus urban residence, and family socioeconomic background.

A follow-up of these children revealed that the morbidity risk for schizophrenia among the high-risk children was 17.1 percent compared with 2.9 percent for the low-risk group (Parnas et al., 1993). Furthermore, although not all diagnosed children satisfied the full DSM criteria for schizophrenia, 42.1 percent of the HR group carried a diagnosis of schizophrenia, a related psychosis, or a personality disorder compared with 7.8 percent of LR group.

Following the work of Mednick and Schulsinger, several other high-risk investigations have been conducted both in the United States (Erlenmeyer-Kimling et al., 1995) and in Israel (Marcus et al., 1987; Mirsky et al., 1995). In general, as Table 10.2 shows, these studies also suggest that being born to a parent with schizophrenia is a reasonably good predictor of developing a serious psychological disorder, including schizophrenia. Do these studies yield any clues about how a risk for schizophrenia is translated into the disorder itself?

Several teams of investigators have continued to follow high- and low-risk subjects and have conducted neuroimaging studies of their brains. They have found that Mednick and Schulsinger's high-risk group had more generalized cortical brain deficits than did low-risk subjects (Cannon et al., 1989; Cannon et al., 1993). In addition, subjects with the greatest genetic risk—that is, those whose fathers and mothers both had schizophrenia or schizotypal personality disorder—had greater brain deficits than those who had only one parent with the disorder (Cannon et al., 1993). Furthermore, the high-risk subjects who developed schizophrenia or schizotypal personality disorder had greater brain deficits than either high-risk subjects who did not develop a schizophrenia spectrum disorder or the low-risk controls (Cannon et al., 1994).

These neurological differences are consistent with several behavioral and academic differences between high-risk and low-risk children. Compared with their low-risk peers, high-risk children tend to show poorer coordination, lower IQ scores, more difficulty concentrating and paying attention, and more problems interacting with other children.

In addition, high-risk studies have shed some light on psychological and environmental factors that

---

TABLE 10.2   High-Risk Studies of Schizophrenia and Other Psychotic Disorders

	New York City (Erlenmeyer-Kimling et al., 1995)	Israel *Kibbutz* (Mirsky et al., 1995)	Israel *Town* (Mirsky et al., 1995)	Denmark (Parnas et al., 1993)
High-risk subjects				
% developing schizophrenia	11.1	8.0	8.0	17.1
% developing any psychosis	22.3	—	—	43.0
Low-risk subjects				
% developing schizophrenia	0.0	0.0	0.0	1.9
% developing any psychosis	2.2	0.0	0.0	7.9

Note that the higher figures from Denmark reflect the older age of participants who have lived through most of the period of risk for developing schizophrenia, whereas participants from New York and Israel were still relatively young.

Source: Based on Erlenmeyer-Kimling et al., 1995; Mirsky et al., 1995; and Parnas et al., 1993.

might help explain the development of schizophrenia. Although no striking psychosocial factors have been isolated that account for which members of a high-risk group ultimately succumb to schizophrenia, a few tentative leads have been suggested. For example, greater levels of family conflict or instability appear to be more prevalent in the backgrounds of high-risk people who ultimately develop predominantly positive-symptom schizophrenia. In contrast, complications during a high-risk baby's gestation or delivery are more predictive of predominantly negative-symptom schizophrenia.

Some of the twin and adoption studies discussed earlier also highlight the causal role of nonbiological factors in the development of schizophrenia. For example, in the Finnish study of twins who had been adopted (Tiernari, 1991), the researchers systematically rated the quality of childrearing by the adoptive parents. Overall, the more disorganized the adoptive family environment, the greater the risk of psychological problems for the adoptees. Consistent with a diathesis–stress model of schizophrenia, the correlation between a faulty family environment and the incidence of mental disorder was greatest among the offspring of schizophrenic mothers. Left unanswered, however, is whether family disorganization preceded or followed the high-risk children's problematic behavior.

Also, studies of identical twins who are discordant for schizophrenia show substantial differences between the basic personalities of the cotwins, although scientists do not know whether these differences result from the harmful effects of schizophrenia on the affected twin or some set of protective or risk factors that differentiates the twins and their vulnerability to schizophrenia (DiLalla & Gottesman, 1995). Perhaps environmental factors or personality differences suppress the tendency to develop schizophrenia in some carriers but fuel it in others.

In Review

The diathesis–stress model argues that certain people are predisposed to schizophrenia but that stressors are usually needed to precipitate its development. Genetic factors predispose some people to develop schizophrenia, as indicated by the results of:

- family aggregation studies;
- twin studies; and
- adoption studies.

However, because the majority of schizophrenic patients do not have close family members who are schizophrenic, nongenetic factors must also be involved. Biological traumas that might contribute to the development of schizophrenia include:

- prenatal viral infections;
- difficulties during delivery that affect brain structures and functions; and
- abnormalities in neurotransmitter systems.

The brain structures and functions most often implicated in schizophrenia involve:

- the frontal and temporal lobes; and
- subcortical areas such as the thalamus and other structures such as the hippocampus and amygdala that are part of the limbic system.

Longitudinal studies of children at risk for schizophrenia as a result of having a parent with the disorder show that high-risk children have more:

- neurological deficits than low-risk controls; and
- academic and behavioral difficulties than low-risk controls.

Psychological and Sociocultural Causes of Schizophrenia

Like biological factors, environmental and psychosocial stressors have long been suspected of being involved somehow in the causation of schizophrenia (Gottesman, 1991). As difficult as it is to document the role of biological factors that might contribute to schizophrenia, it is even harder to isolate the environmental experiences that might help translate a diathesis into actual schizophrenia.

For one thing, most psychological stressors are not single events that can be easily cataloged; rather, they take the form of a long series of events that accumulate to tax a person's coping resources. In addition, these events are themselves probably affected by genes to some extent. A temperamentally withdrawn and shy child is more likely to seek an isolated social environment than is an extroverted and upbeat child. A child with early brain abnormalities faces increased risks of educational failure and possible social rejection. As people grow older, the distinction between genes and environment becomes less meaningful until a point is reached at which the dichotomy no longer makes much sense.

Serious mental disorders such as schizophrenia plague many homeless people. The cognitive and behavioral impairments associated with the disorder put these people at increased risk for physical illnesses and victimization by criminals. They also are hard to treat because they often refuse to take antipsychotic medication.

An intriguing demonstration of how genes may influence experience is provided by a set of studies that examined home movies taken during the childhoods of people who were diagnosed with schizophrenia as adults (Grimes & Walker, 1994; Walker et al., 1993). Observers were asked to rate several aspects of the filmed behavior of these children, as well as the behavior of siblings who also appeared in the movies but did not develop schizophrenia. Even at early ages—sometimes by age 2—the preschizophrenic children were less emotionally expressive (particularly for positive emotions) and displayed more odd or uncoordinated movements than their siblings who did not develop schizophrenia. Early difficulties such as these might be signs of the schizotype diathesis that Meehl hypothesized, and it is reasonable to speculate that, as indications of this diathesis emerge, a child's risk increases for suffering more negative interactions in the social environment. Imagine how other children might react to a child who gives few facial signs of positive emotions or who walks in an odd manner. The schizotypically predisposed child almost certainly will encounter more rejection and other social stressors, at least in part because of the indirect influence of genetic factors.

Another influence is also probable, namely environmental factors that might affect the expression of genetic predispositions. Being raised in an emotionally volatile and unstable family or living in a neighborhood threatened by high levels of violence could aggravate genetically predisposed difficulties in attention or concentration to the point that a person is more easily confused and susceptible to delusional beliefs.

The Role of Social Class and Urbanicity

Stroll through the streets of any American city and you will see shocking examples of how serious mental disorders can ravage people's lives. Whether it's on Broadway, the Sunset Strip, or Michigan Avenue, an astounding number of people with apparent mental disturbances can be found who are homeless and wandering the streets. And the problem appears to be growing. Do such appearances reflect a reality, or are they just a false stereotype about big-city life? Is there a connection between social conditions and the prevalence of schizophrenia?

In the United States, two enduring facts about the prevalence of schizophrenia are that it is highly correlated with (1) living in an urban setting and (2) being a member of a lower social class (Faris & Dunham, 1939; Freeman, 1994; Torrey & Bowler, 1990). Several hypotheses have been proposed to explain the relationship between urban living, social class, and the prevalence of schizophrenia. As explained in Chapter 1, *social drift* hypothesis suggests that, as people develop schizophrenic symptoms, they cannot maintain adequate occupational functioning and thus gradually slip down the socioeconomic ladder. They migrate to the poorer areas of cities where lodging is cheaper and where they become more entrenched in lifestyles of marginal subsistence. Social drift links lower socioeconomic class to schizophrenia as one of the ultimate consequences of the disorder itself (Freeman, 1994). A related explanation, called the *social residue* hypothesis, suggests that, as urban areas decay, people who are more occupationally able and mobile move away, leaving behind the less able, including those with severe mental disorders (Freeman, 1994).

A third explanation, sometimes called the *social causation* or *breeder* hypothesis, suggests that the chronic psychological and social stressors, social disorganization, and greater environmental hazards associated with urban living and poverty breed new cases of schizophrenia (Freeman, 1994). Two lines of evidence are consistent with this idea. First, compared with members of higher social classes, people in lower socioeconomic groups are exposed to higher crime rates, unemployment, physical deterioration of neighborhoods, and medical illnesses (Guerra et al., 1995). Second, in several studies, the onset or relapse of schizophrenia has occurred more often during periods that were preceded by an increase in stressful life events (Brown & Birley, 1968; Day et al., 1987; Ventura et al., 1989).

Thus far, none of these hypotheses is clearly supported over the others (Freeman, 1994), but research on all of them continues. In one novel approach to investigating social factors related to schizophrenia, a group of researchers (Dohrenwend et al., 1992) used the following reasoning: socioeconomic status (SES) depends on one's attainments gained throughout life; therefore, it is hard to determine exactly when an individual's social class becomes stable. However, this is not the case with ethnicity; it is established at birth and does not change. Accordingly, these researchers examined rates of mental disorders among "advantaged" and "disadvantaged" ethnic groups. The social drift hypothesis would predict that healthy members of a disadvantaged ethnic group would be less able to rise above a low socioeconomic status because of the prejudice and discrimination they would face. Equally healthy members of an advantaged ethnic group would face fewer obstacles and should therefore experience more upward mobility. A further implication of social drift is that, as healthy members of the advantaged ethnic group ascend the socioeconomic ladder, they will leave behind less mentally healthy members, producing a higher rate of mental disorder among this group's lower social classes. Thus, if the social drift theory is true, researchers should expect to find a higher rate of mental disorder among lower socioeconomic members of an advantaged ethnic group than among the lower socioeconomic members of a disadvantaged ethnic group.

A test of these predictions was provided by comparing Jews of European background living in Israel (the advantaged ethnic group) with Jews of North African background living in Israel (the disadvantaged ethnic group). The results of this comparison were mixed, depending on the mental disorder stud-

ied (Dohrenwend et al., 1992). In the case of schizophrenia, the social drift hypothesis was supported—among low socioeconomic individuals, the advantaged (European Jews) group showed twice the rate of schizophrenia as the disadvantaged group (North African Jews) did. However, for disorders such as depression, antisocial personality disorder, and substance abuse problems, the data were more consistent with a social causation hypothesis.

Obviously, the factors that are involved in linking poverty, social adversity, and schizophrenia are complex. No single hypothesis can explain all the connections fully, but it is possible that, at least in the United States, the higher concentration of schizophrenic patients in the urban, lower class stems from a combination of breeding and drift effects (Dauncey et al., 1993).

However, even if both social drift and social causation influence the epidemiology of schizophrenia, it is still the case that many schizophrenic patients come from families that are socially and economically advantaged. Furthermore, despite suffering psychotic symptoms for years on end, many schizophrenics do not drift into lives of poverty or marginality. Other forces must be at play in regulating the course of schizophrenia, and family environment turns out to be one of the most important areas to consider.

The Role of Family Environments

Historically, the psychosocial factor most frequently hypothesized to be related to schizophrenia has been some type of family disturbance. One of the earliest views was that certain kinds of mothers (who came to be known as schizophrenogenic mothers) were key to the development of schizophrenia, particularly in boys (Fromm-Reichmann, 1948). The **schizophrenogenic mother** was characterized as domineering, overprotective, cold, rigid, and uncomfortable with sex and physical intimacy—all qualities thought to induce schizophrenia in her offspring.

Another family theory that was influential in the 1950s and 1960s was the **double-bind hypothesis** of Gregory Bateson and his colleagues (Bateson et al., 1956). According to this view, schizophrenia sometimes developed when a child was exposed to parents who communicated incompatible messages to the child. Typically, the parent was thought to send repeated conflicting messages that a child could not possibly answer in a consistent way, leading to anxiety and confused thinking. For example, a mother might complain to her son that he does not show her enough affection but then stiffen or give him the "cold shoulder" whenever he tries to hug her.

Because no one in these families was able to clarify these paradoxical communications, they were thought ultimately to wreak havoc on a child's development.

These theories and others like them never earned much research support, and they are no longer taken seriously by most clinicians. Unfortunately, however, their implications have lingered among the general public. As a result there still tends to be a belief that parents cause schizophrenia by acting aloof or emotionally distant toward their children. This erroneous belief accomplishes little other than casting blame and guilt on family members who, for the most part, strive valiantly to cope with the difficulties that accompany schizophrenia in a loved one.

Although early family-based theories of schizophrenia have been found to have little merit, more recent research has found that certain family interaction styles are related to an increased risk for schizophrenia. One longitudinal study conducted at UCLA (Goldstein, 1985; Goldstein & Rodnick, 1975) followed a group of adolescents who had psychological problems. The communication patterns of the families were observed at the time they entered the study. Deviant, negative communication within families was a significant predictor of which of these adolescents would eventually develop schizophrenia or a schizophrenic spectrum disorder. However, the question remains whether the deviant communication produced the schizophrenia or resulted from genetic factors that also increased the likelihood of schizophrenia in the children, regardless of family communication.

The Role of Expressed Emotion

How do you think you would act if you lived with a person who had schizophrenia? Would you feel afraid? Would you be a nag? Would you challenge the person to become more socially involved or would you feel sorry for the person? Perhaps you would be like the sister of one schizophrenic patient who said, "I can go from tears to rage in a matter of minutes. He either ignores me or threatens to hit me. Nothing I do ever seems to matter."

Life in all families is stressful at times, but some families are more stressful than others. Members of a family in which one member is disruptive and behaves irrationally are especially likely to react with anger and demands for conformity and accountability. What effects might these reactions have?

Years of research on the families of schizophrenic patients show a strong relationship between a family's emotional overinvolvement with the patient, called *expressed emotion (EE)*, and the rate at which

patients suffer relapses of schizophrenia. **Expressed emotion** usually involves high levels of

- criticism ("You don't do anything but sit in front of the TV.")
- hostility ("I'm sick and tired of your craziness.") and
- overinvolvement ("I'll go downtown with you so we can have some time together." or "Don't you realize how hard I try to help you out?").

EE is often assessed through an hour-long interview called the Family Interview Schedule (Vaughn & Leff, 1976). Interviewers rate observed emotions and record the number of positive or critical comments made about the patient during the interview. A family is classified as high EE if, during the interview, its members make six or more negative comments about the patient, if they demonstrate a marked emotional overinvolvement with the patient, or if they earn a high hostility rating (Koenigsberg & Handley, 1986; Vaughn & Leff, 1976).

The results of Vaughn and Leff's (1976) pioneering study show the importance of EE in relation to relapse and the use of antipsychotic drugs. After the patients in this study had entered the hospital, social workers interviewed their families and classified them as high or low EE. Patients who returned to high EE homes were much more prone to relapse within 9 months of release than those returning to low EE families. In addition, the amount of contact with members of high EE families was a critical variable in relapse rate. If patients had more than 35 hours of direct EE family contact per week they relapsed twice as often as patients with less than 35 hours of EE contact. The amount of family contact had no effect on relapse rates among low EE families. Finally, patients' compliance in taking their antipsychotic drugs appeared to protect patients in high EE families against relapse, while compliance had little differential effect on relapse rates of patients from the low EE families.

Note that expressed emotion is not related to the original onset of schizophrenia but to relapses of the disorder. One review of 26 different studies found that the average relapse rate over 9 to 12 months for patients returning to high EE families was 48 percent compared with a relapse rate of 21 percent for patients returning to low EE environments (Kavanagh, 1992). High EE has been found to have similar effects on the relapse of other mental conditions such as mood disorders.

How might EE lead to relapse? One possibility is that people with schizophrenia are sensitive to environmental stimulation, particularly social criticism

(Brown, Birley, & Wing, 1972; Leff, 1994; Tarrier et al., 1988). Social criticism may drive up their levels of psychophysiological arousal (Tarrier et al., 1988). Under this heightened arousal, these patients might lose some of their already-impaired ability to process information accurately. As a result, they feel bombarded with negative stimuli, their symptoms increase, and soon their condition deteriorates into a full-blown episode of psychosis (Brown et al., 1972; Tarrier et al., 1988). Family stressors involving EE could also combine with other life events to heighten the risk of relapse (Brown et al., 1972).

Although EE is a strong predictor of psychiatric relapse, its role as a *cause* of relapse is far from clear (Gottesman, 1991). The most obvious question is whether EE is a cause, a correlate, or a consequence of schizophrenic symptoms. It is entirely possible that patients help bring about their own EE environments. If they display more severe symptoms to begin with, their relatives might become more and more frustrated in attempting to manage such behavior. This frustration might take the form of criticism and hostility, which aggravates patients' symptoms further.

One recent study evaluated this "two-way street" model of EE. The families of 48 schizophrenic patients were interviewed and classified as being high or low EE (Rosenfarb et al., 1995). These families were then videotaped as they discussed a family problem with the patient. Observers coded these videotapes on two variables: the level of symptoms or unusual behaviors displayed by patients and the level of EE expressed within the family. To the researchers' surprise, the only dimension on which the high EE and low EE families differed was that the high EE families made *more* genuinely supportive statements to patients! In addition, the patients in high EE families displayed about 4 times as many symptoms and disruptive behaviors during these interactions.

Next, the researchers looked at the sequence of interactions within the families. They discovered that high EE families were significantly more likely to make a harsh comment following a patient's disruptive behavior than were low EE families. Following such harsh comments, the probability of the patient's engaging in another troubling behavior increased fourfold.

These data indicate that a crucial feature of high EE families is how they respond when their schizophrenic relatives engage in disruptive behavior. High EE relatives are especially prone to respond critically to this behavior—perhaps because they have poor communication skills themselves—which only heightens the risk for more problematic behavior by the patient (Docherty, 1995).

The research reviewed in this section points to the importance of psychological and environmental factors in the development of schizophrenia. Although several exciting discoveries about the genetic, anatomical, and biochemical irregularities involved in schizophrenia have recently been made, scientists should not ignore the role of psychosocial variables. Indeed, biological and psychological factors work hand in hand in bringing about most cases of schizophrenia, as Figure 10.7 shows.

Asking whether schizophrenia is caused by biological *or* psychological factors makes no more sense than asking whether a rectangle is formed by its sides or ends. Both dimensions of schizophrenia must be studied carefully if researchers are to understand this complex disorder fully.

In Review

The two psychosocial factors receiving the most attention in the study of schizophrenia are:

- socioeconomic class and associated stressors; and
- family environments and family communication patterns.

Explanations for the disproportionate rate of schizophrenia among urban and lower SES groups include:

- the *social drift* hypothesis, which suggests that, as patients develop schizophrenic symptoms, they gradually slide down the socioeconomic ladder; and
- the *breeder* or *social causation* hypothesis, which suggests that social strains and environmental hazards breed schizophrenic episodes in vulnerable individuals.

Families high in expressed emotion (EE) are defined by:

- emotional overinvolvement with a patient; and
- a tendency to become hostile and make negative comments to the patient.

High expressed emotion:

- predicts schizophrenic relapse; and
- is probably both a cause and consequence of patients' schizophrenic symptoms.

Treatments for Schizophrenia

Prior to the 1950s there was little hope for successful treatment of schizophrenia. The typical treatment was to confine the mentally ill in large public men-

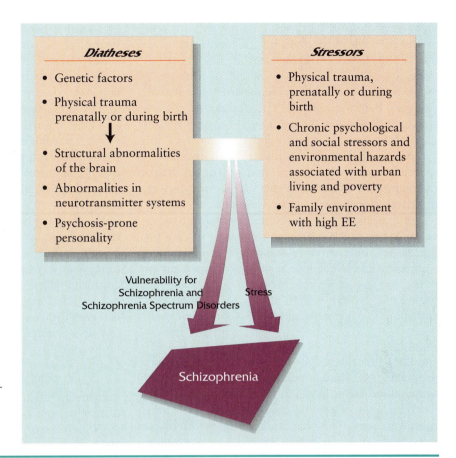

Diatheses
- Genetic factors
- Physical trauma prenatally or during birth
- Structural abnormalities of the brain
- Abnormalities in neurotransmitter systems
- Psychosis-prone personality

Stressors
- Physical trauma, prenatally or during birth
- Chronic psychological and social stressors and environmental hazards associated with urban living and poverty
- Family environment with high EE

Vulnerability for Schizophrenia and Schizophrenia Spectrum Disorders   Stress

Schizophrenia

FIGURE 10.7

Diathesis–Stress Model of Schizophrenia

Any of a set of predisposing factors can contribute to a vulnerability to schizophrenia, and this vulnerability can be aggravated in turn by one or more biological, social, or family stressors. Remember, however, that the role of high expressed emotion appears to be confined largely to relapse rather than onset of schizophrenia.

tal hospitals, where hundreds of patients lived for decades in drab, crowded wards. For the most part, all that this hospitalization accomplished was to segregate patients from the rest of society. Some patients received experimental therapies—psychosurgery, electroconvulsive shock, prolonged isolation, and restraint—but most patients were simply left to languish in the hospital year after year. Their mental abilities, social interests, and self-help skills gradually declined until they became almost totally dependent on the institution. It is difficult to decide which group of patients suffered more harm—the recipients of the aggressive treatments or the victims of neglect. In either case, most patients ended up spending much of their adult lives in these institutions.

Beginning in the 1950s, the bleak outlook for patients with schizophrenia began to change. A new category of drugs—the phenothiazines—was developed that revolutionized the treatment of schizophrenia. These drugs made it possible, for the first time, for many patients to reside outside of mental institutions. Today, they constitute the most common treatment for schizophrenia. Most often, this drug treatment takes place during a 2- to 3-week pe-

riod of hospitalization that (1) gives the patient a respite from the stressors that often precede a rapid worsening of symptoms; (2) allows clinicians to observe how the patient responds to the medication; and (3) permits intensive treatment with methods other than medication.

In comprehensive treatment programs, drug treatment is combined with various kinds of psychosocial treatment—in particular, training in social and stress-coping skills, family-oriented therapy, and community-based psychosocial treatments. In some instances, the psychosocial component may be limited to the time the patient is in the hospital. More commonly, the treatment begins in the hospital and is continued in the community after the patient has been discharged. We will first consider drug treatments and then turn our attention to psychologically oriented treatments.

Biological Treatments

The drugs most commonly used for schizophrenia are called *antipsychotics* or **neuroleptics.** In Chapter 15, we discuss the history, chemical properties, and side effects of these drugs. For now, we will focus on the effects of these drugs on schizophrenia.

Within hours of taking neuroleptics, most patients are calmed. After a few weeks of drug treatment, most patients who entered the hospital with paranoid delusions or with vivid hallucinations are conversing calmly and much more normally. Within days to weeks, many are relieved of most of the symptoms of thought disorder as their incoherent speech becomes more logical and organized. Negative symptoms of schizophrenia such as withdrawal, muteness, and negativism are less dramatically affected, but even these symptoms are reduced somewhat. Many patients become better able to care for themselves and are more responsive to their environments. Overall, between 60 and 70 percent of patients receiving neuroleptic drugs show some improvement, but fewer than 30 percent respond well enough to live in communities entirely on their own.

The Phenothiazines. The major neuroleptics, **chlorpromazine** (sold as Thorazine), **trifluoperazine** (Stelazine), **thioridazine** (Mellaril), and **fluphenazine** (Prolixin) belong to a general chemical group called the phenothiazines. The **phenothiazines** exert their antipsychotic action primarily by blocking the action of the neurotransmitter dopamine. In particular, it is now clear that they block a specific type of dopamine receptor, the D_2 receptor found in the limbic system, basal ganglia, and cortex (List & Cleghorn, 1993; see Table 10.3).

TABLE 10.3   Key Drugs Used in Treating Schizophrenia

Class of drug	Generic name	Brand name
Phenothiazines	Chlorpromazine	Thorazine
	Thioridazine	Mellaril
	Trifluoperazine	Stelazine
	Fluphenazine	Prolixin
	Triflupromazine	Vesprin
	Prochlorperazine	Compazine
Butyrophenones	Haloperidol	Haldol
	Pimozide	Orap
Thioxanthenes	Thiothixene	Navane
Atypical antipsychotics	Clozapine	Clozaril

The antipsychotic benefits of the phenothiazines do not come without cost. These drugs produce a series of side effects that range from controllable nuisances—dry mouth, hypersensitivity to sun, constipation, sleepiness—to incapacitating, irreversible, and even life-threatening complications.

One important group of serious side effects involves abnormalities of movement known as **extrapyramidal symptoms.** Among these are symptoms of *Parkinsonism* (motor disturbances that resemble the difficulties caused by Parkinson's disease), which affect about 50 percent of patients treated with phenothiazines. These symptoms include fine tremor of the hands, a slow shuffling gait, a blank stare, muscular rigidity, and slowness of movement. *Acute dystonia* is an extrapyramidal side effect involving uncontrollable muscle contractions or spasms of the head, neck, tongue, back, and eyes. *Acute akathesia* is a condition in which patients are constantly restless and agitated; they feel they have to keep their limbs moving constantly or they will experience discomfort.

Tardive dyskinesia (TD) is a serious side effect that affects 20 to 30 percent of patients who take phenothiazines over long periods of time; as many as 50 percent of elderly patients may suffer from it (Morgenstern & Glazer, 1993; Yassa et al., 1992). TD symptoms include grotesque and uncontrollable spasmodic jerks, tics, and twitches of the face, tongue, trunk, and limbs. The lips make smacking and sucking sounds, the jaws grind, the limbs may writhe uncontrollably, and speech is progressively impaired (Kahn et al., 1994). As the disorder progresses, larger portions of the body become involved in these involuntary movements. TD typically begins only after patients have been taking phenothiazines for several years, and it usually worsens as long as the drugs are taken.

Neuroleptic malignant syndrome (NMS) is a potentially fatal disorder affecting approximately 1 percent of patients taking neuroleptics. This disorder occurs within the first few days of taking the drug and involves extremely high fever, muscle rigidity, and irregular heart rate and blood pressure. It is fatal in about 20 percent of cases (APA, 1994; Lickey & Gordon, 1991; Velamoor et al., 1994).

Some of the side effects of the phenothiazines can be controlled by taking anti-Parkinsonism medications or by reducing the dose of the phenothiazine. If patients are taken off the phenothiazine early enough, many TD symptoms will diminish (Glazer et al., 1984). However, the side effects of these drugs often prompt many patients to simply stop taking their medication, as Lionel Aldridge did for a time.

This problem is widespread among patients once they leave mental hospitals and have less supervision. In fact, the majority of nonhospitalized schizophrenic patients probably experiment with medication-free periods lasting weeks or months at a time. Most neuroleptics work only for as long as the patient continues to take them, so these drug "holidays" often lead to relapses of schizophrenia.

Atypical Antipsychotic Drugs.

The discovery of several new antipsychotic medications has brought new hope to the treatment of schizophrenia, particularly for those who either do not respond well to standard neuroleptics or who cannot tolerate their side effects.

These drugs are called **atypical antipsychotics** because they do not have the same biochemical or physiological effects as do the standard neuroleptics. One atypical antipsychotic drug is **clozapine** (sold as *Clozaril*). It acts strongly on D_4 dopamine receptors but rather weakly on the D_2 receptors that are targeted by the typical antipsychotics. Because the D_2 receptors are located in several areas of the brain, drugs that affect them less strongly might be expected to produce fewer side effects. This may explain why clozapine produces fewer extrapyramidal side effects such as TD than older medications do. Clozapine appears to be effective in reducing both the positive and negative symptoms of schizophrenia (Kane et al., 1988). It also leads to improvements in 30 to 60 percent of patients who have shown little or no benefit from previous neuroleptic treatments and appears to be more effective than standard neuroleptics in reducing the negative symptoms seen in patients with Type II schizophrenia (Breier et al., 1994; Kane et al., 1988; Pickar et al., 1992).

Clozapine produces side effects such as sedation, dizziness, constipation, dry mouth, and excessive salivation that results in drooling, especially while asleep. Although it does not carry risks for extrapyramidal symptoms, approximately 2 percent of patients taking clozapine develop a potentially fatal blood disease called *agranulocytosis* that involves a loss of white blood cells. Because of this very serious condition patients taking clozapine are required to receive regular blood monitoring tests.

Limitations of Drug Treatments.

Despite evidence that biochemical irregularities and brain dysfunctions are involved in causing schizophrenia and that drug treatments can reduce many of the symptoms of the disorder, most clinicians understand that a complete treatment for schizophrenic patients must include psychosocial interventions (e.g., Bellack &

Mueser, 1993; Hogarty et al., 1986; Strachan, 1986). For one thing, drugs do not teach patients with schizophrenia how to interact more effectively or how to manage stressful situations more successfully. Nor do they help families and friends learn how to cope with the frequent frustrations and conflicts involved in living with a person who has schizophrenia. And even if drugs ameliorate many of the worst symptoms of schizophrenia, they still do not guarantee that patients will feel a sense of really belonging or being connected to people around them.

> *Connections*
>
> What other treatments are compromised by noncompliance? For examples, see Chapter 6, pp. 207–208.

Consider the remarks of Lauran Slater, a clinical psychologist who conducted weekly group therapy with hospitalized and medicated men with schizophrenia. In a memoir of her work with these patients, Slater (1996) describes how she gradually came to believe that her patients craved a meaningful intimacy with others that no medication could ever induce:

> The more I think about it, the clearer it becomes to me that these men's pivotal concerns are with connection—how to get it, how to hold it, how to mourn its loss. Crazy or sane, we all know the desire for skin touching skin or brain rubbing brain. Although their desires are often expressed in lusty ways, I don't believe they are motivated by something as simple as lust. The sensitivity to language and frustration over its loss, the simple touches and aches in their faces—these things lead me to believe their stretches for connections are occurring at more complex levels, are rooted in the need to belong, to participate in the wider world. (Slater, 1996)

The needs that Slater describes illustrate why it is a mistake, in our view, to think about the treatment of schizophrenia in purely biological terms. Drugs are usually necessary for controlling the symptoms of schizophrenia, but they cannot make a new life for patients or teach them how to cope with the negative consequences of the disorder. These goals are more likely to be accomplished through psychosocial treatments.

Psychosocial Treatments

The first well-documented use of psychosocial treatments for psychosis appeared in the Moral Era of the nineteenth century, during which several European and American reformers insisted that institutionalized mental patients could be helped—rather than merely hidden—if they were treated with kindness and taught to take more responsibility for their own lives.

In the United States, the use of psychosocial treatments for schizophrenia has a long history. In the 1920s, Harry Stack Sullivan used a form of psychoanalysis combined with specially organized living arrangements on hospital wards to work with young schizophrenics. His student, Frieda Fromm-Reichmann, continued this tradition, as have other psychoanalytically trained psychiatrists. However, because of a lack of empirical research documenting that psychoanalysis produces significant long-term benefits (Stone, 1986), psychoanalytic treatment is not the treatment of choice for schizophrenics. It is sometimes still combined with medication, but even this use of psychoanalysis is becoming less common, in part because it is so expensive.

During the 1960s and 1970s, as new medications allowed people with schizophrenia to leave hospitals, two important changes occurred in psychosocial interventions. First, psychologists began to design milieu programs to help hospitalized patients develop the self-help skills that years of living in a mental hospital had eroded. **Milieu programs** are intended to resocialize patients in the hospital so that they can learn how to manage their lives and engage in appropriate behavior in the community. These programs attempt to create hospital ward environments that reward patients for resuming independent living.

Many milieu programs took the form of **token economies,** systems of reinforcing desired behaviors with poker chips or other tokens that can be exchanged for access to television, snacks, or other rewards. In essence, token economies use the principles of operant conditioning to teach patients new skills that ideally will generalize to life in the community (Ayllon & Azrin, 1968). In the 1970s, Gordon Paul and his colleagues (Paul & Lentz, 1977) at the University of Illinois compared the effects of standard mental hospital care, milieu therapy, and milieu therapy based on token economy principles. This study, which is widely regarded as the best study of milieu therapy ever conducted, found that, compared with standard hospital treatment, both forms of milieu therapy produced significantly greater improvements in patients' adjustment skills; the token economy milieu program produced the highest rate of improvement.

The second important development in psychosocial treatments was a move toward delivering more treatment outside of hospitals, in community settings known as *therapeutic communities* or *group homes.* In one of the most innovative and effective examples of these programs, a group of patients lived together in the same lodge and successfully supported themselves with a janitorial business that they managed on their own (Fairweather et al., 1969).

Milieu and therapeutic community programs were the predecessors to three kinds of psychosocial therapies that are used today in the comprehensive treatment of schizophrenia: self-management and social skills training, family therapy, and psychosocial rehabilitation. In the usual case, one or more of these treatments is combined with medication.

Self-Management and Social Skills Training. These programs focus on training patients in everyday *self-management skills* such as shopping, cooking, administering and monitoring their medication, and managing their money (e.g., Falloon et al., 1985). Whether offered in the hospital or the community, the aim of these interventions is to help patients become as independent as possible. Ample evidence exists that even severely impaired patients can learn these skills and retain them for as long as a year or more (Wallace, 1993).

A second goal of many of these programs is to help patients learn basic *social skills,* such as carrying on conversations, expressing needs clearly, refusing unreasonable demands, and interacting appropriately with friends and relatives. This training can be tedious because the symptoms of schizophrenia interfere with patients' ability to learn new skills. Patient's attention and concentration are often impaired, memory is sometimes disturbed, and motivation is frequently absent. To counteract these obstacles, a program's staff often break down social skills into simple steps such as making eye contact when greeting others, listening carefully to what others say, taking turns during conversations, and talking in a normal tone of voice (Bellak & Mueser, 1993). Social skills training usually takes place in structured groups that rely on modeling, role playing, lots of practice, and social reinforcement.

Social skills training programs have proved effective in helping patients overcome the impairments of many of their most persistent negative symptoms. However, these improvements often deteriorate after patients move out of the hospital into community living arrangements. To counteract the drop-off in improvements, clinicians often use booster training to reestablish the initial gains. However, even with booster training, the ability of these programs to prevent rehospitalization of patients who have relapsed is not well established (Bellak & Mueser, 1993).

TABLE 10.4	Elements in Effective Psychosocial Family Treatments

Element	Description
Reframing the problem	Provide family members with alternate ways of conceptualizing the patient's disorder so the family does not feel guilty or blamed for it.
Focus on communication	Enhance family and patient communication to prevent arguments and ensure that each other's point of view is understood. This activity changes the family atmosphere from high to low expressed emotion.
Focus on present interactions	Concentrate on current stressors and problems.
Learn behavioral techniques for problem solving	Break problems down into manageable elements and train family members in specific problem-solving strategies.
Create structured, stable programs	Structure all program elements clearly and make them accessible to all family members. The program should be stable and predictable for participants.
Provide psychoeducation	Educate the family about the biological and psychological nature of schizophrenia, what medications are used, and how they affect patients.

Source: After Lam, 1991; and Strachan, 1986.

Family Therapy. Therapy for families of schizophrenic patients focuses on educating them about the nature of schizophrenia and training family members in effective problem-solving and communication skills (see Table 10.4). This approach is based on a bidirectional view of family environments, that is, that a patient's symptoms and erratic behavior can aggravate family members and family members' actions and reactions can exacerbate the patient's condition (e.g., Bellak & Mueser, 1993). Accordingly, families are trained in how to lower their level of expressed emotion by avoiding harshly critical and overinvolved emotional reactions to the patient. There may also be some benefits to treating families in groups so that they can support one another in making changes (McFarlane et al., 1995).

One comprehensive, home-based family treatment program was devised and tested by Ian Falloon and his colleagues (1985). Treatment was tailored to each family member's strengths and weaknesses and included education about schizophrenia and its treatment, training in communication skills and problem-solving strategies, and a plan for rewarding the patient's desirable behaviors. In one study, only 17 percent of patients whose families received this treatment had relapsed after 2 years, compared with an 83 percent relapse for patients who had received standard posthospital treatment (Falloon et al., 1985).

Gerard Hogarty and his research team examined the independent and combined effects of patient-oriented social skills training and family therapy in preventing relapse (Hogarty et al., 1986). They recruited 103 newly admitted patients and their families to participate in the program. All families accepted into the program were high in expressed emotion. Patients in all groups took neuroleptic drugs. One group received *family treatment* focused on decreasing family guilt and family stressors, increasing understanding of the patient's disorder, decreasing expressed emotion, and increasing social networks for the family. In the *social skills* group, treatment focused on helping patients learn how to respond to hostile remarks by family members, express positive feelings, and develop more accurate perceptions of others. A third group received *both* family treatment and social skills training. Patients in a fourth group received only medication from a supportive nurse.

One year after being released from the hospital, 41 percent of the medication-only group had relapsed compared with only 19 percent of the family treatment group and 20 percent of the social skills group. None of the patients in the combined family treatment and social skills group relapsed. The dramatic effect of these treatments, especially the combined treatment, appeared to be largely accounted for by their ability to change the family level of EE. In families that changed from high to low EE, no

Prevention   Stopping Relapse in Young Schizophrenic Patients

Although scientists have discovered no effective ways to prevent schizophrenia, psychosocial rehabilitation coupled with regular medication comes the closest to constituting a form of secondary prevention. For this reason, many programs pay special attention to serving relatively young schizophrenic patients who are not yet chronically disabled from the disorder.

Family therapy and training in social and self-help skills are regular components of psychosocial rehabilitation programs, but the most successful programs offer more services than these. Patients are often assigned to *case managers* who serve as advocates and help patients obtain necessary services involving transportation, housing, medical services, and financial aid. In addition, efforts are made to create social support

that "wraps around" patients and holds them in the community. Peer support groups meet frequently so that patients have a place to engage in recreation and where they can learn from and encourage one another. "Safe houses" or temporary, sheltered living arrangements are also offered to patients who are homeless. Some programs design individualized plans to help clients avoid or manage crises. The plans may include agreements to go to a safe house if family conflict is getting out of hand or to ask a buddy to come stay with the person. In some cases, patients help write what is known as a *proactive crisis plan,* which lists the typical symptoms and warning signs they experience at the beginning of a breakdown. This crisis plan, based on clients' understanding of how their disor-

der usually progresses, specifies the steps that should be taken to help contain or forestall the crisis. A particular emphasis in some crisis planning approaches is to help patients learn how to regulate negative feelings better (Hogarty et al., 1995).

Other programs stress the importance of vocational rehabilitation. A leading example is the Boston University Model, developed by William Anthony and his colleagues (Anthony, Cohen, & Danley, 1988). In this approach, a specific vocational rehabilitation plan identifying occupational goals and needed skills is drawn up for every patient. Sometimes job clubs or transitional employment opportunities are created so that patients can gradually begin returning to the work force. Because finding and keeping a job also requires being able to get along with super-

patient relapsed, but among families showing no change in EE status, relapse prevention occurred only if the family received both the family and social skills interventions.

Psychosocial Rehabilitation. The most comprehensive psychological treatment for schizophrenia involves a set of interventions collectively known as *psychosocial rehabilitation.* **Psychosocial rehabilitation** aims not to cure serious mental disorders such as schizophrenia but to prevent unnecessary hospitalizations, reduce impairments that interfere with a person's daily functioning, strengthen independent living skills necessary to resume normal social roles, and modify environments to make them more supportive (Cook, 1995).

The philosophical origins of psychosocial rehabilitation are found in the Moral Era of the nineteenth century, especially in the view that, if mental patients are treated with kindness and with the ex-

pectation that they can take responsibility for their lives, their overall functioning will improve. The implementation of psychosocial rehabilitation programs in the United States began in the late 1960s and reflects the influence of three groups of people: (1) relatives of patients with severe mental illness who formed advocacy/support groups such as the National Alliance for the Mentally Ill, (2) self-help groups composed of people suffering from severe mental illnesses, and (3) mental health professionals who believed that treatment of the severely mentally ill should take place in community settings whenever possible. Psychosocial rehabilitation interventions try to strengthen patients' competencies to maintain health, get a job, live in stable housing, and be able to take care of daily needs.

Empirical research has now shown that psychosocial rehabilitation can restore some patients' ability to live independently in the community after an initial psychotic episode and can even reduce the

visors and coworkers, a complete vocational rehabilitation plan often addresses interpersonal work skills as well.

A handful of studies have evaluated the success of the Boston University Model. For example, one study reported that the number of patients able to secure a job or enroll in a job-training program increased from 19 to 42 percent following completion of a course on how to choose among available opportunities and how to get a desired job (Unger & Anthony, 1992). Of more interest, participants in this program were hospitalized less often during the training course than before. Other programs have achieved less-positive vocational outcomes, indicating that the best way to improve this aspect of functioning is still unknown (Wallace, 1993).

Learning how to anticipate and manage various crises is crucial to patients' ability to avoid relapses of schizophrenia. Family therapy, social skills training, and vocationally oriented psychosocial rehabilitation have all shown promise in helping young patients prevent some relapses of schizophrenia.

likelihood of relapse (Bond et al., 1990; 1995). As discussed in the Prevention section, psychosocial rehabilitation typically provides a number of related services. What services a given patient needs most is best determined by a careful assessment of the individual's overall circumstances. If the right services can be obtained early enough in the history of a person's disorder, a considerable number of relapses and hospitalizations can be prevented.

In Review

The phenothiazines, the primary treatment for schizophrenia,

- relieve positive symptoms for 60 to 70 percent of patients; and
- cause several kinds of serious side effects.

Newer, atypical antipsychotic drugs:

- relieve negative symptoms as well as positive symptoms; and
- help some patients who are resistant to the phenothiazines.

The most effective psychosocial treatments for schizophrenia focus on:

- training patients in self-help and social skills;
- family therapy in which families are taught how to deal with patients when they return home; and
- psychosocial rehabilitation that helps patients live in communities by strengthening their independent living skills and creating more supportive environments.

In combination with antipsychotic medication, many psychosocial treatments are effective in preventing relapses of schizophrenia.

Irving Gottesman

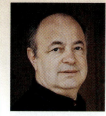

Schizophrenia

Dr. Irving Gottesman is Professor of Psychology at the University of Virginia. He has written extensively on genetic factors in psychopathology and is recognized as one of the leading genetic researchers of schizophrenia in the United States.

Q *Has schizophrenia appeared on the scene only in the past few centuries or has it affected people throughout history?*

A Schizophrenia is not a recent disorder, but we have been able to study it carefully only recently. A number of factors account for this slow progress. Medical schools didn't exist until the mid nineteenth century, and the formal discipline of psychiatry didn't appear until the last half of the nineteenth century. As a result, people were not trained to be alert to psychiatric disorders so they often went undiagnosed. In addition, the life expectancy of humans was much shorter centuries ago so we had less of a chance to observe schizophrenia, which can have an onset even after age 50.

> *We should aspire to treat at least 80 percent of all individuals with schizophrenia as outpatients...*

Q *Is schizophrenia a single disorder, or are there many schizophrenias?*

A Not only is this a key question for schizophrenia, it haunts the study of psychopathology in general, and there is no simple answer to it. Schizophrenia is probably a lot like disorders such as mental retardation or epilepsy. There are several varieties of these disorders. Our research picks away at one variety at a time, but we still have a long way to go before we can identify all the different versions and causes of schizophrenia. I suspect there are a few, rare cases of a single gene leading to schizophrenia, but more often a combination of about a half dozen different genes appear to be involved in a neurodevelopmental, diathesis–stress process yet to be unraveled.

Q *If schizophrenia is a genetic disorder, how can you explain a case such as Lionel Aldridge's, where no one in his family had had schizophrenia?*

A Of course, if you remember that most forms of schizophrenia are under the control of several genes at once, this is really not surprising. An analogy I like to use to illustrate this point is to look at the parents of Michael Jordan. Neither his mother nor his father were as tall or as athletically talented as Michael. Height and coordination are both influenced by genetics, but they are both under multigene control, so we can see the effects of genetics without either parent's manifesting the same physical stature or prowess.

Q *What goals should we have for the treatment of schizophrenia?*

A We should aspire to treat at least 80 percent of all individuals with schizophrenia as outpatients most of the time. About one in five patients will require longer periods of hospitalization. This goal is reasonable because the field has made remarkable improvements in the use of medications. In addition, families of patients with schizophrenia have become increasingly sophisticated in helping their relatives cope with the disorder more effectively. Families need to be heavily involved in treatment, and we must continue to pressure the government and insurance companies to pay the costs of educating family members about schizophrenia.

Q *Do you believe that reducing expressed emotion is a key to effective treatment?*

A The whole literature on expressed emotion is being improved steadily. Although there is no evidence that expressed emotion triggers the initial episode of schizophrenia, I am now convinced that it is an important factor capable of triggering relapses.

Q *What is the key to making more progress in our understanding of schizophrenia?*

A I think the main change the mental health professions need to make is to train students to work in cooperative teams with different kinds of scientists. Currently, there is too much separation between researchers and clinicians and between biological and social factors. We should train psychiatrists, neurochemists, psychologists, immunologists, computer scientists, and epidemiologists to work together. All these perspectives are necessary in understanding schizophrenia.

Revisiting the Case of Lionel Aldridge

ou should now have a much better understanding of the kind of disorder that affected Lionel Aldridge. A hundred years ago, Lionel would not have been diagnosed with schizophrenia. Because his condition did not start at an early age and did not progressively deteriorate, he would not have fit Kraepelin's definition of the disorder. However, clinicians using the DSM diagnosed Lionel with the paranoid type of schizophrenia. Applying other classification schemes, Lionel's case could be described as typical of a reactive Type I schizophrenia.

As Lionel Aldridge discovered, medication alone is not a sufficient treatment for most cases of schizophrenia. The support of friends and the opportunity to relearn how to live successfully in the community are crucial. In the late 1980s, using a combination of medication, community support, and his personal resolve to overcome schizophrenia, Lionel began to put his life back together. He learned to cope with the side effects of his medication and accepted the fact that he had to take it regularly to function adequately. He found that he could "make friends" with the hallucinated voices he sometimes still heard, so he was no longer terrified by them. He also learned—from therapists and from friends—how to stop thinking negative and destructive thoughts when bad things happened to him.

Today, Lionel Aldridge lives in Milwaukee, where he is well known not only for past athletic successes but for his ongoing role in educating the public about severe mental illnesses. His story illustrates how medication, social support, understanding, and constant effort can overcome even the most severe mental disorder.

SUMMARY

What Is Schizophrenia?

Clinicians have formally recognized the disorder of schizophrenia for less than 200 years. Schizophrenia was originally called *dementia praecox* because it was believed to start at a young age and to result in progressive mental deterioration. In the late 1800s, Emil Kraepelin concluded that there were four subtypes of dementia praecox: hebephrenic, catatonic, paranoid, and simple. Bleuler's ideas eventually led to a broadening of the concept to include conditions that did not always start at an early age or deteriorate progressively. Eventually, DSM diagnoses of schizophrenia followed an operational approach to defining the disorder that represented a compromise between the traditions of Kraepelin, Bleuler, and the proposals of German psychiatrist Kurt Schneider.

Life with Schizophrenia: Patterns and Variations

About 1 percent of the world population is diagnosed with schizophrenia. Approximately equal proportions of males and females are affected, but the disorder usually begins earlier in males than in females. Initial onset is usually in the teens and 20s, but schizophrenia can develop at any time, even as late as the 50s or 60s.

Schizophrenia is categorized by two major kinds of symptoms: positive symptoms that include hallucinations, delusions, formal thought disorder, and disordered behavior and negative symptoms that include flattened affect, alogia, and avolition.

The DSM-IV lists five subtypes of schizophrenia: paranoid, disorganized, catatonic, undifferentiated, and residual. Other subclassifications of schizophrenia include the process (long-term, insidious development of symptoms with a poorer prognosis) versus reactive (acute reaction to stressors with a better prognosis) dimension and Type I (prominent positive symptoms) versus Type II schizophrenia (prominent negative symptoms).

In addition to schizophrenia, the DSM-IV lists several other psychotic disorders that involve hallucinations or delusions. These disorders usually involve fragments of a full schizophrenic syndrome or are reactions to specific events that cause a limited episode of psychosis. They seldom cause the intense symptoms and long-term impairment and suffering that are found in many cases of schizophrenia.

Biological Causes of Schizophrenia

It is not possible to pinpoint the causes of any individual case of schizophrenia, but most researchers believe that a diathesis–stress model best explains the disorder's development. Evidence from family aggregation, twin, and adoption studies clearly shows that genes can provide one kind of diathesis to schizophrenia. However, in cases in which one MZ twin has schizophrenia, the cotwin is also diagnosed with schizophrenia only about half the time. Nongenetic factors must be involved as well.

Exactly what is inherited remains unknown. Biological abnormalities, personality patterns, neurological problems involving attentional and cognitive deficits, and structural abnormalities in the brain are all possibilities. Early evidence implicated overactivity of dopamine, but recent studies have cast doubt on this hypothesis as an adequate explanation; other neurotransmitters such as serotonin may also be involved. Brain scanning procedures show that many schizophrenics have significant structural brain deficits, particularly in the frontal lobe and certain subcortical structures under the temporal lobe, including parts of the limbic system. The origin of these deficits is currently unknown; they may be inherited, they may be caused by complications during pregnancy or birth, or they may be the result of early viral infections.

Psychological and Social Causes of Schizophrenia

In the United States, a preponderance of schizophrenic patients come from inner cities and from the lower socioeconomic classes. Whether their disorder causes them to drift down to these levels or whether the stressors of urbanicity and poverty breed schizophrenia is still unresolved.

Family emotional environment, especially high levels of expressed emotion, is a predictor of schizophrenic relapse. However, expressed emotion appears to be both a cause and a consequence of the disorder. Recovery rates for schizophrenia vary considerably between cultures.

Treatments for Schizophrenia

The most common treatments for schizophrenia are antipsychotic drugs, administered initially in the hospital and then continued in the community. The phenothiazines act by blocking dopamine receptors and reduce positive symptoms in about two thirds of patients. These therapeutic effects are offset by potentially serious, sometimes irreversible side effects such as tardive dyskinesia. As a result, many patients stop taking these medications. They then usually suffer relapse. Atypical antipsychotic drugs, which have somewhat different neurotransmitter effects than the phenothiazines, are effective for many patients who do not respond to traditional neuroleptics or who suffer serious side effects from them.

Medication alone is not a sufficient treatment for most cases of schizophrenia. Psychosocial treatments need to be provided as well. Some of these treatments focus on training patients in basic social and survival skills. Others stress family therapy, including educating the family about schizophrenia, enhancing communication among family members, and reducing high levels of expressed emotion in the family. Psychosocial rehabilitation is a broad intervention that teaches patients how to cope with the disabilities of schizophrenia and increases the amount of support available to them in their home communities. All these psychosocial programs have proved to be important in preventing relapses among schizophrenic patients.

Will the causes of schizophrenia eventually be determined so that it can be prevented or at least more successfully treated? That goal is a long way off. Future research will need to address several critical areas. More longitudinal studies that follow patients from the onset of symptoms across all phases of the disorder are needed. Future studies will also need to employ the increasingly sophisticated technology being used in the fields of neuroanatomy and molecular biology so that scientists can learn more about how genetic factors influence schizophrenia. The search for more effective treatment must continue as well. Consistent with the diathesis–stress model, this search must include not only the pursuit of new medications but also the discovery of how psychosocial and cultural stressors and buffers can be changed to lessen the incidence of schizophrenia.

KEY TERMS

active phase, p. 344

alogia, p. 340

atypical antipsychotics, p. 367

avolition, p. 340

brief psychotic disorder, p. 341

catalepsy, p. 348

catatonia, p. 339

catatonic type, p. 348

chlorpromazine, p. 366

clozapine, p. 367

deficit schizophrenia, p. 339

delusional disorder, p. 341

delusions, p. 332

disorganized type, p. 348

double-bind hypothesis, p. 362

expressed emotion, p. 363

extrapyramidal symptoms, p. 366

flat affect, p. 340

fluphenazine, p. 366

formal thought disorder, p. 338

hallucinations, p. 332

hypofrontality, p. 355

illusions, p. 337

milieu programs, p. 368

morbidity risk, p. 345

negative symptoms, p. 334

neuroleptics, p. 365

other psychotic disorders, p. 341

paranoid type, p. 348

phenothiazines, p. 366

positive symptoms, p. 334

postpartum onset, p. 341

process schizophrenia, p. 349

prodromal phase, p. 344

psychosocial rehabilitation, p. 370

psychotic disorder due to a general medical condition, p. 341

reactive schizophrenia, p. 349

residual phase, p. 344

residual type, p. 348

schizoaffective disorder, p. 341

schizophrenia, p. 332

schizophrenic spectrum disorder, p. 341

schizophreniform disorder, p. 341

schizophrenogenic mother, p. 362

schizotaxia, p. 353

season-of-birth effect, p. 354

shared psychotic disorder, p. 341

substance-induced psychotic disorder, p. 342

thioridazine, p. 366

token economies, p. 368

trifluoperazine, p. 366

undifferentiated type, p. 348

ventricles, p. 355

waxy flexibility, p. 348

11

Cognitive Disorders

Colour Machine by Genevieve Burnett, 1978. Oil on canvas, 26" x 24". Courtesy of Sistare.

From the Case of Dorothy

D orothy is a 78-year-old retired laboratory technician. She was almost incoherent when the police picked her up in response to a call about an elderly woman walking in the street in a nightgown and slippers. In her brief moments of clear speech she repeatedly insisted that she must "get to the lab." By the time the squad car reached the hospital, half a mile away, Dorothy was unconscious.

A wrist bracelet identified her as a diabetic and gave the name and telephone number of a neighbor. After an I.V. was started, Dorothy was admitted to the hospital, and her neighbor was notified. The neighbor confirmed that these nocturnal episodes had happened before, but that Dorothy had always been taken to another hospital.

By morning, Dorothy was alert and chatting with the staff. She indicated that she was employed in the chemistry department of a local college and must return to the lab as soon as possible. Several times she told her nurses about the research project in which she was involved. A call to the college revealed that Dorothy had been involved in such a project 15 years earlier, but that she had retired 13 years ago. A CT scan revealed some atrophy of Dorothy's frontal and parietal lobes, but there was no sign of medical problems other than the diabetes and mild osteoporosis. A structured interview revealed that Dorothy was able to correctly state the day's date and the location of the hospital; but she could not recall the names of three objects she had identified minutes earlier, and she had great difficulty counting backward from 100 by 7s. During evening visiting hours Dorothy mistook her roommate's husband for a "spy" from another college; she confided to the nursing assistant that he had been "after her for years" because he wanted to prevent her from completing her research project. Several hours later, the nurses found Dorothy pulling at her I.V. tubing and her bedclothes. The roommate informed the nurses that Dorothy kept muttering about the radioactive fallout spewing from the air vents. After receiving a mild sedative, Dorothy slept through the night. The next morning she was alert, but she showed no memory for the events of the previous day or evening.

Late in the day Dorothy was discharged to the care of her daughter, who had driven several hundred miles to stay with her mother. The daughter admitted that she had been worried about her mother's lapses of attention and memory over the past year, but her mother had refused all offers of help. In fact, she and Dorothy had bickered more with each other in the past few months than at any previous time. The daughter also reported that there was almost no food in her mother's house, there were greasy stains on the living room carpet, and the sink was piled with dirty dishes. This was unlike her usually fastidious mother. During the discharge interview the doctors informed Dorothy and her daughter of their diagnosis: dementia of the Alzheimer's type, with late onset, with delirium. ■

*I*n this chapter we will consider cognitive disorders, a group of mental disorders that, as in Dorothy's case, (1) are directly caused by biological changes in the brain, (2) involve impairments in cognition, and (3) can appear at any age, but are especially common in older people. Injuries to the brain, tumors, infectious diseases, gradual degeneration, poisoning, and substance-induced changes are the most common causes of these conditions. When brain damage underlies these disorders, it is often described as being either focal or diffuse. *Focal damage* involves lesions in specific areas of the brain; closed-head injuries and brain tumors are common causes of focal damage. *Diffuse damage* refers to lesions in brain tissue that are spread across the brain or at least to several areas of it; poisoning and infectious diseases such as AIDS can lead to diffuse damage. Psychological and sociocultural factors also influence the severity and course of the disorders reviewed in this chapter, but, by themselves, they do not cause cognitive disorders.

Research on the functioning of the brain has demonstrated that several mental functions are localized in specific areas and structures and that damage to these areas will result in certain types of cognitive impairment. For example, the left hemisphere controls speech and other language functions for most people, and the right hemisphere specializes in the processing of emotional material. Four different regions, or *lobes,* of the cerebral cortex also have

special responsibilities. The frontal lobes control motor movements and higher-order thinking and planning. The temporal lobes specialize in the processing of language, perception, and memory; beneath the temporal lobes, other structures such as the hippocampus and amygdala are heavily involved in memory and emotions. The parietal lobes help process sensory information about pain, body temperature, and touch. Toward the back of the head, the occipital lobes specialize in vision. Figure 11.1 shows a few of the brain regions that, if damaged, often lead to specific cognitive impairments.

Although the brain is divided into many different components, it must also still function as an integrated system. Most complex mental functions such as perceiving external stimuli, using and understanding language, remembering events, and learning new information require that many brain areas cooperate and communicate. Thus, a breakdown in an area that controls the perception of sounds can also impair language comprehension, learning, memory, and speech. Further complications arise because many forms of brain damage are not limited to a single area or structure. Being struck on one side of the head can cause severe bruising on the opposite side of the brain when it strikes the skull. Conditions such as Alzheimer's disease often produce degeneration across many areas of the brain, producing a mosaic of cognitive problems.

The symptoms of cognitive disorders can take several forms:

- an inability to remember events that happened only minutes earlier;
- loss of the ability to understand written language while still comprehending speech;
- a failure to recognize familiar people or objects;
- loss of the ability to plan simple sequences of behavior;
- a clouding of consciousness that leaves the person with incomplete awareness of what is taking place in the environment;
- profound confusion and disorientation, sometimes to the point of delusional beliefs;
- loss of judgment about the appropriateness of behavior; and
- difficulties in accurately perceiving spatial arrangements or in coordinating motor behaviors.

Although cognitive disorders are found in people of all ages, some of them occur more often in older people, in part because many diseases that cause brain deterioration are more likely to affect the elderly. Because of this association, we will begin our coverage

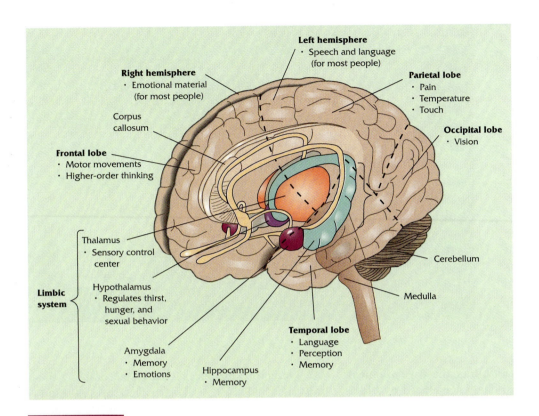

Left hemisphere
· Speech and language
(for most people)

Right hemisphere
· Emotional material
(for most people)

Parietal lobe
· Pain
· Temperature
· Touch

Corpus
callosum

Occipital lobe
· Vision

Frontal lobe
· Motor movements
· Higher-order thinking

Thalamus
· Sensory control
center

Cerebellum

**Limbic
system**

Hypothalamus
· Regulates thirst,
hunger, and
sexual behavior

Medulla

Temporal lobe
· Language
· Perception
· Memory

Amygdala
· Memory
· Emotions

Hippocampus
· Memory

FIGURE 11.1

Brain–Behavior Relationships: Major Structures in the Brain and the Functions
Associated with Each

The organization of the brain is more complicated than figures such as this suggest. Many parts of
the brain are involved in controlling language, thinking, behavior, and emotions so we cannot always
predict how a lesion in a specific part of the brain will affect an individual's overall functioning.

of cognitive disorders with a discussion of aging and
the effects of normal aging on the brain and psychological processes.

Aging

An experienced 60-year-old receptionist with excellent recommendations is denied a job at a health club
because the manager fears his young clientele will not
relate well to her. Neighborhood boys smash eggs on
the front door of a 72-year-old woman because, they
tell police, she "just stares out her window all day."

Ageism, a form of prejudice against the elderly,
exists, like all prejudices, because people fail to appreciate human diversity. Stereotypes of the aged
are often caused by misinformation, such as the mistaken belief that older adults have no interest in (or
capacity for) an active sex life or that intellectual decline in the elderly is inevitable and untreatable. Unfortunately, even providers of health care and mental

health services are not immune to these misconceptions (Gatz & Pearson, 1988).

The need for accurate information about aging
and about the needs of older adults is rising because
the ranks of the elderly are growing rapidly. The elderly (usually defined as those over 65) will soon represent 20 to 25 percent of the U.S. population in the
and a similar percentage in the rest of the world. The
aging of the baby boomers—the approximately 77
million people born in the United States between
1946 and 1964—will accelerate this growth in the
next three decades. Among the elderly, the fastest
growing segment in the American population is the
oldest of the old, those over 85. As more people live
to older ages, new medical and mental health issues
confront us. What factors matter most to older persons' quality of life? Should mandatory retirement be
banned in all occupations or only in some? Should
expensive life-sustaining medical treatments be ra-
tioned to curb health care costs? To answer questions
like these, it is more important than ever that we

For some people, old age is the best of times—for others, the worst. Some spend their "golden years" surrounded by friends, family, or pets whom they love, and who return that love in kind. They worship, work, play, debate, vote, and volunteer their time and talent. Others rarely venture outside their homes and die in solitude— ill, depressed, confused, and forgotten.

learn as much as we can about the psychological and neuropsychological challenges faced by older adults. It is also vital to distinguish changes associated with normal aging from those produced by brain damage.

Normal Aging

In contrast to the assumption that old age is a lonely, unhappy time, recent research shows that, overall, older adults are about as happy as any other age group (Myers & Diener, 1995). For example, one recent survey of 169,776 people in 16 countries found that about 80 percent of adults, regardless of age, report being "satisfied with life" (Inglehart, 1990). Increasingly, researchers are finding that the keys to successful aging include staying physically and mentally active, maintaining some type of religious or spiritual values, and controlling stress by focusing on relationships and commitments that the person finds most fulfilling or pleasing (Margoshes, 1995a; Myers & Diener, 1995). Staying mentally active may even prolong a person's life (Alzheimer's Association, 1994).

Of course, some loss of sensory and motor function seems to be an inevitable consequence of normal aging (Belsky, 1990). Body flexibility, muscular strength and speed, hearing, vision, sensitivity to taste and smell, and vestibular sense (balance) all decline with age. The rate of decline in these capacities is slow from the mid-30s or early 40s through about age 60. Then, for most persons, the rate of decline increases sharply after 65 to 70 years of age.

Numerous metabolic changes accompany these muscular and sensory changes. Decreases in respiratory, cardiac, liver, and kidney function are common. As one important result, older persons metabolize drugs more slowly than they did in younger adulthood. In addition, the sensitivity of the brain's receptors to most classes of drugs increases with age. Consequently, drugs become more effective at a lower dose and are also more likely to be toxic for the elderly (Cummings & Coffey, 1994). To make matters worse, the elderly are prone to using prescribed medications incorrectly. According to one survey (Lamy, 1985), 40 percent of elderly persons taking medications receive prescriptions from more than one physician; 30 percent make serious errors in the way they take their medications; and 12 percent take drugs prescribed for another person. Because the elderly are at a higher risk for many medical disorders and because medications are more frequently given to older adults, the likelihood of drug-induced brain disorder and behavioral abnormalities increases. As Figure 11.2 illustrates, many of the mental disorders observed in older patients (including those discussed in this chapter) are caused by complex interactions of several factors. Older persons become increasingly susceptible to brain diseases, medical illnesses, and drug toxicity (Cummings & Coffey, 1994). These risks then interact with other problems, such as lower levels of social support, in complex ways that can seriously impair mental functioning.

Cognitive functioning also changes with age, but in a complicated way. Average IQ scores tend to de-

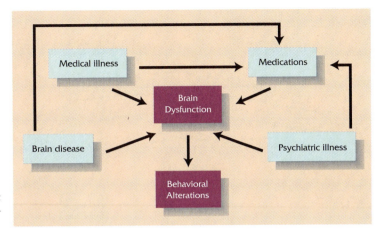

FIGURE 11.2

Multiple Causes of Brain Dysfunctions
in the Aged

The brain dysfunctions and behavioral changes
that are associated with aging are often the result
of interactions between medical illnesses, medications, brain diseases, and psychiatric disorders.

cline a bit starting in the late 50s to early 60s, but
individuals vary greatly in how their intellectual
functioning changes after that. Thanks to the Seattle
Longitudinal Study (Schaie, 1994), which has assessed more than 5,000 adults for as long as 35
years, clinicians now understand more about the intellectual changes that come with aging. All mental
abilities tend to increase modestly from young adulthood to early middle age. Thereafter, different mental abilities tend to peak and decline at different ages
and at different rates. As Figure 11.3 on page 382
shows, the rate of decline becomes steeper with increasing age, but most older persons are just as able
to analyze and understand their daily experiences as
they were in their younger days. In fact, other evidence suggests that certain intellectual processes
such as creativity may increase with age in persons
who exercise their creative gifts throughout their lives
(Margoshes, 1995b).

Performance on tasks that require motor speed,
rapid information processing, or fine motor control
does usually decrease with age (McGuigan, 1994).
However, many persons find ingenious ways to compensate for losses in speed or motor coordination.
For example, concert pianist Artur Rubinstein slowed
his playing of musical passages just before rapid sections to give the illusion of greater speed in the latter
sections (Margoshes, 1995a).

Most older persons also complain of memory
loss, particularly for recent as opposed to more distant events. Short-term memory (memory for events
in the preceding 20 to 30 seconds) is typically somewhat impaired in the elderly (Ratcliff & Saxton,
1994). Some of this memory loss may be a by-product of depression or a side effect of medications prescribed for medical problems, not the result of aging
per se. Many elderly people who believe they are for-

getful show normal memory when tested (Margoshes,
1995a). In fact, clinicians who work with the elderly
recognize that older people who complain the most
about forgetfulness often have the best memories
while those with declining memories often seem not
to notice their impairments.

Some age-related forgetfulness may not be a
problem involving memory retrieval at all. Instead,
it may result from inefficient information storage at
the time of initial learning (Grady et al., 1995). Inefficient storage often results when people are distracted, and distractibility is an increasing problem
as people age. When older persons minimize distraction by focusing closely on important details,
their memory capacity may increase dramatically.

Cognitive Disorders and Aging

Several mental disorders caused primarily by brain lesions and dysfunction are more common or more serious in older adults. These include a group of conditions listed in the DSM-IV as delirium, dementia,
amnestic and other cognitive disorders. Prior to the
DSM-IV, these conditions were classified as **organic
mental disorders** because their etiology was known
or presumed to be some type of brain disease or brain
dysfunction. But this terminology has been changed
in the DSM-IV because, as scientists have learned
more about mental disorders, they have discovered
that most of them have some biological basis. Retaining a separate section for organic disorders implies that other mental disorders are nonorganic; it
also suggests a formal distinction between organic
and nonorganic causes—between mind and body—
that is no longer widely accepted. The World Health
Organization (WHO) still uses the term *organic mental disorders* in the ICD-10 to classify these disorders.

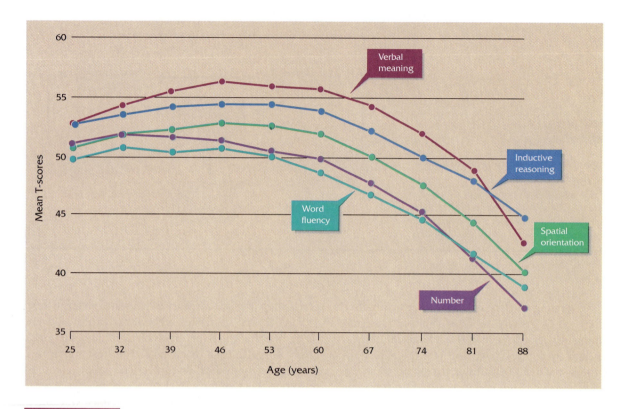

FIGURE 11.3

Age-Related Changes in Mental Abilities

Various mental abilities increase from early adulthood to middle age, after which these abilities (reported here as T-scores) start to decline. The declines begin at different ages depending on the ability being studied, but, the older we become, the steeper the rate of loss tends to be.

Source: From Schaie, 1994.

But the WHO also cautions that this category should not be taken to mean that other classified disorders have no biological foundation; it simply means that "organic" disorders are caused by an "independently diagnosable cerebral or systemic disease or disorder" (WHO, 1992, p. 44).

Central to the definition of all **cognitive disorders** is the presence of biologically caused impairment in one or more of the processes of memory, language, consciousness, perception, and intelligence.

■ **Amnestic disorders** involve memory loss without other serious cognitive impairment. The memory problems may appear as an inability to learn new information or an inability to recall previously acquired information.

■ **Delirium** is a disturbance in consciousness that often develops rapidly and fluctuates dramatically. In many cases the individual loses the ability to focus, sustain, or shift attention. Disorientation, memory and language problems, and hallucinations also often occur. Delirium can occur at any age. Of all the cognitive disorders, it is the least associated with processes of aging.

■ **Dementia,** often called *senility* by laypersons, involves a loss of many cognitive abilities, but memory loss is always involved. At least one of the following additional cognitive impairments must be present for dementia to be diagnosed: **aphasia** (a disturbance in language), **agnosia** (an inability to recognize or interpret objects through one or more of the senses), **apraxia** (an inability to carry out motor activities even though the necessary motor functions are intact), and disturbed **executive functioning** (loss of ability to plan or organize activities or to make good judgments about events and behavior).

Cognitive disorders can be caused by numerous diseases and medical conditions. We will concentrate on a few of the most common or widely studied medical illnesses involved in dementia, the cognitive disorder that involves the most widespread impairments, but first we will describe the amnestic disorders and delirium.

In Review

Normal aging involves:

- gradual changes in physical and mental capabilities;
- little overall change in most individuals' overall levels of happiness and satisfaction with life; and
- heightened risks for mental disorders in which cognitive impairments are prominent.

The cognitive disorders include:

- amnestic disorders, involving memory impairments caused by the physiological effects of a medical condition or substance;
- delirium, characterized by disturbances in consciousness and cognition that develop relatively quickly; and
- dementia, in which memory impairments are prominent along with several other types of cognitive deficits.

Amnestic Disorders and Delirium

Amnestic Disorders

Amnesia, or impairment of memory, characterizes the *amnestic disorders*. These disorders involve pure memory loss; if other cognitive failures are also prominent, delirium or dementia will usually be diagnosed. Amnestic disorders are caused by the direct effects of a general medical condition or the persisting effects of a substance (alcohol or other drug of abuse, medication, or a toxin). To be diagnosed as an amnestic disorder in the DSM-IV, the memory impairment must be serious enough to cause problems with social or occupational functioning, and it must represent a marked decline from previous levels of functioning. In addition, it must not occur only during the course of delirium or dementia.

People with amnestic disorders experience either an inability to learn new information, called **anterograde amnesia,** or the inability to recall information previously learned, called **retrograde amnesia.** The nature of the deficit and of the material that cannot be learned or recalled depends on which areas of the brain are damaged. If the damage is to the medial temporal structures such as the hippocampus or the medial diencephalon (see Figure 11.1 on page 379), the memory disturbance may be permanent.

Most persons with a severe amnestic disorder lack insight into their problems and either deny them or remain apathetic about them. They may be disoriented to time and place, but rarely to their own identity. Interviews with third parties may be required to substantiate information provided by the patient because **confabulation,** making up material to fill in gaps of memory, often occurs in an amnestic disorder.

The prevalence of amnestic disorders is difficult to estimate, partly because, in many cases, they may last no longer than a couple of hours or days, and the affected individual may never come to the attention of a clinician. In other cases, the disorder develops so slowly over the years that it goes unnoticed—especially if there are other more obvious problems. For example, long-term alcohol abusers often develop amnestic disorders because of vitamin deficiencies associated with the heavy use of alcohol. Once established, alcohol-induced amnestic disorder usually persists.

Assessment of amnestic disorders can also be complicated by sociocultural factors. If individuals from certain cultural backgrounds or with limited education are unfamiliar with the information requested on some tests of memory, their poor test performance may have nothing to do with memory loss. Some cultures attach no special significance to birthdays for example; amnesia could be wrongly diagnosed if a person from such a culture could not recall a birthdate.

Some people fake memory problems in order to appear impaired, in need of assistance, or not responsible for their actions. Therefore, it is important to distinguish true amnestic disorder from *factitious disorder* and *malingering* (both of which were discussed in Chapter 6). Making this distinction is often difficult, but factitious disorder or malingering can sometimes be detected by inconsistent results on systematic memory assessment along with the absence of a general medical condition that might account for the memory impairment.

Delirium

An altered or clouded awareness of the environment is the key marker of *delirium;* it may develop in a few hours or less and then fluctuate over the day (Tune & Ross, 1994). Delirious subjects have difficulty sustaining, focusing, or shifting attention. As the following case illustrates, they also experience changes in cognition, such as memory deficits, perceptual or language disturbances, or disorientation.

Connections

How do the amnestic disorders differ from disturbances of memory that are seen in various dissociative disorders? For answers, see Chapter 8, pp. 259–260.

eonard, a 67-year-old retired tool and die maker, had surgery to correct circulatory problems with his feet, caused by chronic diabetes. After awakening in the recovery room, Leonard was agitated and drifted in and out of consciousness. At first, his wife thought her husband was experiencing normal postanesthetic confusion, but when Leonard was still confused after several hours she asked their family doctor to come to the hospital.

Leonard did not appear to recognize his family and repeatedly yelled at his wife, "Who is this woman in my room? Get her out of here!" He insisted on leaving his hospital room as quickly as possible because "they're trying to get my guns out of the basement and someone has to stop them." Leonard became hostile and threatening to the nurses and, when a physician asked Leonard if he knew where he was, he responded, "I'm in jail on my way to the morgue." At other times, Leonard kicked at the folds of the sheet, screaming, "These squirrels are trying to bite me."

These episodes lasted for several hours, after which Leonard began to settle down and finally fell asleep. His physicians diagnosed his problems as an anesthesia-induced delirium.

In general, the DSM-IV and the ICD-10 agree on the characteristics of delirium; however, there are some differences. According to the ICD-10, emotional disturbance, disturbed sleep–wake cycle, and psychomotor disturbance (such as restlessness or lethargy and stupor) must be present for a diagnosis of delirium; the DSM-IV classifies these symptoms as associated features, not core criteria. Also, the ICD-10 stipulates that the total duration of the condition must be less than 6 months; the DSM-IV lists no time limit.

Course, Characteristics, and Prevalence of Delirium. In children, onset of delirium is typically rapid, often coinciding with a high fever. In the elderly, it may develop rapidly or slowly. A common pattern among older patients is for problems of awareness to fluctuate during the day and then worsen at night.

Delirium often begins with warning signs similar to those that precede migraine headaches. Some people become especially sensitive to smells or sounds; others report mild perceptual distortions and changes in mood. In some cases, the person begins to lose the ability to judge the passage of time or to maintain concentration. In addition, signs of autonomic nervous system arousal such as a racing heart, increased blood pressure, sweating, flushed face, and dilated

pupils are common. The normal sleep–wake cycle is often reversed; the person suffers agitation and insomnia at night but is drowsy during the day. Restoration of a more normal sleep–wake cycle is a good sign that the delirium is improving.

Disturbances in consciousness, such as reduced awareness of the environment, are common in delirium. When delirious persons are asked questions, their concentration will wander and they often engage in **perseveration,** meaning that they give the same answer over and over to entirely different questions. At other times, they jump from topic to topic.

As delirious people's inner worlds become increasingly disturbed, they often experience emotional changes including depression, apathy, euphoria, anxiety, or irritability. They may swing rapidly from one emotional extreme to another. Visual hallucinations and paranoid delusions are common. Delusions involving misidentification also frequently occur. For example, as Leonard's case illustrates, **Capgras syndrome,** the delusion that impostors are posing as friends or relatives, is encountered in some cases of delirium. This problem is an especially cruel development for a devoted spouse or friend, and it complicates treatment after the patient is released from the hospital (Faber, 1994).

During delirious delusions a person's memory is usually impaired for events that have just occurred, but memory for events that happened long ago remains intact. After the delusion has passed, memory for events during the delusional period is often absent and is sometimes replaced by false memories.

In most cases of uncomplicated delirium, cognitive losses develop and resolve rapidly, corresponding with the onset and elimination of the medical condition that caused it. Complete recovery from delirium is common once its underlying cause is treated, usually within a few weeks, although recovery tends to be slower in the elderly than in the young. Unfortunately, delirium increases the risk of death at all ages, especially in the elderly. This is because delirium often occurs when the illness that produced it is severe, and because delirium may complicate medical care. The emotional states, delusions, and hallucinations that often accompany delirium can cause patients to refuse treatment. In some cases, fear leads to serious injuries as delirious patients rip out monitors, catheters, and intravenous tubing or fall during an attempt to escape.

Because many cases of delirium develop and resolve so rapidly, it is difficult to estimate the prevalence of the disorder. Mild to moderate cases, in particular, are likely to be missed. Delirium is frequently diagnosed in elderly people who are hospitalized for some other medical condition; prevalence may be as high as 25 percent in this group (APA, 1994). Delirium is especially common in elderly surgical patients, appearing in as many as 80 percent of those who undergo open-heart surgery. However, there is some evidence that preoperative psychiatric intervention may reduce or prevent this type of delirium (Smith & Dimsdale, 1989).

Why is advanced age a risk factor for delirium? Several conditions associated with aging account for the risk, including abnormal sodium levels, severe chronic illnesses, brain disease, fever or hypothermia (subnormal body temperature), impaired kidney function, changes in living circumstances, impaired hearing and vision, and increased use of prescription drugs (Francis et al., 1990; Lipowsky, 1990). Elderly patients tend to take several medications for various ailments, and many commonly prescribed drugs have significant side effects on brain structures, such as the limbic system, that are heavily involved in memory and emotion (Tune & Ross, 1994).

Often, delirium coexists with dementia, especially in the elderly (Lindesay, Macdonald, & Starke, 1990). The cognitive changes in dementia, unlike those of delirium, usually develop slowly and are often irreversible. Also, whereas altered consciousness is the essential symptom for delirium, dementia that is unaccompanied by delirium usually causes no major change of consciousness.

Assessment of Delirium. In order to identify and treat the underlying cause of delirium, clinicians must obtain an accurate assessment of the patient's medical condition and medical history. This assessment can be difficult because even with mild delirium, the patient's reports will often be unreliable. Relatives, friends, or neighbors are often asked to provide information about the onset and progression of symptoms. Table 11.1 outlines an informant interview.

If reliable informants are not available, a brief examination of the patient's home may provide the necessary information. For example, if the home is clean and tidy, the patient's cognitive decline is probably the result of uncomplicated delirium. However, the presence of spoiled food in the refrigerator, trash strewn around the home, and stacks of dirty dishes may indicate more long-standing problems, such as depression or dementia. Sudden bladder or bowel incontinence also points to delirium, especially in older adults. But piles of stained linen or clothing suggest dementia or depression in addition to or instead of delirium (Lindesay et al., 1990).

Assessing cognitive function in delirium is difficult, and formal neuropsychological assessment is often impossible. However, a structured interview—the *Mini-Mental State Examination* (MMSE; Folstein et al., 1975)—is widely used to assess delirium (see Figure 11.4 on page 386). The MMSE is easy to administer and provides a rating of the person's mental state based on brief assessments of attention, memory, language, concentration, figure copying, and orientation to place and time. One simple bedside method for tracking the progression or remission of delirium is the "draw a clock test." The results of this test for one patient are pictured in Figure 11.5 on page 387.

Brain activity is disturbed during attacks of delirium. For example, EEG recordings from the brains

---

TABLE 11.1   An Informant Interview Used to Assess Delirium

How long have you known [the patient]?

When did you last see [the patient] before admission?

How was he/she then?

Do you find [the patient] now confused, or muddled, or forgetful?

IF YES: Can you say when this first became apparent to you? When was the first time you noticed [the patient] was confused/muddled/forgetful?

When, to the best of your knowledge, was [the patient] not confused or muddled at all?

Did it happen suddenly? Over what period (hours, days, years)?

In your opinion, did anything happen to bring about this change? (a fall/an illness/any stress?)

How has [the patient] slept over the past 48 hours? Has [the patient] been drowsy during the day over this period? All of the time? Some of the time? Can [the patient] be woken/roused?

Have you noticed any of the following:
plucking at the bedclothes
misidentifying strangers as familiar
failing to recognize familiar relatives and friends
inexplicable calling out
seeing things that aren't there
unfounded accusations
sudden mood changes or crying
unusual physical aggression

Source: Lindesay et al., 1990.

Patient _____

Examiner _____

Date _____

Maximum score	Score	
		Orientation
5	( )	What is the (year) (day) (month) (season)?
5	( )	Where are we (state) (county) (town) (hospital) (floor)?
		Registration
3	( )	Name 3 objects: 1 second to say each. Then ask the patient all 3 after you have said them. Give 1 point for each correct answer. Then repeat them until he or she learns all 3. Count trial and record.
		Attention and calculation
3	( )	Serial 7s: 1 point for each correct. Stop after 5 answers. Alternately spell "world" backwards.
		Recall
5	( )	Ask for 3 objects repeated above. Give 1 point for each correct answer.
		Language
2	( )	Name a pencil and watch (2 points)
1	( )	Repeat the following: "no ifs, ands, or buts" (1 point)
3	( )	Follow a 3-stage command: "Take a paper in your right hand, fold it in half, and put it on the floor."
1	( )	Read and obey the following: "Close your eyes." (1 point)
1	( )	Write a sentence. Must contain subject and verb and be sensible. (1 point)
		Visual-motor integrity
1	( )	Copy design (2 intersecting pentagons. All 10 angles must be present and 2 must intersect.) (1 point)
		Total score _____
30	( )	Assess level of consciousness along a continuum.
		Alert _____ Drowsy _____ Stupor _____ Coma _____

FIGURE 11.4

Mini-Mental State Examination
Source: Folstein, Folstein, & McHugh, 1975; 189–198.

of delirious persons typically show widespread slow waves, somewhat like those observed during certain stages of sleep. But EEG recordings alone are not necessarily good indicators of delirium because the EEG also slows with normal aging and especially with dementia. Also, delirium induced by drugs or drug withdrawal (e.g., delirium tremens during alcohol withdrawal) can be indicated by bursts of fast EEG activity rather than EEG slowing.

Causes of Delirium. As Table 11.2 indicates, delirium has many physical causes, but the most common causes are head trauma, postoperative states, the effects of using (or withdrawal from) drugs, ex-

FIGURE 11.5

Clock Drawing and Recovery from Delirium

The patient who drew these clocks was recovering from a case of delirium. The improvement in the details and organization of the drawings show a gradual return of the patient's cognitive abilities.

Source: Shulman et al., 1986.

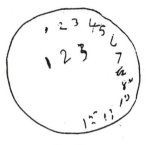

Day One

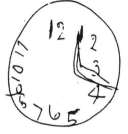

Two weeks later

Five weeks later

posure to toxins, epilepsy, metabolic disturbances, dehydration, and infections. Delirium can affect persons of any age, but the very young and old are most susceptible.

In many cases, delirium is caused by more than one factor. A common combination of causes among the elderly is an infectious disease along with medication-induced side effects. The DSM-IV diagnoses this condition as delirium due to multiple etiologies. Stressful life events can also increase the risk of delirium; bereavement or sudden relocation due to hospitalization can add to the confusion and disorientation felt by the delirious person.

Treatment of Delirium. The most important goal of treatment is to identify and correct the underlying causes of the delirium. It is also critical that treatment be delivered in a supportive environment because delirium can be so frightening. Most patients require repeated reorientation and reassurance because their perception and memory are suddenly impaired. For some recovering patients, the stress of

delirium is such that they require treatment for post-traumatic stress disorder (Tune & Ross, 1994).

Psychosocial interventions that minimize medications and use family members or friends to reassure and reorient the patient are usually helpful. This requires educating all caregivers about delirium, especially delirium that is accompanied by dementia. If education is not provided, the startling symptoms of delirium plus the cognitive deficits of the dementia may lead caregivers to institutionalize the patient prematurely.

Physical restraint of delirious patients should be avoided if possible in order to prevent reinforcement of hallucinations and paranoid delusions that can complicate later treatment. For the same reason, patients should be moved out of "high-tech" environments such as surgical intensive care units as soon as it is safe to do so. Bringing a large clock, calendar, or some familiar items from home into the hospital room can help to comfort and reorient the patient. Patients who used eyeglasses or hearing aids prior to the illness should have them returned as soon as it is

TABLE 11.2   Common Medical Conditions Causing Delirium

Cardiovascular and respiratory	Anticholinergics	Hypoxia or hypercarbia
Anemia	Anticonvulsants	Hypo- or hyperglycemia
Cardiac failure	Antidepressants	Kidney or liver disease
Cardiovascular disease	Antipsychotics/lithium	Protein calorie malnutrition
Pulmonary disease	Cardiovascular	Vitamin deficiency
Central nervous system lesion	Dopamine agonists	
Encephalitis/meningitis	Tranquilizers/hypnotics	Infection
Epilepsy	Drug/alcohol abuse or withdrawal	Intracranial
Head trauma	Surgery/anesthesia	Pneumonia/upper respiratory
Raised intracranial pressure	Metabolic/endocrine/nutritional	Sepsis
Stroke/hemorrhage	Electrolyte imbalance	Urinary tract
Tumor	Fever	Sensory deprivation
Drug therapy	Hypopituitarism	Vision or hearing loss
Analgesics (especially opiates)	Hypothyroidism	
Antibiotics	Hypothermia	

feasible to do so, and their rooms should always be well lighted to reduce perceptual disturbances. The lowest effective doses of antipsychotics, sedatives, or tranquilizers should be used, if they are used at all, and should be discontinued as soon as it is medically safe to do so (Tune & Ross, 1994).

Finally, and perhaps most important, the dignity and personhood of the patient with delirium must be appreciated and protected. Hospitalization can be demeaning, especially to those who are mentally impaired and incapable of understanding what is happening. Insensitivity by caregivers in this setting can threaten the patient's identity and self-esteem. Unfortunately, primary care physicians often show a lack of interest in elderly people's personal histories (Lindesay et al., 1990). When caregivers know patients only by their diseases and know nothing of their unique histories and accomplishments, they are less likely to treat them with respect.

In a pattern known as *looping,* humiliations associated with hospitalization provoke negative reactions by the patient, which then lead to even more humiliating treatments. Looping is especially common with elderly patients. For example, some patients stop eating because they become depressed over their loss of privacy, the removal of personal possessions, and their inability to maintain personal space and prevent invasive physical examinations. They may then suffer the indignity of having feeding tubes forcibly installed. The patients' objections to this procedure may lead to the administration of psychotropic medications that amplify the symptoms of delirium or dementia. In such cases, treatments intended to help or save patients end up degrading them.

In Review

Amnestic disorders are characterized primarily by disturbances in memory that:

- are the direct result of a medical condition or ingested substance;
- involve a failure to learn new information or to remember previously learned information; and
- must be distinguished from malingering and factitious disorder.

In delirium, the primary cognitive impairments:

- consist of disturbances in consciousness, awareness of the environment, attention, and other cognitive functions;
- develop over a short period of time and fluctuate throughout the day;

- are often accompanied by pronounced swings in emotion, sleep disruption, and agitated behavior; and
- can be caused by drug use or withdrawal, metabolic disturbances, infectious diseases, brain injuries, epilepsy, poisoning, and postoperative states.

Treatment of delirium:

- requires identifying and treating the underlying medical cause; and
- is aided by supportive caretakers who provide repeated reassurance, reorientation, and respect for the patient.

Dementia

Dementia refers to an overall loss of several cognitive functions, including memory, thinking, reasoning, and concentration, that is so severe that it interferes with a person's daily functioning, both at work and at home. Dementia is not a single disease. It is a syndrome that may accompany a variety of diseases or physical conditions affecting the central nervous system.

Dementia always includes memory impairment, but, as Dorothy's case reveals, memory loss is often not the first sign of a developing dementia. Changes in personality, increased apathy, social withdrawal, confusion, angry outbursts, loss of social skills, or impaired judgment will often occur before significant memory loss appears. During the early stages of dementia, individuals may have trouble finding the right words to use at certain points in conversations, or their speech may have a vague sound due to their overuse of imprecise words such as *thing* or *stuff.*

Later in the course of the disorder, verbal expression begins to be shortened or repeated; in extreme cases, the person engages in **echolalia,** merely repeating what has just been said by others. Even though people with dementia may maintain adequate eyesight, they frequently lose their ability to recognize family members or to know how common objects such as a shoe or a cup should be used. Because of their memory impairment, they may lose personal possessions or become lost even in their own neighborhoods. Eventually, many patients become unable to complete simple tasks such as washing their hands or unlocking a door. They may forget the names of their relatives or even their own names.

Dementia can occur at any age, but, like delirium, it is much more common among the elderly. The best estimates are that, worldwide, about 5 percent of persons 65 years old or older are affected with dementia, but the risk climbs dramatically with advancing age (Rebok & Folstein, 1993). By age 85, 10 percent or more of the population may suffer from dementia. These figures probably underestimate the magnitude of the problem because some dementias go undiagnosed, and other cases are misdiagnosed (O'Connor, 1994; Roth et al., 1986). In the early stages of dementia, cognitive symptoms such as reduced speech or failed memory may be attributed to sensory or physical difficulties associated with normal aging.

Conversely, mentally intact older adults may occasionally be diagnosed as demented if the role of normal physical or sensory declines is not considered. In fact, the exact nature of the relationship between dementia and the cognitive declines seen in normal aging is uncertain.

Also, some slowly developing cases of delirium may be mistaken for dementia, as might cases in which the gradual development of toxic drug reactions mimic the symptoms of a true dementia (Jorm, 1994). If a misdiagnosis prevents medical steps from being taken to correct drug toxicity, a true dementia may result.

In its early stages, dementia may also be difficult to distinguish from depression (Grossberg & Nakra, 1988); however, several features differentiate the two problems. First, depression is more likely to begin suddenly and progress rapidly and is frequently preceded by a personal or family history of depression. Second, persons with dementia often appear unaware of or unconcerned about their symptoms, while depressed subjects usually communicate strong distress about their problems. Third, symptoms of depression are usually worse in the morning, while symptoms of dementia typically worsen as the day goes on. Fourth, in response to stimulant drugs, depressed persons tend to become more energetic and less confused or withdrawn, but demented people often become even more confused and withdrawn. Finally, persons with dementia continue to deteriorate, whereas persons with depression usually improve or stay about the same (Harvard Medical School, 1995).

Depressed persons also perform differently from demented persons on psychological tests. For example, those with dementia are more likely to guess if they are uncertain of the answers on intelligence tests. Their memory loss for recent events is typically more severe than their remote memory loss; whereas recent and remote memory loss are often equally severe in depressed persons. Depressed persons show widely variable performance on tasks of equal difficulty; whereas those with dementia do about equally well on tasks of similar difficulty but show steady declines on more difficult tasks.

Some persons display both depression and dementia. In the early stages of dementia, patients may develop a reactive depression that makes their symptoms even worse. Also, some of the early brain changes involved in dementia may cause depression directly (Cummings & Coffey, 1994).

Connections

How does dementia differ from psychosis, in which cognitive and perceptual disturbances are also prominent? See Chapter 10, p. 332.

Clinicians still know little about how ethnic or cultural differences affect the prevalence of dementia, but one pattern is clear: the rate of dementia is substantially higher among Blacks than among Whites. At least two factors might account for this difference. First, Blacks, particularly those from earlier generations, tended to complete fewer years of formal education, and years of formal education is negatively correlated with some of the leading causes of dementia in the United States. A second possibility is that, as a result of higher levels of poverty, Blacks receive inferior health care and are therefore more susceptible to the physical diseases that often cause dementia.

A diagnosis of dementia typically specifies the presumed cause of the symptoms. Five main causes are specified in the DSM-IV: dementia of the Alzheimer's type; vascular dementia; dementia due to other medical conditions (common examples are Pick's disease, HIV infection, brain injury, Parkinson's disease, Huntington's disease, brain tumors, and vitamin deficiencies); substance-induced persisting dementias; and dementia due to multiple etiologies.

The most common causes of dementia are

1. Alzheimer's disease (which we will discuss at length later in this chapter);

2. vascular illness, primarily strokes that result in a loss of blood flow and oxygen to the brain; and

3. multiple conditions such as infections, metabolic disturbances, drug reactions, tumors, vitamin deficiencies, and head injuries.

If the dementia arises from cardiovascular problems, certain types of infections, or the side effects of drugs, the disorder may be arrested and even reversed if the underlying cause is properly treated. For most patients, however, the prognosis is more pessimistic; their impairments will remain or progressively worsen (National Institutes of Health, 1987).

Vascular Dementia

Dementia caused by cardiovascular conditions such as strokes or arterial diseases that interrupt blood flow (and oxygen supply) to the brain is called **vascular dementia.** Vascular dementia is the second most common form of dementia after Alzheimer's disease, accounting for about 15 percent of all cases of dementia (Gorelick & Mangone, 1991); Alzheimer's disease coexists with vascular dementia in an additional 15 percent of dementia patients. Vascular dementia is often a progressive disorder.

In the late 1800s, vascular dementia was called "softening of the brain," a term that described the effect of multiple strokes on brain tissue. John Hughlings-Jackson (1875) referred to the "dissolution" of behavior following the destruction of the "higher centers" of the brain by multiple strokes. By the early 1900s there was a tendency to blame all dementias on arteriosclerosis (Southard, 1910), which was viewed as the result of gradual strangulation of the blood supply to the brain; dementia was seen as one behavioral result of this process.

Many symptoms of vascular dementia are similar to those of Alzheimer's disease, but others are different. Unlike Alzheimer's disease, vascular dementia can appear abruptly, and the impairments then progress in a step-wise rather than in a gradual fashion. There is no consistent pattern of symptoms in vascular dementia. Motor impairments may appear first, and memory disturbance may occur relatively late in the course of the disease. The pattern of deficits is often "patchy" and may be confined to one brain hemisphere. Depression and local neurological signs such as palsy or paralysis in one extremity are common, but personality is relatively unaffected. A period of delirium or confusion is typical after each stroke, as are hallucinations or delusions. The life expectancy for patients with vascular dementia is several years shorter than for patients with Alzheimer's type dementia because vascular patients often die suddenly of a heart attack or stroke.

The risk factors for vascular dementia are the same as for cardiovascular disease: age, chronic use of tobacco and alcohol, high blood pressure, high cholesterol and other serum lipids, diabetes, lack of exercise, and previous stroke or heart attack.

Prevention of vascular dementia is usually more effective than treatment is (Gorelick & Mangone, 1991). Prevention requires control of the risk factors for cardiovascular disease. Because great strides have been made in understanding the causes of stroke, it is now much easier to identify persons at risk for heart disease and intervene before dementia has started.

Connections

Can psychologists help prevent cardiovascular disease? For a review of interventions aimed at changing the behavioral risks, See Chapter 6, pp. 204, 210.

Other Medical Conditions Causing Dementia

Pick's disease, like Alzheimer's disease, is a progressive degenerative disease whose most prominent symptoms are those of dementia. Its cause is still unknown. In Pick's disease, brain atrophy is typically restricted to the frontal lobes, and ballooned neurons (Pick cells) are common. These contain protein deposits called *Pick bodies* that differ from the neurofibrillary tangles of Alzheimer's disease (Hodges, 1993).

Early in Pick's disease, memory remains intact, and there is much less disorientation than in Alzheimer's disease. Changes in personality, flamboyant or tactless behavior, uninhibited mood, and emotional reactivity are often the first symptoms, as in the following case.

*D*r. S., a 52-year-old Nobel laureate at a prestigious university, was called into the provost's office to discuss a disturbing call the provost had just received from the dean of a nearby college, where Dr. S. had delivered several lectures. The provost had been informed that Dr. S. had repeatedly used obscene language during the lectures. The provost had also been told that, while attending a reception in his honor at the college president's mansion, Dr. S. had relieved himself behind some bushes in the backyard. At that same reception, Dr. S. had reportedly invited one of the students to spend the night with him. She politely declined his offer, but he persisted, making lewd comments about her attire.

Dr. S. denied none of these allegations but indicated that he could not see what all the fuss was about. After a lengthy and heated argument with the provost, Dr. S. agreed to admit himself to the university's hospital for a complete evaluation.

The medical history revealed that Dr. S. had had some problems with alcohol abuse several years earlier but had moderated his use of alcohol since then. His personality had always been flamboyant, but in recent months he had developed a blunt style of communication and an insensitivity to others that was unusual even for him.

An MRI scan showed mild atrophy of certain regions of the frontal and temporal cortex, and PET and SPECT scans indicated functional impairment of these areas. There were no apparent abnormalities on the EEG or in the results of neuropsychological testing for most skills. However, memory tests showed some mild difficulties, and word fluency was low. On several tests of executive function, Dr. S. showed marked perseveration and poor attention.

Dr. S. expressed his frustration with the assessment process by cursing at the technician giving the tests. By the time he was discharged from the hospital, he had alienated many of the nurses. One member of the housekeeping staff threatened to quit unless she were assigned to another floor where she would not have to deal with "that pig." His roommate also insisted on a transfer after he caught Dr. S. stealing his candy.

The behavioral, neurological, and neuropsychological symptoms led to a diagnosis of dementia due to Pick's disease. The strikingly inappropriate interpersonal behavior and disinhibition were especially important for this diagnosis. The diagnosis came as a surprise to Dr. S., who indicated that an uncle had Pick's disease; but he could not see that his own problems were anything like his uncle's.

The university granted Dr. S. a 6-month sabbatical to write up the final reports of his research findings. By the end of this period, Dr. S. found it impossible to continue writing or lecturing because of growing language impairment. One year later he was admitted to a nursing home because he was incapable of caring for himself, and he had no family. Over the next 2 years his memory worsened, he became mute, he withdrew from all social contact, and he suffered incontinence. Dr. S. died 5 years later.

Pick's disease is much less common than Alzheimer's disease. It is sometimes misdiagnosed as early-onset Alzheimer's because it typically appears when people are in their 40s or 50s.

Lewy body dementia is another rare degenerative dementia that may be misdiagnosed as Alzheimer's disease, despite several distinguishing features (Hansen et al., 1990). Abnormal protein deposits called *Lewy bodies* cause degeneration of the neurons of the cortex and deep in the brain stem. Hallucinations are common early in the disorder, and cognitive abilities fluctuate. Periods of memory loss and confusion may alternate with periods of clear thinking. This fluctuation in symptoms may lead to a misdiagnosis of vascular dementia, but persons with vascular dementia usually have risk factors associated with stroke. Motor signs such as muscular rigidity, slow movement, or immobility are found in Lewy body dementia. Treatment is similar to that of other demen-

In 1995, at age 57, U. S. Attorney General Janet Reno was diagnosed with Parkinson's disease. When she revealed her diagnosis to the American public, she held out a steady left hand for reporters to see and said,

> As I grow old and become a very old lady, I may have limitations in mobility, limitations in muscular response. But I feel fine now. I continue to take long walks. I don't feel like I have any impairments. I feel strong and feel like moving ahead.

tias, but the prominent hallucinations associated with Lewy body dementia may require special care because they often produce strong paranoia.

Dementia due to **Parkinson's disease** shares several features with Lewy body disease. In fact, Lewy bodies are found in the neurons of patients with Parkinson's disease, and the motor symptoms of Parkinson's disease are similar to those of Lewy body disease. One of the first symptoms is often a tremor in one or both hands. Later, the person may develop an unsteady, stiff gait. Movements are usually slow and effortful, and the patient speaks in a voice that is soft and monotonic. In Parkinson's disease, which may affect as many as 1 million Americans, a reduced production of the neurotransmitter dopamine contributes to the uncontrollable tremor and slowing of movements. Not all patients with Parkinson's disease develop dementia, however, and when they

Connections

Certain medications used to treat schizophrenia affect dopamine. Could they also have side effects involving movement? See Chapter 15, p. 548

do it is usually late in the course of the disease. The symptoms of Parkinson's disease can be fairly well controlled with medication, and promising new surgical and tissue transplantation treatments are being developed.

Dementia due to **Huntington's disease,** like that due to Parkinson's disease, involves progressive subcortical degeneration leading to prominent motor disturbances. The primary symptoms include facial grimaces, twitches, and **chorea,** involuntary jerking movements of the limbs. These motor symptoms gradually become more severe until the person has trouble walking or communicating. Onset of Huntington's disease usually occurs in the late 30s to early 40s. Changes in personality are common, and memory loss and depression often occur early in the disease. Later in the disorder, progressive intellectual deterioration, memory problems, disorganized speech, and even psychotic behavior are typical, although not inevitable. Huntington's disease is hereditary, caused by a dominant gene on chromosome 4 (Gusella et al., 1983); the children of a parent with Huntington's disease have a 50 percent chance of developing the disease.

Dementia due to **Creutzfeldt-Jakob disease** is another progressive dementia. It was once thought to be a genetic disorder because it seemed to run in families. But we now know that it is an infectious disease that can be transmitted through eating diseased tissue (Gibbs et al., 1968). "Mad cow disease" is a variant of Creutzfeldt-Jakob disease in which the infection is transmitted from one species to another when people eat infected beef. Lack of motor coordination, rapidly failing memory and attention, and changes in behavior are common in the early stages of Creutzfeldt-Jacob disease. Progression of the disease is rapid, and death usually occurs within a year of diagnosis.

Other dementias caused by infectious agents include dementia due to AIDS or syphilis. Multiple symptoms of dementia, including memory problems, faulty attention, and confusion, are seen in one third or more of people with AIDS. Syphilis was once the most common cause of dementia, but the development of penicillin and public education about the transmission of the disease through unprotected sexual contact have reduced the incidence of this disease dramatically. Unfortunately, public education has not been as effective in controlling HIV infection, and no effective treatment has yet been perfected.

Dementia due to head trauma produces persistent memory impairment along with a variety of other behavioral and cognitive symptoms, depending on the location and severity of the trauma. Young males are at elevated risk for dementia due to head trauma because head injury is strongly associated with their characteristic risk-taking behavior.

Dementia can be caused by several other medical conditions, including hypothyroidism; tumors; subdural hematoma; vitamin deficiencies (thiamine, niacin, vitamin B_{12}); lung, kidney, or liver disease; and other neurological disorders such as multiple sclerosis.

A 1996 outbreak of mad cow disease led to an economic crisis in England, where, because of fears that the infection could be spread to humans, herds of cattle were killed by the government.

In Review

Dementia involves a loss of several cognitive functions that:

- always include memory impairments; and
- impairments in at least one other area such as language, concentration, perception, comprehension, or movement.

Diagnosis of dementia:

- increases with age;
- is often confused with depression; and
- is specified by the medical condition that has caused it.

Causes of dementia include:

- strokes and arterial diseases; and
- Pick's disease, Lewy bodies, Parkinson's disease, Huntington's disease, HIV infection, head trauma, and other medical conditions.

Alzheimer's Disease

An irreversible gradual deterioration of the brain's cerebral cortex called **Alzheimer's disease** is by far the most frequent cause of dementia, accounting for over half of the cases seen in people over 65. Dementia of the Alzheimer's type now affects more than 4 million Americans (Miller et al., 1994), but that number is expected to grow rapidly as the population ages. The incidence of dementia due to Alzheimer's disease doubles with every 5 years of increased age between 65 and 85. This increase has been observed in countries as diverse as the United States, Great Britain, France, Italy, Japan, and China (Katzman & Kawas, 1994) (see Figure 11.6). Because the number of older persons in almost all countries will increase dramatically in the next 50 years, the magnitude of Alzheimer's disease as a health problem is almost certain to reach crisis proportions. When onset of dementia of the Alzheimer's type occurs before 65, it is diagnosed as *with early onset;* when onset occurs after 65, which is much more common, it is diagnosed as *with late onset.*

Alzheimer's disease appears to strike African Americans and European Americans about equally (Lezak, 1995), but there is some dispute about the effects of gender. Several studies have found women to be at higher risk for Alzheimer's disease, but others, using different statistical analyses, have not (Lezak, 1995). If there is a higher risk for females, it does

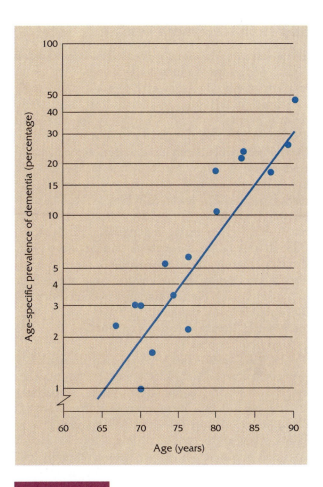

FIGURE 11.6

Dementia and Age

The prevalence of dementia and average age in different countries is represented by the dots. The straight line gives the most accurate summary of the correlation between age and dementia prevalence from these different countries

Source: From Katzman & Saitoh, 1991.

not appear to be explained by the fact that women live longer than men. Some researchers suggest that loss of estrogen after menopause may be involved. Animal experiments show that estrogen stimulates the production of chemicals that promote nerve growth and therefore helps to preserve connections between nerve cells. Recent studies also suggest that women receiving estrogen replacement therapy after menopause are less likely to develop Alzheimer's disease. The longer they took the hormone or the higher the dose, the lower their risk. These results remain controversial, and additional large-scale studies are in progress (Alzheimer's Association, 1995a).

Stages of Alzheimer's Disease

The course of Alzheimer's disease has been divided into as few as three and as many as seven stages. In its early stages, the primary symptoms are usually increased forgetfulness, especially for emotionally neutral events, and a loss of ability to cope with changes in the environment or in routines. Early in the disease, patients can handle routine social situations adequately, but, later, they become increasingly apathetic, emotionally flat, and withdrawn as the disease progresses (Heston & White, 1983). The middle stages of the disease are associated with increasing problems in language, understanding, and perception. At this point, Alzheimer's patients have great difficulty learning new information, and they often ask the same questions and tell the same stories over and over. In later phases, language becomes increasingly simple, until late in the disease when it stops altogether. Ultimately, patients cannot find their way even in familiar places.

Patients' personalities may change dramatically over the course of Alzheimer's disease. They may become hostile or emotionally unstable, sometimes striking out at family members physically or verbally or running away in tears for no apparent reason (Harvard Medical School, 1995). Paranoia is also common and may complicate care. Eventually, patients deteriorate to the point where they are unable to care for themselves. Even routine tasks such as dressing, eating, and using the bathroom become impossible. The rate of deterioration varies dramatically from person to person; the life expectancy of an Alzheimer's patient after the onset of symptoms ranges from 3 to more than 20 years, with an average of about 8 to 12 years.

Neuropathology of Alzheimer's Disease

The brains of patients with Alzheimer's disease usually show atrophy—in the form of neuron and synapse loss—in several areas. Particularly hard hit are areas that mediate language, learning, and memory—the association cortex of the frontal and parietal lobes (Small et al., 1995) and the limbic cortex, hippocampus, and amygdala. The primary sensory and motor cortex is spared. Whether these changes are a more-or-less expected consequence of aging for many individuals or a unique kind of brain pathology is a topic of much debate, as the Controversy section indicates on pages 396–397.

This disease was first identified by German neurologist Alois Alzheimer (1907). During an autopsy of a 51-year-old woman who had suffered serious dementia and deterioration, he discovered two features of her brain that are now recognized as the most distinctive signs of the disease: tangles and plaques. **Neurofibrillary tangles** are twisted clumps of protein fibers found in dying cells. **Neuritic plaques** are composed of the residue of dead neurons and cellular garbage. So characteristic of Alzheimer's disease are plaques and tangles that a definitive diagnosis of the disease depends on finding them during a postmortem examination of the brain.

The death of brain cells in many patients with Alzheimer's disease appears to be caused somehow by **beta-amyloid-4,** an abnormal form of a com-

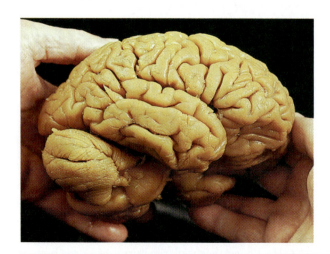 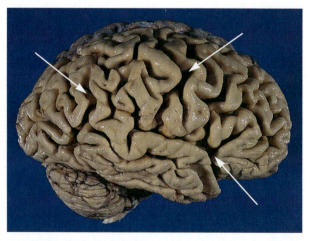

A normal brain (left). *A view of the right side of the brain of a person with Alzheimer's disease* (right); *the arrows point to areas of degeneration in the cortex.*

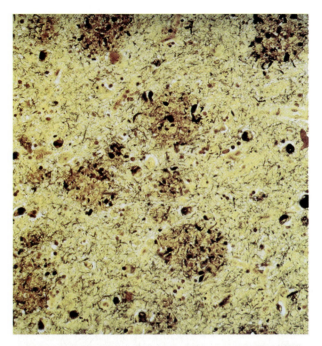

Neuritic plaques (top) *and neurofibrillary tangles* (bottom) *in a silver-stained section of the brain of a patient with Alzheimer's disease. These two brain abnormalities are hallmarks of Alzheimer's disease. (Courtesy of Dr. William Markesbery)*

mon protein that is essential for life (Richards & VanBroeckoven, 1994). The exact mechanism by which beta-amyloid-4 might kill brain cells is not yet known.

Genetic Factors and Alzheimer's Disease

Growing knowledge about a gene on chromosome 21 has led to some intriguing clues about the cause of the rare early-onset form of Alzheimer's disease. Here is what is known so far: People with Down syndrome carry three copies of chromosome 21 and are extremely likely to develop Alzheimer's disease, usually by age 40. Their brains develop large numbers of **amyloid (senile) plaques** almost 50 years before these plaques are seen in such large numbers in normal persons (Rumble et al., 1989). The form of the amyloid protein found in these plaques is an abnormal derivative of **amyloid precursor protein (APP)**, which is produced by a gene on chromosome 21. Persons with one type of early-onset Alzheimer's disease also develop large numbers of amyloid plaques early in life, presumably caused by a mutation of the same APP-producing gene on chromosome 21.

In addition to the APP mutation on chromosome 21, genes on chromosomes 1 and 14 have been linked to early-onset Alzheimer's disease. Gene STM2 on chromosome 1 has been found to be abnormal in family members who develop Alzheimer's disease, but it is normal in those who do not develop the disease (Levy-Lahad et al., 1995a, b). A gene on chromosome 14, S182, has been linked to early-onset Alzheimer's disease in other families (Sherrington et al., 1995). Scientists hypothesize that the proteins produced by these abnormal genes on chromosomes 1 and 14 have similar functions in the brain.

A gene on chromosome 19 has been linked to the much more common late-onset variety of Alzheimer's disease. This gene is known to produce **apolipoprotein E (ApoE)**, a protein that transports cholesterol in the blood and may also have other functions. There are three variants of the ApoE gene: 2, 3, and 4. ApoE-3 is the most common form; it is ApoE-4 that appears to be the form that increases the risk of Alzheimer's disease; ApoE-2 may protect against the disease (Corder et al., 1993). Almost 90 percent of persons with two copies of the ApoE-4 gene (one from each parent) develop Alzheimer's disease compared with 50 percent of persons with only one copy of ApoE-4. Less than 20 percent of persons with no ApoE-4 genes develop Alzheimer's disease, and these people develop Alzheimer's very late in life (Harvard Medical School, 1995). How the ApoE protein leads to the death of nerve cells is not yet known.

Even middle-aged persons carrying the gene for ApoE-4 who show no neurological or neuropsycho-

Controversy

Dementia: Inevitability of Old Age or Special Syndrome?

Is dementia merely an exaggerated form of normal aging? Or are dementia and normal aging distinct entities? Memory loss and other kinds of cognitive deterioration are common results of aging, but do the cognitive losses of dementia differ from those of normal aging? According to one view, the cognitive declines encountered in normal aging are fundamentally different from the severe deterioration seen in most dementias. An alternative model proposes that dementia and normal aging lie along a continuum (e.g., Brayne & Calloway, 1988; Huppert & Brayne, 1994). In this model, the dementias represent behavioral, cognitive, and neural pathology that differs only in degree from the changes that affect all old persons. In other words, dementia is simply accelerated aging; if we live long enough, all of us will suffer its effects.

Most historical definitions of dementia emphasized "discontinuity," in which dementia was seen as an irreversible disorder of intellect that resulted from specific disease processes. In the eighteenth century, for example, *dementia* was defined as "extinction of the imagination" (Blanchard, 1726). Such definitions implied insanity, or a loss of mental function in a person who was previously normal. As noted in Chapter 10, what we now call *schizophrenia* was once known as "dementia praecox."

By the turn of the twentieth century, several distinct causes of dementia were recognized (Berrios & Freeman, 1991), including dementias due to alcoholism, lead poisoning ("crack pot" syndrome), mercury poisoning ("mad hatter" syndrome), syphilis, and hypothyroidism. The evidence for specific organic causes of various types of dementia seemed to settle the argument in favor of the discontinuity principle. However, other evidence complicates the question of how dementia is related to normal aging (Huppert & Brayne, 1994). Most of the current controversy about this question centers on the development of Alzheimer's disease, the most frequent cause of dementia. Several factors point to considerable continuity between Alzheimer's disease and normal aging. For example,

- Most cases of Alzheimer's disease develop after age 65, and the older a person becomes, the more likely he or she is to develop Alzheimer's disease.
- It is often difficult to distinguish between common symptoms of normal aging and early signs of a developing dementia.
- At autopsy, the brains of cognitively normal persons often show signs of pathology that would support a diagnosis of Alzheimer's disease (Crystal et al., 1988).

Arguing against the idea that dementia is an exaggeration of normal aging are other findings about Alzheimer's disease (Berg, 1988). For example,

- Moderate numbers of neurofibrillary tangles are found in the brains of an increasingly large percentage of brains from normal persons as they grow older, until they reach the tenth decade, after which the percentage begins to decline.
- The incidence and prevalence of Alzheimer's disease increase with advancing age until the tenth decade; then there is a decline or at least a stabilization in the rate of increase.
- Neither dementia nor Alzheimer's disease-type changes occur in the brains of persons dying of Werner's syndrome, a disease that accelerates the aging process.
- Dendrites continue to sprout in the hippocampal neurons of the nondemented elderly but not in patients with Alzheimer's disease.

Several scientists have proposed various compromises between the two positions. For example, one model suggests that dementias with distinct biological causes (such as Huntington's disease, hypothyroidism, Creutzfeldt-Jakob disease, alcohol toxicity, and vitamin deficiency) are distinct from normal aging, but that other dementias, such as late-onset Alzheimer's disease, represent severe versions of normal aging (Lishman, 1994).

logical signs suggestive of Alzheimer's disease show decreased blood flow and glucose use in the superior parietal cortex compared with their relatives who do not have the ApoE-4 gene. Because similar reductions in parietal lobe metabolism are seen in dementia patients, the gene associated with ApoE may constitute an early warning of impending Alzheimer's disease in these individuals (Small et al., 1995).

Given the genetic evidence, it should come as no surprise that, next to age, family history is one of the strongest risk factors for Alzheimer's disease (Mortimer, 1994). By the time individuals reach age 90, their risk of developing Alzheimer's disease is almost 50 percent if they had parents or siblings with Alzheimer's disease (Mohs et al., 1987). The risk is lower if the disease appeared only in second-degree

According to Lishman (1994, p. 51), "It is hard, indeed, to point to any feature of the brain of an Alzheimer's patient which does not occur with increasing age alone. . . ."

Another possibility is that dementia occurs whenever a person loses enough reserve brain capacity to fall below a threshold necessary for normal functioning. According to this model, a threshold of brain pathology separates normal, age-related cognitive losses from dementia. Above this level, a person functions with enough reserve capacity to live without substantial impairment. Although all persons progressively lose some capacity as they age, the normal elderly usually die before they reach the threshold for dementia, as the accompanying figure illustrates. Certain persons might have less reserve capacity because of several factors: genetic defects (e.g., Down syndrome), lack of education, or less mental stimulation early in life. Individuals with such limitations may reach the threshold earlier and develop dementia, as do persons who experience any of the risk factors associated with various dementias. One implication of this model is that exposure to risk factors affects not only the age at which clinical symptoms first appear in an individual but also the frequency of dementia in the population.

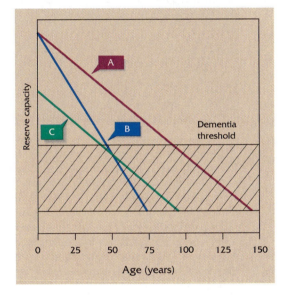

Threshold Model for Dementia

This threshold model for dementia predicts the age at which a person's cognitive capacity will fall below the threshold, resulting in symptoms of dementia. Line A shows normal brain aging, where the threshold for dementia is not reached until after normal life expectancy. Line B shows that the dementia threshold will be reached in middle age for persons who are exposed to risk factors and diseases that cause dementia. Line C shows that early onset of dementia may also occur because of genetic factors or other early influences that limit the development of reserve capacity.

Thinking Critically

We have reviewed findings leading to claims that dementia is either exaggerated aging or a separate and unique syndrome.

- What other similarities or differences might help resolve this controversy?

- Would the possibility of treating or preventing dementia be influenced by whether dementia is an inevitable result of aging or whether it is a distinct condition?

- Should a belief in the inevitability of dementia lead to pessimism about its treatment ("There's nothing we can do; if you live long enough you will get it.") or enthusiasm for prevention ("Since we can't cure dementia, we should try to delay the aging process.")?

relatives (e.g., cousins), but this risk is still much greater than for the general population.

Other Risk Factors for Alzheimer's Disease

Discoveries of possible genetic factors linked to Alzheimer's disease have added to our understanding of this illness and may eventually lead to its prevention. But the exact cause of Alzheimer's disease is not yet known, so scientists continue to pursue leads based on other risk factors.

One well-known risk factor for Alzheimer's disease is head trauma. *Dementia pugilistica*, a form of dementia seen in boxers who have suffered repeated heavy blows to the head, has been recognized for a

Gerry Cooney was once a vigorous heavyweight prize-fighter. Now, after years of absorbing blows to the head, he suffers from "dementia pugilistica."

Although several celebrities have suffered from Alzheimer's disease, Americans' awareness and concern about the disorder was heightened by former President Ronald Reagan's November 12, 1994, handwritten letter to the American public in which he disclosed, "I have recently been told that I am one of the millions of Americans who will be afflicted with Alzheimer's disease. Nancy and I had to decide whether as private citizens we would keep this a private matter or whether we would make this news known in a public way. . . . We feel it is important to share it with you. . . . I now begin the journey that will lead me into the sunset of my life."

long time as a contributor to the disease. But milder and less-frequent head trauma, including a single concussion, has now been linked to Alzheimer's disease (Katzman & Kawas, 1994). This has caused concern over the possible long-term effects of playing soccer and other contact sports. One study (Witol & Webbe, cited by the American Psychological Association, 1995) indicates that hitting soccer balls with one's head leads to impaired performance on neuropsychological tests of cognitive flexibility, attention, concentration, and general intellect. The more frequently a player heads the ball and the more years he or she plays the game, the more serious the impairments.

Coronary artery disease is also associated with Alzheimer's disease. In particular, myocardial infarctions (heart attacks) greatly increase the risk of Alzheimer's disease, especially in women (Katzman & Kawas, 1994).

Environmental toxins have been linked to heightened risk for Alzheimer's disease, and they have been suspected of accelerating brain degeneration initiated by other factors. However, there is little evidence that environmental toxins themselves are a primary cause of Alzheimer's disease. Both aluminum and mercury—neurotoxins seen only in trace amounts in normal brains—have been found in high concentrations in the brains of some Alzheimer's patients (Markesbery & Ehmann, 1994). Aluminum is also highly concentrated in hippocampal neurons of patients who developed dementia in the course of chronic blood dialysis due to kidney failure (Alfrey, 1991). Whether unusual concentrations of these heavy metals precede, accompany, or follow Alzheimer's disease is not yet established.

One other environmental risk linked to Alzheimer's disease is exposure to electromagnetic fields (EMF), often conveyed by certain occupations in which people must work close to electric motors. People who are exposed to high EMF levels on the job —such as seamstresses and carpenters—have about 3 to 5 times the average risk of developing Alzheimer's (Sobel et al., 1995).

The brains of persons with Alzheimer's disease have been found to have dramatically reduced levels of **acetylcholine (ACH),** a neurotransmitter that is critical to movement, physiological arousal, and memory. An acetylcholine deficiency may explain the memory problems encountered with the disease. Alzheimer's patients are also known to be sensitive to drugs that block ACH. Consequently, **tropicamide,** an anticholinergic drug used to dilate pupils during eye examinations, may provide a simple noninvasive test for early detection of Alzheimer's disease. Very dilute drops of this drug will dilate the pupils of persons with suspected Alzheimer's disease but not those of healthy controls or persons with non-Alzheimer's dementias (Scinto et al., 1994).

Among different occupations, seamstresses have one of the highest incidences of Alzheimer's disease, leading to a suspicion that exposure to electromagnetic fields is a risk factor for the disorder.

Finally, low levels of education are linked with Alzheimer's disease. The disease is found significantly more often in persons lacking formal education compared with peers who have completed 6 or more years of schooling. A weaker, but still significant, effect for education exists when people with only elementary school education are compared with those who completed high school (Katzman & Kawas, 1994). Why should education matter? One possibility is that better educated persons enjoy better levels of health care and are better able to avoid other risk factors associated with the disease, such as head trauma, heart disease, and exposure to toxins. Another factor may be that better educated persons maintain higher levels of mental activity early in their lives, which somehow offers protection against developing Alzheimer's disease later on. A third possibility, discussed in the Controversy section on pages 396 and 397, is that people who attain higher educational levels have more cognitive ability to begin with, thus making them less vulnerable to the mental consequences of Alzheimer's disease.

Medical Treatment of Alzheimer's Disease

Most attempts to treat Alzheimer's disease have been disappointing because clinicians do not know enough about the causes of the disease or the biological mechanisms leading to cell death to develop effective interventions. However, several large-scale clinical trials of possible treatments are now being conducted and are suggesting benefits from a number of strategies.

One such treatment is **tacrine** (sold as Cognex), which, as of 1995, was the only drug approved by the Food and Drug Administration for treatment of Alzheimer's disease in the United States. Tacrine slows the breakdown of ACH, which is reduced throughout the brains of Alzheimer's patients. It is useful only in mild to moderately severe cases, but it can temporarily improve the cognitive abilities of some Alzheimer's patients. Tacrine often has negative side effects, which lead many patients to stop taking it. After stopping the medication, patients often lose the cognitive gains they had initially made. Several other drugs with similar actions are also being developed, based on their ability to improve learning and memory in animal studies.

Estrogen, a hormone that promotes synapse formation (McEwen, 1994) and increases ACH synthesis, has been found to improve both mood and cognition in postmenopausal women with Alzheimer's disease.

Deprenyl (also sold as Eldepryl) inhibits monoamine oxidase B, which destroys dopamine, norepinephrine, and serotonin. Therefore, the levels of these neurotransmitters, which, like ACH, tend to be reduced in Alzheimer's disease, are raised to more normal levels by this drug. Deprenyl is now also being used with L-Dopa to treat Parkinson's disease. If the drug is effective, it may slow the development of Parkinson's dementia and may prove useful for other dementias as well.

Vitamin E (alpha-tocopherol) is an antioxidant that inactivates oxygen free radicals, a source of damage to neurons. Clinical trials of vitamin E alone, and,

A Talk with William Markesbery

William R. Markesbery, M.D., is Professor of Pathology and Neurology at the University of Kentucky College of Medicine. He serves as Director of the Sanders-Brown Center on Aging and as Director of the Alzheimer's Disease Research Center at the University of Kentucky. Dr. Markesbery is an expert in the neurological processes involved in Alzheimer's disease.

Alzheimer's Disease

Q *A continuing controversy in this field is the question of whether the changes seen in "normal aging" are the same kind—but not nearly as severe—as we see in Alzheimer's disease. What is your view of this controversy?*

A There are some nondemented older folks whose autopsies are consistent with Alzheimer's disease. They have diffuse senile plaques, indicating that some normal folks have an Alzheimer-type process going on in their brains, and that if they had lived longer they might have shown severe intellectual decline. But I disagree with the theory that Alzheimer's disease is just exaggerated aging.

> *...I disagree with the theory that Alzheimer's ...is just exaggerated aging.*

Q *What changes are distinctive for Alzheimer's disease?*

A Well, if you look at enough of these brains, you find not only an abundance of senile plaques but also the neurofibrillary tangles and neuritic plaques that you discuss in the chapter. You also see many other signs of pathology that are much more marked in Alzheimer's disease. So I think there is a major difference from normal aging. In our own studies and in the Nun Study there are persons who are 85 or 95 years old who have brains without significant alteration. Perhaps they are not genetically programmed to develop the traditional aging changes and are therefore not prone to develop the disease. Perhaps they are people without any of the E-4 allele that may lead to development of Alzheimer's. We don't know the answer. It can't just be exaggerated aging or you would expect the rate of it to go on up after age 90. There are some data from at least two studies suggesting that after age 95 there is a decline in the prevalence of the disease.

Q *What about prevention?*

A The 5-5, 10-10 goal of the National Institute on Aging is to delay institutionalization of demented subjects by 5 years within 5 years and by 10 years within 10 years. The goal arises from a need to have a treatment that will blunt the symptoms and slow the progression of the disease.

This is the most demeaning disease to affect humankind, taking away the very essence of what we are as human beings. If we can push back the age of disease expression, it would free up nursing homes and reduce the expense of the disease.

Q *Have we learned enough about controlling the more disturbing behavioral symptoms of the disease so that we can help caregivers cope better and delay institutionalizing the patient?*

A We have, but it's a double-edged sword because medications that we give for many symptoms often impair the remaining intellectual functions. For example, we do not have drugs yet that can treat some of the psychotic symptoms without affecting memory. The delusions and hallucinations in patients with Alzheimer's can be managed pretty well with modest doses of drugs such as Haldol, and we are trying newer drugs that don't have the side effects of Haldol. The anxiety symptoms can be handled pretty well with antianxiety agents, and our antidepressant armament is much better than it used to be.

Q *Are recent discoveries of several genetic markers, especially for the ApoE-4 allele, the breakthrough they appear to be?*

A I think it has given us the most exciting information we have about Alzheimer's disease yet. The information about mutations in the amyloid precursor protein gene on chromosome 21 is also exciting. But the number of familial cases that have the mutation of the amyloid precursor protein gene is less than 1 percent. Recently, descriptions of mutations on chromosome 14 and 1 were published. The mutations are quite similar. The important thing about them is the resultant proteins. The functions of these proteins aren't yet known, but once we understand them we will know a lot more about the pathology of Alzheimer's disease.

in combination with deprenyl, are determining whether either or both can slow the progression of Alzheimer's disease.

Nimodipine is a calcium channel blocker. It may slow the progression of Alzheimer's disease because calcium is also involved in neuronal degeneration.

Propentofylline enhances blood flow and energy metabolism in the brain. It may improve function in persons with either Alzheimer's disease or vascular dementia.

Finally, anti-inflammatory agents such as prednisone are being tested because there is evidence that an inflammatory response may be involved in Alzheimer's disease. Blocking this response may reduce neural damage.

Psychosocial Interventions for Alzheimer's Disease

Alzheimer's disease is a chronic condition that may involve a long period during which symptoms are not yet obvious or are manageable. Interventions during this period may delay the onset of Alzheimer's disease or may slow its progress. To date, most of these interventions seek to reduce or to control certain Alzheimer's risk factors. For example, reducing head injuries, preventing cardiovascular disease, and controlling blood pressure and stress through exercise and diet should reduce the risk for Alzheimer's disease (as well as for vascular dementia). As highlighted in the Prevention section on pages 402–403, improving education and staying mentally active throughout life have also been proposed as ways to prevent Alzheimer's disease (Katzman & Kawas, 1994; Snowdon, Ostwald, & Kane, 1989), but the evidence for these claims is limited.

Because a cure for Alzheimer's disease is not yet available, treatment of the symptoms and management of the patient's behavior are the best approaches. Medications can play a role in this effort, especially in reducing troubling behaviors such as agitation and depression, but they should be used sparingly and only with careful monitoring of their short- and long-term effects.

A main thrust of treatment involves training caregivers to respond properly to the patient's immediate emotional, psychological, and physical needs. For example, many caregivers are prone to urge the Alzheimer's patient to practice intellectual or social skills so as to hold on to them as long as possible. Once the disease has taken hold, however, these drills accomplish little, other than frustrating the patient and the caregiver.

However, caregivers can take numerous small steps to ease daily problems. Specifically

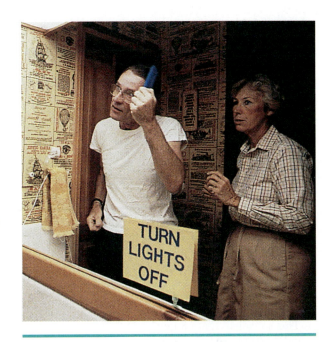

Caregivers for patients with Alzheimer's disease undergo a great deal of stress as they help their family members cope with progressive dementia.

■ offering gentle reminders and making lists can prop up the memories of Alzheimer's patients;

■ sewing labels on their clothing and placing reminders in strategic locations (e.g., "Turn off the stove") can help the patient navigate through confusing environments and maintain some independence;

■ maintaining familiar schedules, keeping personal possessions in the same locations, and adhering to daily routines may reduce stress and help the patient cope with daily demands;

■ providing comfortable, loose-fitting clothing with few buttons, snaps, or zippers is advisable; and

■ maintaining a well-lighted environment, with nightlights and a comfortable auditory environment (e.g., a radio tuned to a station with familiar, favorite music) can reduce such troubling behavior as *sundowning,* that is, the tendency for patients to wander aimlessly or become agitated at night.

It is also important for caregivers to meet the patient's continuing needs for physical and emotional closeness. Although loss of sexual intimacy often occurs as the disease progresses, simple acts of affection—hugs, a gentle touch, handholding—may reassure the patient and help reduce paranoid thoughts (Alzheimer's Association, 1995b). Conversations with patients should be direct, concrete, matter of fact, and

Prevention   Early Cognitive Ability and Alzheimer's Disease

One of the more surprising discoveries about the risks for developing dementias such as Alzheimer's disease is that nonbiological factors in early life, such as education and certain cognitive abilities, may be related to the functioning and even the survival of people in their 70s and 80s. A particularly intriguing demonstration of this possibility is a study of the mortality rates and self-care activities among 306 Roman Catholic nuns who lived together in Mankato, Minnesota.

This so-called "Nun Study" found a strong association between the level of education, mortality, and independent living skills (Snowdon, Ostwald, & Kane, 1989). Sisters who had at least a bachelor's degree lived 89.4 years on average, whereas sisters with less than a college education lived an average of about 82 years. In addition, among sisters who were 75 to 94 years of age, those who had a bachelor's degree were significantly more likely to maintain their ability to perform daily self-care activities and not require daily nursing care than were those with less education. Although the rate of dementias in the sample was not

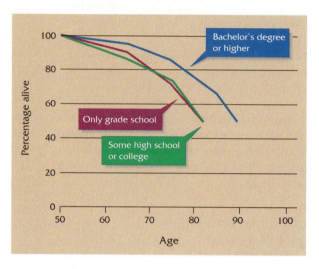

Education and Survival

The probability of death at various ages was reduced substantially by higher educational levels in a group of Catholic sisters who were similar on other social-behavioral factors.

reported, the substantial advantage in independent living was thought to be correlated with a lower rate of dementias among the well-educated sisters.

What makes this study especially interesting is that the advantages of education for this sample could not have been due to any of the factors that are often confounded with higher levels of education. Because they lived together for over 60 years in the same environment, the nuns did not differ in income, diet, access to health care, use of tobacco or alcohol, or expo-

even assertive when necessary. "I am going to church, would you like to go with me?" is better than "Do you want to go to church, take a nap, or watch TV?" If the patient becomes too demanding, it may be necessary to state, "I cannot do everything you want. We will have to discuss how to spend the rest of the evening, and I will do so as soon as I have finished fixing supper." Continued participation in religious practices with family and friends can be calming and meaningful, even for patients who are not otherwise responsive (Alzheimer's Association, 1995c).

Finally, caregivers often need special help themselves. The rate of clinical depression among rela-

tives who care for Alzheimer's patients is extremely high, as are resentment and anger toward the patient. In some cases, anger boils over into physical abuse. Thus, caregivers need time to lead their own lives and may need to learn that their feelings of resentment are normal. However, when necessary, they must also be taught how to control aggressiveness. In most communities, a variety of self-help groups and special agencies provide needed assistance to caregivers. A primary aim of these programs is to help caregivers deal with the almost constant stress imposed by taking care of a loved one with Alzheimer's disease.

sure to toxins. What could account for education's relationship to longer life and better mental functioning?

One possibility is that people who are more educated may have exercised more of their brains' capacities and therefore, have more mental capacity in reserve and are relatively better protected against cognitive impairments in old age. Another possibility is that advanced education is a form of mental exercise that somehow strengthens brains much as vigorous physical exercise builds muscles. As a result, individuals who use their minds actively throughout their lives are less likely to lose cognitive capacity. This advantage may even be strong enough to offset some risk of developing a dementia such as Alzheimer's.

Findings from a couple of studies support the idea that mental activity early in life is negatively correlated with cognitive impairments late in life, as well as with the diagnosis of Alzheimer's disease. First, in the Seattle Longitudinal Study, there were smaller reductions in cognitive ability late in life among people who

had read extensively, traveled frequently, pursued extra educational opportunities, and participated in a range of stimulating intellectual activities (Schaie, 1994).

Additional work by the researcher who conducted the Nun Study has also revealed a negative correlation between dementia and the frequency of complex ideas in autobiographical essays written by the nuns in their 20s, just before they took their vows (Snowdon et al., 1996). A rater analyzed the *idea density* of these essays without knowing the current status of the nuns who wrote them. Essays judged high in idea density contained a greater number of ideas per words than essays judged to have low idea density. For example, the nun with the lowest idea density essay wrote, "I was born in Eau Claire, Wis, on May 24, 1913 and was baptized in St. James Church." The nun with the highest idea density essay wrote, "The happiest day of my life so far was my First Communion Day which was in June nineteen hundred and twenty when I was but eight years of age, and four years later in the same month I was confirmed by Bishop D. D. McGavick." Idea den-

sity in these essays significantly predicted cognitive functioning and presence of Alzheimer's disease 58 year later! All of the nuns who had died of Alzheimer's disease had written low-idea density essays; none of the sisters who had died from other causes had written low-density essays. This pattern was the same regardless of how much education the nuns had received.

What are the implications of these findings? It appears as if the seeds of Alzheimer's disease might be present very early in life, signalled by lower levels of linguistic ability. Low linguistic ability, even early in life, might indicate less mental reserve capacity, which leaves a person more vulnerable to the consequences of Alzheimer's disease. Could efforts at increasing linguistic complexity reduce the risk of Alzheimer's disease? Results from the Nun Study suggest not, but researchers do not know for sure. Involvement in stimulating mental activity is probably not very important once an individual develops Alzheimer's disease, and whether there are any protective effects from exercising the brain in "hard workouts" early in life is still unknown.

In Review

Alzheimer's disease accounts for over half of all cases of dementia. The exact cause of the disorder is not yet fully understood, but:

- abnormal genes on chromosomes 1, 14, 19, and 21 have been linked to the production of proteins that can kill brain cells; and
- family history, brain injuries, exposure to environmental toxins and electromagnetic

fields, heart disease, and depleted levels of acetylcholine are other possible risks.

Alzheimer's disease cannot yet be cured or prevented, but:

- new medications that can temporarily reduce some of its symptoms are being developed; and
- psychosocial interventions can help Alzheimer's patients and their caregivers cope better with many of the disease's impairments.

Revisiting the Case of Dorothy

Dorothy's daughter was devastated by the news that her mother had Alzheimer's disease. It confirmed her worst fears and made her feel extremely guilty for what she now felt was her mistreatment of her mother in the previous few months. The neuropsychologist who was part of the team evaluating Dorothy encouraged her daughter to contact the local chapter of the Alzheimer's Association for information about the disease and about caregiver support groups.

After returning home from the hospital, Dorothy insisted that she was well enough to live on her own. She refused her daughter's offer to stay with her or to move to her daughter's home. Over the next 18 months, she was hospitalized three times; on one occasion she sustained second-degree burns after leaning against her stove and catching her blouse on fire. After this incident, Dorothy's daughter insisted that she sell her house and come live with her. Dorothy bitterly claimed "all you want is to get at my money," but ultimately she relented and moved in with her daughter.

At first, the arrangement worked reasonably well. Dorothy had her own apartment in the basement, so she was able to keep many of her personal possessions, and, because one of her three teenage grandchildren was usually home, she was seldom alone. She had begun taking tacrine, which seemed to restore some of her memory and ability to concentrate, and she was able to help out around the house. Although she missed seeing some of her old friends, she was reasonably content. After about 2 years, however, things took a turn for the worse. Tacrine made Dorothy nauseous, so she stopped taking it. Soon she was more confused and forgetful than ever. She was shaky on her feet and increasingly irritable. Her grandchildren were less and less interested in staying home with her; in fact, Dorothy once overheard them tell their mother they "we're sick and tired of having to look after Grandma all the time; besides, she just sits there and acts like she doesn't even know us."

Soon, Dorothy had to be lifted out of her bed or onto the toilet, and she spent more and more time just lying in bed. After Dorothy scalded her leg by absent-mindedly pouring boiling water on herself, her daughter knew something had to be done. She felt guilty about the thought of moving her mother into an institution, but a couple of sessions with an Alzheimer's support group helped her make that decision. Luckily, the family could afford to keep Dorothy in a full-time nursing home. They watched many other families spend all of their savings and even sell their homes in order to cover the nursing and housing costs required to support their sick, elderly parents.

Once in the nursing home, Dorothy seemed to deteriorate even more quickly. She lost her appetite and became incontinent; ultimately, she was unable to speak. During her final months, Dorothy did not appear to recognize any family members. Her daughter continued to visit her each day, often leaving the nursing home in tears, heartbroken at how ill her mother had become. Dorothy finally died of pneumonia, 15 months after entering the nursing home.

SUMMARY

Aging

Normal aging brings biological changes and gradual declines in sensory and physical abilities. Mental abilities, particularly those that put a premium on speed and memory, also decline with age. After the age of 65 or 70, the declines in mental abilities become steeper, but, in spite of these changes, most elderly people report that they are satisfied with their lives, especially when they have stayed physically and mentally active and involved in important activities and relationships. Several mental disorders caused by physical conditions are associated with aging. The DSM-IV classifies these disorders under the category delirium, dementia, and amnestic and other cognitive disorders.

Amnestic Disorders and Delirium

The primary characteristic of amnestic disorders is an impairment of memory caused by a medical condition. The impairment involves either an ability to learn new information, called anterograde amnesia, or an inability to recall formerly learned information, known as retrograde amnesia. Confabulation, in which people make up information to fill in their memory gaps, is also common.

The primary features of delirium are disturbances in consciousness that often develop quickly and fluctuate throughout the day. Delirious people have trouble maintaining and shifting their attention, and they often also suffer perceptual distortions, memory problems, and disorientation. Delirium is most common in young and old people because both groups are more susceptible to the various illnesses, injuries, and physical conditions that are the most frequent causes of delirium. In many cases, appropriate treatment of the underlying condition will bring about a complete recovery.

Dementia

Dementia refers to a loss of multiple cognitive functions. Memory impairments are always involved and at least one of the following: aphasia, agnosia, apraxia, and disturbance in cognitive functioning. About 5 percent of people 65 or older are affected by dementia, but many cases probably go undetected or are misdiagnosed. In many cases, dementia may be initially difficult to distinguish from depression. Many dementias are progressive disorders for which no effective treatment or prevention is available.

Vascular dementia caused by strokes, heart attacks, and other cardiovascular diseases is the second most common form of dementia after Alzheimer's disease. The life expectancy of vascular dementia patients is shorter than for patients with dementia of the Alzheimer's type. Other, less frequent, medical conditions leading to dementia include Pick's disease, Lewy body disease, Parkinson's disease, Huntington's disease, Creutzfeldt-Jakob disease, head trauma, and HIV infection.

Alzheimer's Disease

The most frequent cause of dementia, accounting for over half the cases, is Alzheimer's disease, a progressive disease of the brain. The specific cause of Alzheimer's disease is not yet known, but various genetic abnormalities appear to be involved. Other factors that may contribute to the risk of developing Alzheimer's disease are head injury, exposure to electromagnetic fields, cardiovascular disease, exposure to toxins, and depleted levels of acetylcholine. Currently, there is no cure for Alzheimer's disease, although new medications and various psychosocial interventions can be useful in managing some of its symptoms.

KEY TERMS

acetylcholine (ACH), p. 398
ageism, p. 379
agnosia, p. 382
Alzheimer's disease, p. 393
amnesia, p. 383
amnestic disorders, p. 382
amyloid (senile) plaques, p. 395
amyloid precursor protein (APP), p. 395
anterograde amnesia, p. 383
aphasia, p. 382
apolipoprotein E (ApoE), p. 395
apraxia, p. 382

beta-amyloid-4, p. 394
Capgras syndrome, p. 384
chorea, p. 392
cognitive disorders, p. 382
confabulation, p. 383
Creutzfeldt-Jakob disease, p. 392
delirium, p. 382
dementia, p. 382
deprenyl, p. 399
echolalia, p. 388
estrogen, p. 399
executive functioning, p. 382
Huntington's disease, p. 392

Lewy body dementia, p. 391
neuritic plaques, p. 394
neurofibrillary tangles , p. 394
nimodipine, p. 401
organic mental disorders, p. 381
Parkinson's disease, p. 391
perseveration, p. 384
Pick's disease, p. 390
propentofylline, p. 401
retrograde amnesia, p. 383
tacrine, p. 399
tropicamide, p. 398
vascular dementia, p. 390

12

Personality Disorders

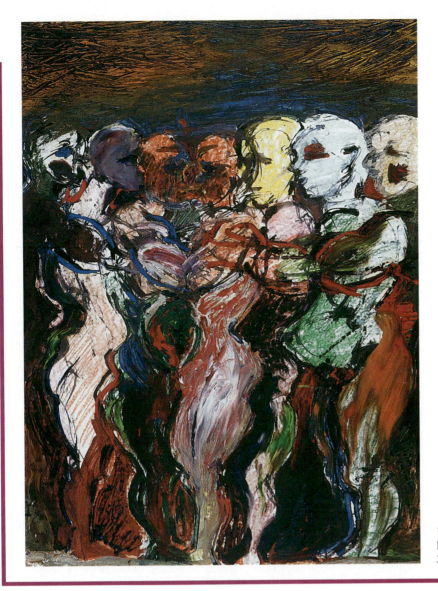

Visitation by Laura Siroog Boyajian, 1994. Mixed media, 28" x 36". Courtesy of Sistare.

From the Case of Ted Bundy

Theodore Robert Bundy seemed destined to live a charmed life; he was intelligent, attractive, and polished. He had been a Boy Scout in his youth and later an honor student in psychology at the University of Washington. He also served as a work-study student in a Seattle crisis clinic. One of Bundy's psychology professors wrote of him: "He conducts himself more like a young professional than a student. I would place him in the top one percent of the undergraduates with whom I have interacted" (quoted in Leyton, 1986). While still in his 20s, Bundy was also named assistant to the chairman of the Washington State Republi-

can Party and was lauded as an "up-and-comer" in political circles.

Of course, this rosy biography omits the fact that Ted Bundy hunted down, raped, and killed young women for the sheer thrill of possessing and controlling them. It was early in January, 1974, when Ted Bundy attacked his first victim: a young woman who Bundy maimed while she was asleep, leaving her with permanent brain damage. From 1974 through 1978, Bundy stalked, sexually assaulted, and killed as many as 36 victims in Washington, Oregon, Utah, Colorado, and Florida. He used his good looks and charm as lures to trap his victims. Looking

407

helpless and harmless—he would walk on crutches or wear a fake cast on his arm—Bundy would enlist the aid of a young woman and, after securing her trust, would choke her to death and mutilate and sexually abuse her body before disposing of it in a remote area. No one knows for sure how many women he killed, because he never gave a complete confession.

Who was the real Ted Bundy? Were there early signs that he was capable of such carnage? Was Bundy mentally ill, and, if so, what diagnosis should he have received?

Beneath the superficial charm of Bundy's overt behavior lurked a far different person, one who was driven by a lust to dominate people and who was incapable of feeling guilt. In Bundy's own words, he was the "most cold-hearted son of a bitch you'll ever meet" who didn't "feel guilt for anything" and felt "sorry for people who feel guilt" (quoted in Jeffers, 1991).

Bundy's quest for domination may have begun with his shame for having been the illegitimate son of his 22-year-old mother and a sailor with whom she had had a brief sexual encounter—Bundy was born in 1946 in the Elizabeth Lund Home for Unwed Mothers in Burlington, Vermont. From an early age he was embarrassed by his illegitimacy and his family's poverty. He told people how humiliated he was to be seen riding in his step-father's run-down Rambler. As a juvenile, he constantly sought to create an impression of being a sophisticated and successful member of the upper class who deserved admiration. He went to great lengths to further this impression, even wearing fake mustaches and makeup to change his appearance. He stole cars in high school to maintain his image and occasionally affected an English accent. He sought out women whose physical appearance satisfied his craving for escaping what he called his "common" origins. He was never interested in an emotionally close relationship with these women; his main desire was to be seen with them and to have other people admire him for being with an attractive woman.

Despite the time he spent creating the right impression, Bundy was not popular in high school, and he knew it. He told interviewers, "In junior high everything was fine, but I got to high school and I didn't make any progress. I felt alienated from my old friends. They just seemed to move on and I didn't . . . I wasn't sure what was wrong and what was right. All I knew was that I felt a bit different" (quoted in Leyton, 1986). As time passed, Bundy's snobbery and social pretensions grew insatiable. He wanted to possess certain women in order to gratify his need for power and control. His preferred victims were upper-class sorority women who became, in their final hours, Bundy's ultimate possessions, mere objects with whom he could do whatever he wished.

In 1980, Bundy was tried for the murder of two sorority sisters at the University of Florida. Appar-

Ted Bundy, one of the United States's most notorious serial killers, was an extreme example of an antisocial personality disorder. Some clinicians still use the terms psychopath *or* sociopath *to describe such people.*

ently convinced of his brilliance and legal acumen obtained while attending two different law schools, Bundy served as his own attorney in the trial. Like many antisocial personalities, Bundy overestimated his skills; he was convicted of the sorority sisters' murders and the kidnapping, murder, and mutilation of a 12-year-old Florida girl. ∎

*I*f we were proposing a moral taxonomy of behavior we would no doubt reserve a particularly ignominious corner for Ted Bundy. But in a formal classification of mental disorders, where should he be placed? Bundy did not hear voices or see visions; he was not out of touch with reality; he did not experience any pronounced physical problems, nor did he suffer attacks of anxiety or bouts of depression. Instead, Ted Bundy's problems seemed to be part and parcel of his **personality,** that unique pattern of consistency in behavior that distinguishes each person from every other. The way we interact with friends and family, the attitudes we hold toward work, and the approach we use to solve life's problems all reveal our personalities. Bundy represented an extreme example of what is called *antisocial personality disorder,* one of ten patterns that the DSM-IV identifies as personality disorders.

A **personality disorder** is an enduring pattern of inner experience and behavior that is extremely inflexible, deviates markedly from the expectations of a person's culture, and causes personal distress or behavioral impairment. These problematic patterns can be traced to adolescence or even childhood. People diagnosed with personality disorders have some consistently distorted ways of thinking, expressing emotions, controlling behavior, or interacting with others that impair their adjustment to everyday demands and often lead to misery for others. People who have antisocial personalities such as Bundy's can maintain a facade of coolness and charm, but behind it lies a long-standing core of aggressiveness and deceit with no regard or empathy for the rights of others.

The degree of damage associated with a personality disorder can be as severe as Bundy's or as mild as the annoyance caused by quirky characters. When Ted Knight of the *Mary Tyler Moore Show* alienated his newsroom colleagues with his self-centered pompousness, he was displaying classic patterns of narcissistic personality disorder. Table 12.1 lists other portrayals of personality disorders in well-known movies.

Because the developers of the DSM worried that personality disorders might be overshadowed by the Axis I disorders, the DSM-IV places personality disorders on a separate axis—Axis II—to draw special attention to them. As shown in Figure 12.1 on page 410, Axis II groups the ten personality disorders in three clusters based on similarities in their characteristics: (1) odd/eccentric, (2) dramatic/emotional/erratic, and (3) anxious/fearful. An eleventh category—*personality disorder not otherwise specified*—is used for personality disturbances that do not meet the criteria for any specific disorder.

In this chapter we will describe the clinical characteristics of each of the ten personality disorders included in the DSM-IV and examine what is known about their causes and treatments. First, though, we will take a closer look at the concept of personality disorder and why these disorders are particularly difficult to diagnose and treat.

Fateful Patterns: An Overview of Personality Disorders

French novelist Andre Malreaux's observation that "character is fate," provides a superb shorthand description of personality disorders. A personality disorder comes to define a person's fate; it is a streak of vulnerability that plagues almost all a person's endeavors. People with personality disorders appear "stuck" in their problems; their behavior is so inflexible that they never seem able to change to a new approach, even when it is obvious that their old strategies are not working.

TABLE 12.1	Axis II Goes to the Movies
Personality disorder	**Role**
Paranoid	Humphrey Bogart's portrayal of Captain Queeg in *The Caine Mutiny* (1954)
Schizotypal	Robert de Niro as the weird cabbie in *Taxi Driver* (1976)
Histrionic	Vivian Leigh's Scarlet O'Hara in *Gone with the Wind* (1939); Jackie Gleason's Ralph Cramden in the TV series *The Honeymooners*
Narcissistic	Warren Beatty in *Shampoo* (1975) and Richard Gere in *American Gigolo* (1980)
Borderline	Diane Keaton in *Looking for Mr. Goodbar* (1977); Jessica Lange in *Frances* (1988)
Antisocial	Alex as played by Malcolm McDowell in *A Clockwork Orange* (1971)
Avoidant	Woody Allen in *Zelig* (1983)
Dependent	Meryl Streep's portrayal of Sophie in *Sophie's Choice* (1982)
Obsessive-Compulsive	Jack Lemon as Felix Unger in *The Odd Couple* (1968)
Schizoid	Hyler presents no cinematic example of a schizoid personality. Can you think of an example? What about William Hurt's character in *The Accidental Tourist*?

Source: Hyler, 1988.

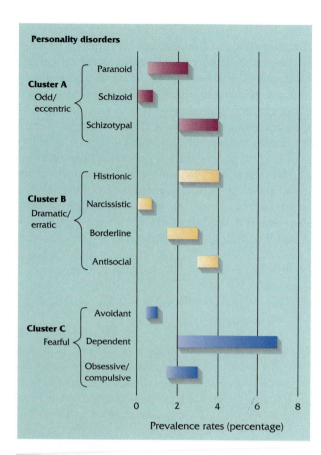

Personality disorders

Cluster A
Odd/
eccentric
- Paranoid
- Schizoid
- Schizotypal

Cluster B
Dramatic/
erratic
- Histrionic
- Narcissistic
- Borderline
- Antisocial

Cluster C
Fearful
- Avoidant
- Dependent
- Obsessive/
  compulsive

0   2   4   6   8

Prevalence rates (percentage)

FIGURE 12.1

**Overview of Personality Disorders and
Their Prevalence**
The DSM-IV describes ten main personality disorders,
organized into three clusters. Because of the nature of
personality disorders, it is difficult to determine their
prevalence accurately. The figures shown here are the best
estimates that current epidemiological research permits.

Defining Characteristics and Prevalence of Personality Disorders

Personality disorders differ in several important ways
from Axis I disorders. Unlike the symptoms of Axis
I mental disorders (which may come and go and
vary in intensity over time) personality disorders do
not usually involve distinct episodes or periods in
which clinical symptoms are obvious. Instead, the
central characteristic of personality disorders is long-
lasting, extreme, and rigid personality traits that are
maladaptive. A **personality trait** is a psychological
attribute that is relatively stable over time and across
different situations. Personality traits distinguish one
person's typical behavior from that of others. For example, people who show a high degree of the trait of

extroversion tend to be outgoing, energetic individuals who feel comfortable in many different social situations and seem to make friends easily.

Everyone knows someone whose personality
seems odd, but personality disorders involve more
than eccentricity. For a personality disorder to be diagnosed, an individual's personality traits must be
maladaptive. Almost any trait, when it becomes too
rigid and extreme, can cause problems for an individual and for society. For example, extroverted people can be too extroverted, becoming annoying pests
who talk too much or fail to respect other people's
privacy. Accordingly, the DSM-IV defines a personality disorder in terms of personality traits that are
"inflexible and maladaptive and [that] cause significant functional impairment and subjective distress"
(APA, 1994, p. 630).

The long-term, ingrained patterns of behavior
seen in personality disorders are related to four other
important features of these disorders.

1. People with personality disorders often do
not see themselves as troubled, let alone as suffering
from a mental disorder. Thus, personality disorders
are sometimes said to be **ego-syntonic**, meaning that
those who display them tend to experience them not
as aberrations but as natural parts of themselves. The
extreme traits associated with the disorder just feel
like part of the person's basic personality structure.
Indeed, many people with personality disorders think
that their only problem is that other people mistreat
or misunderstand them. However, not all personality disorders are ego-syntonic; in some cases individuals are aware that extreme traits are causing
them trouble and feel a desperate need to gain better control of their behavior.

2. Personality disorders are usually difficult to
treat—in many cases, more difficult than Axis I disorders. Part of this difficulty stems from the fact that
clients who believe that their problems are due to the
actions of others are usually reluctant to seek or cooperate in treatment.

3. Personality disorders are often more distressing for others than for the person displaying them.
All mental disorders tax the resources and patience
of friends and relatives, but personality disorders are
particularly troubling to others. As the case of Ted
Bundy illustrates, a severe personality disorder can
leave a trail of disaster in its wake.

4. Personality disorders often appear together
and in combination with Axis I mental disorders,
particularly anxiety disorders, mood disorders, and
substance abuse. For example, 25 to 85 percent of

people diagnosed with one personality disorder also meet the criteria for another one (Widiger & Rogers, 1989; Zimmerman & Coryell, 1989). In terms of Axis I comorbidity, anywhere from 27 to 65 percent of patients with panic disorder or generalized anxiety disorder show a coexisting personality disorder (Brown & Barlow, 1992). Because of this comorbidity, it is often difficult to determine whether a client suffers two or more disorders or whether the problems attributed to an Axis I condition are actually the result of a pervasive personality disorder.

The definition of a personality disorder also implies several things about its course. Just as personality traits begin to stabilize by young adulthood, personality disorders are also usually apparent by that time. By definition, then, the onset of personality disorders occurs no later than young adulthood. However, these disorders often do not come to a clinician's attention until years later, after a series of difficulties have forced clients into treatment or after they have become motivated to change a life of constant, emotional turmoil. Also, by definition, personality disorders are relatively stable through the years, although certain disorders tend to diminish in severity after the age of 40.

The prevalence of personality disorders in the United States is difficult to estimate, in part because many people with these disorders refuse to acknowledge their problems and avoid contact with clinicians. Another complication stems from the fact that the diagnosis of a personality disorder requires establishing a chronic pattern of problems, which is usually more difficult than diagnosing the acute symptoms of an Axis I disorder.

In large-scale epidemiological surveys, the rate of antisocial personality disorder (the most thoroughly studied of the personality disorders) is placed at somewhere around 3 to 4 percent in the United States (Regier et al., 1988). In addition to antisocial personality disorder, the other most prevalent diagnoses are histrionic and schizotypal, each of which may be seen in as many as 4 percent of the population. A recent summary of the epidemiological evidence suggests that somewhere between 10 and 13 percent of the population have met the criteria for at least one type of personality disorder sometime in their lives (Weissman, 1993).

The picture regarding gender differences is complicated. Most of the personality disorders—paranoid, narcissistic, and antisocial personality disorders being the most obvious examples—are diagnosed more often in men than in women. Borderline personality disorder is the prime example of a personality disorder that is diagnosed more often—about 3 times more often—in women than in men. A few disorders, such as avoidant personality disorder and dependent personality disorder, seem to affect men and women about equally.

Scientists still know very little about cultural differences in the prevalence of personality disorders. The approximate 3 to 4 percent rate of antisocial personality disorder holds true for Canada and New Zealand, but, in Taiwan, the prevalence is less than 0.5 percent. Western European countries report a prevalence rate for all personality disorders combined similar to that of the United States. However, the picture is much less clear in non-European nations, where, until recently, clinicians have been less likely than their Western colleagues to diagnose certain types of personality disorders.

Rates of antisocial personality disorder in Taiwan are far lower than in most Western cultures. The factors responsible for this difference are not currently understood, but one possibility is that cultures that help maintain strong bonds to families and schools have a reduced rate of conduct disorder—a forerunner of antisocial personality disorder—among adolescents.

DSM-IV

Diagnostic Criteria for a Personality Disorder

A. An enduring pattern of inner experience and behavior that deviates markedly from the expectations of the individual's culture. This pattern is manifested in two (or more) of the following areas:

   (1) cognition (i.e., ways of perceiving and interpreting self, other people, and events)

   (2) affectivity (i.e., the range, intensity, lability, and appropriateness of emotional response)

   (3) interpersonal functioning

   (4) impulse control

B. The enduring pattern is inflexible and pervasive across a broad range of personal and social situations.

C. The enduring pattern leads to clinically significant distress or impairment in social, occupational, or other important areas of functioning.

D. The pattern is stable and of long duration and its onset can be traced back at least to adolescence or early adulthood.

E. The enduring pattern is not better accounted for as a manifestation or consequence of another mental disorder.

F. The enduring pattern is not due to the direct physiological effects of a substance (e.g., a drug of abuse, a medication) or a general medical condition (e.g., head trauma).

Source: American Psychiatric Association; *Diagnostic and Statistical Manual of Mental Disorders,* Fourth Edition. Washington, DC, American Psychiatric Association, 1994.

Diagnosing Personality Disorders

The DSM table above lists the criteria for diagnosing a personality disorder. Reliable diagnoses of these disorders is complicated by several factors, including their comorbidity with Axis I disorders.

Personality Disorders and Axis I Disorders. By placing personality disorders on Axis II, the DSM-IV encourages clinicians to diagnose personality disorders in addition to any Axis I disorders that are present. However, clinicians often find it difficult to distinguish Axis I and Axis II disorders, and they are uncertain how best to think about clients with diagnoses on both axes.

Comorbidity between Axis I and Axis II disorders can be understood in several ways (Klein, 1993). First, an Axis I disorder and a personality disorder may simply coexist at the same time. When they do, one disorder is likely to aggravate the other. For example, the general suspiciousness of paranoid personality disorder may cause a person to mistrust and shun medication that is necessary for managing an accompanying bipolar disorder. A depressive disorder may lead a person with dependent personality disorder to feel even more desperate for someone else's guidance.

It is also possible that one of the disorders predisposes a person to develop the other. For example,

the emotional instability that is a hallmark of borderline personality disorder may cause a person to react more intensely to major stressors, ultimately leading to a major depressive disorder. In other cases, an Axis I disorder may lead to a personality disorder. A childhood mood disorder may undermine a child's confidence about making new friends or mastering new challenges. As a result, the child may avoid social situations, thereby setting the stage for an avoidant personality disorder.

Another interpretation of comorbidity is that it is an artifact of the criteria used for various diagnoses. Because the diagnostic criteria for several Axis I and Axis II disorders overlap, two diagnoses may be given when only one disorder is present. For example,

- Comorbidity may simply be the result of definitional similarity. Borderline personality disorder shares criteria with mood disorders; the symptoms of antisocial personality disorder and substance abuse are similar; and avoidant personality disorder and the generalized form of social phobia have similar definitions. It is therefore not surprising to find these pairs of disorders often diagnosed together.

- A personality disorder and an Axis I disorder may represent different levels of severity along the same basic dimensions of disturbance. For example, some clinicians believe that schizotypal personality disorder may be a mild form of schizophrenia and that borderline personality disorder is an early or less-severe manifestation of bipolar or cyclothymic disorder. Others argue that each of these conditions is a separate disorder that deserves a unique diagnosis. This controversy has not yet been resolved, but considerable empirical research is being devoted to it.

Other Diagnostic Difficulties. At least three other problems make reliable diagnosis of personality disorders difficult. First, as suggested in the discussion of comorbidity, the criteria used to define different personality disorders often overlap considerably. As a result, the same behavioral characteristics may be associated with several personality disorders. For example, impulsive behavior is symptomatic of both borderline personality disorder and antisocial personality disorder. Distress or impairment due to a lack of close friends and confidants is associated with schizoid, schizotypal, and avoidant personality disorders.

A second obstacle to reliable diagnosis of personality disorders is that, by definition, they refer to long-standing behavior patterns rather than acute, current symptoms. This definition requires that the clinician assess a person's adolescence or childhood to determine whether the individual has been, for example, chronically mistrustful of people (in the case of paranoid personality disorder) or always aloof and emotionally cold (in the case of schizoid personality disorder). Yet an accurate social history of a person's styles of interaction as a child or adolescent may be difficult to obtain. Memory of distant events can be faulty, but even accurate memories are sometimes distorted by clients who put their own "spin" on the past. Such distortions might be particularly likely in the case of personality disorders because of their long-standing nature and their tendency to affect many aspects of behavior, emotion, and thinking simultaneously.

Finally, the problems associated with the DSM-IV's categorical approach to classification are particularly difficult in the case of personality disorders. As noted in Chapter 2, the DSM-IV requires the clinician to assign a diagnosis if a client meets a particular number out of a fixed set of criteria. If this number is met (for example, five out of nine for narcissistic personality disorder) the diagnosis is made. But there is little or no evidence to support a particular cutoff (such as five of nine instead of six of nine criteria) as being the "true" boundary between normal and abnormal personality (Widiger & Trull, 1991). Furthermore, if the rule requires that five of nine criteria be met, two people could be diagnosed as displaying narcissistic personality disorders even though they share only one defining feature. And two other people who share four defining features might receive different diagnoses because they do not share a fifth criterion.

Dimensional Descriptions of Personality Disorders

The difficulties in diagnosing personality disorders have encouraged the development of dimensional approaches (Cloninger, 1987; Costa & Widiger, 1994; Watson, Clark, & Harkness, 1994; Widiger & Costa, 1994; Wiggins & Pincus, 1989). Recall from Chapter 2 that a *dimensional* approach involves describing individuals along various dimensions or traits of personality. These traits span normal and abnormal levels of functioning. Because personality disorders are viewed as extreme, rigid extensions of personality traits, dimensional approaches that rely on reliable, well-validated measures of basic personality are especially appealing. Two systems for measuring personality characteristics have proved particularly useful for distinguishing personality disorders: the Big Five model of personality and the Interpersonal Circumplex. Both these models have been proposed as alternatives to the DSM-IV system of categorizing personality disorders.

The Big Five model is so named because, on the basis of factor analyses and other multivariate methods, various researchers have found that important personality traits can be organized into five basic factors. Individuals can score high or low on any of these factors, based on their answers to a large number of items that assess how they are likely to behave in a wide range of situations. Big Five theorists argue that any personality can be described and distinguished from others in terms of the following five factors:

1. **neuroticism:** the tendency to experience negative emotions such as anxiety, anger, and depression accompanied by disruptions of behavior and distressed thinking. Neuroticism is contrasted with emotional stability, which is typical of people who tend to remain calm even in stressful situations.

2. **extroversion:** a preference for social interaction and a tendency to be active, talkative, optimistic, and affectionate. Introverts tend to prefer solitude and are less active than extroverts. Introverts appear sober, aloof, quiet, and task-oriented. They seem to have less need for stimulation.

Connections

Is comorbidity particularly high for other mental disorders? Consider comorbidity for anxiety disorders in Chapter 7, p. 216, and mood disorders in Chapter 9, pp. 289–290.

3. openness: interest in new experiences and receptivity to new activities and ideas for their own sake. People who score high on this dimension are creative, curious, and untraditional. People who score low on this dimension tend to be more interested in concrete or practical pursuits. They appear set in their ways and emotionally unresponsive.

4. agreeableness: compassionate interest in others. People who score high on this dimension are usually trusting and tender-hearted. They are generous in caring for others, sometimes to the point of putting others' needs before their own or even appearing gullible. People who score low on agreeableness are apt to be competitive and are more likely to be manipulative, cynical, skeptical, and openly hostile or rude.

5. conscientiousness: well-organized dedication to work. People who score high on this dimension are ambitious and persistently strive to be achievers. Those who are low on this dimension are less demanding of themselves and others and may seem unreliable and careless.

According to Big Five theorists, extreme scores on one or more of these dimensions may be sufficient to describe the maladaptiveness of a personality disorder. For example, an extremely high score on neuroticism points to probable adjustment problems. If this score were coupled with an extremely low score on extroversion, suggesting extreme discomfort in most social situations, the essential features of avoidant personality disorder have been captured.

A more elaborate description of two Big Five traits—extroversion and agreeableness—is given with the **Interpersonal Circumplex** or **Circle** created by Timothy Leary (1957). Drawing on Harry Stack Sullivan's view of personality as the enduring pattern of an individual's interpersonal relationships, Leary's model analyzes different personalities as combinations of just two basic dimensions of interpersonal behavior: *dominance/submission* and *love/hate*. The interaction of these dimensions produces the eight personality styles appearing around the outside of the interpersonal circle shown in Figure 12.2.

Individuals diagnosed with personality disorders seem virtually to "live in" one of the wedges of the circle; their behavior is fixed into a narrow and extreme reliance on one personality style. Numerous studies have shown that most personality disorders can be meaningfully described through these

Connections

Is a dimensional approach useful for describing other disorders, possibly even Axis I disorders? See Chapter 3, pp. 81–83.

dimensional models (Costa & McCrae, 1990; Soldz et al., 1993; Trull, 1992; Wiggins & Pincus, 1989). The descriptions of specific personality disorders in the next section takes into account both DSM-IV criteria and dimensional models.

In Review

Unlike most mental disorders, personality disorders:

- do not involve discrete periods of specific clinical symptoms;
- do not come and go or vary widely in intensity;
- are often ego-syntonic (feel normal and natural); and
- are often more distressing for others than for the person displaying them.

Because they involve stable, long-lasting patterns of maladaptive behavior, personality disorders:

- are often diagnosed along with Axis I disorders; and
- are in many cases difficult to treat.

Options for describing people with personality disorders include:

- the categorical approach of the DSM-IV, which identifies ten specific types of personality disorders; and
- the dimensional approach illustrated by the Big Five model and Leary's Interpersonal Circle.

Types of Personality Disorders

Despite some advantages, dimensional descriptions of personality disorders have not replaced the DSM-IV categorical approach. This is partly because no particular dimensional system has gained enough support among clinicians to supplant categorical diagnoses. Another reason is that clinicians are more familiar with the categorical designations, believe they are easier to use, and are therefore reluctant to give them up. Consequently, our descriptions of personality disorders are organized around the DSM-IV categories. However, notice that even this organization implies something of a dimensional approach because the disorders are clustered to emphasize particular personality attributes: odd/eccentric, dramatic/emotional/erratic, and anxious/fearful.

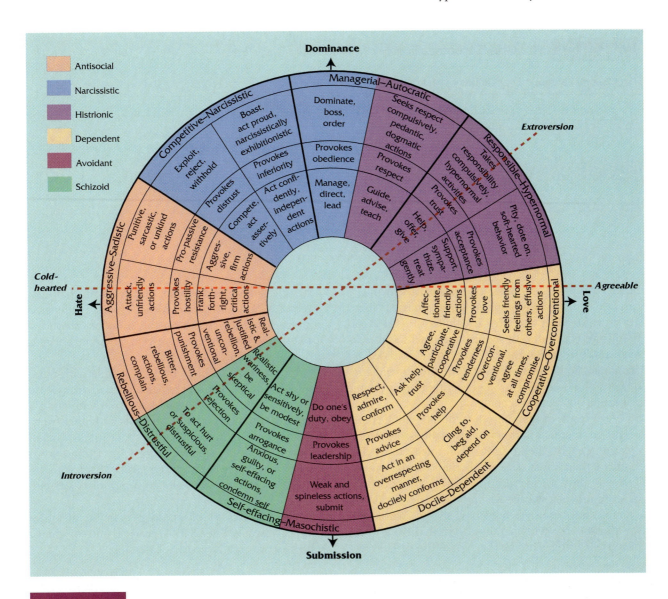

FIGURE 12.2

The Interpersonal Circle and Personality Disorders

Leary's Interpersonal Circle depicts eight different personality styles made up of blends of two basic dimensions—love/hate and dominance/submission. This figure also shows the relationship of the circle to two of the traits in the Big Five model—agreeableness and extroversion—marked by the dotted red lines. Several personality disorders—including the histrionic, narcissistic, dependent, avoidant, antisocial, and schizoid—can be plotted on the interpersonal circle at locations corresponding to the most typical combinations of interpersonal behaviors seen in these disorders. Other personality disorders, such as borderline, schizotypal, and obsessive-compulsive cannot be placed on the circle as reliably.

Source: Based on Wiggins & Pincus, 1992.

Odd/Eccentric Personality Disorders

In the DSM-IV, the *odd/eccentric* personality disorders includes paranoid, schizoid, and schizotypal personality disorders. Table 12.2 on page 416 describes the primary characteristics of these disorders and their relationship to the dimensions of the Big Five model.

The results of empirical studies have consistently supported the dimensional descriptions in this table.

Paranoid Personality Disorder. People with **paranoid personality disorder** are habitually suspicious, constantly on guard, and mistrustful. They assume that

---

TABLE 12.2   The Odd/Eccentric Cluster of Personality Disorders

DSM-IV category	Primary characteristics	Description based on Big Five model
Paranoid	Suspicious, chronically hostile, envious, tense, loners	High neuroticism and low agreeableness
Schizoid	Isolated from others, with a lack of emotional expression	Low extraversion and low agreeableness
Schizotypal	Odd mannerisms, appearances, and experiences; pervasively detached from others	High neuroticism plus low extraversion and low agreeableness

Source: Costa & McCrae (1990); Soldz et al. (1993); Trull (1992); Wiggins & Pincus (1989).

---

others will take advantage of or harm them unless carefully watched and prevented from doing so. They are prone to anger and intense jealousy, and they tend to misinterpret innocent actions or remarks as threats or insults directed at them. Often, these attitudes are accompanied by an air of moral superiority and condescension based on a strong belief that other people are usually corrupt or conniving.

As a result of their chronic irritability and thinly disguised hostility, paranoid personalities succeed at creating exactly the kind of social interactions that confirm their most dire predictions about others. They are drawn toward litigation and other official proceedings as a way of settling their grievances and evening the score over perceived slights. You might say that people with paranoid personality disorder burn their bridges before they get to them. They ap-

pear to dislike other people, and seem incapable of intimacy. Paranoid personalities' loner tendencies, coupled with their chip-on-the-shoulder attitudes, lead others to avoid them, a response that only heightens their paranoid suspicions.

Humorless and unemotional, people with paranoid personality disorder generally avoid groups unless they can lead or otherwise control them. For example, they may be attracted to cults and other fringe organizations either as a leader or as an ambivalent follower of a charismatic figure whose power they covet. Paranoid personalities typically display an undertone of envy toward those in authority or with power.

The features of paranoid personality disorder are illustrated by Bill A., a 45-year-old auto mechanic who worked in a large car dealership.

Individuals with paranoid personality disorder are quick to lose their temper over perceived slights or threats. They hold grudges for a long time and often provoke angry confrontations with neighbors or coworkers. Paranoid personalities share some symptoms with people diagnosed with schizophrenia or delusional disorder, but, unlike these latter disorders, paranoid personality disorder seldom involves delusions or other psychotic symptoms.

For the first two years on the job, Bill performed well, according to his supervisor. But in the next few months, his work and his relationships with coworkers deteriorated. These problems started when Bill accused a fellow mechanic of sabotaging his work by putting grease on his tools. Bill insisted that the coworker was jealous because Bill was a better mechanic. Now, Bill insists that he be given a detailed, written description of every repair job he is to complete and that his supervisor inspect his progress every 20 minutes. Bill believes the other mechanic, whom he calls a "management mole," has turned everyone in the agency against him, and he has asked the police to investigate the telephoned death threats he claims to have received as well as the flat tires that he is convinced have been caused by nails that coworkers have put under his car.

Because of the secretiveness and isolation of persons with paranoid personality disorder, accurate assessment of its prevalence is difficult, but estimates range from 0.5 to 2.5 percent of the general U.S. population (Bernstein, Useda, & Siever, 1993). Its effects are most often observed in occupational settings where, as was the case with Bill A., it leads to frequent conflicts with superiors and coworkers. It is diagnosed more often in men than in women.

Schizoid Personality Disorder. The hallmarks of **schizoid personality disorder** are an indifference to social relationships and a pervasive emotional blandness. People with this disorder usually lack close friends, and they appear to take no pleasure from positive events and to feel no unhappiness after setbacks. It is as though emotional color has been bleached from their lives. They lack social skills and seem to be lethargic and aloof, like the Beatles' "Nowhere Man."

Schizoid personalities prefer solitary activities and occupations. The work of nighttime security guard or lighthouse keeper would be ideally suited to them, although their interpersonal apathy and lack of initiative make it less likely that they would succeed at any job. They prefer mechanical or abstract activities over those that involve working with other people. Often, they drift into marginal living arrangements, such as skid rows, cheap hotels, and rundown boarding houses. Although they may passively accept sexual attention from others, they are typically indifferent to potential romances or friendships.

Diagnosed slightly more often among males, the overall prevalence of schizoid personality disorder is not known, but it is probably less than 1 percent (Weissman, 1993). It is rarely seen in formal clinical treatment settings. Schizoid personality disorder may be a precursor to delusional disorder or schizophrenia in some cases, but the hypothesis that it shares a genetic basis with these serious disorders has not received strong empirical support.

Schizotypal Personality Disorder. The former rock group The Doors captured the schizotypal personality disorder in their song "People Are Strange." People with **schizotypal personality disorder** are like

People with schizoid personality disorder often prefer jobs or lives that allow them almost constant solitude. They seem disinterested in other people and are not bothered by criticism or their own isolation.

schizoids in that they, too, are socially isolated and tend to shun close relationships. However, schizotypal personalities are more noticeable because they tend to act, dress, and talk in odd ways. In addition, schizotypal personalities, unlike schizoids, are socially anxious and apprehensive. This anxiety appears to be tied to general self-consciousness and discomfort with others that does not diminish with further acquaintance. The person with schizotypal personality disorder often appears quirky and reacts stiffly in social situations. Schizotypal people seldom have close friends outside their own families, and other people tend to see them as silly and absurd.

The odd thinking and speech associated with schizotypal personality disorder is not so eccentric as to qualify as psychotic, but they are certainly regressive and strange enough to draw attention and sometimes frighten other people. Schizotypal personalities frequently express superstitions and beliefs in telepathic or extraterrestrial phenomena (Widiger, Frances, & Trull, 1987). *Ideas of reference,* which involve the belief that one is being monitored or talked about by others, are prominent as are associated feelings of paranoia and suspiciousness. People with this disorder also often report bizarre perceptual experiences, such as holding conversations with dead relatives or believing that spirits or nonexistent people are inhabiting a room. They may sometimes talk to themselves or others in vague, confusing, or tangential ways, but their speech is seldom incoherent, as is often the case with schizophrenia.

In his award-winning book about Savannah, Georgia, *Midnight in the Garden of Good and Evil,* John Berendt (1994) describes several examples of schizotypal behavior among the townspeople. One recluse had invented the flea collar and the no-pest strip during his spare moments as a technician whose job it was to test insecticides by injecting them into weevils and beetles. As a hobby, this man would anesthetize flies and glue thread to their backs. Then, when the flies woke up, he would take them on walks through downtown, each fly in tow behind him, on its individual leash. On other occasions, he would trim one wing shorter than the other so the fly would constantly buzz around in a circle. These actions made many Savannahians uneasy, particularly those who feared the man would follow through one day on his threat to poison the city's water supply.

Connections

How much evidence is there for a genetic basis for schizophrenia and the conditions that are part of a schizophrenia spectrum? For answers, see Chapter 10, pp. 349–354.

As the term *schizotypal* implies, this disorder has often been viewed as a mild form of schizophrenia or as part of the schizophrenia *spectrum.* Although there is evidence that schizophrenia and schizotypal disorder are genetically related (Thaker et al., 1996), other studies have found considerable familial and genetic overlap between schizotypal personality disorder and mood disorders as well (Kotsaftis & Neale, 1993). Currently, it appears that schizotypal personality disorder may be a mild or an early form of a psychotic disorder, but we cannot say for sure that it is specific to schizophrenia.

The prevalence of schizotypal personality disorder in the United States is in the 2 to 4 percent range. Most studies suggest that it occurs more frequently among males (Kotsaftis & Neale, 1993). Reliable diagnosis of this personality disorder has proved challenging, in part because of its substantial overlap in symptoms with schizoid, avoidant, and borderline personality disorders.

Dramatic/Emotional/Erratic Personality Disorders

The *dramatic/emotional/erratic* personality disorders includes histrionic, narcissistic, borderline, and antisocial personality disorders. Table 12.3 summarizes the Big Five descriptions of these disorders, which tend to be typified by active, sometimes uncontrolled, behaviors. This cluster contains the two personality disorders—antisocial and borderline personality disorders—that have received the most attention from researchers. This extra attention is given because individuals diagnosed with either of these disorders often get into trouble with legal authorities or are forced into treatment as a result of their socially disruptive behavior.

Histrionic Personality Disorder. The major features of **histrionic personality disorder** are a set of attention-getting behaviors that include seductiveness, exaggerated displays of emotions, and demands for reassurance and praise. Histrionic personalities love to be the center of attention and frequently use physical attractiveness or flamboyant emotionality to gain attention. They describe events with hyperbolic speech that sounds empty in spite of its hyperbole; phrases such as "totally awesome," "incredibly beautiful," and "horribly awful" characterize the speech of histrionic persons. All their actions, even their manner of dress, are designed to make others notice them.

These strategies may at first strike others as creative, entertaining, or even charming, but tend,

TABLE 12.3   The Dramatic/Emotional/Erratic Cluster of Personality Disorders

DSM-IV category	Primary characteristics	Description based on Big Five model
Histrionic	Shallow; always seeking attention; exaggerated emotions; seductive	High extraversion and high neuroticism
Narcissistic	Inflated self-esteem; low empathy for others; feels entitled to special privileges	Low agreeableness
Borderline	Unstable moods; impulsive behaviors; angry; lack of a coherent sense of self; interpersonal turmoil	High neuroticism, low agreeableness, low conscientiousness
Antisocial	Constantly violating rights of others; callous, manipulative, dishonest; does not feel guilt	Low agreeableness and low conscientiousness

Source: Costa & McCrae (1990); Soldz et al. (1993); Trull (1992); Wiggins & Pincus (1989).

in most cultures, to wear thin over time, revealing the strategies to be shallow exhibitions driven by self-centered needs. As the charm wears off and people grow weary of paying constant attention and tribute, histrionic individuals must seek new audiences. When their social charm or physical attractiveness fails to gain the stimulation that these people crave, they may develop attention-getting physical complaints.

The interpersonal style of histrionic people has been described as "actively dependent": "Their clever and often artful social behaviors give the appearance of an inner confidence and independent self-assurance; beneath this guise, however, lies a fear of genuine autonomy and a need for repeated signs of acceptance and approval" (Millon, 1990, p. 121). People with histrionic personality disorder are easily bored and susceptible to group pressures and to joining in fads. They are also suggestible and therefore drawn to strong authority figures whose admiration they especially desire.

Histrionic personality disorder occurs in about 2 to 4 percent of the U.S. population (Weissman, 1993), and it appears to be diagnosed more often in females than in males. The reasons for this gender difference remain controversial. It may reflect cultural influences that lead females, especially, to believe that physical beauty is necessary for a satisfying life, or it may be due to the diagnostic biases described in Chapter 2. Recall the study by Maureen Ford and Tom Widiger in which clinicians were asked to diagnose fictitious cases. One case involved a typical description of antisocial personality disorder for which the person was said to be either a man or a woman; the other described a histrionic personality disorder, again presented as either a man or woman. The results showed that clinicians were more likely to di-

agnose a female with histrionic personality disorder even when she met the criteria for antisocial personality disorder. Likewise, histrionic behavior attributed to a female increased clinicians' use of the histrionic diagnosis. On the other hand, being identified as a male had a smaller effect on the differential use of the two diagnoses.

Researchers' interest in histrionic personality disorder appears to have declined recently; it may be diagnosed less frequently in the future since it overlaps considerably with other personality disorders in the dramatic/emotional/erratic cluster.

Narcissistic Personality Disorder. When Carly Simon sang "You're So Vain," she no doubt had in mind someone who is narcissistic. The term *narcissism* derives from the Greek myth of Narcissus, who was so enthralled with his reflection in a pool that he died of protracted longing after his own beauty. The main feature of **narcissistic personality disorder** is an over-inflated sense of importance and worth leading to a sense of entitlement to special privileges and to exemptions from the rules that apply to others. Narcissists entertain grandiose ideas about their abilities and importance, and they are prone to feelings of rage or humiliation if others overlook or criticize them. Indeed, people with narcissistic personality disorder sometimes behave irresponsibly because they do not feel that normal social constraints should apply to them; at such times, their behavior may turn antisocial.

Like histrionic personalities, those diagnosed with narcissistic personality disorder crave attention and feature themselves as stars in fantasies of success and power. Preoccupied with their own status, narcissistic personalities lack empathy for others and exploit social relationships for their own gain. They are frequently envious or believe that others envy them. If criticized or reprimanded, their arrogance often turns to hostility and even abuse. Unable to admit weaknesses or to appreciate the effect their behavior has on others, narcissists are poor candidates for psychotherapy.

The prevalence of narcissistic personality disorder is not clearly established, but most estimates place it at less than 1 percent of U.S. samples (Zimmerman & Coryell, 1989). This disorder appears to have grown more common over the past decade or so. It is unclear whether the increased incidence represents a genuine upswing in new cases or simply greater clinical interest in and attention to the disorder. Males are diagnosed with narcissistic personality disorder slightly more often than females.

Borderline Personality Disorder. Because it is a frequent disorder that involves potentially destructive behavior, clinicians have studied borderline personality disorder extensively. In fact, it now rivals antisocial personality disorder as the most frequently studied personality disorder. One survey indicated that over 40 percent of journal articles about personality disorders were devoted to borderline personality disorder (Widiger & Frances, 1989).

The clinical term *borderline* has carried different meanings over the years (Widiger, Miele, & Tilly, 1992). Some professionals use it to capture the similarity between borderline personality disorder and brief or mild schizophrenic symptoms. In the DSM-IV, the essential qualities of **borderline personality disorder** are impulsivity and instability in several areas of functioning, including mood, behavior, self-image, and interpersonal relationships. In fact, borderlines are often described as being stable only in their unpredictability. During periods of increased stress, borderlines may display psychotic symptoms for a brief time. Nancy, a 23-year-old veterinary assistant, exemplifies borderline personality disorder.

*T*hree months before Nancy's admission to a hospital, she learned that her mother had become pregnant. She began drinking heavily, ostensibly in order to sleep nights. While drinking, she became involved in a series of "one-night stands." Two weeks before admission, she began feeling panicky and having experiences in which she felt as if she were removed from her body and in a trance. During one of these episodes, she was stopped by the police while wandering on a bridge late at night. The next day, in response to hearing a voice repeatedly telling her to jump off a bridge, Nancy ran to her supervisor and asked

for help. Her supervisor, seeing her distress and also noting scars from a recent wrist slashing, referred her to a psychiatrist, who then arranged for her immediate hospitalization.

In the hospital, Nancy appeared as a disheveled and frail, but appealing, waif. She was cooperative, coherent, and frightened. Although she did not feel that hospitalization was needed, she welcomed the prospect of relief from her anxiety and depersonalization. Nancy acknowledged that she had had feelings of loneliness and inadequacy and brief periods of depressed mood and anxiety since adolescence. Recently she had been having fantasies that she was stabbing herself or a little baby with a knife. She complained that she was "just an empty shell that is transparent to everyone."

Nancy's parents divorced when she was 3, and for the next 5 years she lived with her maternal grandmother and her mother, who had a severe drinking problem. She had night terrors during which she would frequently end up sleeping with her mother. At age 6, she went to a special boarding school for a year and a half. When Nancy was 8, her maternal grandmother died; and she recalls trying to conceal her grief about this from her mother. She spent most of the next 2 years living with various relatives, including a period with her father, whom she had not seen since the divorce. When she was 9, her mother was hospitalized with schizophrenia. From age 10 through college, Nancy lived with an aunt and uncle, but had ongoing and frequent contacts with her mother. Her school record was consistently good.

Since adolescence, Nancy had dated regularly, having an active, but rarely pleasurable, sex life. Her relationships with men usually ended abruptly after she became angry with them when they disappointed her in some apparently minor way. She then concluded that they were "no good to begin with." She had several roommates but had trouble establishing a stable living situation because of her jealousy about sharing her roommates with others and because of her manipulative efforts to keep them from seeing other people.

Since college she worked steadily and, at the time of admission, was working a night shift in a veterinary hospital and living alone. (Based on Spitzer et al., 1994)

As this case illustrates, borderline personality disorder may involve a combination of symptoms that are more severe versions of those seen in several other personality disorders, including the schizotypal, histrionic, narcissistic, and antisocial. Borderlines' interpersonal relationships are especially turbulent.

Glenn Close in a scene from the movie, Fatal Attraction. *Borderline personality disorder is often featured in Hollywood movies. Close's character in* Fatal Attraction *was a particularly startling, but accurate, portrayal. After having a brief but torrid affair with a married man (played by Michael Douglas), Close's character reacted with both rage and desperation when the affair abruptly ended.*

They quickly develop strong, impassioned romances in which they idealize the partner as being almost perfect. However, when negative experiences occur, as they do in any relationship, people with borderline personality disorder overreact with extreme mood swings. They are especially frightened by signs of abandonment or rejection, and will alternate between rage and desperate pleas for the other person to stay with and care for them. They are so sensitive to other people's behavior that they tend to overinterpret its meaning, often in a quasi-paranoid way. Thus, if someone is especially helpful at work, it might be viewed as a sexual overture. Conversely, if someone forgets to say "hello" or says it too matter of factly, this might be seen as a put-down that has to be confronted.

People with borderline personality disorder also have trouble regulating their moods and are particularly unable to tolerate negative emotions. When something bad happens to them, they appear to be unable to say "I'll get over it." Consequently, one negative emotion leads to another. Feeling slighted leads to depression, which leads to rage, which generates some extreme behavior, which ultimately produces guilt. Through such repeated emotional cycles, borderline personalities create most of their own life crises.

Borderlines' instability is also reflected in impulsive, sometimes dangerous, behavior. They often lose control of their tempers and are prone to getting into physical fights. They may go on sprees of spending, eating, drinking, or sex, usually to ward off the feelings of emptiness or loneliness to which they are prone. About 75 percent of borderline personalities make suicidal threats or gestures at least once in their lifetimes. Some engage in self-mutilation such as body-piercing and multiple tattooing. Of course, no single behavior pattern is sufficient to determine a diagnosis, and tatooing or body piercing may also reflect current fads, not a personality disorder.

Borderline personalities also tend to display uncertainty about their self-image and identity. Under extreme stress, they can temporarily lose control of or "forget" their personal identities.

Borderline personality disorder is considered one of the most severe personality disorders because of the intensity, range, and unpredictability of its symptoms. These manifestations tend to be most severe for people in their 20s but ease somewhat as they reach their 30s. Evidence from several studies suggests that the overall prevalence of borderline personality disorder averages about 2 percent (Weissman, 1993). Females are diagnosed with the disorder 2 to 3 times more often than males. Between 15 and 20 percent of psychiatric hospital patients are labeled as borderlines, making it the most common form of diagnosed personality disorder (Widiger & Weissman, 1991).

Antisocial Personality Disorder. **Antisocial personality disorder (APD)** is the latest label for people who are chronically callous and manipulative; who trample on the rights of others; who ignore social rules and laws; who behave impulsively, dishonestly, and irresponsibly; who fail to learn from punishment; and who lack remorse or guilt over crimes and other misdeeds. In decades past, this pattern has been called moral insanity, psychopathy, and sociopathy. Notorious exemplars of this disorder include Ted Bundy, Gary Gilmore, Charles Manson, and Jeffrey Dahmer. Other, less violent, criminals reveal antisocial features

Connections

What other disorders are associated with disturbances in identity or memory? See Chapter 8, pp. 259–262.

through their exploitation of others for personal gain. Examples include swindlers such as financier Charles Keating and evangelist Jim Bakker.

Over two decades ago, the psychiatrist Hervey Cleckley (1976) offered an influential description of individuals then called "psychopathic personalities." According to Cleckley, psychopathic personalities possess superficial charm and intelligence and do not show signs of delusions, irrational thinking, or anxiety about matters that might upset most people. What the psychopath does display is unreliability, insincerity, a disregard for the truth, a lack of remorse over misdeeds, a failure to learn from experience, and an incapacity to feel normal emotional reactions including a genuine love for anyone. In addition, according to Cleckley, psychopaths are manipulative, impulsive, and fail to follow through on any kind of overall life plan. They often have superficial, promiscuous sex lives and are prone to suicide threats that they seldom carry out.

Some psychopaths are sufficiently sophisticated in their manipulations, clever enough in their exploitations, and smooth enough in their mistreatment of others to escape legal sanctions. In fact, some are so successful as to be envied for the power, prestige, and wealth they amass. Society seems to have no shortage of "successful psychopaths," who somehow manage to escape paying for their lives of irresponsibility and deceitfulness.

Robert Hare's Psychopathy Checklist—Revised provides a more recent and highly regarded description of the psychopath. Similar to Cleckley's model, Hare emphasizes two defining characteristics: emotional-cognitive instability and behavioral deviance (Hare, Hart, & Harpur, 1991). The 20 items on this checklist are:

1. glibness/superficial charm
2. grandiose sense of self-worth
3. need for stimulation/proneness to boredom
4. pathological lying
5. conning/manipulative
6. lack of remorse or guilt
7. shallow affect
8. callous/lack of empathy
9. parasitic lifestyle
10. poor behavioral controls
11. promiscuous sexual behavior
12. early behavior problems
13. lack of realistic, long-term goals
14. impulsivity
15. irresponsibility
16. failure to accept responsibility for actions
17. many short-term marital relationships
18. juvenile delinquency
19. revocation of conditional release
20. criminal versatility

Psychopathy and antisocial personality disorder are not synonymous. Many clinicians still use the term *psychopath,* but the DSM-IV's definition of antisocial personality disorder stresses repeated violations of the rights of others and overt criminal behavior more than devious traits and interpersonal tendencies. As a result, some people who might qualify as psychopaths using Cleckley's or Hare's criteria would not be diagnosed as antisocial personality disorders by the DSM-IV. Using the behavioral criteria listed in the DSM table opposite improves the reliability of diagnosis. However, emphasizing only overtly irresponsible behavior may cause some clinicians to overlook less obvious cases of the disorder.

Figure 12.3 outlines the sequence of problems that typically precedes antisocial personality disorder. The disorder begins prior to the age of 15 as symptoms of conduct disorder (see Chapter 3) in which a youngster is repeatedly involved in lying,

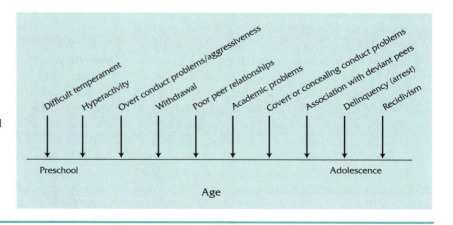

FIGURE 12.3

Precursors of Antisocial Personality Disorder

Signs of antisocial personality disorder are often evident in early childhood. Aggressive children tend to grow up to be aggressive adults, and the precursors of chronic antisocial conduct can frequently be seen in temperamental, interpersonal, and academic problems that show up in the elementary school years.
Source: Based on Loeber, 1990.

Diagnostic Criteria for Antisocial Personality Disorder

A. There is a pervasive pattern of disregard for and violation of the rights of others occurring since age 15 years, as indicated by three (or more) of the following:

(1) failure to conform to social norms with respect to lawful behaviors as indicated by repeatedly performing acts that are grounds for arrest

(2) deceitfulness, as indicated by repeated lying, use of aliases, or conning others for personal profit or pleasure

(3) impulsivity or failure to plan ahead

(4) irritability and aggressiveness, as indicated by repeated physical fights or assaults

(5) reckless disregard for safety of self or others

(6) consistent irresponsibility, as indicated by repeated failure to sustain consistent work behavior or honor financial obligations

(7) lack of remorse, as indicated by being indifferent to or rationalizing having hurt, mistreated, or stolen from another

B. The individual is at least age 18 years.

C. There is evidence of Conduct Disorder with onset before age 15 years.

D. The occurrence of antisocial behavior is not exclusively during the course of Schizophrenia or a Manic Episode.

Source: American Psychiatric Association; *Diagnostic and Statistical Manual of Mental Disorders,* Fourth Edition. Washington, DC, American Psychiatric Association, 1994.

stealing, vandalism, aggressiveness, and even physical cruelty. Ted Bundy, for example, stole cars to impress people. By age 18, when the diagnosis of antisocial personality disorder can officially be made, the antisocial conduct typically includes both crimes against property and assaults against persons. As discussed later, the severity of antisocial personality disorder tends to diminish after age 40.

The overall prevalence of antisocial personality disorder in the United States and other Western countries is about 3 to 4 percent, with men being diagnosed 3 to 4 times more frequently than women. Not surprisingly, the rate is much higher in prisons and jails.

Anxious/Fearful Personality Disorders

The *anxious/fearful* personality disorders include avoidant, obsessive-compulsive, and dependent personality disorders. Table 12.4 on page 424 summarizes the theoretical relationship of these disorders to Big Five dimensions. Empirical research has confirmed most of these predictions. The one exception is that most studies have not found heightened conscientiousness to typify obsessive-compulsive personality disorder, as has been predicted.

Avoidant Personality Disorder. The main characteristics of **avoidant personality disorder** are constant feelings of inadequacy and ineptitude, especially in social situations. Persons with this disorder are afraid of being embarrassed, criticized, or ridiculed by others, and, consequently, they avoid social situations whenever possible. If forced into a social encounter, they are usually very inhibited, afraid at every step of making a mistake that will bring the rejection they are sure is forthcoming. They seek constant reassurance that others will like them and tend to avoid occupations requiring social interaction. However, unlike persons with schizoid personality disorder, who appear indifferent to social interaction, those with avoidant personality disorder long for affection and social acceptance and are distressed by its absence.

People with avoidant personality disorder are inhibited and overly cautious. Afraid that new situations will "throw them a curve" for which they are not prepared, avoidant personalities tend to follow a set routine and try to stay out of situations in which they would be called on to act spontaneously. They are unusually timid, often from childhood on (Windle & Windle, 1993). As substitutes for the real interpersonal contacts they crave but avoid, they may often fantasize about "perfect" relationships that

TABLE 12.4   The Anxious/Fearful Cluster of Personality Disorders

DSM-IV category	Primary characteristics	Description based on Big Five model
Avoidant	Always feels inadequate, needs constant reassurance; timid and cautious	High neuroticism and low extraversion
Dependent	Requires excessive advice and guidance; very submissive; low self-esteem	High neuroticism and high agreeableness
Obsessive-compulsive	Overly conscientious, inhibited, and perfectionistic; preoccupied with staying controlled	High neuroticism, low extraversion, low agreeableness, and high conscientiousness*

*Note: High conscientiousness has not been found to correlate consistently with obsessive-compulsive personality disorder. This may be due to differences in the way researchers measure conscientiousness, because it is difficult to conceive of an obsessive-compulsive personality that does not reflect extreme conscientiousness.

Source: Costa & McCrae (1990); Soldz et al. (1993); Trull (1992); Wiggins & Pincus (1989).

await them in the future. Leon, who came to a clinic complaining of feeling "down" and lonely, is an example of avoidant personality disorder.

*L*eon reveals that he cannot ever remember feeling comfortable socially. Even before kindergarten, if he were asked to speak in front of a group of his parents' friends, his mind would "go blank." He felt overwhelming anxiety at children's social functions, such as birthday parties, which he either avoided or, if he went, attended in total silence. He could answer questions in class only if he wrote down the answers in advance. Even then, he frequently mumbled and couldn't get the answer out . . . .

As he grew up, Leon had a couple of neighborhood playmates, but he never had a best friend. His school grades were good, but suffered when oral classroom participation was expected. As a teenager, he was terrified of girls, and to this day has never gone on a date or even asked a girl for a date . . . .

Leon attended college and did well for a while, then dropped out as his grades slipped. He remained self-conscious and terrified of meeting strangers. He had trouble finding a job because he was unable to answer questions in interviews. . . . He has no friends and avoids all invitations to socialize with coworkers. (Spitzer et al., 1994, pp. 124–125)

Avoidant personality disorder probably affects about 1 percent of the general U.S. population (Maier et al., 1992). It is often difficult to distinguish between avoidant personality disorder and social phobia, a common anxiety disorder discussed in Chapter 6 (Herbert, Hope, & Bellack, 1992).

Dependent Personality Disorder. People with **dependent personality disorder** are unable to make decisions without exorbitant amounts of advice and reassurance. Rather than shunning social contact as is the case with avoidant personality disorder, they cling to others and make excessive self-sacrifices to win the smallest signs of appreciation. Typically, they prefer to have others make decisions for them about where to live, what job to seek, and how to dress and act. Dependent personalities typically behave in a submissive, ingratiating manner to win affection. They dread being alone, and, although their interpersonal strategies may win some temporary friendships, their excessive dependency eventually becomes annoying and ends up driving people away. The chronic submissiveness of the dependent personality was well-described in the lyrics of an American Breed rock song of the 1960s: "Bend Me, Shape Me."

Obviously, people with dependent personality disorder have little self-confidence, and their constant need to lean on others only confirms their sense of being incapable of functioning successfully on their own. Although precise prevalence figures are unknown, a reasonable estimate would be that somewhere between 2 and 7 percent of the U.S. population suffer from this disorder (Weissman, 1993). Dependent personality disorder is common in mental health clinics, and, in these settings, it is diagnosed slightly more often in women, a not-too-surprising finding in light of the fact that women are treated more often in formal clinical settings and that, in some cultures, many women are encouraged to depend on others (usually men) to make major decisions for them.

Obsessive-Compulsive Personality Disorder.

People with **obsessive-compulsive personality disorder** are preoccupied with rules, details, and organization in many aspects of life. They tenaciously manage their lives by always trying to make them predictable and safe. Rigidly committed to the minutiae of life, obsessive-compulsive personalities tend to lack a larger perspective on most activities; they lose sight of the forest because they are so focused on the individual trees. They often hoard worthless possessions, apparently out of a conviction that "some day I might need them." This pack-rat mentality is also reflected in stinginess with money. People tend to refer disdainfully to these individuals as "bean-counters," "nit-pickers," or "worrywarts."

Indeed, obsessive-compulsive personalities are so stubbornly perfectionistic about every task that they may make little or no progress on them, or they take so long at them that they miss important deadlines. At the same time, they are unwilling to delegate tasks to others for fear that the work won't be done to their standards. In such individuals, conscientiousness becomes so extreme as to be a liability. For all their concern about doing things perfectly, most obsessive-compulsive personalities are ineffective and indecisive, often worrying themselves into mediocre performance.

Obsessive-compulsive personalities also tend to be inflexible about moral and ethical matters and, in personal and romantic relationships, to be controlling and aloof, as if emotional spontaneity were too threatening to tolerate. Consequently, they appear cold and insensitive. Describing a character who displayed an obsessive-compulsive personality in "The Man in the Case," playwright Anton Chekov wrote that the man "displayed a constant and insurmountable impulse to wrap himself in a covering, to make himself, so to speak, a case which would isolate and protect himself from external influences."

Estimates of the overall prevalence of obsessive-compulsive personality disorder converge on approximately 2 percent in the United States (Weissman, 1993). It is diagnosed about twice as often in men as in women.

Obsessive-compulsive personality disorder should be distinguished from *obsessive-compulsive disorder*, which was discussed in Chapter 6. Obsessive-compulsive personality disorder is a chronic lifestyle governed by worried busyness, obstinacy, and rigid habits. However, it lacks the specific obsessive thoughts and compulsive rituals that are hallmarks of obsessive-compulsive disorder.

In Review

As diagnosed in the DSM-IV, the ten basic personality disorders are classified under three general clusters:

- paranoid, schizoid, and schizotypal personality disorders involve behavior patterns that appear odd or eccentric;
- histrionic, narcissistic, borderline, and antisocial personality disorders involve behavior that is dramatic, emotionally unstable, or erratic; and
- avoidant, dependent, and obsessive-compulsive personality disorders involve behavior that is anxious and fearful.

Causes of Personality Disorders

Given that extreme, rigid personality traits are the central characteristics of personality disorders, theories of personality development should suggest some causes of these disorders. In this section, we will first consider what theories of personality reveal about personality disorders in general. Then we will examine specific theories about the causes of the two most-studied disorders: borderline and antisocial personality disorders.

Theoretical Perspectives on Personality Disorders

People develop their unique combinations of personality traits through the interaction of inherited tendencies with the experiences they have while adapting to the environmental demands of a particular culture. Although personality does not become fixed at any particular age, most people's main traits develop during childhood and are relatively stable by adolescence or young adulthood. In adulthood, individual qualities become consistent and may not change much across many years (McCrae & Costa, 1994). In particular, extroversion and neuroticism, two traits that are implicated in several personality disorders, remain stable in adulthood.

No one type of personality is best or healthiest. The important question is how well an individual's style fits with environments in which that person most often functions, and how adaptive and flexible the person is in dealing with changing environmental demands. Theories about the causes of personality disorders attempt to explain how people develop styles that do not fit the environment and why those styles are rigidly maintained in spite of the problems they cause. Any general theory of personality could be extended to become a theory of personality disorders, but a few theoretical perspectives dominate the field. Here, we will examine what genetic and psychological theories suggest about the causes of personality disorders.

Genetics and Personality Differences. How important are inherited characteristics in determining personality? Research on identical and nonidentical twins reared apart or together offers a powerful tool for resolving questions about the relative importance of genetic and environmental influence on personality. For example, the Minnesota Study of Twins Reared Apart (Bouchard, 1984; Tellegen et al., 1988) compared 44 identical twin pairs reared apart, 217 identical pairs reared together, 27 nonidentical pairs reared apart, and 114 nonidentical pairs reared together. On average, twins reared apart had been separated in the first year of life and remained separate for an average of more than 30 years. The subjects in the study filled out the Multidimensional Personality Questionnaire, a self-report measure of several personality traits.

Whether identical twins had been reared together or apart had little effect on the similarity of their personalities as measured by this questionnaire. However, identical twins reared apart showed much greater within-pair similarity than did nonidentical twins raised together (see Table 12.5).

Generally, studies that have compared the within-pair personality similarities of identical and nonidentical twin pairs show that an average of about 50 percent of the difference in most personality characteristics is due to genetic influence (McCartney, Harris, & Bernieri, 1990). Environmental circumstances unique to each person (called the *nonshared environment*) appear to be less important

TABLE 12.5   Heritability: Correlations from the Minnesota Twin Study

Scale	Monozygotic twin pairs reared apart (n = 44)	Dizygotic twin pairs reared apart (n = 27)	Monozygotic twin pairs reared together (n = 217)	Dizygotic twin pairs reared together (n = 114)
Well-being	.48	.18	.58	.23
Social potency	.56	.27	.65	.08
Achievement	.36	.07	.51	.13
Social closeness	.29	.30	.57	.24
Stress reaction	.61	.27	.52	.24
Alienation	.48	.18	.55	.38
Aggression	.46	.06	.43	.14
Control	.50	.03	.41	−.06
Harm avoidance	.49	.24	.55	.17
Traditionalism	.53	.39	.50	.47
Absorption	.61	.21	.49	.41
Median correlation	.49	.21	.52	.23

Source: Tellegen et al., 1988.

than genetics in determining personality differences but are considerably more important than the negligible influence of the *shared environment,* which consists of environmental factors shared by offspring within the same family. In other words, the influence of parents' income or education, which is shared by all the children in a family, has less overall impact on personality traits than do factors such as birth order or choice of friends, which are different for each child in a family.

Genetics and Personality Disorders. Data such as these point to a possible role for genetic causes of personality disorders (Nigg & Goldsmith, 1994), but can genetic factors account for these disorders? Are some people genetically predisposed to develop personality disorders associated with extreme versions of certain traits? Are any particular traits more heavily influenced by genetics than others?

For most personality disorders, these questions are difficult to answer because few family, twin, or adoption studies have been published that would shed light on a possible genetic basis for a given disorder (Dahl, 1993). Looking first at the odd/eccentric cluster of personality disorders, we find evidence that the rates of both paranoid and schizoid personality disorders are slightly higher among relatives of individuals diagnosed with schizophrenia than they are among normal controls (Dahl, 1993), but no direct evidence of a genetic risk for either of these two disorders has yet been clearly established. The data suggesting a genetic contribution to schizotypal personality disorder are stronger (Nigg & Goldsmith, 1994). First, most studies indicate that schizotypal personality disorder is more common among relatives of individuals diagnosed with schizophrenia than among the population in general (Dahl, 1993). This finding is consistent with the view discussed in Chapter 10—that some kind of *schizotype* or schizophrenic-like personality constitutes an inherited vulnerability for developing schizophrenia. Second, one twin study found a 33 percent concordance rate of schizotypal personality disorder for identical twins compared with a 4 percent concordance rate for nonidentical twins (Torgersen, 1984). This study has been criticized for several methodological problems, however, so there is some question about the strength of a genetic basis for schizotypal personalities.

For the cluster of dramatic/emotional/erratic personality disorders, the data about genetic influence are mixed. Numerous studies support the role of genetics in antisocial personality disorder. The evidence for a genetic role in borderline, narcissistic, or histrionic personality disorders is not strong.

Very little research has been conducted on the anxious/fearful cluster of personality disorders. What evidence does exist has not supported a genetic vulnerability for these disorders, with the exception of obsessive-compulsive personality disorder, for which some studies suggest a possible genetic influence (Nigg & Goldsmith, 1994).

Psychodynamic Theories of Personality Disorders. Even if we assume that genetics play some role in governing personality traits, the extreme and rigid forms that these traits assume in personality disorders must be shaped by other substantial developmental influences. Freud proposed that problems of personality—his term was "character"—arose from fixations during passage through psychosexual stages of development. Recall that these stages—oral, anal, and phallic—are said to involve a concentration of energy and anxiety on certain areas of the body. As an example, according to traditional Freudian theory, fixation during the anal stage of development was thought to occur when parents were overly strict or unusually permissive in toilet training a child. As adults, some anal characters become overly controlled, highly organized, stingy, and obstinate. These behaviors are similar to the perfectionistic and inflexible patterns of obsessive-compulsive personality disorder. A similar line of reasoning links fixated needs during the oral stage with the excessive concern for nurturance and interpersonal closeness found in dependent personality disorder. But this intriguing account of personality disorders has received little research support, so relatively few clinicians see traditional psychoanalysis as a viable explanation of personality disorders.

More recent psychodynamic formulations, particularly those arising from object relations theories, have received better empirical support (Eagle, 1984). Recall from Chapter 1 that object relations theorists believe that the nature and quality of early attachments between infants and their caregivers largely determine children's expectations about how other people will respond to them. These expectations, in turn, color all other close relationships and help determine a person's strongest needs and vulnerabilities. These needs and vulnerabilities often form the core of personality disorders. Because these expectations are established so early, often before a child has learned to speak, they are very resistant to change, especially through verbal means such as psychotherapy. According to object relations theory, when these expectations become rigid and extreme, the person becomes locked into the troubling behavior patterns that we know as personality disorders.

Interpersonal Learning Theories. If genetics and early relationships cannot by themselves explain personality differences, what other factors are involved? According to interpersonal theorists, most personality traits involve interpersonal themes, such as how outgoing people are, how trusting or dependent they tend to be, how comfortable they feel with different types of people, and how much empathy or warmth they show to others. Differences in these traits may have a genetic basis, and they may also be associated with varying amounts of security in a child's early object relations. But once traits are established, they are solidified into enduring personality patterns as a result of interpersonal learning experiences.

As described in Chapter 1, Harry Stack Sullivan's interpersonal theory of personality suggests that people desire to be with others who reinforce their typical ways of behaving. According to this view, personalities are shaped by the interpersonal experiences that people prefer and seek out. Personality disorders result when an individual relies too heavily on extreme and maladaptive behaviors toward others. How might this happen?

Consider again Leary's circular arrangement of interpersonal styles (shown in Figure 12.2 on page 415). It suggests that segments adjacent to each other are positively correlated, while those that fall on opposite sides of the circle are negatively correlated. Furthermore, Leary's model predicts that encounters between individuals with various interpersonal styles will follow a rule of *complementarity;* the behaviors of two interacting parties should confirm each other's typical personality styles. With respect to dominance, complementarity is *reciprocal;* dominant behavior by one person invites or "pulls for" submissive behavior from another and vice versa. Along the love/hate dimension, complementarity takes the form of *correspondence;* friendliness pulls for friendliness while hostility brings hostility in return. Empirical support for these predictions is mixed; correspondence in nurturance has been supported fairly well, but reciprocity in dominance is less consistently seen (Wiggins & Pincus, 1992). For people who tend toward personality disorders, the effect of complementarity is to entrench them even further in their problematic styles. Their rigid behavior tends to perpetuate itself by evoking behaviors from others that are reinforcing.

Evolutionary Theory. Theodore Millon (1990) has proposed a theory that views personality differences in terms of their evolutionary significance. According to Millon, three fundamental *polarities* underlie the biological structures and psychological processes that constitute human personality. Differences in a person's position along each of these polarities define a unique fit between personality and the demands of the environment. Good fits are adaptive and promote survival; bad fits lead to strain and maladjustment.

The first of these polarities involves the *minimization of pain and the maximization of pleasure.* This polarity involves two basic aims of life: to enhance life through the pursuit of pleasurable activities and to preserve life by protecting against danger. The degrees to which a person pursues pleasure and avoids pain are separate bipolar dimensions; a person can be high or low on either or both. Thus, a person who acts to maximize pleasure may or may not also seek to minimize pain.

The second fundamental polarity is adapting to environmental demands through *passive accommodation or active modification.* Passive accommodation requires little initiative; one can "fit in" by quietly accepting and adjusting to environmental changes. Active modification demands more direct, proactive attempts to make the environment fit an individual's needs. These two poles are mutually exclusive; the more a person tends to use one strategy, the less of the other there is.

The third polarity involves the degree to which a person is oriented toward *advancing the self and/ or caring for others.* As in the first polarity, a person can be high or low on either or both. A major investment in advancing the self is often associated with traditional notions of masculinity, while an orientation toward nurturing others is viewed as a traditional characteristic of femininity.

How do these polarities relate to personality disorders? Millon believes that, as a result of genetic influences, psychodynamics, and learning histories, some people develop deficiencies, imbalances, or conflicts in one or more of the three polarities. When this happens, troubled personalities result, several of which resemble traditional DSM-IV Axis II categories.

For example, persons displaying schizoid personality disorder are deficient in their capacity to feel either pleasure or pain, and they maintain a passively detached style toward most events. They are neither pulled toward the positive nor repelled by the negative. Their overall course is to drift.

Dependent personalities, by contrast, are oriented almost exclusively toward others as a means of producing pleasure and avoiding pain. They passively wait for others to take care of them and believe the best way to secure this guidance is to always assume a submissive role with others.

At the other end of these polarities are the antisocial personalities who actively pursue independence throughout life. They crave autonomy and power for themselves, often at others' expense.

Each of these theories is concerned with explaining the ways in which personality traits, in general, become fixed and maladaptive. These viewpoints do not focus on particular disorders. In the next two sections, we will examine theories and research concerned with specific causes of the two most-studied personality disorders—borderline personality disorder and antisocial personality disorder.

Causes of Borderline Personality Disorder

Theories about the causes of borderline personality disorder have emphasized biological contributions, psychoanalytic factors, and early childhood neglect and abuse. These influences may operate as separate pathways leading to borderline personality disorder or they may interact to produce the condition.

Biological Contributions. There seems to be a plausible sequence leading from neurological impairments to borderline personality disorder. Neurologically impaired children often show hyperactivity, poor attention, unstable moods, fussiness, and impulsivity that are soon translated into interpersonal problems, academic difficulties, and troubles with parents. These problems, in turn, may ultimately lead to the poorly regulated emotions, impulsive behavior, and identity confusion that typify borderline personality disorder.

Does this sequence in fact occur? A few empirical studies have found an association between early organic brain problems and adult borderline personality disorder (Andrulonis et al., 1981). However, many borderlines have no history of neurological problems, so if organic deficits are a significant cause, they may account for only one subtype of the disorder.

One other clue to a possible biological influence on borderline personality disorder is the discovery of a high prevalence of affective disorders among relatives of individuals diagnosed as borderlines (Dahl, 1993). Some clinicians believe this increased prevalence indicates a basic similarity between borderline personality disorder and affective disturbances and a possible shared genetic diathesis for these disorders. Of course, the mere fact that two disorders tend to co-occur does not necessarily mean they are genetically related. As indicated earlier, a genetic risk for borderline personality disorder has not been clearly confirmed.

Psychodynamic Factors. Another plausible progression from early childhood problems to borderline personality is suggested by various psychodynamic theorists. They argue that the seeds of the disorder are sown in the first 2 years of life when excessively aggressive impulses in the child or inadequacies in parenting impair the child's ability to form a stable self-identity. More particularly, many object-relations-oriented theorists believe that borderline personalities are the result of a lack of bonding between infants and primary caregivers. In the absence of a bond that satisfies infants' inherent need for soothing closeness and encourages their growing need for independence and autonomy, they are trapped in a crossfire of emotional needs. The desire for closeness brings fears of being engulfed by an overly involved caregiver, while the desire for independence is undercut by fears of abandonment. The result is that neither a secure sense of self nor an abiding trust in others ever develops. Without a stable self or a belief that relationships can be trusted to last, people are always on the lookout for any sign of rejection or criticism. As a result they typically feel disillusioned and desperate.

Although this theory is intuitively attractive, most empirical research on child development does not support the idea that early parent–child conflicts over dependence and independence lead to adult borderline pathology (Crowell et al., 1993). However, research does suggest a relationship between borderline personality disorder and the occurrence of mistreatment in the first several years of a child's life.

Early Childhood Trauma. Several researchers have focused recently on childhood neglect and abuse as causes of borderline personality disorder. Indeed, separation from parents as a result of death or divorce, physical and sexual abuse, and observation of domestic violence have all been identified as major culprits in borderline personality

Connections

Has childhood abuse been linked with other disorders? See Chapter 8, pp. 264–267, particularly the section on dissociative identity disorder.

disorder (Zanarini et al., 1989). Special attention has focused on the link between early abuse and borderline personality disorder, and several studies have found that as many as 80 percent of individuals diagnosed as borderlines suffered an early history of physical or sexual abuse (Crowell et al., 1993). However, this evidence comes largely from adult borderlines' reports of early traumatic experiences. The reliability and validity of these reports are unknown. Given the characteristics of those with severe personality disorders, clinicians should be skeptical of such reports and cautious in interpreting research based on them.

Causes of Antisocial Personality Disorder

The causes of antisocial personality disorder and repeated criminal conduct have been researched more extensively than those of any other personality disorder (e.g., Andrews & Bonta, 1994). As a result, clinicians now know quite a bit about the precursors of the disorder. For example, men who engage in repeated antisocial behavior tended in early childhood to be more hyperactive, physically clumsy and impulsive, and to have more trouble regulating their emotions than did their prosocial peers. They also had more learning disabilities and speech problems and were prone to break rules frequently both at home and at school. It is easy to see how this cluster of problems soon leads to conflicts with parents, peers, and teachers (Moffitt, 1993). Academic failures and early school dropout often follow as well. Some of these difficulties probably originate from disturbances in the child's nervous system, and this biological diathesis appears to set the stage for a long chain of behavioral and social adversities that ultimately leads to chronic antisocial behavior.

Biological Predispositions. Evidence from twin and adoption studies confirms that genetic factors contribute to the risk of antisocial personality disorder (Dahl, 1993; Nigg & Goldsmith, 1994). Adoption studies consistently show that adopted children whose biological parents were criminals are arrested more frequently for antisocial conduct than children adopted away from noncriminal parents (Mednick, Gabrielli, & Hutchings, 1987). These same studies show, however, that environmental factors are also important contributors to antisocial conduct. As a result, the adopted children who are at highest risk for chronic offending are those who were born and raised in criminal families.

How a genetic risk for psychopathy or chronic antisocial patterns translates into actual antisocial conduct remains unknown; however, some of the biological factors associated with antisocial personality disorder are presumed to be genetically transmitted. The biological factors that have received the greatest attention involve tendencies to be underaroused. This underarousal occurs both in central nervous system and autonomic nervous system functioning and has been related to any of several early precursors of antisocial personality disorder—difficult temperament and moodiness, attention deficits and hyperactivity, and oppositional-defiant and conduct disorders.

Indirect evidence suggests that portions of the cerebral cortex of some antisocial personalities may be slow to develop. Electroencephalographic (EEG) measures of central nervous system activity indicate that psychopaths have a higher rate of EEG abnormalities compared with normal controls; in particular, they are more likely to show low levels of high frequency brain waves and high levels of low frequency brain waves called *theta waves*. Theta waves are typical of the brain activity seen in children, but they usually decrease or disappear in adults. Based on findings such as these, Robert Hare (Hare & McPherson, 1984) suggested that psychopaths suffer from an "immature cortex" that makes it difficult for them to inhibit behavior. One possibility is that a defect in the left hemisphere of the brain impairs the ability of antisocial personalities to plan and regulate behavior carefully. A related idea is Herbert Quay's theory that antisocial personalities suffer chronically low levels of cortical arousal, and they therefore are constantly trying to find ways to "bump up" their arousal. According to Quay's (1965) *stimulation-seeking* theory, the thrill-seeking and disruptive behavior of the psychopath serves to increase sensory input and arousal to a desired level.

Basing their beliefs on the reliable finding that verbal IQ scores tend to be lower among chronic delinquents (e.g., Lynam et al., 1993), other experts have suggested that repeated antisocial conduct may be due to neuropsychological deficits that result in impaired language-based abilities and lower self-control skills (Moffitt & Lynam, 1994).

The other characteristic of antisocial personalities that may result from biological factors is their unusually low anxiety level (as measured by physiological variables such as heart rate or perspiration). They tend to be generally less physiologically aroused than other people, and they are less strongly affected by aversive stimuli such as social rejection or electric shocks (Lykken, 1957). As a result, antisocial per-

A Talk with Paul Costa

Dr. Paul T. Costa is Chief of the Laboratory on Personality and Cognition at the Gerontology Research Center of the National Institute on Aging. With Robert McCrae, he is the author of the leading measure of the Five Factor Model, the Revised NEO Personality Inventory. Dr. Costa is a highly influential scholar in the area of personality assessment and classification, particularly from the perspective of the Five Factor Model.

Personality Disorders

Q *Was it a good idea to assign the personality disorders to a separate axis in the DSM?*

A Originally, I think it was a good idea because it drew attention to the importance of personality in the understanding of mental disorders. Now, I think the Axis I versus Axis II distinction is arbitrary. All mental disorders, including those on Axis I, could probably be described better with a dimensional model.

Q *What about schizophrenia? Doesn't it justify a distinct category?*

A Not necessarily, but it might require us to consider an additional dimension of thought processing that would vary from organized and consensual to disorganized and autistic. The Five Factor Model claims that there are at least five basic dimensions that underlie human personality, but there may be more than five. Intelligence might be a sixth, and style of information processing, which is involved in schizophrenia, could be a seventh.

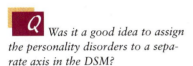

I think the Axis I versus Axis II distinction is arbitrary.

Q *Why do personality disorders tend to show such high levels of overlap or comorbidity?*

A From the perspective of the Five Factor Model, the co-occurrence of personality disorders is not surprising. A person who scores at the extremes of more than one of the five basic dimensions is likely to receive multiple diagnoses, and the more extremes a person shows, the more likely that person is to come to the attention of mental health professionals and be diagnosed. For example, a person who is extremely low on the dimension of agreeableness might be diagnosed as antisocial and/or narcissistic; if that person is also extroverted, (s)he might also meet the criteria for histrionic personality disorder. We get all these multiple diagnoses whenever we try to impose categorical descriptions on five personality dimensions that can assume many different patterns.

Q *Which of the five basic personality dimensions are we most able to change?*

A Neuroticism is probably the most modifiable through deliberate interventions. We have a lot of treatments—drugs and behavioral techniques, for example—for changing neurotic behavior. Conscientiousness is another dimension that can be trained and altered; in fact, that is a major function of schools and the workplace. Openness is fairly hard to change, as are certain temperamental and activity components of extroversion.

Q *How much can a person change his or her basic personality dimensions?*

A Well, we don't really know the answer to that fundamental question yet. What we do know is that just because basic personality dimensions are fairly stable after age 30 does not mean that traits are automatically fixed and unchangeable. We are still in a primitive stage of devising interventions that could have a major impact on most traits. I think the answer to this question depends on our developing and studying interventions designed to change one dimension that are well matched to the rest of a person's basic traits. So, if we want to increase the agreeableness of an abusive father, we need to consider his other basic traits in designing the best intervention. If he is low on extroversion, a group treatment won't work well. On the other hand, if he is highly conscientious, a 12-step program based on a formal structure and public promises might be much more successful.

431

sonalities appear to have difficulty learning to in-hibit their behavior in response to cues that signal punishment or that cause others to feel anxious. By contrast, antisocial individuals do learn how to avoid other aversive stimuli that may be more relevant to them, such as the loss of money, just as well as any-one else (Schmauk, 1970). In fact, they may be par-ticularly quick to escape the negative consequences of their acts by fleeing the scenes of crimes, lying about their behavior, or blaming it on someone else. Other researchers have suggested that antisocial per-sonalities have a heightened sensitivity to rewards that makes it difficult for them to inhibit behavior (Gorenstein & Newman, 1980).

Taken together, these findings paint a picture of the antisocial personality as someone who is impul-sive while being adroit at wriggling out of whatever trouble the disinhibited behavior causes. Add to these factors an enhanced attraction to rewards and ex-citement, and there exist the underpinnings of sev-eral well-known features of this disorder, including impulsivity, callousness, and exploitiveness.

It has been suggested that low autonomic arousal (perhaps in combination with some kind of cortical defect) intensifies the antisocial person's high need for stimulation, as hypothesized by Quay. In fact, one classic study that followed up on psychopaths' inability to learn to avoid aversive shocks found that, when psychopaths are injected with adrenaline in order to bring their level of arousal to a higher level, they are able to learn to avoid electric shocks just as efficiently as normal subjects (Schachter & Latané, 1964).

Chronic underarousal has also been employed as an explanation for antisocial personalties' relative immunity to the social cues that help govern be-havior in other people. For example, Hans Eysenck (1964) proposed that these individuals are bio-logically predisposed to have difficulty developing classically conditioned fear responses to emotional stimuli and, consequently, are unable to learn from punishment or to delay gratification. In Eysenck's theory, the development of a conscience depends on the ability to learn fear and avoidance responses through classical conditioning. If antisocial person-alities are constitutionally less able to learn fear re-sponses, they will not be able to develop normal in-ternal restraints on behavior.

Imagine that a young boy is planning to steal food from a grocery store. If this boy had been caught and punished for similar transgressions in the past, his contemplated theft should lead to fear (signalled by physiological reactions such as sweaty palms or a racing heart) that he will be punished for this act as

well. The emotion of fear should cause the boy to inhibit the theft on his own. Once he decides not to steal, the boy will be reinforced by the reduc-tion in fear that follows, and gradually he will learn that stealing is not worth the fear it engenders. But what if that lesson is not learned, either because his parents have not monitored his behavior close-ly enough or because, even when he is punished, he has a biological tendency to not experience strong fear?

Under these circumstances, the boy will not learn the lessons that fear imparts. Without such restraints, the boy will feel no particular need to engage in self-control or to inhibit antisocial behavior; instead, he will charge ahead with whatever behavior happens to please him at the moment, without considering whether it is appropriate or might hurt someone else.

Family and Childrearing Practices. Historically, fami-lies have been the major social institution for teach-ing conventional moral standards of conduct. Thus, it is not surprising that family factors have been em-phasized in several theoretical accounts of antisocial personality disorder. An early example was provided by Arnold Buss (1966) who claimed that parents who are cold and detached or who are inconsistent and lax in their discipline foster antisocial behavior in their children. These children, said Buss, fail to learn to control their impulsive behavior, and this early deficit in impulse control eventually results in more serious behavioral, academic, and social problems as the child grows older.

Several specific family variables have been con-sistently associated with antisocial behavior (Loeber, 1990; Loeber & Stouthamer-Loeber, 1986; McCord, 1979; Robins, 1966), including:

1. A history of parental criminality (Loeber & Dishion, 1983). Not only does parental criminality, especially by fathers, provide a role model for youth-ful antisocial conduct, it is also likely to disrupt fam-ily stability and limit family resources.

2. Chronic parental uninvolvement, erratic dis-cipline, physical abuse, and poor supervision of chil-dren (Patterson, 1986). Any of these factors will make it more difficult for a child to learn the basic rules of society and to feel committed to obeying these rules. In addition, abusive relationships serve to teach the child that physical violence is an ac-ceptable means of influencing others.

3. Early loss of a parent. When the loss of a parent is due to a bitter divorce or angry separation it can have a more traumatic impact on children than when the loss is due to parental death. In other words, loss *coupled with emotional conflict* is more damaging than loss alone.

4. A tradition of social and health handicaps in the family. Antisocial personality disorder is diagnosed more frequently in lower SES groups (Patterson, 1996), perhaps because several correlates of lower SES such as poverty, educational underattainment, and higher rates of physical illness cause youngsters to feel alienated or hostile toward traditional rules and social expectations.

5. Exposure to deviant peers (Elliott, Huizinga, & Ageton, 1985). Children who become habitually antisocial often learn some of this conduct from peer groups who model antisocial behavior and reinforce it by granting highest status to the most antisocial members of the group.

As summarized in Figure 12.4, when these family and social influences are combined with the biological and temperamental difficulties previously described, they substantially increase the risk of a youngster's developing the early precursors of anti-

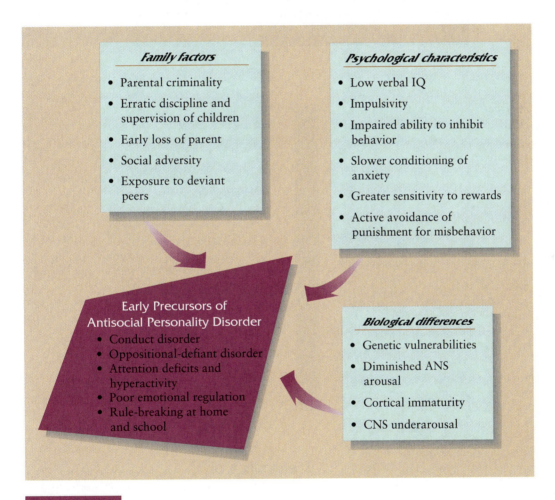

FIGURE 12.4

Biological, Psychological, and Family Contributions to Early Precursors of Antisocial Personality Disorder

Biological differences, psychological characteristics, and family factors often interact to produce a set of childhood problems involving a difficult temperament, aggressive behavior, and childhood behavior disorders. These early precursors often then intensify and harden into antisocial personality disorder.

Chronic antisocial behavior has been linked to a combination of family factors that lessen parents' ability to monitor and effectively discipline their children. Early difficulties by parents in controlling aggressive behavior by their children are predictive of later, more serious problems.

social personality disorder (Nietzel, Hasemann, & Lynam, 1997). Once any of the early precursors are in place, a child is at risk for gradually developing a chronically antisocial pattern of life.

In Review

The major theoretical explanations of extreme, rigid personality traits that make up personality disorders are that:

- genetic factors influence about 50 percent of the differences in major personality traits;
- early developmental disturbances in attachment relationships determine adult personality patterns;
- repeated interpersonal learning experiences solidify personality traits into enduring personality patterns; and
- deficiencies or conflicts in the pursuit of pleasure and avoidance of pain, active or passive adaptation to the environment, and advancing self or others produce disordered personalities.

Theories about the causes of borderline personality disorder have focused on:

- possible organic brain problems;
- genetic links to affective disorders;
- conflicts in early infant–caregiver relationships involving themes of independence and dependence; and
- early childhood trauma, especially in the form of physical or sexual abuse.

Theories about the causes of antisocial personality disorder have focused on interactions between:

- genetically influenced biological differences, including underarousal of the central nervous system, cortical immaturity, and low levels of autonomic arousal;
- psychological characteristics, including lower verbal IQ, impaired ability to inhibit behavior, impulsivity, slower conditioning of anxiety, and heightened sensitivity to rewards and the active avoidance of punishment for misbehavior; and
- family factors, including higher rates of parental criminality, erratic patterns of discipline, loss of a parent, family and socioeconomic hardships, and associations with deviant peers

Treatment of Personality Disorders

We have already mentioned that personality disorders are among the most difficult mental disorders to treat because of their association with other disorders and, especially, because of their status as a long-standing lifestyle. People often become comfortable with their personality disorders, just as many of us become comfortable with an old pair of jeans that may not look attractive to others. And just as we are unwilling to part with those jeans, many people with personality disorders are not motivated to seek treatment. Often, they must be coerced into it by friends or relatives, or even through legal means. Problems in treating personality disorders have increased interest in preventive efforts, but prevention of these disorders is also problematic, as discussed in the Prevention section on pages 436–437.

Ironically, most of the traditional forms of psychotherapy into which clients may be pushed are not well suited to their problems. Therapists have responded to the challenge of treating personality disorders by creating new variations on the standard approaches and by proposing specific treatment goals that are matched to specific personality disorders. For example, Heinz Kohut pioneered a therapeutic approach known as *self psychology* (Kohut, 1977) for treating narcissistic personality disorder. A key element of this approach is Kohut's belief that narcissists' parents failed to meet their normal needs for admiration and protection during infancy. As a result, the children developed incomplete selves and, in self-defense, came to harbor exaggerated beliefs about their own power and importance. The task for the therapist, says Kohut, is to provide the client with a relationship in which needs that were unmet during infancy can be recognized and even gratified; then the person can enjoy a more realistic and healthy sense of self-worth.

Special strategies have been proposed for other personality disorders also. A number of studies have documented that behavioral or cognitive-behavioral treatments can bring about substantial improvements for avoidant personality disorder. In general, these treatments have emphasized reducing clients' avoidance of social encounters through techniques normally used to treat social phobias, including systematic desensitization, gradual exposure to threatening situations, and training clients to develop improved social skills (Alden, 1989; Cappe & Alden, 1986). However, even these improvements leave most clients feeling far less than comfortable in social situations; many clients still report feeling lonely and fearful of interpersonal relationships (Alden, 1989).

Treatment of Borderline Personality Disorder

Borderline personality disorder presents a particularly difficult therapeutic challenge, partly because the clients' interpersonal problems intrude on the process of therapy. Borderline clients often idealize their therapists, only to become enraged at them later because of some disappointment for which they are held responsible. As a result, these clients vacillate between loving and hating their therapists. They also cross boundaries that most other clients honor, often intruding into the therapist's personal life or engaging in dramatic, even dangerous, behavior in an effort to gain extra attention. They will call the therapist in the middle of the night, complaining that they are too upset to sleep. Sometimes, in a crisis, they will show up at the therapist's home and demand to be seen immediately. It is no wonder that some therapists refuse to treat borderline cases, or limit the number they will see at any one time.

Still, specialized psychotherapy approaches for borderline personalities have been developed by interpersonal (Benjamin, 1993), analytic (Marziali & Munroe-Blum, 1987), and cognitive therapists (Beck et al., 1990). And because lithium, various antidepressants, and certain antipsychotic medications have shown some success in controlling the mood swings and erratic behaviors that borderlines often display (Coccaro, 1993; Soloff et al., 1989), therapists of varying theoretical persuasions often combine psychotherapy with drug treatment.

Psychodynamic therapy based on an object-relations model has been a particularly prominent form of treatment. Perhaps the most influential version of this approach is the *expressive psychotherapy* of Otto Kernberg (1984; Kernberg et al., 1989). With borderline clients, Kernberg concentrates on analyzing the *transference* that develops in therapy—the process through which a client transfers to the therapist strong feelings and attitudes that are tied to a significant person from the past. Rather than seeking to uncover childhood conflicts that shape the transference as Freud did, Kernberg focuses on how the borderline client distorts the relationship in the present. A prominent example of this distortion is what Kernberg calls *splitting*, in which the borderline client so exaggerates the negative and positive qualities of the therapist that he or she is unable to see that they are actually just different aspects of the same person. Instead, the client vacillates between seeing the therapist as either all good or all bad. Kernberg also structures treatment sessions and the client's day-to-day environment to help borderline clients maintain firmer controls over their erratic, and often aggressive, behavior.

However, research suggests that the most effective psychotherapy for borderline personality disorder is a form of cognitive-behavioral therapy first pioneered by Marsha Linehan known as **dialectical behavior therapy** or **DBT** (Linehan, 1993; Linehan & Kehrer, 1993). DBT is a comprehensive approach to helping borderlines gain better control of what

Connections

How do various types of psychoanalysts view transference? See Chapter 16, pp. 563–565.

Prevention   Can Personality Disorders Be Prevented?

Personality disorders are difficult to treat, but can they be prevented? Clinicians' answers to this question depend on their theoretical views of personality. Those who believe that genetics are decisive in governing personality traits hold little hope that personality disorders can be prevented to any significant degree. Clinicians who view personality as the combined result of genetic endowment, early childhood learning, and the contemporary influence of culture and society are more optimistic that some personality disturbances can be avoided. In the middle are clinicians who believe that most personality traits are fairly stable, but that changes in these traits, even at their extremes, are still possible.

Considering the personality disorder for which the most research is available—antisocial personality disorder—current knowledge of predisposing risks suggests several prevention goals. First, because some biological vulnerabilities to antisocial personality disorder can be caused by prenatal exposure to drugs or alcohol and by inadequate nutrition for infants, public health programs that improve the health of women during pregnancy and

that teach healthy childrearing practices are essential. Second, programs that treat hyperactivity and help parents and children learn how to control impulsive behavior are critical. Third, keeping children engaged in school and improving their ability to achieve academically is particularly important in the late elementary and middle school years.

Because conduct disorder is a known precursor of antisocial personality disorder, special attention has been given to developing interventions that reduce this problem. In Chapter 3, we reviewed several elements of the FAST Track Program, which was aimed at reducing conduct disorder. The goals of this program were to

1. keep children and their parents involved in and committed to school;
2. help children maintain or increase their levels of academic success;
3. teach children social and cognitive skills that help them make and keep friends;
4. help children learn how to regulate their emotions and control their behavior effectively; and

5. develop a trusting relationship with an adult mentor.

Another excellent example of a multicomponent program designed to prevent early antisocial conduct is the Montreal Longitudinal-Experimental Study (Tremblay et al., 1992, 1995). In this study, a group of kindergarten boys from inner-city, lower socioeconomic neighborhoods in Montreal, Quebec, were identified by their teachers as being at risk for later antisocial behavior because of the disruptive behavior they were already showing at school.

These boys were then randomly assigned to a preventive intervention or a control group. Boys in the control group were repeatedly observed at school, and their parents filled out questionnaires on their behavior over the years, but they received no systematic treatment. Boys in the prevention program received two types of interventions: (1) they were taught new social skills to use at school so they could improve their ability to make friends and solve different kinds of social conflicts, and (2) their parents were trained in more effective child discipline and behavior management practices

Linehan believes is their core problem—namely, difficulty in regulating their emotions and the consequent development of an incoherent self-image. Applying a diathesis–stress model, Linehan sees borderline personality disorder arising when children with emotionally unstable temperaments are raised in *invalidating environments* in which almost all emotions are tightly controlled, ignored, punished, or trivialized. The result is that a person never learns to cope with any intense emotions.

Given that the causes of borderline disorders are multifaceted, Linehan's DBT focuses on several goals. Initially, DBT helps clients develop basic skills in containing erratic behaviors. Clients are taught how to reduce their suicidal preoccupations and gestures, their substance abuse and other high-risk behaviors, as they gradually develop a greater tolerance for painful emotions. After these containment goals have been reached, the therapist helps the client confront traumatizing experiences (such as physical or sexual

using Gerald Patterson's model of parent training, described in Chapter 3. The preventive intervention lasted for 2 years.

The long-term impact of the intervention has now been measured in terms of the boys' adjustment up to age 15, a time when juveniles are at high risk for delinquency. Compared with control group boys, a significantly greater percentage of boys in the prevention program were in an age-appropriate classroom up to the end of elementary school. However, this difference disappeared once the boys entered high school. By age 15, only 40 percent of all the boys in the study were in their age-appropriate grade at school. As the accompanying figure shows, throughout this same time period, the boys receiving the intervention reported significantly less delinquent behavior than the control boys, and their self-reported rates of delinquent behavior did not differ from that reported by a large sample of boys selected at random from other elementary schools in Quebec. However, clinicians must be cautious in judging the clinical significance of this difference. Official court records did not reveal any signifi-

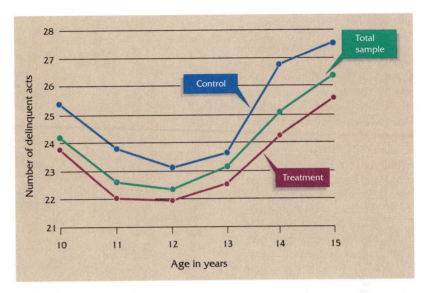

Effects of an Early Prevention Program on Self-Reported Delinquency

At-risk boys who participated in a treatment-prevention program during elementary school reported significantly less delinquent behavior 1 to 6 years later than boys in a control group. Self-reported delinquency did not differ significantly for the boys in the intervention compared to a random sample of peers.

cant advantage for the intervention boys, who, like all youths in the sample, tended to increase their rate of delinquent acts through their early teen years. Perhaps the improvements could

have been more effectively maintained if the boys had received periodic booster treatments during their middle school and high school years.

abuse) that took place in their invalidating environment. This phase of treatment concentrates on recalling memories of past trauma, eliminating self-blame associated with these traumas, reducing post-traumatic stress symptoms, and resolving questions of whom to blame for the trauma (Linehan & Kehrer, 1993).

By consistently helping borderline clients see that almost all events can be looked at from different perspectives, the dialectical therapist tries to en-

courage them to see the world in a more integrated or balanced way. A dialectical attitude by the therapist also balances the goals of accepting clients as they currently are while seeking to promote change in their behavior and thinking.

In comparison with other treatment approaches, DBT has been shown to be associated with better overall adjustment up to 1 year after treatment (Linehan et al., 1991; Linehan, Tutek, & Heard, 1992). Nonetheless, the treatment is intense, it may take

Controversy

Do Antisocial Personalities Burn Out?

Like other personality disorders, antisocial personality disorder tends to persist across the lifespan, but there is evidence that chronic antisocial conduct does decrease a bit with age. In community surveys, the prevalence of antisocial personality disorder is significantly lower among persons over age 45 than among younger individuals (Regier et al., 1988). Furthermore, psychopathic criminals appear to become less involved in overt criminal conduct after they reach age 40 (Hare et al., 1988). Recognition of this burnout process has lead to the only partly facetious claim that the best way to treat antisocial personalities is to help them get older.

Does antisocial personality disorder really burn out, and if so, why? Cross-sectional epidemiological studies showing an age-related decline in antisocial personality disorder does not necessarily prove that burnout exists. The prevalence of the disorder could be lower in older samples because, as antisocial personalities are imprisoned, they are gradually removed from community populations. Another possibility is that researchers might be less likely to diagnose the disorder in older persons because they expect it to become less common with age, a diagnostic bias that could distort the findings.

The best way to study claims of burnout is with a longitudinal design in which offenders are followed over time to determine whether their levels of criminal conduct change as they age. Such a study has been conducted by Robert Hare and his associates (Hare et al., 1988). They examined the conviction rates of 35 psychopathic criminals and 46 nonpsychopathic criminals every 5 years as these men aged from 16 to 45. As the figure shows,

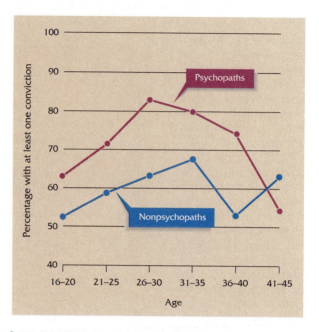

Burnout in Antisocial Personality Disorder

After the age of 40, psychopathic criminals showed a sharp drop in their rate of conviction for crimes. This decline has been interpreted as evidence that antisocial personality disorder tends to burn out with age.

Source: Hare et al., 1988.

the rate of criminal activity declined sharply after the psychopaths reached age 40; crime rates did not decrease for the nonpsychopaths.

Did the basic personality of these psychopaths change or did they just become more adept at dealing with their environments in general and law enforcement, in particular? A second study (Harpur & Hare, 1994) suggests that, although overt antisocial behavior decreases with age, psychopaths' core personality traits of callousness, manipulativeness, and deficient empathy do not decline with age. They remain as sneaky and cold-hearted as ever.

Thinking Critically

The illustration above shows that the rate of convictions increased dramatically between adolescence and age 30 and that more than half of the psychopaths continued to be convicted for crimes even after they turned 40.

- What implications do these patterns have for the concept of burnout?

- What does it say about the process of burnout to find, as the second study did, that only overt antisocial behavior declined with age?

years, and it is not effective for all clients (Linehan & Kehrer, 1993).

Treatment of Antisocial Personality Disorder

Clinicians have suggested several guidelines for treating antisocial personalities: treatment should be in a controlled environment, preferably a residential center; treatment staff must maintain strict limits on clients' antisocial behavior; antisocial personalities must be taught to substitute less deviant means of gaining stimulation and to value cooperation as a basic moral principle (Meyer, 1993). However, even as clinicians suggest these strategies, they also recognize that there are no data supporting the long-

term effectiveness of psychological interventions for antisocial personality disorder.

Antisocial personality disorder is so difficult to alter that most clinicians regard it as essentially untreatable. Persons displaying APD are seldom motivated to change (they are typically in treatment only through legal coercion), and they find it difficult to trust or have genuine rapport with a therapist unless it is part of a manipulation for personal gain (such as release from jail). Indeed, no form of psychotherapy has proved useful in treating APD, nor have drugs or other biological treatments proved to be any better.

Fortunately, the severity of APD tends to decline somewhat after about age 40, even without treatment. Why this phenomenon, termed *burnout*, occurs is not yet known, as discussed in the Controversy section on the opposite page.

Revisiting the Case of Ted Bundy

*I*n an interview shortly before he was executed on January 24, 1989, Ted Bundy expressed remorse for his crimes and blamed them on his addiction to violent pornography. However, most mental health professionals saw Bundy's statements as just one more example of the self-serving justifications that antisocial personalities are so adept at creating, in this case, to buy time and perhaps avoid the electric chair. Antisocial personalities usually feel no real remorse for their actions, and Bundy had never before hinted of an interest in pornography.

Fortunately, not all antisocial personalities are as dangerous as Ted Bundy, but they almost always victimize someone, whether by creating conflict in their families, taking credit for others' achievements, swindling people out of their money, or engaging in other forms of violent or nonviolent crime. Because these violations are chronic and there is no known effective treatment for antisocial personality disorder, incarceration remains the dominant strategy for constraining repeated antisocial conduct.

However, incarceration seems to be no more successful than rehabilitation for the antisocial personality or psychopath. One follow-up study of 231 Canadian male crim-

inals released from prison revealed that almost two thirds of those identified as psychopaths had violated the conditions of their release or had committed a new crime within 1 year. Three years after getting out of prison, 80 percent of the psychopathic criminals had their releases revoked (Hart, Kropp, & Hare, 1988). Regardless of whether the release was through parole (granted after one third of a prison sentence had been completed) or through mandatory supervision (granted after two thirds of a prison term had been served), the psychopathic criminals had significantly higher rates of failure than nonpsychopathic criminals. In short, data such as these suggest that imprisoning psychopaths is unlikely to rehabilitate them; however, it does punish them and offers society a period of protection from their crimes.

For other personality disorders, the prognosis is not quite so dim. Special forms of psychotherapy for avoidant personality disorder and borderline personality disorder have been developed, and initial research indicates that these behaviorally oriented therapies can lead to improvements. Nevertheless, effective treatments for most personality disorders remain more of a future hope than a present reality.

SUMMARY

Fateful Patterns: An Overview of Personality Disorders

According to the DSM-IV, a personality disorder is an enduring pattern of inner experience and behavior that deviates markedly from the expectations of a person's culture, is pervasive and inflexible, begins in childhood or adolescence, lasts a long time, and results in distress or impairment. Personality disorders are listed in ten categories on Axis II of the DSM, and they are often comorbid with one another or with Axis I disorders.

In contrast to the DSM-IV's categorical approach, many clinicians argue that personality disorders can be more thoroughly described and understood as extremes of the basic traits of human personality. The Big Five traits and the axes of the Interpersonal Circle are two-dimensional systems that have been used to describe personality disorders.

Types of Personality Disorders

DSM-IV groups the ten personality disorders into three clusters, based on the similarity of their major symptoms: an odd, eccentric group (paranoid, schizoid, and schizotypal personality disorders); a dramatic/emotional/erratic group (antisocial, borderline, histrionic, and narcissistic personality disorders); and an anxious/fearful group (avoidant, dependent, and obsessive-compulsive personality disorder).

Causes of Personality Disorders

Theories of personality disorders tend to emphasize genetic predispositions, early childhood conflicts and strong emotional experiences, the learning of stable interpersonal patterns of behavior, and interactions among these variables that produce rigid, dysfunctional personality patterns. The suspected causes of borderline personality disorder include brain impairments, genetic ties to affective disorders, infant–caregiver conflicts over dependence and independence, and early childhood sexual or physical abuse. The suspected causes of antisocial personality disorder include biological differences involving underarousal of the central and autonomic nervous systems; psychological characteristics such as lower verbal IQ and impaired ability to inhibit behavior, a heightened sensitivity to rewards, and slower conditioning of anxiety; and a combination of family factors that undermines the ability of parents to control early manifestations of aggressive and rule-breaking behavior.

Treatment of Personality Disorders

Treatment or prevention of personality disorders is difficult because of their long-standing nature and their complicated causation. No single treatment or preventive strategy will be effective for all, or even most, disorders; each disorder requires interventions that are guided by knowledge of specific risk factors. Special forms of psychotherapy have been developed for borderline personality disorder and avoidant personality disorder, and initial research results suggest that they can bring about some positive changes. There is no effective treatment for antisocial personality disorder. Because personality disorders begin to emerge in adolescence, prevention is not likely to be effective unless it targets childhood antecedents to the disorders.

KEY TERMS

agreeableness, p. 414

antisocial personality disorder, p. 421

avoidant personality disorder, p. 423

borderline personality disorder, p. 420

conscientiousness, p. 414

dependent personality disorder, p. 424

dialectical behavior therapy, p. 435

ego-syntonic, p. 410

extroversion, p. 413

histrionic personality disorder, p. 418

Interpersonal Circumplex (Circle), p. 414

narcissistic personality disorder, p. 419

neuroticism, p. 413

obsessive-compulsive personality disorder, p. 425

openness, p. 414

paranoid personality disorder, p. 415

personality, p. 408

personality disorder, p. 409

personality trait, p. 410

schizoid personality disorder, p. 417

schizotypal personality disorder, p. 417

13

Substance-Related Disorders

Sheba by Teino, 1994. Mixed media, 27" x 20". Courtesy of Sistare and NARSAD Artworks.

From the Case of Jerry

It was a typical night at the Blue Ox Bar & Grill. The place was crowded and smoky and every conversation had to be shouted over the pounding bass of the band. Jerry, a junior in college, was there for the fourth time this week. He'd finished only half the assigned reading for his mid-term exam the next morning, but he'd already shared four pitchers of beer with his buddy, Ben. It crossed his mind that, at this time last year, drinking two pitchers would have put him under the table, but now that much beer seemed to have much less effect.

As Jerry wandered home from the bar, he was troubled. Did he have a drinking problem? Could he be an alcoholic? Jerry decided that this was a rather remote possibility. After all, most of his friends drank heavily, and so did his father; they couldn't *all* be alcoholics. Besides, alcoholics were the old guys who drank hard liquor straight out of the bottle and begged money from you on street corners. And he seemed to remember reading that alcoholics were unable to stop drinking until they passed out. He wasn't like that. He drank only beer, and he could stop when he had to.

Or could he? His girlfriend, Alison, had urged him not to drink so much, but, as hard as he tried, Jerry was never able to cut

443

Many experts consider alcohol abuse to be the leading health problem among college students. According to recent surveys, almost half of all college students go on drinking binges and about 4 percent drink alcohol every day.

down on alcohol, and eventually Alison broke up with him. Although Jerry didn't drink every day, he almost always got drunk whenever alcohol was around, often consuming as many as twelve bottles of beer in an evening. Jerry also drank at the worst possible times: when exams were coming up or just before a date. On nights before exams or paper deadlines, he tried to sober up for studying or writing by snorting the stimulant *methamphetamine,* and then smoked marijuana to "round off the edges" of his postamphetamine "crash." Once a high school senior who hated the taste of alcohol and who had tried marijuana only a few times, Jerry had rather quickly developed an entrenched pattern in which his use of these and other drugs put him at risk for flunking out of school. ■

*I*s Jerry correct in assuming that he isn't an alcoholic because he doesn't drink hard liquor, drinks no more than many of his friends, and doesn't ever pass out? What accounts for his heavy drinking and his use of other drugs? Is he just fitting into the college scene, or is Jerry especially vulnerable to alcohol? Does his use of alcohol and other drugs reflect learning or a disease, and will his current use of these substances lead to even more severe problems in the future? Finally, if he wants to lower the risk for such problems, should Jerry give up drinking and taking drugs altogether or should he just try to do so less often and in smaller quantities?

These are just a few of the questions we will discuss in this chapter about disorders associated with alcohol, marijuana, and many other substances.

These substances are called **psychoactive drugs** because they affect users' thinking, emotions, and behavior. They include drugs that

- are widely available and used by many people (such as alcohol, nicotine, and caffeine);
- are legally available only through prescription (such as barbiturates, benzodiazepines, some opioids); or
- are illegal (such as cocaine, marijuana, and LSD).

In most cases, our discussion of these substances will include a description of their physiological and behavioral effects, typical patterns of use and abuse (including DSM-IV criteria for diagnosing substance-related disorders), and methods for changing and preventing these patterns.

No mental disorders create more personal and social disruption than those related to psychoactive substances. The impact of these substances stems in part from the prevalence of their use. Estimates are that 51 percent of Americans between the ages of 15 and 54 have used one or more illegal drugs (marijuana/hashish, cocaine/crack, heroin, hallucinogens, inhalants, and nonmedically obtained sedatives and tranquilizers) at least once in their lives, and that about 15 percent have done so in the past year (Warner et al., 1995). The costs associated with the use of these drugs—and with alcohol—are enormous. For example, according to various surveys of the United States alone, the criminal activities of *each* daily heroin user drains about $55,000 per year from the economy; about 375,000 infants are born annually with mental or physical problems caused by *in utero* exposure to alcohol or drugs; and at least 3 percent of all deaths are directly linked to alcohol (National Institute on Drug Abuse, 1991; National Institute on Alcohol Abuse and Alcoholism, 1990).

In the 1980s, rates of illegal drug use began to level off or even decline from the near-epidemic levels of the previous two decades (National Institute of Drug Abuse, 1991). For example, the rate at which Americans used cocaine declined in this time period, and fewer Americans reported using marijuana, the most common illicit drug in the United States. However, in the 1990s, the picture began to change. Rates of marijuana use have started to creep higher, particularly among juveniles; and heroin use, once concentrated among the urban poor, has surged among more affluent young Americans. Similar trends are found for alcohol. The rate of alcohol use declined between 1979 and 1992, but, since then, alcohol consumption has begun to increase.

Defining Substance-Related Disorders

To understand how the DSM-IV defines substance-related disorders, it is important to know several terms that are used to describe psychoactive drug effects.

Basic Terms and Concepts

Several concepts apply to all substances of abuse. For example, **substance intoxication** refers to a temporary condition in which, as a direct result of ingesting too much of a substance, a person experiences impaired judgment, disturbed perception, pronounced mood changes, altered thinking, or impaired motor behavior. Because certain drugs amplify the effects of other substances, people who abuse several substances are particularly prone to intoxication.

Drug abuse refers to a level of use that is hazardous to a person's health, leads to significant impairment in work or family life, produces personal distress, or leads to legal problems. In many cases, including Jerry's, the impairments result from abusing several substances at the same time, a pattern known as **polysubstance abuse.** But the number or amount of drugs consumed is less important in defining abuse than is the appearance of adverse consequences. Thus, a person who neither experiences nor causes harmful consequences stemming from a drug—even an illegal drug—is a drug user, but not officially a drug abuser.

Prolonged substance abuse usually produces some form of *dependence.* **Psychological dependence** is marked by an intense desire for the drug (called *craving*) and a preoccupation with obtaining it. People who become psychologically dependent devote a large portion of their day to procuring and using drugs, thus reducing the time they can devote to school, work, or social relationships. Indeed, friendships may eventually focus on people who help them find the drug and who, through their own example, support its abuse. Psychologically dependent people continue to consume the drug even when they know it is causing or aggravating stomach ulcers, heart trouble, or other physical problems.

People are said to display **physiological dependence,** often called **addiction,** when excessive and frequent consumption of a substance leads either to tolerance or to a withdrawal syndrome. **Tolerance** refers to a condition in which increasingly larger doses of the drug are required to achieve the same physical effect or subjective state (a "high"). Thus, if the drug is taken repeatedly at the same dose, its effects are significantly reduced (McKim, 1991). A **withdrawal** syndrome is a pattern of physical symptoms that results from discontinuing drug use once the person's body has become used to its presence. Depending on which drug the person has been consuming, withdrawal symptoms can include headaches, nausea, tremors, hallucinations, convulsions, and even death. Physiological dependence creates a vicious cycle in which the person can avoid aversive withdrawal symptoms only by continuing to take the drug.

DSM-IV Diagnosis of Substance-Related Disorders

In the DSM-IV, *substance-related disorders* include substance-induced disorders and substance use disorders. An individual can be diagnosed as displaying either or both. *Substance-induced disorders* involve impaired functioning as a direct result of the physiological effects of the ingested psychoactive substance. Suppose, for example, that a 15-year-old is brought to an emergency room because she displays slurred speech, loss of coordination, and an unsteady gait after drinking beer for the first time. In DSM-IV terms, she is suffering an *alcohol-induced* disorder—specifically, *alcohol intoxication. Substance use disorders* involve repeated, frequent use of substances resulting in problematic behaviors or impairments in personal, social, and occupational functioning. Substance use disorders are further subdivided into those involving abuse versus dependence.

Thus, in the DSM-IV, **substance abuse** is a maladaptive pattern of substance use that results in repeated and significant adverse consequences and maladaptive behaviors. These include (1) failure to fulfill major obligations at work, school, or home; (2) repeatedly using a psychoactive substance in hazardous ways (e.g., while driving an automobile); (3) experiencing recurrent legal problems related to the substance (e.g., arrests for drunken driving); and (4) continuing to use the substance despite its recurrent negative impact on social relationships.

Substance dependence is indicated by a set of behavioral, physiological, and cognitive symptoms and impairments caused by continued use of a substance. The seven criteria for substance dependence are shown in the DSM table below. The first two of these criteria pertain to physiological dependence (tolerance and withdrawal), while the remaining items indicate psychological dependence. Because any three of the seven criteria satisfy the definition of substance dependence, a person need not show signs of physical dependence to be diagnosed as substance dependent using the DSM-IV. A diagnosis of substance dependence can be accompanied by various *course specifiers*. For example, an *early full remission* is diagnosed when the individual has shown no signs of dependence or abuse for at least 1 month but for less than 1 year; a full remission that lasts for at least 1 year is a *sustained full remission*.

The section on substance-related disorders in the DSM-IV includes those associated with 11 classes of substances. These are alcohol, amphetamine (stimulants), caffeine, cannabis (marijuana), cocaine, hallucinogens (e.g., LSD), inhalants (such as glue or spray paint), nicotine, opioids (e.g., heroin), phencyclidine (PCP), and a group of sedatives, hypnotics, and anxiolytics (drugs that reduce anxiety). We emphasize alcohol use disorders in this chapter because they are so common and much is known about their causes and consequences. We also emphasize treat-

---

DSM-IV

Criteria for Substance Dependence

A maladaptive pattern of substance use, leading to clinically significant impairment or distress, as manifested by three (or more) of the following, occurring at any time in the same 12-month period:

(1) tolerance, as defined by either of the following:

    (a) a need for markedly increased amounts of the substance to achieve intoxication or desired effect

    (b) markedly diminished effect with continued use of the same amount of the substance

(2) withdrawal, as manifested by either of the following:

    (a) the characteristic withdrawal syndrome for the substance.

    (b) the same (or a closely related) substance is taken to relieve or avoid withdrawal symptoms

(3) the substance is often taken in larger amounts or over a longer period than was intended

(4) there is a persistent desire or unsuccessful efforts to cut down or control substance use

(5) a great deal of time is spent in activities necessary to obtain the substance (e.g., visiting multiple doctors or driving long distances), use the substance (e.g., chain-smoking), or recover from its effects

(6) important social, occupational, or recreational activities are given up or reduced because of substance use

(7) the substance use is continued despite knowledge of having a persistent or recurrent physical or psychological problem that is likely to have been caused or exacerbated by the substance (e.g., current cocaine use despite recognition of cocaine-induced depression, or continued drinking despite recognition that an ulcer was made worse by alcohol consumption)

Source: American Psychiatric Association; *Diagnostic and Statistical Manual of Mental Disorders,* Fourth Edition. Washington, DC, American Psychiatric Association.

ment of alcohol use disorders because these interventions have been used as models for helping abusers of other drugs.

Alcohol Use and Alcohol-Induced Disorders

The consumption of alcohol is extremely common in the United States, as well as in many other countries (Alvarez, DelRio, & Prado, 1995; Korolenko, Minevich, & Segal, 1994). Its use is fostered by cultural traditions and social conventions and reinforced by intense advertising. Indeed, television and print ads do everything possible to portray the drinking of alcohol in its many forms—beer, wine, or liquor—as a normal part of life and to associate its use with attractive people and happy social situations. Alcohol's popularity stems in part from its perceived ability to lower social inhibitions, facilitate social interaction, and create pleasant feelings. To many people, alcohol is a magic elixir that can increase social competence, sexual prowess, personal confidence, and power.

But alcohol is also a dangerous drug that is associated with hundreds of thousands of deaths each year in the United States alone (Mrazek & Haggerty, 1994). Alcohol contributes to *half* of all fatal traffic accidents (U.S. Department of Transportation, 1991) and to about 25 to 50 percent of all deaths due to fires, falls, and drowning (Institute of Medicine, 1989). Alcohol is also involved in many homicides, suicides, and deaths from alcohol-related illnesses. Indeed, the average life expectancy of people who abuse alcohol is at least 10 years shorter than those of nonabusers, and the total loss of life due to alcohol's effects may exceed that associated with cancer or heart disease.

Over the past 2 decades, the dangers of excessive alcohol consumption have been communicated with increasing clarity by the U.S. Department of Health and Human Services and by organizations such as Mothers Against Drunk Driving (MADD). These efforts have not been in vain. Per capita alcohol consumption by Americans over the age of 14 showed a small but steady decline from an average of 2.65 gallons per year in 1984 to 2.54 gallons in 1987, the lowest amount since 1970 (Rivers, 1994). The percentage of persons using alcohol is highest in the Northeast, where 79 percent of people over 21 drink, and lowest in the South, where 52 percent use alcohol on occasion. People in the West (66 percent) and Midwest (72 percent) fall in between (Rivers, 1994). Recent national surveys not only show fewer

drinkers reporting heavy drinking (more than 14 drinks a week), but that heavy alcohol use is becoming less socially acceptable. Roughly one third of Americans over 18 abstain from alcohol use, one third are light drinkers, and one third are moderate to heavy drinkers (Rivers, 1994). Unfortunately, surveys also contain warning signs that, during the 1990s, alcohol use is again on the upswing among young people in the United States and elsewhere.

Alcohol in the Body

When it enters the stomach, a small amount of *ethanol*—the form of alcohol contained in typical alcoholic beverages—is almost immediately absorbed through the stomach wall and into the bloodstream. The rest passes from the stomach to the small intestine, where most of it is absorbed and carried in the blood to various organs of the body, including the brain, heart, and liver.

When alcohol reaches the liver, it undergoes **oxidation**, through which it is converted to *acetaldehyde* by the enzyme *alcohol dehydrogenase*. Acetaldehyde is further *metabolized*, or chemically decomposed, into other products. The liver can metabolize about a half an ounce to an ounce of alcohol in an hour. Physiological *tolerance* for alcohol results, in part, from the body's capacity to metabolize alcohol more efficiently after repeated exposure to it. When the amount of alcohol consumed exceeds the liver's capacity to oxidize it, ethanol and acetaldehyde begin to accumulate in body cells, disrupting cell structure and functions, and producing several problems. One of these is the faulty metabolism of vitamins, which is why, even if they eat well, people who are heavy abusers of alcohol may suffer deficiencies in vitamin B_1 (thiamine) and other vitamins.

The unmetabolized ethanol absorbed into the blood from the small intestine and stomach can be measured as **blood alcohol concentration**, or **BAC.** Alcohol is absorbed more slowly from drinks with lower alcohol content (such as beer) than from those with higher alcohol content (e.g., whiskey). (A *drink* is defined as 1 ounce of 100-proof alcohol, a 12-ounce beer, or a 4-ounce glass of wine.) In an average-sized person, one or two drinks yields a BAC of 0.02 to 0.05 percent; 3 to 5 drinks produce a BAC of 0.06 to 0.10 percent; and 10 to 13 drinks create BACs of 0.2 to 0.25 percent. In most states in the United States, the legal definition of drunken driving is set in terms of some minimum BAC level, often 0.10 percent. When consumed with food, ethanol remains in the stomach longer, resulting in slower absorption into the bloodstream, lower BAC, and less intoxication than when ingested on its own.

Women metabolize alcohol less efficiently than men, resulting in higher BACs in shorter periods (Frezza et al., 1990). Thus, women are at higher risk than men for liver damage associated with chronic alcohol consumption. Because they have more of a type of isoenzyme (known as a *beta-2* isoenzyme), individuals of Asian descent oxidize ethanol more rapidly than do most Whites (Meier-Tackmann et al., 1990). The beta-2 isoenzyme is also found less often in Caucasian alcoholics than in Caucasian nonalcoholics, for reasons not yet clearly understood (Thomasson et al., 1991).

Unmetabolized alcohol can have devastating effects on bodily organs, particularly the liver, the pancreas, and the heart. Chronic alcohol abuse is the single most frequent cause of liver diseases in the United States. The most serious of these is **alcoholic cirrhosis,** characterized by damaged liver cells, development of scar tissue, and the eventual inability of the liver to filter toxins from the blood. The risk of liver damage is directly related to the amount of alcohol consumed. This risk is significant in men who consume 6 or more ounces of alcohol per day, but women are at risk after daily doses of as little as 1.5 ounces (Grant, DeBakey, & Zobeck, 1991).

The relationship between alcohol use and cardiovascular disease is complex. Male and female nondrinkers seem to have a slightly higher risk of cardiovascular disease than do light or moderate drinkers (Boffetta & Garfinkel, 1990; Razay et al., 1992). It has been suggested that consuming 2 to 3 ounces of alcohol per day may raise HDL cholesterol (the so-called good cholesterol) which, in turn, increases blood flow through the coronary vessels. Heavy drinking, however, is a risk factor for several coronary diseases, including high blood pressure, weakening of the heart muscle, arrhythmias, and strokes. Excessive drinking can also enlarge red blood cells, leading to the anemia seen in at least 10 percent of alcohol abusers.

Numerous other health risks are also linked with alcohol abuse. Heavy drinking commonly results in **pancreatitis,** a condition in which cells in the pancreas are killed. The first sign of this condition is intense stomach pain. Chronic alcohol abuse can suppress the body's immune system, leaving the person vulnerable to infectious diseases, including tuberculosis, pneumonia, and other respiratory illnesses. Among those exposed

Connections

How does maternal alcohol consumption affect fetal development? For descriptions of *fetal alcohol syndrome* and *fetal alcohol effect,* see Chapter 4, pp. 127–128.

to HIV, the effects of alcohol on the immune system may shorten the interval between initial infection and the development of AIDS (Wang & Watson, 1995). Immunosuppression may also explain alcohol abusers' higher risk for developing cancer of the mouth, pharynx, larynx, esophagus, breast, and liver (Gapstur et al., 1992; Longnecker, 1994).

In males, alcohol abuse tends to suppress testosterone levels (Adams & Cicero, 1991). This can lead to testicular abnormalities, sexual dysfunction, and loss of sexual motivation. In women, heavy and prolonged alcohol abuse can contribute to menstrual problems, including cessation of menses and failure to ovulate (Seki, Yoshida, & Okamura, 1991). Drinking during pregnancy also increases the risk of spontaneous abortion and, because alcohol crosses the placental barrier, it can cause problems in infants including low birth weight and mental retardation.

Effects of Alcohol on the Brain and Behavior

When bloodborne alcohol reaches the brain, it interacts with neurotransmitters that provide the chemical basis for communication among brain cells.

Depressant Effects in the Brain. The two neurotransmitters particularly affected by alcohol are glutamate and gamma aminobutyric acid (GABA). **Glutamate** is a major *excitatory* neurotransmitter in the brain; it stimulates activity in the neurons it reaches. *GABA,* the brain's major *inhibitory* neurotransmitter, has the opposite effect—it reduces the activity of the brain cells it reaches. Numerous animal studies show that alcohol reduces the excitatory action of glutamate and increases the inhibitory action of GABA. The net effect is the suppression of brain cell activity, which is why alcohol is considered a central nervous system *depressant.*

Alcohol's effect on GABA is especially strong in two areas of the brain. The first is the *medial septal nucleus* (Givens & Breese, 1990), which connects to the limbic system, a region of the brain involved in the regulation of emotion. Alcohol's enhancement of GABA's inhibitory effects in this area may account for alcohol's sedating and anxiety-reducing action. The second area is the *cerebellum,* which is critical to normal sensory and motor functions. The effect of alcohol on GABA in this region explains why it impairs gait and other aspects of motor coordination.

With continued use, alcohol loses some of its effects on GABA and glutamate, which may be another physiological reason for the development of alcohol tolerance (Allan & Harris, 1987). The processes through which the effects diminish are still

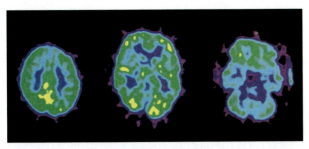

Alcoholic brains

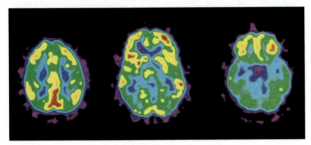

Normal brains

Alcohol's destructive effects on the brain are revealed by brain imaging techniques such as PET scans. These methods have shown that heavy, long-term use of alcohol leads to abnormalities in brain functioning. In this photo, the blood flow and glucose metabolism (shown by the yellow and red areas) is substantially decreased throughout the brain, especially in the frontal lobe, of the alcoholic patient. Recent studies suggest that, if a person abstains from alcohol, some previously alcohol-damaged neurons may be able to repair themselves.

poorly understood, but it may be that neurons compensate for alcohol's inhibitory effects by altering the number or activity of receptors sensitive to GABA and glutamate.

Alcohol affects other neurotransmitters as well. Its effects on **dopamine,** for example, may explain the short-term "rewarding" experience that accompanies alcohol consumption. Neuroscientists believe that certain regions of the brain—such as the *nucleus accumbens*—mediate the experience of pleasure. Research has shown that animals will work hard to maintain electrical stimulation of these "reward centers" (Olds & Milner, 1954). Dopamine is a prominent neurotransmitter in these areas, and alcohol increases the level of dopamine in the nucleus accumbens and other reward centers (e.g., Wozniak, Pert, & Linnoila, 1990). Alcohol also increases neuronal activity in other regions of the brain where dopamine is found in high concentrations (Lewis et al., 1990). The destruction of dopamine-activated nerve cells in rats' nucleus accumbens causes them to increase their alcohol consumption (Quarfordt,

Kalmus, & Myers, 1991), while the administration of drugs that mimic the activity of dopamine in this region diminishes rats' interest in alcohol.

Alcohol's "rewarding" effects may also relate to its ability to increase the level of the neurotransmitter **serotonin** in certain brain regions. When animals are given drugs that increase or mimic the activity of serotonin, they reduce their alcohol intake. Alcohol also increases the release of **endogenous opiates,** also called *endorphins*. These naturally occurring substances are chemically similar to opioid drugs, such as morphine and heroin, that produce a state of euphoria and reduce the experience of pain.

Connections

What other behaviors are affected by the endogenous opiates? See Chapter 5, p. 160.

Effects on Behavior. The behavioral consequences of alcohol intoxication are well known. After a drink or two, most people feel less inhibited, more talkative, and more relaxed. As Figure 13.1 shows, however, as the BAC rises, judgment becomes impaired, self-aware-

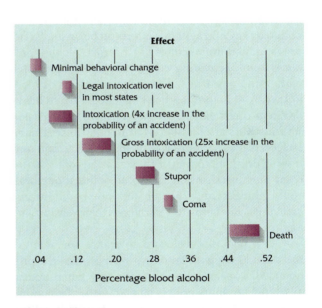

FIGURE 13.1

Blood Alcohol Concentrations and Behavioral Effects

The concentration of alcohol in a person's blood is directly correlated with increased behavioral impairment. Most states use a BAC of 0.10 percent as the legal definition of intoxication. The effects of different BAC levels also depend on factors such as the drinker's weight, how quickly the alcohol was consumed, and whether food was eaten along with the alcohol.

Source: Rivers, 1994.

ness is reduced, and clear thinking becomes more difficult. With BAC in the range of 0.05 to 0.08 percent, slurred speech and mild motor coordination problems are apparent. When the BAC climbs to the 0.10 percent range, motor coordination problems such as unsteady gait, drowsiness, and impaired perception become noticeable enough to mark this level of impairment as "intoxicated" in legal terms. Other typical signs of intoxication include unpredictable mood changes, poor attention and memory, and a lack of inhibition that impairs normal social functioning. Some intoxicated individuals become verbally or physically aggressive (Ito, Miller, & Pollock, 1996) or make uncharacteristic and inappropriate sexual advances. At BAC levels over 0.25 percent, a drinker may lose consciousness and suffer severe respiratory problems that can lead to death.

The behavioral effects of alcohol are determined partly by its physiological impact on the brain, but we will see later that they are also strongly influenced by factors such as the situations in which people drink, their prior drinking experiences, and their expectancies about the effects of alcohol. All of these factors can play a role in shaping the behavior that follows alcohol use.

Even though it is a depressant, alcohol can have both sedating and agitating effects on behavior. By depressing inhibitory centers in the brain, alcohol produces some activating effects like those associated with stimulant drugs. The sedating effects of alcohol wear off before the agitating effects do, so heavy drinkers often experience nervousness and tension several hours after a bout of drinking. This rebound effect sets up a vicious cycle in which the person may resume drinking to reduce the agitation that remains from previous drinking. At some point, though, alcohol abusers find that no amount of additional drinking will completely eliminate their tension and agitation.

As a person develops a tolerance for alcohol, the normal signs of intoxication become less pronounced, appearing in full force only when unusually large amounts are consumed. Other behavioral effects or personality changes worsen with continued alcohol abuse, however. The severity of these effects depends on the drinker's age, education, patterns and duration of drinking, and the presence of medical complications. For example, in some individuals, the aggressiveness characteristic of acute intoxication develops into a brooding, ongoing hostility, often directed at spouses or other family members (Leonard, 1990). Chronic alcohol abusers tend to show a gradual deterioration in problem-solving skills, especially in concentration and flexibility in finding solutions. Visual–motor skills are also impaired (Parsons, Butters, & Nathan, 1987). Short-term memory and learning deficits may result as well, although these are usually mild unless there is alcohol-induced brain damage. As their cognitive abilities become impaired, chronic alcohol abusers may find it even more difficult to communicate effectively with friends and relatives. The resulting deterioration in social relationships and social support exacerbates the alcohol abuser's problems (Steinglass et al., 1987).

Prevalence of Alcohol Use Disorders

Estimates of the prevalence of alcohol use disorders—listed in the DSM-IV as alcohol abuse and alcohol dependence—vary depending on where the line is drawn between use and abuse (Tarter & Vanyukov, 1994). A 1992 survey conducted by the National Institute on Alcohol Abuse and Alcoholism (NIAAA) indicated that 7.4 percent of the adult population in the United States (about 13.7 million people) met the DSM criteria during that year for alcohol abuse (3 percent), alcohol dependence (4.4 percent), or both (Grant et al., 1994). A 1993 report by the U.S. Department of Health and Human Services contained a slightly higher estimate of 15.3 million. Although these estimates are slightly lower than those reported in similar surveys in the 1980s, changes over the years in DSM criteria for alcohol use disorders make it risky to conclude that the overall prevalence of alcohol-related disorders has declined significantly. Indeed, all the surveys point to unacceptably high levels of maladaptive drinking in the United States, and the same story emerges from studies in the United Kingdom, Russia, Australia, Ireland, Korea, and other countries.

Alcohol abuse in the United States is 3 to 4 times more prevalent among males than among females (Rivers, 1994), but this gender gap has been closing rapidly, especially among adolescent girls. Among teenagers, boys and girls are now equally likely to drink alcohol. For both males and females, prevalence is highest in the 18 to 29 age group (NIAAA, 1990). African American teenagers are more likely to abstain from alcohol than European American teens are, regardless of gender (Franklin, 1989). African American men are also less likely to be problem drinkers than European American men are, although African American women who drink are more likely than European American women to drink heavily (Herd, 1989). Alcohol abuse is more prevalent among Hispanic American males, and it is lower among Asian Americans of both genders (NIAAA, 1990), when compared with that of European Americans.

Patterns of Alcohol Abuse and Dependence

The term **alcoholism** has traditionally referred to a pattern of heavy drinking that steadily worsens until the person is thought to have lost control over drinking and become so dependent on alcohol that physical and mental health are jeopardized and social and occupational functioning are impaired. This image of the alcoholic stems partly from an influential survey conducted in the 1940s on a small group of men in Alcoholics Anonymous (AA) (Jellinek, 1946). Based on these men's reported drinking histories, Jellinek proposed a 4-stage model of how alcohol dependence progresses. In the first phase, the *prealcoholic,* individuals drink only occasionally, mostly in social situations and to relieve tension. In the second, or *prodromal* phase, drinking is heavier, sometimes in secret, but with few signs of gross intoxication. In the third, or *crucial,* phase, individuals lose control over their drinking. Even one drink inevitably seems to lead to binge drinking until blackouts result; health is affected, and social lives begin to deteriorate. The final, *chronic,* phase involves daily drinking, often accompanied by malnutrition, physical tolerance, and—when alcohol is unavailable—withdrawal symptoms.

Although Jellinek's model conforms to many stereotypes about alcoholics, scientists now know that his 4 stages do not apply to all alcoholics. Not everyone who drinks heavily suffers blackouts; nor do all alcoholics lose control over their drinking after a single drink. Furthermore, Jellinek's model is not particularly descriptive of female alcoholics. Women with alcohol problems usually start drinking later in life, often after some type of crisis, and they are less likely than men are to go on drinking binges.

Researchers now believe there are multiple "alcoholisms," representing different patterns of drinking and impairment. For example, Robert Cloninger distinguished two types of alcoholics (Cloninger et al., 1981):

■ *Type I alcoholics* show a late onset of problem drinking, are prone to anxiety, engage in binge drinking, and are unlikely to behave antisocially when drinking. They often develop health problems associated with their drinking.

■ *Type II alcoholics* begin their problem drinking in adolescence, experience little anxiety, and frequently show antisocial tendencies as well as disruptions in social and occupational functioning. They tend to have fewer medical complications linked to their drinking.

Other investigators have created similar typologies based on factors such as age of onset, motivation to drink, and the social/psychological consequences of drinking (Babor et al., 1992; Hill, 1992). Robert Zucker (1987), for example, includes a subtype of alcoholic who is not antisocial but who still starts drinking heavily in adolescence, often after being separated from family members.

Disorders Associated with Alcohol Abuse or Dependence

A substantial percentage of individuals who abuse or become dependent on alcohol also show symptoms associated with other psychiatric conditions, especially mood disorders, anxiety disorders, and antisocial personality disorder (Ross, Glaser, & Germanson, 1988). Psychotic symptoms—including delusions or hallucinations—sometimes occur in cases of severe and prolonged alcohol dependence.

The DSM-IV lists 11 alcohol-induced disorders: alcohol intoxication, alcohol withdrawal, alcohol intoxication delirium, alcohol withdrawal delirium, alcohol-induced persisting dementia, alcohol-induced persisting amnestic disorder, alcohol-induced psychotic disorder, alcohol-induced mood disorder, alcohol-induced anxiety disorder, alcohol-induced sexual dysfunction, and alcohol-induced sleep disorder.

The term *alcohol-induced* presupposes that alcohol abuse precedes and causes other comorbid disorders. Is this assumption warranted? As Figure 13.2 on page 452 shows, there are four possible explanations for comorbidity between alcohol-related disorders and other mental disorders: (1) the mental disorder precedes and causes the alcohol disorder; (2) the alcohol disorder precedes and causes the mental disorder; (3) a common factor precipitates both disorders; or (4) both disorders—regardless of which came first—exacerbate each other.

It is often difficult to determine which of these explanations applies to certain instances of comorbidity between alcohol abuse/dependence and other mental disorders. For example, about 20 percent of alcoholics display anxiety disorders (Regier et al., 1990), but it is not clear whether anxiety is the cause of alcohol abuse, or primarily a consequence of it. The answer may vary from case to case because, although low doses of alcohol decrease anxiety and tension, frequent high doses exacerbate anxiety, as noted earlier (Kushner, Sher, & Beitman, 1990). With other kinds of comorbidity, the causal picture may be clearer. For example, when alcohol abusers display cognitive-sensory impairments such as *dementia, delirium,* and *amnesia,* it is usually the case that

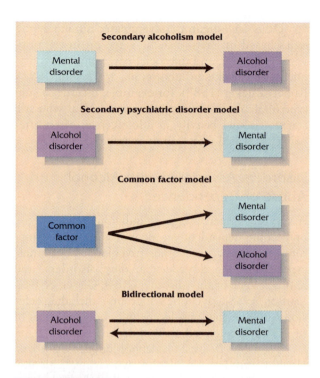

FIGURE 13.2

Four Models of How Alcohol Disorders and Other Mental Disorders May Be Related

these disorders were caused or exacerbated by the alcohol abuse rather than the other way around.

As described in Chapter 11, *delirium* refers to a disturbance of consciousness in which there is profound confusion, agitation, and an inability to attend to the environment. Perceptual or cognitive distortions, such as hallucinations or delusions, may also be present. Alcohol-induced delirium occurs primarily during periods of extreme intoxication or withdrawal following prolonged, heavy drinking. It can be accompanied by muscle tremors, hallucinations, and profuse sweating. The term **delirium tremens** (or **DTs**) is commonly used to identify this particular set of symptoms, as seen in the following case of *alcohol withdrawal delirium.*

*J*oe is a 43-year-old carpenter who, for 5 years, drank more than a fifth of wine daily. He often blacked out during his drinking, ate only one meal a day, and was fired from many jobs because of absenteeism. Recently, Joe ran out of money and, after 3 days with no alcohol, his hands began to shake so severely that he was unable to light a cigarette. He could not sleep and was plagued by panic. Neighbors were concerned because of his rambling, incoherent speech. When taken to the hospital, Joe thought the doctor was his brother; he didn't know where he was, and picked at imaginary insects on his bed sheet. The sound of carts rolling in the hallway provoked intense visual and auditory impressions of "fiery car crashes." (From Spitzer et al., 1994)

Alcohol withdrawal delirium is experienced by less than 5 percent of treated alcoholics and is typically eased with medications that mimic the neurochemical effects of alcohol.

A more severe form of alcohol-induced delirium is *alcohol-induced psychotic disorder,* which resembles delirium but is less episodic and more likely to include well-developed delusions and hallucinations. These delusions and hallucinations are not usually recognized by the psychotic individual as induced by alcohol. For example, one chronic alcoholic believed that TV newscasters were sending him instructions in a "secret language," but he vehemently denied any connection between this belief and his drinking.

Dementia is a more persistent and pervasive condition characterized by significant deterioration in memory, language, motor coordination, or executive functions, such as planning, organizing, and attending to specific tasks. As described in Chapter 11, afflicted individuals are often unable to recognize familiar persons or understand where they are or how they got there. Alcohol-induced dementia can be caused by extremely prolonged, heavy drinking. It is a more persistent condition than delirium, lasting long after the alcoholic's intoxication and withdrawal are over.

A well-known, but rare, alcohol-induced memory disorder called **Wernicke-Korsakoff syndrome** is partly caused by a deficiency in vitamin B_1, or *thiamine.* Thiamine deficiency is related both to the malnourishment commonly seen among chronic alcoholics, and to the fact that alcohol interferes with vitamin metabolism. Wernicke-Korsakoff syndrome occurs in 2 phases. In the first, Wernicke's phase, the individual is suddenly confused and unable to coordinate voluntary muscle movements. In the second, more chronic Korsakoff phase, the individual's memory for personal experiences, even recent ones, is lost while other types of memory remain intact. Individuals with Korsakoff syndrome tend to *confabulate* to compensate for their lost memories. For example, one middle-aged chronic alcoholic with Korsakoff syndrome was asked the name of the nurse with whom he had just spoken. With total confidence, the patient gave an incorrect name and went on to make up a story in which the nurse was his daughter's best friend and former teammate on their college volleyball team.

Causes of Alcohol Use Disorders

Why do people abuse or become dependent on alcohol? Some theorists argue that problem drinking stems from alcohol's ability to stimulate dopamine receptors in the brain's reward centers. But this explanation does not account for why one third of the American population are nondrinkers and one third drink only in moderation. Is there a genetic characteristic that makes certain individuals particularly susceptible to the rewarding effects of alcohol? Or is alcohol abuse shaped by personality, family dynamics, or group norms? No one knows for sure, but biological, psychological, and social factors have all been implicated—singly or in combination—as causes of alcohol abuse and dependence. Some of these factors may be more important in some people than in others. If there are indeed differing alcoholic subtypes, there may be differing combinations of causes underlying each type. It is unlikely that just one or two factors are to blame for all alcohol-related disorders.

Genetic Factors. Problem drinking runs in families. The risk of alcohol abuse is 7 times greater among the first-degree relatives of alcoholics than among first-degree relatives of nonproblem drinkers (Merikangas, 1990). Evidence that genetic factors contribute to this risk comes from both twin and adoption studies.

Most twin studies have found a higher concordance rate among identical twins than among nonidentical twins for level of alcohol consumption, as well as susceptibility to the effects of alcohol (Cadoret, 1990). Concordance rates are generally in the 25 to 75 percent range, but the rates are affected by the type of alcoholism and by factors such as gender. Usually, higher concordance rates appear in males, in people who display severe alcohol abuse, and in those—such as Cloninger's Type II alcoholics—whose problem drinking began early in life (McGue, Pickens, & Svikis, 1992; Pickens et al., 1991).

Adoption studies provide the strongest support for the role of genetic influence on alcohol-related disorders. Reports of research conducted in the United States, Sweden, and Denmark indicate that adopted children born to alcoholic parents are more likely to develop problem drinking as adults than adopted children born to nonalcoholic parents (Cloninger et al., 1981; Schukit, Goodwin, & Winokur, 1972).

What is it that might be inherited by alcoholics? For a time, some scientists thought they had found a gene that produced exceptional vulnerability to the rewarding effects of alcohol. This gene, located on chromosome 11, controls one type of dopamine receptor, the D_2 receptor, which is believed to mediate the reinforcing effects of alcohol (McBride et al., 1990). Early studies of the brains of deceased, extremely hard-drinking alcoholics suggested that there was a higher-than-normal frequency of the D_2 receptor gene in these people (Blum et al., 1990), but several subsequent studies failed to replicate this finding (e.g., Turner et al., 1992). Thus, it is unclear what role, if any, the D_2 receptor gene plays in vulnerability to alcohol's rewarding effects.

Neurobiological Influences. What biological mechanisms might link genetic processes with drinking behavior? Potential answers come from studies comparing certain biological processes in alcoholics, nonproblem drinkers, and the offspring of both. The goal of this research has been to identify *biological markers* of vulnerability to alcohol. Studies comparing the *children* of alcoholics with children of nonproblem drinkers are especially valuable because they allow researchers to study biological vulnerability *before* the onset of problem drinking. This work is still in its infancy, and the results are not yet reliable enough to be used to screen people for risks of becoming alcoholic (Devor, 1994). However, research on these markers does provide several clues about biological processes that might underlie alcohol use disorders.

One possible marker may lie in people's brainwaves, the patterns of electrical activity measured by an electroencephalograph (EEG). Some studies have found that the sons of alcoholic fathers have higher-than-normal rates of a fast-paced brainwave called the *beta wave* (Gabrielli et al., 1982). Sons of alcoholic fathers also show less EEG *change* after alcohol consumption than do sons of nonalcoholics (Ehlers & Schuckit, 1990). Differences also occur in **evoked potentials,** which are small, brief changes in EEG voltage evoked by specific stimuli such as light or sound. One such change—called the *P300* because it occurs about 300 milliseconds after the presentation of a stimulus—is believed to indicate an individual's attentional skills. Some studies have found that sons of alcoholic fathers show smaller P300 amplitude than do sons of nonalcoholic fathers (Begleiter et al., 1984; O'Conner et al., 1987). These results suggest that some individuals might be at risk for drinking problems because they are less aware of the effects of alcohol on their behavior. However, the P300 findings have not always been replicated (Polich & Bloom, 1988), nor are they associated only with alcoholism. Lower P300 amplitudes have also been seen in people diagnosed with schizophrenia and other mental disorders. At the moment, then, researchers still do not know whether or how the brain's neuroelectrical activity increases vulnerability to alcohol abuse.

Another potential biochemical marker for alcohol disorders may lie in the functioning of enzymes and neurotransmitters. One target of research is the enzyme *monoamine oxidase (MAO),* which is involved in the metabolism of the neurotransmitters dopamine and norepinephrine. Recall that dopamine is a suspected mediator of alcohol's effect on reward centers in the brain. Alcoholics tend to show less MAO activity than nonalcoholics do, an effect that is more prominent for Type II alcoholics (Tabakoff, Whelan, & Hoffman, 1990). This finding has been interpreted as indicating that low MAO activity may be a risk factor for alcoholism (Sher, 1991). However, the role of MAO activity is controversial because MAO levels are, themselves, affected by alcohol consumption and by a variety of other psychiatric conditions.

Researchers are also focusing on the neurotransmitter *serotonin* as a possible marker for alcoholism risk. Abnormally low levels of serotonin have been linked to aggression, impulsivity, and antisocial behavior, all of which are associated with Cloninger's Type II alcoholism. Serotonin levels have been found to be related to alcohol craving in both animals and humans. For example, rats bred to desire alcohol have relatively low levels of serotonin in their brains. In addition, drugs that increase serotonin activity decrease alcohol use (Tabakoff & Hoffman, 1991). Unfortunately, serotonin is difficult to extract from the central nervous system, making it rather impractical for use as a marker for alcoholism.

One other potential marker is heart rate change in response to alcohol consumption. The degree to which a substance accelerates the heart rate may reflect an individual's sensitivity to the stimulating properties of that substance, thus providing an index of the reward value of that substance to the user (Wise & Bozarth, 1987). Indeed, men with alcoholic relatives show larger increases in heart rate after drinking than do men from nonalcoholic families (Finn et al., 1990), and those men who show relatively large heart rate increases after using alcohol are more likely to drink alcohol regularly (Pihl & Peterson, 1991). Perhaps the sons of alcoholics are more

susceptible to the stimulating properties of alcohol—and hence more strongly reinforced by its biochemical effects—than are the sons of nonalcoholic fathers.

To summarize, although alcoholics versus nonalcoholics differ in neuroelectrical activity, the functioning of enzymes and neurotransmitters, and postdrinking heart rate changes, only some of these effects (e.g., heart rate changes) have been found to discriminate between the children of alcoholics and the children of nonalcoholics. Furthermore, none of these markers has yet proved to be a consistently reliable indicator of alcohol vulnerability, nor have any of them been conclusively shown to cause alcohol use disorders. Still, the fact that there are biological differences in the way that sons of alcoholic fathers respond to alcohol implicates a biological, potentially heritable, vulnerability. But having this vulnerability does not mean that a person will inevitably become an alcoholic. Psychological and social factors undoubtedly interact with biological variables to elevate the risk of problem drinking.

Psychological Factors. Emotional states, expectancies, and personality characteristics can affect an individual's motivation to drink. For example, the **tension reduction hypothesis**—a mainstay of psychological literature on alcoholism for over 40 years (Conger, 1956)—suggests that drinking alcohol is reinforced by its ability to reduce tension, anxiety, anger, depression, and other unpleasant emotions. Therefore, people who have experienced such reinforcement—either firsthand or by seeing others use alcohol to reduce stress—should increase their drinking in stressful situations.

Many laboratory studies have tested this hypothesis by placing animals and humans in various kinds of stressful conflicts and giving them free access to alcohol. Other studies have correlated the amount of alcohol consumption with the number and intensity of stressors that people report in daily life (e.g., family conflict, job change, death of a loved one). The laboratory studies have generally supported the tension reduction hypothesis, but studies of the results of self-reported, real-life stressors have not been as positive (Cappell & Greeley, 1987). The lack of consistent support from studies of naturally occurring stressors appears to be because (1) drinking can be motivated by many factors besides a desire to reduce tension, (2) alcohol has variable effects on tension depending on how much is consumed, and (3) only certain individuals experience stress reduction after ingesting alcohol.

For example, one study found an association between alcohol use and stress only among individuals who had limited skills for coping with stress and who *believed* that alcohol would relieve their stress (Cooper et al., 1992). This study attests to the power of expectancies in determining the effects of substances on users. **Alcohol expectancies** are an individual's beliefs about the physical and psychological effects of alcohol—for example, that it can enhance sexual performance, reduce tension, restore confidence, or increase social competence (Marlatt, 1987). The development of alcohol expectancies begins early in life, as early as the preschool years, well before children have their first opportunity to actually drink alcohol (Noll, Zucker, & Greenberg, 1990). Children observe adult drinking behaviors and are led by television commercials and other media sources to believe that good things happen when people consume alcohol (Zucker & Fitzgerald, 1991).

According to alcohol expectancy theory, drinking behavior is determined largely by the reinforcement that an individual *expects* to receive from it (Goldman, Brown, & Christiansen, 1987; Thombs, 1994). From this perspective, the physiological effects of alcohol are relatively unimportant in accounting for problem drinking. For example, the fact that high doses of alcohol increase anxiety will probably have little effect on a drinker who is convinced that *any* amount of alcohol will promote relaxation.

How well is this theory supported by research? In a classic study, Alan Marlatt and his colleagues (Marlatt, Demming, & Reid, 1973) compared the drinking behavior of male alcoholics with nonproblem drinkers in the laboratory. Subjects were assigned to one of four groups. Group 1 was told, correctly, that they were being served vodka and tonic. Group 2 was told they were being served vodka and tonic, but they received only tonic. Group 3 was told they were being served tonic alone, but were actually given vodka and tonic. Group 4 was told, correctly, that they were being served only tonic.

The results of this study supported the alcohol expectancy theory: both alcoholics and nonproblem drinkers drank significantly more when told their drinks contained alcohol, *regardless of the beverage's actual alcohol content*. This finding is significant because it challenges models of alcoholism that hold that alcoholic drinking is controlled only by biological mechanisms triggered directly by alcohol's physiological effects on the body. Instead, it appears that how much people drink may be at least partly determined by their expectations about what they are drinking (Thombs, 1994).

Another line of research relies on measures such as the Alcohol Expectancy Questionnaire (AEQ) to compare the alcohol-related beliefs of people who

differ in their use of alcohol. The AEQ assesses expectancies about alcohol's ability to enhance sexual, physical, and social pleasure; to increase social assertiveness and power; to reduce tension; and to promote other positive changes (Brown, Christiansen, & Goldman, 1987). Studies with the AEQ have revealed gender and cultural differences in expectancies about alcohol. In one study of college students, for example, the AEQ scale that best distinguished problem drinkers from nonproblem drinkers among women was the expectancy that drinking would lead to more power. For men it was that drinking would increase physical and social pleasure (cited in Thombs, 1993). In another study, Irish teens were more likely to expect that alcohol would increase power and aggression, whereas American teens tended to expect that alcohol would enhance sexual pleasure and increase social competence (cited in Brown et al., 1987). Overall, alcoholics and heavy social drinkers are more likely than nonproblem drinkers to believe that positive outcomes will follow alcohol use.

However, studies that try to assess the impact of alcohol expectancies in people who have already begun to drink make it difficult to tell whether positive expectations about alcohol shaped drinking behavior—as alcohol expectancy theory suggests—or whether it was drinking that shaped the positive expectancies. To get around this problem, several studies have examined the power of positive alcohol expectancies to predict future drinking patterns in people who have never had alcohol. Research with seventh and eighth graders showed that beliefs that drinking alcohol would reduce tension and increase pleasure predicted the initiation and rate of alcohol use 1 year later (Christiansen et al., 1989). In another study, alcohol expectancies assessed at age 18 predicted alcohol and drug use into the subjects' late 20s (Stacy, Widaman, & Marlatt, 1990).

The expectancy picture is further clarified in a study by Gregory Smith and his colleagues (Smith et al., 1995). Their 3-year assessment of the alcohol expectancies and drinking behavior of 461 12- to 14-year-olds showed that positive expectancies for alcohol predicted higher levels of subsequent alcohol use. They also found, however, that, as these teens began to drink more, their expectancies for positive alcohol effects grew even stronger. In other words, as depicted in Figure 13.3 on page 456, alcohol expectancies and actual drinking experiences work together to increase the risk for developing drinking problems.

Another psychological mechanism thought to contribute to problem drinking is the inability to dis-

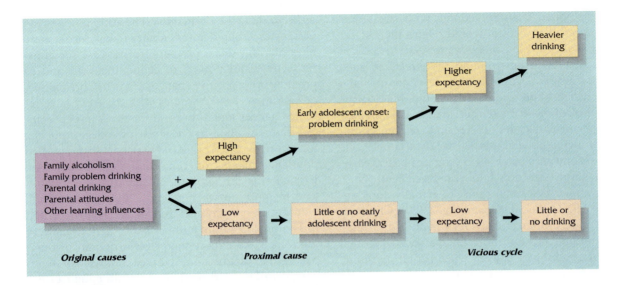

Original causes   Proximal cause   Vicious cycle

FIGURE 13.3

An Expectancy Model of Alcoholism
In Greg Smith's expectancy model of alcoholism, learning experiences transmitted in families influence the expectancies that young children hold about drinking alcohol. High positive expectancies lead children to experiment with drinking at early ages and early drinking tends, in turn, to further increase positive expectancies about drinking.

cern the internal cues that signal intoxication. For many drinkers, these cues—such as dizziness, light-headedness, nausea, and the like—act as warning signs that blood alcohol concentrations are high and serve as a "shut off valve" that inhibits further drinking. Several studies have shown that alcoholics are not very good at detecting these internal cues, tending to estimate their BAC almost exclusively on the basis of such *external* cues as the number of drinks consumed (Brick, 1990). Nonproblem drinkers use both internal and external cues (Huber, Karlin, & Nathan, 1976). The significance of this difference between alcoholics and nonalcoholics is still unclear, however, because researchers still do not know whether poor sensitivity to internal cues is a pre-existing deficit or the consequence of alcohol tolerance in heavy drinkers.

One final psychological factor to consider is personality. Freud contended that alcoholism reflected frustrated oral needs and regression to the oral stage of psychosexual development (see Chapter 1). Other psychoanalysts have suggested that alcoholics have dependent personalities, drink in order to feel powerful, or use their drinking

Connections

What other behaviors are typical of childhood externalizing disorders? See Chapter 3, pp. 83–89.

to disguise homosexual impulses. None of these views has received much empirical support, and, for a time, there was no research showing significant relationships between *any* personality factors and alcoholism (Cox, 1987). However, more recent studies suggest that a particular type of person may be prone to drinking disorders (Sher et al., 1991). In adults, this personality pattern has been variously called "antisocial," "sensation-seeking," "novelty-seeking," and "undersocialized-aggressive." In children, it has been called *externalizing*. All these terms refer to a pattern of impulsive, reckless, hyperactive, and often aggressive behavior.

One study found that an externalizing pattern at age 11 predicted alcohol abuse at age 27 (Cloninger et al., 1988). In another study, the combination of attention-deficit/hyperactivity disorder and aggression in childhood predicted alcohol and drug abuse in a sample of juvenile delinquents (Halikas et al., 1990). Yet another found that externalizing behavior influenced drinking problems in two ways: (1) by directly leading to more exposure to and use of alcohol and (2) by promoting more positive alcohol expectancies (Sher et al., 1991). Adolescents with a history of externalizing behavior problems are more likely to begin drinking early than are children who do not show this pattern (Jessor & Jessor, 1977).

Just how personality fits into the causal chain leading to problem drinking is still not clear. Sons of alcoholics are more likely than the sons of nonalcoholics to manifest externalizing personality patterns (Tarter et al., 1990), but researchers do not yet know whether this is due to genetic effects or to some distinctive manner in which alcoholic parents raise their children.

Sociocultural Factors. Cultural traditions and interpersonal processes such as family interactions, parenting practices, and peer pressure also influence alcohol use disorders. For example, patterns of problem drinking differ from country to country. In England and North America, alcoholism often involves periods of extremely heavy drinking and appears to involve a loss of control over consumption. In wine-drinking countries such as France, however, alcoholics are usually inveterate or steady drinkers who never show a loss of control. In Muslim countries, which discourage alcohol use on religious grounds, the incidence of any kind of alcoholism is very low.

Social processes in the home may be partly responsible for the tendency of alcohol problems to run in families. The quality of parent–child relationships and parenting styles, for example, tend to influence the probability of problem drinking during adolescence. Parents who are nurturant, but still use firm discipline, are less likely than nonsupportive or inconsistent parents to have adolescents who drink (Barnes, Farrell, & Cairns, 1986; Tarter et al., 1993). Adolescents are less likely to drink if they feel close to their parents or are satisfied with the parent–child relationship (Kandel & Andrews, 1987; Tarter et al., 1993). Preliminary evidence also suggests that risks for adult alcohol abuse are lower when a person's family of origin emphasized family "rituals," such as a family dinner hour, vacations, and holiday celebrations. Because these rituals provide opportunities for family communication and shared experiences, they are ideal for fostering the feelings of support and commitment that are linked to a lower probability of problem drinking (Bennett & Wolin, 1990).

Adolescents' drinking tends to mirror that of their parents, suggesting that children imitate the patterns of alcohol use and abuse that they see at home. So, as suggested earlier, if parents use alcohol to deal with stress-induced emotions, adolescents are more likely to believe that alcohol will reduce their own tensions. In general, the more parents drink, the earlier their children begin to drink (Kandel, Kessler, & Marguiles, 1978). When parents' consumption is low to moderate, their adolescent children usually come to match their parents' pattern.

However, when parents are either nondrinkers or very heavy drinkers, there is less linkage between parent and child drinking patterns (Barnes et al., 1986; Harburg, Davis, & Caplan, 1982). For example, the children of parents who drink no alcohol tend to drink either heavily or not at all. For some of these children, parental modeling seems to promote abstinence. For others, the parents' rigid, black-and-white views on alcohol might set up drinking as an issue about which they can rebel against parental authority (Lawson, Peterson, & Lawson, 1983). Linkages between parents' and adolescents' drinking depend on several other factors besides modeling; the quality of interactions with other family members, inherited vulnerabilities to alcohol, and exposure to peers who use alcohol are also important.

Peer group influence is another important social factor in shaping drinking, at least among young people. Indeed, many programs aimed at preventing drinking by young people are based on the assumption that social acceptance is an important reinforcer of drinking, especially during adolescence. However, surprisingly little is known about how peer groups operate in this regard. It is reasonable to assume that many, if not most, adolescents are introduced to drinking by their peers, but it is less clear that the peer group is a primary factor in causing problem drinking. Stress reduction, alcohol expectancies, and inherited vulnerability probably contribute as well. It may be that adolescents who are predisposed to alcohol problems select their friends on the basis of similar attitudes about alcohol use, so that peer processes merely reinforce and solidify the drinking patterns already being developed.

One study of peer influences on drug use in general found that the use of drugs by friends was a better predictor of drug use than the presence of emotional problems (Swaim et al., 1989). Another larger study measured the use of psychoactive substances (including alcohol) by more than 1,000 adolescents as they progressed through the seventh, eighth, and ninth grades (Wills et al., 1996). The youngsters whose drug use increased the most during this 3-year period shared several of the sociocultural risk factors we have discussed. Compared with students who did not increase their use of substances, these individuals

- suffered a greater number of major life stressors;
- had parents who used substances more frequently;
- associated more with substance-using peers; and
- felt less family support.

Controversy

Alcohol Abuse: Sin, Disease, or Habit?

The history of alcohol research and treatment and, to a major extent, approaches to other substances of abuse have been shaped by three broad viewpoints (Thombs, 1994). Advocates of each of these viewpoints have often regarded one another's ideas with suspicion, resulting in heated, sometimes hostile, disagreements about the best way to explain and treat substance abuse.

The *moral* perspective regards alcoholism as a sin or weakness of character. Punishment or repentance is often the treatment of choice, and many advocates of this perspective endorse legal sanctions as the primary strategy for reducing problem drinking.

A second perspective, the *disease model*, sees alcohol abuse and

dependence as symptoms of an illness. According to the disease model, certain individuals have physiological vulnerabilities—probably of genetic origin—that render them unable to control their consumption of alcohol. Treatment based on this perspective consists either of recovery-oriented self-help groups such as Alcoholics Anonymous or care in a hospital or clinic. There is emphasis also on treating the medical complications (e.g., cirrhosis of the liver) often associated with advanced alcohol dependence. Because the disease model emphasizes individuals' inability to control drinking, complete abstinence is usually the treatment goal.

A third, *learning perspective*, contrasts sharply with both previous views in suggesting that alco-

hol abuse and dependence are acquired patterns of maladaptive behavior, harmful habits that anyone can learn if exposed to environmental conditions that support excessive drinking. According to this view, operant learning, classical conditioning, and cognitive expectations lead to and maintain excessive alcohol use. Clinicians adopting a learning perspective are more likely than others to consider alternatives to complete abstinence as a treatment goal.

Currently, alcoholism is usually publically portrayed as an illness. The DSM-IV uses the term *disorder* to describe substance abuse and dependence, and government agencies such as the National Institute on Alcohol Abuse and Alcoholism generally support

---

When several of these factors occur together, they might increase the risk of alcohol abuse by making it generally harder for youths to regulate their emotions and behavior. Increased use of substances might be just one by-product of this impaired coping ability.

A Multifactor Model. As noted in earlier chapters, in relation to most forms of mental disorder, debates about which causal factor is most important eventually give way to models that recognize the combined and interacting roles of several different factors. As the Controversy section above suggests, the field of alcohol abuse was relatively slow to develop this multifactorial perspective, largely because of long-standing, intensely held, and deeply conflicting views about whether alcoholism is a moral failing, a disease, or a learned habit (Thombs, 1994).

Many scientists now argue that alcohol abuse and dependence stem from an interplay of several physiological, psychological, and social factors, all of which must be taken into account to fully explain these disorders (Devor, 1994; Epstein & McCrady, 1994). One such multifactor theory has been proposed by Ralph Tarter and Michael Vanyukov (1994),

who claim that certain genetically determined *temperaments* interact with various *facilitating environments* to produce a heightened risk for alcohol use problems. Their model has a developmental theme: it suggests that, although interactions between high-risk temperaments and environments have their roots in early childhood, well before the emergence of significant alcohol problems, these interactions can raise the risk of alcohol problems at any stage of life.

Table 13.1 lists five temperamental characteristics and four environmental conditions that may interact to promote high risks for alcohol abuse. Some of the proposed high-risk temperamental characteristics are associated with the biological markers and psychological characteristics of alcoholics reviewed earlier. For example, high emotional reactivity is consistent with the high rates of tension and anxiety found in alcoholics and their offspring (Chassin, Rogosch, & Barrera, 1991; Mezzich et al., 1993), while poor attention span fits with the differences in evoked potentials found between sons of alcoholic fathers and sons of nonalcoholic fathers.

In the Tarter and Vanyukov model, neither a "bad" temperament nor a "bad" environment *alone* causes alcohol abuse. It is the combination of specific

the recovery movement and, as a corollary, the disease model. Accordingly, this model is frequently advocated by physicians, whose training emphasizes biological causality. It is also endorsed by alcoholism counselors who follow the 12-step program of Alcoholics Anonymous (AA) and the philosophy that alcoholics lack control over their drinking and must therefore abstain from drinking forever. The popularity of the disease model does have certain advantages. Calling alcoholism a disease makes it less stigmatizing than labeling it a moral problem. Thus, the disease model may reduce guilt, allowing recovering individuals to focus on how to maintain an alcohol-free life (Thombs, 1994).

However, many academic psychologists and some physicians criticize the disease model, contending that empirical data do not support it. They point, for example, to several studies showing that alcohol-dependent drinkers can choose not to drink under laboratory conditions that provide strong reinforcement for abstinence (Fingarette, 1988). Furthermore, and in contradiction to the loss-of-control hypothesis, some alcoholics can ingest alcohol and then limit their subsequent intake. So, although the disease model is a comforting one (and well-suited to motivating alcoholics and their families to seek help in changing alcohol abuse patterns) scientific data on alcoholism suggests that the disease view is by no means the only viable one. Based on this research, recent theorizing about alcohol abuse and dependence seeks to integrate aspects of all three models, bringing the field closer to accepting a diathesis–stress model (e.g., McCrady, 1994; Tarter & Vanyukov, 1994).

Thinking Critically

- Which model do you believe holds the most promise for understanding and treating alcoholism? Why?
- How do each of these models view the likelihood that alcoholics will overestimate or underestimate their ability to control their drinking?
- How likely do you think it is that scientific data—or people's prior beliefs—will be more influential in resolving the controversy over the nature of alcoholism?

TABLE 13.1 Temperaments and Social Environments That Combine to Elevate Risk for Alcoholism

Temperaments

High activity level ("always on the go")

High emotionality ("reacts strongly to the slightest thing")

Low soothability (difficult to calm down after being upset)

Poor attention span/persistence

Disinhibition ("ready to try or say anything, go anywhere")

. . . in combination with . . .

Social environments that include

Infrequent parental stimulation/attention

Excessive parental punishment

Poor parental monitoring of child's or adolescent's whereabouts

Deviant peer group

Source: Tarter & Vanyukov, 1994.

temperamental and environmental characteristics that is critical. Different combinations of high-risk temperaments and environmental liabilities create various *pathways* to an alcohol problem. For example, the combination of *high activity level* and *ineffective parental discipline* constitutes a pathway that is different from *low sociability* and exposure to a *deviant peer group*. One particular pathway has been identified for children of alcoholics (Chassin et al., 1993): high emotional reactivity in the child, combined with family stress and poor parenting skills, leads to a greater likelihood of affiliating with drug-using peers in adolescence and, in turn, to a greater likelihood of alcohol use. In other words, youngsters may be predisposed toward—and may learn to follow—any of several pathways to problem drinking.

Treatment and Prevention of Alcohol Use Disorders

Given the many patterns of alcohol use problems and the multiple factors and pathways that lead to these problems, it should not be surprising to learn that no single treatment is effective in changing the behavior of all, or even most, problem drinkers. But are some treatments more effective than others? Do some treatments work better for certain types of alcohol abusers?

For many years, the most common treatment of alcohol abuse and dependency in the United States was based on the *Minnesota model,* in which alcoholism is viewed as a disease. Named for its place of origin, the Minnesota model typically requires patients to be hospitalized for 4 to 6 weeks, although treatment in outpatient clinics is becoming more popular. For those who show signs of alcohol intoxication or withdrawal, the treatment begins with hospital-based **detoxification,** a supervised period of "drying out," often aided by drugs or other interventions to ease withdrawal symptoms and remedy nutritional deficits. For all patients, the main focus of treatment is on education about the consequences of alcohol use and abuse, individual counseling for psychological problems, group therapy to enhance interpersonal skills, and—at the end of the hospital or clinic program—continued participation in group meetings of Alcoholics Anonymous. Total abstinence from alcohol is nearly always the goal of the Minnesota treatment model and, to emphasize the dangers of relapse, its proponents refer to alcoholics who successfully complete treatment as "in remission" or "recovering," not "cured."

Alcoholics Anonymous. Alcoholics need not complete Minnesota model treatments in order to get help from Alcoholics Anonymous (AA). Indeed, AA works with more alcoholics than any other treatment organization. First organized in 1935 by two alcoholics ("Dr. Bob," a physician, and "Bill W.," a stockbroker), AA is based on the twelve steps to recovery listed in Figure 13.4. Today, thousands of AA groups can be found in countries all around the world.

The AA treatment philosophy is based on the idea that alcoholism is a disease that can be controlled only if the alcoholic strives for complete abstinence. AA members are encouraged to attend self-help meetings with other alcoholics whenever they wish, and many do so several times a week. At first, they are urged merely to accept that they are alcoholics (called "first stepping"), but they are gradually indoctrinated into all aspects of AA's spiritual approach to staying sober. Members who have maintained sobriety for a time serve as sponsors for newcomers. These sponsors answer questions, offer tips on how to stay sober, and maintain frequent personal contact to help the recovery process.

The effectiveness of the AA approach is difficult to assess scientifically because AA group membership is anonymous, and AA has traditionally not been interested in helping researchers conduct outcome studies. Recent reviews (e.g., Emrick et al., 1993) do suggest that members who regularly attend AA meetings have a better chance of maintaining sobriety than those who do not. However, it also appears that many alcoholics who start AA—perhaps

---

Alcoholics Anonymous is a free, nonprofessional, peer-directed counseling program that adheres to a spiritual philosophy defined by these twelve steps.

1. We admitted we were powerless over alcohol—that our lives had become unmanageable.
2. Came to believe that a Power greater than ourselves could restore us to sanity.
3. Made a decision to turn our will and our lives over to the care of God as *we understood Him.*
4. Made a searching and fearless inventory of ourselves.
5. Admitted to God, to ourselves, and to another human being the exact nature of our wrongs.
6. Were entirely ready to have God remove all these defects of character.
7. Humbly asked him to remove our shortcomings.
8. Made a list of all persons we had harmed, and became willing to make amends to them all.

9. Made direct amends to such people wherever possible, except when to do so would injure them or others.
10. Continued to take personal inventory and when we were wrong promptly admitted it.
11. Sought through prayer and meditation to improve our conscious contact with God *as we understood Him,* praying only for knowledge of His will for us and the power to carry that out.
12. Having had a spiritual awakening as a result of these steps, we tried to carry this message to alcoholics, and to practice these principles in all our affairs.

FIGURE 13.4

The Twelve Steps of Alcoholics Anonymous

Tens of thousands of AA chapters with more than a million members have been organized around the world. Most AA members are men between the ages of 30 and 50. Drinkers who feel they have completely lost control over their alcohol use may benefit most from AA.

more than half—discontinue participation in the first year. So the overall efficacy of AA is still unknown. Its advocates believe it is the best alcoholism intervention available, while its detractors argue that other types of treatment are necessary, especially for the many alcoholics who avoid or drop out of AA.

Marital and Family Therapy. Alcohol and other substance abuse patterns are inextricably linked to the close social relationships of the abuser. In many cases, a spouse, parent, or close friend can inadvertently support alcohol abuse by the way he or she responds to it. Sometimes the abuse becomes a preoccupation of another family member whose "job" becomes protecting, monitoring, or censuring the abuser, a role perhaps learned in family relationships during childhood (Koffinke, 1991). Such people, described as **codependents,** can become so enmeshed in another person's drinking problems that they actually prevent changes in the abuse pattern. Even if there is no codependency, marital and family relationships can contribute to abuse, as when marital conflict stimulates bouts of heavy drinking.

Given their potential impact on drinking behavior, it is not surprising that alcoholism treatment programs can be made more effective by involving the patient's spouse and other family members (Bowers & Al-Redha, 1990). In some programs, the spouse may be present as a spectator, participate in alcohol-focused counseling sessions, or take part in marital therapy aimed at teaching communication skills, conflict resolution techniques, and examining the family's role in supporting problem drinking. In one study, alcohol abusers who received marital therapy were found to drink less, report greater marital satisfaction, and experience fewer marital separations 18 months later than did abusers whose spouses participated only in the patient's alcohol-focused counseling sessions (McCrady et al., 1991).

Behavioral Treatments. Alcohol can be thought of as an unconditioned stimulus that elicits unconditioned responses in the form of pleasant physical reactions. Behavior therapists have developed learning-based procedures designed to help alcoholics associate alcohol with *unpleasant* stimuli, and thus make drinking a less pleasant prospect. For example, in aversion therapy, the sight, smell, and taste of alcohol are repeatedly presented while the alcoholic patient is nauseated or vomiting as a result of taking an emetic drug. After repeated trials, these alcohol-related sensory cues should begin to elicit nausea or other unpleasant reactions (see Chapter 1 for a review of classical conditioning principles). By itself, aversion therapy has had limited success in treating alcoholism (Costello, 1975; Nietzel et al., 1977), but it can enhance the effects of more traditional treatments (e.g., Smith, Frawley, & Polissar, 1991).

Behavioral treatments based on operant conditioning (see Chapter 1) attempt to change drinking by manipulating reinforcement contingencies for alcohol use. Nathan Azrin's **community reinforcement** model (Azrin et al., 1994) has proved to be one of the most effective of these operant approaches. In this intervention, several social and environmental influences are used to help substance abusers maintain sobriety. Abusers are taught to recognize the circumstances in which drinking is most likely, as well as the social reinforcers that help support this drinking. They then learn how to arrange reinforcement contingencies to reward sobriety and to avoid situations that encourage drinking.

Behavioral therapy is also used to treat relationship problems that underlie the alcoholic's problems and to help the alcoholic develop the skills needed to deal with vocational and financial difficulties. Finally, special attention is given to helping alcoholics develop new friendships and social contacts so that they spend more time with people who will support sobriety and discourage drinking.

Medication. Prescription drugs have been used both to treat alcohol withdrawal and to curb drinking behavior. Withdrawal effects can be minimized by a variety of drugs that mimic the neurochemical effects of alcohol. *Benzodiazepines* such as Valium or Ativan are the medications of choice for this purpose, and they are given in gradually decreasing doses as withdrawal proceeds. Unfortunately, the benzodiazepines not only have undesirable side effects, but some researchers question their use on the grounds that they are addictive and that most alcoholics do not experience withdrawal symptoms severe enough to warrant this intervention (Wartenberg et al., 1990).

Medications have been used in two ways to discourage drinking. In the first, alcoholics are given drugs such as *disulfiram* (Antabuse) that create increased heart rate, nausea, vomiting, and other unpleasant effects if patients consume alcohol. Controlled studies show that a dose of Antabuse taken in the morning, for example, will be effective in discouraging drinking throughout the day (Fuller et al., 1986), but it has little effect in the long run simply because most alcoholics stop using it whenever they want to drink. Antabuse also has negative side effects (e.g., it can intensify depression) and, if the patient takes too much of it, can create physically dangerous reactions to alcohol. It is not uncommon for suicidal alcoholics to drink heavily after taking an overdose of Antabuse.

The second use of drugs to promote sobriety involves the administration of **antagonists,** which block the effects of other drugs. These anticraving drugs target the neurotransmitters—such as dopamine, serotonin, and the endogenous opiates—that mediate alcohol's effects on the brain and help create the sensation of craving. The most promising of these anticraving drugs is *naltrexone,* which interferes with the production of endogenous opiates. Preliminary studies have shown that naltrexone is more effective than placebos in reducing drinking

during outpatient treatment and in preventing relapse after treatment (O'Malley et al., 1992; Volpicelli et al., 1992). It is not yet clear how effective naltrexone or other anticraving medications will be in the long term. Their success depends on how compliant the individual is in taking the medication and whether the anticraving effects of these medications can outweigh the positive alcohol expectancies, the tension reduction effects, the influence of codependents, and the other psychological factors that support alcohol abuse.

Controlled Drinking Treatments. Some alcoholics avoid AA and other treatment programs because the prospect of living without alcohol is too threatening. Is it possible for alcoholics to learn to drink in moderation? This question was raised as a scientific issue more than 25 years ago, and it has generated some of the most intense controversy ever seen in the field of alcoholism. The controlled drinking debate was sparked by a study by Mark and Linda Sobell, two psychology graduate students, in which they compared a program for teaching alcoholics to drink in moderation with an abstinence-oriented program similar to AA (Sobell & Sobell, 1973, 1976). Their results showed that alcoholics could engage in controlled drinking and that, overall, the moderation group had somewhat better outcomes than the abstinence group. At about the same time, a study by the RAND Corporation (Armor et al., 1976) suggested that not all alcoholics who resumed drinking after treatment inevitably relapsed into problem drinking. In other studies, alcohol abusers were helped to moderate their drinking by becoming more sensitive to bodily cues associated with rising blood alcohol levels and by honing better self-control skills (Lovibond & Caddy, 1970; Miller & Muñoz, 1982).

These results were decried by advocates of the total abstinence camp, and the Sobells were charged with scientific misconduct and ethical violations when follow-up assessments revealed that only one of the 20 alcoholics in the controlled drinking group had been able to maintain his controlled drinking and that four had died from alcohol-induced problems (Pendery, Maltzman, & West, 1982). An independent investigative committee later refuted these charges, and objective reviews of the Sobell's research showed that death from alcohol-related problems were about as frequent in the abstinence group.

The emotional fallout from these bitter disputes has led to continuing mistrust between proponents and opponents of controlled drinking goals. The ferocity of the controversy also led to the virtual disappearance of studies designed to compare the value of treatments aimed at controlled drinking versus total abstinence. What evidence there is suggests that controlled drinking might indeed be an appropriate goal of treatment, especially for those patients who are not physically dependent on alcohol. Even experts who are sympathetic to controlled drinking strategies now tend to agree that abstinence is the proper goal for addicted, chronic alcoholics. Controlled drinking might be the most appropriate goal for younger drinkers who have not become dependent on alcohol (Miller, 1983; Nathan, 1987b).

Relapse Prevention. A study comparing abstinence-oriented treatment with one in which patients could choose the goal of abstinence or controlled drinking found that, as might be expected, abstinence rates 1 year later were significantly higher in the abstinence-oriented program (14 versus 2 percent) (Keso & Salaspuro, 1990). The relatively low percentage of abstainers in *both* groups attests, however, to the difficulty of achieving abstinence even when it is the explicit goal. In one national study of alcoholism treatments, 21 percent of participants remained abstinent for at least 1 year after treatment and 7 percent were abstinent after 4 years, but 54 percent continued to experience alcohol-related difficulties (Polich, Armor, & Braiker, 1981). In other studies, abstinence rates in the year following treatment range from about 20 percent to as high as 75 percent, depending on the length and extent of the patients' alcohol abuse. However, over longer periods of time, the percentage of successful outcomes tends to decline as most treated alcoholics—even in abstinence-oriented programs—eventually begin to use alcohol again, a process known as **relapse.**

According to the disease model, and to proponents of AA, if a treated alcoholic resumes drinking, alcohol abuse or dependency will inevitably follow. However, leading alcoholics to expect that "one drink leads to twenty" may actually create a self-fulfilling prophecy, increasing the likelihood of continued drinking once any drinking occurs. A different approach aims at teaching problem drinkers specific relapse-prevention skills in an effort to prevent isolated drinking episodes from being repeated and eventually escalating into alcohol abuse. The relapse-prevention approach encourages alcoholics to believe that a lapse in abstinence can be a valuable learning experience that can potentially strengthen previous treatment gains (Lewis, Dana, & Blevins, 1988).

Alan Marlatt and his colleagues have been pioneers in the field of relapse prevention (Marlatt & Gordon, 1985). Marlatt believes that relapse is most likely when the recovering alcoholic engages in self-defeating thoughts that bring about "inadvertent" exposures to circumstances that increase the risk of drinking. The case of Jim provides an example.

After 2 or 3 months of abstinence, Jim, a recovering alcoholic, began purchasing cigarettes and groceries at a store next to a bar frequented by his former drinking buddies. Initially, Jim told himself that he went to this store only because it offered easy parking, but this was a dangerous deception because it soon led Jim to stop by the bar to chat with his old friends. After a couple of visits, Jim started to drink again—"just to be friendly." One night, however, he stayed for 3 hours, drank heavily, and was arrested for drunken driving on his way home.

Marlatt and his colleague Judith Gordon (1985) contend that such cases of self-deception result from *apparently irrelevant decisions* that, if unchecked, accumulate and eventually lead to drinking. Cognitions such as "I owe myself a drink" or any number of positive expectancies about the consequences of "one small drink" may set off a chain of faulty decisions. Once there is a lapse, many alcoholics experience intense guilt and shame that generate a cascade of increasingly pejorative self-evaluations ("I've let my family down."; "I'm a complete failure."). These cognitions then increase the probability of continued drinking, an outcome known as the **abstinence violation effect** (Marlatt & Gordon, 1985).

Relapse prevention techniques teach the alcoholic to monitor self-defeating cognitions and to replace them with different thinking strategies. For example, Jim learned that it was better for him to shop at a different store where he did not have to overcome so many temptations to drink. Jogging became a daily ritual, a kind of "positive addiction" that replaced drinking. Finally, Jim learned that he could lessen his urge to drink if, instead of thinking about how good it felt to drink, he focused on how miserable he felt as he sat in jail after his drunken driving arrest. Initial evaluations have shown relapse prevention to be useful for a variety of substance abuse problems, including alcohol dependence (Baer et al., 1992).

Brief Interventions. A preventive focus is evident in a relatively new treatment approach that offers brief intervention programs to problem drinkers who have not yet developed alcohol dependence. Many such programs are aimed at drinkers who consume an average of four or five drinks per day but who experience few adverse social consequences. Other programs aim at helping adolescents or children delay drinking, as the Prevention section on pages 464–465 discusses.

Prevention   Delaying and Deterring Drinking by Adolescents

As noted earlier, the most severe forms of alcoholism in adults begin with drinking during adolescence, so many alcoholism prevention programs are specifically aimed at discouraging teenage drinking. Traditionally, such programs consisted of stricter enforcement of underage drinking laws and warnings about the negative consequences of alcohol and drugs. In the 1980s, for example, young people were told to "just say no" to alcohol and other drugs. Today, prevention programs are becoming more sophisticated. Most are school-based and comprehensive enough to target marijuana, tobacco, and other substances that tend to be associated with the use of alcohol.

These prevention programs employ one or more of four components. The first, *affective education,* attempts to enhance adolescents' self-esteem and clarify their personal values about substance use. The second, called *life skills training,* improves skill at interpersonal communication, conflict resolution, and assertiveness. The third component, *resistance training,* is simi-

lar to life skills training but focuses specifically on teaching youngsters how to resist pressure from peers to use alcohol and other drugs. Finally, *normative education* promotes peer group norms against alcohol and drug use, corrects false impressions about the prevalence of substance use among peers (e.g., challenging the idea that "everyone is doing it"), and encourages youngsters to make public commitments to remain free of alcohol and other drugs. Most programs also provide education about the negative consequences of drug and alcohol use, with an emphasis on important short-term consequences, such as how drinking leads to elevated risk of pregnancy or sexually transmitted diseases stemming from alcohol-induced sexual behavior.

Many well-designed, evaluative studies suggest that these programs can result in a certain amount of change in adolescents' drinking attitudes and behavior (Mrazek & Haggerty, 1994). Overall, affective education tends to be the

least effective approach, while normative education tends to be the most effective (Hansen, 1994; Hansen & Graham, 1991). Some studies suggest that multi-component interventions that combine school-based programs with parental involvement and media coverage may be particularly promising.

Evaluative studies also show, however, just how difficult it is to bring about widespread changes in young people's drinking behavior. Even the most effective programs show only a modest impact on adolescents' alcohol use (Mrazek & Haggerty, 1994). One example is a normative education program for seventh graders called the *Adolescent Alcohol Prevention Trial.* In this program, students conducted television-style interviews with nondrinking peers and discussed them in class; they also wrote and videotaped antidrinking rap songs (Hansen & Graham, 1991). These students showed an average increase of 4 percent in reported alcohol intoxication in the year following the intervention,

---

Participants in brief interventions are usually recruited through primary health care agencies or at their workplace, often following a brief screening that has revealed a problematic level of alcohol consumption. Most of these people have not sought treatment before and often do not regard their drinking as problematic.

Some brief intervention programs teach controlled drinking skills such as goal setting ("no more than two drinks a day"), self-monitoring (counting the number of drinks and slowing the rate of consumption), and self-reinforcement ("I'll buy a new compact disc whenever I go a week with fewer than 10 drinks.") (Harris & Miller, 1990). Other brief interventions include health education seminars, alco-

hol screening interviews by primary-care physicians or nurses, or brief marital counseling.

Dan Kivlahan, Alan Marlatt, and their colleagues have developed a 6-session, cognitive-behavioral program for light-drinking college students, called the Alcohol Skills Training Program (ASTP; Kivlahan et al., 1990). ASTP is designed to meet the special needs of college-age drinkers by deemphasizing (1) the goal of abstinence, (2) long-term health risks of drinking and (3) authoritative messages. The emphasis is placed, instead, on promoting (1) controlled drinking through relapse prevention skills and BAC estimation, (2) avoidance of hangovers and other immediate negative consequences of drinking, and (3) nonconfrontational group discussions about the effects of

compared with an increase of 11 percent among students who did not receive this intervention (Hansen & Graham, 1991). This 7 percent difference is small, but if this program were offered to all junior high school students, it would translate into hundreds of thousands of cases in which the onset of drinking is delayed. The fact that both untreated *and* treated students showed increases in alcohol use also points to the fact that any adolescent prevention program is fighting an uphill battle against culturally supported alcohol use.

With this fact in mind, some alcoholism prevention researchers are trying to intervene well before the teenage years, especially with children at special risk for alcoholism. In one innovative project at Michigan State University, families containing the preschool son of an alcoholic father were invited to participate in a 10-month educational intervention that combined training in parenting, marital communication, and conflict resolution. The intervention improved

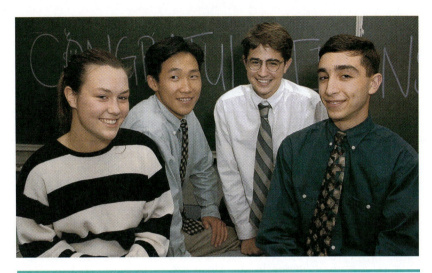

Because of the influence of peers on problem drinking and the fact that youth who begin drinking early in life develop more alcohol-related problems, many prevention programs for problem drinking take place in schools. These students graduated from a 6-week program that taught them how to counsel peers on the dangers of addictive behaviors such as drinking, drug abuse, and gambling.

children's conduct, but only if their families completed the entire program and if their mothers maintained a high investment in it (Nye, Zucker, & Fitzgerald, 1995). It remains to be seen whether these early changes in the boys' behavior will reduce their risks of alcohol abuse in adolescence or adulthood.

drinking on behavior (Fromme et al., 1994). College students taking part in this program have been able to reduce their drinking rates by about 40 percent and maintain these reductions for at least 2 years (Baer et al., 1992). Jerry, our chapter-opening case, responded to a campus newspaper notice about a program much like the ASTP. However, an initial evaluation found that his alcohol and drug problems were too severe for this type of program; he was referred to an off-campus facility that catered to younger drinkers.

Thomas Babor (1994) reviewed 25 well-designed studies evaluating brief interventions and concluded that they are effective, as indicated by self-reports on frequency of alcohol use and alcohol-related problems. In some studies, these reports were confirmed by biological indicators of alcohol consumption. The more intensive versions of these interventions (such as those teaching controlled drinking skills) are usually more effective than less intense interventions (e.g., screening and feedback by a physician), especially for individuals whose drinking is more severe.

Patient–Treatment Matching. Problem drinkers can be differentiated by their alcohol use pattern, their drinking history, and their expectancies about alcohol. They can also be classified in terms of demographic factors (gender, ethnicity, urban versus rural residence), Type I or Type II alcoholism, presence or absence of comorbid psychiatric conditions, and psychological characteristics (Mattson & Allen, 1991).

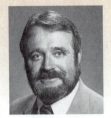

A Talk with Alan Marlatt

Substance Abuse

Dr. Alan Marlatt is Professor of Psychology at the University of Washington in Seattle. He is one of the world's leading experts on substance abuse and pioneered the relapse-prevention approach to treating substance abuse.

Q *In your view, do mood disorders usually lead to problem drinking, or are mood disorders more often a consequence of heavy drinking?*

A I find examples of both in my clinical work. Many problem drinkers drink to "self-medicate" their depression or anxiety, although drinking only exacerbates a mood problem. The other direction of causality, in which heavy drinking leads to depression, is less likely.

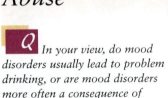

Relapse-prevention training is like... a fire drill...

Q *What were your original goals for relapse prevention as an alcoholism treatment?*

A Relapse prevention was never designed to be a treatment in and of itself, but rather a supplement to help maintain the impact of other treatments. We developed this approach with two goals in mind. The first was to avoid relapses if possible. An equally important second goal was to *manage* a relapse if and when it occurs. Several recent studies have shown that relapse prevention can in fact help contain relapses. Among the alcoholics who relapsed in these studies, those taught cognitive-behavioral skills drank less alcohol overall and had fewer "intoxication days" than alcoholics without this training.

Q *Isn't there a risk that you are increasing the chances of relapse by preparing alcoholics for its occurrence?*

A The probability of a relapse—with or without relapse-prevention training—is extraordinarily high; the vast majority of heavy drinkers eventually experience a return to drinking. The chances of a prolonged relapse are increased by *not* teaching relapse skills. Relapse-prevention training is like participating in a fire drill—it's better to know it and need it than to need it and not know it.

Q *What's your view of the Prochaska, DiClemente, and Norcross "stages-of-change" model?*

A The model has a lot of intuitive appeal, especially the idea that different approaches may be needed, depending on a person's readiness to change. But there have been difficulties in reliably measuring a per-

Several studies have examined the extent to which alcoholics who differ on these dimensions show differing responses to particular treatment approaches. They have found, for example, that interventions such as Marlatt's relapse prevention program, which focus on teaching specific coping skills, tend to produce better outcomes in patients displaying higher levels of psychopathology and more severe alcohol-induced social problems. More conventional, "talking" therapy tends to work better for patients with less severe impairments (Cooney et al., 1991; Litt et al., 1992).

Another factor related to the likelihood of treatment success is the individual's readiness to change. According to a model developed by James Prochaska, Carlo DiClemente, and John Norcross (1992),

the process of changing drinking patterns (or other health-threatening behaviors) occurs in 5 stages, whether professional treatment is involved or not. These stages include:

1. *precontemplation,* in which the person is aware of a problem but has no intention to change;

2. *contemplation,* in which the person is aware of a problem and has begun to think about making changes but has not yet made a commitment to change;

3. *preparation,* in which the person is making small changes in behavior and intends to make more meaningful ones in the future;

son's specific stage of change. For example, classifying someone as "precontemplative" or "contemplative" is not easy to do. Another problem is that the process of change that forms the basis of the model has yet to be studied adequately. To really understand how people change, you need to study them *prospectively* over time, but the stages-of-change model wasn't developed in this way.

Q *Biologically oriented researchers have been searching for the ideal anticraving medication. Will a drug cure ever be found for alcoholism?*

A I very much doubt that medication alone will ever "cure" alcoholism. Naltrexone, for example, certainly does what it is supposed to do: it effectively blocks the action of opioid receptors that probably account for some of alcohol's rewarding effects on the brain. But naltrexone doesn't make the alcoholic *feel* any better, as alcohol can, at least at lower blood levels. As a result, alcoholics on the verge of a relapse may stop taking their naltrexone, so they can maximize reinforcement they get from alcohol.

Q *What about the combined effects of naltrexone and relapse prevention?*

A In theory, relapse prevention should help alcoholics remain on their medication longer by getting them to challenge the seemingly irrelevant cognitions that precede their decision to stop the medication; for example, telling themselves "I don't need meds anymore to not drink." Programs that combine behavior therapy with pharmacotherapy have particular promise, as shown in recent studies for cocaine, nicotine, and opioid dependence.

Q *Are most college students who drink heavily likely to become dependent on alcohol in later years?*

A It depends on family history. College life promotes high rates of alcohol consumption in many students. If the person comes from a family with a history of alcohol dependence, he or she is more likely to continue heavy drinking in later years.

---

4. *action,* in which the person has made substantial efforts to overcome the problem and has already reached a criterion for success in changing the targeted behavior; and

5. *maintenance,* in which the person works to prevent relapse so that positive changes become a new way of life.

As Figure 13.5 on page 468 shows, people often pass through the early phases several times before they are able to make permanent changes in a problem behavior. What implications does this readiness-for-change model have for matching alcoholic patients to various kinds of treatment? For one thing, it suggests that action-oriented programs such as those used by behavior therapists may not be helpful to individuals who are still at the precontemplation or contemplation stages. On the other hand, brief interventions aimed at teaching problem drinkers about the risks they face if they continue drinking and the changes they could make to lessen these risks might be ideal for people at the first two stages of the spiral.

However, not all matching studies have yielded positive results. Preliminary results from an eight-year research program—Project MATCH—has found that matching clients to treatments designed to address specific needs did not lead to better results. Whether they received cognitive-behavior therapy, brief motivational treatment, or a program aimed at helping

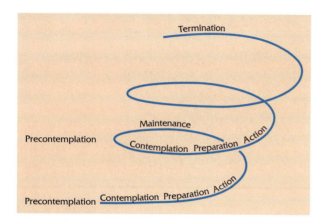

FIGURE 13.5

A Spiral Model of the Stages of Change
Many treatment failures result from a mismatch between the goals of the treatment program and the participant's stage of readiness to change.
Source: Prochaska et al., 1992.

them get involved in AA, alcoholics did about equally well in terms of sobriety (Project MATCH Research Group, 1997). In fact, regardless of the "type" of alcoholic, brief and relatively inexpensive treatment was just as effective as more complex treatment.

In Review

Alcohol abuse and dependence are disorders that:

- are experienced by between 13 and 16 million Americans;
- cost society billions of dollars in crime, illness, absenteeism, and serious accidents; and
- are often comorbid with other mental disorders.

Several factors are involved in causing alcohol abuse and dependence, including:

- genetic risk, especially for males and Type II alcoholics;
- biological irregularities that increase certain individuals' vulnerability to the rewarding effects of alcohol;
- the reinforcing properties of alcohol along with the expectancies that individuals hold about alcohol; and
- family, peer group, and social factors that promote drinking

Interventions for alcohol abuse and dependence:

- include detoxification and inpatient programs, Alcoholics Anonymous, behavioral treatments, family therapy, medication, brief interventions, and prevention efforts;
- differ in whether they aim to promote abstinence or controlled drinking; and
- have, in an attempt to boost their effectiveness, been matched to individual variables such as type of alcoholism, severity and duration of alcohol dependence, and readiness for change.

Other Depressants

Depressants refer to a group of drugs, including alcohol, that inhibit neurotransmitter activity in the central nervous system. These drugs enhance the activity of GABA which, as noted earlier, is the brain's major inhibitory neurotransmitter. The ability of depressants to reduce neural activity leads to several effects, including sedation, enhanced sleep (a *hypnotic* effect), and reduced anxiety (an *anxiolytic* effect). Most of the more than two dozen drugs in this category fall into one of two major types: barbiturates and benzodiazepines.

Barbiturates

Odorless, white, crystalline derivatives of the chemical compound *barbituric acid* make up the class of drugs known as the **barbiturates.** Seconal, Tuinal, and Nembutal are familiar examples. Often called "downs" or "downers," barbiturates are prescribed in tablet form as sedatives or hypnotics for persons suffering from insomnia. Although barbiturates induce sleep in most individuals, they also have certain drawbacks, including reduction of rapid eye movement (REM) sleep. Furthermore, sleep disruptions are common when people stop taking these drugs.

At low doses, barbiturates typically produce relaxation and mild euphoria, but at higher doses they bring about a state similar to alcohol intoxication, including impaired motor coordination and poor judgment and concentration. High doses of barbiturates can also depress respiratory functions and lower blood pressure and body temperature to the point of coma and death, especially if taken with another depressant such as alcohol. Sadly, the ease with which this combination induces loss of conscious-

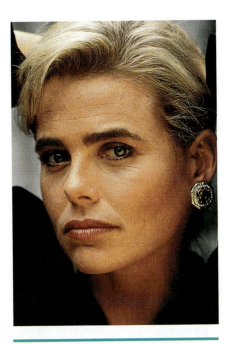

The death of Margaux Hemingway brought renewed attention to the risks of barbiturate abuse. Fatal overdoses of barbiturates claim the lives of many abusers. In some cases, the overdose is deliberate, but in others it may be largely an accident occasioned by the careless use that is so customary among abusers.

ness catches many users by surprise. Accordingly, accidental death is a major risk of barbiturate use, and suicidal people often kill themselves by knowingly combining barbiturates with alcohol.

Benzodiazepines

Drugs derived from *benzoic acid* are called **benzodiazepines.** They are prescribed primarily to alleviate anxiety and panic disorders, although they are sometimes taken to relieve muscle spasms. Commonly prescribed benzodiazepines include Valium, Librium, and Xanax. Like barbiturates, they bring about feelings of relaxation and mild euphoria but are less likely to produce significant toxicity. For this reason, benzodiazepines are regarded by many family doctors as having a low risk for physical dependence, accidental death, and suicide (Dupont & Saylor, 1992; Warneke, 1991). However, this view is probably too optimistic. Toxicity and overdoses do occur when benzodiazepines are taken with other depressants, a common pattern among substance abusers. Autopsies of completed suicides involving

depressant drugs have found equal rates of benzodiazepines and barbiturates as the lethal agents (Mendelson & Rich, 1993). So, although barbiturates, benzodiazepines account for their share of tragic deaths, and prolonged use of both types of drugs can cause dependence and withdrawal.

Depressant Abuse and Dependence

Many Americans have received prescriptions for benzodiazepines or barbiturates at some point in their lives. More than 15 percent get prescriptions for them in any given year (APA, 1994). About 1 percent of these people have also met the criteria for abusing or being dependent on one of these drugs at some point in their lives.

There is substantial variation in the use and abuse patterns associated with benzodiazepines or barbiturates. One pattern is shown by adolescents and young adults who engage in "recreational" use of sedatives, hypnotics, or anxiolytics. These people take the equivalent of two or three therapeutic doses to produce a pleasurable high or reduce social anxiety. Recreational users are typically introduced to these drugs by friends who obtain them illegally. Polydrug use is common in these circumstances; downers are often mixed with alcohol and marijuana. For some recreational users, social use escalates to weekly, then daily, use and leads to high levels of tolerance. Some heavy users may take 10 to 20 times the therapeutic dose of a barbiturate or benzodiazepine daily.

Another pattern of abuse is observed in middle-class individuals, of middle age or older, who initially take prescribed depressants for anxiety, insomnia, or pain. These people then become dependent on the drug and begin to take more than the amount prescribed, as illustrated by the following case.

*B*etty was a well-known attorney in her community. After she suffered a pulled muscle in her leg from a minor skiing accident, Betty's physician prescribed 5 mg of Valium daily to help ease the pain. But Betty gradually became "hooked" on the Valium. Unbeknownst to her family and friends, she steadily increased her use of the drug. Over a 2-year period, she visited 17 doctors and 20 pharmacies to maintain what had grown to a daily intake of 70 mg of Valium. Eventually, she spent more and more time going to doctors and driving to out-of-town pharmacies. By this time, her drug habit seriously interfered with the responsibilities of her work.

Hypnotics are often prescribed for elderly people to control the sleeping problems that tend to increase with age. In one study, 15 percent of men and 23 percent of women over age 70 were taking such medication; for those over 80, use rates increased to 22 percent and 35 percent in men and women, respectively (Asplund, 1995). The elderly suffer especially pronounced impairments in cognition, memory, and coordination as a result of taking depressant medications. In fact, drug-induced confusion may cause them to forget that they have taken the medication and so they take more until intoxication or overdose occurs.

Individuals undergoing withdrawal from a depressant often experience high blood pressure, accelerated heart rate, and rapid breathing. The severity of withdrawal symptoms is determined by the length of drug use, dosage, and type of depressant (Cambor & Millman, 1991). Short-acting drugs whose effects last 10 hours or less (e.g., the benzodiazepine *Atavin*) provoke withdrawal within hours after drug use is stopped, and these symptoms usually ease within a few days. Longer-acting drugs such as Valium lead to withdrawal symptoms that may not develop for more than a week after discontinuing the drug and may take a month or more to disappear.

Even modest therapeutic doses of depressant drugs can lead to withdrawal. Withdrawal from Valium, for example, has been observed in individuals taking as little as 15 mg daily for 6 to 8 months, an amount and duration well within the range that physicians prescribe for several disorders. Following a course of dosages of this amount or somewhat higher, withdrawal symptoms are relatively mild, including anxiety, agitation, tremulousness, and insomnia. Discontinuing daily doses of about 40 mg of Valium can lead to more serious withdrawal symptoms, including increases in coronary activity, sweating, elevated body temperature, nausea, and vomiting. If the dosage had been 100 mg per day, seizures and delirium like those seen in alcohol withdrawal are likely.

Treatment of Depressant Abuse and Dependence

Detoxification after prolonged abuse of a depressant drug is a complicated process that can require weeks of hospitalization. Typically, the patient is initially given about 40 percent of the usual daily dose of the abused drug. This dose is then reduced by about 10 percent each day until the drug is no longer needed to prevent withdrawal (Cambor & Millman, 1991). In some cases, a drug agonist, such as *carbamazepine,* is given instead of the abused drug (Lichtigfeld & Gilman, 1991).

After detoxification, many individuals experience a mild *abstinence syndrome* in which they suffer insomnia, head and body aches, anxiety, and depression (Cambor & Millman, 1991). These symptoms may last for months, making the recovering abuser extremely vulnerable to relapse. Such vulnerability complicates the task of changing the beliefs and behaviors that led to drug abuse. Many of the same psychological and educational procedures used to treat alcoholism are used to rehabilitate persons who have abused other depressant drugs. These treatments include individual and group therapy, drug-specific education, and peer support groups such as AA (Halikas, 1993).

In Review

Depressants:

- reduce neuronal activity, leading to sedating, hypnotic, or anxiolytic effects;
- are often prescribed for a variety of medical and mental disorders, but their use can escalate into abuse;
- can produce strong withdrawal symptoms and dependence; and
- are associated with use or dependence disorders that are usually treated with techniques derived from the alcoholism field.

Stimulants

Drugs that have an excitatory effect on the central nervous system are called **stimulants**. Some stimulants, primarily *amphetamines,* are called "uppers" or "speed." Other stimulants include cocaine, methylphenidate (sold as Ritalin), caffeine, nicotine, and over-the-counter diet pills. Most stimulants create their effects by producing temporary elevations in the neurotransmitter dopamine. Amphetamines do this by increasing the release of dopamine at receptor sites, whereas cocaine primarily blocks the inactivation of dopamine. The net result is the same: increased availability of dopamine at neural synapses. This enhanced dopamine effect is especially apparent in the *nucleus accumbens,* the major reward center in the brain, discussed earlier.

Amphetamines

First used medically to control asthma and nasal congestion, **amphetamines** stimulate the sympathetic branch of the autonomic nervous system, increasing heart rate and blood pressure, constricting blood vessels, and shrinking mucous membranes. Increased sympathetic nervous system arousal also increases alertness and reduces appetite. For this reason, amphetamines have sometimes been used to treat sleep disorders, obesity, and attention-deficit disorders.

For most medical purposes, amphetamines are taken in tablet form. Recreational drug users often take amphetamines by inhaling them nasally, injecting them, or smoking them. In addition to simple amphetamines, many abusers favor two amphetamine variants, *dextroamphetamine* (Dexedrene) and *methamphetamine,* a particularly pure form of amphetamine known as "crystal" or "ice."

Amphetamines produce a wide range of behavioral effects depending on dosage, method of ingestion, frequency of use, and psychological characteristics of the user (Cambor & Millman, 1991). At low doses, amphetamines produce alertness and focused attention that can enhance performance on cognitive tasks such as reading. At higher doses, they lead to feelings of exhilaration and vigor, accompanied by increased talkativeness and extroversion. Generally, amphetamines do not produce the marked euphoria associated with cocaine. At even higher doses, alertness may give way to hypervigilance and restlessness, while extroversion turns into grandiosity and aggressiveness. When high doses are repeatedly taken for a long time, delirium or paranoia may develop, even in previously stable individuals.

---

*J*abbar is a college student who, over a 2-year period, developed a twice-weekly habit of snorting crystal methamphetamine. At first, he enjoyed the rush of energy he got from the drug, bragging to his friends, "I got ice in my veins." Eventually, however, his behavior took an ominous turn. He began to accuse his roommates of trying to disrupt his studying by leaving "Satanic messages" on his answering machine. He was arrested a couple of times for disorderly conduct, once after he ran through the library and ripped up several books because "they had the wrong pages in them." These symptoms stopped immediately after he quit using methamphetamine.

Amphetamine intoxication also brings potentially dangerous physical changes, including an increased or irregular heartbeat, dilation of the pupils, perspiration or chills, nausea, and muscular weakness. Significant weight loss can occur with prolonged use. Frequent users of stimulants often experience a post-intoxication period of marked fatigue, irritability, and dysphoria known as *crashing*. This "crash" suggests a withdrawal syndrome, but there are few empirical studies of amphetamine (or cocaine) abstinence in heavy users, so scientists do not know whether there is a clear-cut physical reaction to terminating stimulants (Lago & Kosten, 1994). Some heavy users experience weeks or months of dysphoria and lethargy after terminating amphetamines, which heightens the risk of clinical depression and suicidal behavior (Cambor & Milman, 1991).

Three groups of individuals are especially vulnerable to becoming amphetamine abusers: (1) those who initially obtain an amphetamine prescription for a disorder; (2) those who obtain the drug, usually through illegal channels, to stay alert while studying or on the job; and (3) recreational users who obtain amphetamines illegally to enjoy a high. Recreational users are typically young people from high-risk backgrounds (living in poverty in an inner city, with high levels of family adversity) who usually smoke amphetamine or inject it intravenously. Intravenous users, who typically inject high doses every few days, are at high risk for HIV infection because of needle sharing and sexual risk-taking (Darke et al., 1995). Individuals in the other two groups are likely to be older, more stable, and to ingest the drug nasally or orally.

Cocaine

An *alkaloid,* or plant-derived, drug, **cocaine** comes from *erythroxylon coca,* a hearty bush indigenous to mountainous areas of South America. Cocaine's active ingredient is found in the leaves of this coca plant and, for centuries, the native peoples of the region, including the Incas as early as the 1500s, chewed these leaves to obtain a stimulating effect (Cambor & Millman, 1991). In the 1800s, cocaine became a popular treatment for various ailments throughout Europe and the United States, partly because of Sigmund Freud's claim that it cured hysteria. In fact, cocaine was regarded as a harmless substance with invigorating properties; as its name implies, Coca Cola contained cocaine until about 1900, after which caffeine was used instead. It was not until 1914, after cocaine's addictive potential was recognized, that the Harrison Narcotics Act limited the availability of cocaine (and opiates) in the United States.

Cocaine was virtually unknown as an illegal recreational drug in the United States until the drug-permissive era of the 1960s and early 1970s, but even then it was not as popular as marijuana or LSD. Later in the 1970s, however, there was a surge in the popularity of cocaine use, especially among middle- and upper-income groups. By the mid 1980s, its expense—and the brevity of its effects—made cocaine a "fashionable" drug for the wealthy. One survey in 1988 indicated that 2.3 million Americans had used cocaine within the previous 30 days (National Institute on Drug Abuse, 1991). The majority of affluent social users snorted cocaine in powder form. Many heavier users either mixed cocaine powder with water and injected it intravenously or experimented with *free-basing,* in which a potent form of cocaine is extracted by heating cocaine powder with a volatile substance such as ether or ammonia. The resulting vapor is then inhaled, producing a rapid and intense infusion of cocaine. As all too many users discovered, this method is especially dangerous because the heated mixture can ignite without warning.

In the late 1980s a form of cocaine known as *crack* became popular, especially among less affluent users. Crack is produced by combining cocaine powder with baking soda and then heating the mixture until brownish crystals settle to the bottom; these are left to harden into "rocks" that can be smoked in a pipe. The term *crack* refers to the noise the rocks make when lit.

Cocaine's physiological and behavioral effects are similar to those of other stimulants. The cardiovascular effects are complicated, but they appear to include rapidly increased blood pressure and irregularities in heart rhythms (Herning et al., 1994). Cocaine intoxication can cause sudden death due to respiratory arrest or heart failure. However, there are two important differences between the effects of cocaine and the amphetamines. First, cocaine produces a more euphoric experience than most am-

phetamines do; the DSM-IV describes it as an "extremely potent" euphoria in which there are instant feelings of well-being and confidence. Second, cocaine produces faster, but less long-lasting effects than amphetamines. Smoking a single piece of crack, for example, can cause a rush that is immediate, but lasts less than 5 minutes. Cocaine users must therefore repeat their doses frequently in order to maintain a cocaine high and forestall the postintoxication crash.

Cocaine's highly pleasurable, but short-lived, effects can lead to extreme psychological dependence in a remarkably short time. Many stable and financially secure individuals have become destitute as a result of their efforts to maintain a cocaine habit that can cost several hundred dollars a week. Cocaine-dependent persons from low-income or impoverished circumstances often turn to theft or prostitution to buy crack. Cocaine has thus contributed to a host of medical and social problems, including sexually transmitted diseases (resulting from both sexual contact and needle exchange), and violence among adolescents who are recruited to distribute crack.

Caffeine

As shown in Figure 13.6, caffeine is found in many foodstuffs, including coffee, tea, some carbonated sodas, and chocolate. Caffeine decreases blood flow to the brain by constricting blood vessels, so it has been used to treat migraine headaches. It also shrinks

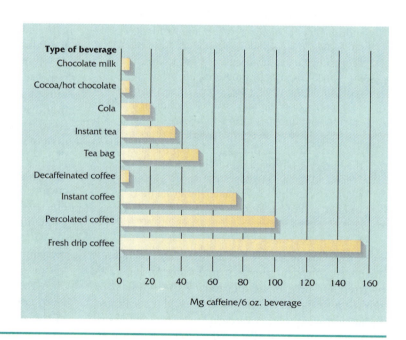

FIGURE 13.6

Average Caffeine Content of Beverages

mucous membranes and widens bronchial airways and is therefore an ingredient in some cold medications and treatments for asthma. It is also contained in over-the-counter diet pills.

Overall, caffeine is less harmful than other stimulant drugs. At low doses (75 to 100 mg), caffeine produces mild stimulation that can improve attention, problem-solving skills, and some aspects of memory, and can induce positive mood (Warburton, 1995). At moderately high doses (100 to 200 mg), most people experience nervousness, insomnia, and gastrointestinal discomfort. At very high doses (more than 1,000 mg a day), caffeine can induce muscle tremor, agitation, excessive talkativeness, disorganized thinking, and rapid or irregular heart rate.

Studies showing a relationship between heavy coffee drinking and increased risk of coronary disease (James, 1994) appear to have been methodologically flawed and have not been replicated (Chou & Benowitz, 1994). Still, regular caffeine use by those with *predispositions* to hypertension is probably a bad idea, especially if these people also smoke cigarettes. Other risks associated with heavy caffeine use include sleeping problems and anxiety. Research has shown that 200 mg of caffeine consumed in the morning can disrupt REM sleep and total sleep time that night (Landolt et al., 1995). Caffeine can also induce panic attacks in persons susceptible to anxiety. Complete abstinence from coffee by heavy coffee drinkers produces some withdrawal effects such as headaches and lethargy (Mitchell, deWit, & Zancy, 1995), but it is not clear that caffeine leads to true dependence.

The DSM-IV describes several caffeine-related disorders, including *caffeine intoxication, caffeine-induced anxiety disorder,* and *caffeine-induced sleep disorder.* These diagnoses are made when caffeine's effects cause significant distress or interfere with social or occupational functioning.

Nicotine

Found in the leaves of the tobacco plant, *nicotiniana tabacum,* **nicotine** is named after the French ambassador to Portugal, Jean Nicot, who began exporting tobacco to Paris in the late sixteenth century. Like the coca plant, tobacco is indigenous to South America. It was first smoked by the ancient Mayans, who passed on the custom to North American Indian tribes. In the fifteenth century, the first Europeans to visit America took up smoking and, by the seventeenth century, European demand for tobacco exports from the Americas was high and the tobacco industry was on its way. Today, tobacco is one of the largest cash crops in the United States, and American cigarette manufacturers export their product to most of the world, earning millions in the process.

In pure form, nicotine is a deadly poison; a few drops on the tongue can cause respiratory failure, paralysis, and death. However, very small amounts of nicotine enter the bloodstream when tobacco leaves are smoked, so the effects of smoking are not immediately lethal. The real danger from nicotine lies in its long-term effects, including its role in making the smoking habit so difficult to break. Many experts consider tobacco smoking to be the number one public-health problem in the United States, where tobacco-related cancer, heart disease, respiratory illness, and other chronic conditions kill nearly half a million people each year. Another 40,000 deaths from heart disease, 3,000 lung cancer deaths, and 26,000 cases of childhood asthma are attributed to the passive smoking that occurs when nonsmokers inhale "secondhand" smoke from smokers' cigarettes (Groth-Marnat & Edkins, 1996). Most of these health problems are not caused by nicotine, but by the carbon monoxide and cancer-causing chemicals found in tobacco smoke. The exception is cardiovascular disease, which is tied more directly to nicotine.

Nicotine dependence develops quickly, partly because of its ability to stimulate the release of dopamine in the nucleus accumbens and its effects on the neurotransmitter *acetylcholine* (ACH); "hooked" smokers must then smoke in order to prevent or postpone the effects of withdrawal. Heavy nicotine use is facilitated by the fact that it is nearly impossible to become intoxicated from the nicotine doses contained in cigarettes. Smokers can thus smoke almost continuously with little or no behavioral impairment. Before the advent of smoking restrictions in the work place and other public settings, heavy smokers could smoke almost anywhere, all day long. Even with such restrictions in place, avid smokers consume 30 or more cigarettes each day for most of their lives. Experienced smokers need a cigarette to start their day; they often smoke more cigarettes than they anticipate, run out sooner, and anxiously look for a place to buy more. They become upset when they encounter smoking restrictions, and many smokers alter their social or recreational plans to accommodate their need to smoke. Virtually all smokers continue to smoke despite knowing that their health is being compromised. All of this adds up to a substance-abuse disorder, as defined by the DSM-IV.

Nicotine produces a clear-cut withdrawal syndrome. The most common symptoms are irritability, depressed mood, lowered heart rate, and weight gain.

The average person gains 7 to 10 pounds after quitting smoking, most of it in the first 6 months after cessation (Perkins, 1993). Women tend to gain more weight following cessation than men do. However, weight gain is not inevitable if the quitter follows a low fat diet and a program of regular exercise (Talcott et al., 1995). Withdrawal symptoms usually begin within hours of quitting, peak in a few days, and last for about a month. Residual effects, such as weight gain, may persist for several months. Certain individuals appear particularly sensitive to the physiological effects of nicotine; as a result, they become dependent on it more easily, develop nicotine tolerance more quickly, and suffer stronger withdrawal symptoms (Pomerleau et al., 1993).

Connections

How have psychologists fought the health risks associated with smoking? See Chapter 6, pp. 208–210.

Treatment of Stimulant Abuse

The epidemic of cocaine abuse during the 1980s created an enormous number of cocaine-dependent persons who needed treatment, but the specialized services needed were virtually nonexistent at the time. As a result, these people were initially treated in inpatient or outpatient programs modeled on traditional treatments for alcoholism. These programs tried to produce total abstinence through group therapy, individual counseling, and training in relapse prevention skills (McLellan et al., 1994). Cocaine Anonymous, a 12-step program similar to Alcoholics Anonymous, was used to provide follow-up support.

The treatment of stimulant abuse became more sophisticated in the 1990s. For example, Azrin's community reinforcement model has been used on an outpatient basis with cocaine abusers. Patients are rewarded with money and social outings with their families or friends if urine tests confirm that they are abstinent from cocaine. The results of this approach have been shown superior to those of a 12-step program (Higgens et al., 1991; 1993).

Another innovation, called **node-link mapping** (Joe, Dansereau, & Simpson, 1994), is intended to correct specific cognitive patterns—including impulsive, distractable, and inattentive behaviors—that interfere with abstinence. In node-link mapping, the abuser draws a large chart depicting the personal problems and behavior patterns that surround his or her use of cocaine. The "nodes" are drawn as interconnected boxes that contain the thoughts, feelings, and actions that precede and follow cocaine abuse. This visual representation helps abusers to better understand the processes that contribute to cocaine dependence and to view their drug use more objectively. At least one study shows that adding node-link mapping to standard cocaine abuse treatments can improve results (Joe et al., 1994).

Two medication strategies have also been used as adjuncts to psychological treatment of stimulant abuse. In the first, antidepressants are prescribed to offset the protracted dysphoria during withdrawal that contributes to relapse. The second aims to reduce drug craving by giving medications such as *bromocriptine* that mimic the dopamine-enhancing effects of stimulants. However, studies comparing antidepressants or bromocriptine with placebos have failed to find that these medications improve outcomes (e.g., Campbell et al., 1994; Eiler et al., 1995). In one study, for example, taking the antidepressant imipramine promoted longer participation in counseling than did a placebo, but it did not decrease drug abuse (Galloway et al., 1994).

The treatment of stimulant abusers is complicated by several factors. For one thing, these people

Women crack users in this residential treatment setting are allowed to have their children live with them as opposed to the standard practice of having the children sent to a relative, friend or foster care. This procedure significantly increased women's participation in treatment.

are especially prone to polydrug use as they attempt to "take the edge off" the crash that follows stimulant intoxication. A study of cocaine users found more than half to be dependent on alcohol (Higgens et al., 1994), while a study of amphetamine users showed that more than half had abused benzodiazepines (Darke, Ross, & Cohen, 1994). Second, these polydrug users are more prone to having comorbid mental disorders and poor health than are people who abuse a single drug (Darke et al., 1994). Whether comorbidity is a cause or effect of polydrug use is uncertain. Third, in treating polydrug users, it is often difficult to decide whether to focus on all the drugs involved, or only on one of them, and, if so, which one?

Finally, many amphetamine or cocaine abusers (especially crack abusers) drop out of treatment prematurely, leading to high rates of relapse. However, different types of risk for relapse are affected by the ethnicity of abusers (Havassy, Wasserman, & Hall, 1995). The availability of strong social relationships and support is more important to relapse prevention for White Americans than for Black Americans, whose relapses tend to be tied more to economic adversity and neighborhood disorganization.

Treatment and Prevention of Nicotine Dependence

Programs that educate the public about nicotine risks, alter smoking attitudes, and restrict smoking in offices and public places have been successful in reducing tobacco smoking in the United States. In the 1970s, more than half of the American population smoked, but today only about 25 percent do so (U.S. Department of Health and Human Services, 1990). Unfortunately, cigarette smoking has increased in most other countries around the world and, even in the United States, smoking continues to be popular among the young. As smokers grow older and begin to take the health risks of their habit seriously, many try to quit. It is a difficult process, however, and most would-be quitters fail 3 or 4 times before achieving long-term success (APA, 1994).

Most of the dozens of formal smoking-cessation treatments available use a variant of behavioral or cognitive-behavioral therapy (self-monitoring, goal-setting, and reinforcement). Some treatments involve abrupt, "cold turkey," cessation, while others seek gradual reduction in smoking. A period of gradual reduction before quitting cold turkey can be especially helpful (Cinciripini et al., 1995). Interventions that involve the most frequent contact with smokers tend to produce the best results (Lichtenstein & Glasgow, 1992). However, even in the most effective programs, abstinence rates after a year rarely exceed 50 percent, and average only about 33 percent (Shiffman, 1993).

Nicotine gum or patches are often used to aid cessation efforts by providing enough replacement nicotine to reduce craving and other withdrawal symptoms. Research on the effects of these nicotine replacement treatments indicates that they can indeed reduce the severity of withdrawal symptoms, including depression and sleep disturbance (Doherty et al., 1995; Fortmann & Killen, 1995). Because nicotine gum and patches are now available over the counter, and because they can improve abstinence rates—particularly when used in combination with intensive behaviorally based treatments (Cepeda-Benito, 1993)—they are likely to play a continuing role in formal and informal smoking cessation efforts. One of the newest uses of nicotine replacement strategies is to combine them with drugs, such as *mecamylamine*, that block nicotine's effects on neurotransmitters. The effect is to ruin the enjoyment of cigarettes through a two-pronged chemical attack that simultaneously eliminates the craving for nicotine and its physiological rewards.

In Review

Stimulants:

- include amphetamines, cocaine, caffeine, and nicotine;
- have excitatory effects on the central nervous system;
- can produce psychological dependence and are often abused in conjunction with other drugs; and
- can cause several dangerous physical changes in the brain and cardiovascular system.

Treatments for stimulant abuse:

- have included innovations such as community reinforcement, node-link mapping, and combinations of behavior therapy; and
- are complicated by high drop-out rates and other factors.

Treatments of nicotine dependence:

- include public education, smoking restrictions, behavior modification programs, and nicotine replacement strategies; and
- are usually more successful when they involve repeated contacts with smokers and aim for gradual reduction prior to abstinence. Most smokers attempt to quit several times before doing so successfully.

Opioids

An **opioid** is an alkaloid containing opium or one of its derivatives, such as morphine, heroin, codeine, or methadone. Opium comes from the seed pods of the poppy plant, which is indigenous to Asia and the Middle East. Opioids, also known as *narcotics*, were used by the ancient Greeks and Romans to relieve pain and induce sleep. During the American Civil War, morphine was used as a surgical anesthetic. Like cocaine, opioids were regarded as relatively harmless until their addictive potential became known, partly as a result of the experiences with opioid-dependent Civil War veterans. As noted earlier, opioids were outlawed by the Harrison Act of 1914. Today, opioids are prescribed for pain relief, as antidiarrheals and cough suppressants, and as antidepressants in rare, intractable cases of depression (Bodkin et al., 1995).

Opioid drugs exert their influence by interacting with the receptor sites used by the body's endogenous opiates including the *endorphins* and *enkephalins*. These receptor sites are located throughout the body—in the brain, spinal cord, and even the bloodstream—and have ties to the immune system (Makman, 1994). The endogenous opiates influence pain and appetite, and they can produce positive moods. There are three types of opioid receptors and several different receptors within each type. One type of receptor, mu_3, is uniquely sensitive to certain *exogenous*, or ingested, opioids.

Because the endogenous and exogenous opiates use the same receptor sites, chronic use of morphine, heroin, or other exogenous opiates may alter the production of endogenous opiates. When the person stops using exogenous opiates, a temporary deficiency in the production of endogenous opiates occurs (Cambor & Millman, 1991). This deficiency may explain why the opioid withdrawal syndrome can include negative mood and increased pain sensitivity.

Opioid Abuse and Dependence

Heroin, a white odorless powder derived from morphine, is the most commonly abused opioid. It was first derived from opium in the late nineteenth century by German physicians who wanted to create a stronger, but less addictive analgesic for use as a substitute for morphine. Heroin was chosen as the trade name for this drug because of its potentially "heroic" effects in the battle against pain. Unfortunately, its creators misjudged heroin's addictive potential: it is one of the most addictive opioids.

Heroin use in the United States has historically been most frequent among lower socioeconomic

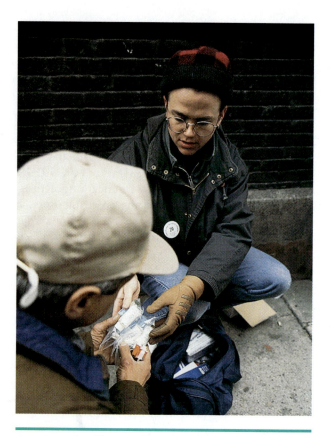

A major risk of heroin abuse is infection and disease spread through the shared use of dirty needles. This problem has given rise to several highly controversial needle distribution programs in which addicts are given clean needles in exchange for used needles.

classes, ethnic minority groups, and people living in inner city areas (Hartnoll, 1994). The same social problems linked to the sale and use of crack cocaine are associated with heroin. It has been estimated that up to 60 percent of heroin users in some inner cities are infected with HIV (APA, 1994), primarily because of their sharing of contaminated needles. In the 1990s, however, the demographics of heroin use have begun to shift; its use has increased dramatically among young, relatively affluent individuals, and it is even considered to be chic in some circles.

In pure form, heroin can be smoked or snorted, but the preferred form of ingestion by most heavy users is intravenous injection ("mainlining"), which produces an almost immediate, intense rush that lasts about 1 minute. After the rush, heroin produces a sedated, dreamlike euphoria in which the senses are dulled, attention to the environment is reduced, and the desire for food is decreased. This condition differs from the euphoria produced by cocaine, which is characterized by high energy and enhanced attention. People experiencing opioid intoxication appear "spacey," drunk, drowsy, and disconnected from their surroundings. Their speech is often slurred, and their pupils are frequently constricted. The intoxicating effects of opioids usually last up to 6 hours.

At high doses, the opioid user can become comatose and suffer respiratory failure. An estimated 1 percent of all heroin addicts die from overdose each year (Thombs, 1994). However, what constitutes an opioid overdose varies from one user to another and, within the same user, from one occasion to another. Heroin addicts sometimes die from a dose that was no stronger than that which they had tolerated in the past. Why? This question was partially answered over 25 years ago by an experimental psychologist named Shepard Siegel. He found that tolerance to a given dose of heroin in rats was partially conditioned to the *physical environment* in which the drug was typically received. Being in a familiar environment appeared to produce learned physiological responses that helped prepare the rat's body for the drug's effects. If an addicted rat received its normal dose of heroin in an unfamiliar cage, death from overdose was very likely (Siegel, 1982).

Another, related explanation for such overdose results involves the fact that opioids block a type of receptor that responds to the acid *N-methyl-D-aspartate* or *NMDA* (Trujillo & Akil, 1995). NMDA, in turn, is believed to mediate learning and memory by bringing about changes in the ease of communication between neurons as learning proceeds. Experiments with animals have found evidence for *environmental-dependent* opioid tolerance mediated by NMDA (Szab'o, Tabakoff, & Hoffman, 1994). An implication of this work is that a heroin overdose depends not only on how much of the drug is taken, but also the tolerance level of the drug user and *where* the drug has typically been taken.

Opioids produce an intense withdrawal syndrome, with symptoms that are almost the opposite of the drug's intoxicating effects. Thus, instead of euphoria, there is dysphoria, and the senses are heightened rather than dulled, leading to anxiety and increased sensitivity to pain. Excessive body secretions (runny nose, watery eyes), pupil dilation, and diarrhea are common, as are fever, insomnia, and "goose bumps." Some of these effects develop within 8 hours after the last opioid dose and gradually decline after about a week. However, anxiety, depression, and craving for the drug may continue for several months.

Relapse of narcotic abuse is extremely common. Many narcotic addicts develop a lifestyle that is centered solely on procuring and using drugs. As part of this lifestyle, addicts often support their habit through theft or prostitution. It is not surprising, then, that antisocial personality disorder is often diagnosed among heroin addicts, but clinicians are uncertain about whether narcotic addiction is a *consequence* of antisocial pathology, or vice versa.

Treatment of Opioid Abuse and Dependence

Medications play a central role in the treatment of opioid abusers. Opioid antagonists such as *naltrexone* are used during initial stages of detoxification to quell withdrawal symptoms (Legarda & Gossop, 1994), and other drugs are used to reduce opioid craving after withdrawal is over. By far the most common—and most controversial—pharmacological approach to treating heroin addiction is the prescription of the synthetic opioid *methadone*. Methadone is a longer-acting drug than heroin and is more active when taken orally. It produces good pain-reducing effects at relatively low doses, even when taken infrequently, thus limiting its addictive potential. However, as with any opioid, higher doses of methadone produce euphoric effects. And, although it can also induce tolerance and withdrawal, the methadone withdrawal syndrome is safer and less painful than withdrawal from heroin.

Methadone was first used in the 1960s as a substitute for heroin as addicts went through withdrawal. The next step was to gradually decrease the methadone dose until the patient achieved complete opioid independence, but this goal proved difficult to achieve. Most addicts simply returned to heroin when their methadone treatment ended. To forestall such relapses, many heroin addicts were eventually placed on **methadone maintenance therapy** in which they continued to receive methadone for as long as they needed it. The daily dosage was regulated by the patient, within limits set by the physician. These patients were also counseled and encouraged to discontinue all drug use, but many remained on methadone for years. As of 1990, approximately 100,000 opioid-dependent persons were receiving methadone maintenance in the United States (U.S. General Accounting Office, 1990, cited in Magura et al., 1994).

The results of the methadone maintenance approach are mixed. Success rates have steadily increased since it was introduced in the early 1970s; current methadone maintenance program participants are reported to reduce illicit opioid use by as much as 80 percent (Bertschy, 1995). They commit fewer crimes because they no longer need to buy heroin (Fontaine & Ansseau, 1995), and, because they no longer share injection needles, addicts on methadone maintenance reduce their risk of HIV infection by about half (Caplehorn & Ross, 1995). Moreover, these people stay in treatment programs longer because those programs serve as the source of their methadone (Rosenbach & Hunot, 1995). Unfortunately, as many as 20 percent of heroin addicts remain dependent on methadone for 10 years or more (Bertschy, 1995). More worrisome is the fact that reductions in heroin use are often offset by increases in nonopioid drug abuse, particularly cocaine. Almost two thirds of the participants in one New York City methadone program tested positive for cocaine (Magura et al., 1994). Cocaine use is especially problematic because it tends to accelerate the body's elimination of methadone (Tennant & Shannon, 1995). Increasing the daily dose of methadone can reduce cocaine use, but the amount needed to do so may be as high as 4 times the normal dose (Tennant & Shannon, 1995). Some programs have combatted drug use by making participants' daily methadone dose contingent on providing clean, drug-free urine tests. In one study, addicts in a dose-contingent group were 4 times more likely to increase their drug-free urine samples as were addicts given methadone noncontingently (Stitzer, Iguchi, & Felch, 1992).

In short, most experts agree that methadone maintenance is preferable to heroin dependence, but few are satisfied with its results. Efforts to provide better treatments have taken several directions. One approach has been to develop methadone substitutes, such as *buprenorphine,* that have fewer reinforcing and addictive properties. Buprenorphine has shown promise (Walsh et al., 1995), but more research is needed before researchers can say whether it can prevent the problems associated with methadone. Other clinicians have focused on combining psychological treatment with methadone maintenance. One example is **supportive-expressive therapy,** a time-limited form of psychoanalysis in which the patient is helped to identify and talk about core relationship patterns and how they relate to drug use (Woody, Higson, & Tannahill, 1984). The effectiveness of this approach has been mixed in some studies, but a recent report involving three community methadone programs was far more positive (Woody et al., 1995). In this study, patients receiving supportive-expressive therapy required less methadone than those who received only standard drug counseling, and, after 6 months of treatment, these patients maintained their gains or showed continuing improvement. Gains tended to dissipate in those re-

ceiving only drug counseling (Woody et al., 1995). The results of this study support the view expressed by most experts that methadone programs achieve better results when combined with high-quality psychological services (Bertschy, 1995).

In Review

Opioids, also known as narcotics:

- contain opium or one of its derivatives, such as morphine, heroin, codeine, or methadone;
- usually produce a pleasurable rush, followed by a dreamy euphoria;
- create strong physical dependence, produce intense withdrawal symptoms, and are associated with lifestyles devoted to drug use; and
- are associated with disorders that have been treated by drug antagonists, methadone maintenance, and various kinds of psychotherapy.

Cannabis and Hallucinogens

Cannabis and hallucinogenic drugs are not members of the same drug category, but we will discuss them together because some of their effects are similar. Using cannabis and hallucinogens produces a range of distorted perceptions—usually mild in the case of cannabis, stronger with hallucinogens. These drugs are also less physiologically addictive than most of the drugs discussed so far, but they can cause psychological dependence and, particularly in the case of cannabis, can lead the user to try other illegal drugs.

Cannabis

The psychoactive drug derived from the hemp plant, *cannabis sativa* is **cannabis.** Originally from Asia, hemp flourishes today in many parts of the world. *Marijuana* (also known as "pot," "weed," "grass," or "boo") is the dried, chopped leaves, tops, and stems of the hemp plant. Typically smoked in cigarette form (called a "joint"), marijuana can also be taken orally by mixing it with food or brewing it as a tea. *Hashish,* which is almost always smoked, is the dried resin from the tops and leaves of the female hemp plant. The psychoactive ingredients of cannabis are called **cannabinoids,** the most important of which is *delta-9-tetrahydrocannabinol*, or *THC*. The concentration of THC in marijuana and hashish varies greatly, depending on the genetic history of the plant and the conditions under which it is grown. Today's marijuana contains nearly 5 times the THC contained in plants cultivated during the 1960s or 1970s.

In the United States, marijuana is the most commonly used illicit drug; at least 5.5 million people report using it weekly (National Institute on Drug Abuse, 1991). Its popularity has waxed and waned with changing legal regulations, political attitudes, and moral and social values. In the first part of the twentieth century, cannabis could be bought and sold without penalty, and was used primarily by jazz and blues musicians and artists. Social concern over the drug materialized in the 1930s, and it was soon outlawed. In the 1950s, marijuana was thought to cause "reefer madness," but, by the late 1960s, it had become such an accepted middle-class recreational drug that some states relaxed criminal codes relating to marijuana, and there were proposals to legalize its use. By 1990 tolerance for cannabis had again declined, despite survey data indicating that about one third of the population had used marijuana at least once (APA, 1994). Use of marijuana among U.S. high school and college students decreased from about 50 to 30 percent between 1979 and 1989, but the figure is once again sharply on the rise. The most recent increases have worried many experts because, as noted earlier, a young person's use of cannabis is believed to be a gateway that increases the chances of trying other, more addictive drugs. Indeed, it does appear that the probability of abusing other, harder drugs is greater if the person has previously used alcohol, smoked cigarettes, and experimented with marijuana (Ellickson, Hays, & Bell, 1992).

The acute physical effects of cannabis include dilation of the blood vessels in the eye, dry mouth, increased appetite (known as the "munchies"), and rapid heartbeat. Cannabis increases cerebral blood flow, especially in the frontal regions of the brain, and it has primarily sedating effects on the central nervous system (Mackie & Hille, 1992). The neurochemical processes by which THC interacts with the brain and other organs are not fully understood, but research in the last decade has begun to piece together a probable scenario. Specific cannabinoid receptors have been identified in the brain (especially the cerebellum and hippocampus), spleen, tonsils, and white blood cells (Bouaboula et al., 1993). Cannabinoids seem to mimic endogenous substances, including the endogenous opiates, suggesting one way by which cannabis exerts its rewarding effects.

THC has several medicinal purposes. Its appetite-enhancing effects have been used to treat anorexia, and, because it reduces pressure within the eye, marijuana is also used to treat glaucoma. Cancer patients undergoing chemotherapy are sometimes given marijuana to reduce the nausea and vomiting caused by anticancer drugs.

Most cannabis users report feelings of mild euphoria, well-being, and relaxation that begin within minutes after the drug is used and last for 2 to 3 hours. Many other users report mildly stimulating effects such as increased heart rate, and still others report feelings of anxiety or even panic on occasion. Emotional reactions to marijuana often seem to involve intensification of whatever mood people are in at the time they use the drug. The effects of cannabis intoxication usually include enhancement of pleasurable physical experiences and mild perceptual distortions: music may sound better, colors may appear more vivid, and time may seem to pass more slowly. During high-dose, acute cannabis intoxication, users may experience hallucinations and other psychotic-like symptoms. In such cases, it is possible that a preexisting mental disorder has been exacerbated by cannabis.

Motor performance—especially on fine motor tasks—is usually impaired by cannabis, as are short-term memory, reaction times, and the ability to sustain attention (Wilson et al., 1994). These effects may be responsible for the fact that cannabis intoxication is frequently implicated in automobile and motorcycle accidents. At one trauma center, nearly one third of all injured motorcyclists tested positive for cannabis in urine samples (Soderstrom et al., 1995).

Tolerance and withdrawal are not usually prominent features of cannabis use. Only a mild withdrawal syndrome, consisting of irritability, restlessness, sleep disturbance, and drug craving has been reported (Cambor & Millman, 1991). However, psychological dependence on cannabis is characterized by preoccupation with and compulsive use of the drug, risk-taking (e.g., driving while "stoned"), interpersonal conflicts, and legal problems.

In other words, the short-term effects of cannabis intoxication are relatively mild compared with those of other drugs discussed in this chapter. But does regular use of cannabis produce significant long-term risks to physical health? A great deal of research with animals and humans has so far failed to produce solid evidence of harmful effects, but several worrisome possibilities are still being investigated. For example, because marijuana smoke contains 50 to 100 times the carcinogens found in tobacco smoke, chronic marijuana smokers might face an increased risk of lung cancer. Pot smokers do suffer deterioration in the linings of the trachea and bronchial tubes; this damage is greatest in people who smoke both marijuana and tobacco. Regular marijuana smoking is also associated with a higher incidence of canker sores and other problems in the mouth (Darling & Arendorf, 1993). THC does lower testosterone levels in males, but the effect is small and may have no measurable effect on health. THC also interferes with immune system functioning, but, again, the effect appears small enough to be of questionable significance (Cambor & Millman, 1991).

Do the acute neuropsychological effects of cannabis—such as deficits in attention, memory, and motor skill—become more permanent with regular use? One review (Pope, Gruber, & Yurgelun-Todd, 1995) found that these deficits occur within 24 hours after cannabis use, but there was no evidence to either support or refute the existence of more prolonged negative effects. **Amotivational syndrome**—a pattern of apathy and inability to meet personal or career goals (Musty & Kaback, 1995)—has been linked to cannabis-induced alteration of brain functioning (Millman & Sbriglio, 1986). Indeed, about one third of daily cannabis users show signs of mild depression (APA, 1994), but it is not clear whether this is a result of cannabis use or a factor that leads to cannabis use. A predisposition to depression could account for the link between regular cannabis use and amotivation (Cambor & Millman, 1991).

Hallucinogens

The drugs discussed thus far have been named after their neurochemical effects (depressants and stimulants) or the plant from which they are derived (opioids and cannabis). **Hallucinogens** are named for the unusual perceptual experiences they produce. Also sometimes called *psychedelics,* these diverse drugs are best known for creating visual effects in which objects appear to shimmer or waver, colorful "halos" appear, or objects emit visual "trails." Users may also experience visual hallucinations of nonexistent objects or people; less often, the hallucinations may be auditory or tactile. Hallucinogens may produce distortions in body image, as when users feel as though their arms are several feet long. In another common perceptual anomaly known as **synesthesia,**

information from different senses is blended so that users claim they can "see" sounds or "feel" colors. In most cases, these perceptual distortions are understood by the person to be drug induced. There have been tragic exceptions, however, as in cases in which people feel that they can fly and then jump off a roof to prove it.

Hallucinogens may also lead to depersonalization, paranoid thinking, and extremely variable moods, in which the user goes from the heights of euphoria to the depths of depression, or from feelings of security to feelings of anxiety and terror. These changes can occur in seconds, often in response to minor events, such as hearing an old song. Hallucinogens' effects usually begin within an hour after ingestion and last from several hours to a day, depending on the type and dose of drug and method of administration.

Lysergic Acid Diethylamide (LSD). The best-known hallucinogen is **lysergic acid diethylamide (LSD)**, which first became popular in the 1960s. Also known as "acid," LSD was discovered in 1943 by Swiss chemist Albert Hofmann, who accidentally ingested a small piece of mold growing on rye grain and then recorded his strange experiences. LSD can be synthesized or derived from *ergot,* a fungus that affects cereal plants such as wheat and rye.

The hallucinogenic experiences during an LSD "trip" are the product of central nervous system excitation. LSD also arouses the sympathetic nervous system, causing dilated pupils, increased heart rate, elevated blood pressure, and increased alertness. LSD mimics the neurotransmitter *serotonin* by interacting with serotonin receptors in the cerebral cortex and brain stem. Because of the similarity between the hallucinogenic effects of LSD and the symptoms of persons with schizophrenia, some researchers have used the effects of LSD as a model from which to develop hypotheses about the causes of schizophrenia (Breier, 1995). For example, individuals with and without schizophrenia have been given LSD in order to compare the number, location, and functioning of serotonin receptor sites. By using brain imaging techniques that trace the interactions of LSD with these receptors (Joyce et al., 1993), researchers have found that schizophrenics have a greater number of serotonin receptors in certain parts of the brain (e.g., the nucleus accumbens) than do persons without this disorder.

LSD can be taken in tablet form or by eating sugar cubes or paper in which a drop of the drug has been placed. Even heavy users usually take LSD only periodically, allowing several days or weeks to pass between episodes. With repeated use, some tolerance develops to LSD's hallucinogenic effects, but tolerance to its effects on the nervous system seldom occurs. LSD has little addictive potential.

LSD produces few direct physical health risks, but LSD-induced behavioral and emotional changes can threaten both physical and psychological well-being. Chief among these problems is panic attacks. When panic occurs, the drug user can usually be "talked down" by a supportive person, although sometimes a sedative must also be given.

Long after LSD's initial effects end, some users report having *flashbacks,* brief recurrences of the perceptual distortions experienced during the LSD "trip." Flashbacks may be triggered by thoughts, by use of other drugs, or by being in an environment with ambiguous or unusual stimuli (e.g., entering a dark room). Some people have reported flashbacks occurring as long as 5 years after their last use of LSD. The DSM-IV lists a new diagnosis, *hallucinogen persisting perception disorder,* to describe the condition in which flashbacks cause clinically significant distress or interfere with day-to-day functioning.

In the United States during the 1960s and 1970s, LSD was primarily used by middle-class White American adolescents and young adults. After the passing of this "hippie" era, the popularity of LSD use declined in favor of such drugs as cocaine and methamphetamine. However, there has recently been an alarming increase in LSD use by young White Americans, many of whom are even younger than the "trippers" of the 1960s—some are preadolescent (Abraham & Aldridge, 1993). According to some survey data, compared with the 1980s, fewer U.S. high school students in the 1990s think that experimentation with LSD is dangerous (Schwartz, 1995).

Other Hallucinogens. Mescaline and psilocybin are alkaloids with hallucinogenic effects similar to those of LSD. **Mescaline** is derived from the *peyote* cactus plant; the crown of the cactus (called the peyote button) is chewed or swallowed with water or food. For centuries, peyote has been used in religious services by Native Americans in South and Central America and in the Southwestern United States, and the practice continues to this day in the Native American church. **Psilocybin** alkaloids are found in several species of Mexican mushrooms, pieces of which are chewed or swallowed with water. Both mescaline and psilocybin produce visual illusions, distorted body image, and depersonalization. "Bad trips" can

Peyote is used as part of some religious ceremonies to heighten the intensity of spiritual experiences. Eating peyote buttons often produces hallucinations. The emotional effects of this experience may be heightened by the constant drum beating that is part of the peyote rite practiced by this American Indian.

often occur because the amount of active hallucinogen varies widely from one peyote button or mushroom to another, so the user can never be certain about the exact dosage.

Methyl-enedioxy-methamphetamine (MDMA), also called *ecstasy,* is a derivative of methamphetamine intentionally designed by unscrupulous chemists. MDMA is reputed to enhance extroversion, making users more open and empathic. Contrary to popular belief, MDMA is *not* a safe drug. It raises the body's temperature to the danger point. There have been several incidents at all-night dance parties in which MDMA users have died from hyperthermia. It appears that certain conditions common to such gatherings—overcrowdedness, extended physical activity, and dehydration—intensify the drug's hyperthermic effects, leading to sudden death (Green, Cross, & Goodwin, 1995). With frequent use, MDMA can

Substances such as gasoline, glue, paint thinners, and spray paints can induce significant hallucinogenic effects when inhaled. Primarily used by adolescents in groups, inhalants can lead to serious abuse and dependence. Extended inhalant abuse can cause permanent damage to the central and peripheral nervous systems.

damage serotonin-sensitive receptors in the brain (Green et al., 1995).

Phencyclidine (PCP), also known as *angel dust,* differs in several ways from other hallucinogens. Originally developed as a medical anesthetic, PCP produces analgesia, respiratory suppression, and seizures when swallowed, smoked, or injected. At high doses, coma results. Unlike LSD, mescaline, and psilocybin, PCP overdoses can be fatal. Its hallucinogenic effects are also different. Perhaps because of PCP's analgesic effects, users report a feeling of superhuman power and invulnerability, sometimes to the point of being delusional. Because of these altered perceptions, PCP users may become so aggressive and violent as to injure themselves or others. The effects of PCP develop quickly, but because it is eliminated from the body slowly, frequent PCP use can lead to confusion and personality changes that last for months. Whereas other hallucinogens are used mostly by middle-class, White American high school and college students, PCP is used most often by members of ethnic minority groups living in poor urban neighborhoods.

Treatment of Cannabis and Hallucinogen Abuse and Dependence

There have been few treatment programs specifically targeted for abusers of marijuana or hallucinogens. One reason, in the case of marijuana, at least, is that most individuals who abuse marijuana also abuse a variety of other drugs. When marijuana abuse is part of a polydrug problem, it is usually the other drugs (e.g., alcohol, cocaine, opioids) that pose a more immediate risk and hence become the focus of treatment.

Still, some 12-step-type support groups have been developed specifically for cannabis abusers (Miller, Gold, & Pottash, 1989). Roger Roffman and his colleagues randomly assigned male marijuana users to a relapse-prevention group based on Alan Marlatt's treatment of alcoholism or to a social support group (Stephens, Roffman, & Simpson, 1994). Immediately after treatment, the relapse-prevention group showed less cannabis use than the social support group, but, a year later, improvement was equivalent in both conditions. The recent discovery of a compound that prevents THC from binding to receptors may soon make it possible to develop a drug that will block THC's effects on the brain.

Treatment of LSD intoxication may require a brief period of hospitalization, but, because the drug is not addictive, most therapies focus on helping abusers curb their psychological dependence on it. Although controlled research on these treatments is lacking, most clinicians believe they are usually successful.

In Review

Cannabis, a psychoactive drug derived from the hemp plant:

- is the main ingredient in marijuana and hashish;
- is the most commonly used illegal drug in the United States;
- usually produces mild euphoria, sedation, and some perceptual distortions;
- does not produce strong tolerance or withdrawal; and
- is often accompanied by other drug use or abuse that is the primary target of treatment.

Hallucinogens are psychoactive drugs that:

- produce perceptual distortions and other unusual sensory experiences;
- include LSD, mescaline, psilocybin, MDMA, and PCP; and
- are not physically addictive but can lead to psychological dependence.

Revisiting the Case of Jerry

*J*ust how severe was Jerry's polydrug problem? Did he have a substance-abuse or dependence disorder? With respect to alcohol use, Jerry more closely fit the criteria for *substance dependence* than *substance abuse*. He had developed tolerance to alcohol (he could "handle" two pitchers now, but not a year ago), often drank more than he wanted to, and had unsuccessfully tried to cut down. Drinking and drug use significantly affected his life; nearly all his friends were heavy drinkers. In short, Jerry was incorrect in assuming that he didn't have an alcohol use disorder because he drank only beer and could stop drinking before passing out.

The best way to describe Jerry's use of marijuana is as substance *abuse,* because he did not show signs of marijuana tolerance or withdrawal. The same is true of Jerry's weekly amphetamine use, which was confined to episodes related to studying. He did not show signs of amphetamine tolerance or withdrawal, nor was he preoccupied with using or obtaining the drug.

There appear to be multiple causes of Jerry's substance abuse and dependence. Jerry's father was an alcoholic, suggesting that a combination of genetic predisposition, parental modeling, and an adverse family environment contributed to his problems. Jerry also drank heavily prior to exams and before going out on a date. These are situations that cause many people to feel anxious, and it could be that Jerry experienced a stress-dampening effect from alcohol, or at least expected the drugs to produce such an effect. Jerry would appear to fall into Cloninger's Type I class of alcoholics who tend to be anxiety prone and who have a relatively late onset of drinking.

Jerry's family history and college-age polydrug pattern placed him at high risk for continuing—and intensifying—his pattern of drug abuse and dependence. Indeed, for a while it appeared that his frequent visits to the Blue Ox tavern would hurt his grades so much that he would have to leave college, and academic failure might well have worsened his substance-use disorder. But Jerry's story has a relatively happy ending. Although his problems were too severe for the university drug abuse prevention program, Jerry was referred to an off-campus, abstinence-oriented, outpatient treatment program whose costs were paid for by his university health insurance. This program combined training in relapse-prevention skills with peer group support. Jerry became very involved in this program. He particularly liked the support group, where he discovered that other students had similar problems, and he appreciated the relapse-prevention approach, where it was possible to "mess up" but still follow a plan for getting his life back together. Although he had several lapses, Jerry eventually graduated from college and, at last report, was working full-time and was not using cannabis, amphetamines, or other drugs, except for an occasional "social" drink. He admitted that alcohol was still—and would probably always be—something to be "very careful about."

SUMMARY

Defining Substance-Related Disorders

Drug abuse involves patterns of use that are hazardous to a person's health, produce personal distress, or lead to occupational, social, or legal difficulties. Prolonged abuse often causes psychological dependence (marked by craving for the drug and a preoccupation with obtaining it) and physiological dependence or addiction. Addiction to a substance is indicated by two physical effects: withdrawal and tolerance. When a person's judgment, thinking, mood, perception, or motor behavior is impaired directly as a result of using a substance, substance intoxication has occurred.

According to the DSM-IV, substance-related disorders involve either problems associated with the direct effects of substances on an individual (substance-induced disorders) or problems associated with patterns of heavy substance use (substance use disorders). The main substances of abuse are alcohol and other depressants (sedatives, hypnotics, and anxiolytics), stimulants (amphetamines, cocaine, caffeine, cannabis, and nicotine), opioids, cannabis, and hallucinogens.

Alcohol Use and Alcohol-Induced Disorders

Alcohol can damage cells, interfere with metabolism, depress brain cell activity, harm the liver and other organs, and suppress the immune system. The initial effects of alcohol consumption on the brain and behavior are sedating, but as blood alcohol concentrations increase, perception, thinking, and behavior become impaired. Between 13 and 16 million Americans meet the criteria for alcohol abuse or dependence, although the term *alcoholism* can refer to varying patterns of drinking and impairment. A substantial percentage of persons with alcohol-related disorders suffer other mental disorders that may cause, follow, or accompany alcohol problems.

Biological, psychological, and social factors help explain who develops an alcohol use disorder, and different causal patterns may be involved depending on the type of alcoholism being explained. Genetics play a role in predisposing some persons to alcoholism, particularly men who start to drink heavily early in life. Several biological vulnerabilities might underlie alcohol use disorders, including abnormal brain cell activity, low MAO activity or serotonin levels, and heightened physical sensitivity to the effects of alcohol. The psychological variables most likely to be causally related to alcoholism are tension reduction, positive expectancies about the effects of alcohol, and a set of antisocial, externalizing, and impulsive personality traits. Cultural traditions, family relationships, parental modeling, and peer associations also influence alcohol use disorders.

The options for treating alcohol use disorders reflect differing philosophies about whether alcohol is a disease, a moral problem, or a learned habit. Some success has been achieved through inpatient treatment and detoxification, Alcoholics Anonymous, training in moderate or controlled drinking, relapse prevention, marital and family therapy, brief educational and counseling interventions, aversion therapy, community reinforcement methods, and medications that minimize alcohol withdrawal symptoms, block alcohol's effects, or cause unpleasant reactions to drinking. Abstinence-oriented treatments are recommended for abusers who are alcohol dependent. Some school-based prevention programs have also achieved positive effects.

Other Depressants

Depressants inhibit neurotransmitter activity in the brain and lead to sedation, sleepiness, and reduced anxiety. In addition to alcohol, the major depressants of abuse are the barbiturates and the benzodiazepines. Both categories of drugs can cause dependence and withdrawal, with the barbiturates posing the more serious risk. Detoxification, personal therapy, peer support groups such as AA, and educationally oriented programs are the primary treatments for depressant abuse.

Stimulants

Stimulants have an excitatory effect on the central nervous system, increasing the availability of dopamine at synapses. These drugs include amphetamines, cocaine, methylphenidate (Ritalin), caffeine, and nicotine. Many stimulant users are prone to polydrug abuse, and they often drop out of treatment. However, newer therapies for cocaine abuse, such as community reinforcement and node-link mapping, have somewhat improved treatment benefits. Behaviorally oriented therapy, nicotine replacement strategies, and a combination of both approaches have had some success in bringing about abstinence from cigarettes.

Opioids

Also known as *narcotics,* the opioids include morphine, heroin, codeine, and methadone. Opioids relieve pain and produce dreamlike states of euphoria. They tend to be highly addictive, can lead to an intense withdrawal syndrome, and are often associated with criminal lifestyles. Treatments for opioid abuse and dependence include antagonist drugs, methadone maintenance, and supportive-expressive therapy.

Cannabis and Hallucinogens

Cannabis and hallucinogens produce some similar effects. Derived from hemp plants, cannabis is a psychoactive drug usually used in the form of marijuana or hashish. Cannabis is the most commonly used illegal drug in the United States. After a period of declining popularity, cannabis use is again on the rise among young people. Cannabis has both sedating and mildly stimulating effects on users, and it produces mild perceptual distortions. Cannabis use can lead to psychological dependence and is often accompanied or followed by abuse of other drugs.

Hallucinogens produce unusual perceptual experiences, visual distortions, and highly variable moods in which users swing from euphoria to depression, sometimes in just a few moments. Paranoia, synesthesia, panic attacks, and flashbacks are other effects. The best known hallucinogen is LSD; others include mescaline, psilocybin, methyl-enedioxy-methamphetamine (MDMA), and phencyclidine.

KEY TERMS

14

Sexual and Gender Identity Disorders

Untitled by Camille Holvoet, 1989. Oil pastel on paper, 18" x 24". Courtesy of Creative Growth Art Center.

From the Case of John

John is a 28-year-old postal employee who works the night shift and lives alone in a one-bedroom apartment in a quiet, middle-class neighborhood. John gets along well with his coworkers but tends to keep to himself most of the time. He has never dated. John remembers that, as a boy, he loved to play with dolls and dress up in female clothes. His favorite toy was a Barbie doll given to him by his grandmother who also let him dress up in her old slips. He often fantasized about being a mother, and at school recess he preferred playing with girls rather than boys. Indeed, John spent most of his primary school years doing art projects and putting on plays with two neighborhood girls, and, while his two older brothers went hunting and fishing with their father, John would stay home with his mother.

His mother called John her "artistic son" and was not bothered by his choice of activities or friends. His father, on the other hand, would become enraged by this talk and blame his wife for babying John. John avoided trouble with his father by participating in scouts and excelling in school, but he was unmercifully teased by other boys who called him a sissy. By the fourth grade, he had learned to keep his feelings to himself.

When John was 10, his father died, and all three boys pitched in to help their mother; John was responsible for household chores. His brothers held after-school jobs and eventually completed high school and left home to marry and raise children. John continued to excel academically, but he had few friends and remembers his junior high and high school years as a very lonely period. The high point of each year was the school play, for which John designed sets or arranged costumes. In John's senior year, his mother remarried, and John decided to live on his own. He considered going to college, but was uncomfortable with the thought of living in a dorm. It was then that the post office job came along.

Soon, John found himself attracted to a male coworker and saw himself as the female in a fantasized relationship with this man. He began dressing as a female in the privacy of his apartment, using a growing wardrobe of female attire, makeup, and wigs. He never felt sexually aroused when dressed as a female, but he did feel at ease and more comfortable with himself. He taped his penis to his leg to minimize its visibility when he dressed as a female and even sometimes when he dressed as a male for work. He never went outside in female attire and never talked to anyone about his feelings until recently, when he told his doctor that, since childhood, he has felt like a woman trapped in a man's body. He wanted to know if it were possible to have surgery to become a woman. ■

Does John have a mental disorder, or does his case represent an extreme variation on the almost endless variability in normal human sexual expression? Is John's dissatisfaction with his gender caused by a biological abnormality, or is it the result of how he was raised? Can he be taught to accept his maleness, or would it be better to help him change his sexual identity? We will consider such questions in this chapter, which focuses on three types of sexual and gender identity problems: *gender identity disorders,* which are characterized by dissatisfaction with one's biological gender; *sexual dysfunction,* in which a person's ability to function sexually is limited or disturbed; and *paraphilias,* which involve sexual arousal that is repeatedly elicited by inanimate objects or other inappropriate stimuli or situations (see Figure 14.1). These disorders can be more fully understood when they are viewed within the context of human sexuality in general.

Human Sexuality

The umbrella of human sexuality encompasses numerous components, including gender identity, gender role, sexual orientation, and patterns of sexual arousal and functioning. In this section we will outline those aspects of human sexuality that influence gender identity, sexual orientation, and sexual behavior patterns.

Aspects of Sexuality

Gender identity refers to a person's sense of being male or female. For the vast majority of people, gender identity is consistent with their biological sex, but in rare cases there is *cross-gender identification,* in which individuals are preoccupied with a desire to live as the other sex. In extreme cases, such as John's, individuals are so uncomfortable with their biological gender that they seek medical help in changing their physical appearance and sexual functioning.

Gender identity is established as early as age 2 and appears in concert with the adoption of consistent gender roles. **Gender** or **sex role** refers to the patterns of behaviors typically expected of males or females in a particular culture. These behaviors may differ from one culture to another. For instance, in preindustrial cultures in which people lived off the land, women gathered food while men hunted game. In contemporary Western cultures, stereotypic masculinity involves assertive behavior aimed at achievement, ascendancy, and power while traditional femininity stresses nurturant behavior aimed at helping others, providing emotional support, and preserving relationships. Although traditional notions of appropriate sex role behavior have loosened in the past two decades, most men and women still conform to the expectations society holds about sex roles.

Sexual orientation refers to a person's tendency or preference for engaging in sexual behavior with

This little girl is not restricted by sex-role stereotypes about appropriate play. These early experiences will shape her ideas about gender roles as she grows older.

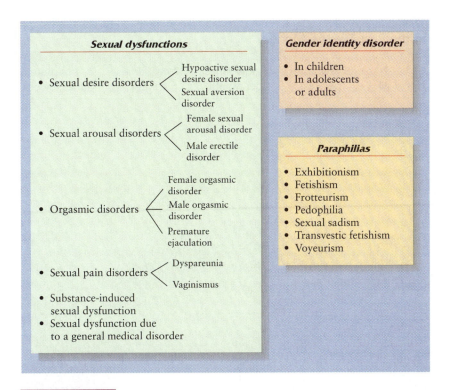

FIGURE 14.1

DSM-IV Sexual and Gender Identity Disorders

male or female partners. **Homosexual behavior** involves sexual intimacies with members of the same sex; homosexual behavior by females is often called **lesbianism.** **Heterosexual behavior** involves sexual activity with members of the opposite sex. **Bisexual behavior** involves sexual activity with members of both sexes. For some people, sexual behaviors are restricted to touching, kissing, and genital intercourse. For others a much wider variety of erotic activities are involved, including masturbation, oral sex, or anal intercourse. Furthermore, although some people engage in sexual activity with only one partner, others have several.

Gender identity, sex roles, sexual orientation, and sexual behavior are all independent aspects of human sexuality; one aspect of a person's sexuality need not, and often does not, determine other aspects of sexuality. Thus, it is common to find that females who behave in accordance with a male gender role may have a secure female gender identity; that a man whose sexual orientation is homosexual (or "gay") has a strong male gender identity; and that a heterosexual male may prefer cooking over football. In short, human sexuality is very complex.

Investigating Sexual Behavior

What is *normal* sexual behavior? Most people have strong opinions on this issue, but it turns out that these opinions vary widely. Some people define *normal* sexual behavior as acts that guarantee the reproduction of the species, while others define it in terms of the moral or religious codes that prevail in their culture. Another approach is to equate sexual normality with that which is most common: if a lot of people engage in a certain pattern of sexual behavior, it is regarded as normal.

How common are various patterns of sexual behavior? In the 1940s, Alfred Kinsey and his associates at Indiana University conducted the first large-scale surveys of sexual behavior in the United States (Kinsey, Pomeroy, & Martin, 1948; Kinsey et al., 1953) by interviewing thousands of volunteers. The results of this survey, like those of subsequent ones, have been viewed with some skepticism because the people studied may not have constituted a representative sample of the adult population about which conclusions are to be drawn. A survey of *Playboy* magazine readers, who are mainly men, will yield different re-

TABLE 14.1   Frequency of Sex in the Past Twelve Months

Social characteristics	Not at all	A few times per year	A few times per month	2 or 3 times a week	4 or more times a week
Gender					
Men	14%	16%	37%	26%	8%
Women	10	18	36	30	7
Age					
Men					
18–24	15	21	24	28	12
25–29	7	15	31	36	11
30–39	8	15	37	33	6
40–49	9	18	40	27	6
50–59	11	22	43	20	3
Women					
18–24	11	16	32	29	12
25–29	5	10	38	37	10
30–39	9	16	36	33	6
40–49	15	16	44	20	5
50–59	30	22	35	12	2
Marital/residential status					
Men					
Noncohabiting	23	25	26	19	7
Cohabiting	0	8	36	40	16
Married	1	13	43	36	7
Women					
Noncohabiting	32	23	24	15	5
Cohabiting	1	8	35	42	14
Married	3	12	47	32	7
Education					
Men					
Less than high school	15	20	28	30	7
High school graduate or equivalent	10	15	34	32	9
Any college	9	18	38	28	7
Women					
Less than high school	19	15	36	23	8
High school graduate or equivalent	11	16	38	30	6
Any college	14	17	37	26	7
Religion					
Men					
None	13	25	25	27	11
Mainline Protestant	8	19	28	27	8
Conservative Protestant	11	15	36	32	7
Catholic	8	17	37	31	8

TABLE 14.1   *(continued)*

Social characteristics	Not at all	A few times per year	A few times per month	2 or 3 times a week	4 or more times a week
Religion (continued)					
Women					
None	10	19	37	26	9
Mainline Protestant	13	17	40	25	5
Conservative Protestant	15	14	36	26	9
Catholic	14	16	37	28	5
Race/ethnicity					
Men					
White	10	17	36	30	8
African American	8	16	38	30	7
Hispanic	9	15	34	29	14
Women					
White	13	16	38	27	7
African American	17	18	33	25	7
Hispanic	11	10	35	33	10

Source: Michael et al., 1994.

sults from one conducted by *Redbook,* whose readers are mainly women (Tavris & Sadd, 1977). And the results of both will differ from those of a study called *The Hite Report,* in which responses were solicited from the National Organization of Women, abortion rights groups, and readers of *Village Voice, Mademoiselle,* and *Ms.* (Hite, 1976). The latest large-scale sex survey in the United States was based on the most representative and scientifically constructed sample of respondents to date. Conducted by the National Opinion Research Center at the University of Chicago, this National Health and Social Life Survey involved interviews with more than 3,000 people between ages 18 and 59 (Michael et al., 1994). Among its more notable findings are the following:

■ about 1.4 percent of women and 2.8 percent of men considered themselves to be homosexual or bisexual;

■ about 60 percent of men and 40 percent of women masturbated in the past year and among those who masturbate, men did so much more frequently than women;

■ by age 22, 90 percent of Americans had engaged in intercourse, and, as Table 14.1 shows, continued to do so regularly for most of their adult lives;

■ only 17 percent of Americans had more than one sexual partner in the previous year. The number of partners varied little by religion or education, but Blacks were about twice as likely as Whites to have more than one partner, who, in turn, were about twice as likely as Asian Americans to have multiple partners. Only 5 percent of married people admitted to having more than one sexual partner.

What kind of sexual behaviors do people in the United States prefer? Several surveys suggest that, if a person has engaged in at least one relatively rare sexual practice, he or she is likely to have engaged in most other forms of sexual behavior as well. This pattern is illustrated in Table 14.2 on page 492, which shows the results for 172 undergraduate women who were asked whether they had ever performed each of 24 sexual activities (Andersen & Cyranowski, 1995).

Another method for investigating sexuality is to study people's sexual fantasies, the mental images that they find sexually arousing. In fact, some researchers believe that sexual fantasies reveal more about sexuality than overt behavior. The famous comment by noted sexologist Helen Kaplan (1974), "Sex is composed of friction and fantasy," confirms what many people already know, namely that

TABLE 14.2   Sexual Experiences of College-Age Women

Ever performed (%)*	How often in past 30 days	Activity
12.3	0.05	Anal intercourse
33.1	0.8	Caressing your partner's anal area
34.9	0.7	Masturbating alone
44.2	0.9	Intercourse: side by side
45.3	1.0	Having your anal area caressed
52.3	1.1	Intercourse: vaginal entry from rear
55.8	1.2	Intercourse: sitting position
63.9	1.8	Mutual petting of genitals to orgasm
67.4	1.7	Mutual oral (mouth) stimulation of genitals
67.8	2.1	Intercourse: female "on top" position
70.3	2.0	Oral stimulation of your partner's genitals
71.3	2.7	Intercourse: male "on top" position
72.1	1.9	Having your genitals orally stimulated
79.7	2.8	Mutual undressing of each other
81.3	3.2	Breast petting while you are nude
86.0	3.3	Stroking and petting your sexual partner's genitals
87.8	3.4	Having your genitals caressed by your partner
88.9	3.4	Your partner kissing your nude breasts
88.9	3.7	Erotic embrace while dressed
90.7	4.1	Kissing of sensitive (nongenital) areas of the body
91.1	4.0	Your partner lying on you while you are clothed
93.0	3.6	Breast petting while you are clothed
95.9	4.8	Deep kissing
98.8	5.6	Kissing on the lips

*For "ever performed," items were scored 0 (*never experienced in my lifetime*) and 1 (*experienced at least once in my lifetime*). Values are percentages of women in the sample who endorsed each item as having been experienced at least once. The following scale was used for the frequency of each behavior in the *past 30 days:* 0 = *this activity did not occur;* 1 = *activity occurred once;* 2 = *activity occurred twice;* 3 = *activity occurred three times;* 4 = *activity occurred four times;* 5 = *activity occurred five times;* 6 = *once a week;* 7 = *two to six times a week;* 8 = *once a day;* and 9 = *two or more times a day.*

Source: Andersen & Cyranowski, 1995.

the brain is the body's most important sex organ. Research suggests that men think about sex a lot; more than half of them say they have sexual fantasies every day, often several times a day (Michael et al., 1994). Most women, on the other hand, think about sex a few times a week or a few times a month (Leitenberg & Henning, 1995; Michael et al., 1994). People usually begin to have sexual fantasies between the ages of 11 and 13, and they tend to occur most often in adolescence and young adulthood.

According to one large-scale review, the most popular sexual fantasies, for both men and women, involve reliving a prior sexually exciting experience or imagining sexual activity, either with a current romantic partner or with another partner. Conventional behavior is the focus of most of these fantasies, but scenes involving multiple partners, sexual dominance or submission, or some "forbidden" sexual behavior were also mentioned rather frequently (Leitenberg & Henning, 1995).

Biological Influences on Sexual Differentiation

All aspects of human sexuality are affected by psychological and sociocultural factors, and these influences distinguish human sexuality from the almost exclusively biological control of sexuality in other species. However, biological factors do play an important role in determining the physical aspects of human sex differences. The vast majority of people have 46 chromosomes in the nucleus of each cell in their bodies, and two of these, known as the X and Y chromosomes, are responsible for determining biological sex. Females inherit two X chromosomes, one from the mother and one from the father; males inherit an X chromosome from the mother and a Y chromosome from the father.

During the first 8 to 12 weeks after conception, the development of males and females is exactly the same. As illustrated in Figure 14.2, each fetus develops genital cells that have an equal chance of becoming male or female sexual structures. It is the Y chromosome that directs differentiation of certain of these cells into testicles, vas deferens, and prostate. The testicles then release testosterone, a hormone that stimulates the development of male external sexual organs. Testicular tissue also produces a substance that suppresses the development of a uterus, a vagina, and other internal female sexual organs. If there is no Y chromosome or if testicular development and hormone secretion are impaired, female sexual structures appear.

Further sexual differentiation occurs beginning at puberty when sex hormones are produced in abundance. While **androgens** (including testosterone) are called *male hormones* and **estrogens** (such as estradiol and progesterone) are called *female hormones,* these labels are oversimplified, because both men and women produce androgens *and* estrogens. The

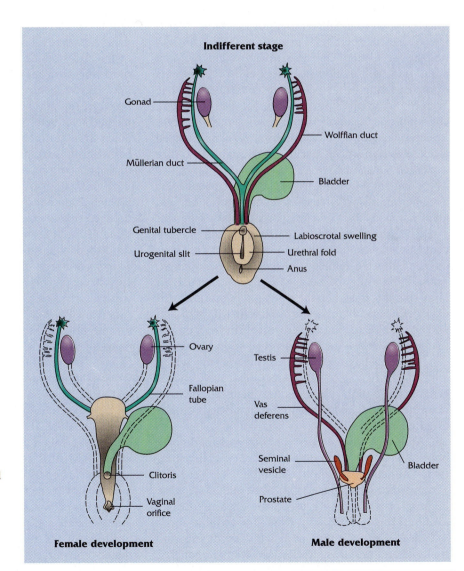

FIGURE 14.2

Differentiation of Internal Sex Organs

At 8 weeks, the internal sex organs of a fetus are not differentiated. Internally, the fetus develops Wolffian ducts, the basis for male internal sex organs, and Müllerian ducts, the basis for female internal sex organs. At this point, the external sex organs consist of the genital tubercle, urogenital slit, labioscrotal swelling, and urethral fold in both males and females. Thereafter, as a result of the presence or absence of testosterone, male and female sexual structures begin to develop.

Source: Galluscio, 1990.

labels reflect the fact that males produce more androgens and females produce more estrogens. These hormones stimulate a variety of general and specific secondary sex characteristics. For example, androgen released from the adrenal gland during adolescence stimulates the growth of underarm and pubic hair in both males and females. Increases in testicular testosterone in males causes penile growth, increased muscle mass, beard development, and a deepening voice. In females, the ovaries increase their output of estradiol and progesterone, and begin the cycling associated with menstruation. The ovaries also increase testosterone production—about 10 percent of that seen in males—that stimulates maturation of the clitoris, breasts, and nipples (Kaplan & Owett, 1993).

Sexual differentiation—and even certain patterns of adult sexual behavior—are also affected by the androgens present during fetal development. Laboratory experiments show, for example, that female mice exposed to high levels of androgens during critical phases of their fetal growth will develop secondary sexual characteristics similar to males and, in adulthood, will exhibit mounting and other aspects of male mating behavior. Similar consequences have been found among humans who, because of genetic, endocrine, or metabolic abnormalities, have an atypical complement of sex chromosomes, were exposed to excessive androgen levels, or are unable to utilize androgens properly.

Congenital adrenal hyperplasia, for instance, is an inherited disorder that leaves the body's adrenal glands unable to synthesize cortisone. To compensate, the adrenals produce an excess of adrenal androgen, which in turn masculinizes the external genitalia of affected females during fetal development. These babies may be born with a clitoris that is so large that it is mistaken for a penis. Diagnosis of this disorder is usually made within the first days of life, and corrective surgery is performed during infancy. In childhood, these girls frequently demonstrate male gender role behaviors (so-called tomboyism), which are thought to reflect the effects of excessive androgens in the womb. Their gender identity, however, remains female, and their later sexual orientation is usually heterosexual.

Androgen insensitivity is another example of a hormonal abnormality affecting sexual differentiation. This condition affects individuals with the XY chromosome complement typical of males but who, because of a defective gene on the Y chromosome, cannot absorb testosterone at the cellular level. Affected babies are thus born with female external genitalia and raised as females. Although, at puberty, breast development occurs, no uterus or ovaries are present. Indeed, this disorder is not usually diagnosed

until, in the teenage years, the youngster fails to begin menstrual periods. These individuals usually live their entire lives as well-adjusted females. Most are happily married to males, and many have adopted children. These relatively rare clinical syndromes remind us again of how the various aspects of sexuality can combine to produce an enormous range of human differences.

Sexual Orientation

Alfred Kinsey saw people's sexual orientation as lying on a continuum that ranged from exclusively heterosexual to exclusively homosexual. Like Kinsey, most current sex researchers believe that trying to define people as gay, straight, or bisexual oversimplifies the concept of sexual orientation, which encompasses many more than three fixed patterns of sexual behavior. For example, most people maintain a consistent sense of themselves as heterosexuals, but many have occasional homosexual fantasies and sometimes feel attracted to members of the same sex. Many adolescents experiment with homosexual behavior as part of their sexual development; the majority of homosexuals have experimented with heterosexual behavior or have tried out being straight for varying periods. A substantial number of homosexuals have entered into heterosexual marriages and have had children.

Sexual Orientation and Mental Health. Should the topic of sexual orientation—and, more specifically, homosexuality—be discussed in relation to mental disorders in an abnormal psychology textbook? Thirty years ago, the answer would have undoubtedly been yes because, until 1973, homosexuality was classified as a mental disorder. In that year, the American Psychiatric Association officially declared that homosexuality is not a mental disorder. A new printing of the then-standard DSM-II was revised to include *sexual orientation disturbance* (with the word *homosexuality* in parenthesis), a category reserved for those homosexuals who were distressed by their orientation and who wanted to change it. When the DSM-III was published in 1980, this condition was called *ego-dystonic homosexuality,* but, when DSM-III-R appeared in 1987, all references to homosexuality as a mental disorder were deleted and are not to be found in the DSM-IV, either.

In short, variations in sexual orientation, and homosexuality in particular, are no longer officially included in the realm of mental disorders. Nevertheless, the outcry over gays in the military, the passage of antihomosexual legislation in some states, the denouncement of gay rights by conservative political groups, and the homophobia displayed by many people—particularly since the outbreak of AIDS—make it obvious that homosexuality remains at the center of moral, political, and social controversy. Accordingly, it is important to discuss homosexuality, not as an example of mental disorder, but as part of a more general consideration of sexual orientation and sexuality.

The historical view of homosexuality as a mental disorder was based largely on the perception that, as a group, homosexuals were not psychologically well adjusted. This impression, in turn, was based mainly on clinical case reports of individuals who felt guilty or embarrassed about their homosexuality. However, objective studies that use structured psychological tests and more representative subject samples have revealed no differences in either the prevalence of mental disorders or the overall quality of psychosocial functioning between homosexuals and heterosexuals (Gadpaille, 1995). One study did find more depression among homosexual than heterosexual men, a difference that may be attributable largely to the rejection, discrimination, hostility, and other hardships encountered by gays in the United States (Pillard, 1988); indeed, gay and lesbian youths are at increased risk for suicidal behavior (Remafedi, Farrow, & Deisher, 1991).

Given the social and legal problems faced by homosexual men and lesbians, a question remains about whether clinicians should try to help them change their sexual orientation. Some therapists argue against "treating" homosexuality, even for clients who request it, because such treatment tacitly supports bias against homosexuals (Davison, 1978). Others claim that therapists should not deny services to clients just because they do not like the social implications of the treatment (Sturgis & Adams, 1978). As the Controversy section on pages 496–497 shows, clinicians remain divided on this issue.

Frequency of Varying Sexual Orientations. Homosexual as well as heterosexual orientations are found in most societies. One study found that 64 percent of non-Western cultures included homosexual activities as an acceptable form of sexual behavior (Gadpaille, 1995). In the other 36 percent, homosexuality was present but not approved. As you might expect, in societies where there are strong religious proscriptions against all but heterosexual orientations, homosexuality is less common, or at least less often reported. Indeed, it is difficult to gauge the prevalence of various sexual orientations wherever certain orientations are censured.

According to Kinsey's initial surveys of sexual behavior in the United States, most people maintain a heterosexual orientation, but 37 percent of men and 13 percent of women had had at least one homosexual experience. A substantial subset of both men (13 percent) and women (1 to 8 percent) indicated predominant to exclusive homosexuality during at least a 3-year period of their late adolescent or adult lives (Pillard & Bailey, 1995). These results were widely interpreted to mean that about 10 percent of Americans are homosexual, a conclusion that Kinsey himself never advocated. Studies conducted during the 1980s and 1990s in the United States have yielded lower rates than those attributed to Kinsey. Reviewers of several of these studies suggest that while 12 to 25 percent of men have had at least one homosexual contact in their lives, mostly during adolescence, only 1 to 6 percent report a homosexual experience in the year preceding the surveys (Seidman & Rieder, 1994). They conclude that 2.4 percent of men are currently exclusively homosexual and that 2.6 percent are bisexual (Berrios, Heart & Perkins, 1992; Seidman & Rieder, 1994). In the University of Chicago sex study mentioned earlier, fewer than 2 percent of women reported having sex with another woman in the previous year, a rate that was about the same as for male homosexual contact in the previous year (Michael et al., 1994). In a health survey completed by 34,706 high school students, about 5 percent of males and females professed "predominantly homosexual attractions" (Remafedi et al., 1993).

Biological Factors in Development of Sexual Orientation. Is sexual orientation a personal choice, a biological leaning, or a learned style of behavior? No one yet knows for sure, but, like most heterosexuals, most homosexuals do not believe that they made a choice to be gay or lesbian; their only choice was whether to disclose their homosexuality (Gonsiorek, Sell, & Weinrich, 1995). Because of the compelling nature of sexual orientation, many scientists believe that it must be at least partially determined by biological factors. Most of the research on this issue is focused on the biological determinants of homosexuality, but the underlying questions can be asked about the origins of heterosexuality or bisexuality, as well. As the data on these questions accumulate, it now appears that there is a moderate degree of *heritability* for sexual orientation, meaning that genetic factors appear partly responsible (Meyer-Bahlburg, 1993). Several hormonal and neuroanatomical factors have also been discovered that could influence sexual orientation.

To what extent is a specific tendency toward homosexuality inherited? Findings vary. One study reported homosexual concordance rates of 52 percent for male and 48 percent for female monozygotic

Controversy

Changing Sexual Orientation

Can people's sexual orientation be changed? If so, should professionals try to change it? When homosexuality was still considered a form of deviant behavior, a variety of procedures were used in an attempt to modify sexual orientation. Physicians gave homosexual men testosterone injections. Behavioral therapists employed desensitization, reconditioning, shaping, and aversive techniques to transfer sexual arousal from homosexual to heterosexual stimuli. Psychodynamic therapists explored their homosexual clients' family dynamics and unresolved unconscious conflicts. Experts disagree on the effects of these interventions. Some reviewers conclude that well-designed, replicated studies have shown that sexual orientation is not amenable to change (Davison, 1978; Mattison & McWhirter, 1995); others claim that intensive behavioral therapies changed sexual preference in 33 to 79

Gay activism has increased in the past two decades as homosexuals have fought to end discrimination and stigmatization of their sexual lifestyles.

percent of cases (Gadpaille, 1995; Schwartz & Masters, 1984).

In the current social and political climate, the idea of trying to

change sexual orientation runs contrary to the official position that sexual orientation is not a mental health issue. Accordingly,

---

twins; in contrast, concordance rates were 22 percent and 16 percent respectively for male and female dizygotic twins, and 11 percent and 6 percent for adopted siblings (Bailey et al., 1991). Another study reported homosexual concordance rates of 65.8 percent for monozygotic and 30.4 percent for dizygotic twins (Whitam, Diamond, & Martin, 1993). However, another, smaller study found much lower rates of concordance and no difference in concordance between monozygotic and dizygotic twin sets (King & McDonald, 1992). Each of these studies has been criticized because the samples were small, were recruited through gay publications rather than through random sampling, and because not all siblings were interviewed. Data from the more exacting method of studying identical twins reared apart are still equivocal (Eckert et al., 1986).

Recently, several research teams have suggested that the long arm of the X chromosome may be the site of a gene related to homosexuality (Hamer et al.,

1993; Turner, 1995). One of these teams (Hamer et al., 1993) studied 32 pairs of exclusively or predominantly homosexual brothers. Of these pairs, 22 (69 percent) shared the same version of a particular gene on the X chromosome, while in 9 of 11 comparison families, heterosexual brothers did not share this version of the gene. Such studies remain controversial and in need of replication; nevertheless, it appears that genetics play a partial, but far from decisive, role in determining homosexuality.

Other recent research points to the possible influence of neuroanatomical differences on sexual orientation. Three findings are noteworthy, although none has yet been replicated and all have been strongly criticized (Byne & Parsons, 1993). First, a study in the Netherlands (Swaab et al., 1993) found the suprachiasmatic nucleus (which governs daily biological rhythms) to be twice as large in a sample of homosexual men when compared with heterosexual men. Second, scientists at the Salk Institute in Cal-

many professionals adamantly oppose any treatments designed to reorient people because they believe that reorientation increases anxiety and shame about homosexual feelings, thereby exacerbating rather than alleviating emotional distress (Mattison & McWhirter, 1995). Opponents of reorientation therapy also argue that it perpetuates a negative image of homosexuality. They believe therapy with homosexuals should focus mainly on facilitating the "coming out" process and helping clients to cope with the social stigmatization they are likely to encounter (Mattison & McWhirter, 1995). To achieve these goals, supportive individual and group therapy is used, along with support groups for friends and relatives of gay and lesbian individuals. Groups such as Parents and Friends of Lesbians and Gays (PFLAG) are especially helpful to parents who are just coming to understand and accept their children's homosexual orientation.

Other therapists persist in advocating sexual reorientation treatments for homosexuals, particularly for those who are profoundly discontented with their sexual orientation. Their methods combine behavioral and psychoanalytic techniques. These therapists have established the National Association for Research and Therapy of Homosexuality (NARTH) as well as support groups for "ex-gays" such as Exodus International, Homosexuals Anonymous, and Love in Action (Nicolosi, 1994). They contend that studies showing a high rate of suicide attempts among gay youth (Hunter & Schaecher, 1995; Rotheram-Borus, Hunter, & Rosario, 1994; 1995) document the need for sexual reorientation methods. In addition, they argue that homosexuals should not be prevented from receiving a treatment they want just because other individuals oppose the goals of this treatment.

Is there a resolution to this controversy? Should clinicians refrain from any attempt to alter sexual orientation because of the possible stigma that such treatment programs could produce? Or should they honor the requests of individual clients and provide requested treatment? Although people on both sides of the debate point to empirical studies supporting their positions, their views often reflect personal values, not hard facts.

Thinking Critically

Imagine that empirical studies showed that current sexual reorientation methods are ineffective.

- Would this mean that such treatment efforts should be ended immediately? Why or why not?

- If research showed sexual reorientation methods to be highly effective, would it be unethical for clinicians to oppose such interventions? Why or why not?

ifornia found that, in homosexual men and heterosexual women, the interstitial nuclei of the anterior hypothalamus were half the size of these structures in heterosexual men (LeVay, 1991). A third study found that a forebrain structure, the anterior commisure, is larger in homosexual men than in women and heterosexual men (Allen & Gorski, 1992).

The influence of prenatal hormones on sexual orientation has also been studied. Females exposed *in utero* to abnormal levels of both androgens and estrogens are more likely than comparison groups to become homosexual or bisexual during adulthood (Meyer-Bahlburg, 1993). However, the vast majority of homosexual individuals show no physical evidence of exposure to atypical prenatal hormones.

One other biological basis for homosexuality has been hinted at by research on birth order and sibling sex ratio. A series of studies (e.g., Blanchard & Sheridan, 1992) documented that male homosexuals tended to be later-born children and to come from families with an overrepresentation of male siblings. Two theories could explain these correlational findings. Prenatal stress could lead to both increased rates of male offspring as well as inadequate androgenization of later-born males. A second possibility is that mothers who have multiple male offspring develop antibodies to testosterone, which in turn leads to underandrogenization of the fetus (Zucker & Green, 1993).

Development of Sexual Orientation: Psychological Factors. Do psychological or environmental factors play any role in the development of sexual orientation? Several theories claim that they do, although most have been applied only to the case of male homosexuals. For example, psychoanalysts traditionally believed that homosexuality was caused by growing up with a dominant mother who failed to establish healthy boundaries between herself and her son. Fathers in this scenario are weak, passive men who fail to help their sons develop positive gender role identities (Bieber et al., 1962). From this perspective, homosexuality develops as a drive to repair or complete oneself through a relationship with another male (Nicolosi, 1991). However, psychoanalytic theory fails to explain why, in most cases, only one child in a family is homosexual, or why the same family constellation would lead to such a diverse group of adult men and women, not all of whom are homosexual.

Homosexuality has also been linked to experiencing sexual abuse during childhood (Gadpaille, 1995), but sexual abuse is also associated with a number of other psychological conditions and disorders, and, in any case, most homosexuals were not sexually abused as children. Exactly how sexual abuse might lead to homosexuality has not yet been clearly explained or carefully researched.

Does growing up in a family with a homosexual parent make it more likely that children will become homosexual? Contrary to popular opinion, the answer, apparently, is no. One study compared 25 children raised by lesbian mothers, most of whom lived with a female partner, with 21 children who grew up with unmarried heterosexual mothers, most of whom lived with a male companion (Golombok & Tasker, 1996). None of the children who lived with heterosexual mothers considered themselves to be homosexual, and only two of the children from the lesbian families became homosexual adults. The difference between the groups was not statistically significant.

In short, numerous empirical studies have found support for biological contributions to sexual orientation, particularly homosexuality, but well-controlled studies have not been able to confirm a clear role for psychological factors. Although the precise reasons why people are homosexual, heterosexual, or bisexual are not clear, genetic and biological factors appear to be the most important influences.

In Review

The study of sexual behavior includes the topics of:

- gender identity, a person's sense of being male or female;
- gender or sex role, patterns of behavior typically expected of men and women;
- sexual orientation, a person's interest in and tendency to engage in sexual behavior with same or opposite sex partners; and
- biological differentiation of sex organs and physical appearance.

Sex surveys, first conducted in the United States in the 1940s, show that:

- fewer than 1 in 5 Americans have had sex with more than one partner in the past year;
- by age 22, 90 percent of Americans have engaged in intercourse, and they continue to do so regularly throughout most of their lives; and
- if a person has engaged in a rare sexual activity, he or she is also likely to have engaged in more common sexual behaviors.

Homosexuality:

- is no longer officially defined as a mental disorder;
- is considered to be the primary sexual orientation of between 4 to 10 percent of adults in the United States; and,
- like other sexual orientations, may be shaped by one or more biological factors, including genetics, neuroanatomical differences, and hormonal influences.

Gender Identity Disorders

The first question inevitably asked after the birth of a baby is whether the child is a boy or a girl. As infants, girls and boys are treated differently; to take but one example, fathers "rough-house" with their sons more often than with their daughters. As a result of these and many other influences, the sense of being male or female is, from the beginning, a deeply felt part of a person's identity. Most toddlers think of themselves as male or female and consistently imitate the male or female models they see at home, school, and on television. By the age of 3, children have a clearly established gender identity even if they think they could temporarily "be" the opposite gender by letting their hair grow or by wearing different clothing.

Few children have an abiding interest in being a member of the opposite sex; most develop gender role behaviors consistent with their gender identifications. However, as children or adults, some people experience **gender identity disorders,** which involve confusion about or dissatisfaction with their biological gender. These disorders always involve two components: (1) a persistent *cross-gender identification,* that is, a person's desire to become the other sex, and (2) a person's profound discomfort or even disgust with his or her biological sex and sexual organs. Adults who experience gender identity disorder are sometimes termed **transsexuals.** As in the case of

Jan Morris before and after undergoing sex reassignment surgery.

I was three or perhaps four years old when I realized that I had been born into the wrong body, and should really be a girl. . . . What triggered so bizarre a thought I have long forgotten, but the conviction was unfaltering from the start. On the face of things it was pure nonsense. . . . by every standard of logic I was patently a boy. I was James Humphry Morris, male child. I had a boy's body. I wore a boy's clothes. It is true that my mother had wished me to be a daughter, but I was never treated as one. It is true that gushing visitors sometimes assembled me into their fox furs and lavender sachets to murmur that, with curly hair like mine, I should have been born a girl. As the youngest of three brothers, in a family very soon to be fatherless, I was doubtless indulged. I was not, however, generally thought effeminate. . . . As I grew older my conflict became more explicit to me, and I began to feel that I was living a falsehood. I was in masquerade, my female reality, which I had no words to define, clothed in male pretense.

Morris, J. (1974). *Conundrum.* New York: Harcourt Brace Jovanovich, Inc.

John, their biological gender feels so foreign to them that they often try to reverse it through surgical and hormonal treatments. It is important to note that transsexuals are not **hermaphrodites**—people who have both female and male sexual organs.

Prevalence

Gender identity disorders are uncommon. No epidemiological studies of gender disorder in childhood have been done, but prevalence rates are estimated to be about 3 percent for boys and less than 1 percent for girls (Green & Blanchard, 1995). Although gender confusion is rare among elementary school children, many children occasionally display some type of gender-atypical behavior, such as playing with toys usually associated with the other sex (Sandberg et al., 1993). A gender disorder is diagnosed only when a child displays a persistent pattern of multiple cross-gender behaviors and seems insistent on becoming the other sex.

Why are more boys than girls diagnosed with gender-identity disorders? One possibility is that gender-atypical behaviors in little girls are less likely to be condemned by parents, teachers, and peers, and are therefore less likely to be brought to the attention of mental health professionals. Having an interest in sports, rough and tumble play, male playmates, and a preference for wearing pants instead of dresses is a common developmental pathway for girls. However, most tomboyish girls do not abhor their female anatomy. Further, they are accepted by both boys and girls, and, by puberty, they typically become interested in being seen as attractive females.

The prevalence of gender identity disorder, or transsexualism, in adults is unknown. Most estimates are based on the extensive medical records kept in some European countries. These records suggest that about 1 in 30,000 males and 1 in 100,000 females seek sex reassignment or request clinical help because of severe gender identity concerns (APA, 1994). Obviously, the much higher rates of gender identity disorder among children suggest that many children outgrow the disorder and go on to establish reasonably conventional gender identities. Interestingly, however, not all adult transsexuals—perhaps only about half—experienced a gender identity disorder in childhood. Some cases of late-onset gender identity disorder involve homosexuals who have decided to alter their biological gender in an attempt to cover up their homosexual preferences.

Gender Identity Disorder in Children

Several characteristics have been associated with early cross-gender identification. Gender-disordered boys tend to show lower activity levels and less interest than their peers in rough-and-tumble play, while gender-disordered girls are more active and more interested in rough-and-tumble play than are their peers (Zucker & Green, 1993). Parents of boys displaying gender identity problems also report them to be highly creative, with artistic and theatrical interests. However, the importance of these characteristics as *causal* factors in gender identity disorders has not been confirmed in well-designed studies (Zucker & Green, 1993).

Gender-disordered boys are more often described as having been beautiful or feminine babies than are non-disordered samples of boys (Stoller, 1975). Furthermore, in one study, college students rated pictures of boys diagnosed with gender identity disorders as more attractive than pictures of boys from a non-disordered comparison group (Zucker et al., 1993). We do not know, of course, whether physical attractiveness is a cause or effect of gender identity disorder, but it has been suggested that a physically pretty male baby engenders responses from caregivers that encourage a female identification.

Many children diagnosed with gender identity disorders began to show a preference for cross-gender toys and activities as early as age 2 or 3. These toy preferences are usually followed by fantasy play in which the child assumes a cross-gender role. In a typical case, a boy will begin at age 3 to ask for dolls and stuffed animals as gifts, to use towels to simulate long hair or a long skirt, and to try on his mother's clothes and high-heeled shoes. Some of these boys will position their penis between their legs when dressing up, or tell their parents they hope their penis goes away when they grow up. At preschool or daycare, these boys spend most of their time playing with girls. Girls who display gender

identity disorders crave acceptance as males, insist on wearing male clothing, ask for extremely boyish haircuts, and introduce themselves to strangers using a male name.

By kindergarten, gender-disordered boys are usually ostracized by traditionally masculine boys, and, when they enter elementary school, they become the target of relentless teasing. In most gender-disordered youngsters, overt cross-gender behaviors are gradually suppressed by negative feedback from parents and peers. For many of these young people, atypical gender behavior becomes even less evident as they resolve questions about their sexual orientation. In one longitudinal study of 66 gender-atypical boys, 80 percent reported being bisexual or homosexual by early adulthood compared with 4 percent of a gender-typical control group (Green, 1987). Thus, only a minority of childhood gender identity disorders persist into adulthood and, even in these cases, the atypical gender behaviors are less overt.

Children with gender identity disorders often develop problems that go beyond gender-related matters. These problems—primarily social avoidance, separation anxiety, and depression—are closely related to the peer ostracism and family criticism these children experience (Zucker & Bradley, 1995). Accordingly, suicidal impulses and suicide attempts are associated with gender identity disorder (Coates & Person, 1985).

Gender Identity Disorder in Adults

Adult transsexuals fall into two major categories. The first consists of individuals who are homosexual (or in a few cases, asexual). Most of these people have experienced gender identity disorders since childhood and, as in the case of John, are now seeking professional help in adopting their desired gender (a process called *sex reassignment*). These clients usually come to clinical attention in their 20s, after becoming independent of their families. Many have had little or no sexual experience, and sexual gratification plays a limited role in their cross-gender desire. After sex-reassignment surgery, these individuals usually identify themselves as heterosexuals.

Members of the second category of gender-disordered adults are almost exclusively male and are heterosexual in orientation. Many in this group report experiencing gender confusion in childhood, mainly in association with secretly dressing in their mother's clothing. Others first experienced gender confusion only in adolescence or adult life, and this confusion is more likely to wax and wane. These men may have married, fathered children, and often engage in heterosexual activity. However, during sex

Connections

In addition to forming a gender identity, what other developmental tasks do children face? See Chapter 3, pp. 78–81.

they imagine themselves as the lesbian lover of a female partner or as a woman making love to man. Because dissatisfaction with their gender (called **gender dysphoria**) fluctuates, these men are less likely to make a good adjustment after sex-reassignment surgery (Green & Blanchard, 1995).

Adults who experience gender identity disorder also often struggle with depression and anxiety as a result of feeling forced into a solitary life. Female-to-male transsexuals generally have fewer psychological problems than male-to-female transsexuals. This may be because the only way some men feel they can live as females is to become prostitutes. The adjustment for female-to-male transsexuals is probably easier because they usually face less social condemnation for their sex conversion and because society values the roles for men more than it values the roles for women.

Causes of Gender Identity Disorders

There are many theories about the causes of gender identity disorders, but there is only limited support for any of them. Part of the problem is that, because these disorders affect so few people and because fear of ostracism causes many affected people to hide their gender confusion or dysphoria, it is difficult to obtain representative samples for study.

The role of genetics in gender identity disorders is uncertain. In one of the few family studies available, there was no increased prevalence of homosexuality among first- or second-degree relatives of gender-disordered youngsters (Zuger, 1989). Likewise, no particular characteristics of brain structure or function have been consistently documented in children or adults diagnosed with gender identity disorders. However, in one study, an area of the hypothalamus known to play a role in animal sexual behavior was smaller in six male-to-female transsexuals than in a comparison group of heterosexual or homosexual men (Zhou et al., 1995). Because gender identity disorders are seldom observed in individuals with endocrine disorders, researchers also have not been able to demonstrate that gender identity disorders depend on early hormonal disturbances.

Could parenting practices and expectations be responsible for gender identity disorders? Is it possible that these children are just trying to please a parent who longed for a child of a different gender? Or is a more complicated pattern of parent–child interaction involved? Richard Green (1974, 1987) has singled out parental indifference toward cross-gender behaviors as a key variable in promoting gender identity disorders. Many families of cross-gender boys report thinking that the boys' behaviors were

cute or represented a temporary phase of development. The relatives of cross-gender boys may not only tolerate gender-atypical behavior, but actively encourage it by dressing the boy in girls' clothing. Finally, many of these boys lacked male playmates and were likely to have fathers who were aloof and uninvolved with their upbringing. It has also been proposed that girls whose mothers are distant may develop gender confusion because their fathers serve as their main role model. Note, however, that parental disengagement might be the result, not the cause, of boys' effeminate behavior and girls' masculine behavior.

Indeed, theories about the causal role of psychological and family influences in gender identity disorders are mostly speculative. For example, Green's descriptions of how a child might learn the "wrong" gender identity are plausible, but clinicians do not yet know how many children exposed to these socialization practices develop a disordered gender identity.

Treatment of Gender Identity Disorders

Gender-disordered children usually first receive professional attention when they start school. Their parents seek help for them because they are concerned that the cross-gender "phase" has not passed and, especially in the case of boys, that it may signal homosexuality. At the same time, some parents worry that treatment will impair their child's creativity or self-esteem. Indeed, some critics charge that treatment of gender identity disorders reinforces narrow definitions of male and female behavior, and others argue that the only reason these individuals are treated is that society is intolerant of variations in sexuality.

Psychological Treatments. While respecting these criticisms, most clinicians recommend treatment for gender dysphoric youngsters. The typical goals of treatment are to maintain self-esteem, minimize behaviors that lead to social rejection and teasing, and teach traditional gender-appropriate behaviors. The child is also helped to develop the social and academic skills needed to function successfully as an adult, regardless of gender identity.

Most psychological attempts to alter gender identity have used behavior therapy for the child, parent training, or both. For example, a 17-year-old male transsexual was systematically trained, using modeling and reinforcement, to alter each component of his gender identity. He was taught to walk and talk more like a traditional male, to fantasize about sexual contacts with females, and to become sexually aroused by women (Barlow, Reynolds, & Agras, 1973).

Parent training involves coaching parents about how to reshape their children's behavior. For example, they are taught how to encourage gender-typical behaviors while gradually discouraging activities such as cross-gender dressing. Thus, one mother worked with a preschool teacher to make a list of boys with whom her son seemed most comfortable. She then arranged for these boys to spend time at her home so that her son could increase his interest in typically masculine activities. Other parents have involved tomboyish girls in girls' sports activities as a way of promoting enjoyable interactions with other girls. Parent training also encourages fathers and mothers to spend more time with their sons and daughters, respectively. At first, these increased-interaction sessions involve pleasant, gender-neutral activities, but parents are then advised to ask the child to adopt a gender-consistent role for a while. They are encouraged as well to tell the child how pleased they are to have a son or a daughter and how much they admire the more gender-appropriate things the child is trying to do. Parents may also be advised to restrict the amount of time their child spends with relatives who encourage cross-gender behavior.

Case studies suggest that interventions to change gender identity can be successful. The 17-year-old mentioned earlier, for example, continued to maintain a male gender identity and a heterosexual orientation 5 years after treatment. Still, there is little well-controlled research on the success of gender identity interventions. One 4-year follow-up study found reductions in cross-gender identification following behavioral treatment of 29 gender dysphoric boys (Rekers, Kilgus, & Rosen, 1990), but the effects of these techniques seldom generalize from one situation to another. That is, cross-dressing may decrease, but gender-inappropriate play will continue unless it is specifically targeted (Zucker & Bradley, 1995). Overall, it appears that psychological interventions are most effective when used with younger children.

Sex Reassignment Surgery. Psychotherapy can help some adults sort out gender confusion, and it is especially useful to those who cling to a cross-gender identity as a way to mask homosexuality. However, most adult transsexuals believe that the best intervention for them is sex reassignment surgery, a procedure that has been offered since the 1930s. In most cases, people are not candidates for this surgery un-

less they have successfully lived for at least 1 year as an ostensible member of their desired gender. Extensive psychological evaluation is also usually conducted to rule out the influence of mental disorders that might make surgery inappropriate. Therapy, not surgery, is recommended for those who display other disorders or for those whose gender dysphoria appears transient.

Female-to-male surgery requires removal of the breasts, but because of the difficulties involved in creating a fully functional artificial penis, many female-to-male transsexuals live as males but do not seek penile surgery. Male-to-female procedures involve removal of the penis, creation of a vagina, and hormone therapy to promote breast growth and more feminine body contours. Electrolysis is employed to permanently remove hair on the face and body.

These radical surgical techniques are considered safe for most patients, and research from around the world indicates that they result in improved psychosocial adjustment and patient satisfaction (Green & Blanchard 1995; Snaith, Tarsh, & Reid, 1993; Tsoi, 1993). One review reported that over 85 percent of the patients were successful, with male-to-female patients faring a bit better than female-to-male patients (Green & Fleming, 1990). However, these results may not justify the unequivocal conclusion that sex reassignment surgery produces a high rate of positive outcomes. First, it is possible that medical centers that conduct the most careful presurgery screenings and collect the most thorough outcome data also provide the best surgical care. Results from other, less diligent treatment centers may not be as good. Second, although it is often done, judging the success of surgery by patients' self-reported satisfaction or adjustment can be problematic. It is likely that, after waiting years for surgery, spending tens of thousands of dollars on it, and withstanding the ridicule that preceded it, patients might overestimate its benefits.

Connections

What methods should be used to judge the effectiveness of a treatment besides patients' reports of success? For some suggestions, see Chapter 16, pp. 575–577.

In Review

Gender identity disorders:

- involve a persistent desire to become the other sex and a strong discomfort with one's biological sex;
- occur in children and, less often, in adults (for whom the term *transsexual* is sometimes used);

- are diagnosed more often in males than in females; and
- appear more likely to be caused by child-rearing practices than by biological abnormalities.

Treatments of gender identity disorders include:

- psychological techniques to help individuals gradually learn and accept new gender behaviors; and
- surgical sex reassignment, which appears to have reasonably good outcomes but is more complicated for female-to-male conversions.

Sexual Dysfunctions

The category of disorders known as **sexual dysfunctions** involves problems in sexual desire, arousal, or response during sexual activity. In the past 30 years, laboratory research on the biological, behavioral, and psychological aspects of sexual activity has shed new light on the nature, causes, and treatment of these dysfunctions.

The Sexual Response Cycle

Sexual responsiveness occurs in a 4-stage sequence of psychological changes and physiological reactions known as the **sexual response cycle** (see Figure 14.3).

The first phase of this cycle begins with a person's *desire* to have sex, often triggered by thoughts and fantasies about a sexual activity or partner. As these fantasies continue, the person starts anticipating emotional and physical reactions, which intensifies the desire.

The second, *excitement phase,* is characterized by several physiological changes in the sexual organs, the skin, and throughout the body. These changes include increased heart rate and respiration, **vasocongestion** (swelling) of the penis or clitoris; lubrication of the vagina; flushing of the abdomen, chest, and face; breast enlargement; and erection of the nipples.

In the third, *orgasmic phase,* sexual pleasure peaks with involuntary rhythmic contractions of the body and a release of sexual tension. For males **orgasm** involves ejaculation of semen; for females, orgasm consists of contractions of the labia minora, vagina, and uterus.

The final, *resolution phase* follows with disengorgement of the blood that has collected in the sexual organs. If orgasm has occurred, resolution happens quickly and is experienced as a sense of well-being. Without orgasm, resolution can take up to 6 hours. During and after resolution in men, there is a *refractory phase* in which they cannot be stimulated to orgasm. Because women do not enter such a phase, some can experience multiple and successive orgasms (Sadock, 1995).

Sexual dysfunctions involve some kind of problem in the first three of these phases—sexual desire,

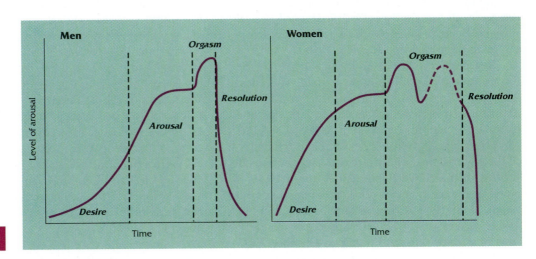

FIGURE 14.3

The Human Sexual Response Cycle
Masters and Johnson (1966) discovered that normal sexual responses follow a similar course for men and women. Some women may not experience an orgasm, but others are able to experience more than one orgasm before the resolution phase.

arousal, or orgasm—and/or pain associated with sexual intercourse.

Changing Views of Sexual Dysfunctions

Psychoanalytic theories about sexual dysfunction were dominant in the late nineteenth and early twentieth centuries. They held that problems with sexual function reflected unresolved conflicts from early childhood. Treatment relied on long-term individual therapy aimed at resolving these conflicts, but the outcomes of these treatments were generally poor and mental health professionals concluded that sexual dysfunctions were difficult to treat (Levine, 1995; Sadock, 1995).

The theory and treatment of sexual dysfunctions changed dramatically in the late 1950s, largely because of the research of William Masters and Virginia Johnson of Washington University in St. Louis. Masters and Johnson (1966, 1970) conducted detailed laboratory studies of the physiological changes that occurred as paid volunteers engaged in various sex acts in their laboratory. They also studied individuals with a wide variety of sexual dysfunctions. Their observations led to a more complete understanding of the course and physiological details of the sexual response cycle, and much of what they learned directly contradicted prevailing psychoanalytic wisdom. For example, psychoanalysts had argued that orgasm arising from vaginal stimulation was more psychosexually mature than orgasm from clitoral stimulation. Masters and Johnson confirmed the importance of clitoral stimulation, direct or indirect, in all female orgasms and showed that the physiological responses were the same regardless of the focus of stimulation (Levine, 1995).

Research by Masters and Johnson also led to a more detailed classification of sexual dysfunctions. They were the first to distinguish between lifelong and acquired sexual disorders and to expand clinicians' understanding of how psychological factors can affect sexual dysfunctions. Prior to publication of their work, the only two sexual dysfunctions described in males were **impotence** (the inability to attain or maintain an erection) and premature ejaculation. Similarly, **frigidity,** or lack of sexual interest and responsivity, was the label used for sexual dysfunctions experienced by women (Levine, 1995). Masters and Johnson identified additional sexual dysfunctions—as did other sex researchers such as Helen Singer Kaplan (1977, 1979)—and described these problems in relation to the phases of the sexual response cycle. These descriptions formed the

basis for the sexual dysfunction categories described in the DSM.

Traditionally, people have been reluctant to talk about sexual dysfunctions, and even today many individuals and couples find it difficult to seek help when these problems occur (Heiman, 1993). This reticence is unfortunate because treatment is often easier and more successful than once believed. Sexual dysfunctions are also more common than many people think. In Western cultures, the majority of people experience brief periods of sexual dysfunction at some point in their lives (Heiman, 1993). Periods of stress or sorrow are often accompanied by temporary disinterest in sex or lessened sexual responsiveness. Sexual desire and response are also sensitive to a host of occupational, familial, social, economic, and other stressors. More enduring sexual dysfunctions may affect as many as 50 percent of all intimate relationships.

Factors Affecting Sexual Responsiveness

Sexual response depends on the interplay of several physiological and psychological factors (Heiman, 1993).

Neurological and Vascular Factors. Any influence that has a negative impact on *neurological* or *vascular* functioning can interfere with sexual response. These influences include, for example, chronic medical conditions such as diabetes mellitus, emotional disorders such as clinical depression, and the use of certain medications. Sexual behavior is also affected by alterations in neurophysiological, vascular, and hormonal systems that occur naturally with age. Thus, while healthy men between the ages of 45 and 75 continue to experience sexual pleasure and satisfaction, there may be age-related decrements in sexual desire, arousal, and activity (Schiavi et al., 1990). Women, too, report decreased frequency of intercourse and orgasm as they grow older. These changes are linked to the decline in estrogen production that comes with menopause. As estrogen levels drop, vaginal lubrication decreases and blood flow to the pelvic area lessens during intercourse. These changes can make sexual intercourse uncomfortable, even painful, but many of them can be reversed with estrogen replacement therapy.

Attitudes and Beliefs. Sexual response is also influenced by *attitudes and beliefs* about sex that have been shaped by cultural heritage, religious training, family traditions, and sexual experiences. In North America, various cultural and religious groups endorse different attitudes toward sexual behavior. Thus, a person with a strong religious background might view extramarital sex as strictly forbidden. Someone raised in a predominantly Hispanic community might value *machismo* sexual behavior for men but maintain conservative ideas about sexual freedoms for women.

More important than either cultural or religious influences is family-based learning about sexuality. When parents punish a young child for masturbating or encourage an adolescent to carry condoms when dating a steady partner, they are passing on to their children certain attitudes about sex. Parents also model sex-related attitudes when they display comfort with physical contact by giving lots of hugs and kisses or when they avoid showing affection for each other in front of their children.

Finally, a person's sexual history can influence comfort with sexual activity. Episodes of criticism, abuse, or coerced sexual activity may inhibit sexual interest or response. Sexual abuse during childhood can have a profound effect on sexual functioning in adulthood (Wyatt, Guthrie, & Notgrass, 1991). Some victims become sexually inhibited and fearful, while others may become sexually promiscuous or flamboyant.

Interpersonal Factors. The relationship between sexual partners also affects sexual behavior. Emotional closeness normally enhances sexual desire, while emotional distance often dampens it. Many couples have relatively equal levels of sexual interest, but, if one partner has a much stronger need for sexual contact than the other, this "desire discrepancy" can cause distress, especially if the desires of one partner are experienced as coercive (Rosen & Leiblum, 1995a). The history of the relationship is also important. Many couples become less sexually active as they age and as they deal with careers, child-rearing, emotional conflicts, and other stressors. Still, among all sexually active adults in the United States, married people report the highest level of pleasure with their sexual relationships: 88 percent of these people say they receive great physical pleasure from sex and 85 percent report receiving great emotional satisfaction (Michael et al., 1994).

In summary, clinicians attempting to treat sexual dysfunctions must first carefully assess each client or couple to understand the role of physical and medical factors, attitudes and beliefs, sexual history, and relationship difficulties in the problems reported. Then, depending on which aspects of the sexual response cycle are most affected, the clinician will describe these problems as falling into one (or more) of four

DSM-IV sexual dysfunction categories: disorders of desire, disorders of arousal, orgasmic disorders, and sexual pain disorders. The DSM-IV further classifies sexual dyfunctions as either a *lifelong type* that has been present since the onset of sexual functioning, or an *acquired type* that began after a period of normal functioning. Problems can also be diagnosed as a *generalized type,* which occurs across partners and situations, or a *situational type,* which arises only in specific situations or with particular partners.

Sexual Desire Disorders

In the DSM-IV, disorders of sexual desire include hypoactive sexual desire disorder and sexual aversion disorder. In **hypoactive sexual desire disorder** (or HSDD), sexual fantasies are infrequent, as is interest in or motivation for sexual activity. In **sexual aversion disorder,** a more extreme version of this problem, the individual fears or is disgusted by the idea of sexual contact. Some people displaying sexual aversion disorder experience panic or revulsion over any kind of sexual behavior.

Connections

What mental disorders have been linked to a history of childhood sexual abuse? See Chapter 8, pp. 264–266 and Chapter 12, pp. 429–430.

*G*ary and Norma were having sex approximately once every 1 to 2 months and only at Gary's insistence. Their sexual activity consisted of Gary's manually stimulating Norma to orgasm while he masturbated. The couple had recently discontinued attempts at penile-vaginal intercourse because Norma often experienced vaginal spasms that made penile penetration painful and difficult. There were other problems in the marriage, as well. Gary worked long hours and spent much of his free time doing errands or household chores for his widowed mother. He also had a compulsive gambling problem, and his gambling losses caused severe financial problems. Norma had always had a strong aversion to looking at or touching her husband's penis. She had no idea where this aversion came from until recently when, at her uncle's funeral, she found herself becoming angry. Her uncle, a famous musician, became her music teacher when she was 9, and his method of teaching rhythm included having her caress his penis in time with the beating of a metronome. Although this repelled her, she was too frightened to tell her parents about it. She finally refused to continue lessons at age 12, without telling her parents why. (Based on Spitzer et al., 1994)

Hypoactive sexual desire disorder can be difficult to diagnose because there is no fixed standard of normal sexual desire. How do we decide when interest in sex becomes abnormally low? Furthermore, how is interest to be measured? Frequency of intercourse is not necessarily a good yardstick because the opportunity to engage in sexual intercourse depends on the availability of a partner and on that partner's desire for sex. Measuring the frequency of sexual fantasies may provide a better alternative; fantasy frequency is indeed lower in HSDD individuals than it is in sexually functional adults (Wincze & Carey, 1991).

In practice, HSDD is diagnosed when an individual feels distressed or when the relationship with a partner is negatively affected, and when no medical problem or other mental disorder can account for the lack of sexual desire. Age of onset can vary; sexual inhibitions learned during childhood or adolescence often carry over into adulthood (Yates, 1993). However, HSDD typically develops after a period of active sexual desire and functioning, often appearing when the intense sexual attraction that initially characterized a relationship declines (Frank, 1981; Kaplan, 1988).

Prevalence. Sexual aversion disorder is not a common problem, but HSDD may affect 15 to 40 percent of adult men and women in the United States. In one report, 17 percent of males and 39 percent of females described a lifelong pattern of low sexual desire (Yates, 1993). Among patients seeking sex therapy, the prevalence of HSDD may reach 65 percent (Beck, 1995). Studies conducted in the United States and in England suggest that about twice as many women as men report HSDD, but the rate appears to be increasing more quickly among men in recent years. Indeed, over the past two decades, the prevalence of hypoactive sexual desire has increased considerably (Rosen & Leiblum, 1995a). Statistics from one sex therapy clinic showed that, from 1974 to 1976, deficits in sexual desire accounted for 32 percent of the cases seen, but from 1982 to 1984, 55 percent of the clinic's clients sought help for inadequate sexual desire (LoPiccolo & Friedman, 1989). In another study (Segraves & Segraves, 1991) 65 percent of patients seeking sex therapy reported difficulty with desire; 40 percent of these patients also had problems with sexual arousal or orgasm. Thus, HSDD may not occur in isolation; it often precedes, accompanies, or follows a problem in sexual arousal or response.

Causal Factors. Like all aspects of sexual behavior, sexual desire is shaped by biological, cognitive, and emotional factors (Levine, 1995). People usually feel sexual desire when a biological drive for sex, determined by neuroendocrine mechanisms and manifested in genital arousal, is joined with positive expectations about sexual behavior and being in the "right mood" to engage in sex with a specific person. In some cases of HSDD, the biological basis of sexual desire may be impaired, sometimes as a result of natural aging.

The gonadal hormones, especially androgens, help maintain sexual desire. Both men and women have testosterone and estrogen receptors in the brain concentrated in areas such as the hypothalamus that control emotional and sexual feelings (McEwen, 1991). For men in particular, adequate levels of testosterone appear necessary for normal sexual desire (Schiavi et al., 1988). We know, for example, that hormone replacement in cases of low testosterone will often alleviate flattened sexual desire (Rosen & Leiblum, 1995a). The role of testosterone is not as consistent in women.

Estrogen in women is important for maintaining vaginal response and comfort during sexual stimulation, but it does not appear to affect sexual desire or arousal (Sherwin & Gelfand, 1987). Barbara Sherwin studied various regimens of hormone replacement therapy for menopausal women and found that a low-dose androgen, along with estrogen, was most effective for increasing sexual desire and enjoyment as well as for promoting an overall sense of well-being. In other studies, women who experienced early menopause following surgical removal of their ovaries reported a return of sexual interest and arousal when placed on a regimen that included both estrogen and androgen (Sherwin, Gelfand, & Brender, 1985).

In most cases of HSDD, however, a clear-cut biological cause cannot be identified. In these cases, the problem appears to stem from one or more of the psychological factors listed in Figure 14.4. For example, Helen Kaplan (1979, 1988) suggested that HSDD results from failures to resolve tasks of early childhood concerned with developing a sense of independence (see Chapter 3). The child who does not develop an adequate sense of independence is left with anxiety or anger about experiences involving intimacy. According to Kaplan, individuals with HSDD have "emotional claustrophobia" that causes them to panic or become angry when faced with the requests for intimacy that occur in sexual relationships. This anxiety and anger squelches sexual desire. Although plausible, this theory has not been confirmed by research findings.

Other psychological problems appear more likely to contribute to loss of sexual desire. In one study of clients with hypoactive sexual desire disorder, 73 percent of the men and 71 percent of the women re-

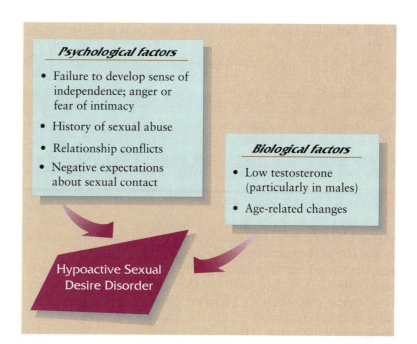

FIGURE 14.4

Possible Causes of Hypoactive Sexual Desire Disorder

Interactions of biological and psychological factors lead to most cases of hypoactive sexual desire disorder. The most important psychological factors derive from negative expectations about sexual contact, a history of unpleasant past relationships, or unresolved conflicts about a romantic relationship, all of which can rob an individual of sexual desire.

ported a history of depression compared with 32 percent of male controls and 27 percent of female controls (Schreiner-Engel & Schiavi, 1986). For many of these clients, sexual desire waned with their first depressive episodes and never fully returned, even if they experienced no further episodes. A history of sexual abuse and the existence of distress in a romantic relationship—both of which are risk factors for difficulties with sexual functioning in general—are also associated with impaired sexual desire (Becker et al., 1986; Rosen & Leiblum, 1995a; Verhulst & Heiman, 1988). Accordingly, clinicians are sensitive to the possibility that HSDD can be a symptom of prior abuse or of a more general problem in the partners' relationship.

Sexual Arousal Disorders

The DSM-IV lists two types of arousal disorders: female sexual arousal disorder and male erectile disorder.

Female Sexual Arousal Disorder. Persistent problems in attaining or maintaining the lubrication and genital swelling normally associated with sexual excitement is the hallmark of **female sexual arousal disorder (FSAD)**. This diagnostic label, which replaces the somewhat demeaning term *frigidity,* is used only when the woman is significantly distressed by the arousal problem and when it is not caused by a medical condition or other mental disorder.

There are two reasons why the prevalence of FSAD is difficult to establish. First, women usually complain of a global problem with sexual desire and response rather than a specific, isolated difficulty with arousal (Heiman, 1993). Second, because the most obvious indicator of FSAD, lack of vaginal lubrication, can be easily remedied by using vaginal lubricants, many women with FSAD never seek professional help.

There is no characteristic profile of women at risk for FSAD, and its causes are not completely understood. Still, clinicians do know some of the causal factors involved. When sexual arousal is impaired by vascular problems, neurological disorders, or medications, the DSM-IV diagnosis is *sexual dysfunction due to a general medical condition* or *substance-induced sexual dysfunction.* In some cases, women's problems with sexual arousal may be due to a lack of sensitivity to those bodily sensations, such as pelvic swelling, that normally increase sexual arousal (Sadock, 1995). In one of the few laboratory studies of FSAD, comparisons were made between the physiological responses to erotic stimuli of 11 women with FSAD and 11 normal controls (Morokoff & Heiman, 1980). Although the physiological responses were about the same in both groups, the FSAD women reported less subjective arousal. Unfortunately, the study design makes it impossible to determine whether the FSAD women were less sensitive than the other group to bodily sensations, or whether the difference was attributable to differences in their sexual histories, romantic relationships, and attitudes about sex.

As with all sexual dysfunctions, a history of sexual abuse may be a factor in FSAD. Victims of childhood sexual abuse often experience adult sexual difficulties that are closely tied to the form of the abuse. For example, women who were sexually fondled as children may fail to become aroused when engaging in foreplay that resembles the abuse pattern. Given a safe and loving relationship, however, these same women may become aroused during sexual intercourse (Becker et al., 1986; Wincze & Carey, 1991).

FSAD can also be caused by a number of cognitive and interpersonal problems. Anxiety about sex can be one of the major threats to adequate arousal. Any time sexual partners worry about whether they are "doing sex the right way" or whether they will satisfy their partners, they may become distracted from the physical sensations of sexual activity that are naturally arousing. The result may be lack of arousal. Hostility or mistrust between partners can also chill sexual arousal. So can guilt. A woman who believes that "too much" sexual arousal is "bad" might remain passive during sexual contact so as to not feel "wicked." For females in particular, feeling emotionally distant from a partner often interferes with sexual arousal. Finally, FSAD occurs in some couples because of a long-term pattern of inadequate or inept sexual foreplay. If one partner is uninterested or uninformed about how to give the other partner sexual pleasure, there may simply be too little stimulation to result in arousal.

Male Erectile Disorder. The most demoralizing sexual dysfunction experienced by men is **male erectile disorder,** in which there is a recurring failure to attain or maintain an erection adequate for sexual activity. Estimates are that over 90 percent of male erectile disorder cases (formerly referred to as *impotence*) are of the acquired subtype, meaning that they develop after a period of normal functioning (Wincze & Carey, 1991).

Erectile difficulties are very common. By one estimate, men make more than 400,000 visits to physicians every year for this problem (U.S. Department of Health and Human Services, 1987), and one of the best prevalence studies reported that 52 percent of men between the ages of 40 and 70 complained of some kind of erectile difficulties at some time in their lives (Feldman et al., 1994). In the NHSLS sex survey described earlier, 10 percent of males reported at least one incident of erectile dysfunction during the prior year and another 15 to 20 percent reported

feeling anxiety about the adequacy of their erections (Laughman et al., 1994). Current estimates are that 10 to 20 million men in the United States experience erectile dysfunction (Althof & Seftel, 1995).

Although erectile problems increase with age, the vast majority of physically healthy men can still perform sexual intercourse even after the age of 80 (Bretschneider & McCoy, 1988). The key word here is *healthy.* More and more cases of erectile problems are now being attributed to a medical condition or to the side effects of medication or other substances. The proper DSM diagnosis in such cases is *sexual dysfunction due to a general medical condition* or a *substance-induced sexual dysfunction.*

Biological Factors. Biological causes of erectile problems have been the focus of extensive clinical and research work over the past three decades (Ackerman & Carey, 1995). An intricate series of neurovascular changes cause the lengthening, stiffening, and realignment of the penis during an erection (Althof & Seftel, 1995). Because endocrine, vascular, and neurological systems all contribute to erections, problems in any of these areas can lead to malfunction. For example, spontaneous erections diminish in frequency and amplitude with the decreases in testosterone that come with aging. Heart disease and vascular problems, such as arteriosclerosis, can impair erections because a normal erection depends on a threefold increase in blood flow to the penis. Neurological disorders also contribute to erectile dysfunction. Problems involving the cerebral hemispheres (such as epilepsy), diseases that alter spinal cord function (such as multiple sclerosis), and disorders that affect the peripheral nervous system (such as diabetes and renal failure) are major neurological culprits in erectile disorder (Wincze & Carey, 1991). Diabetes mellitus is the medical condition most likely to cause erectile problems; over one third of diabetic men are affected (Ackerman & Carey, 1995). Traumatic injuries to the spinal cord or nerve damage can also impair erectile function.

Erectile impairment is a side effect of antihypertension drugs for some individuals, and, although alcohol at low doses may temporarily reduce anxiety and thereby lead to heightened sexual desire and arousal, at higher doses it interferes with erections. Finally, smoking is associated with an increased risk of erectile dysfunction.

Psychological Factors. Even for men whose erectile problems are organically based, cognitive and emotional factors are usually operating as well. One study of over 1,000 men with erectile dysfunction found that only about 30 percent of the problems were attributable "wholly or primarily" to organic causes. About 55 percent were caused wholly or primarily by psychological problems, and the rest were listed as due to unknown causes (Tiefer & Melman, 1989). Performance anxiety, cognitive distractions, stress, and relationship problems are among the psychological factors that contribute to erectile dysfunctions. For many years, the leading theory—popularized by Masters and Johnson—was that men who were anxious about their sexual performance and who worried about how their partners would evaluate them were at greatest risk for erectile problems. It was said that preoccupation with sexual performance turned many men into *spectators* who were so fretful about the adequacy of their sexual functioning that they were unable to experience arousal themselves. Psychotherapist Albert Ellis's pithy summary was that, in most cases of impotence, the man was "scared unstiff."

Anxiety does indeed play a major role in erectile dysfunction, but more recent research has revealed that this role is more complicated than first described. For example, David Barlow and his colleagues have shown that it is not anxiety *per se* that interferes with erections as much as factors that cause a man to become *distracted* and therefore miss out on cues that would sexually arouse him. In one study (Barlow, Sakheim, & Beck, 1983), young males were first given a painful electric shock to their forearms and then watched an erotic film under one of three different conditions: one group was assured that they would not be shocked again, a second group was told that they might be shocked while they watched the film, and a third group was told they would probably be shocked during the film *if* they did not attain adequate erections (as measured by a penile strain gauge; see Figure 14.5). If theories about the debilitating role of performance anxiety were correct, this third condition—intended to mimic the situation in which a man worries about attaining or maintaining erection during sex—should have lead to the weakest erections. To the researchers' surprise, however, men in both of the shock conditions had *stronger* erections than those in the no-shock condition. In fact, the "get-an-erection-or-else" instructions led to the strongest erections of all!

So while anxiety *may* impair erections in some cases, it may not always do so. Indeed, it may be that *any* psychological variable that serves as a distractor from sexual sensations may interfere with the natural process of attaining and maintaining erection.

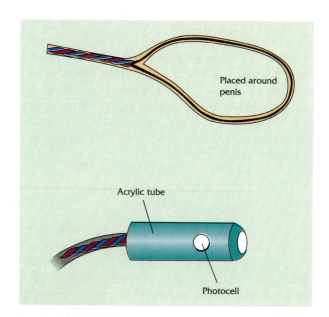

FIGURE 14.5

Measuring Sexual Arousal
Both of these devices measure increased blood flow, a key indication of sexual arousal. The male plethysmograph (*top*) consists of a strain gauge, or thin tube filled with mercury, that is placed around the penis. As the penis enlarges and becomes erect, it stretches the gauge. The female plethysmograph (*bottom*) is inserted in the vagina. It reflects increased light as more blood flows to the vagina.

In one experiment, for example, men who were required to concentrate on a nonerotic narrative while watching an erotic film, developed inferior erections compared with men who were allowed to concentrate on the film (Abrahamson et al., 1985). Other research shows that men with erectile dysfunction are more easily distracted by nonsexual stimuli and less aroused by erotic stimuli than sexually functional men (Rowland, Cooper, & Slob, 1996). They also tend to underestimate the fullness of their erections (Barlow, 1986).

In summary, it appears that men with erectile dysfunction often approach sexual encounters with anxiety and negative expectations. Once in a sexual situation, they are easily distracted from sexual cues so that they underestimate how aroused they might be. Dismayed and embarrassed about what they believe is inadequate arousal that, they fear, is only too obvious to their partners, they engage in more and more negative thinking about themselves and their sexual ability. These negative thoughts further block out sexual cues and increase negative emotions that make sexual arousal all but impossible.

Although there is little research on the role of stressors and significant relationship difficulties in male sexual arousal, these factors are probably important. One of the more destructive myths about male sexuality is that men are always ready to engage in sex regardless of their psychological or emotional state.

Orgasmic Disorders

Orgasm is a very rewarding aspect of sexual activity, but for a significant number people, orgasms are exasperatingly elusive, making sex a source of frustration and disappointment. The DSM-IV lists three types of orgasmic disorders: female orgasmic disorder, male orgasmic disorder, and premature ejaculation.

Female Orgasmic Disorder. Women who experience normal sexual desire and arousal but cannot experience an orgasm or who take an inordinately long time to reach orgasm may be diagnosed with **female orgasmic disorder** (formerly called *inhibited orgasm*). Here is an illustrative case.

---

*L*ola, a 25-year-old laboratory technician, has been happily married to a 32-year-old cab driver for 5 years and has a 2-year-old son. Her only complaint is a lifelong inability to experience orgasm even though she receives what she considers to be sufficient stimulation during sexual activity. She has tried to masturbate, and on many occasions her husband has manually stimulated her for long periods. While these methods have not resulted in orgasm, Lola is strongly attached to her husband, feels erotic pleasure during lovemaking, and lubricates copiously. Her husband reports no sexual difficulty. Clinical interviews reveal that, as she nears orgasm, Lola experiences a sense of dread about some undefined disaster. She fears losing control over her emotions, which she normally keeps closely in check. (Based on Spitzer et al., 1994)

Inhibited orgasm is the most frequent complaint of women who seek sex therapy. One study of predominantly middle-class, White women aged 18 to 73 found that 8.9 percent "always" have difficulty achieving orgasm, 20.7 percent have difficulty about half the time, and 28.8 percent have "occasional" dif-

ficulty (Rosen et al., 1993). Another study suggested that, indeed, most women do not have an orgasm every time they engage in sexual activity, and that about 10 percent have never had an orgasm (Heiman, 1993). Very little is known about the causes of orgasmic problems in women, but four factors have received the most attention: the pubococcygeus muscle, hormonal influences (discussed earlier), alcohol use, and psychosocial factors.

The *pubococcygeus muscle* controls the vagina and urethra. It was once hypothesized that strong muscle tone and increased blood flow in this area would enhance orgasmic response. Accordingly, women were advised to perform exercises to increase the strength and tone of this muscle. These exercises do increase muscle strength and urinary control but do not on their own enhance the likelihood of an orgasm. However, combining vaginal muscle tensing with sexual fantasy appears to increase sexual arousal and may increase a woman's ability to enjoy genital sensations (Heiman & Grafton-Becker, 1989). These effects, in turn, may facilitate orgasm.

Excessive alcohol and drug use is thought to impair a woman's ability to reach orgasm, although research evidence on this point is limited. Higher blood alcohol levels have been associated with longer times to orgasm and subjective reports of diminished orgasmic intensity (Wincze & Carey, 1991).

Of the host of psychosocial factors that have been investigated as possible contributors to a woman's lack of orgasm—age, length of marriage, education, and socioeconomic level—only age is consistently related to orgasmic function (Morokoff, 1978). Simply put, younger women are more likely to be orgasmic. No particular pattern of mental health problems appears in women with orgasmic problems, but it is clear that depression interferes with sexual interest, and antidepressant medications can also diminish sexual response. Although researchers suspect that relationship problems play a role in this disorder, no consistent pattern of conflict has been identified. Surprisingly, even a history of sexual abuse does not necessarily interfere with orgasms.

It may turn out that female orgasmic disorder may be best explained by factors that contribute to diminished desire and arousal. For many women, problems with sexual desire, arousal, and orgasm occur simultaneously and reflect cultural, religious, and social attitudes about how women should express their sexuality. Over the past century, attitudes about women's sexuality have changed dramatically in many parts of the world. Once expected to be passive recipients of sexual activity, women are now far freer to express and act on their sexual interests and needs.

However, they continue to receive mixed messages about sexuality. For example, some women now feel that they have a sexual problem if they are not as sexually assertive as men, or they may feel guilty over preferring a passive sexual role. With these complex psychological crosscurrents in mind, Julia Heiman, a prominent sex researcher and therapist, argues that women's sexual problems, particularly those involving orgasmic difficulties, should be viewed as signals about the influence of sociocultural and interpersonal contexts rather than as indicators of psychological malfunctioning (Heiman & Grafton-Becker, 1989).

Male Orgasmic Disorder and Premature Ejaculation. Men with **male orgasmic disorder** experience an inability to reach orgasm or an inordinately long delay to orgasm during sexual activity. Most of these men still experience orgasms with ejaculation when they masturbate or while asleep during so-called wet dreams. Some men report that their penises feel numb after erection and when intercourse begins. More commonly, they feel sexually excited at the beginning of intercourse, but, as it continues, their desire wanes and the sexual encounter becomes a chore. (Failure to reach orgasm should be distinguished from **retrograde ejaculation,** in which men experience orgasm but release ejaculate into the bladder rather than expelling it from the penis. This problem is usually caused by diabetes, medication, or prostate surgery; Wincze & Carey, 1991).

The prevalence of male orgasmic disorder is estimated to be 1 to 8 percent of men seeking sex therapy and 4 to 10 percent of community samples (Heiman, 1993; Wincze & Carey, 1991). Little research has been done on the causes of this disorder. Currently, the best explanation is that some of the physical and psychological disabilities that lead to erectile problems also play a role in inhibiting orgasms for men. In some cases, men become so frustrated with the delay or absence of an orgasm that they find the act of intercourse to be extremely aversive. Some sex therapists believe this pattern suggests an underlying problem with lack of arousal or conflict with the partner (Heiman, 1993). Others underscore the importance of performance anxiety (McCarthy, 1988) or distractibility. Few men with orgasmic disorder seek treatment.

A much more common orgasmic difficulty for men is **premature ejaculation,** in which a man ejaculates after very little sexual stimulation, usually before or almost immediately after he has achieved penetration. Of course, the "ideal" timing of ejaculation varies depending on the people involved. What is early ejaculation for one couple may be

totally satisfactory for another (McCarthy, 1988). Accordingly, assessment and diagnosis of premature ejaculation must take into account the needs, perceptions, and circumstances of each individual or couple. Still, most men do not want to ejaculate before, or just after, penetrating their partner because it makes satisfactory sexual intercourse nearly impossible. The DSM-IV therefore defines ejaculation as "premature" if it occurs before the person wants it to and if this pattern causes marked distress or interpersonal problems.

Up to 50 percent of young men, and 33 percent of men of all ages, indicate having some problems with premature ejaculation (Heiman, 1993; McCarthy, 1988). The problem occurs in both heterosexual and homosexual couples. Some women also report reaching orgasm too quickly, but this problem is seldom discussed in the clinical literature (Wincze & Carey, 1991).

What factors might lead to premature ejaculation? One possibility is that young men often have their first sexual experiences in places such as parked cars, where concerns about being discovered cause them to want to have an orgasm quickly. Similarly, if a young man feels shame or guilt over masturbation, his goal may be to bring himself to orgasm as quickly as possible. Both kinds of experiences may engender a pattern of rapid progress to orgasm once sexual stimulation begins. Furthermore, some men are simply hypersensitive to sexual stimulation and have a lower threshold for ejaculation (Strassberg et al., 1987). The more these hypersensitive men worry about premature ejaculation, the less likely they are to be able to monitor their levels of sexual excitement, thereby increasing the risk of premature ejaculation.

Men who have not developed techniques for delaying ejaculation may also be more prone to premature ejaculation (McCarthy, 1988). For decades, men have sought to dull sexual sensations by wearing more than one condom or to distract themselves from those sensations with thoughts of sports or the stock market. These efforts can help, but the main requirements for good ejaculatory control include a regular schedule of sexual intercourse, the ability to focus on giving pleasure to the sexual partner, greater intimacy and security with the partner, a desire (shared by the partner) for a slow, prolonged sexual interaction, and comfort using a variety of sexual positions. It is also important for men to accurately perceive sensual cues, especially the approach of ejaculatory inevitability. If they do not recognize these sensations, they will be less able to employ brief cognitive distractions or slow their sexual movement to postpone ejaculation.

Sexual Pain Disorders

Sexual pain disorders include dyspareunia and vaginismus. Neither disorder has been researched extensively, so knowledge and understanding of them are limited.

Dyspareunia. Recurring problems with pain before, during, or after sexual intercourse is the major symptom of **dyspareunia.** Both men and women can experience dyspareunia, but it is more common in women. Women most frequently complain of pain during intercourse, while men are more likely to describe pain during orgasm and ejaculation.

The prevalence of dyspareunia is not well documented. In one survey, 33.5 percent of women in their early 30s said they had persistent problems with painful intercourse, but none had sought professional help (Glatt, Zinner, & McCormack, 1990). Among women seeking sex therapy, about 5 percent report painful intercourse as their primary problem (Renshaw, 1988). Even less is known about the prevalence of sexual pain in men. No general population data are available, although about 1 percent of males seeking sex therapy cite pain as a significant problem (Wincze & Carey, 1991).

Organic pathology often plays a significant role in sexual pain for both men and women. Most male cases are related to a urinary tract infection or chronic diseases such as Peyronie's disease (fibrosis of penile connective tissue), prostatitis, gonorrhea, or herpes (Sadock, 1995). For females, the most common organic causes include infections of the urinary tract, vagina, cervix, or fallopian tubes; scarring following surgery related to childbirth; ovarian cysts or tumors; and **endometriosis** (a painful condition in which the growth of endometrial tissue occurs in the pelvic cavity outside the uterus). The decline in estrogen associated with menopause can lead to a thinning of vaginal tissue, lack of lubrication, and consequent pain during intercourse. This specific problem can be readily treated with estrogen replacement therapy or by the topical use of estrogen cream or lubricants.

Psychosocial factors may also contribute to painful intercourse (Lazarus, 1989). For example, sex may be painful if the woman associates it with negative feelings or with sexual trauma.

Vaginismus. The essential problem in **vaginismus** is an involuntary spasm of the musculature in the outer third of the vagina that makes penile penetration impossible. These muscle spasms usually occur during or just before attempted penetration, but they can also be triggered by gynecological exams.

The prevalence of vaginismus varies across cultures. It affects from 5 to 42 percent of women seen in sex therapy clinics in the United States (Wincze & Carey, 1991), but higher rates are reported in Ireland, Eastern Europe, and Latin America, where there are more restrictive attitudes regarding contraception and sex in general (Barnes, 1986; O'Sullivan, 1979).

Classical conditioning theory suggests that vaginismus might develop in women whose initial experience with intercourse was painful and aversive. Such an experience could lead to avoidance of further sexual contact and an inability to participate if persuaded to have intercourse. Because vaginismus can occur secondary to dyspareunia, organic causes must also be considered. Harsh, demanding behavior by a sexual partner can worsen, if not cause, this problem.

Treatment of Sexual Dysfunctions

For many decades, the most prominent treatment of sexual dysfunctions was long-term, individual, psychodynamically oriented psychotherapy, and the typical outcome was poor. However, with the advent of Masters and Johnson's research in the 1960s and 1970s, this treatment approach was radically transformed. Rather than viewing sexual dysfunction as a symptom of unresolved conflicts, Masters and Johnson argued that inadequate knowledge about sexual functioning, coupled with performance anxiety, was at the root of most sexual problems.

Their treatment model involved working with a couple daily for a 2-week period. First, a male and female cotherapist team conducted an exhaustive history of a couple's sexual functioning and overall relationship. Next, the therapists attempted to dispel various myths about sex and provided the couple with specific information about satisfying sexual functioning. Third, the cotherapists offered the couple an explanation of their sexual problems that stressed how faulty sexual habits can be learned, how successful treatment can eliminate these habits, and how more beneficial habits can be developed. They also coached the couple on how to communicate more clearly about sex and about other topics of importance to their relationship. Couples were then taught —and urged to practice in private—sensate focus, the core therapeutic technique of the Masters and Johnson program.

During **sensate focus** sessions, the partners take turns providing physical pleasure to each other via kissing, massage, or touch without attempting any direct genital stimulation. In fact, in order to reduce performance anxiety and excessive demands for coitus, the couple is told not to have intercourse. Masters and Johnson (1970) saw sensate focus as the first opportunity many couples ever had to "think and feel sensuously and at leisure" without worrying about achieving the goal of sexual satisfaction. After a few days, the couple is given permission to add genital stimulation to their sensate focus sessions, but the ban on intercourse is retained. Finally, the couple is told to attempt brief penetration, but to keep their attention mainly on sensate focus. Masters and Johnson anticipated that, as couples were swept up in their passion, they would break the rules and engage in intercourse.

This approach proved highly effective. Masters and Johnson claimed that over 90 percent of men complaining of premature ejaculation improved, and the majority of couples with more complicated problems such as erectile or orgasmic difficulties also recovered. However, few clients or therapists have the luxury of devoting the intensive 2-week period to treatment that this approach required. Consequently, Masters and Johnson's methods were modified. Cotherapist teams are now seldom used, and most treatment programs meet with couples once or twice a week rather than every day (McConaghy, 1996). Evaluations of these streamlined procedures indicate that they, too, are effective but seldom achieve recovery rates as high as Masters and Johnson originally reported, and relapse is not uncommon. Today's sex therapists often use modified forms of sensate focus or combine it with techniques adopted from traditional individual and couples therapy. New behavioral techniques have been introduced, and medical interventions are increasingly being applied to sexual problems (Ackerman & Carey, 1995; LoPiccolo, 1994; McConaghy, 1996). In the next sections, we consider how some of these treatments are applied to specific sexual dysfunctions.

Treating Disorders of Sexual Desire. Disorders of sexual desire are usually more difficult to treat than problems of arousal or orgasm. On average, positive outcomes are seen in about 50 percent of the cases (Kilmann, Boland & Norton, 1986; Rosen & Leiblum, 1995a). The best results are achieved for disorders of desire when sex therapy techniques are combined with marital or cognitive-behavioral therapy (Hurlbert, 1993; MacPhee, Johnson, & Van Der Veer, 1995).

For example, one treatment approach for low sexual desire contains 4 phases aimed at helping clients become more aware of sexual sensations and understanding why certain sexual feelings might be aversive (LoPiccolo & Friedman, 1989). In the initial phase, patients are trained to fantasize and to associate physical sensations with sexual fantasies. The second phase focuses on understanding how low sexual arousal might have developed by exploring family and relationship histories as well as beliefs about sexuality. Next, irrational thoughts or fears about sex are addressed using cognitive restructuring techniques and coping skills training. Finally, behavioral interventions are used to change behaviors that may interfere with sexual pleasure. These might include assertion training or sensate focus exercises.

Other approaches focus on the quality of the couple's relationship. One of these helps couples explore their sexual scripts as a means of improving sexual desire (Rosen & Leiblum, 1988). **Sexual scripts** consist of expectations about sex that are determined by the roles people play in everyday life and the messages carried over from childhood and from previous sexual encounters. For example, the lack of a sexual script for how to initiate sexual interactions might explain the high prevalence of sexual desire problems in women. Couples may "read" from different sexual scripts, especially as the demands of children or work make it harder to experience sexual desire. As couples explore their sexual scripts together, *script negotiation* can occur. This process helps each partner understand what the other is thinking and encourages communication about sexual preferences.

Can medication enhance sexual desire? Many foods and drugs have been touted for their ability to stimulate sexual desire. For example, the European custom of drinking honeyed wine to foster sexual desire at the beginning of a marriage gave rise to the word *honeymoon* (Segraves, 1988). The effects of traditional aphrodisiacs are mainly placebo effects, but a few clinical reports have described improved sexual desire following the use of drugs that influence the neurotransmitters dopamine, epinephrine, and serotonin. However, these medications are usually prescribed to relieve symptoms of disorders such as depression, so it is difficult to separate their effects on mental health from a specific effect on sexual desire. It does appear that certain antidepressants—Wellbutrin, Desyrel, and Pondimin, in particular—enhance sexual desire in some patients over and above their antidepressant effects (Rosen & Leiblum, 1995b; Segraves, 1988). Yohimbine hydrochloride (which is not an antidepressant) also appears effective in restoring sexual desire in some patients, and it is being investigated as a treatment for hypoactive sexual desire disorder in males (Hollander & McCarley, 1992; Rosen & Leiblum, 1995a). This drug acts quickly to increase heart rate, blood pressure, and blood flow to the penis.

The search for an effective aphrodisiac has been going on for centuries. Shown here is one candidate—the mandrake root. Currently, a number of medications that affect neurotransmitters are being tested to determine if they can stimulate sexual desire, but so far none has consistently increased sexual interest.

Finally, treatment with gonadal hormone therapies is effective for individuals with hormonal deficits. Hormonal augmentation, however, does not usually improve sexual desire in individuals with normal testosterone and estrogen levels.

Treating Female Sexual Arousal Disorder. There are no specific treatments for female sexual arousal disorder beyond the use of vaginal lubricants. This problem tends to be seen as one aspect of other sexual dysfunctions and is thus often treated as part of an overall sex therapy program that addresses relationship problems and includes specific exercises to increase desire, arousal, and orgasmic response.

Treating Male Erectile Disorder. In treating erectile disorders, a mental health professional with expertise in sexual disorders often works closely with a medical specialist, typically a urologist. The results of their assessment of each patient's physiological and psychological status largely determine whether to pursue psychological or medically oriented treatment. If an organic cause is not apparent, a combination of sex therapy and couples therapy is usually

employed. Most therapists try to reduce the man's performance anxiety, improve the couple's overall relationship, and teach the couple specific sex techniques such as sensate focus (Althof, 1989; LoPiccolo, 1994). This combination of treatments reflects current thinking about the complexity of erectile disorders; seldom is the problem due to a single, simple, easily defined cause.

One prominent cognitive-interpersonal treatment model includes five core components (Rosen & Leiblum, 1995b). The first component is an effort to dispel myths about sexual and erectile functioning and to explore the man's thoughts about sexual performance and erectile failure. Many men overgeneralize about their erectile problems, assuming that erectile failure on one occasion means they can never again have or maintain an erection. Others engage in all-or-nothing thinking that tells them that, unless they attain a full erection, sex cannot be pleasurable. The second component of treatment is anxiety reduction. Relaxation techniques, biofeedback, or psychotropic medications are used to reduce performance anxiety, often instead of sensate focus exercises. The third component involves sexual script work designed to help couples understand each other's sexual desires. In conflict resolution, the fourth treatment component, the couple is helped to improve their communication and ability to solve conflicts. Finally, there is relapse prevention, a set of techniques in which couples schedule times for nondemanding, pleasuring interactions; learn how to cope better with disappointing sexual encounters; renew practice of techniques acquired in therapy; and return for follow-up visits with the clinician to improve problem-solving skills (McCarthy, 1993).

When the causes of erectile dysfunction include organic problems, the initial recommendations are simple and practical: reduce the use of alcohol, change medications, or correct endocrine imbalances (Heiman, 1993). Other medical interventions include oral medications, hormone replacement, surgical implants, and various mechanical erectors. Among medications, yohimbine, an alpha-2 adrenergic antagonist, is often used, but evidence for its efficacy is equivocal. L-arginine has proved effective in one small-scale study and warrants further research (Althof & Seftel, 1995), as does trazodone, an antidepressant that has been shown to increase penile tumescence (Rosen & Leiblum, 1995a). Applying topical medications, such as nitroglycerin ointment, to the penis has also been successful in some cases. Hormone therapy is usually effective only when there is a hormone deficiency.

Short-acting vasoactive agents, such as papaverine hydrochloride, phentolamine, and prostaglandin

E1, dilate blood vessels and increase penile blood flow when injected directly into the base of the penis. They can facilitate an erection that lasts 30 to 60 minutes. This treatment leads to improvement rates of up to 90 percent, but as many as half the men starting the treatment discontinue it primarily because it is inconvenient and painful (Althof & Seftel, 1995).

Special devices can also be used to produce erections. One of these includes a plastic tube that is placed over the penis and a hand pump that is used to create a vacuum, thus drawing blood into the penis and causing an erection. The erection is maintained by placing a ring at the base of the penis to hold the blood in place. This device is as effective as injecting vasodilators and is less painful, but it sometime blocks ejaculation, and many men dislike it because it cannot be concealed.

Surgery is another treatment option (Heiman, 1993). Penile prosthesis surgery dates back to the 1930s and involves implanting a semirigid or inflatable rod in the penis. Afterward, the man can bring about erections by using a pump that forces water into the prosthesis. Unfortunately, penile implants often do not measure up to expectations, and many men—and their partners—report being disappointed with them. Surgery can also be performed to correct or bypass vascular blockage preventing erection. Vascular surgery works well in some cases, but the benefits are often only temporary.

Treating Female Orgasmic Disorder. Treatment of female orgasmic disorder often involves a combination of approaches, including dealing with relationship problems and using cognitive techniques to lessen anxiety about sexual encounters and to overcome fears of losing control during orgasm. In many cases, however, direct training in masturbation is the primary intervention. It is designed to educate the woman about her sexual responses, encourage her sexual fantasies, reduce her inhibitions about enjoying sex, and teach her how to experience an orgasm. Indeed, this technique helps up to 80 percent of formerly nonorgasmic women to become orgasmic. Further coaching about sexual stimulation and fantasy helps transfer this private orgasmic ability to situations in which there is a sexual partner. For many women, simply reading about sexual responsiveness and masturbation allows them to learn to become orgasmic (Heiman & LoPiccolo, 1988). No medical treatments have yet been developed for female orgasmic disorder.

Treating Premature Ejaculation. One of the most notable methods developed by Masters and Johnson (1970) for the treatment of premature ejaculation is called the **squeeze technique.** To use this method, the man or his partner firmly squeezes the head of his penis as sexual excitement begins to peak, but before the point of ejaculatory inevitability. This maneuver reduces the man's arousal and prolongs his ability to postpone orgasm. Many sex therapists have replaced the squeeze technique with the stop-and-start technique. In this approach, the man is taught to recognize the sensations leading up to ejaculatory inevitability and to control sexual arousal by simply stopping stimulation and relaxing for a few moments. After mastering this technique during masturbation, the man can use it with a partner to delay his orgasm. Initial reports about the squeeze and stop-and-start techniques were favorable, but more recent studies suggest that improvements gained from these methods alone may fade over a period of years. Accordingly, the techniques are now used in the context of cognitive-behavioral therapy, which seeks also to resolve cognitive distortions and anxieties about sex (McCarthy, 1988).

Medications also offer some promise for premature ejaculation. For example, clomipramine, an antidepressant, can increase ejaculatory latency and improve subjective sexual satisfaction (Althof & Seftel, 1995). Delayed ejaculation is also one of the side effects of selective serotonin reuptake inhibitors (SSRIs) such as fluoxetine (Prozac) and sertraline (Zoloft). Some therapists report the successful use of SSRIs in men with premature ejaculation (Kaplan, 1994), but these case reports must be reinforced by controlled clinical studies.

Treating Sexual Pain Disorders. Treatments for both dyspareunia and vaginismus draw on a combination of behavioral and cognitive techniques. In dyspareunia, after physical problems such as lack of lubrication have been addressed, cognitive and behavioral techniques are used to teach the woman how to relax, first as she imagines sexual involvement and then as she attempts sexual intercourse. Sensate focus and pleasuring exercises are also included, as are efforts to improve communication and reduce conflicts with her partner.

In the treatment of vaginismus, similar techniques are used in combination with special *vaginal insertion* exercises. After practicing how to maintain vaginal relaxation while imagining sexual intercourse, the woman uses a dilator or her finger to practice penetration and relaxation. The size of the dilator can gradually be increased as the woman begins to feel more comfortable. Eventually, a partner may help insert the dilators or finger and, finally, the couple moves on to penile penetration (at first, without thrusting movements by the partner). This treatment—in which the woman has complete control over what steps are taken, how fast, and for how long—can be effective for vaginismus (Heiman, 1993).

In Review

Sexual dysfunctions involve a disturbance in one or more of the 4 phases of the sexual response cycle, consisting of:

- a desire to have sex;
- physiological changes associated with sexual excitement;
- the peaking of sexual pleasure during orgasm; and
- the resolution of sexual arousal following orgasm.

Sexual dysfunctions are:

- prevalent, and most people complain of some temporary sexual dysfunction at some point in their lives;
- caused by an interplay of biological, psychological, and social factors; and
- classified in the DSM in four general categories: sexual desire disorders, sexual arousal disorders, orgasmic disorders, and sexual pain disorders.

Treatment of sexual disorders:

- was revolutionized by the psychoeducational sex therapy program developed by Masters and Johnson in the 1960s and 1970s;
- often involves behavioral or cognitive techniques designed to help a person learn to be less anxious or distracted during sexual activity and to develop a greater awareness of sexual arousal; and
- sometimes employs medical interventions such as medication, hormone supplements, or surgery.

Paraphilias

Everyone has sexual fantasies and preferences for certain kinds of sexual partners, activities, or stimuli, and finding a partner who is willing to share or fulfill such fantasies and preferences adds interest to a person's sex life. However, most people can have satisfactory sex whether or not their partners or the other stimuli in the sexual situation are ideal. The

main feature of **paraphilias** is a repetitive pattern of sexual behavior in which arousal and/or orgasm depends on fantasies or actions involving atypical or socially inappropriate stimuli.

Some paraphilias are harmless, as when a man becomes sexually aroused only if his partner wears black leather or when a woman cannot be orgasmic unless her partner wears cowboy boots. Other paraphilias are far more problematic because they involve forcing partners to have sex, exposing one's genitals in public, secretly watching others' sexual activities, or engaging in other socially disapproved or illegal behavior. In these cases, paraphilias often lead to relationship problems, unemployment, or arrest. For some people, paraphilic stimuli are always necessary, while for others they become important only during periods of stress. Thus, men with paraphilic preferences may routinely engage in sex with a regular adult partner, but periodically seek sexual satisfaction by molesting children, exposing themselves in public, or dressing in women's clothes.

Forms of Paraphilia

The DSM-IV identifies eight specific paraphilias, all of which are seen almost exclusively in men; only about 1 percent of paraphiliacs are women.

Fetishism. In **fetishism,** the person needs or often uses some inanimate object to become sexually aroused. The most common fetishes are shoes (particularly high heels), leather garments, or particular items of underwear. In many cases, the man masturbates while gazing at, rubbing, or sniffing the object. Others coax their partners to don these items during sex. Almost any object can serve as a fetish, whether or not it is normally associated with sex. One 33-year-old man developed a fetish for baby carriages; he hoarded pictures of them and masturbated while looking at them (Raymond, 1956).

Transvestic Fetishism. The diagnosis of **transvestic fetishism** is made if a man dresses in women's clothes in order to experience sexual arousal and satisfaction. This disorder usually occurs among heterosexual men who masturbate or engage in sexual activity while cross-dressed. Others become so aroused by cross-dressing that they ejaculate spontaneously. Some men cross-dress only to become aroused, while others do so more frequently because they find this behavior relaxing, especially during stressful periods. (One highway tollbooth attendant we know of, for example, relaxed after work each evening by lounging around in frilly nightgowns.) Although the partners of trans-

Some transvestites become sexually aroused by cross-dressing. Others feel relaxed by it.

vestites frequently know about these persons' preferences and try to be tolerant, those preferences often disrupt their sexual relations and lead to relationship problems.

Exhibitionism. In **exhibitionism,** the act of exposing one's genitals to an unwilling observer brings sexual excitement and satisfaction. Exhibitionism is the most frequently reported sexual offense in Western cultures and results in about one third of all sex-related court convictions (Rooth & Marks, 1974).

Many exhibitionists follow a consistent pattern, exposing themselves in the same setting or to similar kinds of people, but most attempt no other contact with the observer. Their sexual arousal seems to be stimulated by the surprise or fear that their act causes. Most exhibitionists are not physically aggressive.

Voyeurism. The hallmark of **voyeurism** is that a person achieves sexual arousal and satisfaction through the clandestine observation of others undressing or engaging in sexual activity. These "peeping Toms" typically seek no sexual contact with the people they watch; the thrill seems to come from attempting and

getting away with behavior that is taboo and risky. Voyeurs often masturbate, either while watching others or later as they relive what they saw. Some voyeurs also expose themselves to their victims after watching them for a while.

Frotteurism. The disorder known as **frotteurism** involves recurrent touching or rubbing against a nonconsenting person in order to become sexually aroused and gratified. A common pattern is for a man to approach a female victim in a crowded public place, such as a subway train, bus, or shopping mall. He then moves next to the woman and, while fully clothed, begins to push or brush his penis against her buttocks or legs as he fantasizes about having intercourse with her. Frotteurs are seldom apprehended, in part because their victims are slow to realize what is taking place or are too embarrassed to call attention to it.

Sexual Masochism and Sadism. Obtaining sexual excitement or gratification by inflicting physical pain or humiliation on a sexual partner is the chief feature of **sexual sadism.** When sexual arousal or gratification depends on receiving painful stimulation or being humiliated, **sexual masochism** is the diagnosis. However, sexual fantasies or enactments involving bondage, blindfolds, or minor discomfort do not necessarily constitute paraphilias. It is not uncommon, for example, for individuals to fantasize about a sexual partner overpowering them, and many couples act out shared fantasies in which they bind each other to the bed with a necktie or piece of lingerie. It is only when sexual gratification depends exclusively on pain or humiliation—or when these activities lead to harm or distress when forced on or coerced from a partner—that the diagnosis of sexual sadism or masochism is made.

Sexual masochists act out their urges through masturbatory fantasies or sexual contacts in which they are bound, whipped, cut, electrically shocked, stuck with pins, forced to crawl or imitate animals, or are urinated and defecated on. Sometimes, police find the bodies of men who died accidentally while trying to heighten their arousal during masturbation by self-strangulation.

Sadists derive pleasure from inflicting pain on others, and, although some of these people find willing partners, mainly masochists, others become a public menace because they attain fullest arousal with victims whom they do not know and whom they terrify. Indeed, many serial killers are sexual sadists for whom the act of controlling and hurting victims is intensely pleasurable. This kind of sadist

Some of the equipment that sexual sadists and masochists find attractive or necessary to enjoy sex. Some couples use this paraphernalia in a consensual and safe manner, but in other cases, they lose control over the behavior and cause physical damage or psychological harm.

often chooses victims who are easy targets, such as adolescent runaways or prostitutes.

Most sadists and masochists are heterosexual. In some cases, their sadistic or masochistic acts remain consistent over time, but in others, the desired intensity of pain inflicted or endured gradually increases, placing these people at a growing risk for arrest, injury, or death.

Sadism and Rape. Are sexual sadists responsible for the hundreds of thousands of rapes that occur each year around the world? No. Although an unknown percentage of rapes are committed by true sexual sadists, rape is a crime that is often fueled by motives such as power, hatred, or aggression and may thus have little or no relationship to sexual arousal or satisfaction. Because rape is often a crime of violence, not sex (Brownmiller, 1975), it is not diagnosed as a paraphilia.

Which men are likely to be rapists? Four characteristics appear to differentiate rapists from other men, and may roughly define four subtypes of rapists (Hall & Hirschman, 1991). First, some rapists are more likely to have been sexually aggressive on prior occasions or to have engaged in other patterns of antisocial conduct; in other words, a history of sexual aggression is a good predictor of future sexual aggression (Hall & Proctor, 1987). Ironically, the tendency toward being sexually aggressive may be as-

Connections

What symptoms and behaviors are typical of antisocial personality disorder? Are these individuals always physically dangerous? See Chapter 12, pp. 421–423.

sociated with having been the victim of sexual aggression. Sexually aggressive boys are more likely to have been sexually abused than are normal boys or boys who are delinquent, but not sexually aggressive (Friedrich, Beilke, & Urquiza, 1987, 1988). Some rapists, then, appear to have a generalized difficulty in impulse control and tend to engage in a broader pattern of antisocial conduct.

A second way in which some rapists can be distinguished from other men is on the basis of their beliefs about women and sexual activity. These men are more likely to endorse various rape myths or hold callous attitudes about women that allow them to justify sexual aggression (Briere & Malamuth, 1983; Malamuth, 1981). For example, they believe that women want to be raped, and, after sexually assaulting a victim, may say, "You enjoyed that, didn't you?" These men are prone to blame women for provoking rape by the way they dress or act and are most likely to rape women they know, a pattern known as date rape or acquaintance rape.

The third difference between rapists and other men is that some rapists experience relatively high levels of sexual arousal in response to depictions of rape. Many rapists admit that engaging in rape fantasies, sometimes hundreds of times a day, is their single favorite pastime. Because sex offenders often lie in self-reports about their sexual preferences and behavior, researchers have developed more objective ways of measuring men's sexual arousal to particular stimuli. One of these is to use a strain gauge to measure penile circumference while a man is exposed to audio- or videotapes of various kinds of erotic stimuli and behavior (review Figure 14.5 on page 509). Larger erectile responses are assumed to reflect greater sexual arousal. Several studies have shown that some (but not all) rapists have equal or greater arousal to rape stimuli than to scenes of consensual sex (Hall, 1990). In contrast, men who are not rapists usually show less sexual excitation to rape scenes (Hall, Shondrick, & Hirschman, 1993). These differences may point to a subtype of rapist who finds sexual aggression uniquely arousing, who fantasizes frequently about aggressive sex, and who is very likely to repeat his offenses.

Finally, some rapists experience periodic episodes of depression or hostility during which they lose control and behave aggressively toward women. These men typically do not fantasize about or plan a sexual attack; their assaults are more opportunistic or impulsive, and they are often preceded by alcohol or other substance abuse (Hall & Hirschman, 1991).

Pedophilia. According to the DSM-IV, **pedophilia** involves recurrent and highly arousing fantasies, urges, or behaviors involving sexual activity with a prepubescent child (usually defined as younger than 13) by a person who is at least 16 years of age and is at least 5 years older than the child. Pedophilia toward girls is twice as common as toward boys. Some pedophiles are attracted only to children; others are aroused by adults as well.

Pedophiles typically develop extensive justifications for their behavior, claiming that the child "enjoys it" or that it "teaches the child valuable lessons about love." With the exception of sexual sadists, child molesters are not usually overtly aggressive toward their victims. Typically, they take advantage of the child's trust, or they convince the child that there is nothing wrong with sexual contact. In the case of **incestuous pedophilia,** in which the victims are family members, the pedophile often bribes or intimidates the child to keep her or him from reporting the abuse. Many pedophiles create and take advantage of special opportunities to gain easy access to children, as the following case illustrates.

Dr. Crone, a 35-year-old unmarried child psychiatrist, was prominent in his community and came from a stable family. He had chosen a profession devoted to caring for children, and, for many years, had been a Cub Scout leader and a member of the local Big Brothers organization. Thus, it was a shock to all who knew him when he was arrested, and later convicted, of fondling several young neighborhood boys. In a psychiatric interview following his arrest, Dr. Crone reported that, at the age of 6, a 15-year-old male camp counselor performed fellatio on him several times over the course of the summer. In later years, as his male friends began expressing sexual attraction toward girls, his secret was that he was attracted to boys. As a teenager, he began to realize that he was homosexual, but as he grew older, he noticed that the males who attracted him most were very young boys. Whenever he masturbated, he fantasized about a young boy and, on a couple of occasions, felt himself to be in love with such a youngster. He felt little, if any, sexual attraction toward females of any age or toward adult men. Dr. Crone knew that others would disapprove of his sexual involvement with boys, and he kept promising himself that he would stop, but temptation always got the better of him. (Based on Spitzer et al., 1994)

How widespread is childhood sexual abuse? We can never know for sure because of the enormous problems in documenting these cases. Some clinicians believe that sexual abuse of children has reached epidemic proportions, claiming that one fifth to one third of women and about one seventh of men are sexually abused before their 18th birthday (Finkelhor et al., 1990). Others question these figures, in part because they are based mostly on long-term retrospective reports (Briere, 1992). The situation is complicated by cases in which people claim that their memories of childhood sexual abuse were repressed for many years and then recovered in therapy or in response to some experience that suddenly triggered a recollection of the trauma.

Are such memories valid? Can traumatic memories be repressed and then recovered? One study that attempted to answer this question was conducted by Linda Williams (1994), who interviewed 129 adult women with well-documented cases of sexual abuse during their childhoods. She asked these women detailed questions about their childhood abuse, which had occurred an average of 17 years earlier. Over one third of the women did not disclose the abuse they had experienced. But this figure still does not answer the question of whether the abuse was repressed. It is possible that the women were too young to be fully aware of the abuse initially or that some of them might have been unwilling to report it to the interviewer even though they did remember it.

Connections

How do courts handle the claims of people who allege that they have recovered repressed memories of childhood abuse? See Chapter 18, pp. 635–636.

Prevalence of Paraphilias

It is difficult to estimate the prevalence of paraphilias in the general population because most people whose sex lives are dominated by these problems are not willing to admit them. Furthermore, many paraphiliacs are able to pursue their preferences in private with another consenting adult, and many who are public offenders are never caught. A rough underestimation of the problem can be made from the fact that over 80,000 arrests occur in the United States each year for sexually related crimes (Andreasen & Black, 1991).

After being arrested, these offenders are usually reluctant to disclose the extent of their paraphiliac activities, so to get a glimpse of such behavior patterns, investigators have recently begun offering sex offenders a special Federal Certificate of Confidentiality that guarantees anonymity. Interviews with exhibitionists, frotteurs, and voyeurs under these circumstances have revealed an average of more than 500 paraphilic acts per person, a frequency that is

Judith Becker

Dr. Judith Becker is Professor of Psychology at the University of Arizona. She is nationally recognized for her expertise in the causes and treatment of paraphilias.

Paraphilias

Q *Are sexual offenses discrete disorders or are they different expressions of the same underlying problem?*

A There are some individuals who are exhibitionists as well as frotteurs or who molest children and also engage in sexually aggressive behavior. Other people, whom I call specialists, have just one category of paraphilic behavior. My colleague Gene Abel and I interviewed, under a certificate of confidentiality, over 500 adult sexual offenders. We found that only about 10 percent of them had only one category of paraphilic behavior.

> *... not all sexual offenders have been sexually abused themselves.*

Q *What do you believe causes a person to develop a paraphilia?*

A A number of theories have been proposed to explain why individuals develop paraphilias. Biological theories often focus on levels of androgen. In support of this theory is the fact that some sex offenders, if put on antiandrogen medications that reduce overall sexual drive, experience a cessation or a decrease in sexual offending. Other theorists take a psychoanalytic view and explain paraphilic behavior in relation to conflict or trauma experienced in early childhood. Learning theorists propose that sexual arousal develops when an individual engages in sexual behavior that is subsequently reinforced.

Q *What role does sexual abuse play as a causal factor?*

A It is important to note that not all sexual offenders have been sexually abused themselves. I really want to underscore that because I think we do a disservice to sexual victims when we say, "Because you've been sexually victimized you are at high risk for becoming a sexual offender." In one study of an adult sample of sex offenders, 40 percent of them recalled having been sexually abused; this means that 60 percent of them did not.

Other people have looked at exposure to aggressive models. If you are raised in a home where you see your mother being beaten up, you might develop the belief, "Well I thought women enjoyed being beaten or being forced to do things because

---

much higher than reported in previous studies (Abel et al., 1988). It also became apparent that nearly 40 percent of these men have engaged in five to ten different forms of paraphilic behavior, either concurrently or in sequence (Abel et al., 1988). For example, some reported patterns include a mixture of exhibitionism, voyeurism, making obscene telephone calls, and frotteurism. The findings were especially alarming in relation to pedophiles, who were very likely to have offended several times against both family and nonfamily. Most paraphilias begin in adolescence or early adulthood, peak during adult-

hood, and gradually become less intense as the person ages (Meyer, 1995).

Causes of Paraphilias

Determining the causes of paraphilias is as difficult as estimating their prevalence. Paraphiliacs are reluctant to participate in research, and most enter therapy only when forced to do so after being arrested or threatened with divorce. Once in therapy, they may be only minimally cooperative because they may not be distressed by their behavior and may not

my dad and stepdad did that to my mom and she didn't leave." The other message is that, if you want somebody to do something, you can be coercive with them. So if you want something sexually, it's okay to force a person to do it because you've had models early in your development for that kind of behavior. Other investigators have focused on attachment, bonding, and empathy. If you are neglected, if you have not formed good attachments, then you can grow up thinking that you don't have to show concern and caring for other people.

Q *How effective is treatment for sex offenders?*

A The people with the highest success rate are "pure" incest offenders. I'm talking about men who have engaged in sexual activities only with their own children. Why do these folks have the lowest recidivism rates? Well, it could be that they are in ongoing relationships and have more stability in their lives, or it could also be that the youth has moved out of the home. The people who have the highest reoffense rates are pedophiles, specifically, men who molest prepubescent boys. We're talking about recidivism rates from 13 percent to around 40 percent with adult offenders. Nobody has a 100 percent success rate, but given the chronicity of the behavior for these people, a 13 percent reoffense rate is good. In general, however, the longer you follow these people, the more likely it is that you're going to see the reoffense rates creeping up.

Q *What do you think about the current movement to establish a national registry for sex offenders?*

A I think on the one hand, a registry could help track offenders who move from state to state, which would be useful. Let me tell you where I have some concern, however. Some states are considering, or may have begun, putting juveniles on these registers and keeping them on the registers for the rest of their lives. The reason I have concern is that when we're talking about youths who commit sexual offenses, we don't have enough data to know whether, if a youngster does something one time, he's going to develop a paraphilia and be a risk to the community for the rest of his life. When you're talking about adults who have a history of engaging in these behaviors, I think a registry *may* help to serve and protect the community.

want to change (Meyer, 1995). Indeed, many of these men, especially pedophiles, engage in extensive justification for and rationalization of their sexual behavior (Abel & Rouleau, 1995). Some may even develop false memories about their abusive behavior—in this case incorrectly recollecting their "innocence" (Rubin, 1996).

In short, clinicians know far less than they need to know about why paraphilias develop. A few cases may have an organic basis, and some can probably be traced to extreme childhood trauma, but the vast majority of paraphilias appear to be caused by multiple, interacting factors that are still not well understood.

Biological Factors. Genetic studies have failed to provide evidence that paraphilias are inherited (Hucker & Bain, 1990; LoPiccolo, 1993). The possible role of brain disorders is suggested by studies that show a higher-than-expected incidence of temporal lobe abnormalities in some men who engage in pedophilia, fetishism, and sadism (Langevin, 1993; Meyer, 1995; Wright et al., 1990). Other studies have linked abnormal testosterone levels to pedophilia, but the direction of the abnormality is not consistent. In some cases, testosterone is elevated; in others it is deficient. At this point, not enough is known about these biological influences, but it is extremely unlikely that they can explain most paraphilias.

Psychological Factors. Most psychological explanations of paraphilias suggest that they appear in people whose early experiences (1) undermined their ability to be aroused by consensual sexual activity with another adult, (2) increased their susceptibility to sexual arousal through atypical stimuli, and (3) lowered their ability to empathize with victims and appreciate the harmfulness of their actions.

For example, object relations theorists argue that paraphilias begin early in life when a child fails to establish a secure bond with the mother or other primary caregiver. Failure at this early developmental task may not only lead to separation anxiety when the child enters preschool or elementary school, but may also interfere with the ability to form intimate relationships later in life. If the father was also absent or uncaring, the child (usually a boy) may begin using paraphilic objects such as the mother's shoes or underwear to be comforted or sexually aroused.

John Money and his colleagues (Money & Pranzarone, 1993) have proposed a model of paraphilias that emphasizes the importance of sexual stressors during childhood that shape future patterns of sexual arousal and sexual behavior. Money suggests that children engage in a series of behaviors that serve as "practice" for sexual arousal and sexual activity in adulthood. These behaviors include learning how to approach and initiate social interactions with people who attract them. In early childhood, boys learn to chase or tease girls on the playground, and in middle school boys and girls may start learning how to flirt with each other. Various stressors can interrupt or distort these early sexual learning experiences. For example, children may be punished or humiliated for engaging in normal sexual play or rehearsal, thus making them less likely to continue the normal course of sexual practice that would eventually have led to typical sexual attractions and skills.

A more extreme situation arises for those who are coerced into inappropriate sexual play or otherwise victimized by a pedophile. Money says that these sexually stressed children find themselves in a bind: they feel "in trouble" for engaging in sexual behavior, but they worry about causing even more trouble by reporting it. He believes these children often resolve their dilemma by continuing to endure the sexual stressor. As the inappropriate sexual behavior is repeated, it may gradually seem less unusual or improper, thus helping the child to neutralize or

master the strong emotions that initially accompanied the behavior. Money's theory has been invoked to explain why pedophiles, particularly those who abuse boys, are more likely to have been abused as children than are men who engage in other types of abuse (Worling, 1995).

Still, the most widely accepted psychological explanations of paraphilias are based on the principles of learning, especially on the role of classical conditioning in transforming normal sexual arousal into fetishes or other paraphilias. Learning theorists suggest, for example, that a youngster may become sexually aroused by inappropriate stimuli as the result of a chance association between those stimuli and sexual arousal. Thus, if a young boy is sexually aroused while seeing or touching a certain piece of clothing, that stimulus may become associated with sex. This initial association may be magnified if the boy begins to include the stimulus in his masturbatory fantasies, and after being repeatedly associated with sexual arousal, this originally nonsexual stimulus may acquire the power to elicit that arousal. Eventually, the stimulus becomes a fetish that allows the person to reliably produce sexual arousal, but, as noted earlier, arousal or orgasm may become impossible if the stimulus is absent.

Relying on one object or activity also serves to control sexual arousal. To maintain a sense of control, persons displaying paraphilias develop highly ritualized sexual encounters that must be acted out according to a fixed script in order to achieve satisfaction. These scripts are the focus of masturbatory fantasies and tend to have two other effects as well: (1) they substitute for real people, thereby compensating for shyness, sexual inhibitions, and a lack of social skills; and (2) they tend to reduce attention to the effects that sexual behavior has on real people, thereby minimizing empathy for victims.

One experimental study illustrated how a fetish might be learned. The experimenters showed men pictures of boots along with arousal-eliciting pictures of nude women (Rachman & Hodgson, 1968). After many pairings, the boots themselves elicited sexual arousal. In this laboratory situation, when the boot pictures were no longer paired with the nude photos, they lost their erotic allure for most of the men. However, had the men repeatedly masturbated while fantasizing about boots and if they had had few other sexual outlets, an enduring boot fetish might have developed.

Finally, the social roles expected for men and women, the ways in which sex and aggression are linked in popular media, and social values regarding sex are all factors that might contribute to the distorted sexual arousal seen in paraphilias. Consider, as one example, the differences in how society views masturbation. The fact that masturbation is condoned or accepted more for men than for women results in men more frequently using masturbation to reinforce sexual fantasies. Adding to this the fact that men fantasize about sex more than women—again, perhaps because of social norms—may provide additional clues about why men constitute the vast majority of paraphiliacs.

Treatment of Paraphilias

Because paraphiliacs are seldom motivated to enter or actively participate in programs designed to alter their patterns of sexual arousal and behavior, the successful treatment of paraphilias is not easy. Consequently, many clinicians, and most members of the public, are convinced that paraphilias are nearly untreatable. These beliefs, and the figures suggesting that sexual victimization of children is increasing, have led to several proposed social policies that might prevent sexual offenses. Three of these policies are discussed in the Prevention section on pages 524–525.

Behavioral Methods. Given the apparent learned aspects of many paraphilias, it is not surprising that behavioral therapy is one of the most successful psychological approaches to altering these disorders. The earliest forms of behavior therapy for sex offenders consisted mainly of aversive conditioning techniques designed to reduce arousal to problematic stimuli (Nietzel, 1979). For example, fetishists were given an electrical shock as they fondled a leather handbag, exhibitionists were given drugs that made them nauseous while they thought about exposing themselves, and frotteurs were instructed to imagine rubbing against a woman in the subway and having horrible consequences befall them. This last method, called *covert sensitization* is perhaps the most popular aversive conditioning technique. In covert sensitization, the client imagines a paraphilic stimulus or behavior, and, then, just as he begins to become aroused by these images, the therapist adds images of the client's suddenly developing open sores, of rats crawling all over him, or of other disgusting stimuli. In a variation of this method called **olfactory aversion therapy,** aversive images are accompanied by the presence of a foul odor (Maletsky, 1973). In **shame aversion therapy,** the client imagines his friends or relatives watching his paraphilic acts and expressing their disgust and disapproval. These aversive techniques have helped offenders—particularly those whose paraphilia is isolated and nonaggressive—to control their problematic sexual arousal and behavior (McConaghy, 1990).

Aversive methods remain a common treatment for paraphilias in the United States, but suppressing deviant arousal is only one goal of therapy. The individual must also learn to be aroused by more appropriate stimuli. Otherwise, he may soon return to his paraphilia. **Masturbatory reconditioning** is a primary tool for achieving this second goal. The intent of this procedure is to increase arousal to more appropriate sexual stimuli by associating them with orgasms. Thus, the client is asked to masturbate using fantasies or pictures of his favorite paraphilic stimuli until he is just short of ejaculating. At this point, he is asked to switch to a more appropriate fantasy (or to look at pictures of more appropriate stimuli) and then masturbate to orgasm. Masturbation is also used in a second way, in which the man is required to masturbate to his favorite fantasy until he gets so tired or sore that he can no longer be aroused by the deviant images.

Multimodal Treatment. In many countries today, paraphilias are likely to be treated using a combination of techniques presented in multimodal programs. The model for these treatment packages was developed in the United States and Canada (LoPiccolo, 1993; Marshall & Eccles, 1996) and contains several elements.

The therapist first works to establish rapport with the client and to help him see that he needs to change his behavior. This goal is pursued by countering the sexual myths that many offenders endorse (e.g., that children are not harmed by pedophilia) and by helping them recognize the suffering and damage their victims have endured. The therapist also helps the client to minimize environmental temptations for paraphilic behavior. Thus, pedophiles are asked to have no contact with children, even if this means temporarily leaving home; frotteurs are required to stay away from crowds; and voyeurs are told to avoid places where they have "peeped" before.

The second element of treatment is intensive behavior modification, usually consisting of masturbatory reconditioning and covert sensitization with olfactory aversion. Just as essential is the third treatment element, relapse prevention. Here, the client learns to identify the situations, stressors, or stimuli that lead to paraphilic arousal and then practices better ways of dealing with them. He learns to spot those seemingly irrelevant decisions that, on closer scrutiny, increase the risk of offensive sexual behavior. Voyeurs who know that they are more likely to "peep" when drunk are taught to recognize the significance of agreeing to meet a friend

Connections

How is relapse prevention used for other disorders? Is it effective? See Chapter 13, p. 463.

Prevention

Can Preventive Detention, Public Notification, and Pornography Bans Reduce Sex Crimes?

As fears about sex offenders have skyrocketed in the United States, three kinds of social policies have emerged in an effort to curb repeated sex offenses, if not prevent some of them in the first place.

First, in several states, special legislation is on the books to protect the public from sex offenders. Some of these laws mandate longer prison sentences for people convicted of sex crimes. Others, such as the "sexual predator" bills passed in Washington and Wisconsin, allow convicted sex offenders who are deemed most likely to repeat their offenses to be committed to state mental hospitals after their prison terms expire. This preventive detention can continue as long as authorities judge an offender to be dangerous and, in theory, can last for life. About one third of the states now have some form of sexual predator commitment law.

A second legislative approach to prevention is embodied in *registration and notification* laws that require convicted sex offenders to register with the state immedi-

ately after their release from prison. The goal is to inform the public about where these offenders are living, so that police (and neighbors) can maintain close surveillance of them. The first notification law was passed in New Jersey following the rape and murder of Megan Kanka by a neighbor who had spent 6 years in prison for attempting to murder another little girl. In 1996, President Clinton signed federal legislation known as "Megan's Law" that requires law enforcement authorities in all states to notify communities when convicted sex offenders move into their neighborhoods. It is unclear, however, whether these laws will actually protect the public or make repeat offenses less likely.

A third and even more controversial approach to preventing sex offenses in the United States has taken the form of efforts to ban the availability of pornographic materials. This approach gained prominence in 1986 when it was recommended by a Commission on Pornography appointed by U.S.

Attorney General Edwin Meese. The Meese Commission based its conclusion on evidence that exposure to sexually violent pornography leads to more negative attitudes about women and increased sexual aggression toward them.

Some of this evidence came from an extensive research program by Edward Donnerstein and his colleagues (Donnerstein, 1982; Linz, Donnerstein, & Penrod, 1984, 1987a, 1988; Malamuth & Donnerstein, 1982). In a typical study (Donnerstein & Berkowitz, 1981), male college students were told that they would be paired with either a male or a female partner in an experiment on the effects of stress on learning. At one point, the partner gave the student a number of electrical shocks as a way of indicating that the partner didn't like an essay the student had written earlier in the experiment. The student then watched one of four films: an emotionally neutral talk-show interview, an erotic film depicting nonviolent

for a drink after work. Similarly, pedophiles must understand that deciding to go home by a different route is not a random decision if the new route happens to take them past a schoolyard. Relapse prevention includes paying attention to and avoiding these so-called casual decisions, as well as developing ways to delay gratification when old arousal patterns are triggered. Many sex offenders have a history of giving in to their urges almost immediately, then viewing their transgression as an excuse to give up all efforts to change. In relapse prevention, the client is helped to recognize this phenomenon, known as the *abstinence violation effect* and to learn that isolated slips need not indicate total failure.

Another vital element in most comprehensive treatment programs is the effort to address the social

and emotional deficits that contribute to paraphilias. Clients are trained in the social skills that can help them establish more appropriate sexual contacts and are also helped to overcome depression and problems in existing relationships. In some programs, inappropriate sexual behavior is initially curbed through the use of medication. These medications include *neuroleptics* (major tranquilizers), whose sedating effects tend to reduce sexual arousal, and drugs (such as medroxyprogesterone acetate, sold as Depo-Provera) that lower testosterone levels and the frequency of erections. The selective serotonin reuptake inhibitors have also shown some promise in treating paraphilias (Kafka, 1994). Unfortunately, most of these drugs reduce sexual arousal in general, not just arousal to inappropriate stimuli.

sexual intercourse, or one of two pornographic films that combined sex with aggression (a woman was shown being slapped and sexually assaulted). One of these pornographic films depicted the "rape myth" by showing the woman eventually smiling at her attackers; the other showed the woman suffering throughout. When the film was over, the student was given a chance to administer electric shocks to his partner. Those who had seen either of the *aggressive* pornography films showed high levels of shock-aggression toward their partners, but only if the partner was female. These findings suggest that aggressive pornography specifically promotes aggression toward women, not toward people in general.

Still, the researchers on whose work the Meese Commission relied point to three reasons for caution about banning pornography as a way of preventing or reducing sex offenses (Linz, Donnerstein, & Penrod, 1987b). First, almost all of the research has been conducted in

After she was raped and murdered, Megan Kanka became the impetus for the federal legislation known as "Megan's Law," which requires states to notify communities about the whereabouts of sex offenders who are judged to be particularly dangerous.

laboratories where only artificial forms of aggression are studied. Second, it may well be the depiction of violence, not the portrayal of sex, that promotes aggression toward women. Finally, there is little evidence that long-term exposure to pornographic materials in general creates negative attitudes toward women. Indeed, these researchers have called for more public education about the effects of all media products, not stricter laws about pornography.

Conclusions About Treating Paraphilias. Overall, the results of paraphilia treatments are mixed; anywhere from 10 to 70 percent of convicted sex offenders are rearrested for sexual offenses. Some studies indicate that specialized treatment programs can reduce the likelihood of *recidivism,* or repeat offenses (Marshall & Eccles, 1996), while others suggest that treatment has no significant effect (Furby, Weinrott, & Blackshaw, 1989; Hanson, Steffy, & Gauthier, 1993). These conflicting conclusions may reflect differences in client characteristics. In one study of treated sex offenders, those most likely to be treatment failures had engaged in a higher number of previous sex offenses, had victimized boys more often than girls, and had never been married (Hanson, Steffy, & Gauthier, 1993). In this and other studies, the offenders

most likely to benefit from treatment were incestuous fathers who had had no other criminal history and who were personally committed to making a change. Consistently, the worst treatment candidates are molesters of young boys, sexually sadistic rapists, and exhibitionists.

While many clinicians remain guarded about the effects of paraphilia treatments (Furby et al., 1989), not all experts are pessimistic. A number of specialized programs have reported considerable success, even with sexually aggressive offenders and pedophiles. Programs that combine a variety of cognitive-behavioral techniques and relapse prevention methods appear particularly effective (Maletsky, 1991; Marques et al., 1994; Marshall, Eccles, & Barbaree, 1990).

Revisiting the Case of John

*J*ohn was diagnosed as having a gender identity disorder. After completing an evaluation that ruled out other psychological concerns and mental disorders, he began a trial phase in which he gradually spent more and more time in the female role. He lived as a woman for 2 years and participated in weekly psychotherapy sessions aimed at helping him clarify his desire to become a woman.

After several months of therapy, John decided to begin estrogen therapy, with the ultimate goal of sex reassignment surgery and marriage to a man. John was accepted in a surgical sex reassignment program and, just before starting it, he informed his mother and brothers of his plans. His brothers were appalled and vowed to have nothing more to do with him. His mother was more accepting but admitted to her friends that she did not understand John's decision.

The hormone therapy gradually enlarged John's breasts, and his body took on a softer, more contoured, female shape. During surgery, his penis and scrotum were removed, an artificial vagina was constructed, and his lips and jaws were reconstructed to make his face look more like a woman's. Three years afterward, John, who officially changed his name to Joan, expresses delight with the results. She works as a telemarketer for a credit card company, and, although she occasionally dates men, she is still shy and finds it difficult to meet new people. Still, Joan says that she finally feels like the person she was meant to be.

SUMMARY

Human Sexuality

Human sexuality incorporates several processes that are influenced by biological, psychological, and social factors. Gender identity refers to a person's sense of being either male or female, while gender role refers to patterns of behavior that a culture typically associates with masculinity or femininity. Sexual orientation involves the tendency to engage in sexual behavior with members of the same or opposite sex. Homosexuals prefer sex with members of the same sex; heterosexuals, with members of the opposite sex; and bisexuals, with members of both sexes.

Several surveys of the sexual habits and fantasies of American adults conducted over the past five decades show that most of them engage in intercourse regularly throughout their adult lives, usually in the context of monogamous relationships.

A number of biological factors have been identified as possible determinants of sexual orientation, but none has been established as a definitive cause.

Gender Identity Disorders

The main features of gender identity disorders are a person's persistent desire to become the other sex and a profound discomfort with his or her biological sex. Gender identity disorders are seen in both children and adults; in males more often than in females. Although biological factors may play some role, the primary cause appears to involve a combination of childrearing practices that encourage cross-gender identification. The main treatment for adult transsexuals is surgical sex reassignment.

Sexual Dysfunctions

Normal human sexual responsiveness follows a 4-stage cycle of desire, excitement, orgasm, and resolution. Sexual dysfunctions can occur in any of the first 3 stages of this cycle, and it is not unusual for a person to suffer more than one dysfunction at the same time. The field of sex therapy was revolutionized by Masters and Johnson, who developed several learning-based treatment techniques for various dysfunctions. Many of these behavioral and cognitive-behavioral techniques are still used to treat sexual dysfunctions, along with medical interventions, psychotherapy, and couples therapy.

Paraphilias

In paraphilias, sexual arousal and satisfaction depend on fantasies and behaviors involving atypical or problematic stimuli or activities, including inanimate objects, nonconsenting partners, or mixing sex with pain or humiliation. Paraphilias listed in the DSM-IV include fetishism, transvestic fetishism, exhibitionism, voyeurism, frotteurism, sexual sadism, sexual masochism, and pedophilia. Most paraphilias develop from a combination of experiences that lessen a person's ability to be aroused by consensual sexual stimulation, increase the ability to be aroused by deviant stimuli, and lower the capacity to empathize with victims. Some behaviorally oriented treatments have been successful in decreasing certain paraphilias, but the prognosis for exhibitionism, pedophilia, and sexual sadism is generally not favorable.

KEY TERMS

15

Biological Treatment of Mental Disorders

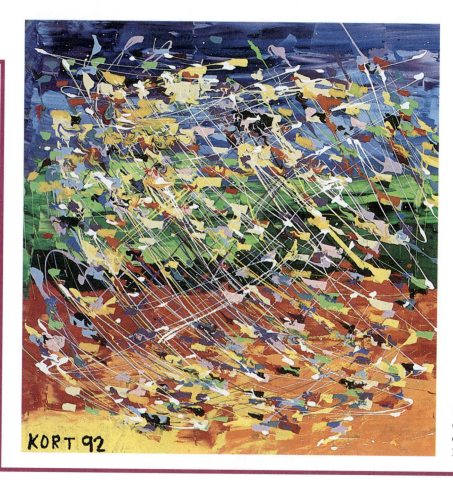

Untitled by Michael Kort, 1992.
Oil on canvas, 24" x 24".
Courtesy of Sistare and
NARSAD Artworks.

From the Case of Christine

Christine remembers feeling depressed for the first time when she was 10 years old. She had overheard her mother telling her father that other kids were avoiding Christine because she was so big and clumsy. Christine ran to her bedroom, tears streaming down her face, and she stayed there for the rest of the afternoon, at first overwhelmed with embarrassment and then just numb.

Afterward, whenever Christine was about to try something new, she recalled her mother's words, and the sense of humiliation was just as strong as when she had first heard them. The pattern was set: through middle school, high school, and even college, Christine kept to herself, always trying to avoid drawing anyone's attention and feeling like a lonely, drab failure. At times her moods were so dark that Christine felt as though she could not move or breathe or speak. She would lie on her bed, promising herself she would get up, but just staying

there for hours. During the worst periods, her appetite all but disappeared and reading, once her favorite pastime, became a dreaded chore.

Christine's parents sent her to therapist after therapist. At 15, it was group therapy with five other girls; in college, it was 4 years of psychoanalysis aimed at exploring Christine's resentment toward her mother. In truth, she enjoyed therapy, but her episodes of depression were undiminished. If anything, the symptoms were getting worse, and Christine began to fear that her whole life would be spent in what she called her "black hole." At 22, after quitting her part-time job as a writer for the local newspaper, Christine finally asked her analyst if there were another treatment they could try. The analyst referred Christine to another psychiatrist.

The new psychiatrist learned that Christine's paternal grandmother and one of her aunts had been diagnosed with depression. She told Christine that her depression was probably due to a chemical imbalance and started her on a daily 75 mg dose of Tofranil, an antidepressant drug. For the first 3 weeks, Christine didn't notice any effects other than constant thirst and some blurred vision in the morning. Then she began to sleep a little better, and her mood brightened. She had more energy and began to feel some enthusiasm for life. Unfortunately, however, Christine gained 10 pounds after 2 months on Tofranil, and she told her psychiatrist that she either had to change the medication or she would stop taking it. The psychiatrist suggested a daily 40 mg dose of another antidepressant, Parnate, but Christine refused to take it because the drug's negative interactions with certain foods meant that she would have to give up eating cheese and drinking wine. Over the next 18 months, Christine tried varying dosages of several other antidepressants. One of them, Norpramin, worked well, but raised her blood pressure and, while the addition of Inderal lowered the blood pressure, it worsened her depression.

The psychiatrist then prescribed Prozac, which greatly improved Christine's mood, but made her feel "spacey" and caused problems in falling asleep. When lowering the Prozac dose did not help, the doctor changed Christine's medication to Zoloft, known to some psychiatrists as "Prozac lite." Christine took Zoloft for 6 months. Her depression improved, she was working regularly, sleeping well, and going out once in a while with a few acquaintances from college. But Christine still felt as if she were missing something; she didn't feel "normal." She wondered if her depression would ever go away for good so that she could stop taking medication. ■

bled minds is reflected in Macbeth's plea for medical help for Lady Macbeth:

> Canst thou not minister to a mind diseased;
> pluck from the memory a rooted sorrow;
> raze out the written troubles of the brain;
> and with some sweet oblivious antidote cleanse
> the stuff'd bosom of that perilous stuff which
> weighs upon the heart?

Over the centuries, biologically based treatments for mental disorder have also included prescriptions for special diets, sleep, exercise, and extreme heat or cold. Patients have been given putrid brews and exposed to leeches in an effort to produce the vomiting and bleeding necessary to rid the body of mental illness that was attributed to toxins and "bad blood." And from prehistoric times, through the middle ages, and even in some cultures today, a surgical procedure called *trephining* has been used to create holes in the skulls of mentally disturbed people to let out the presumed cause of their illness.

Few of these biological treatments are used in Western industrialized societies today, although their legacy can still be seen in the herbal remedies for behavior problems found in health food stores and in the practices of native healers in many cultures. The three main forms of biological treatment now used by Western mental health professionals are psychosurgery, electroconvulsive therapy, and **pharmacotherapy**, or drug treatment. In this chapter, we will consider each of these methods, describe some guide-

*P*rior to 1960, few people received medication for depressive symptoms such as Christine's; today, most depressed people are given drugs as at least part of their treatment. This change is based on four decades of progress in understanding—and developing drugs to alter—the biochemical aspects of a wide range of psychopathology, including mood disorders, anxiety disorders, psychotic conditions such as schizophrenia, and childhood disorders such as attention-deficit/hyperactivity disorder.

Today's drug treatments represent the newest products of a biological approach to mental disorders, an approach whose roots in ancient history were described in Chapter 1. For example, the Roman physician Galen prescribed herbal sedatives and other concoctions designed to restore proper balance among the four bodily humors that his Greek predecessor Hippocrates had proposed as responsible for personality and mental disorders. In Shakespearian times, the continuing desire for magic elixirs to ease trou-

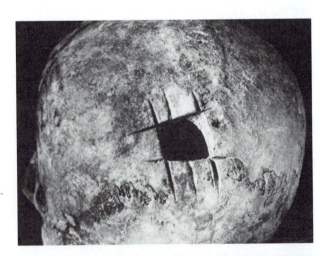

In ancient times, holes were drilled in people's skulls to remove the evil spirits that were supposedly troubling them. This procedure, called trephining, *may have been a predecessor to modern forms of surgery aimed at repairing brain damage or removing diseased brain tissue.*

lines for their use, and summarize their typical effects. We will also discuss some important questions about biological treatments: Are they overused? Do they offer superficial solutions instead of real cures? Will they lead to the disappearance of all other kinds of treatment?

Psychosurgery

Unlike trephining, which simply opened a hole in the skull, modern psychosurgeons make lesions in the brain itself. Thus, **psychosurgery** is surgery designed to alleviate mental disorders by altering or destroying brain tissue.

Psychosurgical Procedures

Modern versions of psychosurgery date from 1891 and the work of Gottlieb Burckhardt, a Swiss neurologist, whose procedure involved destroying a small section of the cerebral cortex. After Burckhardt had operated on six hallucinating mental patients, however, his colleagues forced him to terminate his work because one patient died and another developed epilepsy (Valenstein, 1980). In 1935, the Portuguese neurosurgeon Antonio de Egas Moñiz introduced the *prefrontal leucotomy,* or *lobotomy,* as it was later called. His procedure involved drilling small holes in the skull just over the frontal lobes and then injecting alcohol to destroy tissue in those lobes. Later, in place of alcohol, Moñiz inserted a pick-like instrument (a leucotome) through the skull and destroyed brain tissue by rotating a wire loop that extended from the instrument.

Moñiz and his colleague, Almeida Lima, believed the procedure was quite successful for their first group of patients: 6 were reported as "cured"; 7, "improved"; 6, "unimproved"; and no "failures" (Moñiz, 1948). The degree of improvement in these patients has since been seriously challenged (Valenstein, 1980, 1986). In fact, Moñiz himself was shot and paralyzed by one of his disgruntled surgical patients, but recognition that Moñiz's technique was vastly overrated did not come in time to prevent his receiving the Nobel Prize for Medicine in 1949. In fact, Moñiz's work prompted others to adopt his procedures and to develop new psychosurgery techniques, as well.

Americans Walter Freeman and James Watts developed the *standard lobotomy*—also called the *frontal lobotomy*—in which a cutting instrument was inserted through holes drilled in the side of the skull and then pivoted, severing connections between the frontal lobes and the rest of the brain (Valenstein, 1980). In 1948, Freeman and Watts introduced the *transorbital lobotomy.* In this procedure, an instrument similar to an ice pick was inserted into the eye socket above the eye ball and tapped into the prefrontal tissue. Once in place, the instrument was pivoted back and forth, undercutting the frontal lobes. Because this procedure could be conducted in the doctor's office, it became a popular treatment among psychiatrists at the time. Freeman claimed that he could conduct as many as 50 transorbital lobotomies in a day (Valenstein, 1980).

In the two decades after Moñiz's report, it is estimated that more than 40,000 mental patients were lobotomized (Galluscio, 1990). However, the popularity of psychosurgery declined dramatically in the 1950s following new information about its dangers and the introduction of psychoactive drugs that were capable of controlling the most florid symptoms of severe mental disorders.

Although there was a lack of diagnostic specificity at the time that Moñiz, Freeman, and Watts performed psychosurgery, they seem to have worked mainly with patients displaying schizophrenia and severe mood disorders. The majority of these operations were conducted in mental hospitals and were especially likely when patients were violent and aggressive and the hospital was overcrowded. Indeed, the popularity of psychosurgery was based partly on the fact that, in those days, there was no effective alternative treatment available for severe mental disorders. Eventually, psychosurgery was tried on a wide variety of disorders, including alcoholism and other forms of substance abuse, obesity and anorexia, criminal aggressiveness, mental retardation, and hyperactivity.

Surgeons using these early procedures were often unsure of exactly what areas of the brain were being lesioned, and they ended up destroying a considerable amount of tissue. The side effects from these "blind" procedures included epileptic seizures, impulsiveness, incontinence, lack of foresight or planning, poor judgment, lack of motivation and self-care, extreme lethargy, and impaired thinking and memory (Bridges et al., 1973; Harvey, Mohs, & Davidson, 1993; Mirsky & Orzack, 1980; Valenstein, 1980). Worst of all, as many as 5 percent of patients died during or immediately after the surgery due to hemorrhage from severed cerebral blood vessels.

Criticisms of "blind" lobotomies led to the development of new psychosurgical procedures that continue to be used today. Two modern procedures include the *cingulatomy* (e.g., Corkin, 1980; Jenike

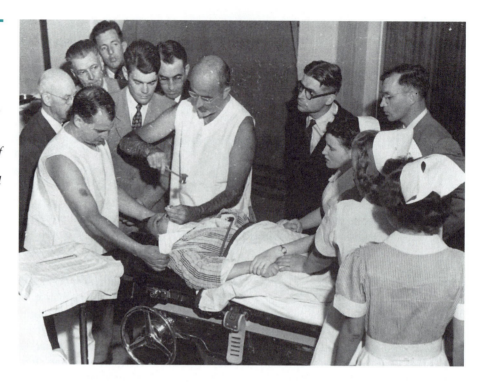

Psychosurgery remained popular into the 1950s, owing in large part to the lack of any careful scientific evaluation of the technique and its side effects. Here, Dr. Freeman performs a lobotomy in 1959. Despite many refinements, current forms of psychosurgery are mostly restricted to very serious mood and anxiety disorders that have not responded to more conservative treatments.

et al., 1991; Sachdev et al., 1992) and the *stereotaxic subcaudate tractotomy* (e.g., Kartsounis et al., 1991; Pangalos et al., 1992). These psychosurgical methods employ stereotaxic equipment and computer-guided imagery (including CT scans and MRI) to place instruments exactly where the surgeon wants them, thus making it possible to lesion more precisely defined and smaller areas of the brain. In most modern forms of psychosurgery, the surgeon attempts to make extremely small and precise cuts in brain tissue.

The advantage of such methods is that smaller lesions tend to create fewer adverse side effects.

Cingulatomy is the most common psychosurgical method used in North America today. It is accomplished by inserting electrodes bilaterally into a portion of the cerebral cortex called the *cingulate gyrus* (Chiocca & Martuza, 1990). As radio frequency waves heat the electrode tip, a lesion is made in fibers that are part of the Papez Circuit, a neural circuit of the limbic system involved in emotional experience. Cingulatomies are used for severe, intractable cases of depression and anxiety disorders, especially obsessive-compulsive disorder. Although cingulatomies lead to fewer adverse side effects compared with lobotomies, recent studies find that as many as 12 percent of cingulatomy patients commit suicide (Jenike et al., 1991; Sachdev et al., 1992) and 9 percent develop postsurgical seizures (Corkin, 1980). Personality changes characteristic of frontal lobe injury are also seen in some patients undergoing this surgery (Jenike et al., 1991; Sachdev et al., 1992).

Stereotaxic subcaudate tractotomy (SST) is procedurally similar to the cingulatomy, but it involves lesioning a different brain area, namely a small region at the base of the frontal lobes immediately below the head of the caudate nucleus. The SST procedure disconnects portions of the frontal lobes from the limbic system and other subcortical areas, such as the hypothalamus, that are involved in emotion and motivation. Like the cingulatomy, SST is used primarily for intractable cases of mood and anxiety disorders (e.g., Kartsounis et al., 1991; Pangalos et al., 1992).

Outcomes of Psychosurgery

Today, a consensus has developed that the patients who are most likely to benefit from psychosurgery are those who suffer mental disorders that involve strong emotion, including severe unipolar and bipolar depression, and serious cases of obsessive-compulsive disorder (OCD) that have not responded to drugs or other treatment (Chiocca & Martuza, 1990; Valenstein, 1980, 1986). Patients whose main symptoms involve thought disorder or flattened emotions are least likely to be helped by psycho-

Connections

What role do brain structures such as the cingulate gyrus play in obsessive-compulsive disorder? For answers, see Chapter 7 p. 236.

surgery. Therefore, schizophrenics are now seldom candidates for it.

The question of whether psychosurgery is an effective treatment for these disorders is not easy to answer. For one thing, psychosurgery today is performed mainly as a last resort on people who have failed to respond to other forms of treatment. In such extreme cases, it may be unrealistic to expect that any treatment will produce dramatic improvements. Second, use of differing diagnostic practices and differing criteria for success or failure makes it difficult to compare the results of various outcome studies on psychosurgery. What one group of researchers considers success might be deemed failure by another research team. Furthermore, because many psychosurgery outcome studies report treating many types of disorders, it is difficult to tell whether overall success rates are affected by the particular mix of clients included in a particular study. Finally, the absence of data comparing psychosurgery with an appropriate placebo control treatment leaves open the question of the degree to which the surgery's effects might be attributable to patients' expectations.

Given these methodological limitations, it is no wonder that the effects of psychosurgery remain uncertain and that the use of these techniques remains controversial. Reviews of worldwide outcome literature indicate, for example, that between 30 and 89 percent of OCD patients can benefit from psychosurgery (Chiocca & Martuza, 1990; Jenike et al., 1991; Sachdev et al., 1992), but the consensus appears to be that only a minority of these people achieve permanent benefits. Some long-time sufferers of severe OCD (and their physicians) believe that, in spite of possible complications, these odds are good enough to justify the surgery. Opponents of psychosurgery argue that the ethical problems associated with destruction of brain tissue outweigh the benefits of the procedure and that it should be discontinued. The resulting controversy has now gone beyond the realm of science and medicine into ethical questions about what interventions should be allowed in the service of alleviating humans' emotional and behavioral disorders (Valenstein, 1980, 1986).

In Review

Psychosurgery, which involves surgery on the brain for the treatment of a mental disorder:

- was practiced widely in the 1940s and 1950s in the form of frontal and transorbital lobotomies; and

- fell into disfavor in the 1950s after the many dangers and minimal benefits of the procedure were realized and more effective drug therapies began to appear.

Modern forms of psychosurgery:

- include the cingulatomy and stereotaxic subcaudate tractotomy, which involve smaller and more precise lesions and therefore fewer negative side effects;

- are usually reserved as a last-resort treatment for refractory cases of severe mood and anxiety disorders; and

- produce major benefits only for some patients and are therefore still an area of ethical concern among clinicians.

Convulsive Therapies

New treatments often arise from serendipitous observations and through theories that are ultimately shown to be incorrect. One such theory, dating back several centuries, held that strong shocks in the form of physical illnesses or extremes of temperature could kill the agents causing a mental disorder. According to this reasoning, **convulsive therapies,** which use physical stimuli to induce an epileptic-like seizure and a brief loss of consciousness, might be an effective treatment for mental disorders. And, as it turns out, a series of such seizures often does result in at least a temporary reduction of mental disorder symptoms in many patients. During the twentieth century, seizures have been induced in several ways. Today, the most common method is to apply electric shock to the brain, but seizures have also been created by injections of chemicals.

Insulin Coma and Metrazol Therapy

In 1933, Viennese psychiatrist Manfred Sakel was treating a diabetic drug addict and accidentally gave her an insulin overdose. The patient went into a convulsion, then into a coma, as her blood sugar dropped dramatically. Upon regaining consciousness, she reported that her craving for morphine was greatly reduced. Attributing her "cure" to the effects of the insulin-induced coma, Sakel used an overdose of insulin on a psychotic addict, and again the patient's mental state appeared to improve following his convulsion. Sakel was soon promoting insulin coma as a treatment for schizophrenia and other severe mental disorders (Valenstein, 1986).

Shortly after Sakel's treatment became popular, postmortem research on human brains led a Hungarian psychiatrist named Ladislas von Meduna to believe (incorrectly, as it turned out) that the neurons of people with epilepsy are different from those who display schizophrenia. He reasoned that seizures and psychosis are therefore incompatible, and, thus, that people with seizure disorders such as epilepsy could not be schizophrenic, and vice versa. This logic led Meduna to assume that, if a seizure could be induced in a schizophrenic patient, it would interfere with and correct schizophrenic brain processes. Working in Germany, Meduna eventually settled on the synthetic drug *metrazol* to induce seizures. Although metrazol-induced seizures were intense and often violent, the treatment soon became quite popular. By the early 1940s, metrazol convulsive therapy was widely used in Europe and the United States for the treatment of schizophrenia and other psychotic conditions (Valenstein, 1986).

As has too often been the case in the history of treating mental disorders, enthusiasm for insulin coma and metrazol therapies preceded a careful assessment of their effectiveness. Once these techniques came under scientific scrutiny, it was clear that they produced no lasting benefits. This outcome, viewed in light of the large number of serious medical side effects associated with these techniques, has led to their virtual disappearance.

Electroconvulsive Therapy

The third type of convulsive treatment, developed in the 1930s, is called **electroconvulsive therapy (ECT)**, and it eventually replaced insulin and metrazol treatment. In ECT, an electric current is applied to the brain, thus inducing a brief seizure. The treatment was pioneered in Italy by two physicians, Ugo Cerletti and Lucio Bini, after observing convulsions in hogs being stunned by an electric shock to the head prior to slaughter. They believed that electricity could induce convulsions more easily and safely than metrazol or other chemicals could.

Cerletti and Bini first used ECT in 1938 on a schizophrenic patient whom police in Rome had found wandering in confusion (Cerletti & Bini, 1938). When electrodes were placed on either side of the patient's forehead and 150 volts of electricity were passed through his brain, his body jolted but did not convulse. The voltage was too low. The next day the experiment was repeated using higher voltage. This time, the patient responded with a full-blown, grand mal epileptic seizure. When he later regained consciousness, he had no memory of the seizure, but

when he heard the doctors discussing the possibility of repeating the treatment, he begged them not to. Since he had shown no such lucidity prior to the treatment, Cerletti and Bini deemed it a success. They were so encouraged, in fact, that they gave the patient another treatment at even higher voltage.

Modern ECT Procedures. Refinements in ECT procedures have minimized the serious (and sometimes fatal) side effects of Cerletti and Bini's original methods. For one thing, although *bilateral* ECT—placing electrodes on both sides of the frontotemporal region—is still used, it is now less common than a *unilateral* procedure in which one electrode is placed on a temple and the other at the top of the head (Abrams, 1993). The hemisphere selected to receive the electrical impulse is usually the nonlanguage hemisphere, typically the right side of the brain, so the patient experiences less memory loss and other side effects following treatment (Calev et al., 1993).

The electrical impulse itself has also been refined to reduce ECT side effects. In the past, the impulse lasted approximately 1 to 2 seconds, but today's practitioners tend to use an impulse that produces a seizure with a third less shock (Kahn et al., 1993; Nobler & Sackeim, 1993). Furthermore, the amount of current applied is adjusted to fit individual patients. For example, because their skulls are less dense, women require 70 to 80 percent less current than males, while the elderly require less than young adults (Nobler & Sackeim, 1993). Indeed, the National Institute of Mental Health (1985) guideline for ECT is to use the lowest current necessary to cause a seizure lasting 20 to 25 seconds. Unfortunately, as treatments are repeated, patients' thresholds for entering convulsions go up, requiring gradually stronger doses of electricity to achieve the same effect (Nobler & Sackeim, 1993).

In early versions of ECT, the patient remained awake until the seizure was induced. Today's ECT patient is given a general anesthetic and muscle relaxants to prevent the severe muscle contractions during seizures that in years past caused broken bones and other bodily injuries (Valenstein, 1986). In modern forms of ECT, the actual convulsion may hardly be visible to observers. The patient is also given supplementary oxygen, which greatly reduces the danger of brain damage and death during ECT. Physicians administering ECT carefully monitor patients' seizures by measuring their brain waves with an *electroencephalogram (EEG)*. Finally, to minimize the uncertainty and fear that continue to surround ECT, patients and their families are usually given detailed descriptions of the treatment (Grunhaus & Pande, 1994).

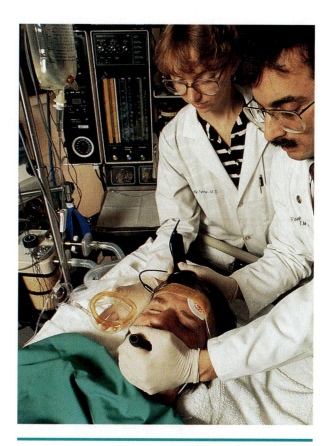

Many modifications in ECT over the past two decades have led to an increased use of this technique. The modern practice of ECT is considered a relatively safe and effective treatment for severe mood disorders.

Today, once the patient is prepared, the entire ECT procedure takes only 3 to 4 minutes, after which the patient awakes with no memory of the treatment session. ECT typically occurs in a series of 10 to 12 sessions on a schedule of 2 to 3 sessions per week over 2 to 4 weeks.

Side Effects of ECT. Injuries that in the past occurred in about 40 percent of ECT patients now appear in only about 1 of every 1,400 ECT treatments. Deaths due to ECT are estimated at between 2.9 to 4.5 per 100,000 administrations, which is about the same as for any medical procedure involving general anesthesia (NIMH, 1985). In spite of these refinements, modern ECT can still result in posttreatment headache, a few hours of confusion, and memory impairment lasting up to 6 months, and, in a few cases, indefinitely (Breggin, 1980; Janicak et al., 1991; NIMH, 1985).

Cognitive impairments usually appear as loss of *episodic memory,* which is memory for events, and tend to be especially pronounced in elderly patients. Typically, memory for the most recently learned infor-

mation is the last to return (Calev et al., 1993). *Semantic memory* (knowledge of vocabulary and other facts), *procedural memory* (about how to type or perform other tasks), and *implicit,* or "automatic," memory, are only minimally affected by ECT (Calev et al., 1993).

Applications and Effects of ECT. In the 1950s, ECT was widely used to treat many mental disorders in the United States. In the 1960s and 1970s, however, ECT's popularity was significantly reduced by growing concern over its adverse side effects and by the advent of promising new antidepressant and antipsychotic drugs. However, many of the optimistic expectations about drug treatment for severe mental disorders have not been realized, and it turns out that drugs have many adverse side effects of their own (Fink, 1990). Accordingly, there has been been a resurgence in the use of modern, safer versions of ECT in the 1990s (Fink, 1993).

Although originally designed for patients diagnosed as schizophrenic, ECT is now most widely and successfully used in the United States for patients displaying severe mood disorders, including bipolar disorder, major depression with melancholia, and psychotic depression with delusions (APA, 1993; Fink, 1993; NIMH, 1985; Shukla, 1989). About 80 percent of patients receiving ECT in the United States have been diagnosed as severely depressed, about 5 percent as bipolar, about 5 percent as schizophrenic, and the rest as having a variety of other problems.

Does ECT help depressed people? Apparently so. Studies comparing the effects of ECT with those of therapeutic drugs show that ECT produces equal or superior benefits, particularly with the most severely disturbed patients (APA, 1993; Fink, 1993; NIMH, 1985). The effects of ECT are considerably more rapid than those of drugs, but they are also more likely to fade with time. Accordingly, a course of ECT is often followed by a regimen of antidepressant drugs or additional ECT sessions to help maintain treatment effects. The rate of relapse within a year of successful ECT is over 50 percent, but as low as 20 percent if ECT is followed by antidepressant medication (Grunhaus & Pande, 1994; Lickey & Gordon, 1991). Because of ECT's rapid effectiveness in treating severe depression, the American Psychiatric Association (1993) has recommended it as the treatment of choice for patients who are severely suicidal or psychotically depressed (e.g., in a stupor and refusing to eat) or who have not responded well to medication (Depression Guideline Panel, 1993; Fink, 1990, 1993). For less severely depressed clients, however, ECT remains a treatment of last resort to be used only following unsuccessful psychotherapy and/or drug treatment.

ECT also appears to have considerable utility in treating manic episodes in patients diagnosed with bipolar disorder. About 80 percent of manic patients obtained marked clinical improvement following ECT (Mukherjee, Sackeim, & Schnur, 1994; Small, 1990), and nearly 70 percent of patients who did not respond to drug treatment were helped by ECT (Mukherjee et al., 1994).

When ECT is used to treat schizophrenic patients in the United States, it tends to be for patients who display catatonic stupor, acute schizophrenic agitation, or schizoaffective disorders (Shukla, 1989; Fink, 1993; APA, 1993). In countries such as India, ECT is used frequently to treat patients with schizophrenia; it may be particularly effective for acute schizophrenic episodes (Shukla, 1989). Patients given ECT tend to be released from the hospital sooner and to require less medication to maintain gains after their release. In contrast, ECT is not usually effective for chronic schizophrenia. Taking all the outcome data together, however, a National Institute of Mental Health Consensus Panel concluded that there are currently insufficient data to recommend ECT for the treatment of schizophrenia (NIMH, 1985).

How Does ECT Work? The mechanism by which ECT works remains a mystery (e.g., Fink, 1990; Kapur & Mann, 1993). Among the most prominent explanatory hypotheses are those suggesting that ECT-induced convulsions correct imbalances or dysregulations in endocrine and neurotransmitter systems. ECT does at least temporarily affect most neurotransmitters in the brain, including serotonin, dopamine, norepinephrine, GABA, and the beta-endorphins (Fink, 1990; Kapur & Mann, 1993). However, there is insufficient evidence that these changes parallel the changes in mood and behavior that often follow a series of ECT treatments. Furthermore, some theories of depression suggest that the changes in neurotransmission brought about by ECT should worsen, not relieve, the disorder. Such inconsistencies make it less likely that ECT's benefits are due only or primarily to its effects on neurotransmitters (Fink, 1990).

Max Fink, an ECT pioneer, believes that repeated convulsions stimulate the production of an undiscovered substance that is responsible for the general regulation of mood states (Fink, 1990; 1993). He has named this elusive substance *antidepressin* and suggests that it must work in a fashion similar to insulin (which regulates sugar metabolism and results in diabetes when not well controlled). There is no direct evidence to support the existence of this substance, and no explanation of how ECT's effects on a single substance could both calm mania and lift the spirits of those displaying severe depression or even catatonia. Obviously, what is known about ECT's mechanisms is dwarfed by what remains to be discovered.

Current Status of ECT. Despite its demonstrated effectiveness in treating certain disorders, ECT remains a controversial therapy. Uncertainty over its mode of action, concern over its side effects, and the fears that linger from its shadowy past make some patients and clinicians uneasy about ECT. In his autobiographical account of being a patient in a mental hospital, psychiatrist N. S. Sutherland reveals the dread that even refined versions of ECT still inspire:

> *O*n my ward, there was usually an unnatural silence when preparations were being made to give ECT, and although one rarely knew beforehand who was to be the recipient, he or she could always be identified afterwards by the small strip of sticking plaster covering the vein on the back of the hand where the anaesthetist had inserted the hypodermic. Patients wearing such sticking plaster were treated with great solicitude by the others. (Sutherland, 1976)

Proponents of ECT in the United States, including the American Psychiatric Association (1993), see it as a valuable therapeutic tool in specific cases; opponents, such as psychiatrist Peter Breggin, argue that ECT cannot be justified under any circumstances (Breggin, 1980). ECT is still the topic of occasional court battles, and some American cities have tried to pass ordinances that would prohibit the use of ECT in local hospitals. In other countries, however, debate about ECT is more muted. ECT is commonly used in the United Kingdom, for example, and in India it has been described as a mainstay of treatment for several types of mental disorder (Shukla, 1989).

ECT is regulated by strict ethical and clinical guidelines in the United States. The NIMH Consensus Conference (1985) guidelines state, "When the physician has determined that clinical indications justify the administration of ECT, the law requires and medical ethics demand, that the patient's freedom to accept or refuse the treatment be fully honored" (1985, p. 3). The guidelines go on to recommend that the benefits as well as the risks—including post-treatment confusion and memory loss—be clearly spelled out for the patient and that alternative treatments be offered. This information is to be repeated as the treatment proceeds to ensure that changes in memory and judgment do not alter the patient's initial willingness to consent.

In Review

The convulsive therapies:

- treat serious mental disorders by inducing a seizure and brief loss of consciousness; and
- first involved administration of drugs such as insulin or metrazol, methods that have now virtually disappeared.

Electroconvulsive therapy (ECT), in which an electric current to the brain induces the convulsion:

- is safer than drug-induced shock;
- has been refined since its introduction in the 1930s so that most serious side effects have been greatly reduced, if not eliminated;
- is used in the United States mostly for severe mood disorders that have not responded well to drug treatment; and
- is a relatively effective treatment, even though how it works is not understood.

Drug Treatments

The introduction in the 1950s of drugs capable of significantly reducing the symptoms of several severe mental disorders was partly responsible not only for the decline of psychosurgery and ECT but also eventually for the release of large numbers of people whose disorders had made long-term hospitalization a necessity (see Figure 15.1 on page 538). These drugs—called **psychoactive** or **psychotropic drugs** because they alter cognitive, emotional, and behavioral processes—are now not only the most common form of biological treatment for mental disorders, but perhaps the most common of all medical treatments. The 1950s also saw the emergence of the new field of **psychopharmacology,** a scientific field devoted to the study of psychoactive drugs and their use in treating mental disorders.

The dramatic growth of drug treatments for mental disorders may have begun in Western societies only about 50 years ago, but the roots of this approach lie in the ancient traditions of herbal medicine. For thousands of years, in cultures all over the world, healers have recommended various plants and plant derivatives for alleviating mental, as well as physical, disorders. The earliest written reference to marijuana (cannabis), for example, is over 4500 years old and describes it as a substance capable of calming the mind (Julien, 1992). It was still being recommended for this purpose in the 1500s by Johann Weyer, a German physician considered to be the first psychiatrist. Other substances with a long history of use in the relief of mental anguish include alcohol, hashish, opium, and chamomile teas, among many others. By the second century A.D., the Roman physician Galen had created a huge pharmacopeia of herbal medicines (Bromberg, 1959).

The development of healing medicines has now evolved into an enormous and influential pharmaceutical industry, and the prescription of psychotropic medication for mental disorders is steadily increasing. In 1975, only 27 percent of psychiatric outpatients were given drugs (Olfson, Pincus, & Sabshin, 1994). By 1988, that figure had grown to 55 percent; today, psychiatrists prescribe psychotropic medication for up to 90 percent of their patients (Olfson et al., 1994). These same drugs are regularly prescribed for many patients by general practice physicians, as well. It is estimated that, in the late 1970s, 8,000 *tons* of benzodiazepines, a type of antianxiety drug, were prescribed annually in the United States alone. By the early 1980s, over 100 million such prescriptions were being written each year in the United States and about 25 million a year in the United Kingdom (Ashton, 1991). During 1995 alone, 19 million prescriptions were filled in the United States for Prozac, the sales leader among antidepressants. Americans currently spend about $3 billion a year for the purchase of antidepressant medications.

There are several reasons for the increasing popularity of drug therapies for mental disorders in the United States. For one thing, drug treatments are effective in reducing the symptoms of many mental disorders; in some cases, these benefits are greater than those of any other form of treatment. Potent economic forces are also at work. The managers of insurance companies, health maintenance organizations, and other managed health care organizations encourage the use of treatments that they believe are the most efficient and cost-effective. Today, despite conflicting evidence, these managers tend to perceive drugs as the preferred treatment for many mental disorders. Furthermore, the pharmaceutical companies that develop and market these drugs (with estimated worldwide sales of $700 billion in 1995) have begun to form their own managed care health organizations, or to purchase existing ones. As a result, these companies are in a position to control treatment decisions. The potential for conflicts of interest in such a situation is obvious, and it raises the

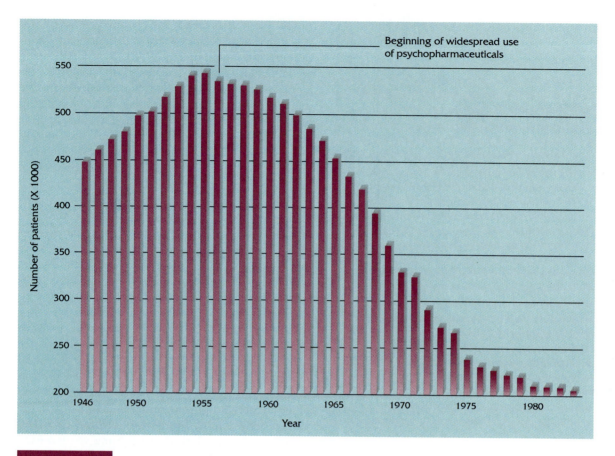

FIGURE 15.1

Mental Hospital Population Before and After the Introduction of Antipsychotic Drugs in the 1950s

Owing in large measure to the introduction of antipsychotic drugs in the 1950s, the number of patients confined to public mental hospitals in the United States dropped by about 75 percent by the 1980s. As a result of this deinstitutionalization movement, most formerly hospitalized patients began living in their communities. However, adequate community care has not always been provided to deinstitutionalized patients, leaving many of them living in poverty and continuing despair.

question of whether it is a wise policy to allow drug manufacturers to control the use of their products.

Psychoactive Drugs and How They Work

Psychoactive prescription drugs can be classified according to their chemical structures, but drugs that are highly similar chemically may have quite different effects. They can also be classified by their expected effects, such as antidepressant or antianxiety. However, drugs in one category sometimes prove effective in treating more than one form of mental disorder. Accordingly, after offering a brief overview of the mechanisms through which psychoactive drugs

exert their effects, we will discuss them in relation to the conditions for which they tend to be prescribed.

Mechanisms of Action. Psychoactive drugs exert their effects on thought, mood, and behavior primarily by altering the biochemical environment of the nervous system. More specifically, they modify the action and availability of neurotransmitters, the chemicals that facilitate or inhibit communication between nerve cells, or neurons, in the brain (see Figure 15.2). Altering any of the processes that affect the availability of neurotransmitters or their ability to influence neurons will affect the mental and behavioral processes mediated by those neurotransmitters.

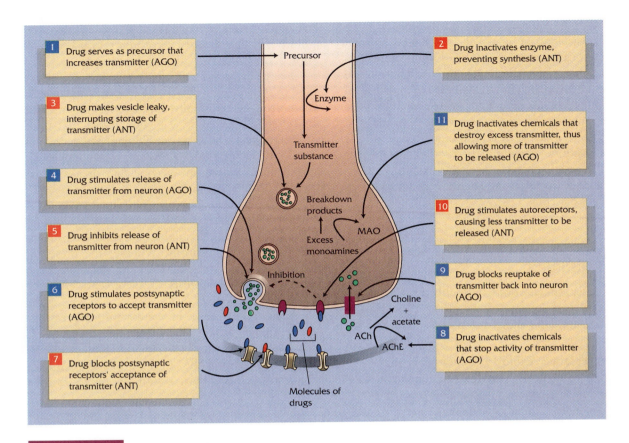

FIGURE 15.2

Typical Agonist and Antagonist Effects
Drugs can change synaptic functioning in two basic ways. Antagonists (ANT, labeled in red) block or inhibit synaptic transmission; agonists (AGO, labeled in blue) facilitate such transmission. This figure shows the various means by which antagonists and agonists can operate.
Source: Adapted from Carlson, 1994.

Some drugs act because they are chemically similar enough to a natural neurotransmitter that they can mimic its effects and thus stimulate neurons to fire. These drugs are called **agonists.** Other drugs, called **antagonists,** are sufficiently similar to a natural neurotransmitter that they occupy receptor sites on neurons that the neurotransmitter would normally stimulate, but are not similar enough to actually stimulate them. Once antagonist drugs occupy receptor sites, they block the action of the natural transmitter. Still other drugs work by prolonging the availability of neurotransmitters in the gaps, or synapses, between neurons, thus amplifying their effects. One group of antidepressants, for example, slows the rate at which the neurotransmitter serotonin is reabsorbed into the neurons that released it. Inhibiting this *reuptake* process makes serotonin more available to operate on receptor sites. A different class of antidepressants increases the availability of neurotransmitters by interfering with the natural process through which certain neurotransmitters are chemically broken down, or inactivated.

Unfortunately, the action of most psychotropic drugs is not specific enough to alter only those neurons involved in a disordered mental or behavioral process. Many drugs have a scattershot impact that affects whole categories of brain cells, thus influencing many parts of the body. Some of these additional, and often undesirable, side effects (such as a dry mouth, insomnia, or urinary retention) are relatively mild. Others, however, can be much more serious, even life threatening. Caution in prescribing psychotropic drugs is also in order because many of them can be physically as well as psychologically addictive (Rickels et al., 1993).

In the following sections we will consider some specific psychoactive drugs currently used to treat four main categories of mental disorder: mood disorders, anxiety disorders, psychotic disorders, and childhood disorders. In all cases, it is important to remember that the effects of psychoactive drugs vary considerably depending on the age, gender, and physical health of patients. A typical or safe dose for one patient could be dangerous for another. The probability and seriousness of side effects from these medications also depend heavily on the characteristics of individual patients.

Drugs for the Treatment of Mood Disorders

The medications most often prescribed for the treatment of depression and other mood disorders are known as antidepressants and mood stabilizers.

Antidepressants. Table 15.1 shows four main categories of antidepressant drugs: (1) monoamine oxidase inhibitors, (2) tricyclics (TCAs) and related compounds, (3) the selective serotonin reuptake inhibitors, and (4) heterocyclic antidepressants.

The antidepressant effects of the *monoamine oxidase (MAO) inhibitors* were discovered by accident. These drugs were initially developed as a treatment for tuberculosis, but it was soon noted that their strongest effect was to relieve TB patients' depressed mood. MAO inhibitors slow down the activity of monoamine oxidase, an enzyme that breaks down neurotransmitters such as serotonin and norepinephrine in the synapse. Since they inhibit MAO, these drugs have the net effect of keeping more serotonin and norepinephrine available in synapses to influence postsynaptic neurons. Whether the preservation of these neurotransmitters in the synapse is the key to the MAO inhibitors' antidepressant effects is still unclear, however.

Although effective in combatting depression, MAO inhibitors create several troublesome side effects. For one thing, they virtually eliminate REM sleep. Furthermore, the combination of MAO inhibitors and foods that contain *tyramine*—a sub-

---

TABLE 15.1 Antidepressants and Mood Elevators

Generic/chemical name	Trade name	Therapeutic dose range (mg/day)
Monoamine oxidase inhibitors (MAO-I)		
Phenelzine	Nardil	45–90
Isocarboxazid	Marplan	30–50
Tranylcypromine	Parnate	20–60
Tricyclic antidepressants (TCA)		
Imipramine	Tofranil	75–300
Amitriptyline	Elavil, Amitid	75–300
Doxepin	Sinequan, Adaptin	75–300
Nortriptyline	Aventyl, Pamelor	40–200
Desipramine	Norpramin, Pertofrane	75–300
Protriptyline	Vivactil	20–60
Clomipramine	Anafranil	75–300
Selective serotonin reuptake inhibitors (SSRI)		
Fluoxetine	Prozac	10–40
Paroxetine	Paxil	20–50
Sertraline	Zoloft	50–150
Others, including the heterocyclics		
Amoxapine	Ascendin	100–600
Buproprion	Wellbutrin	225–450
Trazadone	Desyrel	150–600

Source: U.S. Department of Health and Human Services, 1993.

A number of celebrities and prominent Americans have publicized their use of medications to cope with long-term mood disorders. Mike Wallace and Art Buchwald credit antidepressants with helping them battle depression and continue their careers. Ironically, Dr. Kaye Redfield Jamison (shown above), one of America's leading psychiatrists on mood disorders, suffers bipolar disorder. Discussing her use of lithium in An Unquiet Mind *(1995), Dr. Jamison wrote,*

> *My manias, at least in their early and mild forms, were absolutely intoxicating states that gave rise to great personal pleasure, an incomparable flow of thoughts, and a ceaseless energy that allowed the translation of new ideas into papers and projects. Medication not only cut these fast-flowing, high-flying times, they also brought with them seemingly intolerable side effects. It took me far too long to realize that lost years and relationships cannot be recovered and damage done to oneself cannot always be put right again, and that freedom from control imposed by medication loses its meaning when the only alternatives are death and insanity.*

stance found in aged cheeses, red wine, beer, pickled herring, and chicken livers, for example—can cause rapid, extreme elevation of blood pressure, sometimes resulting in strokes (Julien, 1992). A new, less risky class of "reversible" MAO inhibitors is being tested, but continuing concern over side effects has made alternative medications much more popular.

Among these alternatives are the *tricyclic antidepressants* (TCAs). Named for their three-ring molecular core, TCAs were first synthesized for use in treating schizophrenia, but they turned out to be more beneficial in the treatment of depression. TCAs block the reuptake of norepinephrine and serotonin.

By preventing this reabsorption, the short-term effect of the tricyclics is to increase the level of neurotransmitters available at synapses. Compared with MAO inhibitors, TCAs usually have fewer serious side effects and do not require major dietary changes, but they are by no means problem free. Patients complain of sleepiness, dry mouth, constipation, insomnia, blurred vision, decreased sex drive, dizziness, tremulousness, and nausea. About 40 percent of patients actually terminate treatment because of these side effects (e.g., Rickels et al., 1987). Combining TCAs and alcohol can increase the effects of both, with potentially fatal results. Finally, these antidepressants can stimulate mania in certain depressed people who are predisposed to bipolar disorder.

A second generation of antidepressants primarily affects serotonin rather than norepinephrine. Included among these *selective serotonin reuptake inhibitor* drugs is *fluoxetine,* which is marketed as Prozac. Fluoxetine has become the most widely prescribed antidepressant in the United States, mainly because it is at least as effective as the TCAs but has even milder side effects. About 1.5 million prescriptions for Prozac are written every month in the United States. As discussed in Chapter 9, Prozac is prescribed for an ever-expanding list of complaints. Physicians give it to calm the emotional storms of adolescence, to quell the tempers of abusive husbands, and to reduce the symptoms of PMS.

The SSRIs were specifically designed to increase the availability of just one neurotransmitter—serotonin—to create fewer side effects than those associated with the broader-acting tricyclics. Nevertheless, about 30 percent of patients treated with Prozac report nervousness, insomnia, joint pain, sweating, weight loss, and sexual dysfunction (Hellerstein et al., 1993).

The increasing popularity of *heterocyclic* antidepressants stems from their relative lack of long-term side effects. One example is *bupropion* (Wellbutrin), which blocks the reuptake of dopamine and is much safer for patients with heart disease. New antidepressants are constantly being tested and brought to the market. For example, *nefazodone* (Serzone), introduced in 1994, combines the mechanisms of the tricyclics and SSRIs but with fewer negative effects on sleep and sexual functioning.

The potential dangers of all kinds of antidepressants may be increased in the elderly. The major concern is that drug metabolism slows with age as the

Connections

Does Prozac increase the risk of suicide or violent behavior? See the Controversy section in Chapter 9, p. 314.

gastrointestinal tract, liver, and kidneys function less efficiently. Because drugs do not break down as readily in elderly people, doses that are normal for younger people can accumulate to overdose levels that precipitate psychotic-like symptoms, including delusions, hallucinations, confusion, and delirium (Rockwell et al., 1988; Wood et al., 1988). Physicians and other health care workers face the challenge of distinguishing these drug side effects from the normal processes of aging and the effects of other physical conditions.

As with many other psychotropic drugs, taking antidepressants over a long period can produce physical dependence. When this happens, abrupt withdrawal of the drug can result in malaise, anxiety, nausea and vomiting, headache, chills, sweating, and insomnia (Ceccherini-Nelli et al., 1993). Physicians recommend, therefore, that patients discontinue using these drugs gradually.

Even though scientists do not know exactly how drugs operate to relieve depression, the fact is that they are usually beneficial, at least as long as a person continues to take them. Overall, 60 to 70 percent of patients with major depression or dysthymia who take antidepressants show improved mood, increased physical activity, increased appetite, and associated beneficial weight gain. They report feeling less hopeless and guilty, and they get more sleep without early morning awakening. Furthermore, they report and demonstrate that they can move and think faster. These effects do not usually appear for 1 or 2 weeks after treatment begins and typically do not reach maximum levels for 4 to 6 weeks (APA, 1993).

Antidepressants appear to be most effective for treating major depression and somewhat less so for milder conditions such as dysthymia (Elkin et al., 1989). No single type of antidepressant has been shown to be superior to all others for cases of major depression, and none has been shown to be effective for severe, psychotic depression (APA, 1993; Depression Guidelines Panel, 1993; Lickey & Gordon, 1991). Furthermore, there is little evidence that antidepressant drugs are helpful to depressed children or adolescents. Well-controlled studies have failed to show that either TCAs or SSRIs are superior to placebos for children; in addition, over half the children taking antidepressants have been reported to suffer negative side effects (Sommers-Flanagan & Sommers-Flanagan, 1996).

Mood Stabilizers. About 1949, Australian psychiatrist John Cade found that the mineral salt *lithium* calmed manic patients. Now administered as lithium carbonate, regular doses of this salt stabilize severe mood swings and can prevent the recurrence of both the depression and mania associated with bipolar disorder.

How lithium exerts its effects on both mania and depression remains a matter of speculation. Current theories emphasize its ability to reduce the availability of dopamine and norepinephrine but in ways that differ from antidepressant drugs. Lithium is thought to alter **secondary messengers,** which are biochemical changes that take place in the neurons after they have initially been stimulated by a neurotransmitter. Another possibility is that lithium affects electrolyte balances in the neurons, thereby stabilizing neurons' reactions to various neurotransmitters and making the postsynaptic neurons less likely to fire (Julien, 1992; Lickey & Gordon, 1991; Risby et al., 1991).

Whatever the mechanism, lithium is effective, at least in the short run, for up to 80 percent of treated bipolar patients (Coppen, Mendelwicz, & Kielholz, 1986; Prien & Potter, 1993). The typical untreated bipolar patient experiences a manic episode about every 14 months and a depressive episode about every 17 months. With lithium, attacks of mania occur much less often, sometimes as rarely as every 9 years (Lickey & Gordon, 1991). Because lithium's effects tend to appear relatively slowly over a 1- to 3-week period, patients in a manic state are often given an antipsychotic drug to achieve quicker temporary control.

Lithium is often used as a *prophylactic* drug, meaning that bipolar patients take it even when they are symptom free in order to prevent future episodes. Taking maintenance doses during nonmanic periods is now probably the most common pattern of lithium use by bipolar patients.

The usual daily dose of lithium is 900–1800 mg, sometimes taken in three to six small administrations to prevent negative side effects on the stomach. Lithium can also have other bothersome, and sometimes serious, side effects, including tremor, weight gain, diarrhea, cramps, weakness and fatigue, increased thirst, memory loss, and impaired concentration. Some of these problems subside over the first few weeks of treatment, but the amount of lithium in the patient's blood must be regularly monitored because if it reaches toxic levels, the results can be confusion, loss of balance, vomiting, nausea, slurred speech and, in severe overdoses, renal disease, coma, or death. Women must avoid taking lithium during the early stages of pregnancy and while breastfeeding.

In *Prozac Nation,* Elizabeth Wurtzel (1995) vividly describes some of the negative effects she experienced with lithium.

*M*y dreams are polluted with paralysis. I regularly have night visions where I try to walk somewhere—to the grocery store or the pharmacy, nowhere special, routine errands—and I just can't do it. I am exhausted in the dream and I become more exhausted in my sleep, if that's possible. I wake up tired, amazed that I can even get out of bed. And often I can't. I usually sleep ten hours a night, but often it's many more. I am trapped in my body as I have never been before. I am perpetually zonked.

In my waking life, I am almost this tired. People say, "Maybe it's Epstein-Barr." But I know it's the lithium, the miracle salt that has stabilized my moods but is draining my body. And I want out of this life on drugs.

Combining lithium with psychotherapy is rapidly becoming the standard treatment for bipolar disorder. Indeed, if psychotherapy and educational programs for the patient's family are not included in treatment, lithium's side effects can lead 20 to 47 percent of patients to stop taking it and thus to risk relapse into a depressive or manic episode (Frank et al., 1985; 1990). Psychotherapy can also deal with another problem: some bipolar patients actually miss the excitement associated with their manic periods and stop taking lithium in order to reexperience these elevated moods.

Two antiepileptic drugs—*carbamazepine* (Tegretol) and *valproic acid* (Depakote or Depakene)—are increasingly being used as adjunctive or alternative treatments for the 20 to 25 percent of bipolar patients who do not respond to lithium alone (APA, 1993; Lickey & Gordon, 1991). Carbamazepine, which is structurally similar to the TCAs, appears especially helpful in enhancing lithium's antidepressant effects when the two are administered together (APA, 1993).

Drugs for the Treatment of Anxiety Disorders

Given that anxiety disorders are the most prevalent of all mental disorders (see Chapter 7), it is not surprising that antianxiety medications, also called *anxiolytics,* are the most widely prescribed category of psychoactive drugs. We will describe three types of anxiolytics: the benzodiazepines, buspirone, and certain antidepressants. Each type has somewhat different biochemical actions, but all have been found useful in the treatment of various anxiety disorders.

The Benzodiazepines. Once known as *minor tranquilizers,* the *benzodiazepines* are a group of chemically related drugs used primarily for the relief of anxiety (see Table 15.2). The benzodiazepines were discovered in Poland in the 1930s (McKim, 1991),

---

TABLE 15.2 Antianxiety Drugs (Anxiolytics)

Generic/chemical name	Trade name	Therapeutic dose range (mg/day)
Benzodiazepines		
Long-acting benzodiazepines		
Diazepam	Valium	4–40
Clorazepate	Tranxene	15–60
Chlordiazepoxide	Librium	15–100
Intermediate-acting benzodiazepines		
Lorazepam	Ativan	2–6
Clonazepam	Klonopin	1–4
Short-acting benzodiazepines		
Oxazepam	Serax	30–180
Triazolam	Halcion	0.125–0.250
Alprazolam	Xanax	.75–4
Novel antianxiety drugs		
Buspirone	BuSpar	5–40

Source: Hollister & Csernansky, 1991; p. 28; *Physicians' Desk Reference.*

but it was not until the late 1950s that scientists at the Hoffman LaRoche drug company discovered the sedating properties of the first benzodiazepine, Librium. By the early 1970s, Librium, and another benzodiazepine called Valium, were the most widely prescribed of all drugs in North America (Blackwell, 1973). By 1990, about 60 million prescriptions for benzodiazepines were being written annually, and overall they are the fourth most widely prescribed class of drugs in the United States (Julien, 1992; Lickey & Gordon, 1991).

The benzodiazepines were developed in part because of concerns over the safety of previously available antianxiety drugs, including *barbiturates* such as phenobarbital. When barbiturate drugs first appeared in the early 1900s, their sedating and anticonvulsant properties made them enormously popular for the treatment of everything from arthritis to bedwetting. They are highly addicting, however, and overdoses can cause death. Because there are fewer dangers associated with benzodiazepine overdoses, most physicians today favor them over barbiturates to combat anxiety. Unfortunately, various barbiturates are still sold illicitly on the streets as "goofballs," "dolls," "downers," "blues" (Amytal), "yellow jackets" (Nembutal), and "reds" (Seconal).

Benzodiazepines act by facilitating the postsynaptic binding of central nervous system neurotransmitters such as GABA, the brain's major inhibitory agent. By facilitating the action of GABA, these drugs serve as a kind of "braking system," reducing nerve transmissions that would otherwise result in anxiety and tension. Patients using benzodiazepines report physical relaxation along with calmer mental processes, less worry, mild euphoria, and less catastrophic thinking. These effects have made benzodiazepines popular in the treatment of many anxiety disorders, and their frequent use would suggest that they are highly effective. In fact, as described by one Valium user, they do produce reductions in anxiety.

*W*hen I was 27 and my youngest child was 18 months old, I mentioned to the doctor that he was sleeping very little and though he did not seem tired in any way, I certainly was! After a course of vitamins I still felt worn out and this was when I was first prescribed Valium. I remember instantly feeling a lot better—all the irritability and tiredness seemed to disappear and I became a lot more relaxed and content. The next 3 years seemed to fly over; the eldest child began school, my husband gained a promotion, and we bought a new house. Any problems which cropped up during this time could always be wiped out just by taking a Valium. (Based on Ashton, 1984; cited in McKim, 1991)

However, benzodiazepine-induced reductions in anxiety are usually short-lived. For example, alprazolam (Xanax) is widely used to treat panic disorder and agoraphobia (Greenblatt et al., 1993; Klosko et al., 1990; Lesser et al., 1992; Schweizer et al., 1993). Studies have consistently found that, after 8 weeks of treatment, 50 to 60 percent of patients taking Xanax are free of panic attacks (Ballenger et al., 1988; Klosko et al., 1990; Schweizer et al., 1993). Unfortunately, the benefits tend to last only as long as the medication continues; the majority of users suffer a relapse of anxiety when they stop taking the drug.

The benzodiazepines' short-term antianxiety and antipanic effects must also be viewed in light of the side effects caused by their amplification of GABA's inhibitory effects. Patients often report drowsiness, fatigue, dizziness, impaired psychomotor functioning, and clouded thinking (see Figure 15.3). These problems are made worse if the patient consumes alcohol while taking benzodiazepines: the combined effects of these two drugs can result in severe impairment of motor skills, which can be dangerous or fatal while driving (Mattila, Aranko, & Seppala, 1982; Moskowitz & Smiley, 1982) (see Figure 15.4). Extended use of the benzodiazepines can lead to physical dependence and, if they are discontinued abruptly, can result in a withdrawal syndrome including panic and anxiety that are worse than ever (Rickels et al, 1993). The body also develops a tolerance for benzodiazepines, requiring increased dosages to obtain reductions in anxiety. In one study of Xanax

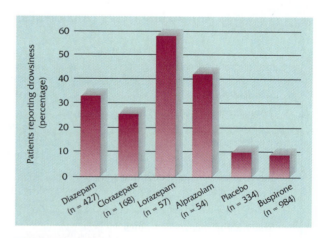

FIGURE 15.3

Drowsiness and the Benzodiazepines

The incidence of drowsiness reported in controlled clinical studies is much greater for the benzodiazepines than for either buspirone or placebo.

Source: Adapted from Feighner, 1987.

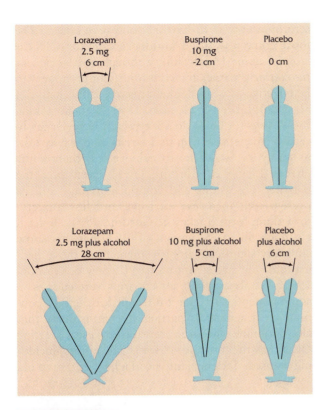

Lorazepam 2.5 mg 6 cm	Buspirone 10 mg -2 cm	Placebo 0 cm

Lorazepam 2.5 mg plus alcohol 28 cm	Buspirone 10 mg plus alcohol 5 cm	Placebo plus alcohol 6 cm

FIGURE 15.4

Effects of Benzodiazepines on Motor Coordination

The body sway effects of buspirone alone or combined with alcohol are essentially the same as when alcohol is taken alone. The body sway effect with the benzodiazepine lorazepam (Ativan) alone, but especially when combined with alcohol, results in much greater instability.

Source: From Shuckit, based on Mattila et al., 1982.

treatment for panic disorder, 96 percent of patients taking the drug for 8 months experienced withdrawal symptoms when the drugs were discontinued, making it impossible for 33 percent of them to stop taking it (Rickels et al., 1993).

The woman mentioned above who started taking Valium when she was 27 to help her deal with the stress of her first baby ultimately described how she became dependent on the drug and how she suffered when she tried to discontinue it.

My problems did not go away like in the early days on the pills—they seemed greater. I started to become withdrawn, insecure, and confused and suffered bouts of depression together with uncontrollable outbursts of rage.... I saw a doctor who told me it was not the pills I needed but psychotherapy. The pills were only covering up the mental turmoil. The next year involved extensive analysis and although at times this was mentally distressing, it seemed to help. During the weekly sessions it was suggested I drop my dose of Valium so I quickly agreed; at first it was easy—a bit jumpy when I dropped 1 mg—but then things became much worse. My confidence began to wane dramatically—I could not go out or be left on my own. My husband finally had to give up his job, as I spent most of the time begging him to come home as I was frightened. I started to feel very ill, and even going to the shops was a mammoth task. My doctor advised me not to drop the Valium any more (I was down from 15 mg to 4 mg) as I was suffering from chronic anxiety and needed some form of sedation. What both of us did not realize was—I was in tranquilizer withdrawal. I begged the doctor to help me—I could not go on any more like this—it was like a "living death." He suggested another form of tranquilizer and took the remaining Valium away—I thought I had gone mad. That was 9 weeks ago and during that time I have not touched a tablet. This brought on a series of symptoms that I had experienced only mildly before. Noises jarred every fibre in my body and my eyes seemed to shun the light of day. I shook from head to foot and enormous panic attacks would sweep through my body, leaving me exhausted and totally afraid. Complete fatigue took over the feeling of tiredness and sleep no longer came with the night. Many times I thought it would be best to die. (Ashton, 1984; pp. 1135–1136; cited in McKim, 1991)

Many of the long-term problems associated with the benzodiazepines can be traced to the overwillingness of physicians to prescribe (and patients' eagerness to take) these drugs at the first sign of tension or discomfort. Because the benzodiazepines act quickly, are initially easy to take, and are relatively inexpensive, they are consumed at an alarming rate in the United States and in many other countries.

Buspirone. The side effects and addictive potential of the benzodiazepines made clear the need for an alternative class of anxiolytic drugs. For people with anxiety disorders other than panic disorder, one of the newest nonbenzodiazepine anxiolytics, *buspirone* (BuSpar), may provide such an alternative. Buspirone acts primarily by affecting receptors of serotonin and dopamine rather than GABA and appears to be effective for treating generalized anxiety symptoms without creating serious side effects, physical or psychological dependence, or dangerous interactions with alcohol (see Figure 15.4).

Unlike the benzodiazepines, however, buspirone produces not an immediate calming effect, but a gradual reduction in tension and anxiety over a period of a few weeks. Indeed, the improvement is so subtle that some patients stop taking the drug because they think its only effects are minor dizziness and headache (Lickey & Gordon, 1991; Schnabel, 1987). However, comparative studies consistently show that, in cases of generalized anxiety disorder, buspirone has antianxiety effects equal to or greater than those of the benzodiazepines (e.g., Feighner, Merideth, & Hendrickson, 1982; Schnabel, 1987).

Antidepressants Used to Treat Anxiety Disorders. Several drugs initially developed to treat depression are also effective at relieving some symptoms of anxiety disorders. In particular, monoamine oxidase inhibitors such as phenelzine (Nardil) and tricyclic antidepressants such as imipramine (Tofranil) can successfully abort many panic attacks. After taking these drugs for several weeks, panic disorder patients may experience the increased autonomic arousal associated with the beginnings of an attack, but the symptoms then diminish and panic never materializes (Klein, Ross, & Cohen, 1987). Several studies show that about 8 weeks of treatment with these antidepressants allow up to 50 percent of patients to be panic free. In patients who are able to tolerate the side effects associated with higher doses, success rates are even higher (e.g., Mavissakalian, 1990; Mavissakalian & Perel, 1995; Schweizer et al., 1993). Interestingly, these drugs appear to specifically affect panic attacks; they do not produce general feelings of relaxation, nor do they necessarily reduce feelings of agoraphobia, which are often the most debilitating feature of panic disorder.

Other antidepressants—especially the SSRIs—have also been shown to have significant antipanic effects, with relatively few side effects. Approximately three quarters of patients with panic disorder can be essentially free of symptoms after 8 weeks of treatment with an SSRI (Black et al., 1993).

Antidepressants have also been used to treat agoraphobia, but, when used without some form of behavioral or cognitive-behavioral retraining, they have little effect on the avoidance components of the disorder. When medication is combined with gradual exposure techniques, the two treatment approaches appear to enhance each other's benefits, leading to reduced agoraphobic avoidance (Klein et al., 1987; Mavissakalian, 1990).

Finally, certain antidepressants have been found useful in treating obsessive-compulsive disorder, one of the most resistant of the anxiety disorders. In particular, antidepressants that inhibit the reuptake of serotonin appear to have antiobsessive effects. The most commonly used antidepressant for OCD is *clomipramine* (Anafranil), although SSRIs such as *fluoxetine* (Prozac) and *sertraline* (Zoloft) appear to be effective as well (Behkelfat et al., 1989; Jenike et al., 1990; Lickey & Gordon, 1991). Patients taking these drugs for OCD do not typically experience observable benefits for up to 5 weeks, and it may take as many as 10 weeks to achieve full therapeutic effects (Lickey & Gordon, 1991). Even then, the patients' obsessions and compulsions may still be present, but in a less intrusive and less anxiety-provoking form (Lickey & Gordon, 1991). Indeed, although 50 to 75 percent of OCD patients show clinically significant improvement from these medications, few are symptom free (Lickey & Gordon, 1991). As always, side effects are severe enough in some patients to make it difficult for them to continue treatment. It is particularly unfortunate that clomipramine, the drug most effective for treating OCD, has the most bothersome side effects, including nausea, fatigue, and headache (Jenike et al., 1990).

Drugs for the Treatment of Schizophrenia and Other Psychoses

The discovery in the early 1950s of a group of drugs variously called *antipsychotics, major tranquilizers,* or *neuroleptics* revolutionized the treatment of severe mental disorders. The various names used for this class of drugs refer to various aspects of their effects on behavior: they reduce the symptoms of psychosis, have a sedating effect on agitated behavior, and sometimes create neuroleptic side effects involving rigidity and movement difficulties.

When given to severely disturbed mental patients—especially those diagnosed as schizophrenic—these drugs dramatically reduce the intensity of schizophrenia's positive symptoms, such as hallucinations, delusions, paranoia, disordered thinking, and incoherence. Patients who enter the hospital hearing hallucinated voices or feeling driven by intense delusions can be free of most of these symptoms within a few weeks of drug therapy. In addition, their fears are often reduced dramatically, and their incoherent speech becomes more logical and organized. In some cases, intense agitation diminishes within a matter of hours. The negative symptoms of schizophrenia, such as withdrawal, muteness, and negativism, are less dramatically affected, but even these symptoms can be reduced somewhat by these drugs.

Decades of research show that, overall, 60 to 70 percent of patients receiving antipsychotic drugs show some improvement. Thousands of patients, many of whom had been hospitalized for decades, have at last been able to leave the institution, largely because of drug-induced improvements (review Figure 15.1 on page 538). For those who have remained hospitalized, neuroleptic drugs have all but eliminated the need for straightjackets, padded cells, and other once-common restraints. However, antipsychotic drugs are not a panacea; fewer than 30 percent of schizophrenic patients respond well enough to live entirely on their own.

As Table 15.3 shows, there are several general classes of antipsychotic drugs. The first widely used antipsychotic drug, *chlorpromazine,* is one of the *phenothiazines,* the best-known of these classes. Chlorpromazine was used by French surgeon Henri Labroit as a preoperative medicine to reduce surgical shock. Labroit then recommended it to French psychiatrists who began to use it to treat mental patients in the 1950s. Chlorpromazine appeared in the United States as Thorazine in 1955. A second type of antipsychotic compound, called *reserpine* (Serpasil), was discovered at about the same time as chlorpromazine, but the severity of its side effects

made it a seldom-used alternative. Yet another antipsychotic drug, called haloperidol (Haldol), was developed in the 1960s. Haloperidol has much the same antipsychotic effects as the phenothiazines but produces less sedation.

Typical Neuroleptics. The phenothiazines are the largest class of antipsychotics and include such widely used drugs as thioridazine (Mellaril), fluphenazine (Prolixin), and trifluoperazine (Stelazine). These drugs, along with other classes of antipsychotics, are called *typical neuroleptics.* They are thought to exert their therapeutic benefits by blocking the action of the neurotransmitter dopamine. They do so by acting as dopamine antagonists, that is, they block the neurotransmitter's effect on a specific type of receptor called the D_2 receptor (List & Cleghorn, 1993). The more effective an antipsychotic drug is at blocking these dopamine receptors, the more potent are its antipsychotic effects.

Side Effects of the Typical Neuroleptics. The seemingly miraculous ability of the typical neuroleptics to reduce psychotic symptoms does not come without a

TABLE 15.3   Antipsychotics (Neuroleptics)

Generic/chemical name	Trade name	Therapeutic dose range (mg/day)
Phenothiazines		
Chlorpromazine	Thorazine	50–2000
Perphenazine	Trilafon	8–64
Trifluperazine	Stelazine	4–60
Fluphenazine	Prolixin	2–60
Mesoridazine	Serentil	25–400
Thioridazine	Mellaril	200–600
Thioxanthenes		
Clorprothixene	Taractan	75–600
Thiothixene	Navane	6–120
Butyrophenones		
Haloperidol	Haldol	2–100
Pimozide	Orap	2–20
Dibenzoxazepines		
Loxapine	Loxitane	20–120
Other and atypical neuroleptics		
Molindone	Moban	15–225
Clozapine	Clozaril	100–600
Risperidone	Risperdal	4–8

Source: Hollister & Csernansky, 1991, p. 108; *Physicians' Desk Reference.*

cost in side effects that range from treatable nuisances to incapacitating, irreversible, even life-threatening conditions. Many of these side effects are attributable to the fact that the typical neuroleptics block the action of dopamine and other neurotransmitters in *all* areas of the brain, not just those associated with psychotic symptoms.

The merely bothersome side effects include dry mouth, blurred vision, constipation, postural hypotension, and urinary retention, among others. For some patients, these side effects remain troublesome enough to result in treatment termination and the subsequent return of psychotic symptoms. In many cases, however, these problems are treatable, or eventually diminish on their own.

Unfortunately, blockage of dopamine often results in more severe side effects. Dopamine blockage in the basal ganglia, for example, brings about a number of movement disorders known as *extrapyramidal symptoms.* One of these is **Parkinsonism,** a condition that mimics some of the symptoms of Parkinson's disease such as a fine tremor of the hands; a slow, shuffling gait; a blank facial expression; muscular weakness and rigidity; and slowed movement. Parkinsonism, which affects up to 50 percent of outpatients treated with typical neuroleptics, results when the dopamine level drops enough to be out of balance with another neurotransmitter, *acetylcholine.* These side effects can be reduced or eliminated by administering *anticholinergic* drugs that lower the level of acetylcholine and thus restore its balance with dopamine.

A second set of extrapyramidal side effects involves **acute dystonia,** a syndrome of uncontrollable contractions of muscles in the head, neck, tongue, back, and eyes. Patients with this syndrome exhibit a rapid series of spasmodic body contortions; their eyes may roll back into their heads, giving the appearance of a seizure. A third pattern of extrapyramidal symptoms is called **acute akathesia,** in which the patient appears uncontrollably restless and agitated. People suffering this disorder feel the constant need to keep their limbs moving and experience a sense of discomfort if they remain still for too long. Dystonia and akathesia are largely reversed by anti-Parkinsonism medications or by reducing the dose of the neuroleptic causing them (Lickey & Gordon, 1991).

Tardive dyskinesia, or TD, is perhaps the most serious movement disorder associated with the typical

Connections

What are the implications of the typical antipsychotic medications for the dopamine theory of schizophrenia? See Chapter 10, p. 358.

neuroleptics. The symptoms of tardive dyskinesia include grotesque spasmodic jerks, tics, and twitches of the face, tongue, trunk, and limbs. The lips make smacking and sucking sounds, the jaw moves laterally, the limbs may writhe uncontrollably, and speech is progressively impaired (Kahn et al., 1994). As the disorder progresses, these involuntary movements spread to larger portions of the body. Although the cause of TD is not fully understood, it is thought to result when long-term blockage of dopamine receptors in the basal ganglia causes more movement-relevant dopamine receptors to develop. These additional receptors appear to become ever more sensitive until they generate virtually uncontrollable movements.

Unfortunately, TD symptoms typically do not appear until after patients have taken neuroleptics for several years, at which point the disorder is essentially irreversible. TD tends to intensify as neuroleptic treatment continues, but abrupt termination of the drug only makes the TD symptoms worse. Only if TD is identified in its early stages, and if patients can be kept off of neuroleptic medication for as long as 18 months, are many of the TD symptoms likely to diminish (APA, 1994; Glazer et al., 1984). One of the most unfortunate aspects of TD is that, in the process of bringing patients' schizophrenic symptoms under control, the movement disorders sometimes caused by neuroleptics can leave patients so socially disabled that they are no better able to function in public than when they displayed schizophrenia (APA, 1994; Lickey & Gordon, 1991).

Age is the most consistent predictor of which patients will develop TD. Older patients are more likely to develop the disorder, regardless of how long they have taken the drug. Accordingly, while TD affects about 20 to 30 percent of all hospitalized patients on neuroleptics, it is seen in as many as 50 percent of elderly patients (APA, 1994; Morgenstern & Glazer, 1993; Yassa et al., 1992). The *severity* of TD tends to increase as treatment progresses and with higher neuroleptic doses, regardless of which neuroleptic is prescribed (Morgenstern & Glazer, 1993).

A final, thankfully rare, side effect of neuroleptic drugs is **neuroleptic malignant syndrome,** a potentially fatal disorder involving extremely high fever, muscle rigidity, and irregular heart rate and blood pressure. This disorder appears in approximately 1 percent of treated patients within the first few days of taking neuroleptics and is fatal for about 20 percent of those who develop it (APA, 1994; Lickey & Gordon, 1991; Velamoor et al., 1994).

With all these side effects in mind, physicians are well advised to use the lowest effective dosage of neuroleptic medication for the shortest time possible; long-term medication is recommended only for patients for whom there is no safer alternative.

Atypical Neuroleptics. Concern over the potentially devastating side effects of the typical neuroleptics has motivated psychopharmacologists to search for safer drugs to treat schizophrenia and other forms of severe psychosis. One recent discovery, *clozapine* (Clozaril), appears to be an extremely effective alternative for treating patients who either do not respond to standard neuroleptics or who cannot tolerate their side effects. Clozapine reduces both positive and negative symptoms of schizophrenia for 30 to 60 percent of patients who had shown little or no response to previous treatment with neuroleptics (Breier et al., 1994; Kane et al., 1988; Pickar et al., 1992). Furthermore, some studies show clozapine to be more effective than other neuroleptics at reducing negative symptoms such as apathy and withdrawal (Breier et al., 1994; Kane et al., 1988; Pickar et al., 1992).

Clozapine's mechanism of action is not yet completely understood. It differs from the other neuroleptics in that it has a greater effect on the D_4 dopamine receptors, but only a weak effect on D_2 receptors. It is also a potent antagonist of several other neurotransmitters including serotonin, norepinephrine, histamine, and muscarinic acid (Lieberman, 1993; Pickar et al., 1992). It may be that these combined effects bring about a rebalancing of all these neurotransmitters, which, in turn, accounts for clozapine's impact on both positive and negative symptoms of schizophrenia (Tandon & Kane, 1993). If supported by future research, this hypothesis would offer another challenge to the dopamine theory of schizophrenia (see Chapter 10).

Clozapine does not appear to create the extrapyramidal symptoms or the tardive dyskinesia associated with other antipsychotic drugs, but it does have some negative side effects, including sedation, dizziness, constipation, and excessive salivation that results in drooling, especially during sleep. Of greatest concern, however, is that approximately 1 to 2 percent of those who take clozapine develop a potentially fatal blood disease called **agranulocytosis,** in which there is a loss of white blood cells. The risk of agranulocytosis is increased in women and older patients. To prevent this disease, patients are required to have weekly white cell counts before being given the next week's medication. As a result of this careful monitoring, the worldwide incidence of clozapine-related fatalities has been kept extremely low.

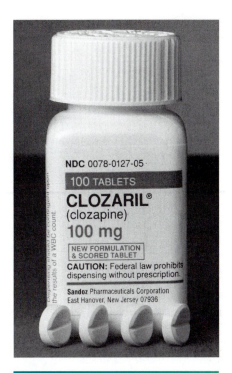

Clozapine (sold as Clozaril) is called an atypical antipsychotic because it acts on a different pattern and type of dopamine receptor (along with serotonin) than most antipsychotic drugs. Because it has fewer negative side effects and helps a significant percentage of schizophrenics who have not responded to typical antipsychotics, Clozaril is regarded as one of the most promising drug treatments for schizophrenia.

However, the extensive testing of patients' blood, along with the price of the medication itself, has put the cost of a clozapine program at $4,000 to $10,000 per patient per year (Breier et al., 1994; Lickey & Gordon, 1991). For many of the patients who need it most, clozapine treatment is unaffordable, and, although competition among drug manufacturers will ultimately bring the cost down, it may still remain too expensive for many patients.

New antipsychotic drugs are constantly under development. In 1994, a drug called *risperidone* (Risperdal) was approved by the U.S. Food and Drug Administration. Risperdal blocks both serotonin and D_2 dopamine receptors, and it has been reported to lessen both positive and negative symptoms of schizophrenia. Another new antipsychotic— *olanzapine* (Zyprexia)—was approved by the FDA in 1996.

David L. Dunner

Psychoactive Drugs

David Dunner, M.D., is Professor and Vice-Chairman of Clinical Services in Psychiatry and Behavioral Sciences and Director of Outpatient Psychiatry at the University of Washington Medical School.

Q *Do psychotropic drugs exert their therapeutic effects primarily by altering basic causal processes or by altering symptoms?*

A I don't think it matters. It's clear to me we don't know how any treatment works. We don't know how drugs work. We don't know how psychotherapy works. We have a lot of outcome data that says if you have this kind of depression, of this severity, treat it this way. I'm pragmatic. I like to find what helps people get better. Use it and don't worry about why or how.

> *I'm pragmatic. I like to find what helps people get better.*

Q *With all the treatments available today, how do you choose which treatment to administer?*

A In the case of depression, for example, several types of information can help guide that decision. First, you need to know what type of depression it is. Is it bipolar or unipolar? Acute episode or chronic? How severe is the disorder? If someone has an acute first episode depression that's mild, I would recommend psychotherapy alone, perhaps cognitive-behavior therapy. If it's an acute episode of moderate severity, I would recommend a medication. If it's an

acute episode that's severe, I recommend hospitalization and perhaps ECT. If the patient has chronic depression, I would recommend a medication *and* psychotherapy. And if the depression is recurrent and requires maintenance psychotherapy, I would suggest that the patient get medication and therapy with the idea that the medication would be continued long term and that the patient would get psychotherapy for recurrences. If the patient is treatment-resistant, I would recommend sequential drug treatments coupled with psychotherapy and ECT.

Q *A lot of concerns have been raised about Prozac because it is so effective and seems to be increasingly prescribed. Are you concerned about overprescription of Prozac?*

A No. I think that only one third of patients with depression are being correctly diagnosed. So, if anything, not enough antidepressants are being prescribed, rather than people getting antidepressants for inappropriate reasons. One of the interesting things about medication is that the milder the illness, the less tolerated the medication because of its side effects.

Q *What's your feeling about ECT in general?*

A I think ECT is a terrific treatment for severe depression, for psychotic depression, and

for treatment-resistant depression. One problem is that ECT was administered badly in the early days. It's handled much better now so there are really few complications. If I had a serious, psychotic depression, I'd want ECT over medication. In general, it's a safe, effective, and well-tolerated treatment.

Q *What changes can we expect to see in the biological treatment of mental disorders in the next decade?*

A Overall, I think that treatments are going to need to be more focused. For example, I think the emphasis is going to be on recognizing the patient who's depressed, making a determination of how he or she might best be treated, and how long that treatment needs to last. I think it's clear that drug treatments need to be continued longer than they usually have been. Very few people are being treated for an acute depressive episode for 6 to 9 months even though that may be how much treatment it takes; likewise, very few people with recurrent depression are being treated with maintenance therapy.

Psychotherapy is going to need to be more focused as well. Cost constraints make it less practical to deliver 12 to 20 weeks of a therapy. You need to offer psychotherapies that are briefer and more specific, like cognitive-behavioral therapy.

Drugs for the Treatment of Attention-Deficit/Hyperactivity Disorder

The use of stimulant drugs for children displaying attention-deficit/hyperactivity disorder (ADHD) is both the most prevalent and the most controversial form of treatment for childhood mental disorders (Henker & Whalen, 1989). Estimates suggest that by the mid-1990s more than 2 million children in the United States were taking some form of psychostimulant to control ADHD symptoms.

The psychostimulant most frequently used for children with ADHD is *methylphenidate* (Ritalin). A chemical variant of amphetamine, Ritalin facilitates the release of norepinephrine and dopamine and blocks their reuptake, making them more available in the synapse. A less commonly used stimulant called *pemoline* (Cylert) differs chemically from Ritalin in that it mimics rather than facilitates dopamine. However, by activating neural circuits that use dopamine, Cylert creates behavioral effects similar to those of Ritalin (Kroft & Cole, 1992). Another, less often prescribed, psychostimulant for ADHD is *dextroamphetamine* (Dexedrine) whose chemical structure and effects are similar to those of methylphenidate.

Stimulant drugs are popular for ADHD because most studies show them to be effective at decreasing disruptive behaviors in school and in free play for 75 percent of treated children (Henker & Whalen, 1989). Other behavioral changes attributed to stimulant drug treatment include decreases in demanding behaviors, increases in "on-task" behavior, and greater classroom productivity (Evans & Pelham, 1991; Henker & Whalen, 1989). As treated children become more attentive, they appear calmer and more able to inhibit inappropriate behaviors, thus allowing teachers and other adults to interact with them in more meaningful ways (Henker & Whalen, 1989).

It was once thought that giving hyperactive children a stimulant that calmed them down involved a paradoxical effect. It was further believed that this paradoxical effect was a sign of an abnormality peculiar to ADHD children. It now appears that, particularly at relatively low doses, these drugs help attention and concentration in most users, not just ADHD children. Thus, children and adults receiving Ritalin and related drugs are better able to focus on academic tasks.

As with many other psychoactive drugs, the effects of stimulants last only while they are present in the body—in this case, about 4 to 5 hours. Indeed, if the drug is discontinued, ADHD children often experience a *rebound effect* in which inattention, hyperactivity, and impulsivity are stronger than ever (Evans & Pelham, 1991). Thus, it is common for ADHD children to continue taking stimulant medication into adolescence and even adulthood (Evans & Pelham, 1991).

Such extended medication programs are controversial because, although there is little question about the short-term benefits of stimulant drugs on ADHD symptoms, there is concern over their long-term effects (Henker & Whalen, 1989). Among these are the possible psychological and social consequences of keeping children on drugs. Telling children they must take a drug because they cannot control their own behavior might make them feel different from, and perhaps inferior to, their peers. If they come to think of self-control as something that requires a pill, they might never develop a secure sense of their own abilities, leaving them vulnerable to later behavioral and psychological problems (Schwartz & Johnson, 1985; Henker & Whalen, 1989). These are real possibilities, but proponents of stimulant medication point out that ADHD children's confidence and social development could also be undermined if, without drugs, their behavior is so poorly controlled that they fail in school or are shunned by other children.

Another concern about Ritalin, in particular, relates to the fact that its use is not limited to children. An increasing number of college students and other adults are taking the drug to help them concentrate better and be more efficient at work. In fact, it is now estimated that about as many adults as children are taking Ritalin. Furthermore, abuse and recreational use of Ritalin are also on the upswing, particularly among teenagers who buy the drug on the street or from other youngsters for whom it has been prescribed.

Critics also point out that, although drugs can inhibit ADHD children's impulsive behavior, increase their attentional skills, and allow teachers and family members to interact with them more normally, they cannot teach the social and academic skills many of these children need to learn (Henker & Whalen, 1989). Accordingly, many psychologists recommend combining stimulant drug treatment with psychological and educational programs that focus on teaching academic strategies and social and personal control skills (Evans & Pelham, 1991; Henker & Whalen, 1989).

Side Effects of Psychostimulants. As with any drug treatment, the benefits of psychostimulants for ADHD children must be weighed against their side effects.

> *Connections*
>
> Do children taking Ritalin have increased or decreased feelings of self-confidence and control? See Chapter 3, pp. 96–97.

Most investigators agree that these side effects are mild compared with those of the other drugs described in this chapter. But even these mild effects may have special consequences for children as young as 3 who are just beginning their physical, social, and emotional development. For example, because these drugs tend to reduce food intake, the rate of weight and height gains among children taking the drugs often lags behind those of their age-mates. In order to allow treated children to catch up, the drugs may be discontinued during occasional *drug holidays* that correspond to school vacations (Klein & Mannuzza, 1988; Schwartz & Johnson, 1985).

The other side effects of methylphenidate (pemoline) and dextroamphetamine are essentially the same as those of any stimulant. They include insomnia, abdominal pain, headache, proneness to crying, nervous habits and tics, and increased heart rate and blood pressure (Gadow, 1992; Julien, 1992). There is also some evidence associating stimulant drugs with the development of Tourette's disorder, with its tic-like actions, but it is unclear whether the relationship is causal. The drugs may simply facilitate the appearance of a preexisting condition.

Ethnicity, Gender, and the Psychology of Drug Treatments

The American population is over 50 percent female and contains a growing proportion of ethnic minorities, but the vast majority of research on psychoactive drugs has focused on White males. As a result, these drugs are being prescribed for all kinds of people everywhere even though knowledge about their effects and ideal dosages is based on data from people who represent only about 20 percent of the world's population (Lin, Poland, & Nakasaki, 1993). This state of affairs is particularly troubling because there are many reasons to believe that ethnicity and gender can lead to important differences in how a person responds to a psychoactive drug. These individual differences can affect **pharmacokinetics**—the way drugs are metabolized, absorbed, distributed in the body, and excreted—as well as **pharmacodynamics,** how drugs interact with receptors and ultimately what effects they have on cognitive, behavioral, and emotional processes.

For example, biologically based differences in body weight, fat distribution, hormonal fluctuations, and metabolizing enzymes in the liver, can all affect how long a drug remains active in the body, how rapidly it is eliminated, and how long its effects linger (Lin et al., 1993). Culturally based ethnic differences—such as diet and use of indigenous herbal medicines, alcohol, and tobacco—can also have an impact on a drug's effects. So can cultural beliefs about the nature of health, illness, and medicine. People who do not believe that medicine can work are unlikely to comply with instructions to take prescribed drugs, thus rendering them ineffective (Smith, Lin, & Mendoza, 1993). The Controversy section discusses another example of how psychological factors influence drug therapies.

Ethnicity. Until recently, the need to explore gender and ethnic differences in the pharmacokinetics and pharmacodynamics of drug treatments was largely ignored. A major stimulus for the study of human diversity and drug effects came from Dr. Keh-Ming Lin, who established the Center on the Psychobiology of Ethnicity at Harbor-UCLA Medical Center Research and Education Institute in Torrance, California (Lin et al., 1993). At this center and others, scientists are now examining similarities and differences in drug responses across ethnic groups.

Some of the research shows consistent ethnic differences in responses to the tricyclic antidepressants. Studies of Chinese patients in China, for example, have indicated that they require only half the dose of TCAs to obtain the same antidepressant effect seen in Whites in the United States (Kleinman, 1981; Silver, Poland, & Lin, 1993). Other data show that Blacks seem to accumulate TCAs more quickly than Whites and thus experience quicker and more effective drug responses, but they also experience more side effects (Strickland et al., 1991).

Several other studies have demonstrated that Asians and Caucasians differ in the rate at which they metabolize benzodiazepines. Asians from China did not differ from Chinese Americans born in the United States, but both groups metabolized benzodiazepines more slowly than Caucasians from the United States (Lin, Poland, & Fleishaker, 1993).

Cross-ethnic studies of the neuroleptics, especially haloperidol, have consistently shown that Asians achieve a higher blood concentration of these drugs from a given dose than do African Americans or European Americans (Jann, Lam, & Chang, 1993). This greater blood concentration means that Asians can obtain treatment effects at lower drug doses, but extrapyramidal side effects are more prevalent as well (Strickland et al., 1991).

These results are obviously important, but there is some uncertainty about what they mean. Differences in pharmacokinetics among ethnic groups could come from various sources, including genetic

Controversy

How Important Are Placebo Effects in Drug Treatments?

Not only do personal expectations affect whether individuals continue to take prescribed drugs, but they also affect the degree to which medications bring about improvement. The power of positive expectations is revealed by the well-known **placebo effect,** in which individuals experience improvements in their physical and mental functioning even when taking a *placebo,* a pill that has no chemical effect. For example, studies comparing anxiolytics or antidepressants with placebos routinely find that at least 25 percent of patients receiving the placebo show improvements comparable with those seen in patients in the drug group. These results suggest that some of the benefits of drug therapies are due to (1) patients' belief that the drug will be helpful and (2) having an opportunity to talk to a doctor about their problems.

Indeed, one recent study suggests that having a good relationship with a therapist is as important to the success of drug treatment as it is to the success of psychotherapy. In this study, the investigators videotaped early treatment sessions and rated the quality of the therapeutic relationship for depressed clients who were taking part in the NIMH Treatment of Depression Collaborative Research Program (Krupnick et al., 1996). As described in Chapter 9, these clients had been randomly assigned to one of four treatments: cognitive therapy, interpersonal therapy, the antidepressant imipramine (plus discussions with a physician), or placebo medication (plus discussions with a physician). The results showed that the quality of the relationship with the therapist or physician was significantly related to the amount of improvement patients experienced, no matter what form of psychotherapy—or what type of medication—they received. In other words, successful drug therapy involved more than just giving the correct dosage of an actual drug. It also appeared to require a relationship that allowed patients to feel comfortable about taking a drug and discussing their reactions to it with the physician.

These findings are consistent with a conclusion reached by many clinicians, namely, that the best treatment for many mental disorders is a combination of drug therapy and psychotherapy. Such combinations are increasingly used in the treatment of schizophrenia, depression, bipolar disorder, anxiety disorders, and childhood problems, and evidence is accumulating about which combinations work best (e.g., Gould, Otto, & Pollack, 1995; Hollon, Shelton, & Loosen, 1991). Generally, a specific benefit of medications is that they bring about relatively quick relief of severe symptoms. The greatest advantages of psychotherapy are that it sometimes decreases the number of clients dropping out of treatment and it can lead to more durable changes than those achieved by drugs alone.

Thinking Critically

The study by Krupnick et al. (1996) showed that a good therapy relationship was equally important to the success of drug therapy and psychotherapy.

- What are some of the mechanisms through which the therapy relationship could affect the impact of psychoactive drugs?

- How would you design a study that could test whether client factors or therapist factors have the greater impact on the therapy relationship?

- What implications does this study have for the way psychiatrists should be trained?

---

differences in body composition or liver enzymes and differences in dietary habits. Unfortunately, the design of some studies of ethnic differences in drug responses makes it difficult to determine the degree to which these differences are due to genetic as opposed to behavioral variables.

Gender. There are clear male/female differences in drug metabolism. For example, there are gender differences in how much of a drug is absorbed through the gastrointestinal tract and into the bloodstream and how much accumulates in fat tissue. It should not be surprising, then, that several studies have found that lower doses of benzodiazepines and neuroleptics are needed to produce therapeutic responses in females compared with males and that females may also show greater side effects, including tardive dyskinesia. Furthermore, drug effects for female patients can be significantly different depending on where they are in their menstrual cycles and whether they are taking birth control pills (Yonkers et al., 1992). Flaws in research designs leave the exact relationship between gender and psychoactive drugs somewhat murky, but the fact that nearly twice as many females as males receive prescriptions for psychotropic drugs makes it imperative that research be directed to understanding this relationship more fully.

Whether in relation to gender or ethnicity, then, one dose does not fit all when it comes to drug treatment of mental disorders. As data from ever-improved research designs accumulate, mental health clinicians will be able to more precisely adjust psychoactive drug dosages to individual differences in both gender and ethnicity. The result should be maximal therapeutic effects and minimal side effects.

Revisiting the Case of Christine

Christine's dissatisfaction with antidepressants is typical of how many depressed patients feel while taking these drugs. They begin to wonder what sort of person they are without the drugs and whether they could "make it" without medication. Also typical is the fact that Christine's doctor experimented with many different drugs, trying to find the one that would work best. Drug therapy is often a process of trial and error in which, as was the case with Christine, several drugs are prescribed at the same time. Such augmentation therapy is becoming increasingly common, a testimony as much to the aggressive marketing efforts of the pharmaceutical industry as to the boldness of physicians.

Christine's continuing difficulties ultimately led her depression to be termed "treatment-resistant." Her physician raised the possibility of ECT, citing its effectiveness in such cases, but Christine adamantly refused to consider this alternative. For the past year, she has being doing reasonably well on Serzone, a relatively new antidepressant. It has had few negative side effects for Christine, and on most days she feels fairly contented with her life. She also began to see a cognitive therapist twice a month to talk about her tendencies to be shy and self-critical. As a result, Christine has gradually become more accepting of the fact that she takes antidepressants and that they can be of some help to her.

SUMMARY

Psychosurgery

In the 100 years since Burckhardt used brain surgery to treat mental illness, psychosurgery has changed considerably. Moñiz's crude leucotomy procedure was revised by Freeman, Watts, and others around the world, and evolved into various forms of the frontal and transorbital lobotomy. These procedures were initially reported to be effective, but careful evaluations ultimately showed they had minimal benefits and produced numerous adverse side effects, including about a 5 percent immediate death rate.

Modern psychosurgery procedures—particularly the cingulatomy and the stereotaxic subcaudate tractotomy—reduced the most serious side effects and allowed surgeons to make more accurate and less extensive lesions. These procedures, which

were aimed at disrupting nerve tracts that affect emotional responses, are used today primarily in cases of severe mood and anxiety disorders. Overall, 30 to 89 percent of some groups of patients who have been unresponsive to other treatments show significant improvement following psychosurgery. Unfortunately, irreversible side effects—including epileptic seizures, suicide, and personality changes—can still occur.

Convulsive Therapies

The convulsive therapies were originally developed from observations that chemically induced comas and seizures improved mental patients' conditions. By 1937, electrically induced seizures (known eventually as ECT) were being used to treat severe depressive disorders and acute manic and schizophrenic conditions. Patients risked adverse side effects ranging from memory loss and confusion to broken bones, brain damage, and death. Procedural refinements have significantly reduced, but not eliminated, side effects.

In the United States, ECT is used primarily for severe psychotic and depressive disorders that do not respond well to drug treatment and in some cases of mania and acute schizophrenic episodes. The mechanism through which ECT exerts its effects remains a mystery. Current theories focus on ECT's effects on neurotransmitters or other chemicals in the brain. Although ECT's side effects can be significant, the American Psychiatric Association and National Institute of Mental Health have concluded that its benefits (for severe mood disorders, in particular) outweigh its risks, especially if precise guidelines are observed.

Drug Treatments

Drugs are by far the most widely used biological treatment procedure for mental disorders. Antidepressant drugs are widely and successfully used to treat mood disorders such as major depression. Bipolar disorder is typically treated with lithium, which acts to diminish mania and to prevent recurrence of both manic and depressive episodes. Anticonvulsant drugs are sometimes used for patients who do not respond to lithium.

Antianxiety drugs such as the benzodiazepines are effective for short-term calming of various anxiety disorders. Unfortunately, the extended use of benzodiazepines such as Xanax can result in physical dependence, and many patients experience an anxiety rebound effect and withdrawal symptoms upon discontinuing treatment. A widely used alternative, buspirone, reduces anxiety more slowly but does not have addictive potential.

Antipsychotic or neuroleptic drugs reduce the hallucinations, incoherence, and delusions of schizophrenia and related psychotic conditions. Drugs such as the phenothiazines have allowed many former mental patients to live outside of hospitals, but these drugs can cause severe side effects, including several varieties of extrapyramidal movement disorders, tardive dyskinesia, and neuroleptic malignant syndrome. Clozapine is a newer antipsychotic drug that can help some patients who do not respond to the phenothiazines and related compounds. It has fewer side effects than traditional neuroleptics, but it can cause a potentially fatal blood disorder.

Psychostimulants such as methylphenidate are the most widely used drugs for treating children who display attention-deficit/hyperactivity disorder. These drugs reduce hyperactivity and inattention by stimulating attentive processes. Side effects of these stimulants include diminished appetite, slowed growth, and anxiety. A temporary rebound in activity occurs when the child stops taking the drug.

In spite of all that has been learned about drug treatment, there is still too little research on the differences in drug effects among people of different ethnic backgrounds and genders. Preliminary data suggest that antidepressant, antianxiety, and neuroleptic drugs are metabolized differently in men and women and in people of differing genetic and cultural backgrounds.

KEY TERMS

16

Psychotherapy

The Journey by Camille Holvoet, 1989. Oil pastel on paper, 30" x 36". Courtesy of Creative Growth Art Center.

From the Case of Marilyn

Marilyn, a married mother of two daughters, is about to meet with a clinical psychologist to talk about the nightmarish secrets that have made her so depressed that she has missed 2 weeks of work in the past month.

She has run out of excuses to give her boss about why she can't get out of bed before noon and why she feels exhausted just 2 hours later. Twice in the last week, Marilyn has locked herself in the bathroom, poured out a handful of sleeping pills, and considered ending her life. She has told no one of her despair—not her husband, not her coworkers, and certainly not her children, who think their mother just has a bad case of the flu.

Marilyn has struggled with feelings of depression ever since high school, but they have never been this bad before. Increasingly, she has felt demoralized and suicidal, but part of Marilyn isn't ready to quit yet. She called an old high school friend who had once been very depressed and asked for the name of her friend's therapist. She telephoned the therapist, but, unwilling to admit her problems, Marilyn said she was calling on behalf of a neighbor. She ultimately made an appointment with Dr. Linda Barnett but later cancelled it. She told herself she was too upset to talk. Now, she is finally at Dr. Barnett's office. Sick to her stomach with nervousness, she can barely walk through the door.

Marilyn (M), sitting down: Well I made it here, but I can hardly stand this.

Dr. Barnett (B): I'm glad you came. Sounds as if you're feeling pretty nervous about talking to me.

M: It's horrible. I can't believe I'm in this mess, and I can't imagine talking about it with anyone. No offense.

B: Well, let's give it a try. Tell me what's been happening to you.

M: I can't seem to think straight anymore. I can't concentrate. I feel like giving up. I'm too scared to know what to do. I'm 43 years old, and I'm like a little kid.

B: You've already done something; you've come to talk with me. We have some time today where I can learn a little more about what's gone wrong in your life.

M: I'm so embarrassed. I can't get a hold of myself, and I need to for my family's sake. I know I'm coming undone.

B: Sounds like you feel as if your life has slipped out of your control. Maybe you could tell me some more about what's taken place.

M: I feel like life has passed me by. I'm depressed every morning. I can't eat. All I do is sleep and cry. What am I supposed to do? This just can't be me.

B: For now, let's you and I talk some more about you. Maybe we can understand a little better what's happening. Before you leave today, we'll also talk a little about what we'll be doing after today. ■

Marilyn has begun her first session of psychotherapy. Like millions of others before her, she has finally decided to share her deepest feelings with a therapist in order to survive a personal crisis that has brought her to the brink of despair. She has begun a uniquely intimate journey in which she and her therapist will work to find ways for her to cope with her problems more effectively and to regain confidence in her life.

In previous chapters, we have offered brief discussions of how various forms of psychotherapy have been used to treat specific mental disorders. Here, we will focus more directly on psychotherapy as a general intervention, including what psychotherapy is and how it differs from, say, the advice of friends or the support of family. We will describe in some detail the various methods used by psychotherapists; we will consider research showing that psychotherapy works; and we will examine the debate about how and why therapy helps people. In doing so, we will deal with such questions as whether the effects of psychotherapy are due to specific techniques, therapists' personal qualities, or factors common to any close relationship. We will also explore whether therapists need special training to be effective and, finally, what research reveals about whether some forms of therapy are better than others.

What Is Psychotherapy?

Psychotherapy literally means "treatment of the psyche." A less colorful, but more contemporary and specific definition of psychotherapy would be "treatment of an individual's behavior disorders by a therapist using psychological methods." **Psychotherapy** is an enterprise in which a client with psychological problems interacts with a *psychotherapist* who helps the client change certain behaviors, thoughts, or emotions so that the client feels and functions better.

Psychotherapists can be psychiatrists, psychologists, clinical social workers, pastoral counselors, psychiatric nurses, or other counselors, all of whom have had some kind of special training and experience in treating people with psychological problems. As a result, they are expected to have special skills that enable them to understand their clients' problems and to intervene to alleviate those problems. These skills include specific methods that are derived from some theory about how people develop behavior disorders and how those disorders can best be addressed. In addition to specialized professional training, psychotherapists are expected to possess personal qualities that make them especially helpful. One of these qualities is the ability to show empathy with clients; that is, to listen to them with a sense of understanding and sensitivity without being judgmental. Another is the capacity for warmly supporting clients while at the same time challenging them to examine and change their behavior.

Psychotherapy Clients and Their Problems

People from all walks of life, all age groups and ethnic backgrounds, and all social classes and educational levels can benefit from psychotherapy. With a few exceptions, clients' demographic characteristics are not related to the success of therapy. For example, although Freud believed that older clients were less suitable for psychoanalysis than younger persons, empirical research suggests that—among adults at least—age has little influence on whether clients stay in therapy or benefit from it (Garfield, 1994). It is the case, however, that children and adolescents are less likely to receive psychotherapy than are adults; only about 13 percent of youngsters suffering a mental disorder receive any professional treatment during the year in which they experience the problem (Human Capital Initiative Coordinating Committee, 1996). Clients' gender is related to the use of psychotherapy services but not to its general effectiveness. Women are more likely than men to seek therapy for their problems, but males and females improve in therapy about equally overall (Garfield, 1994).

One client characteristic that *is* related to the outcome of psychotherapy is socioeconomic status. People from lower social class backgrounds tend to seek psychotherapy less often and to terminate it earlier than do clients with higher socioeconomic status (Lorion, 1978). However, for those who stay, there does not appear to be any clear-cut relationship between social class and the success of therapy. Likewise, people with higher levels of education continue in therapy longer than less-educated clients.

Poor people who also are members of ethnic minority groups are the least likely to take part in psychotherapy, but available research suggests that client ethnicity is not consistently related to psychotherapy outcome. Some studies show that people of color fare less well in therapy, while other reports indicate no ethnic differences (Sue, Zane, & Young, 1994). There is still too little research on this question, so it is premature to say whether a client's ethnic background is a significant predictor of the effects of psychotherapy, or whether members of certain ethnic groups might benefit from certain kinds of therapy. However, because there is so much variability among people—even among those from the same ethnic background—it appears unlikely that membership in a particular group is the primary determining factor of the outcome of treatment. Such differences are likely to be small compared with the effects of the type of problem the person has and the particular therapist and therapy methods that the person encounters.

For the most part, psychotherapy is an intervention that embodies values usually associated with Western cultures and traditions, including an emphasis on personal autonomy and the importance of individual achievements as a key to self-esteem. However, clients from different cultural backgrounds may exhibit different patterns of values, beliefs, and behaviors. The growing diversity of the American population, in particular, makes it incumbent on therapists to be aware that some treatment techniques and goals might not be appropriate for every client. For example, techniques that require disclosure of emotional feelings will be particularly difficult for clients from cultures that discourage such expressions, and goals that emphasize gaining emotional independence from parents might be hard to achieve for clients from cultures that discourage independence or independent thinking. In short, it is essential that therapists conduct psychotherapy in a culturally sensitive manner. More research is needed on how therapists can best address cultural factors in psychotherapy, but it is always essential that therapists consider the potential role of their clients' cultural backgrounds in planning and conducting treatment.

Indeed, cultural values are even influential in determining whether people enter psychotherapy. As already noted, there are significant differences in the degree to which members of various ethnic groups use psychotherapy and other mental health services. Studies that control for socioeconomic status show that, in general, African Americans tend to receive mental health services more frequently than European Americans, while Hispanic Americans and Asian Americans tend to receive them less frequently (Sue et al., 1994). This pattern is true for both outpatient services and for hospitalization, but the differences are greater for inpatient services, especially for involuntarily hospitalized clients, where African Americans are greatly overrepresented (Lindsey & Paul, 1989).

What problems do clients bring to therapy? One survey of 6,500 psychologists found that the most commonly treated problems in psychotherapy are (in order of frequency): (1) anxiety and depression, (2) interpersonal problems, (3) marital problems, (4) school difficulties, (5) physical complaints, (6) job-related difficulties, (7) substance abuse, (8) psychotic conditions, and (9) mental retardation (VandenBos & Stapp, 1983).

Therapist Training and Experience

The average psychotherapist sees five to ten clients per day. Some therapists specialize in one or two kinds of problems; others accept a wider range. Does their professional training help these people do a better job? Most people assume that it does, but several researchers have claimed that untrained helpers do just as well as professional therapists (Dawes, 1994; Durlak, 1979; Hattie, Sharpley, & Rogers, 1984). If this claim were true, it would be difficult to justify the many years of training that professionals undergo, or the $50 to $150 per hour fees they charge. Surprisingly, most research does indicate that clients treated by nonprofessional counselors do about as well as those treated by professionals. These results are clouded, however, by possible flaws in the research studies that have examined this issue. For example, in several studies, the nonprofessionals were supervised by professional clinicians (Nietzel & Fisher, 1981), a factor that might be critical to their success. A related finding concerns the fact that the *type* of professional training is unrelated to therapy outcome. Psychologists, social workers, and psychiatrists, for example, all do about equally well.

Training aside, do more-experienced therapists achieve better outcomes than their less-experienced colleagues? Once again, the answer is surprising: Available evidence suggests that novice therapists do about as well as seasoned therapists. What novices lack in finesse, they seem to make up for with enthusiasm. Any advantages associated with greater experience are due mainly to the fact that more senior therapists keep clients in therapy longer than less-experienced practitioners and that they do a little better with more seriously disturbed clients (Beutler, Machado, & Neufeldt, 1994; Stein & Lambert, 1995).

The results we have summarized do not mean that professional training and experience are irrelevant to the success of psychotherapy but that their impact may be less important than other factors, especially the quality of the client–therapist relationship.

The Psychotherapy Relationship

Indeed, the client–therapist relationship is probably the single most crucial component of successful psychotherapy. This is one reason why all therapists, regardless of their training or theoretical approach, attempt to build a positive therapeutic relationship or *working alliance* with their clients (Horvath & Luborsky, 1993). Carl Rogers (1951), founder of client-centered therapy, claimed that "the process of therapy is . . . synonymous with the experiential relationship between client and therapist" (p. 172). According to Sigmund Freud, the therapy relationship is the primary vehicle for showing clients how early experiences cause current problems. Other psychodynamic therapists, such as Heinz Kohut, use the therapeutic relationship to offer clients a new chance at soothing past insecurities and fears. Interpersonal therapists see the therapy relationship as a safe context in which clients have an opportunity to try out new ways of interacting with others. For behavioral and cognitive-behavioral therapists, a positive therapeutic relationship helps to encourage clients' cooperation with specific treatment techniques and recommendations.

The therapeutic relationship flourishes when client and therapist have a strong personal commitment to the therapy effort, when they communicate

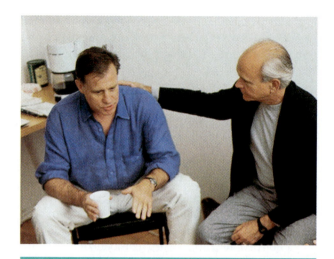

All major theoretical approaches to psychotherapy agree that a trusting, supportive relationship between therapist and client is critical to the success of psychotherapy.

clearly with each other, and when the therapist shows a genuine concern for the client's well-being (Orlinsky, Grawe, & Parks, 1994). Therapists can foster the development of this positive therapeutic bond by giving clients information early on about what to expect from therapy, especially about what the therapist's and client's responsibilities will be. In addition to developing this initial *therapeutic contract*, therapists seek to create and maintain conditions that facilitate the continued growth of a strong therapeutic relationship. For example, professional therapists are pledged to keep confidential what clients reveal in therapy. They also maintain a professional demeanor toward clients, even when the intensity and intimacy of therapy creates feelings of sexual attraction, resentment, or pity for clients. The relationship should be attentive to and supportive of the client's attempts to change, but it must never become romantic and certainly not sexually intimate. Nor should it provide an outlet for therapists' frustrations, parenting needs, or other impulses. The best therapeutic relationships develop when the *client's* welfare is the therapist's primary concern.

Hans Strupp (1989) provides additional advice for nurturing working alliances:

> a therapist (must be) human—keenly attentive, interested, caring, respectful, and empathic. . . . A therapist should never criticize, never diminish the patient's self-esteem and self-worth, and should leave no doubt about his or her commitment and willingness to help. . . . The therapist's language should be simple, straightforward, and understandable. The patient should feel that the therapist understands his or her feelings, at least a good part of the time. (p. 723)

Connections

What other important, ethical obligations do psychotherapists have? For answers, see Chapter 18, p. 637.

Methods of Psychotherapy

The work of many psychotherapists is guided by one of five theoretical models: psychoanalytic/psychodynamic, phenomenological/experiential, interpersonal, behavioral, or cognitive-behavioral. However, most therapists do not adhere rigidly to a single theoretical point of view or to its methods. The largest category of therapists—30 to 55 percent in various surveys—identify themselves as *eclectic* or *integrationist,* meaning that they combine the assumptions and procedures associated with two or more theoretical points of view (Conway, 1988; Garfield & Kurtz, 1976; Zook & Walton, 1989). Eclectics are not necessarily *anti*theoretical; they simply prefer to draw on various approaches when choosing therapeutic strategies to meet their clients' individual needs (Goldfried, 1980).

Certain methods are especially popular components of eclectic therapy strategies. One national survey in the United States found that 72 percent of eclectic therapists reported using psychodynamic principles in their version of therapy, 54 percent included cognitive methods, and 45 percent incorporated behavioral techniques (Jensen, Bergin, & Greaves, 1990). The fourth most popular component was phenomenological/experiential methods. Recently, another kind of integrated treatment—which combines psychotherapy with psychoactive medications—has become popular for dealing with mood disorders, anxiety disorders, certain childhood disorders, and schizophrenia.

Psychoanalysis

The primary goal of Freudian psychoanalysis is to help clients understand the unconscious reasons why they act in maladaptive ways, so that, after being convinced that these reasons are no longer valid, they can behave in new and more constructive ways. According to Freud (1938), the analyst helps the client make these discoveries by coming to the aid of the client's weakened ego to

> combine against the enemies, the instinctual demands of the id, and the moral demands of the superego. We form a pact with each other. [Analysts] assure [the client] of our strictest discretion and put at his service our experience in interpreting material that has been influenced by the unconscious. Our knowledge shall compensate for his ignorance and shall give his ego once more mastery over the lost provinces of his mental life.

Analysts help clients to unveil the unconscious causes of their problems by showing them how to uncover repressed material and then helping them understand what emerges. In psychoanalysis, full self-understanding is a gradual process requiring years of treatment and two types of self-exploration. First, clients must achieve conscious *insight* or recognition of the long-hidden nature of their problems. Second, they must emotionally *work through,* or examine, these insights to see how old, unconscious conflicts are still affecting their daily lives.

If Marilyn, the depressed woman described earlier, were in psychoanalysis, her analyst might sus-

Sigmund Freud (1856–1939) pioneered psychoanalysis, a form of psychotherapy that aims to help clients gain insight into long-repressed emotional conflicts. Although most research-oriented clinicians are skeptical about the effectiveness of psychoanalysis, it remains popular among many practicing therapists.

pect that her current problems stem from unconscious feelings of anger toward her mother that have their roots in her childhood. If this were true, it would not be enough for Marilyn to *intellectually* understand that she has these feelings. To be of benefit to her, this insight would have to be accompanied by an *emotional* understanding that she treats other women as if they were her mother and then repeatedly feels hurt and rebuffed by them.

Psychoanalysts use various combinations of five basic techniques to help clients gain intellectual insight into the unconscious and then work through the emotional meaning of what they find.

Free Association. The method of *free association* requires the client to say everything that comes to mind without censoring it. The rationale for this procedure is that, by removing the restrictions imposed by logic, propriety, and other rules, expressions of unconscious material will rise to consciousness. To foster relaxation and reduce distractions that might interfere with the stream of free association, the client lies on a couch while the analyst sits out of the client's view.

Free association does not eliminate all psychological defenses, so the client's speech may contain only glimpses into the unconscious. It is the analyst's task to help the client see a sensible pattern in the bits and pieces that emerge. Here is an example of a client's free association:

> My dad called last night, and, though it was nice to hear from him, I never know what to talk about once we get beyond the usual "how are you doing" part. (Long silence). I almost fell asleep for a minute there. That's something I used to do in college a lot, sleep through my classes. I remember waking up one time, and there was the professor standing right over me with the whole class laughing.

The analyst would notice that thoughts about father led to a memory about a threatening authority figure and thus may have special significance for this client, particularly if this theme is repeated in later sessions and if conflicts with authority are a source of the client's problems.

Dream Interpretation. Freud once called dreams the "royal road to an understanding of the unconscious mind" because he believed that they contain disguised expressions of unconscious wishes and conflicts. The client's description of a dream's *manifest content,* or obvious features, is seen as less important than the dream's *latent content,* the unconscious ideas and impulses symbolized by the man-

ifest content. Analysts typically look for clues to latent content as the client free associates to a dream's manifest content.

Interpretation of Everyday Behavior. In his book *The Psychopathology of Everyday Life,* Freud (1901) suggested that our day-to-day behavior often reflects unconscious conflicts and defenses. Accordingly, psychoanalysts try to maintain an "evenly divided" or "free-floating" attention to all client behaviors, whether trivial or momentous, purposeful, or apparently accidental. Slips-of-the-tongue ("I hurt you" rather than "I heard you") or jokes, for example, may reveal a client's unconscious impulses, conflicts, or defenses.

Analysts often interpret "accidental" events, especially those in which the client has at least partial responsibility, as fulfilling an unconscious, perhaps forbidden wish. The waiter who accidentally spills hot soup on an elderly male customer may be guided to insights about his lingering hostility toward his father, symbolized by the older men he must please.

Forgetfulness is another kind of "mistake" that analysts believe expresses unconscious motivation. For example, when clients forget the manifest content of a dream they were about to report, or forget certain parts when repeating the dream, the analyst may suspect that the client is trying to defend against threatening material symbolized in the dream. Even temporarily forgetting the name of a friend the client sees at a party may suggest to an analyst that the friend is linked to some unconscious feeling or impulse such as jealousy or revenge.

Analysis of Resistance. Analysts contend that clients find ways to resist coming to conscious grips with previously unconscious material, especially the most threatening or conflict-filled material. Because resistance strategies are thought to reveal habitual psychological defenses, they are a major target of psychoanalytic interpretations. Analysts interpret many behaviors as resistance, even those that appear on the surface to be unrelated to anything. Examples include cancelling a session, being late, stating a preference not to recline during treatment and, of course, unwillingness to talk about certain topics. Analysts also believe that resistance appears in *intellectualization,* a psychological defense in which the client substitutes logic and reason for the expression of emotion. Clients who talk about a parent's death only in cold, clinical terms might be seen as resistant.

Other forms of resistance are more subtle, as when a client develops a persistent cough or cold that makes it difficult to respond to the analyst's probing just as important unconscious material is about to emerge. In other cases, resistance takes the form of *acting out,* in which the client behaves in reckless or impulsive ways to escape the anxiety triggered by previously repressed material. Substance abuse, spending sprees, and other dramatic life changes signal possible acting out.

Analysis of the Transference. Freud believed that, as the client–therapist relationship develops (especially if the therapist remains neutral and detached and reveals no personal information), the client begins to unconsciously transfer to the analyst certain characteristics of significant people from the past, usually a parent. This process is known as **transference,** and as it develops, the client begins to reenact reactions, conflicts, and impulses associated with these important figures, many of whom remain at the heart of the client's difficulties. Transference reactions can appear as intense hatred or passionate love for the therapist, to name just the extremes.

Because the transference provides a glimpse into the nature of early conflicts, therapists typically analyze its meaning as a way of helping clients become aware of the origins of their current problems. This is especially true when the transference turns into **transference neurosis,** a miniature version of the client's essential problems. In such cases, the transference neurosis itself becomes the focus of treatment. If the analyst and client can correctly decode the unconscious meaning of transference reactions, the client will gradually become aware of and work through the unconscious material that the transference has vividly revealed. Because sensitive handling of the transference is thought to be so crucial to psychoanalysis, analysts are trained to be keenly alert to their own unconscious feelings toward clients—known as **countertransference**—so that these feelings do not distort the analytic process.

Variations on Psychoanalysis

Freud's views on psychotherapy were challenged as soon as he articulated them in the late 1800s, and they have continued to be the subject of heated debate. Particularly in the past 25 years, a number of scholars have subjected the major claims of psychoanalysis to careful scientific scrutiny and concluded that much of Freud's theorizing is devoid of any scientific merit and that his treatment methods often ended up doing more harm than good (e.g., Crews, 1994; Macmillan, 1991). Research-oriented therapists tend to be particularly skeptical that psychoanalysis produces any unique improvements or that it works in the ways that Freud described.

Decades before the current round of criticism emerged, many of Freud's contemporaries and followers had already broken with him and had gone on to revise or replace the principles and techniques of classic psychoanalysis with their own forms of psychodynamic therapies. Next, we will briefly review four of these variations.

Psychoanalytically Oriented Psychotherapy. Developed primarily by Franz Alexander and his colleagues (Alexander, 1956; Alexander & French, 1946) at the Chicago Psychoanalytic Institute during the 1930s and 1940s, psychoanalytically oriented psychotherapy uses basic Freudian techniques in a flexible and active manner. (More recent examples of this approach are seen in the work of Davanloo, 1994; Sifneos, 1979; and Strupp, 1989.) Clients in psychoanalytically oriented psychotherapy sit and face the therapist instead of lying on a couch, and they have one or two sessions a week rather than every day. Conversation about present problems often replaces free association. Rather than encouraging transference by maintaining a detached neutrality, the therapist offers an empathic relationship in which the client can reexperience old conflicts and, with help from the therapist, resolve them in an emotionally satisfying way. Alexander called these outcomes *corrective emotional experiences* and claimed they were the "secret of every penetrating therapeutic result" (Alexander & French, 1946, p. 338). Psychoanalytically oriented treatment usually takes much less time than traditional analysis, often lasting only 20 to 30 sessions.

Ego Analysis. Another group of analysts—including Heinz Hartman (1958), Erik Erikson (1946), and Freud's oldest daughter Anna (A. Freud, 1946)—argued that Freudian analysis was too preoccupied with unconscious sexual and aggressive motivation and that people are more capable of controlling and guiding their behavior than Freud believed. They chose to emphasize the importance of the ego and the ability of people to direct their behavior toward adaptive goals. Ego analysts employ many of Freud's techniques to explore clients' egos rather than focusing primarily on the id. They help clients understand how they have relied on various defense mechanisms to cope with personal conflicts and environmental demands.

Adler's Individual Psychology. By personal temperament and style, Alfred Adler was the early psychoanalyst who stood in most striking contrast to Sigmund Freud. Adler's main theoretical argument with Freud was that sexual and aggressive instincts are less

One of the original psychoanalysts, Alfred Adler (1870–1937) ultimately broke with Freud and developed a different analytic treatment that shares several features with modern cognitive therapies.

important forces in personality than is the striving by each individual to overcome what that person sees as personal inferiority or weakness. In Adler's Individual Psychology, mental disorders are seen as the consequence of deep-seated mistaken beliefs, leading people to develop a maladaptive *style of life* aimed at protecting themselves from perceiving their own imperfections and weaknesses.

Suppose a student has an upset stomach every day before class. Where Freud would help the client explore the defensive and unconscious significance of the stomach trouble through free association and dream interpretation, Adler would try to show the client that the symptom illustrates a neurotic lifestyle founded on mistaken attitudes and basic fictions (e.g., "If I don't do better than everyone else, my stupidity will be discovered."). Adler would also suggest alternative beliefs and attitudes on which he believed the client could build a more adaptive lifestyle and then he would encourage the client to adopt these new ideas.

Adlerian therapists interpret clients' dreams and resistances, but they concentrate on what these experiences mean in terms of current behavior and future intentions rather than in terms of unconscious conflicts. For example, Adlerians usually interpret trans-

ference as an example of mistaken beliefs leading to a faulty lifestyle, not as a sign of unconscious infantile conflicts. Adlerians also offer direct advice about the thoughts and behaviors a client might try in order to build a new lifestyle. Adler's emphasis on changing beliefs and encouraging new behaviors are strategies that subsequently became mainstays in many of the cognitive and behavioral therapies described later.

Object Relations and Self Therapy.   A popular derivative of psychoanalysis is *object relations therapy*, which has been promoted by British analysts Ronald Fairbairn (1952), Donald Winnicott (1965), and Melanie Klein (1975) and by American analysts Otto Kernberg (1976) and Heinz Kohut (1977). Object relations theorists believe that interactions between caregivers and infants in the first 3 years of life are the building blocks of adult personality and that infant–caregiver relationships guide children's expectations about close relationships for the rest of their lives.

In Kohut's view, for example, certain personality disorders are the result of an infant's receiving inadequate nurturance and empathy from a caregiver, usually the mother. In his **self psychology** approach, the analyst's task is to be a responsive, empathic therapist who, through transference, allows the client's self to be "completed" by having early unmet needs fulfilled. To Kohut, three types of special transferences are essential: (1) the *mirror transference*, in which early needs to be admired are met; (2) the *idealizing transference*, in which needs for protection and soothing are finally acknowledged; and (3) the *twinship transference*, in which needs for being close to another person who is like oneself are fulfilled.

In short, object relations therapists view the therapeutic relationship as a new opportunity for clients to obtain the emotional gratifications they were denied as infants and in later life. Rather than analyzing these needs as a Freudian would, object relations therapists offer a special type of better-late-than-never parenting to clients who were damaged by emotional deprivation in infancy. Their emphasis on empathic support, acceptance, and on providing a psychologically "holding" relationship bears a striking resemblance to many of Carl Rogers's ideas about psychotherapy (Kahn, 1985), as will be discussed later.

Interpersonal Therapies

Harry Stack Sullivan was influenced by Freud but believed that mental disorders resulted not so much from unconscious conflicts as from disturbances in interpersonal relationships, disturbances that developed out of early interactions between children and their parents and peers. A number of interpersonally oriented clinicians since Sullivan have followed his lead, arguing that mental disorders consist of "rigid, constricted, and extreme patterns of interpersonal behaviors" (Kiesler, 1986).

Because troubled clients tend to perpetuate maladaptive behaviors by provoking others to behave in ways that reinforce these behaviors, a major goal for interpersonal therapists is to counteract the clients' usual ploys. For example, the hostile dominance of an antisocial client typically influences others to be angrily submissive. The therapist tries to avoid this trap by acting in a consistently friendly and dominant manner toward the client so that ultimately the client will attempt some less coercive way of dealing with other people.

The interpersonal therapist must also help clients understand how they perpetuate conflicts by displaying extreme interpersonal styles, such as exaggerated dependence or hostility. They point out that these styles probably originated in childhood as a way of gaining acceptance and security from parents and peers, but have now become a dysfunctional and self-defeating style. To help clients recognize their maladaptive interpersonal styles, the therapist offers continuous feedback about how their actions tend to create negative interactions. The therapist also seeks to help clients learn to interact with people in more flexible and positive ways.

A different form of interpersonal therapy was developed by Myrna Weissman and Gerald Klerman for the treatment of depression (Klerman et al., 1984). This version of interpersonal treatment was one of the psychotherapies found effective in the NIMH Treatment of Depression Collaborative Research Program mentioned in Chapter 9 (Elkin, 1994). Instead of focusing on general interpersonal patterns, this approach concentrates on four interpersonal problems that constitute the social context for many cases of depression. Depending on which problems are most prominent in an individual case, the client will be helped to develop new strategies for coping with (1) prolonged grieving over the loss of a loved one; (2) conflicts between social roles (e.g., parenting versus career); (3) difficult transitions between roles (e.g., high school student living at home to college student on an unfamiliar campus); and (4) lack of interpersonal skills. The therapist attempts to help clients improve their functioning in one or more of these problem areas to reduce feelings of dependency and increase self-esteem.

Phenomenological/Experiential Therapies

Phenomenological/experiential (P/E) therapies vary considerably in their specific methods, but they share five distinguishing features that stem from the assumptions of the phenomenological approach to psychopathology (Greenberg, Elliott, & Lietaer, 1994; Fischer, 1989; see Chapter 1).

First, P/E therapists assume that a client's life is comprehensible only when viewed from the point of view of that client. Phenomenologists believe that to understand another person's behavior one must perceive the world as if looking through that person's eyes. This theme can be traced to the philosophies of Edmund Husserl, Martin Heidegger, Sören Kierkegaard, and Jean-Paul Sartre, all of whom emphasized that the meaning of life is not intrinsic but is constructed by the perceiver. The theme of individually construed reality was sharpened by a group of German psychologists—including Koffka, Köhler, and Wertheimer—who came to be known as the *Gestalt* school.

Second, many P/E therapists view human beings not as instinct-driven creatures but as naturally good people who are able to make choices about their lives and determine their own destinies. This optimistic perspective has led some versions of P/E therapies—especially those arising in North America—to be described as *humanistic* therapies. Those P/E therapists committed to European existential philosophies are less likely to insist that all clients will naturally strive toward positive goals (Fischer, 1989), but all P/E therapies aim to promote each client's growth as a unique person. This goal is referred to as **self-actualization**. The assumption is that, once clients are allowed to reach their full potentials, they will find their own solutions to personal problems.

Third, P/E therapists view the therapeutic relationship as the primary vehicle by which therapy achieves its benefits. It must be a real relationship that guarantees honest, emotionally open, interpersonal experiences for both client and therapist. Focusing on the immediate, moment-to-moment experiences in this relationship is what helps clients perceive themselves more accurately.

A fourth characteristic of P/E therapies is that clients are regarded as equals. Therapists treat them as responsible individuals who are experts on their own experiences and who must ultimately be the ones to make decisions about their lives.

Connections

To what extent does the treatment relationship influence the effects of drug therapies? See Chapter 15, p. 553.

Finally, many phenomenological/existential therapists emphasize the importance of experiencing and exploring emotions that are confusing or painful. They use several techniques to encourage emotional awareness. As research documenting the effectiveness of these techniques has accumulated (Greenberg et al., 1994), many therapists beyond the P/E school have employed them.

One popular method, known as the **empty chair technique,** is designed to increase awareness of unresolved conflicts and emotions from the past by asking the client to imagine that the person associated with the conflict (a parent, child, or spouse, for example) is sitting in an empty chair nearby. The client is then instructed to talk to the imagined person and to express—perhaps for the first time—true feelings about him or her and about events or conflicts in which that person played a part. The idea is to help clients become aware of and understand more fully some of their strongest feelings in an environment in which they feel safe and supported. It is hoped that, in the process, clients will learn to take responsibility for and master these feelings.

Prominent examples of phenomenological/existential therapies include Carl Rogers's (1951) *client-centered therapy,* Fritz Perls's *Gestalt therapy* (Perls, 1969), *existential therapy* (Bugental, 1978; May, 1969), *logotherapy* (Frankl, 1967), and *experiential therapy* (Gendlin, 1981).

Client-Centered Therapy. The best-known form of phenomenological treatment is client-centered therapy, pioneered by Carl Rogers (1942, 1951, 1954). **Client-centered therapy** emphasizes "the warmth and permissiveness of the therapist, a permissive climate in which the feelings of the client could be freely expressed, and a freedom for the client from all coercion or pressure" (Rogers, 1942).

As noted in Chapter 1, Rogers believed that the self-actualization of troubled clients had been thwarted by judgments imposed by other people. These judgments, he said, create *conditions of worth,* a sense that a person is not worthwhile unless he or she meets other people's standards. When meeting conditions of worth requires people to distort their feelings and actions, symptoms of disorder appear. Thus, in the initial case example, a client-centered therapist would not have been surprised to find that Marilyn really wanted to pursue a career in art but put aside her feelings in deference to family pressures to become an accountant. The resulting impairment in her personal growth would have been seen as a major cause of her depression. After discovering these things about Marilyn, the therapist

Carl Rogers (1902–1987) in a group treatment session. Although initially trained in psychoanalysis, Rogers (upper right) ultimately abandoned that approach and pioneered the development of client-centered therapy.

would probably encourage her to explore her original aspirations, trust them as valid motives, and consider whether to begin pursuing them.

To provide new experiences that allow personal growth to resume, the client-centered therapist tries to create a supportive and nonjudgmental relationship that does not impose conditions of worth on the client. Success in creating such a relationship requires the therapist to communicate three related attitudes, known as facilitative conditions. First, the therapist must convey *unconditional positive regard,* a willingness to accept clients as they are. Accordingly, clients are not diagnosed, evaluated, or given advice, rather, they are valued as unique individuals, no matter how problematic their behavior might be. Second, the therapist strives for *empathic understanding* by trying to see the world as the client sees it. Therapists communicate **empathy** by reflecting what they perceive of the client's feelings. Often, reflection takes the form of rephrasing the client's statements in terms that show that the therapist has recognized the emotions that underlie the words. Finally, the therapist must be *genuine* in relating to the client; all actions and feelings must be *congruent.* Being congruent and genuine requires therapists to say what they feel, tactfully, but free from hypocrisy and pretense. Ideally, once clients begin to experience, perhaps for the first time, a relationship in which someone offers nonjudgmental support, empathy, and genuineness, their confidence will increase and their progress toward self-actualization should resume.

Here is an edited portion of a treatment session in which Carl Rogers (R) works with a 28-year-old man hospitalized for schizophrenia (Meador & Rogers, 1973; pp. 139–144). At the time of this session, he had been treating "Jim" (J) for about 11 months. Even though some progress had occurred, Jim was still withdrawn.

R: Do you look kind of angry this morning, or is that my imagination? (Jim shakes his head slightly.) Not angry, huh? (silence of 1 minute, 26 seconds)

R: Feel like letting me in on what is going on? (silence of 12 minutes, 52 seconds)

R: I kind of feel like saying that "If it would be of any help at all I'd like to come in." On the other hand if it's something you'd rather—if you just feel more like being within yourself, why that's okay too—I guess another thing I'm saying, really, in saying that is, "I do care. I'm not just sitting here like a stick." (silence of 1 minute, 11 seconds)

R: And I guess your silence is saying to me either you don't want to or can't come out right now and that's okay. So I won't pester you but I just want you to know, I'm here. (silence of 17 minutes, 41 seconds)

[After two more unanswered comments over the next minute or so, Rogers continues.]

R: Maybe this morning you just wish I'd shut up—and maybe I should, but I just keep feeling I'd like to—I don't know, be in touch with you in some way. (silence of 2 minutes, 21 seconds)

[Jim yawns.]

R: Sounds discouraged or tired. (silence of 41 seconds)

J: No. Just lousy.

R: Everything's lousy, huh? You feel lousy? . . .

J: No.

R: No? (silence of 20 seconds)

J: No, I just ain't no good to nobody, never was, and never will be.

R: Feeling that now, hm? That you're just no good to yourself, no good to anybody. Just that you're completely worthless, huh? . . .

J: Yeah. That's what this guy I went to town with just the other day told me . . .

R: I guess the meaning of that, if I get it right, is that here's somebody that—meant something to you and what does he think of you? Why, he's told you that he thinks you're no good at all. And that really knocks the props out from under you. [Jim weeps quietly.] It just brings the tears.

J: I don't care though.

R: You tell yourself you don't care at all, but somehow I guess some part of you cares because some part of you weeps over it . . .

J: I guess I always knew it.

R: If I'm getting that right, it is that what makes it hurt worst of all is that when he tells you you're no good, well shucks, that's what you've always felt about yourself. Is that—the meaning of what you're saying? Jim nods in [agreement]. . . So that between his saying so and your perhaps feeling it underneath, you just feel about as no-good as anybody could feel.

[Jim continues to cry and, after several more minutes of reflecting the sad, hopeless feelings being expressed, Rogers ends the interview. Three days later another session takes place. After some initial comments by Rogers, Jim breaks in]:

J: I'm gonna take off.

R: You're going to take off? Really run away from here? . . . I know you don't like the place but it must be something special came up or something?

J: I just want to run away and die.

R: M-hm, m-hm, m-hm. It isn't even that you want to get away from here *to* something. You just want to leave here and go away and die in a corner, hm? . . . Can't help but wonder whether it's still true that some things this friend said to you—are those still part of the thing that makes you feel so awful?

J: In general, yes.

[The next 30 minutes are taken up in further reflection of Jim's negative feelings and in silences of up to 13 minutes.]

J: I might go today. Where, I don't know, but I don't care.

R: Just feel your mind is made up and that you're going to leave. (silence of 53 seconds)

J: That's why I want to go, 'cause I don't care what happens.

R: M-hm, m-hm. That's why you want to go, because you really don't care about yourself. You just don't care *what* happens. And I guess I'd just like to say—I care about you. And I care what happens.

[After a 30-second silence, the client bursts into violent sobs. For the next 15 minutes or so, Rogers reflects on the intense emotions that pour forth.]

According to Rogers, this is an important moment of change.

> Jim Brown, who sees himself as stubborn, bitter, mistreated, worthless, useless, hopeless, unloved, unlovable, experiences my caring. In that moment his defensive shell cracks wide open, and can never again be quite the same. (Meador & Rogers, 1973, p. 145)

This client left the hospital after several more months of treatment; 8 years later he reported to Rogers that he was happy, employed, and living on his own.

Gestalt Therapy. Another form of phenomenological treatment, known as Gestalt therapy, was developed by Fritz Perls, a psychoanalytically trained therapist who eventually rejected psychodynamic theories to found a tradition of his own. Perls emphasized the idea that there are gaps or distortions in peoples' awareness of their genuine feelings and that these gaps are primarily responsible for impaired personal growth and consequent behavioral disturbances. He noted, for example, that people often find it difficult to directly experience and express emotions like anger or the need for love. Instead, they develop manipulative social games or phony roles to try—usually unsuccessfully—to satisfy their needs indirectly. As people devote more and more energy to distorted roles and burdensome

Fritz Perls (1893–1970). After Carl Rogers, Friedrich S. (Fritz) Perls was the best-known phenomenologically oriented therapist. Perls introduced Gestalt therapy, which aims at helping clients increase their awareness and acceptance of genuine feelings that they had come to deny.

games, their lives become more and more limited and unhappy.

Worse still, said Perls, these ploys lead people to believe that they are not responsible for their own behavior. They become so ready to blame their problems on other people or on circumstances that they eventually feel powerless. Marilyn's complaint that she feels like a little kid might be an example of this perceived helplessness. Perls warned that the problems created by clients' lack of awareness of genuine feelings and consequent game-playing usually invade the therapy room. For example, while most clients deny it, many really want the therapist to solve their problems for them.

Like other P/E clinicians, Gestalt therapists try to reestablish clients' personal growth and sense of responsibility for change. **Gestalt therapy** focuses on helping clients to (1) become aware of the feelings and needs that they have disowned and (2) recognize that these feelings and needs are a genuine part of themselves that should be accepted and even celebrated. Perls believed that, by reexamining what he called "unfinished business," clients will be more likely to take responsibility for the way they really are instead of maintaining a phony self-image.

The growth-enhancing potential of the client–therapist relationship is strongly emphasized in Gestalt therapy, but the therapist is more active and confrontive than in client-centered therapy. For example, rather than listening and waiting for clients to gradually confront genuine feelings, Gestalt therapists challenge clients whenever they suspect them of being defensive or disingenuous.

An important assumption underlying this approach is that talking about the past gets clients nowhere; they must reexperience old hurts, resentments, jealousies, and fears if these feelings are ever to be understood, accepted, and defanged. Gestalt therapists use a variety of techniques to activate past experiences and help clients work through them. For example, as the client speaks, the therapist might point out certain postures or other nonverbal behavior—such as twisting a handkerchief or tapping a foot. The therapist might then instruct the client to "become" the clasping hands or the tapping foot and to say what these body parts are trying to express about the person or event the client had been talking about. Clients are also often asked to role-play significant people in their lives or to enact one of their own typical, game-playing manipulations. They might be asked, too, to give voice to internal dialogs in which they express the feelings of the part of them that wants to take a new job and the part that is afraid of failing at it. Indeed, empty chair dialogs are a hallmark of Gestalt therapy.

These methods not only help people to become more aware of genuine feelings, they may also reduce emotional upset. In one laboratory study, college students spent 20 minutes expressing their feelings about an upsetting event to an empty chair (Conoley et al., 1983). The students' blood pressure and self-reports of anger were measured before and after the experience. Compared with a group of students who spent the same amount of time expressing their feelings to an experimenter, the "empty chair" students showed lower blood pressure and reduced anger. Similar results have been reported with clients in psychotherapy sessions (Greenberg et al., 1994).

Behavioral Therapies

The term *behavior therapy* was first used in a 1953 paper, coauthored by B. F. Skinner, that described an operant conditioning treatment for psychotic patients (Lindsley, Skinner, & Solomon, 1953). Over the next 20 years, several other therapists, including Arnold Lazarus, Joseph Wolpe, and Hans Eysenck used the term (or similar designations, such as *behavior modification*) to describe an approach to psychotherapy that viewed disordered behavior as learned and that aimed to literally teach clients to behave more adaptively.

Originally, behavior therapy was guided primarily by empirical research on the basic learning principles associated with classical and operant conditioning. Over the last 20 years, however, behavior therapy methods have broadened to reflect the latest research on perception, cognition, and biological bases of behavior (Viken & McFall, 1994). As a result, **behavior therapy** now includes techniques aimed at helping clients to (1) decrease maladaptive behaviors and develop or increase more adaptive ones; (2) replace self-defeating or counterproductive thoughts with more rational ones; and (3) control disruptive emotions. Like Gestalt therapy, behavior therapy focuses on the here and now. Less attention is paid to early childhood history than to what current skills the client does or doesn't have and what environmental conditions serve to maintain maladaptive thoughts, actions, and emotions. Behavior therapy interventions, in turn, are aimed at specific, measurable targets, such as improving particular social skills, reducing phobias, or practicing self-rewarding thoughts to improve job performance under stress. We will briefly describe some of the many behavioral techniques used to bring about these changes.

Systematic Desensitization. Developed by Joseph Wolpe in the 1950s, **systematic desensitization** is a treatment for phobias and other forms of maladaptive anxiety. Wolpe based this treatment on methods he had developed for reducing cats' fear of cages in which they had previously received electric shocks. The cats refused to eat in those cages but, relying on a principle called *reciprocal inhibition*, Wolpe was able to reduce their anxiety by hand-feeding the animals in places that were closer and closer to the feared cages. Wolpe reasoned that an animal could not be anxious and relaxed at the same time and that the relaxation associated with eating could inhibit fear if the feared situation were approached gradually enough. Applying reciprocal inhibition to human fears, Wolpe began desensitization by teaching phobic clients a set of relaxation exercises that bring about reduced sympathetic nervous system arousal (Bernstein & Borkovec, 1973; see Chapter 1). Next, the client is exposed to a hierarchy of gradually more anxiety-arousing stimuli. In *in vivo* desensitization, clients are gradually exposed to the actual stimuli they fear; in *imaginal* desensitization, clients merely visualize increasingly frightening stimuli. In either case, it is crucial that the client learn to be relaxed at one level of the hierarchy before attempting to deal with the next one. As progress is made, clients are encouraged to consolidate their gains by exposing themselves to newly conquered stimuli outside of therapy.

One of the best-researched psychotherapy techniques in use today, systematic desensitization is effective for phobias of well-defined stimuli such as dogs or heights. It is less successful for the diffuse anxiety seen in panic attacks, obsessive-compulsive disorder, agoraphobia, or social phobias. These problems are usually more successfully treated with exposure treatments.

Exposure Treatments. Like *in vivo* desensitization, **exposure treatments** entail direct exposure to frightening stimuli, but the idea behind exposure methods is to allow anxiety to occur and to continue until it eventually disappears through the process of extinction. In a procedure known as **flooding**, for example, exposure to a feared stimulus is intense and prolonged, lasting as long as 2 hours in some cases. Some therapists prefer more gradual, self-paced exposures but, either way, the goal is to help clients stay in contact with a feared stimulus in order to learn that it holds no real danger. When appropriate, exposure methods are accompanied by **response prevention**, meaning that clients are not

Connections

How successful are exposure and response prevention techniques in the treatment of obsessive-compulsive disorder? See Chapter 7, p. 237.

allowed to perform any rituals they might normally use to reduce anxiety. Such rituals dilute the exposure to the feared stimulus and serve to maintain the false belief that the stimulus is harmful.

Social Skills Training. Behavior therapists believe that deficiencies in social skills contribute to some mental disorders. For example, severe social skills deficits can lead a person to feel demoralized, anxious, resentful, or depressed. Social skills training includes many techniques, one of the most common of which is **assertiveness training,** which helps people express their feelings and wants more clearly and effectively. Unlike aggressiveness, assertiveness is defined as the appropriate expression of feeling in ways that do not infringe on the rights of others (Alberti & Emmons, 1974; Wolpe & Lazarus, 1966). Refusing your boss's unreasonable request requires assertiveness, as does telling your friends that you appreciated their recent show of support. All too often, people know how they would *like* to act in social situations, but, because of thoughts such as "I shouldn't make a fuss," they suffer in silence. Increased social awkwardness, self-blame, and varying degrees of depression are common results.

Assertiveness training usually has four components: (1) distinguishing assertiveness from aggression and submissiveness; (2) discussing personal rights and the rights of others in a variety of situations; (3) identifying and eliminating cognitive obstacles to assertiveness; and (4) practicing assertive behavior. This last component usually begins with a rehearsal of difficult social interactions in which the therapist demonstrates appropriately assertive behavior for the client. Next, the client tries the same behavior, and suggestions are made for improvement. After additional rehearsals, the client tries the new thoughts and actions in real-life settings. Successes and failures are then analyzed, and new or revised skills are developed and practiced.

Although initially focused on the "refusal skills" needed to ward off pushy people, assertiveness training now aims at developing many other aspects of effective interpersonal functioning, including conversational skills (Hansen, St. Lawrence, & Christoff, 1989), social problem solving (Kazdin et al., 1987), and responding appropriately to emotional provocations (Tisdelle & St. Lawrence, 1988). Accordingly, assertiveness training is offered to couples experiencing marital discord, college students with interpersonal problems, shy and introverted adults, alcoholics, drug abusers, socially awkward adolescents, and even to people who rely on aggression as an interpersonal strategy. Most research shows that clients who receive assertiveness training show im-

proved social skills compared with clients who receive no treatment, but it is not clear that assertiveness skills always transfer to real-life situations.

Modeling. Albert Bandura (1969) claimed, "virtually all learning phenomena resulting from direct experiences can occur on a vicarious basis through observation of other persons' behavior and its consequences for them" (p. 118). In fact, learning new behaviors through modeling is often more efficient than learning through direct reinforcement. For one thing, observation of competent models can eliminate the hazards of trial and error. Imagine if everyone had to be hit by a car before knowing how to cross streets safely! In addition to guiding the development of new behaviors, modeling can inhibit imitative behavior in someone who sees a model punished. Observing a model can also trigger behavior that might not have occurred otherwise.

Behavior therapists use the power of modeling to promote adaptive behavior in people displaying a variety of problems, including social withdrawal, obsessive-compulsive disorder, unassertiveness, antisocial conduct, physical aggressiveness, and early infantile autism (Rosenthal & Steffek, 1991). Modeling is also commonly used in fear reduction treatments. Typically, the fearful client observes models performing a behavior the client avoids—riding in a

Stanford University psychologist Albert Bandura's research on modeling has shown that it is an extremely effective technique for developing new skills and overcoming strong fears.

glass elevator, perhaps—and sees that the consequences are positive, or at least not negative. In a procedure known as **participant modeling**, this live modeling of fearless behavior is supplemented by therapist-guided sessions in which the client is given increasingly close contact with the feared situation under protected circumstances. For an elevator phobia, the therapist might ride with the client for one floor, then two, then three, and so on. In **covert modeling**, clients imagine fearless models rather than watching them live or on videotape.

Donald Meichenbaum (1971) proposed that observing models who display some initial fearful behavior can further enhance modeling effects if the model ultimately copes with and overcomes the fear. He argued that this technique, called **coping modeling**, may strengthen treatment effects by enhancing observer–model similarity and providing clients with information on how to cope with fear, not just how to behave fearlessly. Some studies, but not others, have replicated Meichenbaum's finding that coping models produce stronger effects than models who display utter fearlessness (e.g., Kazdin, 1973).

Research on the use of modeling for fear reduction and other goals has shown it to be effective when combined with other techniques (Bandura, 1986; Rosenthal, 1982). The apparent benefits of modeling treatments may be linked to their effects on clients' *self-efficacy*, the belief that clients can successfully perform important behaviors. When clients lack crucial behavioral skills, modeling methods appear to quickly improve competence and, in turn, provide the basis for increased self-efficacy (Williams & Zane, 1989).

Contingency Management. Based on the principles of operant conditioning, **contingency management** is a generic term for deliberately presenting or withdrawing reinforcers or aversive stimuli following behaviors that clients and therapists want to change. Contingency management has been applied in the treatment of adults and children with a variety of problems including autism, temper tantrums, learning difficulties, hyperactivity, retardation, juvenile delinquency, aggression, hallucinations, delusions, depression, phobias, sexual disorders, and physical and psychosomatic complaints.

In some cases, clients are taught to use contingency management to modify their own behaviors, a process known as **self-control**. As a form of contingency management, clients using self-control arrange and carry out planned reinforcement contingencies on their own. For example, an overweight person might decide to eat only at specified times, only in the kitchen, and only in the presence of family members.

Contingency contracting is a form of contingency management in which a formal, often written, agreement between therapist and client spells out the consequences of certain client behaviors. Behavioral contracting has been applied to marital problems (Wood & Jacobson, 1985), family disruptions (Alexander & Parsons, 1973), drug abuse (Boudin, 1972), obesity (Brownell & Foreyt, 1985), and other problems (Walker et al., 1981). Some therapy contracts include information about therapists' ethical obligations and about the benefits and risks of therapy (Handelsman & Galvin, 1988). Therapeutic contracts may also help safeguard depressed or reckless clients by including terms that require the client to take specific precautionary actions (e.g., calling the therapist) before doing anything dangerous or potentially self-destructive (Bongar, 1991).

Perhaps the best-known contingency management procedure is the **token economy**, which uses reinforcement contingencies to alter the behaviors of individuals or groups. A scaled-down monetary system, token economies pay clients in a special currency (tokens) when they perform designated behaviors. Creation of a token economy occurs in 4 steps. First, desired target behaviors, such as increased social interaction or improved self-help skills, are specified. Second, contingency rules are established so that participants earn tokens or other reinforcers by performing any of a designated list of target behaviors. Third, an exchange system is established in which tokens may be exchanged for food, recreational privileges, "vacations" from the hospital, more luxurious living conditions, or other desired rewards. Finally, exchange rates are set to govern the number of tokens that can be earned by performing particular target behaviors and the number of tokens necessary to purchase each kind of reward.

In the first report of a token economy, hospitalized chronic mental patients showed a significant increase in self-care behaviors and completed work assignments (Ayllon & Azrin, 1965). Token economies soon became a popular method for improving the self-help and social skills of schizophrenic patients. There was also a dramatic increase in the application of token economies to other populations, including youngsters who displayed inattentive, disruptive, delinquent, or antisocial behavior in institutions (Burchard, 1967; Cohen, 1968) and in elementary school classrooms (O'Leary & Becker, 1967). Other token economies were tailored for use with Head Start participants, retarded persons, alcoholics, drug ad-

Connections

What are some other contingency management techniques? For a review, see Chapter 1, p. 24.

dicts, and autistic children. Token economies have even been used to increase community activism among the poor (Miller & Miller, 1970) and to promote conservation and environmental protection efforts (Nietzel et al., 1977).

With surprisingly few exceptions, contingency management techniques are effective in modifying specific behaviors in desired directions. Their main limitations are that their effects are often not very durable and do not consistently generalize to new situations (Woods, Higson, & Tannahill, 1984).

Biofeedback. The use of operant contingencies to control biological processes is known as **biofeedback** because the behaviors to be changed include heart rate, blood pressure, brain waves, or other biological responses that were once thought to be beyond a person's control. Target behaviors can also include responses over which the client has lost control because of disease or injury. Biofeedback requires special equipment that monitors the response to be modified and provides the client with information about the intensity or frequency of that response in the form of a meter reading, graph, or auditory signal.

Neal Miller (1969) was one of the first psychologists to show that autonomic nervous system activity could be modified through operant conditioning. He demonstrated, for example, that rats could learn to increase and decrease the output of their kidneys on the basis of reinforcement provided by

pleasurable brain stimulation. Despite the fact that Miller and other researchers had difficulty replicating the results of these early animal studies, throughout the 1960s and 1970s many investigators reported that humans could gain some control over numerous biological functions. As a result, biofeedback has been used to treat several clinical disorders, including high blood pressure, bruxism (nocturnal clenching and grinding of the teeth), seizures, incontinence, migraine headaches, and Reynaud's disease (a circulatory disorder). Unfortunately, although biofeedback can produce significant improvements in clinical conditions, it is still not clear that it reliably leads to lasting improvements. Furthermore, simpler procedures such as relaxation training appear capable of producing effects that often equal or exceed those of biofeedback (Reed, Katkin, & Goldband, 1986).

Aversion Therapy. **Aversion therapy** involves the use of painful or unpleasant stimuli to decrease such unwanted behaviors as drug abuse, alcoholism, overeating, smoking, and disturbing sexual practices. Most aversion methods are based on classical conditioning principles, pairing stimuli that elicit or give rise to problem behaviors with a noxious stimulus such as electric shock or nausea. For example, an alcoholic seeking help in abstaining might be exposed to a foul odor while reaching for a bottle of Scotch or be required to drink after having taken a drug that causes a nauseous reaction to alcohol. Ideally, contin-

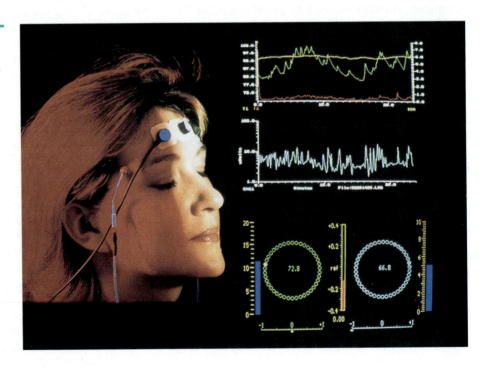

In biofeedback, a monitor and a feedback apparatus are attached to a client, who then uses a mental or physical strategy to change some biological process such as blood pressure or body temperature in a desired direction.

ued pairings of the odor or feelings of sickness with the sight or smell of alcohol will decrease alcohol's appeal so that drinking is reduced if not eliminated.

Aversion therapy may also employ operant conditioning techniques, particularly punishment. Here, the aversive stimulus (an electric shock, perhaps) is delivered shortly *after* the client drinks alcohol or performs some other problematic behavior. In a cognitive variant on aversion therapy called **covert sensitization,** the therapist delivers a long narrative to help the client imagine aversive consequences of unwanted behavior that are far more intense and horrifying than anything that could ethically be delivered in reality (Little & Curren, 1978).

There is considerable debate among mental health professionals about aversion therapy methods. First, many clinicians doubt that aversion therapy produces changes that are significant, long-lasting, or likely to generalize beyond the treatment situation. Second, clinicians recognize that aversion therapy alone does not teach clients adaptive behaviors to use in place of the maladaptive acts that aversive methods suppress. As noted in Chapter 14, for example, sexual disorders known as paraphilias usually reappear if clients are not helped to develop alternative sexual outlets that are both satisfying and socially acceptable. Third, in spite of its effectiveness in some cases, many therapists find aversive therapy offensive, and some have called for abolition of aversion techniques.

Partly because of these concerns, aversion therapy is usually employed either as a last resort in cases of dangerous behavior, such as self-abuse, that has not responded to nonaversive methods, or in conjunction with techniques aimed at promoting more adaptive, rewardable behaviors. The aversive component in these packages usually employs the mildest effective noxious stimulus and is discontinued as soon as possible.

Despite concerns over aversive methods, behavior therapy methods in general have enjoyed a tremendous surge in popularity that is unmatched by any other formal system of psychotherapy. This reaction is partly because behavioral methods are, by and large, quite effective and even superior to other approaches for certain forms of anxiety disorders, certain childhood disorders, and many habitual behaviors. Behavioral methods are also efficient, often leading to significant changes in problematic behaviors in a relatively short time compared with other methods. In an era when the cost of mental health services is of ever-increasing concern, the more efficient the technique, the more likely it is to be used. Finally, behavior therapy is popular because many

of its methods can be effectively used by nonprofessional counselors and self-help groups.

Cognitive Therapies

Therapies that use learning principles to alter not only overt behavior problems but also the maladaptive thoughts and beliefs that accompany those problems are known as **cognitive therapies** or cognitive-behavioral therapies. This focus on changing specific thoughts and beliefs reflects ideas seen in the psychodynamic and interpersonal approaches of Alfred Adler and Harry Stack Sullivan, but today, the two most influential cognitively oriented treatments are Aaron Beck's cognitive therapy and Albert Ellis's rational emotive therapy.

Beck's Cognitive Therapy.   Much of the research on Aaron Beck's therapy has focused on its use in the treatment of depression (Dobson, 1989; Robins & Hayes, 1993), but his methods have also been applied to anxiety, personality disorders, and substance abuse problems (Beck et al., 1990; Linehan, 1993). Cognitive therapy for depression seeks to correct depressed clients' negatively biased beliefs and assumptions about themselves, the future, and the world. Cognitive therapists teach clients to identify these cognitive distortions and then ask them to examine whether there is any valid evidence for their negative views. Ideally, clients discover that no such evidence exists or that they have been exaggerating the importance of negative events or the significance of potential threats—a process called *catastrophizing.* Clients are then helped to develop more realistic thoughts to substitute for their pessimistic beliefs. The next step is to complete "homework assignments" that require clients to practice their new thinking strategies in the situations that have led to their strongest distortions and most problematic emotional reactions.

In dealing with generalized anxiety disorder, for example, the cognitive therapist seeks to alter clients' beliefs that even relatively minor negative events are major threats, while cognitive treatment of obsessive-compulsive disorder might focus on exploring the belief that chaos and danger will occur unless the client performs elaborate mental or behavioral rituals.

Ellis's Rational Emotive Therapy.   The core principles of Albert Ellis's **rational emotive therapy (RET)** are literally as simple as ABC (Ellis, 1973). Ellis believes that people suffer anxiety, depression, and other psychological problems when activating events (A) are followed by upsetting emotional consequences (C). However, he says that A does not actually cause C.

Instead, emotional consequences are the result of problems in how a person *thinks* about activating events, in other words, in his or her personal *belief system* (B). Specifically, Ellis says that anxiety, depression, and other problems are the result of beliefs that are extreme, irrational, and self-defeating. Rational emotive therapy challenges these irrational beliefs and helps clients replace them with more logical thoughts. Shakespeare anticipated RET when he had Hamlet say that "There is nothing either good or bad but thinking makes it so."

In RET, the therapist is active, challenging, demonstrative, and even abrasive. Ellis urged therapists to use strong language and vivid examples to persuade clients to give up the irrational ideas with which they have indoctrinated themselves into misery. His methods are illustrated in this excerpt from a first session of RET in which the therapist (T) meets a young female client (C) seeking help with several problems, including alcohol abuse.

C: . . . I want to change everything; I'm depressed about everything; et cetera.

T: Give me a couple of things, for example.

C: What I'm depressed about? I, uh, don't know that I have any purpose in life. I don't know what I—what I am. And I don't know in what direction I'm going.

T: Yeah, but that's—so you're saying, "I'm ignorant?" (client nods) Well what's so awful about being ignorant? It's too bad you're ignorant. It would be nicer if you weren't—if you *had* a purpose and *knew* where you were going. But just let's suppose the worst: for the rest of your life you didn't have a purpose, and you stayed this way. Let's suppose that. Now why would you be so bad?

C: Because everyone *should* have a purpose!

T: Where did you get the *should*?

C: 'Cause it's what I believe in. (silence for a while)

T: I know. But think about it for a minute. You're obviously a bright woman; now, where did that *should* come from?

C: I, I don't know! I'm not thinking clearly at the moment. I'm too nervous! I'm sorry.

T: Well, but you *can* think clearly. Are you now saying, "Oh, it's hopeless! I can't think clearly. What a _____ I am for not thinking clearly!" You see: You're blaming yourself for *that*.

C: (visibly upset; can't seem to say anything; then nods)

T: Now you're perfectly *able* to think.

C: Not at the moment!

T: Yes you are! Want to bet?

C: (begins to sob)

T: What are you crying about now?

C: Because I feel so stupid! And I'm afraid!

T: Yeah, but "stupid" means "I'm putting myself down for acting stupidly."

C: All right! I didn't expect to be put on so *fast*. I expected a moment to catch my breath and see who you *were;* and to establish some different kind of rapport.

T: Yeah. And that would be nice and easier; but we would really waste our time.

C: Yes, I guess we would.

T: But you're really upset because you're not giving the right answers—and isn't that *awful!*

C: Yes. And I don't think that anybody likes to be made a fool, a fool of!

T: You *can't* be made a fool of!

C: (chokes a little)

T: You see, that's the *point:* That's impossible. Now why *can't* you be made a fool of?

C: (angry outburst) Why don't you stop asking me?

T: (interrupting) No! You'll never get better unless you *think*. And you're saying, "Can't we do something *magical* to get me better? And the answer is "No!"

In Review

Psychotherapy is a psychological intervention:

- in which a psychotherapist tries to help a client change behaviors, cognitions, or emotions so that the client functions more adequately; and
- that benefits men and women of all ages, cultural backgrounds, and social classes even though these demographic variables do affect the extent to which individuals participate in therapy.

Most psychotherapists do not adhere strictly to one theoretical approach but integrate principles and techniques from the following major approaches:

- psychoanalysis/psychodynamic therapy;
- interpersonal therapy;
- phenomenological/experiential therapies;
- behavior therapy; and
- cognitive therapy.

Evaluating Psychotherapy

How can clinicians know whether psychotherapy is effective? There are several possibilities. Researchers could ask clients and therapists whether they think a treatment has been helpful. They could give clients psychological tests before and after therapy to measure changes. They could ask clients' friends or relatives whether clients are acting differently since having had therapy. Indeed, all these perspectives are important in assessing the effects of psychotherapy because each of them taps different types of change (Strupp & Hadley, 1977). Tests can measure whether specific symptoms have been altered. Self-reports reflect the degree to which clients actually feel better. Therapist reports suggest the degree to which clients have progressed toward an ideal level of functioning. Reports from friends, relatives, and others provide information about the socially important question of whether the client's behavior has become less disruptive and disturbing.

Methods of Evaluating Psychotherapy

It is one thing for clients, therapists, relatives, and test scores to show that a client has improved after psychotherapy, but it is quite another to demonstrate scientifically that the psychotherapy *caused* the improvements. Of all the research designs that can evaluate the presence of a cause–effect relationship between therapy and improvement, the most powerful is the controlled *experiment*. Experiments are scientific research methods that systematically manipulate one factor, the *independent variable*, then measure the effect of this manipulation on another factor, the *dependent variable*. In psychotherapy studies, the independent variable is usually whether (or what type) of therapy is given. The dependent variable is the amount and direction of change seen in clients.

Experimental Group Designs. In the most basic type of psychotherapy outcome experiment, clients displaying the same kind of disorder are randomly assigned to either an experimental group that receives psychotherapy or a no-treatment control group that does not. Randomly assigning clients to conditions is important because, given a large enough number of clients, this procedure makes it likely that the treatment and control groups will be approximately equivalent in age, severity of disorder, socioeconomic status, and other important *client variables*. If clients are not randomly assigned to conditions, any between-group differences in client behavior seen at the end of the experiment might have been due to differences that existed between groups before the experiment began. If, for example, the most disturbed clients were put in the no-treatment group, the cards are stacked in favor of the treatment that is being evaluated. Thus, treated clients might improve much more than untreated clients, but, because they were less disturbed to begin with, the treated clients might have improved even without treatment. When experimental designs are flawed, or *confounded,* in this way, researchers do not know whether to attribute improvement to treatment itself or to other uncontrolled factors.

After random assignments are made, the dependent variables (such as anxiety level or depression) are measured in both groups. These same measures are repeated at various intervals, perhaps during treatment, shortly after treatment ends, and at several follow-up points months or even years later.

In practice, psychotherapy evaluation experiments often require more than two groups because investigators are usually interested in questions that go beyond whether treatment is better than no treatment. Even large differences in improvement between clients in experimental and control groups reveal little or nothing about what *components* of the total psychotherapy package might be responsible for the superiority of treatment over no treatment. Was the improvement due to the therapists' characteristics, specific therapy techniques, or simply the opportunity for clients to talk to someone who paid special attention to them? Moreover, the simple treatment versus no-treatment design cannot show whether the therapy being tested is more or less effective than other forms of treatment.

To answer these more sophisticated questions, researchers often add groups and conditions to the experiment that allow for comparisons to be made between types of treatments as well as between treatment and no treatment. These more elaborate experiments are called *factorial designs* because they allow researchers to manipulate more than one factor, or variable, within the same experiment and to examine whether these variables act separately or in varying combinations (called *interactions*) to affect dependent variables.

Thus, if researchers want to determine whether a particular component of treatment is important in creating improvement, they might randomly assign one group of subjects to receive the "complete" treatment package (e.g., systematic desensitization) while another group gets a partial version (e.g., desensitization minus relaxation training). In order to assess how much posttreatment change could have been due to clients' positive expectations about therapy, a third group might be assigned to a *psychological placebo* treatment that generates strong expectations for benefit, but offers nothing that could reasonably be expected to produce improvement. A fourth, no-treatment group might also be included to assess the effects of the mere passage of time.

By comparing results from all four groups, the experimenter begins to discover whether the whole treatment package is (1) superior to a version that is more streamlined or perhaps devoid of one of its components, (2) more effective than a placebo, and (3) better than no treatment at all. If clients had been assigned to a different form of psychotherapy altogether, the experimenter could also learn which of the two therapies was more effective.

Placebo Groups in Psychotherapy Research. The placebo group has often been used as a control for the effects of the so-called nonspecific factors thought to be common to all kinds of therapy (Frank, 1973). These factors include not only positive expectations for improvement, but also just the opportunity to talk with an understanding person, the chance to express emotions in a safe environment and to receive encouragement to change.

However, there are several reasons why many researchers question the usefulness of placebo controls in psychotherapy outcome research (e.g., Critelli & Neumann, 1984). First, it is virtually impossible to create a psychotherapy placebo that is truly inert from every theoretical perspective. For example, listening attentively to clients (a common placebo treatment) is a primary ingredient in many forms of psychotherapy. Second, the term *placebo* carries the connotation that placebo effects are trivial or short-lived. Such a connotation is clearly incorrect; the factors that different therapies share—including the ability to activate client expectations for improvement—might be more powerful in creating change than are the specific procedures that differentiate one therapy from the next. In fact, subjects in placebo groups consistently show significantly better outcomes than do clients in no-treatment control groups, although they usually do not do as well as clients who receive some form of active psychotherapy (Barker, Funk, & Houston, 1988). Finally, there are ethical objections to psychotherapy placebos. Is the relatively small methodological benefit provided by placebo controls worth the cost to the placebo group members who might be at least temporarily denied the most effective treatment available? Because of these concerns, many psychotherapy researchers no longer use psychotherapy placebos, preferring instead to randomly assign clients to one or more alternative forms of therapy and perhaps to a temporary no-treatment group.

Within-Subject Designs. Another scientific approach to evaluating the effects of psychotherapy measures changes that occur in the same clients at different times rather than making comparisons between groups of clients at the same time. These *within-subject* experiments begin by repeatedly observing dependent variables such as aggression or depression or fear before the independent variable—treatment—is manipulated. In the simplest within-subject designs, these *baseline* measurements are followed by the *intervention* phase, in which the experimenter introduces the treatment and then repeatedly measures the dependent variable to detect changes from the baseline.

However, little would be learned from this design if the experiment ended after improvement was observed. That improvement might have been due to treatment, but it might also have been due to many other factors, including the possibility that the client was about to improve anyway. Accordingly, within-subject designs commonly employ additional strategies, the most common of which are the *ABAB*, or *reversal*, design and the *multiple baseline* design. In the **ABAB design,** the no-treatment baseline condition (A) is alternated with the intervention phase (B) at least twice (see Figure 16.1). If the dependent measure changes *only* during the intervention phase, the experimenter can be more confident that the intervention caused the changes.

In the **multiple baseline design,** therapy is evaluated by applying it sequentially to each of several treatment targets (see Figure 16.2). The experimenter gains confidence in the causal impact of a therapy if each target changes when, *and only when,* the therapy is applied to it.

Within-subject research is sometimes conducted with only one subject. Several practical advantages make *single subject,* or *N=1,* research a popular psychotherapy research strategy (Barlow & Hersen, 1984). For one thing, it allows clinicians to evaluate the treatment of rare disorders, an enterprise that would be difficult if they had to assemble the large number of clients required by between-subjects designs. Second, N=1 research encourages practicing therapists to conduct empirical research on their own treatment methods, thus providing them an objective, empirically based look at their own effectiveness. Third, N=1 research allows for research on specific techniques or different sequences of techniques as they are actually employed with a given client. N=1 research also allows clients a better opportunity to see for themselves whether desired changes are occurring in therapy. Finally, N=1 research is generally less expensive than between-group designs because it does not require large numbers of clients or therapists.

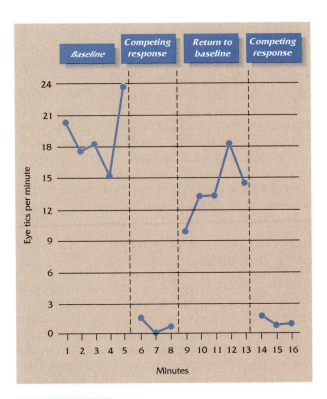

FIGURE 16.1

An ABAB Design

The client in this study was a 9-year-old girl with a severe eye tic. The frequency of tics observed during the initial baseline declined dramatically during the intervention, which consisted of teaching the girl to blink softly every 5 seconds as a competing response to the tic. Notice that, when the baseline condition was returned, the eye tics again increased. When the competing response intervention was resumed, eye tics decreased to low levels again.

Source: From Azrin & Peterson, 1989.

The Validity of Experiments on Psychotherapy

The ideal experiment is designed to maximize **internal validity,** the degree to which an experiment allows a researcher to be confident that the results are due to the independent variable (therapy) rather than confounding factors such as the passage of time or group differences in client variables (Cook & Campbell, 1979). Thus, a treatment outcome experiment that does not randomly assign clients to conditions has low internal validity.

Researchers also try to design experiments that have high external and statistical validity. **External validity** is a measure of the degree to which an experiment's results can be generalized to situations and clients beyond those included in the experiment.

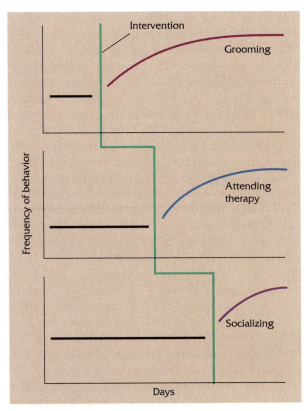

FIGURE 16.2

A Multiple Baseline Design

Suppose researchers want to investigate the effects of social praise on the behavior of severely disturbed patients in a mental hospital. Three behaviors are examined in this hypothetical experiment—grooming, attending group therapy, and socializing with other patients. The intervention (giving social praise) is introduced at different times for each of the three behaviors. Each "new" intervention begins on the day following termination of the baseline phase for the targeted behavior. As this figure shows, each behavior improves when, and only when, the intervention is applied to it. The fact that a behavior changes only when social praise is given for it makes it unlikely that some other uncontrolled factor (e.g., the influence of other patients) is responsible for the changes observed.

If, for example, only male subjects participated in a treatment experiment, its results might not apply to females. **Statistical validity** refers to whether there were enough subjects in the experiment to allow statistical analyses to detect any significant between-group differences that might have occurred.

Psychotherapy researchers have several options for dealing with threats to the validity of their experiments. Some use single-subject designs to study therapy with individual clients (Greenberg, 1986; Kazdin, 1994b; Mahrer, 1988), but, although they take pains to use the most rigorous methodology (Persons 1991), external validity may be limited. Another alternative is to combine the resources, clients, and talents of many therapy researchers into a large cooperative outcome study conducted simultaneously at several sites. A leading example of this strategy is the NIMH Collaborative Study on the treatment of depression (Elkin, 1994; Elkin et al., 1989; see Chapter 9). Similar multisite studies are currently evaluating the treatment of other mental disorders.

Researchers can also bring psychotherapy research into the laboratory, buying the experimental control needed for internal validity but losing much of the external validity afforded by real-life clinical settings. In a strategy called **analogue research**, researchers attempt to approximate in the laboratory the subject populations, psychological problems, therapists, and psychotherapy procedures seen in real clinical settings. If the laboratory analogy is a close one, the external validity of the research is enhanced. If not, the gain in internal validity offered by analogue research may become insignificant when viewed in light of the loss of external validity.

Finally, researchers can conduct evaluations that deliberately place a higher premium on external rather than internal validity. These evaluations are not well-controlled laboratory experiments on the effects of specific therapies, but are surveys of how clients fare after receiving psychotherapy as it is practiced in the community. The best example of this approach is the *Consumer Reports Survey,* in which over 7,000 readers of *Consumer Reports* magazine answered a series of questions about the kinds of assistance and treatment they sought for mental health problems in the previous 3 years (Seligman, 1995).

Notice the dilemma inherent in trying to design psychotherapy research that will be high on internal, external, *and* statistical validity: by exerting the experimental control necessary for internal validity, researchers may be forced to study clients, therapists, and treatment settings that may not allow for high external validity, and vice versa. Thus, random assignment of volunteer clients to groups (including a no-treatment control group) is relatively easy in a laboratory study of therapy with college student research volunteers, but those volunteers might not be representative of the general population or of the full range of severity in the behavior disorder under study. Likewise, it is relatively easy to train university-affiliated therapists to use a special technique, but it is usually much more difficult to train a large number of therapists working in diverse community settings. A representative sample of clients and problem severity could be found in a community mental health center but—even after gaining informed consent—there might be ethical concerns over even temporarily assigning clients to a no-treatment control group when they came in expecting immediate help. Similarly, it is often difficult to find, at one time and place, enough clients with a particular kind of problem to ensure that analyses of therapy outcome will have sufficient statistical power. For all these reasons, it is often unclear to what extent the results of therapy evaluated in well-controlled experiments can be used to draw conclusions about therapy as it is conducted in clinical practice (Weisz, Weiss, & Donenberg, 1992; Shadish et al., in press).

Research on the Outcome of Psychotherapy

The modern era of outcome research on psychotherapy began in 1952 when Hans J. Eysenck, a prominent British psychologist, reviewed a number of studies on the effects of therapy. His analyses led him to conclude that troubled people who receive psychotherapy are no more likely to improve than those who do not. More specifically, Eysenck reported that the rate of improvement over a 2-year period was 44 percent for clients receiving psychoanalysis and 64 percent for those receiving eclectic therapy. He calculated the rate of **spontaneous remission**—improvement without any treatment—to be 72 percent.

Eysenck's conclusions sparked intense debate among clinicians. Many critics attacked the thoroughness of his review, objected to the way he defined improvement, and quarreled with his statistical analyses. Other reviewers, using different criteria and reviewing other therapy outcome studies, reached more optimistic conclusions. For example, Allen Bergin (1971, p. 228) concluded, "psychotherapy on the average has mostly positive effects," while others reported positive outcomes in more than 80 percent of the outcome studies they reviewed (Meltzoff & Kornreich, 1970). In fact, the 1970s and early 1980s saw many reviews concluding that psychotherapy generally produced better outcomes than no treatment and that different types of therapy were about equally effective (Bergin & Lambert, 1978; Luborsky, Singer, & Luborsky, 1975). Still other reviewers in this period were pessimistic about the benefits of psychotherapy in general, although they tended to conclude that, for certain disorders at least, behavior therapy was effective (Kazdin & Wilson, 1978; Rachman & Wilson, 1980).

In retrospect, it is no wonder that clinicians had trouble reaching consensus about the value of psychotherapy. Different reviewers used different standards and methods in selecting studies for review, in evaluating the quality of those studies, in deciding whether the results actually favored psychotherapy, and in combining the results of many studies into a summary index of therapy outcomes. There was an obvious need for an alternative to these qualitatively oriented narrative reviews, an alternative that would allow reviewers to quantify and statistically summarize the effects of each study, separately and in the aggregate.

Meta-Analysis. A procedure called **meta-analysis** offers just such a technique for statistically combining the results of several studies into an overall average or estimate. In 1977, Mary Smith and Gene Glass published the first meta-analysis of outcome studies and concluded that psychotherapy was very effective, on the average. Later, these reviewers published a monumental book, *The Benefits of Psychotherapy*, which covered the results of 475 psychotherapy studies (Smith, Glass, & Miller, 1980). To summarize this mass of data, Smith and her colleagues computed the average difference in outcome between treated and untreated groups in each study. These average differences, or **effect sizes,** were computed for several types of dependent measures, including clients' self-reports of how they felt, therapists' opinions about how much a client had changed, psychological test scores, and observers' ratings of how well clients were doing. Looking at effect sizes measured immediately after therapy ended, or, in some cases, months after treatment, indicates how much better off the average treated client was compared with the average person in a no-treatment control group.

The main conclusion of this meta-analysis was that "the average person receiving psychotherapy was better off at the end of it than 80 percent of the persons who did not" (Smith, Glass, & Miller, 1980, p. 29). In other words, on average, a person receiving psychotherapy has a 2 to 1 chance of doing better than a person not receiving therapy. Furthermore, only 9 percent of the effect sizes were negative, indicating that deterioration following psychotherapy was infrequent. Effect sizes tended to be larger immediately after therapy than at follow-up assessments, but, even months later, improvement was still evident.

Smith, Glass, and Miller's (1980) meta-analysis was important not only for what it said about the effectiveness of psychotherapy, but also for those aspects of therapy it suggested might not be particularly important (Dawes, 1994). As noted earlier, the nature of therapists' professional training was not related to treatment success; psychologists, psychiatrists, social workers, and other mental health workers did about equally well. The type or level of therapist training did not matter much, either; in terms of outcomes, it did not make a difference whether the therapists had a Ph.D., an M.D., or no advanced training. Not even length of treatment was strongly related to outcome; longer courses of therapy were not uniformly associated with better results. Finally, and perhaps most controversial, was the fact that the specific type of therapy used was not as strongly related to outcome as most therapists might have expected. Across all types of problems, psychoanalytically oriented, Rogerian, behavioral, and cognitive therapies all tended to yield essentially equivalent effect sizes. The one exception to this pattern was that behavioral therapies were a bit more effective than other approaches in treating certain well-defined problems such as phobias and panic attacks.

Some clinicians and researchers have criticized meta-analytic summaries on several counts. For example, they charge that using aggregate figures to summarize, combine, and compare results from a large volume of vastly different therapies is as inappropriate and misleading as comparing apples and oranges. These critics further contend that by failing to distinguish well-designed studies from poorly designed ones, meta-analyses run the risk of letting less-well-controlled studies spuriously inflate the apparent benefits of treatment. In the world of computing, this criticism is described as "garbage in, garbage out."

In our view, neither criticism is particularly compelling. Meta-analysis is currently the most reliable technique available for summarizing the effects of a large body of research literature. Any review, whether it uses statistical or qualitative methods, compares or combines results from different types of treatment, and there is nothing wrong with comparing apples and oranges if your concern is with fruit in general. Further, when meta-analysts have rated the research quality of the studies in their reviews, they consistently find that the better-designed studies yield stronger effects (Landman & Dawes, 1982). It simply is not the case that including lower-quality research inflates effect sizes.

Conclusions About Psychotherapy's Effectiveness. Following publication of Smith, Glass, and Miller's (1980) pioneering study, other reviewers of outcome research performed meta-analyses to reevaluate their original conclusions or to investigate other aspects of psychotherapy. In general, these second- and third-generation meta-analyses have confirmed that psychotherapy is an effective treatment for a wide variety of mental disorders (Brown, 1987; Lambert & Bergin, 1994; Lipsey & Wilson, 1993).

A similar conclusion is suggested by the *Consumer Reports Survey* of mental health treatment described earlier (Seligman, 1995). In that survey, about 4,100 of the 7,000 respondents had seen a mental health professional in the previous 3 years. As a group, these clients were well educated and predominantly middle class; about half were women, and their average age was 46. Although these characteristics are not representative of the United States population as a whole, they are a reasonably good approximation of the type of client who normally seeks out professional treatment for psychological problems. The respondents were asked to rate (1) the degree to which formal treatment had helped with the problem that led them to therapy; (2) how satisfied they were with the treatment they received; and (3) how they judged their "overall emotional state" after treatment. Responses indicated that about 90 percent of these clients felt better after treatment; that there was no difference in the improvement of clients who had psychotherapy alone versus psychotherapy plus medication; that no particular approach to psychotherapy was rated more highly than others; and that, although all types of professionals appeared to help their clients, greater improvements were associated with treatments by psychologists, psychiatrists, and social workers compared with family physicians or marriage counselors (see Figure 16.3).

Continued meta-analyses have reached numerous additional conclusions about psychotherapy. For one thing, they suggest that its effects are reasonably durable. Although Smith, Glass, and Miller (1980) found larger therapy effect sizes at the end of

therapy than at follow-up, subsequent meta-analyses have consistently reported that clients tend to maintain their end-of-treatment gains over periods as long as 18 months (Andrews & Harvey, 1981; Nicholson & Berman, 1983; Robinson, Berman, & Neimeyer, 1990). In fact, some studies suggest that clients make continuing improvements over follow-up periods (Gallagher-Thompson, Hanley-Peterson, & Thompson, 1990).

Second, the amount of professional experience therapists have—and even whether they are professional or nonprofessional therapists—appears largely unrelated to the success of treatment (Berman & Norton, 1985; Hattie, Sharpley, & Rogers, 1984; Stein & Lambert, 1984). This conclusion supports the results of the Smith, Glass, and Miller (1980) meta-analysis, which found that nonprofessionals and professionals with less experience did about as well overall as experienced professional therapists. True, experienced professionals sometimes produce outcomes that are superior to those of novice or nonprofessional therapists (Stein & Lambert, 1995), but the fact that most studies fail to find consistent advantages associated with professional training or experience is remarkable. Of course, in many of the studies reviewed, nonprofessional therapists worked under the supervision of experienced professionals, and, in others, professional therapists were assigned more difficult cases. Similarly, in some studies, a therapist described as "more experienced" might have been practicing only a year longer than one described

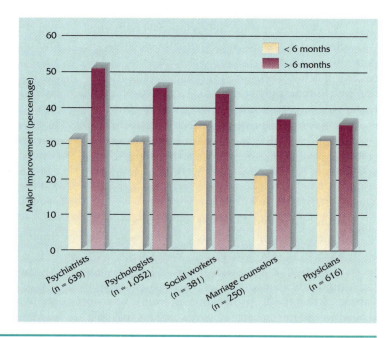

FIGURE 16.3

Consumer Reports **Evaluation of Psychotherapy**

The *Consumer Reports Survey* of mental health treatments showed that people treated for more than 6 months were more likely to experience "major improvements" than were people who were treated for less than 6 months. In addition, compared with clients treated by marriage counselors or physicians, a larger percentage of clients receiving treatment from psychiatrists, psychologists, and social workers reported experiencing major improvement in their presenting problem.

as "less experienced." Still, after years of research, the most obvious conclusion is that therapist training and experience do not affect the success of therapy as much as most clinicians assume. In fact, intensive training in specific therapy techniques may initially lead some therapists to become less effective, perhaps because they are so preoccupied with correctly executing techniques that they begin to pay less attention to the quality of the therapeutic relationship (Henry et al., 1993).

Third, it appears that, for about half of treated clients, the benefits of psychotherapy begin to appear after the first 6 to 8 sessions, and that 75 percent of clients who show improvement typically do so by the 26th session (Howard et al., 1986). Continued benefits occur as treatment continues, but the rate of progress tends to slow, probably because the client's most difficult problems tend to be addressed in later sessions. The relatively quick response to psychotherapy by most clients has led to the increased use of "brief therapies" that aim to produce benefits in 25 sessions or less (Koss & Shiang, 1994).

Finally, and again in line with the original Smith, Glass, and Miller (1980) study, most meta-analyses have found that the type of therapy clients receive makes little difference to overall treatment effectiveness. When differences are found, cognitive and behavioral therapies usually show slight-to-moderate advantages over traditional verbal or insight treatments (e.g., Shapiro & Shapiro, 1982; Svartberg & Stiles, 1991). This meta-analytic conclusion is supported by experimental studies demonstrating that certain well-defined therapies are particularly beneficial in the treatment of specific mental disorders. These **empirically validated treatments** are summarized in Table 16.1.

TABLE 16.1   Empirically Validated Treatments

A special task force of the Clinical Psychology Division of the American Psychological Association reviewed the literature to identify those psychological therapies that empirical research had validated as effective interventions for specific disorders. "Well-established treatments" had been found effective by a body of research studies; "probably efficacious treatments" were those shown to be effective in an initial, smaller number of studies.

Treatment	Source for evidence of efficacy
Well-established treatments	
Beck's cognitive therapy for depression	Dobson (1989)
Behavior modification for developmentally disabled individuals	Scotti, Evans, Meyer, & Walker (1991)
Behavior modification for enuresis and encopresis	Kupfersmid (1989); Wright & Walker (1978)
Behavior therapy for headache and for irritable bowel syndrome	Blanchard, Schwarz, & Radnitz (1987); Blanchard, Andrasik, Ahles, Teders, & O'Keefe (1980)
Behavior therapy for female orgasmic dysfunction and for male erectile dysfunction	LoPiccolo & Stock (1986); Auerbach & Kilmann (1977)
Behavioral marital therapy	Azrin, Bersalel, et al. (1980); Jacobson & Follette (1985)
Cognitive behavior therapy for chronic pain	Keefe, Dunsmore, & Burnett (1992)
Cognitive behavior therapy for panic disorder with and without agoraphobia	Barlow, Craske, Cerny, & Klosko (1989); Clark et al. (1989)
Cognitive behavior therapy for generalized anxiety disorder	Butler, Fennell, Robson, & Gelder (1991); Borkovec et al. (1987); Chambless & Gillis (1993)

(continued)

TABLE 16.1 *(continued)*

Treatment	Source for evidence of efficacy
Exposure treatment for phobias (agoraphobia, social phobia, simple phobia) and posttraumatic stress disorder	Mattick, Andrews, Hadzi-Pavlovic, & Christensen (1990); Trull, Nietzel, & Main (1988); Foa, Rothbaum, Riggs, & Murdock (1991)
Exposure and response prevention for obsessive-compulsive disorder	Marks & O'Sullivan (1988); Steketee, Foa, & Grayson (1982)
Family education programs for schizophrenia	Hogarty et al. (1986); Falloon et al. (1985)
Group cognitive behavioral therapy for social phobia	Heimberg, Dodge, Hope, Kennedy, & Zollo (1990); Mattick & Peters (1988)
Interpersonal therapy for bulimia	Fairburn, Jones, Peveler, Hope, & O'Conner (1993); Wilfley et al. (1993)
Klerman and Weissman's interpersonal therapy for depression	DiMascio et al. (1979); Elkin et al. (1989)
Parent training programs for children with oppositional behavior	Wells & Egan (1988); Walter & Gilmore (1973)
Systematic desensitization for simple phobia	Kazdin & Wilcoxin (1976);
Token economy programs	Liberman (1972)
Probably efficacious treatments	
Applied relaxation for panic disorder	Öst (1988); Öst & Westling (1991)
Brief psychodynamic therapies	Piper, Azim, McCallum, & Joyce (1990); Shefler & Dasberg (1989); Thompson, Gallagher, & Breckenridge (1987); Winston et al. (1991); Woody, Luborsky, McLellan, & O'Brien (1990)
Behavior modification for sex offenders	Marshall, Jones, Ward, Johnston, & Barbaree (1991)
Dialectical behavior therapy for borderline personality disorder	Linehan, Armstrong, Suarez, Allmon, & Heard (1991); Johnson & Greenberg (1985)
Emotionally focused couples therapy	Azrin, Nunn, & Frantz (1980)
Habit reversal and control techniques	Azrin, Nunn, & Frantz-Renshaw (1980)
Lewinsohn's psychoeducational treatment for depression	Lewinsohn, Hoberman, & Clarke (1989)

Source: Division of Clinical Psychology, American Psychological Association, 1995.

The finding that different therapies appear to produce similar outcomes has appeared with such regularity that psychotherapy researchers jokingly refer to it as the "Dodo bird verdict" (Luborsky et al., 1975). They are referring, of course, to Lewis Carroll's tale *Alice in Wonderland,* in which Alice and several other characters run a race to dry themselves off after being soaked with water. But they run in different directions, so when they ask the Dodo bird to name the winner, he answers diplomatically: "Everybody has won and all must have prizes." In the race among various psychotherapies, too, all appear to have crossed the outcome finish line together. As most close races do, this one has sparked arguments among the contestants and raised new questions about how psychotherapy works, as discussed in the Controversy section on pages 583–584.

Clinical Significance. Most studies of psychotherapy have focused on the question of whether the outcome of a specific treatment differs in a statistically significant way from what is seen following other types of

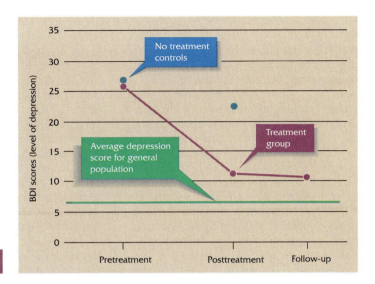

FIGURE 16.4

Clinical Significance of Psychotherapy for Depression

This figure summarizes the clinical significance of psychotherapy outcomes for more than 1,000 depressed clients examined in 31 separate studies. Before they entered treatment, clinically depressed clients reported far higher levels of depressed symptoms than did non-depressed controls. However, immediately after treatment and then at long-term follow-ups, the level of depression reported by treated clients was no longer significantly different from the nondepressed controls. Depressed clients assigned to control groups continued to show significantly higher levels of depression.

Source: Based on Nietzel et al., 1987

treatment or in various control conditions. Although this is an important question, it is not the one that concerns most clients, nor the only one that interests researchers. Equally important is the question of whether psychotherapy produces changes that are great enough to show **clinical significance,** or to be socially meaningful. As Figure 16.4 shows, one way that researchers have defined clinical significance is to compare the behavior or test scores of treated clients to those of people who do not suffer from the disorder under study. If the treated clients now resemble members of a normative group, treatment can be said to be clinically significant. It is encouraging to report that the results of psychotherapy for many kinds of mental disorders appear to be clinically as well as statistically significant (Nietzel et al., 1987; Nietzel & Trull, 1988).

Controversy

Does Psychotherapy Work Through Specific Processes or General Factors?

One of the most perplexing questions about psychotherapy is this: If the training and experience of therapists do not affect the success of therapy, if longer treatment adds diminishing returns to brief therapy, and, if one type of therapy is about as successful as another, what factors *do* influence the success of therapy?

Numerous answers to this question have been proposed (Stiles, Shapiro, & Elliott, 1986), but two have received the most attention.

According to the *specific processes* explanation, all therapists, regardless of their theoretical backgrounds, first facilitate a positive therapeutic alliance and then use a variety of specific treatment techniques. Although different in style

(continued)

Controversy *(continued)*

and form, these techniques help clients achieve at least one of the following: (1) a better cognitive understanding of their lives and behavior, (2) a clearer experience and acceptance of their emotions, and (3) a greater ability to regulate their behavior.

The "specific processes" position assumes that all forms of therapy achieve their effects by emphasizing one of these objectives. For example, behavior therapists help clients regulate behavior more effectively, while psychoanalysts enhance clients' insight into the causes of their behavior. Cognitive therapists emphasize the correction of distorted beliefs, while experiential therapists promote the experience and acceptance of strong emotions. The specific processes explanation of therapy suggests that reaching any or all of these objectives will lead to similar levels of improvement, although there may be occasional advantages for one approach over the others with clients who tend to use particular problem-solving styles (Beutler, Machado, & Neufeldt, 1994).

The second answer to the question of what underlies therapy effects emphasizes the *common factors* that are shared by all therapies. Advocates of this position argue that certain therapist characteristics and client qualities, along with a few core features of all forms of psychotherapy, lead to successful outcomes (Orlinsky, Grawe, & Parks, 1994). The most important common factor determining therapy effectiveness is thought to be a strong therapeutic alliance (Orlinsky et al., 1994). As a result of being actively engaged with one another and communicating clearly, clients and therapists work closely together to resolve clients' problems. When therapists are able to make clients feel supported and ac-

cepted, clients feel more committed to and more capable of changing their behavior for the better.

The client characteristics most commonly associated with successful therapy include openness and self-relatedness. **Self-relatedness** refers to clients' ability to experience and understand internal states such as thinking and emotions. Clients who are high in self-relatedness tend to be open minded and flexible, to listen carefully to their therapists, and to constructively use what they hear. As clients with these characteristics feel themselves making progress, they tend to gain further confidence about making overall lifestyle changes that will prevent future problems (Howard et al., 1993).

Having formed a strong therapeutic alliance with a cooperative, motivated client, effective therapists may all tend to use a common set of therapeutic operations that will enhance the outcome of therapy. These may include focusing therapy on clients' core problems and emotional reactions, offering clients alternative ways of interpreting their behavior, and encouraging clients to express and understand their true feelings.

Deciding whether specific processes or common features are more important in psychotherapy is a little like trying to decide why people feel better after a vacation. Is it because different kinds of vacations lead to specific benefits? Surely, hiking in the mountains improves physical conditioning, camping brings the peace and quiet of nature, and travel broadens cultural horizons. Or is it because all good vacations share common features, such as a break from the stress of everyday routines and a chance to revitalize interpersonal relationships. Answering these

questions is difficult, so it should not be surprising that psychotherapy researchers have not yet resolved the question of whether specific processes, common features, or a combination of both are responsible for therapy benefits (Beutler & Crago, 1991; Orlinsky & Howard, 1987; Shadish & Sweeney, 1991). What does seem clear is that, for psychotherapy to be effective, clients must be committed to the therapeutic enterprise and therapists must be skilled in engaging their clients in actively exploring the problems that brought them to therapy. When therapists succeed in helping clients consider—and attempt—new ways of thinking and behaving, the outcome of therapy is usually positive. The specific approach and the particular procedures used in therapy may be important mainly as a roadmap that gives both therapists and clients confidence that they are on the right track.

Thinking Critically

In one sense, it appears that the Dodo bird's verdict was misleading. The success of therapy does depend in part on a therapist skillfully using specific methods with the active collaboration of a client.

- Do you think that every type of client will respond equally well to all kinds of therapy?
- How would you design a study to test whether different types of clients received greater benefits from different forms of therapy?
- If different types of clients do fare better with different types of therapy, would this favor the specific processes or the common factors perspective?

David Orlinsky

Psychotherapy

Dr. David Orlinsky is Professor, Committee on Human Development, at the University of Chicago. Recognized as one of the world's leading psychotherapy researchers, Dr. Orlinsky has long studied the question of what makes psychotherapy effective.

Q *Is there enough evidence at this point to conclude that psychotherapy is an effective form of treatment for mental disorders?*

A Absolutely. After almost 40 years of research, we have documented beyond any reasonable doubt that psychotherapy, on average, is an effective form of treatment for many clients. When I say "psycho- therapy," I am referring to psychodynamic, interpersonal, phenomenological/experiential, and behavioral or cognitive-behavioral therapies. Therapists who have been trained in and work within these general traditions—and who are able to maintain supportive, understand- ing relationships with clients—are likely to be effective.

> *. . . clients need . . . to be well- informed consumers.*

Q *How can people estimate how valuable a particular kind of psychotherapy will be in their own cases?*

A A potential psychotherapy client should try to be as well in- formed as possible about this ser- vice. There are three important steps clients need to take to be well- informed consumers. First, they need to know what the large body of avail- able research has to say about ther-

apy. Second, they should be skepti- cal of all therapists who promise miracle cures for psychological prob- lems, who insist that they know the exact causes of disorders, or who claim they can reveal the deep se- crets or mysteries of a person's life. Finally, clients should never aban- don their common sense. If a thera- pist says or does things that seem harmful, disrespectful, or risky, clients should trust their common sense and be very cautious before entering into, or proceeding any fur- ther with, therapy with this person.

Q *Do you think therapy is effective primarily because of spe- cific techniques or strategies that therapists use or because of the general benefits of being in a ther- apy relationship?*

A This, of course, is one of the main questions psychotherapy re- searchers have been studying over the years. I believe there is no real con- flict between the two positions. Psy- chotherapy is effective both because of specific techniques that therapists use and because of the relationship that should develop between a thera- pist and a client that makes it possi- ble for the client to explore his or her life thoroughly and attempt to make some changes in it. Effective psychotherapy is never just the appli- cation of techniques to a recipient; it also always requires a relationship in which the therapist proves to be a

good listener and a sensitive coun- selor who helps clients discover how they can change.

Q *Why is it that professional therapists don't appear to do better than nonprofessionals, and why don't more experienced therapists do better than novice therapists?*

A There are a couple of an- swers to this. First, as I just men- tioned, therapy involves more than procedures; it also requires the therapist to have certain special qualities that are helpful: being a good listener and being able to keep the client's needs as the priority in the relationship are two obvious ex- amples. Some people simply have these qualities more strongly than others, and I doubt whether profes- sional training can do much about it. The second answer is that much of the research on this topic does not define "professional" and "nonpro- fessional" or "experienced" and "in- experienced" in meaningful ways. In some studies, the professional thera- pists have actually overseen or super- vised the work of the nonprofession- als; in others, the nonprofessionals spend much more time with the clients than do the professionals. Fi- nally, the "experienced" therapists in some studies are brand new Ph.D.s, while the inexperienced therapists are advanced graduate students. This is hardly the difference people have in mind when they think about sea- soned versus beginning therapists.

Revisiting the Case of Marilyn

Marilyn saw Dr. Barnett once a week for 3 months. Marilyn's therapy concentrated on helping her understand how she had come to apply perfectionistic standards to every area of her life until she believed that she was a total failure if she did anything less than the best in her job or as a mother. She learned that, as she put more and more pressure on herself, she became increasingly discouraged and depressed. Although the sessions were hard work and often left Marilyn feeling drained, she felt that Dr. Barnett was a good listener and genuinely understood how she felt. Gradually, Marilyn realized that one of her core assumptions was that people would like or respect her only if she could prove to them that she was worthwhile. Dr. Barnett helped Marilyn see how her perfectionistic demands, and her depression, ultimately grew out of this assumption. She asked Marilyn to keep a diary of how many times a day she entertained thoughts such as "My kids are waiting for me to get home on time and I can't let them down," or "By this age, my older sister

had already gotten three promotions, and I still haven't had one." She also helped Marilyn develop some thoughts that she could substitute for her usual self-demands; these included more reasonable statements such as "My kids will be happy to see me when I get home" and "I'm glad my work leaves me time to spend with the kids."

After 3 months, Marilyn had made enough progress that her treatment sessions were scheduled only once every 2 weeks. During the next 2 months she concentrated on reducing the number of times she upset herself with perfectionistic thinking. She ultimately came to understand that a great deal of her depressed mood depended on her distorted thinking patterns, and she became increasingly able to stop such thinking before it depressed her. After a total of 20 sessions, Marilyn felt well enough to terminate regular therapy, but she continued to schedule a session with Dr. Barnett every few months to review her status and to receive reminders on how to control her tendencies toward negative thinking.

SUMMARY

What Is Psychotherapy?

Psychotherapy is an intervention in which a client with personal problems interacts with a psychotherapist who helps the client change certain behaviors, thoughts, or emotions so that the client feels better and functions better. Psychiatrists, psychologists, clinical social workers, pastoral counselors, psychiatric nurses, and other counselors offer psychotherapy to the public. Psychotherapists usually receive some type of specialized training in how to understand and treat psychological problems. In addition, they are expected to possess certain personal qualities, such as the ability to empathize and communicate clearly, that make them especially likely to be helpful.

Methods of Psychotherapy

All traditional approaches to psychotherapy emphasize the importance of a positive therapeutic relationship or working alliance. In addition to building good therapeutic relationships, many therapists follow one of five theoretical frameworks to guide treatment: (1) psychoanalysts try to help clients gain insight into the main conflicts and themes that influence them; (2) interpersonal therapists emphasize understanding the recurring patterns in clients' important relationships and how these patterns, if they become too rigid, can be harmful; (3) phenomenological/experiential therapists focus on helping clients reexperience and gain mastery over strong feelings; (4) behavior therapists try to reduce emotions that interfere with effective behavior and teach clients new, more adaptive behaviors; and (5) cognitive therapists strive to help clients replace the biased assumptions and distorted beliefs that accompany mental disorder. In the course of treating many different clients, most therapists employ principles from more than one of these theoretical approaches in an eclectic or integrated treatment. Combining psychotherapy and drug treatments is becoming more common.

Evaluating Psychotherapy

Research on the effectiveness of psychotherapy has established that psychotherapy is a reasonably successful intervention for clients suffering from many kinds of mental disorders. On average, a person receiving psychotherapy is twice as likely to improve as a person not receiving therapy, and these changes are often large enough to be considered clinically as well as statistically significant.

Clinicians have reached several additional conclusions about psychotherapy. The effects of psychotherapy tend to be greater in better-controlled empirical studies. Most improvements usually appear within the first 6 to 8 sessions of treatment and these effects are generally well maintained for as long as 18 months after treatment. Clinicians who differ in experience or professional training do not differ much in their overall rate of success, nor does their theoretical approach to therapy make a large difference in the success of psychotherapy. For certain mental disorders, however, specific treatments—especially those using behavioral and cognitive techniques—have been shown to be particularly effective.

Factors that do appear to influence the effectiveness of psychotherapy include the presence of a strong therapeutic alliance between client and therapist, the client's capacity to talk about and understand thoughts and feelings, and the therapist's ability to use any of several techniques to guide clients toward a more complete understanding of themselves.

KEY TERMS

ABAB design, p. 576
analogue research, p. 578
assertiveness training, p. 570
aversion therapy, p. 572
behavior therapy, p. 569
biofeedback, p. 572
client-centered therapy, p. 566
clinical significance, p. 583
cognitive therapy, p. 573
contingency management, p. 571
contingency contracting, p. 571
coping modeling, p. 571
countertransference, p. 563
covert modeling, p. 571
covert sensitization, p. 573

effect size, p. 579
empathy, p. 566
empirically validated treatment, p. 581
empty chair technique, p. 566
exposure treatment, p. 569
external validity, p. 577
flooding, p. 569
Gestalt therapy, p. 568
internal validity, p. 577
meta-analysis, p. 579
multiple baseline design, p. 576
participant modeling, p. 571
psychotherapy, p. 558

rational emotive therapy (RET), p. 573
response prevention, p. 569
self-control, p. 571
self psychology, p. 564
self-actualization, p. 565
self-relatedness, p. 584
spontaneous remission, p. 578
statistical validity, p. 577
systematic desensitization, p. 569
token economy, p. 571
transference, p. 563
transference neurosis, p. 563

17

Alternatives to Individual Psychotherapy

3 Eyes #5 by Kate Monson, 1995. Acrylic on paper, 19" x 22". Courtesy of Sistare.

From the Case of Juan

When he was 13, Juan emigrated from Honduras to the United States with his parents and three sisters. Life in his homeland had been plagued by extreme poverty; he had had to drop out of second grade—before learning to read or write—in order to work in the coffee fields. Things did not improve much in the United States. His father was unable to find steady employment, and the family was forced to live in one run-down apartment after another, sometimes with people they did not know. They lived in four different cities in the first 2 years and were often barely able to scrape together enough money to put food on the table.

Always a loner and shunned by other boys his age, Juan never went to school in the United States, nor could he find a job. He spent most of his time in bed, complaining of fatigue, depression, and tingling sensations in his spine. Eventually, he came to believe that his spine had been removed and replaced with one that had belonged to his uncle. When he wasn't in bed, Juan hung out in bus and train stations where he would ask strangers for money. His parents knew something was seriously wrong with Juan, but they did not know how to help. They could not afford health care, and besides, they didn't particularly trust Anglo doctors.

At around the age of 16, Juan started hearing hallucinated voices that kept him awake all night. As these hallucinations became more intense, Juan became more irritable and his general demeanor became more menacing. At 17, he got in a fight with a man at the bus station who refused Juan's shouted demand, "Give me five bucks or Satan will eat your dog." On that occasion, Juan was arrested and taken to the state psychiatric hospital, an event that was to be repeated six times in the next 4 years. At first his diagnosis was schizoaffective disorder, then schizophrenia, undifferentiated type. During each hospitalization, which usually lasted less than 3 weeks, he refused psychotherapy, but would sometimes participate in a therapy group that included a few Spanish-speaking patients.

After being stabilized in the hospital on phenothiazines, Juan was discharged with orders to take medication daily and to report for psychotherapy at a community mental health center every 2 weeks. He never showed up there, and no one from the center came to check on him. After a day or two he stopped taking his medication because it made him constipated and thirsty. Soon, he was back at the train station, his life now deteriorating into days of boredom and mental chaos. When his parents grew weary of what they called his "craziness" and the endless shouting matches it caused, they kicked Juan out of their apartment. When a social worker from the mental health center called to ask whether they would like to start family therapy with Juan in order to "learn how to help him more," they were deeply offended. They believed they had already done everything they could.

After 5 years of intermittent hospitalization and sporadic drug treatment, Juan's mental condition was worse than ever. Why? Did the mental health system offer him too little, or were the treatments just not what he needed or could accept? What else could have been done? ■

*I*n this chapter we will consider various forms of psychological treatment other than individual psychotherapy and will suggest interventions that, had they been available to Juan, might have helped him more.

Although individual psychotherapy is the best-known and most widely used form of psychological treatment for mental disorders, it is by no means the only one. Some alternative psychological approaches,

such as *group therapy, marital, or couples, therapy,* and *family therapy,* employ techniques that are similar to those used in individual psychotherapy and, in some cases, are derived from the same theories that guide certain kinds of psychotherapy. Other alternative interventions—such as *psychosocial rehabilitation* and *primary prevention*—bear almost no resemblance to psychotherapy. They rely on different techniques, embrace different assumptions about mental disorders, and often pursue different goals. Some advocates of primary prevention even argue that preoccupation with offering psychotherapy is counterproductive because it distracts mental health professionals—and society as a whole—from working to eliminate the underlying social causes of the mental disorders that affect millions of people around the world.

To varying degrees, all five of these alternatives to individual psychotherapy are more *social* therapy than psychotherapy in the sense that each seeks to change how other people contribute to or are affected by disturbed behavior. Thus, couples therapy addresses these issues through understanding and changing interactions in an intimate dyad. Family therapy focuses on how forces within a family affect the functioning of each of its members. Group therapy seeks changes in the way individuals tend to interact in a wide range of interpersonal relationships. Psychosocial rehabilitation aims to help people who display mental disorders to cope with the occupational, economic, family, and environmental effects of those disorders. Finally, primary prevention attempts to modify social, economic, and environmental factors that lead to dysfunction among vulnerable populations or to strengthen positive qualities that can protect individuals from developing disorders (see Table 17.1).

TABLE 17.1 Psychological Interventions with a Social Emphasis

Treatment	Emphasis
Group therapy	Understand and change disturbances in interpersonal relationships as they are exposed in a special group
Couples therapy	Help couples in intimate relationships improve problem-solving and communication skills in order to improve their relationship
Family therapy	Change harmful interaction patterns within a family so that the family system or a person in the family functions better
Psychosocial rehabilitation	Improve patients' ability to cope with a mental disorder, limit the impairments of the disorder, and help patients live in community
Prevention	Reduce mental disorders by counteracting risk factors or strengthening protective factors

The Limits of Psychotherapy

Why do we need alternative psychological interventions if, as discussed in Chapter 16, research shows that individual psychotherapy tends to be effective for most clients? The answer is that individual psychotherapy is not the answer to *all* mental health problems. Cases such as Juan's reveal that the individual psychotherapy approach is subject to several important limitations.

Accessibility

For one thing, individual psychotherapy is simply not available to many people who need it. For some, the obstacle is financial. At costs ranging as high as $150 per session, psychotherapy may simply be too expensive. In the United States there are 30 million people who have no health insurance to help offset these costs, and even sliding scale fees may still exceed the resources of many poor and working-class people.

Second, even if psychotherapy were free, many people would still be reluctant to utilize it. For example, some men may think it is weak or unmanly to discuss their personal problems or intense feelings with another person, especially a stranger. Similarly, family members may discourage potential clients from seeking therapy because they think that doing so stigmatizes the family as being unable to solve its own problems.

Cultural expectations about mental health and illness also influence willingness to enter individual therapy. Although adults from different ethnic groups in the United States appear to suffer similar rates of serious mental disorders (e.g., Burnam et al., 1987), some groups are more likely than others to seek individual psychotherapy. Indeed, differing world views and cultural traditions affect the way people think about their problems and about what kinds of help (if any) they feel are appropriate (see Table 17.2). It is not surprising, therefore, that some individuals—especially those from some non-Western cultures and some ethnic minority groups—view individual psychotherapy as a pointless, shameful, or selfish option to be avoided at all costs (Foulks, Bland, & Shervington, 1995).

Third, even if everyone wanted it and could afford it, it has been predicted that there will never be enough mental health professionals available to provide individual psychotherapy to all those who need it (Albee, 1959). Although experts in the United States now disagree with this opinion (Robiner, 1991; Pion, 1991; Schneider, 1991), they do agree that the geographical distribution of mental health professionals is uneven. Psychotherapists tend to be concentrated in the affluent sections of larger cities, especially along the east and west coasts, making psychotherapy services less accessible to people in rural areas and in poorer urban neighborhoods.

Focus on Individuals

A basic assumption of most forms of individual psychotherapy is that something problematic *inside* the

---

TABLE 17.2 Cultural Influences on Psychological Processes

Several psychological processes involved in psychotherapy and behavior change are strongly influenced by cultural differences. Below are four basic processes that have been defined largely by research conducted with individuals from Western cultures. These processes are often experienced differently in other cultures.

Basic process	In Western cultures	In other cultures
Sense of self	Seen as independent of others, based on internal attributes	Seen in relation to others, based on group qualities
Sense of false uniqueness	Tendency to enhance self-esteem by viewing self as better than others	Promote supportive ties and relationships as basis for self-esteem
Emotional expression	Emotions can be created through enacting facial expressions and noticing bodily changes	Tend to view facial and other bodily changes as signs of somatic states instead of emotions
Fundamental attribution error	Using personal, internal factors to explain behavior of others	Using social roles and relationships to explain behavior of others

Source: Basic Behavioral Science Task Force of the National Advisory Mental Health Council, 1996.

client needs to change. As described in Chapter 16, this might involve changes in the ways clients think, in the emotions they experience, or in the behaviors they display. Critics believe this emphasis on internal psychological factors limits the value of individual psychotherapy because it pays too little attention to the social aspects of mental disorders. They note, for example, that there are cases in which disorders are best treated by changing the way family members interact with one another or by improving a couple's ability to communicate with each other. Indeed, some mental health professionals believe that, to be most effective, interventions must address the social conditions and environmental stressors that, in a diathesis–stress model, are likely to trigger or worsen mental disorders.

Emphasis on Pathology

Critics also see individual psychotherapy as limited by its emphasis on psychopathology—what is wrong with people—and its corresponding lack of attention to people's competencies. An alternative goal, often pursued by those who see prevention as ultimately more important than treatment, is to maximize positive outcomes in people's lives by building their strengths and promoting wellness for everyone, not just those diagnosed with mental disorders or exposed to risks for developing them. Wellness is marked by occupational effectiveness, satisfying interpersonal relationships, and feelings of belongingness, control, and self-esteem (Cowen, 1994). This **psychological wellness** orientation calls for mental health professionals to be more proactive and less reactive—to design programs that promote wellness from the start of people's lives rather than intervening only after problems have been identified.

In Review

Psychological interventions are not restricted to individual psychotherapy. Common alternatives are:

- more social in their focus and methods; and
- seek to overcome some perceived limits of psychotherapy.

Those perceived limits include:

- its inaccessibility to many people;
- its focus on individual instead of social factors; and
- its concern with relieving pathology rather than encouraging competence.

Alternative Forms of Psychological Treatment

Group Therapy

First practiced in the United States by Joseph Pratt at the turn of the 20th century, **group therapy** is designed to allow several unrelated people to discuss their (usually similar) problems with one another under the guidance and leadership of a therapist. The group approach grew in popularity later in the century because it provided a partial answer to the problem of having too few mental health professionals available to treat the flood of mental disorders stemming from World War II. Group therapy is now regarded as an effective intervention in its own right; every major theoretical approach to individual treatment is currently also offered in a group format. Group treatment is also popular with nonprofessional and self-help organizations that focus on everything from weight loss and assertiveness to alcoholism and recovery from sexual abuse.

Some therapy groups are guided by the principles of a specific form of individual psychotherapy. In such cases, the treatment methods do not differ substantially from those seen in the individual therapy from which the group version was derived—psychodynamic, client-centered, or cognitive, for example. The main special feature of this kind of treatment is that clients can talk to one another and can observe each other's progress as treatment proceeds. Among the many examples of this kind of therapy are cognitive-behavioral group treatments for depression or anxiety disorders.

In other kinds of group therapy, therapists place less emphasis on applying techniques derived from individual psychotherapy and focus instead on facilitating the group interactions that they believe provide the essential ingredients for clients' improvement. These therapists see eight factors in the group format as creating an ideal environment in which clients can recognize, understand, and correct their interpersonal problems (Bednar & Kaul, 1994; Yalom, 1985).

1. *sharing new information.* Therapy groups provide each client with new information, coming not only from the group leader's suggestions and interpretations, but also from the much richer range of insights and advice provided by the other members of the group.

2. *consensuality.* Group feedback is especially powerful when it shows *consensuality,* or agreement, among group members. While a client might discount

Group therapy usually involves more than the simultaneous treatment of several individuals. It offers several distinctive curative factors that depend on the interactions of group members.

the accuracy of a therapist's perceptions, it is much harder to dismiss feedback from six or seven people, especially when all of them say the same things.

3. *instilling hope.* Groups make it especially easy for clients to develop the positive outcome expectancies that are often so important to the success of treatment. For example, watching a shy or hostile group member try new and better ways of thinking about and behaving toward others in the group confirms that change is possible. Furthermore, seeing group members change at different rates can reassure clients who might otherwise have been impatient with slow improvement.

4. *universality.* Group members learn that they are not the only ones who have problems in general or their kind of problem in particular. They may even discover that they are better off than many other people. These revelations may help overcome the kind of secretiveness that, in individual therapy, might have prevented them from opening themselves to the treatment process. As they share their experiences, group members become more aware of the universality of human problems and may worry less about "going crazy" or "falling apart."

5. *altruism.* Therapy groups give their members a chance to help others in ways that also help themselves. For example, the experience of offering suggestions during group sessions that prove helpful to another participant cannot help but make clients feel that, whatever their own problems, they still have

substantial strengths and still have something to offer others. These experiences tend to increase feelings of self-esteem.

6. *interpersonal learning.* Therapy sessions provide a natural arena for the development of new interpersonal skills. A properly conducted group fosters feelings of mutual trust among members that help them to feel safe, not silly or subject to ridicule, when learning and trying out new behaviors. Furthermore, each group session presents a new opportunity to practice—and to immediately receive constructive feedback about—new or revised social skills and interaction styles with a number of different people. Finally, each group member can also serve as a model for adaptive behaviors that other members may want to emulate.

7. *recapitulation of the primary family.* Some group therapists believe that the interactions taking place in therapy groups may symbolically recreate important aspects of their clients' families of origin. This recapitulation process allows clients to reexamine and better understand the lingering effects of early family experiences that may be hampering their current functioning. Recapitulation of the primary family is group therapy's counterpart to the transference relationship in individual psychoanalytic therapy.

8. *group cohesiveness.* Group cohesiveness has been defined as the "attractiveness of a group for its members" (Frank, 1957). Members of cohesive groups accept each other; they are committed to the group and are willing to be influenced by it. They feel secure enough to participate freely in the group and will defend it against outside threats or disruptions. Therapy groups with high levels of cohesion permit their members to express hostility as well as warmth, criticism as well as praise, challenges as well as support. Participants in cohesive groups sometimes attempt to live up to the group's expectations, a kind of *group fulfilling prophecy*. Indeed, group cohesiveness is regarded by many as the single most important curative factor in group therapy and, although questions remain about how to define and measure cohesion (Bednar & Kaul, 1994), group therapists typically view it as a necessary precondition to the operation of all the other curative factors in group therapy.

The Practice of Group Therapy. Therapy groups usually consist of 6 to 12 members. Some groups are *homogeneous*, consisting of members who are similar in age, gender, or type of problem; in *heterogeneous* groups, different types of clients and problems are treated together. Groups that operate mainly as multiclient administrations of individual psychotherapy are usually homogeneous, at least in terms of the problems addressed. For example, cognitive-behavioral treatment groups are usually made up of people seeking help with a particular problem, such as depression or an eating disorder. Groups that emphasize interpersonal dynamics may be either homogeneous or heterogeneous.

Group sessions are usually about twice as long as the 1-hour sessions that are typical of individual psychotherapy. The longevity of group treatment varies considerably, depending on its goals and membership. Some groups continue to meet for years, adding new members as older ones depart. Other groups meet for as few as 6 sessions. In fact, brief group therapy is becoming increasingly popular because it is less costly and thus often a preferred treatment among health maintenance organizations.

As is the case in individual psychotherapy (see Chapter 16), group leaders' experience, training, leadership style, and theoretical backgrounds do not consistently affect the outcome of group treatments. And like individual psychotherapists, effective group leaders must to be able to accurately monitor the therapy process, communicate clearly with clients, and convey warm support for them all. Beyond these qualities, effective group therapists usually try to be a "first among equals," steering the group in constructive directions and preventing any clients from getting lost along the way. The following vignette provides an illustration of how group therapy might actually operate.

The group consisted of five women and three men in their late 20s and 30s, all unmarried or separated. This was the fifth session in a group treatment designed to help singles cope more effectively with the unique stressors they face. As the group members settled into their places on the carpet or on chairs, Harriet, the group therapist, welcomed them and asked each to review what he or she had done throughout the week to complete the "homework" assignment from the previous week's session. One at a time, the members described their social achievements, their success in coping with anxiety, and the frequency with which they used a newly learned relaxation exercise. Several told of unusually stressful situations they had experienced during the week.

After these reports, and amid a great deal of praise and support from group members for achievements, Delores volunteered to describe a situation in which her ever-present feelings of helplessness were intensified. She said that her supervisor at work was always giving her instructions about trivial things. "It was as if she thought I was stupid and, frankly, I'm beginning to believe it." She also noted that in a previous job no one gave her more than the briefest instructions, and she did fine. The others inquired about the nature of her job, which was quite complicated. They noted that her description of her job showed that she received good feedback from her peers, and that she was often consulted by them about various work-related problems. Charles wondered whether the problem she described reflected a conflict between her and her supervisor, not necessarily a problem with her as a person. There was just no evidence, he said, that she was dumb in any way; in fact, she appeared to be uniquely qualified to do her job. The others agreed. Delores said she guessed they were right, but she didn't know what to do about the conflict, and that it was making her miserable. She had thought about quitting, but she liked her job overall, and besides, she added, "Good jobs are hard to get these days."

After the other clients carefully questioned Delores to further clarify what was going on with her supervisor, they suggested a number of strategies she could employ to deal with the situation and a number of specific things that she could say to herself and to her supervisor when future conflicts arose. She evaluated and selected several from among these for practice in the group. (Rose & LeCroy, 1991)

Effectiveness of Group Therapy. Empirical evidence confirms that group therapy can be an effective form of treatment, especially when members clearly understand how the group will be run and what will be expected of them (Bednar & Kaul, 1994). Better outcomes are achieved when the group is cohesive, provides accurate feedback to members, and encourages interpersonal learning and supportive interactions. There is little evidence that treatments delivered as individual psychotherapy are superior to similar treatments in a group format (Orlinsky, Grawe, & Parks, 1994), a result that will probably lead to an increased use of group therapy because of its potential for cost savings.

Marital Therapy

About half of all marriages in the United States end in divorce, and many of those that endure are racked with conflict and distress. This epidemic of marital discord not only creates widespread personal unhappiness and millions of broken homes, it has also been associated with startling increases in social problems such as spousal and child abuse, school problems, conduct disorder, adolescent suicide, and substance abuse. No wonder the goal of intervening in troubled marriages holds a high priority in psychological treatment efforts today.

Marital therapy, also known as **couples therapy,** is the psychological treatment of problems in marriages or other intimate relationships. Marital or couples therapy is sometimes called **conjoint therapy** when both members of the couple see the same therapist(s) in the same sessions. Couples therapy can be the main intervention when relationship difficulties are the primary treatment target, or it can be combined with other methods designed to address other problems. For example, because depression, alcoholism, and severe anxiety disorders may be related to or affected by the quality of a client's marriage or intimate relationship, some mental health experts recommend couples therapy—or at least the involvement of the client's partner—in the treatment of these disorders (Jacobson, Holtzworth-Monroe, & Schmaling, 1989). Couples therapy may also be recommended when the effects of a partner's alcoholism or depression threaten the integrity of an intimate relationship. Some couples even obtain therapy to help them end a marriage or long-term relationship with a minimum of conflict. Such *separation counseling* is often desirable when questions about child custody must be resolved.

In contrast to individual psychotherapy, the client in marital therapy is usually the couple's *disturbed relationship,* not disturbed individuals who happen to be in a relationship. Indeed, the need for marital therapy usually arises out of conflicting expectations and needs of a particular *couple* which might not have arisen had these two people paired with other partners. For example, a wife who was initially attracted to her husband because of his dashing charm may find that this quality now leaves her feeling insecure about his commitment to her. Similarly, a husband who once admired his wife's

Marital therapy focuses on disturbed intimate relationships. Almost all marital therapies investigated empirically have brought about short-term improvements for treated couples, but long-term gains and a restoration of marital happiness have been harder to achieve.

"spunkiness" might now see her independence as a threat to his need for dominance. Intimate relationships are usually beset by conflicts and problems in several domains, including sexual satisfaction, personal autonomy, dominance/submission, responsibility for child rearing, communication, emotional or psychological intimacy, money management, fidelity, and expressions of disagreement and hostility.

Marital Therapy Techniques. The specific techniques and goals of marital therapy depend partly on the couple's problems and partly on the therapist's theoretical approach. For example, a behaviorally oriented marital therapist would be likely to help with a couple's communication problems by teaching the partners to replace hostile, unconstructive criticism with comments that express feelings clearly and convey requests forthrightly for the behaviors that each wants from the other. To bring about quick changes in a troubled relationship, *behavioral exchange contracts* may be established. Using such agreements, one partner who does something on the other's "wish list" (e.g., listening without interrupting) will be rewarded when the other partner reciprocates by doing something that is desired by the first partner (e.g., paying a compliment).

Cognitive-behavioral marital therapists work to help couples change the ways they think about their relationship and modify the attributions they make about each other (Baucom et al., 1989; Bradbury & Fincham, 1990). When couples become preoccupied with deciding who is to blame for their relationship problems and especially when each member begins to attribute dishonorable motives to everything the other one says or does, it becomes almost impossible for the couple to even work on, let alone solve, their problems. Accordingly, the cognitive-behavioral therapist may teach each member of a couple to recognize, for example, that the other member's anger may reflect anxiety about the future of the relationship, not necessarily an intention to end it.

Other marital therapists may focus on restoring the emotional bond and sense of intimacy the couple once enjoyed. Thus, the goal of *emotionally focused* couples therapy is to help partners become more comfortable expressing and accepting each others' emotional needs (Greenberg & Johnson, 1988). To reach this goal, the therapist may use techniques from client-centered and Gestalt therapies that allow partners to become aware of and resolve, or at least disarm, the lingering resentments or other emotional problems that always seem to be resurfacing in their relationship.

Insight-oriented couples therapy is also designed to help partners understand and resolve areas of con-

flict, but here the therapist suggests that the problems may be unconscious. Accordingly, the partners work to understand that the actions of each that cause unhappiness for the other may arise out of unresolved unconscious conflicts experienced in their families of origin or may stem from unmet emotional needs that impair their ability to handle intimacy. The partners may also come to realize that the *pairing* of their individual characteristics may have tended to bring out the worst in each other. Following such insights, the partners are helped to work through the emotional meaning of their problems and to work on conscious efforts to solve them.

Communication Training. Although the theoretical orientation of marital therapists influences the techniques they use, almost all of these therapists employ *communication training* to help couples work more closely together to solve the problems that arise in their relationship. In the following example of communication training, the therapist (T) is trying to help a wife (W) learn new ways of communicating negative feelings to her husband:

T: I do think that what Pete is saying is an important point. There are things that are going to be different about you and each of you is going to think the things you do maybe make more sense than the other person's, and that's probably going to be pretty much of a reality. You're not going to be able to change all those. You may not be able to change very many of them. And everybody is different. They have their own predilections to do things a certain way and again what's coming through from you is sort of like damning those and saying those are wrong; they're silly, they don't make sense, I don't understand them or whatever. You may not understand them but they are a reality of each of you. That's something you have to learn how to deal with in some way. . . . The reason I'm stressing this is I think it plays a large part in your criticalness.

W: Well, I do find it difficult to cater to, I guess that's the word, cater to some idiosyncrasies that I find or think are totally foolish. I am intolerant. I am, and I find it very difficult. I find it almost impossible to do it agreeably and without coming on as "Oh, you're ridiculous."

T: I guess what would be helpful would be if you could come on honestly enough to say "I don't like them" or "It doesn't sit well with me" without having to add the additional value judgment of whether they're foolish or ridiculous or whatever. That's the part that hurts. It's when you damn him because of these things— that's gonna hurt. I'm sure from Pete's point of view they make sense for his total economy of functioning. There's some sense to why he does things the way he does, just as there is for why you do things the way you do. It's not that they're foolish. They make sense in terms of where you are, what you're struggling with, and what's the best way you can deal with right now. I'm not trying to say that means you have to like them, but when you come across and say "It's ridiculous or foolish"—that's the part that makes it hurt.

W: Well, tell me again how to say it, because I find it hard to say anything except "That's really stupid—that's silly." I know you said it a minute ago but I lost it.

T: Well, anytime you can say it in terms of how it affects you and say with it, like "It's hard— I find it hard to take," that doesn't say "I find you're an ass for wanting to do that such and such a way. It's just that, I find it hard to take—I get upset in this circumstance" or whatever. Stay with what your feelings are rather than trying to evaluate Pete. (Ables & Brandsma, 1977, pp. 92–94)

Effectiveness of Couples Therapy. Compared with no-treatment control groups, almost all forms of marital therapy can produce significant improvements in couples' happiness and adjustment (Alexander, Holtzworth-Monroe, & Jameson, 1994). However, the magnitude or clinical significance of these improvements is frequently disappointing. As many as half of treated relationships remain distressed, and, even among couples who show improvement, the changes are often not large enough to allow them to view their marriage or relationship as successful or happy. Furthermore, the few available long-term follow-ups on the effects of successful marital therapy indicate that 30 to 40 percent of couples treated with behavioral marital techniques, at least, relapse into marital discord or divorce (Jacobson, Schmaling, & Holtzworth, 1987; Snyder, Wills, & Grady-Fletcher, 1991).

Programs aimed at *enriching* marital relationships or *preventing* marital problems from arising in new marriages generally show positive initial effects relative to no-treatment controls (Giblin, 1986; Halweg & Markman, 1988). However, as with most forms of marital therapy, marital enrichment programs have not demonstrated that they can produce lasting changes in long-term relationships (Bradbury & Fincham, 1990).

Studies comparing the effects of different theoretical approaches to marital therapy have not found significant advantages for any of them in terms of immediate benefits. In one of the most comprehensive of these comparative outcome studies, Doug Snyder and his colleagues assessed the fate of 79 unhappily married couples who had been randomly assigned to behavioral marital therapy, insight-oriented marital therapy, or a wait-list control group (Snyder & Wills, 1989; Snyder et al., 1991; Wills, Faitler, & Snyder, 1987). All therapy sessions were conducted by well-trained and closely supervised clinicians. After 25 treatment sessions, both behavioral and insight couples reported significant improvements in marital satisfaction and individual adjustment compared with their pretreatment status and with couples on the wait list. At a follow-up assessment six months later, these improvements tended to be well maintained. In short, both therapies proved to be about equally effective (Snyder & Wills, 1989).

Unfortunately, the picture changed after 4 years (Snyder et al., 1991). Although the results of the two types of therapy did not differ at termination or at the 6-month follow-up, at the 4-year follow-up, 38 percent of behaviorally treated couples had divorced compared with only 3 percent of the couples in the insight-oriented treatment (see Figure 17.1). About half the couples in both treatments reported substantial marital difficulties following the termination of treatment.

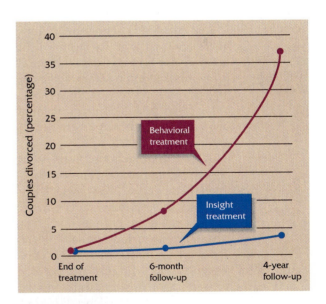

FIGURE 17.1

Long-Term Effects of Different Marital Therapies
Although both behavioral and insight-oriented marital therapy were effective in keeping divorce rates low at the end of treatment, the picture was very different 4 years later. Significantly more divorces had taken place among couples who had received behavioral marital therapy.

Although these results call into question the long-term benefits of behavioral marital therapy, critics of the study have claimed that the form of behavioral therapy used in Snyder's research excluded many contemporary behavioral techniques, including some procedures that were included in the insight-oriented treatment (Jacobson, 1991). Still, these results suggest to many that achieving long-term gains in a couple's happiness requires understanding and resolving persistent emotional conflicts, not just negotiating solutions to specific problems.

Family Therapy

Just as marital therapy is aimed at changing a couple's relationship, **family therapy** is psychological treatment aimed at changing patterns of family interaction to correct family disturbances. And, like couples therapy, family therapy arose from observations that problems seen in individual psychotherapy clients have social contexts and social consequences. For example, family dynamics affect the functioning of people who display childhood behavior problems, eating disorders, schizophrenia, affective disorders, and various medical conditions. In fact, several early theories of psychopathology, including those of Freud, emphasized the family environment and parent–child interactions as causes of maladaptive behavior (Bateson et al., 1956; Lidz & Lidz, 1949; Sullivan, 1953). The role of family interaction patterns in mental disorder can also be seen when individuals show marked improvements after being hospitalized for schizophrenia or other severe mental disorders, then suffer a relapse when they return to their families.

Most approaches to family therapy are grounded in *systems theory* (von Bertalanffy, 1968), which emphasizes three principles. The first is *circular causality,* meaning that events are interrelated and mutually dependent rather than fixed in a simple cause–effect sequence. Thus, no one member of a family is the cause of another's problems. Instead, the behavior of each family member depends to some degree on that of each of the others. The second principle is that of *ecology,* which says that systems can be understood only as integrated patterns, not as collections of component parts. In a family system, a change in the behavior of one member will affect all the other members. The third principle of systems theory is *subjectivity,* which means that there are no objective views of events, only subjective perceptions filtered by the experiences of perceivers within a system. In other words, each member of the family has his or her own perception of family events.

Family therapy often begins by focusing on one member of the family who is having the most obvious problems; therapists speak of this person as the *identified client* or as the family's "ticket of entry" to treatment. The identified client is often an adolescent male whose parents have declared him "umanageable," or a teenage girl who displays an eating disorder. Relying on systems theory, the family therapist encourages the family to consider the role each member might play in the problem and what each might be able to do to help solve it.

As in couples therapy, family therapy often aims at improving communication among family members. For example, in many disturbed families, the main communication methods involve threats or other coercive messages (Patterson, 1982). In one way or another, parents and children are saying to each other, "Do what I want or you'll be sorry." Because these strategies are often successful in meeting short-term goals—such as getting a child to stop whining, or a parent to stop yelling—they gradually evolve into a pattern in which family members give in to coercive demands in order to avoid more severe conflict. When coercion and intimidation become the predominant forms of family interaction, long-term problems are inevitable.

Techniques of Family Therapy. Family therapists operating from a *behavioral* point of view try to teach family members alternative, noncoercive ways of communicating their needs. These therapists teach parents to be firm and consistent in their child discipline practices, encourage each family member to communicate clearly with one another, educate family members in behavior-exchange principles, discourage blaming the identified client for all family problems, and help each member of the family to consider whether their expectations of other members are reasonable.

Another influential approach is called *strategic,* or *structural* family therapy (Minuchin, 1974; Satir, 1967). Here, the therapist seeks to reframe the main problems of the identified client as a disturbed *family* process rather than as an individual defect. The goal is to minimize the blame being directed at a person who has become a convenient family scapegoat. For example, the therapist might suggest that an adolescent son's aggressive and defiant behavior may be a sign of teenage insecurity or a plea for more attention from his father.

The structural family therapist also helps families communicate more clearly and directly. In many

Connections

What effects do family processes have on the course of schizophrenia? See Chapter 10, pp. 362–364.

Family therapists try to help members of a family communicate more effectively with one another and understand how their problems are interrelated.

distressed families, emotional messages are so disguised or distorted that family members frequently talk *at* rather than *with* each other. Often they assume they can "read each others' minds," as when a daughter accuses her mother of "never believing anything I say" or when a father accuses his son of "never caring about anyone but yourself."

Virginia Satir, a well-known pioneer in structural family therapy, offers the following example of how a family therapist helps parents and children communicate better.

Mother: His pleasure is doing things he knows will get me up in the air. Every minute he's in the house . . . constantly.

Therapist: There's no pleasure to that.

Mother: Well, there is to him.

Therapist: No, you can't see his thoughts. You can't get inside his skin. All you can talk about is what you see and hear. You can say it looks as though it's for pleasure.

Mother: All right. Well, it looks as though, and that's just what it looks like constantly.

Therapist: He could be trying to keep your attention, you know. It is very important to Johnny what Mother thinks.

Next, the therapist helps the child understand family situations that precipitate anger.

Therapist: Do you kind of get mad at Daddy when he gets mad at you?

Son: Yeah, and sometimes he gets real mad and pinches my ear.

Therapist: He pinches your ear. Do you feel like hitting him back?

Son: Yeah, I get real mad sometimes.

Therapist: So what keeps you from hitting him?

Son: Well he's, uh, he's bigger than me. (Satir, 1967, pp. 151–152)

One of the most distinctive structural family techniques is the **paradoxical directive.** In this procedure, which has been incorporated into many forms of therapy, the therapist asks clients to purposely perform, even exaggerate, problematic behaviors. For example, one family therapist described a situation in which an adolescent son was repeatedly stealing (Minuchin, 1974). The therapist believed that this behavior reflected a more fundamental family problem, namely the lack of any effective parental control. Therefore, he told the boy to continue, and even escalate his stealing, "I want to see if you are skillful enough to steal from your father." The directive was intended, of course, to force the parents to increase their supervision of and control over the boy's behavior, which it did.

Why might such an apparently illogical method be helpful? One possibility is that, by deliberately performing a problem behavior, clients learn that they control it rather than the other way around. Second, paradoxes challenge clients' assumptions about certain problems, helping them see that a specific problem might not have to be overcome before anything good can happen in the family. Third, paradoxes shift the focus from the individual to the family system, where structural therapists believe problems are usually determined. Finally, paradoxes pose a "win–win" situation for therapists. If clients follow the directive to increase the symptom, they learn a valuable lesson about it; if they don't follow the instruction, the symptom has come under better control!

Recently, structural family therapy has been adapted to take into account cultural factors that might interfere with the treatment of families from certain ethnic groups. The role of such factors was illustrated at the opening of this chapter in the reaction of Juan's parents, who refused to enter family therapy. José Szapocznik and his colleagues in Miami commonly encountered this reaction when they used structural family therapy to treat drug abuse among adolescents in Hispanic, largely Cuban, families (Szapocznik et al., 1986).

To get these families into treatment, and to keep them in treatment, Szapocznik evaluated a set of "family engagement" procedures (Szapocznik et al., 1990). These methods were designed to counter four strategies these families tended to use to resist treatment: (1) adolescents identified as suspected drug abusers were unwilling to start treatment; (2) mothers were ambivalent about having their families in treatment even when they realized their children needed it; (3) fathers were often disengaged from their families and refused to be involved in treatment; and (4) family members were worried that their secrets would be disclosed and therefore did not want to come to treatment.

In this study, families were randomly assigned to receive either a standard invitation to begin treatment or an experimental program that used structural family techniques to overcome the family's initial resistance to therapy. Results indicated that the experimental engagement technique was highly successful; 93 percent of families receiving the culturally sensitive engagement methods began treatment compared with 42 percent of the standard invitation families. Furthermore, those families receiving the structured engagement method were 3 times more likely to complete treatment than were families in the control condition (see Figure 17.2).

Effectiveness of Family Therapy. Regardless of how the families in Szapocznik's study were recruited, those that *completed* treatment experienced significant improvements in their adolescents' behavior. This outcome is typical of empirical research showing that family therapy is an effective treatment for several kinds of disorders and family problems (Hazelrigg, Cooper, & Boudin, 1987). Certain types of family therapy do appear more successful than oth-

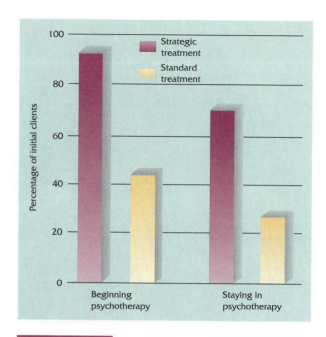

FIGURE 17.2

Culturally Sensitive Family Therapy
When family therapists use culturally sensitive techniques to overcome common resistances to therapy, the rates of beginning and staying in family therapy can be significantly increased.

Source: Based on Szapocznik et al., 1990.

ers, however. Behavioral and structural family therapies have received the strongest empirical support. Each of these approaches emphasizes pragmatic changes in the way families interact and go about solving problems. Psychodynamic or humanistic family therapies that do not stress direct modification of specific symptoms and problems tend to show smaller effects.

Self-Help Groups

It has been estimated that 10 to 15 million people in the United States and another half a million in Canada participate in **self-help groups** that meet regularly, without professionally trained leaders, to address members' psychological problems (Gottlieb & Peters, 1991; Jacobs & Goodman, 1989). This number rivals the number of clients in psychotherapy and suggests that self-help groups, or SHGs, have become a major method of mental health care delivery. Indeed, SHGs are growing in popularity, partly because of an apparent backlash against the idea that professional therapists are needed to help people solve all types of psychological problems. This is not a new idea. In earlier times, people facing adversity could turn to relatives, friends, and neighbors for comfort and aid. Today, with many people living far from their families in neighborhoods of strangers, self-help groups provide some of this support and nurturance.

Several features are common to most of the SHGs operating around the world today (Jacobs & Goodman, 1989). First, their members usually share a relatively well-defined problem or set of life experiences, such as alcoholism, severe mental illness, or the recent death of a spouse or child. Second, self-help group meetings focus on exchanging information, providing feelings of togetherness and belonging, and discussing mutual problems. All of these activities are forms of social support provided by peers who are struggling with similar problems. Third, most self-help groups charge no fees, or low fees; their goal is to provide mutual aid, not to make a profit. Finally, self-help groups are largely member governed, and, although some use professional consultants, they rely mainly on group members as primary caregivers.

Although SHGs differ in size, organization, and goals (Powell, 1987), they fall into five general types. *Habit disturbance* groups emphasize a specific behavior problem that all members share; examples include Alcoholics Anonymous and Gamblers Anonymous. *General-purpose groups* address a wider range of difficulties, such as dealing with the death of a child (e.g., Compassionate Friends) or helping psychiatric patients cope with crises (e.g., GROW, or

Recovery, Inc.). *Lifestyle organizations* support individuals—such as single parents (Parents Without Partners) or the elderly (Gray Panthers)—who feel they are being treated unfairly by society. *Significant-other* organizations provide advocacy, education, support, and partnership for relatives of disturbed persons; examples include Gam-Anon (for relatives of compulsive gamblers) and Al-Anon (for relatives of alcoholics). Finally, several *physical handicap organizations* offer support to people with heart disease (Mended Hearts) and other medical conditions.

Effectiveness of Self-Help Groups. The effectiveness of SHGs is seldom evaluated empirically. Most SHG members are simply convinced that their groups are valuable and thus see formal outcome research on them as unnecessary or even undesirable. Evaluation is further complicated by the fact that the goals of SHGs are often hard to describe precisely. The few outcome evaluations that are available have produced mixed results (Nietzel, Guthrie, & Susman, 1991), but it generally appears that active members value their involvement in the group and experience moderate improvements in some areas of their lives. It would be helpful if SHGs would become more receptive to empirical research so that clinicians could learn more about their beneficial effects and how they are brought about.

Connections

The best-known self-help group in the world is Alcoholics Anonymous (AA). How effective is AA? See Chapter 13, pp. 460–461.

Self-help groups such as Alcoholics Anonymous, Parents Without Partners, GROW, and the cancer support group shown here are becoming increasingly popular around the world. These groups provide support, a sense of connectedness, and valuable information to individuals who often feel alone and bewildered by their personal problems.

In Review

The curative factors in group therapy include:

- sharing new information;
- consensual feedback;
- instilling hope;
- universality;
- altruism;
- interpersonal learning;
- recapitulating primary families; and
- group cohesiveness.

Marital, or couples, therapy:

- typically aims to improve a couple's ability to solve problems and to communicate with each other;
- has been shown to bring about positive changes in a large percentage of couples, although these changes are often not enough to make the relationship a happy one; and
- is often followed by relapse into distress.

Family therapy:

- seeks to change the way the members of a family interact with one another; and
- is particularly effective when it employs behavioral and structural techniques.

Self-help groups:

- rely on individuals who have some problem in common to support and help one another; and
- are an increasingly popular intervention for people with habit disturbances, physical handicaps, difficult or unpopular lifestyles, and problems in coping with stressors such as relatives who have a physical or mental disorder.

Psychosocial Rehabilitation

The effectiveness of antipsychotic medications has allowed an increasing number of severely mentally ill people to be discharged from public mental institutions into local communities in recent decades. This trend was also encouraged by the community mental health center movement of the 1960s, which presented evidence that severely mentally ill people could receive more beneficial (and less expensive) care as outpatients at neighborhood mental health centers (Kiesler & Sibulkin, 1987). As a result of these two innovations, the number of mental patients confined in public mental hospitals has declined from approximately 550,000 in 1955 to only about 100,000 in the 1990s (Lamb, 1992).

This shifting of patients from public hospitals to the community is known as **deinstitutionalization.** In theory, deinstitutionalization should have been a great success for the field of mental health, but, for many former mental patients, release from hospitals did not improve the quality of their lives, at least not on a permanent basis (Moscarelli & Capri, 1992).

What has happened to all the patients who once made up the bulk of public mental hospital populations? Very few are being treated in general hospitals or private psychiatric hospitals because these facilities usually provide only short-term care to those who can afford it. And too few are being treated in community mental health centers or other social service agencies, because these facilities often lack the resources to handle the severe and chronic problems presented by former mental patients. Sadly, thousands of deinstitutionalized patients have simply been left to fend for themselves and are not receiving any kind of regular treatment. Many have drifted into unemployment and homelessness, often becoming the unwanted responsibility of the police and criminal justice system.

Because deinstitutionalization and community-based mental health care failed to fulfill many of their initial promises, severe mental disorders such as schizophrenia and major mood disorders continue to take an enormous toll on many people's lives. Severe mental illness leads to chronic unemployment and homelessness for millions of people across the United States and the rest of the world. For example, in the United States, more than 70 percent of individuals with schizophrenia are unemployed at any given time. The severely mentally ill also face higher than normal risks for physical illness, criminal victimization, and premature death due to injuries and accidents (e.g., Greenberg, Shah, & Seide, 1993). In many cases, the families of these people also suffer as they attempt to care for their loved ones, and the costs of this care are enormous. Estimates are that the overall financial costs of schizophrenia—about $19 billion a year in the United States—exceed those of cancer (National Foundation for Brain Research, 1992; cited by Andreasen & Carpenter, 1993).

Obviously, these severely mentally ill people are unlikely to enter individual psychotherapy and, even if pushed into it by family members, may not benefit much. Although psychotherapy was a primary treatment for schizophrenia earlier in this century, it is no longer considered a sufficient treatment (Schooler & Keith, 1993). An alternative intervention called **psychosocial rehabilitation** teaches patients who display schizophrenia, major mood disorders, or other severe mental disorders how to cope better with the effects of these disorders and especially how to prevent or lessen the crises that often threaten their ab-

Individuals with severe mental illness have trouble performing basic life skills. The cornerstone of psychosocial rehabilitation is teaching patients new skills to lessen the impairments associated with mental disorders.

ility to function in society. In other words, rather than trying to cure serious mental disorders, psychosocial rehabilitation helps patients normalize their lives, compensate for their impairments, and achieve the highest possible quality of life in the community (Hunter, 1995).

Psychosocial rehabilitation has emerged from the cooperative efforts of three groups interested in improving the lives of the severely mentally ill. The first of these is the National Alliance for the Mentally Ill (NAMI), a support group for the families of the mentally ill, which, since the early 1980s, has educated the public about mental illness and has advocated for more effective services for seriously mentally ill people in the community. These efforts have been supplemented by similar educational and political activity by self-help groups of seriously mentally ill people. At the same time, scores of community-oriented mental health professionals have designed treatment programs to help maintain seriously mentally ill clients in local communities. The collaborative efforts of these three groups has been recognized in federal legislation (P. L. 99-660) mandating that each of them must be represented on mental health planning councils in every state in the United States.

One major goal of psychosocial rehabilitation is **empowerment** (Rappaport, 1981, 1987), that is, the development of a belief among formerly dependent and powerless people that they can have mastery and control over their lives. Empowerment requires both an adequate understanding of the environment and skills for living effectively in it. It also includes the abilities to maintain stable housing and engage in regular, meaningful employment. Thus, psychosocial re-

habilitation programs are designed to teach formerly hospitalized mental patients the basic competencies they need to live successfully and independently in the community (Stroul, 1993). These programs, which are often started when the patient is still in the hospital and then continued in the community, typically involve four components.

The first component of psychosocial rehabilitation is the effort to help patients understand their disorder so that they can cope with it more effectively. For example, Assertive Community Treatment (ACT)—a multicomponent program developed in Madison, Wisconsin, in the late 1960s—uses mental health teams to teach patients how to recognize the early warning signs of psychological deterioration in time to avoid high-risk situations and to obtain social support to avert a crisis. When patients and their families are able to detect specific symptoms, such as insomnia or auditory hallucinations, that precede psychotic "breaks" and lead to hospitalization or arrest, they can call on treatment staff for help in managing the situation (Herz & Melville, 1980). Doing so can significantly reduce the necessity for hospitalization and the likelihood of arrest (Bond et al., 1990).

Second, psychosocial rehabilitation programs help patients identify, then learn, the skills they need for community living. The targeted skills often involve practical, day-to-day tasks such as making change, using public transportation, obtaining medical care, buying groceries, cooking meals, and, most important, interacting with other people. Patients are also helped to understand how their symptoms may affect others. They are told, for example, that it is frightening to the average person on the street to see someone who is disheveled or is talking back to hallucinated voices. Once patients understand onlookers' reactions, they can learn to cope with them better. Note that the goal here is not to eliminate the symptoms of mental disorder, but to help patients cope better with their consequences.

A third component of most psychosocial rehabilitation programs is **case management,** in which a single staff person assists the client in obtaining services related to employment, housing, nutrition, transportation, recreation, medical care, and finances. Having one case manager act as the client's advocate and resource broker in all these areas makes it easier for the client to gain access to a sometimes bewildering range of social services.

Finally, psychosocial rehabilitation promotes treatment efforts by maintaining a coalition among mental health professionals, family members, and patients. Often, treatment occurs in self-help groups. Organizations such as GROW and Recovery, Inc., have demonstrated that severely mentally ill people are capable of providing mutual support and effective crisis intervention services (Galanter, 1988; Rappaport et al., 1985). Members of these self-help groups challenge and encourage each other to actively participate in their own treatment, sometimes using **therapeutic contracting,** in which they commit themselves to work toward improvement in specific areas (Heinssen, Levendusky, & Hunter, 1995).

Effectiveness of Psychosocial Rehabilitation. Several studies have shown that psychosocial rehabilitation programs can help severely mentally ill patients learn new skills such as administering their own medications, monitoring their symptoms, engaging in appropriate social conversations, and caring for their own health and safety (Benton & Schroeder, 1990). The evidence is less clear that patients regularly use the skills they have learned to cope with problems in the community (Wallace, 1993). Patients who have received special skill training perform better in their home environments than they did before training but not as well as they did in the training environments.

Comprehensive psychosocial rehabilitation programs have also been shown to reduce relapse rates and other crises such as arrests or imprisonment (Bond et al., 1990; Olfson, 1990). In some cases, these outcomes are achieved even though the overall rate of symptoms has not declined significantly. In one well-conducted evaluation of Assertive Community Treatment, severely mentally ill patients were randomly assigned to either ACT or to a drop-in center where they could socialize with other patients, obtain food, and engage in recreational activities (Bond et al., 1990). Outcome assessments after 1 year suggested that there were large differences in how often clients actually participated in their assigned services; 76 percent of ACT patients were active in treatment, compared with only 7 percent of drop-in center patients. Furthermore, ACT patients were admitted to the state mental hospital significantly less often during the treatment year than were the drop-in center clients, they had significantly fewer contacts with the legal system, and they maintained more stable housing arrangements in the community.

Other research indicates, however, that, if rehabilitation programs are not continued for at least 2 years, clients' conditions often deteriorate, rehospitalization rates increase, and overall quality of life declines (Wallace, 1993). These results are not particularly surprising. Given that disorders such as schizophrenia impair almost all aspects of functioning, it is to be expected that, to be effective, treatment should be comprehensive and continuous.

Connections

Can psychosocial rehabilitation help prevent relapse in schizophrenia? See Chapter 10, pp. 370–371.

In Review

Psychosocial rehabilitation teaches patients how to cope better with their mental disorders by:

- teaching them about their disorders;
- empowering them with new skills and competencies;
- providing case managers who can help patients locate and utilize various services, and
- combining professionals, family members, and patients into cooperative treatment teams.

Severely mentally ill people can benefit from psychosocial rehabilitation, especially if:

- multiple services are included; and
- the program is continued for a sufficient length of time.

Prevention: The Legacy of Community Psychology

Several influences came together in the 1960s to bring about the birth of community psychology as well as several radically new ideas about how to combat mental disorders. Within the mental health professions, there was growing disenchantment with traditional forms of assessment and treatment. Many clinical psychologists, in particular, began to question whether traditional models of psychopathology were sufficiently comprehensive and whether psychotherapy was an adequate treatment for serious psychological problems.

The 1960s also saw a spreading distrust of many traditional institutions and practices in society. The civil rights movement, black separatist ideologies, antiwar protests, urban crises, and the War on Poverty all marked the 1960s as a decade of social upheaval and change. These social forces, too, prompted many psychologists to consider whether mental health could be promoted more effectively through positive social change rather than through individual therapy.

The 1962 Community Mental Health Centers Act authorized the construction of a nationwide network of community mental health centers in the United States and gave socially and politically active psychologists a base from which to launch a volley of new ideas for treating—and even preventing—mental disorders. **Community psychology** soon emerged as a new subdiscipline within which to develop and test these new ideas. It was born in the spring of 1965 at a conference attended by about 30 psychologists in Swampscott, Massachusetts. They called for psychologists to become "change agents, social system analysts, consultants in community affairs, and students generally of the whole man in relation to all his environment" (Bennett, 1965, p. 833).

Principles of Community Psychology

Four principles set community psychology apart from traditional clinical psychology. First, community psychologists believe that behavior cannot be explained solely on the basis of biological factors or psychological dynamics. Instead, they view behavior from an **ecological perspective,** which means that they look for the causes of behavior in the *interactions* between individuals and the economic, social, and physical aspects of the environment. Taking this ecological perspective means developing interventions that are designed to maximize the "fit" between individuals and specific environments in ways that promote their adjustment. The ecological perspective also allows psychologists to go beyond strictly psychological variables in explaining and treating mental disorders. Thus, where the traditional clinical perspective might see a young child's constant misbehavior in school as indicative of attention-deficit/hyperactivity disorder or some neurological impairment, the ecological view would consider other possible explanations. Perhaps the child's classroom is inadvertently organized to reward underachievement and inattentiveness. Perhaps the curriculum is either too easy or too hard for the child's level of development. Or perhaps the child's family or peer group devalues academic achievement.

A second principle of community psychology is a corollary of the ecological perspective: interventions should take place in the settings where clients live, work, or go to school. Accordingly, community psychology interventions are implemented in homes, schools, and neighborhoods. Some are even transmitted through mass media in order to influence whole communities.

The ecological perspective is also evident in the third principle of community psychology, namely, that mental health interventions should aim at the goal

The ecological perspective of community psychology argues that, rather than helping people adjust to harmful environments, it is often preferable to bring about change in the environment itself. Because residential instability is especially hard on children's adjustment, the construction of stable, low-cost housing may be important to protecting mental health.

of *social-system change*, not merely *person-oriented change,* as is typical of individual psychotherapy. Community psychologists do not ignore the need for individual changes, but they prefer social-system changes because such changes present the best opportunity for improving the lives of large numbers of people. Thus, community psychology interventions for mental health address how social institutions might be changed to eliminate school failure, family discord, unemployment, community disorganization, and other harmful influences on mental health. These changes can occur at the local level, as when a public school teacher introduces a token economy to increase class participation by shy children, but they can happen on a broader scale, as well. Thus, parents who are dissatisfied with the quality of public education in their communities might start an alternative school, or a state seeking to promote cooperative learning and reduce students' grade-related stress might decide to merge first-, second-, and third-grade classrooms and to eliminate all letter grades.

Community psychologists sometimes stimulate broad social-system changes by conducting **action research,** which involves empirically testing the effects of some deliberate change in the normal operation of a social institution or system (Seidman, 1988). If the tested change proves beneficial, it can then be disseminated to other settings where additional evaluative research can be done.

The fourth, and most important, principle of community psychology is its emphasis on prevention. Prevention is such an important aspect of community psychology that it deserves a more detailed discussion.

Prevention in Community Psychology

Using principles borrowed from the field of public health, Gerald Caplan (1964) described three different types of programs for preventing mental health problems.

1. *Tertiary prevention* seeks to lessen the severity of a disorder and to reduce its short-term and long-term consequences. Tertiary prevention is really prevention in name only because any form of treatment seeks to minimize the severity and reduce the adverse consequences of being ill. Tertiary interventions have also been called *indicated* prevention because they focus on persons who have already indicated that they have the early signs of disorder (Institute of Medicine, 1994).

2. *Secondary prevention* involves interventions for groups of people who are at risk for developing a disorder. This approach is sometimes called *selective* prevention because it focuses on specific individuals. Effective secondary prevention requires knowledge about how risk factors culminate in specific disorders. It also usually requires assessment methods that reliably and validly detect the initial signs of a disorder so that attempts can be made to stop the development of the disorder at the earliest possible point. One example of secondary prevention is the early family interventions that are used to prevent relapse and deterioration among young schizophrenic patients (see Chapter 10).

3. *Primary prevention* involves eliminating disorders by either modifying environments or strengthening individuals so that they are not susceptible to disorders in the first place. Also referred to as *universal prevention,* this approach is intended to affect the well-being of the general population. Primary prevention programs seek one of two main goals: *counteracting risk factors* and *reinforcing protective factors* (Coie et al., 1993). There are five basic methods through which effective programs for the primary prevention of mental illness seek to accomplish these goals.

Encouraging Secure Attachments and Reducing Family Violence. One method is to help parents and their children form the kind of warm, nurturant, and secure early attachments that are associated with mental health as the children grow. As discussed in other chapters, insecure or disrupted attachments are one of the earliest and most pernicious risk factors for many mental disorders. The absence of a warm and secure attachment between infant and caregiver seriously threatens a child's healthy development and increases the child's risk for short-term difficulties, problematic relationships, and anxiety and mood disorders in adulthood. Why don't healthy attachments form naturally? For one thing, some parents do not understand the importance of such attachments or may believe that if they are too responsive their baby will be "spoiled." In other cases, substance abuse or depression might leave parents unable to care properly for a child. Severe poverty can also make it difficult for parents to properly nurture children. Various types of preventive interventions can be devised to deal with these and other sources of attachment problems and, if applied early enough, can reduce the harm they might otherwise have done.

Another family-related primary prevention tactic is the reduction of family violence. It is difficult to determine the precise incidence of family violence—including physical and sexual abuse of children and the battering of spouses—but available figures for the United States alone are staggering. At least 1 million children a year are victims of physical or sexual abuse or severe neglect, and 3 to 4 million households may experience other forms of family violence every year (Gelles & Straus, 1988). Family violence is disturbing enough on its own to warrant anger and moral outrage, but there is also increasing evidence that children reared in violent homes are more likely to become aggressive, abusive, or criminal adults themselves. In short, it appears that violence begets violence, as the Controversy section on page 608 suggests.

Teaching Effective Problem Solving. A second approach to primary prevention of mental disorder involves teaching children and adolescents cognitive and interpersonal skills that are crucial to later development and adjustment. Included among these skills are those that children need to solve the problems they repeatedly face at home and at school.

As early as kindergarten, children who lack such skills tend to display a pattern of behavior that has been shown to increase their risk for later delinquency (Farrington, 1991). A core element of this pattern is frequent disruptions and impulsivity, which are manifested by children's refusing to wait their turn in line, being disrespectful and defiant toward teachers, and constantly interrupting others. In other words, these children have trouble regulating their behavior to abide by rules and accommodate others. However, there is evidence that, if these children can be taught to control their impulses (Kendall & Braswell, 1985), to use effective problem-solving strategies (Spivack & Shure, 1974), and to respond nonaggressively to provocation and teasing by peers (Dodge, McClaskey, & Feldman, 1985), they can avoid developing the academic and peer-interaction problems that are common in the backgrounds of conduct-disordered youngsters (see Chapter 3).

An example of the cognitive/interpersonal skills approach with older children is the Teen Outreach Program. Operating in middle schools and high schools at over 130 different sites, this program attempts to prevent problem behaviors such as teenage pregnancy, school failure, and school dropout. This program has reduced these problems by an average of 10 to 15 percent (Philliber & Allen, 1992). It places teens as volunteers in various community service agencies and links this activity with a special curriculum in which the youngsters discuss family conflict, human development, and social problem solving. The program helps youths understand and gain an increasing sense of autonomy at a time in their lives when autonomy is often forged through rebellion and conflict. The volunteer work allows this autonomy to develop in the context of positive relationships with adults and peers.

Most programs that have focused on preventing mental disorders by changing a single causal factor—such as children's social skills—have achieved positive, but modest, short-term results. Some prevention scientists argue, therefore, that multiple-component programs are necessary to achieve major, long-term preventive effects (Borduin et al., 1995). In one such program, the Montreal Longitudinal Experimental Study, parents were trained in childrearing practices and children were taught improved social skills. The children were kindergarten boys, averaging 7 years of age, from poor, inner-city areas of Montreal, Canada. All were identified by their teachers as being among the most disruptive children in their classes, and were therefore at risk for serious delinquency. The boys were randomly assigned to one of three conditions: (1) 2 years in the multicomponent treatment (parent training at home; social skill training at school); (2) 2 years of frequent psychological assessments and referral for treatment at a mental health center, if requested by their parents; or (3) a no-treatment control group.

After the treatment period ended, all three groups were followed for several years to determine how each was doing in school and how often they were engaging in delinquent behavior (Tremblay et al., 1995). The boys in the multicomponent treatment group were more likely to be in a classroom appropriate to their age than were boys in either of the two control groups. However, this difference disappeared by the middle of high school, at about age 15 (see Figure 17.3 on page 609). Boys in the treatment group reported significantly lower rates of delinquent behavior up to age 15, but they did not differ from the control boys in the number of times they had actually been arrested (see Figure 17.3). And in spite of the parent training component of the treatment program, boys in that program did not report any lasting differences in their parents' disciplinary practices. In short, the effects of this multicomponent program were modest, at best. Perhaps its impact would have been greater if treated boys had received "booster sessions" as they entered early adolescence. Future studies will need to evaluate this possibility as well as the relative costs and benefits of multicomponent prevention programs.

Changing Environments. A third approach to primary prevention entails analyzing environments, then changing them to make them more supportive. Prime targets for such environmental reengineering

Controversy   Can Violence Be Socially Inherited?

If violence is indeed socially inherited through abuse experiences in childhood, the need for early interventions to prevent family violence becomes all the more obvious. But does being abused as a child actually cause criminal behavior or mental disorders in later years, or are such problems merely correlated with abuse?

Controversy over this point arises partly because studies reporting a higher incidence of abuse experiences in the childhoods of aggressive, abusive adults (Milner, 1994) have usually relied on retrospective methods, often using potentially biased or faulty self-reported memories of abuse. It would be much better to base conclusions about relationships between childhood abuse and violence in adulthood on long-term prospective studies in which abused children are identified, then repeatedly assessed as they grow into adulthood.

Just such a study has been conducted by Cathy Spatz Widom (1989, 1992). She used court records to identify a group of 908 children in a midwestern American city who had suffered abuse (i.e., sexual abuse or physical assault leading to injury) or severe neglect (i.e., inadequate food, clothing, shelter, or medical care) between 1967 and 1971. This "abuse/neglect" group was matched to a group of 667 children who had not been exposed to abuse or neglect but who were similar in sex ratio, age, ethnicity, and family socioeconomic status. Matching the abused versus non-abused groups on these variables was important because it allowed Widom to assure that any differences between the groups in terms of violent behavior in adolescence or adulthood were not due to the effects of differences in demographic characteristics.

Extent of Involvement in Delinquency, Adult Criminality, and Violent Criminal Behavior

Type of arrest	Abused and neglected (n = 908)	Comparison group (n = 667)
Juvenile	26.0%	16.8%
Adult	28.6	21.1
Violent crime	11.2	7.9

Note: All differences between groups are statistically significant.
Source: From Widom, 1992.

Widom's analysis of police and court records showed that, as earlier research had suggested, abused or neglected children were significantly more likely than the comparison group to have been arrested for violent crimes as juveniles or as adults (see the table above). In addition, the abused or neglected individuals were, on average, 1 year younger than comparison subjects at the time of their first arrest and had committed twice as many total offenses over the 15- to 20-year period studied. These differences were seen in boys and girls and in European Americans and African Americans; however, the relationship between abuse and violence was particularly strong among African Americans.

As disturbing as these results are, they may actually *underestimate* the risks created by childhood abuse. For one thing, only incidents that resulted in arrest or trial were included in this study. Many other undetected or unreported crimes may have been committed by the abused/neglected group. Furthermore, this aspect of the study did not assess group differences in mental disorders, substance abuse, educational and occupational difficulties, or other possible long-term consequences of childhood abuse. In a second phase of Widom's research, the groups are being interviewed about such consequences, and preliminary results indicate that they may be as common in the abused/neglected group as the delinquency and violent crime already identified. In short, it would appear that programs aimed at preventing mental disorders would do well to focus on preventing family violence.

Thinking Critically

Based on this research it appears that violence can be socially inherited, but the mechanisms responsible for transmitting it across generations are still unknown.

- What factors could account for this transmission effect?

- Is it possible that an aggressive temperament in some children might have triggered abusiveness in their parents as well as their own later criminality?

- How would you design a research study to test this possibility?

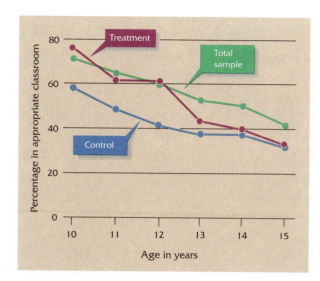

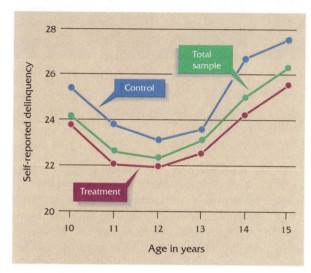

FIGURE 17.3

Long-Term Effects of a Delinquency Prevention Program

In the Montreal Longitudinal Experimental Study, at-risk boys who received a combination of social skills training with childrearing training for their parents showed some gains in school progress and reductions in delinquency. However, these effects tended to fade with time, suggesting that effective prevention requires a continuing investment.

Source: Tremblay et al., 1995.

are settings that powerfully shape human development, namely families, schools, neighborhoods, and the criminal justice system. For example, programs such as Head Start that expand preschool opportu-

nities and increase the commitment of parents and children to academic success have been shown to decrease antisocial behavior in the long run, even though this was not their original goal (Schweinhart, Barnes, & Weikhart, 1993; Zigler, Taussig, & Black, 1992). Programs that help children and adolescents adjust to the transition from elementary to middle school or from middle school to high school have also been found to prevent school dropout and antisocial behavior in school (Olweus, 1995; Seidman et al., 1994).

Reengineering within the criminal justice system is seen in programs known as diversion (e.g., Davidson et al., 1977). **Diversion** involves requiring youthful (often first-time) offenders to engage in community-based alternatives to imprisonment, such as attending special classes, performing community service, or compensating crime victims. The rationale for diversion is that labeling and processing youngsters as "delinquent" creates a self-fulfilling prophesy that almost always leads to further criminal behavior. Diversion prevents young offenders from being officially labeled as criminals and, by keeping them out of jail, avoids their being exposed to seasoned offenders who would train and encourage them to engage in more serious forms of violence and aggression after their release. (Note that, by targeting people who have already shown signs of disorder, diversion programs actually aim at secondary rather than primary prevention.)

Enhancing Stress-Coping Skills. A fourth approach to primary prevention takes the form of reducing environmental stressors and/or helping people cope more effectively with the major stressors they must endure. In either case, harmful mental and physical stress reactions are likely to decrease, along with the incidence of the disorders associated with them (see Chapter 5).

For example, increasing the availability of affordable housing can reduce the frequency of household moves, a major stressor for poor families that has been linked to psychological maladjustment. Furthermore, strengthening or creating social support for the elderly, for immigrants, and for other people facing social isolation can help protect against future problems (Felner, Farber, & Primavera, 1983). So too might efforts to help people develop new strategies for coping with the ethnic discrimination faced by millions of people every day in the form of unfair employment and housing practices, verbal abuse, and social rejection. The anticipation of discrimination by minority children in schools has led some

Diversion of juveniles from the criminal justice system has been considered a promising form of secondary prevention because it lessens exposure of youths to more seasoned criminals. Several states are now lowering the age at which they treat juvenile offenders as adults, however, making the future status of diversion programs uncertain.

of them to devalue and withdraw from academic activities. Interventions designed to prevent this counter-productive coping strategy could improve these youngsters' academic performance, bolster their self-esteem, and keep them on the path to success (Basic Behavioral Science Task Force of the National Advisory Mental Health Council, 1996).

Promoting Empowerment. Finally, there are primary prevention programs designed to empower the powerless and to help those for whom old age, poverty, homelessness, ethnic minority status, physical disability, or other factors have left them without the ability or confidence to take control of their own lives. Many psychologists believe that the disproportionately high levels of mental disorder seen in these groups is due largely to the psychological and physical problems that often accompany their chronic sense of *disempowerment*. Accordingly, prevention programs or social changes that help these groups gain a sense of control over their lives can be expected to decrease their risk for developing mental disorders. There is already some evidence, for example, that empowering minority parents to influence school policies or empowering neighborhoods to control crime can have long-term mental health benefits (Comer, 1987).

Connections

How do stressful events increase the risk of physical illness? See Chapter 6, pp. 197–199.

Designing Effective Prevention Programs

Over the past 30 years, prevention programs have been aimed at almost every conceivable cause of pschological problems (Trickett, Dahiyal, & Selby, 1994). Parents have been taught to cuddle infants, read to toddlers, and closely supervise middle schoolers. Children have been trained to control their aggressive conduct, become more creative problem solvers, strengthen their social skills, cope with negative life events, and resist harmful peer pressures. School curricula have been expanded, contracted, specialized, and decentralized. The criminal justice system has experimented with decriminalization, diversion, and neighborhood watches, while the mental health care system has attempted deinstitutionalization, community consultation, and stress management. Teenagers have been educated about the dangers of unprotected sex, single parenthood, substance abuse, and other risky behaviors, and they have been encouraged to turn their energies to prosocial pursuits. Communities have been reorganized, recapitalized, and empowered. Job training, affirmative action, welfare reforms, and new public housing programs have all been justified, in part, by their potential for preventing mental disorders.

Prevention programs differ in many ways. Some aim at one causal variable, while others address a multitude of influences. Some are small-scale innovations funded on a shoestring, while others are multibillion dollar national initiatives such as Head Start. Most important, some of these programs have failed, while others have produced impressive successes (Edelstein & Michelson, 1986; Mrazek & Haggerty, 1994; Trickett, Dahiyal, & Selby, 1994; Price et al., 1988). As a result of increasingly sophisticated prevention-centered research, mental health professionals have learned several important lessons about what makes prevention programs work (Coie et al., 1993).

They have learned, first, that the especially damaging risk factors listed in Table 17.3 have widespread effects on human development and must therefore receive the highest priority in prevention planning and programming.

Second, it is now clear that most mental disorders are caused by a host of social, economic, and psychological risk factors, including poor infant–parent attachment, family adversity, school failure, peer pressure, and the ready availability of harmful substances and adverse influences (Petraitis, Flay, & Miller, 1995). Thus, to be most effective, prevention programs should be multifaceted and address all the major risks for the kinds of disorders being targeted. When people face a multitude of adversities, collab-

orative, multidisciplinary efforts are necessary to accomplish meaningful preventive effects. For example, preventing school failures among low-income children might require study-skill tutoring programs, but these programs will not help children whose parents cannot bring them to the sessions because they lack reliable transportation or cannot afford child care for their younger children or have no way of communicating with the program to schedule follow-up tutoring. An effective prevention program for these families would have to go beyond tutoring and arrange transportation to and from sessions, provide for child care during the tutoring, and buy a telephone for the family so that ongoing communication about their children's progress is possible.

Researchers have also learned that risk factors for mental disorders tend to have cumulative effects; the longer they operate in peoples' lives, the more serious are their consequences. This "domino theory" of vulnerability is seen in many contexts. For example, severe parental conflicts or other family problems early in a child's life may reduce parents' supervision of the child and thus make it harder for the child to achieve success in the early school years. As school performance declines, the child may begin to suffer rejection by more successful peers, thus

TABLE 17.3 Risk Factors That Have Widespread Effects on Development

General domain	Specific risks	General domain	Specific risks
Family circumstances	Low social class Family conflict Mental illness in the family Large family size Poor bonding to parents Family disorganization Communication deviance	Ecological context	Neighborhood disorganization Racial injustice Unemployment Extreme poverty
Emotional difficulties	Child abuse Apathy or emotional blunting Emotional immaturity Stressful life events Low self-esteem Emotional dyscontrol	Constitutional handicaps	Perinatal complications Sensory disabilities Organic handicaps Neurochemical imbalances
		Interpersonal problems	Peer rejection Alienation and isolation
School problems	Academic failure Scholastic demoralization	Delays in skill development	Subnormal intelligence Social incompetence Attentional deficits Reading disabilities Poor work skills and habits

Source: Coie et al., 1993.

A Talk with Melvin Wilson

Prevention

Dr. Melvin Wilson is Associate Professor of Psychology at the University of Virginia. He specializes in designing clinical services for ethnic minorities, particularly African Americans. Dr. Wilson has recently developed a therapy program for families in which a batterer has been physically violent toward other family members.

Q *What do you think is psychotherapy's major limitation?*

A I agree with the chapter's description of psychological interventions falling along a social continuum. Of these interventions, psychotherapy is the most individualized and the least concerned with social context. The consequence of this fact is that psychotherapy is often not well suited for people who lack resources. When I speak of lacking resources, I mean more than just not having money. I mean a lack of decent housing, meaningful employment, reliable transportation, and a sense of physical safety. Members of the so-called urban underclass—whole communities of people who are cut off and isolated and have no linkages to resources—must first be helped to develop some of these resources.

> *. . . prevention can be a bargain.*

Q *Do psychologists have anything to offer this urban underclass?*

A Therapists need to help these people become better linked to resources by increasing their ability to make interpersonal connections and by advising them on how to obtain tangible resources. Traditionally, clinical psychologists have farmed these tasks out to social workers, but I think that might be a mistake.

We should be demonstrating our understanding that psychological well-being depends on adequate social support and tangible resources as well as better psychological understanding.

Q *In this decade, the cost of psychological interventions is becoming an increasingly important factor. Are prevention programs cost-effective? Can society really afford them?*

A Prevention does cost a lot. We think in terms of how expensive it is, but we have not measured long-term outcomes very well so we don't know much about prevention's overall cost-effectiveness. Mostly, we just guess about long-term benefits. Only in the past few years, for example, have we discovered that Head Start, psychology's most ambitious prevention program, produces strong benefits. The initial evaluation studies found that most kids lost the academic gains from Head Start after just 3 years. More recent studies, completed 20 years after the program's beginning, have uncovered long-term effects such as staying in school and staying out of legal trouble. When we discover effects such as these, we also learn that prevention can be a bargain.

Q *Can prevention have any negative effects?*

A Prevention is usually directed at people who are selected because of certain risk factors. Many risk factors create ecologies of their own. By that I mean they lead to their own set of associated consequences, some of which we do not anticipate very well. For example, when you design a preventive intervention for a primary school child with learning or behavior problems, you may require the teacher to spend more time with that child. Inevitably, this takes the teacher away from the other children in the class and may create resentment among them. Similarly, mainstreaming disabled students into regular classrooms is an element of many prevention programs, but it does carry risks. Mainstreaming itself may lead to social rejection and interpersonal problems as the other children in these classrooms become less tolerant of disabled children.

Another possible negative effect of prevention programs is that they may involve unwarranted assumptions about recipients who may sometimes be given a label they do not deserve. Thus, not every African American child in a single-parent family necessarily needs a specially assigned mentor or an after-school educational program. It is hard to distinguish those children who need such interventions from those for whom it may not be appropriate. However, I still think that a good prevention program is worth this risk. We can usually catch children who don't really need a service, but it is much harder to make up for a missed opportunity to intervene.

leading the child to affiliate with other children who are doing poorly in school. By early adolescence, these groups of unsuccessful, disaffected youngsters tend to increasingly reject prosocial expectations, thus putting themselves at risk for antisocial behavior and substance abuse. Patterns such as these have led psychologists to the conclusion that prevention programs should target risk factors early, before their impact spreads (Zigler et al., 1992).

Prevention scientists have found that, partly because of the domino effect, certain risk factors are particularly dangerous during particular developmental stages. For example, the appearance of antisocial behavior disorders is most closely linked to inadequate parental monitoring and discipline in the preschool years; to disengagement, misbehavior, and poor academic performance in the primary school years; and to peer influences in adolescence. This shifting of risk factors over time presents a gradually moving target for prevention programs. To be effective, these programs must be designed to address the right risk factor at the right time in clients' lives (Yoshikawa, 1994).

The design of prevention programs must also take into account the various cultural norms and traditions of the people they aim to help. People of color—African Americans, Hispanic Americans, Asian Americans, and Native Americans—now constitute about 18 percent of the population of the United States; by the year 2050, it is estimated that this figure will be nearly 50 percent. These demographic changes pose a fundamental challenge to preventionists because, as the case of Juan shows, programs that work well in one culture may not work well in another. Accordingly, a general rule of thumb has evolved in the prevention field: interventions should be designed to capitalize as much as possible on people's natural strengths, existing resources, and cultural traditions rather than trying to change people's coping methods to match the program planners' idealized vision. This *continuity principle* (Omer & Alon, 1994) has been particularly useful in organizing programs to prevent mental disorders in communities that have been struck by natural disasters.

It is also becoming clearer that the development of preventive interventions should be guided by risk factor theories that have been tested by rigorous research conducted in the natural environments where targeted disorders occur. In 1982, the National Institute of Mental Health began funding a series of Prevention Intervention Research Centers (PIRCs) to stimulate this kind of research. PIRCs bring together scientists from fields such as psychology, anthropology, sociology, epidemiology, and psychiatry to collaborate on research on the early causes of specific disorders. The centers focus on experiments with at-risk, but not yet disordered, groups such as children living in high-stress environments (Sandler et al., 1991) or adults facing the threat of unemployment (Turner, Kessler, & House, 1991). PIRC research is geared toward first discovering the incidence of disorders, then investigating the causal mechanisms that are responsible for them. Prevention programs aimed at modifying risk factors for the disorders are then developed and assessed. The programs that prove effective can then be transferred to new settings where their impact is again evaluated. Prevention-centered research is of great benefit to the entire field of mental health because its longitudinal nature leads to a clearer picture of the way mental disorders emerge and develop (see Figure 17.4).

Finally, prevention scientists have learned that primary prevention efforts introduce a special set of dilemmas and problems. For example, many of the people for whom prevention programs are intended

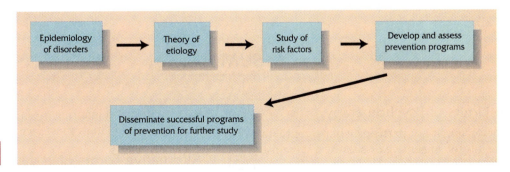

FIGURE 17.4

Science-Based Prevention
The sequence of research steps involved in a scientific model of prevention.
Source: Based on Tolan, Guerra, & Kendall, 1995.

do not acknowledge that they are at risk for anything and may view preventive services as unnecessary or intrusive. In other words, those most in need are sometimes the least interested in what prevention scientists have to offer. Should prevention scientists try to convince people of their high-risk status? Doing so can have unintended consequences that raise serious ethical questions. For example, educating people about their mental health risks might create an exaggerated fear of mental illness and might even become a self-fulfilling prophecy. In any case, the reluctance of some high-risk people to take part in prevention programs means that the people who *do* participate may be at lower overall risk for dis-

order than the population for which the programs were intended (Stein, Bauman, & Ireys, 1991). Using these less-endangered samples may thus lead to overestimates of what a prevention program can accomplish in the community as a whole.

Even when a new prevention program demonstrates success with high-risk groups, its results may not be replicable. The sad reality is that demonstration projects—with their full funding and large and enthusiastic staffs—are often hard to duplicate in less-well-funded agencies where overworked, underpaid, and unappreciated staffers do not have the time or commitment to follow through on the project (Bauman, Stein, & Ireys, 1991).

Revisiting the Case of Juan

Even if Juan's parents had been able to afford individual therapy for him, it is doubtful that he, or they, would have felt comfortable with this form of treatment. Juan was a better candidate for a psychosocial rehabilitation program or a self-help group of other schizophrenic individuals, but in his city there were few, if any, Spanish-speaking people, so Juan refused both alternatives. For a year after his parents kicked him out of their home, Juan lived on the streets. He began drinking heavily and was arrested repeatedly for petty crimes such as disturbing the peace and indecent exposure. Unfortunately, the city jail was the closest Juan ever got to a mental health program; it was only there that he got adequate food and was made to take his medication. Juan's struggle with mental ill-

ness ended at the age of 25 when the police found his body in an alley where he had been stabbed to death by an unknown killer.

Would Juan's life have been different if his community had provided programs for reducing the economic and social stressors that contributed to his deterioration? Very possibly. Could his disorder have been prevented by such programs? Maybe not, because scientists do not yet know enough about schizophrenia to offer primary prevention for it. Still, had he entered a program aimed at improving his social skills, increasing his social support, and decreasing the stressors he had to endure, Juan might have been more likely to stay on his medication and thus less likely to have relapsed into florid schizophrenia.

SUMMARY

The Limits of Psychotherapy

A person might not participate in psychotherapy because it is too expensive or because a therapist might not be available nearby. Some potential clients might resist psychotherapy because of cultural beliefs that are incompatible with it, while others avoid psychotherapy because it focuses too much on individ-

ual mental states, ignoring the larger social problems that many individuals must face.

Alternative Forms of Psychological Treatment

Group, marital (couples), and family therapy—along with self-help groups—are all psychological treatments that focus on the social aspects of mental disorders. Group therapy emphasizes disturbances in interpersonal relationships, and it attempts to change such problems in a unique environment where interpersonal relationships are constantly being explored. Couples therapy focuses on helping people involved in disturbed intimate relationships develop better problem-solving and communication skills so that they can manage conflicts more effectively. Family therapy aims at changing harmful interactions among all family members as it seeks to improve the functioning of an identified individual and to aid the family as a whole. Self-help groups are composed of individuals who share certain problems and who try to help one another cope with them.

Psychosocial Rehabilitation

Psychosocial rehabilitation programs aim to teach people how to cope better with a severe mental disorder and to develop living skills that will lessen their impairments. Such programs also usually employ case managers who help patients obtain the many different services they need to live successfully in the community. Comprehensive psychosocial rehabilitation programs have been found to reduce relapse and other crises suffered by individuals with severe mental disorders.

Prevention: The Legacy of Community Psychology

Primary prevention, the major goal of community psychology, seeks to counteract risk factors and reinforce protective factors. Five general strategies have been used in the best prevention programs: (1) teaching parents to form warm, nurturant, and secure early attachments with their children and to reduce family violence; (2) teaching children and adolescents the cognitive and interpersonal skills that are crucial for later development and adjustment; (3) changing family, school, workplace, and neighborhood environments to make them more supportive and helpful; (4) teaching people new and more effective strategies for coping with stressors; and (5) empowering dependent and powerless groups—especially those who are poor, homeless, discriminated against, or disabled—to increase their sense of control over their lives.

The prospects for primary prevention improve when prevention scientists (1) examine multiple risk factors shown to affect many aspects of adjustment; (2) target these risks for change as early as possible; (3) aim at risks that are most powerful at certain developmental stages; (4) design programs that are sensitive to cultural factors; and (5) use sound psychological theory to guide prevention programs that are evaluated in natural environments.

KEY TERMS

action research, p. 606

case management, p. 604

community psychology, p. 605

conjoint therapy, p. 595

couples therapy, p. 595

deinstitutionalization, p. 602

diversion, p. 609

ecological perspective, p. 605

empowerment, p. 603

family therapy, p. 598

group therapy, p. 592

marital therapy, p. 595

paradoxical directive, p. 599

psychological wellness, p. 592

psychosocial rehabilitation, p. 602

self-help group, p. 600

therapeutic contracting, p. 604

18

Legal and Ethical Issues in Mental Disorders

State Hospital by Genevieve Burnett, 1966. Oil on canvas,
20" x 16". Courtesy of Sistare.

From the Case of Wilson

At the age of 22, Wilson was diagnosed with paranoid schizophrenia. For the next 10 years, he was in and out of public mental hospitals where his treatment consisted mainly of various kinds of psychoactive drugs. Starting at the age of 32, Wilson spent 15 months living with his girlfriend, after which time he went home to live with his mother and father. As long as Wilson received his monthly injection of Prolixin, he had no hallucinations or delusions, and he stayed almost completely out of trouble. But he said the injections hurt, and Wilson ultimately refused to take them. He promised that, if his doctors would stop the injections, he would take Prolixin orally every day instead. The doctors agreed, but just 2 weeks after making this promise, Wilson stopped taking his medication and stopped seeing his case worker at the local community mental health center. In a matter of days, Wilson's behavior began to dete-riorate. He heard voices telling him that his mother was having sex with his former doctors and was stealing his social security check. He developed the delusion that his father was lacing his meals with Prolixin, causing Wilson to search the garbage cans in his neighborhood for "untainted food." When he heard voices from the trash cans accusing him of stealing, Wilson would retaliate by setting the cans afire, then urinating on them. His neighbors grew so afraid of him they would hide indoors if they saw him nearby. They begged Wilson's parents to do something "before it was too late."

One evening, as his father was cooking dinner, Wilson picked up a chair and threw it at him in order to, as he later told police, "stop the SOB and his whore-wife from putting that crap in my food." His mother called 911 and when the police arrived minutes later, they found Wilson huddled in a corner of the kitchen, hallucinating and terrified. When they told him they were going to take him to the state hospital, Wilson did not resist, but he continued to shout at his father, threatening to kill him at his first opportunity. A hospital psychiatrist concluded that Wilson was mentally ill and dangerous and ordered him committed to the hospital on an emergency basis for a 72-hour observation period. ■

*T*hroughout this book, we have concentrated on describing the diagnosis, symptoms, causes, and treatments of specific mental disorders. We have emphasized the ways in which various kinds of disorders differ from one another and how these disorders affect the lives of those who suffer from them. We have also pointed out that all mental disorders occur in a social and cultural context, but in this chapter we focus more directly on that context by considering some of the ways in which mental disorders can affect society at large, not just the diagnosed clients and the mental health professionals who work with them.

The effects are numerous, and they can be intense. One obvious example is that relatives and friends of mentally disturbed people suffer the burden of caring for troubled loved ones, many of whom have nowhere else to turn for support. Businesses, schools, and factories are also affected when employees' mental disorders result in absenteeism or impaired productivity. The costs of schizophrenia alone in the United States have been estimated at about $19 billion a year, and this doesn't include direct costs such as lost productivity (Human Capital Initiative Coordinating Committee, 1996). About 1 of every 4 days that people spend in American hospitals is for mental health reasons (Kiesler & Simpkins, 1991); indeed, about 10 percent of the approximately $1 trillion spent annually for health care in the United States goes for mental health care. In short, mental disorders are a major problem for every individual in a society, whether that individual experiences them personally or not.

It is no wonder that there is worldwide concern about finding the most socially beneficial way of dealing with people who have mental disorders. At the same time, there is great concern for treating these people humanely. In the United States, for example, elaborate policies and procedures are designed to ensure that the constitutional rights of severely disturbed patients are protected. These policies and procedures reflect just one of the legal and ethical issues surrounding the care of mentally disordered people. Leaders and policymakers in government, business and industry, law, and the mental health professions play a central role in deciding these issues

and their choices reveal society's values regarding people with mental disorders. Those choices are continually being examined and changed because the legal and ethical issues associated with mental disorders are complex and not easily resolved by a single "correct" solution that satisfies everyone.

For example, in Chapter 17 we examined the question of whether is it better to focus society's resources on the treatment of individuals with mental disorders or on efforts to prevent these disorders in the first place. Treatment and prevention often compete for limited funds, so if resources are consistently directed toward one approach, support for the other will ultimately decline. Such competition need not result in only one winner, but some tension between advocates of prevention versus treatment is inevitable.

At issue, too, is the need to balance the rights of individuals with mental disorders against the rights of citizens to be protected from potentially dangerous people. To what extent, if any, should the right of all people to feel safe be constrained in order to preserve freedoms for those who display mental disorders? And who should make decisions about limiting the freedoms of the mentally ill? Is it better to allow mental health professionals to decide the type, length, and setting for treatment, or should the courts regulate, or even decree, the nature of professional mental health services?

The impact of mental disorders on society is also seen in controversies about whether and in what ways mental health professionals should participate in the legal system. For example, should they offer opinions about the mental status of defendants who claim they were insane at the time of an alleged offense or who appear mentally ill at the time of their trials? Should mental health professionals' predictions about the likelihood of future dangerousness be used in deciding whether to release someone from a prison or psychiatric hospital? In civil trials, can mental health professionals accurately assess the psychological suffering or emotional damage one person has inflicted on another? If mental health professionals testify about such matters, should they be advocates for one side or the other, or should they dispassionately summarize for the court the scientific evidence about a certain topic?

In this final chapter, we focus on three of the most important issues that arise as modern societies attempt to deal humanely and responsibly with the legal and ethical aspects of mental disorders:

1. Whose rights are paramount: those of mentally disturbed individuals to have autonomy over their behavior or those of the general public to en-

Despite concerted efforts by police and a priest to save this man's life, he ultimately jumped from this fifth-floor fire escape and was killed instantly. Shortly before jumping, the man (who had also cut his wrists) told the priest he felt he had no reason to live. How much power should the state have to hospitalize mentally ill people against their will? Under current laws, mentally ill people cannot be involuntarily committed to a hospital just because they suffer a mental disorder that could be helped by treatment, or because they are seen by others as a nuisance.

joy a collective sense of welfare and safety? Can the proper balance ever be found?

2. How much formal regulation of mental health services should the legal system provide, and how are these regulations related to other forms of social control (such as professional ethics and economic realities)?

3. What is the proper role of mental health professionals who participate as experts in formal legal disputes relating to mental disorders?

Because it would be virtually impossible to provide a complete description of how these issues are being addressed in every country around the world, we will focus largely on the United States and other Western countries where the most heated debates about the legal and ethical aspects of mental illness have occurred.

The Rights of Individuals Versus the Rights of Society

The past 30 years have seen especially intense debate in the United States over how to balance the rights of mentally disordered citizens against society's concern for the safety and protection of all citizens.

The debate tends to focus on two areas: (1) should the state hospitalize people against their will, and (2) should people with mental disorders be allowed to refuse treatment ordered by mental health professionals?

The arguments on both sides of these issues appeal to personal values and beliefs. Maximum freedom for individuals is one of the most cherished ideals in the United States, proclaimed boldly in its constitutional preamble's call for the "Blessings of Liberty" and in the 14th Amendment's guarantee of due process. Indeed, the United States prides itself on being the most individualist society in the world today. At the same time, it is a society governed by laws that decree everything from how fast people can drive to whether and when a woman can have an abortion. Many of these laws represent compromises that grant individuals considerable personal freedom while denying them the right to behave in ways that are disruptive to the overall social order. Just such a compromise is evident in the way the rights of mentally disordered people are both protected and restricted.

Mental health laws and policies can have significant positive or negative effects on patients, leading many mental health professionals and attorneys to consider the therapeutic implications of legal rulings in this area, not just the effects of such rulings on individual versus social rights. This perspective, known as **therapeutic jurisprudence** (Wexler & Winnick, 1991), views the law as having the potential for being helpful to patients and argues that all mental health laws should be evaluated to determine their potential therapeutic impact. In other words, therapeutic jurisprudence frames the issues discussed in this section not solely in terms of conflicting rights but also in terms of how individual patients are likely to be affected.

Civil Commitment

In the United States in the 1950s and 1960s it was relatively easy for people displaying serious mental disorders to be committed to a psychiatric hospital against their will through a legal order known as **civil commitment**. Such orders were issued whenever the state believed an individual required psychiatric treatment, and the length of hospital confinement—which in many cases extended for decades—was determined by the hospital's staff; patients were released only when their doctors thought the time was right. This approach to civil commitment began around the time of the Civil War, when the United States first started to construct large public mental hospitals. It was based on the tradition of *parens patriae* ("the country as parent"), which holds that certain types of weakness or impairment can render people incapable of deciding what is best for them. In such cases, the state will, like the parent of a young child, act in what it sees as the best interests of these people.

In the late 1960s, states began to reform their rules for involuntary commitment to expand the rights of mentally ill people. The new rules allowed patients to resist psychiatric hospitalization and to be protected against indefinite periods of commitment. These reforms were part of the social upheaval that occurred in the United States during a period of intense debate about the wisdom of virtually all government policies, including the principle of police power. Civil-liberties activists were concerned, for example, that patients were being deprived of legal due process during commitment proceedings. A strong bias against psychiatry also developed during this period, and critics argued that psychiatrists' lack of success in treating mental disorders made involuntary hospitalization little more than imprisonment without trial (Appelbaum, 1994).

The new civil commitment laws required that, before a person could be involuntarily placed in a mental hospital, the state had to prove that the following four conditions existed: (1) the person is mentally ill, (2) the person poses an imminent risk of dangerousness to self or to others as a result of mental illness, (3) treatment for the person's mental illness is available at the proposed hospitalization site, and (4) hospitalization is the *least restrictive alternative* available for this treatment.

Public Mental Hospitals and Deinstitutionalization. By the end of the 1970s, every state and the District of Columbia had passed laws that allowed involuntary hospitalization of mentally ill citizens *only* if some version of these four conditions were met. These new rules, combined with new psychoactive medications capable of controlling psychotic behavior, led to the release of large numbers of mental patients. As mentioned in Chapter 17, the number of patients in state and county mental hospitals peaked at around 550,000 in the mid-1950s. By 1970, this number had fallen below 400,000; by 1979, fewer than 150,000 psychiatric inpatients were in state hospitals; and, by the late 1980s, the number was around 100,000 (Manderscheid & Sonnenschein, 1990).

This dramatic decline in mental hospital populations over the past three decades has generally been described as a shift from inpatient to outpatient treatment of mental disorders in the United States. This shift, known as *deinstitutionalization,* was an important goal of the community mental health movement described in Chapter 17. As promising as deinstitutionalization appeared on paper, however, its implementation has turned out to be a combination of myth and missed opportunity (Kiesler, 1991; Kiesler & Simpkins, 1991). There are three reasons for this disappointing assessment.

First, most statistics on inpatient treatment count the number of patients in mental hospitals on a given or average day. This figure is determined by two factors: how many patients are admitted to a mental hospital and how long they stay. However, considering the number of patients admitted to *all types* of hospitals for mental health care, the number of total admissions actually increased by more than 30 percent from the late 1960s to the late 1980s (Manderscheid & Sonnenschein, 1990). This is because, although people now stay in inpatient facilities for shorter periods than before, admissions and readmissions are more frequent. The current pattern has been described as a revolving door.

Second, the fact that there are decreased numbers of patients in state mental hospitals or Veterans Administration (VA) hospitals does not mean that inpatient care is a thing of the past. After carefully studying trends in mental health care in the United States, psychologist Charles Kiesler points out that much inpatient mental health care now takes place in many other kinds of facilities. General hospitals devote some of their beds to psychiatric care. In addition, many private, usually for-profit, psychiatric hospitals have been constructed in the past 10 years, specialized chemical dependency units have been set up to treat people who once would have gone to state or VA hospitals, residential treatment units have been opened in some communities to treat troubled adolescents and children, and there are inpatient facilities run by the military and the Indian Health Service. Statistics on treatment provided in *all* these inpatient facilities contradicts the notion of widespread deinstitutionalization: the total number of inpatient cases has actually increased somewhat, with most of the increase appearing in general medical and private psychiatric hospitals (see Figure 18.1). In other words, mental health care in the United States has not been deinstitutionalized to the extent that is often claimed; the decline in the population of patients committed to public psychiatric hospitals has been offset to some extent by increased use of other inpatient settings (Kiesler & Simpkins, 1991).

Third, there is a difference between just being deinstitutionalized and receiving adequate treatment in the community. It is easy to release severely mentally ill people from hospitals, but it is much more difficult

Too often deinstitutionalization has resulted in formerly hospitalized patients receiving little or no treatment. Shelters for the homeless, such as the one pictured above, simply substitute one form of institutionalization for another.

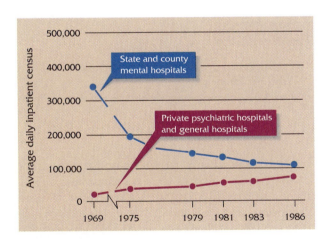

FIGURE 18.1

Changes in Hospitalization Patterns for the Mentally Ill

Although the number of patients in public mental hospitals declined dramatically beginning in the early 1970s, hospitalization of the mentally ill in private mental hospitals or general hospitals has steadily increased over this same period. In general, the people being treated in private or general hospitals tend to suffer less severe or chronic forms of mental disorders than do those who had been housed in public hospitals.

to ensure that they receive the continuing care and training necessary for adequate adjustment in the community. The overall failure of the deinstitutionalization movement is suggested by the large percentage of severely mentally ill persons who, during the past 10 years, have either drifted into homelessness or have become wards of the criminal justice system.

Mental Illness and the Homeless. As many as 1 million American citizens were homeless by the beginning of the 1990s, and it is estimated that up to one third of them suffer from severe mental illnesses such as schizophrenia or bipolar disorder (Tessler & Dennis, 1989). About half of these severely mentally ill homeless people are also alcohol or drug abusers. In other words, homelessness has become an enormous public health crisis in the United States.

The homeless mentally ill struggle with many disadvantages. Their mental disorders frequently impair their judgment and ability to comply with treatment. They lack adequate shelter and nutrition. Many suffer serious physical illnesses. They are seldom employed and, if they do hold jobs, their incomes average less than $5,000 a year. Beyond all this, they suffer almost daily rejection by members of the general public who both pity and fear them (Federal Task Force on Homelessness and Severe Mental Illness, 1992). The policy of confining these people in state mental hospitals was obviously not the answer, but at least it usually assured them a minimum level of safety and shelter. Today, with public mental hospitals a less-ready refuge, there is a continuing struggle to provide the broad range of services these individuals need.

Should they all be put back in hospitals? The problem of mental illness among the homeless is too complex and profound to be solved through any single program or idea. The National Institutes of Mental Health Task Force on Homelessness and Severe Mental Illness has proposed creation of an integrated system of care with three main components (see Figure 18.2). The first would be its *assertive outreach orientation,* meaning that service providers would seek out and bring treatment to the homeless mentally ill on the streets and in shelters rather than waiting for these clients to ask for help. Service providers would also offer *integrated case management,* helping clients obtain necessary health and welfare benefits, arranging appointments with health care providers, and making sure they are receiving appropriate services.

The second major component of this system would be to provide adequate housing. Many of the homeless mentally ill need *safe havens* from their confusing and frightening lives on the street or in mass shelters. These facilities would provide semiprivate living conditions and basic services (such as food, showers, and clothing) for small groups of people whose mental illness has kept them out of larger shelters. Safe havens would provide temporary help until more permanent housing could be found in a special-residence hotel, halfway house, group home, foster home, nursing home, board-and-care home, or apartment.

The final component in this integrated system of care would consist of a collection of income support, health care, psychosocial rehabilitation, mental health and substance abuse treatment, education, and vocational services. The specific package of services offered would depend on the particular needs of a given client, as assessed by a case manager. Because some severely mentally ill persons re-

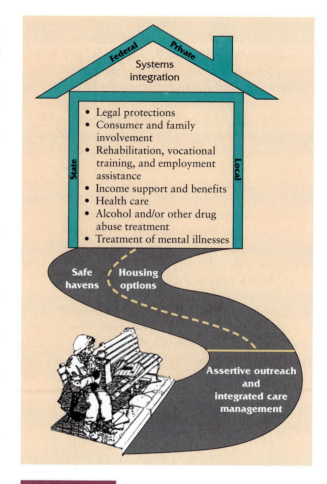

FIGURE 18.2

An Integrated System of Care for the Mentally Ill Who Are Homeless

Connections

Do services such as psychosocial rehabilitation successfully maintain patients in the community? See Chapter 17, pp. 602–604.

sist or avoid psychiatric treatment, one strategy would be to "bundle" services so that mental health treatment and rehabilitation are always paired with necessities such as food and shelter. Proponents of bundled services see them as a reasonable, efficient way to reach an often-inaccessible population; opponents view bundling as coercing people into treatment that they may not want and should be free to refuse. The debate highlights again the enduring conflict in the United States between personal autonomy and the rights of society at large.

The Mentally Ill in the Criminal Justice System. The process of deinstitutionalization has placed ever-greater responsibility for supervising the severely mentally ill on police and the criminal justice system.

Police officers have wide discretion in their response to disruptive people who may also be mentally ill. They can arrest them or force them into a hospital. They can attempt on-the-spot counseling, refer them to a mental health agency, or return them to the care of friends or relatives. Research suggests that the police are reluctant to arrest or hospitalize mentally ill people unless they create an obvious public danger (Bittner, 1967). This reluctance is part of a general tendency for police to avoid arrests in minor encounters unless the suspect is disrespectful or a complainant insists on pressing charges. Consider, for example, the research of Linda Teplin (1984), a sociologist at Northwestern University, who trained a team of psychology graduate students to observe police–citizen interactions over a 14-month period in two Chicago precincts. Using a symptom checklist and a global rating of mental disorders, the researchers studied more than 800 police–citizen encounters. In these encounters, over 500 citizens were considered suspects eligible for arrest, but only 29.4 percent of them were actually arrested. However, of the 30 suspects rated by the observers as mentally ill, 46.7 percent were arrested, a significantly higher rate than for suspects who did not appear to display a mental disorder. Similar results have been reported in other cities.

In other words, when something must be done about a disruptive mentally ill person, police officers may prefer arrest over hospitalization, partly because arrest often involves less red tape, and also because hospitals often refuse to accept these people because they are too dangerous, not dangerous enough, or suffer a disorder that the hospital does not treat. Thus, the homeless mentally ill are being "criminalized" to a certain extent because society does not know what else to do with them. They are often treated like petty criminals and, for many, local jails have become their major source of shelter, food, medical treatment, detoxification, remedial education, and other services. Not surprisingly, rates of severe mental disorders and substance abuse are now alarmingly high among jail populations (Abram & Teplin, 1991). Commenting on this situation as it affects Black youngsters, the Reverend Jesse Jackson noted that, for many teenagers, "Jail is a step up; once they are jailed, they are no longer homeless . . . they have balanced meals . . . they will no longer be hit by drive-by shootings."

By the 1980s, it was apparent to most thoughtful observers that an exclusive concern for protecting the rights of mentally disordered patients often meant ignoring their needs for adequate care, housing, and treatment. Ironically, the legislative reforms of the 1970s inadvertently helped create a situation in which it was too hard to get mentally ill people into a hospital for needed treatment and too easy for them to be released before they were ready to cope effectively with the outside world. These people had been protected from hospitalization only to be relegated to the streets, jails, or "psychiatric slums" that offered neither treatment nor protection from hunger, crime, disease, and other dangers. Had adequate attention been given to providing community-based services to deinstitutionalized patients, the results

Partly as a result of laws that make it harder to hospitalize the mentally ill against their will, increasing numbers of individuals with mental disorders are being detained in local jails where they can be observed for a day or two to determine whether a hospital commitment is justified. One jailer, commenting on individuals who are repeatedly arrested for this reason, said "it is as if they are serving a life sentence a few days at a time."

might have been different. But the fact is that most communities have not assured the services that a proper deinstitutionalization program requires.

As activism by mental health professionals and patients' families awakened interest in these concerns, the social policy pendulum began to swing back toward making it a bit easier to commit people to a hospital without their permission. Many states altered their laws to permit involuntary commitment, not only of people whose mental illnesses poses a danger to themselves or others, but also of people who are *gravely disabled* by their disorder or are in danger of *deteriorating* if they are not hospitalized. These revised laws recognized that a small percentage of people may be so severely incapacitated by mental illness that, although they pose no real danger to others, they will be unable to survive for long unless they receive custodial care and protection.

Even before legislators began to pass these revised state laws, clinicians and judges had informally started to use commitment criteria that anticipated them. Their decisions were based on a common-sense model of commitment that did not "place rights above suffering" (Applebaum, 1994). Sometimes called the "thank-you theory" of commitment, this model assumed that patients whose disorders render them unable to make reasonable decisions about their lives will ultimately be grateful for the treatment that a mental health professional or judge insists they receive. This practice amounted to an informal return to the *parens patriae* logic for commitment.

Types of Commitment in Use Today. Most state laws now permit three types of involuntary commitment of mentally ill persons: (1) commitment without a court order, (2) commitment by court order, and (3) outpatient commitment.

Commitment without a court order is allowed under emergency circumstances. Because most commitments arise in emergency situations, this is the most frequent means by which patients are committed to hospitals. Family members, police officers, mental health professionals, or, sometimes, just concerned citizens can initiate this type of commitment by alerting law enforcement officials when people appear mentally disturbed and about to harm themselves or others. This was the basis for the commitment of Wilson, whose case opened this chapter. A few states require approval by a judge before allowing an emergency commitment but, in most cases, the decision is left up to a mental health professional at the hospital to which the person is taken by the police. Upon being committed, the person is read a list of legal rights pertaining to commitment. Patients are told, for example, that they can be detained in the hospital for only a limited time—usually from 24 hours to a few days—before a court hearing must be conducted to determine whether more extended confinement is necessary.

Commitment with a court order requires that a family member, police officer, or other concerned party petition a court to have the allegedly mentally ill person examined by a mental health professional. A court hearing is then conducted to determine whether the criteria for commitment are satisfied. The person whose commitment is being sought has the right to be represented at this hearing by an attorney who can call and cross-examine witnesses. The judge or a jury then decides whether the commitment criteria have been met. Although "dangerousness" is the standard discussed as the formal basis for most involuntary commitments, proof of "grave disability" is actually the criterion that usually determines the court's decision (Turkheimer & Parry, 1992). Regardless of the formal criteria, if the judge or jury thinks a person is mentally ill and in obvious need of care, commitment is usually ordered.

Outpatient commitment is a procedure allowed in most states, but, until recently, it has not been used very often. It allows the state to commit a patient to mandatory treatment in an outpatient setting— a community mental health center, or day center, for example. Outpatient commitment often occurs when patients are given conditional release from a mental hospital: they are ordered to continue to receive medication or other treatment in the community and, if they fail to do so, they can be returned to an inpatient institution.

Although outpatient commitment appears to be an attractive alternative for treating some severely mentally ill persons, it carries several complications. For example, are therapists liable for any dangerous acts performed by patients while on outpatient commitment? Is effective, community-based treatment readily available? Finally, the vast majority of outpatient commitments require that patients continue to take prescribed medication. Can patients be forced to take these medications? This last question, the thorniest of all, involves patients' right to refuse treatment.

The Right to Refuse Treatment

Several fundamental questions about patients' rights are raised when a patient does not want to take medication that a physician believes would be beneficial. Should society "help" patients by giving them treatment against their will? Does the need for treatment outweigh patients' rights to protection against invasion of privacy and against interference with decisions about what goes into their bodies? Does it make sense to commit people to an institution and then allow them to refuse the very treatment that may be necessary for them to regain their freedom?

For many years the treatment of medical patients has been governed by rules that require patients to give informed consent before receiving medication, surgery, or other procedures. The rules of **informed consent** presume that medical patients are competent to decide whether they want to receive a treatment after being told about its potential benefits and risks and the alternative treatments available (see Figure 18.3 on page 626). For many decades, however, informed consent rules were not usually applied in the treatment of the seriously mentally ill because it was assumed that their disorders made them incompetent to render such decisions. In short, the mentally ill were expected to simply follow doctors' orders.

By the late 1970s, however, courts in Massachusetts (*Rogers* v. *Okin*, 1979) and New Jersey (*Rennie* v. *Klein*, 1978), among others, had decided that committed mental patients should not be automatically presumed incompetent and that they therefore retained the right to refuse medication, even if it were likely to be beneficial. Still, the right to refuse treatment is not recognized in all states; some state courts have decided that committed patients can be ordered to comply with treatment that a professional has deemed necessary.

Indeed, the U.S. Supreme Court has never held that the mentally ill have a constitutional right to refuse all treatment. Instead, it has mostly followed the principle of deferring to the professional judgment of physicians who are treating a patient. For example, in the 1982 case of *Youngberg* v. *Romeo*, which involved a profoundly retarded young man who was involuntarily committed, the court held that honoring the rights of patients cannot unnecessarily restrict the judgment of the treating professionals. Likewise, in *Washington* v. *Harper*, a 1990 case involving a mentally ill prisoner, the court stated that the prisoner could not be medicated against his will *unless* treating professionals concluded that medication was necessary to ensure the safety of the prisoner or others. The Supreme Court reached a similar decision in the 1992 case of *Riggins* v. *Nevada*, when it ruled that it was unconstitutional to force a defendant on trial for murder to be medicated *unless* it could be shown that such medication was necessary to ensure the defendant's safety (or the safety of others) or that the trial could not be conducted unless the defendant were medicated.

Even in states that recognize a patient's right to refuse treatment, that right is not absolute. A patient's refusal can be overridden if the patient is behaving dangerously and medication is likely to lessen the emergency, or if the patient is judged to be incompetent to make a decision about treatment. In the latter instance, a judge or a panel of clinicians and citizens can give "substituted" consent on the patient's behalf if they conclude that the patient would have consented to treatment had he or she been mentally competent to do so.

Despite these exceptions, many mental health professionals were alarmed about the implications of allowing patients even limited rights to refuse treatment, especially psychoactive medications. They predicted that, because the mentally ill often deny their problems, few of them would consent to treatment and that mental hospitals would thus not be able to do their job. They warned that hordes of unmedicated patients would make hospital wards increasingly chaotic, violent, and dangerous, and they suggested that the nearly constant hearings required to determine the competency of each nonconsenting patient would place a substantial drain on their time and money.

In fact, these predictions have generally not come true. Formal refusals of treatment are surprisingly infrequent. On average, in jurisdictions recognizing the right to refuse treatment, only about 10 percent of patients actually do so (Appelbaum, 1994). Even fewer refuse medication for very long, and those who do almost always have their refusal overridden eventually by a judge or review panel (Appelbaum & Hoge, 1986). And while states that allow patients to refuse treatment have seen some increases in aggression in hospital wards, these increases have been less than feared.

Predictions about increased costs *have* come true. Taking into consideration the clinicians' time, judicial and court costs, waiting periods, and review panel obligations, it is clear that allowing patients to refuse treatment is an expensive process. However, these costs must be viewed in light of their benefits in giving patients a feeling of control over their lives. Typically, a patient's refusal of treatment comes as an initial *objection* to treatment. Then, the patient and physician usually begin to negotiate (Appelbaum, 1994). If the patient refuses one drug, the clinician may prescribe a different one. If the patient refuses medication because of feared side effects, the clinician may prescribe a lower dose. In some cases, patient and therapist come to an understanding and the therapist may agree to suspend medication for a while in order to see how well the patient functions. If symptoms return, the patient agrees to go back on the medicine. If the symptoms do not return, the doctor does not insist on continued treatment.

CONSENT TO TREATMENT AND RELEASE OF INFORMATION

Consent to Treatment: I/we voluntarily authorize the rendering of such care, including diagnostic procedures and medical treatment, by authorized agents and employees of the University _____ Hospital (hereafter referred to as the Hospital), and _____ and the medical staff, or their designees, as may in their professional judgment be deemed necessary or beneficial, and may include testing for HIV (the virus that causes AIDS) and other blood borne diseases. I/we acknowledge that no guarantees have been made as to the effect of such examination or treatment on my condition or the condition of the person for whom I am duly authorized to sign. I/we understand that I/we have the right to make decisions concerning my health care or the health care of the person for whom I am duly authorized to make such decisions, including the right to refuse medical and surgical procedures.

☐ I have formulated Advance Directives (living will, health care surrogate declaration, durable power of attorney) and request that these directives govern my course of care, in as much as is possible under state or federal law. I understand that it is my responsibility to provide the Hospital with a copy of my Advance Directives and that those directives will not govern my course of care until they have been filed in my medical record.
  ☐ Advance Directives attached ☐ Advance Directives not attached

☐ I have not formulated Advance Directives (living will, health care surrogate declaration, durable power of attorney), but I understand that it is my right to make decisions regarding my course of treatment, including the executing of advance directives.

Release of Information: I authorize the release from my medical records or the records of the person for whom I am duly authorized to do so, of such medical and/or psychiatric information as may be required by:
1. Any health, sickness, and accident insurance carrier, workman's compensation, or agency (social welfare, governmental) which is legally responsible, or which the Hospital has good cause to believe is legally responsible for all or any part of the Medical Center's charges and/or professional fees.
2. Physicians or health care facilities rendering professional care to the patient.
3. The Peer Review Organization responsible for reviewing medical care under Public Law 92-603.

Procurement of Information: I/we authorize the release of any medical records from other physicians, hospitals or health care facilities that the Hospital needs for my present medical care or the present medical care of the person for whom I am duly authorized to sign.

*This consent may be revoked at any time, except to the extent that action has already been taken, by the patient/duly authorized agent and will expire automatically one year from the date below.

_____   _____   _____
Signature of Patient or Next of Kin, Legal   Signature of Witness   Date
Agent/Guardian and Relationship to Patient

FIGURE 18.3

Informed Consent

Under normal conditions, patients are treated only after they have been made familiar with the potential risks and benefits of a medical or psychological procedure and have explicitly agreed to it. In cases of individuals with severe mental disorders, the capacity to give informed consent may be impaired, requiring special procedures designed to protect the rights of such people.

As is true in the process of civil commitment, day-to-day decisions about allowing committed patients to refuse treatment are usually adjusted in light of the common sense idea that hospitals are for treatment. These decisions seldom ignore the reality of a committed patient's serious disability. If a judge or jury believes someone is disturbed enough to be confined in a mental hospital, it is unlikely that the person will be allowed to endlessly refuse the very treatment the commitment was intended to provide.

Other Legal Rights of the Mentally Ill

In addition to rules and regulations covering involuntary hospitalization and refusal of treatment, state and federal courts have decided a number of cases that give mental patients other basic rights.

The Right to Treatment. Several courts have held that people committed to mental hospitals have the right to be *treated*, not merely confined. In the landmark 1966 case of *Rouse* v. *Cameron,* Charlie Rouse had been confined to a hospital for 4 years after being found not guilty by reason of insanity on a weapons charge. Rouse petitioned the court for his release, claiming that he had been confined, without receiving treatment, for longer than the 1-year maximum prison sentence he could have received had he been found guilty. The court of appeals agreed and ruled that involuntary commitment required hospitals to make at least a reasonable effort to treat committed patients.

Standards of Treatment. The case of *Youngberg* v. *Romeo* involved a profoundly retarded, 33-year-old man named Nicholas Romeo who was committed to the Pennhurst State Hospital in Pennsylvania after his father died and his mother was no longer able to care for him. Nicholas frequently engaged in self-mutilation and was injured several times during his first few years in the hospital, both through his own actions and by other patients who reacted to his provocations. As a protective measure, he was restrained in bed for long periods. Upset with the conditions of her son's lack of proper treatment at Pennhurst, Nicholas's mother filed suit, alleging that Pennsylvania was violating Nicholas's 14th Amendment due process rights by not keeping him in a safe environment and by failing to train him to the limits of his abilities. The case ultimately reached the U.S. Supreme Court, which held that the Constitution guarantees involuntarily committed patients the following rights: (1) adequate food, shelter, and clothing; (2) adequate medical care; (3) a safe environment; (4) freedom from restraint, unless restraint is necessary to protect the patient or others; and (5) such training as may be required to ensure the above rights. As mentioned earlier, however, the Court also concluded that the form of training or treatment provided should remain largely a matter of professional judgment.

The constitutional rights established in *Youngberg* set minimal standards of care below which no state can fall in treating patients committed to its institutions. However, individual states are free to insist on higher standards of care for the mentally ill, and several states have done so. Some federal courts have also mandated additional specific treatment rights for patients, but the Supreme Court has not yet ruled these to be constitutionally required. For example, in the celebrated 1971 case of *Wyatt* v. *Stickney,* a federal court in Alabama ruled that involuntarily committed patients have the right to individualized treatment that they can help plan, to clothing of their choice, and to enough mental health professionals per patient to ensure that treatment will be more than an empty promise. Various other state and federal courts have ruled that mental patients have the right to receive visitors, to enjoy a zone of personal privacy (except in emergencies), to receive reasonable payment for work they do in the hospital and, within the limits already described, to refuse treatment.

Rights of Nondangerous Patients. In 1975, the U.S. Supreme Court considered the case of *O'Connor* v. *Donaldson.* Kenneth Donaldson was a 49-year-old man who had been diagnosed with paranoid schizophrenia and confined in the Florida State Hospital at Chattahoochee for about 15 years. His father had had him committed because he was supposedly delusional and dangerous, but the evidence for his alleged dangerousness at the time of commitment was questionable. Indeed, hospital staff notes and testimony later revealed that he was never dangerous to himself or anyone else. Donaldson repeatedly asked to be released from the hospital on the grounds that he was not receiving treatment, that he was not a threat to anyone, and that he could live independently outside the hospital. When his requests were denied, Donaldson filed a lawsuit against Dr. J. B. O'Connor, who had been superintendent of the hospital for most of the time Donaldson was confined there. A jury agreed with Donaldson that he had been improperly confined and awarded him $38,500 in damages. The wisdom of this decision was supported by the fact that, immediately upon his release, Donaldson obtained a job in hotel administration.

The state of Florida appealed the jury's verdict to the U.S. Supreme Court. *O'Connor* was a landmark case because it marked the first time the Supreme Court agreed to hear arguments about the constitutional rights of a civilly committed mental patient, and it required the court to evaluate the state's justifications for involuntarily committing the mentally ill to a hospital. Its ruling seriously undercut the *parens patriae* rationale for involuntary commitment.

Kenneth Donaldson, the plaintiff in the landmark case O'Connor v. Donaldson, *won his freedom from hospital confinement after the Supreme Court ruled that nondangerous patients who could survive in the community cannot be involuntarily confined in a hospital.*

Writing for the Court, Justice Potter Stewart ruled that a "state cannot constitutionally confine . . . a nondangerous individual who is capable of surviving safely in freedom by himself or with the help of willing and responsible family and friends." In other words, the Supreme Court decided that mental illness and the need for treatment alone were not enough to justify involuntary commitment. The effect of this decision and others since then (e.g., *Foucha v. Louisiana,* 1992) was to limit states' powers so that they cannot force hospitalization of persons who, even though mentally ill, are not dangerous and can live outside the hospital on their own or with the support of others.

The *O'Connor v. Donaldson* decision also illustrates the Supreme Court's tendency to reach conclusions that are no broader than necessary. Notice that the court did not rule that *any* mentally ill patient who was not receiving treatment had to be released from the hospital; it restricted its ruling to nondangerous patients who could function adequately outside the hospital.

Housing Rights. The opportunity to obtain affordable housing in the community is a basic need of severely mentally ill people, including those who, as part of the deinstitutionalization movement, have been discharged from state hospitals. Several federal laws (such as the Fair Housing Amendments Act of 1988 and the Americans with Disabilities Act of 1990) prohibit housing discrimination against people with mental disorders, but some cities have discouraged the establishment of group homes or halfway houses for these people—especially in residential neighborhoods—by requiring such facilities to have special zoning permits. One such city was Cleburne, Texas, which passed an ordinance restricting group homes for mentally retarded patients. In the case of *Cleburne Living Center, Inc. v. City of Cleburne, Texas,* the Supreme Court ruled in favor of the retarded citizens, stating that cities cannot pass laws requiring special permits for homes for retarded citizens just because a community opposes such homes.

Rights of Mentally Ill or Mentally Retarded Criminal Defendants. The Supreme Court has also recognized the need for extra protection of mentally disordered people who are accused of crimes. For example, in the case of *Ake v. Oklahoma* (1985), the Court ruled that a poor person who uses insanity as a defense must be provided a psychiatrist, at state expense, who might later testify as an expert witness at the defendant's trial. Writing the majority opinion, the late Thurgood Marshall noted that "without the assistance of a psychiatrist to conduct a professional examination on issues relevant to the defense, to help determine whether the insanity defense is viable, to present testimony, and to assist in preparing cross-examination of a state's psychiatric witness, the risk of an inaccurate resolution of sanity issues is extremely high."

Mentally ill convicts have been granted other special protections. In 1986, for example, the U.S. Supreme Court ruled that the Eighth Amendment of the Constitution forbids the execution of any inmate who is mentally incompetent at the time of execution. Definitions of mental incompetence for execution vary, but, in most states, a condemned prisoner is considered incompetent if he or she is judged to be insane or if, as the result of a mental disorder, the prisoner is unaware of the nature of the death penalty and the reasons it is being imposed.

This ruling came in *Ford v. Wainwright,* a 1974 Florida case in which Alvin Bernard Ford had been sentenced to death for killing a police officer during an attempted robbery. After 8 years on death row, he began to manifest symptoms of a mental disorder. Reading about Ku Klux Klan activities in nearby Jacksonville, Florida, Ford began to develop an obsession about the organization. In letters to various people, he claimed to be the target of a complex conspiracy involving the Klan and others that would ultimately force him to kill himself. He believed that his prison guards, whom he saw as part of this conspiracy, were killing people and burying their bodies in concrete. He thought that female members of his family were being tortured and sexually abused in the prison and that up to 135 of his relatives had been taken hostage. At about the time the hostage list grew to include Senator Edward Kennedy and other government leaders, Ford informed prison officials that several of them had been fired, began calling himself Pope John Paul III, and said that he had appointed nine new judges to the Florida Supreme Court. Ford's mental condition eventually deteriorated to the point that he spoke mostly in a private code, saying things such as "Hands one, face one. Mafia one. God one, father one, Pope one. Pope one. Leader one."

Ford's lawyers raised the question of whether he had become incompetent and, thus, ineligible for execution. When they asked for an evaluation of Ford's mental competence, Dr. Jamal Amin, a psychiatrist who had been seeing him in prison, stated that Ford suffered a mental disorder similar to paranoid schizophrenia and was not capable of appreciating what was happening to him. A second doctor hired by Ford's lawyers reached a similar conclusion. However, the Governor of Florida appointed three psychiatrists to evaluate Ford's competence, and after a single 30-minute meeting with Ford, they unanimously pronounced him competent for execution. The Governor signed Ford's death warrant, but Ford's lawyers appealed to the Supreme Court, which ruled that it is unconstitutional to execute insane people and that the state of Florida had not given Ford sufficient due process in assessing his mental condition. Alvin Ford ultimately died in prison, of natural causes, but other inmates have been executed despite indications that they might have been suffering from serious mental disorders at the time.

Questions about a death row inmate's competence to be executed do not arise very often, but, when they do, they represent one of the most difficult ethical dilemmas a clinician can face. Should the clinician refuse to participate in an assessment process that might increase the probability of an execution? If an inmate is found mentally incompetent, should a clinician agree to treat the inmate in order to restore the competency necessary for the execution to proceed? Clinicians continue to debate whether it is ethical for them to participate in competence-to-be-executed proceedings (Appelbaum, 1986; Heilbrun, 1987).

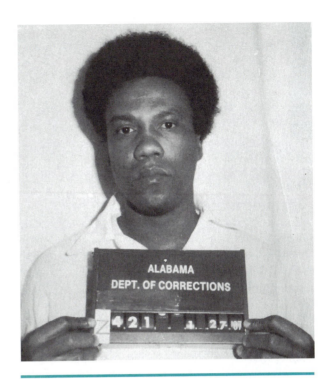

Varnall Weeks, described by prosecution and defense experts alike as seriously mentally ill, was executed in Alabama's electric chair on May 13, 1995. Even though Weeks was apparently racked by delusions (e.g., he believed that after his death he would take the form of a godlike turtle and rule all of mankind), the courts held that Weeks was competent for execution because he was capable of understanding that he was being executed for his crime of murder.

In Review

The conflict between autonomy rights of individuals with mental disorders and society's rights to be protected is revealed most clearly:

- in the changing principles and procedures for involuntarily hospitalizing patients with mental disorders; and
- in the debate over whether patients have a right to refuse treatment.

Commitment of the mentally ill can be accomplished through:

- commitment with a court order;
- emergency commitment without a court order; and
- outpatient commitment.

(continued)

Other legal rights of persons with mental illness concern:

- the right to effective treatment;
- public housing rights; and
- special rights for criminal defendants with mental disorders.

The Regulation of Mental Health Professionals

As the mental health professions have grown in size and influence, they have come under increasing scrutiny and control from several sources. Many of these controls involve the legal system, including, for example, laws that restrict participation in mental health professions to those who are licensed or certified to practice them.

All states have laws that regulate the ability of people to call themselves psychiatrists, psychologists, or social workers and to offer the services associated with these professions. **Certification laws** restrict the use of a professional title to people who have met certain requirements for education, practical training, and supervised experience. **Licensure laws** restrict the use of a professional title *and* prohibit unlicensed people from offering the traditional services of a given profession. The primary purpose of such regulations is to protect the public from impostors or unskilled professionals. Although no one would argue with this goal, some have questioned whether it is the public or the professionals who benefit most from these regulations. By denying some people the opportunity to offer mental health services, these regulations give licensed or certified professionals an economic edge over those with mental health–related training and experience that do not fit the criteria established by mainstream mental health service providers.

A more controversial form of legal regulation of the mental health professions involves court oversight of their treatment techniques and services. Recognizing the hazards of second-guessing mental health professionals, courts have historically been reluctant to pass judgment on mental health care. In the past two decades, however, judges have been more willing to evaluate the legality of certain aspects of professional practice and to impose special obligations on clinicians. Some courts have ruled that a therapist's obligation to try to protect potential victims of a client's dangerous actions takes prece-dence over the obligation to protect that client's privacy.

Confidentiality

The laws of most states recognize several types of **privilege,** which protects certain people from public disclosure in court of what they have said in confidence to certain other people. Privilege exists, for example, between a minister and parishioner, a husband and wife, a lawyer and client, and a doctor and patient. Most states have laws that also establish privileged communications between a psychotherapist and client. These communications are considered privileged because society believes that the relationships in which they occur could not survive without the assurance of nondisclosure, even if it means that the whole truth about some matters may never be revealed.

Privilege is similar, but not identical, to *confidentiality.* **Confidentiality** is not a legal requirement but an *ethical* obligation that therapists owe their clients. Indeed, most therapists believe that confidential communication is absolutely essential to effective therapy because without it, clients might be unwilling to talk about the embarrassing, terrifying, or socially inappropriate things that hold the key to understanding and addressing their problems. Furthermore, as in other close relationships, confidentiality helps cement the bond of trust between a client and a therapist; people tend to trust those they know will keep their secrets.

A 1996 Supreme Court decision was the first to ensure protection of confidential communications between a therapist and a client in federal cases. Prior to this ruling, federal judges were free to decide on a case-by-case basis whether to force therapists to reveal the contents of their communications with a client. The decision was based on the case of *Jaffee v. Redmond,* in which Ricky Allen was killed by Mary Lu Redmond, an Illinois police officer. Called to an apartment to break up a fight, Redmond shot Allen when she saw him about to stab another man with a knife. Allen's family claimed that he was unarmed and sued officer Redmond and the police department for violating his civil rights. The family discovered that, after the shooting, Redmond had entered therapy, and they petitioned to have the therapy notes made available to them. When the therapist refused to turn over the notes, the trial judge told the jury that they could assume the notes contained material unfavorable to officer Redmond. The jury returned a verdict for the plaintiff and awarded Allen's family $545,000. In its review of the case, the Supreme

Court overturned the verdict and ruled that therapists could not be forced to testify about confidential communications. Writing for the court, Justice John Paul Stevens stated, "Effective psychotherapy . . . depends upon an atmosphere of confidence and trust in which the patient is willing to make a frank and complete disclosure of facts, emotions, memories, and fears."

As desirable as it may be, a client's right to privileged or confidential communication—like the right to refuse treatment—is not absolute. A therapist may be forced to breach confidentiality in the following situations.

1. If the therapist believes that a client needs to be involuntarily committed to a hospital.

2. If a client raises the issue of his or her mental condition in a trial and the therapist is called on to testify on the client's behalf.

3. If a client has undergone a court-ordered psychological evaluation.

4. If the therapist learns from the client that the client is abusing other people.

5. If the client tells a therapist of an intent to harm another person.

The Tarasoff Decision. This last exception to maintaining confidentiality creates a particularly thorny problem: should a therapist be required to break confidentiality whenever a client threatens to harm another person? Since the now-famous case of *Tarasoff* v. *Regents of the University of California*, the answer, in several states at least, is yes. In *Tarasoff*, the parents of a University of California student sued the University, psychotherapists employed by the University, and the campus police to recover damages for the murder of their daughter by a client of one of the psychotherapists. After a lower court found for the university, the parents appealed to the Supreme Court of California, which in two separate, but similar, decisions found for the plaintiffs (*Tarasoff II*, 1976).

Here are the facts of the case. Prosenjit Poddar was a client of psychologist Lawrence Moore. Poddar confided to Moore that he intended to kill Tatiana Tarasoff because she had rebuffed his romantic interest in her. Moore told his supervisor Dr. Harvey Powelson of this threat and then called and wrote the campus police, requesting that they detain Poddar. They did so but then released him because they were convinced that he was rational and would keep his promise to stay away from Tatiana (who was out

of the country at the time). Poddar didn't keep his promise. About 2 months after terminating therapy with Dr. Moore, Poddar went to Tatiana's home and stabbed her to death. He was subsequently convicted of murder. No one had warned Tatiana or her parents of Poddar's threats. In fact, Dr. Powelson had told the campus police to return Moore's written request for their intervention and had ordered the destruction of all copies of this letter and Moore's therapy notes.

In deciding for the parents, the California Supreme Court weighed the importance of a client's right to confidentiality in psychotherapy against society's interest in protecting itself from dangerous people. The court tipped the scales in society's favor because it viewed Moore's situation as being like that of a physician who would be held liable for failing to warn people about a contagious disease carried by one of the physician's patients. In the court's words, "The protective privilege ends where the public peril begins." As a result, therapists in California are required to take steps to protect victims from clients who the therapists believe, or should believe, are dangerous. The "steps to protect" can include warning victims, informing the police of the danger, seeking the voluntary or involuntary commitment of the client, or a combination of these actions.

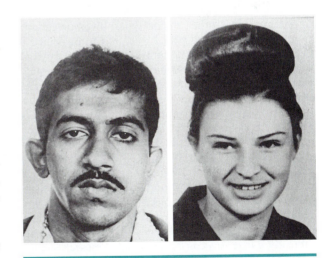

Prosenjit Poddar (left) *told his psychotherapist he intended to hurt Tatiana Tarasoff* (right). *After Tatiana was stabbed to death by Prosenjit about two months later, her parents sued the therapist and the University of California, where he was employed, for failing to take steps to protect Tatiana. This case established a precedent, now observed in many states, that requires therapists to break confidentiality when their clients tell them they intend to harm someone.*

The precedent set by *Tarasoff* had a mixed reception elsewhere. Several state courts reached decisions similar to the California ruling. Other states imposed no special obligation on therapists to break confidentiality to protect potential victims. In the case of *Brady et al.* v. *Hopper,* for example, the psychiatrist who had been treating John Hinckley, Jr., prior to his attempt to assassinate President Ronald Reagan was not held liable for damages. In still other states, courts have gone even further than California did, by extending therapists' responsibility not only to protect a specifically targeted victim, but "anyone who might forseeably be endangered" by a client (*Peterson* v. *State*).

The *Tarasoff* decision raised an outcry from psychotherapists. Many called it antitherapeutic, claiming that without the promise of confidentiality clients would not discuss their most troubling problems—or would avoid therapy altogether (Stone, 1976)—and that therapists might not want to explore and treat clients' violent impulses. The net result, they said, would be disastrous for society. Furthermore, clinicians argued that the *Tarasoff* decision ignored years of research showing that mental health professionals cannot accurately predict who

will and will not be dangerous in the future (Klassen & O'Connor, 1988; Monahan, 1981; Mulvey & Lidz, 1984). Finally, critics argued that the *Tarasoff* mandates were hopelessly vague. How dangerous does the client have to be before a therapist has to act? Is the need to warn triggered, for example, when an HIV-positive client tells a therapist he or she is having sex with an unprotected partner? How forseeable must the endangerment of a third party be? What steps are adequate to protect a potential victim in a given situation? Although none of these questions has clear-cut answers, debate has centered on the issue of dangerousness and clinicians' ability to predict it. As the Controversy section suggests, accurate assessment and prediction of dangerousness are among the most difficult challenges faced by mental health professionals.

The Impact of Tarasoff. Now that more than 20 years have passed since the *Tarasoff* case, it is possible to assess its effects on clinical practice. First, *Tarasoff* made therapists more alert to the potential for dangerous behavior by their clients. Survey after survey has indicated that, since *Tarasoff*, therapists are more

Controversy

Can Clinicians Predict Dangerousness?

In one form or another, the question of whether an individual will behave dangerously in the future is at the heart of many assessments that clinicians make in the legal system. Assessments and predictions of dangerousness can have a major impact on therapy clients and criminal defendants. In *Tarasoff*-type situations, for example, predicting that a client is dangerous can result in breached confidentiality and efforts to protect potential victims. Mentally ill people who are judged to be imminently dangerous can be involuntarily committed to a hospital. A convicted murderer's predicted dangerousness is a factor that can be considered by juries in some states in recommending a death sentence. Other criminal defendants found not guilty by reason of insanity can be forced into a hospital if they are judged to pose a risk for future dangerousness.

Even defendants awaiting trial can be denied bail if they are considered dangerous.

Can mental health professionals accurately predict whether such individuals will be dangerous? Can they say with certainty when the dangerous behavior might occur and how serious it might be in a particular case? During the 1970s and 1980s, most scholars concluded that clinicians' predictions about violence were usually incorrect (Monahan, 1984; Perlin, 1989). More recent, better-designed research suggests a slightly more optimistic picture (Borum, 1996). A thorough review of 44 studies on predicting dangerousness concluded that (1) clinicians do better than chance, sometimes much better, in distinguishing patients who will become violent from those who will not; (2) clinicians who are given information about whether a person has been violent in the past

do better than those not given such information; (3) predictions about behavior during 1- or 2-week periods are no more accurate than those made about periods as long as a year; and (4) there are no data that would allow mental health clinicians to claim they are better than others in making these predictions (Mossman, 1994). In other words, clinicians can anticipate dangerousness with some degree of accuracy, but they still make many errors and they are not uniquely skillful in predicting dangerousness (Lidz, Mulvey, & Gardner, 1993; Mossman, 1994).

Several factors combine to make the prediction of dangerousness difficult. First, because the rate of dangerous behavior in a population is usually very low (most people are not violent), clinicians are being asked to predict a phenomenon that is relatively rare. The cost of failing to detect dangerousness

aware of potential complications involving client dangerousness, are more concerned about their legal liability in such situations, and have changed the way they practice in order to reduce their legal risks (Shapiro, 1984; Wise, 1978).

At the same time, there is considerable evidence that *Tarasoff* has not had the adverse impact that many clinicians predicted. Researchers have found little evidence that *Tarasoff* has deterred many clinicians from treating potentially dangerous clients or has caused such clients to avoid therapy (Givelber, Bowers, & Blitch, 1984). Even more surprisingly, even when a therapist breaks confidentiality by warning a potential victim or the police, this act typically does *not* have a negative effect on the client, particularly if the therapist first discusses with the client the need to give the warning. In fact, under these conditions, warning a third party sometimes has positive effects on clients. Why? Perhaps the need to warn helps establish for the client clear limits on what behavior is acceptable or not acceptable, perhaps the warning stimulates the client's involvement in self-control, or perhaps the warning demonstrates the therapist's willingness to take decisive action.

Two factors help explain why *Tarasoff* did not bring all the negative consequences that had been predicted. First, even before *Tarasoff*, many therapists—up to 50 percent in one survey (Wise, 1978)—had been breaking confidentiality to warn victims or the police about dangerous clients. Second, many states have passed statutes to clarify the confusing obligations that therapists face with a *Tarasoff*-type client. As a result, therapists now have a clearer understanding of their options for managing such situations. California was the first state to pass a law limiting therapists' liability to a few, narrowly defined situations, namely those in which a client, in the course of therapy, makes a threat against a specific victim or states an intention to perform a dangerous act. About a third of the states now have statutes limiting therapist liability.

Regulation of Treatment Through Malpractice Lawsuits

Another important way in which mental health services are legally regulated is through civil lawsuits brought by clients who allege that they were harmed

---

is high, however, so clinicians tend to overpredict it, leading to many "false positive" cases in which expected violent behavior never occurs. Second, clinicians must usually base their assessments of dangerousness on what they learn about people in hospital or prison settings. That information might not help to predict people's behavior at home, at work, or on the street where dangerousness poses the greatest threat. Finally, even though they know that dangerousness is the product of individual characteristics *and* environmental triggers, clinicians usually have little opportunity to learn about the environments in which clients normally function. As a result, their predictions must often be made without a full understanding of the environmental factors that might make violence more, or less, likely in a given case.

In summary, dangerousness can never be predicted perfectly, but clinicians can improve the accuracy of their predictions if they adhere to a few basic principles (Gardner et al., 1996; Klassen & O'Connor, 1988; Litwack & Schlesinger, 1987; Monahan, 1984).

1. Assess the correct personal risk factors. The best predictor of future dangerousness is dangerousness in the past; a history of violence is correlated with greater risk for future violence. Additional factors that elevate the risk of dangerousness are ongoing substance abuse, current psychotic delusions, and frequent affiliation with others who behave aggressively.

2. Learn as much as possible about the environment in which the person has functioned and will be functioning in the future. Among individuals with a history of violent behavior, those at highest risk for future violence live in places where the base rates for violence are the highest.

3. Collect data on the accuracy of previous predictions. Individual

clinicians cannot learn about, and correct for, their tendency to make certain types of predictive mistakes unless they monitor their own track records.

Thinking Critically

Research suggests that a history of past violence is the single best predictor of future violence.

- Can we expect accurate information about previous violence to be gathered in the typical emergency room evaluation of a patient?

- What sorts of inaccuracies about patients' history might be most likely when obtaining this information from patients themselves?

- If there is misinformation about patients' violence history, what kind of predictive errors would clinicians most often make?

by the malpractice of mental health professionals. If a jury agrees with the client's claim, it may order the mental health professional to pay the client monetary damages to compensate for the harm suffered. To prove a claim of professional malpractice, four elements must be established.

1. A *special professional relationship* had to exist between the client/plaintiff and the therapist. Generally, this requires proving that the plaintiff was rceiving formal services from the professional in exchange for payment of a fee.

2. It must be shown that the professional was *negligent* in treating the client. Negligence does not simply mean that a bad outcome occurred; nor does it require that the therapist intended any harm to occur. Negligence involves an unintended violation of the **standard of care,** which is defined as the treatment that a reasonable practitioner facing circumstances similar to those of the plaintiff's case would be expected to give.

3. Even if the professional was negligent, it must be shown that the client suffered *harm.*

4. The therapist's negligence must then be shown to be the *cause* of the client's harm.

Until the mid-1960s, malpractice claims against clinical psychologists were almost nonexistent. Plaintiffs were reluctant to sue a therapist if it meant that they might have to talk about their psychological problems on the witness stand. Furthermore, there were few agreed-upon standards of care for treating mental disorders, so it was difficult to show that a therapist had violated principles of accepted practice.

The number of lawsuits involving malpractice began to increase, however, as the previously mentioned wave of skepticism about the mental health professions grew during the turbulent 1960s. As a result, malpractice charges against psychologists and psychiatrists are now much more common even though they are still not nearly as frequent as those against medical specialists in obstetrics, gynecology, and surgery.

Psychotherapists face the possibility of malpractice actions arising out of several kinds of situations, including (1) failing to prevent a client from committing suicide, (2) failing to carry out *Tarasoff* duty-to-protect obligations, (3) failing to make a proper referral for a client when the therapist terminates treatment, and (4) misrepresenting professional qualifications (Smith, 1996). However, the most common basis for malpractice claims against psychotherapists involves charges that they engaged in sexual intimacies with a current or recently terminated client.

Malpractice Related to Sexual Contact with Clients. The ethical codes of all mental health professions strictly forbid sexual intimacies between therapist and client (e.g., APA, 1992), so plaintiffs who prove that such sexual contact took place sometimes win large monetary awards. In spite of such outcomes and of the ethical injunctions against it, from 2 to 10 percent of mental health professionals report having engaged in intercourse or other sexually intimate behavior with clients (see Table 18.1). The rate of reported sexual contact with clients is about 4 to 5 times higher for male therapists than for female therapists, and therapists who have engaged in sex with their clients once are likely to repeat the offense with other clients (Pope & Vasquez, 1991).

Sexual contact between therapist and client is unethical for many reasons. First, most clients who

TABLE 18.1 Sexual Intimacy Between Therapists and Clients

Study	Sample	Rate of sexual intimacy*
Pope & Tabachnick (1994)	476 psychologists who had been in therapy	6%
Bouhoutsos et al. (1983)	704 California psychologists	3
Holroyd & Brodsky (1977)	703 psychologists	8
Pope & Feldman-Summers (1992)	290 psychologists	6
Pope, Tabachnick, & Keith-Spiegel (1987)	456 psychologists	2–3
Pope, Levenson, & Schover (1979)	481 psychologists	7
Kardener et al. (1973)	114 California psychologists	10

*Sexual intimacy defined as intercourse or other erotic physical contact.

have engaged in sex with their therapists report it to have been harmful (Feldman-Summers & Jones, 1984; Pope & Tabachnick, 1994). Second, giving in to a sexual attraction toward a client means that the therapist is putting his or her own needs before those of the client, which is fundamentally unethical behavior. Third, a therapist who engages in sexual contact with a client is not likely to be objective in making judgments about the proper care for that client. Fourth, therapy clients are often in the midst of psychological crises that impair their ability to make fully informed, independent judgments about how to behave. Finally, sexual relationships between therapist and client are exploitive because the therapist's power and control in the relationship is always much greater than the client's.

These ethical concerns are obvious, but should sexual intimacy between a therapist and a *former* client also be prohibited? If the therapy relationship is over, if the contact involves two freely consenting adults, and if no spouses or other third parties are involved, could there be any harm? The APA ethical standards say yes. These standards make it clear that psychologists should not engage in sexual intimacies with former therapy clients "for at least two years after cessation or termination of professional services" (APA, 1992, p. 1605). Even then, psychologists should not engage in sexual behavior with a former client unless they can clearly demonstrate that such activity would not be exploitive or harmful. Many clinicians believe that a sexual relationship with a former client *at any time* is unethical, is likely to be harmful to the former client, and should therefore always be avoided.

Malpractice Related to Repressed Memory Therapy. Malpractice verdicts (and judgments for substantial monetary damages) have also been returned in cases in which therapists have been accused of influencing clients to falsely recall allegedly repressed memories of physical or sexual abuse in childhood. Such "derepression" techniques have been advocated by popular books on incest (e.g., Bass & Davis, 1988) and by therapists who believe that, unless severe childhood traumas are recalled and defused, they will continue to cause mental problems (Blume, 1990). In addition to being asked to dredge up memories of traumatic incidents, suspected victims are often encouraged by therapists to join special support groups such as Survivors of Incest Anonymous. These groups urge their members to aggressively search for repressed memories of abuse.

Many researchers are skeptical about the accuracy of clients' memories of trauma that are reported years after the alleged incidents, especially when the reports come only *after* contact with aggressive practitioners of memory therapy (Loftus, 1993; Wakefield & Underwager, 1992). These skeptics point out that most people who suffer severe trauma do not lose their memories of the event; in fact, many of them suffer intrusive recollections of it for years afterward. Skepticism is also fueled by the fact that some alleged victims claim to have recalled traumas that happened when they were less than a year old, a feat contradicted by almost all research on childhood memory and amnesia.

If such recollections do not stem from actual traumatic events, how do they originate? There are several possible sources, including fantasies, distorted recollections, or even the unintentional *planting* of memories by therapists who try (perhaps too hard) to find reasons for clients' unhappiness or other problems. In one highly publicized trial, Gary Ramona—once a highly paid executive in the California wine industry—sued family counselor Marche Isabella and psychiatrist Richard Rose for allegedly planting false memories of trauma in his 19-year-old daughter, Holly, when she was their patient. In his suit, Ramona claimed that the therapists told Holly that her bulimia and depression were the result of having been repeatedly raped by him when she was a child. He claimed that they also told her that the memory of this molestation was so traumatic that she had repressed it for years. According to Ramona, Dr. Rose then gave Holly sodium amytal (a so-called truth serum) to confirm the validity of her "recovered memory." Isabella was said to have told Holly's mother that up to 80 percent of all bulimics had been sexually abused (a statement for which there is no scientific support).

At their trial, the therapists claimed that Holly suffered flashbacks of what seemed to be real sexual abuse. She also became increasingly depressed and bulimic as she reported these frightening images. In addition, Holly's mother, Stephanie, who had divorced her husband after Holly's allegations came to light, testified that she had suspected her husband might have abused Holly and listed several pieces of supposedly corroborating evidence. During his testimony, Gary Ramona emotionally denied ever sexually abusing his daughter. The mental health experts who testified on Romana's behalf criticized the therapists for engaging in dangerous techniques. Elizabeth Loftus (1993), a leading critic of therapists who claim the ability to recover long-buried traumatic memories, charged that these therapists often either

Connections

What evidence is there for the validity of repressed memory techniques and the role of such memories in mental disorders? See Chapter 8, pp. 266–268, 270–271.

Gary Ramona won the first lawsuit in the United States in which a therapist was found negligent in the use of memory-recovery therapy techniques.

suggest the idea of trauma to their clients or are too uncritical in accepting the validity of trauma reports that occur spontaneously. Another defense witness, Martin Orne, a renowned authority on hypnosis, condemned the use of sodium amytal interviews as "inherently untrustworthy and unreliable" and concluded that Holly's memory had been so distorted by her therapists that she no longer knew what the truth was.

The jury decided that Holly's therapists had, indeed, planted false memories in her mind and, in May 1994, awarded damages to Gary Ramona in the amount of $500,000. Since then, according to the False Memory Syndrome Foundation, a group devoted to uncovering abuses associated with memory recovery therapy, the number of "false memory" cases against therapists appears to be growing.

The increase in false memory litigation adds to the already difficult challenges therapists face when trying to help adult clients who have suffered a traumatic childhood. It is obvious that recovered memory therapy has led to some very bad outcomes and some very real damage to clients and their families (Ofshe & Watters, 1993). It is also obvious that the trauma of child abuse does occur and that it can leave deep, painful, and long-lasting emotional scars. Accordingly, therapists must be sympathetic listeners and helpful counselors when clients remember only too well real horrors from childhood. Such

clients need support to be able to talk about and cope with what they remember. At the same time, therapists must be cautious and avoid suggesting that clients' problems come from traumas that might never have happened.

Regulation of Treatment Through Economic Controls

Cases such as Gary Ramona's grab headlines, but they usually do not affect many therapists or clients. In fact, court decisions or malpractice verdicts are actually inefficient ways of regulating mental health treatment. *Tarasoff* requirements, for example, do not apply in many states, and even when they do they are not relevant to the treatment of most clients.

Much broader and stronger influences on mental health treatment—especially on the type and duration of treatment clients receive—are exerted by those who pay the therapy bills. In the United States, the practice of psychotherapy is more and more often regulated by the insurance companies or health maintenance organizations that are responsible for all or part of clients' therapy costs. These "third-party payers" want to make sure that they pay only for treatments that are effective, efficient, and necessary. They want to know which treatments, delivered for how long, and to which types of clients they should pay for, and when they should refuse to pay.

The type and length of treatment that clients have access to are increasingly controlled by **managed care systems,** which use methods of allocating health services to a group of people in order to contain the overall cost of these services. (In contrast to fee-for-service plans, most managed health care systems provide health care to their subscribers for a fixed, prepaid price.) Managed care plans thus exert far greater control over the way psychotherapy is practiced in the United States than any court decision or malpractice verdict ever has.

Here is how a simple managed care system might work. The Acme Insurance Company agrees to pay a mental health corporation $3.00 per month for every subscriber to its Positive Mental Health Plan. Such *capitation* systems limit the insurance company's financial risk by putting a cap on its costs. If the Positive Mental Health Plan enrolls 60,000 members, Acme will pay it $180,000 every month out of the insurance premiums Acme collects from its customers. Obviously, the fewer treatment sessions Positive Plan clients receive from professionals working for the Plan, the more profit Positive will make. The more clients treated, or the longer treatments last, the smaller Positive's profits will be.

A main mechanism that Positive will use to contain costs is the *utilization review,* in which one of their case managers will review a client's problem, the therapist's treatment plan, and the therapy progress notes. The case manager (who is *not* likely to be a mental health professional) then determines whether Positive will pay for the treatment and, if so, for how many sessions, and for which specific types of therapy. In other words, it is the case manager, not just the therapist, who determines the clinical needs and the level of care appropriate for each client. Generally, managed care reviewers favor treatments that involve medication and short-term therapy, thus discouraging comprehensive clinical assessments and insight-oriented, longer-term therapies. A case manager may decide, for example, that a depressed client can receive no more than 8 sessions of psychotherapy, even when the therapist says the client's problems require more extensive treatment.

While most clinicians welcome incentives that encourage them to use the most effective and efficient treatments available, they oppose incentives that (1) put profits before high quality treatment and (2) are determined by case managers who know very little about mental disorders and their treatment. Indeed, a major concern about managed care is that it usually focuses on management of costs, not quality, of health care. If cost containment is promoted over treatment quality, if inappropriate limits are set on the duration of psychotherapy, and if case managers intrude too often into the confidentiality of therapy, managed mental health care systems will ultimately fail to bring about the cost-effective treatment they promise.

Regulation of Treatment Through Ethical Standards

In addition to legal and economic controls, mental health practice is also regulated by **ethical standards,** the principles endorsed by a profession that encourage and forbid certain types of conduct and express the profession's norms and aspirations. All mental health professions have developed their own ethical standards. These standards tend to overlap and support some of the legal controls that have already been discussed. As noted earlier, for example, the legal protection of privileged communication is consistent with the ethical obligation of all mental health professionals to keep their communications with clients confidential. Similarly, the legal liability ther-

apists might incur if they have sexual contact with clients is reinforced by ethical prohibitions against sexual intimacies between therapist and client.

A wide array of behavior is covered by professional ethics. For example, the current version of the *Ethical Principles of Psychologists and Code of Conduct* (APA, 1992) addresses issues such as limiting practice to areas of demonstrated competence; maintaining proper clinical records; using and interpreting tests properly; protecting the privacy and confidentiality of client communications; consulting and cooperating with other mental health professionals; eliminating bias based on cultural, ethnic, religious, or socioeconomic factors; and protecting clients' welfare.

The largest number of ethical violations among psychologists occur in three general areas: breach of confidentiality, sexual intimacies between therapist and client, and disputes over financial matters. In one survey about the ethical dilemmas they most often face (Pope & Vetter, 1992), 14 to 18 percent of more than 600 psychologists responding mentioned problems in at least one of these areas. Here are three examples of the psychologists' descriptions (Pope & Vetter, 1992):

> One girl underwent an abortion without the knowledge of her foster parents. . . . I fully evaluated her view of the adults' inability to be supportive and agreed but worried about our relationship being damaged if I was discovered to know about the pregnancy and her action. (p. 599)

> I was conducting therapy with a child and soon became aware that there was a mutual attraction between myself and the child's mother. The strategies I had used and my rapport with the child had been positive. Nonetheless, I felt it necessary to refer to avoid a dual relationship (at the cost of the gains that had been made). (p. 400)

> A 7-year-old boy was severely sexually abused and severely depressed. I evaluated the case and recommended 6 months treatment. My recommendation was evaluated by a managed health care agency and approved for 10 sessions by a nonprofessional in spite of the fact that there is no known treatment program that can be performed in 10 sessions on a 7-year-old that has demonstrated efficacy. (p. 401)

Ethical standards do not have the force of law, but violations of these standards can still result in serious consequences for offenders. Clinicians found to have violated the ethics of their professions can be publicly reprimanded, censured, or expelled from their professional organizations. As a result, they may also end up losing their state licensure or certification.

Mental Health Professionals in the Legal System

Mental health professionals generally provide the legal system with one or more of four main services (Wrightsman, Nietzel, & Fortune, 1994):

1. As *basic scientists,* they study a phenomenon to learn as much as they can about it, with no regard for whether their work has relevance to the legal system. For example, a psychologist studying the development of cognitive ability tests might examine whether the predictive validity of the test is affected by the ethnicity or gender of the people being tested. This research might subsequently play a role in litigation about the legally acceptable use of the test in hiring decisions (Gottfredson, 1994).

2. As *trial consultants* to attorneys, mental health professionals participate, for example, in jury selection or trial preparation in order to help one side win the trial.

3. As *policy evaluators or researchers,* they study the effects of changes in correctional programs, legislation, or social services.

4. As *expert witnesses,* they testify on a wide variety of subjects in civil and criminal trials.

From the public's point of view, the mental health professional's role as expert witness is surely the most controversial. Psychologists and psychiatrists have testified in some of the most notorious trials in recent American history, including those of the Menendez brothers, Jeffrey Dahmer, Susan Smith, and John Hinckley. In his 1994 book *The Abuse Excuse,* Harvard law professor Alan Dershowitz denounced much of this type of testimony as providing obviously guilty defendants a way to avoid being held responsible for their crimes. One commentator summed up the skepticism of many Americans when he referred to trial testimony by mental health experts as the time to "send in the clowns."

The Scope of Expert Testimony

Despite public skepticism about it, psychological and psychiatric expert testimony in the United States has grown rapidly. It is estimated that psychologists and psychiatrists testify in approximately 8 percent of all trials held in federal civil courts and that mental health witnesses participate in as many as a million cases each year (O'Connor, Sales, & Shuman, 1996). Three factors appear especially responsible for the expansion of **forensic psychology** and **forensic psychiatry,** two specialty fields that apply mental health knowledge to questions about individuals involved in legal proceedings.

Expert testimony is frequently used, first, because, as shown in Table 18.2, there are many topics about which mental health experts can testify. As scientists learn more about human behavior, attorneys are likely to find this information helpful in court cases. Our discussion of expert testimony focuses on the questions of criminal competence and responsibility, but these are only two of many subjects about which psychological experts testify, and they are relatively rare, at that. Expert testimony is also given in areas such as developmental, industrial/organizational, experimental, and social psychology, as well as in many areas of medicine.

Second, expert testimony flourishes because the law permits it and may even encourage it. Since the mid-1970s, American courts have relaxed their standards for the admissibility of expert testimony. In general, a qualified expert can testify on a topic if "scientific, technical, or other specialized knowledge will assist the trier of fact to understand the evidence or to determine a fact in issue" (Federal Rule of Evidence 702). In 1993, the U.S. Supreme Court ruled in *Daubert* v. *Merrell Dow Pharmaceutical, Inc.* that judges are allowed to decide when expert testimony is based on sufficiently relevant and reliable scien-

TABLE 18.2 Topics for Expert Testimony

Topic	Main question addressed
Insanity	What is the relationship between the defendant's mental condition at the time of the alleged offense and the defendant's responsibility for the crime with which he or she is charged?
Criminal competencies	Does the defendant have an adequate understanding of the legal proceedings?
Sentencing	What are the prospects for the defendant's rehabilitation? What deterrent effects do certain sentences have?
Eyewitness identification	What factors affect the accuracy of eyewitness identification?
Trial procedure	What effects are associated with variations in pretrial and/or trial procedures?
Civil commitment	Does a mentally ill person present a danger or a threat of danger that requires treatment no less restrictive than hospitalization?
Psychological damages in civil cases	What psychological consequences has an individual suffered as a result of someone's wrongful conduct? To what extent are the psychological problems attributable to a preexisting condition?
Psychological autopsies	In equivocal cases, do the person's personality and the circumstances under which he or she died indicate a likely mode of death?
Negligence and product liability	How do environmental factors and human perceptual abilities affect an individual's use of a product?
Trademark litigation	Is a certain product name or trademark confusingly similar to a competitor's?
Class-action suits	What psychological evidence is there that effective treatment is being denied or that testing procedures are discriminatory?
Guardianship and conservatorship	Does an individual possess the necessary mental ability to make decisions concerning living conditions, financial matters, health, etc.?
Child custody	What psychological factors will affect the best interests of a child whose custody is in dispute?
Adoption and termination of parental rights	What psychological factors affect the best interests of a child whose parents' disabilities may render them unfit to raise and care for the child?
Professional malpractice	Did a defendant's professional conduct fail to meet the standard of care owed to the plaintiff?
Social issues in litigation	What are the effects of pornography, violence, spousal abuse, etc., on the behavior of a defendant who claims that his or her misconduct was caused by one of these influences?

Source: Based on Nietzel & Dillehay, 1986.

tific evidence to be admitted. This opinion encourages the consideration of innovative opinions, and many critics, including experts themselves, fear that it will lead judges—especially those who cannot accurately distinguish valid from invalid research—to occasionally expose jurors to testimony based on "junk science" rather than standard empirical methods.

Finally, expert testimony thrives because, quite simply, it can be very lucrative. At hourly rates ranging from $100 to $400, forensic experts can earn thousands of dollars per case.

Criminal Competence and Responsibility

No area of law illustrates the controversies surrounding expert testimony as dramatically as testimony about whether a defendant was insane during the commission of an illegal act. Proving insanity can result in a defendant's acquittal or protect the individual from the punishment that would otherwise follow conviction.

Why do courts allow defendants' mental condition to be introduced at trial? The fundamental reason is that, in most societies, it is seen as immoral to punish people who, as a result of a mental disorder, either do not know that their actions are wrong or are unable to control their conduct. Societies see punishment as fully deserved only by those who can comprehend the nature and wrongness of their criminal behavior.

Criminal Competence. Indeed, in the United States it is not even permissible to continue criminal proceedings against a defendant who is unable to understand the nature and purpose of those proceedings. Thus, before a court ever considers whether a defendant was sane or insane during the commission of a crime, it must first decide about the defendant's **competence to stand trial.** Defendants are considered incompetent if, as a result of a mental disorder, they cannot (1) understand the nature of the trial proceedings, (2) participate meaningfully in their own defense, or (3) consult with their attorney. Note that competence refers to the defendant's mental condition *at the time of the trial,* whereas insanity, described next, refers to the defendant's mental condition *at the time of an alleged offense.*

The question of criminal competence can be raised at any point in the criminal process by the prosecutor, the defense attorney, or the presiding judge. In practice, this question is usually raised by defense attorneys who have reason to believe that their client may be suffering from a mental disorder. Typically, when the judge orders a competency assessment, the defendant is taken to a special forensic hospital for observation and examination. In fact, the majority of mentally disordered offenders who have been committed to hospitals are there either because they are awaiting a competency evaluation or they have been found incompetent and are receiving treatment to restore their competence. In most states, psychiatrists, psychologists, and social workers are authorized to perform competency evaluations, and they often use special structured interviews to do so. More than 70 percent of defendants referred for such evaluations are ultimately found competent to stand trial (Nicholson & Kugler, 1991). Defendants found to be not competent may be committed to a hospital for medication and other treatment. In most states, this mandatory treatment can last up to 6 months, after which, if a person is still judged incompetent, a different form of hospitalization might be arranged, or the person might be released.

The Insanity Defense. In all states, defendants are initially presumed to be mentally responsible for the crimes with which they are charged. Therefore, if defendants plead not guilty by reason of **insanity,** they must present evidence to show that they lacked a state of mind necessary to be held responsible for the crimes with which they are charged. Because insanity is a legal term, not a psychological concept, it is defined in the United States by legal standards that have evolved over time and vary from state to state.

These standards had their origins in 1843, when Englishman Daniel McNaughton tried to assassinate the British prime minister, Robert Peel. McNaugthon suffered the paranoid delusion that Peel was conspiring against him, so he waited outside the prime minister's house at Number 10 Downing Street, and he shot and killed Peel's secretary, whom he mistook for the prime minister. McNaughton was charged with murder, but pleaded not guilty by reason of insanity (NGRI), essentially claiming that he did not know the difference between right and wrong. Nine medical experts testified that McNaughton was insane and, after hearing instructions from the judge, the jury did not even leave the courtroom before deciding that McNaughton was not guilty by reason of insanity. This verdict infuriated the British public. Queen Victoria, particularly upset because she herself had been the target of several assassination attempts, demanded that Britain toughen its definition of insanity.

After extended debate in the House of Lords and among the nation's highest judges, a definition of insanity known as the **McNaughton rule** was enacted that states, " . . . to establish a defense on the grounds of insanity it must be clearly proved that, at the time of committing the act, the accused was laboring under such a defect of reason, from disease of the mind, as not to know the nature and quality of the act he was doing or, if he did know it, that he did not know what he was doing [was] wrong" (quoted in Post, 1963, p. 113).

McNaughton became the rule in Great Britain, and it remains the standard for insanity in about 20 states in the United States. It essentially "excuses" criminal conduct by defendants whose mental illness either (1) causes them to not know what they are doing (e.g., believing they are stabbing the devil rather than a person) or (2) leaves them incapable of knowing that what they are doing is wrong (e.g., having the delusion that the victim is about to kill them). However, the McNaughton rule has been severely criticized over the years because it focuses only on cognition—knowing right from wrong—and ignores how mental illness might affect motivation and control.

An alternative to McNaughton appeared in response to a 1954 case involving Monte Durham. Durham had been in and out of prisons and mental hospitals for most of his life. He was a car thief, a burglar, and a bad check artist. At one of his trials for residential burglary, Durham's plea of not guilty by reason of insanity was rejected by the judge, who obviously thought the defendant knew right from wrong. His lawyers appealed this decision, claiming that the McNaughton rule was obsolete. Judge David Bazelon of the United States Court of Appeals in Washington, D.C., reviewed objections to McNaughton and ruled that Durham should have a new trial in which the standard for judging insanity would be "that an accused is not criminally responsible if his unlawful act was the product of a mental disease or mental defect." This became known as the **Durham rule,** or the *product test.*

Initially, the Durham rule was popular with mental health professionals, but it soon ran into trouble with attorneys and judges who believed that it gave far too much weight to the testimony of psychiatrists and psychologists about any kind of mental illness that could cause criminal behavior. As a result, the Durham rule was never accepted by more than a few states, and in 1972, it was replaced by the same Bazelon court with the Brawner rule, also known as the ALI rule.

The **ALI rule** was developed by the American Law Institute (ALI) in an appellate case in which the defendant, Archie Brawner, Jr., had been convicted of the murder of Billy Ford. This rule holds that a defendant is not responsible for criminal conduct if, "at the time of such conduct as a result of mental disease or defect [the defendant] lack[s] substantial capacity either to appreciate the criminality [wrongfulness] of his conduct or to conform his conduct to the requirements of the law." The ALI rule, or some-

thing close to it, is used in about half the states, and one part of it is now used in all federal courts as the test of insanity. The ALI rule differs from McNaughton in three main ways.

1. By using the term *appreciate* instead of *know,* the ALI rule acknowledges that emotional factors as well as cognitive ones can influence criminal conduct.

2. The ALI rule does not require that offenders have a total lack of appreciation for the wrongfulness of their conduct—only that they lack "substantial capacity."

3. The ALI rule defines insanity in both cognitive and volitional terms. Under this rule, defendants can be considered insane even if they appreciated that certain conduct was wrong, as long as a mental illness rendered them unable to control their conduct.

The Insanity Defense Under Fire. After John Hinckley was found not guilty by reason of insanity for shooting President Ronald Reagan, Press Secretary James Brady, and three other people in 1982, an ABC News poll showed that 67 percent of Americans believed that justice had not been served in the case. Highly publicized cases such as Hinckley's (and McNaughton's) tend to be followed by widespread public dissatisfaction and cynicism about the insanity defense. Among the greatest concerns are that a large number of defendants successfully use the insanity defense, that defendants found NGRI are quickly released from the hospital after their trials, and that insane criminals are more dangerous than other criminals. There is also concern that the insanity defense favors the rich and that court decisions about it rely too much on the testimony of expert witnesses. How realistic are these concerns?

Prevalence and Success of the Insanity Defense. The insanity defense is employed much less frequently than most people assume and with far less success than defendants would wish. One study in Wyoming found that the public assumed that the insanity defense was used in about half of all criminal cases and was successful about 20 percent of the time. In fact, the insanity defense was used by only 102 of 22,102 felony defendants studied (less than .005 percent) and was successful only once (Pasewark & Pantle, 1981). Across the United States, experts estimate that fewer than 1 percent of all criminal cases result in a finding of NGRI; in general the more often the insanity defense is used, the lower its rate of success (Appelbaum, 1994). Simply put, juries are reluctant to find violent offenders NGRI, mainly out of fear that these offenders will be prematurely released and will repeat their violence.

The Likelihood of Early Release. Defendants found NGRI seldom go free. One study found that NGRI defendants in New York were hospitalized for an average of 3.5 years (Steadman & Braff, 1983). The same study showed that defendants who had committed more serious offenses tended to be confined longer. In many states, the norm is to keep NGRI defendants in mental institutions until a judge is convinced that it is safe to release them.

Do hospital confinement and treatment have any clear benefits for defendants found NGRI? No one knows for sure. Some studies show that individuals who complete their hospital treatment do better than those who run away from the institution (Nicholson, Norwood, & Enyart, 1991), but another study found no difference in the posthospitalization behavior between NGRI defendants who were officially discharged and those who escaped (Pasewark et al., 1982). Robert Nicholson and his colleagues (1991) collected data on all NGRI defendants in Oklahoma who had been treated in the state forensic hospital over a 5-year period. Within two-and-a-half years of their release, half of these patients had been rearrested or rehospitalized, a rate that is about the same as for criminals in general. These data confirm the results of earlier studies (Melton et al., 1987).

In an effort to err on the side of caution, judges often use criteria for releasing NGRI defendants that are, stricter than those set for noncriminal involuntary commitments. In the 1992 case of *Foucha* v. *Louisiana,* the U.S. Supreme Court acted to eliminate this discrepancy, ruling that it is unconstitutional to keep a defendant in an institution who no longer meets the standard for involuntary civil commitment—that is, who is no longer mentally ill *and* dangerous. Although the ruling seems fair, cases such as that of E. E. Kemper III raise doubts about it. Kemper was released from a California hospital for the insane after spending 5 years there for murdering his grandparents. He then petitioned a court to seal his psychiatric records, which it did after psychiatrists pronounced him sane. What neither the court nor the examining psychiatrists knew was that, since his release, Kemper had killed his mother and seven other women. The last murder occurred 3 days before the court hearing that sealed his records (Gleick, 1978).

Dangerousness of Insane Defendants. Cases such as Kemper's are rare, but they add weight to the argument that the insanity defense places the public at risk of violence by NGRI defendants. The dangerousness of NGRI defendants is difficult to determine, partly because, as already noted, it is often difficult to know how dangerous *anyone* might be. Assessing the public dangerousness of NGRI defendants is also complicated by the fact that most of them are immediately removed from public life and confined in a hospital where they usually receive drugs and other treatment. Although people with serious mental disorders (including NGRI defendants) are somewhat more likely to be violent than people without such disorders, this relationship is typically found *only for people who are currently experiencing psychotic symptoms* (Link, Cullen, & Andrews, 1993; Monahan, 1992). If drugs or other treatments reduce these symptoms, the potential for violence is reduced as well.

The Economics of the Insanity Defense. The parents of John Hinckley, Jr., reportedly spent between $500,000 and $1,000,000 on psychiatric evaluations and expert testimony in support of their son's insanity plea. Cases such as this contribute to the perception that the insanity defense is so costly that the average defendant cannot afford to use it. There are almost no data to support this view. A series of studies has found no socioeconomic or ethnic bias in the use or success of the insanity plea (Boehnert, 1989; Howard & Clark, 1985; Nicholson et al., 1991; Pasewark & Pantle, 1981; Steadman et al., 1983).

As mentioned earlier, equal access to the insanity plea is assured by a 1985 U.S. Supreme Court decision in *Ake* v. *Oklahoma* that poor defendants who plead insanity are entitled to the assistance of mental health professionals at state expense. Of course, a person who can afford more than one expert or the most expensive expert is likely to mount a more impressive insanity defense than a less affluent defendant, but this economic reality applies to any kind of defense. Defendants who can afford to hire a squadron of attorneys, detectives, DNA experts, or ballistics specialists have advantages over poor defendants, but no one would suggest that this fact justifies eliminating defenses based on mistaken identity or ballistics tests.

The Role of Expert Witnesses. There is considerable public concern that testifying about insanity allows mental health experts to give opinions for which they lack proper competence or certainty. The debate centers on three issues. First, can experts reliably and validly diagnose mental illness and therefore identify the conditions that qualify as legal insanity? Second, can experts accurately discern a defendant's criminal responsibility for acts that were

Connections

What are the two kinds of mistakes that clinicians make in predicting or diagnosing behavior? See Chapter 2, p. 49.

committed in the past, sometimes in the distant past? Third, even assuming that the answer to the first two questions is "yes," are clinicians any more capable than nonprofessionals of making these judgments?

Many psychologists and psychiatrists doubt that professionals in their fields have any special expertise in determining a defendant's sanity at the time of an alleged offense (Dawes, Faust, & Meehl, 1989; Ziskin & Faust, 1988). They are also concerned that experts have too much influence on the outcomes of insanity trials. These critics contend that decisions about criminal responsibility are legal questions that are best answered by juries or judges. Finally, they worry that public confidence in the behavioral sciences is eroded when juries see, and the media report, a parade of mental health experts who contradict each other about a defendant's sanity. Loss of credibility for mental health professionals' expertise is especially likely when such contradictory testimony occurs in high profile trials such as those of John Hinckley or Jeffrey Dahmer.

Revisions and Reforms in the Insanity Defense

Of all the reforms introduced in insanity defense rules and procedures over the past 20 years, three have received the most attention.

The Guilty But Mentally Ill Verdict. For many decades, juries deliberating cases in which the insanity defense is raised could reach only verdicts of guilty, not guilty, or not guilty by reason of insanity. Since 1976, however, about a quarter of the states in the United States have passed laws giving juries a fourth possible verdict: **guilty but mentally ill (GBMI).** A defendant found GBMI is usually sentenced to the same period of confinement as would any other defendant convicted of the same crime. Ideally, however, the GBMI prisoner's confinement begins in a treatment facility, and transfer to a prison occurs only after treatment is complete. The primary intent behind GBMI laws is to offer a compromise verdict that would decrease the number of defendants found NGRI. It is unclear whether these laws are successful in this respect; there have been decreases in NGRI verdicts in some states but not in others (Callahan et al., 1992; Roberts & Golding, 1991).

Several other problems have led to growing skepticism about the value of the GBMI verdict. For one thing, it complicates an already confusing situation for juries who must evaluate insanity pleas. GBMI laws require jurors to distinguish between mental illness that results in insanity and mental illness that does not. In addition, the notion that the GBMI ver-

dict would result in more treatment for mentally ill prisoners has proved to be unfounded. Overcrowding at most facilities prevents adequate treatment from ever taking place. In one Michigan study, 75 percent of GBMI offenders went directly to prison without any treatment (Sales & Hafemeister, 1984). Finally, the GBMI verdict and the opportunity for treatment that it might bring is available only to the relatively small proportion of defendants who raise an insanity defense. Thus, a severely disturbed defendant who does not claim insanity cannot be found GBMI.

The Insanity Defense Reform Act. In 1984, in the wake of the John Hinckley trial, Congress passed the *Insanity Defense Reform Act (IDRA)*. Its main purpose was to limit the number of defendants in federal courts who could successfully claim insanity as a defense. Although not abolishing the insanity defense, the IDRA changed its use in the federal courts in three important ways. First, it placed the burden on the defendant to prove insanity, rather than on the prosecution to prove sanity, which had previously been the case.

Second, it did away with the volitional section of the ALI rule. Lack of behavioral control because of mental illness is no longer a basis for insanity in federal cases. Insanity is restricted to the cognitive part of the ALI rule, namely that as a result of mental illness the defendant could not appreciate the nature or wrongfulness of his acts. Removing the volitional section essentially makes the federal test of insanity the same as the McNaughton rule. This reform was introduced because of the view that (1) a person's ability to control his or her actions cannot be assessed reliably and (2) the issue of volition provided a loophole through which too many criminal offenders were walking to freedom. This change in federal insanity rules came about in spite of empirical research that tended to contradict both these claims.

Third, the IDRA prohibited experts from giving *ultimate opinion* testimony about insanity. As a result of this change, experts may describe a defendant's mental condition and the effects it might have on behavior, but they may not state any conclusions about a defendant's insanity. The reformers acted in the hope that this change would prohibit experts from having too much control over verdicts, but there is some evidence that the prohibition might not have much effect on juries. In one study, for example, subjects read one of several versions of a trial in which a defendant pleaded NGRI in the killing of his boss (Fulero & Finkel, 1991). One group of subjects read a transcript in which mental health experts for both sides offered only *diagnostic* testimony, that is, that the defendant was mentally ill at the time of the offense. A second group read a version in which the

A Talk with Ron Roesch

Dr. Ron Roesch is Professor of Psychology and Director of the Clinical Psychology Program at Simon Fraser University in Vancouver, British Columbia. A past president of the American Psychological Association's Division 41 (American Psychology-Law Society) and former editor of Law and Human Behavior, *Dr. Roesch has conducted several influential studies on the assessment of legal issues such as competency to stand trial and on the treatment of mentally disordered offenders in the criminal justice system.*

Legal Controversies and Mental Disorders

Q *What is your current reading on how the legal system is balancing the autonomy rights of individuals and the safety interests of society?*

A There is no question that the system has been heading toward greater protection of social interests. A major reason for this shift has been that public perceptions of crime and criminals are shaped more quickly now by the media. Because the media pay so much attention to notorious cases such as Colin Ferguson (who shot several people on a New York commuter train), Jeffrey Dahmer, or O. J. Simpson, the public bases its opinions about the criminal justice system on these cases. But these cases are usually extreme, often resulting in policies that are inappropriate for most cases.

> *I would like to see the adversary structure abolished when it comes to expert testimony.*

Q *What is an example of a criminal justice system policy that might be unnecessary for most defendants?*

A Most evaluations of a defendant's competency or criminal responsibility are conducted in special institutions when they could be performed quicker, with less expense, and just as validly in community mental health centers or even local jails. A major reason why defendants are sent to these special institutions is that they often have mental health problems that the personnel in local jails are not equipped to handle.

Q *What does your own research suggest about the incidence of mental disorders in jails?*

A We recently surveyed about 700 people confined in the Vancouver city jail. About 15 percent were diagnosed with a major mental disorder such as schizophrenia or mood disorders, and, if we included substance abuse disorders and less serious mental disorders, the percentage rose to 85 percent. Several were subsequently sent off to a forensic facility for competency evaluations. This pattern illustrates my previous point: competency exams performed in other institutions are often just a short-term solution for the problem of mental illness in jails. We need long-term solutions to this problem, and that inevitably means that we need prevention programs.

Q *Are mental health professionals making positive contributions to the criminal justice system?*

A I think that many courts do not pay sufficient attention to the research on forensic questions, and often the end result is negative. In recent years, the Supreme Court in particular has acted indifferently to the results of psychological research. If research findings do not agree with the preferences of certain judges, they either ignore the research or declare it irrelevant.

Q *What's your opinion about mental health professionals' testifying as expert witnesses?*

A Michael Saks once classified expert witnesses into three categories: hired guns who will say anything to help the side paying their bills, advocates who argue strongly for their position and tend to minimize conflicting opinions or data, and educators who try to accurately portray what is known about a particular subject matter. While the last role is, in my mind, the only proper one for experts to play, the adversary system makes it hard for experts to maintain a neutral educator position.

Q *Can this problem be solved?*

A I would like to see the adversary structure abolished when it comes to expert testimony. Keep it for the rest of litigation, but when it comes to expert testimony, have the judge appoint two experts to come to court and tell the jury what they believe is the scientific consensus about a topic in question. Have the experts paid by the court, not the lawyers for each side. This should reduce the tendency for experts to develop opinions that serve the interests of only one side in a court dispute—the side that paid them.

experts testified about their diagnosis and also gave a *penultimate* opinion about how the disorder might have affected the defendant's understanding of the wrongfulness of his act. A third group read a transcript in which the experts discussed diagnosis, gave penultimate opinions, and then offered an *ultimate opinion* as to whether the defendant was sane or insane at the time he killed his boss. In this study, subjects' verdicts were not affected by the type of testimony they read. These results could mean that a ban on ultimate opinion testimony does not accomplish much (Rogers & Ewing, 1989), but it could also mean that the ban can shorten expert testimony without sacrificing essential information. Further research on this issue is needed.

Most mock jury studies of the IDRA have found that verdicts are little affected by whether jurors hear ALI instructions, IDRA instructions, or no instructions at all about the definition of insanity (Finkel, 1989). Jurors appear to depend on their own views about what constitutes insanity and interpret the evidence according to those views, regardless of the formal instructions judges give them (Roberts & Golding, 1991).

Abolition of the Insanity Defense. A few states, such as Idaho and Montana, have abolished the insanity defense. Has this drastic step solved the problem of holding mentally ill people responsible for criminal acts? Not really. Issues associated with insanity remain because, to be convicted of a crime in any state, one must have intended the illegal act. Defendants can be found guilty of theft, for example, only if it can be proved that they intended to steal. Accordingly, even states in which there is no insanity defense must allow evidence to be introduced at trial about a defendant's *mens rea*, or guilty mind, during alleged crimes. If, as a result of a mental disorder, defendants lack the *mens rea* for a crime, they should be found not guilty. And so, to help juries decide, experts continue to offer testimony about the effects of mental illness on defendants' *mens rea*.

In short, a defendant's mental state can never be entirely eliminated from jurors' consideration, simply because it makes no sense to talk about guilt without knowing something about a person's state of mind at the time of their alleged crime. In one form or another, then, the issue of insanity is likely to remain a part of court decisions about criminal responsibility.

Revisiting the Case of Wilson

During his short-term commitment to the hospital for observation, Wilson once again promised the staff that he would take his antipsychotic medication. Based on this promise, plus the fact that Wilson responded quickly and favorably to the medication he started in the hospital, he was discharged after 5 days. Over the next 6 months, Wilson took his medication sporadically, and he managed to keep only about half of his scheduled appointments at the community mental health center that was responsible for supervising his treatment.

During the last of these appointments, he told a psychiatrist at the center that his medication was making him sick and that he didn't need it anymore. The psychiatrist tried to reason with him, but to no avail. Wilson stalked out of the office, vowing never to "come back to you witch doctors again." The psychiatrist took no further action. Two nights later, Wilson's parents called the police to ask for help because they feared that Wilson was again becoming unmanageable. A police officer arrived at Wilson's home the next day to take him to the hospital, but as they walked to the patrol car, Wilson attacked the officer, took his service revolver, and shot him three times in the chest, killing him instantly.

At his murder trial, Wilson pleaded not guilty by reason of insanity, but the jury found him guilty but mentally ill and recommended a sentence of life in prison. The family of the slain police officer filed a civil suit against Wilson's psychiatrist and the community mental health center, claiming that they should have known that Wilson was dangerous and should have taken steps to protect their son, either by immediately committing Wilson to the hospital or compelling him to take his medication. The case was settled out of court. Wilson continues to serve his sentence, and, according to prison psychiatrists, takes his medication without incident.

1

SUMMARY

The Rights of Individuals Versus the Rights of Society

The involuntary commitment of mentally ill citizens illustrates one of the most fundamental controversies surrounding the treatment of abnormal behavior. Commitment procedures raise the question of how to balance the rights of individuals to be left alone and the rights of society to be protected from harm. In the United States, the rationale for involuntary commitment has been either *parens patriae* (deciding what is best for incapacitated people) or police power (protecting society against dangerous people). In the late 1960s and 1970s, commitment procedures were reformed throughout the United States, making it much more difficult to commit the mentally ill on the basis of a *parens patriae* doctrine. The populations of public mental hospitals declined throughout this period, although this deinstitutionalization process left many seriously disturbed patients without adequate treatment or protection. Beginning in the 1980s and continuing to the present, the procedures for involuntary commitments have attempted to balance concerns about patients' rights while realizing that some people are so seriously disabled that society should insist on their treatment even if they pose no danger to others. Commitment through a court order, commitment without a court order, and outpatient commitment are three procedures for civil commitment.

Other examples of the tension between individual and societal rights are revealed in questions about whether mental patients should have the right to refuse treatment. As of now, the Supreme Court has not recognized such a right, but in many situations patients are able to object to certain types of medication and thereby influence the kind of treatment they receive. American courts have established other basic rights for mental patients that guarantee treatment, fair housing, and professional assistance in criminal proceedings.

The Regulation of Mental Health Professionals

Mental health professionals and the techniques they employ are increasingly regulated through legal, economic, and ethical controls. Access to and the practice of the mental health professions is controlled through certification and licensure laws. The courts also control mental health professionals' practice by placing limits on certain privileges and ethical obligations typically honored by these professions. For example, the right to confidential mental health treatment can be abridged in certain circumstances, such as when a therapy client threatens to harm a third party. Mental health services are also regulated through malpractice suits brought by clients who believe they have been harmed by a professional who does not live up to the prevailing standards of care. The most common cause of malpractice suits against mental health professionals is the allegation of sexual contact with current or former clients. However, the most widespread control over mental health services is exerted by third-party payers and managed care plans, which decide how much the companies will pay for certain kinds of mental health treatment.

Mental Health Professionals in the Legal System

No psycholegal topic has generated more controversy than the question of what is the proper role for mental health professionals who are asked to testify in court about a defendant's mental state as it relates to the insanity defense. Insanity is a legal term that has been defined in various ways over the past two centuries. The current definition most in favor in the United States is the ALI rule, which states that defendants are not criminally responsible if, as the result of mental illness, they lack a substantial capacity either to appreciate the criminality of their conduct or to conform their conduct to the requirements of the law.

Although the public tends to believe that the insanity defense is used frequently in criminal cases, is often successful, and leads to large numbers of dangerous people being released from custody, the insanity defense is actually used rarely, and is seldom successful in setting defendants free. Most defendants found not guilty by reason of insanity (NGRI) serve lengthy periods of hospital confinement. Several reforms—such as the guilty-but-mentally-ill (GBMI) verdict—have been introduced in recent years, and a few states have abolished the insanity defense. None of these changes has been shown to substantially change the ways juries evaluate insanity defenses. Even states that have done away with the insanity defense still find it necessary to consider the effects mental illness might have had on defendants' capacity to understand the crimes with which they are charged.

KEY TERMS

References

Abel, G. G., Becker, J. V., Cunningham-Rather, J., Mittelman, M. & Rouleau, J. L. (1988). Multiple paraphilic diagnoses among sex offenders. *Bulletin of the American Academy of Psychiatry and the Law, 16*, 153–168.

Abel, G. G., & Rouleau, J. L. (1995). Sexual abuses. *Psychiatric Clinics of North America, 18*, 139–153.

Abikoff, H., & Klein, R. G. (1992). Attention-deficit hyperactivity and conduct disorder: Comorbidity and implications for treatment. *Journal of Consulting and Clinical Psychology, 60*, 881–892.

Abikoff, H., Klein, R. G., Klass, E., & Ganeles, D. (1987, October). Methylphenidate in the treatment of conduct disordered children. In H. Abikoff (Chair), *Diagnosis and treatment issues in children with disruptive behavior disorders*. Symposium conducted at the annual meeting of the American Academy of Child and Adolescent Psychiatry, Washington, DC.

Ables, B. S., & Brandsma, J. M. (1977). *Therapy for couples*. San Francisco: Jossey-Bass.

Abood, L. G. (1960). A chemical approach to the problem of mental illness. In D. D. Jackson (Ed.), *The etiology of schizophrenia* (pp. 91–119). New York: Basic Books.

Abraham, H. D., & Aldridge, A. M. (1993). Adverse consequences of lysergic acid diethylamide. *Addiction, 88*, 1327–1334.

Abraham, K. (1911). Notes on the psychoanalytic investigation and treatment of manic-depressive insanity and allied conditions. In *Selected papers on psychoanalysis*. New York: Basic Books (1960).

Abrahamson, D. J., Barlow, D. H., Beck, J. C., Sakheim, D. K., & Kelly, J. P. (1985). The effects of attentional focus and partner responsiveness on sexual responding: Replication and extension. *Archives of Sexual Behavior, 14*, 361–371.

Abram, K. M., & Teplin, L. A. (1991). Co-occuring disorders among mentally ill jail detainees: Implications for public policy. *American Psychologist, 46*, 1036–1045.

Abrams, R. (1993). ECT technique: Electrode placement, stimulus type and treatment frequency. In C. E. Coffey, *The clinical science of electroconvulsive therapy* (pp. 17–28). Washington, DC: American Psychiatric Press.

Abramson, L. Y., Metalsky, G. I., & Alloy, L. B. (1989). Hopelessness depression: A theory-based subtype of depression. *Psychological Review, 96*, 358–372.

Abramson, L. Y., Seligman, M. E. P., & Teasdale, J. D. (1978). Learned helplessness in humans: Critique and reformulation. *Journal of Abnormal Psychology, 87*, 49–74.

Achenbach, T. M. (1974). *Developmental psychopathology*. New York: Ronald Press.

Achenbach, T. M. (1997). *Empirically based assessment of child and adolescent psychopathology*. Thousand Oaks, CA.: Sage.

Achenbach, T. M., Howell, C. T., Quay, H. C., & Conners, C. K. (1991). National survey of problems and competencies among four- to sixteen-year-olds: Parents' reports for normative and clinical samples. *Monographs of the Society for Research in Child Development, 56*(3).

Ackerman, M. D. & Carey, M. P. (1995). Psychology's role in the assessment of erectile dysfunction: Historical precedents, current knowledge, and methods. *Journal of Clinical and Consulting Psychology, 63*, 862–876.

Adam, K. S. (1990). Environmental, psychosocial, and psychoanalytic aspects of suicidal behavior. In S. J. Blumenthal & D. J. Kupfer (Eds.), *Suicide over the life cycle: Risk factors, assessment, and treatment of suicidal patients* (pp. 39–96). Washington, DC: American Psychiatric Press.

Adams, M. L., & Cicero, T. J. (1991). Effects of alcohol on beta-endorphin and reproductive hormones in the male rat. *Alcoholism in Clinical and Experimental Research, 15*(4), 685–692.

Adelstein, A. M. (1980). Life-style in occupational cancer. *Journal of Toxicology and Environmental Health, 6*, 953–962.

Ader, R. A., & Cohen, N. (1982). Behaviorally conditioned immunosuppression and murine systemic lupus erythematosus. *Science, 215*, 1534–1536.

Ader, R. A., & Cohen, N. (1993). Psychoneuroimmunology: Conditioning and stress. *Annual Review of Psychology, 44*, 53–85.

Adler, N. E., Boyce, T., Chesney, M. A., Cohen, S., Folkman, S., Kahn, R. L., & Syme, S. L. (1994). Socioeconomic status and health: The challenge of the gradient. *American Psychologist, 49*, 15–24.

Adler, N. E., & Matthews, K. (1994). Health psychology: Why do some people get sick and some stay well. *Annual Review of Psychology, 45*, 229–259. Palo Alto, CA: Annual Reviews.

Agras, W. S., Chapin, H., & Oliveau, D. (1972). The natural history of phobia. *Archives of General Psychiatry, 26*, 315–317.

Agras, W. S., Sylvester, D. & Oliveau, D. (1969). Epidemiology of common fears and phobias. *Comprehensive Psychiatry, 10*, 151–156.

Ainsworth, M. D. S., Blehar, M. C., Waters, E., & Wall, S. (1978). *Patterns of attachment*. Hillsdale, NJ: Erlbaum.

Ake v. Oklahoma, 105 S. Ct. 977 (1985).

Akiskal, H. S. (1992). Delineating irritable and hyperthymic variants of the cyclothymic temperament. *Journal of Personality Disorders, 6*, 326–342.

Al-Issa, I. (1977). Social and cultural aspects of hallucinations. *Psychological Bulletin, 84*, 570–587.

Albee, G. (1959). *Mental health manpower trends*. New York: Basic Books.

Alberti, R. E., & Emmons, M. L. (1974). *Your perfect right: A guide to assertive behavior*. San Luis Obispo, CA: Impact.

Alcohol, Drug Abuse, and Mental Health Administration. (1989). *Report of the Secretary's Task Force on Youth Suicide: Vols. I–IV.* (DHSS Publication No. ADM 89-1621-1624). Washington, DC: U.S. Government Printing Office.

Alden, L. (1989). Short-term structured treatment for avoidant personality disorder. *Journal of Consulting and Clinical Psychology, 57*, 756–764.

Alexander, A., Andersen, H., Heilman, P., Voeller, K., & Torgesen, J. (1991). Phonological awareness training and remediation of analytic decoding deficits in a group of severe dyslexics. *Annals of the Orton Society, 41*, 193–206.

Alexander, F. M. (1950). *Psychosomatic medicine*. New York: W. W. Norton.

Alexander, F. M. (1956). *Psychoanalysis and psychotherapy*. New York: W. W. Norton.

Alexander, F. M., & French, T. M. (1946). *Psychoanalytic therapy*. New York: Ronald Press.

Alexander, J. F., Holtzworth-Monroe, A., & Jameson, P. B. (1994). The process and outcome of marital and family therapy: Research review and evaluation. In A. E. Bergin & S. L. Garfield (Eds.), *Handbook of psychotherapy and behavior change* (pp. 595–630). New York: John Wiley & Sons.

Alexander, J. F., & Parsons, B. V. (1973). Short-term behavioral intervention with delinquent families: Impact on family process and recidivism. *Journal of Abnormal Psychology, 81,* 219–225.

Alfrey, A. C. (1991). Aluminum intoxication, recognition and treatment. In M. Nicolini, P. F. Zatta, & B. Corain (Eds.), *Aluminum in chemistry, biology, and medicine* (pp. 73–84). New York: Raven Press.

Allan, A. M., & Harris, R. A. (1987). Involvement of neuronal chloride channels in ethanol intoxication, tolerance, and dependence. In M. Galanter (Ed.), *Recent developments in alcoholism* (pp. 313–322). New York: Plenum.

Allen, J. P., & Litten, R. Z. (1993). Psychometric and laboratory measures to assist in the treatment of alcoholism. *Clinical Psychology Review, 13,* 223–240.

Allen, L. S., & Gorski, R. A. (1992). Sexual orientation and the size of the anterior commissure in the human brain. *Proceedings of the National Academy of Science, USA, 89,* 7199–7202.

Alloy, L. B., & Abramson, L. Y. (1979). Judgment of contingency in depressed and nondepressed students: Sadder but wiser? *Journal of Experimental Psychology: General, 108,* 441–485.

Alloy, L. B., & Abramson, L. Y. (1988). Depressive realism: Four theoretical perspectives. In L. B. Alloy (Ed)., *Cognitive processes in depression* (pp. 223–265). New York: Guilford Press.

Alper, J. S., & Natowicz, M. R. (1993). On establishing the genetic basis of mental disease. *Trends in Neuroscience, 16,* 387–389.

Alphs, L. D., Summerfelt, A., Lann, H., Muller, R. J. (1989). The negative symptom assessment: A new instrument to assess negative symptoms of schizophrenia. *Psychopharmacology Bulletin, 25,* 159–163.

Althof, S. E. (1989). Psychogenic impotence: Treatment of men and couples. In S. R. Leiblum & R. C. Rosen (Eds.) *Principles and practice of sex therapy: Update for the 1990s* (pp 237–268). New York: Guilford Press.

Althof, S. E., & Seftel, A. D. (1995). The evaluation and management of erectile dysfunction. *Psychiatric Clinics of North America, 18,* 171–192.

Alvarez, F. J., Del Rio, M. C., & Prada, R. (1995). Drinking and driving in Spain. *Journal of Studies on Alcohol, 56,* 403–407.

Alvir, J., Lieberman, J., & Safferman, A. Z. (1994). The incidence of clozapine associated agranulocytosis in the United States. *Psychopharmacology Bulletin, 30,* 73.

Alzheimer, A. (1907). Uber eine eigenartige Erkrankungder Hirnrinde. *Allgemeine Zeitscrift fur Psychiatrie und Psychisch-Gerichtlich Medizine, 64,* 146–148.

Alzheimer's Association. (1994). Understanding the second leading cause of dementia. *Advances in Alzheimer Research, 3,* 1–4.

Alzheimer's Association. (1995a, summer). Researchers look to women for clues. *Advances in Alzheimer Research, 5,* 1A–4A.

Alzheimer's Association. (1995b, summer). Alzheimer's challenges couples' closest ties. *Alzheimer's Association National Newsletter, 15,* 1, 7.

Alzheimer's Association. (1995c, fall). Spirituality and Alzheimer's. *Alzheimer's Association National Newsletter, 15,* 3.

Ambrosini, P. J., Bianchi, M. D., Rabinovich, H., & Elia, J. (1993). Antidepressant treatments in children and adolescents. I. Affective disorders. *Journal of the American Academy of Child Adolescent Psychiatry, 32,* 1–6.

American Psychiatric Association. (1952). *Diagnostic and statistical manual of mental disorders.* Washington, DC: Author.

American Psychiatric Association. (1968). *Diagnostic and statistical manual of mental disorders* (2nd ed.). Washington, DC: Author.

American Psychiatric Association. (1980). *Diagnostic and statistical manual of mental disorders* (3rd ed.). Washington, DC: Author.

American Psychiatric Association. (1987). *Diagnostic and statistical manual of mental disorders* (3rd ed. Rev.). Washington, DC: Author.

American Psychiatric Association. (1993). Practice guide for major depressive disorder in adults. *American Journal of Psychiatry, 150* (Suppl. April), 1–26.

American Psychiatric Association. (1994). *Diagnostic and statistical manual of mental disorders* (4th ed.). Washington, DC: Author.

American Psychological Association. (1992). Ethical principles of psychologists and code of conduct. *American Psychologist, 47,* 1597–1611.

American Psychological Association. (1995, October). Warning: Soccer can be harmful to your head's health. *The APA Monitor, 26,* 12–13.

American Psychological Association. (1995). Training in and dissemination of empirically-validated psychological procedures: Report and recommendations. *The Clinical Psychologist, 48,* 22–23.

Amering, M., & Katschnig, H. (1990). Panic attacks and panic disorder in cross-cultural perspective. *Psychiatric Annals, 20,* 511–516.

Amundson, M. E., Hart, C. A., & Holmes, T. H. (1986). *Manual for the schedule of recent experience.* Seattle: University of Washington Press.

Anastasiow, N. J. (1990). Implications of the neurobiological model for early intervention. In S. J. Meisels & J. P. Shonkoff (Eds.), *Handbook of early childhood intervention* (pp. 196–216). New York: Cambridge University Press.

Andersen, B. L., & Cyranowski, J. M. (1995). Women's sexuality: Behaviors, responses, and individual differences. *Journal of Consulting and Clinical Psychology, 63,* 891–906.

Andersen, B. L., Kielcolt-Glaser, J. K., & Glaser, R. (1994). A biobehavioral model of cancer stress and disease course. *American Psychologist, 49,* 389–404.

Anderson, G. M., & Hosino, Y. (1987). Neurochemical studies of autism. In D. Cohen & A. Donnellan (Eds.), *Handbook of autism and pervasive developmental disorders* (pp. 166–191). New York: John Wiley & Sons.

Anderson, K. E., Lytton, H., & Romney, D. M. (1986). Mothers' interactions with normal and conduct-disordered boys: Who affects whom? *Developmental Psychology, 22*(5), 604–609.

Anderson, L. T., Campbell, M., Adams, P., Small, A. M., Perry, R., & Shell, J. (1989). The effects of haloperidol on discrimination learning and behavioral symptoms in autistic children. *Journal of Autism and Developmental Disorders, 19,* 227–239.

Anderson, N. B. (1989). Racial differences in stress-reduced cardiovascular reactivity and hypertension: Current status and substantive issues. *Psychological Bulletin, 105,* 89–105.

Andreasen, N. C. (1982). Negative symptoms in schizophrenia: Definition and reliability. *Archives of General Psychiatry, 39,* 784–788.

Andreasen, N. C. (1987). Creativity and mental illness: Prevalence rates in writers and their first-degree relatives. *American Journal of Psychiatry, 144,* 1288–1292.

Andreasen, N. C. (1988). Brain imaging: Applications in Psychiatry. *Science, 239,* 1381–1388.

Andreasen, N. C., Arndt, S., Alliger, R., Miller, D., & Flaum, M. (1995). Symptoms of schizophrenia: Method, meaning and mechanisms. *Archives of General Psychiatry, 53,* 341–351.

Andreasen, N. C., Arndt, S., Swayze, V., Cozadlo, T., Flaum, M., O'Leary, D., Ehrhardt, J., & Yuh, W. T. C. (1994). Thalamic abnormalities in schizophrenia visualized through magnetic resonance imaging averaging. *Science, 266,* 294–298.

Andreasen, N. C., & Black, D. W. (1991). *Introductory textbook of psychiatry.* Washington, DC: American Psychiatric Press.

Andreasen, N. C., & Carpenter, N. T. (1993). Diagnosis and classification of schizophrenia. *Schizophrenia Bulletin, 19,* 199–214.

Andreasen, N. C., Erhardt, J, Swayze, V., Alliger, R., Yuh, W. T. C., Cohen, G., & Ziebell, S. (1990). Magnetic resonance imaging of the brain in schizophrenia. *Archives of General Psychiatry, 47,* 35–44.

Andreasen, N. C., Nasrullah, H., Dunn, V., Olson, S., Grove, W., Erhardt, J, Coffman, J., & Crosett, J. (1986). Structural abnormalities in the frontal system in schizophrenia. *Archives of General Psychiatry, 43,* 136–144.

Andreasen, N. C., Rezai, K., Alliger, R., Swayze, V., Flaum, M., Kirchner, P., Cohen, G., & O'Leary, D. (1992). Hypofrontality in neuroleptic-naive patients and in patients with chronic schizophrenia: Assessment with xenon-133 single proton emission computed tomography and the Tower of London. *Archives of General Psychiatry, 49,* 943–958.

Andrews, D. A., & Bonta, J. (1994). *The psychology of criminal conduct.* Cincinnati, OH: Anderson Publishing Co.

Andrews, G., & Harvey, R. (1981). Does psychotherapy benefit neurotic patients? A re-analysis of the Smith, Glass, and Miller data. *Archives of General Psychiatry, 38,* 1203–1208.

Andrulonis, P. A., Glueck, B. C., Stroebel, C. F., Vogel, N. G., Shapiro, A. L., & Aldridge, D. M. (1981). Organic brain dysfunctions and the borderline syndrome. *Psychiatric Clinics of North America, 4,* 47–66.

Andrykowski, M. A., & Redd, W. H. (1987). Longitudinal analysis of the development of anticipatory nausea. *Journal of Consulting and Clinical Psychology, 55,* 36–41.

Angst, J., Felder, W., & Frey, R. (1979). The course of unipolar and bipolar affective disorders. In M. Schou & E. Stromgren (Eds.), *Origin, prevention, and treatment of affective disorders.* New York: Academic Press.

Anthony, W. A., Cohen, M. R., & Danley, K. S. (1988). The psychiatric rehabilitation model as applied to vocational rehabilitation. In J. A. Ciardiello & M. D. Bell (Eds.), *Vocational rehabilitation of persons with prolonged psychiatric disorders.* Baltimore: Johns Hopkins University Press.

Antoni, M. H., Baggett, L., Ironson, G., Laperriere, A., August, S., Klimas, N., Schneiderman, N., & Fletcher, M. A. (1991). Cognitive-behavioral stress management intervention buffers distress responses and immunologic changes following notification of HIV-1 seropositivity. *Journal of Consulting and Clinical Psychology, 59,* 906–915.

Antonuccio, D. O., Danton, W. G., & DeNelsky, G. Y. (1995). Psychotherapy versus medication for depression: Challenging the conventional wisdom with data. *Professional Psychology: Research and Practice, 6,* 574–585.

Appelbaum, P. S. (1986). Competence to be executed: Another conundrum for mental health professionals. *Hospital and Community Psychiatry, 37,* 682–684.

Appelbaum, P. S. (1994). *Almost a revolution: Mental health law and the limits of change.* New York: Oxford University Press.

Appelbaum, P. S. & Hoge, S. K. (1986). The right to refuse treatment: What the research reveals. *Behavioral Sciences and the Law, 4,* 279–292.

Appels, A., & Otten, F. (1992). Exhaustion as precursor of cardiac death. *British Journal of Clinical Psychology, 31,* 351–356.

Appels, A., & Schouten, E. (1991). Burnout as a risk factor for coronary heart disease. *Behavioral Medicine, 17,* 53–59.

Arieti, A., & Bemporad, J. (1978). *Severe and mild depression: A psychotherapeutic approach.* New York: Basic Books.

Armor, D. J., Polich, J. M., & Stambul, H. B. (1976). *Alcoholism and treatment.* Prepared for the National Institute on Alcohol Abuse and Alcoholism. Santa Monica, CA: Rand Corp.

Arrindell, W. A. (1993). The fear of fear concept: Stability, retest artifact, and predictive power. *Behaviour Research and Therapy, 31,* 139–148.

Ashton, H. (1991). Psychotropic-drug prescribing for women. *British Journal of Psychiatry, 158* (Suppl. 10). 30–35.

Asmundson, G. J., & Norton, G. R. (1993). Anxiety sensitivity and its relationship to spontaneous and cued panic attacks in college students. *Behaviour Research and Therapy, 31,* 199–201.

Asperger, H. (1944). Die autistischen Psychopathen im Kindesalter. *Archiv fur Psychiatrie und Nervenkrankheiten, 117,* 76–136.

Asplund, R. (1995). Sleep and hypnotics among the elderly in relation to body weight and somatic disease. *Journal of Internal Medicine, 238(1),* 65–70.

Aston-Jones, G., & Bloom, F. E. (1981). Activity of norepinephrine-containing neurons in behaving rats anticipates fluctuations in the sleep-waking cycle. *The Journal of Neuroscience, 1,* 876–886.

Auerbach, R., & Kilmann, P. R. (1977). The effects of group systematic desensitization on secondary erectile failure. *Behavior Therapy, 8,* 330–339.

Averill, J. R. (1973). Personal control over aversive stimuli and its relationship to stress. *Psychological Bulletin, 80,* 286–303.

Avery, D. H. (1993). Electroconvulsive therapy. In D. D. Dunner (Ed.), *Current psychiatric therapy* (pp. 524–528). Philadelphia: W. B. Saunders Co.

Avery, D. H., Dahl, D., Savage, M., Brengelmann, G., Larsen, L., Vitiello, M., & Prinz, P. (1990). Bright light treatment of winter depression: AM compared to PM light. *Acta Psychiatric Scandinavica, 82,* 335–338.

Avery, D. H., Bolte, M. A., Wolfson, J. K., & Kazaras, A. L. (1994). Dawn simulation compared with dim red signal in treatment of winter depression. *Biological Psychiatry, 36,* 180–188.

Avery, D. H., & Winoker, G. (1976). Mortality in depressed patients treated with electroconvulsive therapy and antidepressants. *Archives of General Psychiatry, 33,* 1029–1037.

Ayllon, T., & Azrin, N. H. (1965). The measurement and reinforcement of behavior of psychotics. *Journal of the Experimental Analysis of Behavior, 8,* 357–383.

Ayllon, T., & Azrin, N. H. (1968). *The token economy: A motivational system for therapy and rehabilitation.* New York: Appleton-Century-Crofts.

Azrin, N. H., Bersalel, A., Bechtel, R., Michalicek, A., Mancera, M., Carroll, D., Shuford, D., & Cox, J. (1980). Comparison of reciprocity and discussion-type counseling for marital problems. *American Journal of Family Therapy, 8,* 21–28.

Azrin, N. H., Hontos, P. T., & Besalel-Azrin, V. A. (1979). Elimination of enuresis without a conditioning apparatus: An extension by office instruction of the child and parents. *Behavior Therapy, 18,* 14–19.

Azrin, N. H., McMahon, P.T., Donohue, B., Besalel, V. A., & Lapinski, K. J. (1994). Behavior therapy for drug abuse: A controlled treatment outcome study. *Behaviour Research and Therapy, 32,* 857–866.

Azrin, N. H., Nunn, R. G., & Frantz, S. E. (1980). Habit reversal vs. negative practice treatment of nailbiting. *Behaviour Research & Therapy, 18,* 281–285.

Azrin, N. H., Nunn, R. G., & Frantz-Renshaw, S. (1980). Habit reversal treatment of thumbsucking. *Behaviour Research and Therapy, 18,* 395–399.

Azrin, N. H., & Peterson, A. L. (1989). Reduction of an eye tic by controlled blinking. *Behavior Therapy, 20,* 467–473.

Babor, T. F. (1994). Avoiding the horrid and beastly sin of drunkenness: Does dissuasion make a difference? *Journal of Consulting and Clinical Psychology, 62*(6), 1127–1140.

Babor, T. F., Hofmann, M., DelBoca, F. K., Hesselbrock, V., Meyer, R. E., Dolinsky, Z. S., & Rounsaville, B. (1992). Types of alcoholics I: Evidence for an empirically-derived typology based on indicators of vulnerability and severity. *Archives of General Psychiatry, 8*, 599–608.

Bachmann, G. A., Leiblum, S. R., & Grill, J. (1989). Brief sexual inquiry in gynecologic practice. *Obstetrics and Gynecology, 73*, 425–427.

Baer, J. S., Marlatt, G. A., Kivlahan, D. R., Fromme, K., Larimer, M. E., & Williams, E. (1992). An experimental test of three methods of alcohol risk reduction with young adults. *Journal of Consulting and Clinical Psychology, 60*(6), 974–979.

Baer, L., Rauch, S. L., Ballantine, T., Martuza, R., Cosgrove, R., Cassem, E., Girunas, I., Manzo, P. A., Domino, C., & Jenike, M. A. (1995). Cingulotomy for intractable obsessive-compulsive disorder: Prospective long-term follow-up of 18 patients. *Archives of General Psychiatry, 52*, 384–392.

Baer, R. A., & Nietzel, M. T. (1991). Cognitive and behavioral treatment of impulsivity in children: A meta-analytic review of the outcome literature. *Journal of Clinical Child Psychology, 20*(4), 400–412.

Bailey, J. M., & Pillard, R. C. (1991). A genetic study of male sexual orientation. *Archives of General Psychiatry, 48*, 1089–1091.

Bailey, J. M., Pillard, R. C., Neale, M. C., & Agyei, Y. (1993). Heritable factors influence sexual orientation in women. *Archives of General Psychiatry, 50*, 217–223.

Bailey, J. S. (1992). Gentle teaching: Trying to win friends and influence people with euphemism, metaphor, smoke, and mirrors. *Journal of Applied Behavior Analysis, 25*, 879–883.

Ball, E., & Blackman, B. (1991). Does phoneme awareness training in kindergarten make a difference in early word recognition and developmental spelling? *Reading Research Quarterly, 26*, 49–66.

Ballenger, J., Burrows, G. D., DuPont, R., Lesser, I., Noyes, R., Pecknold, J., Rifkin, A., & Swinson, R. (1988). Alprazolam in panic disorder and agoraphobia: Results from a multicenter trial. *Archives of General Psychiatry, 45*, 413–422.

Bandura, A. (1969). *Principles of behavior modification.* New York: Holt, Rinehart & Winston.

Bandura, A. (1977). Self-efficacy: Toward a unifying theory of behavioral change. *Psychological Review, 84*, 191–215.

Bandura, A. (1982). Self-efficacy mechanism in human agency. *American Psychologist, 33*, 344–358.

Bandura, A. (1986). *Social foundations of thought and action: A social cognitive theory.* Englewood Cliffs, NJ: Prentice Hall.

Bandura, A., Blanchard, E., and Ritter, B. (1969). Relative efficacy of desensitization and modeling approaches for inducting behavioral, affective, and attitudinal changes. *Journal of Personality and Social Psychology, 13*, 173–199.

Barbaree, H. E., Marshall, W. L. (1991). The role of male sexual arousal in rape: Six models. *Journal of Consulting and Clinical Psychology, 59*, 621–630.

Barker, S. L., Funk, S. C., & Houston, B. K. (1988). Psychological treatment versus nonspecific factors: A meta-analysis of conditions that engender comparable expectations for improvement. *Clinical Psychology Review, 8*, 579–594.

Barkley, R. A. (1990). A critique of current diagnostic criteria for attention deficit-hyperactive disorder: Clinical and research implications. *Developomental Behavioral Pediatrics, 11*, 343–352.

Barkley, R. A., DuPaul, G. J., & Costello, A. (1993). Stimulants. In J. S. Werry & M. G. Aman (Eds.), *Practitioner's guide to psychoactive drugs for children and adolescents* (pp. 205–237). New York: Plenum.

Barkley, R. A., DuPaul, G. J., & McMurray, M. B. (1990). Comprehensive evaluation of attention deficit disorder with and without hyperactivity as defined by research criteria. *Journal of Consulting and Clinical Psychology, 58*, 775–789.

Barkley, R. A., Guevremont, D. C., Anastopoulos, A. D., & Fletcher, K. E. (1992). A comparison of three family therapy programs for treating family conflicts in adolescents with attention-deficit hyperactivity disorder. *Journal of Consulting and Clinical Psychology, 60*(3), 450–462.

Barlow, D. H. (1986). Causes of sexual dysfunction: The role of anxiety and cognitive interference. *Journal of Consulting and Clinical Psychology, 54*, 140–148.

Barlow, D. H. (1988). *Anxiety and its disorders.* New York: Guilford Press.

Barlow, D. H., Craske, M. G., Cerny, J. A., & Klosko, J. S. (1989). Behavior treatment of panic disorder. *Behavior Therapy, 20*, 261–282.

Barlow, D. H., & Hersen, M. (1984). *Single-case experimental designs: Strategies for studying behavior* (2nd ed.). New York: Pergamon Press.

Barlow, D. H., Rapee, R. M., & Brown, T. A. (1992). Behavioral treatment of generalized anxiety disorder. *Behavior Therapy, 23*, 551–570.

Barlow, D. H., Reynolds, E. J., & Agras, W. S. (1973). Gender identity change in a transsexual. *Archives of General Psychiatry, 28*, 569–576.

Barlow, D. H., Sakheim, D. K., & Beck, J. G. (1983). Anxiety increases sexual arousal. *Journal of Abnormal Psychology, 92*, 49–54.

Barlow, J., & Kirby, N. (1991). Residential satisfaction of persons with an intellectual disability living in an institution or in the community. *Australia and New Zealand Journal of Developmental Disabilities, 17*(1), 7–23.

Barnard, K. E., Hammond, M. A., Booth, C. L., Bee, H. L., Mitchell, S. K., & Spieker, S. J. (in press). Measurement and meaning of parent-child interaction. In F. Morrison, C. Lord, & D. Keating (Eds.), *Applied developmental psychology* (Vol. 3). New York: Academic Press.

Barnard, K. E., & Kelly, J. F. (1990). Assessment of parent-child interaction. In S. J. Meisels & J. P. Shonkoff (Eds.), *Handbook of early childhood intervention* (pp. 278–302). New York: Cambridge University Press.

Barnes, G. M., Farrell, M. P., & Cairns, A. L. (1986). Parental socialization factors and adolescent drinking behaviors. *Journal of Marriage and the Family, 48*, 27–36.

Barnes, J. (1986). Primary vaginismus (Part 2): Aetiological factors. *Irish Medical Journal, 79*, 62–65.

Baron, M., Risch, N., Hamburger, R., Mandel, B., Kushner, S., Newman, M., Drumer, D., & Belmaker, R. H. (1987). Genetic linkage between X-chromosome markers and bipolar affective illness. *Nature, 326*, 289–292.

Baron-Cohen, S. (1989). Are autistic children "behaviorists"? An examination of their mental-physical and appearance-reality distinctions. *Journal of Autism and Developmental Disorders, 19*, 579–600.

Baron-Cohen, S., Ring, H., Moriarity, J., Schmitz, B., et al. (1994). Recognition of mental state terms: Clinical findings in children with autism and a functional neuroimaging study of normal adults. *British Journal of Psychiatry, 165*, 640–649.

Barondes, S. H. (1993). Molecules and mental illness. *Scientific American Library* (p. 128). New York: Freeman.

Barsky, A. J. (1989). Somatoform disorders. In H. I. Kaplan and B. J. Sadock (Eds.), *Comprehensive Textbook of Psychiatry V* (pp. 1009–1027). Baltimore: Williams & Wilkins.

Barsky, A. J. (1992). Amplification, somatization, and the somatoform disorders. *Psychosomatics, 33*, 28–34.

Barsky, A. J., Barnett, M. C., & Cleary, P. D. (1994). Hypochondriasis and panic disorder. Boundary and overlap. *Archives of General Psychiatry, 51,* 918–925.

Barsky, A. J., Wyshak, G., Klerman, G. L., & Latham, K. S. (1990). The prevalence of hypochondriasis in medical outpatients. *Social Psychiatry and Psychiatric Epidemiology, 25,* 89–94.

Barta, P., Pearlson, G., Powers, R., Richards, S., & Tune, L. (1990). Auditory hallucinations and smaller superior temporal gyral volume in schizophrenia. *American Journal of Psychiatry, 147,* 1457–1463.

Bashore, T. R., & Rapp, P. E. (1993). Are there alternatives to traditional polygraph procedures? *Psychological Bulletin, 113,* 3–22.

Basic Behavioral Science Task Force of the National Advisory Mental Health Council (1996). Basic behavioral science research for mental health. *American Psychologist, 51,* 722–731.

Bass, E., & Davis, L. (1988). *The courage to heal: A guide for women survivors of childhood sexual abuse.* New York: Harper & Row.

Bateson, G., Jackson, D. D., Haley, J., & Weakland, J. (1956). Toward a theory of schizophrenia. *Behavioral Science, 1,* 251–264.

Baucom, D. H., Epstein, N., Sayers, S., & Sher, T. G. (1989). The role of cognitions in marital relationships: Definitional, methodological, and conceptual issues. *Journal of Consulting and Clinical Psychology, 57,* 31–38.

Bauer, W. D., & Twentyman, C. T. (1985). Abusing, neglectful, and comparison mothers' responses to child-related and non-child stressors. *Journal of Consulting and Clinical Psychology, 53,* 335–343.

Baum, A., & Fleming, I. (1993). Implications of psychological research on stress and technological accidents. *American Psychologist, 48,* 665–672.

Baum, A., Gatchel, R. J., & Schaeffer, M. A. (1983). Emotional, behavioral, and physiological effects of chronic stress at Three Mile Island. *Journal of Consulting and Clinical Psychology, 51,* 565–572.

Bauman, L. J., Stein, R. E. K., & Ireys, H. T. (1991). Reinventing fidelity: The transfer of social technology among settings. *American Journal of Community Psychology, 19,* 619–640.

Baumeister, A. A., Kupstas, F. D., & Klindworth, L. M. (1991). The new morbidity: A national plan of action. *American Behavioral Scientist, 34,* 468–500.

Baumeister, R. F., & Leary, M. R. (1995). The need to belong: Desire for interpersonal attachments as a fundamental human motivation. *Psychological Bulletin, 117,* 497–529.

Baumrind, D. (1971). Current patterns of adult authority. *Developmental Psychology Monograph, 4*(1).

Baxter, L. M., Schwartz, J., Bergman, K., Szuba, M., Guze, B., Mazziotta, J. C., Alazaki, A., Selin, C., Ferng, H-G., Munford, P., & Phelps, M. (1992). Caudate glucose metabolic rate changes with both drug and behavior therapy for obsessive-compulsive disorder. *Archives of General Psychiatry, 49,* 681–689.

Beardsley, R. S., Gardocki, G. J., Larson, D., & Hidalgo, J. (1988). Prescribing of psychotropic medication by primary care physicians and psychiatrists. *Archives of General Psychiatry, 45,* 1117–1119.

Beck, A. T. (1976). *Cognitive therapy and the emotional disorders.* New York: International Universities Press.

Beck, A. T. (1983). Cognitive therapy of depression: New Perspectives. In P. J. Clayton & J. E. Barrett (Eds.), *Treatment of depression: Old controversies and new approaches* (pp. 265–284). New York: Raven Press.

Beck, A. T. (1987). Cognitive models of depression. *Journal of Cognitive Psychotherapy: An International Journal, 1,* 5–37.

Beck, A. T., & Emery, G. (1985). *Anxiety disorders and phobias: A cognitive perspective.* New York: Basic Books.

Beck, A. T., Freeman, A., & Associates (1990). *Cognitive therapy of personality disorders.* New York: Guilford Press.

Beck, A. T., Rush, A. J., Shaw, B. F., & Emery, G. (1979). *Cognitive therapy of depression.* New York: Guilford Press.

Beck, J. G. (1995). Hypoactive sexual desire disorder: An overview. *Journal of Consulting and Clinical Psychology, 63,* 919–927.

Becker, J., & Schmaling, K. (1991). Interpersonal aspects of depression from psychodynamic and attachment perspectives. In J. Becker & A. Kleinman (Eds.), *Psychosocial aspects of depression* (pp. 131–138). Hillsdale, NJ: Erlbaum.

Becker, J. V., Skinner, L., Abel, G., & Cichon, R. (1986). Level of postassault sexual functioning in rape and incest victims. *Archives of Sexual Behavior, 15,* 37–49.

Becker, M. H., & Maiman, L. A. (1975). Sociobehavioral determinants of compliance with health and medical care recommendations. *Medical Care, 13,* 10–24.

Beckwith, L., & Parmelee, A. H. (1986). EEG patterns of preterm infants, home environment, and later IQ. *Child Development, 57*(3), 777–789.

Bednar, R. L., & Kaul, T. (1994). Experiential group research. In A. E. Bergin & S. L. Garfield (Eds.), *Handbook of psychotherapy and behavior change* (pp. 631–663). New York: John Wiley & Sons.

Begleiter, H., Porjesz, B., Bihari, B., & Kissin, B. (1984). Event-related brain potentials in boys at risk for alcoholism. *Science, 225*(4669), 1493–1496.

Behkelfat, C., Murphy, D., Zohar, J., Hill, J., Grover, G., & Insel, T. (1989). Clomipramine in obsessive-compulsive disorder. *Archives of General Psychiatry, 46,* 23–28.

Beitchman, J. H., Inglis, A., & Schachter, D. (1992). Child psychiatry and early intervention: IV. The externalizing disorders. *Canadian Journal of Psychiatry, 37,* 245–249.

Bellack, A. S., & Hersen, M. (Eds.). (1988). *Behavioral assessment: A practical handbook* (3rd ed.). New York: Pergamon Press.

Bellack, A. S., & Mueser, K. (1993). Psychosocial treatment for schizophrenia. *Schizophrenia Bulletin, 19,* 143–163.

Belsky, J. K. (1990). *The psychology of aging: Theory, research and interventions* (2nd ed.). Pacific Grove, CA: Brooks/Cole.

Ben-Porath, Y. S., Butcher, J. N., & Graham, J. R. (1991). Contribution of the MMPI-2 scales to the differential diagnosis of schizophrenia and major depression. *Psychological Assessment: A Journal of Consulting and Clinical Psychology, 3,* 634–640.

Ben-Porath, Y. S., & Waller, N. G. (1992). "Normal" personality inventories in clinical assessment: General requirements and potential for using the NEO Personality Inventory. *Psychological Assessment, 4,* 14–19.

Benbow, S. (1989). The role of electroconvulsive therapy in the treatment of depressive illness in old age. *British Journal of Psychiatry, 155,* 147–152.

Benjamin. L. S. (1993). *Interpersonal diagnosis and treatment of personality disorders.* New York: Guilford Press.

Bennett, C. C. (1965). Community psychology: Impressions of the Boston conference on the education of psychologists for community mental health. *American Psychologist, 20,* 832–835.

Bennett, L. A., & Wolin, S. J. (1990). Family culture and alcoholism transmission. In R. L. Collins, K. E. Leonard, & J. S. Searles (Eds.), *Alcohol and the family: Research and clinical perspectives* (pp. 194–219). New York: Guilford Press.

Bentall, R. P. (1990). The illusion of reality: A review and integration of psychological research on hallucinations. *Psychological Bulletin, 107,* 82–95.

Benton, M. K., & Schroeder, H. E. (1990). Social skills training with schizophrenics: A meta-analytic evaluation. *Journal of Consulting and Clinical Psychology, 58,* 741–747.

Berenbaum, H., & Oltmanns, T. F. (1992). Emotional experience and expression in schizophrenia and depression. *Journal of Abnormal Psychology, 101*, 37–44.

Berendt, J. (1994). *Midnight in the garden of good and evil.* New York: Random House.

Berg, L. (1988). The aging brain. In R. Strong, W. G. Wood, & W. J. Burke (Eds.), *Aging: Vol. 33. Central nervous system disorders of aging: Clinical interventions and research* (pp. 1–16). New York: Raven Press.

Bergin, A. E. (1971). The evaluation of therapeutic outcomes. In A. E. Bergin & S. L. Garfield (Eds.), *Handbook of psychotherapy and behavior change: An empirical analysis* (pp. 217–270). New York: John Wiley & Sons.

Bergin, A. E., & Lambert, M. J. (1978). The evaluation of therapeutic outcomes. In S. L. Garfield & A. E. Bergin (Eds.), *Handbook of psychotherapy and behavior change: An empirical analysis* (2nd ed., pp. 139–190). New York: John Wiley & Sons.

Berk, L. E. (1991). *Child development* (2nd ed.). Boston: Allyn & Bacon.

Berman, J. S., & Norton, N. C. (1985). Does professional training make a therapist more effective? *Psychological Bulletin, 98*, 401–406.

Berney, T., Kolvin, I., Bhate, S. R., Garside, R. F., Jeans, J., Kay, B., & Scarth, L. (1981). School phobia: A therapeutic trial with clomipramine and short-term outcome. *British Journal of Psychiatry, 138*, 110–118.

Berninger, V. W. (1994). *Reading and writing acquisition: A developmental neuropsychological perspective.* Dubuque, IA: Wm. C. Brown Communications.

Bernstein, D. A., & Borkovec, T. D. (1973). *Progressive relaxation training.* Champaign, IL: Research Press.

Bernstein, D. P., Useda, D., & Siever, L. J. (1993). Paranoid personality disorder: Review of the literature and recommendations for DSM-IV. *Journal of Personality Disorders, 7*, 53–62.

Bernstein, G. A., & Borchardt, C. M. (1991). Anxiety disorders of childhood and adolescence: A critical review. *Journal of the American Academy of Child and Adolescent Psychiatry, 30*(4), 519–532.

Bernstein, G. A., Garfinkel, B. D., & Borchardt, C. M. (1990). Comparative studies of pharmacotherapy for school refusal. *Journal of the American Academy of Child and Adolescent Psychiatry, 29*(5), 773–781.

Berrios, D. C., Heart, N., & Perkins, L. L. (1992). HIV antibody testing in young, urban adults. *Archives of Internal Medicine, 152*, 397–402.

Berrios, G. E. (1994). Dementia and aging since the nineteenth century. In G. A. Huppert, C. Brayne, & D. W. O'Connor (Eds.), *Dementia and normal aging* (pp. 15–40). Cambridge: Cambridge University Press.

Berrios, G. E., & Freeman, H. (1991). *Alzheimer and the dementias.* London: Royal Society of Medicine.

Berry, C. A., Shaywitz, S. E., & Shaywitz, B. A. (1985). Girls with attention deficit disorder: A silent minority? A report on behavioral and cognitive characteristics. *Pediatrics, 76*, 801–809.

Bertschy, G. (1995). Methadone maintenance treatment: An update. *European Archives of Psychiatry and Clinical Neuroscience, 245*(2), 114–124.

Beutler, L. E., & Crago, M. (Eds.), (1991). *Psychotherapy research: An international review of programmatic studies.* Washington, DC: American Psychological Association.

Beutler, L. E., Machado, P. P. P., & Neufeldt, S. A. (1994). Therapist variables. In A. E. Bergin, & S. L. Garfield (Eds.), *Handbook of psychotherapy and behavior change* (pp. 229–269). New York: John Wiley & Sons.

Beyreuther, K., & Masters, C. L. (1991). Amyloid precursor protein (APP) and beta-amyloid-4 amyloid in the etiology of Alzheimer's disease: Precursor-product relationships in the derangement of neuronal function. *Brain Pathology, 1*, 241–252.

Bieber, I., Dain, H. J., Dince, P. R., Orellich, M. G., Grand, H. C., Gundlach, R. H., Kremer, M. W., Rifkin, A. H., Wilbur, C. B., & Bieber, T. B. (1962). *Homosexuality: A psychoanalytic study.* New York: Random House.

Biederman, J., Milberger, S., Farone, S.V., et al. (1995). Impact of adversity on functioning and comorbidity in children with attention-deficit hyperactivity disorder. *Journal of American Academy of Child and Adolescent Psychiatry, 34*, 1498–1502.

Biederman, J., Rosenbaum, J. F., Hirshfeld, D. R., Faraone, S. V., Bolduc, E. A., Gersten, M., Meminger, S. R., Kagan, J., Snidman, N., & Reznick, J. S. (1990). Psychiatric correlates of behavioral inhibition in young children of parents with and without psychiatric disorders. *Archives of General Psychiatry, 47*(1), 21–26.

Biklen, D. (1990). Communication unbound: Autism and praxis. *Harvard Educational Review, 60*(3), 291–314.

Biklen, D., et al. (1992). Facilitated communication: Implications for individuals with autism. *Topics in Language Disorders, 12*(4), 1–28.

Biklen, D., & Schubert, A. (1991). New words: The communication of students with autism. *Remedial and Special Education, 12*(6), 46–57.

Billings, A. G., & Moos, R. H. (1985). Children of parents with unipolar depression: A controlled 1-year follow-up. *Journal of Abnormal Child Psychology, 14*, 149.

Bittner, E. (1967). Police discretion in emergency apprehension of mentally ill persons. *Social Problems, 14*, 278–292.

Blacher, R. S. (1972). The hidden psychosis of open-heart surgery. *Journal of the American Medical Association, 222*, 305–308.

Black, D. W., Noyes, R., Goldstein, R., & Blum, N., (1992). A family study of obsessive-compulsive disorder. *Archives of General Psychiatry, 49*, 362–368.

Black, D. W., & Winokur, G. (1990). Suicide and psychiatric diagnosis. In S. J. Blumenthal & D. J. Kupfer (Eds.), *Suicide over the life cycle: Risk factors, assessment, and treatment of suicidal patients* (pp. 135–154). Washington, DC: American Psychiatric Press.

Black, D., Wesner, R., Bowers, W., & Gabel, J. (1993). A comparison of fluvoxamine, cognitive therapy, and placebo in the treatment of panic disorder. *Archives of General Psychiatry, 50*, 44–50.

Black, F. W. (1973). Reversal and rotation errors by normal and retarded readers. *Perceptual and Motor Skills, 36*, 895–898.

Blackburn, H., Luepker, R. V., Kline, F. G., Bracht, N., Carlaw, R., Jacobs, D., Mittelmark, M., Stauffer, L., & Taylor H. L. (1984). The Minnesota Heart Health Program: A research and demonstration project in cardiovascular disease prevention. In J. D. Matarazzo et al. (Eds.), *Behavioral health: A handbook of health enhancement and disease prevention* (pp. 1171–1178). New York: John Wiley & Sons.

Blackwell, B. (1973). Psychotropic drugs in use today. *Journal of the American Medical Association, 225*, 1637–1641.

Blanchard, E. B. (1992). Psychological treatment of benign headache disorders. *Journal of Consulting and Clinical Psychology, 60*, 537–551.

Blanchard, E. B. (1994). Behavioral medicine and health psychology. In A. E. Bergin & S. L. Garfield (Eds.), *Handbook of psychotherapy and behavior change* (pp. 701–733). New York: John Wiley & Sons.

Blanchard, E. B., Andrasik, F., Ahles, T. A., Teders, S. J., & O'Keefe, D. (1980). Migraine and tension headache: A meta-analytic review. *Behavior Therapy, 11*, 613–631.

Blanchard, E. B., Schwarz, S. P., & Radnitz. C L. (1987). Psychological assessment and treatment of irritable bowel syndrome. *Behavior Modification, 11*, 348–372.

Blanchard, R., & Sheridan, P. M. (1992). Sibship size, sibling sex ratio, birth order, and parental age in homosexual and nonhomosexual gender dysphorics. *Journal of Nervous and Mental Disease, 180,* 40–47.

Blanchard, R., Zucker, K. J., Bradley, S. J., & Hume, C. S. (1995). Birth order and sibling sex ratio in homosexual male adolescents and probably prehomosexual feminine boys. *Developmental Psychology, 31,* 22–30.

Blanchard, S. (1726). *The physical dictionary wherein the terms of anatomy, the names and causes of diseases, chirurgical instruments, and their use, are accurately described.* London: John & Benjamin Sprint.

Blatt, S. J. (1982). Depression and self criticism: Psychological dimensions of depression. *Journal of Clinical and Consulting Psychology, 50,* 113–124.

Blatt, S. J. (1995). The destructiveness of perfectionism. *American Psychologist, 50,* 1003–1020.

Blatt, S. J., Quinlan, D. M., Pilkonis, P. A., & Shea, M. T. (1995). Impact of perfectionism and need for approval on the brief treatment of depression: The National Institute of Mental Health Depression Collaborative Research Program. *Journal of Clinical and Consulting Psychology, 63,* 125–132.

Blatt, S. J., & Zuroff, D. C. (1992). Interpersonal relatedness and self-definition: Two prototypes for depression. *Clinical Psychology Review, 12,* 527–550.

Blazer, D. G., Hughes, D., George, L. K., Swartz, M., & Boyer, R. (1991). Generalized anxiety disorder. In L. N. Robins & D. A. Regier (Eds.), *Psychiatric disorders in America: The epidemiologic catchment area study.* New York: Maxwell MacMillan International.

Bleuler, E. (1911). *Dementia praecox or the group of schizophrenias* (J. Zinkin, Trans. 1950). New York: International Universities Press.

Bliss, E. L. (1986). *Multiple personality, allied disorders and hypnosis.* New York: Oxford University Press.

Blum, K., Noble, E. P., Sheridan, P. J., Montgomery, A., Ritchie, T., Jagadeeswaran, P., Nogami, H., Briggs, A. H., & Cohn, J. B. (1990). Allelic association of human dopamine D2 receptor gene in alcoholism. *Journal of the American Medical Association, 263*(15), 2055–2060.

Blume, E. S. (1990). *Secret survivors: Uncovering incest and its aftereffects in women.* New York: Ballantine.

Blumenthal, S. J. (1994). Introductory remarks. In S. J. Blumenthal, K. Matthews, & S. M. Weiss (Eds.), *New research frontiers in behavioral medicine* (pp. 9–15). Washington, DC: National Institute of Mental Health.

Blumenthal, S. J., Matthews, K., & Weiss, S. W. (Eds.). (1994). *New research frontiers in behavioral medicine.* Washington, DC: National Institute of Mental Health.

Boddy, J. (1988). Spirits and selves in northern Sudan: The cultural therapeutics of possession and trance. *American Ethnologist, 15,* 4–27.

Bodkin, J. A., Zornberg, G. L., Lukas, S. E., & Cole, J. O. (1995). Buprenorphine treatment of refractory depression. *Journal of Clinical Psychopharmacology, 15*(1), 49–57.

Bodmer, W., & McKie, R. (1994). *The book of man: The human genome project and the quest to discover our genetic heritage.* New York: Scribner.

Boehnert, C. (1989). Characteristics of successful and unsuccessful insanity pleas. *Law and Human Behavior, 13,* 31–40.

Boffetta, P., & Garfinkel, L. (1990). Alcohol drinking and mortality among men enrolled in an American Cancer Society prospective study. *Epidemiology, 1*(5), 342–348.

Bond, G. R., Clark, R. E., & Drake, R. E. (1995, summer). Cost effectiveness of psychiatric rehabilitation. *Psychotherapy & Rehabilitation Research Bulletin,* 26–31.

Bond, G. R., Witheridge, T. F., Dincin, J., Wasmer, D., Webb, J., & Graff-Kaser, R. (1990). Assertive community treatment for frequent users of psychiatric hospitals in a large city: A controlled study. *American Journal of Community Psychology, 18,* 865–891.

Boney-McCoy, S., & Finkelhor, D. (1995). Psychosocial sequelae of violent victimization in a national youth sample. *Journal of Consulting and Clinical Psychology, 63,* 726–736.

Bongar, B. (1991). *The suicidal patient: Clinical and legal standards of care.* Washington, DC: American Psychological Association.

Boon, S., & Draijer, N. (1993). Multiple personality disorder in the Netherlands: A clinical investigation of 71 patients. *American Journal of Psychiatry, 150,* 489–491.

Booth-Kewley, S., & Friedman, H. S. (1987). Psychological predictors of heart disease: A quantitative review. *Psychological Bulletin, 101,* 343–362.

Borduin, C. M., Mann, B. J., Cone, L. T., Henggeler, S. W., Fucci, B. R., Blaske, D. M., & Williams, R. A. (1995). Multisystemic treatment of serious juvenile offenders: Long-term prevention of criminality and violence. *Journal of Consulting and Clinical Psychology, 63,* 569–578.

Borkovec, T. D., Abel, J. L., & Newman, H. (1995). Effects of psychotherapy on comorbid conditions in generalized anxiety disorder. *Journal of Consulting and Clinical Psychology, 63,* 479–483.

Borkovec, T. D., & Costello, E. (1993). Efficiency of applied relaxation and cognitive behavioral theory in the treatment of generalized anxiety disorders. *Journal of Consulting and Clinical Psychology, 61,* 611–619.

Borkovec, T. D., Hopkins, M., Lyonfields, J., Lytle, R., Posa, S., Roemer, L., & Shadick, R. (1991, November). *Efficacy of nondirective therapy, applied relaxation, and combined cognitive behavioral therapy for generalized anxiety disorder.* Paper presented at the 25th annual convention of the Association for the Advancement of Behavior Therapy, New York.

Borkovec, T. D., & Hu, S. (1990). The effect of worry on cardiovascular response to phobic imagery. *Behaviour Research and Therapy, 28,* 69–73.

Borkovec, T. D., & Mathews, A. (1988). Treatment of nonphobic anxiety disorders: A comparison of nondirective, cognitive, and coping desensitization therapy. *Journal of Consulting and Clinical Psychology, 56,* 877–884.

Borkovec, T. D., Mathews, A. M., Chambers, A., Ebrahimi, S., Lytle, R., & Nelson, R. (1987). The effects of relaxation training with cognitive or nondirective therapy and the role of relaxation-induced anxiety in the treatment of generalized anxiety. *Journal of Consulting and Clinical Psychology, 55,* 883–888.

Bornstein, M. H., & Sigman, M. D. (1986). Continuity in mental development from infancy. *Child Development, 57*(2), 251–274.

Borum, R. (1996). Improving the clinical practice of violence risk assessment: Technology, guidelines, and training. *American Psychologist, 51,* 945–956.

Bouaboula, M., Rinaldi, M., Carayon, P., Carillon, C., Delpech, B., Shire, D., Le-Fur, G., & Casellas, P. (1993). Cannabinoid-receptor expression in human leukocytes. *European Journal of Biochemistry, 214*(1), 173–180.

Bouchard, T. J. (1984). Twins reared together and apart: What they tell us about human diversity. In S. W. Fox (Ed.), *Individuality and determinism.* New York: Plenum.

Boudin, H. (1972). Contingency contracting as a therapeutic tool in the deceleration of amphetamine use. *Behavior Therapy, 3,* 604–608.

Bouhoutsos, J. C., Holyrod, J., Lerman, H., Forer, B., & Greenberg, M. (1983). Sexual intimacies between therapists and patients. *Professional Psychology: Research and Practice, 14,* 185–196.

Bourdon, K. H., Boyd, J. H., Rae, D. S., Burns, B. J., Thompson, J. W., & Locke, B. Z. (1988). Gender differences in phobias: Results of the ECH community survey. *Journal of Anxiety Disorders, 2,* 227–241.

Bourgeois, M., Duhamel, P., & Verdoux, H. (1992). Delusional parasitosis: Folie à deux and attempted murder of a family doctor. *British Journal of Psychiatry, 161,* 709–711.

Bowers, K. S., & Farvolden, P. (1996). Revisiting a century-old Freudian slip—from suggestion disavowed to the truth repressed. *Psychological Bulletin, 119,* 355–380.

Bowers, T. G., & Al-Redha, M. R. (1990). A comparison of outcome with group/marital and standard/individual therapies with alcoholics. *Journal of Studies on Alcohol, 51,* 301–309.

Bowlby, J. (1980). *Attachment and loss. Vol. III: Loss, sadness and depression.* New York: Basic Books.

Bowlby, J. (1988a). *A secure base: Parent-child attachment and healthy human development.* New York: Basic Books.

Bowlby, J. (1988b). Developmental psychiatry comes of age. *American Journal of Psychiatry, 145,* 1–10.

Bowman, E. S., & Nurnberger, J. I. (1993). Genetics of psychiatry diagnosis and treatment. In D. L. Dunner (Ed.), *Current psychiatric therapy* (pp. 46–56). Philadelphia: W. B. Saunders Co.

Boyce, W. T., Jensen, E. W., Cassel, J. C., Collier, A. M., Smith, A. H., & Ramey, C. T. (1977). Influence of life events and family routines on childhood respiratory tract illness. *Pediatrics, 60,* 609–615.

Bradbury, T., & Miller, G. A. (1985). Season of birth in schizophrenia: A review of evidence, methodology, and etiology. *Psychological Bulletin, 98,* 569–594.

Bradbury, T. N., & Fincham, F. D. (1990). Attributions in marriage: Review and critique. *Psychological Bulletin, 107,* 3–33.

Brady et al v. Hopper, 570 F. Supp. 1333, 1339 (1983).

Brady, E. U., & Kendall, P. C. (1992). Comorbidity of anxiety and depression in children and adolescents. *Psychological Bulletin, 111*(2), 244–255.

Brayne, C., & Calloway, P. (1988). Normal ageing, impaired cognitive function, and senile dementia of the Alzheimer's type: A continuum? *Lancet, ii,* 1265–1267.

Breggin, P. (1980). Brain disabling therapies. In E. S. Valenstein (Ed.), *The psychosurgery debate: Scientific, legal, and ethical perspectives.* San Francisco: Freeman.

Breggin, P. (1994). *Talking back to Prozac.* New York: Saint Martin's Press.

Breier, A. (1995). Serotonin, schizophrenia and antipsychotic drug action. *Schizophrenia Research, 14*(3), 187–202.

Breier, A., Buchanan, R., Kirkpatrick, B., Davis, O., Irish, D., Summerfelt, A., & Carpenter, W. (1994). Effects of clozapine on positive and negative symptoms in outpatients with schizophrenia. *American Journal of Psychiatry, 151,* 20–26.

Bremner, J. P., Southwick, S. M., Darnell, A., & Charney, D. S. (1996). Chronic PTSD in Vietnam combat veterans: Course of illness and substance abuse. *American Journal of Psychiatry, 153,* 369–375.

Brems, C., Thevenin, D. M., & Routh, D. K. (1991). The history of clinical psychology. In C. E. Walker (Ed.), *Clinical psychology: Historical and research foundations* (pp. 3–36). New York: Plenum.

Bretschneider, J. G., & McCoy, N. L. (1988). Sexual interest and behavior in healthy 80- to 102-year-olds. *Archives of Sexual Behavior, 17,* 109–129.

Brewerton, T. D. (1994). Hyperreligiosity in psychotic disorders. *Journal of Nervous and Mental Disease, 182,* 302–304.

Brick, J. (1990). Learning and motivational factors in alcohol consumption. In W. M. Cox (Ed.), *Why people drink: Parameters of alcohol as a reinforcer.* New York: Gardner Press.

Bridges, K. W., & Goldberg, D. P. (1985). Somatic presentation of DSM-III psychiatric disorders in primary care. *Journal of Psychosomatic Research, 29,* 563–569.

Bridges, P. K., Goktepe, E. O., Maratos, J., Browne, A., Young, L. (1973). A comparative review of patients with obsessional neurosis and depression treated by psychosurgery. *British Journal of Psychiatry, 123,* 663–674.

Briere, J. (1992). Methodological issues in the study of sexual abuse effects. *Journal of Consulting and Clinical Psychology, 60,* 196–203.

Briere, J., & Malamuth, N. M. (1983). Self-reported likelihood of sexually aggressive behaviors: Attitudinal versus sexual explanation. *Journal of Research in Personality, 17,* 315–323.

Briggs, D. (1991). Preventing ICU psychosis. *Nursing Times, 87,* 30–31.

Brislin, R. (1991). *Understanding culture's influence on behavior.* Fort Worth, Texas: Harcourt, Brace, Jovanovich.

Brna, T. G., & Wilson, C. C. (1990). Psychogenic amnesia. *American Family Physician, 41,* 229–234.

Bromberg, W. (1959). *The mind of man: A history of psychotherapy and psychoanalysis.* New York: Harper & Row.

Browerman, C. P., Gordon, G. C., Tepas, D. I., & Walsh, J. K. (1977). Reported sleep and drug use of workers: A preliminary report. *Sleep Research, 6,* 111.

Brown, E. S., & Lambert, M. T. (1995). Delusional electronic dental implants: Case reports and literature review. *Journal of Nervous and Mental Disease, 183,* 603–604.

Brown, G. L., Ebert, M. H., Goyer, P. F., Jimerson, D. C., Klein, W. J., Bunney, W. E., & Goodwin, F. K. (1982). Aggression, suicide, and serotonin: Relationships to CSF amine metabolites. *American Journal of Psychiatry, 139,* 741–746.

Brown, G. L., & Goodwin, F. K. (1986). Cerebrospinal fluid correlates of suicide attempts and aggression. *Annals of the New York Academy of Science, 487,* 175–188.

Brown, G. L., Goodwin, F. K., & Bunney, W. E. (1982). Human aggression and suicide: Their relationship to neuropsychiatric diagnoses and serotonin metabolism. *Advances in Biochemical Psychopharmacology, 34,* 287–307.

Brown, G. W., Adler, Z., & Bifulco, A. (1988). Life events, difficulties and recovery from chronic depression. *British Journal of Psychiatry, 152,* 487–498.

Brown, G. W., & Birley, J. L. T. (1968). Crises and life changes and the onset of schizophrenia. *Journal of Health and Social Behavior, 9,* 203–214.

Brown, G. W., Birley, J. L. T., & Wing, J. K. (1972). Influence of family life on the course of schizophrenic disorders: A replication. *British Journal of Psychiatry, 121,* 241–258.

Brown, G. W., & Harris, T. (1978). *Social origins of depression: A study of psychiatric disorder in women.* New York: The Free Press.

Brown, J. (1987). A review of meta-analyses conducted on psychotherapy outcome research. *Clinical Psychology Review, 7,* 1–24.

Brown, S. A., Christiansen, B. A., & Goldman, M. S. (1987). The Alcohol Expectancy Questionnaire: An instrument for the assessment of adolescent and adult alcohol expectancies. *Journal of Studies on Alcohol, 48*(5), 483–491.

Brown, T. A., Antony, M. M., & Barlow, D. H. (1995). Diagnostic comorbidity in panic disorder: Effect on treatment outcome and course of comorbid diagnoses following treatment. *Journal of Consulting and Clinical Psychology, 63,* 408–418.

Brown, T. A., & Barlow, D. H. (1992). Comorbidity among anxiety disorders: Implications for treatment and DSM-IV. *Journal of Consulting and Clinical Psychology, 60,* 835–844.

Brown, T. A., & Barlow, D. H. (1995). Long-term outcome in cognitive-behavioral treatment of panic disorder: Clinical predictors and alternative strategies for assessment. *Journal of Consulting and Clinical Psychology, 63,* 754–765.

Brown, T. A., Moras, K., Zinbarg, R. E., & Barlow, D. H. (1993). Diagnostic and symptom distinguishability of generalized anxiety disorder and obsessive-compulsive disorder. *Behavior Therapy, 24,* 227–240.

Brownell, K. D., & Foreyt, J. P. (1985). Obesity. In D. H. Barlow (Ed.), *Clinical handbook of psychological disorders* (pp. 299–343). New York: Guilford Press.

Brownell, K. D., & Wadden, T. A. (1992). Etiology and treatment of obesity: Understanding a serious, prevalent, and refractory disorder. *Journal of Consulting and Clinical Psychology, 60,* 505–517.

Brownmiller, S. (1975). *Against our will: Men, women, and rape.* New York: Bantam Books.

Brugge, K. L., Nichols, S. L., Salmon, D. P., Hill, L. R., Delis, D. C., Aaron, L., & Trauner, D. A. (1994). Cognitive impairment in adults with Down's syndrome: Similarities to early cognitive changes in Alzheimer's disease. *Neurology, 44*(2), 232–238.

Bruton, C., Crow, T. J., Firth, C. D., Johnson, E. C., Owens, D. G., & Roberts, G. W. (1990). Schizophrenia and the brain: A prospective clinico-neuropathological study. *Psychological Medicine, 20,* 285–304.

Bugental, J. F. T. (1978). *Psychotherapy and process: The fundamentals of an existential-humanistic approach.* Reading, MA: Addison-Wesley.

Buka, S., Tsaung, M. T., & Lipsitt, L. (1993). Pregnancy/delivery complications and psychiatric diagnosis. *Archives of General Psychiatry, 50,* 151–156.

Bunney, W. E., & Garland, B. L. (1983). Possible receptor effects of chronic lithium administration. *Neuropharmacology, 22,* 367–372.

Burchard, J. D. (1967). Systematic socialization: A programmed environment for the habilitation of antisocial retardates. *Psychological Record, 17,* 461–476.

Burchard, S. N., et al. (1991). An examination of lifestyle and adjustment in three community residential alternatives. *Research in Developmental Disabilities, 12*(2), 127–142.

Buhrmester, D., Whalen, C. K., Henker, B., MacDonald, V. et al. (1992). Prosocial behavior in hyperactive boys: Effects of stimulant medication and comparison with normal boys. *Journal of Abnormal Child Psychology, 20,* 103–121.

Burish, T. G., & Carey, M. P. (1986). Conditioned aversive responses in cancer chemotherapy patients: Theoretical and developmental analysis. *Journal of Consulting and Clinical Psychology, 54,* 593–600.

Burish, T. G., Carey, M. P., Krozely, M. G., & Greco, F. A. (1987). Conditioned side effects induced by cancer chemotherapy: Prevention through behavioral treatment. *Journal of Consulting and Clinical Psychology, 55,* 42–48.

Burnam, M. A., Hough, R., Escobar, J. I., & Karno, M. (1987). Six months prevalence of specific psychiatric disorders among Mexican Americans and non-Hispanic whites in Los Angeles. *Archives of General Psychiatry, 44,* 687–694.

Buschbaum, M., Haier, R., Potkin, S., Nuechterlein, K., Bracha, H., Katz, M., Lohr, J. M., Wu, J., Lottenberg, S., Jerabek, P., Trenary, M., Tafalla, R., Reynolds, C., & Bunney, W. (1992). Frontostriatal disorder of cerebral metabolism in never-medicated schizophrenics. *Archives of General Psychiatry, 49,* 935–942.

Buss, A. H. (1966). *Psychopathology.* New York: John Wiley & Sons.

Buss, D. M. (1995). Evolutionary psychology: A new paradigm for psychological science. *Psychological Inquiry, 6,* 1–30.

Butcher, J. N., Dahlstron, W. G., Graham, J. R., Tellegen (1989). *Minnesota Multiphasic Personality Inventory-2 (MMPI-2): Manual for administration and scoring.* Minneapolis: University of Minnesota Press.

Butcher, J. N., Williams, C. L., Graham, J. R., Archer, R., Tellegen, A., Ben-Porath, Y. S., & Kaemmer, B. (1992). *MMPI-A: Manual for administration, scoring and interpretation.* Minneapolis: University of Minnesota Press.

Butler, G., Fennell, M., Robson, P., & Gelder, M. (1991). Comparison of behavior therapy and cognitive behavior therapy in the treatment of generalized anxiety disorder. *Journal of Consulting and Clinical Psychology, 59,* 167–175.

Butler, L., Miezitis, S., Friedman, R., & Cole, E. (1980). The effect of two school-based intervention programs on depressive symptoms in preadolescents. *American Educational Research Journal, 17,* 111–119.

Buzsaki, G., & Gage, F. H. (1988). Mechanisms of action of neural grafts in the limbic system. *Canadian Journal of Neurological Sciences, 15,* 99–105.

Byne, W., & Parsons, B. (1993). Human sexual orientation: The biologic theories reappraised. *Archives of General Psychiatry, 50,* 228–239.

Cabay, M. (1994). A controlled evaluation of facilitated communication using open-ended and fill-in questions. *Journal of Autism and Developmental Disorders, 24*(4), 517–527.

Cadoret, R. J. (1990). Genetics of alcoholism. In R. L. Collins, K. E. Leonard, & J. S. Searles (Eds.), *Alcohol and the family: Research and clinical perspectives* (pp. 39–78). New York: Guilford Press.

Caldwell, C. B., & Gottesman, I. I. (1990). Schizophrenics kill themselves too: A review of risk factors for suicide. *Schizophrenia Bulletin, 16,* 571–589.

Calev, A., Pass, H., Shapira, B., Fink, M., Tubi, N., & Lerer, B. (1993). In C. E. Coffey, (Ed.), *The clinical science of electroconvulsive therapy* (pp. 125–142). Washington, DC: American Psychiatric Press.

Callahan, V. A., McGreevey, M. A., Cirnicione, C., & Steadman, H. J. (1992). Measuring the effects of the guilty but mental ill (GBMI) verdict: Georgia's 1982 GBMI reform. *Law and Human Behavior, 16,* 447–462.

Cambor, R., & Millman, R. B. (1991). Alcohol and drug abuse in adolescents. In M. Lewis (Ed.), *Child and adolescent psychiatry: A comprehensive textbook* (pp. 736–754). Baltimore: Williams & Wilkins.

Campbell, D. T., & Stanley, J. C. (1966). *Experimental and quasi-experimental designs for research.* Chicago: Rand McNally & Co.

Campbell, J. L., Thomas, H. M., Gabrielli, W., Liskow, B. I., & Powell, B. J. (1994). Impact of desipramine or carbamazepine on patient retention in outpatient cocaine treatment: Preliminary findings. *Journal of Addictive Diseases, 13*(4), 191–199.

Campbell, M., Anderson, L. T., Small, A. M., Adams, P., Gonzalez, N. M., & Ernst, M. (1993). Naltrexone in autistic children: Behavioral symptoms and attentional learning. *Journal of the American Academy of Child and Adolescent Psychiatry, 32*(6), 1283–1291.

Campbell, S. B. (1990). *Behavior problems in preschool children: Clinical and developmental issues.* New York: Guilford Press.

Campbell, S. B., Ewing, L. J., Breaux, A. M., & Szumowski, E. K. (1986). Problem three-year-olds: Follow-up at school entry. *Journal of Child Psychology and Psychiatry, 27,* 473–488.

Canino, G., Bird, H., Shrout, P., Rubio-Stipec, M., Bravo, M., Martinez, R., Sesman, M., & Guevara, L. (1987). The prevalence of specific psychiatric disorders in Puerto Rico. *Archives of General Psychiatry, 44,* 727–735.

Cannon, T., Mednick, S., Parnas, J. (1989). Genetic and perinatal determinants of structural brain deficits in schizophrenia. *Archives of General Psychiatry, 46,* 883–888.

Cannon, T., Mednick, S., Parnas, J., Schulsinger, F., Praestholm, J., & Vestergaard, A. (1993). Developmental brain abnormalities in the offspring of schizophrenic mothers. I: Contributions of genetic and perinatal factors. *Archives of General Psychiatry, 50,* 551–564.

Cannon, T., Mednick, S., Parnas, J., Schulsinger, F., Praestholm, J., & Vestergaard, A. (1994). Developmental brain abnormalities in the offspring of schizophrenic mothers: II: Structural brain characteristics of schizophrenia and schizotypal personality disorder. *Archives of General Psychiatry, 51,* 955–962.

Cantor-Graae, E., McNeil, T., Sjostrom, K., Nordstrom, L. G., & Rosenlund, T. (1994). Obstetric complications and their relationship to other etiological risk factors in schizophrenia. *Journal of Nervous and Mental Disease, 182,* 645–650.

Cantwell, D. P., & Baker, L. (1989). Stability and natural history of DSM-III childhood diagnoses. *Journal of the American Academy of Child and Adolescent Psychiatry, 28,* 691–700.

Cantwell, D., Baker, L., & Rutter, M. (1978). Family factors. In M. Rutter & E. Schopler (Eds.), *Autism: A reappraisal of concepts and treatment* (pp. 269–296). New York: Plenum.

Caplan, G. (1964). *Principles of preventive psychiatry.* New York: Basic Books.

Caplan, G. (1964). *An approach to community mental health.* New York: Grune & Stratton.

Caplehorn, J. R., & Ross, M. W. (1995). Methadone maintenance and the likelihood of risky needle-sharing. *Internation Journal of Addictions, 30,* 685–698.

Cappe, R. F., & Alden, L. E. (1986). A comparison of treatment strategies for clients functionally impaired by extreme shyness and social avoidance. *Journal of Consulting and Clinical Psychology, 54,* 796–801.

Cappell, H., & Greeley, J. (1987). Alcohol and tension reduction: An update on research and theory. In H. T. Blane & K. E. Leonard (Eds.), *Psychological theories of drinking* (pp. 15–51). New York: Guilford Press.

Capute, A. J., & Accardo, P. J. (1996). *Developmental disabilities in infancy and childhood* (2nd edition). Baltimore: Paul Brookes Publishing.

Cardon, L. R., Smith, S. D., Fulker, D. W., Kimberling, W. J., Pennington, B. F., & DeFries, J. C. (1994). Quantitative trait locus for reading disability on chromosome 6. *Science, 266,* 276–279.

Carey, M. P., & Burish, T. G. (1988). Etiology and treatment of the psychological side effects associated with cancer chemotherapy. *Psychological Bulletin, 104,* 307–325.

Carlson, C. L., Pelham, W. E., Jr., Milich, R., & Dixon, J. (1992). Single and combined effects of methylphenidate and behavior therapy on the classroom performance of children with attention-deficit hyperactivity disorder. *Journal of Abnormal Child Psychology, 20*(2), 213–232.

Carroll, B. J. (1986). Informed use of the dexamethasone suppression test. *Journal of Clinical Psychiatry, 47 (Suppl. 1),* 10–12.

Carson, R. C. (1969). *Interaction concepts of personality.* Chicago: Aldine Publishing Co..

Carson, R. C. (1991). Dilemmas in the pathway of the DSM-IV. *Journal of Abnormal Psychology, 100,* 302–307.

Carter, M. M., Hollon, S. D., Carson, R., & Shelton, R. C. (1995). Effects of a safe person on induced distress following a biological challenge in panic disorder with agoraphobia. *Journal of Abnormal Psychology, 104,* 156–163.

Carver, C., & Scheier, M. (1981). *Attention and self-regulation.* New York: Springer-Verlag.

Case, R. B., Moss, A. J., Case, N., McDermott, M., & Eberly, S. (1992). Living alone after myocardial infarction: Impact on prognosis. *Journal of the American Medical Association, 267,* 515–519.

Cassidy, J. (1988). Child–mother attachment and the self in six-year-olds. *Child Development, 59,* 121–134.

Castle, D. J., & Murray, R. M.(1993). The epidemiology of late-onset schizophrenia. *Schizophrenia Bulletin, 19,* 691–700.

Ceccherini-Nelli, A., Bardellilni, L., Cur, A., Guazelli, M., Maggini, C., & Dilsaver, S. (1993). Antidepressant withdrawal: Prospective findings. *American Journal of Psychiatry, 150,* 165.

Centers for Disease Control Viet Nam Experience Survey (VES) (1988). Psychosocial Characteristics. *Journal of the American Medical Association, 259,* 2701–2707.

Cepeda-Benito, A. (1993). Meta-analytical review of the efficacy of nicotine chewing gum in smoking treatment programs. *Journal of Consulting and Clinical Psychology, 61*(5), 822–830.

Cerletti, U., & Bini, L. (1938). Electroshock. *Archives of General Neurology, Psychiatry, and Psychoanalysis, 19,* 266–268.

Chambers, M. J., & Keller, B. (1992). Alert insomniacs: Are they really sleep deprived? *Clinical Psychology Review, 13,* 649–666.

Chambless, D. L., & Gillis, M. (1993). Cognitive therapy with anxiety disorders. *Journal of Consulting and Clinical Psychology, 61,* 248–260.

Champion, V. L. (1990). Breast self-examination in women 35 and older: A prospective study. *Journal of Behavioral Medicine, 13,* 523–538.

Chandler, W., Schuster, J. W., & Stevens, K. B. (1993). Teaching employment skills to adolescents with mild and moderate disabilities using a constant time delay procedure. *Education and Training in Mental Retardation, 28*(2), 155–168.

Chaney, C. (1994). Language development, metalinguistic awareness, and emergent literacy skills of 3-year-old children in relation to social class. *Applied Psycholinguistics, 15*(3), 371–394.

Chapman, L. J., & Chapman, J. P. (1980). Scales for rating psychotic and psychotic-like experiences as continua. *Schizophrenia Bulletin, 6,* 476–489.

Chapman, L. J., Chapman, J. P., Kwapil, T. R., Eckblad, M., & Zinser, M. C. (1994). Putatively psychosis-prone subjects 10 years later. *Journal of Abnormal Psychology, 103,* 171–183.

Charcot, J. M. (1881). *Clinical lectures on senile and chronic diseases.* London: New Sydenheim Society.

Chassin, L., Pillow, D., Curran, P., Molina, B., & Barrera, M. (1993). Relation of parental alcoholism to early adolescent substance use: A test of three mediating mechanisms. *Journal of Abnormal Psychology, 102,* 3–19.

Chassin, L., Rogosch, F., & Barrera, M. (1991). Substance use and symptomatology among adolescent children of alcoholics. *Journal of Abnormal Psychology, 100*(4), 449–463.

Chen, C. N., Wong, J., Lee, N., Chan-Ho, M. W., Lau, J., & Fung, M. (1993). The Shatin community mental health survey in Hong Kong. II. Major findings. *Archives of General Psychiatry, 50,* 125–132.

Chiocca, E. A., & Martuza, R. (1990). Neurosurgical therapy of obsessive compulsive disorder. In M. A. Jenike, L. Baer, & W. Minichiello (Eds.) *Obsessive-compulsive disorders: Theory and management.* St. Louis: Mosby-Yearbook.

Chou, T. M., & Benowitz, N. L. (1994). Caffeine and coffee: Effects on health and cardiovascular disease. Comparative Biochemistry and Physiology. *Pharmacology, Toxicology and Endocrinology, 109*(2), 173–189.

Christiansen, B. A., Roehling, P. V., Smith, G. T., & Goldman, M. S. (1989). Using alcohol expectancies to predict adolescent drinking behavior after one year. *Journal of Consulting and Clinical Psychology, 57*(1), 93–99.

Chrousos, G. P., & Gold, P. W. (1992). The concepts of stress and stress system disorders. *Journal of the American Medical Association, 267,* 1244–1252.

Chung, R. C.-Y., & Singer, M. K. (1995). Interpretation of symptom presentation and distress: A southeast Asian refugee example. *Journal of Nervous and Mental Disease, 183,* 639–648.

CIBA-GEIGY Corporation (1991). OCD: *When a habit isn't just a habit: A guide to obsessive-compulsive disorder.* Summit, NJ: Author.

Cicchetti, D., & Beeghly, M. (Eds.). (1990). *Children with Down syndrome: A developmental approach.* New York: Cambridge University Press.

Cicchetti, D., & Toth, S. L. (1991). A developmental perspective on internalizing and externalizing disorders. In D. Cicchetti & S. L. Toth (Eds.), *Internalizing and externalizing expressions of dysfunction: Rochester symposium on developmental psychopathology* (Vol. 2, pp. 1–19). Hillsdale, NJ: Erlbaum.

Cinciripini, P. M., Lapitsky, L. G., Seay, S., Wallfisch, A., Kitchens, K., & Van Vunakis, H. (1995). The effects of smoking schedules on cessation outcome: Can we improve on common methods of gradual and abrupt nicotine withdrawal? *Journal of Consulting and Clinical Psychology, 63,* 388–399.

Clark, D. M. (1986). A cognitive approach to panic. *Behavioral Research & Therapy, 24,* 461–470.

Clark, D. M., Salkovskis, P. M., Hackman, A., Middleton, H., Anastasiades, P., & Gelder, M. (1994). A comparison of cognitive therapy, applied relaxation, and imipramine in the treatment of panic disorder. *British Journal of Psychiatry, 164,* 759–769.

Clark, L. A., Watson, D., & Reynolds, S. (1995). Diagnosis and classification of psychopathology: Challenges to the current system and future directions. *Annual Review of Psychology, 46,* 121–153. Palo Alto, CA: Annual Reviews.

Clarkin, J. F., Glick, I D., Haas, G. L., Spencer, J. H., Lewis, A. B., Peyser, J., Demane, N., Good-Ellis, M., Harris, E., & Lestelle, V. (1990). A randomized clinical trial of inpatient family intervention. V: Results for affective disorders. *Journal of Affective Disorders, 18,* 17–28.

Clarkin, J. F., & Kendall, P. C. (1992). Comorbidity and treatment planning: Summary and future directions. *Journal of Consulting and Clinical Psychology, 60,* 904–908.

Clayton, P. J. (1986). Bipolar illness. In G. Winokur & P. Clayton (Eds.), *The medical basis of psychiatry* (pp. 39–59). Philadelphia: W. B. Saunders Co.

Clayton, P. J., Herjanic, M., Murphy, G. E., Woodruff, R. (1974). Mourning and depression: Their similarities and differences. *Journal of the Canadian Psychiatric Association, 19,* 309–312.

Cleburne Living Center, Inc. v. City of Cleburne, Texas, 52 L. W. 2515, 726 F. 3d 191 (1985).

Cleckley, H. (1976). *The mask of sanity* (5th ed). St. Louis: Mosby.

Clementz, B. A., & Sweeney, J. A. (1990). Is eye movement dysfunction a biological marker for schizophrenia? A methodological review. *Psychological Bulletin, 108,* 77–92.

Cloninger, C. R. (1987). A systematic method for clinical description and classification of personality variants: A proposal. *Archives of General Psychiatry, 44,* 573–588.

Cloninger, C. R., Bohman, M., & Sigvardsson, S. (1981). Inheritance of alcohol abuse: Cross-fostering analysis of adopted men. *Archives of General Psychiatry, 38,* 861–868.

Cloninger, C. R., & Gottesman, I. (1987). Genetic and environmental factors in antisocial behavior disorders. In S. A. Mednick, T. E. Moffitt, & S. A. Stack (Eds.), *Causes of crime: New biological approaches.* Cambridge: Cambridge University Press.

Cloninger, C. R., Sigvardsson, S., & Bohman, M. (1988). Childhood personality predicts alcohol abuse in young adults. *Alcoholism in Clinical and Experimental Research, 12*(4), 494–505.

Clozapine Study Group (1993). The safety and efficacy of clozapine in severe treatment-resistant schizophrenics in the UK. *British Journal of Psychiatry, 163,* 150–155.

Clum, G. A., Clum, G. A., & Surls, R. (1993). A meta-analysis of treatments for panic disorder. *Journal of Consulting and Clinical Psychology, 61,* 317–326.

Coates, S. (1990). Ontogenesis of boyhood gender identity disorder. *Journal of the American Academy of Psychoanalysis, 18,* 414–438.

Coates, S., & Person, E. S. (1985). Extreme boyhood femininity: Isolated behavior or pervasive disorder? *Journal of the American Academy of Child Psychiatry, 24,* 702–709.

Coccaro, E. F. (1993). Psychopharmacologic studies in patients with personality disorders: Review and perspective. *Journal of Personality Disorders, 7,* 181–192.

Coffey, C. E. (Ed.). (1993). *The clinical science of electroconvulsive therapy.* Washington DC: American Psychiatric Press.

Cohen, C. I. (1993). Poverty and the course of schizophrenia: Implications for research and policy. *Hospital and Community Psychiatry, 44,* 951–958.

Cohen, H. L. (1968). Educational therapy: The design of learning environments. *Research in Psychotherapy, 3,* 21–58.

Cohen, J. B., & Reed, D. (1985). Type A behavior and coronary heart disease among Japanese men in Hawaii. *Journal of Behavioral Medicine, 8,* 343–352.

Cohen, J., & Servan-Schreiber, D. (1992). Context, cortex, and dopamine: A connectionist approach to behavior and biology in schizophrenia. *Psychological Review, 99,* 45–77.

Cohen, S., Tyrell, D. A. J., & Smith, A. P. (1991). Psychological stress and susceptibility to the common cold. *New England Journal of Medicine, 325,* 606–612.

Cohen, S., & Wills, T. A. (1985). Stress, social support, and the buffering hypothesis. *Psychological Bulletin, 98,* 310–357.

Cohn, J. F., Campbell, S. B., Matias, R., & Hopkins, J. (1990). Face-to-face interactions of postpartum depressed and nondepressed mother-infant pairs at two months. *Developmental Psychology, 26,* 15–23.

Coie, J. D., Lochman, J. E., Terry, R., & Hyman, C. (1992). Predicting early adolescent disorder from childhood aggression and peer rejection. *Journal of Consulting and Clinical Psychology, 60,* 783–792.

Coie, J. D., Watt, N. F., West, S. G., Hawkins, J. D., Asarnow, J. R., Markman, H. J., Ramey, S. L., Shure, M. B., & Long, B. (1993). The science of prevention: A conceptual framework and some directions for a national research program. *American Psychologist, 48,* 1013–1022.

Cole, D. A., & White, K. (1993). Structure of peer impressions of children's competence: Validation of the peer nomination of multiple competencies. *Psychological Assessment, 5,* 449–456.

Cole, J. O., & Bodkin, J. A. (1990). Antidepressant drug side effects. *Journal of Clinical Psychiatry, 51* (Suppl.), 21–26.

Coles, G. (1987). *The learning mystique: A critical look at "learning disabilities."* New York: Fawcett Columbine.

Colvin, C. R., & Block, J. (1994). Do positive illusions foster mental health? An examination of the Taylor and Brown formulation. *Psychological Bulletin, 116,* 3–20.

Comer, J. P. (1987). New Haven's school-community connection. *Educational Leadership, 44,* 13–16.

Comings, D. E., Comings, B. G., Muhleman, D., Dietz, G., Shahbahrami, B., Tast, D., Knell, E., Kocsis, P., Baumgarten, R., Kovacs, B. W., Levy, D. L., Smith, M., Borison, R. L., Evans, D. D., Klein, D. N., Macmurray, J., Tosk, J. M., Sverd, J., Gysin, R., & Flanagan, S. D. (1991). The dopamine D2 receptor locus as a modifying gene in neuropsychiatric disorders. *Journal of the American Medical Association, 266*(13), 1793–1800.

Conduct Problems Prevention Research Group (1994). A developmental and clinical model for the prevention of conduct disorder: The FAST Track Program. *Development and Psychopathology, 4,* 509–527.

Conger, J. J. (1956). Alcoholism: Theory, problem and challenge: II. Reinforcement theory and the dynamics of alcoholism. *Quarterly Jouranl of Studies on Alcohol, 101*(1), 139–152.

Conoley, C. W., Conoley, J. C., McConnell, J. A., & Kimzey, C. E. (1983). The effect of the ABCs of rational emotive therapy and the empty-chair technique of Gestalt therapy on anger reduction. *Psychotherapy: Theory, Research, and Practice, 20,* 112–117.

Consensus Development Conference Statement (1985). *Electroconvulsive therapy.* National Institutes of Health OM-00–4018. vol 5, (11).

Conte, H. R., Plutchik, R., Wild, K., & Karasau, T. B. (1986). Combined psychotherapy and pharmacotherapy for depression: A systematic analysis of evidence. *Archives of General Psychiatry, 43,* 471–479.

Conway, J. B. (1988). Differences among clinical psychologists: Scientists, practitioners, and scientist-practitioners. *Professional Psychology: Research and Practice, 19,* 642–655.

Cook, C. C. H. (1988). The Minnesota model in the management of drug and alcohol dependency: Miracle, method or myth? Part II. Evidence and conclusions. *British Journal of Addictions, 83,* 735–748.

Cook, J. A. (1995, summer). Research on psychosocial rehabilitation services for persons with psychiatric disabilities. *Psychotherapy and Rehabilitation Research Bulletin,* 5–11.

Cook, M., & Mineka, S. (1987). Second-order conditioning and overshadowing in the observational conditioning of fear in monkeys. *Behaviour Research and Therapy, 25,* 349–364.

Cook, T. D., & Campbell, D. T. (1979). *Quasi-experimentation: Design and analysis issues for field settings.* Chicago: Rand-McNally & Co.

Cooney, N. L., Kadden, R. M., Litt, M. D., & Getter, H. (1991). Matching alcoholics to coping skills or interactional therapies: Two-year follow-up results. *Journal of Consulting and Clinical Psychology, 59*(4), 598–601.

Coons, P. M. (1986). Treatment progress in 20 patients with multiple personality disorder. *Journal of Nervous and Mental Disease, 174,* 715–721.

Coons, P. M., Milstein, V., & Marley, C. (1982). EEG studies of two multiple personalities and a control. *Archives of General Psychiatry, 39,* 823–825.

Cooper, G. L. (1988). The safety of fluoxetine—An update. *British Journal of Psychiatry, 153,* (Suppl. 3), 77–86.

Cooper, J. E., Kendell, R., Gurland, B., Sharpe, L., Copeland, J. R., & Simon, R. (1972). *Psychiatric Diagnosis in New York and London.* London: Oxford University Press.

Cooper, M. L., Russell, M., Skinner, J. B., Frone, M. R., & Mudar, P. (1992). Stress and alcohol use: The moderating effects of gender, coping, and alcohol expectancies. *Journal of Abnormal Psychology, 101*(1), 139–152.

Coplan, J., Sharama, T., Rosenblum, L., Friedman, S., Bassoff, T., Barbour, R., & Gorman, J. (1992). Effects of sodium lactate infusion on cisternal lactate and carbon dioxide levels in nonhuman primates. *American Journal of Psychiatry, 149,* 1369–1373.

Coppen, A., Mendelwicz, J., & Kielholz, P. (1986). *Pharmacotherapy of depressive disorders: A consensus statement.* Geneva: World Health Organization.

Corder, B., Saunders, A. M., Strittmatter, W. J., Schmechel, D. E., Gaskell, P. C., & Small, G. N. (1993). Gene dose of apolipoprotein E type 4 allele and the risk of Alzheimer's disease in late onset families. *Science, 261,* 921–923.

Corkin, S. (1980). A prospective study of cingulatomy. In E. S. Valenstein (Ed.), *The psychosurgery debate: Scientific, legal and ethical perspectives* (pp. 164–204). San Francisco: Freeman.

Coryell, W., Lavori, P., Endicott, J., Keller, M., & Van-Eerdewegh, M. (1984). Outcome in schizoaffective, psychotic and nonpsychotic depression. *Archives of General Psychiatry, 41,* 787–791.

Cosgrove, G. R., Baer, L., Rauch, S., Ballantine, R., Casuem, E., Manzo, P., & Jenihy, M. (1995). Cingulatomy for intractable obsessive-compulsive disorder: A prospective long-term follow-up study. *Stereotactic and Functional Neurosurgery, 65,* 67–71.

Costa, P. T., Jr., & McCrae, R. R. (1986). Personality stability and its implications for clinical psychology. *Clinical Psychology Review, 6,* 407–424.

Costa P. T., Jr., & McCrae, R. R. (1990). Personality disorders and the five-factor model of personality. *Journal of Personality Disorders, 4,* 362–371.

Costa, P. T., Jr., & McCrae, R. R. (1992a). *Manual for the Revised NEO Personality Inventory (NEO-PIR) and the NEO Five-Factor Inventory (BEO-FFI).* Odessa, FL: Psychological Assessment Resources.

Costa, P. T., Jr., & McCrae, R. R. (1992b). Normal personality assessment in clinical practice: The NEO Personality Inventory. *Psychological Assessment, 11,* 5–13.

Costa, P. T., Jr., & Widiger, T. A. (1994) (Eds.) *Personality disorders and the five factor model of personality.* Washington, DC: American Psychological Association.

Costello, E., Costello, A., Edelbrock, C., Burns, B., Dulcan, M., Brent, D., & Janiszewski, S. (1988). Psychiatric disorders in pediatric primary care. *Archives of General Psychiatry, 45,* 1107–1116.

Costello, R. M. (1975). Alcoholism treatment and evaluation: In search of methods. *International Journal of the Addictions, 10,* 251–275.

Courchesne, E., Yeung-Courchesne, R., Press, G. A., Hesselink, J. R., & Jernigan, T. L. (1988). Hypoplasia of cerebellar vermal lobules VI and VII in autism. *New England Journal of Medicine, 318,* 1349–1354.

Cowdry, R. W., & Gardner, D. L. (1988). Pharmacotherapy of borderline personality disorder: Alprazolam, carbamazepine, trifluoperazine, and tranylcypromine. *Archives of General Psychiatry, 45,* 111–119.

Cowen, E. L. (1994). The enhancement of psychological wellness: Challenges and opportunities. *American Journal of Community Psychology, 22,* 149–180.

Cowen, E. L., Gesten, E. L., & Wilson, A. B. (1979). The primary mental health project (PMHP): Evaluation of current program effectiveness. *American Journal of Community Psychology, 7,* 293–303.

Cox, W. M. (1987). Personality theory and research. In H. T. Blane & K. E. Leonard (Eds.), *Psychological theories of drinking and alcoholism: The Guilford Alcohol Studies Series G* (pp. 55–89). New York: Guilford Press.

Coyne, J. C. (1976). Toward an interactional description of depression. *Psychiatry, 39,* 28–40.

Coyne, J. C., & Downey, G. (1991). Social factors in psychopathology: Stress, social support, and coping processes. *Annual Review of Psychology, 42,* 401–425.

Coyne, J. C., Kessler, R. C., Tal, M., Turnbull, J., Wortman, C., & Greden, J. (1987). Living with a depressed person: Burden and psychological distress. *Journal of Clinical and Consulting Psychology, 55,* 347–352.

Crapper-McLachlan, D. R., Dalton, A. J., Kruck, T. P. A., Bell, M. Y., Smith, W. L., Kalow, W., & Andrews, D. F. (1991). Intramuscular desferrioxamine in patients with Alzheimer's disease. *Lancet, 337,* 1304–1308.

Craske, M., & Barlow, D. H. (1993). Panic disorder and agoraphobia. In D. H. Barlow (Ed.), *Clinical handbook of psychological disorders: A step-by-step treatment manual* (2nd ed.). New York: Guilford Press.

Craske, M., Zarate, R., Burton, T., & Barlow, D. (1993). Specific fears and panic attacks: A survey of clinical and nonclinical samples. *Journal of Anxiety Disorders, 7,* 1–19.

Creamer, M., Burgess, P., & Pattison, P. (1992). Reactions to trauma: A cognitive processing model. *Journal of Abnormal Psychology, 101,* 452–459.

Crews, F. (1994). *The memory wars: Freud's legacy in dispute.* New York: New York Review Imprints.

Crisp, A. H., Norton, K., Gowers, S., Halek, C., Bowyer, C., Yeldham, D., Levett, G., & Bhat, A. (1991), A controlled study of the effect of therapies aimed at adolescent and family psychopathology in anorexia nervosa. *British Journal of Psychiatry, 159,* 325–333.

Critelli, J. W., & Neumann, K. F. (1984). The placebo: Conceptual analysis of a construct in transition. *American Psychologist, 39,* 32–39.

Crnic, K. A., Greenberg, M. T., Ragozin, A. S., Robinson, N. M., & Basham, R. B. (1983). Effects of stress and social support on mothers and premature and full-term infants. *Child Development, 54,* 209–217.

Crockenberg, S., & Littman, C. (1990). Autonomy as competence in 2-year olds: Maternal correlates of child defiance, compliance, and self assertion. *Developmental Psychology, 26,* 961–971.

Cronbach, L. J., & Meehl, P. E. (1955). Construct validity in psychology tests. *Psychological Bulletin, 52,* 281–302.

Cross, D. G., Sheehan, P. W., & Khan, J. A. (1980). Alternative advice and counsel in psychotherapy. *Journal of Consulting and Clinical Psychology, 48,* 615–625.

Cross-National Collaborative Group (1992). The changing rate of major depression: Cross-national comparisons. *Journal of the American Medical Association, 268,* 3098–3105.

Crow, T. (1980). Positive and negative schizophrenia symptoms and the role of dopamine. *British Journal of Psychiatry, 137,* 383–386.

Crow, T. (1985). The two-syndrome concept: Origins and current status. *Schizophrenia Bulletin, 11,* 471–486.

Crowe, R., Noyes, R., Pauls, D., & Slyman, D. (1983). A family study of panic disorder. *Archives of General Psychiatry. 40,* 1065–1069.

Crowell, J. A., Waters, E., Kring, A., & Riso, L. P. (1993). The psychosocial etiologies of personality disorders: What is the answer like? *Journal of Personality Disorders, 7,* 118–128.

Cryan, M. J., & Ganter, K. (1992). Childhood hallucinations in the context of parental psychopathology. *Irish Journal of Psychological Medicine, 9,* 120–122.

Crystal, H., Fuld, P., Masur, D., Scott, R., Mehler, M., Masdeu, J., Kawas, C., Aronson, M., & Wolfson, L. (1988). Clinico-pathological studies in dementia: Non-demented subjects with pathologically confirmed Alzheimer's disease. *Neurology, 38,* 1682–1687.

Cumins, R. A., et al. (1990). Deinstitutionalization of St. Nicholas Hospital. IV: A four-year follow-up of resident life-style. *Australia and New Zealand Journal of Developmental Disabilities, 16*(4), 305–321.

Cummings, J. L., & Coffey, C. E. (1994). Geriatric neuropsychiatry. In C. E. Coffey & J. L. Cummings (Eds.). *Textbook of geriatric neuropsychiatry* (pp. 3–15). Washington, DC: American Psychiatric Press.

Cunningham, J., Dockery, D. W., & Speizer, F. E. (1994). Maternal smoking during pregnancy as a predictor of lung function in children. *American Journal of Epidemiology, 139*(12), 1139–1152.

Curran, S. L., Sherman, J. J., Cunningham, L. C., Okeson, J. P., Reid, K. I., & Carlson, C. R. (1995). Physical and sexual abuse among orofacial pain patients: Linkages with pain and psychologic distress. *Journal of Orofacial Pain, 9,* 340–346.

Dahl, A. A. (1993). The personality disorders: A critical review of family, twin, and adoption studies. *Journal of Personality Disorders, 7,* 86–99.

Darke, S., Ross, J., & Cohen, J. (1994). The use of benzodiazepines among regular amphetamine users. *Addiction, 89,* 1683–1690.

Darke, S., Ross, J., Cohen, J., Hando, J., & Hall, W. (1995). Injecting and sexual risk-taking behaviour among regular amphetamine users. *AIDS Care, 7,* 19–26.

Darling, M. R., & Arendorf, T. M. (1993). Effects of cannabis smoking on oral soft tissues. *Community Denistry and Oral Epidemiology, 21,* 78–81.

Daubert v. Merrell Dow Pharmaceutical, Inc., 509 U.S. 113 S. Ct. 2786 (1993).

Dauncey, K., Giggs, J., Baker, K., & Harrison, K. (1993). Schizophrenia in Nottingham: Lifelong residential mobility of a cohort. *British Journal of Psychiatry, 163,* 613–619.

Davanloo, H. L. (1994). *Basic principles and techniques in short-term dynamic psychotherapy.* Northdale, NJ: Jason Aronson.

Davidson, R. J. (1991). Cerebral asymmetry and affective disorders: A developmental perspective. In D. Cicchetti & S. L. Toth (Eds.), *Internalizing and externalizing expressions of dysfunction: Rochester symposium on developmental psychopathology* (Vol. 2, pp. 123–154). Hillsdale, NJ: Erlbaum.

Davidson, R. J., & Fox, N. A. (1989). Frontal brain asymmetry predicts infants' response to maternal separation. *Journal of Abnormal Psychology, 98,* 127–131.

Davidson, W. S., Rappaport, J., Seidman, E., Berck, P., Rapp, C., Rhodes, W., & Herring, J. (1977). A diversion program for juvenile offenders. *Social Work Research and Abstracts, 1,* 47–56.

Davila, J., Hammen, C., Burge, D., & Paley, B. (1995). Poor interpersonal problem solving as a mechanism of stress generation in depression among adolescent women. *Journal of Abnormal Psychology, 104,* 592–600.

Davis, D. (1993). Multiple personality, fugue, and amnesia. In D. L. Dunner (Ed.), *Current psychiatric therapy* (pp. 328–334). Philadelphia: W. B. Saunders Co.

Davis, J. O., Phelps, J. A., & Bracha, H. S. (1995). Prenatal development of monozygotic twin and concordance in schizophrenia. *Schizophrenia Bulletin, 21,* 357–366.

Davis, K., Kahn, R., Ko, G., & Davidson, M. (1991). Dopamine in schizophrenia: A review and reconceptualization. *American Journal of Psychiatry, 148,* 1474–1486.

Davis, M. (1994). The role of the amygdala in emotion-learning. *International Review of Neuroscience, 36,* 225–266.

Davison, G. C. (1978). Not can but ought: The treatment of homosexuality. *Journal of Clinical and Consulting Psychology, 46,* 170–172.

Dawes, R. M. (1994). *House of cards.* New York: The Free Press.

Dawes, R. M., Faust, D., & Meehl, P. (1989). Clinical versus actuarial judgment. *Science, 243,* 1668–1674.

Dawson, G., & Lewy, A. (1989). Arousal, attention, and the socioemotional impairments of individuals with autism. In G. Dawson (Ed.), *Autism: Nature, diagnosis, and treatment.* New York: Guilford Press.

Dawson, G., & Osterling, J. (1996). Early intervention in autism. In M. J. Guralnick (Ed.), *The effectiveness of early intervention.* Baltimore: Paul Brookes.

Day, N. L., Richardson, G. A., Geva, D., & Robles, N. (1994). Alcohol, marijuana, and tobacco: Effects of prenatal exposure on offspring growth and morphology at age six. *Alcoholism: Clinical and Experimental Research, 18*(4), 786–794.

Day, R., Nielsen, J. A., Korten, A., Ernberg, G., Dube, K. C., Gebhart, J., Jablensky, A., Leon, C., Marsella, A., Olatawura, M., Sartorius, N., Stromgren, E., Takahashi, R., Wig, N., & Wynne, L. C. (1987). Stressful life events preceding the acute onset of schizophrenia: A cross-national study from the World Health Organization. *Cultural Medicine and Psychiatry, 11,* 123–205.

de Beurs, E., van Balkon, A. J., Lange, A., Koele, P., & van Dyke, R. (1995). Treatment of panic disorder with agoraphobia: Comparison of fluvoxamine, placebo, and psychological panic management combined with exposure and of exposure in vivo alone. *American Journal of Psychiatry, 152,* 683–691.

DeFries, J., Fulker, D., & LaBuda, M. (1987). Evidence for a genetic aetiology in reading disability of twins. *Nature, 329,* 537–539.

Deger, S. R., Strauss, W. L., Marro, K. I., Richards, T. L., Metzger, G. D., & Artru, A. A. (1995). Proton magnetic resonance spectroscopy investigation of hyperventilation in subjects with panic disorder and comparison subjects. *American Journal of Psychiatry, 152,* 666–672.

Dembroski, T. M., MacDougall, J. M., Williams, R. B., Haney, T. L., & Blumenthal, J. A. (1985). Components of Type A, hostility, and anger-in: Relationship to angiographic findings. *Psychosomatic Medicine, 47,* 219–233.

Denicola, J., & Sandler, J. (1980). Training abusive parents in child management and self-control skills. *Behavior Therapy, 11,* 263–270.

Depression Guideline Panel (1993). *Depression in primary care. Vol. 1: Detection and diagnosis.* Rockville, MD: U.S. Department of Health and Human Services.

Depue, R. A., & Iacono, W. G. (1989). Neurobehavioral aspects of affective disorders. *Annual Review of Psychology, 40,* 457–492.

Depue, R. A., Slater, J. F., Wolfstetter-Kausch, Klein, D., Goplerud, E., & Farr, D. (1981). A behavioral paradigm for identifying persons at risk for bipolar depressive disorder: A conceptual framework and five validation studies. *Journal of Abnormal Psychology Monograph, 90,* 5, 381–437.

deSilva, P., & Rachman, S. (1992). *Obsessive-compulsive disorder: The facts.* Oxford: Oxford University Press.

Deutsch, J. A. (1983). The cholinergic synapse and the site of memory. In J. A. Deutsch (Ed.), *The physiological basis of memory.* New York: Academic Press.

Devor, E. J. (1994). A developmental-genetic model of alcoholism: Implications for genetic research. *Journal of Consulting and Clinical Psychology, 62*(6), 1108–1115.

Diener, E. (1984). Subjective well-being. *Psychological Bulletin, 95,* 542–575.

DiLalla, D. L., & Gottesman, I. I. (1995). Normal personality characteristics in identical twins discordant for schizophrenia. *Journal of Abnormal Psychology, 104,*490–499.

DiMascio, A., Weissman, M. M., Prusoff, B. A., Neu, C., Zwilling, M., & Klerman, G. L. (1979). Differential symptom reduction by drugs and psychotherapy in acute depression. *Archives of General Psychiatry, 36,* 1450–1456.

Dobson, K. S. (1989). A meta-analysis of the efficacy of cognitive therapy for depression. *Journal of Consulting and Clinical Psychology, 57,* 414–419.

Docherty, N. M. (1995). Expressed emotion and language disturbances in parents of stable schizophrenic patients. *Schizophrenia Bulletin, 21,* 411–418.

Dodge, K. A., & Coie, J. D. (1987). Social information-processing factors in reactive and proactive aggression in children's peer groups. *Journal of Personality and Social Psychology, 53,* 389–409.

Dodge, K. A., McClaskey, C. L., & Feldman, E. (1985). Situational approach to the assessment of social competence in children. *Journal of Consulting and Clinical Psychology, 53,* 344–353.

Dodge, K. A., Pettit, G. S., McClaskey, C. L., & Brown, J. (1986). Social competence in children. *Monographs of the Society for Research in Child Development, 44* (2, Serial No. 213).

Doerfler, L. A., & Chaplin, W. F. (1985). Type III error in research on interpersonal models of depression. *Journal of Abnormal Psychology, 94,* 227–230.

Doherty, K., Kinnunen, T., Militello, F. S., & Garvey, A. J. (1995). Urges to smoke during the first month of abstinence: Relationship to relapse and predictors. *Psychopharmacology, 119*(2), 171–178.

Dohrenwend, B. S. (1978). Social stress and community psychology. *American Journal of Community Psychology, 6,* 1–14.

Dohrenwend, B. P., Levav, I., Shrout, P. E., Schwartz, S., Naveh, G., Link, B. G., Skodol, A. E., & Stueve, A. (1992). Socioeconomic status and psychiatric disorders: The causation-selection issue. *Science, 255,* 946–952.

Doman, R. J., Spitz, E. B., Zucman, E., Delacato, C. H., & Doman, G. (1960). Children with severe brain unjuries. *Journal of the American Medical Association, 174,* 219–223.

Donnelly, D. A., & Murray, E. J. (1991). Emotional changes in written essays and therapy interviews. *Journal of Social and Clinical Psychology, 10,* 334–350.

Donnerstein, E. (1982). Erotica and human agression. In R. G. Green & E. Donnerstein (Eds.), *Aggression: Theoretical and empirical views.* Orlando, FL: Academic Press.

Donnerstein, E., & Berkowitz, L. (1981). Victim reactions in aggressive erotic films as a factor in violence against women. *Journal of Personality and Social Psychology, 41,* 710–724.

Dowart, R. A., & Chartock, L. (1989). Suicide: A public health perspective. In D. G. Jacobs & H. N. Brown (Eds.), *Suicide: Understanding and responding: Harvard Medical School perspectives on suicide* (pp. 31–55). Madison, CT: International Universities Press.

Downey, G., & Coyne, J. C. (1990). Children of depressed parents: An integrative review. *Psychological Bulletin, 108,* 50–76.

Dube, K. C., Kumar, N., & Dube, S. (1984). Long term course and outcome of the Agra cases in the International Pilot Study of Schizophrenia. *Acta Psychiatrica Scandanavica, 70,* 170–179.

Dunkell, S. (1994). *Goodbye insomnia, hello sleep.* New York: Dell.

Dunn, L. M. (1968). Special education for the mildly retarded: Is much of it justifiable? *Exceptional Children, 35,* 5–22.

DuPaul, G. J., & Barkley, R. A. (1990). Medication therapy. In R. A. Barkley (Ed.), *Attention deficit hyperactivity disorder: A handbook for diagnosis and treatment* (pp. 573–612). New York: Guilford Press.

DuPaul, G. J., & Rapport, M. D. (1993). Does methylphenidate normalize the classroom performance of children with attention deficit disorder? *Journal of the American Academy of Child and Adolescent Psychiatry, 32*(1), 190–198.

Dupont, R. L., & Saylor, K. E. (1992). Depressant substances in adolescent medicine. *Pediatrics in Review, 13*(10), 381–386.

Durand, V. M., & Carr, E. G. (1987). Social influences on "self-stimulatory" behavior: Analysis and treatment application. *Journal of Applied Behavior Analysis, 20,* 119–132.

Durlak, J. (1979). Comparative effectiveness of para-professional and professional helpers. *Psychological Bulletin, 86,* 80–92.

Dworkin, R. H. (1994). Pain insensitivity in schizophrenia: A neglected phenomenon and some implications. *Schizophrenia Bulletin, 20,* 235–248.

Dworkin, S. F., & Wilson, L. (1993). Somatoform pain disorder and its treatment. In D. L. Dunner (Ed.), *Current psychiatric therapy* (pp. 320–328). Philadelphia: W. B. Saunders Co.

Dykens, E. M., Hodapp, R. M., & Leckman, J. F. (1994). *Behavior and development in fragile X syndrome. Sage Series on Developmental Clinical Psychology and Psychiatry (No. 28).* Newbury Park, CA: Sage.

Dykens, E. M, Hodapp, R. M., & Evans, D. W. (1994). Profiles and development of adaptive behavior in males with fragile X syndrome. *Journal of Autism and Developmental Disorders, 23,* 135–145.

D'Zurilla, T. J., & Goldfried, M. R. (1971). Problem solving and behavior modification. *Journal of Abnormal Psychology, 78,* 107–126.

Eagle, M. (1984). *Recent developments in psychoanalysis: A critical evaluation.* New York: McGraw-Hill.

Eaker, E. D., Abbott, R. D., Kannel, W. B. (1989). Frequency of uncomplicated angina pectoris in Type A compared with Type B persons (the Framingham Study). *American Journal of Cardiology, 63,* 1042–1045.

Eaker, E. D., Pinsky, J., Castelli, W. P. (1992). Maintenance of safer sexual behaviors and predictors of risky sex: The San Francisco Men's Health Study. *American Journal of Public Health, 80,* 973–977.

Earls, F., Escobar, J. I., Manson, S. M. (1990). Suicide in minority groups: Epidemiologic and cultural perspectives. In S. J. Blumenthal & D. J. Kupfer (Eds.), *Suicide over the life cycle: Risk factors, assessment, and treatment of suicide patients* (pp. 571–598). Washington, DC: American Psychiatric Press.

Eaton, W. W. (1986). Epidemiology of schizophrenia. *Epidemiology Review, 7,* 105–126.

Eaton, W. W., & Keyl, P. M. (1990). Risk factors for the onset of Diagnostic Interview Schedule/DSM-III agoraphobia in a prospective, population-based study. *Archives of General Psychiatry, 47,* 819–824.

Eberlin, M., McConnachie, G., Ibel, S., & Volpe, L. (1993). Facilitated communication: A failure to replicate the phenomenon. *Journal of Autism and Developmental Disorders, 23*(3), 507–530.

Eckert, E. D., Bouchard, T. J., Bohlen, J., & Heston, L. L. (1986). Homosexuality in monozygotic twins reared apart. *British Journal of Psychiatry, 148,* 421–425.

Edelstein, B. A., & Michelson, L. (Eds.) (1986). *Handbook of prevention.* New York & London: Plenum.

Egbert, L., Battit, G., Welch, C., & Bartlett, M. (1964). Reduction of postoperative pain by encouragement and instruction of patients. *New England Journal of Medicine, 270,* 825–827.

Egel, A. L., & Powers, M. D. (1989). Behavioral parent training: A view of the past and suggestions for the future. In M. J. Begab (Ed.), *The treatment of severe behavior disorders: Behavior analysis approaches* (pp. 153–173). Washington, DC: American Association on Mental Retardation.

Egeland, J. A., Gerhard, D. S., Pauls, D. L., Susses, J. N., Kidd, K. K., Allen, C. R., Hostetter, A. M., & Housman, D. E. (1987). Bipolar affective disorders linked to DNA markers on chromosome 11. *Nature, 325,* 783–787.

Ehlers, C. L., & Schuckit, M. A. (1990). EEG fast frequency activity in sons of alcoholics. *Biol Psychiatry, 27*(6), 631–641.

Eiler, K., Schaefer, M. R., Salstrom, D., & Lowery, R. (1995). Double-blind comparison of bromocriptine and placebo in cocaine withdrawal. *American Journal of Drug and Alcohol Abuse, 21*(1), 65–79.

Ekstrand, M. L., & Coates, T. J. (1990). Maintenance of safer sexual behaviors and predictors of risky sex: The San Francisco Men's Health Study. *American Journal of Public Health, 80,* 973–977.

Elia, J., Gulotta, C., Rose, S. R., Marin, G., & Rapoport, J. L. (1994). Thyroid function and attention-deficit hyperactivity disorder. *Journal of the American Academy of Child and Adolescent Psychiatry, 33*(2), 169–172.

Elkin, I. (1994). The NIMH treatment of depression collaborative research program: Where we began and where we are. In A. E. Bergin & S. L. Garfield (Eds.), *Handbook of psychotherapy and behavior change* (4th ed., pp. 114–139). New York: John Wiley and Sons.

Elkin, I., Gibbons, R. D., Shea, M. T., & Sotsky, S. M. (1995). Initial severity and different treatment outcomes in the National Institute of Mental Health Treatment of Depression Collaborative Research Program. *Journal of Clinical and Consulting Psychology, 63,* 841–847.

Elkin, I., Shea, M. T., Watkins, J. T., Imber, S. D., Sotsky, S. M., Collins, J. F., Glass, D. R., Pilkonis, P. A., Leber, W. R., Docherty, J. P., Fiester, S. J., & Parloff, M. B. (1989). National Institute of Mental Health Treatment of Depression Collaborative Research Program. General ef-

fectiveness of treatments. *Archives of General Psychiatry, 46,* 971–982.

Ellickson, P. L., Hays, R. D., & Bell, R. M. (1992). Stepping through the drug use sequence: Longitudinal scalogram analysis of initiation and regular use. *Journal of Abnormal Psychology, 101*(3), 441–451.

Ellinwood, E. H., Easier, M. E., Linnoila, M., Molter, D., Heatherly, D., & Bjornsson, T. (1983). Effects of oral contraceptives and diazepam-induced psychomotor impairment. *Clinical Pharmacology and Therapeutics, 35,* 360–366.

Elliott, D., Huizinga, D., & Ageton, S.S. (1985). *Multiple problem youth: Delinquency, substance use, and mental health problems.* New York: Springer-Verlag.

Ellis, A. (1962). *Reason and emotion in psychotherapy.* New York: Lyle Stuart.

Ellis, A. (1973). Rational-emotive therapy. In R. Corsini (Ed.), *Current psychotherapies* (pp. 167–206). Itasca, IL: F. E. Peacock.

Emerich, D. F., Cahill, D. W., and Sanberg, P. R. (1994). Excitotoxic lesions of the neostriatum as an animal model of Huntington's disease. In M. L. Woodruff & A. J. Nonneman (Eds.), *Neurotoxin-induced animal models of neurological disorders.* New York: Plenum.

Emmelkamp, P. (1982). *Phobic and obsessive-compulsive disorders: theory, research and practice.* New York: Plenum.

Emrick, C., Tonigan, J. S., Montgomery, H., & Little, L. (1993). Alcoholics Anonymous: What is currently known? In B. S. McCrady & W. R. Miller (Eds.), *Research on Alcoholics Anonymous: Opportunities and alternatives* (pp. 41–76). New Brunswick, NJ: Alcohol Research Documentation, Rutgers, The State University of New Jersey.

Epstein, E. E., & McCrady, B. S. (1994). Introduction to the special section: Research on the nature and treatment of alcoholism—Does one inform the other? *Journal of Consulting and Clinical Psychology, 62*(6), 1091–1095.

Erikson, E. (1946). Ego development and historical change. *The psychoanalytic study of the child* (Vol. 2, pp. 359–396). New York: International Universities Press.

Erlenmeyer-Kimling, L. E., & Cornblatt, B. (1987). The New York high-risk project: A follow-up report. *Schizophrenia Bulletin, 13,* 451–461.

Erlenmeyer-Kimling, L. E., Squires-Wheeler, E., Adamo, U., Bassett, A. S., Cornblatt, B., Kestenbaum, C. J., Rock, D., Roberts, S. A., & Gottesman, I. I. (1995). The New York High Risk Project: Psychoses and cluster A personality disorders in offspring of schizophrenic patients at 23 years of follow-up. *Archives of General Psychiatry, 52,* 857–865.

Ernst, N. D., & Harlan, W. R. (1991). Obesity and cardiovascular disease in minority populations: Executive summary. Conference highlights, conclusions, and recommendations. *American Journal of Clinical Nutrition, 53,* 1507S-1511S.

Escobar, J. I., Burnam, M. A., Karno, M., Burnam, M. A., & Wells, K. B. (1987). Somatization in the community. *Archives of General Psychiatry, 44,* 713–718.

Esterling, B. A., Antoni, M. H., Fletcher, M. A., Margulies, S., & Schneiderman, N. (1994). Emotional disclosure through writing or speaking modulates latent Epstein-Barr virus antibody titers. *Journal of Consulting and Clinical Psychology, 62,* 130–140.

Evans, S. W., & Pelham, W. (1991). Psychostimulant effects on academic and behavioral measures of ADHD junior high school students in a lecture format classroom. *Journal of Abnormal Child Psychology, 19,* 537–552.

Exner, J. E. (1993). *The Rorschach: A comprehensive system: Basic foundations* (3rd ed). New York: John Wiley & Sons.

Eyberg, S. (1988). Parent-child interaction therapy: Integration of traditional and behavioral concerns. *Child and Family Behavior Therapy, 10*(1), 33–46.

Eysenck, H. J. (1964). *Crime and personality.* Boston: Houghton Mifflin.

Eysenck, H. J., & Grossarth-Maticek, R. (1991). Creative novation behaviour therapy as a prophylactic treatment for cancer and coronary heart disease (Part II): Effects of treatment. *Behaviour Research & Therapy, 29,* 17–31.

Eysenck, H. J., & Rachman, S. (1965). *The causes and cures of neurosis.* San Diego, CA: Knapp.

Ezquiaga, E., Gutierrez, J. L. A., & Lopez, A. G. (1987). Psychosocial factors and episode number in depression. *Journal of Affective Disorders, 12,* 135–138.

Faber, R. (1994). Neuropsychiatric assessment. In C. E. Coffey & J. L. Cummings (Eds.). *Textbook of geriatric neuropsychiatry* (pp. 99–109). Washington, DC: American Psychiatric Press.

Fahey, T. A., Abas, M., & Brown, J. C. (1989). Multiple personality: A symptom of psychiatric disorder. *British Journal of Psychiatry, 154,* 99–101.

Fairbairn, W. R. D. (1952). *Psychoanalytic studies of the personality.* London: Tavistock Publications/Routledge & Kegan Paul.

Fairbanks, J. A., & Brown, T. A. (1987). Current behavioral approaches to the treatment of post-traumatic stress disorder. *The Behavior Therapist, 3,* 57–64.

Fairburn, C. G., Jones, R., Peveler, R. C., Hope, R. A., & O'Connor, M. (1993). Psychotherapy and bulimia nervosa: Longer-term effects of interpersonal psychotherapy, behavior therapy, and cognitive behavior therapy. *Archives in General Psychiatry, 50*(6), 419–428.

Fairweather, G., Sanders, D., Maynard, H., Cressler, D. L., & Bleck, P. S. (1969). *Community life for the mentally ill: An alternative to institutional care.* Chicago: Aldine Publishing Co.

Fallon, A., & Rozin, P. (1985). Sex differences in perception of desirable body size. *Journal of Abnormal Psychology, 94,* 102–105.

Falloon, I., Boyd, J., McGill, C., Williamson, M., Razani, J., Moss, H., Gilderman, A., & Simpson, G. (1985). Family management in the prevention of morbidity of schizophrenia: Clincial outcome of a two year longitudinal study. *Archives of General Psychiatry, 42,* 887–896.

Fals-Stewart, W., Marks, A., & Schafer, J. (1993). A comparison of behavioral group therapy and individual behavior therapy in treating obsessive-compulsive disorder. *Journal of Nervous and Mental Disease, 181,* 189–193.

Faravelli, C., Pallanti, S., Biondi, F., & Parerniti, S. (1992). Onset of panic disorder. *American Journal of Psychiatry, 149,* 827–828.

Faris, R. E. L., & Dunham, H. W. (1939). *Mental disorders in urban areas.* Chicago: University of Chicago Press.

Farrington, D. P. (1991). Childhood aggression and adult violence: Early precursors and later-life outcomes. In D. J. Pepler & K. H. Rubin (Eds.), *The development of childhood aggression* (pp. 5–29). Hillsdale, NJ: Erlbaum.

Fawzy, F. I., Cousins, N., Fawzy, N., Kemeny, M. E., Elashoff, R., & Morton, D. (1990). A structured psychiatric intervention for cancer patients. I: Changes over time in methods of coping and affective disturbance. *Archives of General Psychiatry, 47,* 720–725.

Fawzy, F. I., Fawzy, N. W., Arndt, L. A., & Pasnau, R. O. (1995). Critical review of psychosocial interventions in cancer care. *Archives of General Psychiatry, 52,* 100–113.

Fawzy, F. I., Fawzy, N. W., Hyun, C. S., Guthrie, D., Fahey, J. L., & Morton, D. (1993). Malignant melanoma: Effect of an early structured psychiatric intervention, coping and affective state on recurrence and survival 6 years later. *Archives of General Psychiatry, 50,* 681–689.

Federal Task Force on Homelessness and Severe Mental Illness (1992). *Outcasts on Main Street.* Washington, DC: Interagency Council on the Homeless.

Feighner, J. (1987). The impact of anxiety therapy on patients' quality of life. *The American Journal of Medicine, 82,* (Suppl. 5A), 14–19.

Feighner, J., Merideth, C., & Hendrickson, G. (1982). A double blind comparison of buspirone and diazepam in outpatients with generalized anxiety disorder. *Journal of Clinical Psychiatry, 43,* 103–107.

Feldman, H. A., Goldstein, I., Hatzichristou, D. G., Krane, R. J., & Mckinlay, J. (1994). Impotence and its medical and psychological correlates: Results of the Massachusetts Male Aging Study. *Journal of Urology, 151,* 54–61.

Feldman, H. A., Goldstein, I., Hatzichristou, D. G. (1994). Impotence and its medical and psychosocial correlates: Results of the Massachusetts male aging study. *Journal of Urology, 151,* 54.

Feldman-Summers, S., & Jones, G. (1984). Psychological impacts of sexual contact between therapists and other health care professionals and their clients. *Journal of Consulting and Clinical Psychology, 52,* 1054–1061.

Felner, R. D., Farber, S. S., & Primavera, J. (1983). Transitions and stressful life events: A model for primary prevention. In R. D. Felner, L. A. Jason, J. N. Moritsugu, & S. S. Farber (Eds.), *Preventive psychology: Theory, research, and prevention* (pp. 191–215). New York: Pergamon Press.

Felner, R. D., Jason, L. A., Moritsugu, J. N., & Farber, S. S. (Eds.). (1983). *Preventive psychology: Theory, research and practice.* New York: Pergamon Press.

Fenton, W., & McGlashan, T. (1991a) Natural history of schizophrenia subtypes: I. Longitudinal study of paranoid, hebephrenic, and undifferentiated schizophrenia. *Archives of General Psychiatry, 48,* 969–977.

Fenton, W., & McGlashan, T. (1991b) Natural history of schizophrenia subtypes II: Positive and negative symptoms and long term course. *Archives of General Psychiatry, 48,* 978–986.

Ferretti, R. P., Cavalier, A. R., Murphy, M. J., & Murphy, R. (1993). The self-management of skills by persons with mental retardation. *Research in Developmental Disabilities, 14*(3), 189–205.

Fichter, M. M., Leibl, K., Rief, W., Brunner, E., Schmidt-Auberger, S., & Engel, R. R. (1991). Fluoxetine versus placebo: A double-blind study with bulimic inpatients undergoing intensive psychotherapy. *Pharmacopsychiatry, 24*(1), 1–7.

Field, T. M., Schanberg, S. M., Scafidi, F., Bauer, C. R., Vega-Lahr, N., Garcia, R., Nystrom, J., & Kuhn, C. M. (1986). Tactile/kinesthetic stimulation effects on preterm neonates. *Pediatrics, 77*(5), 654–658.

Filipek, P., & Kennedy, D. (1991). Magnetic resonance imaging: Its role in the developmental disorders. In D. Duane & D. Gray (Eds.), *The reading brain: The biological basis of dyslexia* (pp. 133–160). Parkton, MD: York Press.

Fine, S., Forth, A., Gilbert, M., Haley, G. (1991). Group therapy for adolescent depressive disorder: A comparison of social skills and therapeutic support. *Journal of American Academy of Child Adolescent Psychiatry, 30,* 79–85.

Fingarette, H. (1988). *Heavy drinking: The myth of alcoholism as a disease.* Berkeley: University of California Press.

Fink, M. (1990). How does convulsive therapy work? *Neuropsychopharmacology, 3,* 73–82.

Fink, M. (1993). Who should get ECT? In C. E. Coffey (Ed.), *The clinical science of electroconvulsive therapy* (pp. 3–16). Washington, DC: American Psychiatric Press.

Fink, M. (1994). Indications for the use of ECT. *Psychopharmacology Bulletin, 30,* 269–275.

Finkel, N. J. (1989). The Insanity Defense Reform Act of 1984—Much ado about nothing. *Behavioral Sciences and the Law, 7,* 403–419.

Finkelhor, D. (1994). The international epidemiology of child sexual abuse. *Child Abuse and Neglect, 18,* 409–418.

Finkelhor, D., Hotaling, G., Lewis, I. A., & Smith, C. (1990). Sexual abuse in a national survey of adult men and women: Prevalence, characteristics, and risk factors. *Child Abuse and Neglect, 14,* 19–28.

Finn, P. R., Zeitouni, N. C., & Pihl, R. O. (1990). Effects of alcohol on psychophysiological hyperreactivity to non-aversive and aversive stimuli in men at high risk for alcoholism. *Journal of Abnormal Psychology, 99*(1), 79–85.

Fischer, C. T. (1989). A life-centered approach to psychodiagnostics: Attending to lifworld, ambiguity, and possibility. *Person-Centered Review, 4,* 163–170.

Fischer, M., Barkley, R. A., Fletcher, K. E., & Smallish, L. (1993). The adolescent outcome of hyperactive children: Predictors of psychiatric, academic, social, and emotional adjustment. *Journal of the American Academy of Child and Adolescent Psychiatry, 32*(2), 324–332.

FitzGerald, S. (1995, August 22). Nuns find way to keep giving—after death. *The Philadelphia Inquirer,* pp. A1, A6.

Fleming, I., Baum, A., Davidson, L. M., Rectanus, E., & McArdle, S. (1987). Chronic stress as a factor in psychologic reactivity to challenge. *Health Psychology, 6,* 221–238.

Foa, E. B., & Kozak, M. J. (1986). Emotional processing of fear: Exposure to corrective information. *Psychological Bulletin, 99,* 20–35.

Foa, E. B., Hearst-Ikeda, D., & Perry, K. J. (1995). Evaluation of a brief cognitive-behavioral program for the prevention of chronic PTSD in recent assault victims. *Journal of Consulting and Clinical Psychology, 63,* 948–955.

Foa, E. B., Riggs, D. S., Massie, E. D., & Yarczower, M. (1995). The impact of fear activation and anger on the efficacy of exposure treatment for posttraumatic stress disorder. *Behavior Therapy, 26,* 487–500.

Foa, E. B., Rothbaum, B. O., Riggs, D. S., & Murdock, T. B. (1991). Treatment of posttraumatic stress disorder in rape victims: A comparison between cognitive-behavioral procedures and counseling. *Journal of Consulting and Clinical Psychology, 59,* 715–723.

Foa, E. B., Steketee, G., & Olasov-Rothbaum, B. (1989). Behavioral/cognitive conceptualizations of post-traumatic stress disorder. *Behavior Therapy, 20,* 155–176.

Foa, E. B., Steketee, G., & Rothbaum, B. O. (1989). Behavior/cognitive conceptualization of PTSD. *Behavior Therapy, 20,* 155–176.

Foa, E. B., Zinbarg, R., & Olasov-Rothbaum, B. (1992). Uncontrollability and unpredictability in post-traumatic stress disorder: An animal model. *Psychological Bulletin, 112,* 218–238.

Folkman, S., & Lazarus, R. S. (1980). An analysis of coping in a middle-aged community sample. *Journal of Health & Social Behavior, 21,* 251–262.

Folstein, M. F., Folstein, S. E., & McHugh, P. R. (1975). 'Mini-Mental State': A practical method for grading the cognitive state of patients for the clinician. *Journal of Psychiatric Research, 12,* 189–198.

Folstein, S., & Rutter, M. (1977). Infantile autism: A genetic study of 21 twin pairs. *Journal of Child Psychology and Psychiatry, 18,* 297–321.

Fontaine, P., & Ansseau, M. (1995). Pharmaco-clinical aspects of methadone: Literature review of its importance in treatment of substance dependence. *Encephale, 21,* 167–179.

Ford, C. V. (1995). Dimensions of somatization and hypochondriasis. *Neurologic Clinics, 12,* 241–253.

Ford, D. E., & Kamerow, D. B. (1989). Epidemiologic study of sleep disturbances and psychiatric disorder: An opportunity for prevention? *Journal of the American Medical Association, 262,* 1479–1484.

Ford, M., & Widiger, T. (1989). Sex bias in the diagnosis of histrionic and antisocial personality disorders. *Journal of Consulting and Clinical Psychology, 57,* 301–305.

Ford v. Wainwright, 477 U.S. 399 (1986).

Fordyce, W. E. (1976). *Behavioral methods for chronic pain and illness.* St. Louis: Mosby.

Forehand, R. L., & McMahon, R. J. (1981). *Helping the noncompliant child: A clinician's guide to parent training.* New York: Guilford Press.

Fortmann, S. P., & Killen, J. D. (1995). Nicotine gum and self-help treatment for smoking relapse prevention: Results from a trial using population-based recruitment. *Journal of Consulting and Clinical Psychology, 63,* 460–468.

Foster, G. D., & Kendall, P. C. (1994). The realistic treatment of obesity: Changing the scales of success. *Clinical Psychology Review, 14,* 701–736.

Foucha v. Louisiana, 112 S. Ct. 1780 (1992).

Foulks, F. F., Bland, I. J., & Shervington, D. (1995). Psychotherapy across cultures. *Review of Psychiatry, 14,* 511.

Fowler, A. (1988). Determinants of rate of language growth in children with Down syndrome. In L. Nadel (Ed.), *The psychobiology of Down syndrome* (pp. 217–245). Cambridge: MIT Press.

Foy, D., Sipprelle, R., Rueger, D., & Carroll, E. (1984). Etiology of post-traumatic stress disorder in Vietnam veterans: Analysis of premilitary, military, and combat exposure influences. *Journal of Consulting and Clinical Psychology, 52,* 79–87.

France, K. G., & Hudson, S. M. (1992). Management of infant sleep disturbance: A review. *Clinical Psychology Review, 13,* 635–648.

Francis, J., Martin, D., & Kapoor, W. N. (1990). A prospective study of delirium in hospitalized elderly. *Journal of the American Medical Association, 263,* 1097–1101.

Frank, E. (1981). How prevalent is lack of sexual desire in marriage? *Medical Aspects of Human Sexuality, 15,* 74–79.

Frank, E., Kupfer, D., Perel, J., Cornes, C., Jarrett, D. Mallinger, A., Thase, M., McEachran, A., & Grochocinski, V. (1990). Three-year outcomes for maintenance therapies in recurrent depression. *Archives of General Psychiatry, 47,* 1093–1099.

Frank, E., Prien, R., Kupfer, D., & Alberts, L. (1985). Implications of non-compliance on research in affective disorders. *Psychopharmacology Bulletin, 21,* 37–42.

Frank, J. D. (1957). Some determinants, manifestations, and effects of cohesiveness in therapy groups. *International Journal of Group Psychotherapy, 7,* 53–63.

Frank, J. D. (1973). *Persuasion and healing* (rev. ed.). Baltimore: Johns Hopkins University Press.

Frankl, V. (1967). *Psychotherapy and existentialism: Selected papers on logotherapy.* New York: Washington Square Press.

Franklin, J. E. (1989). Alcoholism among Blacks. *Hospital and Community Psychiatry, 40,* 1120–1127.

Frassica, J. J., Orav, E. J., Walsh, E. P., & Lipshultz, S. E. (1994). Arrhythmias in children prenatally exposed to cocaine. *Archives of Pediatrics and Adolescent Medicine, 148*(11), 1163–1169.

Free, N., Winget, C., & Whitman, R. (1993). Separation anxiety in panic disorder. *American Journal of Psychiatry, 150,* 595–599.

Freeman, H. (1994). Schizophrenia and city residence. *British Journal of Psychiatry, 164* (Suppl. 23), 39–50.

Freeman, T. (1971). Observations on mania. *International Journal of Psychoanalysis, 52,* 479–486.

Freud, A. (1946). *The ego and mechanisms of defense.* New York: International Universities Press.

Freud, S. (1901). *The psychopathology of everyday life.* New York: Macmillan.

Freud, S. (1917/1957). Mourning and melancholia. In J. Strachey (Ed.), *Collected works of Sigmund Freud: Third standard edition.* Vol. 14. London: Hogarth Press.

Freud, S. (1933/1965). *New introductory lectures on psychoanalysis.* New York: W. W. Norton.

Freud, S. (1936/1963). *The problem of anxiety.* New York: W. W. Norton.

Freud, S. (1938). *The basic writings of Sigmund Freud.* New York: Modern Library.

Freund, B., Foa, E., Kozak, M., & Hembree, E. (1991, November). *Comparisons of OCD treatment outcome among* clomipramine, fluvoxamine, placebo, and behavior therapy. Presented at the 25th annual meeting of the Association for Advancement of Behavior Therapy, New York.

Frezza, M., Di Padova, C., Pozzato, G., Terpin, M., Baraona, E., & Lieber, C. S. (1990). High blood alcohol levels in women: The role of decreased gastric alcohol dehydrogenase activity and first-pass metabolism. *New England Journal of Medicine, 322*(2), 95–99.

Friedman, H. S., & Booth-Kewley, S. (1987). The "disease-prone personality." *American Psychologist, 42,* 539–555.

Friedman, H. W., Tucker, J. S., Schwartz, J. E., Tomlinson-Keasey, C., Martin, L. R., Wingard, D. L., & Criqui, M. H. (1995). Psychosocial and behavioral predictors of longevity: The aging and death of the "Termites." *American Psychologist, 50,* 69–78.

Friedman, M. J., & Southwick, S. M. (1995). Towards pharmacotherapy for post-traumatic stress disorder. In M. J. Friedman, D. S. Charney, & A. Y. Deutch (Eds.), *Neurobiological and clinical consequences of stress: From normal adaptation to PTSD* (pp. 465–481). Philadelphia: Lippincott-Raven.

Friedman, M., & Rosenman, R. H. (1974). *Type A behavior and your heart.* New York: Knopf.

Friedman, M., Thoresen, C. E., Gill, J., Ulmer, D., Powell, L. H., Price, V. A., Brown, B., Thompson, L., Rabin, D. D., Breall, W. S., Bourg, W., Levy, R., & Dixon, T. (1986). Alteration of Type A behavior and its effect on cardiac recurrences in post-myocardial infarction patients: Summary results on the Recurrent Coronary Prevention Project. *American Heart Journal, 112,* 653–665.

Friedman, M., & Ulmer, D. (1984). *Treating type A behavior and your heart.* New York: Fawcett Crest.

Friedman, R., Sandler, J., Hernandez, M., & Wolfe, D. (1981). Child abuse. In E. J. Marsh & L. G. Terdal (Eds.), *Behavioral assessment of childhood disorders* (pp. 221–255). New York: Guilford Press.

Friedrich, W. N., Beilke, R. L., & Urquiza, A. J. (1987). Children from sexually abusive families: A behavior comparison. *Journal of Interpersonal Violence, 2,* 391–402.

Friedrich, W. N., Beilke, R. L., & Urquiza, A. J. (1988). Behavior problems in young sexually abused boys: A comparison study. *Journal of Interpersonal Violence, 3,* 21–28.

Frischholz, E. J., Lipman, L. S., Braun, B. G., & Sachs, R. G. (1992). Psychopathology, hypnotizability, and dissociation. *American Journal of Psychiatry, 149,* 1521–1525.

Fromm-Reichmann, F. (1948). Notes on the development of treatment of schizophrenics by psychoanalytic psychotherapy. *Psychiatry, 11,* 263–273.

Fromme, K., Marlatt, G. A., Baer, J. S., & Kivlahan, D. R. (1994). The Alcohol Skills Training Program: A group intervention for young adult drinkers. *Journal of Substance Abuse Treatment, 11*(2), 143–154.

Fuchs, D., & Fuchs, L. S. (1994). Inclusive schools movement and the radicalization of special education reform. *Exceptional Children, 60*(4), 294–309.

Fulero, S., & Finkel, N. J. (1991). Barring ultimate issue testimony: An "insane" rule? *Law and Human Behavior, 15,* 495–508.

Fuller, R. K., Branchey, L., Brightwell, D. R., Derman, R. M., James, K. E., Lacoursiere, R. B., Lee, K. K., Lowenstam, I., Maany, I., Neiderheiser, D., Nocks, J. J., & Shaw, S. (1986). Disulfiram treatment of alcoholism: A Veterans Administration cooperative study. *Journal of the American Medical Association, 256*(11), 1449–1455.

Fuller, S. C. (1912). Alzheimer's disease (senium praecox): The report of a case and review of published cases. *Journal of Nervous and Mental Disease, 39,* 440–455; 536–557.

Furby, L., Weinrott, M. R., Blackshaw, L. (1989). Sex offender recidivism: A review. *Psychological Bulletin, 105,* 3–30.

Gabrielli, W. F., Jr., Mednick, S. A., Volavka, J., Pollock, V. E., Schulsinger, F., & Itil, T. M. (1982). Electroencephalograms in children of alcoholic fathers. *Psychophysiology, 19*(4), 404–407.

Gadow, K. D. (1992). Pediatric psychopharmacotherapy: A review of recent research. *Journal of Child Psychology and Psychiatry and Allied Disciplines, 33*(1), 281–300.

Gadow, K. D. (1993). Prevalence of drug therapy. In J. S. Werry & M. G. Aman (Eds.), *Practitioner's guide to psychoactive drugs for children and adolescents* (pp. 57–74). New York: Plenum.

Gadow, K. D., Sverd, J., Sprafkin, J., Nolan, E. E., & Ezor, S. N. (1995). Efficacy of methylphenidate for attention-deficit hyperactivity disorder in children with tic disorder. *American Journal of Psychiatry, 152,* 444–455.

Gadpaille, W. J. (1995). Homosexuality and homosexual behavior. In H. I. Kaplan & B. J. Sadock (Eds.), *Comprehensive textbook of psychiatry/VI* (pp. 1321–1333). Baltimore: Williams & Wilkins.

Gaffney, G. R., Kuperman, S., Tsai, L. Y., & Minchin, S. (1989). Forebrain structure in infantile autism. *Journal of the American Academy of Child and Adolescent Psychiatry, 28,* 534–537.

Galaburda, A. M., Menard, M. T., & Rosen, G. D. (1994). Evidence for aberrant auditory anatomy in developmental dyslexia. *Proceedings of the National Academy of Sciences of the United States of America, 91*(17), 8010–8013.

Galaburda, A. M., Wang, P. P., Bellugi, U., & Rossen, M. (1994). Cytoarchitectonic anomalies in a genetically based disorder: Williams syndrome. *Neuroreport, 5*(7), 753–757.

Galanter, M. (1988). Zealous self-help groups as adjuncts to psychiatric treatment: A study of Recovery, Inc. *American Journal of Psychiatry, 145,* 1248–1253.

Galin, D., Diamond, R., & Braff, D. (1977). Lateralization of conversion symptoms: More frequent on the left. *American Journal of Psychiatry, 134,* 578–580.

Gallagher-Thompson, D., Hanley-Peterson, P., & Thompson, L. W. (1990). Maintenance of gains versus relapse following brief psychotherapy for depression. *Journal of Consulting and Clinical Psychology, 58,* 371–374.

Galloway, G. P., Newmeyer, J., Knapp, T., Stalcup, S. A., & Smith, D. (1994). Imipramine for the treatment of cocaine and methamphetamine dependence. *Journal of Addictive Diseases, 13*(4), 201–216.

Galluscio, E. H. (1990). *Biological psychology.* New York: Macmillan.

Gapstur, S. M., Potter, J. D., Sellers, T. A., & Folsom, A. R. (1992). Increased risk of breast cancer with alcohol consumption in postmenopausal women. *American Journal of Epidemiology, 136,* 1221–1231.

Garber, J., Braafladt, N., & Zeman, J. (1991). The regulation of sad affect: An information-processing perspective. In J. Garber & K. A. Dodge (Eds.), *The development of emotion regulation and dysregulation* (pp. 208–242). New York: Cambridge University Press.

Gardner, H. (1993). *Multiple intelligences: The theory in practice.* New York: Basic Books.

Gardner, W., Lidz, C. W., Mulvey, E. P., & Shaw, E. C. (1996). A comparison of actuarial methods for identifying repetitively violent patients. *Law and Human Behavior, 20,* 35–48.

Garfield, S. L. (1994). Research on client variables in psychotherapy. In A. E. Bergin & S. L. Garfield, *Handbook of psychotherapy and behavior change* (pp. 190–228). New York: John Wiley & Sons.

Garfield, S. L., & Kurtz, R. (1976). Clinical psychologists in the 1970s. *American Psychologist, 31,* 1–9.

Garland, A. F., & Zigler, E. (1993). Adolescent suicide prevention: Current research and social policy implications. *American Psychologist, 48,* 169–182.

Garner, D. M., Garfinkel, P. E., Schwartz, D., & Thompson, M. (1980). Cultural expectations of thinness in women. *Psychological Reports, 47,* 483–491.

Gath, A. (1977). The impact of an abnormal child upon the parents. *British Journal of Psychiatry, 130,* 405–410.

Gatz, M., & Pearson, C. G. (1988). Ageism revised and the provision of psychological services. *American Psychologist, 43,* 184–188.

Geller, B., Fox, L. W., Fletcher, M. (1993). Effect of tricyclic antidepressants on switching to mania and on the onset of bipolarity in depressed 6- to 12-year olds. *Journal of American Academy Child Adolescent Psychiatry, 32,* 43–50.

Gelles, R. (1980). A profile of violence toward children in the United States. In G. Gerbner, C. J. Ross, & E. Ligler (Eds.), *Child abuse: An agenda for action* (pp. 82–105). New York: Oxford University Press.

Gelles, R. J., & Straus, M. A. (1988). *Intimate violence.* New York: Simon & Schuster.

Gendlin, E. T. (1981). *Focusing* (2nd ed.). New York: Bantam Books.

George, M., Trimble, M., Ring, H., Sallee, F., & Robertson, M. (1993). Obsessions in obsessive-compulsive disorder with and without Gilles de la Tourette's syndrome. *American Journal of Psychiatry, 150,* 93–97.

Gershon, E. S., Berretini, W. H., & Goldin, L. R. (1989). Mood disorders: Genetic aspects. In H. I. Kaplan & B. J. Sadock (Eds.), *Comprehensive textbook of psychiatry V* (pp. 879–887). Baltimore: Williams & Wilkins.

Gershon, E. S., Hamovit, J. H., Guroff, J. J., Nurnberger, J. I. (1987). Birth-cohort changes in manic and depressive disorders in relatives of bipolar and schizoaffective patients. *Archives of General Psychiatry, 44,* 314–319.

Geschwind, N., & Levitsky, W. (1968). Human brain: Left-right asymmetries in temporal speech region. *Science, 161,* 186–187.

Gibbons, F. X. (1986). Social comparison and depression: Company's effect on misery. *Journal of Personality and Social Psychology, 51,* 140–149.

Gibbs, C. J., Gajdusek, D. C., Asher, D. M., Alpers, M. P., Beck, E., Daniel, P. M., & Matthews, W. B. (1968). Creutzfeldt-Jacob disease (spongiform encephalopathy): Transmission to the chimpanzee. *Science, 161,* 388–389.

Giblin, P. (1986). Research and assessment in marriage and family enrichment: A meta-analysis study. *Journal of Psychotherapy and the Family, 2,* 79–96.

Gilbert, P. (1992). *Depression: The evaluation of powerlessness.* New York: Guilford Press.

Gilbert, P. L., Harris, M. J., McAdams, L. A., & Jeste, D. (1995). Neuroleptic withdrawal in schizophrenic patients. *Archives of General Psychiatry, 52,* 173–187.

Gislason, I. L. (1988). Eating disorders in childhood (ages 4 through 11 years). In B. J. Blinder, B. F. Chaitin, & R. Goldstein (Eds.), *The eating disorders* (pp. 285–293). PMA Publishing Corporation.

Gittelman, R., & Klein, D. F. (1980). Separation anxiety in school refusal and its treatment with drugs. In L. Hersov & I. Berg (Eds.), *Out of school.* New York: John Wiley & Sons.

Gittelman, R. & Klein, D. F. (1985). Childhood separation anxiety and adult agoraphobia. In A. Tuma & J. Maser (Eds.), *Anxiety and the anxiety disorders.* Hillsdale, NJ: Erlbaum.

Givelber, D. J., Bowers, W. J., & Blitch, C. L. (1984). *Tarasoff,* myth and reality: An empirical study of private law reaction. *Wisconsin Law Review, 1984,* 443–497.

Givens, B. S., & Breese, G. R. (1990). Electrophysiological evidence that ethanol alters function of medial septal area without affecting lateral septal function. *Journal of Pharmacology and Experimental Therapeutics, 253*(1), 95–103.

Glaser, R., Rice, J., Sheridan, J., Fertel, R., Stout, J. C., Speicher, C. E., Pinsky, D., Kotur, M., Post, A., Beck, M., & Kiecolt-Glaser, J. K. (1987). Stress-related immune suppression: Health implications. *Brain, Behavior, and Immunity, 1,* 7–20.

Glatt, A. E., Zinner, S. H. & McCormack, W. M. (1990). The prevalence of dyspareunia. *Obstetrics and Gynecology, 75,* 433–436.

Glazer, W., Moore, D., Schooler, N., Brenner, L., & Morgenstern, H. (1984). Tardive dyskinesia: A discontinuation study. *Archives of General Psychiatry, 41,* 623–627.

Gleaves, D. H. (1996). The sociocognitive model of dissociative identity disorder: A reexamination of the evidence. *Psychological Bulletin, 120,* 42–59.

Gleick, J. (1978, August 21). Getting away with murder. *New Times,* 21–27.

Goetz, R., Klein, D., Gully, R., Kahn, J., Leibowitz, M., Fyer, A., & Gorman, J. (1993). Panic attacks during placebo procedures in the laboratory. *Archives of General Psychiatry, 50,* 280–295.

Goisman, R. M., Warshaw, M. G., Steketee, G. S., Fierman, E. J., Rogers, M. P., Goldenberg, I., Weinshenker, N. J., Vasile, R. G., & Keller, M. B. (1995). DSM-IV and the disappearance of agoraphobia without a history of panic disorder: New data on a controversial diagnosis. *American Journal of Psychiatry, 152,* 1438–1443.

Gold, N. (1993). Depression and social adjustment in siblings of boys with autism. *Journal of Autism and Developmental Disorders, 23,* 147–164.

Goldbloom, D. S., & Olmsted, M. P. (1993). Pharmacotherapy of bulimia nervosa with fluoxetine: Assessment of clinically significant attitudinal change. *American Journal of Psychiatry, 150*(5), 770–774.

Golden, C. J., Purisch, A. D., & Hammeke, T. A. (1985). *Luria-Nebraska Neuropsychological Battery: Forms I and II Manual.* Los Angeles: Western Psychological Services.

Golden, D. (1994, July). Building a better brain. *Life,* 63–70.

Golden, G. (1987). Neurological functioning. In D. Cohen & A. Donnellan (Eds.), *Handbook of autism and pervasive developmental disorders* (pp. 133–147). New York: John Wiley & Sons.

Goldfried, M. R. (1980). Toward the delineation of therapeutic change principles. *American Psychologist, 24,* 991–999.

Goldman, M. S., Brown, S. A., & Christiansen, B. A. (1987). Expectancy theory: Thinking about drinking. In H. T. Blane & K. E. Leonard (Eds.), *Psychological theories of drinking and alcoholism* (pp. 181–226). New York: Guilford Press.

Goldsmith, S. J., Fyer, M., & Frances, A. (1990). Personality and suicide. In S. J. Blumenthal & D. J. Kupfer (Eds.), *Suicide over the life cycle: Risk factors, assessment, and treatment of suicidal patients* (pp. 155–176). Washington, DC: American Psychiatric Press.

Goldstein, A. & Chambless, D. (1978). A reanalysis of agoraphobia. *Behavior Therapy, 9,* 47–59.

Goldstein, M. J. (1985). Family factors that antedate the onset of schizophrenia and related disorders: The results of a 15-year prospective longitudinal study. *Acta Psychiatrica Scandinavica Suppl.um, 319,* 7–18.

Goldstein, M. J. (1988). Gender differences in the course of schizophrenia. *American Journal of Psychiatry, 145,* 684–689.

Goldstein, M. J., & Rodnick, E. (1975). The family's contribution to the etiology of schizophrenia: Current status. *Schizophrenia Bulletin, 14,* 48–63.

Golombok, S., & Tasker, F. (1996). Do parents influence the sexual orientation of their children? Findings from a longitudinal study of lesbian families. *Developmental Psychology, 32,* 3–11.

Gonsiorek, J. C., Sell, R. L., & Weinrich, J. D. (1995). Definition and measurement of sexual orientation. *Suicide and Life Threatening Behavior* (Suppl. 25), 40–51.

Goodman, G., & Poillion, M. J. (1992). ADD: Acronym for any dysfunction or difficulty. *The Journal of Special Education, 26*(1), 37–56.

Goodwin, F. K., & Jamison, K. R. (1990). *Manic-depressive illness.* New York: Oxford University Press.

Goodyear, P., & Hynd, G. W. (1992). Attention-deficit disorder with (ADD/H) and without (ADD/WO) hyperactivity: Behavioral and neuropsychological differentiation. *Journal of Clinical Child Psychology, 21*(3), 273–305.

Gorelick, P. B., & Mangone, C. A. (1991). Vascular dementias in the elderly. In J. Biller (Ed.), *Clinics in geriatric medicine: Cerebrovascular disorders in the 1990's, 7*, 599–615. Philadelphia: W. B. Saunders Co.

Gorenstein, E. E., & Newman, J. P. (1980). Disinhibitory psychopathology: A new perspective and a model for research. *Psychological Review, 87*, 301–315.

Gorman, J., Leibowitz, M., Fryer, A., & Stein, J. (1989). A neuroanatomical hypothesis for panic disorder. *American Journal of Psychiatry, 146*, 148–161.

Gottesman, I. I. (1991). *Schizophrenia genesis: The origins of madness.* New York: Freeman.

Gottesman, I. I., & Bertelsen, A. (1989). Confirming unexpressed genotypes for schizophrenia: Risks in the offspring of Fischer's Danish identical and fraternal discordant twins. *Archives of General Psychiatry, 46*, 867–872.

Gottesman, I. I., & Shields, J. (1972). *Schizophrenia and genetics: A twin study vantage point.* New York: Academic Press.

Gottfredson, L. S. (1994). The science and politics of race-norming. *American Psychologist, 49*, 955–963.

Gottlieb, B. H., & Peters, L. (1991). A national demographic portrait of mutual aid group participants in Canada. *American Journal of Community Psychology, 19*, 651–666.

Gough, H. (1987). *California Psychological Inventory: Administrator's guide.* Palo Alto, CA: Consulting Psychologists Press.

Gould, M. A., Otto, M. W., & Pollack, M. H. (1995). A meta-analysis of treatment outcome for panic disorder. *Clinical Psychology Review, 15*, 819–844.

Gould, M. S. (1990). Suicide clusters and medial exposure. In S. J. Blumenthal & D. J. Kupfer (Eds.), *Suicide over the life cycle: Risk factors, assessment, and treatment of suicidal patients* (pp. 517–532). Washington, DC: American Psychiatric Press.

Gould, R. A., & Clum, G. A. (1995). Self-help plus minimal therapist contact in the treatment of panic disorder: A replication and extension. *Behavior Therapy, 26*, 533–546.

Graden, J., Thurlow, M., & Ysseldyke, J. (1983). Instructional ecology and academic responding time for students at three levels of teacher-perceived behavioral competence. *Journal of Experimental Child Psychology, 36*, 241–256.

Grady, C. L., McIntosh, A. R., Horwitz, B., Maisog, J. M., Ungerleider, L. G., Mentis, M. J., Pietrini, P., Schapiro, M. B., & Haxby, J. V. (1995). Age-related education in human recognition memory due to impaired encoding. *Science, 269*, 218–221.

Grant, B. F., DeBakey, S., & Zobeck, T. S. (1991). *Liver cirrhosis mortality in the United States, 1973–1988.* (NIAAA Surveillance Report No. 18. DHHS Pub. No. (ADM) 281-89-0001.) Washington, DC: Supt. of Docs., U.S. Government Printing Office.

Grant, B. F., Harford, T. C., Dawson, D. A., Chou, P., Dufour, M., & Pickering, R. (1994). Prevalence of DSM-IV alcohol abuse and dependence: United States, 1992. *NIAAA's Epidemiologic Bulletin No. 35, 18*(3), 243–248.

Gray, J. (1981). A critique of Eysenck's theory of personality. In H. Eysenck (Ed.), *A model for personality* (pp. 246–276). New York: Springer-Verlag.

Green, A. R., Cross, A. J., & Goodwin, G. M. (1995). Review of the pharmacology and clinical pharmacology of 3,4-methylenedioxymethamphetamine (MDMA or "Ecstasy"). *Psychopharmacology, 119*(3), 247–260.

Green, B., Grace, M., Lindy, J., Gleser, G., & Leonard, A. C. (1990). Risk factors for PTSD and other diagnoses in a general sample of Vietnam Veterans. *American Journal of Psychiatry, 147*, 729–733.

Green, B. L., Grace, M. C., & Lindy, J. D., Titchener, J. L., & Lindy, J. G. (1983). Levels of functional impairment following a civilian disaster: The Beverly Hills Supper Club fire. *Journal of Consulting and Clinical Psychology, 51*, 573–580.

Green, R. (1974). *Sexual identity conflict in children and adults.* New York: Basic Books.

Green, R. (1987). *The "sissy boy syndrome" and the development of homosexuality.* New Haven, CT: Yale University Press.

Green, R., & Blanchard (1995). Gender identity disorders. In H. I. Kaplan & B. J. Sadock (Eds.), *Comprehensive textbook of psychiatry/VI* (pp. 1345–1360). Baltimore: Williams & Wilkins.

Green, R. & Fleming, D. T. (1990). Transsexual surgery follow-up: Status in the 1990s. *Annual Review of Sex Research, 1*, 163–174.

Greenberg, L. S. (1986). Change process research. *Journal of Consulting and Clinical Psychology, 54*, 4–9.

Greenberg, L. S., Elliott, R. K., & Lietaer, G. (1994). Research on experiential psychotherapies. In A. E. Bergin & S. L. Garfield (Eds.), *Handbook of psychotherapy and behavior change* (pp. 509–539). New York: John Wiley & Sons.

Greenberg, M. T., Speltz, M. L., DeKlyen, M., & Endriga, M. C. (1991). Attachment security in preschoolers with and without externalizing problems: A replication. *Developmental Psychopathology, 3*, 413–430.

Greenberg, M. T., Speltz, M. L., & DeKlyen, M. (1993). The role of attachment in the early development of disruptive behavior problems. *Development and Psychopathology, 5*, 191–213.

Greenberg, L. S., & Johnson, S. M. (1988). *Emotionally focused couples therapy.* New York: Guilford Press.

Greenberg, W. M., Shah, P. J., & Seide, M. (1993). Recidivism on an acute psychiatric forensic service. *Hospital & Community Psychiatry, 44*, 583–585.

Greenblatt, D., Harmatz, J., & Shader, R. I. (1993). Plasma alprazolam concentrations: Relation to efficacy and side effects in the treatment of panic disorder. *Archives of General Psychiatry, 50*, 715–732.

Grimes, K., & Walker, E. F. (1994). Childhood emotional expressions, educational attainment, and age at onset of illness in schizophrenia. *Journal of Abnormal Psychology, 103*, 784–790.

Grof, P., Angst, J., Haines, T. (1974). The clinical course of depression: Practical issues. In J. Angst (Ed.), *Classification and prediction of outcome of depression.* New York Symposia Medical Hoeschst 8, F. K. Schattauer Verlag.

Grossarth-Maticek, R., & Eysenck, H. J. (1991). Creative novation behaviour therapy as a prophylactic treatment for cancer and coronary heart disease. Part I: Description of treatment. *Behaviour Research & Therapy, 29*, 1–16.

Grossberg, G. T., & Nakra, R. (1988). The diagnostic dilemma of depressive pseudodementia. In R. Strong, W. G., Wood & W. J. Burke (Eds.), *Aging: Vol. 33. Central nervous system disorders of aging: Clinical intervention and research.* (pp. 107–115). New York: Raven Press.

Grossman, H. J. (Ed.). (1973). *Manual on terminology and classification in mental retardation.* Washington, DC: American Association on Mental Deficiency.

Grossman, P. B., & Hughes, J. N. (1992). Self-control interventions with internalizing disorders: A review and analysis. *School Psychology Review, 21*(2), 229–245.

Groth-Marnat, G., & Edkins, G. (1996). Professional psychologists in general health care settings: A review of the financial efficacy of direct treatment interventions. *Professional Psychology: Research and Practice, 27*, 161–174.

Grunhaus, L., & Pande, A. C. (1994). Electroconvulsive therapy for severe depressive disorder. In L. Grunhaus & J. F. Greden (Eds.), *Severe depressive disorders* (pp. 297–330). Washington, DC: American Psychiatric Press.

Guerra, N. G., Huesmann, L. R., Tolan, P. H., Acker, R. V., Eron, L. D. (1995). Stressful events and individual beliefs as correlates of economic disadvantage and aggression among urban children. *Journal of Consulting and Clinical Psychology, 63,* 518–528.

Gur, R. C., & Gur, R. E. (1995). Hypofrontality in schizophrenia: RIP. *The Lancet, 345,* 1383–1384.

Gur, R. E., & Pearlson, G. D. (1993). Neuroimaging in schizophrenia research. *Schizophrenia Bulletin, 19,* 337–353.

Gusella, J. F., Wexler, N. S., Conneally, P. M. et al. (1983). A polymorphic DNA marker genetically linked to Huntington's disease. *Nature, 306,* 234–238.

Guze, S. B. (1993). Genetics of Briquets' syndrome and somatization disorder. A review of family, adoption, and twin studies. *Annals of Clinical Psychiatry, 5,* 225–230.

Haaga, D. A., Dyck, M. J., Ernst, D. (1991). Empirical status of cognitive theory of depression. *Psychological Bulletin, 110,* 215–236.

Hafner, H., Maurer, K., Fatkenheuer, B., An Der Heiden, W., Riecher-Rossler, A., Behrens, S., & Gattz, W. (1994). The epidemiology of early schizophrenia: Influence of age and gender on onset and early course. *British Journal of Psychiatry, 164* (Suppl.), 29–38.

Halikas, J. A. (1993). Treatment of drug abuse syndromes. *Psychiatric Clinics of North America, 16*(4), 693–702.

Halikas, J. A., Meller, J., Morse, C., & Lyttle, M. D. (1990). Predicting substance abuse in juvenile offenders: Deficit disorder versus aggressivity. *Child Psychiatry & Human Development, 21,* 49–55.

Hall, G. C., & Hirschman, R. (1991). Toward a theory of sexual aggression: A quadripartite model. *Journal of Consulting and Clinical Psychology, 59,* 662–669.

Hall, G. C., Shondrick, D. D., & Hirschman, R. (1993). The role of sexual arousal in sexually aggressive behavior: A meta-analysis. *Journal of Consulting and Clinical Psychology, 61,* 1091–1095.

Hall, G. C., & Proctor, W. C. (1987). Criminological predictors of recidivism in a sexual offender population. *Journal of Consulting and Clinical Psychology, 55,* 111–112.

Hall, G. C. (1990). Prediction of sexual aggression. *Clinical Psychology Review, 10,* 229–245.

Halvorsen, J. G., & Metz, M. E. (1992). Sexual dysfunction. Part I: Classification, etiology, and pathogenesis. *Journal of the American Board of Family Practitioners, 5,* 51–61.

Halweg, K., & Markman, H. J. (1988). Effectiveness of behavioral marital therapy: Empirical status of behavioral techniques in preventing and alleviating marital distress. *Journal of Consulting and Clinical Psychology, 56*(3), 440–447.

Hamer, D. H., Hu, S., Magnuson, V. L., Hu, N., & Pattatucci, A. M. L. (1993). A linkage between DNA markers on the X chromosome and the male sexual orientation. *Science, 261,* 321–327.

Hamilton, M. (1989). Mood disorders: Clinical features. In H. I. Kaplan and B. J. Sadock (Eds.), *Comprehensive textbook of psychiatry V* (Vol. 1). Baltimore: Williams & Wilkins.

Hammen, C. (1992). Cognitive, life stress, and interpersonal approaches to a developmental psychopathology model of depression. *Development and Psychopathology, 4,* 189–206.

Hammen, C., & Goodman-Brown, T. (1990). Self-schemas and vulnerability to specific life stress in children at risk for depression. *Cognitive Therapy and Research, 14,* 215–227.

Hammen, C., Marks, T., Mayol, A., & deMayo, T. (1985). Depressive self-schemas, life stress, and vulnerability to depression. *Journal of Abnormal Psychology, 94,* 308–319.

Hammill, D. D., Leigh, J. E., McNutt, G., & Larsen, S. C. (1981). A new definition of learning disabilities. *Learning Disabilities Quarterly, 4,* 336–342.

Handelsman, M. M., & Galvin, M. D. (1988). Facilitating informed consent for outpatient psychotherapy: A suggested written format. *Professional Psychology: Research and Therapy, 19,* 223–225.

Hansen, D. J., St. Lawrence, J. S., & & Christoff, K. A. (1989). Group conversational-skills training with inpatient children and adolescents. *Behavior Modification, 3,* 4–31.

Hansen, L., Salmon, D., Mashliah, E., Katzman, R., DeTeresa, R., Thal, L., Pay, M., Hoffstetter, R., Klauber, M., Rice, V., Butters, N. & Alford, M. (1990). The Lewy body variant of Alzheimer's disease: A clinical and pathological entity. *Neurology, 40,* 1–8.

Hansen, W. B. (1994). School-based substance abuse prevention: A review of the state of the art in curriculum. *Health Education Research.*

Hansen, W. B., & Graham, J. W. (1991). Preventing alcohol, marijuana, and cigarette use among adolescents: Peer pressure resistance training versus establishing conservative norms. *Preventive Medicine, 20*(13), 414–430.

Hanson, K. A., & Gidycz, C. A. (1993). Evaluation of a sexual assault prevention program. *Journal of Consulting and Clinical Psychology, 61,* 1046–1052.

Hanson, R. K., Steffy, R. A., & Gauthier, R. (1993). Long-term recidivism of child molesters. *Journal of Consulting and Clinical Psychology, 61,* 646–652.

Harbin, T. J. (1989). The relationship between the Type A behavior pattern and physiological responsivity: A quantitative review. *Psychophysiology, 26,* 110–119.

Harburg, E., Davis, D. R., & Caplan, R. (1982). Parent and offspring alcohol use. *Journal of Studies on Alcohol, 43,* 497–516.

Hare, R. D., Hart, S. D., & Harpur, T. J. (1991). Psychopathy and the DSM-IV criteria for antisocial personality disorder. *Journal of Abnormal Psychology, 100,* 391–398.

Hare, R. D., & McPherson, L. M. (1984). Psychopathy and perceptual asymmetry during verbal dichotic listening. *Journal of Abnormal Psychology, 93,* 141–149.

Hare, R. D., McPherson, L. M., & Forth, A. E. (1988). Male psychopaths and their criminal careers. *Journal of Consulting and Clinical Psychology, 56,* 710–714.

Harpur, T. J., & Hare, R. D. (1994). Assessment of psychopathy as a function of age. *Journal of Abnormal Psychology, 103,* 604–609.

Harrington, R. (1992). Annotation: The natural history and treatment of child and adolescent affective disorders. *Journal of Child Psychology and Psychiatry, 33*(8), 1287–1302.

Harris, K. B., & Miller, W. R. (1990). Behavioral self-control training for problem drinkers: Components of efficacy. *Psychology of Addictive Behaviors, 4*(2), 82–90.

Harris, M. J., & Jeste, D. V. (1988). Late-onset schizophrenia: An overview. *Schizophrenia Bulletin, 14,* 39–55.

Hart, S. D., Kropp, P. R., & Hare, R. D. (1988). Performance of male psychopaths following conditional release from prison. *Journal of Consulting and Clinical Psychology, 56,* 227–232.

Hartman, H. (1958). *Ego psychology and the problem of adaptation.* New York: International Universities Press.

Hartnoll, R. L. (1994). Opiates: Prevalence and demographic factors. *Addiction, 89*(11), 1377–1383.

Harvard Medical School. (1995, February, March). Update on Alzheimer's disease. Part I, Part II. *The Harvard Mental Health Letter, 11,* 1–5, 1–5.

Harvey, P. D., Mohs, R., & Davidson, M. (1993). Leukotomy and aging in chronic schizophrenia: A follow-up study 40 years after psychosurgery. *Schizophrenia Bulletin, 19,* 723–732.

Hattie, J. A., Sharpley, C. F., & Rogers, H. J. (1984). Comparative effectiveness of professional and paraprofessional helpers. *Psychological Bulletin, 95,* 534–541.

Havassy, B. E., Wasserman, D. A., & Hall, S. M. (1995). Social relationships and abstinence from cocaine in an American treatment sample. *Addiction, 90*(5), 699–710.

Haynes, S. G., Feinleib, M., & Kannel, W. B. (1980). The relationahip of psychosocial factors to coronary heart disease in the Framingham study: III. Eight-year incidence of coronary heart disease. *American Journal of Epidemiology, 111,* 37–58.

Hazelrigg, M. D., Cooper, H. M., & Boudin, C. M. (1987). Evaluating the effectiveness of family therapies: An integrative review and analysis. *Psychological Bulletin, 101,* 428–442.

Hazlett, E. A., Dawson, M. E., Buchsbaum, M. S., & Nuechterlein, K. H. (1993). Reduced regional brain glucose metabolism assessed by positron emission tomography in electrodermal nonresponder schizophrenics: A pilot study. *Journal of Abnormal Psychology, 102,* 39–46.

Heber, R. (1961). Modifications in the manual on terminology and classification in mental retardation. *American Journal on Mental Deficiency, 65,* 499–500.

Heckler, S. (1994). Facilitated communication: A response by Child Protection. *Child Abuse and Neglect: The International Journal, 18*(6), 495–503.

Heilbrun, A. B. (1993). Multifactorial theories of hallucinations. In C. G. Costello (Ed.), *Symptoms of Schizophrenia* (pp. 56–91). New York: John Wiley & Sons.

Heilbrun, K. S. (1987). The assessment of competence for execution: An overview. *Behavioral Sciences and the Law, 5,* 383–396.

Heiman, J. (1993). Sexual dysfunctions. In D. L. Dunner (Ed.), *Current psychiatric therapy* (pp. 346–353). Philadelphia: W. B. Saunders Co.

Heiman, J., & Grafton-Becker, V. (1989). Orgasmic disorders in women. In S. R. Leiblum & R. C. Rosen (Eds), *Principles and practice of sex therapy: Update for the 1990s* (pp. 51–88). New York: Guilford Press.

Heiman J., & LoPiccolo, J. (1988). *Becoming orgasmic: A sexual and personal growth program for women* (2nd ed.). New York: Prentice Hall.

Heimberg, R. G., Dodge, C. S., Hope, D. A., Kennedy, C. R., & Zollo, I. J. (1990). Cognitive behavioral group treatment for social phobia: Comparison with a credible placebo control. *Cognitive Therapy & Research, 14,* 1–23.

Heinssen, R. K., Levendusky, P. G., & Hunter, R. H. (1995). Client as colleague: Therapeutic contracting with the seriously mentally ill. *American Psychologist, 50,* 522–532.

Heller, K. A., Holtzman, W. H., & Messick, S. (Eds.). (1982). *Placing children in special education: A strategy for equity.* Washington, DC: National Academy Press.

Heller, K. A., Swindle, R. W., Jr., & Dusenbury, L. (1986). Component social support processes: Comments and integration. *Journal of Consulting and Clinical Psychology, 54,* 466–470.

Hellerstein, D., Yanowitch, P., Rosenthal, J., Samstag, L. W., Maurer, M., Kasch, K., Burrows, L., Poster, M., Cantillon, M., & Winston, R. (1993). A randomized double-blind study of fluoxetine versus placebo in the treatment of dysthymia. *American Journal of Psychiatry, 150,* 1169–1175.

Helmes, E., & Reddon, J. R. (1993). A perspective on developments in assessing psychopathology: A critical review of the MMPI and MMPI-2. *Psychological Bulletin, 113,* 453–471.

Helzer, J. E., Canino, G. J., Yeh, E. K., Bland, R. C., Lee, C. K., Hwu, H. G., & Newman, S. (1990). Alcoholism—North America and Asia: A comparison of population surveys with the Diagnostic Interview Schedule. *Archives of General Psychiatry, 47,* 313–319.

Helzer, J. E., Robins, L. N., & McEvoy, L. (1987). Posttraumatic stress disorder in the general population. *New England Journal of Medicine, 317,* 1630–1634.

Henker, B., & Whalen, C. (1989). Hyperactivity and attention deficits. *American Psychologist, 44,* 216–223.

Henn, F. A. (1986). The neurobiologic basis of psychiatric illness. In G. Winokur and P. Clayton (Eds.), *The Medical Basis of Psychiatry* (pp. 461–485). Philadelphia: W. B. Saunders Co.

Henry, W. P., Strupp, H. H., Butler, S. F., Schacht, T. E., & Binder, J. L. (1993). Effects of training in time-limited dynamic psychotherapy: Changes in therapist behavior. *Journal of Consulting and Clinical Psychology, 61,* 434–440.

Herbert, T. B., & Cohen, S. (1993a). Stress and immunity in humans: A meta-analytic review. *Psychosomatic Medicine, 55,* 364–379.

Herbert, T. B., & Cohen, S. (1993b). Depression and immunity: A meta-analytic review. *Psychological Bulletin, 113,* 472–486.

Herbert, J. D., Hope, D. A., & Bellack, A. S. (1992). Validity of the distinction between generalized social phobia and avoidant personaltiy disorder. *Journal of Abnormal Psychology, 101,* 332–339.

Herd, D. (1989). The epidemiology of drinking patterns and alcohol-related problems among U.S. blacks. In D. Spiegler, D. Tate, S. Aitken, & C. Christian (Eds.), *Alcohol use among U.S. ethnic minorities: Proceedings of a conference on the epidemiology of alcohol use and abuse among ethnic minority groups* (NIAAA Research Monograph No. 18, DHHS Pub. No. (ADM) 89-1435, pp. 3–50). Washington, DC: Supt. of Docs., U.S. Government Printing Office.

Hermann, E. C., Dorwart, R. A., Hoover, C. W. & Brody, J. (1995). Variation in ECT use in the United States. *American Journal of Psychiatry, 152,* 869–875.

Herning, R. I., Glover, B. J., Koeppl, B., Phillips, R. L., & London, E. D. (1994). Cocaine-induced increases in EEG alpha and beta activity: Evidence for reduced cortical processing. *Neuropsychopharmacology, 11*(1), 1–9.

Herrnstein, R. J., & Murray, C. (1994). *The bell curve: Intelligence and class structure in American life.* New York: Free Press.

Hersen, M., & Bellack, A. S. (1976). Social skills training for chronic psychiatric patients: Rationale, research findings, and future directions. *Comprehensive Psychiatry, 17,* 559–580.

Herz, M. I., & Melville, C. (1980). Relapse in schizophrenia. *American Journal of Psychiatry, 137,* 801–805.

Hess, R. D., & McDevitt, T. M. (1984). Some cognitive consequences of maternal intervention techniques: A longitudinal study. *Child Development, 55*(6), 2017–2030.

Heston, L. L. (1966). Psychiatric disorders in foster home reared children of schizophrenic mothers. *British Journal of Psychiatry, 112,* 819–825.

Heston, L. L., & White, J. A. (1983). *Dementia: A practical guide to Alzheimer's disease and related illnesses.* New York: W. H. Freeman & Co.

Hibbard, J., & Pope, C. (1993). The quality of social roles as predictors of morbidity and mortality. *Social Science and Medicine, 36,* 217–225.

Higgins, S. T., Budney, A. J., Bickel, W. K., Foerg, F. E., & Badger, G. J. (1994). Alcohol dependence and simultaneous cocaine and alcohol use in cocaine-dependent patients. *Journal of Addictive Diseases, 13*(4), 177–189.

Higgins, S. T., Budney, A. J., Bickel, W. K., Hughes, J. R., Foerg, F., & Badger, G. (1993). Achieving cocaine abstinence with a behavioral approach. *American Journal of Psychiatry, 150,* 763–769.

Higgins, S. T., Delaney, D. D., Budney, A. J., Bickel, W. K., Hughes, J. R., Foerg, F., & Fenwick, J. W. (1991). A behavioral approach to achieving initial cocaine abstinence. *American Journal of Psychiatry, 148*(9), 1218–1224.

Hill, S. Y. (1992). Absence of paternal sociopathy in the etiology of severe alcoholism: Is there a Type III alcoholism? *Journal of Studies on Alcohol, 53*(2), 161–169.

Hinshaw, S. P. (1987). On the distinction between attentional deficits/hyperactivity and conduct problems/aggression in child psychopathology. *Psychological Bulletin, 101,* 443–463.

Hiroto, D. S., & Seligman, M. E. P. (1975). Generality of learned helplessness in man. *Journal of Personality and Social Psychology, 31,* 311–327.

Hirshfeld, D. R., Rosenbaum, J. F., Biederman, J., Bolduc, E. A., Faraone, S. V., Snidman, N., Reznick, F. S., & Kagan, J. (1992). Stable behavioral inhibition and its association with anxiety disorder. *Journal of the American Academy of Adolescent Psychiatry, 31*(1), 103–111.

Hirshfeld, R. M., & Goodwin, F. K. (1988). Mood disorders. In J. A. Talbot, R. E. Hales, & S. C. Yudofsky (Eds.), *Textbook of psychiatry*. Washington, DC: American Psychiatric Press.

Hite, S. (1976). *Hite report: A nationwide study on female sexuality*. New York: Macmillan.

Hobbs, S., & Goswick, R. (1977). Behavioral treatment of self-stimulation: An examination of alternatives to physical punishment. *Journal of Clinical Child Psychology, 6,* 20–23.

Hobson, R. P. (1989). On sharing experiences. *Development and Psychopathology, 1,* 197–205.

Hodapp, R. M. (1994). Cultural-familial mental retardation. In R. Sternberg (Ed.), *Encyclopedia of intelligence* (pp. 711–717). New York: Macmillan.

Hodapp, R. M., Burack, J. A., & Zigler, E. (Eds.). (1990). *Issues in the developmental approach to mental retardation*. New York: Cambridge University Press.

Hodapp, R. M., & Dykens, E. M. (1994). The two cultures of behavioral research in mental retardation. *American Journal on Mental Retardation, 97,* 675–687.

Hodapp, R. M., & Krasner, D. V. (1995). Families of children with disablties: Findings from a national sample of eighth-grade students. *Exceptionality, 5*(2), 71–81.

Hodapp, R. M., Leckman, J. F., Dykens, E. M., Sparrow, S. S., Zelinsky, D. G., & Ort, S. I. (1992). K-ABC profiles in children with fragile X syndrome, Down syndrome, and nonspecific mental retardation. *American Journal on Mental Retardation, 97,* 39–46.

Hodges, J. R. (1993). Pick's disease. In A. Burns & R. Levy (Eds.). *Dementia* (pp. 737–750). London: Chapman and Hall.

Hodges, J. R. (1994). Neurological aspects of dementia and normal aging. In F. A. Huppert, C. Brayne, & D. W. O'-Connor (Eds.), *Dementia and normal aging* (pp. 118–129). Cambridge: Cambridge University Press.

Hodgkinson, S., Sherrington, R., Gurling, H., Marchbanks, R., Reeders, S., Mallet, J., McInnis, M., Perursson, H., & Brynjolfsson, J. (1987). Molecular genetic evidence for heterogeneity in manic depression. *Nature, 325,* 805–806.

Hodiamont, P. (1991). How normal are anxiety and fear? *International Journal of Sociological Psychiatry, 37*(1), 43–50.

Hoelscher, T. J., Lichstein, K. L., & Rosenthal, T. L. (1986). Home relaxation practice in hypertension treatment: Objective assessment and compliance induction. *Journal of Consulting and Clinical Psychology, 54,* 217–221.

Hogarty, G., Anderson, C., Reiss, D., Kornblith, S., Greenwald, D., Javna, C., and Madonia, M. (1986). Family psychoeducation, social skills training, and maintenance chemotherapy in the aftercare treatment of schizophrenia. I: One-year effects of a controlled study on relapse and expressed emotion. *Archives of General Psychiatry, 43,* 633–642.

Hogarty, G. E., Kornblith, S. J., Greenward, D., DiBarry, A. L., Cooley, S., Flesher, S., Reiss, D., Carter, M., & Ulrich, R. (1995). Personal therapy: A disorder-relevant psychotherapy for schizophrenia. *Schizophrenia Bulletin, 21,* 379–393.

Hoien, T., Lundberg, I., Larsen, J., & Tonnessen, F. (1989). Profiles of reading related skills in dyslexic families. *Reading and Writing. An Interdisciplinary Journal, 1,* 381–392.

Hollander, E. & McCarley, A. (1992). Yohimbine treatment of sexual side effects induced by serotonin reuptake blockers. *Journal of Clinical Psychiatry, 53,* 207–209.

Hollister, L. E., & Csernansky, J. G. (1990). *Clinical pharmacology of psychotherapeutic drugs* (3rd ed.). New York: Churchill Livingstone.

Hollon, S. D. (1993). Review of psychosocial treatments for mood disorders. In D. D. Dunner (Ed.), *Current psychiatric therapy* (pp. 240–246). Philadelphia: W. B. Saunders Co.

Hollon, S. D., Shelton, R. C., & Davis, D. D. (1993). Cognitive therapy for depression: Conceptual issues and clinical efficacy. *Journal of Clinical and Consulting Psychology, 61,* 270–275.

Hollon, S. D., Shelton, R. C., & Loosen, P. T. (1991). Cognitive therapy and pharmacotherapy for depression. *Journal of Consulting and Clinical Psychology, 59,* 88–99.

Holmes, T. H., & Rahe, R. H. (1967). The social readjustment rating scale. *Journal of Psychosomatic Research, 11,* 213–218.

Holroyd, J., & Brodsky, A. M. (1977). Psychologists' attitudes and practices regarding erotic and nonerotic physical contact with patients. *American Psychologist, 32,* 843–849.

Holroyd, S., Rabins, P., Finkelstein, D., and Lavrisha, M. (1994). Visual hallucinations in patients from an ophthalmology clinic and medical clinic population. *Journal of Nervous and Mental Disease, 182,* 273–276.

Holtzman, P. S., Kringlen, E., Matthysse, S., Flanagan, S. D., Lipton, R. B., Cramer, S., Levin, S., Lange, K., & Levy, D. L. (1988). A single dominant gene can account for eye tracking dysfunctions and schizophrenia in offspring of discordant twins. *Archives of General Psychiatry, 45,* 641–647.

Holzer, C. E., Shae, B. M., Swanson, J. W. (1986). The increased risk for specific psychiatric disorders among persons of low socioeconomic status. *American Journal of Social Psychiatry, 4,* 259–271.

Homan, S., Lachenbruch, P., Winokur, G., Clayton, P. (1982). An efficacy study of electroconvulsive therapy and antidepressants in treatment of primary depression. *Psychological Medicine, 12,* 615–624.

Hooley, J. M. (1987). The nature and origins of expressed emotion. In K. Hahlweg & M. J. Goldstein (Eds.), *Understanding major mental disorder: The contribution of family interaction research* (pp. 176–194). New York: Family Process.

Horn, W. F., Ialongo, N. S., Pascoe, J. M., Greenberg, G., Packard, T., Lopez, M., Wagner, A., & Puttler, L. (1991). Additive effects of psychostimulants, parent training, and self-control therapy with ADHD children. *Journal of the American Academy of Child and Adolescent Psychiatry, 30*(2), 233–240.

Horvath, A. O., & Luborsky, L. (1993). The role of the therapeutic alliance in psychotherapy. *Journal of Consulting and Clinical Psychology, 61,* 561–573.

Horwath, E., Johnson, J., & Hornig, C. (1993). Epidemiology of panic disorder in African-Americans. *American Journal of Psychiatry, 150,* 465–469.

House, J. S., Landis, K. R., & Umberson, D. (1988). Social relationships and health. *Science, 241,* 540–545.

House, J. S., Robbins, C., & Metzner, H. L. (1982). The association of social relationships and activities with mortality: Prospective evidence from the Tecumseh Community Health Study. *American Journal of Epidemiology, 116,* 123–140.

Houts, A. C. (1991). Nocturnal enuresis as a biobehavioral problem. *Behavior Therapy, 22,* 133–151.

Houts, A. C., Peterson, J. K., & Whelan, J. P. (1986). Prevention of relapse in full-spectrum home training for primary enuresis: A components analysis. *Behavior Therapy, 17,* 462–469.

Howard, A., Pion, G. M., Gottfredson, G. D., Flattau, P. E., Oskamp, S., Pfafflin, S. M., Bray, D. W. (1986). The changing face of American psychology: A report from the Committee on Employment and Human Resources. *American Psychologist, 41,* 1311–1327.

Howard, K. I., Lueger, R. J., Maling, M. S., & Martinovich, Z. (1993). A phase model of psychotherapy outcome:

Causal mediation of change. *Journal of Consulting and Clinical Psychology, 61,* 678–685.

Howard, R. (1992). Folie à deux involving a dog. *American Journal of Psychiatry, 149,* 414.

Howard, R. C., & Clark, C. R. (1985). When courts and experts disagree: Discordance between insanity recommendations and adjudications. *Law and Human Behavior, 9,* 385–395.

Hsu, L. K. G. (1988). The etiology of anorexia nervosa. In B. J. Blinder, B. F. Chaitin, & R. Goldstein (Eds.), *The eating disorders* (pp. 239–246). PMA Publishing Corporation.

Huber, H., Karlin, R., & Nathan, P. E. (1976). Blood alcohol level discrimination by non-alcoholics: The role of internal and external cues. *Journal of Studies on Alcohol, 37,* 27–39.

Hucker, S. J. & Bain, J. (1990). Androgenic hormones and sexual assault. In W. L. Marshall, D. R. Laws, & H. E. Barbaree (Eds.), *Handbook of sexual assault* (pp. 93–102). New York: Plenum.

Hudson, A., Melita, B., & Arnold, N. (1993). A case study assessing the validity of facilitated communication. *Journal of Autism and Developmental Disorders, 23*(1), 165–173.

Hughes, P. H., Coletti, S. D., Neri, R. L., Urmann, C. F., Stahl, S., Sicilian, D. M., & Anthony, J. C. (1995). Retaining cocaine-abusing women in a therapeutic community: The effect of a child live-in program. *American Journal of Public Health, 85*(8), 1149–1152.

Hughlings-Jackson, J. (1875). A lecture on softening of the brain. *Lancet, ii,* 335–339.

Human Capital Initiative Coordinating Committee (1996). Reducing mental disorders: A behavioral science research plan for psychopathology. *American Psychological Society Observer,* February special issue.

Hunter, J., & Schaecher, R. (1995). Gay and lesbian adolescents. In R. L. Edwards & J. G. Hopps (Eds.), *Encyclopedia of Social Work, 19th Ed.* (pp. 1055–1063). Washington, DC: National Association of Social Workers.

Hunter, R. H. (1995). Benefits of competency-based treatment programs. *American Psychologist, 50,* 509–513.

Huppert, F. A., & Brayne, C. (1994). What is the relationship between dementia and normal aging? In F. A. Huppert, C. Brayne, & D. W. O'Connor (Eds.), *Dementia and normal aging* (pp. 3–14). Cambridge: Cambridge University Press.

Hurlbert, D. F. (1993). A comparative study using orgasm consistency training in the treatment of women reporting hypoactive sexual desire. *Journal of Sex and Marital Therapy, 19,* 41–55.

Hurt, H., Brodsky, N. L., Betancourt, L., Braitman, L. E., Malmud, E., & Giannetta, J. (1995). Cocaine-exposed children: Follow-up through 30 months. *Developmental and Behavioral Pediatrics, 16*(1), 29–35.

Hyler, S. E. (1998). DSM III at the cinema: Madness in the movies. *Comprehensive Psychiatry, 29,* 195–206.

Hynd, G. W., Hern, K. L., Voeller, K. K., & Marshall, R. M. (1991). Neurobiological basis of attention-deficit hyperactivity disorder (ADHD). *School Psychology Review, 20*(2), 174–186.

Hynd, G. W., & Semrud-Clikeman, M. (1989). Dyslexia and brain morphology. *Psychological Bulletin, 106,* 447–482.

Hynd, G. W., Semrud-Clikeman, M., Lorys, A. R., Novey, E. S., & Eliopulos, D. (1990). Brain morphology in developmental dyslexia, attention deficit disorder/hyperactivity. *Archives of Neurology, 47,* 919–926.

Hynd, G. W., Semrud-Clikeman, M., & Lyytinen, H. (1991). Brain imaging in learning disabilities. In J. E. Obrzut & G. W. Hynd (Eds.), *Neuropsychological foundations of learning disabilities: A handbook of issues, methods and practice* (pp. 475–511). New York: Academic Press.

Iacono, W. G. (1988). Eye movement abnormalities in schizophrenic and affective disorders. In C. W. Jhohnson & F. J. Pirozzolo (Eds.), *Neuropsychology of eye movements* (pp. 115–145). Hillsdale, NJ: Erlbaum.

Iacono, W. G., Moreau, M., Beiser, M., Fleming, J. A. E., & Lin, T. Y. (1992). Smooth-pursuit eye movement dysfunction and liability for schizophrenia: Implications for genetic modeling. *Journal of Abnormal Psychology, 101,* 104–116.

Inglehart, R. (1990). *Culture shift in advanced industrial society.* Princeton, NJ: Princeton University Press.

Ingram, R. E. (1990). Self-focused attention in clinical disorders: Review and a conceptual model. *Psychological Bulletin, 107,* 156–176.

Insel, T. R. (1992). Toward a neuroanatomy of obsessive-compulsive disorder. *Archives of General Psychiatry, 49,* 739–744.

Institute of Medicine. (1989). *Prevention and treatment of alcohol problems: Research opportunities.* Washington, DC: National Academy of Sciences.

Institute of Medicine (1994). *Reducing risks for mental disorders: Frontiers for prevention.* Washington, DC: National Academy Press.

Isen, A. M., Daubman, K. A., & Nowicki, G. P. (1987). Positive affect facilitates creative problem solving. *Journal of Personality and Social Psychology, 52,* 1122–1131.

Ito, T. A., Miller, N., & Pollock, V. E. (1996). Alcohol and aggression: A meta-analysis on the moderating effects of inhibitory cues, triggering events, and self-focused attention. *Psychological Bulletin, 120,* 60–82.

Jackson, D. N. (1989). *Basic Personality Inventory manual.* Port Huron, MI: Sigma Assessment Systems.

Jacobs, G. A. (1995). The development of a national plan for disaster mental health. *Professional Psychology: Research and Practice, 26,* 543–549.

Jacobs, M. K., & Goodman, G. (1989). Psychology and self-help groups: Predictions on a partnership. *American Psychologist, 44,* 536–545.

Jacobson, J. W., Mulick, J. A., & Schwartz, A. A. (1995). A history of facilitated communication: Science, pseudoscience, and antiscience. Science working group on facilitated communication. *American Psychologist, 50*(9), 750–765.

Jacobson, N. S. (1991). Behavioral versus insight-oriented marital therapy: Labels can be misleading. *Journal of Consulting and Clinical Psychology, 59*(1), 142–145.

Jacobson, N. S., & Follette, W. C. (1985). Clinical significance of improvement resulting from two behavioral marital therapy components. *Behavior Therapy, 16,* 249–262.

Jacobson, N. S., Holtzworth-Monroe, A., & Schmaling, K. B. (1989). Marital therapy and spouse involvement in the treatment of depression, agoraphobia, and alcoholism. *Journal of Consulting and Clinical Psychology, 57,* 5–10.

Jacobson, N. S., Schmaling, K. B., & Holtzworth-Munroe, A. (1987). Component analysis of behavioral marital therapy: 2-year follow-up and prediction of relapse. *Journal of Marital and Family Therapy, 13*(2), 187–195.

Jacobvitz, D., & Sroufe, L. A. (1987). The early caregiver-child relationship and attention-deficit disorder with hyperactivity in kindergarten: A prospective study. *Child Development, 58,* 1488–1495.

Jaffee v. *Redmond,* 133 L. 2d 758 (1996).

James, J. E. (1994). Chronic effects of habitual caffeine consumption on laboratory and ambulatory blood pressure levels. *Journal of Cardiovascular Risk, 1*(2), 159–164.

Jamison, K. R. (1989). Mood disorders and patterns of creativity in British writers and artists. *Psychiatry, 52,* 125–134.

Janicak, P., Sharma, R., Israni, T., Dowd, S., Altman, E., & Davis, J. (1991). Effects of unilateral-non-dominant vs. bilateral ECT on memory and depression: A preliminary report. *Psychopharmacology Bulletin, 27,* 353–357.

Janis, I. (1958). *Psychological stress: Psychoanalytic and behavioral studies of surgical patients.* New York: John Wiley & Sons.

Jann, M., Lam, T. W., & Chang, W. H. (1993). Haloperidol and reduced haloperidol plasma concentrations in different ethnic populations and interindividual variabilities in haloperidol metabolism. In K. M. Lin, R. Poland, & G. Nakasaki (Eds.), *Psychopharmacology and psychobiology of ethnicity.* Washington, DC: American Psychiatric Association Press.

Jarvis, E. (1844). Insanity among the coloured population of the free states. *American Journal of Mental Science, 7,* 71–83.

Jeffers, H. P. (1991). *Who killed precious.* New York: Pharos Books.

Jeffery, R. W. (1988). Dietary risk factors and their modification in cardiovascular disease. *Journal of Consulting and Clinical Psychology, 56,* 350–357.

Jellinek, E. M. (1946). The problem of alcohol. In Yale Studies on Alcohol (Ed.), *Alcohol, science, and society* (pp. 13–30). Westport, CT: Greenwood Press.

Jenike, M. A., Baer, L., Ballentine, T., Martuza, R., Tynes, S., Giriunas, I., Buttolph, M., & Cassem, N. (1991). Cingulotomy for refractory obsessive-compulsive disorder: A long-term follow-up of 33 cases. *Archives of General Psychiatry, 48,* 548–555.

Jenike, M. A., Hyman, S., Baer, L., Holland, A., Minichiello, W., Buttolph, L., Summergrad, P., Seymour, J. & Ricciardi, J. (1990). A controlled trial of fluvoxamine in obsessive-compulsive disorder: Implications for a serotonergic theory. *American Journal of Psychiatry, 147,* 1209–1215.

Jenkins, C. D., Zyzanski, S., & Rosenman, R. H. (1979). *The Jenkins Activity Survey.* New York: Psychological Corporation.

Jensen, J. P., Bergin, A. E., & Greaves, D. W. (1990). The meaning of eclecticism: New survey and analysis of components. *Professional Psychology: Research and Practice, 21,* 124–130.

Jessor, R., & Jessor, S. L. (1977). *Problem behavior and psychosocial development: A longitudinal study of youth.* San Diego: Academic Press.

Joe, G. W., Dansereau, D. F., & Simpson, D. D. (1994). Node-link mapping for counseling cocaine users in methadone treatment. *Journal of Substance Abuse, 6(4),* 393–406.

Johnson, S. L., & Roberts, J. E. (1995). Life events and bipolar disorder: Implications from biological theories. *Psychological Bulletin, 117,* 434–449.

Johnson, S. M., & Greenberg, L. S. (1985). Differential effects of experiential and problem-solving interventions in resolving marital conflict. *Journal of Consulting and Clinical Psychology, 53,* 175–184.

Jones, M. C. (1924). A laboratory study of fear. The case of Peter. *Pedagogical Seminary, 31,* 308–315.

Jorm, A. F. (1994). A method for measuring dementia as a continuum in community surveys. In F. A. Huppert, C. Brayne, & D. W. O'Connor (Eds.), *Dementia and normal aging* (pp. 244–253). Cambridge: Cambridge University Press.

Joseph, S., Williams, R., & Yule, W. (1995). Psychosocial perspectives on post-traumatic stress. *Clinical Psychology Review, 15,* 515–544.

Joyce, J. N., Shane, A., Lexow, N., Winokur, A., Casanova, M. F., & Kleinman, J. E. (1993). Serotonin uptake sites and serotonin receptors are altered in the limbic system of schizophrenics. *Neuropsychopharmacology, 8(4),* 315–336.

Julien, R. (1992). *A primer of drug action* (6th ed.). New York: Freeman.

Julien, R. (1995). *A primer of drug action* (7th ed.). New York: Freeman.

Kafka, M. P. (1994). Sertraline pharmacotherapy for paraphilias and paraphilia-related disorders: An open trial. *Annals of Clinical Psychiatry, 3,* 189–95.

Kagan, J. (1989). Temperamental contributions to social behavior. *American Psychologist, 44,* 668–674.

Kahn, A., Mirolo, H., Lai, H., Claypoole, K., Bierut, L., Malik, R., & Bhang, J. (1993). ECT and TRH: Cholinergic involvement in a cognitive deficit state. *Psychopharmacology Bulletin, 29,* 345–352.

Kahn, E. (1985). Heinz Kohut and Carl Rogers: A timely comparison. *American Psychologist, 40,* 893–904.

Kahn, J. S., Kehle, T. J., Jenson, W. R., & Clark, E. (1990). Comparison of cognitive-behavioral, relaxation and self-modeling interventions for depression among middle-school students. *School Psychology Review, 19,* 196–211.

Kahn, R., Jampala, V. C., Dong, K., & Vedak, C. (1994). Speech abnormalities in tardive dyskinesia. *American Journal of Psychiatry, 151,* 760–762.

Kahn, R. J., McNair, D., Lipman, R., Covi, L., Rickels, K., Fisher, S., & Frankenthaler, L. (1986). Imipramine and chlordiazepoxide in depressive and anxiety disorders. II: Efficacy in anxious outpatients. *Archives of General Psychiatry, 43,* 79–85.

Kaler, S. R., & Freeman, B. J. (1994). Analysis of environmental deprivation: Cognitive and social development in Romanian orphans. *Journal of Child Psychology and Psychiatry and Allied Disciplines, 35(4),* 769–781.

Kandel, D. B., & Andrews, K. (1987). Processes of adolescent socialization by parents and peers. *International Journal of Addiction, 22(4),* 319–342.

Kandel, D. B., Kessler, R. C., & Marguiles, R. Z. (1978). Antecedents of adolescent initiation into stages of drug use: A developmental analysis. In D. B. Kandel (Ed.), *Longitudinal research on drug use.* Washington, DC: Hemisphere.

Kandel, E. R., Schwartz, J. H., & Jessell, J. M. (1995). *Essentials of neural science and behavior.* Norwalk, CT: Prentice Hall.

Kane, J. M., Honigfeld, G., Singer, J. & Melzer, H., (1988). Clozapine for the treatment-resistant schizophrenic: A double-blind comparison with chlorpromazine. *Archives of General Psychiatry, 45,* 789–796.

Kane, J. M., & Lieberman, J. A. (1992). *Adverse effects of psychotropic drugs.* New York: Guilford Press.

Kanner, A. D., Coyne, J. C., Schaefer, C., & Lazarus, R. S. (1981). Comparison of two modes of stress measurement: Daily hassles and uplifts versus major life events. *Journal of Behavioral Medicine, 14,* 1–39.

Kanner, L. (1943). Autistic disturbances of affective contact. *Nervous Child, 2,* 217–230.

Kanner, L., & Lesser, L. (1958). *Early infantile autism: The pediatric clinics of North America.* Philadelphia: W. B. Saunders Co.

Kaplan, A. S., Garfinkel, P. E., Darby, P. L., & Garner, D. M. (1983). Carbamazepine in the treatment of bulimia. *American Journal of Psychiatry, 140,* 1225–1226.

Kaplan, H. I., Saddock, B. J., & Grebb, J. A. (1994). *Synopsis of psychiatry: Behavioral sciences, clinical psychiatry.* Baltimore: Williams & Wilkins.

Kaplan, H. S. (1974, October). Fiction and fantasy: Nonsense therapy for six sexual malfunctions. *Psychology Today,* 77–86.

Kaplan, H. S. (1977). Hypoactive sexual desire. *Journal of Sex and Marital Therapy, 3,* 3–9.

Kaplan, H. S. (1979). *Disorders of sexual desire.* New York: Brunner/Mazel.

Kaplan, H. S. (1988). Intimacy disorders and sexual panic states. *Journal of Sex and Marital Therapy, 14,* 3–12.

Kaplan, H. S., & Owett, T. (1993). The female androgen deficiency syndrome. *Journal of Sex & Marital Therapy, 19,* 3–24.

Kaplan, H., Wamboldt, R., & Barnhardt, R. (1986). Behavioral effects of dietary sucrose in disturbed children. *American Journal of Psychology, 7,* 143.

Kaplan, M. (1983). A woman's view of DSM-III. *American Psychologist, 38,* 786–792.

Kaplan, P. M. (1994). The use of serotonergic uptake inhibitors in the treatment of premature ejaculation. *Journal of Sex and Marital Therapy, 20,* 321–324.

Kapur, S., & Mann, J. J. (1993). Antidepressant action and the neurobiologic effects of ECT: Human studies. In C. E. Coffey (Ed.), *The clinical science of electroconvulsive therapy* (pp. 235–250). Washington, DC: American Psychiatric Press.

Karasek, R. A. (1979). Job demands, job decision latitude and mental strain: Implications for job redesign. *Administrative Science Quarterly, 24,* 285–308.

Karasu, T. B. (1990). Toward a clinical model of psychotherapy for depression. I: Systematic comparison of three psychotherapies. *American Journal of Psychiatry, 147,* 133–147.

Kardener, S. H., Fuller, M., & Mensch, I. N. (1973). A survey of physicians' attitudes and practices regarding erotic and non-erotic contact with patients. *American Journal of Psychiatry, 130,* 1077–1081.

Kartsounis, L. D., Poynton, A., Bridges, P. K., & Bartlett, J. R. (1991). Neuropsychological correlates of stereotaxic subcaudate tractotomy. *Brain, 114,* 2657–2673.

Katerndahl, D. A., & Realini, J. P. (1993). Lifetime prevalence of panic states. *American Journal of Psychiatry, 150,* 246–249.

Katon, W. (1993). Somatization disorder, hypochondriasis, and conversion disorder. In D. L. Dunner (Ed.), *Current psychiatric therapy* (pp. 314–320). Philadelphia: W. B. Saunders Co.

Katon, W., & Russo, J. (1989). Somatic symptoms and depression. *Journal of Family Practice, 29,* 65–69.

Katon, W., Von Korff, M., Lin, E., Liscomb, P., Russo, J., Wagner, E., & Polk, E. (1990). Distressed high utilizers of medical care. DSM-III-R diagnosis and treatment needs. *General Hospital Psychiatry, 12,* 355–362.

Katz, J. L., Boyar, R., Roffwarg, H., Hellman, L., & Weiner, H. (1978). Weight and circadian luteinizing hormone secretory pattern in anorexia nervosa. *Psychosomatic Medicine, 40,* 549–567.

Katzman, R., & Kawas, C. (1994). The epidemiology of dementia and Alzheimer's disease. In R. D. Terry, R. Katzman, & K. L. Bick (Eds.), *Alzheimer's disease* (pp. 105–121). New York: Raven Press.

Katzman, R., & Saitoh, T. (1991). Advances in Alzheimer's disease. *FASEB Journal, 5,* 278–286.

Kaufman, H. S., & Biren, P. L. (1977). Persistent reversers: Poor readers, writers, spellers? *Academic Therapy, 12,* 209–217.

Kavanagh, D. J. (1992). Recent developments in expressed emotion in schizophrenia. *British Journal of Psychiatry, 148,* 601–620.

Kawachi, I., Colditz, G. A., Ascherio, A., Rimm, E. B., Giovannucci, E., Stampfer, M. J., & Willett, W. C. (1993). Prospective study of phobic anxiety and risk of coronary heart disease in men. *Circulation, 89,* 1992–1997.

Kaye, W. H., & Weltzin, T. E. (1991). Neurochemistry of bulimia nervosa. *Journal of Clinical Psychiatry, 52,* 21–28.

Kazdin, A. E. (1973). Covert modeling and reduction of avoidance behavior. *Journal of Abnormal Psychology, 81,* 87–95.

Kazdin, A. E. (1994a). Psychotherapy for children and adolescents. In A. E. Bergin & S. L. Garfield (Eds.), *Handbook of psychotherapy and behavior change* (pp. 543–594). New York: John Wiley & Sons.

Kazdin, A. E. (1994b). Methodology, design, and evaluation in psychotherapy research. In A. E. Bergin & S. L. Garfield (Eds.), *Handbook of psychotherapy and behavior change* (pp. 19–71). New York: John Wiley & Sons.

Kazdin, A. E., Bass, D., Siegel, T., & Thomas, C. (1989). Cognitive-behavioral therapy and relationship therapy in the treatment of children referred for antisocial behavior. *Journal of Consulting and Clinical Psychology, 26, 57,* 522–535.

Kazdin, A. E., Esveldt-Dawson, K., French, N. H., & Unis, A. S. (1987). Problem-solving skills training and relationship therapy in the treatment of antisocial child behavior. *Journal of Consulting and Clinical Psychology, 55,* 76–85.

Kazdin, A. E., & Wilcoxin, L. A. (1976). Systematic desensitization and nonspecific treatment effects: A methodological evaluation. *Psychological Bulletin, 83,* 729–758.

Kazdin, A. E., & Wilson, G. T. (1978). *Evaluation of behavior therapy: Issues, evidence and research strategies.* Cambridge, MA: Ballinger.

Keane, T. M., Fairbank, J. A., Caddell, J. M., & Zimering, R. T. (1989). Implosive (flooding) therapy reduces symptoms of PTSD in Vietnam combat veterans. *Behavior Therapy, 20,* 245–260.

Keane, T. M., Zimering, R. T., & Caddell, J. (1985). A behavioral formulation of post-traumatic stress disorder in Vietnam veterans. *The Behavior Therapist, 8,* 9–12.

Keefe, F. J., Dunsmore, J., & Burnett, R. (1992). Behavioral and cognitive-behavioral approaches to chronic pain: Recent advances and future directions. *Journal of Consulting and Clinical Psychology, 60,* 528–536.

Keller, L. S., & Butcher, J. N. (1991). *Assessment of chronic pain patients with the MMPI-2.* Minneapolis: University of Minnesota Press.

Keller, M. B., Baker, L. A., & Russell, C. W. (1993). Classification and treatment of dysthymia. In D. D. Dunner (Ed.), *Current psychiatric therapy* (pp. 210–214). Philadelphia: W. B. Saunders Co.

Keller, M. B., Lavori, P. W., Mueller, T. I., Endicott, J., Coryell, W., Hirschfeld, R. M. A., Shea, T. (1992). Time to recovery, chronicity, and levels of psychopathology in major depression. A 5-year prospective follow-up of 431 subjects. *Archives of General Psychiatry, 49,* 809–816.

Kellner, C., Nixon, D., & Bernstein, H. (1991). ECT-drug interactions: A review. *Psychopharmacology Bulletin, 27,* 595–609.

Kelly, J. A., & Murphy, D. A. (1992). Psychological interventions with AIDS and HIV: Prevention and treatment. *Journal of Consulting and Clinical Psychology, 60,* 576–585.

Kelly, J. A., St. Lawrence, J. S., Hood, H. V., & Brashfield, T. L. (1989). Behavioral intervention to reduce AIDS risk activities. *Journal of Consulting and Clinical Psychology, 57,* 60–67.

Keltner, B. (1994). Home environments of mothers with mental retardation. *Mental Retardation, 32,* 123–127.

Kendall, P. C. (1994). Treating anxiety disorders in children: Results of a randomized clinical trial. *Journal of Consulting and Clinical Psychology, 62,* 100–110.

Kendall, P. C., & Braswell, L. (1985). *Cognitive behavioral modification with impulsive children.* New York: Guilford Press.

Kendall, P. C., & Clarkin, J. F. (1992). Introduction to Special Section: Comorbidity and treatment implications. *Journal of Consulting and Clinical Psychology, 60,* 833–834.

Kendall, P. C., & Watson, D. (1989). *Anxiety and depression: Distinctive and overlapping features.* San Diego: Academic Press.

Kendler, K. S., & Diehl, S. R. (1993). The genetics of schizophrenia: A current genetic-epidemiologic perspective. *Schizophrenia Bulletin, 19,* 87–112.

Kendler, K. S., Gruenberg, A. M., & Strauss, J. S. (1981). An independent analysis of the Copenhagen sample of the Danish adoption study of schizophrenia. *Archives of General Psychiatry, 38,* 982–974.

Kendler, K. S., McGuire, M., Gruenberg, A., O'Hare, A., Spellman, M., & Walsh, D. (1993a). The Roscommon family study. I: Methods, diagnosis of probands, and risk of schizophrenia in relatives. *Archives of General Psychiatry, 50,* 527–540.

Kendler, K. S., McGuire, M., Gruenberg, A., O'Hare, A., Spellman, M., & Walsh, D. (1993b). The Roscommon family study. III: Schizophrenia-related personality disorders in relatives. *Archives of General Psychiatry, 50,* 781–788.

Kendler, K. S., McGuire, M., Gruenberg, A., O'Hare, A., Spellman, M., & Walsh, D. (1993c). The Roscommon family study. IV: Affective illness, anxiety disorders, and alcoholism in relatives. *Archives of General Psychiatry, 50,* 952–960.

Kendler, K. S., Neale, M., Kessler, R. C., Heath, A., & Eaves, L. (1992a). The genetic epidemiology of phobias in women: The interrelationship of agoraphobia, social phobia, situational phobia, and simple phobia. *Archives of General Psychiatry, 49,* 273–281.

Kendler, K. S., Neale, M., Kessler, R. C., Heath, A., & Eaves, L. (1992b). Major depression and generalized anxiety disorder: Same genes, (partly) different environments. *Archives of General Psychiatry, 49,* 716–725.

Kendler, K. S., Neale, M., Kessler, R. C., Heath, A., & Eaves, L. (1992c). Generalized anxiety disorder in women: A population-based twin study. *Archives of General Psychiatry, 49,* 267–272.

Kendler, K. S., Walters, E. E., Neale, M. C., Kessler, R. C., Heath, A. C., & Eaves, L. J. (1995). The structure of the genetic and environmental risk factors for six major psychiatric disorders in women: Phobia, generalized anxiety disorder, panic disorder, bulimia, major depression, and alcoholism. *Archives of General Psychiatry, 52,* 374–383.

Kent, D. A., Tomasson, K., & Coryell, W. (1995). Course and outcome of conversion and somatization disorders: A four-year follow-up. *Psychosomatics, 36,* 138–144.

Kernberg, O. F. (1976). *Object relations, theory and clinical psychoanalysis.* New York: Jason Aaronson.

Kernberg, O. F. (1984). *Severe personality disorders.* New Haven, CT: Yale University Press.

Kernberg, O. F., Selzer, M. A., Koenigsberg, H. W., Carr, A. C., & Appelbaum, A. H. (1989). *Psychodynamic psychotherapy of borderline patients.* New York: Basic Books.

Keso, L., & Salaspuro, M. (1990). Inpatient treatment of employed alcoholics: A randomized clinical trial on Hazelden-type and traditional treatment. *Alcoholism in Clinical and Experimental Research, 14*(4), 584–589.

Kessler, R. C., McGonagle, K. A., Zhao, S., Nelson, C. B., Hughes, M., et al. (1994). Lifetime and 12-month prevalence of *DSM-III-R* psychiatric disorders in the United States: Results from the National Comorbidity Study. *Archives of General Psychiatry, 51,* 8–19.

Kettlewell, P. W., Mizes, J. S., & Wasylyshyn, N. A. (1992). A cognitive-behavioral group treatment of bulimia. *Behavior Therapy, 23,* 657–670.

Kety, S. S. (1990). Genetics factors in suicide: Family, twin, and adoption studies. In S. J. Blumenthal & D. J. Kupfer (Eds.), *Suicide over the life cycle: Risk factors, assessment, and treatment of suicidal patients* (pp. 127–134). Washington, DC: American Psychiatric Press.

Keyes, D. (1981). *The minds of Billy Milligan.* New York: Random House.

Khachaturian, Z. S., Phelps, C. H., & Buckholtz, N. S. (1994). The prospect for developing treatments for Alzheimer's disease. In R. D. Terry, R. Katzman, & K. L. Bick (Eds.). *Alzheimer's disease* (pp. 445–454). New York: Raven Press.

Kiecolt-Glaser, J. K., & Glaser, R. (1987). Chronic stress and immunity in family caregivers of Alzheimer's disease victims. *Psychosomatic Medicine, 49,* 523–535.

Kiecolt-Glaser, J. K., & Glaser, R. (1992). Psychoneuroimmunology: Can psychological interventions modulate immunity? *Journal of Consulting and Clinical Psychology, 60,* 569–575.

Kiecolt-Glaser, J. K., Malarkey, W. B., Chee, M. A., Newton, T., Cacioppo, J. T., Mao, H.-Y, & Glaser, R. (1993). Negative behavior during marital conflict is associated with immunological down-regulation. *Psychosomatic Medicine, 55,* 395–409.

Kiesler, C. A., & Sibulkin, A. E. (1987). *Mental hospitalization: Myths and facts about a national crisis.* Beverly Hills, CA: Sage.

Kiesler, C. (1991). Changes in general hospital psychiatric care, 1980–1985. *American Psychologist, 46,* 416–421.

Kiesler, C., & Simpkins, C. (1991). The de facto national system of psychiatric inpatient care: Piecing together the national puzzle. *American Psychologist, 46,* 579–584.

Kiesler, D. J. (1986). Interpersonal methods of diagnosis and treatment. In J. O. Cavenar, Jr. (Ed.), *Psychiatry* (Vol. 1, pp. 1–23). Philadelphia: J. B. Lippincott.

Kilmann, P. R., Boland, J. P., Norton, S. C. (1986). Perspectives on sex therapy outcome: A survey of AASECT providers. *Journal of Sex and Marital Therapy, 12,* 116–138.

Kilpatrick, D., Saunders, B., Amick-McMullan, A., Best, C., Vernonen, L., & Resnick, H. (1989). Victim and crime factors associated with the development of crime-related post-traumatic stress disorder. *Behavior Therapy, 20,* 199–214.

King, D. A., & Heller, K. (1984). Depression and the response of others. A re-evaluation. *Journal of Abnormal Psychology, 93,* 477–480.

King, M., & McDonald, E. (1992). Homosexuals who are twins: A study of 46 probands. *British Journal of Psychiatry, 160,* 407–409.

King, N. J., & Ollendick, T. H. (1989). Children's anxiety and phobic disorders in school settings: Classification, assessment, and intervention issues. *Review of Educational Research, 59*(4), 431–470.

Kinsey, A. C., Pomeroy, W. B., & Martin, C. E. (1948). *Sexual behavior in the human male.* Philadelphia: W. B. Saunders Co.

Kinsey, A. C., Pomeroy, W. B., Martin, C. E., Gebhardt, P. H. (1953). *Sexual behavior in the human female.* Philadelphia: W. B. Saunders Co.

Kirch, D. G. (1993). Infection and autoimmunity as etiologic factors in schizophrenia: A review and reappraisal. *Schizophrenia Bulletin, 19,* 181–255.

Kirmayer, L. J. (1994). Pacing the void: Social and cultural dimensions of dissociation. In D. Spiegel (Ed.), *Dissociation: Culture, mind, and body* (pp. 91–122). Washington DC: American Psychiatric Press.

Kirmayer, L. (1991). The place of culture in psychiatric nosology: *Taijin Kyofusho* and DSM-III-R. *The Journal of Nervous and Mental Disease, 179,* 19–28.

Kirschenbaum, D. S., & Fitzgibbon, M. L. (1995). Controversy about the treatment of obesity: Criticisms or challenges? *Behavior Therapy, 26,* 43–68.

Kissen, D. M., & Eysenck, H. J. (1962). Personality in male lung cancer patients. *Journal of Psychosomatic Research, 6,* 123–127.

Kitagawa, E. M., & Hauser, P. M. (Eds.). (1973). *Differential mortality in the United States: A study in socioeconomic epidemiology.* Cambridge: Harvard University Press.

Kivlahan, D. R., Marlatt, G. A., Fromme, K., Coppel, D. B., & Williams, E. (1990). Secondary prevention with college drinkers: Evaluation of an alcohol skills training program. *Journal of Consulting and Clinical Psychology, 58,* 805–810.

Klassen, D., & O'Connor, W. A. (1988). A prospective study of predictors of violence in adult male mental health admissions. *Law and Human Behavior, 12,* 143–158.

Klein, D. F. (1990). NIMH collaborative research on the treatment of depression. *Archives of General Psychiatry, 47,* 682–688.

Klein, D., Ross, D., & Cohen, P. (1987). Panic and avoidance in agoraphobia: Application of path analysis to treatment studies. *Archives of General Psychiatry, 44,* 377–385.

Klein, M. (1975). *The writings of Melanie Klein* (Vol. III). London: Hogarth Press.

Klein, M. H. (1993). Issues in the assessment of personality disorders. *Journal of Personality Disorders,* (Suppl.), 18–33.

Klein, R. G. (1988). Hyperactive boys almost grown-up. III: Methylphenidate effects on ultimate height. *Archives of General Psychiatry, 45,* 1131–1134.

Klein, R., & Mannuzza, S. (1988). Hyperactive boys almost grown up III: Methylphenidate effects on ultimate height. *Archives of General Psychiatry, 45,* 1131–1134.

Klein, R. G., & Mannuzza, S. (1991). Long-term outcome of hyperactive children: A review. *Journal of the American Academy of Child and Adolescent Psychiatry, 30*(3), 383–387.

Kleinknecht, R. A., (1991). *Mastering anxiety: The nature and treatment of anxious conditions.* New York: Plenum.

Kleinknecht, R. A. (1993). Rapid treatment of blood and injection phobia with eye movement desensitization. *Journal of Behavior Therapy and Experimental Psychiatry, 24,* 2211–2217.

Kleinknecht, R. A., & Lenz, J. (1989). Blood/injury fear, fainting and avoidance of medical treatment: A family correspondence study. *Behaviour Research and Therapy, 27,* 537–547.

Kleinknecht, R. A., & Morgan, M. (1992). Treatment of posttraumatic stress disorder using eye movement desensitization. *Journal of Behavior Therapy and Experimental Psychiatry, 23,* 43–49.

Kleinman, A. (1981). Culture and patient care: Psychiatry among the Chinese. *Drug Therapy, 11,* 134–140.

Klerman, G. L. (1988). The current age of youthful melancholia: Evidence for increase in depression among adolescents and young adults. *British Journal of Psychiatry, 152,* 4–7.

Klerman, G. L., Weissman, M. M., & Rounsaville, B. J. (1984). *Interpersonal psychotherapy of depression.* New York: Basic Books.

Klin, A. (1993). Asperger syndrome. *Child and Adolescent Psychiatric Clinics of North America, 3*(1), 131–148.

Klin, A., Volkmar, F. R., Naylor, S., Sparrow, S. S., & Rourke, B. P. (1993, October). *Asperger syndrome: Diagnosis, neuropsychological aspects, and interventions.* Poster presented at the 40th Annual Meeting of the American Academy of Child and Adolescent Psychiatry, San Antonio, TX.

Klosko, J. S., Barlow, D. H., Tassinari, R., & Cerny, J. A. (1990). A comparison of alprazolam and behavior therapy in the treatment of panic disorder. *Journal of Consulting and Clinical Psychology, 58,* 77–84.

Kluft, R. P. (1984). Multiple personality in childhood. *Psychiatric Clinics of North America, 7,* 121–134.

Kluft, R. P. (1995). Current controversies surrounding dissociative identity disorder. In L. M. Cohen, J. N. Berzoff, & M. R. Elin (Eds.), *Dissociative identity disorder: Theoretical and treatment controversies* (pp. 347–4378). Northvale, NJ: Jason Aronson.

Kobak, R. R., & Sceery, A. (1988). Attachment in late adolescence: Working models, affect regulation, and representations of self and others. *Child Development, 59,* 135–146.

Kochanek, T. T., Kabacoff, R. I., & Lipsitt, L. P. (1990). Early identification of developmentally disabled and at-risk preschool children. *Exceptional Children, 56,* 528–538.

Koegel, R. L., & Koegel, L. K. (1989). Community-referenced research on self-stimulation. In M. J. Begab (Ed.), *The treatment of severe behavior disorders: Behavior analysis approaches* (pp. 129–149). Washington, DC: American Association on Mental Retardation.

Koenigsberg, H., & Handley, R. (1986). Expressed emotion: From predictive index to clinical construct. *American Journal of Psychiatry, 143,* 1361–1373.

Koffinke, C. (1991). Family recovery issues and treatment resources. In D. C. Daley & M. S. Raskin (Eds.), *Treating the chemically dependent and their families.* Newbury Park, CA: Sage.

Kohlenberg, R. J. (1973). Behavioristic approach to multiple personality: A case study. *Behavior Therapy, 4,* 137–140.

Kohut, H. (1977). *The restoration of the self.* New York: International Universities Press.

Kolata, G. (1987). Manic-depression gene tied to chromosome 11. *Science, 235,* 1139–1140.

Kolb, L. (1968). *Noyes' Modern Clinical Psychiatry* (7th ed.). Philadelphia: W. B. Saunders Co.

Kolko, D. J., Loar, L. L., & Sturnick, D. (1990). Inpatient social-cognitive skills training groups with conduct disordered and attention deficit disordered children. *Journal of Child Psychology and Psychiatry, 31,* 737–748.

Korolenko, C., Minevich, V., & Segal, B. (1994). The politicalization of alcohol in the USSR and its impact on the study and treatment of alcoholism. *International Journal of the Addictions, 29,* 1269–1285.

Koss, M. P., Gidycz, C. A., & Wisniewski, N. (1987). The scope of rape: Incidence and prevalence of sexual aggression and victimization in a national sample of higher education students. *Journal of Consulting and Clinical Psychology, 55,* 162–170.

Koss, M. P. & Shiang, J. (1994). Research on brief psychotherapy. In A. E. Bergin & S. L. Garfield (Eds.), *Handbook of psychotherapy and behavior change* (pp. 664–700). New York: John Wiley & Sons.

Kotsaftis, A., & Neale, J. M. (1993). Schizotypal personality disorder. I: The clinical syndrome. *Clinical Psychology Review, 13,* 451–472.

Kovacs, M., Gatsonis, C., Paulauskas, S. L., & Richards, C. (1989). Depressive disorders in childhood. IV. A longitidinal study of comorbidity with and risk for anxiety disorders. *Archives of General Psychiatry, 46,* 776–782.

Kovacs, M., Goldston, D., & Gatsonis, C. (1993). Suicidal behaviors and childhood-onset depressive disorders: A longitudinal investigation. *Journal of the American Academy of Child and Adolescent Psychiatry, 32,* 8–20.

Kramer, P. (1993). *Listening to Prozac.* New York: Penguin Books.

Krantz, D. S., & Manuck, S. B. (1984). Acute psychophysiologic reactivity and risk of cardiovascular disease—A review and methodologic critique. *Psychological Bulletin, 96,* 435–464.

Kraepelin, E. (1910). *Dementia praecox and paraphrenia* (R. M. Barclay & G. M. Robertson, trans.). Edinburgh: E. & S. Livingstone (1971).

Kroft, C., & Cole, J. (1992). Adverse behavioral effects of psychostimulants. In J. M. Kane & J. A. Lieberman (Eds.), *Adverse effects of psychotropic drugs.* New York: Guilford Press.

Kruesi, M. J., Hibbs, E. D., Zahn, T. P., Keysor, C. S., Hamburger, S., Bartko, J. J., & Rapoport, J. L. (1992). A 2-year prospective follow-up study of children and adolescents with disruptive behavior disorders. *Archives of General Psychiatry, 49,* 429–435.

Krupnick, J. L., Sotsky, S. M., Simmens, S., Moyer, J., Elkin, I., Watkins, J., & Pilkonis, P. A. (1996). The role of the therapeutic alliance in psychotherapy and pharmacotherapy outcome: Findings in the National Institute of Mental Health Treatment of Depression Collaborative Research Program. *Journal of Consulting and Clinical Psychology, 64*, 532–539.

Kuechler, J., & Hampton, R. (1988). Learning and behavioral approaches to the treatment of anorexia nervosa and bulimia. In B. J. Blinder, B. F. Chaitin, & R. Goldstein (Eds.), *The eating disorders* (pp. 423–431). PMA Publishing Corporation.

Kulik, J. A., & Mahler, H. I. (1989). Social support and recovery from surgery. *Health Psychology, 8*, 221–238.

Kupfersmid, J. (1989). Treatment of nocturnal enuresis: A status report. *The Psychiatric Forum, 14*, 37–46.

Kushner, M., Riggs, D., Foa, E., & Miller, S. (1992). Perceived controllability and the development of posttraumatic stress disorder (PTSD) in crime victims. *Behaviour Research and Therapy, 31*, 105–110.

Kushner, M., Sher, K., & Beitman, B. (1990). The relation between alcohol and the anxiety disorders. *American Journal of Psychiatry, 147*, 685–695.

Kutcher, S., Malkin, D., Silverberg, J., Marton, P., Williamson, P., Malkin, A., Szalai, J., & Katic, M. (1991). Nocturnal cortisol, thyroid stimulating hormone, and growth hormone secretory profiles in depressed adolescents. *Journal of the American Academy of Child Psychiatry, 30*, 407–414.

Lacks, P., & Morin, C. M. (1992). Recent advances in the assessment and treatment of insomnia. *Journal of Consulting and Clinical Psychology, 60*, 586–594.

Lago, J. A., & Kosten, T. R. (1994). Stimulant withdrawal. *Addiction, 89*(11), 1477–1481.

Lam, D. H. (1991). Psychosocial family intervention in schizophrenia: A review of empirical studies. *Psychological Medicine, 21*, 423–441.

Lamb, H. R. (1992). Is it time for a moratorium on deinstitutionalization? *Hospital and Community Psychiatry, 43*, 669.

Lambert, M. C., Weisz, J. R., & Knight, F. (1989). Over- and undercontrolled clinic referral problems of Jamaican and American children and adolescents: The culture general and the culture specific. *Journal of Consulting and Clinical Psychology, 57*, 467–472.

Lambert, M. J., & Bergin, A. E. (1994). The effectiveness of psychotherapy. In A. E. Bergin & S. L. Garfield (Eds.), *Handbook of psychotherapy and behavior change* (pp. 143–189). New York: John Wiley & Sons.

Lamy, P. P. (1985). Patterns of prescribing and drug use. In R. N. Butler & A. D. Beard (Eds.), *The aging process: Therapeutic implications* (pp. 53–82). New York: Raven Press.

Landman, J. T., & Dawes, R. (1982). Experimental outcome: Smith and Glass' conclusions stand up under scrutiny. *American Psychologist, 37*, 504–516.

Landolt, H. P., Werth, E., Borb'ely, A. A., & Dijk, D. J. (1995). Caffeine intake (200 mg) in the morning affects human sleep and EEG power spectra at night. *Brain Research, 675*(1–2), 67–74.

Lang, P. J. (1985). The cognitive psychophysiology of emotion: Fear and anxiety. In A. H. Tuma & J. D. Maser (Eds.), *Anxiety and the anxiety disorders* (pp. 131–170). Hillsdale, NJ: Erlbaum.

Langevin, R. (1993). A comparison of neurendocrine and genetic factors in homosexuality and in pedophilia. *Annals of Sex Research, 1*, 67–76.

LaPerriere, A. R., Antoni, M. H., Schneiderman, N., Ironson, G., Klimas, N., Caralis, P., & Fletcher, M. A. (1990). Exercise intervention attenuates emotional distress and natural killer cell decrements following notification of positive serologic status for HIV-1. *Biofeedback and Self-Regulation, 15*, 229–242.

Laruelle, M., Ai-Dargham, A., Casanova, M., Toti, R., Weinberger, D., & Kleinman, J. (1993). Selective abnormalities of prefrontal serotonergic receptors in schizophrenia. *Archives of General Psychiatry, 50*, 810–818.

Last, C. G., Barlow, D. H., & O'Brien, G. (1984). Precipitants of agoraphobia: Role of stressful life events. *Psychological Reports, 54*, 567–570.

Last, C. G., Francis, G., Hersen, M., Kazdin, A. E., & Strauss, C. C. (1987). Separation anxiety and school phobia: A comparison using DSM-III criteria. *American Journal of Psychiatry, 144*, 653–657.

Last, C. G., & Strauss, C. C. (1990). School refusal in anxiety-disordered children and adolescents. *Journal of the American Academy of Child and Adolescent Psychiatry, 29*, 31–35.

Laughman, E., Gagnon, J. H., Michael, R., & Michaels, S. (1994). *Sex in America.* Chicago: University of Chicago Press.

Lawson, G., Peterson, J. S., & Lawson, A. (1983). *Alcoholism and the family: A guide to treatment and prevention.* Rockville, MD: Aspen.

Lazarus, A. A. (1989). Dyspareunia: A multimodal psychotherapeutic perspective. In S. R. Leiblum & S. R. Rosen (Eds.), *Principles and practices of sex therapy* (2nd ed., pp 89–112). New York: Guilford Press.

Lazarus, R. S. (1993). From psychological stress to the emotions: A history of changing outlooks. *Annual Review of Psychology, 44*, 1–21.

Lazarus, R. S., & Folkman, S. (1984). *Stress, appraisal, and coping.* New York: Springer-Verlag.

Leahey, T. H. (1992). *History of psychology* (3rd ed.). Englewood Cliffs, NJ: Prentice Hall.

Leary, T. (1957). *Interpersonal diagnosis of personality. A functional theory and methodology for personality evaluation.* New York: Ronald Press.

Lecci, L., Karoly, P., Ruehlman, L. S., & Lanyon, R. I. (1996). Goal-relevant dimensions of hypochondriacal tendencies and their relation to symptom manifestation and psychological distress. *Journal of Abnormal Psychology, 105*, 42–52.

Leckman, J. F., & Cohen, D. J. (1994). Tic disorders. In M. Rutter, E. Taylor, & L. Hersou (Eds.), *Child and adolescent psychiatry.* Oxford: Blackwell Scientific Publications.

Leekam, S., & Perner, J. (1991). Does the autistic child have a theory of representation? *Cognition, 40*, 203–218.

Leff, J. (1994). Working with families of schizophrenic patients. *British Journal of Psychiatry, 164*, (Suppl. 23), 71–76.

Legarda, J. J., & Gossop, M. (1994). A 24-hour inpatient detoxification treatment for heroin addicts: A preliminary investigation. *Drug and Alcohol Dependence, 35*(2), 91–93.

Leibowitz, S. F., Weiss, G. F., Yee, F., and Tretter, J. B. (1985). Noradrenergic innervation of the paraventricular nucleus: Specific role in control of carbohydrate ingestions. *Brain Research Bulletin, 14*, 561–567.

Leichner, P., & Gertler, A. (1988). Prevalence and incidence studies of anorexia nervosa. In B. J. Blinder, B. F. Chaitin, & R. Goldstein (Eds.), *The eating disorders* (pp. 131–149). PMA Publishing Corporation.

Leitenberg, H., & Henning, K. (1995). Sexual fantasy. *Psychological Bulletin, 117*, 469–496.

Leonard, C., Voeller, K., Lombardino, L., Alexander, A., Andersen, H., Morris, M., Garofalakis, M., Hynd, G., Honeyman, J., Mao, J., Agee, F., & Staab, E. (1993). Anomalous cerebral structure in dyslexia revealed with magnetic resonance imaging. *Archives of Neurology, 50*, 461–469.

Leonard, K. E. (1990). Marital functioning among episodic and steady alcoholics. In R. L. Collins, K. E. Leonard, & J. S. Searles (Eds.), *Alcohol and the family: Research and clinical perspectives* (pp. 220–243). New York: Guilford Press.

Leonard, H., Swedo, S., Rapoport, J., Koby, E., Lenane, M., Cheslow, D., & Hamberger, S. (1989). Treatment of obsessive-compulsive disorder with clomipramine and desipramine in children and adolescents. *Archives of General Psychiatry, 46*, 1088–1092.

Lesser, I., Lydiard, R. B., Antal, A., Rubin, R., Ballenger, J., & DuPont, R. (1992). Alprazolam plasma concentrations and treatment response in panic disorder and agoraphobia. *American Journal of Psychiatry, 149*, 1556–1562.

Lester, D. (1993). The effectiveness of suicide prevention centers. *Suicide and Life-Threatening Behavior, 23*, 263–267.

Lester, D. (1988). Gun control, gun ownership, and suicide prevention. *Suicide and Life-Threatening Behavior, 18*, 176–180.

Lester, D., & Murrell, M. E. (1980). The influence of gun control laws on suicidal behavior. *American Journal of Psychiatry, 137*, 121–122.

LeVay, S. (1991). A difference in hypothalamic structure between heterosexual and homosexual men. *Science, 253*, 1034–1037.

Levin, J., & Fox, J. A. (1985). *Mass murder: America's growing menace*. New York: Plenum.

Levine, A. G., & Stone, R. A. (1986). Threats to people and what they value: Residents' perceptions of the hazards of Love Canal. In A. H. Lebovits, A. Baum, & J. E. Singer (Eds.), *Advances in environmental psychology: Vol. 6. Exposure to hazardous substances: Psychological parameters* (pp. 109–130). Hillsdale, NJ: Erlbaum.

Levine, K., Shane, H. C., & Wharton, R. H. (1994). What if . . . : A plea to professionals to consider the risk-benefit ratio of facilitated communication. *Mental Retardation, 32*(4), 300–304.

Levine, S. B. (1995). What is clinical sexuality? *Psychiatric Clinics of North America, 18*, 1–6.

Levy-Lahad, E., Wasco, W., Poorkaj, P., Romano, D. M., Oshima, J., Pettingell, W., Yu, Chang-en, Jondro, P. D., Schmidt, S. D., Wang, K., Crowley, A. C., Fu, Ying-Hui, Guenette, S., Galas, D., Nemens, E., Wijsman, E. M., Bird, T. D., Schellenberg, G. D., & Tanzi, R. (1995a). Candidate gere for the chromosome I familial Alzheimer's disease locus. *Science, 269*, 973–977.

Levy-Lahad, E., Wijsman, E. M., Nemens, E., Anderson, L., Goddard, K. A. B., Weber, J. L., Bird, T. D. & Schellenberg, G. D. (1995b). A familial Alzheimer's disease locus on chromosome 1. *Science, 269*, 970–973.

Lewinsohn, P. M. (1974). A behavioral approach to depression. In R. J. Freidman & M. M. Katz (Eds.), *The psychology of depression: Contemporary theory and research* (pp. 157–170). Washington, DC: Winston-Wiley.

Lewinsohn, P. M., & Clarke, G. N. (1984). Group treatment of depressed individuals: The "coping with depression" course. *Advances in Behavior Research and Therapy, 6*, 99–114.

Lewinsohn, P. M., Clarke, G. N., Hops, H., & Andrews, J. (1990). Cognitive-behavioral treatment for depressed adolescents. *Behavior Therapy, 21*, 385–401.

Lewinsohn, P. M., Hoberman, H. M., & Clarke, G. N. (1989). The Coping With Depression Course: Review and future directions. *Canadian Journal of Behavioural Science, 21*, 470–493.

Lewinsohn, P. M., Rohde, P., & Seeley, J. R. (1993). Psychosocial characteristics of adolescents with a history of suicide attempt. *Journal of the American Academy of Child and Adolescent Psychiatry, 31*, 60–68.

Lewinsohn, P. M., Rohde, P., & Seeley, J. R. (1996). Adolescent suicidal ideation and attempts: Prevalence, risk factors, and clinical implications. *Clinical Psychology: Science and Practice, 3*, 25–46.

Lewinsohn, P. M., Youngren, M. A., & Grosscup, S. J. (1979). Reinforcement and depression. In R. A. Depue (Ed.), *The psychobiology of depressive disorders: Implications for the effects of stress*. New York: Academic Press.

Lewis, G., Davis, A., Andreason, S., & Allebek, P. (1992). Schizophrenia and city life. *The Lancet, 340*, 137–140.

Lewis, J. A., Dana, R. Q., & Blevins, G. A. (1988). *Substance abuse counseling: An individualized approach*. Pacific Grove, CA: Brooks/Cole.

Lewis, M. J., Perry, L. B., June, H. L., Garnett, M. L., & Porrino, L. J. (1990). Regional changes in functional brain activity with ethanol stimulant and depressant effects. *Soc Neurosci Abstracts, 16*(1), 459.

Lewis-Fernandez, R. (1994). Culture and dissociation: A comparison of Ataque de Nervios among Pureto Ricans and possession syndrome in India. In D. Spiegel (Ed.), *Dissociation: Culture, mind, and body* (pp. 123–170). Washington DC: American Psychiatric Press.

Lewontin, R. C., Rose, S., & Kamin, L. J. (1984). *Not in our genes*. New York: Pantheon.

Lewy, A. J. (1993). Seasonal mood disorders. In D. D. Dunner (Ed.), *Current psychiatric therapy* (pp. 220–225). Philadelphia: W. B. Saunders Co.

Lewy, A. J., Sack, R. L., Miller, S., Hoban, T. M. (1987). Antidepressant and circadian phase-shifting effects of light. *Science, 235*, 352–354.

Ley, R. (1985). Blood, breathe, and fears: A hyperventilation theory of panic attacks and agoraphobia. *Clinical Psychology Review, 5*, 171–285.

Leyton, E. (1986). *Compulsive killers: The story of modern multiple murder*. New York: New York University Press.

Lezak, M. (1995). *Neuropsychological assessment* (3rd ed.). New York: Oxford University Press.

Liberman, R. P. (1972). Behavioral modification of schizophrenia: A review. *Schizophrenia Bulletin, 1*, 37–48.

Lichtenstein, E., & Glasgow, R. E. (1992). Smoking cessation: What have we learned over the past decade? *Journal of Consulting and Clinical Psychlogy, 60*(4), 518–527.

Lichtigfeld, F. J., & Gilman, M. A. (1991). Combination therapy with carbamazepine/benzodiazepine for polydrug analgesic/depressant withdrawal. *Journal of Substance Abuse Treatment, 8*(4), 293–295.

Lickey, M., & Gordon, B. (1991). *Medicine and mental illness: The use of drugs in psychiatry*. New York: W. H. Freeman & Co.

Liddle, P. F., Friston, K., Frith, C., Hirsh, S., Jones, T., & Frackowiak, S. J. (1992). Patterns of blood flow in schizophrenia. *British Journal of Psychiatry, 160*, 179–186.

Lidz, C., Mulvey, E., & Gardner, W. (1993). The accuracy of predictions of violence to others. *Journal of the American Medical Association, 269*, 1007–1011.

Lidz, R. W., & Lidz, T. (1949). The family environment of schizophrenic patients. *American Journal of Psychiatry, 106*, 332–345.

Lieberman, J. A. (1993). Understanding the mechanism of action of atypical antipsychotic drugs: A review of compounds in use and development. *British Journal of Psychiatry, 63*, 7–18.

Lieberman, J. A., & Koreen, A. R. (1993). Neurochemistry and neuroendocrinology of schizophrenia. *Schizophrenia Bulletin, 19*, 197–256.

Lilienfeld, S. O. (1992). The association between antisocial personality and somatization disorders: A review and integration of theoretical models. *Clinical Psychology Review, 12*, 641–662.

Lilienfeld, S. O., & Marino, L. (1995). Mental disorder as a Roschian concept: A critique of Wakefield's "Harmful Dysfunction" analysis. *Journal of Abnormal Psychology, 104*, 411–420.

Lilienfeld, S. O., & Waldman, I. D. (1990). The relationship between childhood attention-deficit hyperactivity disorder and adult antisocial behavior reexamined: The problem of heterogeneity. *Clinical Psychology Review, 10*, 699–725.

Lin, K. L., & Kleinman, A. M. (1988). Psychopathology and course of schizophrenia: A cross-cultural perspective. *Schizophrenia Bulletin, 14*, 555–567.

Lin, K. M., Poland, R., & Nakasaki, G. (Eds.). (1993). *Psychopharmacology and psychobiology of ethnicity*. Washington, DC: American Psychiatric Press.

Lin, K. M., Poland, R., & Fleishaker, J. (1993). Ethnicity and differential response to benzodiazepines. In K. M. Lin, R. Poland, & G. Nakasaki (Eds.), *Psychopharmacology and psychobiology of ethnicity*. Washington, DC: American Psychiatric Press.

Lin, K. M., Poland, R., & Nakasaki, G. (1993). Introduction: Psychopharmacology, psychobiology, and ethnicity. In K. M. Lin, R. Poland, & G. Nakasaki (Eds.), *Psychopharmacology and psychobiology of ethnicity*. Washington, DC: American Psychiatric Press.

Lindesay, J., Macdonald, A. & Starke, I. (1990). *Delirium in the elderly*. Oxford: Oxford University Press.

Lindsay, D. & Read, J. (1995). Memory work and recovered memories of childhood sexual abuse: Scientific evidence and public, professional, and personal issues. *Psychology, Public Policy, and Law, 1*, 846–908.

Lindsey, K. P., & Paul, G. L. (1989). Involuntary commitments to public mental institutions: Issues involving the overrepresentation of Blacks and assessment of relevant functioning. *Psychological Bulletin, 106*, 171–183.

Lindsley, O. R., Skinner, B. F., & Solomon, H. C. (1953). *Studies in behavior therapy. Status report 1*. Waltham, MA: Metropolitan State Hospital.

Linehan, M. M. (1993). *Cognitive behavioral treatment of borderline personality disorder*. New York: Guilford Press.

Linehan, M. M., Armstrong, H. E., Suarez, A., Allmon, D., & Heard, H. L. (1991). Cognitive-behavioral treatment of chronically parasuicidal borderline patients. *Archives of General Psychiatry, 48*, 1060–1064.

Linehan, M. M., & Kehrer, C. A. (1993). Borderline personality disorder. In D. H. Barlow (Ed.), *Clinical handbook of psychological disorders* (pp. 396–441). New York: Guilford Press.

Linehan, M. M., Tutek, D., & Heard, H. L. (1992, November). *Interpersonal and social treatment outcomes for borderline personality disorder*. Poster presented at the annual meeting of the Association for the Advancement of Behavior Therapy, Boston, MA.

Link, B., Cullen, F., & Andrews, H. (1993). Reconsidering the violent and illegal behavior of mental patients. *American Sociological Review, 57*, 1229–1236.

Linnoila, M., Virkkunen, M., Scheinin, M., Nuutila, A., Rimon, R., & Goodwin, F. K. (1983). Low cerebrospinal fluid 5-hydroxindoleacetic acid concentration differentiates impulsive from nonimpulsive violent behavior. *Life Sciences, 33*, 2609–2614.

Linz, D., Donnerstein, E., & Penrod, S. (1984). The effects of long-term exposure to filmed violence against women. *Journal of Communication, 34*, 130–147.

Linz, D., Donnerstein, E., & Penrod, S. (1987a). Sexual violence in the news media: Social psychological implications. In P. Shaver & C. Hendrick (Eds.), *Sex and gender*. Newbury, CA: Sage.

Linz, D., Donnerstein, E., & Penrod, S. (1987b). The findings and recommendations of the Attorney General's Commission on Pornography: Do the psychological facts fit the political fury. *American Psychologist, 42*, 946–953.

Linz, D., Donnerstein, E., & Penrod, S. (1988). Effects of long-term exposure to violent and sexually degrading depictions of women. *Journal of Personality & Social Psychology, 55*, 758–768.

Lipowski, Z. J. (1990). *Delirium: Acute confusional states*. New York: Oxford University Press.

Lipsey, M. W., & Wilson, D. B. (1993). The efficacy of psychological, educational, and behavioral treatment: Confirmation from meta-analysis. *American Psychologist, 48*, 1181–1209.

Lishman, W. A. (1994). The history of research into dementia and its relationship to current concepts. In F. A. Huppert, C. Brayne, & D. W. O'Connor (Eds.), *Dementia and normal aging* (pp. 41–56). Cambridge: Cambridge University Press.

List, S. M., & Cleghorn, J. M. (1993). Implications of positron emission tomography research for the investigation of the action of antipsychotic drugs. *British Journal of Psychiatry, 163*, 25–30.

Litt, M. D., Babor, T. F., DelBoca, F. K., Kadden, R. M., & Cooney, N. (1992). Types of alcoholics: II. Application of an empirically derived typology to treatment matching. *Archives of General Psychiatry, 49*, 609–614.

Little, L. M., & Curren, J. P. (1978). Covert sensitization: A clinical procedure in need of some explanation. *Psychological Bulletin, 85*, 513–531.

Litwack, T. R., & Schlesinger, L. B. (1987). Assessing and predicting violence: Research, law and applications. In I. B. Weiner & A. K. Hess (Eds.), *Handbook of forensic psychology*. New York: John Wiley & Sons.

Litz, B. T., & Keane, T. M. (1989). Information processing in anxiety disorders: Application to the understanding of post-traumatic stress disorder. *Clinical Psychology Review, 12*, 417–432.

Lochman, J. E., & Dodge, K. A. (1994). Social-cognitive processes of severely violent, moderately aggressive and nonaggressive boys. *Journal of Consulting and Clinical Psychology, 62*, 366–374.

Lochman, J. E., & Lenhart, L. A. (1993). Anger coping intervention for aggressive children: Conceptual models and outcome effects: Disinhibition disorders in childhood [Special issue]. *Clinical Psychology Review, 13*(8), 785–805.

Loeber, R. (1990). Development and risk factors of juvenile antisocial behavior and delinquency. *Clinical Psychology Review, 10*, 1–42.

Loeber, R., & Dishion, T. (1983). Early predictors of male delinquency: A review. *Psychological Bulletin, 94*, 68–99.

Loeber, R., & Stouthamer-Loeber, M. (1986). Family factors as correlates and predictors of juvenile conduct problems and delinquency. In M. Tonry & N. Morris (Eds.), *Crime and justice: An annual review of research* (Vol. 7, pp. 29–149). Chicago, IL: University of Chicago Press.

Loehlin, J. C. (1989). Partitioning environmental and genetic contributions to behavioral development. *American Psychologist, 44*, 1285–1292.

Loening-Baucke, V. A. (1990). Modulation of abnormal defecation dynamics by biofeedback treatment in chronically constipated children with encopresis. *Journal of Pediatrics, 116*, 214–221.

Loening-Baucke, V. A., & Cruikshank, B. M. (1986). Abnormal defecation dynamics in chronically constipated children with encopresis. *Journal of Pediatrics, 108*, 562–566.

Loftus, E. (1993). The reality of repressed memories. *American Psychologist, 48*, 518–537.

Loftus, E. F., & Ketcham, K. (1994). *The myth of repressed memory*. New York: St. Martin's Press.

Longnecker, M. P. (1994). Alcohol consumption and the risk of cancer in humans: An overview. *Alcohol, 12*(2), 87–96.

Lopez, S. R. (1989). Patient variable biases in clinical judgement: Conceptual overview and methodological considerations. *Psychological Bulletin, 106*, 184–203.

LoPiccolo, J. (1993). Paraphilias. In D. L. Dunner (Ed.), *Current psychiatric therapy* (pp. 339–346). Philadelphia: W. B. Saunders Co.

LoPiccolo, J. (1994). The evolution of sex therapy. *Sexual and Marital Therapy, 9*, 5–7.

LoPiccolo, J., & Friedman, J. M. (1989). Broad-spectrum treatment of low sexual desire: Integration of cognitive, behavioral, and systemic therapy. In S. R. Leiblum & R. C. Rosen (Eds), *Principles and practice of sex therapy: Update for the 1990s* (pp. 107–144). New York: Guilford Press.

LoPiccolo, J., & Stock, W. E. (1986). Treatment of sexual dysfunction. *Journal of Consulting and Clinical Psychology, 54*, 158–167.

Lord, J., & Pedlar, A. (1991). Life in the community: Four years after the closure of an institution. *Mental Retardation, 29*(4), 213–221.

Lorion, R. (1978). Research on psychotherapy and behavior change with the disadvantaged. In A. E. Bergin & S. L. Garfield (Eds.), *Handbook of psychotherapy and behavior change*. New York: John Wiley & Sons.

Lou, H. C., Henrikson, L., & Bruhn, P. (1984). Focal cerebral hypo-perfusion in children with dysphasia and/or attention deficit disorders. *Archives of Neurology, 41,* 825–829.

Lovaas, O. I. (1987). Behavioral treatment and normal educational and intellectual functioning in young autistic children. *Journal of Consulting and Clinical Psychology, 55,* 3–9.

Lovaas, O. I., & Smith, T. (1989). Intensive behavioral treatment with young autistic children. In B. B. Lahey & A. E. Kazdin (Eds.), *Advances in clinical child psychology* (Vol. 11, pp. 285–324). New York: Plenum.

Loveland, K. A., Tunali-Kotoski, B., Pearson, D. A., Brelsford, K. A., Ortegon, J., & Chen, R. (1994). Imitation and expression of facial affect in autism. *Development and Psychopathology, 6,* 433–444.

Lovell, M. R., & Nussbaum, P. D. (1994). Neuropsychological assessment. In C. E. Coffey & J. L. Cummings (Eds.), *Textbook of geriatric neuropsychiatry* (pp. 129–144). Washington, DC: American Psychiatric Press.

Lovibond S. H., & Caddy, G. (1970). Discriminated aversive control in the moderation of alcoholics' drinking behavior. *Behavior Therapy, 1,* 437–444.

Luborsky, L. (1984). *Principles of psychoanalytic psychotherapy: A manual for supportive-expressive treatment.* New York: Basic Books.

Luborsky, L., Singer, B., & Luborsky, L. (1975). Comparative studies of psychotherapies: Is it true that "Everyone has won and all must have prizes"? *Archives of General Psychiatry, 32,* 995–1008.

Luckasson, R., Coulter, D. L., Polloway, E. A., Reiss, S., Schalock, R. L., Snell, M. E., Spitalnik, D. M., & Stark, J. A. (1992). *Mental retardation: Definition, classification, and systems of supports.* Washington, DC: American Association on Mental Retardation.

Lykken, D. T. (1957). A study of anxiety in the sociopathic personality. *Journal of Abnormal and Social Psychology, 55,* 6–10.

Lynam, D., Moffitt, T., & Stouthamer-Loeber, M. (1993). Explaining the relation between IQ and delinquency: Class, race, test motivation, school failure, or self-control? *Journal of Abnormal Psychology, 102,* 187–196.

Lyness, S. A. (1993). Predictors of differences between Type A and B individuals in heart rate and blood pressure reactivity. *Psychological Bulletin, 114,* 266–295.

Lynn, S. J., & Ruhe, J. W. (1986). The fantasy-prone person: Hypnosis, imagination, and creativity. *Journal of Personality and Social Psychology, 51,* 404–408.

Lyon, G. R. (1985). Identification and remediation of learning disability subtypes: Preliminary findings. *Learning Disabilities Focus, 1,* 21–35.

Lyonfields, J. D., Borkovec, T. D., & Thayer, J. F. (1995). Vagal tone in generalized anxiety disorders and the effects of aversive imagery and worrisome thinking. *Behavior Therapy, 26,* 457–465.

Mackie, K., & Hille, B. (1992). Cannabinoids inhibit N-type calcium channels in neuroblastomaglioma cells. *Proceedings of the National Academy of Sciences USA, 89*(9), 3825–3829.

MacMillan, D. L., Gresham, F. M., & Siperstein, G. N. (1993). Conceptual and psychometric concerns about the 1992 AAMR definition of mental retardation. *American Journal on Mental Retardation, 98*(3), 325–335.

Macmillan, M. (1991). *Freud evaluated: The completed arc.* Amersterdam: North-Holland.

MacPhee, D. C., Johnson, S. M., & Van Der Veer, M. M. (1995). Low sexual desire in women: The effects of marital therapy. *Journal of Sex and Marital Therapy, 21,* 159–182.

Madakasira, S., & O'Brien, K. F. (1987). Acute post-traumatic stress disorder in victims of a natural disaster. *Journal of Nervous and Mental Disease, 175,* 286–290.

Magrab, P., & Papadopoulou, Z. L. (1977). The effect of a token economy on dietary compliance for children on hemodialysis. *Journal of Applied Behavioral Analysis, 10,* 573–578.

Magura, S., Rosenblum, A., Lovejoy, M., Handelsman, L., Foote, J., & Stimmel, B. (1994). Neurobehavioral treatment for cocaine-using methadone patients: A preliminary report. *Journal of Addictive Diseases, 13*(4), 143–160.

Maher, B. (1968). *Abnormal psychology.* New York: McGraw-Hill.

Maher, B., & Spitzer, M. (1993). Delusions. In C. G. Costello (Ed.), *Symptoms of schizophrenia* (pp. 92–120). New York: John Wiley & Sons.

Mahler, M. S., Pine, F., & Bergman, A. (1975). *The psychological birth of the human infant.* New York: Basic Books.

Mahoney, M. J. (1993). Introduction to Special Section: Theoretical developments in the cognitive psychotherapies. *Journal of Consulting and Clinical Psychology, 61,* 187–193.

Mahrer, A. R. (1988). Discovery-oriented psychotherapy research: Rationale, aims, and methods. *American Psychologist, 43,* 694–702.

Maier, S. F., Watkins, L. R., & Fleshner, M. (1994). Psychoneuroimmunology: The interface between behavior, brain, and immunity. *American Psychologist, 49,* 1004–1017.

Maier, W., Lichtermann, D., Klingler, T., Heun, R., & Hallmayer, J. (1992). Prevalences of personality disorders (DSM-III-R) in the community. *Journal of Personality Disorders, 6,* 187–196.

Main, M., & Hesse, E. (1990). Parents' unresolved traumatic experiences are related to infant disorganized attachment status: Is frightened and/or frightening parental behavior the linking mechanism? In M. T. Greenberg, D. Cicchetti, & M. Cummings (Eds.), *Attachment in the preschool years: Theory, research, and intervention* (pp. 161–182). Chicago, IL: The University of Chicago Press.

Makman, M. H. (1994). Morphine receptors in immunocytes and neurons. *Advances in Neuroimmunology, 4*(2), 69–82.

Malamuth, N. M. (1981). Rape proclivity among males. *Journal of Social Issues, 37,* 138–157.

Malamuth, N. M., & Donnerstein, E. (1982). The effects of aggressive-pornographic mass media stimuli. In L. Berkowitz (Ed.), *Advances in experimental social psychology.* Orlando, FL: Academic Press.

Maletsky, B. M. (1973). "Assisted" covert sensitization: A preliminary report. *Behavior Therapy, 4,* 117–119.

Maletsky, B. M. (1991). *Treating the sexual offender.* Newbury Park, CA: Sage.

Mallon, G. P. (1995). *Suicide and the gay and lesbian adolescent.* Workshop presentation. Western Regional Meeting on Youth Suicide, Salt Lake City, UT.

Manderscheid, R. W., & Sonnenschein, M. A. (1990). *Mental health, United States 1990.* Rockville, MD: National Institute of Mental Health.

Mann, J. J., & Kapur, S. (1991). The emergence of suicidal ideation and behavior during antidepressant pharmacotherapy. *Archives of General Psychiatry, 48,* 1027–1033.

Mannuzza, S., Klein, R. G., Bonagura, N., Malloy, P., Giampino, T. L., & Addalli, K. A. (1991). Hyperactive boys almost grownup: V. Replication of psychiatric status. *Archives of General Psychiatry, 48,* 77–83.

Manschreck, T. C. (1993). Psychomotor abnormalities. In C. G. Costello (Ed.), *Symptoms of schizophrenia* (pp. 261–290). New York: John Wiley & Sons.

Manuck, S. B., Kaplan, J. R., Adams, M. R., & Clarkson, T. B. (1988). Effects of stress and the sympathetic nervous system on coronary artery atheroslerosis in the cynomolgus macaque. *American Heart Journal, 116,* 328–333.

Manuck, S. B., Kaplan, J. R., & Clarkson, T. B. (1983). Behaviorally induced heart rate reactivity and atheroslerosis in cynomolgus monkeys. *Psychosomatic Medicine, 49,* 95–108.

Marchi, M., & Cohen, P. (1990). Early childhood eating behaviors and adolescent eating disorders. *Journal of the American Academy of Child and Adolescent Psychiatry, 29*(1), 112–117.

Marcus, J., Hans, S. L., Nagier, S., Auerbach, J. G., Mirsky, A. F., & Aubrey, A. (1987). Review of the NIMH Israeli Kibbutz-City and the Jerusalem infant development study. *Schizophrenia Bulletin, 13,* 425–438.

Marengo, J., Harrow, M., & Edell, W. S. (1993). Thought disorder. In C. G. Costello (Ed.), *Symptoms of schizophrenia* (pp. 56–91). New York: John Wiley & Sons.

Margoshes, P. (1995a, May). For many, old age is the prime of life. *The APA Monitor, 26,* 36–37.

Margoshes, P. (1995b, May). Creative spark lives on, can increase with age. *The APA Monitor, 26,* 37.

Margraf, J., Barlow, D., Clark, D., & Telch, M. (1993). Psychological treatment of panic: Work in progress on outcome, active ingredients, and follow-up. *Behaviour Research and Therapy, 31,* 1–8.

Markesbery, W. R., & Ehmann, W. D. (1994). Brain trace elements in Alzheimer's disease. In R. D. Terry, R. Katzman, & K. L. Bick (Eds.). *Alzheimer's disease* (pp. 353–367). New York: Raven Press.

Markowitz, J., Weissman, M., Ouellette, R., Lish, J., & Klerman, G. (1989). Quality of life in panic disorder. *Archives of General Psychiatry, 46,* 984–992.

Markowitz, J. H., Matthews, K. A., Wing, R. R., Kuller, L. H., & Meilahn, E. (1991). Psychological, biological and health behavior predictors of blood pressure changes in middle-aged women. *Journal of Hypertension, 9,* 399–406.

Marks, I. M. (1987). *Fears, phobias, and rituals.* Oxford: Oxford University Press.

Marks, I. M., & O'Sullivan, G. (1988). Drugs and psychological treatments for agoraphobia/panic and obsessive-compulsive disorders: A review. *British Journal of Psychiatry, 153,* 650–658.

Marks, I. M., Swinson, R. P., Basoglu, M., Kuch, K., Noshirvani, H., O'Sullivan, G., Lelliot, P. T., Kirby, M., McNamee, G., Sengun, S., & Wickwire, K. (1993). Alprazolam and exposure alone and combined in panic disorder with agoraphobia. *British Journal of Psychiatry, 162,* 776–787.

Marlatt, G. A. (1987). Alcohol, the magic elixir: Stress, expectancy, and the transformation of emotional states. In E. Gottheil, K. A. Druly, S. Pashko, S. P. Weinstein (Eds.) *Stress and Addiction.* (pp. 302–322). New York: Brunner/Mazel.

Marlatt, G. A., Demming, B., & Reid, J. B. (1973). Loss of control drinking in alcoholics: An experimental analogue. *Journal of Abnormal Psychology, 81,* 223–241.

Marlatt, G. A., & Gordon, J. R. (Eds.). (1985). *Relapse prevention maintenance strategies in the treatment of addictive behaviors.* New York: Guilford Press.

Marques, J., Nelson, C., West, M. A., & Day, D. M. (1994). The relationship between treatment goals and recidivism among child molesters. *Behaviour Research and Therapy, 32,* 577–588.

Marshall, W. L., & Eccles, A. (1996). Cognitive-behavioral treatment of sex offenders. In V. B. Van Hasselt & M. Hersen (Eds.), *Sourcebook of psychological treatment manuals for adult disorders.* New York: Plenum.

Marshall, W. L., Eccles, A., & Barbaree, H. E. (1990). The treatment of exhibitionists: A focus on sexual deviance versus cognitive and relationship features. *Behaviour Research and Therapy, 29,* 129–135.

Marshall, W. L., Jones, R., Ward, T., Johnston, P., & Barbaree, H. E. (1991). Treatment outcome with sex offenders. *Clinical Psychology Review, 11,* 465–485.

Martin, A. D. (1982). Learning to hide: The socialization of the gay adolescent. In J. G. Looney, A. Z. Schwartburg, & A. D. Sorosky (Eds), *Adolescent psychiatry* (Vol. 10, pp. 52–65). Chicago: University of Chicago Press.

Martin, R. (1994). *Out of silence: A journey into language.* New York: Holt.

Marziali, E. A., & Munroe-Blum, H. (1987). A group approach: The management of projective identification in group treatment of self-destructive borderline patients. *Journal of Personality Disorders, 1,* 340–343.

Maslow, A. H. (1954). *Motivation and personality.* New York: Harper.

Maslow, A. H. (1962). *Toward a psychology of being.* Princeton, NJ: Van Nostrand.

Massion, A., Warshaw, M., & Keller, M. (1993). Quality of life and psychiatric morbidity in panic disorder and generalized anxiety disorder. *American Journal of Psychiatry, 150,* 600–607.

Masson, J. M. (1983). *The assault on the truth: Freud's suppression of the seduction theory.* New York: Farrar, Straus & Giroux.

Masters, W. H., & Johnson, V. E. (1966). *Human sexual response.* Boston: Little, Brown and Company.

Masters, W. H. & Johnson, V. E. (1970). *Human sexual inadequacy.* Boston: Little, Brown and Company.

Masur, F. T. (1981). Adherence to health care regimens. In C. K. Prokop & L. A. Bradley (Eds.), *Medical psychology: Contributions to behavioral medicine* (pp. 442–470). New York: Academic Press.

Matthews, K. A. (1982). Psychological perspectives on the Type A behavior pattern. *Psychological Bulletin, 91,* 293–323.

Matthews, K. A. (1988). Coronary heart disease and Type A behavior: Update on and alternative to the Booth-Kewley and Friedman (1987) quantitative review. *Psychological Bulletin, 104,* 373–380.

Matthews, K. A., & Haynes, S. G. (1986). Type A behavior pattern and coronary risk: Update and critical evaluation. *American Journal of Epidemiology, 123,* 923–960.

Mattick, R. P., & Peters, L. (1988). Treatment of severe social phobia: Effects of guided exposure with and without cognitive restructuring. *Journal of Consulting and Clinical Psychology, 56,* 251–260.

Mattick, R. P., Andrews, G., Hadzi-Pavlovic, D., & Christensen, H. (1990). Treatment of panic and agoraphobia: An integrative review. *Journal of Nervous and Mental Disease, 178,* 567–576.

Mattila, M., Aranko, K., & Seppala, T. (1982). Acute effects of buspirone and alcohol on psychomotor skills. *Journal of Clinical Psychiatry, 43,* 56–61.

Mattison, A. M. & McWhirter, D. P. (1995). Lesbians, gay males, and their families: Some therapeutic issues. *Psychiatric Clinics of North America, 18,* 123–137.

Mattson, M. E., & Allen, J. P. (1991). Research on matching alcoholic patients to treatments: Findings, issues, and implications. *Journal of Addictive Diseases, 11*(12), 33–49.

Matz, P. A., Altepeter, T. S., & Perlman, B. (1992). MMPI-2 reliability with college students. *Journal of Clinical Psychology, 48,* 330–334.

Mavissakalian, M. R. (1989). Imipramine dose-response relationship in panic disorder with agoraphobia: Preliminary findings. *Archives of General Psychiatry, 46,* 127–131.

Mavissakalian, M. R. (1990). Differential efficacy between tricyclic antidepressants and behavior therapy of panic disorder. In J. Ballenger (Ed.), *Clinical aspects of panic disorder* (pp. 195–209). New York: Wiley-Liss.

Mavissakalian, M. R., & Michelson, L. (1986). Agoraphobia: Relative and combined effectiveness of therapist-assisted in vivo exposure and imipramine. *Journal of Clinical Psychiatry, 47,* 117–122.

Mavissakalian, M. R., & Perel, J. M. (1995). Imipramine treatment of panic disorder with agoraphobia: Dose ranging and plasma level-response relationships. *American Journal of Psychiatry, 152,* 673–682.

May, R. (1969). *Love and will.* New York: W. W. Norton.

McAdoo, W., & DeMeyer, M. (1978). Personality characteristics of parents. In M. Rutter & E. Schopler (Eds.), *Autism: A reappraisal of concepts and treatment* (pp. 251–267). New York: Plenum.

McBride, W. J., Murphy, J. M., Lumeng, L., & Li, T.-K. (1990). Serotonin, dopamine, and GABA involvement in alcohol drinking of selectively bred rats. *Alcohol, 7,* 199–205.

McCarthy, B. (1988). *Male sexual awareness.* New York: Carroll and Graf.

McCarthy, B. (1993). Relapse prevention strategies and techniques in sex therapy. *Journal of Sex and Marital Therapy, 19,* 142–146.

McCartney, K., Harris, M. J., & Bernieri, F. (1990). Growing up and growing apart: A developmental meta-analysis of twin studies. *Psychological Bulletin, 107,* 226–237.

McCauley, E., & Myers, K. (1992). The longitudinal clinical course of depression in children and adolescents. *Child and Adolescent Psychiatric Clinics of North America, 1(1),* 183–196.

McCauley, E., Reid, M., Kerns, K., & Calderon, R. (1991, April). *Perceptions of parent and peer relationships in depressed youth.* Paper presented at the meeting of the Society for Research in Child Development, Seattle, WA.

McConaghy, N. (1990). Assessment and treatment of sex offenders: The Prince of Wales Programme. *Australian and New Zealand Journal of Psychiatry, 24,* 175–181.

McConaghy, N. (1996). Treatment of sexual dysfunctions. In V. B. Van Hasselt & M. Hersen (Eds.), *Sourcebook of psychological treatment manuals for adult disorders.* New York: Plenum.

McCord, J. (1979). Some child rearing antecedents of criminal behavior in adult men. *Journal of Personality and Social Psychology, 9,* 1477–1486.

McCrady, B. S. (1994). Alcoholics Anonymous and behavior therapy: Can habits be treated as diseases? Can diseases be treated as habits? *Journal of Consulting and Clinical Psychology, 62(6),* 1159–1156.

McCrady, B. S., Stout, R., Noel, N., Abrams, D., & Nelson, H. F. (1991). Effectiveness of three types of spouse-involved behavioral alcoholism treatments. *British Journal of the Addictions, 86(11),* 1415–1424.

McCrae, R. R., & Costa, P. T. (1994). The stability of personality: Observation and evaluations. *Current Directions in Psychological Science, 3,* 173–175.

McCubbin, J. A. (1993). Stress and endogenous opioids: Behavioral and circulatory interventions. *Biological Psychology, 35,* 91–122.

McEachin, J. J., Smith, T., & Lovaas, O. I. (1993). Longterm outcome for children with autism who received early intensive behavioral treatment. *American Journal on Mental Retardation, 97(4),* 359–372.

McEwen, B. S. (1991). Sex differences in the brain: What are they and how do they arise? In M. T. Notman & C. C. Nadelson (Eds.), *Women and men: New perspectives on gender differences,* (pp. 35–41). Washington, DC: American Psychiatric Press.

McEwen, B. S. (1994). How do sex and stress hormones affect nerve cells? In V. N. Luine & C. F. Harding (Eds.), *Hormonal restructuring of the adult brain: Basic and clinical perspectives.* New York: Annals of the New York Academy of Sciences.

McFarlane, W. R., Lukens, E., Link, B., Dushay, R., Deakins, S. A., Newmark, M., Dunne, E. J., Horen, B., & Toran, J. (1995). Multiple-family groups and psychoeducation in the treatment of schizophrenia. *Archives of General Psychiatry, 52,* l, 679–687.

McGee, J. J. (1992). Gentle teaching's assumptions and paradigm. *Journal of Applied Behavior Analysis, 25,* 869–872.

McGlashan, T., & Fenton, W. (1991). Classical subtypes for schizophrenia: Literature review for DSM-IV. *Schizophrenia Bulletin, 17,* 610–632.

McGrath, M. J., & Cohen, D. B. (1978). REM sleep facilitation of adaptive waking behavior: A review of the literature. *Psychological Bulletin, 85,* 24–57.

McGue, M., Pickens, R. W., & Svikis, D. S. (1992). Sex and age effects on the inheritance of alcohol problems: A twin study. *Journal of Abnormal Psychology, 101(3),* 3–17.

McGuigan, F. J. (1994). *Biological psychology: A cybernetic science.* Englewood Cliffs, NJ: Prentice Hall.

McGuinness, D. (1985). *When children don't learn: Understanding the biology and psychology of learning disabilities.* New York: Basic Books.

McGuire, P. K., Shah, G. M. S., & Murray, R. M. (1993). Increased blood flow in Broca's area during auditory hallucinations in schizophrenia. *Lancet, 342,* 703–706.

McKeon, R. (Ed.) (1941). *The basic works of Aristotle.* New York: Random House.

McKey, R. H., Condelli, L., Ganson, H., Barrett, B., McConkey, C., & Plantz, M. (1985). *The impact of Head Start on children, family, and communities: Final report of the Head Start Evaluation, Synthesis and Utilization Project* (DHHS Publication No. OHDS 85–31193). Washington, DC: U.S. Government Printing Office.

McKim, W. A. (1991). *Drugs and behaviors: An introduction to behavioral pharmacology.* Upper Saddle River, NJ: Prentice Hall.

McKinnon, W., Weisse, C. S., Reynolds, C. P., Bowles, C. A., & Baum, A. (1989). Chronic stress, leukocyte subpopulations, and hormonal response to latent viruses. *Health Psychology, 8,* 399–402.

McLellan, A. T., Alterman, A. I., Metzger, D. S., Grissom, G. R., Woody, G. E., Luborsky, L., & O'Brien, C. P. (1994). Similarity of outcome predictors across opiate, cocaine, and alcohol treatments: Role of treatment services. *Journal of Consulting and Clinical Psychology, 62,* 1141–1158.

McLeod, J. D., & Kessler, R. C. (1990). Socioeconomic status differences in vulnerability to undesirable life events. *Journal of Health and Social Behavior, 31,* 162–172.

McLeskey, J., & Pacchiano, D. P. (1994). Mainstreaming students with learning disabilities: Are we making progress? *Exceptional Children, 60,* 508–517.

McNally, R. (1987). Preparedness and phobias: A review. *Psychological Bulletin, 101,* 283–303.

McNally, R. (1994). *Panic disorder: A critical analysis.* New York: Guilford.

McNeal, E. T., & Cimbolic, P. (1986). Antidepressants and biochemical theories of depression. *Psychological Bulletin, 99,* 361–374.

McNeil, D. W., Vrana, S. R., Melamed, B. G., Cuthbert, B. N., & Lang, P. J. (1993). Emotional imagery in simple and social phobia: Fear versus anxiety. *Journal of Abnormal Psychology, 102,* 212–225.

McReynolds, P. (1989). Diagnosis and clinical assessment: Current status and major issues. In M. R. Rosenzweig & L. W. Porter (Eds.), *Annual Review of Psychology* (pp. 83–108). Palo Alto, CA: Annual Reviews.

Meador, B. D., & Rogers, C. R. (1973). Client-centered therapy. In R. Corsini (Ed.), *Current psychotherapies* (pp. 119–165). Itasca, IL: F. E Peacock.

Mednick, S. A., Gabrielli, W. F., & Hutchings, B. (1984). Genetic influences in criminal convictions: Evidence from an adoption cohort. *Science, 224,* 891–894.

Mednick, S., Gabrielli, W. F., & Hutchings, B. (1987). Genetic influences in the etiology of criminal behavior. In S. A. Mednick, T. Moffit, & S. Stack (Eds.), *The causes of crime: New biological approaches* (pp. 74–91). Cambridge: Cambridge University Press.

Mednick, S. A., Machon, R. A., & Huttunen, M. O. (1990). An update on the Helsinki influenza project [Letter to the editor]. *Archives of General Psychiatry, 47,* 292.

Mednick, S. A., Machon, R. A., Huttunen, M. O., & Bonett, D. (1988). Adult schizophrenia following prenatal exposure to an influenza epidemic. *Archives of General Psychiatry, 45,* 189–192.

Mednick, S. A., & Schulsinger, F. (1968). Some premorbid characteristics related to breakdown in children with schizophrenic mothers. In D. Rosenthal & S. S. Kety (Eds.), *The transmission of schizophrenia* (pp. 267–291). Oxford: Pergamon Press.

Meehl, P. (1962). Schizophrenia, schizotypy and schizophrenia. *American Psychologist, 17,* 827–838.

Meehl, P. (1990). Toward an integrated theory of schizotaxia, schizotypy, and schizophrenia. *Journal of Personality Disorders, 4,* 1–99.

Meichenbaum, D. (1971). Examination of model characteristics in reducing avoidance behavior. *Journal of Personality and Social Psychology, 17,* 298–307.

Meier-Tackmann, D., Leonhardt, R. A., Agarwal, D. P., & Goedde, H. W. (1990). Effect of acute ethanol drinking on alcohol metabolism in subjects with different ADH and ALDH genotypes. *Alcohol, 7*(5), 413–418.

Melloni, R. H., Delville, Y., & Ferris, C. E. (1995). Vasosuppression/serotonin interactions in the anterior hypothalamus control aggressive behavior in golden hamsters. *Society for Neuroscience Abstracts,* p. 1695.

Melton, G., Petrila, J., Poythress, N., & Slobogin, C. (1987). *Psychological evaluation for the courts.* New York: Guilford Press.

Meltzoff, A. N., & Gopnik, A. (1993). The role of imitation in understanding persons and developing a theory of mind. In S. Baron-Cohen, H. Tager-Flusberg, & D. Cohen (Eds.), *Understanding other minds: Perspectives from autism* (pp. 335–366). New York: Oxford University Press.

Meltzoff, J., & Kornreich, M. (1970). *Research in psychotherapy.* New York: Atherton Press.

Mendelson, W. B., & Rich, C. L. (1993). Sedatives and suicide: The San Diego study. *Acta Psychiatrica Scandinavica, 88*(5), 337–341.

Mendelwicz, J., & Rainer, J. D. (1977). Adoption study supporting genetic transmission in manic-depressive illness. *Nature, 268,* 327–329.

Menzies, R. G., & Clarke, J. C. (1995). The etiology of phobias: A nonassociative account. *Clinical Psychology Review, 15,* 23–48.

Merckelbach, H., deJong, P. J., Muris, P., & van den Hout, M. A. (1996). The etiology of specific phobias: A review. *Clinical Psychology Review, 16,* 337-361.

Merikangas, K. R. (1990). The genetic epidemiology of alcoholism. *Psychological Medicine, 20,* 11–22.

Mersky, H. (1995). The manufacture of personalities: The production of multiple personality disorder. In L. M. Cohen, J. N. Berzoff, & M. R. Elin (Eds.), *Dissociative identity disorder: Theoretical and treatment controversies* (pp. 3–32). Northvale, NJ: Jason Aronson.

Metalsky, G. I., Joiner, T. E., Hardin, T. S., & Abramson, L. Y. (1993). Depressive reactions to failure in a naturalistic setting: A test of the hopelessness and self-esteem theories of depression. *Journal of Abnormal Psychology, 103,* 101–109.

Meyer, A. J., Nash, J. D., McAlister, A. L., Maccoby, N., & Farquhar, J. W. (1980). Skills training in a cardiovascular education campaign. *Journal of Consulting and Clinical Psychology, 48,* 129–142.

Meyer, J. (1995). Paraphilias. In H. I. Kaplan & B. J. Sadock (Eds.), *Comprehensive textbook of psychiatry/VI* (pp. 1334–1346). Baltimore: Williams & Wilkins.

Meyer, R. B. (1993). *The clinician's handbook: Integrated diagnostics, assessment, and intervention in adult and adolescent psychopathology.* Boston: Allyn & Bacon.

Meyer-Bahlburg, H. F. L. (1993). Psychobiologic research on homosexuality. *Child and Adolescent Psychiatric Clinics of North America, 2,* 489–500.

Meyerowitz, B. E., Heinrich, R. L., & Schag, C. C. (1983). A competency-based approach to coping with cancer. In T. G. Burish & L. A. Bradley (Eds.), *Coping with chronic disease* (pp. 137–158). New York: Academic Press.

Mezzich, J. E., Fabrega, H., Coffman, G. A., & Haley, R. (1989). DSM-III disorders in a large sample of psychiatric patients: Frequency and specificity of diagnoses. *American Journal of Psychiatry, 146,* 212–219.

Mezzich, J. A., & von Cranach, M. (Eds.). (1988). *International classificaion in psychiatry.* Cambridge: Cambridge University Press.

Mezzich, A., Tarter, R., Kirisci, L., Clark, D., Bukstein, O., & Martin, C. (1993). Subtypes of early age onset alcoholism. *Alcoholism in Clinical and Experimental Research, 17,* 767–770.

Michael, R. I., Gagnon, J. H., Laumann, E. O., Kolata, G. (1994). *Sex in America: A definitive survey.* Boston: Little, Brown and Company.

Miller, B. L., Chang, L., Oropilla, G., & Mena, I. (1994). Alzheimer's disease and frontal lobe dementias. In C. E. Coffey & J. L. Cummings (Eds.). *Textbook of geriatric neuropsychiatry.* (pp. 389–404). Washington, DC: American Psychiatric Press.

Miller, H. L., Combs, D. W., Leeper, J. D., & Bartan, S. N. (1984). An analysis of the effects of suicide prevention facilities on suicide rates in the United States. *American Journal of Public Health, 74,* 340–343.

Miller, I. W., Keitner, G. E., Whisman, M. A., Ryan, C. E., Epstein, N. B., & Bishop, D. S. (1992). Depressed patients with dysfunctional families: Description and course of illness. *Journal of Abnormal Psychology, 101,* 637–646.

Miller, L. K., & Miller, O. (1970). Reinforcing self-help group activities of welfare recipients. *Journal of Applied Behavior Analysis, 3,* 57–64.

Miller, N. E. (1969). Learning of visceral and glandular responses. *Science, 163,* 434–445.

Miller, N. S., Gold, M. S., & Pottash, A. C. (1989). A 12-step treatment approach for marijuana (cannabis) dependence. *Journal of Substance Abuse Treatment, 6,* 241–250.

Miller, T. Q., Turner, C. W., Tindale, R. S., Posavac, E. J., & Dugoni, B. L. (1991). Reasons for the trend toward null findings in research on Type A behavior. *Psychological Bulletin, 110,* 469–485.

Miller, W. R. (1983). Motivational interviewing with problem drinkers. *Behavioral Psychotherapy, 11,* 147–172.

Miller, W. R., & Muñoz, R. F. (1982). *How to control your drinking* (2nd ed.). Albuquerque: University of New Mexico Press.

Millman, R. B., & Sbriglio, R. (1986). Patterns of use and psychopathology in chronic marijuana users. *Psychiatric Clinics of North America, 9,* 533–545.

Millon, T. (1987). *Manual for the MCMI-II* (2nd ed.). Minneapolis: National Computer Systems.

Millon, T. (1990). *Toward a new personology.* New York: John Wiley & Sons.

Millon, T. (1991). Classification in psychopathology: Rationale, alternatives, and standards. *Journal of Abnormal Psychology, 100,* 245–261.

Millon, T., & Klerman, G. L. (Eds.). (1986). *Contemporary directions in psychopathology: Toward the DSM-IV.* New York: Guilford Press.

Milner, J. S. (1994). Assessing physical child abuse risk: The child abuse potential inventory. *Clinical Psychology Review, 14,* 547–583.

Mineka, S., & Cook, M. (1986). Immunization against the observational conditioning of snake fear in Rhesus monkeys. *Journal of Abnormal Psychology, 95,* 307–318.

Mineka, S., Davison, M., Cook, M., & Keir, R. (1984). Observational conditioning of snake fear in Rhesus monkeys. *Journal of Abnormal Psychology, 93,* 355–372.

Minichiello, W., Baer, L., Jenike, M. A., & Holland, A. (1990). Age of onset and major subtypes of obsessive-compulsive disorder. *Journal of Anxiety Disorders, 4,* 147–150.

Minuchin, S. (1974). *Families and family therapy.* Cambridge: Harvard University Press.

Minuchin, S., Rosman, R., & Baker, L. (1978). *Psychosomatic families: Anorexia nervosa in context.* Cambridge: Harvard University Press.

Mirsky, A., Kugelmass, S., Ingraham, L. J., Frenkel, E., & Nathan, M. (1995). Overview and summary: Twenty-five years follow-up of high-risk children. *Schizophrenia Bulletin, 21,* 227–239.

Mirsky, A., & Orzack, M. H. (1980). Two retrospective studies of psychosurgery. In E. S. Valenstein (Ed), *The psychosurgery debate: Scientific, legal and ethical perspectives* (pp. 205–244). San Francisco: W. C. Freeman & Co.

Mitchell, J. E., Pyle, R. L., Eckert, E. D., Hatsukami, D., Pomeroy, C., & Zimmerman, R. (1990). A comparison study of antidepressants and structured intensive group psychotherapy in the treatment of bulimia nervosa. *Archives in General Psychiatry, 47*(2), 149–157.

Mitchell, J., McCauley, E., Burke, P. M., & Moss, S. J. (1988). Phenomenology of depression in children and adolescents. *Journal of American Academy of Child Adolescence Psychiatry, 27,* 12–20.

Mitchell, R. E., Billings, A. G., & Moos, R. H. (1982). Social support and well-being: Implications for prevention programs. *Journal of Primary Prevention, 3,* 77–98.

Mitchell, S. H., deWit, H., & Zancy, J. P. (1995). Caffeine withdrawal symptoms and self-administration following caffeine deprivation. *Pharmacology, Biochemistry and Behavior, 51*(4), 941–945.

Modestin, J. (1992). Multiple personality disorders in Switzerland. *American Journal of Psychiatry, 149,* 88–91.

Moffitt, T. E. (1990). Juvenile delinquency and attention-deficit disorder: Developmental trajectories from age 3 to 15. *Child Development, 61,* 893–910.

Moffitt, T. E. (1993). Adolescence-limited and life-course persistent antisocial behavior: A developmental taxonomy. *Psychological Review, 100,* 674–701.

Moffitt, T. E., & Lynam, D. R. (1994). The neuropsychology of conduct disorder and delinquency: Implications for understanding antisocial behavior. In D. Fowles, P. Sutker, & S. Goodman (Eds.), *Psychopathy and antisocial personality: A developmental perspective* (pp. 233–262). New York: Springer.

Mohs, R. C., Breitner, J. C. S., Silverman, J. M., & Davis, K. L. (1987). Alzheimer's disease. Morbid risk among first-degree relatives approximates 50 percent by 90 years of age. *Archives of General Psychiatry, 44,* 405–408.

Monahan, J. (1981). *The clinical prediction of violent behavior.* Washington, DC: National Institutes of Health.

Monahan, J. (1984). The prediction of violent behavior: Toward a second generation of theory and practice. *American Journal of Psychiatry, 141,* 10–15.

Monahan, J. (1992). Mental disorder and violent behavior: Perceptions and evidence. *American Psychologist, 47,* 511–521.

Money, J., & Pranzarone, R.. (1993). Development of paraphilia in childhood and adolescence. *Child and Adolescent Psychiatric Clinics of North America, 2,* 463–476.

Moniz, E. (1948). *How I came to perform prefrontal leucotomy* (pp. 7–18). Proceedings of the First International Congress of Psychosurgery, Lisboa, Edicoes Atica.

Monroe, S. M., & Depue, R. A. (1991). Life stress and depression. In J. Becker & A. Kleinman (Eds.), *Psychosocial aspects of depression* (pp. 101–130). Hillsdale, NJ: Erlbaum.

Morey, L. (1991). *Personality Assessment Inventory manual.* Odessa, FL: Psychological Assessment Resources.

Morgenstern, H., & Glazer, W. (1993). Identifying risk factors for tardive dyskinesia among long-term outpatients maintained with neuroleptic medications: Results of the Yale Tardive Dyskinesia Study. *Archives of General Psychiatry, 50,* 723–733.

Morokoff, P. J. (1978). Determinants of female orgasm. In J. LoPiccolo & L. LoPiccolo (Eds.), *Handbook of sex therapy.* New York: Plenum.

Morokoff, P. J., & Heiman, J. (1980). Effects of erotic stimuli on sexually functional and dysfunctional women: Multiple measures before and after sex therapy. *Behaviour Research and Therapy, 18,* 127–137.

Morrison, J. (1989). Childhood sexual histories of women with somatization disorder. *American Journal of Psychiatry, 146,* 239–241.

Morrow, J., & Nolen-Hoeksema, S. (1990). Effects of responses to depression on the remediation of depressive affect. *Journal of Personality and Social Psychology, 58,* 519–527.

Mortimer, J. A. (1994). What are the risk factors for dementia? In F. A. Huppert, C. Brayne, & D. W. O'Connor (Eds.). *Dementia and normal aging* (pp. 208–229). Cambridge: Cambridge University Press.

Moscarelli, M., & Capri, S. (1992). The cost of schizophrenia: Editors' introduction. *Schizophrenia Bulletin, 17,* 367–369.

Moskowitz, H., & Smiley, A. (1982). Effects of chronically administered buspirone and diazepam on driving-related skills performance. *Journal of Clinical Psychiatry, 43,* 45–55.

Mossman, K. (1994). Assessing predictions of violence: Being accurate about accuracy. *Journal of Consulting and Clinical Psychology, 62,* 783–792.

Mowrer, O. H. (1939). A stimulus-response analysis of anxiety and its role as a reinforcing agent. *Psychological Review, 46,* 553–565.

Mrazek, P. J., & Haggerty, R. J. (Eds.). (1994). *Reducing risks for mental disorders: Frontiers for preventive intervention research.* Washington, DC: National Academy Press.

MRFIT (Multiple Risk Factors Intervention Trial Research Group). (1982). Multiple risk factor intervention trial: Risk factor changes and mortality results. *Journal of the American Medical Association, 248,* 1465–1477.

Mukerjee, M. (1995). Hidden scares: Sexual and other abuse may alter a brain region. *Scientific American,* October, 14–15.

Mukherjee, S., Sackeim, H., & Schnur, D. (1994). Electroconvulsive therapy of acute manic episodes: A review of 50 years experience. *American Journal of Psychiatry, 151,* 169–176.

Mullen, B., & Suls, J. (1982). The effectiveness of attention and rejection as coping styles. *Journal of Psychosomatic Research, 26,* 43–49.

Mulvey, E. P., & Lidz, C. W. (1984). Clinical considerations in the prediction of dangerousness in mental patients. *Clinical Psychology Review, 4,* 379–401.

Mundy, P., Sigman, M., & Kasari, C. (1994). Joint attention, developmental level, and symptom presentation in autism. *Development and Psychopathology, 6,* 389–401.

Muñoz, R. F., Hollon, S. D., McGrath, E., Rehm, L. P., & VandenBos, G. R. (1994). On the AHCPR *Depression in Primary Care Guidelines:* Further considerations for practitioners. *American Psychologist, 49,* 42–61.

Munroe, R. (1955). *Schools of psychoanalytic thought.* New York: Dryden Press.

Murphy, J. M. (1976). Psychiatric labeling in cross-cultural perspective. *Science, 191,* 1019–1028.

Musty, R. E., & Kaback, L. (1995). Relationships between motivation and depression in chronic marijuana users. *Life Sciences, 56,* 2151–2155.

Myers, D. G., & Diener, E. (1995). Who is happy? *Psychological Science, 6,* 10–19.

Myers, J., Weissman, M., Tischler, G., Holzer, C. E., Leaf, P., Oravaschel, H., Anthony, J., Boyd, J., Burke, J., Kramer, M., & Stoltzman, R. (1984). Six-month prevalence of psychiatric disorders in three communities. *Archives of General Psychiatry, 41,* 959–967.

Nathan, P. E. (1987a). DSM-III-R and the behavior therapist. *Behavior Therapy, 10,* 203–205.

Nathan, P. E. (1987b). What do behavioral scientists know and what can they do about alcoholism? In C. P. Rivers (Ed.), *Alcohol and addictive behavior: Vol. 34. Nebraska Symposium on Motivation.* Lincoln: University of Nebraska Press.

Nathan, S. (1986). The epidemiology of the DSM-III psychosexual dysfunctions. *Journal of Sex and Marital Therapy, 12,* 267–281.

National Institutes of Health. (1987). Differential diagnosis of dementing diseases. *Journal of the American Medical Association, 258,* 3411–3416.

National Center for Health Statistics. (1992). *Vital statistics of the United States, 1992.* Washington, DC: U.S. Government Printing Office.

National Institute on Drug Abuse (1991). *National household survey on drug abuse. Populations estimates 1990.* Rockville, MD: U.S. Department of Health and Human Services.

National Institute of Mental Health. (1985). *Consensus development conference statement on electroconvulsive therapy,* Vol. 5 (11, pp. 1–8). Bethesda, MD: Author.

National Institute on Alcohol Abuse and Alcoholism. (1990). *Alcohol and health: Seventh special report to the U.S. Congress* (DHHS Publication No. ADM 90-1656). Washington, DC: U.S. Government Printing Office.

Neal, A. M., & Turner, S. M. (1991). Anxiety disorders research with African Americans: Current status. *Psychological Bulletin, 109,* 400–410.

Newman, E., Orsillo, S. M., Herman, D. S., Niles, B. L., & Litz, B. T. (1995). Clinical presentation of disorders of extreme stress in combat veterans. *Journal of Nervous and Mental Disease, 183,* 628–632.

Newman, D. L., Moffitt, T. E., Caspi, A., Magdol, L., Silva, P., & Stanton, W. R. (1996). Psychiatric disorder in a birth cohort of young adults: Prevalence, comorbidity, clinical significance, and new case incidence from ages 11 to 21. *Journal of Consulting and Clinical Psychology, 64,* 552–562.

Neziroglu, F., Anemone, R., & Yaryura-Tobias, J. A. (1992). Onset of obsessive-compulsive disorder in pregnancy. *American Journal of Psychiatry, 149,* 947–950.

Neziroglu, F., McKay, D., Fodaro, J., & Yaryura-Tobias, J. A. (1996). Effect of cognitive behavior therapy on persons with body dysmorphic disorder and co-morbid Axis II diagnoses. *Behavior Therapy, 27,* 67–68.

Nicholson, R. A., & Berman, J. S. (1983). Is follow-up necessary in evaluating psychotherapy? *Psychological Bulletin, 93,* 261–278.

Nicholson, R. A., & Kugler, K. E. (1991). Competent and incompetent criminal defendants: A quantitative review of comparative research. *Psychological Bulletin, 109,* 355–370.

Nicholson, R. A., Norwood, S., & Enyart, C. (1991). Characteristics and outcomes of insanity acquitees in Oklahoma. *Behavioral Sciences and the Law, 9,* 487–500.

Nicolosi, J. (1991). *Reparative therapy of male homosexuality.* Northvale, NJ: Aronson.

Nicolosi, J. (1994). Objections to AAP statement on homosexuality and adolescence (letter). *Pediatrics, 92,* 631–634.

Nietzel, M. T. (1979). *Crime and its modification: A social learning perspective.* New York: Pergamon Press.

Nietzel, M. T., Bernstein, D. A., & Milich, R. (1998). *Introduction to clinical psychology* (4th ed.). Englewood Cliffs, NJ: Prentice Hall.

Nietzel, M. T., & Dillehay, R. C. (1986). *Psychological consultation in the courtroom.* New York: Pergamon Press.

Nietzel, M. T., & Fisher, S. G. (1981). Effectiveness of professional and paraprofessional helpers. A reply to Durlak. *Psychological Bulletin, 89,* 555–565.

Nietzel, M. T., Guthrie, P. R., & Susman, D. T. (1991). Utilization of community and social support services. In F. H. Kanfer & A. P. Goldstein (Eds.), *Helping people change* (4th ed., pp. 396–421). New York: Pergamon Press.

Nietzel, M. T., & Harris, M. (1990). Relationship of dependency and achievement/autonomy to depression. *Clinical Psychology Review, 10,* 279–297.

Nietzel, M. T., Hasemann, D. M., & Lynam, D. R. (1997). Behavioral perspectives on violent behavior. In V. B. Van Hasselt & M. Hersen (Eds.), *Handbook of psychological approaches with violent criminal offenders: Contemporary strategies and issues.* New York: Plenum.

Nietzel, M. T., & Himelein, M. (1986). Prevention of crime and delinquency. In L. Michelson & B. Edelstein (Eds.), *Handbook of prevention* (pp. 195–221). New York: Plenum.

Nietzel, M. T., Russell, R. L., Hemmings, K. A., & Gretter, M. L. (1987). The clinical significance of psychotherapy for unipolar depression: A meta-analytic approach to social comparison. *Journal of Consulting and Clinical Psychology, 55,* 156–161.

Nietzel, M. T., & Trull, T. J. (1988). Meta-analytic approaches to social comparisons: A method for measuring clinical significance. *Behavioral Assessment, 10,* 159–169.

Nietzel, M. T., Winett, R. A., Macdonald, M. L., & Davidson, W. S. (1977). *Behavioral approaches to community psychology.* New York: Pergamon Press.

Nigg, J. T., & Goldsmith, H. H. (1994). Genetics of personality disorders: Perspectives from personality and psychopathology research. *Psychological Bulletin, 115,* 346–380.

Nihira, K., Leland, H., & Lambert, N. (1993). *Adaptive behavior scales: Residential and community.* Austin, *Texas: Pro-Ed.*

Nobler, M., & Sackeim, H. (1993). ECT stimulus dosing: Relations to efficacy and adverse effects. In C. E. Coffey (Ed.), *The clinical science of electroconvulsive therapy* (pp. 29–52). Washington, DC: American Psychiatric Press.

Nobler, M. S., Sackeim, H. A., Prohovnik, I., Moeller, J. R., Schnur, D. B., Prudic, J., & Devanand, D. P. (1994). Regional cerebral blood flow in mood disorders. III: Treatment and clinical response. *Archives of General Psychiatry, 51,* 884–897.

Nolen-Hoeksema, S. (1987). Sex differences in unipolar depression: Evidence and theory. *Psychological Bulletin, 101,* 259–282.

Nolen-Hoeksema, S., Morrow, J., Fredrickson, B. (1993). Response styles and the duration of episodes of depressed mood. *Journal of Abnormal Psychology, 102,* 20–28.

Noll, R. B., Zucker R. A., & Greenberg, G. S. (1990). Identification of alcohol by smell among preschoolers: Evidence for early socialization about drugs occurring in the home. *Child Development, 61*(5), 1520–1527.

North, C. S., Ryall, J. E. M., Ricci, D. A., & Wetzsel, R. D. (1993). *Multiple personalities, multiple disorders: Psychiatric classification and media influence.* New York: Oxford University Press.

Noyes, R., Crowe, R. R., Harris, E. L., Hamra, B. J., McChesney, C. M., & Chandry, D. R. (1986). Relationship between panic disorder and agoraphobia: A family study. *Archives of General Psychiatry, 43,* 227–232.

Noyes, R., Garvey, M., & Cook, B. (1990). Benzodiazepines other than alprazolam in the treatment of panic disorder. In J. Ballenger (Ed.), *Clinical aspects of panic disorder* (pp. 251–258). New York: Wiley-Liss.

Noyes, R., Garvey, M., Cook, B., & Sulzer, M. (1991). Controlled discontinuation of benzodiazepine treatment for patients with panic disorder. *American Journal of Psychiatry, 148,* 517–523.

Noyes, R., Kathol, R. G., Fisher, M. M., Phillips, B. M., Suelzer, M. T., Woodman, C. L. (1994). One-year follow-up of medical outpatients with hypochondriasis. *Psychosomatics, 35,* 533–545.

Noyes, R., Woodman, C., Garvey, M., Cook, B., Sulzer, M., Clancy, J., & Anderson, D. (1992). Generalized anxiety disorder *vs.* panic disorder: Distinguishing characteristics and patterns of comorbidity. *Journal of Nervous and Mental Diseases, 180,* 369–379.

Nunes, E. V., Frank, K. A., & Kornfeld, S. D. (1987). Psychologic treatment for Type A behavior pattern and for coronary heart disease: A meta-analysis of the literature. *Psychosomatic Medicine, 48,* 159–173.

Nurnberger, J. I., & Gershon, E. S. (1992). Genetics. In E. S. Paykel (Ed.), *Handbook of affective disorders.* New York: Guilford Press.

Nye, C. L., Zucker, R. A., & Fitzgerald, H. E. (1995). Early intervention in the path to alcohol problems through conduct problems: Treatment involvement and child behavior change. *Journal of Consulting and Clinical Psychology, 63*(5), 831–840.

O'Conner, S., Hesselbrock, V., Tasman, A., & DePalma, N. (1987). P3 amplitude in two distinct tasks are decreased in young men with a history of paternal alcoholism. *Alcohol, 4,* 323–330.

O'Connor, D. W. (1994). Mild dementia: A clinical perspective. In F. A. Huppert, C. Brayne, & D. W. O'Connor (Eds.), *Dementia and normal aging* (pp. 91–117). Cambridge: Cambridge University Press.

O'Connor, M., Sales, B. D., & Shuman, D. (1996). Mental health professional expertise in the courtroom. In B. D. Sales & D. W. Shuman (Eds.), *Law, mental health, and mental disorder.* Pacific Grove, CA: Brooks/Cole.

O'Connor v. Donaldson, 422 U.S. 563 (1975).

O'Hara, M. W., Zekoski, E. M., Phillipps, L. H., & Wright, E. J. (1990). Controlled prospective study of postpartum mood disorders: Comparison of childbearing and non-childbearing women. *Journal of Abnormal Psychology, 99,* 3–15.

O'Leary, A. (1990). Stress, emotion, and human immune function. *Psychological Bulletin, 108,* 363–382.

O'Leary, K. D., & Becker, W. C. (1967). Behavior modification of an adjustment class: A token reinforcement program. *Exceptional Children, 33,* 637–642.

O'Malley, S. S., Jaffe, A., Chang, G., Witte, G., Schottenfeld, R. S., & Rounsaville, B. J. (1992). Naltrexone in the treatment of alcohol dependence: Preliminary findings. In C. A. Naranjo & E. M. Sellars (Eds.), *Novel pharmacological interventions for alcoholism* (pp. 148–157). New York: Springer-Verlag.

O'Sullivan, K. (1979). Observations on vaginismus in Irish women. *Archives of General Psychiatry, 36,* 824–826.

Obrist, P. (1981). *Cardiovascular psychophysiology: A perspective.* New York: Plenum.

Odom, S. L., et al. (1982). Promoting social integration of young children at risk for learning disabilities. *Learning Disability Quarterly, 5*(4), 379–387.

Offer, D., & Sabshin, M. (1991). *The diversity of normal behavior.* New York: Basic Books.

Ofshe, R., & Watters, E. (1993, March/April). Making monsters. *Society,* 4–16.

Öhman, A. (1985). Face the beast and fear the face: Animal and social phobia as prototypes for evolutionary analyses of emotion. *Psychophysiology, 23,* 123–145.

Okazaki, S., & Sue, S. (1995). Methodological issues in assessment research with ethnic minorities. *Psychological Assessment, 7,* 367–375.

Olds, J., & Milner, P. (1954). Positive reinforcement produced by electrical stimulation of septal area and other regions of rat brain. *Journal of Comparative and Physiological Psychology, 47,* 419–427.

Olfson, M. (1990). Assertive community treatment: An evaluation of the experimental evidence. *Hospital and Community Psychiatry, 41,* 634–641.

Olfson, M., Pincus, H., & Sabshin, M. (1994). Pharmacotherapy in outpatient psychiatric practice. *American Journal of Psychiatry, 151,* 580–585.

Olin, J. T., & Zelinski, E. M. (1991). The 12-month reliability of the Mini-Mental State Examination. *Psychological Assessment: A Journal of Consulting and Clinical Psychology, 3,* 427–432.

Olson, R., Wise, B., Conners, F., Rack, J., & Fulker, D. (1989). Specific deficits in component reading and language skills: Genetic and environmental influences. *Journal of Learning Disabilities, 22,* 339–348.

Olweus, D. (1995). Bullying or peer abuse at school: Facts and intervention. *Current Directions in Psychological Science, 4,* 196–200.

Omer, H., & Alon, N. (1994). The continuity principle: A unified approach to disaster and trauma. *American Journal of Community Psychology, 22,* 273–287.

Onstad, S., Skre, I., Torgersen, S., & Kringlen, E. (1991). Twin concordance for DSM-III-R schizophrenia. *Acta Psychiatrica Scandinavica, 83,* 395–401.

Orlinsky, D. E., Grawe, K., & Parks, B. K. (1994). Process and outcome in psychotherapy—Noch Einmal. In A. E. Bergin & S. L. Garfield, *Handbook of psychotherapy and behavior change* (pp. 270–376). New York: John Wiley & Sons.

Orlinsky, D. E., & Howard, K. I. (1987). A generic model of psychotherapy. *Journal of Integrative and Eclectic Psychotherapy, 6,* 6–27.

Orr, S. P., Lasko, N. B., Shalev, A. Y., & Pittman, R. (1995). Physiological responses to loud tones in Vietnam veterans with posttraumatic stress disorder. *Journal of Abnormal Psychology, 104,* 75–82.

Osgood, N. J., & Thielman, S. (1990). Geriatric suicidal behavior: Assessment and treatment. In S. J. Blumenthal & D. J. Kupfer (Eds.), *Suicide over the life cycle: Risk factors, assessment, and treatment of suicidal patients* (pp. 341–379). Washington, DC: American Psychiatric Press.

Osman, O. T., & Loschen, E. L. (1992). Self-injurious behavior in the developmentally disabled: Pharmacologic treatment. *Psychopharmacology Bulletin, 28*(4), 439–449.

Osofsky, J. D. (1995). The effects of exposure to violence on young children. *American Psychologist, 50,* 782–788.

Öst, L-G. (1988). Applied relaxation vs. progressive relaxation in the treatment of panic disorder. *Behaviour Research and Therapy, 26,* 13–22.

Öst, L-G., & Westling, B. E. (1991). *Treatment of panic disorder by applied relaxation versus cognitive therapy.* Paper presented at the meeting of the European Association of Behaviour Therapy, Oslo.

Öst, L-G. (1987). Age of onset in different phobias. *Journal of Abnormal Psychology, 96,* 223–229.

Öst, L-G. (1992). Blood and injection phobia: Background and cognitive, physiological, and behavioral variables. *Journal of Abnormal Psychology, 101,* 68–74.

Öst, L-G., & Hugdahl, K. (1984). Acquisition of blood and dental phobia and anxiety response patterns in clinical patients. *Behaviour Research and Therapy, 23,* 27–34.

Osterling, J., & Dawson, G. (1994). Early recognition of children with autism: A study of first birthday home videotapes. *Journal of Autism and Developmental Disorders, 24,* 247–257.

Otto, M., Pollack, M., Sachs, G., Reiter, S., Meltzer-Brody, B. S., & Rosenbaum, J. (1993). Discontinuation of benzodiazepine treatment: Efficacy of cognitive-behavioral therapy for patients with panic disorder. *American Journal of Psychiatry, 150,* 1485–1490.

Ozonoff, S., Strayer, D. L., McMahon, W. M., & Filloux, F. (1994). Executive function abilities in autism and Tourette syndrome: An information processing approach. *Journal of Child Psychology and Psychiatry and Allied Disciplines, 35*(6), 1015–1032.

Ozonoff, S., & McEvoy, R. E. (1994). A longitudinal study of executive function and theory of mind development in autism. *Development and Psychopathology, 6,* 415–431.

Palazzoli, M. S. (1985). *Self-starvation.* New York: Aronson.

Paliast, E., Jongbloet, P., Straatman, H., & Zielhuis, G. (1994). Excess seasonality of births among patients with schizophrenia and seasonal ovopathy. *Schizophrenia Bulletin, 20,* 269–276.

Pangalos, M. N., Malizia, A. L., Francis, P. T., Lowe, S., Bertolucci, P., Procter, A., Bridges, P., Bartlett, J., Bowen, D. (1992). Effect of psychotropic drugs on excitatory amino acids in patients undergoing psychosurgery for depression. *British Journal of Psychiatry, 160,* 638–642.

Papp, L., Klein, D., Martinez, J., Schneier, F., Cole, R., Liebowitz, M., Hollander, E., Fryer, A., Jordan, F., & Gorman, J. (1993). Diagnostic and substance specificity of carbon-dioxide-induced panic. *American Journal of Psychiatry, 150,* 250–257.

Parkin, A. J. (1987). *Memory and amnesia: An introduction.* New York: Blackwell.

Parmar, R. S., Cawley, J. F., & Miller, J. H. (1994). Differences in mathematics performance between students with learning disabilities and students with mild retardation. *Exceptional Children, 60,* 549–563.

Parnas, J., Cannon, T., Jacobsen, B., Schulsinger, H., Schulsinger, F., & Mednick, S. (1993). Lifetime DSM-III-R diagnostic outcomes in the offspring of schizophrenic mothers: Results of the Copenhagen high-risk study. *Archives of General Psychiatry, 50,* 707–714.

Parsons, O. A., Butters, N., & Nathan, P. E. (Eds.). (1987). *Neuropsychology of alcoholism: Implications for diagnosis and treatment.* New York: Guilford Press.

Pascual, R., Fern'andez, V., Ruiz, S., & Kuljis, R. O. (1993). Environmental deprivation delays the maturation of motor pyramids during the early postnatal period. *Early Human Development, 33,* 145–155.

Pasewark, R. A., & Pantle, M. L. (1981). Opinions about the insanity plea. *Journal of Forensic Psychology, 8,* 63.

Pasewark, R. A., Bieber, S., Bosten, K. J., Kiser, M., & Steadman, H. J. (1982). Criminal recidivism among insanity acquitees. *International Journal of Law and Psychiatry, 5,* 365–374.

Patterson, E. B. (1996). Poverty, income inequality, and community crime rates. In D. G. Rojet & G. F. Jensen (Eds.), *Exploring delinquency: Causes and control* (pp. 142–149). Los Angeles, CA: Roxbury Publishing Co.

Patterson, G. R. (1982). *A social learning approach to family intervention: III. Coercive family process.* Eugene, OR: Castalia.

Patterson, G. R. (1986). Performance models for antisocial boys. *American Psychologist, 41,* 432–444.

Patterson, G. R., Chamberlain, P., & Reid, J. B. (1982). A comparative evaluation of a parent training program. *Behavior Therapy, 13,* 638–650.

Patterson, G. R., DeBaryshe, D., & Ramsey, E. (1989). A developmental perspective on antisocial behaviour. *American Psychologist, 44,* 329–335.

Paul, G. L., & Lentz, R. J. (1977). *Psychosocial treatment of chronic mental patients: Milieu versus social-learning programs.* Cambridge: Harvard University Press.

Pauls, D. L., Raymond, C. L., & Robertson, M. (1991). The genetics of obsessive-compulsive disorder: A review. In J. Zohar, I. Insel, & S. Rasmussen (Eds.), *The psychobiology of obsessive-compulsive disorder.* New York: Springer.

Pelham, W. E., & Murphy, H. A. (1986). Behavioral and psychopharmacological treatment of attention deficit and conduct disorders. In M. Hersen (Ed.), *Pharmacological and behavioral treatment: An integrative approach* (pp. 108–148). New York: John Wiley & Sons.

Pelham, W. E., Murphy, D. A., Vannatta, K., Milich, R., Licht, B. G., Gnagy, E. M., Greenslade, K. E., Greiner, A. R., & Vodde-Hamilton, M. (1992). Methylphenidate and attributions in boys with attention-deficit hyperactivity disorder. *Journal of Consulting and Clinical Psychology, 60,* 282–292.

Penderey, M. L., Maltzman, I. M., & West, L. J. (1982). Controlled drinking by alcoholics?: New findings and reevaluation of a major affirmative study. *Science, 217,* 169–174.

Pennebaker, J. W., Barger, S. D., & Tiebout, J. (1989). Disclosure of traumas and health among Holocaust survivors. *Psychosomatic Medicine, 51,* 577–589.

Pennebaker, J., & Beall, S. (1986). Confronting a traumatic event: Toward an understanding of inhibition and disease. *Journal of Abnormal Psychology, 95,* 274–281.

Pennebaker, J., Kiecolt-Glaser, J. K., & Glaser, R. (1988). Disclosure of traumas and immune function: Health implications for psychotherapy. *Journal of Consulting and Clinical Psychology, 56,* 239–245.

Perkins, K. A. (1993). Weight gain following smoking cessation. *Journal of Consulting and Clinical Psychology, 61(5),* 768–777.

Perlin, M. (1989). *Mental disability law: Civil and criminal.* Charlottesville, VA: Michie.

Perls, F. S. (1969). *Gestalt therapy verbatim.* Lafayette, CA: Real People Press.

Perner, J., Frith, U., Leslie, A. M., & Leekam, S. R. (1989). Exploration of the autistic child's theory of mind: Knowledge, belief and communication. *Child Development, 60,* 689–700.

Perry, C. L., Klepp, K., & Schultz, J. M. (1988). Primary prevention of cardiovascular disease: Community-wide strategies for youth. *Journal of Consulting and Clinical Psychology, 56,* 358–364.

Perry, J. C. (1993). Longitudinal studies of personality disorders. *Journal of Personality Disorders, 7,* 63–85.

Perry, S., Difede, J., Musngi, G., Frances, A., & Jacobsberg, L. (1992). Predictors of posttraumatic stress disorder after burn injury. *American Journal of Psychiatry, 149,* 931–935.

Persons, J. B. (1991). Psychotherapy outcome studies do not accurately represent current models of psychotherapy: A proposed remedy. *American Psychologist, 46,* 99–106.

Peterson, C., Seligman, M. E. P., & Vaillant, G. E. (1988). Pessimistic explanatory style is a risk factor for physical illness: A thirty-five-year longitudinal study. *Journal of Personality and Social Psychology, 55,* 23–27.

Peterson, L., & Brown, D. (1994). Integrating child injury and abuse-neglect research: Common histories, etiologies, and solutions. *Psychological Bulletin, 116,* 293–315.

Peterson v. State, 100 Wn2d 421, 671 P.2d 320 (1983).

Petraitis, J., Flay, B. R., & Miller, T. Q. (1995). Reviewing theories of adolescent substance use: Organizing pieces in the puzzle. *Psychological Bulletin, 117,* 67–86.

Petrie, K. J., Booth, R. J., Pennebaker, J. W., & Davison, K. P. (1995). Disclosure of trauma and immune response to a Hepatitis B vaccination program. *Journal of Consulting and Clinical Psychology, 63,* 787–792.

Pettinati, H. M., Tamburello, T. A., Ruetsch, C., & Kaplan, F. (1994). Patient attitudes toward electroconvulsive therapy. *Psychopharmacology Bulletin, 30,* 471–475.

Pettit, G. S., & Bates, J. E. (1989). Family interaction patterns and children's behavior problems from infancy to 4 years. *Developmental Psychology, 25,* 413–420.

Phelps, L., Cox, D., & Bajorek, E. (1992). School phobia and separation anxiety: Diagnostic and treatment comparisons. *Psychology in the Schools, 29,* 384–394.

Philliber, S., & Allen, J. P. (1992). Life options and community services: Teen Outreach Program. In B. C. Miller, J. J. Card, R. L. Paikoff, & J. L. Peterson (Eds.), *Preventing adolescent pregnancy: Model programs and evaluation* (pp. 139–155). Newbury Park, CA: Sage.

Phillips, K. A., McElroy, S. L., Keck, P. E., Pope, H. G., & Hudson, J. I. (1993). Body dysmorphic disorder: 30 cases of imagined ugliness. *Amercian Journal of Psychiatry, 150,* 302–308.

Pickar, D., Owen, R., Litman, R., Konicki, P., Guiterrez, R., & Rapaport, M. (1992). Clinical and biologic response to clozapine in patients with schizophrenia. *Archives of General Psychiatry, 49*, 345–353.

Pickens, R. W., Svikis, D. S., McGue, M., Lykken, D. T., Hesten, L. L., & Clayton, P. J. (1991). Heterogeneity in the inheritance of alcoholism. *Archives of General Psychiatry, 48*(1), 19–28.

Pierce, K. A., & Kirkpatrick, D. R. (1992). Do men lie on fear surveys? *Behavior Research and Therapy, 30*, 415–418.

Pigott, T., Pato, M., Bernstein, S., Grover, G., Hill, J., Tolliver, T., & Murphy, D. (1990). Controlled comparisons of clomipramine and fluoxetine in treatment of obsessive-compulsive disorder. *Archives of General Psychiatry, 47*, 926–932.

Pihl, R. O., & Peterson, J. B. (1991). Attention-deficit hyperactivity disorders, childhood conduct disorder and alcoholism: Is there an association? *Alcohol Health Research World, 15*, 25–31.

Pillard, R. C. (1988). Sexual orientation and mental disorder. *Psychiatric Annals, 18*, 52–56.

Pillard, R. C. & Bailey, J. M. (1995). A biologic perspective on sexual orientation. *Psychiatric Clinics of North America, 18*, 71–84.

Pion, G. M. (1991). A national human resources agenda for psychology: The need for a broader perspective. *Professional Psychology: Research and Practice, 22*, 449–455.

Piper, A. (1994). Multiple personality disorder. *British Journal of Psychiatry, 164*, 600–612.

Piper, W. E., Azim, H. F., McCallum, M., & Joyce, A. S. (1990). Patient suitability and outcome in short-term individual psychotherapy. *Journal of Consulting and Clinical Psychology, 58*, 475–481.

Piven, J., Simon, J., Chase, G. A., Wzorek, M., Landa, R., Gayle, J., & Folstein, S. (1993). The etiology of autism: Pre-, peri- and neonatal factors. *Journal of the American Academy of Child and Adolescent Psychiatry, 32*, 1256–1263.

Plomin, R. (1989). Environment and genes: Determinants of behavior. *American Psychologist, 44*, 105–111.

Polich, J. M., Armor, D. J., & Braiker, H. B. (1981). Stability and change in drinking patterns. In J. M. Polich (Ed.), *The course of alcoholism: Four years after treatment* (pp. 159–200). New York: John Wiley & Sons.

Polich, J., & Bloom, F. E. (1988). Event-related brain potentials in individuals at high and low risk for developing alcoholism: Failure to replicate. *Alcoholism in Clinical and Experimental Research, 12*, 368–373.

Pollard, C. A., Detrick, P., Flynn, T., & Frank, M. (1990). Panic attacks and related disorders in alcohol-dependent, depressed, and non-clinical samples. *Journal of Nervous and Mental Disease, 178*, 180–185.

Pollock, B., Perel, J. M., Paradis, C. F., Fasiczka, A. L., & Reynolds, C. F. (1994). Metabolic and physiologic consequences of nortriptyline treatment in the elderly. *Psychopharmacology Bulletin, 30*, 80.

Pomerleau, O. F., Collins, A. C., Shiffman, S., & Sanderson, C. S. (1993). Why some poeple smoke and others do not: New perspectives. *Journal of Consulting and Clinical Psychology, 61*, 723–731.

Pope, H. G., Jr., Gruber, A. J., & Yurgelun-Todd, D. (1995). The residual neuropsychological effects of cannabis: The current status of research. *Drug and Alcohol Dependence, 38*(1), 25–34.

Pope, H. G., Jr., McElroy, S. L., Keck, P. E., Hudson, J. I. (1991). Valproate in the treatment of acute mania. A placebo-controlled study. *Archives of General Psychiatry, 48*, 62–68.

Pope, K. S., & Feldman-Summers, S. (1992). National survey of psychologists' sexual and physical abuse history and their evaluation of training and competence in these areas. *Professional Psychology: Research and Practice, 23*, 353–361.

Pope, K. S., Levenson, H., & Schover, L. R. (1979). Sexual intimacy in psychology training: Results and implication of a national survey. *American Psychologist, 34*, 682–689.

Pope, K. S., & Tabachnick, B. G. (1994). Therapists as patients: A national survey of psychologists' experiences, problems, and beliefs. *Professional Psychology: Research and Practice, 25*, 247–258.

Pope, K. S., Tabachnick, B. G., & Keith-Spiegel, P. (1987). Ethics of practice: The beliefs and behaviors of psychologists as therapists. *American Psychologist, 42*, 993–1006.

Pope, K. S., & Vasquez, M. J. T. (1991). *Ethics in psychotherapy and counseling: A practical guide for psychologists.* San Francisco, CA: Jossey-Bass.

Pope, K. S., & Vetter, V. A. (1992). Ethical dilemmas encountered by members of the American Psychological Association: A national survey. *American Psychologist, 47*, 397–411.

Posner, M. I., & Raichle, M. C. (1994). *Images of mind.* New York: Scientific American Library.

Post, C. G. (1963). *An introduction to the law.* Englewood Cliffs, NJ: Prentice Hall.

Post, R. M. (1990). Non-lithium treatment for bipolar disorder. *Journal of Clinical Psychiatry, 51*, (Suppl.), 9–16.

Post, R. M. (1992). Transdirection of psychosocial stress into the neurobiology of recurrent affective disorder. *American Journal of Psychiatry, 149*, 999–1010.

Post, R. M. (1993). Mood disorders: Acute mania. In D. D. Dunner (Ed.), *Current psychiatric therapy* (pp. 204–210). Philadelphia: W. B. Saunders Co.

Powell, T. J. (1987). *Self-help organizations and professional practice.* Silver Springs, MD: National Association of Social Workers.

Power, K. G., Simpson, R., Swanson, V., & Wallace, L. (1990). A controlled comparison of cognitive-behavioral therapy, diazepam, and placebo, alone and in combination for the treatment of generalized anxiety disorder. *Journal of Anxiety Disorders, 4*, 267–292.

Preston, R. (1994). *The hot zone.* London: Doubleday.

Price, R. H., Cowen, E. L., Lorion, R. L., & Ramos-McKay, J. (1988). *Fourteen ounces of prevention: A casebook for practitioners.* Washington, DC: American Psychological Association.

Prien, R. F., & Potter, W. Z. (1993). Maintenance treatment for mood disorders. In D. L. Dunner (Ed.), *Current psychiatric treatments* (pp. 255–260). Philadelphia: W. B. Saunders Co.

Prigatano, G. P., Parsons, O. A., & Bortz, J. J. (1995). Methodological considerations in clinical neuropsychological research: 17 years later. *Psychological Assessment, 7*, 396–403.

Prochaska, J. O., DiClemente, C. C., & Norcross, J. C. (1992). In search of how people change: Applications to addictive behaviors. *American Psychologist, 47*(9), 1102–1114.

Project MATCH Research Group (1997). Matching alcoholism treatments to client heterogeneity: Project MATCH posttreatment drinking outcomes. *Journal of Studies on Alcohol, 58*, 7–29.

Pueschel, S. M., Gallagher, P. L., Zartler, A. S., & Pezzullo, J. C. (1987). Cognitive and learning processes in children with Down syndrome. *Research in Developmental Disabilities, 8*, 21–37.

Putnam, F. W. (1988). The switch process in multiple personality disorder and other state-change disorders. *Dissociation, 1*, 24–32.

Putnam, F. W. (1989). *Diagnosis and treatment of multiple personality disorder.* New York: Guilford Press.

Putnam, F. W., Helmers, K., Horowitz, L. A., & Trickett, P. K. (1995). Hypnotizability and dissociativity in sexually abused girls. *Child Abuse and Neglect, 19*, 645–655.

Pyzczynski, T., & Greenberg, J. (1987). Self-regulatory perseveration and the depressive self-focusing style: A self-awareness theory of reactive depression. *Psychological Bulletin, 102,* 122–138.

Quarfordt, S. D., Kalmus, G. W., & Myers, R. D. (1991). Ethanol drinking following 6-OHDA lesions of nucleus accumbens and tuberculum olfactorium of the rat. *Alcohol, 8*(3), 211–217.

Quay, H. C. (1965). Psychopathic personality as pathological stimulus-seeking. *American Journal of Psychiatry, 122,* 180–183.

Rachman, S. J. (1990). *Fear and courage* (2nd ed.) New York: W. F. Freeman.

Rachman, S. J. (1993). Obsessions, responsibility, and guilt. *Behavior Research and Therapy, 31,* 149–154.

Rachman, S. J., & Hodgson, R. (1968). Experimentally induced "sexual fetishism": Replication and development. *Psychological Record, 18,* 25–27.

Rachman, S. J. & Hodgson, R. (1980). *Obsessions and compulsions.* Englewood Cliffs, NJ: Prentice Hall.

Rachman, S. J., & Wilson, G. T. (1980). *The effects of psychological therapy.* Oxford: Pergamon Press.

Ragland, D. R., & Brand, R. J. (1988). Type A behavior and mortality from coronary heart disease. *New England Journal of Medicine, 318,* 65–69.

Raine, A., & Jones, F. (1987). Attention, autonomic arousal, and personality in behaviorally disordered children. *Journal of Abnormal Child Psychology, 15,* 583–599.

Raine, A., Venebles, P. H., & Williams, M. (1990). Relationships between central and autonomic measures of arousal at age 15 years and criminality at age 24 years. *Archives of General Psychiatry, 47,* 1003–1007.

Ramey, C. T. (1993). High-risk children and IQ: Altering intergenerational patterns. *Intelligence, 16,* 239–256.

Ramey, C. T., & Ramey, S. L. (1992). Effective early intervention. *Mental Retardation, 30,* 337–345.

Ramey, C. T., & Smith, B. J. (1977). Assessing the intellectual consequences of early intervention with high-risk infants. *American Journal of Mental Deficiency, 81,* 318–324.

Rapee, R., Brown, T., Antony, M., & Barlow, D. (1992). Response to hyperventilation and inhalation of 5.5% carbon dioxide-enriched air across the DSM-III-R anxiety disorders. *Journal of Abnormal Psychology, 101,* 538–552.

Rapoport, J. (1989). The biology of obsessions and compulsions. *Scientific American, 260,* (3), 83–89.

Rapoport, J., Elkins, R., Langer, D. H., Sceery, W., Buschbaum, M. S., Gillin, J. C., Murphy, D., Zahn, T. P., Ludlow, C., & Mendelson, W. (1981). Childhood obsessive compulsive disorder. *American Journal of Psychiatry, 138,* 1545–1554.

Rapoport, J., Ryland, D. H., & Kriete, M. (1992). Drug treatment of canine acral lick: An animal model of obsessive-compulsive disorder. *Archives of General Psychiatry, 49,* 517–521.

Rappaport, J. (1977). *Community psychology: Values, research and action.* New York: Holt, Rinehart & Winston.

Rappaport, J. (1981). In praise of paradox: A social policy of empowerment over prevention. *American Journal of Community Psychology, 9,* 1–25.

Rappaport, J. (1987). Terms of empowerment/exemplars of prevention: Toward a theory for community psychology. *American Journal of Community Psychology, 15,* 121–148.

Rappaport, J., Seidman, E., Toro, P., McFadden, L., Reischel, T., Roberts, L., Salem, D., & Zimmerman, M. (1985). Collaborative research with a mutual help organization. *Social Policy, 15,* 12–24.

Ratcliff, G., & Saxton, J. (1994). Age-associated memory impairment. In C. E. Coffey & J. L. Cummings (Eds.), *Textbook of geriatric neuropsychiatry* (pp. 145–158). Washington, DC: American Psychiatric Press.

Rauschenberger, S. L., & Lynn, S. J. (1995). Fantasy proneness, DSM-II-R Axis 1 psychopathology, and dissociation. *Journal of Abnormal Psychology, 104,* 373–380.

Raymond, M. J. (1956). Case of fetishism treated by aversion therapy. *British Medical Journal 2,* 854–857.

Raz, S., & Raz, N. (1990). Structural brain abnormalities in the major psychoses: A quantitative review of the evidence from computerized imaging. *Psychological Bulletin, 89,* 93–108.

Razay, G., Heaton, K. W., Bolton, C. H., & Hughes, A. O. (1992). Alcohol·consumption and its relation to cardiovascular risk factors in British Women. *British Medical Journal, 304*(6819), 80–82.

Rebok, G. W., & Folstein, M. F. (1993). Dementia. *Journal of Neuropsychiatry and Clinical Neurosciences, 5,* 265–276.

Reed, S. D., Katkin, E. S., & Goldband, S. (1986). Biofeedback and behavioral medicine. In F. H. Kanfer & A. P. Goldstein (Eds.), *Helping people change: A textbook of methods* (3rd ed., pp. 381–436). New York: Pergamon Press.

Regal, R. A., Rooney, J. R., & Wandas, T. (1994). Facilitated communication: An experimental evaluation. *Journal of Autism and Developmental Disorders, 24*(3), 345–355.

Regier, D. A., Boyd, J. H., Burke, J. D., Rae, D. S., Myers, J. K., Kramer, M., Robins, L. N., George, L. K., Karno, M., & Locke, B. Z. (1988). One-month prevalence of mental disorders in the United States. *Archives of General Psychiatry, 45,* 977–986.

Regier, D. A., Farmer, M. E., Rae, D. S., Locke, B. Z., Keith, S. J., Judd, L. J., & Goodwin, F. K. (1990). Comorbidity of mental disorders with alcohol and other drug abuse. *Journal of the American Medical Association, 264*(19), 2511–2518.

Regier, D. A., Hirschfeld, R. M. A., Goodwin, F. K., Burke, J. D. Jr., Lazar, J. B., & Judd, L. L. (1988). The NIMH Depression Awareness, Recognition, and Treatment program: Structure, aims and scientific basis. *American Journal of Psychiatry, 145,* 1351–1357.

Rehm, L. P. (1977). A self-control model of depression. *Behavior Therapy, 8,* 787–804.

Rehm, L. P. (1984). Self-management therapy for depression. *Advances in Behavior Research and Therapy, 6,* 83–98.

Reifman, A., & Windle, M. (1995). Adolescent suicidal behaviors as a function of depression, hopelessness, alcohol use, and social support: A longitudinal investigation. *American Journal of Community Psychology, 23,* 329–354.

Reilly, M., Klima, E., & Bellugi, U. (1990). Once more with feeling: Affect and language in atypical populations. *Development and Psychopathology, 2,* 367–391.

Reisberg, B., Ferris, S. H., DeLeon, M. J., & Crook, T. (1982). The global deterioration scale for assessment of primary degenerative dementia. *American Journal of Psychiatry, 139,* 1136–1139.

Rekers, G. A., Kilgus, M., & Rosen, A. C. (1990). Long-term effect of treatment for gender identity disorder of childhood. *Journal of Psychology and Human Sexuality, 3,* 121–153.

Remafedi, G., Farrow, J., & Deisher, R. (1991). Risk factors for attempted suicide in gay and bisexual youth. *Pediatrics, 87,* 869–876.

Remafedi, G., Resnick, M., Blum, R., & Harris, L. (1993). Demography of sexual orientation in adolescents. *Pediatrics, 89,* 714–721.

Remschimdt, H., Schulz, E., Martin, M., Warnke, A., & Trott, G. E. (1994). Childhood onset schizophrenia: History of the concept and recent studies. *Schizophrenia Bulletin, 20,* 727–745.

Rennie v. Klein, 462 F. Supp. 1131 (D. N.J. 1978).

Renouf, A. G. & Harter, S. (1990). Low self-worth and anger as components of the depressive experience in young adolescents. *Development and Psychopathology, 2,* 293–310.

Renshaw, D. C. (1988). Profile of 2376 patients treated at Loyola Sex Clinic between 1972 and 1987. *Social and Marital Therapy, 3,* 111–117.

Resick, P. & Schnicke, M. (1992). Cognitive processing therapy for sexual assault victims. *Journal of Consulting and Clinical Psychology, 60,* 748–756.

Resnick, H. S., Kilpatrick, D. G., Dansky,, B. S., Saunders, B., & Best, C. L. (1993). Prevalence of civilian trauma and posttraumatic stress disorder in a representative national sample of women. *Journal of Consulting and Clinical Psychology, 61,* 984–991.

Reveley, M., Reveley, A., & Baldy, R. (1987). Left cerebral hemisphere hypodensity in discordant schizophrenic twins. *Archives of General Psychiatry, 44,* 625–632.

Revenson, T. A., & Felton, B. J. (1989). Disability and coping as predictors of psychological adjustment to rheumatoid arthritis. *Journal of Consulting and Clinical Psychology, 57,* 344–348.

Rey, J. M., Bashir, M. R., Schwarz, M., Richards, I. N., Plapp, J. M., & Stewart, G. W. (1988). Oppositional disorder: Fact or fiction? *Journal of the American Academy of Child and Adolescent Psychiatry, 27,* 157–162.

Reynolds, W. M., & Coats, K. I. (1986). A comparison of cognitive-behavioral therapy and relaxation training for the treatment of depression in adolescents. *Journal of Consulting and Clinical Psychology, 54,* 653–660.

Richards, S. J., & VanBroeckoven, C. (1994). Genetic linkage in Alzheimer's disease. In F. A. Huppert, C. Brayne, & D. W. O'Connor (Eds.), *Dementia and normal aging* (pp. 492–518). Cambridge: Cambridge University Press.

Richelson, E. (1993). Treatment of acute depression. *Psychiatric Clinics of North America, 16,* 461–478.

Richters, J. E., Arnold, L. E., Jensen, P. S., Abikoff, H., Conners, C. K., Greenhill, L. L., Hechtman, L., Hinshaw, S. P., Pelham, W. E., and Swanson, J. M. (1995). NIMH collaborative multisite multimodal treatment study of children with ADHD: I. Background and rationale. *Journal of the American Academy of Child and Adolescent Psychiatry, 34,* 987–1000.

Rickels, K., Chung, H., Csanalosi, I., Hurowitz, A., London, J., Wiseman, K., Kaplan, M., & Amsterdam, J. (1987). Alprazolam, diazepam, imipramine, and placebo in outpatients with major depression. *Archives of General Psychiatry, 44,* 862–866.

Rickels, K., Schweizer, E., Weiss, S., & Zavodnick, S. (1993). Maintenance drug treatment of panic disorder. II: Short and long-term outcome after drug taper. *Archives of General Psychiatry, 50,* 61–68.

Riether, A. M., & Stoudemire, A. (1988). Psychogenic fugue states: A review. *Southern Medical Journal, 82,* 568–571.

Riggins v. Nevada, 112 S. Ct. 1810 (1992).

Risby, W., Hsiao, J., Manji, H., Bitran, J., Moses, F., Zhou, D., & Potter, W. (1991). The mechanism of action of lithium II: Effects of adenylate cyclase activity and beta-adrenergic receptor binding in normal subjects. *Archives of General Psychiatry, 48,* 513–523.

Ritenbaugh, C., Shisslak, C., Teufal, N., & Leonard-Green, T. K. (1996). A cross-cultural review of eating disorders in regard to DSM-IV. In J. E. Mezzick, A. Kleinman, H. Fabrega, & D. L. Parron (Eds.), *Culture and psychiatric diagnosis: A DSM-IV perspective.* Washington, DC: American Psychiatric Press.

Rivara, F. P., Booth, C. L., Bergman, A. B., Rogers, L. W., & Weiss, J. (1991). Prevention of pedestrian injuries to children: Effectiveness of a school training program. *Pediatrics, 88*(4), 770–775.

Rivers, P. C. (1994). *Alcohol and human behavior: Theory, research, and practice.* Englewood Cliffs, NJ: Prentice Hall.

Roback, A. A. (1961). *History of psychology and psychiatry.* New York: Philosophical Library.

Roberts, C. F., & Golding, S. (1991). The social construction of criminal responsibility and insanity. *Law and Human Behavior, 15,* 349–376.

Robiner, W. N. (1991). How many psychologists are needed? A call for a national psychology human resource agenda. *Professional Psychology: Research and Practice, 22,* 427–440.

Robins, C. J., & Hayes, A. M. (1993). An appraisal of cognitive therapy. *Journal of Consulting and Clinical Psychology, 61,* 205–214.

Robins, L. N. (1966). *Deviant children grown up: A sociological and psychiatric study of sociopathic personality.* Baltimore: Williams & Wilkins.

Robins, L. N. (1991). Conduct disorder. *Journal of Child Psychology and Psychiatry, 32*(1), 193–212.

Robins, L. N., Helzer, J. E., Weissman, M. M., Orvaschel, H., Gruenberg, E., Burke, J. K., & Regier, D. H. (1984). Lifetime prevalence of specific psychiatric disorders in three cities. *Archives of General Psychiatry, 41,* 949–958.

Robins, L. N., & Regier, D. A. (1991). *Psychiatric disorders in America: The epidemiological catchment area study.* New York: The Free Press.

Robins, L. N., & Rutter, M. (1990). Childhood prediction of psychiatric status in the young adulthood of hyperactive boys: A study controlling for chance associations. In L. Robins & M. Rutter (Eds.), *Straight and deviant pathways from childhood to adulthood* (pp. 279–299). Cambridge, MA.: Cambridge University Press.

Robins, L. N., Tipp, J., & Przybeck, T. (1991). Antisocial personality. In L. N. Robins & D. A. Regier (Eds.), *Psychiatric disorders in America* (pp. 258–290). New York: Free Press.

Robinson, L. A., Berman, J. S., & Neimeyer, R. A. (1990). Psychotherapy for the treatment of depression: A comprehensive review of controlled outcome research. *Psychological Bulletin, 108,* 30–49.

Rockwell, E., Lam, E. R., & Zisook, S. (1988). Antidepressant drug studies in the elderly. *Psychiatric Clinics of North America, 11,* 215–321.

Rodin, J., & Salovey, P. (1989). Health psychology. *Annual Review of Psychology, 40,* 533–579.

Rodriguez, J. G. (1990). Childhood injuries in the United States: A priority issue. *American Journal of Diseases of Children, 144,* 625–626.

Roffwarg, H. P., Muzio, J. N., & Dement, W. C. (1966). Ontogenetic development of the human sleep-dream cycle. *Science, 152,* 604–619.

Rogeness, G. A., Javors, M. A., & Pliszka, S. R. (1992). Neurochemistry and child and adolescent psychiatry. *Journal of the American Academy of Child and Adolescent Psychiatry, 31,* 765–781.

Rogers, C. R. (1942). *Counseling and psychotherapy.* Boston: Houghton Mifflin.

Rogers, C. R. (1951). *Client-centered therapy.* Boston: Houghton Mifflin.

Rogers, C. R. (1954). *Psychotherapy and personality change.* Chicago: University of Chicago Press.

Rogers, R. (1995). *Diagnostic and structured interviewing: A handbook for psychologists.* New York: Psychological Assessment Resources.

Rogers, R., & Ewing, C. (1989). Ultimate opinion proscriptions: A cosmetic fix and a plea for empiricism. *Law and Human Behavior, 13,* 357–374.

Rogers, S. J., Ozonoff, S., & Maslin-Cole, C. (1991). A comparative study of attachment behavior in children with autism and children with other disorders of behavior and development. *Journal of the American Academy of Child and Adolescent Psychiatry, 30,* 433–438.

Rogers v. Okin, 478 F. Supp. 1342, 1369 (Mass. 1979).

Rogoff, B., & Chavajay, P. (1995). What's become of research on the cultural basis of cognitive development? *American Psychologist, 50,* 859–877.

Rokeach, M. (1964). *The three Christs of Ypsilanti.* New York: Knopf.

Rooth, F. G., & Marks, I. M. (1974). Persistent exhibitionism: Short-term response to aversion, self-regulation, and relaxation treatments. *Archives of Sexual Behavior, 3,* 227–248.

Rose, S. D., & LeCroy, C. W. (1991). Group methods. In F. H. Kanfer & A. P. Goldstein (Eds.), *Helping people change* (4th ed., pp. 422–453). New York: Pergamon Press.

Rosen, R. C., & Leiblum, S. R. (1988). A sexual scripting approach to inhibited sexual desire. In S. R. Leiblum & R. C. Rosen (Eds.), *Sexual desire disorders* (pp. 168–191). New York: Guilford Press.

Rosen, R. C. & Leiblum, S. R. (1995a). Hypoactive sexual desire. *Psychiatric Clinics of North America, 18,* 107–121.

Rosen, R. C., & Leiblum, S. R. (1995b). Treatment of sexual disorders in the 1990s: An integrated approach. *Journal of Consulting and Clinical Psychiatry, 63,* 877–890.

Rosen, R. C., Taylor, J. F., Leiblum, S. R., & Bachmann, G. A. (1993). Prevalence of sexual dysfunction in women: Results of a survey study of 329 women in an outpatient gynecological clinic. *Journal of Sex and Marital Therapy, 19,* 171–188.

Rosenbach, A., & Hunot, V. (1995). The introduction of a methadone prescribing programme to a drug-free treatment service: Implications for harm reduction. *Addiction, 90,* 815–821.

Rosenbaum, J. F., Biederman, J., Hirshfeld, D. R., Bolduc, E. A., & Chaloff, J. (1991). Behavioral inhibition in children: A possible precursor to panic disorder or social phobia. *Journal of Clinical Psychiatry, 52* (Suppl.), 5–9.

Rosenberg, M. L., Smith, J. C., & Davidson, L. E. (1987). The emergence of youth suicide: An epidemiologic analysis and public health perspective. *Annual Review Public Health, 8,* 417–440.

Rosenfarb, I. S., Goldstein, M.J., Mintz, J., & Nuechterlein, K. H. (1995). Expressed emotion and subclinical psychopathology observable within transactions between schizophrenia patients and their family members. *Journal of Abnormal Psychology, 104,* 259–267.

Rosenhan, D. L. (1973). On being sane in insane places. *Science, 179,* 250–258.

Rosenman, R. H. (1978). The interview method of assessment of the coronary-prone behavior pattern. In T. M. Dembroski, S. M. Weiss, J. L. Shields, S. G. Haynes, & M. Feinleib (Eds.), *Coronary-prone behavior* (pp. 55–69). New York: Springer-Verlag.

Rosenman, R. H., Brand, R. J., Jenkins, D. D., Friedman, M., Straus, R., & Wurm, M. (1975). Coronary heart disease in the Western Collaborative Group Study: Final follow-up experiences after 8½ years. *Journal of The American Medical Association, 233,* 872–877.

Rosenstock, I. M. (1966). Why people use health services. *Milbank Memorial Fund Quarterly, 44,* 94–127.

Rosenthal, T. L. (1982). Social learning theory. In G. T. Wison & C. M. Franks (Eds.), *Contemporary behavior therapy: Conceptual and empirical foundations* (pp. 339–363). New York: Guilford Press.

Rosenthal, T. L., & Steffek, B. D. (1991). Modeling methods. In F. H. Kanfer & A. P. Goldstein (Eds.), *Helping people change* (4th ed. pp. 70–121). New York: Pergamon Press.

Ross, C. A. (1989). *Multiple personality disorder: Diagnosis, clinical features, and treatment.* New York: John Wiley & Sons.

Ross, C. A. (1991). Epidemiology of multiple personality disorder and dissociation. *Psychiatric Clinics of North America, 14,* 596–600.

Ross, C. A. (1995). Current treatment of dissociative identity disorder. In L. M. Cohen, J. N. Berzoff, & M. R. Elin (Eds.), *Dissociative identity disorder: Theoretical and treatment controversies* (pp. 413–434). Northvale, NJ: Jason Aronson.

Ross, H. E., Glaser, F. B., & Germanson, T. (1988). The prevalence of psychiatric disorders in patients with alcohol and other drug problems. *Archives of General Psychiatry, 45*(11), 1023–1031.

Ross, R. T., Begab, M. J., Dondis, E. H., Giampiccolo, J., & Meyers, C. E. (1985). *Lives of the retarded: A forty-year follow-up study.* Stanford, CA: Stanford University Press.

Roth, M. (1994). The relationship between dementia and normal aging of the brain. In F. A. Huppert, C. Brayne, & D. W. O'Connor (Eds.), *Dementia and normal aging* (pp. 57–78). Cambridge: Cambridge University Press.

Roth, M., Huppert, F. A., Tym, E., & Mountjoy, C. Q. (1988). *CAMDEX: The Cambridge Examination for Mental Disorders in the Elderly.* Cambridge: Cambridge University Press.

Roth, M., Tym, E., Mountjoy, C. Q., Huppert, F. A., Hendrie, H., Verma, S., & Goddard, R. (1986). CAMDEX: A standardized instrument for the diagnosis of mental disorder in the elderly with special reference to the early detection of dementia. *British Journal of Psychiatry, 149,* 698–709.

Rothbaum, B. O., Hodges, L. F., Kooper, R., Opdyke, D., Wilford, J. S., & North, M. (1995). Virtual reality graded exposure in the treatment of acrophobia: A case report. *Behavior Therapy, 26,* 547–554.

Rotheram-Borus, M. J., Hunter, J., & Rosario, M. (1995). Coming out as lesbian or gay in the era of AIDS. In G. M. Herek & B. Greene (Eds.), *AIDS, identity, and community: The HIV epidemic and lesbians and gay men: Psychological perspectives on lesbian and gay issues* (Vol. 2, pp. 150–168). Thousand Oaks, CA: Sage.

Rotheram-Borus, M. J., Hunter, J., & Rosario, M. (1994). Suicidal behavior and gay-related stress among gay and bisexual male adolescents. *Journal of Adolescent Research, 9,* 498–508.

Rotter, J. (1954). *Social learning and clinical psychology.* New Jersey: Prentice Hall.

Rottwarg, H. P., Rottwarg, Muzio, J. N., & Dement, W. C. (1966). Ontogenetic development of the human sleep-dream cycle. *Science, 152,* 604–619.

Rouse v. Cameron, 373 F. 2d 451 (1966).

Rowland, D. L., Cooper, S. E., & Slob, A. K. (1996). Genital and psychoaffective response to erotic stimulation in sexually functional and dysfunctional men. *Journal of Abnormal Psychology, 105,* 194–203.

Rubin, K. H., Hymel, S., Mills, R. S. L., & Rose-Krasnor, L. (1991). In D. Cicchetti & S. L. Toth (Eds.), *Internalizing and externalizing expressions of dysfunction: Rochester symposium on developmental psychopathology* (Vol. 2, pp. 91–122). Hillsdale, NJ: Erlbaum.

Rubin, L. J. (1996). Childhood sexual abuse: False accusations of "false memory"? *Professional Psychology: Research and Practice, 27,* 447–451.

Rumble, B., Retallack, R., Hilbich, C., Simms, G., Multhaup, G., Martins, R., Hockey, A., Montgomery, P., Beyreuther, K., & Masters, C. L. (1989). Amyloid A4 protein and its precursor in Down's syndrome and Alzheimer's disease. *New England Journal of Medicine, 320,* 1446–1452.

Rush, A. J. (1993). Mood disorders in DSM-IV. In D. L. Dunner (Ed.), *Current psychiatric treatments* (pp. 189–195). Philadelphia: W. B. Saunders Co.

Russell, J., Mauthner, N., Sharpe, S., & Tidswell, T. (1991). The "windows task" as a measure of strategic deception in preschoolers and autistic children. *British Journal of Developmental Psychology, 9,* 331–349.

Russo, J., Katon, K., Sullivan, M., Clark, M., & Buchwald, D. (1994). Severity of somatization and its relationship to psychiatric disorders and personality. *Psychosomatics, 35,* 546–556.

Rutter, M. (1970). Autistic children: Infancy to adulthood. *Seminal Psychiatry, 2,* 435–450.

Rutter, M., Macdonald, H., Le Couteur, A., Harrington, R., Bolton, P., & Bailey, A. (1990). Genetic factors in child psychiatric disorders. II: Empirical findings. *Journal of Child Psychology and Psychiatry, 31,* 39–83.

Rutter, M., & Quinton, D. (1984). Parental psychiatric disorder: Effects on children. *Psychological Medicine, 14,* 853.

Rutter, M., & Schopler, E. (1992). Classification of pervasive developmental disorders: Some concepts and practical considerations. *Journal of Autism and Developmental Disorders, 22,* 459–482.

Rutter, M., Tizard, J., & Whitmore, K. (1970). *Education, health, and behavior.* London: Longman.

Ryan, N. D. (1992). The pharmacologic treatment of child and adolescent depression. *Psychiatric Clinics of North America, 15,* 29–40.

Rydelius, P. A. (1988). The development of antisocial behavior and sudden violent death. *Acta Psychiatrica Scandinavica, 77,* 398–403.

Sachar, E. J., Hellman, L., Roffwarg, H. P. Halpern, F. S., Fukushima, D. K., Gallagher, T. F. (1973). Disrupted 24-hour patterns of cortisol secretion in psychotic depression. *Archives of General Psychiatry, 28,* 19–24.

Sachdev, P. & Hay, P. (1995). Does neurosurgery for obsessive-compulsive disorder produce personality changes? *Journal of Nervous and Mental Disease, 183,* 408–413.

Sachdev, P., Hay, P., & Cumming, S. (1992). Psychosurgical treatment of obsessive-compulsive disorder. *Archives of General Psychiatry, 49,* 582–583.

Sack, R. L., Lewy, A. J., White, D. M., Singer, C. M., Fireman, M. J., & Vandiver, R. (1990). Morning vs evening light treatment for winter depression: Evidence that the therapeutic effects of light are mediated by circadian phase shifts. *Archives of General Psychiatry, 47,* 343–351.

Sadock, V. A. (1995). Normal Human Sexuality. In H. I. Kaplan & B. J. Sadock (Eds.), *Comprehensive textbook of psychiatry/VI* (pp. 1295–1321). Baltimore: Williams & Wilkins.

Safer, D. J., & Krager, J. M. (1988). A survey of medication treatment for hyperactive/inattentive students. *Journal of the American Medical Association, 260,* 2256–2258.

Sagan, C. (1977). *The dragons of Eden.* New York: Random House.

Sales, B., & Hafemeister, T. (1984). Empiricism and legal policy on the insanity defense. In L. A. Teplin (Ed.), *Mental health and criminal justice.* Newbury Park, CA: Sage.

Salzman, C. (1991). The APA task force report on benzodiazepine dependence, toxicity, and abuse. *American Journal of Psychiatry, 148,* 151–152.

Sameroff, A. J., Seifer, R., Zax, M., & Barocas, R. (1987). Early indicators of developmental risk: Rochester longitudinal study. *Schizophrenia Bulletin, 13,* 383–394.

Samuels, A. (1995). Somatization disorder: A major public health issue. *The Medical Journal of Australia, 163,* 147–149.

Sandberg, D. E., Meyer-Bahlburg, H. F. L., Ehrhardt, A. A., Yager, T. J. (1993). The prevalence of gender-atypical behavior in elementary school children. *Journal of the American Academy of Child and Adolescent Psychiatry, 32,* 306–314.

Sanderson, W., Rapee, R., & Barlow, D. (1989). The influence of perceived control on panic attacks induced via inhalation of 5.5% CO_2-enriched air. *Archives of General Psychiatry, 46,* 157–162.

Sandler, I., Wolchik, S., Braver, S., & Fogas, B. (1991). Stability and quality of life events and psychological symptomatology in children of divorce. *American Journal of Community Psychology, 19,* 501–520.

Sarason, I. G., Johnson, J. H., & Siegel, J. M. (1978). Assessing the impact of life changes: Development of the life experiences survey. *Journal of Consulting and Clinical Psychology, 46,* 932–946.

Sarbin, T. R. (1969). The scientific status of the mental illness metaphor. In S. G. Plog & R. B. Edgerton (Eds.),

Changing perspectives in mental illness. New York: Holt, Rinehart, & Winston.

Sartorius, N., Üstün, T. B., Korten, A., Cooper, J. E., & van Drimmelen, J. (1995). Progress toward achieving a common language in psychiatry. II: Results from the international field trials of the ICD-10 diagnostic criteria for research for mental and behavioral disorders. *The American Journal of Psychiatry, 152,* 1427–1437.

Satir, V. (1967). *Conjoint family therapy* (rev. ed.). Palo Alto, CA: Science and Behavior Books.

Satterfield, J. H., & Dawson, M. E. (1971). Electrodermal correlates of hyperactivity in children. *Psychophysiology, 8,* 191–197.

Schachter, S., & Latane, B. (1964). Crime, cognition, and the autonomic nervous system. In D. Levine (Ed.), *Nebraska Symposium on motivation* (Vol. 12, pp. 221–273). Lincoln: University of Nebraska Press.

Schaie, K. W. (1994). The course of adult intellectual development. *American Psychologist, 49,* 304–313.

Scheff, T. J. (1966). *Being mentally ill.* Chicago: Aldine.

Scheier, M. F., & Carver, C. S. (1985). Optimism, coping, and health: Assessment and implications of generalized outcome expectancies. *Health Psychology, 4,* 219–247.

Scherwitz, L. W., Perkins, L. L., Chesny, M. A., Hughes, G. H., & Sidney, S. (1992). Hostility and health behaviors in young adults: The CARDIA Study. *American Journal of Epidemiology, 136,* 136–145.

Schiavi, R. C., Schreiner-Engel, P., Mandeli, J., Schanzer, H., & Cohen, E. (1990). Healthy aging and male sexual function. *American Journal of Psychiatry, 174,* 766–771.

Schiavi, R. C., Schreiner-Engel, P., White, D., & Mandeli, J. (1988). Pituitary-gonadal function during sleep in men with hypoactive sexual desire and in normal controls. *Psychosomatic Medicine, 50,* 304–318.

Schmauck, F. J. (1970). Punishment, arousal, and avoidance learning in sociopaths. *Journal of Abnormal Psychology, 76,* 443–453.

Schnabel, T. (1987). Evaluations of the safety and side effects of antianxiety agents. *The American Journal of Medicine, 82,* (Suppl. 5A), 7–13.

Schneider, K. (1959). *Clinical Psychopathology.* New York: Grune & Stratton.

Schneider, S. F. (1991). No fluoride in our future. *Professional Psychology: Research and Practice, 22,* 456–460.

Schnurr, P., Friedman, M. J., & Rosenberg, S. D. (1993). Preliminary MMPI scores as predictors of combat-related PTSD symptoms. *American Journal of Psychiatry, 150,* 479–483.

Schooler, N. R., & Keith, S. J. (1993). The clinical research base for the treatment of schizophrenia. *Psychopharmacology Bulletin, 29,* 431–446.

Schradle, S. B., & Dougher, M. J. (1985). Social support as a mediator of stress: Theoretical and empirical issues. *Clinical Psychology Review, 5,* 641–662.

Schreiber, F. R. (1973). *Sybil.* Chicago: Henry Regnery.

Schreiner-Engel, P., & Schiavi, R. C. (1986). Lifetime psychopathology in individuals with low sexual desire. *Journal of Nervous and Mental Diseases, 174,* 646–651.

Schukit, M. A., Goodwin, D. W., & Winokur, G. (1972). Biological vulnerability to alcoholism. *American Journal of Psychiatry, 128,* 1132–1136.

Schwartz, M. F., & Masters, W. H. (1984). The Masters and Johnson treatment program for dissatisfied homosexual men. *American Journal of Psychiatry, 141,* 173–181.

Schwartz, R. H. (1995). LSD: Its rise, fall, and renewed popularity among high school students. *Pediatric Clinics of North America, 42(2),* 403–413.

Schwartz, S., & Johnson, J. H. (1985). *Psychopathology of childhood: A clinical-experimental approach* (2nd ed.). New York: Pergamon Press.

Schwarzwald, J., Weisenberg, M., Waysman, M., Solomon, Z., & Klingman, A. (1993). Stress reaction of school-age children to the bombardment by SCUD missiles. *Journal of Abnormal Psychology, 102,* 404–410.

Schweinhart, L. L., Barnes, H. V., & Weikhart, D. P. (1993). *Significant benefits. The High/Scope Perry School Study through age 27.* Ypsilanti, MI: High/Scope Press.

Schweinhart, L. J., Weikart, D. P., & Larner, M. B. (1986). Consequences of three preschool curriculum models through age 15. *Early Childhood Research Quarterly, 1*(1), 15–45.

Schweizer, E., Rickels, K., Weiss, S., & Zavodnick, S. (1993). Maintenance drug treatment of panic disorder: I. Results of a prospective, placebo-controlled comparison of alprazolam and imipramine. *Archives of General Psychiatry, 50,* 51–60.

Scinto, L. F. M., Daffner, K. R., Dressler, D., Ransil, B. I., Rentz, D., Weintraub, S., Mesulam, M., & Potter, H. (1994). A potential noninvasive neurobiological test for Alzheimer's disease. *Science, 266,* 1051–1054.

Scott, A. (1989). Which depressed patients will respond to electroconvulsive therapy? The search for biological predictors of recovery. *British Journal of Psychiatry, 154,* 8–17.

Scotti, J. R., Evans, I. M., Meyer, L. H., & Walker, P. (1991). A meta-analysis of intervention research with problem behavior: Treatment validity and standards of practice. *American Journal on Mental Retardation, 96,* 233–256.

Seeman, P. (1987). Dopamine receptors and the dopamine hypothesis of schizophrenia. *Synapse, 1,* 133–152.

Segraves, K. B., & Segraves, R. T. (1991). Hypoactive sexual desire disorder: Prevalence and comorbidity in 906 subjects. *Journal of Sex and Marital Therapy, 17,* 55–58.

Segraves, R. T. (1988). Drugs and desire. In S. R. Leiblum & R. C. Rosen (Eds.), *Sexual desire disorders* (pp. 313–347). New York: Guilford Press.

Seidman, E. (1988). Back to the future, community psychology: Unfolding a theory of social intervention. *American Journal of Community Psychology, 16,* 3–24.

Seidman, E., Allen, L., Aber, J. L., Mitchell, C., & Feinman, J. (1994). The impact of school transitions in early adolescence on the self-system and perceived social context of poor urban youth. *Child Development, 65,* 507–522.

Seidman, S. N., & Rieder, R. O. (1994). A review of sexual behavior in the United States. *The American Journal of Psychiatry, 151,* 330–341.

Seki, M., Yoshida, K., & Okamura, Y. (1991). A study on hyperprolactinemia in female patients with alcoholism. *Arukoru Kenkyu-to Yakubutsu Ison, 26*(1), 49–89.

Seligman, M. E. P. (1971).Phobias and preparedness. *Behavior Therapy, 2,* 307–320.

Seligman, M. E. P. (1975). *Helplessness: On depression, development, and death.* San Francisco: Freeman.

Seligman, M. E. P. (1995). The effectiveness of psychotherapy: The *Consumer Reports* study. *American Psychologist, 50,* 965–974.

Seligman, M. E. P., & Maier, S. F. (1967). Failure to escape traumatic shock. *Journal of Experimental Psychology, 74,* 1–9.

Selye, H. (1936). A syndrome produced by diverse noxious agents. *Nature, 38,* 32–36.

Selye, H. (1982). History and present status of the stress concept. In L. Goldberger and S. Breznitz (Eds.), *Handbook of stress: Theoretical and clinical aspects* (pp. 7–17). New York: The Free Press.

Semrud-Clikeman, M., & Hynd, G. W. (1991). Specific nonverbal and social-skills deficits in children with learning disabilities. In J. E. Obrzut & G. W. Hynd (Eds.), *Neuropsychological foundations of learning disabilities: A handbook of issues, methods and practice* (pp. 603–629). New York: Academic Press.

Serpell, R. (1979). How specific are perceptual skills? A cross-cultural study of pattern reproduction. *British Journal of Psychology, 70,* 365–380.

Sexton, M. M. (1979). Behavioral epidemiology. In O. F. Pomerleau & J. P. Brady (Eds.), *Behavioral medicine:*

Theory and practice (pp. 3–22). Baltimore: Williams & Wilkins.

Shadish, W. R., Jr., Matt, G. E., Navarro, A. M., Liegle, G., Crits-Christoph, P., Hazelrigg, M., Jorm, A., Lyons, L. S., Nietzel, M. T., Prout, H. T., Robinson, L., Smith, M. L., Svartberg, M., & Weiss, B. (in press). The generalization of psychotherapy research to clinically representative conditions. *Journal of Consulting and Clinical Psychology.*

Shadish, W. R., Jr., & Sweeney, R. B. (1991). Mediators and moderators in meta-analysis: There's a reason we don't let dodo birds tell us which psychotherapies should have prizes. *Journal of Consulting and Clinical Psychology, 59,* 763–765.

Shaffer, D. (1990). Adolescent suicide. *Presentation at the ADAMHOL Clinical training meetings,* Reston, VA.

Shaffer, D., Garland, A., Gould, M., Fisher, P., & Trautman, P. (1988). Preventing teenage suicide: A critical review. *Journal of the American Academy of Child and Adolescent Psychiatry, 27,* 675–687.

Shapiro, D. (1984). *Psychological evaluation and expert testimony: A practical guide to forensic work.* New York: Van Nostrand Reinhold Co.

Shapiro, D. A., & Shapiro, D. (1982). Meta-analysis of comparative therapy outcome research: A critical appraisal. *Behavioral Psychotherapy, 10,* 4–25.

Shariff, H. (1995). Mother-child HIV transmission: Prevention options for women in developing countries. *AIDcaptions, 25*–27.

Shefler, G., & Dasberg, H. (1989, June). *A randomized controlled outcome and follow-up study of James Mann's time-limited psychotherapy in a Jerusalem community mental health center.* Paper presented at the meeting of the Society for Psychotherapy Research, Toronto.

Shelley, Queen Mab (1813), Canto 9, 1, 76.

Sher, K. J. (1991). *Children of alcoholics: A critical appraisal of theory and research.* Chicago: University of Chicago Press.

Sher, K. J., Walitzer, K. S., Wood, P. K., & Brent, E. F. (1991). Characteristics of children of alcoholics: Putative risk factors, substance use and abuse, and psychopathology. *Journal of Abnormal Psychology, 100,* 427–448.

Sherman, S. (1992, June). *Epidemiology and screening.* Paper presented at the Third International Fragile X Conference, Snowmass Resort, CO.

Sherrington, R., Rogaev, E. I., Liang, Y., Rogaev, E. A., Levesque, G., Ikeda, M., Chi, H., Lin, C., Li, G., Holman, K., Tsuda, T., Mar, L., Foncin, J.-F., Bruni, A. C., Montesi, M. P., Sorbi, S., Rainero, I., Pinessi, L., Nee, L., Chumakov, I., Pollen, D., Brookes, A., Sanseau, P., Polinsky, R. J., Wasco, W., Da Silva, H. A. R., Haines, J. L., Pericak-Vance, M. A., Tanzi, R. E., Roses, A. D., Fraser, P. E., Rommens, J. M., & St. George-Hyslop, P. H. (1995). Cloning of a gene bearing missense mutations in early-onset familial Alzheimer's disease. *Nature, 375,* 754–760.

Sherwin, B. B. (1985). Changes in sexual behavior as a function of plasma sex steroid levels in post-menopausal women. *Maturity, 7,* 225–233.

Sherwin, B. B., & Gelfand, M. M. (1987). The role of androgen in the maintenance of sexual functioning in oophorectomized women. *Psychosomatic Medicine, 49,* 397–409.

Sherwin, B. B., Gelfand, M. M., & Brender, W. (1985). Androgen enhances sexual motivation in females: A prospective, crossover study of sex steroid administration in the surgical menopause. *Psychosomatic Medicine, 47,* 339–351.

Shiffman, S. (1993). Smoking cessation treatment: Any progress? *Journal of Consulting and Clinical Psychology, 61*(5), 718–722.

Shonkoff, J. P., & Marshall, P. C. (1990). Biological bases on developmental dysfunction. In S. J. Meisels & J. P. Shonkoff (Eds.), *Handbook of early childhood intervention* (pp. 35–52). New York: Cambridge University Press.

Shorter, E. (1994). *From the mind into the body: The cultural origins of psychosomatic symptoms.* New York: Free Press.

Shukla, G. D. (1989). Electroconvulsive therapy: A review. *Indian Journal of Psychiatry, 31,* 97–115.

Shulman, C., Yirmiya, N., & Greenbaum, C. W. (1995). From categorization to classification. A comparison among individuals with autism, mental retardation, and normal development. *Journal of Abnormal Psychology, 104,* 601–609.

Shulman, I., Cox, B., Swinson, R., Kuch, K., & Reichman, J. (1994). Precipitating events, locations, and reactions associated with initial unexpected panic attacks. *Behaviour Research and Therapy, 32,* 17–20.

Shulman, K. I., Shedletsky, R., & Silver, I. L. (1986). The challenge of time: Clock-drawing and cognitive functions in the elderly. *International Journal of Geriatric Psychiatry, 1,* 135–140.

Shumaker, S. A., & Czajkowski, S. M. (1994). *Social support and cardiovascular disease.* New York: Plenum.

Siegel, J. M., & Kuykendall, D. H. (1990). Loss, widowhood, and psychological distress among the elderly. *Journal of Consulting and Clinical Psychology, 58,* 519–524.

Siegel, S. (1982). Drug dissociation in the nineteenth century. In F. C. Colpaert & J. L. Slangen (Eds.), *Drug discrimination: Applications in CNS pharmacology.* Amsterdam: Elsevier.

Sifneos, P. E. (1979). *Short-term dynamic psychotherapy: Evaluation and technique.* New York: Plenum.

Silver, B., Poland, R., & Lin, K. M. (1993). Ethnicity and pharmacology of tricyclic antidepressants. In K. M. Lin, R. Poland, & G. Nakasaki (Eds.), *Psychopharmacology and psychobiology of ethnicity.* Washington, DC: American Psychiatric Press.

Silver, L. B. (1992). Psychological and family problems associated with learning disabilities: Assessment and intervention. *Journal of the American Academy of Child and Adolescent Psychiatry, 28*(3), 319–325.

Sirkin, M. I. (1992). The role of network therapy in the treatment of relational disorders: Cults and Folie à deux. *Contemporary Family Therapy, 14,* 211–224.

Sitaram, N., Moore, A. M., and Gillin, J. C. (1978). Experimental acceleration and slowing of REM ultradian rhythm by cholinergic agonist and antagonist. *Nature, 274,* 490–492.

Slade, P. D. & Bentall, R. P. (1988). *Sensory deception: A scientific analysis of hallucination.* Baltimore: Johns Hopkins University Press.

Slater, L. (1996). *Welcome to my country.* New York: Random House.

Slipp, S. (Ed.). (1981). *Curative factors in psychodynamic therapy.* New York: McGraw-Hill.

Small, G. W., Mazziotta, J. C., Collins, M. T., Baxter, L. R., Phelps, M. E., Mandelkern, M. A., Kaplan, A., LaRue, A., Adamson, C. F., & Chang, L. (1995). Apolipoprotein E type 4 allele and cerebral glucose metabolism in relatives at risk for familial Alzheimer's disease. *Journal of the American Medical Association, 273,* 942–947.

Small, J. (1990). Anticonvulsants in affective disorders. *Psychopharmacology Bulletin, 26,* 25–36.

Small, J., Klapper, M., Kellams, J., Miller, M., Milstein, V., Sharpley, P., & Small, I. (1988). Electroconvulsive treatment compared with lithium in the management of manic states. *Archives of General Psychiatry, 45,* 727–732.

Smalley, S. L., Asarnow, R. F., & Spence, M. A. (1988). Autism and genetics: Decade of research. *Archives of General Psychiatry, 45,* 953–961.

Smith, D. W., & Wilson, A. A. (1973). *The child with Down's syndrome (mongolism).* Philadelphia: W. B. Saunders Co.

Smith, E. M., North, C. S., & Price, P. C. (1988). Response to technological accidents. In M. Lystad (Ed.), *Mental health response to mass emergencies* (pp. 52–95). New York: Brunner/Mazel.

Smith, G. T., Goldman, M., Greenbaum, P. E., Christiansen, B. A. (1995). Expectancy for social facilitation from drinking: The divergent paths of high-expectancy and low-expectancy adolescents. *Journal of Abnormal Psychology, 104,* 32–40.

Smith, J., Frawley, P. J., & Polissar, L. (1991). Six- and twelve-month abstinence rates in inpatient alcoholics treated with aversion therapy compared with matched inpatients from a treatment registry. *Alcoholism in Clinical and Experimenta Research, 15*(5), 862–870.

Smith, L. W., & Dimsdale, J. E. (1989). Postcardiotomy delirium: Conclusions after 25 years? *American Journal of Psychiatry, 146,* 452–458.

Smith, M., Lin, K. M., & Mendoza, R. (1993). Non-biological issues affecting psychopharmacotherapy: Cultural considerations. In K. M. Lin, R. Poland, & G. Nakasaki (Eds.), *Psychopharmacology and psychobiology of ethnicity.* Washington, DC: American Psychiatric Press.

Smith, M. D., & Belcher, R. G. (1993). Facilitated communication with adults with autism. *Journal of Autism and Developmental Disorders, 23*(1), 175–183.

Smith, M. L., & Glass, G. V. (1977). Meta-analysis of psychotherapy outcome studies. *American Psychologist, 32,* 752–777.

Smith, M. L., Glass, G. V., & Miller, T. I. (1980). *The benefits of psychotherapy.* Baltimore: Johns Hopkins University Press.

Smith, R. E., & Winokur, G. (1991). Mood disorders (bipolar). In M. Hersen & S. M. Turner (Eds.), *Adult psychopathology and diagnosis.* New York: John Wiley & Sons.

Smith, S. R. (1996). Malpractice liability of mental health professionals and institutions. In B. D. Sales & D. W. Shuman (Eds.), *Law, mental health, and mental disorders.* Pacific Grove, CA: Brooks/Cole.

Snaith, P., Tarsh, M. J., & Reid, R. (1993). Sex reassignment surgery. A study of 141 Dutch transsexuals. *British Journal of Psychiatry, 162,* 681–685.

Snowdon, D. A., Ostwald, S. K., & Kane, R. L. (1989). Education, survival, and independence of elderly Catholic sisters, 1936–1988. *American Journal of Epidemiology, 42,* 1055–1066.

Snowdon, D. A., Kemper, S. J., Mortimer, J., Greiner, L., Wekstein, D., & Markesbery, W. R. (1996). Linguistic ability in early life and cognitive function and Alzheimer's disease in later life. *Journal of the American Medical Association, 275,* 528–532.

Snyder, D. K., & Wills, R. M. (1989). Behavioral versus insight-oriented marital therapy: Effects on individual and interspousal functioning. *Journal of Consulting and Clinical Psychology, 57,* 39–46.

Snyder, D. K., Wills, R. M., & Grady-Fletcher, A. (1991). Long-term effectiveness of behavioral versus insight-oriented marital therapy: A 4-year follow-up study. *Journal of Consulting and Clinical Psychology, 59,* 138–141.

Sobel, E. et al. (1995). Occupations with exposure to electromagnetic fields: A possible risk factor for Alzheimer's disease. *American Journal of Epidemiology, 142,* 515–519.

Sobell, L. C., Toneatto, T., & Sobell, M. B. (1994). Behavioral assessment and treatment planning for alcohol, tobacco, and other drug problems: Current status with an emphasis on clinical applications. *Behavior Therapy, 25,* 533–580.

Sobell, M. B., & Sobell, L. C. (1973). Alcoholics treated by individualized behavior therapy: One year treatment outcome. *Behavior Research and Therapy, 11,* 599–618.

Sobell, M. B., & Sobell, L. C. (1976). Second year treatment outcome of alcoholics treated by individualized behavior therapy: Results. *Behaviour Research and Therapy, 14,* 195–215.

Sobin, C., Sackeim, H., Prudic, J., Devanand, D. P., Moody, B. J., & McElhiney, M. C. (1995). Predictors of retrograde amnesia following ECT. *American Journal of Psychiatry, 152,* 995–1001.

Soderstrom, C. A., Dischinger, P. C., Kerns, T. J., & Trifillis, A. L. (1995). Marijuana and other drug use among automobile and motorcycle drivers treated at a trauma center. *Accident Analysis and Prevention, 27*(1), 131–135.

Sodian, B., & Frith, U. (1992). Deception and sabotage in autistic, retarded and normal children. *Journal of Child Psychology and Psychiatry and Allied Disciplines, 33*(3), 591–605.

Soldz, S., Budman, S., Demby, A., & Merry, J. (1993). Representation of personality disorders in circumplex and five-factor space: Explorations with a clinical sample. *Psychological Assessment, 5,* 41–52.

Soloff, P. D., George, A., Nathan, R. S., Schulz, P. M., Cornelius, J. R., Herring, J., & Perel, J. M. (1989). Amitriptyline versus haloperidol in borderlines: Final outcomes and predictors of response. *Journal of Clinical Psychopharmacology, 9,* 238–246.

Sommers-Flanagan, J., & Sommers-Flanagan, R. (1996). Efficacy of antidepressant medication with depressed youth: What psychologists should know. *Professional Psychology: Research and Practice, 27,* 145–153.

Southard, E. E. (1910). Anatomical findings in "senile dementia": A diagnostic study bearing especially on the group of cerebral atrophies. *American Journal of Insanity, 61,* 673–708.

Southwick, S. M., Yehuda, R., & Morgan, C. A. (1995). Clinical studies of neurotransmitter alterations in post-traumatic stress disorder. In M. J. Friedman, D. S. Charney, & A. Y. Deutch (Eds.), *Neurobiological and clinical consequences of stress: From normal adaptation to PTSD* (pp. 335–349). Philadelphia: Lippincott-Raven.

Spake, A. (1992). Breaking the silence. *Teacher Magazine, 3*(9), 14–21.

Spanos, N. P. (1978). Witchcraft in histories of psychiatry: A critical analysis and an alternative conceptualization. *Psychological Bulletin, 85,* 417–439.

Spanos, N. (1994). Multiple identity enactments and multiple personality disorder. *Psychological Bulletin, 116,* 143–165.

Spanos, N. P., Weekes, J. R., Bertrand, L. D. (1985). Multiple personality: A social psychological perspective. *Journal of Abnormal Psychology, 94,* 362–376.

Spanos, N. P., Weekes, J. R., Menary, E., & Bertrand, L. D. (1986). Hypnotic interview and age regression procedures in the elicitation of multiple personality symptoms: A simulation study. *Psychiatry, 49,* 298–311.

Sparrow, S. S., Balla, D. A., & Cicchetti, D. V. (1984). *Vineland Adaptive Behavior Scales.* Circle Pines, MN: American Guidance Service.

Sparrow, S., & Zigler, E. (1978). Evaluation of patterning treatment for retarded children. *Pediatrics, 62,* 137–150.

Speltz, M. L. (1990). The treatment of preschool conduct problems: An integration of behavioral and attachment concepts. In M. T. Greenberg, D. Cicchetti, & M. Cummings (Eds.), *Attachment in the preschool years: Theory, research, and intervention* (pp. 399–426). Chicago, IL: University of Chicago Press.

Speltz, M. L., Shimimura, J., & McReynolds, W. T. (1982). Procedural variations in group contingencies: Effects on children's academic and social behavior. *Journal of Applied Behavior Analysis, 15,* 533–544.

Spencer, T. (1996). Pharmacotherapy of attention-deficit hyperactivity disorder across the life cycle. *Journal of the American Academy of Child and Adolescent Psychiatry, 35,* 409–432.

Spiegel, D., & Bloom, J. R. (1983). Group therapy and hypnosis reduce metastatic breast carcinoma pain. *Psychosomatic Medicine, 45,* 333–339.

Spiegel, D., Bloom, J. R., Kraemer, H. C., & Gottheil, E. (1989, October 14). Effect of psychosocial treatment on survival of patients with metastatic breast cancer. *Lancet, 14,* 888–891.

Spiegel, D., Bloom, J. R., & Yalom, I. (1981). Group support for patients with metastatic cancer: A randomized outcome study. *Archives of General Psychiatry, 38,* 527–533.

Spiegel, D., & Vermutten, E. (1994). Physiological correlates of hypnosis and dissociation. In D. Spiegel (Ed.), *Dissociation: Culture, mind, and body* (pp. 185–210). Washington DC: American Psychiatric Press.

Spiegler, M. D., & Guevremont, D. C. (1993). *Contemporary behavior therapy* (2nd ed.). Belmont, CA: Brooks/Cole.

Spierings, C., Poels, P. J., Sijben, N., Babreels, F. J., & Renier, W. O. (1990). Conversion disorders in childhood: A retrospective follow-up study of 84 inpatients. *Developmental Medicine and Child Neurology, 32,* 865–871.

Spitzer, R. L. (1975). On pseudoscience in science, logic in remission and psychiatric diagnosis: A critique of Rosenhan's "On being sane in insane places." *Journal of Abnormal Psychology, 84,* 442–452.

Spitzer, R. L., Gibbon, M., Skodol, A. E., Williams, J. B. W., & First, M. B. (Eds.). (1994). *DSM-IV Casebook: A learning companion to the Diagnostic and Statistical Manual of Mental Disorders* (4th ed.). Washington, DC: American Psychiatric Press.

Spivack, G., & Shure, M. B. (1974). *Social adjustment of young children: A cognitive approach to solving real-life problems.* San Francisco: Jossey-Bass.

Srole, L., Langner, T. S., Michael, S. T., Opler, M. K., & Rennie, T. A. C. (1962). *Mental health in the metropolis: The midtown Manhattan study.* New York: McGraw-Hill.

Sroufe, L. A., & Fleeson, J. (1986). Attachment and the construction of relationships. In W. Hartup & Z. Rubin (Eds.), *Relationships and development* (pp. 51–71). Hillsdale, NJ: Erlbaum.

Sroufe, L. A., & Rutter, M. (1984). The domain of developmental psychopathology. *Child Development, 55,* 17–29.

St. Lawrence, J. S., Brasfield, T. L., Jefferson, K. W., Alleyne, E., & O'Bannon, R. E., III (1995). Cognitive-behavioral intervention to reduce African American adolescents' risk for HIV infection. *Journal of Consulting and Clinical Psychology, 63,* 221–237.

Stacy, A. W., Widaman, K. F., & Marlatt, G. A. (1990). Expectancy models of alcohol use. *Journal of Personality and Social Psychology, 58,* 918–928.

Stainback, S., & Stainback, W. (1992). *Curriculum considerations in inclusive classrooms: Facilitating learning for all students.* Baltimore: Paul Brookes.

Stark, K. D., Reynolds, W., & Kaslow, N. J. (1987). A comparison of the relative efficacy of self-control therapy and a behavioral problem-solving therapy for depression in children. *Journal of Abnormal Child Psychology, 15,* 91–113.

Starr, E. (1994). Facilitated communication: A response by Child Protection: Commentary. *Child Abuse and Neglect: The International Journal, 18,* 515–527.

Steadman, H. J., & Braff, J. (1983). Defendants not guilty by reason of insanity. In J. Monahan & H. Steadman (Eds.), *Mentally disordered offenders: Perspectives from law and social science.* New York: Plenum.

Steadman, H. J., Keitner, L., Braff, J., & Arvanites, T. M. (1983). Factors associated with a successful insanity plea. *American Journal of Psychiatry, 140,* 401–405.

Stein, D. M., & Lambert, M. J. (1984). On the relationship between therapist experience and psychotherapy outcome. *Clinical Psychology Review, 4,* 127–142.

Stein, D. M., & Lambert, M. J. (1995). Graduate training in psychotherapy: Are therapy outcomes enhanced? *Journal of Consulting and Clinical Psychology, 63,* 182–196.

Stein, M. B., Walker, J. R., Anderson, G., Hazen, A. L. Ross, C. A., Eldridge, G., & Forde, D. R. (1996). Childhood physical and sexual abuse in patients with anxiety disorders and in a community sample. *American Journal of Psychiatry, 153,* 275–277.

Stein, R. E. K., Bauman, L. J., & Ireys, H. T. (1991). Who enrolls in prevention trials? Discordance in perception of risk by professionals and participants. *American Journal of Community Psychology, 19,* 603–618.

Steinberg, M. (1994). Systematizing dissociation: Symptomatology and diagnostic assessment. In D. Spiegel (Ed.), *Dissociation: Culture, mind, and body* (pp. 59–90). Washington, DC: American Psychiatric Press.

Steinglass, P., Bennett, L. A., Wolin, S. J., & Reiss, D. (1987). *The alcoholic family.* New York: Basic Books.

Steketee, G., Foa, E. B., & Grayson, J. B. (1982). Recent advances in the behavioral treatment of obsessive-compulsives. *Archives of General Psychiatry, 39,* 1365–1371.

Steketee, G., & White, K. (1990). *When once is not enough: Help for obsessive compulsives.* Oakland, CA: New Harbinger Press.

Stengel, E. (1943). Further studies on pathological wanderings. *Journal of Mental Science, 89,* 224–241.

Stephens, R. S., Roffman, R. A., & Simpson, E. E. (1994). Treating adult marijuana dependence: A test of the relapse prevention model. *Journal of Consulting and Clinical Psychology, 62,* 92–99.

Stewart, J. W., Rabkin, J. G., Quitkin, F. M., McGrath, P. J., & Klein, D. F. (1993). Atypical depression. In D. L. Dunner (Ed.), *Current psychiatric therapy* (pp. 215–220). Philadelphia: W. B. Saunders Co.

Stiles, W. A., Shapiro, D. A., & Elliott, R. (1986). "Are all psychotherapies equivalent?" *American Psychologist, 41,* 165–180.

Stitzer, M. L., Iguchi, M. Y., & Felch, L. J. (1992). Contingent take-home incentives: Effects on drug use of methadone maintenance patients. *Journal of Consulting and Clinical Psychology, 60*(6), 927–934.

Stoller, R. J. (1968). Male childhood transsexualism. *Journal of the American Academy of Child Psychiatry, 7,* 193–209.

Stoller, R. J. (1975). *Sex and gender: Vol. 2. The transsexual experiment.* London: Hogarth Press.

Stone, A. (1976). The *Tarasoff* decision: Suing psychotherapists to safeguard society. *Harvard Law Review, 90,* 358–378.

Stone, A. A., & Neale, J. M. (1984). New measures of daily coping: Developments and preliminary results. *Journal of Personality and Social Psychology, 46,* 892–906.

Stone, M. H. (1986). Exploratory psychotherapy in schizophrenia-spectrum patients: A reevaluation in the light of long-term follow-up of schizophrenic and borderline patients. *Bulletin of the Menninger Clinic, 50,* 287–306.

Strachan, A. (1986). Family intervention for the rehabilitation of schizophrenia: Toward protection and coping. *Schizophrenia Bulletin, 12,* 678–698.

Strassberg, D. S., Kelly, M. P., Carroll, C., & Kircher, J. C. (1987). The psychophysiological nature of premature ejaculation. *Archives of Sexual Behavior, 16,* 327–336.

Strauss, C. C. (1990). Anxiety disorders of childhood and adolescence. *School Psychology Review, 19*(2), 142–157.

Strauss, M. E. (1993). Relations of symptoms to cognitive deficit in schizophrenia. *Schizophrenia Bulletin, 19,* 41–57.

Streissguth, A. P. (1994). A long-term perspective of FAS. *Alcohol Health and Research World, 18,* 74–81.

Streissguth, A. P., Barr, H. M., & Sampson, P. D. (1990). Moderate prenatal alcohol exposure: Effects on child IQ and learning problems at age 7½ years. *Alcoholism: Clinical and Experimental Research, 14,* 662–669.

Strickland, T., Ranganath, V., Lin, K. M., Poland, R., Mendoza, R., & Smith, M. (1991). Psychopharmacologic considerations in the treatment of Black American populations. *Psychopharmacology Bulletin, 27,* 441–448.

Strober, M., Freeman, F., & Rigali, J. (1990). The pharmacotherapy of depressive illness in adolescence: I. An open label trial of imipramine. *Psychopharmacology Bulletin, 26,* 80–84.

Strober, M., Lampert, C., Schmidt, S., & Morrell, W. (1993). The course of major depressive disorder in adolescents: I. Recovery and risk of manic switching in a follow-up of psychotic and nonpsychotic subtypes. *Journal of the American Academy of Child and Adolescent Psychiatry, 32,* 34–42.

Strober, M., Morrell, W., Burroughs, J., Lampert, C., Danforth, H., & Freeman, R. (1988). A family study of bipolar I disorder in adolescence: Early onset of symptoms linked to increased familial loading and lithium resistance: Childhood affective disorders [Special Issue]. *Journal of Affective Disorders, 15,* 255–268.

Stroul, B. (1993). *Psychiatric crisis response systems: A descriptive study.* Rockville, MD: Substance Abuse and Mental Health Services Administration.

Strupp, H. H. (1989). Psychotherapy: Can the practitioner learn from the researcher? *American Psychologist, 44,* 717–724.

Strupp, H. H., Binder, J. L. (1984). *Psychotherapy in a new key: A guide to time-limited dynamic psychotherapy.* New York: Basic Books.

Strupp, H. H., & Hadley, S. W. (1977). A tripartite model of mental health and therapeutic outcomes. *American Psychologist, 32,* 187–196.

Stuart, M., & Masterson, J. (1992). Patterns of reading and spelling in 10-year-old children related to prereading phonological abilities. *Journal of Experimental Child Psychology, 54,* 168–187.

Stunkard, A., Sorensen, T., & Shulsinger, F. (1980). Use of the Danish adoption register for the study of obesity and thinness. In S. Kety (Ed.), *The genetics of neurological and psychiatric disorders.* New York: Raven Press.

Sturgis, E. T., & Adams, H. E. (1978). The right to treatment: Issues in the treatment of homosexuality. *Journal of Consulting and Clinical Psychology, 46,* 165–169.

Styron, W. (1990). *Darkness visible: A memoir of madness.* New York: Random House.

Suddath, R. L., Christison, G. W., Torrey, E. F., Casanova, M. F., & Weinberger, D. (1990). Anatomical abnormalities in the brains of monozygotic twins discordant for schizophrenia. *New England Journal of Medicine, 322,* 789–794.

Sue, S., Fujino, D. C., Hu, L. T., Takeuchi, D. T., & Zane, N. W. S. (1991). Community mental health services for ethnic minority groups: A test of the cultural responsiveness hypothesis. *Journal of Counseling Psychology, 59,* 533–540.

Sue, S., Zane, N., & Young, K. (1994). Research on psychotherapy with culturally diverse populations. In A. E. Bergin & S. L. Garfield (Eds.), *Handbook of psychotherapy and behavior change* (pp. 783–820). New York: John Wiley & Sons.

Sukhai, R. N., Mol, J., & Harris, A. S. (1989). Combined therapy of enuresis alarm and desmopressin in the treatment of nocturnal enuresis. *European Journal of Pediatrics, 148,* 465–467.

Sullivan, H. S. (1953). *The interpersonal theory of psychiatry.* New York: W. W. Norton.

Suls, J., & Wang, C. K. (1993). The relationship between trait hostility and cardiovascular reactivity: A quantitative review and analysis. *Psychophysiology, 30,* 1–12.

Sulser, F., & Sanders-Bush, E. (1989). From neurochemical to molecular pharmacology of antidepressants. In E. Costa (Ed.), *Tribute to B. B. Brodie.* New York: Raven Press.

Sundberg, N. (1977). *Assessment of persons.* Englewood Cliffs, NJ: Prentice Hall.

Suomi, S. J. (1991). Early stress and adult emotional reactivity in rhesus monkeys. *CIBA Foundation Symposium, 156,* 171–183.

Suppes, T., Baldessarini, R. J., Faedda, G. L., & Tohen, M. (1991). Risk of recurrence following discontinuation of lithium in treatment of bipolar disorder. *Archives of General Psychiatry, 48,* 82–88.

Susser, E., & Wanderling, J. (1994). Epidemiology of nonaffective remitting psychosis vs schizophrenia: Sex and sociocultural setting. *Archives of General Psychiatry, 51,* 294–301.

Sutherland, N. S. (1976). *Breakdown.* New York: Signet.

Sutker, P., Davis, J. M., Uddo, M., & Ditta, S. (1995). War zone stresses, personal resources, and PTSD in Persian Gulf returnees. *Journal of Abnormal Psychology, 104,* 444–452.

Svartberg, M., & Stiles, T. C. (1991). Comparative effects of short-term psychotherapy: A meta-analysis. *Journal of Consulting and Clinical Psychology, 59,* 704–714.

Sveinsson, I. S. (1975). Postoperative psychosis after heart surgery. *The Journal of Thoracic and Cardiovascular Surgery, 70,* 717–726.

Swaab, D. F., Hofman, M. A., Lucasen, P. D., Purba, J. S., Raadsheer, F. L., & van der Nas, J. A. P. (1993). Functional neuroanatomy and neuropathology of the human hypothalamus. *Anatomical Embryology, 187,* 317–330.

Swaim, R. C., Oetting, E. R., Edwards, R. W., & Beauvais, F. (1989). Links from emotional distress to adolescent drug use: A path model. *Journal of Consulting and Clinical Psychology, 57,* 227–231.

Swain, M. A., & Steckel, S. B. (1981). Influencing adherence among hypertensives. *Research Nursing and Health, 4,* 213–218.

Swedo, S., Pietrini, P., Leonard, H., Schapiro, M., Rettew, D., Goldberger, E., Rapoport, J., & Grady, C. (1992). Cerebral glucose metabolism in childhood-onset obsessive-compulsive disorder: Revisualization during pharmacotherapy. *Archives of General Psychiatry, 49,* 690–694.

Syvalahti, E. K. G. (1994). Biological factors in schizophrenia: Structural and functional aspects. *British Journal of Psychiatry, 164* (Suppl. 23), 9–14.

Szab'o, G., Tabakoff, B., & Hoffman, P. L. (1994). The NMDA receptor antagonist dizocilpine differentially affects environment-dependent and environment-independent ethanol tolerance. *Psychopharmacology, 113*(3–4), 511–517.

Szapocznik, J., Kurtines, W. M., Foote, F., Perez-Vidal, A., & Hervis, O. (1986). Conjoint versus one-person family therapy: Further evidence for the effectiveness of conducting family therapy through one person with drug-abusing adolescents. *Journal of Consulting and Clinical Psychology, 54,* 395–397.

Szapocznik, J., Kurtines, W., Santisteban, D. A., & Rio, A. T. (1990). Interplay of advances between theory, research, and application in treatment interventions aimed at behavior problem children and adolescents. *Journal of Consulting and Clinical Psychology, 58,* 696–703.

Szasz, T. S. (1961). *The myth of mental illness: Foundations of a theory of personal conduct.* New York: Hoeber-Harper.

Szasz, T. S. (1986). The case against suicide. *American Psychologist, 41,* 806–812.

Szatmari, P., Jones, M. B., Tuff, L., Bartolucci, G., Fisman, S., & Mahoney, W. (1993). Lack of cognitive impairment in first-degree relatives of children with pervasive developmental disorders. *Journal of the American Academy of Child and Adolescent Psychiatry, 32,* 1264–1273.

Szatmari, P., Offord, D., & Boyle, M. H. (1989). Ontario Health Study: Prevalence of attention deficit disorders with hyperactivity. *Journal of Child Psychology and Psychiatry, 30,* 219–230.

Tabakoff, B., & Hoffman, P. L. (1991). Neurochemical effects of alcohol. In R. J. Frances & S. I. Muller (Eds.), *Clinical textbook of addictive disorders* (pp. 501–525). New York: Guilford Press.

Tabakoff, B., Whelan, J. P., & Hoffman, P. L. (1990). Two biological markers of alcoholism. In C. R. Cloninger & H. Begleiter (Eds.), *Genetics and biology of alcoholism*

(pp. 195–204). Cold Spring Harbor, NY: Cold Spring Harbor Laboratory Press.

Takahashi, T. (1989). Social phobia syndrome in Japan. *Comprehensive Psychiatry, 30,* 45–52.

Takahashi, Y. (1990). Is multiple personality disorder really rare in Japan? *Dissociation, 3,* 57–59.

Talcott, G. W., Fiedler, E. R., Pascale, R. W., Klesges, R. C., Peterson, A. L., & Johnson, R. S. (1995). Is weight gain after smoking cessation inevitable? *Journal of Consulting and Clinical Psychology, 63,* 313–316.

Tandon, R., & Kane, J. M. (1993). Neuropharmacologic basis for clozapine's unique profile. *Archives of General Psychiatry, 50,* 158–159.

Tarasoff v. Regents of the University of California, 17 Cal. 3d 425,551 P.2d 334, 131 Cal. Reptr. 14 (1976).

Tarrier, N., Barrowclough, C., Porceddu, K. & Watts, S. (1988). The assessment of psychophysiological reactivity to expressed emotion of relatives of schizophrenic patients. *British Journal of Psychiatry, 152,* 618–624.

Tartre, R., Blackson, T., Martin, C., Seilhamer, R., Pelham, W., & Loeber, R. (1993). Mutual dissatisfaction between mother and son in substance abuse and normal families: Association with child behavior problems. *American Journal on Addiction, 2,* 1–10.

Tartre, R. E., Kabene, M., Escallier, E. A., Laird, S. B., & Jacob, T. (1990). Temperament deviation and risk for alcoholism. *Alcoholism in Clinical and Experimental Research, 14,* 380–382.

Tartre, R. E., & Vanyukov, M. (1994). Alcoholism: A developmental disorder. *Journal of Consulting and Clinical Psychology, 62,* 1096–1107.

Tavris, C., & Sadd, S. (1977). *The Redbook report on female sexuality: 100,000 married women disclose the good news about sex.* New York: Delacorte Press.

Taylor, P. J., & Kopelman, M. D. (1984). Amnesia for criminal offenses. *Psychological Medicine, 14,* 581–588.

Taylor, S. E. (1983). Adjustment to threatening events: A theory of cognitive adaptation. *American Psychologist, 38,* 1161–1173.

Taylor, S. E. (1989). *Postive illusions: Creative self-deception and the healthy mind.* New York: Basic Books.

Taylor, S. E. (1994). Asymmetrical effects of positive and negative events: The mobilization-minimization hypothesis. *Psychological Bulletin, 110,* 67–85.

Taylor, S. E. (1995). *Health psychology.* New York: McGraw-Hill.

Taylor, S. E., & Brown, J. D. (1988). Illusion and well-being: A social psychological perspective on mental health. *Psychological Bulletin, 103,* 193–210.

Taylor, C. B., Ironson, G., & Burnett, K. (1990). Adult medical disorders. In A. S. Bellack, M. Hersen, & A. E. Kazdin (Eds.), *International handbook of behavior modification and therapy* (pp. 371–398). New York: Plenum.

Telch, M., Lucus, J., Schmidt, N., Hanna, H., Jaimez, T., & Lucas, R. (1993). Group cognitive-behavioral treatment of panic disorder. *Behaviour Research and Therapy, 31,* 279–287.

Tellegen, A., Lykken, D. T., Bouchard, T. J., Jr., Wilcox, K. J., Segal, N. L., & Rich, S. (1988). Personality similarity in twins reared apart and reared together. *Journal of Personality and Social Psychology, 54,* 1031–1039.

Tennant, F., & Shannon, J. (1995). Cocaine abuse in methadone maintenance patients is associated with low serum methadone concentrations. *Journal of Addictive Disorders, 14,* 67–74.

Tennen, H., & Affleck, G. (1990). Blaming others for threatening events. *Psychological Bulletin, 108,* 209–232.

Teplin, L. (1984). The criminalization of the mentally ill: Speculation in search of data. In L. A. Teplin (Ed.), *Mental health and criminal justice.* Newbury Park, CA: Sage.

Teri, L, & Gallagher, T. D. (1991). Cognitive therapy and depression in Alzheimer's patients. *Gerontologist, 31,* 413–416.

Terman, L. M., & Oden, M. H. (1947). *Genetic studies of genius: The gifted child grows up* (Vol. 4). Stanford, CA: Stanford University Press.

Tessler, R. C., & Dennis, D. L. (1989). *A synthesis of NIMH-funded research concerning persons who are homeless and mentally ill.* Rockville, MD: National Institute of Mental Health.

Thaker, G. K., Cassady, S., Adami, H., Moran, M., & Ross, D. E. (1996). Eye movements in spectrum personality disorders: Comparison of community subjects and relatives of schizophrenic patients. *The American Journal of Psychiatry, 153,* 362–368.

Thapar, A., Davies, G., Jones, T., & Rivett, M. (1992). Treatment of childhood encopresis—A review. *Child: Care, Health and Development, 18,* 343–353.

Thigpen, C. H., & Cleckley, H. (1957). *The three faces of Eve.* New York: McGraw-Hill.

Thoits, P. A. (1986). Social support as coping assistance. *Journal of Consulting and Clinical Psychology, 54,* 416–423.

Thomasson, H. R., Edenberg, H. J., Crabb, D. W., Mai, X. L., Jerome, R. E., Li, T.-K., Wang, S.-P., Lin, Y.-T., Lu, R.-B., & Yin, S.-J. (1991). Alcohol and aldehyde dehydrogenase genotypes and alcoholism in Chinese men. *American Journal of Human Genetics, 48,* 677–681.

Thombs, D. L. (1993). The differentially discriminating properties of alcohol expectancies for female and male drinkers. *Journal of Counseling and Development, 71,* 321–325.

Thombs, D. L. (1994). *Introduction to addictive behaviors.* New York: Guilford Press.

Thompson, J. W., Weiner, R. D., & Myers, C. P. (1994). Use of ECT in the United States in 1976, 1980, and 1986. *American Journal of Psychiatry, 151,* 1657–1661.

Thompson, L. W., Gallagher, D., & Breckenridge, J. S. (1987). Comparative effectiveness of psychotherapies for depressed elders. *Journal of Consulting and Clinical Psychology, 55,* 385–390.

Thompson, T., Hackenberg, T., Cerutti, D., Baker, D., & Axtell, S. (1994). Opioid antagonist effects on self-injury in adults with mental retardation: Response form and location as determinants of medication effects. *American Journal on Mental Retardation, 99*(1), 85–102.

Thoresen, C. E., & Powell, L. H. (1992). Type A behavior pattern: New perspectives on theory, assessment and intervention. Special issue: Behavioral medicine: An update for the 1990s. *Journal of Consulting and Clinical Psychology, 60,* 595–604.

Thorndike, R. L., Hagen, E. P., & Sattler, J. M. (1986). *The Stanford-Binet Intelligence Scale: Fourth Edition, Guide for administering and scoring.* Chicago: Riverside Publishing Co.

Thyer, B., Nesse, R., Curtis, G., & Cameron, O. (1986). Panic disorder: A test of the separation anxiety hypothesis. *Behaviour Research and Therapy, 24,* 209–211.

Thyer, B. A. (1991). Diagnosis and treatment of child and adolescent anxiety disorders. *Behavior Modification, 15*(3), 310–325.

Tiefer, L., & Melman, A. (1989). Comprehensive evaluation of erectile dysfunction and medical treatments. In S. R. Leiblum & R. C. Rosen (Eds.), *Principles and practice of sex therapy: Update for the 1990s* (pp. 207–236). New York: Guilford Press.

Tiernari, P. (1991). Interaction between genetic vulnerability and family environment: The Finnish adoptive family study of schizophrenia. *Acta Psychiatrica Scandanavica, 84,* 460–465.

Timbrook, R. E., & Graham, J. R. (1994). Ethnic differences on the MMPI-2? *Psychological Assessment, 6,* 212–217.

Tisdelle, D. A., & St. Lawrence, J. S. (1988). Adolescent interpersonal problem-solving skill training: Social validation and generalization. *Behavior Therapy, 19,* 171–182.

Tolan, P. H., Guerra, N. G., & Kendall, P. C. (1995). A developmental-ecological perspective on antisocial behavior in children and adolescents: Toward a unified risk and intervention framework. *Journal of Consulting and Clinical Psychology, 63,* 579–584.

Tollefson, G. D. (1993). Major depression. In D. L. Dunner (Ed.), *Current Psychiatric Practice* (pp. 196–204). Philadelphia: W. B. Saunders Co.

Tollefson, G. D., Rampey, A. H., & Genduso, L. A., (1994). A fixed-dose, placebo-controlled trial in OCD. *Psychopharmacology Bulletin, 30,* 84.

Tollefson, G. D., Rampey, A. H., Potvin, J., Jenike, M. A., Rush, J., Dominguez, R. A., Koran, L. M., Shear, K., Goodman, W., & Genduso, L. A. (1994). A multicenter investigation of a fixed-dose fluoxetine in the treatment of obsessive-compulsive disorder. *Archives of General Psychiatry, 51,* 559–563.

Tomarken, A. J. (1995). A psychometric perspective on psychophysiological measures. *Psychological Assessment, 7,* 387–395.

Tomasson, K., Kent, D., & Coryell, W. (1991). Somatization and conversion disorders: Comorbidity and demographics at presentation. *Acta Psychiatrica Scandinavica, 84,* 288–293.

Torgersen, S. G. (1983). Genetic factors in anxiety disorders. *Archives of General Psychiatry, 40,* 1065–1069.

Torgersen, S. G. (1984). Genetic and nosological aspects of schizotypal and borderline personality disorders. *Archives of General Psychiatry, 41,* 546–554.

Torgersen, S. G. (1986). Genetics of somatoform disorder. *Archives of General Psychiatry, 43,* 502–505.

Torrey, E. F. (1987). Prevalence studies of schizophrenia. *British Journal of Psychiatry, 164,* 589–608.

Torrey, E. F. (1988). *Nowhere to go: The tragic odyssey of the homeless mentally ill.* New York: Harper & Row.

Torrey, E. F., & Bowler, A. (1990). Geographical distribution of insanity in America: Evidence for an urban factor. *Schizophrenia Bulletin, 16,* 591–604.

Torrey, E. F., Bowler, A. E., Rawlings, R., & Terrazas, A. (1993). Seasonality of schizophrenia and stillbirths. *Schizophrenic Bulletin, 19,* 557–562.

Torrey, E. F. Taylor, E. H. J., Bracha, H., Bowler, A., McNeil, T., Rawlings, R., Quinn, P., Biglow, L., Rickler, K., Sjostrom, K., Higgins, E., & Gottesman, I. (1994). Prenatal origin of schizophrenia in a subgroup of discordant monozygotic twins. *Schizophrenia Bulletin, 20,* 423–431.

Torrey, E. F., & Yolkin, R. H. (1995). Could schizophrenia be a viral zoonosis transmitted from house cats? *Schizophrenia Bulletin, 21,* 167–171.

Tremblay, R. E., Pagani-Kurtz, L., Masse, L. C., Vitaro, F., & Pihl, R. O. (1995). A bimodal preventive intervention for disruptive kindergarten boys: Its impact through mid-adolescence. *Journal of Consulting and Clinical Psychology, 63,* 560–568.

Tremblay, R. E., Masse, B., Perron, D., Leblanc, M., Schwartzman, A. E., & Ledingham, J. E. (1992). Early disruptive behavior, poor school achievement, delinquent behavior, and delinquent personality: Longitudinal analyses. *Journal of Consulting and Clinical Psychology, 60,* 64–72.

Trickett, E. J., Dahiyal, C., & Selby, P. M. (1994). *Primary prevention in mental health: An annotated bibliography 1983–1991.* Rockville, MD: National Institute of Mental Health.

Trickett, P. K., & Putnam, F. W. (1993). Impact of child sexual abuse on females: Toward a developmental, psychobiological integration. *Psychological Science, 4,* 81–87.

True, W. R., Rice, J., Eisen, S. A., Heath, A. C. et al. (1993). A twin study of genetic and environmental contributions to liability for posttraumatic stress symptoms. *Archives of General Psychiatry, 50,* 257–264.

Trujillo, K. A., & Akil, H. (1995). Excitatory amino acids and drugs of abuse: A role for N-methyl-D-aspartate receptors in drug tolerance, sensitization and physical dependence. *Drug and Alcohol Dependence, 38,* 139–154.

Trull, T. J. (1992). DSM-III-R personality disorders and the five-factor model of personality: An empirical comparison. *Journal of Abnormal Psychology, 101,* 553–560.

Trull, T. J., Nietzel, M. T., & Main, A. (1988). The use of meta-analysis to assess the clinical significance of behavior therapy for agoraphobia. *Behavior Therapy, 19,* 527–538.

Tsai, L. Y. (1987). Pre-, peri-, and neonatal factors in autism. In E. Schopler & G. G. Mesibov (Eds.), *Neurobiological issues in autism* (pp. 180–187). New York: Plenum.

Tsoi, W. F. (1993). Follow-up study of transsexuals after sex-reassignment surgery. *Singapore Medical Journal, 34,* 515–517.

Tsuang, D. & Coryell, W. (1993). An 8-year follow-up of patients with DSM-III-R psychotic depression, schizoaffective disorder and schizophrenia. *American Journal of Psychiatry, 150,* 1182–1188.

Tune, L., & Ross, C. (1994). Delirium. In C. E. Coffey & J. L. Cummings (Eds.), *Textbook of geriatric neuropsychiatry* (pp. 351–365). Washington, DC: American Psychiatric Press.

Turk, D. C., & Rudy, T. E. (1990). Pain. In A. S. Bellack, M. Hersen, & A. E. Kazdin (Eds), *International handbook of behavior modification and therapy.* New York: Plenum.

Turkheimer, E., & Parry, C. D. H. (1992). Why the gap? Practice and policy in civil commitment hearings. *American Psychologist, 47,* 646–655.

Turner, E., Ewing, J., Shilling, P., Smith, T. L., Irwin, M., Schuckit, M., & Kelsoe, J. R. (1992). Lack of association between an RFLP near the D2 dopamine receptor gene and severe alcoholism. *Biological Psychiatry, 31,* 285–290.

Turner, J. B., Kessler, R. C., & House, J. S. (1991). Factors facilitating adjustment to unemployment: Implications for intervention. *American Journal of Community Psychology, 19,* 521–542.

Turner, M. J. (1995). Homosexuality, Type 1: An Xq28 phenomenon. *Archives of Sexual Behavior, 24,* 109–134.

Turner, S. M., Beidel, D. C., & Jacob, R. G. (1994). Social phobia: A comparison of behavior therapy and atenolol. *Journal of Consulting and Clinical Psychology, 62,* 350–358.

Tyrka, A. R., Cannon, T. D., Haslam, N., Mednick, S. A., Schulsinger, F., Schulsinger, H., & Parnas, J. (1995). The latent structure of schizotypy. I: Premorbid indicators of a taxon of individuals at risk for schizophrenia-spectrum disorders. *Journal of Abnormal Psychology, 104,* 173–183.

U.S. Department of Health and Human Services. (1987). *National Center for Health Statistics: Detailed diagnoses and procedures for patients discharged from short-stay hospitals: United States, 1985.* Hyattsville, MD: Author.

U.S. Department of Health and Human Services. (1990). *The health benefits of smoking cessation: A report of the Surgeon General* (DHHS Publication No. CDC 90-8416). Washington, DC: U.S. Government Printing Office.

U.S. Department of Transportation, National Highway Traffic Safety Administration. (1991). *Fatal accident reporting system (FARS) 1990: A review of information on fatal traffic crashes in the United States.* (DOT HS 807 794). Washington, DC: Supt. of Docs., U.S. Government Printing Office.

U.S. General Accounting Office (1990). *Methadone maintenance: Some treatment programs are not effective; greater federal oversight needed.* Washington, DC: U.S. General Accounting Office.

Ullmann, L. P., & Krasner, L. (1975). *A psychological approach to abnormal behavior.* Englewood Cliffs, NJ: Prentice Hall.

Unger, K. V., & Anthony, W. A. (1992). A supported education program for young adults with long-term mental illness. *Hospital and Community Psychiatry, 42,* 838–842.

Urban, J., Carlson, E., Egeland, B., & Sroufe, A. L. (1991). Patterns of individual adaptation across childhood: Attachment and developmental psychopathology [Special Issue]. *Developmental Psychology, 3,* 445–460.

Vaillant, G. E. (1984). The disadvantages of DSM-III outweigh its advantages. *American Journal of Psychiatry, 141,* 542–545.

Vaillant, G. E. (1994a). Ego mechanisms of defense and personality psychopathology. *Journal of Abnormal Psychology, 103,* 44–50.

Vaillant, G. E. (1994b). Behavioral medicine over the life span. In S. J. Blumenthal, K. Mathews, & S. M. Weiss (Eds.), *New research frontiers in behavioral medicine: Proceedings of the national conference.* Washington, DC: National Institutes of Health.

Valenstein, E. S. (Ed.). (1980). *The psychosurgery debate: Scientific, legal and ethical perspectives.* San Francisco: Freeman.

Valenstein, E. S. (1986). *Great and desperate cures: The rise and decline of psychosurgery and other radical treatments for mental illness.* New York: Basic Books.

Van Hoesen, G. W., & Damasio, A. R. (1987). Neural correlates of cognitive impairment in Alzheimer's disease. In F. Blum (Ed.), *Handbook of Physiology: Section I. The Nervous System: Vol. V. Higher Functions of the Brain,* Bethesda, MD: American Physiological Society.

van Ijzendoorn, M. H., & Kroonenberg P. M. (1988). Cross-cultural patterns of attachment: A meta-analysis of the strange situation. *Child Development, 59,* 147–156.

VandenBos, G. R., & Stapp, J. (1983). Service providers in psychology: Results of the 1982 APA human resources survey. *American Psychologist, 38,* 1330–1352.

Varadaraj, R., Norman, R. C., Caroff, S. N., Mann, S., Sullivan, K., & Antelo, E. (1994). Progression of symptoms in neuroleptic malignant syndrome. *Journal of Nervous and Mental Disease, 182,* 168–173.

Vaughn, C., & Leff, J. (1976). Measurement of expressed emotion in the families of psychiatric patients. *British Journal of Social and Clinical Psychology, 15,* 1069–1177.

Vaughn, C., Sorenson, K., Jones, S., Freeman, W., & Falloon, I. (1984). Family factors in schizophrenia relapse: Replication in California of British research on expressed emotion. *Archives of General Psychiatry, 41,* 1069–1177.

Vaughan, E. (1993). Individual and cutural differences in adaptation to environmental risks. *American Psychologist, 48,* 673–680.

Velamoor, V. R., Norman, R. M., Caroff, S. N., Mann, S. C., Sullivan, K., & Antelo, R. E. (1994). Progression of symptoms in neuromalignant syndrome. *The Journal of Nervous and Mental Disease, 182,* 168–173.

Vellutino, F., & Scanlon, D. (1985). Verbal memory in poor and normal readers: Developmental differences in the use of linguistic codes. In D. B. Gray & J. F. Kavanagh (Eds.), *Biobehavioral measures of dyslexia* (pp. 117–214). Parkton, MD: York Press.

Venables, P. H. (1996). Schizotypy and maternal exposure to influenza and to cold temperature: The Mauritius study. *Journal of Abnormal Psychology, 105,* 53–60.

Ventura, J., Nuechterlein, K. H., Lukoff, D., & Hardesty, J. P. (1989). A prospective study of stressful life events and schizophrenic relapse. *Journal of Abnormal Psychology, 98,* 407–411.

Verhulst, F. C., Eussen, M. L. J. M., Berden, G. F. M. G., Sanders-Woudstra, J., & Van Der Ende, J. (1993). Pathways of problem behaviors from childhood to adolescence. *Journal of the American Academy of Child Adolescence Psychiatry, 32,* 388–396.

Verhulst, J., & Heiman, J. (1988). A systems perspective on sexual desire. In S. R. Leiblum & R. C. Rosen (Eds.), *Perspectives on sexual desire* (pp. 168–191). New York: Guilford Press.

Vernberg, E. M., La Greca, A. M., Silverman, W. K., & Prinstein, M. J. (1996). Prediction of posttraumatic stress symptoms in children after Hurricane Andrew. *Journal of Abnormal Psychology, 105*, 237–248.

Viken, R. J., & McFall, R. M. (1994). Paradox lost: Implications of contemporary reinforcement theory for behavior therapy. *Current Directions in Psychological Science, 3*, 121–125.

Virkkunen, M., & Narvanen, S. (1987). Plasma insulin, tryptophan and serotonin levels during the glucose tolerance test among habitually violent and impulsive offenders. *Neuropsychobiology, 17*, 19–23.

Volkmar, F. R. (1992). Autism and the pervasive developmental disorders. In M. Lewis (Ed.), *Child and adolescent psychiatry: A comprehensive textbook* (pp. 499–508). Baltimore: Williams & Wilkins.

Volpicelli, J. R., Alterman, A. I., Hayashida, M., & O'Brien, C. P. (1992). Naltrexone in the treatment of alcohol dependence. *Archives of General Psychiatry, 49*, 876–880.

von Bertalanffy, L. (1968). *General systems theory.* New York: Braziller.

Von Korff, M., Dworkin, S. F., & LeResche, L. (1990). Graded chronic pain status: An epidemiologic evaluation. *Pain, 40*, 2791.

Von Knorring, A. L., Cloninger, C. R., Boham, M., & Sigvardsson, S. (1983). An adoption study of depressive disorders and substance abuse. *Archives of General Psychiatry, 40*, 943–950.

Wakefield, H., & Underwager, R. (1992). Recovered memories of alleged sexual abuse: Lawsuits against parents. *Behavioral Sciences and the Law, 10*, 483–507.

Wakefield, J. C. (1992). The concept of mental disorder: On the boundary between biological facts and social values. *American Psychology, 47*, 373–388.

Walker, C. E., Hedberg, A., Clement, P. W., & Wright, L. (1981). *Clinical procedures for behavior therapy.* Englewood Cliffs, NJ: Prentice Hall.

Walker, D., Greenwood, C. R., Hart, B., & Carta, J. (1994). Prediction of school outcomes based on early language production and socioeconomic factors: Children and poverty [Special Issue]. *Child Development, 65*, 606–621.

Walker, E. F., Grimes, K. E., Davis, D., & Smith, A. (1993). Childhood precursors of schizophrenia: Facial expressions of emotion. *American Journal of Psychiatry, 150*, 1654–1660.

Walker, L. S., Garber, J., & Greene, J. W. (1994). Somatic complaints in pediatric patients: A prospective study of the role of negative life events, child social and academic competence, and parental somatic symptoms. *Journal of Consulting and Clinical Psychology, 62*, 1213–1221.

Wallace, C. J. (1993). Psychiatric rehabilitation. *Psychopharmacology Bulletin, 29*, 537–548.

Walsh, B. T. (1988). Pharmacotherapy of eating disorders. In B. J. Blinder, B. F. Chaitin, & R. Goldstein (Eds.), *The eating disorders* (pp. 469–476). PMA Publishing Corporation.

Walsh, S. L., June, H. L., Schuh, K. J., Preston, K. L., Bigelow, G. E., & Stitzer, M. L. (1995). Effects of buprenorphine and methadone in methadone-maintained subjects. *Psychopharmacology, 119*, 268–276.

Walter, H. I., & Gilmore, S. K. (1973). Placebo versus social learning effects in parent training procedures designed to alter the behavior of aggressive boys. *Behavior Therapy, 4*, 361–377.

Wang, Y., & Watson, R. R. (1995). Is alcohol consumption a cofactor in the development of acquired immunodeficiency syndrome? *Alcohol, 12*, 105–109.

Warburton, D. M. (1995). Effects of caffeine on cognition and mood without caffeine abstinence. *Psychopharmacology, 119*, 66–70.

Warneke, L. B. (1991). Benzodiazepines: Abuse and new use. *Canadian Journal of Psychiatry, 36*, 194–205.

Warner, L. A., Kessler, R. C., Hughes, M., Anthony, J. C., & Nelson, C. B. (1995). Prevalence and correlates of drug use and dependence in the United States. *Archives of General Psychiatry, 52*, 219–229.

Warner, M. D., Peabody, C., Boutros, N., & Whiteford, H. (1990). Alprazolam and withdrawal seizures. *Journal of Nervous and Mental Disease, 178*, 208–209.

Wartenberg, A. A., Nirenberg, T. D., Liepman, M. R., Silvia, L. Y., Begin, A. M., & Monti, P. M. (1990). Detoxification of alcoholics: Improving care by symptom-triggered sedation. *Alcoholism in Clinical and Experimental Research, 14*, 71–75.

Washington v. Harper, 494 U.S. 210 (1990).

Waterhouse, B. D., Sessler, F. M., Cheng, J. G., Woodward, D. J., Azizi, S. A., and Moises, H. C. (1988). New evidence for a gating action of norepinephrine in central neuronal circuits of mammalian brain. *Brain Research Bulletin, 1*, 425–432.

Waterman, B., & Lewandowski, L. (1993). Phonologic and semantic processing in reading-disabled and nondisabled males at two age levels. *Journal of Experimental Child Psychology, 55*, 87–103.

Watkins, J. (1984). The Bianchi (L. A. Hillside Strangler) case: Sociopath or multiple personality? *The International Journal of Clinical and Experimental Hypnosis, 2*, 67–101.

Watson, C. G., Anderson, P., Gearhart, L. P. (1995). Posttraumatic stress disorder (PTSD) symptoms in PTSD patients' families of origin. *Journal of Nervous and Mental Disease, 183*, 633–638.

Watson, D., Clark, L. A., & Harkness, A. R. (1994). Structures of personality and their relevance to psychopathology. *Journal of Abnormal Psychology, 103*, 18–31.

Watson, D., & Kendall, P. C. (1989). Understanding anxiety and depression: Their relation to negative and positive affective states. In P. C. Kendall & D. Watson (Eds.), *Anxiety and depression: Distinctive and overlapping features* (pp. 3–26). San Diego: Academic Press.

Watson, J. B., & Rayner, R. (1920). Conditioned emotional reaction. *Journal of Experimental Psychology, 3*, 1–14.

Watt, N. F., & Saiz, C. (1991). Longitudinal studies of premorbid development of adult schizophrenics. In P. F. Walker (Ed.), *Schizophrenia: A life-course in developmental perspective.* San Diego: Academic Press.

Webster-Stratton, C. (1984). Randomized trial of two parent training programs for families with conduct disordered children. *Journal of Consulting and Clinical Psychology, 52*, 666–678.

Wechsler, D. (1981). *Wechsler Adult Intelligence Scale-Revised.* New York: Psychological Corporation.

Wechsler, D. (1991). *WISC-III: Manual.* San Antonio, TX: Psychological Corporation.

Weinberger, D., Berman, K., & Torrey, E. F. (1992). Evidence of dysfunction of a prefrontal-limbic network in schizophrenia: A magnetic resonance imaging and blood flow study of discordant monozygotic twins. *American Journal of Psychiatry, 149*, 890–897.

Weisenberg, M., Schwarzwald, J., Waysman, M., Solomon, Z., & Klingman, A. (1993). Coping of school-age children in the sealed room during scud missile bombardment and postwar stress reactions. *Journal of Consulting and Clinical Psychology, 61*, 462–467.

Weishaar, M. E., & Beck, A. T. (1990). Cognitive approaches to understanding and treating suicidal behavior. In S. J. Blumenthal & D. J. Kupfer (Eds.), *Suicide over the life cycle: Risk factors, assessment, and treatment of suicidal patients* (pp. 469–498). Washington, DC: American Psychiatric Press.

Weiss, R. E., Stein, M. A., Trommer, B., & Refetoff, S. (1993). Attention-deficit hyperactivity disorder and thyroid function. *Journal of Pediatrics, 123*, 539–45.

Weisse, C. S. (1992). Depression and immunocompetence: A review of the literature. *Psychological Bulletin, 111*, 475–489.

Weissman, M. M. (1993). The epidemiology of personality disorders: A 1990 update. *Journal of Personality Disorders* (Suppl.), 44–62.

Weissman, M. M., Bruce, M. L., Leaf, P. J., Florio, L., & Holzer, C. (1991). Affective disorders. In L. N. Robins & D. A. Regier (Eds.), *Psychiatric disorders in America* (pp. 53–80). New York: The Free Press.

Weissman, M. M., Klerman, G. L., Markowitz, J. S., & Ouellette, R. (1989). Suicidal ideation and suicide attempts in panic disorder and attacks. *New England Journal of Medicine, 321,* 1209–1214.

Weisz, J. R., Suwanlert, S., Chaiyasit, W., & Walter, B. R. (1987). Over- and undercontrolled clinic-referral problems among Thai and American children and adolescents: The *wat* and *wai* of cultural differences. *Journal of Consulting and Clinical Psychology, 55,* 719–726.

Weisz, J. R., Weiss, B., & Donenberg, G. R. (1992). The lab versus the clinic: Effects of child and adolescent psychotherapy. *American Psychologist, 47,* 1578–1585.

Wells, K. B., Burnam, A., Rogers, W., Hays, R., & Camp, P. (1992). The course of depression in adult outpatients: Results from the Medical Outcome Study. *Archives of General Psychiatry, 49,* 788–794.

Wells, K. C., & Egan, J. (1988). Social learning and systems family therapy for childhood oppositional disorder: Comparative treatment outcome. *Comprehensive Psychiatry, 29,* 138–146.

Wells, K., Katon, W., Rogers, B., & Camp, P. (1994). Use of minor tranquilizers and antidepressant medications by depressed outpatients: Results from the medical outcome studies. *American Journal of Psychiatry, 151,* 694–700.

Welner, A., Welner, Z., & Leonard, M. A. (1977). Bipolar manic-depressive disorder: A reassessment of course and outcome. *Comprehensive Psychiatry, 18,* 327–332.

Wender, P. H., Kety, S. S., Rosenthal, D., Schulsinger, F., Ortmann, J., & Lunde, I. (1986). Psychiatric disorders in the biological and adoptive families of adopted individuals with affective disorders. *Archives of General Psychiatry, 43,* 923–929.

Wetzel, R. D., Guze, S. B., Cloninger, R., Martin, R. L., & Clayton, P. J. (1994). Briquet's syndrome (hysteria) is both a somatoform and a "psychoform" illness: A Minnesota Multiphasic Personality Inventory Study. *Psychosomatic Medicine, 56,* 564–569.

Wesolowski, M. D., & Zawlocki, R. J. (1982). The differential effects of procedures to eliminate an injurious self-stimulating behavior (digito-ocular sign) in blind retarded twins. *Behavior Therapy, 13,* 334–345.

Westermeyer, J. (1987). Cultural factors in clinical assessment. *Journal of Consulting and Clinical Psychology, 55,* 472–478.

Wexler, B. E., & Cicchetti, D. V. (1992). The outpatient treatment of depression. Implications of outcome research for clinical practice. *Journal of Nervous and Mental Diseases, 180,* 277–286.

Wexler, D., & Winnick, B. J. (1991). *Essays in therapeutic jurisprudence.* Durham, NC: Carolina Academic Press.

Whalen, C. K., & Henker, B. (1991). Therapies for hyperactive children: Comparisons, combinations, and compromises. *Journal of Consulting and Clinical Psychology, 59,* 126–137.

Whalen, C. K., Henker, B., & Hinshaw, S. P. (1985). Cognitive-behavior therapies for hyperactive children: Premises, problems, and prospects. *Journal of Abnormal Child Psychology, 13,* 391–410.

Whiffen, V. E. (1992). Is postpartum depression a distinct diagnosis? *Clinical Psychology Review, 12,* 485–508.

Whiffen, V. E., & Gotlib, I. H. (1993). Comparison of postpartum and nonpostpartum depression: Clinical presentation, psychiatric history, and psychosocial functioning. *Journal of Clinical and Consulting Psychology, 61,* 485–494.

Whitam, F. L., Diamond, M., & Martin, J. (1993). Homosexual orientation in twins: A report on 61 pairs and three triplet sets. *Archives of Sexual Behavior, 22,* 187–206.

White, J., Moffitt, T. E., Earls, F., Robins, L., & Silva, P. (1990). How early can we tell? Preschool predictors of conduct disorder. *Criminology, 28,* 507–533.

WHO (World Health Organization). (1968). *Manual of the international statistical classification of diseases, injuries, and causes of death (ICD-8).* Geneva, Switzerland: Author.

WHO (World Health Organization). (1978). *Schizophrenia: An international follow-up study.* London: John Wiley & Sons.

WHO (World Health Organization). (1992). *International Classification of Diseases (ICD-10).* Geneva, Switzerland: Author.

WHO (World Health Organization). (1992). *The ICD-10 classification of mental disorders: Clinical descriptions and diagnostic guide.* Geneva, Switzerland: Author.

WHO (World Health Organization). (1993). *The ICD-10 chapter V: Mental and behavioral disorders: Diagnostic criteria for research.* Geneva, Switzerland: Author.

Widiger, T. A., & Costa, P. T., Jr. (1994). Personality and personality disorders. *Journal of Abnormal Psychology, 103,* 78–91.

Widiger, T., & Frances, A. (1989). Epidemiology, diagnosis, and comorbidity of borderline personality disorder. In A. Tasman, R. Hales, & A. Frances (Eds.), *American Psychiatric Press Review of Psychiatry* (Vol. 8, pp. 8–24). Washington, DC: American Psychiatric Press.

Widiger, T. A., Frances, A. J., Pincus, H. A., Davis, W. W., & First, M. B. (1991). Toward an empirical classification for the DSM-IV. *Journal of Abnormal Psychology, 100,* 280–288.

Widiger, T. A., Frances, A. J., Pincus, H. A., First, M., Ross, R., & Davis, W. (Eds.). (1994). *DSM-IV Sourcebook* (Vol 1). Washington, DC: American Psychiatric Press.

Widiger, T., Frances, A., & Trull, T. (1987). A psychometric analysis of the social-interpersonal and cognitive-perceptual items for the schizoptypal personality disorder. *Archives of General Psychiatry, 44,* 741–745.

Widiger, T. A., Mangine, S., Corbitt, E. M., Ellis, C. G., & Thomas, G. V. (1995). *Personality Disorder Interview-IV: A semistructured interview for the assessment of personality disorders.* Odessa, FL: Psychological Assessment Resources.

Widiger, T., Miele, G., & Tilly, S. (1992). Alternative perspectives on the diagnosis of borderline personality disorder. In J. Clarkin, E. Marziali, & H. Munroe-Blum (Eds.), *Borderline personality disorder: Clinical and empirical perspectives* (pp. 89–115). New York: Guilford Press.

Widiger, T. A., & Rogers, J. H. (1989). Prevalence and comorbidity of personality disorders. *Psychiatric Annals, 19,* 132–136.

Widiger, T., & Spitzer, R. (1991). Sex bias in the diagnosis of personality disorders. *Clinical Psychology Review, 11,* 1–22.

Widiger, T., & Trull, T. (1991). Diagnosis and clinical assessment. *Annual Review of Psychology, 42,* 109–133.

Widiger, T. A., Trull, T. J., Hurt, S. W., Clarkin, J., & Frances, A. (1987). A multidimensional scaling of the DSM-III personality disorders. *Archives of General Psychiatry, 44,* 557–563.

Widiger, T., & Weissman, M. (1991). Epidemiology of borderline personality disorder. *Hospital and Community Psychiatry, 42,* 1015–1021.

Widom, C. S. (1989). Child abuse, neglect, and adult behavior: Research design and findings on criminality, violence, and child abuse. *American Journal of Orthopsychiatry, 59,* 355–367.

Widom, C. S. (1992). The cycle of violence. *National Institute of Justice Research in Brief.* Washington, DC: U.S. Department of Justice.

Wiggins, J., & Pincus, A. (1989). Conceptions of personality disorders and dimensions of personality. *Psychological*

Assessment: Journal of Consulting and Clinical Psychology, 1, 305–316.

Wiggins, J. S., & Pincus. L. (1992). Personality: Structure and assessment. *Annual Review of Psychology, 43,* 473–504.

Wilfley, D. E., Agras, W. S., Telch, C. F., Rossiter, E. M., Schneider, J. A., Cole, A. G., Sifford, L., & Raeburn, S. D. (1993). Group cognitive-behavioral therapy and group interpersonal psychotherapy for the nonpurging bulimic individual: A controlled comparison. *Journal of Consulting and Clinical Psychology, 61,* 296–305.

Williams, C. L., Arnold, C. B., & Wynder, E. L. (1977). Primary prevention of chronic disease beginning in childhood: The Know Your Body Program: Design of study. *Preventive Medicine, 6,* 344–357.

Williams, L. M. (1994). Recall of childhood trauma: A prospective study of women's memories of child sexual abuse. *Journal of Consulting and Clinical Psychology, 62,* 1167–1176.

Williams, R. B., Jr., & Barefoot, J. C. (1988). Coronary-prone behavior: The emerging role of the hostility complex. In B. K. Houston & C. R. Snyder (Eds.), *Type A behavior pattern: Research, theory, and intervention* (pp. 189–211). New York: John Wiley & Sons.

Williams, S. L., & Zane, G. (1989). Guided mastery and stimulus exposure treatments for severe performance anxiety in agoraphobics. *Behaviour Research and Therapy, 27,* 237–246.

Wills, R. M., Faitler, S. L., & Snyder, D. K. (1987). Distinctiveness of behavioral versus insight-oriented marital therapy: An empirical analysis. *Journal of Consulting and Clinical Psychology, 55,* 685–690.

Wills, T. A., McNamara, G., Vaccaro, D, & Hirky, A. E. (1996). Escalated substance abuse: A longitudinal grouping analysis from early to middle adolescence. *Journal of Abnormal Psychology, 105,* 166–180.

Wilson, C. P. (1988). The psychoanalytic treatment of anorexia nervosa and bulimia. In B. J. Blinder, B. F. Chaitin, & R. Goldstein (Eds.), *The eating disorders* (pp. 433–446). PMA Publishing Corporation.

Wilson, W. H., Ellinwood, E. H., Mathew, R. J., & Johnson, K. (1994). Effects of marijuana on performance of a computerized cognitive-neuromotor test battery. *Psychiatry Research, 51,* 115–125.

Winchel, R. M., Stanley, B., & Stanley, M. (1990). Biochemical aspects of suicide. In S. J. Blumenthal & D. J. Kupfer (Eds.), *Suicide over the life cycle: Risk factors, assessment, and treatment of suicide patients* (pp. 96–127). Washington, DC: American Psychiatric Press.

Wincze, J. P., Bansal, S., & Malamud, M. (1986). Effects of medroxyprogesterone acetate on subjective arousal, arousal to erotic stimulation, and nocturnal penile tumescence in male sex offenders. *Archives of Sexual Behavior, 15,* 293–305.

Wincze, J. P., & Carey, M. P. (1991). *Sexual dysfunction: A guide for assessment and treatment.* New York: Guilford Press.

Windle, M., & Windle, R. C. (1993). The continuity of behavioral expression among disinhibited and inhibited childhood subtypes. *Clinical Psychology Review, 13,* 741–762.

Winett, R. A. (1995). A framework for health promotion and disease prevention programs. *American Psychologist, 50,* 341–350.

Winnicott, D. W. (1965). *The maturational processes and the facilitating environment.* New York: International Universities Press.

Winokur, G. (1986). Unipolar depression. In G. Winokur & P. Clayton (Eds.), *The medical basis of psychiatry* (pp. 60–79). Philadelphia: W. B. Saunders Co.

Winston, A., Pollack, J., McCullough, L., Flegenheimer, W., Kestenbaum, R., & Trujillo, M. (1991). Brief dynamic psychotherapy of personality disorders. *Journal of Nervous and Mental Disease, 179,* 188–193.

Wise, R. A., & Bozarth, M. A. (1987). A psychomotor stimulant theory of addiction. *Psychological Review, 94,* 469–492.

Wise, T. (1978). Where the public peril begins: A survey of psychotherapists to determine the effect of *Tarasoff. Stanford Law Review, 31,* 165–190.

Wolf, E. M., & Crowther, J. H. (1992). An evaluation of behavioral and cognitive-behavioral group interventions for the treatment of bulimia nervosa in women. *International Journal of Eating Disorders, 11,* 3–15.

Wolfensberger, W. (1972). *Normalization: The principle of normalization in human services.* Toronto, Canada: National Institute of Mental Retardation.

Wolkin, A., Sanfilpo, M., Wolf, A., Angrist, B., Brodie, J., & Rotrosen, J. (1992). Negative symptoms and hypofrontality chronic schizophrenia. *Archives of General Psychiatry, 49,* 959–965.

Wolpe, J. (1958). *Psychotherapy by reciprocal inhibition.* Stanford, CA: Stanford University Press.

Wolpe, J., & Lazarus, A. A. (1966). *Behavior therapy techniques: A guide to the treatment of neuroses.* New York: Pergamon Press.

Wolraich, M. L., Lindgren, S. D., Stumbo, P. J., Stegink, L. D., Appelbaum, M. I., Kiritsy, M. C. (1994). Effects of diets high in sucrose or aspartame on the behavior and cognitive performance of children. *New England Journal of Medicine, 330,* 301–307.

Wood, J. A., Bootzin, R. R., Rosenhan, D., Nolen-Hoeksema, S., & Jourden, F. (1992). Effects of the 1989 San Francisco earthquake on frequency and content of nightmares. *Journal of Abnormal Psychology, 101,* 219–224.

Wood, J. M., Nezworski, M. T., & Stejskal, W. J. (1996). The comprehensive system for the Rorschach: A critical examination. *Psychological Science, 7,* 3–10.

Wood, K., Harris, M. J., Morreale, A., & Rizos, A. (1988). Drug-induced psychosis and depression in the elderly. *Psychiatric Clinics of North America, 11,* 167–191.

Wood, L. F., & Jacobson, N. S. (1985). Marital distress. In D. Barlow (Ed.), *Clinical handbook of psychological disorders* (pp. 344–416). New York: Guilford Press.

Woods, P. A., Higson, P. J., & Tannahill, M. M. (1984). Token-economy programmes with chronic psychotic patients: The importance of direct measurement and objective evaluation for long-term maintenance. *Behaviour Research and Therapy, 22,* 41–51.

Woody, G. E., Luborsky, L., McLellan, A. T., & O'Brien, C. P. (1990). Corrections and revised analyses for psychotherapy in methadone maintenance patients. *Archives of General Psychiatry, 47,* 788–789.

Woody, G. E., McLellan, A. T., Luborsky, L., & O'Brien, C. P. (1995). Psychotherapy in community methadone programs: A validation study. *American Journal of Psychiatry, 152,* 1302–1308.

Workman, E. A., & LaVia, M. F. (1987). T-lymphocyte polyclonal proliferation: Effects of stress and stress response style on medical students taking national board examinations. *Clinical Immunology and Immunopathology, 43,* 308–313.

Worling, J. R. (1995). Sexual abuse histories of adolescent male sex offenders: Differences on the basis of the age and gender of their victims. *Journal of Abnormal Psychology, 104,* 610–613.

Wortman, C. B., & Lehman, D. R. (1985). Reactions to victims of life crises: Support attempts that fail. In I. G. Sarason & B. R. Sarason (Eds.), *Social support: Theory, research, and applications* (pp. 463–489). Dordrecht, The Netherlands: Martinus Nijhoff.

Wozniak, K. M., Pert, A., & Linnoila, M. (1990). Antagonism of 5-HT3 receptors attenuates the effects of ethanol on extracellular dopamine. *European Journal of Pharmacology, 187,* 287–289.

Wright, L., & Walker, C. E. (1978). A simple behavioral treatment program for psychogenic encopresis. *Behaviour Research and Therapy, 16,* 209–212.

Wright, P., Nobrega, J., Langevin, R., & Wortzman, G. (1990). Brain density and symmetry in pedophilic and sexually aggressive offenders. *Annals of Sex Research, 3,* 319–328.

Wrightsman, L. S., Nietzel, M. T., & Fortune, W. H. (1994). *Psychology and the legal system* (3rd ed.). Pacific Grove, CA: Brooks/Cole.

Wurtzel, E. (1995). *Prozac nation.* Boston: Houghton-Mifflin.

Wyatt, G. E., Guthrie, D., & Notgrass, C. M. (1991). Differential effects of women's child sexual abuse and subsequent sexual revictimization. *Journal of Consulting and Clinical Psychology, 60,* 167–173.

Wyatt v. Stickney, 325 F. Supp. 781 (1971).

Yalom, I. D. (1985). *The theory and practice of group psychotherapy* (3rd ed.). New York: Basic Books.

Yassa, R., Nastase, C., Dupont, D., & Thibeau, M. (1992). Tardive dyskinesia in elderly psychiatric patients: A 5-year study. *American Journal of Psychiatry, 149,* 1209–1211.

Yates, A. (1993). Sexually inhibited children. *Child and Adolescent Psychiatric Clinics of North America, 2,* 451–461.

Yee, A. H., Fairchild, H. H., Weizmann, F., & Wyatt, G. E. (1993). Addressing psychology's problems with race. *American Psychologist, 48,* 1132–1140.

Ying, Y. (1989). Nonresponse on the Center for Epidemiological Studies-Depression scale in Chinese Americans. *International Journal of Social Psychiatry, 35,* 156–163.

Yonkers, K., Kando, J., Cole, J., & Blumenthal, S. (1992). Gender differences in pharmacokinetics and pharmacodynamics of psychotropic medication. *The American Journal of Psychiatry, 149,* 587–595.

Yoshikawa, H. (1994). Prevention as cumulative protection: Effects of early family support and education on chronic delinquency and its risks. *Psychological Bulletin, 115,* 28–54.

Young, L. D. (1992). Psychological factors in rheumatoid arthritis. *Journal of Consulting and Clinical Psychology, 60,* 619–643.

Youngberg v. Romeo, 457 U.S. 307 (1982).

Ysseldyke, J. E., Algozzine, B., & Epps, S. (1983). A logical and empirical analysis of current practice in classifying students as handicapped. *Exceptional Children, 50,* 160–166.

Zanarini, M. C., Gunderson, J. G., Frankenburg, F. R., & Chauncey, D. L. (1989). The revised diagnostic interview for borderlines: Discriminating BPD from other axis II disorders. *Journal of Personality Disorders, 3,* 10–18.

Zhou, J., Hofman, M. A., Gooren, L. J. G., & Swaab, D. F. (1995). A sex difference in the human brain and its relation to transsexuality. *Nature, 378,* 68–70.

Zigler, E., & Hodapp, R. M. (1986). *Understanding mental retardation.* New York: Cambridge University Press.

Zigler, E., & Styfco, S. J. (1993). Head Start: Criticisms in a constructive context. *American Psychologist, 49,* 127–132.

Zigler, E., Levine, I., & Zigler, B. (1976). The relation between premorbid competence and paranoid-nonparanoid status in schizophrenia. *Psychological Bulletin, 83,* 303–313.

Zigler, E., Taussig, C., & Black, K. (1992). Early childhood intervention: A promising preventative for juvenile delinquency. *American Psychologist, 47,* 997–1006.

Zimmerman, M. (1983). Methodological issues in the assessment of life events: A review of issues and research. *Clinical Psychology Review, 3,* 339–370.

Zimmerman, M., & Coryell, W. (1989). DSM-III personality disorder diagnoses in a non-patient sample. *Archives of General Psychiatry, 46,* 682–689.

Zinbarg, R. E., & Mineka, S. (1991). Animal models of psychopathology: II. Simple phobia. *Behavior Therapy, 14,* 61–65.

Zinbarg, R., Barlow, D., Brown, T., & Hertz, R. (1992). Cognitive-behavioral approaches to the nature and treatment of anxiety disorders. *Annual Review of Psychology, 43,* 235–267.

Ziskin J., & Faust, D. (1988). *Coping with psychiatric and psychological testimony.* Marina del Rey, CA: Law and Psychology Press.

Zitrin, C. M., Klein, D. F., & Woerner, M. G. (1980). Treatment of agoraphobia with group exposure in vivo and imipramine. *Archives of General Psychiatry, 37,* 63–72.

Zook, A. H., & Walton, J. M. (1989). Theoretical orientations and work settings of clinical and counseling psychologists: A current perspective. *Professional Psychology: Research and Practice, 20,* 23–31.

Zubin, J., & Spring, B. (1977). Vulnerability: A new view of schizophrenia. *Journal of Abnormal Psychology, 86,* 103–126.

Zucker, K. J. & Bradley, S. J. (1995). *Gender identity disorder and psychosexual problems in children and adolescents.* New York: Guilford Press.

Zucker, K. J. & Green, R. (1992). Psychosexual disorders in children and adolescents. *Journal of Child Psychology and Psychiatry and Allied Disciplines, 33,* 107–151.

Zucker, K. J., & Green, R. (1993). Psychological and familial aspects of gender identity disorder. In A. Yates (Ed.), Sexual and gender identity disorders, *Child and Adolescent Psychiatric Clinics of North America, 2,* 513–542.

Zucker, K. J., Wild, J., Bradley, S. J., & Lowry, C. B. (1993). Physical attractiveness of boys with gender identity disorder. *Archives of Sexual Behavior, 22,* 23–34.

Zucker, R. A. (1987). The four alcoholisms: A developmental account of the etiologic process. In P. C. Rivers (Ed.), *Nebraska Symposium on Motivation, 1986: Vol. 34, Alcohol and addictive behaviors.* Lincoln: University of Nebraska Press.

Zucker, R. A., & Fitzgerald, H. E. (1991). Early developmental factors and risk for alcohol problems. *Alcohol Health Research World, 15,* 18–24.

Zuger, B. (1989). Homosexuality in families of boys with early effeminate behavior: An epidemiological study. *Archives of Sexual Behavior, 18,* 155–166.

Glossary

ABAB design: A research design in which a baseline condition (A) is alternated with an intervention phase (B) at least twice to determine whether there are behavior changes that can be attributed to the intervention.

abnormal behavior: A pattern of behavioral, psychological, or physical functioning that is not culturally expected and that leads to psychological distress, behavioral disability, or impaired overall functioning.

absorption: A dimension of personality that describes a person's tendency to become caught up in private reveries, imaginings, or a current task to the exclusion of surrounding stimuli; also known as fantasy proneness, or imaginative involvement.

abstinence violation effect: A situation in which expectancies about using a drug may set off a chain of faulty decisions for an abuser that then increase the probability of resumed abuse.

acetylcholine (ACH): A neurotransmitter that is critical to movement, physiological arousal, memory, learning, and sleep.

achievement test: A measure of how much a person has learned about a specific area. One example is the Wide Range Achievement Test-Revised (WRAT-3).

action research: Empirically testing the effects of some deliberate change in the operation of a social institution or system.

active phase (of schizophrenia): The stage of schizophrenia where one or more psychotic symptoms such as delusions or hallucinations appear.

acute akathesia: An extrapyramidal side effect of some neuroleptics involving uncontrollable restlessness and agitation.

acute dystonia: An extrapyramidal side effect of some neuroleptics involving tics in the head, neck, and face.

acute stress disorder: A mental disorder in which a person who has undergone a traumatic event experiences trauma-related symptoms similar to PTSD that begin within 1 month of the trauma and last less than 1 month.

adaptive behavior: Behavior that enables an individual to meet the cultural expectations for independent functioning associated with a particular age.

addiction: *See* physiological dependence.

adjustment disorder: Maladaptive behavioral and psychological reactions to a stressor occurring within 3 months of the stressor.

adoption study: A method of systematically examining traits and disorders in persons who were separated from their biological parents at early ages; the method compares similarities between adopted individuals and their biological and adoptive parents.

adrenal corticosteroid: A chemical messenger, also known as a stress hormone, that intensifies alarm and prepares the body to cope with a stressor.

adrenocorticotrophic hormone (ACTH): A hormone that, in response to a stressor, directs the adrenal glands to release adrenal corticosteroids.

affect regulation: The process by which individuals use thought and action to prevent or reduce strong negative emotions.

ageism: A form of prejudice against the elderly.

agnosia: Inability to recognize or interpret objects through one or more of the senses.

agonist: A drug that stimulates neurons to fire.

agoraphobia: A fear of open spaces or of being separated from a safe place.

agranulocytosis: A potentially fatal blood disease in which there is a loss of white blood cells; a possible side effect of the drug clozapine.

agreeableness: A personality trait involving compassionate interest in others.

AIDS (Acquired Immune Deficiency Syndrome): An immune disease caused by transfer of HIV, resulting in the destruction of the immune system. Affected persons are left susceptible to secondary, opportunistic infections, central nervous system damage, and malignancies that ultimately result in death.

alcohol expectancy: An individual's belief about the physical and psychological effects of alcohol.

alcoholic cirrhosis: A disease characterized by damaged liver cells, development of scar tissue, and the eventual inability of the liver to filter toxins from the blood.

alcoholism: A pattern of heavy drinking in which the person loses control over drinking and becomes so dependent on alcohol that physical and mental health are jeopardized and social and occupational functioning are impaired.

ALI rule: A legal rule that holds that a defendant is not responsible for criminal conduct if he or she lacks substantial capacity to either appreciate the wrongfulness of the act or to control his or her conduct as required by law.

allele: Any of the alternative forms a gene may take.

alogia: A negative symptom of schizophrenia involving the failure to say much, if anything, in response to questions or comments.

alter personality (alter): In dissociative identity disorder, one of the different "personalities" that seem to assume control over the individual's functioning in different situations.

altruistic suicide: One of four suicide types proposed by Emile Durkheim, committed by people who choose suicide because they place a social goal or group ahead of personal survival.

Alzheimer's disease: The most frequent cause of dementia, characterized by memory loss, apathy, cognitive difficulties, language problems, and personality changes.

amnesia: Loss or impairment of memory.

amnestic disorder: A disorder that involves primarily memory loss.

amniocentesis: The medical procedure of extracting amniotic fluid for the purpose of screening for potential fetal problems.

amniotic fluid: The fluid surrounding the fetus.

amotivational syndrome: A pattern of apathy and inability to meet personal or career goals, linked to cannabis-induced alteration of brain functioning.

amphetamines: A class of drugs that stimulate the sympathetic nervous system, increasing alertness and reducing appetite.

amygdala: A structure in the forebrain that is part of the limbic system and is linked to emotions.

amyloid (senile) plaque: A deposit found in large numbers in the brains of people who are likely to develop Alzheimer's disease.

amyloid precursor protein (APP): A form of protein produced by a gene on chromosome 21, thought to mutate in people with Alzheimer's disease.

anal stage: In psychoanalytic theory, the second of five stages of psychosexual development, occuring during the second year of life when stimuli associated with elimination and retention of feces become the main source of pleasure.

analogue research: A research strategy in which subject populations, problems, and therapeutic procedures that are seen in real clinical settings are approximated in the laboratory.

androgen insensitivity: A condition in which a person with X and Y chromosomes is unable to absorb testosterone at the cellular level, resulting in feminization of external genitalia and assumption of a feminine identity.

androgen: A hormone that stimulates the development of male characteristics, sometimes called the male hormone although it is produced by both males and females.

aneurysm: A bulge in the artery walls that can rupture.

angina pectoris: A condition that results from insufficient oxygen to the heart and involves periodic chest pains that sometimes radiate out the left arm or up the neck.

anhedonia: Loss of the ability to enjoy activities central to a person's life.

anomic suicide: One of four suicide types proposed by Emile Durkheim; committed by people who feel lost or abandoned by society, often because of social upheaval such as divorce or job loss.

anorexia nervosa: A disorder whose main characteristics are an unreasonable fear of gaining weight, disturbances in the perception of one's body shape or size, and the relentless pursuit of thinness, no matter what the consequences.

antagonist: A drug that blocks the effects of neurotransmitters or other drugs.

anterograde amnesia: The inability to learn new information, usually following brain injury.

antibody: A biochemical substance that circulates in the bloodstream and detects and binds to foreign substances in order to neutralize them.

anticipatory nausea: A condition in which cancer patients who have been undergoing chemotherapy vomit or become nauseated during the time period preceding subsequent drug administrations.

antidiuretic hormone (ADH): A chemical that controls the kidney's regulation of urine production in relation to bladder capacity.

antigen: Any foreign substance that enters the body.

antisocial personality disorder: A personality disorder characterized by repeated rule breaking, chronic manipulativeness, a callous outlook toward the rights of others and society, and tendencies to behave impulsively, dishonestly and irresponsibly, and to lack remorse.

anxiety: A diffuse or vague sense of apprehension accompanied by fearful behavior and physiological arousal.

anxiety disorder: A group of mental disorders in which fear or anxiety and associated maladaptive behaviors are the core of the disturbance.

anxiety hierarchy: A graded list of fear-provoking stimuli or situations ranging from the least to most threatening; used in systematic desensitization.

aphasia: A loss of or an impairment in language.

apolipoprotein E (ApoE): A protein that transports cholesterol in the blood.

applied behavior analysis: The study of the stimulus events and reinforcment contingencies that control operant behavior; often used as part of a teaching process in which complex skills are broken down and learned as a series of smaller units.

appraisal: An evaluation of our own behavior and the behavior of others.

apraxia: An inability to carry out motor activities even though the necessary motor functions are intact.

aptitude test: A measure of the accumulated effects of educational or training experiences that attempts to forecast future performance. One example is the Scholastic Aptitude Test (SAT).

Asperger's disorder: A disorder similar to autism except that higher intellectual skills and normal or near-normal expressive language are seen in the affected individual.

assertiveness training: Techniques that help people express their feelings and wants more clearly and effectively.

assessment: The collection of information for the purpose of making an informed decision.

atherosclerosis: The main cause of coronary heart disease; the flow of blood to the heart is reduced due to cholesterol and other fatty substances forming plaque inside the walls of blood vessels.

attention-deficit/hyperactivity disorder (ADHD): A childhood mental disorder marked by inattention, impulsivity, and/or high motor activity.

attitude and interest tests: Tests that measure the range and strength of a person's interests, attitudes, preferences, and values.

attribution: An individual's explanation for behavior or other events.

atypical antipsychotics: Drugs that do not have the same biochemical or physiological effects as standard neuroleptics.

autoimmune disease: A condition in which the cells that normally fight off antigens turn against the body itself.

autonomy-oriented (achievement) personality: A personality characterized by perfectionism, guilt over failure and shortcomings, frequent self-criticism, and a feeling of not living up to standards.

aversion therapy: Treatment that uses painful or unpleasant stimuli to decrease unwanted behaviors.

avoidant personality disorder: A personality disorder characterized by constant feelings of inadequacy, especially in social situations.

avolition: A negative symptom of schizophrenia in which patients may sit for hours making no attempt to do anything.

Axis I: In DSM-IV, the dimension that contains 16 general groupings of major mental disorders.

Axis II: In DSM-IV, the dimension that contains 10 personality disorders and mental retardation.

Axis III: In DSM-IV, the dimension that lists general medical conditions that could be relevant to understanding or treating a person's mental disorder.

Axis IV: In DSM-IV, the dimension that records psychosocial and environmental stressors that could affect the diagnosis, treatment, and course of a mental disorder.

Axis V: In DSM-IV, the dimension on which clinicians rate a person's overall level of functioning at the time of the evaluation, giving a summary assessment of the person's general clinical status and providing a gauge for how well the person has responded to treatment.

axon: A long fiber extension of a neuron from which neurotransmitters are released.

B cell: A lymphocyte that destroys pathogens.

barbiturates: A class of drugs that are addictive and produce relaxation and mild euphoria at low levels, and have an effect similar to alcohol intoxication at higher levels.

behavior modification (behavior therapy): Behavioral treatments based on learning theory that are aimed at helping people decrease specific maladaptive behaviors and increase adaptive behaviors.

behavioral genetics: A scientific field that examines genetic influences on behavior and their interaction with the environment.

behavioral medicine: A discipline that integrates behavioral science and biomedical knowledge in an effort to understand, treat, and prevent illness.

behavioral theory: A theory of behavior that explains how normal and abnormal behaviors are shaped by people's experiences with the world, and how people learn to behave as a result of these experiences.

benzodiazepines: A class of drugs derived from benzoic acid that are prescribed to alleviate anxiety and panic; includes Valium and Xanax.

bereavement: Feelings of sadness that follow the death of a loved one and are best characterized as normal grief reactions to loss.

beta-amyloid-4: An abnormal form of a common protein that is essential for life.

biofeedback: A treatment technique in which a person learns to control biological processes as a result of being given explicit feedfack about the occurence or intensity of that process.

biological model: A model of abnormal behavior that explains how biological factors influence thought and behavior, both normal and abnormal.

biopsychosocial model: A view that explains illness as the outgrowth of biological vulnerability, psychological processes, and social conditions.

bipolar disorder: A mood disorder marked by alternating periods of depression and mania.

bipolar I disorder: A mood disorder in which severe, full-blown manic symptoms are accompanied by one or more periods of major depression.

bipolar II disorder: A mood disorder in which a major depressive episode has occurred in addition to manic episodes that are mild, or hypomanic.

bisexual behavior: Sexual attraction to and activity with members of both sexes.

blood alcohol concentration (BAC): The amount of unmetabolized ethanol absorbed into the blood.

body dysmorphic disorder: A mental disorder in which a person becomes so preoccupied with his or her physical appearance or a real or imagined physical defect that it interferes significantly with social contact, employment, or other functioning.

borderline personality disorder: A personality disorder characterized by impulsivity and instability in several areas of functioning, including mood, behavior, self-image and interpersonal relationships.

brief psychotic disorder: The sudden onset of psychotic symptoms marked by intense emotional turmoil and confusion.

Briquet's syndrome: Named after physician Pierre Briquet, this disorder involves a seemingly endless list of physical complaints without medical explanations; now called somatization disorder.

bulimia nervosa: A mental disorder characterized by recurrent binge eating in which large quantities of food are consumed in one sitting, followed by purging or other efforts to prevent weight gain.

buspirone: A nonbenzodiazepine drug that produces slow but durable reductions in anxiety and tension.

cannabinol: Psychoactive ingredient of cannabis, the most important of which is THC.

cannabis: A psychoactive drug derived from the hemp plant, causing a variety of intoxicating and hallucinatory effects.

Capgras syndrome: The delusion that impostors are posing as friends or relatives.

case management: A component of psychosocial rehabilitation in which a staff person helps a client obtain services related to employment, housing, nutrition, transportation, recreation, medical care and finances.

catalepsy: Immobility.

cataplexy: A period of muscle paralysis that causes the person to collapse and be immobile for several seconds to a few minutes.

catatonia: A dimension of disordered behavior ranging from great excitement, extreme motor activity, repetitive gestures or mannerisms, and undirected violent behaviors to immobility where a person may maintain awkward body positions for hours at a time, appearing stuporous.

catatonic schizophrenia: A type of schizophrenia marked by extreme psychomotor symptoms.

catecholamine theory: The idea that low levels of norepinephrine lead to depression and high levels of norepinephrine lead to mania.

cerebral asymmetry: Differential activity between the two hemispheres of the brain; decreased activity in the left frontal region of the brain relative to that in the right frontal region is often found in individuals experiencing depressive symptoms.

cerebral palsy: A group of motor disorders that result from cerebral insult or injury, usually during the peri- or postnatal period or early childhood when brain development is most active.

cerebrum: Main part of human brain, covered by the cerebral cortex; responsible for integrative processes such as thought, language, and emotion. It is divided into two hemispheres, which are further divided into lobes.

certification law: A law that restricts the use of a professional title to people who have met certain requirements for education, practical training, and supervised experience.

childhood disintegrative disorder: A mental disorder in which, after a period of normal development for at least the first 2 years of life, autistic symptoms begin to appear.

chlorpromazine: A type of neuroleptic drug, sold as Thorazine.

chorea: Involuntary jerking movements of the limbs.

cingulatomy: A type of psychosurgery used for severe, intractable mental disorders; electrodes are inserted bilaterally into the cerebral cortex to make a lesion.

circadian rhythm: An internally cued rhythmic schedule of biological activity that repeats roughly every 24 hours.

circadian rhythm sleep disorder: A sleep disturbance involving a mismatch between a person's natural circadian sleep/wake cycle and the demands of the environment.

civil commitment: The legal order by which an individual can be involuntarily committed to a psychiatric hospital.

classical conditioning: A form of learning in which a formerly neutral stimulus is able to elicit a new response. This learning occurs after repeated associations between the neutral stimulus and an unconditioned stimulus that automatically elicits a response that resembles the learned one.

classical method of classification: A method of classification in which every disorder is assumed to be a distinct and unique condition for which each and every attribute must be present for a diagnosis to be made.

client-centered therapy: Therapy developed by Carl Rogers that emphasizes empathy and nondirectiveness by the therapist and a climate in which the client feels free from coercion or pressure.

clinical psychology: The branch of psychology devoted to studying, assessing, diagnosing, treating and preventing abnormal behavior.

clinical significance: Changes in a target behavior that are large enough to be not only statistically significant but also socially meaningful.

clomipramine: A drug that blocks reuptake of serotonin and is used in the treatment of obsessive-compulsive disorder.

clozapine: An atypical antipsychotic drug, sold as Clozaril.

comorbidity: The co-occurrence of two or more mental disorders in the same person.

cocaine: A psychoactive, pain-reducing, stimulant drug.

codependent: A person who protects, monitors, or censures a substance abuser, becoming enmeshed in the abuser's problems and preventing change in the abuse pattern.

cognition: Mental processes involved in an individual's capacity to learn, understand, retain, and use information.

cognitive disorder: A disorder marked by impairment in one or more of the processes of memory, language, consciousness, perception and intelligence.

cognitive reappraisal: An attempt to reduce stress by thinking about a stressor in ways that make it less upsetting.

cognitive restructuring: A treatment in which the individual is taught to identify distorted and biased thoughts and replace them with more adaptive self-statements.

cognitive theory: A theory that explains behavior primarily in terms of the way people process information about the world—what they attend to, perceive, think about, and remember.

cognitive therapy: A therapy that uses learning principles to alter maladaptive thoughts and beliefs that accompany behavior problems.

cognitive triad: Automatic, repetitive, and negative thoughts about the self, the world, and the future that are characteristic of depressed people.

community psychology: A subdiscipline of psychology that focuses on promoting mental health through positive social change in the community.

community reinforcement: A treatment for substance abuse in which social and environmental influences are used to help maintain sobriety.

competence to stand trial: A legal decision that an individual is mentally able to understand the nature of trial proceedings, participate meaningfully in the trial, and consult with an attorney at the time of the trial.

compulsion: A repetitive, nearly irresistible act that a person performs, often in response to some obsessive thought.

computerized axial tomography (CT): A neurodiagnostic procedure that provides computer-enhanced, three-dimensional pictures of the brain.

concordance rate: The rate at which a trait or disorder is shared with close relatives, such as a twin.

conduct disorder: A childhood mental disorder involving a pattern of antisocial behavior at home or in the community, including significant physical aggression, property damage, deceitfulness, or rule violations.

confabulation: The process of making up material to fill in memory gaps; common in amnestic disorder.

confidentiality: The ethical obligation of a therapist to keep in confidence the information that is discussed with a client.

confounding variable: A variable that confuses or distorts research results, making it difficult to be sure whether the independent variable, confounding variable, or some combination of the two was responsible for observed effects on the dependent variable.

congenital adrenal hyperplasia: An inherited disorder that leaves the body's adrenal glands unable to synthesize cortisone, resulting in masculinization of the external genitalia.

conjoint therapy: Couple or marital therapy in which both members of a couple see the same therapist in the same sessions.

conscientiousness: A personality trait involving well-organized dedication to fulfilling obligations or expectations.

contingency contracting: A form of contracting in which a formal agreement between therapist and client spells out the consequences of certain client behaviors.

contingency management: Deliberately presenting or withdrawing reinforcers or aversive stimuli following changeworthy behaviors.

continuous amnesia: The loss of memory for events from a particular time or trauma up to the present.

control group: A group of subjects included in an experiment to control for some variable that could provide an alternative explanation for observed effects on a dependent variable.

conversion disorder: A mental disorder in which a person experiences problems with motor or sensory abilities that suggest a neurological impairment, but no such impairment exists.

convulsive therapy: A treatment that uses physical stimuli to induce a seizure and a brief loss of consciousness.

coping: A person's efforts to modify, manage, or tolerate stressors.

coping modeling: A procedure used in fear reduction treatments in which the client watches a model display some initial fearful behavior before coping with and overcoming the fear.

coping skills training: A treatment in which the individual is taught to use a cognitive plan and a behavioral strategy to cope with a problem.

coprolalia: The involuntary shouting or repeating of obscene words.

coronary heart disease (CHD): Disease of the heart.

correlation: A measure of the degree to which one variable is related to another.

correlation coefficient: A number that quantifies the size of relationship between two variables, noted by the symbol r, and ranging from +1.00 to -1.00. The larger the absolute value of the correlation, the stronger the relationship between the variables.

corticotropin-releasing hormone (CRH): A hormone that starts a chain of coordinated physiological and biochemical defenses against a stressor, and signals the pituitary gland to secrete adrenocorticotrophic hormone (ACTH).

countertransference: In psychotherapy, the process by which a therapist's own unconscious feelings are directed toward clients.

couples therapy: *See* marital therapy.

covert modeling: A type of fear-reduction treatment in which a client imagines a model engaging in fearless behavior, supplemented by sessions in which the client is brought into increasingly close contact with the feared situation under protected circumstances.

covert sensitization: A cognitive version of aversion therapy in which the client associates aversive images and narratives with an unwanted behavior.

Creutzfeldt-Jakob disease: An infectious and rapidly progressive dementia that is transmitted through eating diseased tissue; marked by the lack of motor coordination, failing memory and attention, and changes in behavior.

culture-bound syndrome: A pattern of abnormal behavior that appears only in certain localities or cultures.

cyclothymic disorder: A mood disorder in which moods fluctuate over a long period, but neither the depressive nor the manic episodes are as severe as in bipolar I or II disorder.

defense mechanism: In psychoanalytic theory, psychological processes that operate unconsciously to minimize conflicts between the id, ego, and superego.

deficit schizophrenia: Another name for negative symptoms of schizophrenia.

deinstitutionalization: A social policy of moving patients with severe mental disorders out of mental institutions and into the community for treatment.

delirium: A disturbance in consciousness involving impairments in attention, disorientation, memory and language problems, and hallucinations.

delirium tremens (DTs): A set of symptoms including muscle tremors, hallucinations, and profuse sweating that result from withdrawal from heavy alcohol use.

delta sleep: The most restorative period of sleep in which slower brain waves called delta waves are predominant; it accounts for 10 to 20 percent of sleep time.

delusional disorder: A mental disorder in which the main symptom is the presence of at least one systematic delusional belief.

delusion: An extreme, false belief that is so firmly held that no evidence or argument can convince the person to give it up.

dementia: A deterioration in cognitive functioning involving memory loss and one of the following: aphasia, agnosia, apraxia, or disturbed executive functioning.

dendrite: A branchlike structure on a neuron that receives information from other neurons.

deoxyribonucleic acid (DNA): The substance that is the primary component of genes.

dependent personality disorder: A personality disorder characterized by excessive self-sacrifice, an inability to make decisions without exorbitant help, and a dread of being alone.

dependent variable: The variable in an experiment that is observed in order to determine the effect of the independent variable.

depersonalization: A feeling that a person has become detached from his or her real self, as if the person were observing him- or herself from outside the body.

depersonalization disorder: A disorder in which a person experiences both depersonalization and derealization in the absence of other physical and mental disorders.

deprenyl: A chemical that inhibits monoamine oxidase B, which destroys dopamine, norepinephrine, and serotonin.

depression: A extremely low, miserably unhappy mood.

derealization: A feeling that objects or events are strange or unreal, or have suddenly changed shape, size, or location.

detoxification: A supervised period of "drying out" from an abused substance, often aided by drugs or other interventions to ease withdrawal symptoms and remedy nutritional deficits.

developmental disability: A disability based on three criteria: lifelong impairment in mental or physical functioning first evident prior to adulthood, substantial limitations in daily living skills such as communication and self-care, and the necessity for extended specialized care.

developmental psychopathology: A field of study that focuses on how problems that first appear in childhood or adolescence are linked to disorders occurring later in life.

developmental task: A psychological or cognitive task to be mastered during the course of development from infancy through adolescence; these tasks form a foundation for later learning and adjustment.

dexamethasone: A substance that temporarily suppresses the production of cortisol in healthy adults.

diagnosis: The classification of mental disorders by determining which of several possible descriptions best fits the nature of the problem(s).

dialectical behavior therapy: A comprehensive form of cognitive behavioral therapy designed specifically for the treatment of borderline personality disorder; it focuses on increasing self-regulation skills.

diathesis: A biological or psychological predisposition for a disorder.

diathesis–stress model: A model that explains how a mental disorder can result from the interaction of a pre-disposition (diathesis) for a disorder with a trigger (stressor) that converts the predisposition into the actual disorder.

dimensional approach: An approach to describing mental disorders in which disorders are portrayed along different personality dimensions that produce a profile summarizing the person's functioning.

disorganized schizophrenia: A type of schizophrenia marked by grossly inappropriate and disorganized speech, behavior and affect.

dispositional optimism: A tendency for an individual to think optimistically.

dissociative disorder: A mental disorder that involves disruptions in a person's normally integrated sense of memory, consciousness, or identity.

dissociated fugue: A dissociative state in which a person travels to a new location without remembering the pre-fugue life, often also becoming confused about his or her identity.

dissociation: The process by which the normally integrated elements of consciousness, memory, and personal identity become splintered.

dissociative amnesia: Sudden loss of memory for personally important information that is not caused by a medical condition or other mental disorder, usually following a stressful event.

dissociative identity disorder: Formerly called *multiple personality disorder;* a mental disorder in which individuals experience a shattering of a unified identity into at least two separate but coexisting personalities with different memories, behavior patterns, and emotions.

dissociative trance disorder: A mental disorder involving involuntary trance states that are not an accepted expression of cultural or religious beliefs.

diversion: Diverting offenders from official processing in the criminal justice system by finding community-based alternatives to imprisonment.

dominant allele: A gene that will be expressed whenever present.

dopamine: A neurotransmitter that is prominent in several areas of the brain and is linked with several types of mental disorder.

double depression: A condition in which both major depression and dysthymia are experienced.

double-bind hypothesis: An early theory suggesting that schizophrenia could arise from the confusion produced when a child is raised by parents who communicated incompatible messages.

double-blind study: An experimental design in which only the director of the experiment knows which participants are in the experimental group and which are in the control group.

Down syndrome: A form of mental retardation caused by a genetic malfunction on chromosome 21.

drug abuse: A level of drug use that is hazardous to a person's health, leads to significant impairment in work or family life, produces personal distress, or leads to legal problems.

dual diagnosis: A term used for individuals who meet the criteria for two disorders at the same time; often involves mental retardation or substance abuse and some other psychiatric disorder.

Durham rule: A former legal standard for insanity that states that, if an unlawful act were the product of a mental disease or defect, the accused should not be held responsible for the act.

dyspareunia: Recurring problems with pain before, during, or after sexual intercourse.

dyssomnia: One of the two categories of primary sleep disorders involving disturbances in the amount, quality, or timing of a person's sleep.

dysthymic disorder: A mood disorder characterized by chronic depressed mood and related symptoms that last at least two years but that is not as disabling as major depression.

echolalia: A symptom found in serious mental disorders in which the person merely repeats what has just been said by others.

ecological model: Another name for the sociocultural model.

ecological perspective: The view that behavior is influenced by interactions between individuals and the economic, social, and physical aspects of their environment.

effect size: The magnitude of impact or influence one variable has on another; often reported in meta-analyses.

ego: One of the three structures in the psychoanalytic concept of personality; it seeks compromise between the id and the superego by following the reality principle.

ego analyst: A psychoanalytically oriented theorist who differs from Freud by assigning more importance to conscious personality factors.

ego-dystonic: Experiences that seem in conflict with the self.

ego-syntonic: Experiences that seem a natural part of the self.

egoistic suicide: One of four suicide types proposed by Durkheim, committed by those who are poorly integrated into society.

electroconvulsive therapy (ECT): A treatment for severe depression that induces brief seizures through the use of an electric current.

electroencephalogram (EEG): A measure of changes in the electrical activity of the brain.

emotion-focused coping: Attempts to reduce stress by changing a person's emotional responses to a stressor.

empathy: The ability to appreciate and share the feelings of another person.

empirically validated treatment: A treatment that is supported by scientific studies as being beneficial for specific mental disorders.

empowerment: Developing the belief among formerly dependent and powerless people that they can have mastery and control over their lives.

empty chair technique: A therapeutic technique designed to increase awareness of unresolved conflicts and emotions by asking clients to engage in imaginary conversations with significant people in their lives.

encopresis: A disorder involving repeated passage of feces in one's clothing after the age of four.

endocrine system: A network of glands that affects organs throughout the body by releasing hormones into the bloodstream.

endogenous opiate: A naturally occurring chemical, similar to an opioid drug that produces a state of euphoria and reduces the experience of pain.

endometriosis: A painful condition in which the growth of endometrial tissue occurs in the pelvic cavity outside the uterus.

endorphin: An endogenous opioid that helps regulate cardiovascular activity, relieve pain, and facilitate psychological coping.

enuresis: A disorder involving repeated release of urine into bedding or clothes, after the age of five.

epidemiology: The scientific study of the onset and frequency of disorders in certain populations.

essential hypertension: High blood pressure that does not have an obvious organic cause.

estrogen: A hormone that stimulates the development of female characteristics, sometimes called the female hormone, although it is produced by both males and females.

ethical standards: Principles endorsed by a profession that encourage or forbid certain types of conduct and express the profession's norms and aspirations.

etiological factor: A specific cause of disorders.

evoked potential: A small, brief change in EEG voltage evoked by specific stimuli such as light or sound.

executive functioning: The cognitive ability to attend to relevant information, plan or organize activities, and make good judgments about events in the environment.

exhibitionism: A disorder in which a person gains sexual excitement and satisfaction by exposing one's genitals to an unwilling observer.

experiment: A scientific process of determining cause and effect wherein subjects are randomly assigned to conditions manipulated by a researcher who measures the effect of this manipulation on other variables, while holding all other influences constant.

experimental group: The group that receives an active treatment or manipulation in an experiment.

exposure treatment: A behavioral treatment involving direct exposure to frightening stimuli to decrease anxiety through the process of extinction.

expressed emotion: Emotional overinvolvement with a person, usually taking the form of high levels of criticism and hostility; a risk factor for relapse of mental disorders such as schizophrenia.

expressive language: Language that is used to communicate thoughts or needs.

external validity: The degree to which an experiment's results can be generalized to situations beyond those included in the experiment.

externalizing problem: A disruptive childhood behavior that is a nuisance to others, such as aggression, hyperactivity, impulsivity, or inattention.

extinction: The decrease in a behavior caused by the absence of reinforcers for that behavior.

extrapyramidal symptoms: A group of side effects that result from neuroleptic drugs, consisting of movement abnormalities such as tremor, rigidity, spasms, and agitation.

extroversion: A personality trait involving preference for social interaction and tendencies to be active, talkative, optimistic and affectionate.

facilitated communication: A controversial treatment in which a "facilitator" physically assists a developmentally disabled child to communicate by typing or pointing to letters.

family adversity index: An index of six risk factors quantifying the negative experiences of a family (severe marital discord, low socioeconomic class, large family size, criminality by the father, mental disorder in the mother, placement of the child in foster care); these factors are associated with antisocial behavior.

family study: A technique used by behavioral geneticists to examine patterns of a disorder in members of a family.

family therapy: Psychological treatment aimed at changing patterns of family interaction to correct family disturbances.

fantasy proneness: *See* absorption.

fatalistic suicide: One of four suicide types proposed by Durkheim, committed by people such as prisoners or slaves who experience severe isolation or rejection and who hold little hope for social integration.

fear: A set of emotional, behavioral, and physical responses to danger.

fear network: A memory network that connects fear stimuli and fearful responses.

female orgasmic disorder: A sexual disorder that involves an inability to experience orgasm, although the woman experiences normal sexual desire and arousal.

female sexual arousal disorder (FSAD): A sexual disorder characterized by persistent problems in attaining or maintaining the lubrication and genital swelling normally associated with sexual excitement.

fetal alcohol syndrome (FAS): A pattern of abnormalities resulting from maternal ingestion of alcohol during pregnancy. FAS is associated with mild to severe mental retardation, distinctive physical abnormalities, and social and emotional difficulties.

fetishism: The focusing of sexual interest on an inanimate object in order to become aroused.

field trial: A research study conducted in the natural environment.

fight-or-flight response: The immediate response to a stressor in which the individual's autonomic nervous system is activated to fight or to flee from the stressor.

flat affect: Blunted emotionality, often consisting of minimal eye contact, an emotionless face, little or no tone in the voice, and a drab or listless demeanor.

flooding: A treatment technique to extinguish phobias or overcome anxiety by exposing persons to prolonged presentations of the most intense version of the feared stimulus.

fluphenazine: A type of neuroleptic drug, sold as Prolixin.

forebrain: The largest of the three main parts of the brain, it includes structures that are responsible for processing sensory information, guiding body movements, and thinking.

forensic psychology (psychiatry): Specialty fields that apply mental health knowledge to questions about individuals involved in legal proceedings.

formal thought disorder: Symptoms involving disturbances in the way thinking is organized.

fragile X syndrome: A heritable genetic aberration involving chromosome 23 that results in moderate mental retardation and physical anomalies.

frontal lobe: The area of the cerebral cortex that controls executive functions such as planning and carrying out goal-directed activities.

frotteurism: A sexual disorder involving recurrent touching or rubbing against a nonconsenting person in order to become sexually aroused and gratified.

gamma aminobutyric acid (GABA): A neurotransmitter that inhibits postsynaptic activity.

gender dysphoria: Profound dissatisfaction with one's gender.

gender identity: A person's sense of being male or female.

gender identity disorder: Disorders involving a person's confusion about or dissatisfaction with his or her biological gender.

gender role: The pattern of behaviors typically expected of males or females in a particular culture.

gene: Strands of DNA that are located along a chromosome and are the basic units of heredity.

general adaptation syndrome (GAS): A three-stage physiological reaction to a stressor, consisting of alarm, resistance, and exhaustion.

general paresis: A deteriorative brain syndrome caused by syphilis; it involves ever-worsening delusions, muscle paralysis, and ultimately, death.

generalization: The process by which a learned behavior tends to occur in novel situations.

generalized amnesia: Loss of memory of a person's entire life.

generalized anxiety disorder: A mental disorder in which anxiety is experienced as "free floating," not connected to any specific stimulus, and is pervasive enough to interfere with daily functioning.

genital stage: In psychoanalytic theory, the last of five stages of psychosexual development; it begins in adolescence and continues through adulthood.

genotype: A person's genetic makeup.

gestalt therapy: A therapy that focuses on helping clients become more aware and accepting of feelings and needs.

glove anesthesia: A type of conversion disorder in which the person experiences a loss of sensation and sometimes paralysis only in a hand, contrary to what is physically possible given the underlying nerve structure.

glucocorticoid: A steroidal hormone the body uses to fight stress.

glutamate: A major excitatory neurotransmitter in the brain.

graduated exposure: A treatment technique for extinguishing phobias in which persons are exposed to progressively more frightening items from an anxiety hierarchy.

gross motor skill: The ability to control large muscle movements and body posture.

group therapy: A therapy approach in which several people discuss their problems with one another under the guidance of a therapist.

guilty but mentally ill (GBMI): A legal verdict that results in a defendant's conviction for a crime even though the jury concludes that the defendant suffers a mental illness.

habituation speed: The amount of time it takes to habituate, or lose interest in, a repetitively presented stimulus.

hallucination: A sensory experience that seems real but is not based on external stimulation of the relevant sensory organ.

hallucinogen: A drug that produces unusual perceptual experiences.

haloperidol: A type of neuroleptic drug, sold as Haldol.

health belief model: A theory that explains why people do or do not engage in healthy behaviors.

health psychology: A specialized area of study devoted to understanding psychological influences on health and sickness.

hermaphrodite: An individual who possesses both male and female sexual organs.

heroin: A white, odorless powder derived from morphine; it is one of the most addictive and commonly abused opioids.

heterosexual behavior: Sexual attraction to and activity with members of the opposite sex.

heterozygous: Having different alleles of a certain gene.

hindbrain: One of the three main parts of the brain, it includes structures such as the medulla, the reticular formation, and the cerebellum, which maintain activities essential to life.

histrionic personality disorder: A personality disorder characterized by extreme attention-getting behaviors, flamboyance, and suggestibility.

homosexual behavior: Sexual attraction to and activity with members of the same sex.

homozygous: Having similar alleles of a certain gene.

hopelessness: A chronic tendency to view negative events as inevitable and positive events as unlikely, with no prospect for changing this pattern.

hormone: A chemical messenger secreted by the adrenal glands or other parts of the endocrine system.

host personality: In dissociative identity disorder, the primary identity that is in charge of the person's functioning most of the time.

human immunodeficiency virus type 1 (HIV-1): The virus that causes AIDS.

humanistic model: Any of several theories of human behavior that explain how behavior is influenced by each person's unique perception of the world rather than instincts, conflicts, or environmental consequences.

Huntington's disease: A dementia involving progressive subcortical degeneration that leads to motor disturbances, changes in personality, and cognitive difficulties.

hypertension: High blood pressure.

hypnotizability: The ease with which a person can be hypnotized; suggestibility.

hypoactive sexual desire disorder: A sexual disorder characterized by low or infrequent interest in or motivation for sexual activity and infrequent sexual fantasies.

hypochondriasis: A mental disorder in which the person focuses on select symptoms and is preoccupied with the fear of having a serious medical illness.

hypofrontality: Diminished activity in the frontal lobe of the brain.

hypomania: A mild form of mania.

hypothalamic-pituitary-adrenocortical (HPAC) axis: A chemical relay system that helps the body respond to sudden stressors.

hypothalamus: A key structure in the forebrain that aids in regulating hunger, thirst, sex drive, and other motivated behavior, as well as activity of various internal organs.

hypothesis: A theoretical proposition describing how two or more variables are related.

hypoxia: Oxygen deprivation.

hysteria: A mental disorder in which patients with normal physical abilities appear unable to see or hear or walk.

id: One of three structures in the psychoanalytic conception of personality; it represents basic, unconscious instincts and provides the energy, or libido, to satisfy those instincts.

identification: In psychoanalytic theory, the process of imitating an adult, usually the same-sex parent.

identity alteration: Behavioral patterns suggesting that a person has assumed a new identity.

identity confusion: A person's uncertainty about the nature of his or her own identity, of who he or she is.

illusion: The misperception or misinterpretation of actual sensory experiences.

imaginative involvement: *See* absorption.

immunosupression: A decrease in immune system effectiveness that sometimes follows sustained stress.

impotence: The inability to attain or maintain an erection.

incestuous pedophilia: Sexual activity by an adult with a child family member.

incidence: The number of people who develop a disorder in a specific time period, usually the previous six or twelve months.

inclusion: Similar to mainstreaming, this process involves keeping students with disabilities in regular classrooms.

independent variable: The variable in an experiment that is manipulated by the experimenter.

infant sleep disturbance: A sleep disorder that affects infants and involves trouble falling asleep, nighttime waking, and distress.

informed consent: Obtaining agreement from individuals to participate in research or receive treatment after they have been informed of the procedure's potential benefits and risks and the alternatives that are available.

inhibition: A pattern of unusually shy, quiet, and withdrawn behavior, usually regarded as a temperamental characteristic.

insanity: A legal term that describes a state of mind and implies that a defendant cannot be held responsible for his or her illegal conduct.

insecure attachment: A pattern of infant–parent attachment in which infants show minimal separation distress, coupled with avoidance of the parent during reunions.

insomnia: A condition in which a person complains of difficulty falling asleep or staying asleep.

intelligence test: A measure of general mental ability and various specific intellectual abilities such as verbal reasoning, quantitative skills, abstract thinking, visual recognition, and memory.

interleukin-1: A chemical messenger used by macrophages to summon various kinds of T cells and activate them.

internal validity: The degree to which an experiment allows a researcher to be confident that the results are due to the independent variable rather than confounding factors.

internalizing problem: A deficit in desired child behaviors, usually accompanied by subjective distress in the child.

Interpersonal Circumplex (Circle): A model of personality based on combinations of the dimensions of extroversion and agreeableness.

interpersonal theory: A theory that explains personality as the result of consistent styles of interaction.

joint attention: The process of coordinating attention with another person.

kuru: A fatal disease of the central nervous system found in cannibalistic tribes in the highlands of New Guinea, similar to Huntington's disease.

la belle indifference: An attitude of indifference or nonchalance toward symptoms by persons with conversion disorder.

latency stage: In psychoanalytic theory, the fourth stage of psychosexual development during which instinctual conflicts are subdued. It begins around age 6 and lasts until adolescence.

learned helplessness model: An explanation of depression suggesting that, if people feel chronically unable to control life events, they learn a sense of helplessness that leads to depressive symptoms.

learning disorder: A disorder in which a discrepancy exists between an individual's achievements in reading, writing, or mathematics and his or her expected achievements based on age, schooling, and level of intelligence.

learning readiness: The level of cognitive and emotional factors that aid or deter the learning process; includes expectations of success or failure, motivation, and emotional response to corrective feedback.

learning theories: Explanations of how new behaviors are acquired, retained, and used.

lesbianism: Homosexual behavior by females.

Lewy body dementia: A rare degenerative dementia distinguished by abnormal protein deposits, hallucinations, and fluctuating memory loss and confusion.

libido: In psychoanalytic theory, the energy that motivates people to satisfy their basic needs.

licensure law: A law that restricts the use of a professional title and prohibits unlicensed people from offering the services of a given profession.

life records: Documents associated with important events and milestones in a person's life, such as school grades, court records, police reports, and medical histories.

light therapy: Exposing patients to a bright light source during the early morning hours to reduce symptoms of seasonal depression and correct problems in body temperature or hormone output.

limbic system: A complex circuit of brain structures (including the thalamus, hippocampus, cingulate gyrus, hypothalamus, amygdala, septum, and parts of the cortex) that help regulate emotions, memory, and certain aspects of movement.

linkage analysis: A study of the linked occurrence of a disorder and some genetic marker across several generations.

lithium carbonate: A drug used to treat mania, commonly known as lithium.

localized amnesia: Loss of memory for a distinct period of time, usually the few hours immediately after a specific trauma.

locus coeruleus: A small area of the brain stem in which abnormalities are associated with alarm or panic.

longitudinal study: A study in which an investigator repeatedly assesses the same individuals or variables over a period of time.

lysergic acid diethylamide (LSD): A hallucinogenic drug that excites the central nervous system.

macrophage: A white blood cell responsible for the detection of pathogens.

magnetic resonance imaging (MRI): A neurodiagnostic procedure that tracks the activity of atoms in the body as they are "excited" by magnets in a chamber or coil placed around the patient.

magnetic resonance spectroscopy (MRS): A newer version of magnetic resonance imaging that allows the simultaneous study of brain structure and function.

mainstreaming: An educational policy in which children with disabilities spend part of their school time in regular classrooms.

maintenance: The persistence of a learned behavior.

major depressive disorder: One of the most severe forms of depression, characterized by constant sadness or despair, irritability, guilt, physical symptoms, insomnia, and lack of energy.

male erectile disorder: A sexual disorder characterized by a recurring failure to attain or maintain an erection adequate for sexual activity.

male orgasmic disorder: A sexual disorder involving difficulty in or complete inability to experience orgasm during sexual activity.

managed care system: An organization that allocates health services to a group of people in order to contain the overall cost of these services.

mania: An excited mood in which a person feels excessively and unrealistically positive and energetic.

marital therapy: Psychological treatment of problems in marriages or other intimate relationships, also called couples or conjoint therapy.

masturbatory reconditioning: A procedure intended to increase arousal to appropriate sexual stimuli by associating them with orgasms reached through masturbation.

McNaughton rule: A legal definition of insanity requiring that at the time the wrongful act was committed, the person accused was, as a result of a mental disorder, unable to know the nature and quality of the act or to know that the act was wrong.

medical model: A model that explains abnormal behavior as symptoms resulting from an underlying illness.

melatonin: A hormone that affects the hypothalamus and helps prepare the body for sleep.

memory T cells: Cells of the immune system that help the body continue its immune response after antigens have been neutralized.

mental age: A measure of a person's level of cognitive functioning relative to normative standards.

mental disorder: A behavioral or psychological syndrome that produces harmful dysfunction in an individual, causing objective impairment and/or subjective harm.

mental retardation: Significantly subaverage intellectual functioning occurring before the age of 18 that is associated with significant limitations in adaptive functioning.

mental status examination (MSE): A brief, specialized, and focused interview designed to assess a person's memory, mood, orientation, thinking, and concentration.

mescaline: A hallucinogenic drug derived from the peyote cactus, causing effects similar to LSD.

meta-analysis: A statistical technique that combines the results of several studies into an overall average or estimate.

methadone maintenance therapy: A treatment designed to help opioid-dependent persons avoid relapses by giving them methadone until they can achieve complete opioid independence.

midbrain: One of the three main parts of the brain, it helps coordinate head and eye movements, controls gross body movements, and is involved in basic responses to visual, auditory, and tactile stimuli.

milieu program: A hospital program that intends to resocialize patients with severe mental disorders so that they can learn how to manage their lives better and engage in appropriate behavior in the community.

model of abnormality: A comprehensive account of how and why abnormal behaviors develop and how best to treat them.

monoamine oxidase inhibitor (MAO): A drug that blocks monoamine oxidase, an enzyme that breaks down neurotransmitters such as serotonin and norepinephrine, resulting in greater availability of these neurotransmitters at neural synapses.

mood disorders: A group of mental disorders associated with serious and persistent difficulty maintaining an even, productive emotional state.

morbidity risk: The risk for a person's developing a disorder over his or her lifetime.

multiaxial classification: A system for diagnosing mental disorders and describing a person along several dimensions, or axes, including physical health, psychosocial and environmental problems, and global functioning.

multiple baseline design: A research design in which an intervention is evaluated by applying it sequentially to each of several treatment targets to see whether the target changes when, and only when, the intervention is applied.

multiple personality disorder: Name for dissociative identity disorder used prior to DSM-IV.

myocardial infarction: A condition commonly known as a heart attack, in which the supply of blood to the heart muscle is cut off, resulting in serious damage.

narcissistic personality disorder: A personality disorder characterized by an overinflated sense of self-importance and worth that leads to a sense of entitlement to special privileges and exemptions from the rules that apply to others.

narcolepsy: A sleep disturbance in which a person suffers sudden attacks of REM sleep, usually accompanied by temporary muscle paralysis and immobility.

negative affect: An emotional state that is a mixture of anxious and depressive symptoms.

negative attributional style: A tendency to interpret successes in life as the result of external, temporary, and specific factors beyond a person's control, and to interpret failures in life as the result of internal, stable, and global factors within a person.

negative symptom: A diminution, absence, or loss of normal psychological functions; apathy, flat emotions, lack of self-help skills, and social withdrawal; found in many cases of schizophrenia.

neuritic plaque: The residue of dead neurons and cellular debris; found in patients diagnosed with Alzheimer's disease.

neurofibrillary tangles: Twisted clumps of protein fibers found in dying brain cells.

neuroleptic: A drug that blocks the action of neurotransmitters in the brain, thereby relieving many positive symptoms of schizophrenia.

neuroleptic malignant syndrome: A rare side effect of neuroleptic drugs that is potentially fatal and involves extremely high fever, muscle rigidity, and irregular heart rate and blood pressure.

neuron: A nerve cell in the brain that specializes in transmitting information.

neuropsychological test: A psychological assessment tool that measures deficits in behavior, cognition, or emotion known to correlate with brain dysfunction and damage, and helps to determine whether a person is suffering from brain damage or deterioration.

neuroscience: A set of disciplines that study the structure, organization, functions, and chemistry of the nervous system, especially the brain.

neurosis: A term often used to describe chronic anxiety, unhappiness, and guilt that reduces a person's overall effectiveness; historically, it was thought to be a disorder brought about by unconscious emotional conflicts and expressed mainly through anxiety-related symptoms.

neuroticism: A personality trait involving the tendency to experience negative emotions such as anxiety, anger, and depression, accompanied by disrupted behavior and distressed thinking.

neurotransmitter: A chemical released by neurons that acts on other neurons.

nicotine: A stimulant drug found in the leaves of the tobacco plant and usually ingested by smoking.

nightmare disorder: A sleep disturbance that involves repeated frightening dreams that interrupt sleep, usually during REM stages.

nimodipine: A calcium channel blocker that may slow the progression of Alzheimer's disease.

node-link mapping: A method of correcting specific cognitive patterns such as impulsivity, distractibility, and inattention that interfere with abstinence from drugs.

non-REM (NREM) sleep: Sleep stages 1 to 4, in which REM sleep is not experienced.

norepinephrine: A neurotransmitter involved in sleep and arousal, attention, mood, and eating.

normalization: A social policy based on the idea that persons with mental retardation should experience mainstream society in their everyday lives; associated with deinstitutionalization and an emphasis on family care, community-based facilities, and public school education of children with disabilities.

norm: A score obtained from large numbers of people who have taken a test previously under similar conditions.

nosology: A classification system containing categories of disorders and rules for categorizing disorders depending on observable signs and symptoms.

nucleotide: Any of several biochemical compounds that make up DNA and contain sugar, phosphate, and a nitrogen base.

object relations theory: A modern variant of psychoanalytic theory that explains how adult personality is based on the nature and quality of early interactions between infants and their caregivers.

objective test: A personality test that requires answers or ratings to specific questions or statements that are scored quantitatively.

observational learning: In social learning theory, the view that behavior develops as a result of observing other people's behavior and its consequences.

obsession: An unwanted, disturbing, often irrational thought, feeling, or image that people cannot get out of their minds.

obsessive-compulsive disorder (OCD): An anxiety disorder that involves recurrent obsessions or compulsions that are serious enough to adversely affect a person's life.

obsessive-compulsive personality disorder: A personality disorder characterized by a preoccupation with rules, details, and organization in many aspects of life, so much so that the person is stubbornly perfectionistic.

Oedipus complex: In psychoanalytic theory, the conflict young boys feel between sexual desire for their mothers, the wish to eliminate their fathers as sexual competitors, and the resultant fear that these impulses will be discovered and punished.

olfactory aversion therapy: Treatment sometimes used for paraphilic behavior in which the client imagines a paraphilic stimulus or behavior in association with aversive images and the presence of a foul odor.

openness: A personality trait involving interest in new experiences and a receptivity to new activities and ideas.

operant conditioning: A form of learning in which the consequences of a behavior influence the probability of its being performed in the future.

operational definition: A statement that equates a concept with the exact methods used to represent or measure it.

opioid: An alkaloid containing opium or one of its derivatives, such as morphine, heroin, codeine or methadone.

oppositional defiant disorder (ODD): A childhood mental disorder involving a pattern of negativistic, disobedient, and defiant behavior, usually shown at home and sometimes at school.

oral stage: In psychoanalytic theory, the first stage of psychosexual development; it occurs in the first year of life when eating, sucking, and biting are the main sources of pleasure.

organic mental disorders: A group of mental disorders that are caused by brain disease or dysfunction.

orgasm: The phase of sexual response in which sexual pleasure peaks with involuntary rhythmic muscle contractions and a release of sexual tension; in males this involves ejaculation of semen, in females this involves contractions of the labia minora, vagina, and uterus.

other psychotic disorders: A group of mental disorders whose psychotic symptoms are usually more limited in duration and less intense than those of schizophrenia; includes schizophreniform disorder, schizoaffective disorder, delusional disorder, brief psychotic disorder, and shared psychotic disorder.

overpathologizing: A tendency to mistakenly construe some behavior as a symptom of a mental disorder when in fact the behavior is culturally appropriate.

oxidation: The process by which alcohol is converted to acetylaldehyde and metabolized.

pain disorder: A disorder in which the predominant clinical complaint is pain, and psychological factors are thought to play a significant role in causing or maintaining the pain.

pancreatitis: A condition in which cells in the pancreas are killed, commonly caused by heavy drinking.

panic attack: A period of unexpected, intense, terrifying anxiety that leaves victims feeling as if they are going crazy or are about to die.

panic disorder: An anxiety disorder marked by panic attacks coupled with persistent anxiety that another attack will occur.

panic disorder with agoraphobia: Panic disorder that results in or is accompanied by a fear of being in public or being trapped in a place that is not safe.

paradoxical directive: A treatment technique in which the therapist asks clients to purposely perform and even exaggerate problematic behaviors in order to ultimately reduce them.

paranoid personality disorder: A personality disorder characterized by habitual suspicion, mistrust, irritability, and hostility.

paranoid schizophrenia: A type of schizophrenia marked by persistent and elaborate delusions involving themes of persecution and grandiosity.

paraphilia: A repetitive pattern of sexual behavior in which arousal and/or orgasm depends on atypical or socially inappropriate stimuli.

parasomnias: One of the two categories of primary sleep disorders, they involve unusual behaviors or abnormal physiological events during sleep.

parasuicidal behavior: A behavior suggestive of suicide attempts, such as mild drug overdosing, mixing alcohol and other drugs, or minor cutting of the wrists.

parasympathetic nervous system: A division of the autonomic nervous system that balances the sympathetic nervous system by decreasing arousal, slowing heart rate, and decreasing blood pressure, conserving the body's energy and resources.

Parkinson's disease: A degenerative dementia characterized by tremor, difficulty in movement, and reduced production of dopamine.

Parkinsonism: An extrapyramidal side effect of some neuroleptic drugs, leading to symptoms that mimic Parkinson's disease such as tremor, shuffling gait, blank facial expression, muscular weakness and rigidity, and slowed movement.

participant modeling: A treatment technique in which a model demonstrates fearless behavior while a client is given increasingly close contact with the feared situation under protected circumstances.

pathogen: An invading virus or bacterium.

pedophilia: Sexual activity with a prepubescent child by a person who is at least 16 years of age and at least 5 years older than the child.

penetrance: The degree to which a genetic predisposition is actually expressed in behavior or physical features.

perseveration: Repeating the same answer over and over to different questions.

personality: The unique pattern of consistency in behavior that distinguishes each person from every other person.

personality disorder: An enduring pattern of inner experience and behavior that is inflexible, deviates markedly from the expectations of a person's culture, and causes personal distress, behavioral impairment, or discomfort for others.

personality fragment: In dissociative identity disorder, a condition that is similar to, but not as well-developed as, an alter personality; it typically represents an emotion that a person displays only in certain situations.

personality test: A standardized psychological assessment of an individual's predominant personality traits and characteristics.

personality trait: A psychological attribute that is relatively stable for an individual over time and across different situations.

pervasive developmental disorder (PDD): Severe childhood mental disorders with autistic features, including autism.

phallic stage: In psychoanalytic theory, the third stage of psychosexual development; it occurs between ages 3 and 6 when the genitals become the focus of pleasure.

pharmacodynamics: How drugs interact with receptors and what effects they eventually have on cognitive, behavioral, and emotional processes.

pharmacokinetics: The way drugs are metabolized, absorbed, distributed in the body, and excreted.

pharmacotherapy: Treatment of disorders with medication.

phenomenological model: Any of several theories of human behavior that explain how behavior is influenced by each person's unique perception of the world rather than by instincts, conflicts, or environmental consequences.

phenothiazines: A chemically similar group of neuroleptic drugs that act by blocking specific neurotransmitter receptors.

phenotype: The characteristics displayed by a person that result from the interaction of genetic makeup and the environment.

phenylketonuria (PKU): A genetic cause of mental retardation that results from an abnormality in protein metabolism.

phobia: An irrational, excessive fear that causes intense emotional distress and interferes significantly with everyday life.

physiological dependence: Excessive or frequent consumption of a drug resulting in drug tolerance or withdrawal.

Pick's disease: A progressive degenerative disease marked by dementia and atrophy of the frontal lobes of the brain.

pituitary gland: A structure in the forebrain that controls the endocrine system and plays a key role in physiological responses to stressful events.

placebo control group: In an experiment, a control group that receives an impressive, but inactive or theoretically inert, treatment.

placebo effect: Improvements that result from expectations or other psychological factors rather than from a treatment's active ingredients.

plaque: Deposits of fatty substances on the walls of blood vessels.

pleasure principle: In psychoanalysis, the premise that immediate gratification of desires and impulses is a primary motive for behavior.

polysomnographic (PSG) assessment: A measurement process in which a person sleeps in a laboratory while sleep variables are observed and monitored.

polysubstance abuse: The abuse of several substances at the same time.

polythetic approach: An approach to classification that requires a person to meet a particular number of criteria out of a larger set of criterion symptoms in order to be diagnosed with a specific mental disorder.

positive symptoms: Symptoms associated with schizophrenia, involving distorted or excess behaviors such as hallucinations, delusions, bizarre behavior, confused thinking, and disorganized speech.

positron emission tomography (PET): A neurodiagnostic procedure that shows changes in the structure of the brain and in its metabolic functioning by tracking the rate at which injected radioactive glucose is consumed by brain cells.

postpartum onset: Beginning of a disorder shortly after giving birth.

posttraumatic stress disorder (PTSD): An anxiety disorder in which a person experiences a pattern of intense, fear-related reactions after being exposed to a highly stressful event.

prednisone: An antiinflammatory agent.

premature ejaculation: A condition in which a man ejaculates after very little sexual stimulation, usually before or almost immediately after penetrating a partner.

preparedness theory: The hypothesis that people are biologically prepared to develop fears of certain classes of stimuli, such as snakes and spiders, that were potentially dangerous to our evolutionary ancestors.

prevalence: The total number of people who suffer from a disorder in a specific population.

primary gain: According to Freud, the reduction of anxiety accomplished by the conversion of psychological conflict into physical symptoms.

primary hypersomnia: A sleep disturbance in which an individual complains of excessive sleepiness and engages in prolonged sleep on an almost daily basis.

primary insomnia: A sleep disturbance in which individuals have such trouble falling asleep or staying asleep that they suffer significant distress or impairment.

primary prevention: An attempt to reduce the onset of disorders or eliminate them entirely by bringing about changes that either eliminate risk factors or promote psychological health.

primary sleep disorders: A group of sleep disturbances that arise from the interaction of biological, psychological, behavioral, and cultural factors; they are divided into the categories dyssomnia and parasomnia.

primitive thinking: Simplistic thinking that is absolute and invariant.

private self-consciousness: A tendency to concentrate on internal sensations and private thoughts.

privilege: The protection from being made to publicly disclose in court what individuals have said in confi-dence to certain other people (e.g., between a lawyer and client or doctor and patient).

problem-focused coping: An attempt to reduce stress by directly changing the stressor itself.

process schizophrenia: A form of schizophrenia characterized by early onset and progressive deterioration in functioning.

prodromal phase: The usual first phase of schizophrenia in which there is an insidious onset of problems suggesting psychological deterioration.

projective tests: Personality tests that require the person to respond to ambiguous stimuli such as inkblots, incomplete sentences, or vague drawings. The responses are thought to reveal important characteristics about people by the way they project meaning onto the ambiguous stimuli.

propentofylline: A chemical that enhances blood flow and energy metabolism in the brain.

psilocybin: Substances found in several species of Mexican mushrooms that produce visual illusions, distorted body image, and depersonalization.

psychiatrist: A medical doctor who specializes in the study and treatment of mental disorders.

psychoactive (psychotropic) drugs: Drugs that alter cognitive, emotional, and behavioral processes.

psychoanalysis: A theory of human behavior and a therapeutic approach based on the idea that both normal and abnormal behaviors are influenced by conflicting unconscious forces, especially sexual and aggressive instincts.

psychological dependence: Intense desire for a drug and preoccupation with obtaining it.

psychological factors affecting medical condition: A set of psychological influences that can trigger or lead to a worsening of physical illnesses.

psychological test: A systematic procedure for observing and describing a person's behavior in a standardized situation.

psychological wellness: A general approach toward mental health that calls for professionals to design programs that promote health rather than intervening after problems have started.

psychoneuroimmunology: A field of study that focuses on how the brain, the immune system, and psychological processes affect one another.

psychopharmacology: The scientific field devoted to the study of psychoactive drugs and their use in treating mental disorders.

psychosexual stages of development: In psychoanalytic theory, stages that all children pass through corresponding to the part of the body most involved with pleasurable experiences at the time. They include the oral, anal, phallic, latency, and genital stages.

psychosis: A general term describing mental disorders that produce severe disorganization in behavior and gross impairment in the ability to comprehend and accurately perceive events.

psychosocial rehabilitation: A set of interventions focused on preventing unnecessary hospitalizations, reducing impairments in daily functioning, and strengthening independent living skills by teaching patients with severe mental disorders how to cope with these disorders.

psychosurgery: Surgery designed to alleviate mental disorders by altering or destroying brain tissue.

psychotherapy: Treatment of an individual's mental disorders or behavioral problems by a therapist using psychological methods.

psychotic disorder due to a general medical condition: A mental disorder involving psychotic symptoms caused by a medical illnesses or condition.

punishment: The operant learning process that decreases the frequency of a preceding behavior.

quasi-experiment: A study that resembles or "comes close" to being a true experiment, but lacks one or more elements of a true experiment such as random assignment, manipulation of the independent variable, or a control group.

random assignment: A method of assigning members to experimental and control groups such that they have an equal chance of being in either. Random assignment decreases the chance that variables other than the independent variable will influence the result of the experiment.

rapid eye movement (REM) sleep: A phase of sleep in which the eyes dart back and forth quickly under closed lids; often associated with dreaming.

rational emotive therapy (RET): Therapy developed by Albert Ellis based on the theory that psychological problems are caused by irrational thinking; the therapy challenges irrational beliefs and helps clients replace them with more logical beliefs.

reactive schizophrenia: A form of schizophrenia characterized by sudden onset of symptoms, often in reaction to a traumatic situation.

reality principle: In psychoanalysis, a process used by the ego to reach rational compromises between the instincts of the id and the moral demands the superego.

receptive language: The understanding of language.

recessive allele: A gene inherited from one parent that can be expressed only when paired with a similar allele from the other parent.

reinforcement: The operant learning process that increases the frequency of a preceding behavior.

relapse: The return or worsening of a disorder after recovery.

reliability: Consistency or agreement among assessment data; includes test-retest reliability, internal consistency, and interrater reliability.

remission: When symptoms of a previously present disorder are no longer apparent, implying improvement or recovery.

replication: Repeating a research study with a new group of subjects and/or in a different situation to assess whether prior findings will be found under new circumstances.

representative sample: A sample in which participants are selected to represent levels of important subject variables such as age, gender, and ethnicity; a small group selected from a larger group in such a way that it approximates the characteristics of the larger group.

repression: A psychoanalytic defense mechanism that involves motivated forgetting of anxiety-arousing thoughts, images, or impulses.

residual phase (of schizophrenia): A stage of schizophrenia during which most psychotic symptoms have subsided in frequency and intensity; the affected person may still be withdrawn and apathetic, behave strangely at times, and continue to show social and occupational impairments.

residual schizophrenia: A type of schizophrenia in which patients have had at least one prior episode of schizophrenia but are not currently displaying major positive symptoms.

resilience: The ability to solve problems effectively, cope with stressors, and overcome adversity.

response prevention: A treatment in which clients are kept from performing the compulsive rituals they normally use to reduce anxiety.

reticular activating system (RAS): A complex network of neurons in the midbrain that connects the reticular formation with higher brain centers and is responsible for arousal processes.

retrograde amnesia: The inability to recall previously learned information.

retrograde ejaculation: A condition in which a man experiences orgasm but releases ejaculate into the bladder rather than expelling it from the penis.

retrospective research: Research done by asking respondents about past experiences.

Rett's disorder: A mental disorder in which children who have previously developed normally for their first 6 to 18 months suddenly lose previously acquired skills, decelerate in head growth, and show autistic behaviors.

reuptake: A process by which neurotransmitters are reabsorbed into the neurons that released them.

risk/rescue ratio: A comparison of the riskiness of a person's suicidal behavior to the availability of rescue or help in the situation.

Ritalin: A drug that facilitates the release, and blocks the reuptake, of norepinephrine and dopamine, amplifying the impact of these neurotransmitters in the brain; commonly used to treat attention-deficit/hyperactivity disorder.

schizoaffective disorder: A mental disorder in which the person displays symptoms of both schizophrenia and a mood disorder without satisfying the full criteria for either diagnosis.

schizoid personality disorder: A personality disorder characterized by extreme indifference to social relationships and a pervasive emotional blandness.

schizophrenia: A psychotic mental disorder marked by serious impairments in basic psychological functions—attention, perception, thought, emotion, and behavior.

schizophrenic spectrum disorders: Disorders that are schizophrenic-like but do not meet all the diagnostic criteria for schizophrenia and tend to be less severe.

schizophreniform disorder: A disorder in which people experience symptoms of schizophrenia for only a few months.

schizophrenogenic mother: A formerly popular term for a type of mother thought to cause schizophrenia in her children by her domineering, overprotective, cold, and rigid manner and her discomfort with physical intimacy.

schizotaxia: A hypothetical vulnerability to schizophrenia that is thought to be inherited.

schizotypal personality disorder: A personality disorder characterized by odd ways of talking, thinking, acting, and dressing, as well as social isolation and a lack of close relationships.

scientific method: A systematic process of studying, observing, and recording data in order to assess the validity of hypotheses.

season-of-birth effect: The finding that a greater proportion of schizophrenics are born in the winter or early spring months, when they are presumably more likely to be exposed to viral infections that may affect brain development.

seasonal affective disorder: Mood disorders that are linked to a particular season of the year; probably caused by shifts in overall exposure to light.

secondary gain: Possible benefits of somaticized illness, such as gaining attention or avoiding stressful responsibilities, that may play a major role in maintaining somatization.

secondary messenger: A biochemical change that takes place in neurons after they have initially been stimulated by a neurotransmitter.

secondary prevention: A selective attempt to reduce the onset of disorders in persons who are judged to be at risk for these disorders.

secure attachment: A pattern of infant–parent attachment in which infants show moderate separation distress, coupled with a strong approach to the parent during reunions.

selective amnesia: Ability to remember only some of the events surrounding a trauma; the remainder are forgotten.

selective serotonin reuptake inhibitor (SSRI): A type of drug used to treat mental disorders such as depression; it works by slowing the reuptake of serotonin.

self psychology: A therapy developed by Kohut in which the therapist's task is to be responsive and empathic and to permit a transference that will allow the client's self to be "completed" by having early unmet needs fulfilled.

self-actualization: The growth of each client as a unique person; a goal of phenomenological/experiential therapies.

self-awareness theory: An explanation of depression that emphasizes the role of excessive, sustained self-focused attention.

self-control: Processes by which individuals use contingency management and other behavior-change techniques to modify their own behaviors.

self-efficacy: A person's belief that he or she can successfully perform a given behavior.

self-focused attention: The tendency to engage in private self-reflection and evaluation.

self-help group: A group of people who meet regularly to address members' psychological problems without a professionally trained leader.

self-monitoring: A special form of observation in which people record the frequency, duration, intensity, or quality of their own behaviors, such as smoking, eating, moods, or thoughts.

self-regulation: Actions taken by individuals to regulate their own feelings and thoughts.

self-reinforcement: An individual's regulation of reinforcers for the purpose of increasing his or her own desirable behavior.

self-relatedness: A person's ability to experience and understand internal states such as thoughts and emotions.

self-schema: Core assumptions and beliefs about the self.

sensate focus: A method of increasing sensuality and the ability to experience physical pleasure by focusing on kissing, massage, or touch without attempting direct genital stimulation of a partner.

sensitivity: The probability that a person with a mental disorder is diagnosed as having that disorder.

separation anxiety disorder: A mental disorder of childhood in which there is developmentally inappropriate fear of separation from home or from those to whom the child is most closely attached, usually parents.

serotonin: A neurotransmitter that influences emotion, sleep, and behavioral control.

sex role: *See* gender role.

sex-linked chromosome: Chromosome 23 is known as the sex-linked chromosome because it consists of duplicate chromosomes in the female (designated XX) but not in the male (designated XY).

sexual aversion disorder: A more extreme version of hypoactive sexual desire disorder wherein the affected individual fears or is disgusted by the idea of sexual contact.

sexual dysfunctions: A category of disorders involving problems in sexual desire, arousal, or response during sexual activity.

sexual masochism: When sexual arousal or gratification depends on receiving painful stimulation or being humiliated.

sexual orientation: A person's tendency or preference for engaging in sexual behavior with same- or opposite-sex partners.

sexual response cycle: A four-stage sequence of psychological changes and physiological reactions, consisting of desire, excitement, orgasm, and resolution.

sexual sadism: When sexual arousal or gratification depends on inflicting physical pain or humiliation on a sexual partner.

sexual script: An expectation about sex that is determined by the social roles and messages carried over from childhood and from previous sexual encounters.

shame aversion therapy: A treatment technique often used for paraphilias; the client imagines engaging in paraphilic acts while imagining or experiencing his friends or relatives expressing their disgust and disapproval.

shaping: An operant learning technique in which successive approximations of a target behavior are reinforced until the final target behavior is performed or learned.

shared psychotic disorder: A condition in which one person develops a psychotic disorder and then influences another person or persons to behave in a similar fashion.

single photon emission computed tomography (SPECT): Similar to positron emission tomography (PET), a SPECT scan uses a radioactive chemical that allows pictures of the brain from several angles.

sleep disorder due to a general medical condition: A problem of sleep that is the direct physiological result of a medical problem.

sleep disorder related to another mental disorder: A sleep disturbance that is a symptom of some other diagnosed mental problem, most often a mood disorder or an anxiety disorder.

sleep paralysis: A symptom associated with panic disorder; it occurs when a person is waking up or falling asleep, and involves a brief inability to move.

sleep terror disorder: A sleep disturbance in which the person awakes with a terrified scream or panicky cry, and usually remains extremely upset for several minutes.

sleepwalking disorder: A sleep disturbance that involves the person's leaving the bed and moving about, or sitting up in bed, talking, or gesturing. During the episode, the person is unresponsive and can be awakened only with great difficulty.

social causation theory: A theory suggesting that stress, poverty, racism, inferior education, unemployment, and social changes are sociocultural risk factors leading to mental disorders.

social drift: Also called the *social selection hypothesis*, it explains higher rates of mental disorders among lower socioeconomic groups as the consequence of disordered people sinking to lower socioeconomic levels because of their disorders.

social history: Obtained as part of clinical interviews, it includes assessment of educational achievements, occupational positions, family history, marital status, physical health, and prior contacts with mental health professionals.

social learning theory: A theory that explains how behavior is learned through observation (vicarious learning), direct experiences, and cognitive processes such as expectancies.

social phobia: Excessive and inappropriate fear of situations in which a person might be evaluated and possibly embarrassed.

social relativism: The idea that the same standards and definitions of abnormal behavior do not apply in all cultures.

social selection hypothesis: *See* social drift.

social support: The feeling that one is cared for by others or belongs to a valued group.

sociocultural model: Explanations of mental disorders that emphasize external factors, such as harmful environments, unfortunate social policies, lack of personal power, and cultural traditions; also called the *ecological model*.

sociocultural model of dissociative disorder: The claim that dissociative identity disorder is not a genuine mental disorder but rather a diagnosis given to patients who have learned to enact a role that emphasizes multiple personalities, often in response to suggestions from therapists.

sociotropic (dependent) personality: A personality characterized by a heightened sensitivity to isolation, fear of abandonment, and a strong need for love from others.

sodium amytal: A drug supposedly capable of inducing a person to tell the truth, also referred to as "truth serum."

somaticizing: A tendency to express psychological problems through physical complaints.

somatization: A process in which physical symptoms that suggest a medical disorder appear without an adequate medical explanation, or by which emotional distress is converted into physical symptoms.

somatization disorder: A disorder in which a person shows a chronic pattern of physical complaints that cannot be medically explained but are severe enough to interfere with the person's functioning.

somatoform disorders: A group of disorders that involve physical complaints or disabilities that suggest a medical problem but have no known biological cause and are not voluntarily produced by the patient.

somatosensory amplifier: A person who exaggerates normal bodily sensations and is prone to be disturbed by them.

specific phobia: Intense, persistent fear of specific objects or situations that pose little or no actual threat.

specificity: The probability that a person without any mental disorder will be diagnosed as having no disorder.

specifier: A descriptor used in the DSM-IV to indicate the likely course, severity, and specific symptom characteristics of certain mental disorders.

spectrum disorder: A disorder, such as autism, that is manifested in variations ranging from typical presentations to incomplete or atypical presentations of the disorder.

spontaneous remission: Improvement without any treatment.

squeeze technique: A method of treating premature ejaculation by firmly squeezing the head of the penis as sexual excitement begins to peak but before the point of ejaculatory inevitability, thus prolonging the time to ejaculation.

stage of exhaustion: The third stage of the general adaptation syndrome, in which breakdown of organ systems appears.

stage of resistance: The second stage of the general adaptation syndrome, in which various coping mechanisms are used to defend against a stressor.

standard of care: Treatment that a reasonable practitioner would be expected to give a patient.

standardization: Administering and scoring a test using uniform procedures for all respondents.

standardized mortality ratio: The ratio of deaths that actually occur to deaths that are naturally expected.

statistical validity: Whether the statistical methods used to analyze data are likely to yield valid conclusions about the effects of the independent variable.

stereotaxic subcaudate tractotomy (SST): Psychosurgery used for severe, intractable mental disorders; it involves disconnecting portions of the frontal lobes from the limbic system and other subcortical areas.

stimulant: A drug that has an excitatory effect on the central nervous system.

strange situation: A laboratory assessment of infant–parent attachment that allows observation of how an infant responds to separations from parents.

stress: An ongoing process that occurs when environmental or social threats place demands on individuals.

stress hormone: *See* adrenal corticosteroid.

stressor: Any event that requires a person to adjust.

stroke: A condition in which brain tissue and functioning are damaged by a loss of blood supply resulting in a loss of oxygen to the brain.

structured interview: An interview in which the interviewer asks questions in a predetermined sequence so that the procedure is essentially the same from one interview to another.

substance abuse: A maladaptive pattern of substance use resulting in repeated and significant adverse consequences and maladaptive behaviors.

substance dependence: A condition indicated by a set of behavioral, physiological, and cognitive symptoms and impairments caused by continued or excessive use of a substance.

substance intoxication: A temporary condition in which, as a direct result of ingesting too much of a substance, a person experiences impaired judgment, altered thinking, pronounced mood changes, disturbed perception, or impaired motor behavior.

substance-induced psychotic disorder: A mental disorder in which a person experiences psychotic symptoms beyond what is expected from intoxication or withdrawal from a substance, and in which the person is not aware that the substance is producing the psychotic symptoms.

substance-induced sleep disorders: Problems of sleep that are the direct physiological result of ingestion of medication or a drug of abuse.

superego: One of the three components of the psychoanalytic conception of personality; it is the repository of cultural rules, models of ideal behavior, and moral values.

supportive-expressive therapy: A time-limited form of psychoanalysis in which the patient is helped to identify and talk about core relationship patterns and how they relate to problems; often used in treatment of drug abuse.

suppressor T cells: Cells that signal the immune system to stop killer cell activity.

suprachiasmatic nucleus (SCN): A brain structure found in the hypothalamus that maintains the body's circadian rhythms.

switching: In dissociative identity disorder, the process of changing from one personality to another, thought to be stimulated by anxiety.

sympathetic nervous system: A division of the autonomic nervous system that prepares the body for action by increasing physiological arousal (e.g., stimulating the heart rate and increasing blood pressure) as preparation for fighting or fleeing a threat.

synapse: The tiny gap between neurons where neurotransmitters are released or received.

synesthesia: A drug-induced perceptual anomaly in which information from different senses is blended so that users "see" sounds or "feel" colors.

systematic desensitization: A behavioral treatment for phobias and anxiety disorders in which the client learns to use an anxiety-inhibiting technique while simultaneously being exposed to gradually increasing levels of the feared object or situation.

systematized amnesia: Loss of memory for certain classes of information.

T cells: Lymphocytes that destroy pathogens.

tacrine: A drug treatment approved for Alzheimer's disease, it slows the breakdown of acetylcholine.

tardive dyskinesia: An extrapyramidal side effect of some neuroleptic drugs; it involves spasmodic jerks, tics, and twitches of the face, tongue, trunk, and limbs, and causes speech impairment.

tension reduction hypothesis: The idea that drinking alcohol is reinforced by its ability to reduce tension, anxiety, anger, depression, and other unpleasant emotions.

teratogen: A substance that crosses the placenta and damages the fetus.

tertiary prevention: Attempts to reduce the severity or consequences of a disorder in people who have already been diagnosed with the disorder.

thalamus: A key structure in the forebrain that receives, analyzes, and sends on information from all the senses except smell.

theory: A set of propositions used to predict and explain certain phenomena.

theory of mind: A cognitive process that allows an individual to infer the mental states of others.

therapeutic contracting: Formal commitments by clients to work toward improvement in specific areas.

therapeutic jurisprudence: Consideration of the therapeutic implications of legal rulings on patients.

thioridazine: A type of neuroleptic drug, sold as Mellaril.

token economy: A procedure that uses operant reinforcement principles to alter the behaviors of individuals or groups by giving tokens (such as poker chips) that can be exchanged for other tangible rewards.

tolerance: A condition in which increasingly larger doses of a drug are required to achieve the same physical effect or subjective state.

Tourette's disorder: A disorder characterized by both repetitive vocal tics or vocalizations and motor acts and tics.

transference: The process by which the client begins to unconsciously transfer to the therapist certain feelings or conflicts that were experienced with significant people from the past, usually a parent.

transference neurosis: A psychoanalytic term describing a miniature version of the client's essential problems, now evident in the transference relationship between the client and therapist.

transsexual: A common term for adults with gender identity disorder.

transvestic fetishism: A sexual disorder in which a man dresses in women's clothes in order to experience sexual arousal and satisfaction.

trauma-dissociation model: A theory that explains dissociative identity disorder as the result of severe trauma during childhood that produced a splitting of personalities as a defense against the trauma.

trifluoperazine: A type of neuroleptic drug, sold as Stelazine.

trisomy 21: Three chromosomes instead of the normal two on pair 21; another name for Down syndrome.

tropicamide: An anticholinergic drug showing promise as an early screening test for Altheimer's disease.

tryicyclics: Drugs used primarily to treat depression; they increase levels of neurotransmitters such as norepinephrine and serotonin by blocking their reuptake.

twin study: A method of systematically comparing the traits of monozygotic twins reared together or apart with the traits of dizygotic twins reared together or apart.

two-factor conditioning: A model that combines classical conditioning and operant conditioning to explain disorders such as PTSD and phobias.

Type A behavior pattern: A specific emotional and behavioral pattern characterized by high levels of competitiveness, drive, hostility, need for control, a heightened sense of time urgency, and an overall pressured tempo of life.

Type B behavior pattern: A specific emotional and behavioral pattern characterized by a relaxed, nonhostile, or noncompetitive lifestyle.

Type C behavior pattern: A personality and behavioral pattern, allegedly associated with cancer proneness, despite the lack of replicated evidence linking its emotional features to cancer.

typical autism: A childhood mental disorder marked by severe disturbances in social relationships, language, and stereotypical autistic behavior (e.g., rocking or unusual hand movements); often involves mental retardation and tends to be a lifelong condition.

underpathologizing: A tendency for clinicians to mistakenly construe some behavior as merely reflecting a cultural difference when in fact it is the symptom of a mental disorder.

undifferentiated somatoform disorder: A type of somatoform disorder similar to somatization but with fewer unexplained physical complaints.

undifferentiated schizophrenia: A type of schizophrenia in which the symptoms do not satisfy criteria for the paranoid, disorganized, or catatonic subtypes.

vaginismus: An involuntary spasm of the musculature in the outer third of the vagina that makes penile penetration impossible.

validity: The degree to which an assessment instrument measures what it is supposed to measure, thereby providing an estimate of accuracy or meaning.

vascular dementia: Dementia caused by cardiovascular conditions that interrupt blood flow to the brain.

vasocongestion: An excessive accumulation of blood in tissue.

ventricle: A cavity in the center of the brain that is filled with cerebrospinal fluid.

visual–motor skills: The ability to control eye–hand coordination.

vital exhaustion: A condition commonly called *burnout* that is characterized by fatigue, dejection, defeat, and increased irritability.

voyeurism: A sexual disorder in which a person achieves sexual arousal and satisfaction through the clandestine observation of others.

waxy flexibility: Molding and holding the body in bizarre positions, characteristic of catatonic schizophrenia.

Wernicke-Korsakoff syndrome: A rare, alcohol-induced memory disorder in which the affected individual becomes confused and unable to coordinate voluntary muscle movements, and then loses memory for personal experiences.

Williams syndrome: A rare childhood mental disorder resulting from a deleted gene on chromosome 7; the symptoms include a puzzling combination of intellectual strengths and weaknesses, exceptional hearing ability, and physical anomalies.

withdrawal: A pattern of physical symptoms that results from discontinuing drug use once the person has become physically dependent on it.

Name Index

Green, B.L., 175
Green, R., 497, 499-502
Greenbaum, P.E., 455, 456
Greenberg, G., 96
Greenberg, G.S., 455
Greenberg, J., 304, 307, 309
Greenberg, L.S., 178, 565, 566, 569, 577, 582, 596
Greenberg, M., 634
Greenberg, M.T., 81, 88, 128
Greenberg, W.M., 602
Greenblatt, D., 544
Greene, J.W., 281
Greenhill, L.L., 92, 96
Greenslade, K.E., 97
Greenwald, D., 367, 369, 582
Greenward, D., 370
Greenwood, C.R., 128
Greiner, A.R., 97
Gresham, F.M., 120, 121
Gretter, M.L., 583
Griesinger, Wilhelm, 60
Grimes, K., 361
Grissom, G.R., 474
Grochocinski, V., 543
Grof, P., 296
Grossarth-Maticek, R., 206, 207
Grossberg, G.T., 389
Grosscup, S.J., 304
Grossman, H.J., 121
Grossman, P.B., 101, 102, 103
Groth-Marnat, G., 274, 279, 473
Grove, W., 355
Grover, G., 237, 546
Gruber, A.J., 480
Gruenberg, A., 351, 354
Gruenberg, E., 227, 228, 235, 241
Guazelli, M., 542
Guenette, S., 395
Guerra, N.G., 48, 362, 613
Guevara, L., 227, 228
Guevremont, D.C., 97, 178
Guiterrez, R., 367, 549
Gull, William, 110
Gully, R., 229
Gulotta, C., 94
Gunderson, J.G., 430
Gundlach, R.H., 498
Gunhaus, L., 534, 535
Gur, R.C., 356
Gur, R.E., 14, 356
Gurland, B., 334
Gurling, H., 298
Guroff, J.J., 309
Gusella, J.F., 392
Guthrie, D., 504
Guthrie, P.R., 179, 601
Gutierrez, J.L.A., 309
Guze, B., 236
Guze, S.B., 275, 280

Haaga, D.A., 306
Haas, G.L., 319
Hackenberg, T., 133
Hadley, S.W., 575
Hadzi-Pavlovic, 582
Hafemeister, T., 643
Hafner, H., 346, 358
Hagen, E.P., 51, 120
Haggerty, R.J., 447, 464, 611
Haier, R., 355, 358
Haines, J.L., 395
Haines, T., 296
Halek, C., 111
Haley, G., 315
Haley, J., 362, 598

Haley, R., 174
Halikas, J.A., 456, 470
Hall, G.C., 518
Hall, G.L., 58, 518
Hall, S.M., 475
Hall, W., 471
Halpern, F.S., 301
Halstead, Ward, 52
Halweg, K., 597
Hamberger, S., 237
Hamburger, R., 298
Hamburger, S., 87
Hamer, D.H., 496
Hamilton, M., 289, 290, 295
Hammeke, T.A., 52
Hammen, C., 103, 306, 309, 311, 318
Hammill, D.D., 146
Hamovit, J.H., 309
Hampton, R., 111
Hamra, B.J., 228
Handel, George Frederick, 288
Handelsman, L., 477, 478
Handelsman, M.M., 571
Handley, R., 363
Hando, J., 471
Haney, T.L., 193
Hanley-Peterson, P., 580
Hanna, H., 231
Hans, S.L., 359
Hansen, D.J., 570
Hansen, L., 391
Hansen, W.B., 464, 465
Hanson, K.A., 156
Hanson, R.K., 525
Harbin, T.J., 193
Harburg, E., 457
Hardesty, J.P., 362
Hardin, T.S., 305
Hare, R.D., 422, 430, 438, 439
Harford, T.C., 450
Harkness, A.R., 413
Harlan, W.R., 200
Harmatz, J., 544
Harpur, T.J., 422, 438
Harrington, R., 103, 105, 138
Harris, A.S., 112
Harris, E., 319
Harris, E.L., 228
Harris, K.B., 464
Harris, L., 495
Harris, M., 311
Harris, M.J., 346, 426, 542
Harris, Marty, 153-54
Harris, R.A., 448
Harris, T., 309
Harrison, K., 362
Harrow, M., 338
Hart, B., 128
Hart, C.A., 158
Hart, S.D., 422, 439
Harter, S., 103
Hartman, H., 563
Hartnoll, R.L., 476
Harvey, P.D., 531
Harvey, R., 580
Hasemann, D.M., 434
Haslam, John, 333
Haslam, N., 353
Hatsukami, D., 110
Hattie, J.A., 559, 580
Hatzichristou, D.G., 508
Hauser, P.M., 199
Havassy, B.E., 475
Hawkins, J.D., 606, 611
Haxby, J.V., 381
Hay, P., 237, 532, 533

Hayashida, M., 462
Hayes, A.M., 573
Haynes, S.G., 192, 193
Hays, R., 290, 292
Hays, R.D., 479
Hazelrigg, M., 578, 600
Hazlett, E.A., 58
Heard, H.L., 437, 582
Hearst-Ikeda, D., 247
Heart, N., 495
Heath, A., 218, 222, 238
Heaton, K.W., 448
Heber, R., 121
Hechtman, L., 92, 96
Heckler, S., 145
Hedberg, A., 571
Heidegger, Martin, 565
Heilbrun, A.B., 337
Heilbrun, K.S., 629
Heilman, P., 149
Heiman, J., 504, 507, 510, 511, 514, 515, 516
Heimberg, R.G., 582
Heinrich, R.L., 166
Heinssen, R.K., 604
Heller, K., 134, 165, 303
Hellerstein, D., 541
Hellman, L., 109, 301
Helmes, E., 54
Helzer, J.E., 27, 28, 217, 227, 228, 235, 241
Hembree, E., 237
Hemingway, Ernest, 288
Hemingway, Margaux, 469
Hemmings, K.A., 583
Hendrickson, G., 546
Hendrie, H., 389
Henggeler, S.W., 48, 607
Henker, B., 96, 97, 551
Henn, F.A., 299
Henning, K., 492
Henriksen, L., 95
Henry, W.P., 581
Herbart, Johann, 9
Herbert, J.D., 424
Herbert, T.B., 163, 291
Herd, D., 450
Herjanic, M., 293
Hern, K.L., 95, 148
Hernandez, M., 270
Herning, R.I., 472
Herring, J., 435, 608
Herrnstein, R.J., 35, 131
Hersen, M., 61, 99-100, 576
Hertz, R., 231, 246
Hervis, O., 600
Herz, M.I., 603
Hess, R.D., 148
Hesse, E., 81
Hesselbrock, V., 451, 453
Hesselink, J.R., 138
Heston, L.L., 352, 394, 453, 496
Hibbard, J., 166
Hibbs, E.D., 87
Higgins, E., 354, 355
Higgins, S.T., 474, 475
Higson, P.J., 478, 572
Hilbich, C., 395
Hill, J., 237, 546
Hill, L.R., 125
Hill, S.Y., 451
Hille, B., 479
Himelein, M., 270
Hinckley, John, Jr., 632, 638, 641, 642, 643
Hinshaw, S.P., 84, 92, 96
Hippocrates, 5-6, 60, 530
Hirky, A.E., 457

Hiroto, D.S., 304
Hirschfeld, R.M.A., 292, 438
Hirschman, R., 518
Hirsh, S., 356
Hirshfeld, D.R., 100
Hirshfield, R.M., 288, 301
Hite, S., 491
Hoban, T.M., 315
Hobbs, S., 133
Hoberman, H.M., 582
Hobson, R.P., 138
Hockey, A., 395
Hodapp, R.M., 123, 125, 126, 127, 128, 130, 142, 144, 145, 149, 150
Hodges, J.R., 390
Hodgkinson, S., 298
Hodgson, R., 232, 233, 235, 236, 241, 522
Hodiamont, P., 98
Hoelscher, T.J., 208
Hoffman, P.L., 454, 477
Hoffstetter, R., 391
Hofman, M.A., 496, 501
Hofmann, Albert, 480
Hofmann, M., 451
Hogarty, G., 367, 369, 370, 582
Hoge, S.K., 625
Hoien, T., 147
Holland, A., 235, 546
Hollander, E., 229, 513
Hollister, L.E., 543, 547
Hollon, S.D., 69, 229, 315, 316, 317, 553
Holman, K., 395
Holmes, T.H., 158, 177
Holroyd, J., 634
Holroyd, S., 337
Holtzman, P.S., 354
Holtzman, W.H., 134
Holtzworth-Monroe, A., 595, 597
Holyrod, J., 634
Holzer, C., 289, 295
Holzer, C.E., 216, 218, 220, 346
Homan, S., 315
Honeyman, J., 147, 148
Honigfeld, G., 367, 549
Hontos, P.T., 112
Hood, H.V., 204
Hooley, J.M., 309
Hope, D.A., 424
Hope, R.A., 111, 582
Hopkins, J., 105
Hopkins, M., 239
Hops, H., 105, 315
Horen, B., 369
Horn, W.F., 96
Hornig, C., 218, 225, 227
Horowitz, Ralph, 195
Horvath, A.O., 560
Horwath, E., 218, 225, 227
Horwitz, B., 381
Hosino, Y., 138
Hostetter, A.M., 298
Hotaling, G., 519
Hough, R., 227, 591
House, J.S., 166, 199, 203, 613
Housman, D.E., 298
Houston, B.K., 576
Houts, A.C., 111, 112
Howard, A., 581
Howard, K.I., 584
Howard, R.C., 642
Hsiao, J., 542
Hsu, L.K.G., 108, 109

Subject Index

Fair Housing Amendments Act of 1988, 628
Faith healing, 5
False alarms, panic attacks as, 229, 230
False memories, 272
False Memory Syndrome Foundation, 636
False-negative diagnosis, 49, 67
False-positive diagnosis, 49, 67
"False positive" in predicting dangerousness, 633
False uniqueness, sense of, 591
Family. *See also* Environmental factors
    alcohol use disorders and, 457
    anorexia and, 108–9
    antisocial personality disorder and, 432–34
    childhood depression and, 105
    environmental reengineering in, 608
    recapitulation of, in group therapy, 593
    reducing violence in, 606–7, 609
    role in shaping somatoform disorders, 281
    schizophrenia and, 360, 362–63, 364
    sex-related attitudes and, 505
Family adversity index, 88–89
Family counselors, 10
Family education programs, empirically-validated uses of, 582
"Family engagement" procedures, 600
Family Interview Schedule, 363
Family studies, 16–18. *See also* Adoption studies; Twin studies
    of gender identity disorders, 501
    of mood disorders, 298, 299
    of schizophrenia, 350–52
Family therapy
    for alcohol use disorders, 461
    as alternative to individual psychotherapy, 590, 598–600
    for eating disorders, 111
    effectiveness of, 600
    for pain disorder, 283
    for schizophrenics, 369–70
    techniques of, 598–600
Fantasies
    as mild dissociation, 253
    sexual, 491, 506, 513, 517, 523
Fantasy proneness, 263, 264
FAST Track Program, 91, 436
Fatal Attraction (movie), 421
Fatalistic suicides, 323
Fear, 216–18. *See also* Anxiety disorders
    ability to learn, 432
    anxious/fearful personality disorders, 410, 423–25, 427
    defined, 216
    vicarious conditioning of, 222
Fear networks, 246
Fear reduction treatments, modeling in, 570–71
Federal Certificate of Confidentiality, 519
Federal Rule of Evidence 702, 638
Federal Task Force on Homelessness and Severe Mental Illness, 622
Feedback
    biofeedback, 112, 202, 283, 572
    in group therapy, 593
    negative feedback loop, 161
Feeding and eating disorders, 65, 106–11
    anorexia nervosa, 28, 106–9, 110–11
    bulimia nervosa, 106, 107, 109, 110–11
    longitudinal course of, 109–10
    treatment of, 110–11
Female hormones. *See* Estrogens
Female orgasmic disorder, 510–11, 515
Female sexual arousal disorder (FSAD), 507–8, 514
Femininity, 488

Fenfluramine, 143
Fertilization, 14
Fetal alcohol effect (FAE), 128
Fetal alcohol syndrome (FAS), 94, 127–28
Fetal development, sexual differentiation and, 494
Fetishism, 516–17, 522, 523
Field trial, 61
Fight-or-flight reaction, 12, 159, 164
Fine motor skills, 119
Finger tapping test, 52
Firearms, teen suicide and availability of, 325
Five Factor Model. *See* Big Five model of personality
Fixation, 20
Flashbacks, 246, 256, 481
Flat affect, schizophrenia and, 340
Flexibility, waxy, 292, 339, 348
Flooding, 224, 569
Fluoxetine (Prozac), 110, 235, 300, 312, 313, 314, 515, 530, 540, 541, 546, 550
Fluphenazine (Prolixin), 366, 547, 617
Focal brain damage, 378
Folie à deux or *folie à trois* (shared psychotic disorder), 341–42
Ford v. *Wainwright*, 628–29
Forebrain, 12, 13
Forensic psychiatry, 638
Forensic psychology, 638
Foreplay, sexual, 408
Forgetfulness, psychoanalytic interpretation of, 562. *See also* Memory loss
Formal thought disorder, 338
Formication, 338
Foucha v. *Louisiana*, 628, 642
14th Amendment, 619, 627
Fragile X syndrome, 124, 125–26, 138, 150
Framingham (Massachusetts) Heart Study, 193
Frank Porter Graham Child Development Center, 131
Fraternal (dizygotic) twins, 16, 18. *See also* Twin studies
Free association, 21, 562, 564
Free-basing of cocaine, 472
Free-floating anxiety, 225, 237–38
Freudian personality structures, 19–20
Friendship, childhood depression and, 103
Frigidity, 504, 507. *See also* Female sexual arousal disorder (FSAD)
Frontal cortex of autistic persons, 138, 139
Frontal lobe, 12
    attention-deficit/hyperactivity disorder and deficits in, 95
    functions of, 378, 379
    hypofrontality, schizophrenia and, 355–56, 357
    panic and anxiety experiences and, 228
Frontal lobotomy, 531
Frotteurism, 517, 523
FSAD (Female sexual arousal disorder), 507–8, 514
Fugue, dissociative, 255, 261–62, 272
Functional brain imaging, 142
Fundamental attribution error, 591

Gam-Anon, 601
Gamblers Anonymous, 601
Gamma aminobutyric acid (GABA), 222, 231
    alcohol's effect on, 448–49
    benzodiazepines' effect on, 544
    depressants' effects on, 468

Gay men, HIV prevention efforts among, 204
Gay rights, 494–95
GBMI (guilty but mentally ill), 643
Gender bias in DSM, 67
Gender confusion, 500
Gender differences
    in alcohol metabolism, 448
    in alcohol use disorder prevalence, 449–50
    in Alzheimer's disease, 393
    in anorexia prevalence, 108
    in anxiety, 240–41
    in cancer rates, 198, 199
    in cardiovascular disease, 191
    in coping styles, 310
    in depressive disorders, 289, 318
    in drug metabolism, 553–54
    in exposure to stressors, 157–58
    in frequency of sex, 490
    in histrionic personality disorder, 419
    in morbidity risk for schizophrenia, 346
    in personality disorders, 411
    in psychotherapy clients, 558–59
    in suicide, 319–20
Gender dysphoria, 501
Gender identity, 488
Gender identity disorders, 487–88, 489, 498–503, 526. *See also* Paraphilias; Sexual dysfunctions
    in adults, 500–501
    causes of, 501
    in children, 500
    defined, 498
    in DSM-IV, 64
    prevalence of, 499–500
    treatment of, 501–2
Gender role, 488
Gender role expectations, 240–41
General adaptation syndrome (GAS), 155, 159–63, 168
General factors vs. specific processes explanation of psychotherapy, 583–84
Generalization, 130
    stimulus, 244
Generalized amnesia, 259
Generalized anxiety disorder (GAD), 74, 237–40
    causes of, 238–39
    in children and adolescents, 99
    prevalence of, 72, 238
    treatment of, 239–40, 573
Generalized social phobia, 220
Generalized type sexual dysfunctions, 505
General paresis, 9
General-purpose self-help groups, 601
Genes, 14–16, 17, 34
Genetic counseling, 129
Genetic factors in abnormality, 14–18, 34–35
    in alcohol use disorders, 453
    Alzheimer's disease and, 395–97
    in antisocial personality disorder, 427, 430–32
    childhood depression and, 105
    controversy over studying, 34–35
    in gender identity disorders, 501
    in generalized anxiety disorder, 238
    mental retardation caused by genetic additions or deletions, 125–27
    in mood disorders, 298–99
    in obsessive-compulsive disorder, 235
    personality differences and, 426–27
    in personality disorders, 427
    in reading disabilities, 147–48
    in schizophrenia, 349–54, 360, 361, 372

Credits

Chapter 2

Table 2.3 From *Assessment of Persons* by Norman D. Sundberg, © 1977. Reprinted by permission of Prentice-Hall, Inc., Upper Saddle River, NJ.

Figure 2.4 *Minnesota Multiphasic Personality Inventory-2 (MMPI-2) Profile for Basic Scales.* Copyright © 1989 the Regents of the University of Minnesota. All rights reserved. "MMPI" and "Minnesota Multiphasic Personality Inventory-2" are trademarks owned by the University of Minnesota. Reprinted by permission.

DSM Table, p. 62. Reprinted with permission from the *Diagnostic and Statistical Manual of Mental Disorders,* Fourth Edition. Copyright © 1994 American Psychiatric Asociation.

Table 2.6 Adapted with the permission of The Free Press, a division of Simon & Schuster from *Psychiatric Disorders in America: Epidemiological Catchment Area Study* by Lee N. Robins and Darrel A. Regier. Copyright © 1991 by Lee N. Robins and Darrel A. Regier.

Figure 2.6 Reprinted with permission from the *Diagnostic and Statistical Manual of Mental Disorders,* Fourth Edition. Copyright © 1994 American Psychiatric Association.

Chapter 3

Table 3.1 Adapted from Sroufe & Rutter, *Child Development,* Vol. 55, 1984, with permission of Society for Research in Child Development.

Figure 3.1 Copyright T.M. Achenbach. Reproduced by permission.

DSM Table, p. 82. Reprinted with permission from the *Diagnostic and Statistical Manual of Mental Disorders,* Fourth Edition. Copyright © 1994 American Psychiatric Association.

DSM Table, p. 86. Reprinted with permission from the *Diagnostic and Statistical Manual of Mental Disorders,* Fourth Edition. Copyright © 1994 American Psychiatric Association.

Figure 3.3 From Raine, Venables, Williams in *Archives of General Psychiatry,* Vol. 47, 1990, p. 1005. Reprinted by permission of Dr. Adrian Raine.

DSM Table, p. 93. Reprinted with permission from the *Diagnostic and Statistical Manual of Mental Disorders,* Fourth Edition. Copyright © 1994 American Psychiatric Association.

DSM Table, p. 107. Reprinted with permission from the *Diagnostic and Statistical Manual of Mental Disorders,* Fourth Edition. Copyright © 1994 American Psychiatric Association.

Chapter 4

Table 4.1 Adapted from Eric R. Kandel, James H. Schwartz and Thomas M. Jessell, *Essentials of Neural Science and Behavior* (Norwalk, CT: Appleton & Lange, 1995). Reprinted by permission.

DSM Table, p. 136. Reprinted with permission from the *Diagnostic and Statistical Manual of Mental Disorders,* Fourth Edition. Copyright © 1994 American Psychiatric Association.

Chapter 5

Figure 5.4 From "Ontogenetic Development of the Human Sleep-Dream Cycle" by H.P. Roffwarg, J.N. Muzio and W.C. Dement in *Science,* 152, 1966, with permission from Science. Copyright © 1966 American Association for the Advancement of Science. Reprinted by permission.

Figure 5.5 From "Reported Sleep and Drug Use of Workers" by Brownman et al. in *Sleep Research,* 1977, Vol. 6, p. 111. Reprinted by permission of the Brain Research Institute.

Chapter 6

Figure 6.4 From Adler et al., *American Psychologist,* 1994, Vol. 49, pp. 15-24. Reprinted by permission of Nancy E. Adler.

Figure 6.5 From Kirschenbaum & Fitzgibbon, *Behavior Therapy,* Vol 26 1995, p. 59. Copyright © 1995 by the Association for Advancement of Behavior Therapy. Reprinted by permission.

Controversy figure, p. 203. From Friedman et al. in *American Psychologist,* Vol. 50, 1995, pp. 69. Copyright © Howard S. Friedman and Joseph E. Schuartz. Reprinted by permission of Dr. Howard S. Friedman.

Prevention figure, p. 210. From Meyer, *Journal of Consulting and Clinical Psychology,* Vol 48, p. 137.

Chapter 7

DSM Table, p. 226. Reprinted with permission from the *Diagnostic and Statistical Manual of Mental Disorders,* Fourth Edition. Copyright © 1994 American Psychiatric Association.

DSM Table, p. 233. Reprinted with permission from the *Diagnostic and Statistical Manual of Mental Disorders,* Fourth Edition. Copyright © 1994 American Psychiatric Association.

DSM Table, p. 242. Reprinted with permission from the *Diagnostic and Statistical Manual of Mental Disorders,* Fourth Edition. Copyright © 1994 American Psychiatric Association.

Figure 7.4 Barlow, D.H. From *Anxiety and its Disorders* by D.H. Barlow, Guilford Press, 1988. Reprinted by permission.

Prevention figure, p. 247. From Foa, et al. in *Journal of Consulting Psychology,* Vol. 63, 1995, p. 952. Reprinted by permission.

Chapter 8

DSM Table, p. 256. Reprinted with permission from the *Diagnostic and Statistical Manual of Mental Disorders,* Fourth Edition. Copyright © 1994 American Psychiatric Association.

DSM Table, p. 274. Reprinted with permission from the *Diagnostic and Statistical Manual of Mental Disorders,* Fourth Edition. Copyright © 1994 American Psychiatric Association.

DSM Table, p. 277. with permission from the *Diagnostic and Statistical Manual of Mental Disorders,* Fourth Edition. Copyright © 1994 American Psychiatric Association.

Prevention figure, p. 270. From Denicola & Sander, *Behavior Therapy,* Vol 11, 1980. Copyright © 1980 by the Association for Advancement of Behavior Therapy. Reprinted by permission of the publisher and the author.

Chapter 9

DSM Table, p. 290. Reprinted with permission from the *Diagnostic and Statistical Manual of Mental Disorders,* Fourth Edition. Copyright © 1994 American Psychiatric Association.

DSM Table, p. 294. Reprinted with permission from the *Diagnostic and Statistical Manual of Mental Disorders,* Fourth Edition. Copyright © 1994 American Psychiatric Association.

DSM Table, p. 296. Reprinted with permission from the *Diagnostic and Statistical Manual of Mental Disorders,* Fourth Edition. Copyright © 1994 American Psychiatric Association.

Figure 9.2 From *Manic Depressive Illness* by Goodman and Jamison. New York: Oxford University Press, p. 82.

Figure 9.3 From *Molecules and Mental Illness* by Samuel H. Barondes. Copyright © 1993 by Scientific American Library. Used with permission of W.H. Freeman and Company.

Table 9.1 From Rogeness, et al., "Neurochemistry and Child and Adolescent Psychiatry" in Journal Of The American Academy of Child And Adolescent Psychiatry, Vol. 31, pp.765-781. Copyright © 1992 Williams & Wilkins. Reprinted by permission of Waverly.

Tables 9.2 and 9.3 Excerpts from *Cognitive Therapy of Depression* by Beck, Rush, Shaw and Emery, The Guilford Press, 1979. Reprinted by permission.

Table 9.4 From *Suicide Over the Life Cycle: Risk Factors, Assessments and Treatment of Suicidal Patients* by Blumenthal and Kupfer, American Psychiatric Press, 1990, p. 494. Reprinted by permission of the American Psychiatric Association.

Chapter 10

DSM Table, p. 335. Reprinted with permission from the *Diagnostic and Statistical Manual of Mental Disorders,* Fourth Edition. Copyright © 1994 American Psychiatric Association.

Figure 10.1 From *Schizophrenia Genesis: The Origins of Madness* by Gottesman © 1991 by Irving I. Gottesman. Used with permission of W.H. Freeman and Company.

Figure 10.2 Adapted from p. 117 from *Surviving Schizophrenia: A Family Manual* by E. Fuller Torrey. Copyright © 1988 by E. Fuller Torrey. Reprinted by permission of HarperCollins Publishers, Inc.

Figures 10.3 and 10.4 From *Schizophrenia Genesis: The Origins of Madness* by Gottesman © 1991 by Irving I. Gottesman. Used with permission of W.H. Freeman and Company.

Chapter 11

Figure 11.3 From K.W. Schaie in *American Psychologist*, Vol. 49, pp. 304-313. Reprinted by permission of the author.

Table 11.1 From *Delirium in the Elderly*, Lindsay, MacDonald and Starke, Oxford University Press, 1990, p. 24. Reprinted by permission of Oxford University Press.

Figure 11.4 From "Mini-Mental State: A Practical Method for Grading the Cognitive State of Patients for the Clinician" by M.F. Folstein, S.E. Folstein and P.R. McHugh in *Journal of Psychiatric Research*, 12:189-198, 1975, Elsevier Science Ltd., Oxford England. Reprinted by permission.

Figure 11.6 From *F.A.S.E.B. Journal*, 1991, Vol. 5. Reprinted by permission of F.A.S.E.B. Journal.

Controversy figure, p. 397. From *Dementia And Normal Aging* by Felicia A. Huppert, Carol Brayne and D.W. O'Connor. Reprinted with the permission of Cambridge University Press.

Chapter 12

DSM Table, p. 412. Reprinted with permission from the *Diagnostic and Statistical Manual of Mental Disorders,* Fourth Edition. Copyright © 1994 American Psychiatric Association.

Figure 12.2 From *Interpersonal Diagnosis of Personality-A Functional Theory and* Methodology for Personality Evaluation by Timothy Leary, Ronald Press, 1957. Copyright 1957 by Timothy Leary.

Figure 12.3 Reprinted from *Clinical Psychology Review* by Loeber, 1990, Vol. 10, p. 6. Copyright ©1990, with kind permission from Elsevier Science Ltd., The Boulevard, Langford Lane, Kidlington OX5 1GB, United Kingdom.

DSM Table, p. 423. Reprinted with permission from the *Diagnostic and Statistical Manual of Mental Disorders,* Fourth Edition. Copyright © 1994 American Psychiatric Association.

Table 12.5 From Tellegen et al. in *Journal Of Personality and Social Psychology*, Vol. 54, 1988, pp. 1031-1039. Reprinted by permission of Dr. Auke Tellegen.

Controversy figure, p. 438. From Robert D. Hare, Leslie M. McPherson and Adelle E. Forth, "Male Psychopaths and Their Criminal Careers" in *Journal of Consulting Psychology*, Vol. 56. No. 5, 710-714. Copyright © 1988 by the American Psychological Association, Inc. Reprinted by permission.

Chapter 13

DSM Table, p. 446. Reprinted with permission from the *Diagnostic and Statistical Manual of Mental Disorders,* Fourth Edition. Copyright © 1994 American Psychiatric Association.

Figure 13.4 The Twelve Steps are reprinted with permission of Alcoholics Anonymous World Services, Inc. Permission to reprint *The Twelve Steps* does not mean that A.A. has reviewed or approved the contents of this publication, nor that A.A. agrees with the view expressed herein. A.A. is a program of recovery from alcoholism only - use of *The Twelve Steps* in connection with programs and activities which are patterned after A.A., but which address other problems, or in any other non-A.A. context, does not imply otherwise.

Figure 13.5 From Prochaska et al., in *American Psychologist*, Vol. 47, pp. 1102-1114. Reprinted by permission of Dr. James O. Prochaska.

Figure 13.6 Adapted from "Human Consumption of Caffeine" in *Caffeine*, ed. P.B. Dews, Springer-Verlag, 1984. Reprinted by permission.

Chapter 14

Table 14.1 From *Sex in America* by Michael et al. Copyright © 1994 by CSG Enterprises, Inc., Edward O. Laumann, Robert T. Michael, and Gina Kolata. By permission of Little, Brown and Company.

Table 14.2 From Anderson & Cyranowski, *Journal of Consluting Psychology*, 1995. Copyright 1995 by the American Psychological Association. Reprinted by permission.

Chapter 15

Figure 15.3 Reprinted by permission of the publisher from Feighner, "Symposium on Buspirone" in American Journal Of Medicine, Vol. 82 (suppl 5A), p. 1. Copyright © 1987 by Excerpta Medica Inc.

Figure 15.4 Reprinted by permission of the publisher from Schuckit, "Symposium on Buspirone" in *American Journal Of Medicine*, Vol. 82 (suppl 5A), p. 29. Copyright © 1987 by Excerpta Medica Inc.

Chapter 16

Figure 16.1 From Azrin & Peterson, *Behavior Therapy*, Vol 20, 1989, pp. 467-473. Copyright © 1989 by the Association for Advancement of Behavior Therapy. Reprinted by permission of the publisher and the author.

Table 16.1 From "Training and Dissemination of Empirically-Validated Psychological Procedures: Report and Recommendations" by Task Force on Promotion and Dissemination of Psychological Procedures, 1995 in *The Clinical Psychologist*, 48, pp. 22-23. Copyright 1995 by Division of Clinical Psychology, American Psychological Association. Reprinted by permission.

Figure 16.2 From Kazdin & Kopel, *Behavior Therapy*, Vol 6, 1975, pp. 601-608. Copyright © 1975 by the Association for Advancement of Behavior Therapy. Reprinted by permission of the publisher and the author.

Chapter 17

Figure 17.2 From Szapocznik et al. in *Journal of Consulting and Clinical Psychology*, Vol. 58, 1990. Copyright 1990 by the American Psychological Association. Reprinted by permission.

Figure 17.3 From Tremblay et al., *Journal of Consulting Psychology*, Vol 63, 1995. Reprinted by permission of Richard E. Tremblay.

Table 17.3 "Some Generic Risk Factors" from Coie, et al., *American Psychologist*, Vol 48, 1993, p. 1013. Reprinted by permission of Professor John D. Coie.

Pages 596-597 Exerpted from *Therapy for Couples*, Ables and Brandsma, Jossey-Bass, Inc., 1997, pp. 92-94.

Page 599 From *Conjoint Family Therapy* by Virginia Satir, Science & Behavior Books, Inc., Palo Alto CA, 800-547-9982. Reprinted by permission of the author and publisher.

Chapter 18

Figure 18.1 From "Episodic Rate of Mental Hospitalization: Stable or Increasing?" by C.A. Kiesler and A.E. Sibulkin in *American Journal of Psychiatry*, 141. Copyright by the American Psychiatric Association. Reprinted by permission.

PHOTO CREDITS

Chapter 1
Page 4, N. Richmond/The Image Works; p. 7, The Granger Collection; p. 8, North Wind Picture Archives; p. 19, The Granger Collection; p. 25, Paul Chesley/Tony Stone Images; p. 29, Untitled by George Kellogg, 1990. Water color and ink on paper, 22" x 30". Courtesy of Creative Growth Art Center; p. 32, Bob Daemmrich/The Image Works.

Chapter 2
Page 45, Mobile Press Register/Gamma Liaison; p. 48, Will Faller; p. 51, Michael Siluk/The Picture Cube; p. 59 (left), Science Photo Library/Science Source/Photo Researchers; p. 59 (center), Larry Mulvehill/Photo Researchers; p. 59 (right), NIH/Science Source/Photo Researchers; p. 60, The Granger Collection; p. 70, Paul Chesley/Tony Stone Images.

Chapter 3
Page 80, Elizabeth Crews/The Image Works; p. 85, Maggie Leonard/Rainbow; p. 91, Will Faller; p. 95, Myrleen Ferguson Cate/PhotoEdit; p. 99, Michael Nichols/Magnum Photos; p. 100, Steve Winter/Black Star; p. 106, Mary Kate Denny/PhotoEdit; p. 110, Farrell Grehan.

Chapter 4
Page 120, FujiFotos/The Image Works; p. 125 (left), CNRI Science Library/Photo Researchers; p. 125 (right), Jim Pickerell; p. 126, Mike Greenlar/The Image Works; p. 128, George Steinmetz; p. 134, Jim Pickerell; p. 139 (both), Courtesy of Julie Osterling; p. 144, Alan Carey/The Image Works.

Chapter 5
Page 157, AP/Wide World Photos; p. 159, Reuters/Corbis-Bettmann; p. 165, John Coletti; p. 166, Lisa Rudy Hoke/Black Star; p. 172, Kindra Clineff/The Picture Cube; p. 175, AP/Wide World Photos.

Chapter 6
Page 185, Corbis-Bettmann; p. 186, Barry King/Gamma Liaison; p. 190, Phyllis Picardi/Stock, Boston; p. 191, Courtesy of Dr. Norman Anderson; p. 192, Tony Freeman/PhotoEdit; p. 196, NIBSC/Science Photo Library/Photo Researchers; p. 197, Joe Carini/The Image Works; p. 198, Dan McCoy/Rainbow; p. 201, Owen Franken/Stock, Boston; p. 205, Jeremy Hartley/Panos Pictures.

Chapter 7
Page 216, Courtesy of Human Interaction Laboratory; p. 221, Archive Coll./Offshoot; p. 224 (left), Georgia Tech Telephoto; p. 224 (right), Dr. Larry F. Hodges, Thomas C. Meyer, and Rob Kooper/Georgia Tech Telephoto; p. 227, AP/Wide World Photos; p. 234, UPI/Corbis-Bettmann; p. 244, Phyllis Picardi/Stock, Boston.

Chapter 8
Page 252, The Granger Collection; p. 254, Steve Winter/Black Star; p. 257, Photofest; p. 261, R. L. Oliver/Los Angeles Times; p. 269, Philippe Plailly/Science Photo Library/Photo Researchers; p. 278, Bob Daemmrich/Stock, Boston.

Chapter 9
Page 289, Inge Morath/Magnum Photos; p. 293, Myrleen Ferguson Cate/PhotoEdit; p. 301, Drevets, et al., Journal of Neuroscience, vol. 12, pp. 3628–3641. Photo Courtesy of Dr. Wayne C. Drevets; p. 303, Richard T. Nowitz/Photo Researchers; p. 312, Oskar Reinhart Collection "Am Römerholz," Winterthur, Switzerland; p. 316, Toni Michaels/The Image Works; p. 323, AP/Wide World Photos; p. 325, Joe Rodriquez/Black Star.

Chapter 10
Page 332, Courtesy of Lionel Aldridge; p. 333, The Granger Collection; p. 337, "Untitled" by Viktor Orth (Clemens Von Oertzen). All rights reserved by Prinzhorn-Sammlung der Psyciatrischen Universit„tsklinik Heidelberg; p. 339, Will Hart; p. 340, Vincent Oliver/Tony Stone Images; p. 351, Courtesy of Edna Morlok; p. 355, Courtesy of Dr. Nancy Andreasen and the Mental Health Clinical Research Center, The University of Iowa Hospitals and Clinics; p. 357, Archives of General Psychiatry, December 1992, Vol. 49, p. 951. Copyright 1992, American Medical Association. Photo courtesy of Dr. Nancy Andreasen; p. 361, Jeff Lawrence/Stock, Boston; p. 371, Bill Stanton/Rainbow.

Chapter 11
Page 380, David Young Wolff/Tony Stone Images; p. 391, AP/Wide World Photos; p. 392, Reuters/Gloucestershire Echo/Archive Photos; p. 394 (left), Dan McCoy/Rainbow; p. 394 (right), Martin Rotker; p. 395 (both), Courtesy of Dr. William Markesbery, Sanders-Brown Center on Aging, University of Kentucky; p. 398 (left), UPI/Corbis-Bettmann; p. 398 (right), AP/Wide World Photos; p. 399, Michael Grecco/Stock, Boston; p. 401, Stephen Marks/Black Star;.

Chapter 12
Page 408, AP/Wide World Photos; p. 411, Alexis Duclos/Gamma Liaison; p. 416, PhotoEdit; p. 417, Steve Maines/Stock, Boston; p. 421, Photofest; p. 434, Billy E. Barnes/PhotoEdit.

Chapter 13
Page 444, Rick Friedman/Black Star; p. 449 (both), Courtesy of Dr. Gene-Jack Wang, Brookhaven National Laboratory; p. 461, John Boykin/The Picture Cube; p. 465, AP/Wide World Photos; p. 469, Archive Photos; p. 474, PhotoEdit; p. 476, Steve Leonard/Black Star; p. 481, Edward S. Curtis/National Geographic Image Collection; p. 482, Corbis-Bettmann.

Chapter 14
Page 488, Elizabeth Crews/The Image Works; p. 496, Jonathon Nourok/Tony Stone Images; p. 499 (both), UPI/Corbis-Bettmann; p. 514, The Granger Collection; pp. 517, 525, AP/Wide World Photos.

Chapter 15
Page 530, The Granger Collection; p. 532, UPI/Corbis-Bettmann; p. 535, Will & Demi McIntyre/Photo Researchers; p. 541, Tom Wolff/Courtesy of Random House; p. 549, Courtesy of Sandoz Pharmaceuticals Corporation.

Chapter 16
Page 560, David Harry Stewart/Tony Stone Images; p. 561, Archive Photos; p. 564, The Granger Collection; p. 566, Michael Rougier/Life Magazine; p. 568, Archive Coll./Offshoot; p. 570, Courtesy of Dr. Albert Bandura; p. 572, William McCoy/Rainbow.

Chapter 17
Page 593, Zigy Kaluzny/Tony Stone Images; p. 595, Will Hart; p. 599, David Young Wolff/PhotoEdit; p. 601, James Wilson/Woodfin Camp & Associates; p. 603, Rhoda Sidney/Stock, Boston; p. 605, Rob Nelson/Time/Black Star; p. 610, P. F. Bentley/Black Star.

Chapter 18
Page 619, P. Chauvel/Sygma; p. 621, Richard Kalvar/Magnum Photos; p. 623, Gale Zucker/Stock, Boston; pp. 628, 629, 631, AP/Wide World Photos; p. 636, Jim Wilson/New York Times Pictures.